The Teacher's Calendar

School Year 2005–2006

The Day-by-Day Almanac to Historic Events, Holidays, Famous Birthdays and More!

McGraw-Hill
New York Chicago San Francisco Lisbon London Madrid Mexico City Milan New Delhi San Juan Seoul Singapore Sydney Toronto

1 2 3 4 5 6 7 8 9 0 QPD/QPD 0 9 8 7 6 5

ISBN 0-07-145099-8
ISSN 1533-0362

NOTICE
Events listed herein are not necessarily endorsed by the editors or publisher. Every effort has been made to assure the correctness of all entries, but neither the authors nor the publisher can warrant their accuracy. IT IS IMPERATIVE, IF FINANCIAL PLANS ARE TO BE MADE IN CONNECTION WITH DATES OR EVENTS LISTED HEREIN, THAT PRINCIPALS BE CONSULTED FOR FINAL INFORMATION.

This book is printed on acid-free paper.

TABLE OF CONTENTS

How to Use This Book .... Inside front cover
Welcome to *The Teacher's Calendar* iv
Calendar of Events: Aug 1, 2005–July 31, 2006........ 1
- August 2005........ 1
- September 2005 22
- October 2005........ 44
- November 2005........ 69
- December 2005........ 92
- January 2006 112
- February 2006........ 133
- March 2006 151
- April 2006 173
- May 2006........ 196
- June 2006........ 218
- July 2006 235

Resources........ 252
Some Facts About the United States........ 253
Some Facts About the Presidents 255
Contact Information for State Governors and US Senators 257
Some Facts About Canada........ 264
Some Facts About Mexico 264
Calendar Information for 2005........ 265
Calendar Information for 2006........ 266
2005 and 2004 American Library Association Awards for Children's Books 267
Coretta Scott King Awards and Honor Books 1970–2003 269
Newbery Medal Winners and Honor Books 1933–2003........ 272
Caldecott Medal Winners and Honor Books 1944–2003 276
Index........ 280

WELCOME TO *THE TEACHER'S CALENDAR*

Welcome to The Teacher's Calendar

This edition of *The Teacher's Calendar* contains more than 4,500 events that you can use in planning the school calendar, creating bulletin boards and developing lesson plans. Some of the entries were taken from the 2005 edition of *Chase's Calendar of Events*, the standard reference book that for 48 years has provided librarians and the media with events arranged day-by-day. Hundreds of entries were written especially for *The Teacher's Calendar*. For example, among the "Birthdays Today" entries are birthdays for authors of children's books. We've also added the dates of national professional meetings for teachers, children's book conferences and other events of interest to professional educators.

Types of Events

Presidential Proclamations: We have included in the day-by-day chronology proclamations that have continuing authority with a formula for calculating the dates of observance and those that have been issued consistently since 1995. The president issues proclamations only a few days before the actual event so it is possible that some dates may vary slightly for 2005–2006. The most recent proclamations can be found on the Federal Register Online: www.access.gpo.gov. ★ in the text indicates presidential proclamations.

National Holidays and State Days: Public holidays of other nations are gleaned from United Nations documents and from information from tourism agencies. Technically, the United States has no national holidays. Those holidays proclaimed by the president apply only to federal employees and to the District of Columbia. Governors of the states proclaim holidays for their states. In practice, federal holidays are usually proclaimed as state holidays as well. Some governors also proclaim holidays unique to their state but not all state holidays are commemorated with the closing of schools and offices.

Religious Observances: Principal observances of the Christian, Jewish and Muslim faiths are presented with background information from their respective calendars. For dates of Jewish observances, we refer to Arthur Spier's *Comprehensive Hebrew Calendar*. We use anticipated dates for Muslim holidays. There is no single Hindu or Buddhist calendar; therefore, we are able to provide only a limited number of religious holidays for these faiths.

Historic Events and Birth Anniversaries: Dates for these entries have been gathered from a wide range of reference sources. Most birth anniversaries here are for people who are deceased. Birthdays of living people are usually listed under "Birthdays Today."

Astronomical Phenomena: Information about eclipses, equinoxes and solstices, and moon phases is calculated from the annual publication, *Astronomical Phenomena*, from the US Naval Observatory. Dates for these events in *Astronomical Phenomena* are given in Universal Time (i.e., Greenwich Mean Time). We convert these dates and times into Eastern Standard or Eastern Daylight Time.

Sponsored Events: We obtain information on these events directly from their sponsors and provide contact information for the sponsoring organization.

Other Special Days, Weeks and Months: Information on these events is also obtained from their sponsors.

Process for Declaring Special Observances

How do special days, weeks and months get created? The president of the United States has the authority to declare a commemorative event by proclamation, but this is done infrequently. In 2000, for example, the president issued about 100 proclamations. Many of these, such as Mother's Day and Bill of Rights Week, were proclamations for which there was legislation giving continuing authority for a proclamation to be issued each year.

Until 1995, Congress was active in seeing that special observances were commemorated. Members of the Senate and House could introduce legislation for a special observance to commemorate people, events and other activities they thought worthy of national recognition. Because these bills took up a lot of time on the part of members of Congress, when Congress met in January 1995 to reform its rules and procedures, it was decided to discontinue this practice. Today, the Senate passes resolutions commemorating special days, weeks and months but these resolutions do not have the force of law.

It is not necessary to have the president or a senator declare a special day, week or month; many of the events in *The Teacher's Calendar* have been declared only by their sponsoring organizations.

Websites

Web addresses have been provided when relevant. These URLs were checked the first week in January 2005. Although we have tried to select sites maintained by the government, universities and other stable organizations, some of these sites inevitably change or disappear.

Curriculum Connections

These sidebars were written by Sally Walker, Denise Frank, Elizabeth Van Buren, Johnny Loftus, Adrienne van den Beemt and Luisa Gerasimo, as well as the editors to give teachers ideas for integrating some of the events in *The Teacher's Calendar* into the classroom.

Acknowledgements

Thanks to Bill and Helen Chase, the founders of *Chase's Calendar of Events*, who, as always, are wonderful inspiration. Thanks to the staff at the Chicago, Evanston and Skokie public libraries who helped in the process of compiling *The Teacher's Calendar*. Special thanks to our colleagues at Contemporary Books: Marisa L'Heureux, Martha Best, Denise Fieldman, Gigi Grajdura, Terry Stone, Jeanette Wojtyla and John Kwasek. And now Associate Editor Kathy Keil and I invite you to join us in the celebration of the coming school year.

March 2005 — Holly McGuire, Editor in Chief
Chase's Calendar of Events

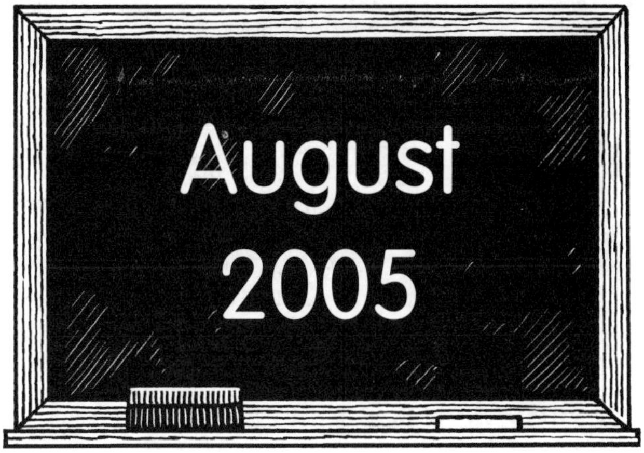

AUGUST 1 — MONDAY

Day 213 — 152 Remaining

AMERICAN HISTORY ESSAY CONTEST. Aug 1–Dec 15. American History Committee activities are promoted throughout the year with the essay contest conducted in grades 5–8 beginning in August. Essays are submitted for judging by Dec 15, with the winners announced in April at the Daughters of the American Revolution Continental Congress. Events vary, but include programs, displays, spot announcements and recognition of essay writers. Essay topic can be obtained from DAR Headquarters. For info: Daughters of the American Revolution, Office of the Historian-General, Admin Bldg, 1776 D St NW, Washington, DC 20006-5392. Phone: (202) 628-1776 or (812) 337-2331. Web: www.dar.org.

ANTIGUA AND BARBUDA: AUGUST MONDAY. Aug 1–2. The first Monday in August and the day following form the August Monday public holiday in this Caribbean nation.

AUSTRALIA: PICNIC DAY. Aug 1. The first Monday in August is a bank holiday in New South Wales and Picnic Day in Northern Territory, Australia.

BAHAMAS: EMANCIPATION DAY. Aug 1. Public holiday in Bahamas. Annually, the first Monday in August. Commemorates the emancipation of slaves by the British in 1834.

BENIN, PEOPLE'S REPUBLIC OF: NATIONAL DAY. Aug 1. Public holiday. Commemorates independence from France in 1960. Benin at that time was known as Dahomey.

BURK, MARTHA (CALAMITY JANE): DEATH ANNIVERSARY. Aug 1, 1903. Known as a frontierswoman and companion to Wild Bill Hickock, Calamity Jane Burk was born Martha Jane Cannary at Princeton, MO, in May 1852. As a young girl living in Montana, she became an excellent markswoman. She went to the Black Hills of South Dakota as a scout for a geological expedition in 1875. Several opposing traditions account for her nickname, one springing from her kindness to the less fortunate, while another attributes it to the harsh warnings she would give men who offended her. She died Aug 1, 1903, at Terry, SD, and was buried at Deadwood, SD, next to Wild Bill Hickock.

CANADA: CIVIC HOLIDAY. Aug 1. The first Monday in August is observed as a holiday in seven of Canada's ten provinces. Civic Holiday in Manitoba, Northwest Territories, Ontario and Saskatchewan; British Columbia Day in British Columbia; New Brunswick Day in New Brunswick; Natal Day in Nova Scotia and Heritage Day in Alberta.

CHILDREN'S VISION AND LEARNING MONTH. Aug 1–31. A monthlong campaign reminding Americans of the important role that good vision plays in a child's ability to read and learn. For info: College of Optometrists in Vision Development, 243 N Lindbergh Blvd, Ste 310, St. Louis, MO 63141. Phone: (314) 991-4007. Web: www.covd.org.

CLARK, WILLIAM: BIRTH ANNIVERSARY. Aug 1, 1770. Coleader with Meriwether Lewis on the Corps of Discovery expedition that explored the Louisiana Territory from 1804–06. Clark was an able leader and contributed detailed maps and animal illustrations on the journey. A grateful President Thomas Jefferson made Clark brigadier general of militia for the Louisiana Territory (1807–13) and superintendent of Indian Affairs (1807–38). Clark was also governor of the Missouri Territory (1813–20) and surveyor general for Illinois, Missouri and Arkansas (1824–25). Born at Caroline County, VA, Clark died at St. Louis, MO, Sept 1, 1838.

COLORADO: ADMISSION DAY: OBSERVED. Aug 1. Colorado. Annually, the first Monday in August. Commemorates Admission Day when Colorado became the 38th state, Aug 1, 1876.

COLORADO: ADMISSION DAY. Aug 1, 1876. Colorado became the 38th state. Observed on the first Monday in August in Colorado (Aug 1 in 2005).

DIARY OF ANNE FRANK: THE LAST ENTRY: ANNIVERSARY. Aug 1, 1944. To escape deportation to concentration camps, the Jewish family of Otto Frank hid for two years in the warehouse of his food products business at Amsterdam. Gentile friends smuggled in food and other supplies during their confinement. Thirteen-year-old Anne Frank, who kept a journal during the time of their hiding, penned her last entry in the diary Aug 1, 1944: "[I] keep on trying to find a way of becoming what I would like to be, and what I could be, if . . . there weren't any other people living in the world." Three days later (Aug 4, 1944) Grüne Polizei raided the "Secret Annex" where the Frank family was hidden. Anne and her sister were sent to Bergen-Belsen concentration camp where Anne died at age 15, two months before the liberation of Holland. Young Anne's diary, later found in the family's hiding place, has been translated into 30 languages and has become a symbol of the indomitable strength of the human spirit. See also: "Frank, Anne: Birth Anniversary" (June 12). For more info: www.annefrank.com.

EMANCIPATION OF 500: ANNIVERSARY. Aug 1, 1791. Virginia planter Robert Carter III confounded his family and friends by filing a deed of emancipation for his 500 slaves. One of the wealthiest men in the state, Carter owned 60,000 acres over 18 plantations. The deed included the following words: "I have for some time past been convinced that to retain them in Slavery is contrary to the true principles of Religion and Justice and therefore it is my duty to manumit them." The document established a schedule by which 15 slaves would be freed each Jan 1, over a 21-year period, plus slave children would be freed at age 18 for females and 21 for males. It is believed this was the largest act of emancipation in US history and predated the Emancipation Proclamation by 70 years.

FIRST US CENSUS: ANNIVERSARY. Aug 1, 1790. The first census revealed that there were 3,939,326 citizens in the 16 states and the Ohio Territory. The US has taken a census every 10 years since 1790. The most recent one was taken in April 2000. For the population of the US today, calculated to the minute, go to www.census.gov/main/www/popclock.html.

GRENADA: EMANCIPATION DAY. Aug 1. Grenada observes this public holiday annually on the first Monday in August. Commemorates the emancipation of slaves by the British in 1834.

ICELAND: AUGUST HOLIDAY. Aug 1. National holiday. Commemorates the constitution of 1874. The first Monday in August.

ICELAND: SHOP AND OFFICE WORKERS' HOLIDAY. Aug 1. In Iceland an annual holiday for shop and office workers is observed on the first Monday in August.

INTERNATIONAL CLOWN WEEK. Aug 1–7. To call public attention to the charitable activities of clowns and the wholesome entertainment they provide. Annually, Aug 1–7. For info: Clowns of America International, PO Box CLOWN, Richeyville, PA 15358-0532. Phone: (888) 52-CLOWN. Web: www.coai.org/.

JAMAICA: INDEPENDENCE DAY OBSERVED: ANNIVERSARY. Aug 1. National holiday observing achievement of Jamaican independence from Britain Aug 6, 1962. Annually, the first Monday in August.

KEY, FRANCIS SCOTT: BIRTH ANNIVERSARY. Aug 1, 1779. American attorney, social worker, poet and author of the US national anthem. While on a legal mission during the War of 1812, Key was detained on shipboard off Baltimore, during the British bombardment of Fort McHenry on the night of Sept 13–14, 1814. Thrilled to see the American flag still flying over the fort at daybreak, Key wrote the poem "The Star Spangled Banner." Printed in the *Baltimore American*, Sept 21, 1814, it was soon popularly sung to the music of an old English tune, "Anacreon in Heaven." It did not become the official US national anthem until 117 years later when, on Mar 3, 1931, President Herbert Hoover signed into law an act for that purpose. Key was born at Frederick County, MD, and died at Baltimore, MD, Jan 11, 1843.

MELVILLE, HERMAN: BIRTH ANNIVERSARY. Aug 1, 1819. American author, best known for his epic novel of the white whale: *Moby-Dick*. Also an acclaimed poet of the Civil War, Melville wrote in "The March into Virginia": "All wars are boyish, and are fought by boys." Born at New York, NY, Melville died there Sept 28, 1891.

MITCHELL, MARIA: BIRTH ANNIVERSARY. Aug 1, 1818. An interest in her father's hobby and an ability for mathematics resulted in Maria Mitchell's becoming the first female professional astronomer. In 1847, while assisting her father in a survey of the sky for the US Coast Guard, Mitchell discovered a new comet and determined its orbit. She received many honors because of this, including being elected to the American Academy of Arts and Sciences—its first woman. Mitchell joined the staff at Vassar Female College in 1865—the first US female professor of astronomy—and in 1873 was a cofounder of the Association for the Advancement of Women. Born at Nantucket, MA, Mitchell died June 28, 1889, at Lynn, MA. For more info: *Maria's Comet*, by Deborah Hopkinson (Simon & Schuster, 0-689-81501-8, $16 Gr. K–3).

NATIONAL INVENTORS' MONTH. Aug 1–31. To educate the American public about the value of creativity and inventiveness and the importance of inventions and inventors to the quality of our lives. This will be accomplished through specially designed displays for libraries, an interactive website and the placement of media stories about living inventors in most of the top national, local and trade publications. Sponsored by the United Inventors Association of the USA (UIA-USA), the Academy of Applied Science and *Inventors' Digest*. For info: Joanne Hayes-Rines, *Inventors' Digest*. Phone: (617) 367-4540. Fax: (617) 723-6988. E-mail: joanne@inventorsdigest.com. Web: www.inventorsdigest.com.

August 2005

S	M	T	W	T	F	S
	1	2	3	4	5	6
7	8	9	10	11	12	13
14	15	16	17	18	19	20
21	22	23	24	25	26	27
28	29	30	31			

OAK RIDGE ATOMIC PLANT BEGUN: ANNIVERSARY. Aug 1, 1943. Ground was broken at Oak Ridge, TN, for the first plant built to manufacture the uranium 235 needed to build an atomic bomb. The plant was largely completed by July of 1944 at a final cost of $280 million. By August 1945 the total cost for development of the A-bomb ran to $1 billion.

SWITZERLAND: CONFEDERATION DAY. Aug 1. National holiday. Anniversary of the founding of the Swiss Confederation. Commemorates a pact made in 1291. Parades, patriotic gatherings, bonfires and fireworks. Young citizens' coming-of-age ceremonies. Observed since the 600th anniversary of Swiss Confederation was celebrated in 1891.

TRINIDAD AND TOBAGO: EMANCIPATION DAY. Aug 1. Public holiday.

WORLD WIDE WEB: 15th ANNIVERSARY. Aug 1, 1990. The creation of what would become the World Wide Web was suggested this month by Tim Berners-Lee at CERN, the European Laboratory for Particle Physics at Switzerland. By October, he had designed a prototype Web browser. By early 1993, there were 50 Web servers worldwide.

ZAMBIA: YOUTH DAY. Aug 1. National holiday. Focal point is Lusaka's Independence Stadium. Annually, the first Monday in August.

BIRTHDAYS TODAY

Gail Gibbons, 61, author and illustrator (*Fire! Fire!*), born Oak Park, IL, Aug 1, 1944.

Edgerrin James, 27, football player, born Immokalee, FL, Aug 1, 1978.

AUGUST 2 — TUESDAY

Day 214 — 151 Remaining

ALBERT EINSTEIN'S ATOMIC BOMB LETTER: ANNIVERSARY. Aug 2, 1939. Albert Einstein, world-famous scientist, a refugee from Nazi Germany, wrote a letter to US President Franklin D. Roosevelt, first mentioning a possible "new phenomenon . . . chain reactions . . . vast amounts of power" and "the construction of bombs." "A single bomb of this type," he wrote, "carried by boat and exploded in a port, might very well destroy the whole port together with some of the surrounding territory." A historic letter that marked the beginning of atomic weaponry. Six years and four days later, Aug 6, 1945, the Japanese city of Hiroshima was destroyed by the first atomic bombing of a populated place.

COSTA RICA: FEAST OF OUR LADY OF THE ANGELS. Aug 2. National holiday. In honor of Costa Rica's patron saint.

DECLARATION OF INDEPENDENCE: OFFICIAL SIGNING: ANNIVERSARY. Aug 2, 1776. Contrary to widespread misconceptions, the 56 signers did not sign as a group and did not do so July 4, 1776. John Hancock and Charles Thomson signed only draft copies that day, the official day the Declaration was adopted by Congress. The signing of the official declaration occurred Aug 2, 1776, when 50 men probably took part. George Washington, Patrick Henry and several others were not in Philadelphia and thus were unable to sign. Later that year, five more signed separately and one added his name in a subsequent year. (From "Signers of the Declaration . . ." US Dept of the Interior, 1975.) See also: "Declaration of Independence: Approval and Signing" (July 4). For more info: *Give Me Liberty! The Story of the Declaration of Independence*, by Russell Freedman (Holiday House, 0-8234-1448-5, $24.95 Gr. 5 & up).

AUGUST
ADOPTING AN ANIMAL

As you begin your school year, you might want to investigate animal "adoptions" for your class for yearlong education. Animal adoptions from zoos and other organizations are a powerful way for young people to connect with animals, geography and conservation efforts around the world. It is an opportunity to focus on and learn about one animal's biology and habitat while at the same time supporting conservation, education and care of animals. Students derive a sense of pride and satisfaction from knowing that they are helping an animal to survive, whether it be in a zoo or in the wild. Zoos, aquariums, animal rehabilitation centers and conservation groups offer many different programs which are easy to integrate into any unit on animals or habitats.

It is important to be very clear with the students so that they understand that adopting an animal doesn't mean that they actually get to bring the animal home. Many a student has been disappointed to find that they wouldn't be keeping a tiger or manatee in their classroom. The adoption is symbolic. So where does the money go, if not into a pet giraffe? Many zoos put your donation into the care, medication, feeding and housing of the animals they keep, as well as for educational programs that teach visitors about animals and conservation. Some organizations use the donations to preserve habitat for animals in the wild. The World Wildlife Fund, for example, uses donations for cold-weather animals like polar bears and snow leopards by fighting the causes of global warming that threaten their habitats.

Almost all organizations have similar sliding scale for the cost of adopting an animal. For around $30, you often receive a personalized adoption certificate, animal fact sheet and sometimes a photo of your animal. From $50–$250, benefits can include a plush toy, tote bag, T-shirt or more photos. Above the $250 level, a tour, visit or complimentary tickets are offered, sometimes to a limited number of people. You should investigate the perks of different levels of giving when you visit the organization's website. Some organizations offer benefits that do not seem that enticing to a child, like being listed in the group's annual report, or being invited to the director's reception. Others, like the Cincinnati Zoo, offer kid-friendly benefits, such as 32 wallet-sized photos, 32 trading cards or a grade-level-specific animal book with a personalized inscription.

You may want to choose an animal based on a unit that you already teach. In this case, you should search for that animal's name plus "adoption" on a search engine like Google. This way you can find specific organizations that are committed to the conservation of that animal. Conservation groups exist that focus exclusively on gorillas, sea turtles, manatees and whales, to name a few. You can also even adopt an entire habitat, such as a rainforest or coral reef.

If you have a specific animal in mind, however, your local zoo may not offer an adoption for that species. Some organizations only offer adoptions on attention-grabbers like the giant panda, cheetah, orangutan and elephant. Others open up their entire collection, offering close to 100 different choices, from the Andean condor to the naked mole rat to the hissing cockroach. A good place to start is the website of the American Zoo and Aquarium Association (www.aza.org). Out of the 2,400 "animal exhibitors" in the United States, only 212 are currently licensed by the AZA. Affiliation with the AZA ensures that your donation is going to an organization with high standards of animal care, education and conservation.

While your local zoo or conservation group might not have the exact animal you're looking for, there is great benefit in working locally. Your students can actually meet "their" animal up close and in person. A visit to a local organization helps form bonds between child and animal, and it makes their stewardship more real. It will be something that your students will remember for the rest of their lives.

—Adrienne van den Beemt

DISABILITY DAY IN KENTUCKY. Aug 2.

HOLLING, HOLLING C.: BIRTH ANNIVERSARY. Aug 2, 1900. Author and illustrator (*Paddle-to-the-Sea;* Newbery Honors for *Seabird* and *Minn of the Mississippi*), born Holling Allison Clancy at Holling Corners, MI. Died Sept 7, 1973.

IRAQ INVADES KUWAIT: 15th ANNIVERSARY. Aug 2, 1990. Iraq invaded Kuwait. President Saddam Hussein claimed that Kuwait presented a serious threat to Iraq's economic existence by overproducing oil and driving prices down on the world market. After conquering the capital, Kuwait City, Hussein annexed the country to Iraq on the claim that Kuwait was historically part of Iraq. The US and most other nations immediately condemned the aggression and the UN passed measures calling for broad economic sanctions against Iraq. As Iraqi forces began to mass along the border with Saudi Arabia, the US and other nations sent troops to Saudi Arabia to protect that country from invasion. This US military operation, named Desert Shield, was the largest mobilization of forces since the Vietnam War. The following January, Desert Shield became Operation Desert Storm as the Allied forces went to war against Iraq.

L'ENFANT, PIERRE CHARLES: BIRTH ANNIVERSARY. Aug 2, 1754. The architect, engineer and Revolutionary War officer who designed the plan for the city of Washington, DC, Pierre Charles L'Enfant was born at Paris, France. He died at Prince Georges County, MD, June 14, 1825.

MACEDONIA, FORMER YUGOSLAV REPUBLIC OF: NATIONAL DAY. Aug 2. Commemorates the nationalist uprising against the Ottoman Empire in 1903. Also known as St. Elias Day, the most sacred and celebrated day of the Macedonian people.

NATIONAL NIGHT OUT. Aug 2. Designed to heighten crime prevention awareness and to promote police-community partnerships. Annually, the first Tuesday in August. For info: Matt A. Peskin, Dir, National Assn of Town Watch, PO Box 303, Wynnewood, PA 19096. Phone: (610) 649-7055 or (800) 648-3688. Fax: (610) 649-5456. E-mail: info@natw.org. Web: www.natw.org.

US VIRGIN ISLANDS NATIONAL PARK ESTABLISHED: ANNIVERSARY. Aug 2, 1956. Areas on St. John and St. Thomas in the Virgin Islands were established as a national park and preserve. On Oct 5, 1962, Virgin Islands National Park was extended to offshore areas, including coral reefs, shorelines and sea grass beds. For more info: www.nps.gov/viis/index.htm.

BIRTHDAYS TODAY

Hallie Kate Eisenberg, 13, actress (*Beautiful, The Miracle Worker*), born East Brunswick, NJ, Aug 2, 1992.

James Howe, 59, author (the Bunnicula series), born Oneida, NY, Aug 2, 1946.

John Snow, 66, US Secretary of the Treasury, born Toledo, OH, Aug 2, 1939.

Michael Weiss, 29, figure skater, born Washington, DC, Aug 2, 1976.

★ ★ ★

AUGUST 3 — WEDNESDAY

Day 215 — 150 Remaining

COLUMBUS SAILS FOR THE NEW WORLD: ANNIVERSARY. Aug 3, 1492. Christopher Columbus, "Admiral of the Ocean Sea," set sail half an hour before sunrise from Palos, Spain. With three ships, the *Niña*, the *Pinta* and the *Santa Maria*, and a crew of 90, he sailed "for Cathay" but found instead a New World of the Americas, first landing at Guanahani (San Salvador Island in the Bahamas), Oct 12. See also: "Columbus Day (Traditional)" (Oct 12).

EQUATORIAL GUINEA: ARMED FORCES DAY. Aug 3. National holiday.

GUINEA-BISSAU: COLONIZATION MARTYR'S DAY. Aug 3. National holiday is observed.

MUSTANG LEAGUE WORLD SERIES. Aug 3–6. Irving, TX. International youth baseball World Series for players of league ages 9 and 10. Est attendance: 6,000. For info: PONY Baseball, Inc, PO Box 225, Washington, PA 15301. Phone: (724) 225-1060. Fax: (724) 225-9852. E-mail: info@pony.org. Web: www.pony.org.

NIGER: INDEPENDENCE DAY. Aug 3. Commemorates the independence of this West African nation from France on this date in 1960.

OHIO STATE FAIR. Aug 3–14. Columbus, OH. Family fun, amusement rides, games, food booths, parades, entertainment, agricultural exhibits and educational displays. Est attendance: 900,000. For info: Ohio State Fair, 717 E 17th Ave, Columbus, OH 43211. Phone: (614) 644-4000. Fax: (614) 644-4031. Web: www.ohiostatefair.com.

SCOPES, JOHN T.: BIRTH ANNIVERSARY. Aug 3, 1900. Central figure in a cause célèbre (the "Scopes Trial" or the "Monkey Trial"), John Thomas Scopes was born at Paducah, KY. An obscure 24-year-old schoolteacher at the Dayton, TN, high school in 1925, he became the focus of world attention. Scopes never uttered a word at his trial, which was a contest between two of America's best-known lawyers (William Jennings Bryan and Clarence Darrow). The trial, July 10–21, 1925, resulted in Scopes's conviction "for teaching evolution" in Tennessee. He was fined $100. The verdict was upset on a technicality and the statute he was accused of breaching was repealed in 1967. Scopes died at Shreveport, LA, Oct 21, 1970. For more info: *The Scopes Monkey Trial: A Headline Court Case*, by Freya Ottem Hanson (Enslow, 0-7660-1388-X, $19.95 Gr. 8 & up) or www.umkc.edu/famoustrials.

August 2005

S	M	T	W	T	F	S
	1	2	3	4	5	6
7	8	9	10	11	12	13
14	15	16	17	18	19	20
21	22	23	24	25	26	27
28	29	30	31			

SCOTLAND: ABERDEEN INTERNATIONAL YOUTH FESTIVAL. Aug 3–13. Aberdeen, Scotland. Talented young people from all areas of the performing arts come from around the world to participate in this festival. Est attendance: 30,000. For info: Stephen Stenning, Linksfield Community Centre, 520 King St, Aberdeen, Scotland, AB24 5SS. Phone: (44) (1224) 484-400. Fax: (44) (1224) 484-114. E-mail: admin@aiyf.org. Web: www.aiyf.org.

BIRTHDAYS TODAY

Tom Brady, 28, football player, born San Mateo, CA, Aug 3, 1977.

Mary Calhoun, 79, author (*High-Wire Henry*), born Keokuk, IA, Aug 3, 1926.

Troy Glaus, 29, baseball player, born Tarzana, CA, Aug 3, 1976.

Blaine Wilson, 31, Olympic gymnast, born Columbus, OH, Aug 3, 1974.

AUGUST 4 — THURSDAY

Day 216 — 149 Remaining

ARMSTRONG, LOUIS: BIRTH ANNIVERSARY. Aug 4, 1900. Jazz musician extraordinaire, born at New Orleans, LA. (Some sources list 1901.) Asked to define jazz, Armstrong reportedly replied, "Man, if you gotta ask, you'll never know." The trumpet player was also known as Satchmo. He appeared in many films. Popular singles included "What a Wonderful World" and "Hello, Dolly" (with Barbra Streisand). Died at New York, NY, July 6, 1971.

BRONCO LEAGUE WORLD SERIES. Aug 4–9. Monterey, CA. International youth baseball World Series for players of league ages 11 and 12. Est attendance: 15,000. For info: PONY Baseball, PO Box 225, Washington, PA 15301. Phone: (724) 225-1060. Fax: (724) 225-9852. E-mail: info@pony.org. Web: www.pony.org.

BURKINA FASO: REVOLUTION DAY. Aug 4. National holiday. Commemorates a 1983 coup.

COAST GUARD DAY. Aug 4. Celebrates anniversary of founding of the US Coast Guard in 1790.

MANDELA, NELSON: ARREST: ANNIVERSARY. Aug 4, 1962. Nelson Rolihlahla Mandela, charismatic black South African leader, was born in 1918, the son of the Tembu tribal chief, at Umtata, Transkei territory of South Africa. A lawyer and political activist, Mandela, who in 1952 established the first black law partnership in South Africa, had been in conflict with the white government there much of his life. Acquitted of a treason charge after a trial that lasted from 1956 to 1961, he was apprehended again by security police, Aug 4, 1962. The subsequent trial, widely viewed as an indictment of white domination, resulted in Mandela's being sentenced to five years in prison. In 1963 he was taken from the Pretoria prison to face a new trial—for sabotage, high treason and conspiracy to overthrow the government—and in June 1964 he was sentenced to life in prison. See also: "Mandela, Nelson: Prison Release: Anniversary" (Feb 11).

MOON PHASE: NEW MOON. Aug 4. Moon enters New Moon phase at 11:05 PM, EDT.

SCHUMAN, WILLIAM HOWARD: BIRTH ANNIVERSARY. Aug 4, 1910. Born at New York, NY, American composer who won the first Pulitzer Prize for composition and founded the Juilliard School of Music. His compositions include *American Festival Overture*, the baseball opera *The Mighty Casey* and *On Freedom's Ground*, written for the centennial of the Statue of Liberty in 1986. He was instrumental in the conception of the Lincoln Center for the Performing Arts and served as its first president. In 1985 he was awarded a special Pulitzer Prize. He also received a National Medal of Arts in 1985 and a Kennedy Center Honor in 1989. Schuman died at New York City, Feb 15, 1992.

WISCONSIN STATE FAIR. Aug 4–14. State Fair Park, Milwaukee, WI. Wisconsin celebrates its rural heritage at the state's most popular and most historic annual event. Features giant midway, 26 free stages, livestock, food and flower judging and top-name entertainment. (Call 24-hour recorded information line at 1-800-884-FAIR for up-to-date information.) Est attendance: 910,000. For info: PR Dept, Wisconsin State Fair Park, PO Box 14990, West Allis, WI 53214-0990. Phone: (414) 266-7000. Fax: (414) 266-7007. E-mail: wsfp@sfp.state.wi.us. Web: www.wistatefair.com.

BIRTHDAYS TODAY

Nancy White Carlstrom, 57, author (*Jesse Bear, What Will You Wear?, Does God Know How to Tie Shoes?*), born Washington, PA, Aug 4, 1948.
Roger Clemens, 43, baseball player, born Dayton, OH, Aug 4, 1962.
Jeff Gordon, 34, race car driver, born Pittsboro, IN, Aug 4, 1971.
Barack Obama, 44, US Senator (D, Illinois), born Honolulu, HI, Aug 4, 1961.

AUGUST 5 — FRIDAY

Day 217 — 148 Remaining

BATTLE OF MOBILE BAY: ANNIVERSARY. Aug 5, 1864. A Union fleet under Admiral David Farragut attempted to run past three Confederate forts into Mobile Bay, AL. After coming under fire, the Union fleet headed into a maze of underwater mines, known at that time as torpedos. The ironclad *Tecumseh* was sunk by a torpedo, after which Farragut is said to have exclaimed, "Damn the torpedos, full steam ahead." The Union fleet was successful and Mobile Bay was secured.

BURKINA FASO: REPUBLIC DAY. Aug 5. Burkina Faso (formerly Upper Volta) gained autonomy from France in 1960.

CROATIA: HOMELAND THANKSGIVING DAY. Aug 5. National holiday.

ELIOT, JOHN: BIRTH ANNIVERSARY. Aug 5, 1604. American "Apostle to the Indians," translator of the Bible into an Indian tongue (the first Bible to be printed in America), was born at Hertfordshire, England. He died at Roxbury, MA, May 21, 1690.

FIRST ENGLISH COLONY IN NORTH AMERICA: FOUNDING ANNIVERSARY. Aug 5, 1583. Sir Humphrey Gilbert, English navigator and explorer, aboard his sailing ship, the *Squirrel*, sighted the Newfoundland coast and took possession of the area around St. John's harbor in the name of the Queen, thus establishing the first English colony in North America. Gilbert was lost at sea, in a storm off the Azores, on his return trip to England.

LYNCH, THOMAS: BIRTH ANNIVERSARY. Aug 5, 1749. Signer, Declaration of Independence, born Prince George's Parish, SC. Died 1779 (lost at sea, exact date of death unknown).

NEW JERSEY STATE FAIR/SUSSEX COUNTY FARM AND HORSE SHOW. Aug 5–14. Augusta, NJ. The state's largest livestock and horse show also includes educational exhibits, amusements, commercial exhibits and entertainment. Located off Rt 206 and Plains Rd. Gate opens 1 PM Friday and closes 7 PM Sunday. For info: New Jersey State Fair, PO Box 2456, Branchville, NJ 07826. Phone: (973) 948-5500. Fax: (973) 948-0147. E-mail: thefair@njstatefair.com. Web: www.njstatefair.com.

WALLENBERG, RAOUL: BIRTH ANNIVERSARY. Aug 5, 1912. Swedish architect Raoul Gustaf Wallenberg was born at Stockholm, Sweden. He was the second person in history (Winston Churchill was the first) to be voted honorary American citizenship (US House of Representatives 396–2, Sept 22, 1981). He is credited with saving 100,000 Hungarian Jews from almost certain death at the hands of the Nazis during WWII. Wallenberg was arrested by Soviet troops at Budapest, Hungary, Jan 17, 1945, and, according to the official Soviet press agency Tass, died in prison at Moscow, July 17, 1947.

BIRTHDAYS TODAY

Neil Alden Armstrong, 75, former astronaut (first man to walk on moon), born Wapakoneta, OH, Aug 5, 1930.
Brendon Ryan Barrett, 19, actor (*Casper*), born Roseville, CA, Aug 5, 1986.
Patrick Aloysius Ewing, 43, former basketball player, born Kingston, Jamaica, Aug 5, 1962.
Lorrie Fair, 27, soccer player, born Los Altos, CA, Aug 5, 1978.
Eric Hinske, 28, baseball player, born Menasha, WI, Aug 5, 1977.
John Olerud, 37, baseball player, born Seattle, WA, Aug 5, 1968.

AUGUST 6 — SATURDAY

Day 218 — 147 Remaining

ATOMIC BOMB DROPPED ON HIROSHIMA: 60th ANNIVERSARY. Aug 6, 1945. At 8:15 AM, local time, an American B-29 bomber, the *Enola Gay*, dropped an atomic bomb named "Little Boy" over the center of the city of Hiroshima, Japan. The bomb exploded about 1,800 ft above the ground, killing more than 105,000 civilians and destroying the city. It is estimated that another 100,000 persons were injured and died subsequently as a direct result of the bomb and the radiation it produced. This was the first time in history that such a devastating weapon had been used by any nation.

BOLIVIA: INDEPENDENCE DAY. Aug 6. National holiday. Gained freedom from Spain in 1825. Named after Simon Bolivar.

COONEY, BARBARA: BIRTH ANNIVERSARY. Aug 6, 1917. Children's author and illustrator, born at Brooklyn, NY. Cooney won Caldecott Medals for *Ox-Cart Man* and *Chanticleer and the Fox*. Her 1982 publication *Miss Rumphius* received the National Book Award for 1983. She died at Portland, ME, Mar 14, 2000.

FARBER, NORMA: BIRTH ANNIVERSARY. Aug 6, 1909. Poet (*How the Hibernators Came to Bethlehem*), born at Boston, MA. Died Mar 21, 1984, at Boston.

FIRST WOMAN SWIMS THE ENGLISH CHANNEL: ANNIVERSARY. Aug 6, 1926. The first woman to swim the English Channel was 19-year-old Gertrude Ederle of New York, NY. Her swim was completed in 14 hours and 31 minutes. For more info: *America's Champion Swimmer: Gertrude Ederle*, by David A. Adler (Harcourt/Gulliver, 0-15-201969-3, $16 Gr. K–3). See also: "Ederle, Gertrude: Birth Anniversary" (Oct 23).

FLEMING, ALEXANDER: BIRTH ANNIVERSARY. Aug 6, 1881. Sir Alexander Fleming, Scottish bacteriologist, discoverer of penicillin and 1954 Nobel Prize recipient, was born at Lochfield, Scotland. He died at London, England, Mar 11, 1955.

"GREAT DEBATE": ANNIVERSARY. Aug 6–Sept 10, 1787. The Constitutional Convention engaged in the "Great Debate" over the draft constitution, during which it determined that Congress should have the right to regulate foreign trade and interstate commerce, established a four-year term of office for the president and appointed a five-man committee to prepare a final draft of the Constitution.

HIROSHIMA DAY. Aug 6. There are memorial observances in many places for victims of the first atomic bombing of a populated place, which occurred at Hiroshima, Japan, in 1945, when an American B-29 bomber dropped an atomic bomb over the center of the city. More than 205,000 civilians died either immediately in the explosion or subsequently of radiation. A peace festival is held annually at Peace Memorial Park at Hiroshima in memory of the victims of the bombing.

JAMAICA: INDEPENDENCE ACHIEVED: ANNIVERSARY. Aug 6, 1962. Jamaica attained its independence this date after centuries of British rule. Independence Day is observed on the first Monday in August (Aug 1 in 2005).

NATIONAL MUSTARD DAY. Aug 6. Mustard lovers across the nation pay tribute to the king of condiments by slathering their favorite mustard on hot dogs, pretzels, circus peanuts and all things edible. The Mount Horeb Mustard Museum holds the world's largest collection of prepared mustards and mustard memorabilia. Activities include mustard games, street music and lots of great food (with mustard, of course!). Join in the mustard college fight song with the "POUPON U" marching band. Annually, the first Saturday in August. Est attendance: 1,000. For info: Barry M. Levenson, Curator, The Mount Horeb Mustard Museum, 100 W Main St, Mount Horeb, WI 53572. Phone: (608) 437-3986. Fax: (608) 437-4018. E-mail: curator@mustardmuseum.com. Web: www.mustardmuseum.com.

ROOSEVELT, EDITH KERMIT CAROW: BIRTH ANNIVERSARY. Aug 6, 1861. Second wife of Theodore Roosevelt, 26th president of the US, whom she married in 1886. Born at Norwich, CT, she died at Long Island, NY, Sept 30, 1948.

VOTING RIGHTS ACT OF 1965 SIGNED: 40th ANNIVERSARY. Aug 6, 1965. Signed into law by President Lyndon Johnson, the Voting Rights Act of 1965 was designed to thwart attempts to discriminate against minorities at the polls. The act suspended literacy and other disqualifying tests, authorized appointment of federal voting examiners and provided for judicial relief on the federal level to bar discriminatory poll taxes. Congress voted to extend the Act in 1975, 1984 and 1991.

WORLD'S LARGEST, SMELLIEST FLOWER DISCOVERED BY SCIENCE. Aug 6, 1878. Exploring the rainforests of Sumatra in Indonesia, Italian botanist Dr. Odoardo Beccari found the titan arum (*Amorphophallus titanum*), or "corpse flower." Growing from a tuber that can weigh as much as 170 pounds, this plant sports a single leaf that can reach 20 feet by 15 feet. It flowers seldomly in its long life, but the bloom can reach 6 to 10 feet. (Precisely, it is not a flower but an inflorescence, or cluster of blooms.) As it blooms, for 8 hours it releases an incredibly foul odor that attracts pollinating insects. It first bloomed in cultivation at the Royal Botanic Gardens at Kew in England in 1889, and in the US at the New York Botanic Garden in 1937. For more info: see the Fairchild Tropical Garden page on "Mr Stinky's" 2001 blooming at www.fairchildgarden.org/blooms/amorphophallus01.html.

★ ★ ★

August 2005

S	M	T	W	T	F	S
	1	2	3	4	5	6
7	8	9	10	11	12	13
14	15	16	17	18	19	20
21	22	23	24	25	26	27
28	29	30	31			

BIRTHDAYS TODAY

Frank Asch, 59, author and illustrator (*Mooncake*), born Somerville, NJ, Aug 6, 1946.

Catherine Hicks, 54, actress ("7th Heaven"), born Scottsdale, AZ, Aug 6, 1951.

David Robinson, 40, former basketball player, born Key West, FL, Aug 6, 1965.

AUGUST 7 — SUNDAY

Day 219 — 146 Remaining

AMERICAN FAMILY DAY IN ARIZONA. Aug 7. Commemorated on the first Sunday in August.

BUNCHE, RALPH JOHNSON: BIRTH ANNIVERSARY. Aug 7, 1904. American statesman, UN official, Nobel Peace Prize recipient (the first black to win the award), born at Detroit, MI. Died Dec 9, 1971, at New York, NY. For more info: *Ralph J. Bunche: Peacemaker*, by Patricia and Fredrick McKissack (Enslow, 0-8949-0300-4, $14.95 Gr. K–3).

COLOMBIA: BATTLE OF BOYACÁ DAY. Aug 7. National holiday. Commemorates 1819 victory over Spanish forces.

CÔTE D'IVOIRE: NATIONAL DAY. Aug 7. Commemorates the independence of the Ivory Coast from France in 1960.

SPACE MILESTONE: FIRST PICTURE OF EARTH FROM SPACE. Aug 7, 1959. US satellite *Explorer VI* transmitted the first picture of Earth from space. For the first time we had a likeness of our planet based on more than projections and conjectures. For a current view of Earth from a satellite, visit Earth Viewer: www.fourmilab.to/earthview.

ISING, RUDOLF C.: BIRTH ANNIVERSARY. Aug 7, 1903. Cocreator (with Hugh Harman) and producer of the cartoons "Looney Tunes" and "Merrie Melodies," Ising was born at Kansas City, MO. Their production *Bosko the Talk-Ink Kid* (1929) was the first talkie cartoon synchronizing dialogue on the soundtrack with the action on screen. Ising received an Academy Award in 1948 for *Milky Way*, a cartoon about three kittens. He died July 18, 1992, at Newport Beach, CA.

NATIONAL KIDSDAY. Aug 7. A day to celebrate and honor children by spending meaningful time with them. Sponsored by the Boys and Girls Clubs of America and KidsPeace®. Annually, the first Sunday in August. For info: National Kidsday Mgmt, c/o Boys and Girls Clubs of America, 1230 W Peachtree St NW, Atlanta, GA 30309-3447. Phone: (404) 487-5700. Fax: (404) 487-5787. E-mail: kidsday@bgca.org. Web: www.kidsday.net.

PURPLE HEART: ANNIVERSARY. Aug 7, 1782. At Newburgh, NY, General George Washington ordered the creation of a Badge of Military Merit. The badge consisted of a purple cloth heart with silver braided edge. Only three are known to have been awarded during the Revolutionary War. The award was reinstituted on the bicentennial of Washington's birth, Feb 22, 1932, and recognizes those wounded in action.

SISTERS' DAY. Aug 7. Celebrating the spirit of sisterhood—sisters nationwide show appreciation and give recognition to one another for the special relationship they share. Send a card, make a phone call, share memories, photos, flowers, candy, etc. Sisters may include biological sisters, sisterly friends, etc. Annually, the first Sunday in August. For info: Tricia Eleogram, 5112 Normandy Ave, Memphis, TN 38117. Phone: (901) 681-2145 or (901) 755-0751. Fax: (901) 754-9923. E-mail: MySistersDay@aol.com.

US WAR DEPARTMENT ESTABLISHED: ANNIVERSARY. Aug 7, 1789. The second presidential cabinet department, the War Department, was established by Congress. In 1947 it became part of the Department of Defense. See also: "US Department of Defense Created" (July 26).

BIRTHDAYS TODAY

Betsy Byars, 77, author (*The Summer of the Swans*, the Bingo Brown series), born Charlotte, NC, Aug 7, 1928.

Joy Cowley, 69, author (*Red-Eyed Tree Frog*), born New Zealand, Aug 7, 1936.

Édgar Rentería, 30, baseball player, born Barranquilla, Colombia, Aug 7, 1975.

AUGUST 8 — MONDAY

Day 220 — 145 Remaining

BHUTAN: NATIONAL DAY. Aug 8. National holiday observed commemorating independence from India in 1949.

BONZA BOTTLER DAY™. Aug 8. To celebrate when the number of the day is the same as the number of the month. Bonza Bottler Day™ is an excuse to have a party at least once a month. For info: Gail M. Berger, 14 Fernwood Dr, Taylors, SC 29687. Phone: (864) 609-9874. E-mail: gberger5@aol.com.

HENSON, MATTHEW A.: BIRTH ANNIVERSARY. Aug 8, 1866. American black explorer, born at Charles County, MD. He met Robert E. Peary while working in a Washington, DC, store in 1888 and was hired to be Peary's valet. He accompanied Peary on his seven subsequent Arctic expeditions. During the successful 1908–09 expedition to the North Pole, Henson and two of the four Inuit guides reached their destination on Apr 6, 1909. Peary arrived minutes later and verified the location. Henson's account of the expedition, *A Negro Explorer at the North Pole*, was published in 1912. In addition to the Congressional medal awarded all members of the North Pole expedition, Henson received the Gold Medal of the Geographical Society of Chicago and, at 81, was made an honorary member of the Explorers Club at New York, NY. Died Mar 9, 1955, at New York, NY. For more info: *Matthew Henson and the North Pole Expedition*, by Ann Graham Gaines (Child's World, 1-56766-743-0, $25.64 Gr. 4–6).

ODIE: BIRTHDAY. Aug 8, 1978. Commemorates the birthday of Odie, Garfield's sidekick, who first appeared in the "Garfield" comic strip on Aug 8, 1978. "Garfield" was created by Jim Davis.

RAWLINGS, MARJORIE KINNAN: BIRTH ANNIVERSARY. Aug 8, 1896. American short-story writer and novelist (*The Yearling*), born at Washington, DC. Rawlings died at St. Augustine, FL, Dec 14, 1953. For a study guide to *The Yearling*: glencoe.com/sec/literature/litlibrary.

SPACE MILESTONE: *GENESIS* (US). Aug 8, 2001. The robotic explorer *Genesis* was launched on a mission to gather tiny particles of the sun. Its three-year, 20 million-mile round-trip mission was to shed light on the origin of the solar system. It traveled to a spot where the gravitational pulls of the sun and the Earth are equal and gathered atoms from the solar wind hurtling by. In 2004 a capsule carrying the solar samples crashed to Earth.

TANZANIA: FARMERS' DAY. Aug 8. National holiday. Also called "Nane Nane" or "8-8."

BIRTHDAYS TODAY

JC Chasez, 29, singer ('N Sync), born Joshua Scott, Washington, DC, Aug 8, 1976.

Rashard Lewis, 26, basketball player, born Pineville, LA, Aug 8, 1979.

AUGUST 9 — TUESDAY

Day 221 — 144 Remaining

ATOMIC BOMB DROPPED ON NAGASAKI: 60th ANNIVERSARY. Aug 9, 1945. Three days after the atomic bombing of Hiroshima, an American B-29 bomber named *Bock's Car* left its base on Tinian Island carrying a plutonium bomb nicknamed "Fat Man." Its target was the Japanese city of Kokura, but because of clouds and poor visibility the bomber headed for a secondary target, Nagasaki, where at 11:02 AM, local time, it dropped the bomb, killing an estimated 70,000 persons and destroying about half the city. The next day the Japanese government surrendered, bringing WWII to an end.

COCHRAN, JACQUELINE: 25th DEATH ANNIVERSARY. Aug 9, 1980. American pilot Jacqueline Cochran was born at Pensacola, FL, in 1910. She began flying in 1932 and by the time of her death she had set more distance, speed and altitude records than any other pilot, male or female. She was founder and head of the WASPs (Women's Air Force Service Pilots) during WWII. She also won the Distinguished Service Medal in 1945 and the US Air Force Distinguished Flying Cross in 1969. She died at Indio, CA.

LASSEN VOLCANIC NATIONAL PARK ESTABLISHED: ANNIVERSARY. Aug 9, 1916. California's Lassen Peak and Cinder Cone National Monument, proclaimed May 6, 1907, and other wilderness land were combined and established as a national park. For more info: www.nps.gov/lavo/index.htm.

NIXON RESIGNS: ANNIVERSARY. Aug 9, 1974. Richard Milhous Nixon's resignation from the presidency of the US, which he had announced in a speech to the American people on Thursday evening, Aug 8, became effective at noon. Nixon, under threat of impeachment as a result of the Watergate scandal, became the first person to resign the presidency. He was succeeded by Vice President Gerald Rudolph Ford, the first person to serve as vice president and president without having been elected to either office. Ford granted Nixon a "full, free and absolute pardon" Sept 8, 1974. Although Nixon was the first US president to resign, two vice presidents had resigned: John C. Calhoun, Dec 18, 1832, and Spiro T. Agnew, Oct 10, 1973.

PERSEID METEOR SHOWERS. Aug 9–13. Among the best-known and most spectacular meteor showers are the Perseids, peaking about Aug 10–12. As many as 50–100 may be seen in a single night. Wish upon a "falling star"!

★ ★ ★

PIAGET, JEAN: BIRTH ANNIVERSARY. Aug 9, 1896. Born at Neuchâtel, Switzerland, Piaget is the major figure in developmental psychology. His theory of cognitive development still influences educators today. Piaget died at Geneva, Switzerland, Sept 16, 1980.

SINGAPORE: NATIONAL DAY: 40th ANNIVERSARY. Aug 9, 1965. Most festivals in Singapore are Chinese, Indian or Malay, but celebration of national day is shared by all to commemorate the withdrawal of Singapore from Malaysia and its becoming an independent state in 1965. Music, parades, dancing.

SOUTH AFRICA: NATIONAL WOMEN'S DAY. Aug 9. National holiday. Commemorates the march of women in Pretoria to protest the pass laws in 1956.

TRAVERS, P.L.: BIRTH ANNIVERSARY. Aug 9, 1899. Famous for her Mary Poppins series, Pamela L. Travers was born at Maryborough, Queensland, Australia. *Mary Poppins* was made into a movie by Disney in 1964. Travers died at London, England, Apr 23, 1996.

VEEP DAY. Aug 9. Commemorates the day in 1974 when Richard Nixon's resignation let Gerald Ford succeed to the presidency of the US. This was the first time the new Constitutional provisions for presidential succession in the Twenty-Fifth Amendment of 1967 were used. For info: Bob Birch, The Puns Corps, PO Box 2364, Falls Church, VA 22042-0364. Phone: (703) 533-3668.

WEBSTER-ASHBURTON TREATY SIGNED: ANNIVERSARY. Aug 9, 1842. The treaty delimiting the eastern section of the Canadian-American border was negotiated by the US Secretary of State, Daniel Webster, and Alexander Baring, president of the British Board of Trade. The treaty established the boundaries between the St. Croix and Connecticut rivers, between Lake Superior and the Lake of the Woods and between Lakes Huron and Superior. The treaty was signed at Washington, DC.

BIRTHDAYS TODAY

Chamique Holdsclaw, 28, basketball player, born Flushing, NY, Aug 9, 1977.

Whitney Houston, 42, singer ("And I Will Always Love You"), actress (*Waiting to Exhale*), born Newark, NJ, Aug 9, 1963.

Brett Hull, 41, hockey player, born Belleville, ON, Canada, Aug 9, 1964.

Hazel Hutchins, 53, author (*One Duck*), born Calgary, AB, Canada, Aug 9, 1952.

Patricia McKissack, 61, author, (*Christmas in the Big House, Goin' Someplace Special, A Picture of Freedom*), born Nashville, TN, Aug 9, 1944.

Deion Sanders, 38, former football and baseball player, born Ft Meyers, FL, Aug 9, 1967.

Seymour Simon, 74, author (*Earthquakes, The Universe*), born New York, NY, Aug 9, 1931.

August 2005

S	M	T	W	T	F	S
	1	2	3	4	5	6
7	8	9	10	11	12	13
14	15	16	17	18	19	20
21	22	23	24	25	26	27
28	29	30	31			

AUGUST 10 — WEDNESDAY

Day 222 — 143 Remaining

ECUADOR: INDEPENDENCE DAY. Aug 10. National holiday. Celebrates declaration of independence in 1809. Freedom from Spain attained May 24, 1822.

HOOVER, HERBERT CLARK: BIRTH ANNIVERSARY. Aug 10, 1874. The 31st president (Mar 4, 1929–Mar 3, 1933) of the US was born at West Branch, IA. Hoover was the first president born west of the Mississippi River and the first to have a telephone on his desk (installed Mar 27, 1929). "Older men declare war. But it is youth that must fight and die," he said at Chicago, IL, at the Republican National Convention, June 27, 1944. Hoover died at New York, NY, Oct 20, 1964. The Sunday nearest Aug 10th is observed in Iowa as Herbert Hoover Day (Aug 7 in 2005). For info: www.ipl.org/ref/POTUS.

INDIANA STATE FAIR. Aug 10–21. Indiana State Fairgrounds, Indianapolis, IN. Top-rated livestock exhibition, world-class harness racing, top country music, giant midway and Pioneer Village. Est attendance: 750,000. For info: Andy Klotz, Public Relations Dir, Indiana State Fair, 1202 E 38th St, Indianapolis, IN 46205-2869. Phone: (317) 927-7524. Fax: (317) 927-7578. Web: www.indianastatefair.com.

JAPAN'S UNCONDITIONAL SURRENDER: 60th ANNIVERSARY. Aug 10, 1945. A gathering to discuss surrender terms took place in Emperor Hirohito's bomb shelter; the participants were stalemated. Hirohito settled the question, believing continuation of the war would only result in further loss of Japanese lives. A message was transmitted to Japanese ambassadors in Switzerland and Sweden to accept the terms issued at Potsdam, July 26, 1945, except that the Japanese emperor's sovereignty must be maintained. The Allies devised a plan under which the emperor and the Japanese government would administer under the rule of the Supreme Commander of the Allied Powers, and the Japanese surrendered.

MICHIGAN STATE FAIR. Aug 10–21. State Fairgrounds, Detroit, MI. 2005 marks the centennial of the Michigan State Fair. Est attendance: 450,000. For info: State of Michigan, Dept of Agriculture, State Fairgrounds, Eight Mile Rd and Woodward Ave, Detroit, MI 48203. Phone: (313) 369-8250. Fax: (313) 369-8410. Web: www.michiganstatefair.com.

MISSOURI: ADMISSION DAY: ANNIVERSARY. Aug 10. Became 24th state in 1821.

SMITHSONIAN INSTITUTION FOUNDED: ANNIVERSARY. Aug 10, 1846. Founding of the Smithsonian Institution at Washington, DC, designed to hold the many scientifc, historical and cultural collections that belong to the US. The National Museum of Natural History, the National Zoo, the National Museum of American Art, the National Air and Space Museum and the National Gallery of Art are among the museums in the Smithsonian Institution. For info for teachers from the Smithsonian on the Web: educate.si.edu. For info: Smithsonian Institution, 900 Jefferson Dr SW, Washington, DC 20560. Phone: (202) 357-2700.

BIRTHDAYS TODAY

Thomas J. Dygard, 74, author of sports books (*Game Plan*), born Little Rock, AR, Aug 10, 1931.

AUGUST 11 — THURSDAY

Day 223 — 142 Remaining

ATCHISON, DAVID R.: BIRTH ANNIVERSARY. Aug 11, 1807. Missouri legislator who was president of the US for one day. Born at Frogtown, KY, Atchison's strong pro-slavery opinions made his name prominent in legislative debates. He served as president pro tempore of the Senate a number of times, and he became president of the US for one day—Sunday, Mar 4, 1849—pending the swearing in of President-elect Zachary Taylor, Mar 5, 1849. The city of Atchison, KS, and the county of Atchison, MO, are named for him. He died at Gower, MO, Jan 26, 1886.

CHAD: INDEPENDENCE DAY. Aug 11. National holiday. Commemorates independence from France in 1960.

FREDERICK DOUGLASS SPEAKS: ANNIVERSARY. Aug 11, 1841. Having escaped from slavery only three years earlier, Frederick Douglass was legally a fugitive when he first spoke before an audience. At an antislavery convention on Nantucket Island, Douglass spoke simply but eloquently about his life as a slave. His words were so moving that he was asked to become a full-time lecturer for the Massachusetts Anti-Slavery Society. Douglass became a brilliant orator, writer and abolitionist who championed the rights of blacks as well as the rights of all humankind.

FREEMAN, DON: BIRTH ANNIVERSARY. Aug 11, 1908. Author and illustrator (*Corduroy*), born at San Diego, CA. Died Feb 1, 1978.

HALEY, ALEX PALMER: BIRTH ANNIVERSARY. Aug 11, 1921. Born at Ithaca, NY, Alex Haley was raised by his grandmother at Henning, TN. In 1939 he entered the US Coast Guard and served as a cook, but eventually he became a writer and college professor. His first book, *The Autobiography of Malcolm X*, sold six million copies and was translated into eight languages. *Roots*, his Pulitzer Prize–winning book published in 1976, sold millions, was translated into 37 languages and was made into an eight-part TV miniseries in 1977. The story generated an enormous interest in family ancestry. Haley died at Seattle, WA, Feb 13, 1992.

IOWA STATE FAIR. Aug 11–21. Iowa State Fairgrounds, Des Moines, IA. One of America's oldest and largest state fairs. Since 1854, the Iowa State Fair is "still the one" for showcasing Iowa pride, talent and tradition. The Fair boasts one of the world's largest livestock shows. Ten-acre carnival, superstar grandstand stage shows, track events, spectacular free entertainment. 160-acre campgrounds. Est attendance: 1,008,000. For info: Kathie Swift, Mktg Dir, Iowa State Fair, PO Box 57130, Des Moines, IA 50317-0003. Phone: (515) 262-3111. Fax: (515) 262-6906. E-mail: info@iowastatefair.org. Web: www.iowastatefair.org.

MISSOURI STATE FAIR. Aug 11–21. Sedalia, MO. Livestock shows, commercial and competitive exhibits, horse show, car races, tractor pulls, carnival and headline musical entertainment. Economical family entertainment. Est attendance: 360,000. For info: Kimberly Allen, PR Dir, Missouri State Fair, 2503 W 16th, Sedalia, MO 65301. Phone: (800) 422-FAIR. Fax: (660) 827-8160. Web: www.mostatefair.com.

"RUGRATS" TV PREMIERE: ANNIVERSARY. Aug 11, 1991. This animated cartoon features the toddler children of several suburban families. One-year-old Tommy Pickles and his dog Spike play with 15-month-old twins Phil and Lil DeVille. Other characters include Tommy's three-year-old cousin Angelica, two-year-old Chuckie and Tommy's new brother Dil. Created by the animators of "The Simpsons." *The Rugrats Movie* was released in 1998 and *The Rugrats in Paris* in 2000.

SAINT CLARE OF ASSISI: FEAST DAY. Aug 11, 1253. Chiara Favorone di Offreduccio, a religious leader inspired by St. Francis of Assisi, was the first woman to write her own religious order rule. Born at Assisi, Italy, July 16, 1194, she died there Aug 11, 1253. A "Privilege of Poverty" freed her order from any constraint to accept material security, making the "Poor Clares" totally dependent on God.

ZIMBABWE: HEROES' DAY. Aug 11. National holiday. Followed by Defense Forces Day on Aug 12.

BIRTHDAYS TODAY

Joanna Cole, 61, author (the Magic School Bus series), born Newark, NJ, Aug 11, 1944.

Hulk Hogan, 52, wrestler, actor, born Terry Gene Bollea, Augusta, GA, Aug 11, 1953.

George Sullivan, 78, author (*Mathew Brady: His Life and His Photographs; Lewis and Clark; Helen Keller*), born in Massachusetts, Aug 11, 1927.

Stephen Wozniak, 55, Apple computer cofounder, born Sunnyvale, CA, Aug 11, 1950.

AUGUST 12 — FRIDAY

Day 224 — 141 Remaining

IBM PERSONAL COMPUTER INTRODUCED: ANNIVERSARY. Aug 12, 1981. Although IBM was one of the pioneers in making mainframe and other large computers, this was the company's first foray into the desktop computer market. The first PC cost the equivalent of $3,000 in today's dollars. Eventually, more IBM-compatible computers were manufactured by IBM's competitors than by IBM itself.

ILLINOIS STATE FAIR. Aug 12–21. Springfield, IL. Amusement rides, food booths, parade, various types of entertainment and tractor pulls. Est attendance: 1,100,000. For info: Bud Ford, Illinois State Fair, PO Box 19427, Springfield, IL 62794. Phone: (217) 782-6661. Fax: (217) 782-9115. Web: www.illinoisstatefair.com.

KING PHILIP ASSASSINATION: ANNIVERSARY. Aug 12, 1676. Philip, son of Massasoit, chief of the Wampanog tribe, was killed near Mt Hope, RI, by a renegade Indian of his own tribe, bringing to an end the first and bloodiest war between American Indians and white settlers of New England, a war that had raged for nearly two years and was known as King Philip's War.

MOON PHASE: FIRST QUARTER. Aug 12. Moon enters First Quarter phase at 10:38 PM, EDT.

SPACE MILESTONE: *ECHO I* (US): 45th ANNIVERSARY. Aug 12, 1960. First successful communications satellite in Earth's orbit launched, used to relay voice and TV signals from one ground station to another.

THAILAND: BIRTHDAY OF THE QUEEN. Aug 12. The entire kingdom of Thailand celebrates the birthday of Queen Sirikit.

UNITED NATIONS: INTERNATIONAL YOUTH DAY. Aug 12. A day to increase public awareness of calls for action in 10 priority areas: education, employment, hunger and poverty, health, environment, drug abuse, juvenile delinquency, leisure-time activities, girls and young women, and full and effective participation of youth (15 to 24 years old) in the life of society and in decision making. For info: United Nations, Dept of Public Info, New York, NY 10017. Web: www.un.org.

WEST VIRGINIA STATE FAIR. Aug 12–20. Lewisburg, WV. For info: The State Fair of West Virginia, PO Drawer 986, Lewisburg, WV 24901. Phone: (301) 645-1090. Web: www.statefairofwv.com.

BIRTHDAYS TODAY

Ruth Stiles Gannett, 82, author (*My Father's Dragon, Elmer and the Dragon*), born New York, NY, Aug 12, 1923.

Mary Ann Hoberman, 75, author (*One of Each; You Read to Me, I'll Read to You*), born Stamford, CT, Aug 12, 1930.

Ann M. Martin, 50, author (*A Corner of the Universe,* The Baby-Sitters Club series), born Princeton, NJ, Aug 12, 1955.

Fredrick McKissack, 66, author, with his wife Patricia (*Christmas in the Big House*), born Nashville, TN, Aug 12, 1939.

Walter Dean Myers, 68, author (*Slam!, Glory Field, Monster, Fallen Angels*), born Martinsburg, WV, Aug 12, 1937.

Kyla Pratt, 17, actress (*Dr. Dolittle,* "The Baby-Sitters Club"), born North Kansas City, MO, Aug 12, 1988.

Pete Sampras, 34, former tennis player, born Washington, DC, Aug 12, 1971.

Antoine Walker, 29, basketball player, born Chicago, IL, Aug 12, 1976.

AUGUST 13 — SATURDAY

Day 225 — 140 Remaining

BERLIN WALL ERECTED: ANNIVERSARY. Aug 13, 1961. Early in the morning, the East German government closed the border between the east and west sectors of Berlin with barbed wire fence to discourage further population movement to the west. Telephone and postal services were interrupted, and, later in the week, a concrete wall was built to strengthen the barrier between official crossing points. The dismantling of the wall began Nov 9, 1989. See also: "Berlin Wall Opened: Anniversary" (Nov 9). For more info: *The Berlin Wall*, by R.G. Grant (Raintree, 0-8172-5017-4, $28.55 Gr. 5–7).

BUD BILLIKEN PARADE. Aug 13. Chicago, IL. A parade especially for children begun in 1929 by Robert S. Abbott. The second largest parade in the US, it features bands, floats, drill teams and celebrities. Annually, the second Saturday in August. For info: Michael Brown, PR Dir, Chicago Defender Charities, 2400 S Michigan, Chicago, IL 60616. Phone: (312) 225-2400. Fax: (312) 255-9231.

August 2005

S	M	T	W	T	F	S
	1	2	3	4	5	6
7	8	9	10	11	12	13
14	15	16	17	18	19	20
21	22	23	24	25	26	27
28	29	30	31			

CAXTON, WILLIAM: BIRTH ANNIVERSARY. Aug 13, 1422. First English printer, born at Kent, England. Died at London, England, 1491. Caxton produced the first book printed in English (while working for a printer at Bruges, Belgium), the *Recuyell of the Histories of Troy*, in 1476, and in the autumn of 1476 set up a print shop at Westminster, becoming the first printer in England.

CENTRAL AFRICAN REPUBLIC: INDEPENDENCE DAY. Aug 13. Commemorates Proclamation of Independence from France of the Central African Republic in 1960.

NATIONAL UNDERWEAR DAY. Aug 13. A day for all Americans to show pride for their undergarments. Underwear doesn't get the recognition it properly deserves, and, considering the amount of time people spend picking them out each morning, they should be able to show off those undies a little bit more. Visit Freshpair.com to electronically sign a petition permanently designating Aug 13 National Underwear Day. For info: Sean Evans, 594 Broadway, Suite 506, New York, NY 10012. Phone: (212) 431-7900. Fax: (212) 202-4754. E-mail: sean@freshpair.com. Web: www.nationalunderwearday.com.

OAKLEY, ANNIE: BIRTH ANNIVERSARY. Aug 13, 1860. Annie Oakley was born at Darke County, OH. She developed an eye as a markswoman early as a child, becoming so proficient that she was able to pay off the mortgage on her family farm by selling the game she killed. A few years after defeating vaudeville marksman Frank Butler in a shooting match, she married him and they toured as a team until joining Buffalo Bill's Wild West Show in 1885. She was one of the star attractions for 17 years. She died Nov 3, 1926, at Greenville, OH. For more info: *Shooting for the Moon: The Amazing Life and Times of Annie Oakley*, by Stephen Krensky (Farrar, Straus and Giroux, 0-3743-6843-0, $17 Gr. K–3).

SPACE MILESTONE: *HELIOS* SOLAR WING. Aug 13, 2001. The solar-powered plane *Helios* broke the altitude records for propeller-driven aircraft and non-rocket planes, soaring as high as 96,500 feet. The plane was launched this day on the Hawaiian island of Kauai and returned to Earth on Aug 14, 2001. The plane has a wingspan longer than a Boeing 747 and uses solar-powered motors to power 14 propellers, flying at speeds as high as 170 MPH. NASA plans to develop similar craft for unmanned flights on Mars.

STONE, LUCY: BIRTH ANNIVERSARY. Aug 13, 1818. American women's rights pioneer, born near West Brookfield, MA, Lucy Stone dedicated her life to the abolition of slavery and the emancipation of women. A graduate of Oberlin College, she had to finance her education by teaching for nine years because her father did not favor college education for women. An eloquent speaker for her causes, she headed the list of 89 men and women who signed the call to the first national Woman's Rights Convention, held at Worcester, MA, October 1850. On May 1, 1855, she married Henry Blackwell. She and her husband aided in the founding of the American Suffrage Association, taking part in numerous referendum campaigns to win suffrage amendments to state constitutions. She died Oct 18, 1893, at Dorchester, MA.

TUNISIA: WOMEN'S DAY. Aug 13. General holiday. Celebration of independence of women.

WYOMING STATE FAIR & RODEO. Aug 13–20. Douglas, WY. Recognizing the products, achievements and cultural heritage of the people of Wyoming. Bringing together rural and urban citizens for an inexpensive, entertaining and educational experience. Features livestock show for beef, swine, sheep and horses, junior livestock show for beef, swine, sheep, horses, goats, dogs and rabbits, competitions and displays for culinary arts, needlework, visual arts and floriculture, 4-H and FFA county/chapters state qualifications competitions, youth talent show, Demo Derby, live entertainment, midway, PRCA rodeo and an all-woman rodeo (rough stock). Est attendance: 48,000. For info: Wyoming State Fair, Drawer 10, Douglas, WY 82633. Phone: (307) 358-2398. Fax: (307) 358-6030. E-mail: wyomingstatefair@netcommander.com. Web: www.wystatefair.com.

BIRTHDAYS TODAY

Michael Bennett, 27, football player, born Milwaukee, WI, Aug 13, 1978.

Fidel Castro, 78, President of Cuba, born Mayari, Cuba, Aug 13, 1927.

Bobby Clarke, 56, Hall of Fame hockey player, born Flim Flon, MB, Canada, Aug 13, 1949.

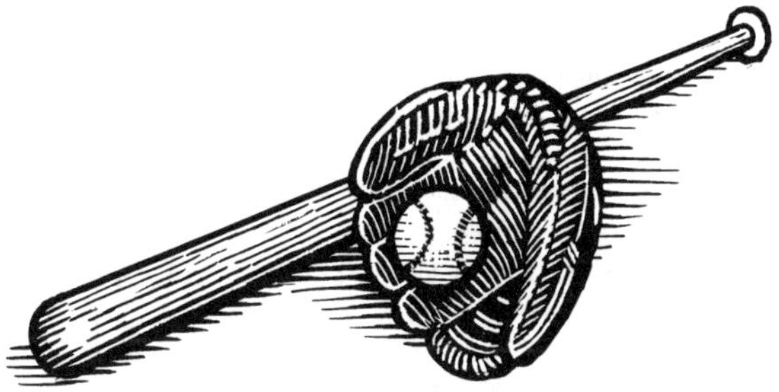

AUGUST 14 — SUNDAY

Day 226 — 139 Remaining

ATLANTIC CHARTER SIGNING: ANNIVERSARY. Aug 14, 1941. The charter grew out of a three-day conference aboard ship in the Atlantic Ocean, off the Newfoundland coast, and stated policies and goals for the postwar world. The eight-point agreement was signed by US President Franklin D. Roosevelt and British Prime Minister Winston S. Churchill.

INTERNATIONAL FEDERATION OF LIBRARY ASSOCIATIONS ANNUAL CONFERENCE. Aug 14–18. Oslo, Norway. The 71st annual conference. For info: IFLA 2005 Organizing Committee, Malerhaugveien 20, N-0661 Oslo, Norway. Phone: (47) 23 24 34 30. Fax: (47) 22 67 23 68. E-mail: ifla2005@norskbibliotekforening.no. Web: www.ifla.org.

SOCIAL SECURITY ACT: 70th ANNIVERSARY. Aug 14, 1935. The Congress approved the Social Security Act, which contained provisions for the establishment of a Social Security Board to administer federal old-age and survivors' insurance in the US. By signing the bill into law, President Franklin D. Roosevelt was fulfilling a 1932 campaign promise. For more info: www.ssa.gov.

V-J (VICTORY OVER JAPAN) DAY: 60th ANNIVERSARY. Aug 14, 1945. Anniversary of President Truman's announcement that Japan had surrendered to the Allies, setting off celebrations across the nation. Official ratification of surrender occurred aboard the USS *Missouri* at Tokyo Bay, Sept 2 (Far Eastern time).

BIRTHDAYS TODAY

Lynne Cheney, 64, Second Lady, wife of Richard Cheney, 46th vice president of US, born Casper, WY, Aug 14, 1941.

Terin Humphrey, 19, gymnast, born St. Joseph, MO, Aug 14, 1986.

Magic Johnson, 46, former basketball player, born Earvin Johnson, Jr, at Lansing, MI, Aug 14, 1959.

Gary Larson, 55, cartoonist ("The Far Side"), born Tacoma, WA, Aug 14, 1950.

Alice Provensen, 87, author and illustrator, with her husband Martin (Caldecott for *The Glorious Flight: Across the Channel with Louis Bleriot*), born Chicago, IL, Aug 14, 1918.

AUGUST 15 — MONDAY

Day 227 — 138 Remaining

ASSUMPTION OF THE VIRGIN MARY. Aug 15. Greek and Roman Catholic churches celebrate Mary's ascent to Heaven.

BONAPARTE, NAPOLEON: BIRTH ANNIVERSARY. Aug 15, 1769. Anniversary of the birth of French emperor Napoleon Bonaparte on the island of Corsica. He died in exile May 5, 1821, on the island of St. Helena. Public holiday at Corsica, France.

CANADA: YUKON DISCOVERY DAY. Aug 15. In the Klondike region of the Yukon, at Bonanza Creek (formerly known as Rabbit Creek), George Washington Carmack discovered gold Aug 16 or 17, 1896. During the following year more than 30,000 people joined the gold rush to the area. Anniversary is celebrated as a holiday (Discovery Day) in the Yukon, on nearest Monday.

CHAUVIN DAY. Aug 15. A day named for Nicholas Chauvin, French soldier from Rochefort, France, who idolized Napoleon and who eventually became a subject of ridicule because of his blind loyalty and dedication to anything French. Originally referring to bellicose patriotism, chauvinism has come to mean blind or absurdly intense attachment to any cause. Observed on Napoleon's birth anniversary because Chauvin's birth date is unknown.

CONGO (BRAZZAVILLE): NATIONAL HOLIDAY. Aug 15. National day of the People's Republic of the Congo. Commemorates independence from France in 1960.

DORMITION OF THEOTOKOS. Aug 15. According to New Calendar (Gregorian), the Dormition Fast is observed Aug 1–14, followed by Dormition of Theotokos Aug 15.

EQUATORIAL GUINEA: CONSTITUTION DAY. Aug 15. National holiday. Commemorates a 1982 revision of the constitution.

HARDING, FLORENCE KLING DeWOLFE: BIRTH ANNIVERSARY. Aug 15, 1860. Wife of Warren Gamaliel Harding, 29th president of the US, born at Marion, OH. Died at Marion, OH, Nov 21, 1924.

INDIA: INDEPENDENCE DAY. Aug 15. National holiday. Anniversary of Indian independence from Britain in 1947.

KOREA: LIBERATION DAY. Aug 15. National holiday commemorates acceptance by Japan of Allied terms of surrender in 1945, thereby freeing Korea from 36 years of Japanese domination. Also marks formal proclamation of the Republic of Korea in 1948. Military parades and ceremonies throughout country.

LIECHTENSTEIN: NATIONAL DAY. Aug 15. Public holiday.

NESBIT, E. (EDITH): BIRTH ANNIVERSARY. Aug 15, 1858. Born at London (some sources say Aug 19), Edith Nesbit wrote enduring works of fiction for children in several genres. Her realistic fiction included stories about the Bastable children (*The Wouldbegoods, The Story of the Treasure Seekers*) as well as standalone novels like *The Railway Children*. Some of her most famous fantasy novels included *The Enchanted Castle, The Five Children and It* and *The Phoenix and the Carpet*. She died at New Romney, Kent, England, May 4, 1924.

PANAMA CANAL OPENS: ANNIVERSARY. Aug 15, 1914. After years of delay and diplomatic maneuvering, construction began in 1904 on a waterway to pass through the country of Panama that would connect the Atlantic and the Pacific. The US controlled the rights, as directed by the Hay-Bunau-Varilla treaty, in a newly created Panama Canal Zone. On Jan 7, 1914, a self-propelled crane boat made the first passage through the canal. The first ocean steamer, the SS *Ancon,* passed through Aug 3, 1914, and the canal officially opened Aug 15, 1914.

TRANSCONTINENTAL US RAILWAY COMPLETION: ANNIVERSARY. Aug 15, 1870. The Golden Spike ceremony at Promontory Point, UT, May 10, 1869, was long regarded as the final link in a transcontinental railroad track reaching from an Atlantic port to a Pacific port. In fact, that link occurred unceremoniously on another date in another state. Diaries of engineers working at the site establish "the completion of a transcontinental track at a point 928 feet east of today's milepost 602, or 3,812 feet east of the present Union Pacific depot building at Strasburg (formerly Comanche)," CO. The final link was made at 2:53 PM, Aug 15, 1870. Annual celebration at Strasburg, CO, on a weekend in August. See also: "Golden Spike Driving: Anniversary" (May 10).

BIRTHDAYS TODAY

Ben Affleck, 33, actor (*Good Will Hunting, Daredevil*), born Berkeley, CA, Aug 15, 1972.

Stephen G. Breyer, 67, Associate Justice of the US Supreme Court, born San Francisco, CA, Aug 15, 1938.

Linda Ellerbee, 61, journalist, host of "Nick News," born Bryan, TX, Aug 15, 1944.

Jenny Kirk, 21, figure skater, born Newton, MA, Aug 15, 1984.

Jane Resh Thomas, 69, author (*Saying Good-bye to Grandma, Behind the Mask: The Life of Queen Elizabeth I*), born Kalamazoo, MI, Aug 15, 1936.

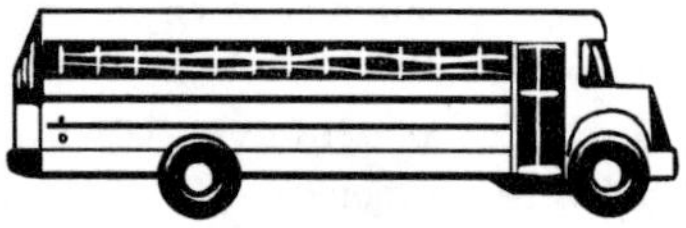

AUGUST 16 — TUESDAY

Day 228 — 137 Remaining

BENNINGTON BATTLE DAY: ANNIVERSARY. Aug 16, 1777. Anniversary of this Revolutionary War battle is a legal holiday in Vermont.

CHRISTOPHER, MATT: BIRTH ANNIVERSARY. Aug 16, 1917. Children's author known for his sports-related fiction and athlete biographies, he was born at Bath, PA. Some of his most popular titles include *The Kid Who Only Hit Homers, The Dog That Pitched a No-Hitter* and *The Basket Counts.* The series of sports biographies that bears his name features some of today's most popular athletes, including Sammy Sosa, Kobe Bryant and Tony Hawk. Christopher died in 1997, at Charlotte, NC.

DOMINICAN REPUBLIC: RESTORATION OF THE REPUBLIC. Aug 16. The anniversary of the Restoration of the Republic in 1863 is celebrated as an official public holiday.

SCHENK de REGNIERS, BEATRICE: BIRTH ANNIVERSARY. Aug 16, 1914. Author who perfectly captured the emotions of the young, she was born at Lafayette, IN. Her books included *May I Bring a Friend?* and *A Little House of Your Own,* and she edited the poetry collection *Sing a Song of Popcorn.* Died at Washington, DC, Mar 1, 2000.

August 2005

S	M	T	W	T	F	S
	1	2	3	4	5	6
7	8	9	10	11	12	13
14	15	16	17	18	19	20
21	22	23	24	25	26	27
28	29	30	31			

BIRTHDAYS TODAY

Diana Wynne Jones, 71, author (*Dark Lord of Derkholm, The Chronicles of Chrestomanci*), born London, England, Aug 16, 1934.

LL Cool J, 37, rap singer, born James Todd Smith, Queens, NY, Aug 16, 1968.

AUGUST 17 — WEDNESDAY

Day 229 — 136 Remaining

ARGENTINA: DEATH ANNIVERSARY OF SAN MARTÍN. Aug 17. National holiday. Commemorates the death in 1850 of the hero of the struggle for independence from Spain.

BALLOON CROSSING OF ATLANTIC OCEAN: ANNIVERSARY. Aug 17, 1978. Three Americans—Maxie Anderson, 44, Ben Abruzzo, 48, and Larry Newman, 31—all of Albuquerque, NM, became the first people to complete a transatlantic trip in a balloon. Starting from Presque Isle, ME, Aug 11, they traveled some 3,200 miles in 137 hours, 18 minutes, landing at Miserey, France (about 60 miles west of Paris), in their craft, named the *Double Eagle II.*

CROCKETT, DAVID "DAVY": BIRTH ANNIVERSARY. Aug 17, 1786. American frontiersman, adventurer and soldier, born at Hawkins County, TN. Died during final heroic defense of the Alamo, Mar 6, 1836, at San Antonio, TX. In his *Autobiography* (1834), Crockett wrote, "I leave this rule for others when I'm dead, be always sure you're right—then go ahead."

FORT SUMTER SHELLED BY NORTHERN FORCES: ANNIVERSARY. Aug 17, 1863. In what would become a long siege, Union forces began shelling Fort Sumter at Charleston, SC. The site of the first shots fired during the Civil War, Sumter endured the siege for a year and a half before being returned to Union hands. For more info: *The Firing on Fort Sumter: A Splintered Nation Goes to War,* by Nancy Colbert (Morgan Reynolds, 1-883846-51-X, $19.95 Gr. 6 & up).

FULTON SAILS STEAMBOAT: ANNIVERSARY. Aug 17, 1807. Robert Fulton began the first American steamboat trip between Albany and New York, NY, on a boat later called the *Clermont.* After years of promoting submarine warfare, Fulton engaged in a partnership with Robert R. Livingston, the US minister to France, allowing Fulton to design and construct a steamboat. His first success came in August 1803 when he launched a steam-powered vessel on the Seine. That same year the US Congress granted Livingston and Fulton exclusive rights to operate steamboats on New York waters during the next 20 years. The first Albany-to-New York trip took 32 hours to travel the 150-mile course. Although his efforts were labeled "Fulton's Folly" by his detractors, his success allowed the partnership to begin commercial service the next year, Sept 4, 1808.

GABON: NATIONAL DAY. Aug 17. National holiday. Commemorates independence from France in 1960.

INDONESIA: INDEPENDENCE DAY. Aug 17. National holiday. Republic proclaimed in 1945. It was only after several years of fighting, however, that Indonesia was formally granted its independence by the Netherlands, Dec 27, 1949.

SANDCASTLE DAY. Aug 17. Making sandcastles at the beach is a time-honored family tradition. Today is a day to recognize this tradition and celebrate it at beaches everywhere! For info: David Benson, 13116 Frog Hollow Ct, Oak Hill, VA 20171. Phone: (703) 471-5784. E-mail: David.C.Benson@saic.com.

TURKISH EARTHQUAKE: ANNIVERSARY. Aug 17, 1999. An earthquake with a magnitude of 7.4 struck northwestern Turkey where 45 percent of the population lives. More than 17,000 people died and thousands more remained missing. Many of the deaths were due to the shoddy construction of apartment buildings. On Nov 12, 1999, a magnitude 7.2 earthquake struck Turkey, killing more than 800 people. Also in 1999 there were earthquakes in Greece (139 dead) and Taiwan (2,200 dead). For more info go to the National Earthquake Information Center: wwwneic.cr .usgs.gov.

BIRTHDAYS TODAY

Norm Coleman, 56, US Senator (R, Minnesota), born Brooklyn, NY, Aug 17, 1949.

Christian Laettner, 36, basketball player, born Angola, NY, Aug 17, 1969.

Myra Cohn Livingston, 79, poet (*Sky Songs, Space Songs*), born Omaha, NE, Aug 17, 1926.

Donnie Wahlberg, 36, actor (*Band of Brothers*), singer (New Kids on the Block), born Boston, MA, Aug 17, 1969.

AUGUST 18 — THURSDAY

Day 230 — 135 Remaining

CLEMENTE, ROBERTO: BIRTH ANNIVERSARY. Aug 18, 1934. National League baseball player, born at Carolina, Puerto Rico. Drafted by the Pittsburgh Pirates in 1954, he played his entire major league career with them. Clemente died in a plane crash Dec 31, 1972, while on a mission of mercy to Nicaragua to deliver supplies he had collected for survivors of an earthquake. He was elected to the Baseball Hall of Fame in 1973.

DARE, VIRGINIA: BIRTH ANNIVERSARY. Aug 18, 1587. Virginia Dare, the first child of English parents to be born in the New World, was born to Ellinor and Ananias Dare, at Roanoke Island, NC. When a ship arrived to replenish their supplies in 1591, the settlers (including Virginia Dare) had vanished, without leaving a trace of the settlement.

KENTUCKY STATE FAIR (WITH WORLD CHAMPIONSHIP HORSE SHOW). Aug 18–28. Kentucky Fair and Expo Center, Louisville, KY. Held since 1904. Midway, concerts by nationally known artists and the World Championship Horse Show. Est attendance: 650,000. For info: KY Fair and Expo Center, Box 37130, Louisville, KY 40233. Phone: (502) 367-5000 or (502) 367-5291. Web: www.kyfairexpo.org or www.kystatefair.org.

LEWIS, MERIWETHER: BIRTH ANNIVERSARY. Aug 18, 1774. American explorer (of Lewis and Clark expedition), born at Albemarle County, VA. Died Oct 11, 1809, near Nashville, TN. For more info: *How We Crossed the West: The Adventures of Lewis & Clark*, by Rosalyn Schanzer (National Geographic, 0-79-223738-2, $18 Gr. 3–7).

MAIL-ORDER CATALOG: ANNIVERSARY. Aug 18, 1872. The first mail-order catalog was published by Montgomery Ward. It was only a single sheet of paper. By 1904, the Montgomery Ward catalog weighed four pounds. In 1985, Montgomery Ward closed its catalog business; in 2000, it announced it was closing its retail stores.

NINETEENTH AMENDMENT TO US CONSTITUTION RATIFIED: VOTES FOR WOMEN: 85th ANNIVERSARY. Aug 18, 1920. The 19th Amendment extended the right to vote to women.

BIRTHDAYS TODAY

Rosalynn Smith Carter, 78, former First Lady, wife of President Jimmy Carter, 39th president of the US, born Plains, GA, Aug 18, 1927.

Mike Johanns, 55, Secretary of Agriculture, born Osage, IA, Aug 18, 1950.

Shannon Johnson, 31, basketball player, born Hartsville, SC, Aug 18, 1974.

AUGUST 19 — FRIDAY

Day 231 — 134 Remaining

AFGHANISTAN: INDEPENDENCE DAY. Aug 19. National day. Commemorates independence from British control over foreign affairs in 1919. ***See Curriculum Connection.***

CALIFORNIA STATE FAIR. Aug 19–Sept 5. Sacramento, CA. Top-name entertainment, fireworks, California counties exhibits, livestock nursery, culinary delights, carnival rides and award-winning wines and microbrews. For info: California State Fair, PO Box 15649, Sacramento, CA 95852. Phone: (916) 263-FAIR. Web: www.bigfun.com.

CHINA: FESTIVAL OF HUNGRY GHOSTS. Aug 19. Important Chinese festival, also known as Chung Yuan Festival. According to Chinese legend, during the seventh lunar month the souls of the dead are released from purgatory to roam the Earth. Joss sticks are burned in homes; prayers, food and "ghost money" are offered to appease the ghosts. Market stallholders combine to hold celebrations to ensure that their businesses will prosper in the coming year. Wayang (Chinese street opera) and puppet shows are performed, and fruit and Chinese delicacies are offered to the spirits of the dead. Chung Yuan is observed on the 15th day of the seventh lunar month. Date in other countries will differ from China's.

CLINTON, WILLIAM JEFFERSON: BIRTHDAY. Aug 19, 1946. The 42nd president of the United States (1993–2001), born at Hope, AR. For info: www.ipl.org/ref/POTUS.

GINZA HOLIDAY: JAPANESE CULTURAL FESTIVAL. Aug 19–21. Midwest Buddhist Temple, Chicago, IL. Experience the Waza (National Treasures tradition) by viewing 300 years of Edo craft tradition and seeing it come alive as master craftsmen from Tokyo demonstrate their arts. Japanese folk and classical dancing, martial arts, taiko (drums), flower arrangements and cultural displays. Chicken teriyaki, sushi, udon, shaved ice, corn on the cob and refreshments. Annually, the third weekend in August. Est attendance: 15,000. For info: Office Secretary, Midwest Buddhist Temple, 435 W Menomonee St, Chicago, IL 60614. Phone: (312) 943-7801. Fax: (312) 943-8069.

LITTLE LEAGUE BASEBALL WORLD SERIES. Aug 19–28. Williamsport, PA. Sixteen teams from the US and foreign countries compete for the World Championship. Est attendance: 315,000. For info: Little League Baseball HQ, Box 3485, Williamsport, PA 17701. Phone: (570) 326-1921. Web: www.little league.org.

AUGUST 19
AFGHANISTAN

Today is the day the nation of Afghanistan celebrates its independence from the United Kingdom. Considering its importance lately in world affairs, you might spend some time introducing Afghanistan to your class.

The mountainous, landlocked region of Central Asia where Afghanistan is located has been a part of the world's cultural and political landscape for thousands of years. Its present-day neighbors include Iran to the west and Pakistan to the east and south, and further map study will show how it's also connected to three former Soviet republics, and even China via a strip of mountainous terrain to the northeast (*Afghanistan International Travel Map* by Viet Hoa Pham, ITMB Publishing, 1-553-41102-1, $9.95).

But Afghanistan's borders have always shifted to reflect the efforts made to rule it, from ancient times (Alexander the Great, Genghis Khan) to the more recent (the British Empire and the Soviet Union). Stephen Tanner's *Afghanistan: A Military History from Alexander the Great to the Fall of the Taliban* (0-306-81233-9, Perseus Books Group, $17.95 Adult) illustrates well the sheer scope of rule in the region. You might talk with your class about how near-mythic historical figures like Alexander can be made real in the context of a country as wise and ancient as Afghanistan, and how the country is still striving to define itself.

The years of political upheaval and unrest have also shaped the culture of Afghanistan, which in the 21st century blends centuries of religious growth, varying linguistics and tribal migration for a vibrant, though fractious, society. Afghanistan's major ethnic groups include the Pashtun (42 percent), Tajik (27 percent), Uzbek (9 percent) and Turkoman (3 percent). (For more information see the CIA World Factbook for Afghanistan at www. cia.gov/cia/publications/factbook/geos/af. html.) The majority of Afghans practice Islam, first brought to the region by the Arabs in AD 652, but faiths such as Hinduism and Judaism are also represented. Likewise, Afghanistan has two official languages, Afghan Persian and Pashtu, but there are nearly 30 other languages spoken within its borders. Erinn Banting's *Afghanistan: The Culture* (Crabtree Publishing, 0-778-79705-8, $7.95 Ages 9–12) provides a solid overview, while *Afghanistan (Many Cultures, One World)* by Barbara Knox (Blue Earth Books, 0-736-82448-0, $23.93) does the same for students grades 2–4.

Additional books include *Afghanistan (Cultures of the World)* by Sharifah Enayat Ali (Benchmark Books, 0-761-40177-6, $37.07 Gr. 5–8) and journalist Asne Seierstad's *The Bookseller of Kabul* (Little, Brown, 0-316-73450-0, $19.95 Adult), which traces the efforts of one Afghan to save literature in the face of a brutal political regime. You might also consult for in-classroom play *Afghanistan Untouched* (Traditional Crossroads, 630785393X, $17.98), a two-disc set of audio recordings capturing Afghani folk and street musicians in 1968, before political hostilities once again silenced art. —Johnny Loftus

★ ★ ★

August 2005

S	M	T	W	T	F	S
	1	2	3	4	5	6
7	8	9	10	11	12	13
14	15	16	17	18	19	20
21	22	23	24	25	26	27
28	29	30	31			

MOON PHASE: FULL MOON. Aug 19. Moon enters Full Moon phase at 1:53 PM, EDT.

★**NATIONAL AVIATION DAY.** Aug 19. Presidential Proclamation 2343, of July 25, 1939, covers all succeeding years. Always Aug 19 of each year since 1939. Observed annually on anniversary of birth of Orville Wright, who piloted "first self-powered flight in history" on Dec 17, 1903. First proclaimed by President Franklin D. Roosevelt.

PERIGEAN SPRING TIDES. Aug 19. Spring tides, the highest possible tides, occur when New Moon or Full Moon falls within 24 hours of the moment the Moon is nearest Earth (perigee) in its monthly orbit. These tides are not named for the season of spring but for the German word *springen*, "to rise up."

SPACE MILESTONE: *SPUTNIK 5* (USSR): 45th ANNIVERSARY. Aug 19, 1960. Space menagerie satellite with dogs Belka and Strelka, mice, rats, houseflies and plants launched. These passengers became first living organisms recovered from orbit when the satellite returned safely to Earth the next day.

WESTERN IDAHO FAIR. Aug 19–27. Boise, ID. 108th annual. Largest fair in the state, including four stages of entertainment on the grounds with local and regional talent, seven nights of grandstand concerts, two days of Idaho Cowboy Association Rodeo finals, carnival midway, 70 food booths and a power equipment display. Est attendance: 254,000. For info: Western Idaho Fair, 5610 Glenwood, Boise, ID 83714. Phone: (208) 287-5650. Fax: (208) 375-9972. Web: www.idahofair.com.

WRIGHT, ORVILLE: BIRTH ANNIVERSARY. Aug 19, 1871. Aviation pioneer (with his brother Wilbur), born at Dayton, OH, and died there Jan 30, 1948.

BIRTHDAYS TODAY

Victor Ambrus, 70, author (*The Three Poor Tailors*), born Budapest, Hungary, Aug 19, 1935.

William Jefferson (Bill) Clinton, 59, 42nd president of the US (1993–2001), born Hope, AR, Aug 19, 1946.

John Stamos, 42, actor ("Full House"), born Cypress, CA, Aug 19, 1963.

AUGUST 20 — SATURDAY

Day 232 — 133 Remaining

BROWN, JEFF: BIRTH ANNIVERSARY. Aug 20, 1926. Born Richard Chester Brown at New York, NY, this author worked as a writer and editor in Hollywood and New York before becoming known for his book for beginning readers, *Flat Stanley*, published in 1964. Many sequels followed, including *Stanley in Space, Invisible Stanley,* and *Stanley and the Magic Lamp.* His books have sold nearly a million copies. He died at New York, NY, Dec 1, 2003.

COLORADO STATE FAIR. Aug 20–Sept 4. State Fairgrounds, Pueblo, CO. One of the nation's oldest western fairs, it is also Colorado's largest single event. Family fun, top-name entertainment, lots of food and festivities. Est attendance: 650,000. For info: Colorado State Fair, 1001 Beulah Ave, Pueblo, CO 81004. Phone: (719) 561-8484. Web: www.coloradostatefair.com.

HARRISON, BENJAMIN: BIRTH ANNIVERSARY. Aug 20, 1833. The 23rd president of the US, born at North Bend, OH. He was the grandson of William Henry Harrison, 9th president of the US. His term of office, Mar 4, 1889–Mar 3, 1893, was preceded and followed by the presidential terms of Grover Cleveland (who thus became the 22nd and 24th president of the US). Harrison died at Indianapolis, IN, Mar 13, 1901. For info: www.ipl.org/ref/POTUS.

HUNGARY: ST. STEPHEN'S DAY. Aug 20. National holiday. Commemorates the canonization of St. Stephen in 1083. Under the Communists it was celebrated as Constitution Day.

O'HIGGINS, BERNARDO: BIRTH ANNIVERSARY. Aug 20, 1778. First ruler of Chile after its declaration of independence. Called the "Liberator of Chile." Born at Chillan, Chile. Died at Lima, Peru, Oct 24, 1842.

SPACE MILESTONE: *VOYAGER 2* (US). Aug 20, 1977. This unmanned spacecraft journeyed past Jupiter in 1979, Saturn in 1981, Uranus in 1986 and Neptune in 1989, sending photographs and data back to scientists on Earth.

BIRTHDAYS TODAY

Tara Dakides, 30, snowboarder, born Mission Viejo, CA, Aug 20, 1975.
Todd Helton, 32, baseball player, born Knoxville, TN, Aug 20, 1973.
Al Roker, 51, TV meteorologist ("Today Show"), born Brooklyn, NY, Aug 20, 1954.

AUGUST 21 — SUNDAY

Day 233 — 132 Remaining

CHAMBERLAIN, WILT: BIRTH ANNIVERSARY. Aug 21, 1936. Basketball Hall of Fame center, born at Philadelphia, PA. Died Oct 12, 1999, at Los Angeles, CA.

HAWAII: ADMISSION DAY: ANNIVERSARY. Aug 21, 1959. President Dwight Eisenhower signed a proclamation admitting Hawaii to the Union. The statehood bill had passed the previous March with a stipulation that statehood should be approved by a vote of Hawaiian residents. The referendum passed by a huge margin in June and Eisenhower proclaimed Hawaii the 50th state Aug 21. The third Friday in August is observed as a state holiday in Hawaii, commemorating statehood (Aug 19 in 2005).

MONARCH BUTTERFLY FALL MIGRATION. Aug 21–Nov 7 (approximate). The monarch butterfly (*Danaus plexippus*) of North America begins an amazing migration of up to 3,000 miles in late August to escape the northern winter. Some 140 million insects travel to small forests in southern California (west of the Rocky Mountains) and Mexico (east of the Rockies, via central and coastal Texas) from as far as Minnesota and New England. In late spring, they will journey north again. Given that their lifespan is 4 to 6 weeks, the butterflies making the same annual migration are the grandchildren of the grandchildren of the butterflies that overwintered 10 months previously. For more information: www.monarchwatch.org and www.monarchlab.umn.edu (with resources for K–12 teachers).

BIRTHDAYS TODAY

Steve Case, 47, former president, America Online, born Honolulu, HI, Aug 21, 1958.
Sharon M. Draper, 57, author (*Tears of a Tiger, Forged by Fire*), born Ohio, Aug 21, 1948.
Akili Smith, 30, former football player, born San Diego, CA, Aug 21, 1975.
Arthur Yorinks, 52, author (*Hey, Al*), born Roslyn, NY, Aug 21, 1953.

AUGUST 22 — MONDAY

Day 234 — 131 Remaining

BE AN ANGEL DAY. Aug 22. A day to do "one small act of service for someone. Be a blessing in someone's life." Annually, Aug 22. For info: Angel Heights Healing Center, Rev Jayne M. Howard-Feldman, PO Box 95, Upperco, MD 21155. Phone: (410) 833-6912. E-mail: earthangel4peace@aol.com. Web: earthangel4peace.com.

CAMEROON: VOLCANIC ERUPTION: ANNIVERSARY. Aug 22, 1986. Deadly fumes from a presumed volcanic eruption under Lake Nios at Cameroon killed more than 1,500 persons. A similar occurrence two years earlier had killed 37 persons. For more info visit Volcano World: volcano.und.nodak.edu.

DEBUSSY, CLAUDE: BIRTH ANNIVERSARY. Aug 22, 1862. (Achille) Claude Debussy, French musician and composer, especially remembered for his impressionistic "tone poems," was born at St. Germain-en-Laye, France. He died at Paris, France, Mar 25, 1918.

NATIONAL PUNCTUATION DAY. Aug 22. A celebration of the lowly comma, the correctly used quote and other proper uses of periods, semicolons and the ever mysterious ellipsis. For info: Jeff Rubin, Put It in Writing Newsletter Publishers, 1517 Buckeye Court, Pinole, CA 94564. Phone: (877) 588-1212 (toll-free). Fax: (510) 741-8698. E-mail: jeff@put-it-in-writing.com. Web: www.put-it-in-writing.com.

VIETNAM CONFLICT BEGINS: 60th ANNIVERSARY. Aug 22, 1945. Less than a week after the Japanese surrender ended WWII, a team of Free French parachuted into southern Indochina in response to a successful coup by a Communist guerrilla named Ho Chi Minh in the French colony.

★ ★ ★

BIRTHDAYS TODAY

Ray Bradbury, 85, author (*Dandelion Wine, Fahrenheit 451, Something Wicked This Way Comes*), born Waukegan, IL, Aug 22, 1920.
Howie Dorough, 32, singer (Backstreet Boys), born Orlando, FL, Aug 22, 1973.
Will Hobbs, 58, author (*Downriver, Far North*), born Pittsburgh, PA, Aug 22, 1947.
Paul Molitor, 49, Hall of Fame baseball player, born St. Paul, MN, Aug 22, 1956.

AUGUST 23 — TUESDAY

Day 235 — 130 Remaining

BUSHMILLER, ERNIE: 100th BIRTH ANNIVERSARY. Aug 23, 1905. Comic strip artist famous for the "Nancy" strip featuring spiky-haired Nancy, her pal Sluggo and glamorous Aunt Fritzi. Born at the Bronx, NY, Bushmiller died Aug 15, 1982, at Stamford, CT.

FIRST MAN-POWERED FLIGHT: ANNIVERSARY. Aug 23, 1977. At Schafter, CA, Bryan Allen pedaled the 70-lb *Gossamer Condor* for a mile at a "minimal altitude of two pylons" in a flight certified by the Royal Aeronautical Society of Britain, winning a £50,000 prize offered by British industrialist Henry Kremer.

PERRY, OLIVER HAZARD: BIRTH ANNIVERSARY. Aug 23, 1785. American naval hero, born at South Kingston, RI. Died Aug 23, 1819, at sea. Best remembered is his announcement of victory at the Battle of Lake Erie, Sept 10, 1813, during the War of 1812: "We have met the enemy, and they are ours."

VIRGO, THE VIRGIN. Aug 23–Sept 22. In the astronomical/astrological zodiac, which divides the sun's apparent orbit into 12 segments, the period Aug 23–Sept 22 is identified, traditionally, as the sun sign of Virgo, the Virgin. The ruling planet is Mercury.

BIRTHDAYS TODAY

Kobe Bryant, 27, basketball player, born Philadelphia, PA, Aug 23, 1978.

Natalie Coughlin, 23, Olympic swimmer, born Concord, CA, Aug 23, 1982.

Rik Smits, 39, former basketball player, born Eindhoven, The Netherlands, Aug 23, 1966.

AUGUST 24 — WEDNESDAY

Day 236 — 129 Remaining

HURRICANE ANDREW HITS AMERICAN COAST: ANNIVERSARY. Aug 24, 1992. Hurricane Andrew hit the coast at Homestead Air Force Base in southern Florida. Winds averaged 145 MPH, with gusts of up to 175 MPH. Fifteen people were killed. In its wake, Andrew left destruction totaling $26.5 billion, making it the second most costly weather disaster in US history. For more info about hurricanes: www.fema.gov/kids/hurr.htm. For more info about Andrew: www.nhc.noaa.gov/1992andrew.html.

LIBERIA: FLAG DAY. Aug 24. National holiday.

NEVADA STATE FAIR. Aug 24–28. Reno Livestock Events Center, Reno, NV. State entertainment and carnival, with home arts, agriculture and commercial exhibits. Est attendance: 60,000. For info: Nevada State Fair, 1350-A N Wells Ave, Reno, NV 89512. Phone: (775) 688-5767. Fax: (775) 688-5763. E-mail: info@nvstatefair.com. Web: www.nvstatefair.com.

UKRAINE: INDEPENDENCE DAY. Aug 24. National day. Commemorates independence from the Soviet Union in 1991.

VESUVIUS ERUPTION DESTROYS POMPEII: ANNIVERSARY. Aug 24, AD 79. Anniversary of the eruption of Vesuvius, an active volcano in southern Italy, which destroyed the Roman cities of Pompeii, Stabiae and Herculaneum. Pliny the Younger, who escaped the disaster, wrote of it to the historian Tacitus: "[B]lack and horrible clouds, broken by sinuous shapes of flaming winds, were opening with long tongues of fire . . ." For more info: *In Search of Pompeii* (Peter Bedrick, 0-87226-545-5, $18.95 Gr. 5 & up) or visit Volcano World: volcano.und.nodak.edu.

WARNER WEATHER QUOTATION: ANNIVERSARY. Aug 24, 1897. Charles Dudley Warner, American newspaper editor for the *Hartford Courant*, published this now-famous and oft-quoted sentence, "Everybody talks about the weather, but nobody does anything about it." The quotation is often mistakenly attributed to his friend and colleague Mark Twain. Warner and Twain were part of the most notable American literary circle during the late 19th century. Warner was a journalist, essayist, novelist, biographer and author who collaborated with Mark Twain in writing *The Gilded Age* in 1873.

WASHINGTON, DC: INVASION ANNIVERSARY. Aug 24–25, 1814. During the War of 1812, British forces briefly invaded and raided Washington, DC, burning the Capitol, the president's house and most other public buildings. President James Madison and other high US government officials fled to safety until British troops (not knowing the strength of their position) departed the city two days later.

BIRTHDAYS TODAY

Kenny Guinn, 69, Governor of Nevada (R), born Garland, AR, Aug 24, 1936.

Mike Huckabee, 50, Governor of Arkansas (R), born Hope, AR, Aug 24, 1955.

Joe Manchin III, 58, Governor of West Virginia (D), born Farmington, WV, Aug 24, 1947.

Reginald (Reggie) Miller, 40, basketball player, born Riverside, CA, Aug 24, 1965.

Calvin Edward (Cal) Ripken, Jr, 45, former baseball player, born Havre de Grace, MD, Aug 24, 1960.

Tim Salmon, 37, baseball player, born Long Beach, CA, Aug 24, 1968.

Merlin Tuttle, 64, scientist who works with bats, author (*Bats for Kids*), born Honolulu, HI, Aug 24, 1941.

AUGUST 25 — THURSDAY

Day 237 — 128 Remaining

ALASKA STATE FAIR. Aug 25–Sept 5. Palmer, AK. Cows and critters, music and dancing, rides, excitement and family fun at the state's largest summer extravaganza. See 100-lb cabbages, native art and more than 500 events including demonstrations, high-caliber entertainment, rodeos, horse shows, crafts and agricultural exhibits. Est attendance: 300,000. For info: Alaska State Fair, Inc, 2075 Glenn Hwy, Palmer, AK 99645. Phone: (907) 745-4827 or (800) 850-FAIR. Fax: (907) 746-2699. Web: www.alaskastatefair.org.

BE KIND TO HUMANKIND WEEK. Aug 25–31. 17th annual observance. All of the negative news that you read about in the paper each day and hear on your local news station is disheartening—but the truth is the positive stories outweigh the negative stories by a long shot! We just don't hear about them as often. Take heart . . . most people are caring individuals. Show you care by being kind. For info: Lorraine Jara, PO Box 586, Island Heights, NJ 08732-0586. Phone: (732) 255-0553. E-mail: LsaysBeKind@comcast.net.

BERNSTEIN, LEONARD: BIRTH ANNIVERSARY. Aug 25, 1918. American conductor and composer, born at Lawrence, MA. One of the greatest conductors in American music history, he first conducted the New York Philharmonic Orchestra at age 25 and was its director from 1959 to 1969. His musicals include *West Side Story* and *On the Town*, and his operas and operettas include *Candide*. He died Oct 14, 1990, at New York, NY, five days after his retirement.

GIBSON, ALTHEA: BIRTH ANNIVERSARY. Aug 25, 1927. Born at Silver, SC, Althea Gibson learned paddle tennis by chance as a child when her block of West 143rd St in New York was designated as a Police Athletic League play street. She overcame great financial and social adversity, and eventually won 10 consecutive national titles in the American Tennis Association, a league for black players. On Aug 28, 1950, she became the first black player to compete in the national tennis championship at Forest Hills, NY. A few years later, she became the first black woman to win the singles championship at Wimbledon. In her prime, she was ranked as high as 7th in the United States, winning titles at the French Open, Wimbledon and US Nationals at Forest Hills. She died at East Orange, NJ, Sept 28, 2003.

KELLY, WALT: BIRTH ANNIVERSARY. Aug 25, 1913. American cartoonist and creator of the comic strip "Pogo" was born at

August 2005

S	M	T	W	T	F	S
	1	2	3	4	5	6
7	8	9	10	11	12	13
14	15	16	17	18	19	20
21	22	23	24	25	26	27
28	29	30	31			

Philadelphia, PA. It was Kelly's character Pogo who paraphrased Oliver Hazard Perry to say, "We has met the enemy, and it is us." Kelly died at Hollywood, CA, Oct 18, 1973. See also: "Perry, Oliver Hazard: Birth Anniversary" (Aug 23).

MINNESOTA STATE FAIR. Aug 25–Sept 5. St. Paul, MN. Twelve days of fun ending on Labor Day. Major entertainers, agricultural displays, arts, crafts, food, carnival rides, animal judging and performances. Est attendance: 1,700,000. For info: Minnesota State Fair, 1265 Snelling Ave N, St. Paul, MN 55108-3099. Phone: (651) 288-4400. E-mail: fairinfo@mnstatefair.org. Web: www.mnstatefair.org.

NEW YORK STATE FAIR. Aug 25–Sept 5. Syracuse, NY. Agricultural and livestock competitions, top-name entertainment, the International Horse Show, business and industrial exhibits, the midway and ethnic presentations. Est attendance: 1,000,000. For info: Joseph LaGuardia, Dir of Mktg, NY State Fair, 581 State Fair Blvd, Syracuse, NY 13209. Phone: (315) 487-7711. Fax: (315) 487-9260.

PARIS LIBERATED: ANNIVERSARY. Aug 25, 1944. As dawn broke, the men of the 2nd French Armored Division entered Paris, ending the long German occupation of the City of Light. That afternoon General Charles de Gaulle led a parade down the Champs Elysées. Though Hitler had ordered the destruction of Paris, German occupying-officer General Dietrich von Choltitz refused that order and instead surrendered to French Major General Jacques Leclerc.

SMITH, SAMANTHA: 20th DEATH ANNIVERSARY. Aug 25, 1985. American schoolgirl whose interest in world peace drew praise and affection from people around the world. In 1982, the 10-year-old wrote a letter to Soviet leader Yuri Andropov asking him, "Why do you want to conquer the whole world, or at least our country?" The letter was widely publicized in the USSR and Andropov replied personally to her. Samantha Smith was invited to visit and tour the Soviet Union. On Aug 25, 1985, the airplane on which she was riding to the USSR crashed at Maine, killing all aboard, including Samantha and her father. In 1986, minor planet No 3147, an asteroid between Mars and Jupiter, was named Samantha Smith in her memory.

URUGUAY: INDEPENDENCE DAY. Aug 25. National holiday. Gained independence from Brazil in 1828.

***THE WIZARD OF OZ* FIRST RELEASED: ANNIVERSARY.** Aug 25, 1939. This film classic featured Dorothy and her dog Toto. The two were swept into a tornado and landed in a fictional place called Munchkinland. To get home she must go and see the Wizard of Oz and on the way meets the Scarecrow, the Tin Man and the Cowardly Lion. The cast included Judy Garland as Dorothy, Frank Morgan as the Wizard, Ray Bolger as the Scarecrow, Bert Lahr as the Lion, Jack Haley as the Tin Man and Margaret Hamilton as the Wicked Witch of the West.

BIRTHDAYS TODAY

Albert Belle, 39, former baseball player, born Shreveport, LA, Aug 25, 1966.

Marvin Harrison, 33, football player, born Philadelphia, PA, Aug 25, 1972.

Kel Mitchell, 27, actor ("All That," "Kenan & Kel"), born Chicago, IL, Aug 25, 1978.

Lane Smith, 46, author, illustrator (Caldecott Honor for *The Stinky Cheese Man and Other Fairly Stupid Tales; The Happy Hocky Family*), born Tulsa, OK, Aug 25, 1959.

Virginia Euwer Wolff, 68, author (*Make Lemonade*, National Book Award for *True Believer*), born Oregon, Aug 25, 1937.

AUGUST
ELOISE TURNS 50!

In 1955, author Kay Thompson's six-year-old Eloise, who lives in a hotel in New York, whirled onto the children's literature stage with the power of a tornado. Her mischievous, sometimes downright naughty, antics and free-spirited approach to life enchanted children, even as they dismayed some adults. It seems hard to believe that the young lady who shook up children's literature turns 50 in 2005.

Eloise (Simon & Schuster, reissue edition, 0-671-22350-X, $18 Ages 4–8) paved the way for books in which young protagonists were given the freedom to behave like children. Prior to that, main characters in picture books and novels for primary grade readers behaved like "good" little boys and girls. Today, children know and love characters such as Junie (Junie B. Jones series by Barbara Park), Joey Pigza (*Joey Pigza Swallowed the Key* by Jack Gantos [Harper Trophy, 0-06-440833-7, $5.99 Ages 9–12]) and David (*David Gets in Trouble* by David Shannon [Blue Sky Press, 0439050227, $15.95 Ages 4–8]). These characters, who regularly misuse language and/or misbehave, have endeared themselves to children precisely because they recognize themselves—or at least an aspect of themselves—in their fictional peers.

Although parts of the Eloise books are out of date—few children today have rotary dial telephones—others still ring true, no pun intended: who wouldn't like to have room service regularly deliver meals on demand? Oddly enough, Eloise's behavior creates a perfect opportunity to discuss appropriate behaviors and good choices.

Just-for-fun is the best reason to read any book, including *Eloise* and its sequels, but Thompson's books can be used in the language arts curriculum too. One way, suitable for second- through fifth-grade readers, is to read and compare them with novels such as the Junie B. Jones and Joey Pigza books. Students can diagram the character traits of the three different protagonists and then compare and contrast them. As a reality check, students could compare actions and consequences as well. Junie and Joey have to deal with the consequences of their actions, something Eloise rarely, if ever, does.

Word play is another way to incorporate Eloise into language arts. She regularly uses words such as "skibble," "slomp" and "sklathe." You won't find these words in the dictionary, but they surely do sound great when Eloise uses them. Challenge your students to make up fun new words—then read *Frindle* by Andrew Clements (Aladdin, 0-689-81876-9, $4.99 Ages 9–12).

Eloise refers to Nanny as her "mostly companion." Ask students to write about what this means. What qualities would they look for in a perfect "mostly companion"?

Eloise's pet turtle Skipperdee wears sneakers, or so Eloise claims. What outfits would your students' pets wear if they wore clothes? And where would they go wearing them? Read *The Night I Followed the Dog*, by Nina Laden (Chronicle Books, 0-8118-0647-2, $16.95 Ages 4–8), for a hilarious tale of one dog's adventures away from home.

Other Eloise books include her escapades in Paris and Moscow, an adventure in the "bawth" and a Christmas story. The website www.eloisewebsite.com has information about the books, author and illustrator, and recently issued movies.

—Sally Walker

★ ★ ★

AUGUST 26 — FRIDAY

Day 238 — 127 Remaining

De FOREST, LEE: BIRTH ANNIVERSARY. Aug 26, 1873. American inventor of the electron tube, radio knife for surgery and the photoelectric cell and a pioneer in the creation of talking pictures and television. Born at Council Bluffs, IA, De Forest was holder of hundreds of patents but perhaps best remembered by the moniker he gave himself in the title of his autobiography, *Father of Radio*, published in 1950. So unbelievable was the idea of wireless radio broadcasting that De Forest was accused of fraud and arrested for selling stock to underwrite the invention that later was to become an essential part of daily life. De Forest died at Hollywood, CA, June 30, 1961.

FIRST BASEBALL GAMES TELEVISED: ANNIVERSARY. Aug 26, 1939. WXBS television, at New York City, broadcast the first major league baseball games—a doubleheader between the Cincinnati Reds and the Brooklyn Dodgers at Ebbets Field. Announcer Red Barber interviewed Leo Durocher, manager of the Dodgers, and William McKechnie, manager of the Reds, between games.

KRAKATOA ERUPTION: ANNIVERSARY. Aug 26, 1883. Anniversary of the biggest explosion in historic times. The eruption of the Indonesian volcanic island, Krakatoa (Krakatau) was heard 3,000 miles away, created tidal waves 120 ft high (killing 36,000 persons), hurled five cubic miles of earth fragments into the air (some to a height of 50 miles) and affected the oceans and the atmosphere for years.

MARYLAND STATE FAIR. Aug 26–Sept 5. Timonium, MD. Home arts, agricultural and livestock presentations, midway rides, live entertainment and thoroughbred horse racing. Est attendance: 500,000. For info: Maryland State Fair, Publicity Dept, State Fairgrounds, PO Box 188, Timonium, MD 21094. Phone: (410) 252-0200. E-mail: msfair@msn.com. Web: www.maryland statefair.com.

MONTGOLFIER, JOSEPH MICHEL: BIRTH ANNIVERSARY. Aug 26, 1740. French merchant and inventor, born at Annonay, France, who, with his brother Jacques Etienne in November 1782, conducted experiments with paper and fabric bags filled with smoke and hot air which led to the invention of the hot-air balloon and man's first flight. Died at Balaruc-les-Bains, France, June 26, 1810. See also: "Montgolfier, Jacques Etienne: Birth Anniversary" (Jan 7), "First Balloon Flight: Anniversary" (June 5) and "Aviation History Month" (Nov 1).

MOON PHASE: LAST QUARTER. Aug 26. Moon enters Last Quarter phase at 11:18 AM, EDT.

NAMIBIA: HEROES' DAY. Aug 26. National holiday. Commemorates the beginning of the struggle for independence in 1966.

OREGON STATE FAIR. Aug 26–Sept 5. Salem, OR. Exhibits, products and displays illustrate Oregon's role as one of the nation's major agricultural and recreational states. Floral gardens, carnival, big-name entertainment, horse show and food. Est attendance: 400,000. For info: Oregon State Fair, 2330 17th St NE, Salem, OR 97303-3201. Phone: (503) 947-3247.

August 2005

S	M	T	W	T	F	S
	1	2	3	4	5	6
7	8	9	10	11	12	13
14	15	16	17	18	19	20
21	22	23	24	25	26	27
28	29	30	31			

PHILIPPINES: NATIONAL HEROES' DAY. Aug 26. National holiday. Commemorates the 1896 start of the revolution for independence from Spain.

SABIN, ALBERT BRUCE: BIRTH ANNIVERSARY. Aug 26, 1906. American medical researcher, born at Bialystok, Poland. He is most noted for his oral vaccine for polio, which replaced Jonas Salk's injected vaccine because Sabin's provided lifetime protection. He was awarded the US National Medal of Science in 1971. Sabin died Mar 3, 1993, at Washington, DC.

★**WOMEN'S EQUALITY DAY.** Aug 26. Presidential Proclamation issued in 1973 and 1974 at request and since 1975 without request.

WOMEN'S EQUALITY DAY. Aug 26. Anniversary of certification as part of US Constitution, in 1920, of the 19th Amendment, prohibiting discrimination on the basis of sex with regard to voting. Congresswoman Bella Abzug's bill to designate Aug 26 of each year as "Women's Equality Day" in August 1974 became Public Law 93–382.

BIRTHDAYS TODAY

Patricia Beatty, 83, author (*Charley Skedaddle; Turn Homeward, Hannalee*), born Portland, OR, Aug 26, 1922.
Macaulay Culkin, 25, actor (*Home Alone, My Girl*), born New York, NY, Aug 26, 1980.
Jamal Lewis, 26, football player, born Atlanta, GA, Aug 26, 1979.

AUGUST 27 — SATURDAY

Day 239 — 126 Remaining

DAWES, CHARLES GATES: BIRTH ANNIVERSARY. Aug 27, 1865. The 30th vice president of the US (1925–29), born at Marietta, OH. Won the Nobel Peace Prize in 1925 for the "Dawes Plan" for German reparations. Died at Evanston, IL, Apr 23, 1951.

FIRST COMMERCIAL OIL WELL: ANNIVERSARY. Aug 27, 1859. W.A. "Uncle Billy" Smith discovered oil in a shaft being sunk by Colonel E.L. Drake at Titusville, in western Pennsylvania. Drilling had reached 69 feet, 6 inches when Smith saw a dark film floating on the water below the derrick floor. Soon 20 barrels of crude were being pumped each day. At first, oil was refined into kerosene and used for lighting in place of whale oil. Only later was it refined into gasoline for cars. The first gas station opened in 1907.

FIRST PLAY PRESENTED IN NORTH AMERICAN COLONIES: 350th ANNIVERSARY. Aug 27, 1655. Acomac, VA, was the site of the first play presented in the North American colonies. The play was *Ye Bare and Ye Cubb*, by Phillip Alexander Bruce. Three local residents were arrested and fined for acting in the play. At the time, most colonies had laws prohibiting public performances; Virginia, however, had no such ordinance.

HAMLIN, HANNIBAL: BIRTH ANNIVERSARY. Aug 27, 1809. The 15th vice president of the US (1861–65), born at Paris, ME. Died at Bangor, ME, July 4, 1891.

JOHNSON, LYNDON BAINES: BIRTH ANNIVERSARY. Aug 27, 1908. The 36th president of the US succeeded to the presidency following the assassination of John F. Kennedy and then was elected to one term on his own. Johnson's term of office: Nov 22, 1963–Jan 20, 1969. In 1964, he said: "The challenge of the next half-century is whether we have the wisdom to use [our] wealth to enrich and elevate our national life—and to advance the quality of American civilization." Johnson was born near Stonewall, TX, and died at San Antonio, TX, Jan 22, 1973. For info: www.ipl.org/ref/POTUS.

MOLDOVA: INDEPENDENCE DAY. Aug 27. Republic of Moldova declared its independence from the Soviet Union in 1991.

MOTHER TERESA: BIRTH ANNIVERSARY. Aug 27, 1910. Albanian Roman Catholic nun, born Agnes Gonxha Bojaxhiu at Skopje, Macedonia. She founded the Order of the Missionaries of Charity, which cared for the destitute of Calcutta, India. She won the Nobel Peace Prize in 1979. She died at Calcutta, Sept 5, 1997.

NEBRASKA STATE FAIR. Aug 27–Sept 5 (tentative). Lincoln, NE. Food booths, variety of entertainment, amusement rides, concerts, livestock shows and tractor pulls. Est attendance: 300,000. For info: Nebraska State Fair, PO Box 81223, Lincoln, NE 68501. Phone: (402) 474-5371. Fax: (402) 473-4114. E-mail: nestatefair@statefair.org.

BIRTHDAYS TODAY

Suzy Kline, 62, author (the Horrible Harry series), born Berkeley, CA, Aug 27, 1943.

Carlos Moya, 29, tennis player, born Palma de Mallorca, Aug 27, 1976.

Ann Rinaldi, 71, author (*Time Enough for Drums, A Stitch in Time*), born New York, NY, Aug 27, 1934.

Suzanne Fisher Staples, 60, author (*Shabanu: Daughter of the Wind, Haveli*), born Philadelphia, PA, Aug 27, 1945.

Sarah Stewart, 67, author (*The Library, The Gardener*), born Corpus Christi, TX, Aug 27, 1938.

AUGUST 28 — SUNDAY

Day 240 — 125 Remaining

DUVOISIN, ROGER: BIRTH ANNIVERSARY. Aug 28, 1904. Author and illustrator, born at Geneva, Switzerland. His drawings made Alvin Tresselt's *White Snow, Bright Snow* and *Hide and Seek Fog* unforgettable, and *Petunia*, which he wrote and ilustrated, is considered a classic. He died at Morristown, NJ, June 30, 1980.

FEAST OF SAINT AUGUSTINE. Aug 28. Bishop of Hippo, author of *Confessions* and *The City of God*, born Nov 13, 354, at Tagaste, in what is now Algeria. Died Aug 28, 430, at Hippo, also in North Africa.

HAYES, LUCY WARE WEBB: BIRTH ANNIVERSARY. Aug 28, 1831. Wife of Rutherford Birchard Hayes, 19th president of the US, born at Chillicothe, OH. Died at Fremont, OH, June 25, 1889. She was nicknamed "Lemonade Lucy" because she and the president, both abstainers, served no alcoholic beverages at White House receptions.

MARCH ON WASHINGTON: ANNIVERSARY. Aug 28, 1963. More than 250,000 people attended this Civil Rights rally at Washington, DC, at which Reverend Dr. Martin Luther King, Jr, made his famous "I have a dream" speech. For the text of his speech: *I Have a Dream*, by Dr. Martin Luther King, Jr (Scholastic, 0-590-20516-1, $16.95 All ages). An audio version of Dr. King's speech is available at www.historychannel.com/speech/index.html. For more info on the march: *Martin Luther King, Jr, and the March on Washington*, by Frances E. Ruffin (Grosset & Dunlap, 0-448-42424 X, $13.89 Gr. 1–3).

PETERSON, ROGER TORY: BIRTH ANNIVERSARY. Aug 28, 1908. Naturalist, author of *A Field Guide to Birds*, born at Jamestown, NY. Peterson died at Old Lyme, CT, July 28, 1996.

RADIO COMMERCIALS: ANNIVERSARY. Aug 28, 1922. Broadcasters realized radio could earn profits from the sale of advertising time. WEAF in New York ran a commercial "spot," which was sponsored by the Queensboro Realty Corporation of Jackson Heights to promote Hawthorne Court, a group of apartment buildings at Queens. The commercial rate was $100 for 10 minutes.

SETON, ELIZABETH ANN BAYLEY: BIRTH ANNIVERSARY. Aug 28, 1774. First American-born saint was born at New York, NY. Seton died Jan 4, 1821, at Emmitsburg, MD. The founder of the American Sisters of Charity, the first American order of Roman Catholic nuns, she was canonized in 1975.

TILL, EMMETT: 50th DEATH ANNIVERSARY. Aug 28, 1955. Emmett Till, a 14-year-old African-American teenager from Chicago visiting relatives in Money, MS, was murdered on this date by a group of white men angry at Till's reported flirtation with a white woman. The Till murder and the acquittal of two of the men involved brought the nation's attention to racial tensions in the South and helped spark civil rights protests later that year—most famously, Rosa Parks's refusal to give up her seat to a white man on a municipal bus in Montgomery, AL, in December of that year.

BIRTHDAYS TODAY

Mamadou Diallo, 34, soccer player, born Dakar, Senegal, Aug 28, 1971.

Michael Galeota, 21, actor (*Can't Be Heaven, Clubhouse Detectives*), born Long Island, NY, Aug 28, 1984.

Scott Hamilton, 47, Olympic gold medal figure skater, born Toledo, OH, Aug 28, 1958.

Paul Martin, 67, 21st prime minister of Canada, born Windsor, ON, Canada, Aug 28, 1938.

J. Brian Pinkney, 44, illustrator (*Duke Ellington: The Piano Prince and His Orchestra; The Dark Thirty: Southern Tales of the Supernatural; Happy Birthday, Martin Luther King*), born Boston, MA, Aug 28, 1961.

LeAnn Rimes, 23, singer, born Jackson, MS, Aug 28, 1982.

Allen Say, 68, illustrator and author (*How My Parents Learned to Eat, Stranger in the Mirror*, Caldecott for *Grandfather's Journey*), born Yokohama, Japan, Aug 28, 1937.

Tasha Tudor, 90, illustrator (*A Little Princess, A Child's Garden of Verses*), author (*Corgiville Fair*), born Starling Burgess at Boston MA, Aug 28, 1915.

AUGUST 29 — MONDAY

Day 241 — 124 Remaining

"ACCORDING TO HOYLE" DAY (EDMOND HOYLE DEATH ANNIVERSARY). Aug 29, 1769. A day to remember Edmond Hoyle and a day for fun and games *according to the rules*. He is believed to have studied law. For many years he lived at London, England, and gave instructions in the playing of games. His "Short Treatise" on the game of whist (published in 1742) became a model guide to the rules of the game. Hoyle's name became synonymous with the idea of correct play according to the rules, and the phrase "according to Hoyle" became a part of the English language. Hoyle was born about 1672, at London and died there.

AMISTAD SEIZED: ANNIVERSARY. Aug 29, 1839. In January 1839, 53 Africans were seized near modern-day Sierra Leone, taken to Cuba and sold as slaves. While being transferred to another part of the island on the ship *Amistad*, led by the African, Cinque, they seized control of the ship, telling the crew to take them back to Africa. However, the crew secretly changed course and the ship landed at Long Island, NY, where it and its "cargo" were seized as salvage. The *Amistad* was towed to New Haven, CT, where the Africans were imprisoned and a lengthy legal battle began to determine if they were property to be returned to Cuba or free men. John Quincy Adams took their case all the way to the Supreme Court, where on Mar 9, 1841, it was determined that they were free and could return to Africa. For more info: *Amistad: A Long Road to Freedom*, by Walter Dean Myers (Dutton, 0-525-45970-7, $16.99 Gr. 7 & up) or *Freedom's Sons: The True Story of the Amistad Mutiny*, by Suzanne Jurmain (Lothrop, 0-688-11072-X, $15 Gr. 4–8). A replica of the *Amistad* was built at the Mystic Seaport Museum, Mystic, CT (amistad.mysticseaport.org). For more info on the trial: www.umkc.edu/FamousTrials.

HONG KONG: LIBERATION DAY. Aug 29. Public holiday to celebrate liberation from the Japanese in 1945. Annually, the last Monday in August.

PARKER, CHARLIE: BIRTH ANNIVERSARY. Aug 29, 1920. Jazz saxophonist Charlie Parker was born at Kansas City, KS. He earned the nickname "Yardbird" (later "Bird") from his habit of sitting in the backyard of speakeasies, fingering his saxophone. His career as a jazz saxophonist took him from jam sessions in Kansas City to New York, where he met Dizzy Gillespie and others who were creating a style of music that would become known as bop or bebop. He struggled throughout his career with schizophrenia and drug addictions, and died at Rochester, NY, Mar 12, 1955. For more info: *Charlie Parker Played Be Bop*, by Chris Raschka (Orchard, 0-531-05999-5, $15.95 Gr. K–1).

SHAYS REBELLION: ANNIVERSARY. Aug 29, 1786. Daniel Shays, veteran of the battles of Lexington, Bunker Hill, Ticonderoga and Saratoga, was one of the leaders of more than 1,000 rebels who sought redress of grievances during the depression days of 1786–87. They prevented general court sessions and they prevented Supreme Court sessions at Springfield, MA, Sept 26. On Jan 25, 1787, they attacked the federal arsenal at Springfield; Feb 2, Shays' troops were routed and fled. Shays was sentenced to death but pardoned June 13, 1788. Later he received a small pension for services in the American Revolution.

SLOVAKIA: NATIONAL UPRISING DAY. Aug 29. National holiday. Commemorates the beginning of the 1944 resistance to Nazi occupation.

SOVIET COMMUNIST PARTY SUSPENDED: ANNIVERSARY. Aug 29, 1991. The Supreme Soviet, the parliament of the USSR, suspended all activities of the Communist Party, seizing its property and bringing to an end the institution that ruled the Soviet Union for nearly 75 years. The action followed an unsuccessful coup Aug 19–21 that sought to overthrow the government of Soviet President Mikhail Gorbachev but instead prompted a sweeping wave of democratic change. Gorbachev quit as party leader Aug 24.

August 2005

S	M	T	W	T	F	S
	1	2	3	4	5	6
7	8	9	10	11	12	13
14	15	16	17	18	19	20
21	22	23	24	25	26	27
28	29	30	31			

BIRTHDAYS TODAY

Karen Hesse, 53, author (*The Music of Dolphins, Letters from Rifka*, Newbery for *Out of the Dust*), born Baltimore, MD, Aug 29, 1952.

Michael Jackson, 47, singer, songwriter ("We Are the World," *Bad, Thriller, Beat It*), born Gary, IN, Aug 29, 1958.

Pablo Mastroeni, 29, soccer player, born Mendoza, Argentina, Aug 29, 1976.

John McCain III, 69, US Senator (R, Arizona), born Panama Canal Zone, Aug 29, 1936.

Roy Oswalt, 28, baseball player, born Weir, MS, Aug 29, 1977.

AUGUST 30 — TUESDAY

Day 242 — 123 Remaining

ARTHUR, ELLEN LEWIS HERNDON: BIRTH ANNIVERSARY. Aug 30, 1837. Wife of Chester Alan Arthur, 21st president of the US, born at Fredericksburg, VA. Died at New York, NY, Jan 12, 1880.

BURTON, VIRGINIA LEE: BIRTH ANNIVERSARY. Aug 30, 1909. Author and illustrator, born at Newton Centre, MA. Her book *The Little House* won the Caldecott Medal in 1942. Other works include *Choo, Choo* and *Mike Mulligan and His Steam Shovel*. Burton died at Boston, MA, Oct 15, 1968.

FIRST WHITE HOUSE PRESIDENTIAL BABY: BIRTH ANNIVERSARY. Aug 30, 1893. Frances Folsom Cleveland (Mrs Grover Cleveland) was the first presidential wife to have a baby at the White House when she gave birth to a baby girl (Esther). The first child ever born in the White House was a granddaughter to Thomas Jefferson in 1806.

PERU: SAINT ROSE OF LIMA DAY. Aug 30. Saint Rose of Lima was the first saint of the western hemisphere. She lived at the time of the colonization by Spain in the 16th century. Patron saint of the Americas and the Philippines. Public holiday in Peru.

RUTHERFORD, ERNEST: BIRTH ANNIVERSARY. Aug 30, 1871. Physicist, born at Nelson, New Zealand. He established the nuclear nature of the atom, the electrical structure of matter and achieved the transmutation of elements, research that later resulted in the atomic bomb. Rutherford died at Cambridge, England, Oct 19, 1937.

SHELLEY, MARY WOLLSTONECRAFT: BIRTH ANNIVERSARY. Aug 30, 1797. English novelist Mary Shelley, daughter of the philosopher William Godwin and the feminist Mary Wollstonecraft and wife of the poet Percy Bysshe Shelley, was born at London and died there Feb 1, 1851. In addition to being the author of the famous novel *Frankenstein*, Shelley is important in literary history for her role in the editing and publishing of her husband's unpublished work after his early death.

SPACE MILESTONE: _DISCOVERY_ (US). Aug 30, 1984. Space shuttle *Discovery* was launched from Kennedy Space Center, FL, for its maiden flight with a six-member crew. During the flight the crew deployed three satellites and used a robot arm before landing at Edwards Air Force Base, CA, Sept 5.

SUPERCROC DISCOVERED: 5th ANNIVERSARY. Aug 30, 2000. A 40-ft dinosaur crocodile fossil, *Sarcosuchus imperator*, was discovered in the Sahara Desert in Niger in West Africa by a team led by paleontologist Paul Sereno. This croc wasn't new to science—some of its teeth and vertebrae had been discovered earlier—but Sereno's team found about 50 percent of the skeleton, including the entire six-ft-long skull. The croc is estimated to have weighed 10 tons. SuperCroc lived 110 million years ago. For more info: www.supercroc.org.

TURKEY: VICTORY DAY. Aug 30. Commemorates victory in War of Independence in 1922. Military parades, performing of the Mehtar band (the world's oldest military band), fireworks.

WILKINS, ROY: BIRTH ANNIVERSARY. Aug 30, 1901. Roy Wilkins, grandson of a Mississippi slave, civil rights leader, active in the National Association for the Advancement of Colored People (NAACP), retired as its executive director in 1977. Born at St. Louis, MO, he died at New York, NY, Sept 8, 1981.

BIRTHDAYS TODAY

Helen Craig, 71, illustrator (the Angelina Ballerina series, *This Is the Bear*), born London, England, Aug 30, 1934.

Donald Crews, 67, author, illustrator (*Bigmama's, Freight Train*), born Newark, NJ, Aug 30, 1938.

Cameron Diaz, 33, actress (*Shrek, Charlie's Angels*), born San Diego, CA, Aug 30, 1972.

Andy Roddick, 23, tennis player, born Omaha, NE, Aug 30, 1982.

AUGUST 31 — WEDNESDAY

Day 243 — 122 Remaining

CANADA: KLONDIKE ELDORADO GOLD DISCOVERY: ANNIVERSARY. Aug 31, 1896. Two weeks after the Rabbit/Bonanza Creek claim was filed, gold was discovered on Eldorado Creek, a tributary of Bonanza. More than $30 million worth of gold (worth some $600–$700 million in today's dollars) was mined from the Eldorado Claim in 1896. For more info: *Gold Rush Fever: A Story of the Klondike*, by Barbara Greenwood (Kids Can, 1-55074-852-1, $18.95 Gr. 4–7).

KAZAKHSTAN: CONSTITUTION DAY. Aug 31. National holiday. Commemorates the constitution of 1995.

KYRGYZSTAN: INDEPENDENCE DAY. Aug 31. National holiday. Commemorates independence from the Soviet Union in 1991.

MALAYSIA: FREEDOM DAY: ANNIVERSARY. Aug 31. National holiday. Merdeka (Freedom) Day commemorates independence from Britain in 1957.

MOLDOVA: NATIONAL LANGUAGE DAY. Aug 31. National holiday. Commemorates the 1991 replacement of the Cyrillic alphabet with the Roman alphabet.

MONTESSORI, MARIA: BIRTH ANNIVERSARY. Aug 31, 1870. Italian physician and educator, born at Chiaraville, Italy. Founder of the Montessori method of teaching children. She believed that children need to work at tasks that interest them and if given the right materials and tasks, they learn best through individual attention. Montessori died at Noordwijk, Holland, May 6, 1952.

POLAND: SOLIDARITY FOUNDED: 25th ANNIVERSARY. Aug 31, 1980. The Polish trade union Solidarity was formed at the Baltic Sea port of Gdansk. Outlawed by the government, many of its leaders were arrested. Led by Lech Walesa, Solidarity persisted in its opposition to the Communist-controlled government, and on Aug 19, 1989, Polish president Wojcieck Jaruzelski astonished the world by nominating for the post of prime minister Tadeusz Mazowiecki, a deputy in the Polish Assembly, 1961–72, and editor-in-chief of Solidarity's weekly newspaper, bringing to an end 42 years of Communist Party domination.

SPAIN: LA TOMATINA. Aug 31. Buñol (near Valencia). The world's biggest food fight takes place today as 35,000 revelers hurl 120 tons of tomatoes at each other (and the town) for 2 hours. La Tomatina ("Tomato Festival") occurs annually the last Wednesday of August. Festivities kick off with a competition to see who can reach a ham at the top of a greased pole. With the ham secured, the trucks arrive with tomatoes.

TRINIDAD AND TOBAGO: INDEPENDENCE DAY: ANNIVERSARY. Aug 31. National holiday. Became an independent nation within the British Commonwealth in 1962. Trinidad became a republic Sept 24, 1976.

BIRTHDAYS TODAY

Jennifer Azzi, 37, former basketball player, born Oak Ridge, TN, Aug 31, 1968.

Ian Crocker, 23, Olympic swimmer, born Portland, ME, Aug 31, 1982.

Edwin Corley Moses, 50, Olympic gold medal track athlete, born Dayton, OH, Aug 31, 1955.

Hideo Nomo, 37, baseball player, born Osaka, Japan, Aug 31, 1968.

Kenneth Oppel, 38, author (*Silverwing, Firewing*), born Port Albernia, BC, Canada, Aug 31, 1967.

Itzhak Perlman, 60, violinist, born Tel Aviv, Israel, Aug 31, 1945.

SEPTEMBER 1 — THURSDAY

Day 244 — 121 Remaining

BACKPACK SAFETY AMERICA MONTH. Sept 1–30. Thousands of school-age children are straining in pain under backpacks that are too heavy for their growing bodies. Backpack Safety America Month was founded to educate and remind students, parents and teachers about the safe and proper ways to choose, pack, lift and carry a backpack. For info: Backpack Safety America, c/o John Carroll, PO Box 2430, Mt Pleasant, SC 29465. Phone: (800) 672-4277. Fax: (843) 881-6746. E-mail: info@backpacksafe.com. Web: www.backpacksafe.com.

BRAZIL: INDEPENDENCE WEEK. Sept 1–7. The independence of Brazil from Portugal in 1822 is commemorated with civic and cultural ceremonies promoted by federal, state and municipal authorities. On Sept 7, a grand military parade takes place and the National Defense League organizes the Running Race in Honor of the Symbolic Torch of the Brazilian Nation.

BURROUGHS, EDGAR RICE: BIRTH ANNIVERSARY. Sept 1, 1875. US novelist (*Tarzan of the Apes*), born at Chicago, IL. Correspondent for the *Los Angeles Times*, he died at Encino, CA, Mar 19, 1950. For more info: *Edgar Rice Burroughs: Creator of Tarzan*, by William J. Boerst (Morgan Reynolds, 1-883846-56-0, $19.95 Gr. 5–8).

CARTIER, JACQUES: DEATH ANNIVERSARY. Sept 1, 1557. French navigator and explorer who sailed from St. Malo, France, Apr 20, 1534, in search of a northwest passage to the Orient. Instead, he discovered the St. Lawrence River, explored Canada's coastal regions and took possession of the country for France. Cartier was born at St. Malo, about 1491 (exact date unknown) and died there.

CHILDREN'S GOOD MANNERS MONTH. Sept 1–30. Starts the school year with a national program of teachers and parents encouraging good manners in children. The yearlong program includes monthly objectives that work in conjunction with a reinforcing home program. ***See Curriculum Connection.*** For info: "Dr. Manners," Fleming Allaire, PhD, 35 Eastfield St, Manchester, CT 06040. Phone: (860) 643-0051. E-mail: dr.manners@cox.net. Web: www.goodmannersclub.com or www.askdrmanners.com.

September 2005

S	M	T	W	T	F	S
				1	2	3
4	5	6	7	8	9	10
11	12	13	14	15	16	17
18	19	20	21	22	23	24
25	26	27	28	29	30	

CHILE: NATIONAL MONTH. Sept 1–30. A month of special significance in Chile: arrival of spring, Independence of Chile anniversary (proclaimed Sept 18, 1810), anniversary of the armed forces rising of Sept 11, 1973, to overthrow the government and celebration of the 1980 Constitution and Army Day, Sept 19.

D.A.R.E. LAUNCHED: ANNIVERSARY. Sept 1, 1983. D.A.R.E. (Drug Abuse Resistance Education) is a police officer–led series of classroom lessons that teaches students how to resist peer pressure and lead productive drug- and violence-free lives. The program, which was developed jointly by the Los Angeles Police Department and the Los Angeles Unified School District, initially focused on elementary school children but has now been expanded to include middle and high school students. D.A.R.E. has been implemented in 75 percent of US school districts and in 44 other countries. For info: D.A.R.E. America, PO Box 512090, Los Angeles, CA 90051-0090. Phone: (800) 223-DARE. Web: www.dare-america.com.

EMMA M. NUTT DAY. Sept 1. A day to honor the first woman telephone operator, Emma M. Nutt, who reportedly began her professional career at Boston, MA, Sept 1, 1878, and continued working as a telephone operator for some 33 years.

ISRA AL MI'RAJ: ASCENT OF THE PROPHET MUHAMMAD. Sept 1. Islamic calendar date: Rajab 27, 1426. Begins at sunset on the previous day. Commemorates the journey of the Prophet Muhammad from Mecca to Jerusalem, his ascension into the Seven Heavens and his return on the same night. Muslims believe that on that night Muhammad prayed together with Abraham, Moses and Jesus in the area of the Al-Aqsa Mosque at Jerusalem. The rock from which he is believed to have ascended to heaven to speak with God is the one inside The Dome of the Rock. Different methods for "anticipating" the visibility of the new moon crescent at Mecca are used by different Muslim groups. US date may vary. Began at sunset the preceding day.

LIBRARY CARD SIGN-UP MONTH. Sept 1–30. This observance was launched in 1987 to meet the challenge of then Secretary of Education William J. Bennett who said, "Let's have a national compaign. . . . every child should obtain a library card—and use it." Since then, thousands of public and school libraries join each fall in a national effort to ensure every child does just that. Annually, the month of September. For info: American Library Assn, Public Information Office, 50 E Huron St, Chicago, IL 60611. Phone: (312) 280-5043 or (312) 280-5042. E-mail: pio@ala.org. Web: www.ala.org.

LIBYA: REVOLUTION DAY: ANNIVERSARY. Sept 1. Commemorates the revolution in 1969 when King Idris I was overthrown by Colonel Qaddafi. National holiday.

MEXICO: PRESIDENT'S STATE OF THE UNION ADDRESS. Sept 1. National holiday.

NATIONAL CHILDHOOD INJURY PREVENTION WEEK. Sept 1–7. Injuries continue to be the #1 killer of American children. This month promotes prevention and intervention of unintentional injuries to children and emphasizes community involvement. Although money cannot buy social change, no significant change can happen without it. We invite you to join our mission. "Because the worst kind of childhood injury is the one that could have been prevented."® For info on our strategic partnership and sponsorship opportunities to help us mobilize the necessary human and financial resources to accomplish our objectives, contact The Safe As Possible Campaign, PO Box 715, Richboro, PA 18954. E-mail: nobooboos@AsSafeAsPossible.org. Web: www.AsSafeAsPossible.org.

NATIONAL 5-A-DAY MONTH. Sept 1–30. To encourage all Americans to increase the amount of fruits and vegetables they eat to five or more servings per day, to better their health and reduce their risk of cancer and other chronic diseases. For information on the US Department of Agriculture's Food Pyramid, go to www.nal.usda.gov/fnic/Fpyr/pyramid.html. For more info: *The Edible Pyramid: Good Eating Every Day*, by Loreen Leedy (Holiday House, 0-8234-1126-5, $15.95 Gr. 5–7) and *The Food Pyramid*, by Joan Kalbacken (Children's Press, 0-516-20756-3, $21 Gr. 2–4). For info: Produce for Better Health Foundation, 5301 Limestone Rd, Ste 101, Wilmington, DE 19808. Web: www.5aday.com.

NATIONAL FOOD ALLERGY AWARENESS MONTH. Sept 1–30. A month for all to learn about the seriousness of food allergies. For info: Robyn Rogers, 41 Massachusetts Ave, Norfolk, MA 02056. Phone: (508) 553-3858. E-mail: rrhearts@attbi.com. Web: www.seafoodallergy.com.

NATIONAL HONEY MONTH. Sept 1–30. To honor the US's 211,600 beekeepers and 2.63 million colonies of honeybees, which produce more than 220 million pounds of honey each year. For info: National Honey Board, 390 Lashley St, Longmont, CO 80501-6045. Phone: (303) 776-2337. Web: www.honey.com.

NATIONAL PEDICULOSIS PREVENTION MONTH. Sept 1–30. To promote awareness of how to prevent pediculosis and protect against unneccesary and potentially harmful pesticide treatments for head lice. For info: National Pediculosis Assn, 50 Kearney Rd, Needham, MA 02494. Phone: (781) 449-NITS. Fax: (781) 449-8129. Web: www.headlice.org or www.licemeister.org.

NATIONAL PIANO MONTH. Sept 1–30. Recognizes America's most popular instrument and its more than 20 million players; also encourages piano study by people of all ages. For info: Donald W. Dillon, Exec Dir, National Piano Foundation, 13140 Coit Rd, Ste 320, LB 120, Dallas, TX 75240-5737. Phone: (972) 233-9107. Fax: (972) 490-4219. E-mail: don@dondillon.com. Web: www.pianonet.com.

NATIONAL SCHOOL SUCCESS MONTH. Sept 1–30. Today's young people have many distractions from school and are sometimes overwhelmed when it comes to academics. Parents are often unskilled at effectively redirecting the attention of their children, especially their teenagers. This observance is to recognize parents who want to support and encourage their children to succeed in school and to explore ways to do that. Annually, the month of September. For info send SASE to: Teresa Langston, Dir, Parenting Without Pressure, 1330 Boyer St, Longwood, FL 32750-6311. Phone: (407) 767-2524. Web: www.parentingwithoutpressure.com.

NEW MEXICO STATE FAIR. Sept 1–18. Albuquerque, NM. Nationally known recording artists perform at Tingley Coliseum. PRCA rodeo competitions, thoroughbred and quarter horse racing, Villa Hispana and Native American villages, free entertainment. Est attendance: 725,000. For info: New Mexico State Fair, PO Box 8546, Albuquerque, NM 87198. Phone: (505) 265-EXPO. Fax: (505) 266-6753. Web: www.exponm.com.

PEDIATRIC CANCER AWARENESS MONTH. Sept 1–30. Cancer is the chief cause of death by disease in children. More than 2,300 children in the US die of cancer every year, more than die of AIDS. For info: Bear Necessities Pediatric Cancer Foundation, 23 W Hubbard St, 3rd Fl, Chicago, IL 60610. Phone: (312) 836-1284. Web: www.bearnecessities.org.

PHILLIS WHEATLEY'S POETRY COLLECTION PUBLISHED: ANNIVERSARY. Sept 1, 1773. On this date in 1773, the first book of poetry composed by an African American was published. Phillis Wheatley's *Poems on Various Subjects, Religious and Moral* was published at London, England. This publication came only 12 years after her arrival in America as a child slave from Senegal. In those 12 years, she learned to read and write English and studied literature in English and Latin. Feted in America and England, Wheatley eventually gained her freedom but died in poverty. See also: "Wheatley, Phillis: Death Anniversary" (Dec 5).

SEPTEMBER 1–30

CELEBRATING GOOD MANNERS WITH MUNRO LEAF

September is Children's Good Manners Month, and what better way to observe this month than by paging through two etiquette classics by Munro Leaf. 2005 marks the centennial of other Leaf's birth. Leaf, born Dec 4, 1905, is best known as the author of *The Story of Ferdinand* but also wrote and illustrated dozens of other children's books before his death in 1976. Two of his classics for young readers, *Manners Can Be Fun* (Universe, 0-7893-1061-9, $14.95) and *How To Behave and Why* (Universe, 0-7893-0684-0, $14.95), have recently been reissued for a new generation of children to love.

Both books, which feature simple illustrations in cheerful primary colors, adopt a friendly, accessible tone for a topic—etiquette—that can often be rendered severely. In *Manners Can Be Fun* (1936), Leaf doesn't just offer a list of etiquette do's and don't's. He also discusses *why* manners are important. "Having good manners is really just living with other people pleasantly," he explains. To bring the point home, Leaf introduces readers to the Pigs, the Whineys, the Noiseys, the Me Firsts, Smash, Rip and Ruin—people who don't make life pleasant. The gentle good humor of this book will delight any child.

Leaf followed *Manners Can Be Fun* with *How To Behave and Why* (1946), a book about "how to have the most fun in living." He suggests that children ask themselves, "Are most of the people I know glad that I am here?" This book will help them answer "Yes!" with discussions of how to be honest, fair, strong, and wise. And Leaf explains that it won't be easy, but that it is worth it. The concept of strength in *How To Behave and Why* will probably provoke a good classroom discussion. Leaf points out that strength is not about having muscles like a gorilla. Ask your class what strength may have to do with good manners or good behavior.

Whether you're celebrating good manners or Munro Leaf's 100th birthday, these two timeless books will be wonderful classroom resources. —Holly McGuire

SEA CADET MONTH. Sept 1–30. Nationwide year-round youth program for boys and girls 11–17 teaches leadership and self-discipline with emphasis on nautically oriented training without military obligation. Est attendance: 10,000. For info: US Naval Sea Cadet Corps, 2300 Wilson Blvd, Arlington, VA 22201. Phone: (703) 243-6910. Fax: (703) 243-3985. E-mail: mford@NAVYLEAGUE.org. Web: www.seacadets.org.

SLOVAKIA: CONSTITUTION DAY: ANNIVERSARY. Sept 1. Anniversary of the adoption of the Constitution of the Slovak Republic in 1992.

***TITANIC* DISCOVERED: 20th ANNIVERSARY.** Sept 1, 1985. Almost 75 years after the *Titanic* sank in the North Atlantic after striking an iceberg, a joint American-French expedition force led by marine geologist Dr. Robert Ballard located the wreck. The luxury liner was resting on the ocean floor 12,500 feet down—about 350 miles southeast from Newfoundland, Canada. In July 1986, Ballard returned in an expedition aboard the *Atlantis II*. A submersible craft, *Alvin*, descended to the deck of the *Titanic* and with underwater robot "Jason, Jr," explored the ship. Two memorial bronze plaques were left on the deck of the ship. See also: "Sinking of the *Titanic*: Anniversary" (Apr 15).

UZBEKISTAN: INDEPENDENCE DAY. Sept 1. National holiday. Commemorates independence after the breakup of the Soviet Union in 1991.

"THE WILD THORNBERRIES" TV PREMIERE: ANNIVERSARY. Sept 1, 1998. From the production company that created "Rugrats," this show follows the not-so-typical Thornberry family as they travel around the world in an RV. Parents Nigel and Marrianne are famous nature show hosts and daughter Eliza has the magical ability to talk with and understand animals. The show centers around Eliza, and she has many adventures involving her teenage sister, Debbie; pet monkey, Darwin; and her wild-boy foster brother Donnie. Featuring the voice talents of Lacey Chabert, Tim Curry, Jodi Carlisle and Flea (of The Red Hot Chili Peppers). A feature-length film was released in theaters in December 2002.

WORLD WAR II BEGINS: GERMANY INVADES POLAND: ANNIVERSARY. Sept 1, 1939. After securing a nonagression pact with the USSR (which secretly allowed for the partition of Poland by the Soviet Union and Germany) on Aug 23, Germany invaded Poland without a declaration of war at 4:45 AM. Two days later, Britain and France declared war, with Canada, Australia, New Zealand and South Africa soon following with their own declarations. Poland, overwhelmed by German air and land power, was in German and Soviet hands before the month concluded.

BIRTHDAYS TODAY

Jim Arnosky, 59, author and illustrator (*Watching Water Birds*, the Crinkleroot series, *Every Autumn Comes the Bear*), born New York, NY, Sept 1, 1946.

Rosa Guy, 77, author (*Billy the Great*), born Trinidad, West Indies, Sept 1, 1928.

Tim Hardaway, 39, former basketball player, born Chicago, IL, Sept 1, 1966.

Jane Hissey, 53, author, illustrator (*Old Bear, Old Bear's Trousers*), born Norfolk, England, Sept 1, 1952.

Zach Thomas, 32, football player, born Pampa, TX, Sept 1, 1973.

SEPTEMBER 2 — FRIDAY

Day 245 — 120 Remaining

CALENDAR ADJUSTMENT DAY: ANNIVERSARY. Sept 2, 1752. Pursuant to the British Calendar Act of 1751, Britain (and the American colonies) made the "Gregorian Correction" in 1752. The Act proclaimed that the day following Wednesday, Sept 2, should become Thursday, Sept 14, 1752. There was rioting in the streets by those who felt cheated and who demanded the eleven days back. The Act also provided that New Year's Day (and the change of year number) should fall Jan 1 (instead of Mar 25) in 1752 and every year thereafter. See also: "Gregorian Calendar Day: Anniversary" (Feb 24, Oct 4).

DAYS OF MARATHON: ANNIVERSARY. Sept 2–9, 490 BC. Anniversary of the event during the Persian Wars from which the marathon race is derived. Phidippides, "an Athenian and by profession and practice a trained runner," according to Herodotus, was dispatched from Marathon to Sparta (26 miles), Sept 2 to seek help in repelling the invading Persian army. Help being unavailable by religious law until after the next full moon, Phidippides ran the 26 miles back to Marathon Sept 4. Without Spartan aid, the Athenians defeated the Persians at the Battle of Marathon Sept 9. According to legend Phidippides carried the news of the battle to Athens and died as he spoke the words, "Rejoice, we are victorious." The marathon race was revived at the 1896 Olympic Games at Athens. Course distance, since 1924, is 26 miles, 385 yards.

ENGLAND: GREAT FIRE OF LONDON: ANNIVERSARY. Sept 2–5, 1666. The fire generally credited with bringing about our system of fire insurance started Sept 2, 1666, in the wooden house of a baker named Farryner, at London's Pudding Lane, near the Tower. During the ensuing three days more than 13,000 houses were destroyed, though it is believed that only six lives were lost in the fire.

FORTEN, JAMES: BIRTH ANNIVERSARY. Sept 2, 1766. James Forten was born of free black parents at Philadelphia, PA. As a powder boy on an American Revolutionary warship, he escaped being sold as a slave when his ship was captured due to the intervention of the British commander's son. While in England he became involved with abolitionists. On his return to Philadelphia, he became an apprentice to a sailmaker and eventually purchased the company for which he worked. He was active in the abolition movement, and in 1816, his support was sought by the American Colonization Society for the plan to settle American blacks at Liberia. He rejected their ideas and their plans to make him the ruler of the colony. From the large profits of his successful sailmaking company, he contributed heavily to the abolitionist movement and was a supporter of William Lloyd Garrison's antislavery journal, *The Liberator*. Died at Philadelphia, PA, Mar 4, 1842.

McAULIFFE, CHRISTA: BIRTH ANNIVERSARY. Sept 2, 1948. Christa McAuliffe, a 37-year-old Concord, NH, high school teacher, was to have been the first "ordinary citizen" in space. Born Sharon Christa Corrigan at Boston, MA, she perished with six crew members in the space shuttle *Challenger* explosion Jan 28, 1986. See also: "*Challenger* Space Shuttle Explosion: Anniversary" (Jan 28).

SHERMAN ENTERS ATLANTA: ANNIVERSARY. Sept 2, 1864. After a four-week siege, Union General William Tecumseh Sherman entered Atlanta, GA. The city had been evacuated on the previous day by Confederate troops under General John B. Hood. Hood had mistakenly assumed Sherman was ending the siege Aug 27, when actually Sherman was beginning the final stages of his attack. Hood then sent troops to attack the Union forces at Jonesboro. Hood's troops were defeated, opening the way for the capture of Atlanta.

US TREASURY DEPARTMENT: ANNIVERSARY. Sept 2, 1789. The third presidential cabinet department, the Treasury Department, was established by Congress.

VERMONT STATE FAIR. Sept 2–11. Fairgrounds, Rutland, VT. Annually, the Friday before Labor Day to the weekend after Labor Day. Est attendance: 100,000. For info: Vermont State Fair, 175 S Main St, Rutland, VT 05701. Phone: (802) 775-5200. Web: www.vermontstatefair.net.

September 2005

S	M	T	W	T	F	S
				1	2	3
4	5	6	7	8	9	10
11	12	13	14	15	16	17
18	19	20	21	22	23	24
25	26	27	28	29	30	

VIETNAM: INDEPENDENCE DAY. Sept 2. Ho Chi Minh formally proclaimed the independence of Vietnam from France and the establishment of the Democratic Republic of Vietnam in 1945. National holiday.

V-J (VICTORY OVER JAPAN) DAY: 60th ANNIVERSARY. Sept 2, 1945. Official ratification of Japanese surrender to the Allies occurred aboard the USS *Missouri* at Tokyo Bay Sept 2 (Far Eastern time) in 1945, thus prompting President Truman's declaration of this day as Victory-over-Japan Day. Japan's initial, informal agreement of surrender was announced by Truman and celebrated in the US Aug 14.

BIRTHDAYS TODAY

John Bierhorst, 69, author (*The Woman Who Fell from the Sky*), born Boston, MA, Sept 2, 1936.

Demi, 63, author (*One Grain of Rice, The Empty Pot*), born Charlotte Dumaresque Hunt, Cambridge, MA, Sept 2, 1942.

Jim DeMint, 54, US Senator (R, South Carolina), born Greenville, SC, Sept 2, 1951.

Elizabeth Borton de Trevino, 101, author (*I, Juan de Pareja*), born Bakersfield, CA, Sept 2, 1904.

Barbara Dillon, 78, author (*The Teddy Bear Tree, The Beast in the Bed*), born Montclair, NJ, Sept 2, 1927.

Bernard Most, 68, author and illustrator (*Where to Look for a Dinosaur, If the Dinosaurs Came Back*), born New York, NY, Sept 2, 1937.

Carlos Valderrama, 44, soccer player, born Santa Marta, Colombia, Sept 2, 1961.

Ellen Stoll Walsh, 63, author and illustrator (*Pip's Magic, Mouse Magic*), born Baltimore, MD, Sept 2, 1942.

SEPTEMBER 3 — SATURDAY

Day 246 — 119 Remaining

DOUGLASS ESCAPES TO FREEDOM: ANNIVERSARY. Sept 3, 1838. Dressed as a sailor and carrying identification papers borrowed from a retired merchant seaman, Frederick Douglass boarded a train at Baltimore, MD, a slave state, and rode to Wilmington, DE, where he caught a steamboat to the free city of Philadelphia. He then transferred to a train headed for New York City where he entered the protection of the Underground Railway network. Douglass later became a great orator and one of the leaders of the antislavery struggle.

EASTERN IDAHO STATE FAIR. Sept 3–10. Blackfoot, ID. Family fun, amusement rides, food booths, entertainment, tractor pulls and more. Est attendance: 212,000. For info: Manager, Eastern Idaho State Fair, PO Box 250, Blackfoot, ID 83221. Phone: (208) 785-2480. Fax: (208) 785-2483. E-mail: theFair@idaho-state-fair.com. Web: www.idaho-state-fair.com.

ITALY SURRENDERS: ANNIVERSARY. Sept 3, 1943. General Giuseppe Castellano signed three copies of the "short armistice," effectively surrendering unconditionally for the Italian government in World War II. That same day the British Eighth Army, commanded by General Bernard Montgomery, invaded the Italian mainland.

MOON PHASE: NEW MOON. Sept 3. Moon enters New Moon phase at 2:45 PM, EDT.

QATAR: INDEPENDENCE DAY. Sept 3. National holiday. Commemorates the severing in 1971 of the treaty with Britain, which had handled Qatar's foreign relations.

SAN MARINO: NATIONAL DAY. Sept 3. Public holiday. Honors St. Marinus, the traditional founder of San Marino.

★ ★ ★

SOUTH DAKOTA STATE FAIR. Sept 3–10. Huron, SD. Grandstand entertainment nightly, 10 free stages with multiple shows daily, hundreds of commercial exhibits and thousands of livestock exhibits. One of the largest agricultural fairs in the US. Est attendance: 250,000. For info: South Dakota State Fair, PO Box 1275, Huron, SD 57350-1275. Phone: (605) 353-7340. Fax: (605) 353-7348. E-mail: statefair@state.sd.us. Web: www.sdstatefair.com.

TREATY OF PARIS ENDS AMERICAN REVOLUTION: ANNIVERSARY. Sept 3, 1783. Treaty between Britain and the US, ending the Revolutionary War, signed at Paris, France. American signatories: John Adams, Benjamin Franklin and John Jay.

WORLD WAR II DECLARATION: ANNIVERSARY. Sept 3, 1939. British ultimatum to Germany, demanding halt to invasion of Poland (which had started at dawn on Sept 1), expired at 11 AM, GMT, Sept 3, 1939. At 11:15 AM, in a radio broadcast, Prime Minister Neville Chamberlain announced the declaration of war against Germany. France, Canada, Australia, New Zealand and South Africa quickly issued separate declarations of war. Winston Churchill was named First Lord of the Admiralty.

BIRTHDAYS TODAY

Aliki, 76, author and illustrator (*Manners; Corn is Maize: The Gift of the Indians; Three Gold Pieces*), born Aliki Liacouras Brandenberg, Wildwood Crest, NJ, Sept 3, 1929.

Damon Stoudamire, 32, basketball player, born Portland, OR, Sept 3, 1973.

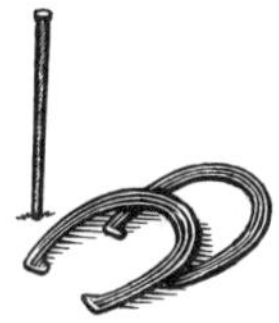

SEPTEMBER 4 — SUNDAY

Day 247 — 118 Remaining

FIRST ELECTRIC LIGHTING: ANNIVERSARY. Sept 4, 1882. Four hundred electric lights came on in offices on Spruce, Wall, Nassau and Pearl streets in lower Manhattan as Thomas Edison hooked up lightbulbs to an underground cable carrying direct current electrical power. Edison had demonstrated his first incandescent lightbulb in 1879. See also: "Incandescent Lamp Demonstrated: Anniversary" (Oct 21).

HOFF, SYD: BIRTH ANNIVERSARY. Sept 4, 1912. Author of more than 60 books, Syd Hoff was born at New York, NY. He began drawing cartoons in high school and was first published in *The New Yorke*r at age 18. His most popular titles for children include *Sammy the Seal* and *Danny and the Dinosaur.* He died at Miami Beach, FL, May 12, 2004.

LOS ANGELES, CALIFORNIA FOUNDED: ANNIVERSARY. Sept 4, 1781. Los Angeles founded by decree and called "El Pueblo de Nuestra Senora La Reina de Los Angeles de Porciuncula." For more info: *City of Angels: In and Around Los Angeles*, by Julie Jaskol and Brian Lewis (Dutton, 0-525-46214-7, $16.99 All ages).

NEWSPAPER CARRIER DAY. Sept 4. Anniversary of the hiring of the first "newsboy" in the US, 10-year-old Barney Flaherty, who is said to have answered the following classified advertisement which appeared in *The New York Sun*, in 1833: "To the Unemployed—a number of steady men can find employment by vending this paper. A liberal discount is allowed to those who buy to sell again."

POLK, SARAH CHILDRESS: BIRTH ANNIVERSARY. Sept 4, 1803. Wife of James Knox Polk, 11th president of the US. Born at Murfreesboro, TN, and died at Nashville, TN, Aug 14, 1891.

WRIGHT, RICHARD: BIRTH ANNIVERSARY. Sept 4, 1908. African-American novelist and short story writer whose works included *Native Son, Uncle Tom's Children* and *Black Boy*. Born at Natchez, MS, Wright died at Paris, France, Nov 28, 1960. For more info: *Richard Wright and the Library Card*, by William Miller (Lee & Low, 1-88000-057-1, $6.95 Gr. 1–4).

BIRTHDAYS TODAY

Mike Piazza, 37, baseball player, born Norristown, PA, Sept 4, 1968.

SEPTEMBER 5 — MONDAY

Day 248 — 117 Remaining

BE LATE FOR SOMETHING DAY. Sept 5. To create a release from the stresses and strains resulting from a consistent need to be on time. For info: Les Waas, Pres, Procrastinators' Club of America, Inc, Box 712, Bryn Athyn, PA 19009. Phone: (215) 947-9020. Fax: (215) 947-7210. E-mail: procrastinators_club_of_america@yahoo.com.

CANADA: LABOR DAY. Sept 5. Annually, the first Monday in September.

FIRST CONTINENTAL CONGRESS ASSEMBLY: ANNIVERSARY. Sept 5, 1774. The first assembly of this forerunner of the US Congress took place at Philadelphia, PA. All 13 colonies were represented except Georgia. Peyton Randolph, delegate from Virginia, was elected president. The second Continental Congress met beginning May 10, 1775, also at Philadelphia.

JAMES, JESSE: BIRTH ANNIVERSARY. Sept 5, 1847. Western legend and bandit Jesse Woodson James was born at Centerville (now Kearney), MO. His criminal exploits were glorified and romanticized by writers for Eastern readers looking for stories of Western adventure and heroism. After the Civil War, James and his brother, Frank, formed a group of eight outlaws who robbed banks, stagecoaches and stores. In 1873 the James gang began holding up trains. The original James gang was put out of business Sept 7, 1876, while attempting to rob a bank at Northfield, MN. Every member of the gang except for the James brothers was killed or captured. The brothers formed a new gang and resumed their criminal careers in 1879. Two years later, the governor of Missouri offered a $10,000 reward for their capture, dead or alive. On Apr 3, 1882, at St. Joseph, MO, Robert Ford, a member of the gang, shot 34-year-old Jesse in the back of the head and claimed the reward.

LABOR DAY. Sept 5. Legal public holiday. Public Law 90–363 sets Labor Day on the first Monday in September. Observed in all states. First observance believed to have been a parade at 10 AM, Tuesday, Sept 5, 1882, at New York, NY, probably organized by Peter J. McGuire, a Carpenters and Joiners Union secretary. In 1883, a union resolution declared "the first Monday in September of each year a Labor Day." By 1893, more than half of the states were observing Labor Day on one or another day, and a bill to establish Labor Day as a federal holiday was introduced in Congress. On June 28, 1894, President Grover Cleveland signed into law an act making the first Monday in September a legal holiday for federal employees and the District of Columbia. Canada also celebrates Labor Day on the first Monday in September. In most other countries, Labor Day is observed May 1. For links to Labor Day websites, go to: www.dol.gov/opa/aboutdol/laborday.htm or www.usinfo.pl/aboutusa/holidays/labor.htm.

September 2005

S	M	T	W	T	F	S
				1	2	3
4	5	6	7	8	9	10
11	12	13	14	15	16	17
18	19	20	21	22	23	24
25	26	27	28	29	30	

SPACE MILESTONE: *VOYAGER 1* (US). Sept 5, 1977. Twin of *Voyager 2* which was launched Aug 20. On Feb 18, 1998, *Voyager 1* set a new distance record when after more than 20 years in space it reached 6.5 billion miles from Earth.

BIRTHDAYS TODAY

Paul Fleischman, 53, author, poet (*Seedfolks, Whirligig*, Newbery for *Joyful Noise: Poems for Two Voices*), born Monterey, CA, Sept 5, 1952.

Roxie Munro, 60, author (*The Inside-Outside Book of Libraries*), born Mineral Wells, TX, Sept 5, 1945.

Brian Schweitzer, 50, Governor of Montana (D), born Havre, MT, Sept 5, 1955.

SEPTEMBER 6 — TUESDAY

Day 249 — 116 Remaining

ADDAMS, JANE: BIRTH ANNIVERSARY. Sept 6, 1860. American worker for peace, social welfare and the rights of women. The founder of Chicago's Hull House settlement house, she was cowinner of the Nobel Peace Prize in 1931. Born at Cedarville, IL, she died May 21, 1935, at Chicago, IL.

BALTIC STATES' INDEPENDENCE RECOGNIZED: ANNIVERSARY. Sept 6, 1991. The Soviet government recognized the independence of the Baltic states—Latvia, Estonia and Lithuania. The action came 51 years after the Baltic states were annexed by the Soviet Union. All three Baltic states had earlier declared their independence, and many nations had already recognized them diplomatically, including the US, Sept 2, 1991.

BULGARIA: UNIFICATION DAY. Sept 6. National holiday. Commemorates the 1885 reunification of the South and the rest of Bulgaria.

LAFAYETTE, MARQUIS DE: BIRTH ANNIVERSARY. Sept 6, 1757. French general and aristocrat, Lafayette, whose full name was Marie-Joseph-Paul-Yves-Roch-Gilbert du Motier, came to America to assist in the revolutionary cause. He was awarded a major-generalship and began a lasting friendship with the American commander-in-chief, George Washington. After an alliance was signed with France, he returned to his native country and persuaded Louis XVI to send a 6,000-man force to assist the Americans. On his return, he was given command of an army at Virginia and was instrumental in forcing the surrender of Lord Cornwallis at Yorktown, leading to the end of the war and American independence. Born at Chavaniac, he died at Paris, May 20, 1834. For more info: *Why Not, Lafayette?*, by Jean Fritz (Putnam, 0-399-23411-X, $16.99 Gr. 3–7).

SAINT PETERSBURG NAME RESTORED: ANNIVERSARY. Sept 6, 1991. Russian legislators voted to restore the name Saint Petersburg to the nation's second largest city. The city had been known as Leningrad for 67 years in honor of the Soviet Union's founder, Vladimir I. Lenin. The city, founded in 1703 by Peter the Great, has had three names in the 20th century with Russian leaders changing its German-sounding name to Petrograd at the beginning of WWI in 1914 and Soviet Communist leaders changing its name to Leningrad in 1924 following their leader's death.

SWAZILAND: INDEPENDENCE DAY: ANNIVERSARY. Sept 6. National holiday, commemorates attainment of independence from Britain in 1968. Also called Somhlolo Day in honor of the great 19th-century Swazi leader.

BIRTHDAYS TODAY

Tim Henman, 31, tennis player, born Oxford, England, Sept 6, 1974.
Chad Scott, 31, football player, born Washington, DC, Sept 6, 1974.

SEPTEMBER 7 — WEDNESDAY

Day 250 — 115 Remaining

BRAZIL: INDEPENDENCE DAY. Sept 7. Declared independence from Portugal in 1822. National holiday.

ELIZABETH I: BIRTH ANNIVERSARY. Sept 7, 1533. Queen of England, after whom the "Elizabethan Age" was named, born at Greenwich Palace, daughter of Henry VIII and Anne Boleyn. She succeeded to the throne in 1558 and ruled England until her death on May 24, 1603. Her reign was one of the most dynamic in English history and she was held in great affection by her people. The British defeated the Spanish Armada and England became a world power during her reign. For more info: *Good Queen Bess: The Story of Elizabeth I of England*, by Diane Stanley and Peter Vennema (HarperCollins, 0-688-17961-4, $16.95 Ages 4–8).

GRANDMA MOSES DAY. Sept 7. Anna Mary Robertson Moses, modern primitive American painter, born at Greenwich, NY, Sept 7, 1860. She started painting at the age of 78. Her 100th birthday was proclaimed Grandma Moses Day in New York state. Died at Hoosick Falls, NY, Dec 13, 1961. For info: *Grandma Moses*, by Zibby O'Neal (Puffin, 0-14-032220-5, $4.99 Gr. 4–8).

LAWRENCE, JACOB: BIRTH ANNIVERSARY. Sept 7, 1917. African-American painter, born at Atlantic City, NJ. Lawrence was best known for his series of historical paintings on John Brown and on the migration of African Americans out of the South. He also illustrated children's books. A recipient of the NAACP's Spingarn Medal, he won many other awards during his lifetime. Lawrence died June 9, 2000, at Seattle, WA. For more info: *Story Painter: The Life of Jacob Lawrence*, by John Duggleby (Chronicle, 0-8118-2082-3, $16.95 Gr. 4–7) and *The Great Migration: An American Story*, by Jacob Lawrence (Harper Trophy, 0-06-443428-1, $8.95 Gr. 4–7). ***See Curriculum Connection.***

NEITHER SNOW NOR RAIN DAY: ANNIVERSARY. Sept 7, 1914. Anniversary of the opening to the public, on Labor Day, 1914, of the New York Post Office Building at Eighth Avenue between 31st and 33rd Streets. On the front of this building was an inscription supplied by William M. Kendall of the architectural firm that planned the building. The inscription, a free translation from Herodotus, reads: "Neither snow nor rain nor heat nor gloom of night stays these couriers from the swift completion of their appointed rounds." This has long been believed to be the motto of the US Post Office and Postal Service. They have, in fact, no motto . . . but the legend remains. (Info from: New York Post Office, Public Info Office and US Postal Service.)

SEPTEMBER 7
JACOB LAWRENCE

Jacob Lawrence is one of America's best-known artists. Born this day in 1917, in Atlantic City, NJ, he was the eldest of three children. When his mother moved the family to Harlem, NY, in the 1930s, Lawrence joined an after-school art class. His talent was quickly recognized by the teacher, and several years later he was awarded a scholarship to attend the American Artists School in New York City.

In his early years, Lawrence was influenced by many artists, including Diego Rivera, Goya and Brueghel. He also met Romare Bearden, a prominent artist who also lived in Harlem. At first, Lawrence painted on brown wrapping paper, using poster and tempura paints. Later, he worked in several different mediums, including prints and drawing. He used a narrative style, developed by creating groups of paintings that reflected the struggle of oppressed people and African Americans. He is well known for his series of paintings that illustrate Toussaint L'Ouverture's life and the 1791 slave rebellion in Haiti. Similarly, Lawrence created a group of 63 pieces to illustrate the lives of Harriet Tubman, Frederick Douglass and others who actively aided the abolition of slavery in the United States. Seventeen of his paintings were used to illustrate his children's book *Harriet and the Promised Land* (Simon & Schuster, 0-689-80965-4, $6.99 All ages).

Lawrence's 60-painting work "Migration" depicts the story of African Americans as they moved to northern states, hoping to find freedom, equality and better jobs.

The best way to introduce students to Jacob Lawrence is by bringing his art into the classroom. His paintings are readily accessible in a number of books. *The Great Migration* (HarperCollins, 0-064-43428-1, $8.99 All ages) reproduces 60 of his works. Paintings of Haiti's slave rebellion can be found in *Toussaint L'Ouverture: The Fight for Haiti's Freedom* by Walter Dean Myers (Simon & Schuster, 0-689-80126-2 All ages).

Lawrence's colorful images appear flat on paper, yet they vividly convey tension and immediacy. At times the images seem almost as if they'd been cut out of paper and pasted onto the panel. Students may enjoy experimenting with Lawrence's style using paint or paper to create pictures of their own. They could be encouraged to produce a series of images that tell a narrative relating to their own lives or the history of their school or town. They may want to paint on brown paper bags that have been cut open, which would parallel Lawrence's use of wrapping paper. Comparing and contrasting Lawrence's work with that of Romare Bearden would also be fun.

Two biographies that young readers will enjoy are *Jacob Lawrence* by Mike Venezia (Children's Press, 0-516-26533-4, $6.95 Ages 8–11) and *Story Painter: The Life of Jacob Lawrence* by John Duggleby (Chronicle Books, 0-8118-2082-3, $16.95 All ages), which is illustrated with Lawrence's work.

Jacob Lawrence died at age 82 in June 2000, at his home in Seattle, WA.

—Sally Walker

BIRTHDAYS TODAY

Alexandra Day, 64, author and illustrator (*The Teddy Bears' Picnic; Good Dog, Carl; Carl's Afternoon in the Park*), born Cincinnati, OH, Sept 7, 1941.
Eric Hill, 78, author (*Where's Spot?, Spot Goes to School, Spot Visits His Grandparents*), born London, England, Sept 7, 1927.
Daniel Ken Inouye, 81, US Senator (D, Hawaii), born Honolulu, HI, Sept 7, 1924.

SEPTEMBER 8 — THURSDAY

Day 251 — 114 Remaining

ANDORRA: NATIONAL HOLIDAY. Sept 8. Honors our Lady of Meritxell.

CORN ISLAND STORYTELING FESTIVAL. Sept 8–10. Louisville, KY. Est. attendance: 10,000. For info: Corn Island Storytelling Festival, 651 S. Fourth St, Louisville, KY 40202. Web: www.cornislandstorytellingfestival.org.

GALVESTON HURRICANE: ANNIVERSARY. Sept 8, 1900. The worst national disaster in US history in terms of lives lost. More than 6,000 people were killed when a hurricane struck Galveston, TX. For more info about hurricanes: www.fema.gov/kids/hurr.htm.

INCA ICE MAIDEN DISCOVERED: 10th ANNIVERSARY. Sept 8, 1995. Climbing Mount Ampato in the Peruvian Andes, Dr. Johan Reinhard and Miguel Zarate discovered at 20,500 feet the best preserved Incan mummy: a girl, about 14 years old, who had been offered as a precious *capacocha* sacrifice to the gods. The girl had been frozen for about 500 years and has given scientists much information on Incan life. The "ice maiden" now resides in a specially constructed freezer unit at Arequipa, Peru. Reinhard discovered more sacrificial mummies in the Andes in 1999. For more info: *Discovering the Inca Ice Maiden* by Johan Reinhard (National Geographic, 0-7922-7142-4, $17.95 Gr. 4 & up).

NORTHERN PACIFIC RAILROAD COMPLETED: ANNIVERSARY. Sept 8, 1883. After 19 years of construction, the Northern Pacific Railroad became the second railroad to link the two coasts. The Union Pacific and Central Pacific lines met at Utah in 1869.

"STAR TREK" TV PREMIERE: ANNIVERSARY. Sept 8, 1966. The first of 79 episodes of the TV series "Star Trek" was aired on the NBC network. Although the science fiction show set in the future only lasted a few seasons, it has remained enormously popular through syndication reruns. It has been given new life through six motion pictures, a cartoon TV series and the very popular TV series "Star Trek: The Next Generation," "Star Trek: Deep Space Nine," "Star Trek: Voyager" and "Enterprise." It has consistently ranked among the biggest titles in the motion picture, television, home video and licensing divisions of Paramount Pictures.

UNITED NATIONS: INTERNATIONAL LITERACY DAY. Sept 8. An international day observed by the organizations of the United Nations system. Info from: United Nations, Dept of Public Info, New York, NY 10017.

UTAH STATE FAIR. Sept 8–18. Utah State Fairpark, Salt Lake City, UT. PRCA Rodeo, exhibits, livestock, family contests, cook-offs, concerts and entertainment. Annually, beginning the first Thursday after Labor Day. Est attendance: 277,000. For info: Utah State Fairpark, 155 N 1000 W, Salt Lake City, UT 84116. Phone: (801) 538-8440. Fax: (801) 538-8455. E-mail: utstfair@fiber.net.

September 2005

S	M	T	W	T	F	S
				1	2	3
4	5	6	7	8	9	10
11	12	13	14	15	16	17
18	19	20	21	22	23	24
25	26	27	28	29	30	

BIRTHDAYS TODAY

Michael Hague, 57, illustrator (*The Children's Book of Virtues, The Wind in the Willows, The Hobbit*), born Los Angeles, CA, Sept 8, 1948.

Jack Prelutsky, 65, poet (*The New Kid on the Block, A Pizza the Size of the Sun*), born Brooklyn, NY, Sept 8, 1940.

Jon Scieszka, 51, author (*The Stinky Cheese Man and Other Fairly Stupid Tales, Math Curse*), born Flint, MI, Sept 8, 1954.

Latrell Sprewell, 35, basketball player, born Milwaukee, WI, Sept 8, 1970.

Jonathan Taylor Thomas, 24, actor ("Home Improvement," voice of Simba in *The Lion King*), born Bethlehem, PA, Sept 8, 1981.

SEPTEMBER 9 — FRIDAY

Day 252 — 113 Remaining

ATLANTA BOOK FESTIVAL. Sept 9–11. Various sites throughout metropolitan Atlanta, GA. For info: The Atlanta Book Fest, 1710 DeFoor Ave, Atlanta, GA 30318. Phone: (404) 683-0388. Web: www.atlantabookfestival.com.

BONZA BOTTLER DAY™. Sept 9. To celebrate when the number of the day is the same as the number of the month. Bonza Bottler Day™ is an excuse to have a party at least once a month. For info: Gail M. Berger, 14 Fernwood Dr, Taylors, SC 29687. Phone: (864) 609-9874. E-mail: gberger5@aol.com.

CALIFORNIA: ADMISSION DAY: ANNIVERSARY. Sept 9. Became 31st state in 1850.

COLONIES BECOME UNITED STATES: ANNIVERSARY. Sept 9, 1776. The Continental Congress resolved that the name United States was to replace United Colonies.

IRISH FAMINE BEGINS: ANNIVERSARY. Sept 9, 1845. On this day, *The Dublin Evening Post* reported the partial failure of the potato crop in Ireland. A blight caused by a fungus destroyed 30 percent of the crop; in 1846, 1848 and 1849 nearly the entire potato crop failed. Out of a population of 8 million, about 1 million people died in the resulting famine and 1.5 million emigrated to the US, Canada and Australia. The 1850 US census showed that more than 40 percent of the country's foreign-born population was Irish. For more info: *Feed the Children First: Irish Memories of the Great Hunger*, ed by Mary E. Lyons (Simon & Schuster, 0-689-84226-0, $17 Gr. 4–8).

KANSAS STATE FAIR. Sept 9–18. Hutchinson, KS. Commercial and competitive exhibits, entertainment, carnival, car racing and other special attractions. Annually, beginning the first Friday after Labor Day. Est attendance: 400,000. For info: Denny Stocklein, Gen Mgr, Kansas State Fair, 2000 N Poplar, Hutchinson, KS 67502. Phone: (316) 669-3600. E-mail: info@kansasstatefair.com. Web: www.kansasstatefair.com.

KOREA, DEMOCRATIC PEOPLE'S REPUBLIC OF: NATIONAL DAY. Sept 9. National holiday in the Democratic People's Republic of [North] Korea.

LUXEMBOURG: LIBERATION ANNIVERSARY CEREMONY. Sept 9. Petange. Commemoration of liberation of Grand-Duchy by the Allied forces in 1944. Ceremony at monument of the American soldier.

★**NATIONAL DAYS OF PRAYER AND REMEMBRANCE.** Sept 9–11 (tentative). In remembrance of the victims of the terrorist attacks of Sept 11, 2001.

TAJIKISTAN: INDEPENDENCE DAY. Sept 9. National holiday commemorating independence from the Soviet Union in 1991.

TENNESSEE STATE FAIR. Sept 9–18. Nashville, TN. A huge variety of exhibits, carnival midway, animal and variety shows, live stage presentations, livestock, agricultural and craft competitions and food and game booths. Annually, beginning the first Friday after Labor Day. Est attendance: 200,000. For info: Tennessee Fair Office, PO Box 40208, Melrose Station, Nashville, TN 37204. Phone: (615) 862-8980. Fax: (615) 862-8992. Web: www.tennesseestatefair.org.

WILLIAM, THE CONQUEROR: DEATH ANNIVERSARY. Sept 9, 1087. William I, The Conqueror, King of England and Duke of Normandy, whose image is portrayed in the Bayeux Tapestry, was born about 1028 at Falaise, Normandy. Victorious over Harold at the Battle of Hastings (the Norman Conquest) in 1066, William was crowned King of England at Westminster Abbey on Christmas Day of that year. Later, while waging war in France, William met his death at Rouen, Sept 9, 1087.

BIRTHDAYS TODAY

Benjamin Roy (BJ) Armstrong, 38, former basketball player, born Detroit, MI, Sept 9, 1967.
Shane Battier, 27, basketball player, born Birmingham, MI, Sept 9, 1978.
Kimberly Willis Holt, 45, author (*When Zachary Beaver Came to Town*), born Pensacola, FL, Sept 9, 1960.
Kazuhisa Ishii, 32, baseball player, born Chiba, Japan, Sept 9, 1973.
Alphonso Jackson, 60, US Secretary of Housing and Urban Development, born Marshall, TX, Sept 9, 1945.
Adam Sandler, 39, actor (*The Waterboy, Big Daddy, Happy Gilmore*), born Brooklyn, NY, Sept 9, 1966.
Mildred Pitts Walter, 83, author (*Justin and the Best Biscuits in the World*), born De Ridder, LA, Sept 9, 1922.

SEPTEMBER 10 — SATURDAY

Day 253 — 112 Remaining

BELIZE: SAINT GEORGE'S CAYE DAY. Sept 10. Public holiday celebrated in honor of the battle between the European Baymen Settlers and the Spaniards for the territory of Belize.

BRAXTON, CARTER: BIRTH ANNIVERSARY. Sept 10, 1736. American revolutionary statesman and signer of the Declaration of Independence. Born at Newington, VA, he died Oct 10, 1797, at Richmond, VA.

FESTIVAL OF BOOKS FOR YOUNG PEOPLE. Sept 10. Iowa Memorial Union, Iowa City, IA. Annual festival will feature talks by children's authors, booktalk sessions and exhibits of new books for young people. For info: School of Library and Information Science, University of Iowa, Iowa City, IA 52242-1420. Phone: (319) 335-5707. E-mail: jane-bradbury@uiowa.edu.

KEIKO RETURNS TO ICELAND: ANNIVERSARY. Sept 10, 1998. Keiko, the killer whale or orca who starred in the 1993 film *Free Willy*, was returned to his home in waters off Iceland after spending 19 years in captivity. Keiko was to be kept in a specially built cage in the ocean until it was determined if he could return to the wild. He was moved to Taknes, Norway, but did not adjust well to independence and needed to be in the company of humans. He died of pneumonia on Dec 12, 2003, and was buried on a beach nearby. For more info: *Keiko's Story: A Killer Whale Goes Home*, by Linda Moore Kurth (Millbrook, 0-7613-1500-4, $23.90 Gr. 4–8).

LAURA INGALLS WILDER DAYS. Sept 10–11. Pepin, WI. 15th annual. Experience life in the mid-1800s with demonstrations of blacksmithing, woodworking, ironworking, weaving, quilting and wool-spinning by individuals dressed in period costumes. Stories and songs cited in Little House books are also performed and there's a Laura Ingalls look-alike contest. Additional attractions include a traveling exhibit of Wilder's written materials, sanctioned horse-pull, Civil War encampment, children's games from the period, parade, crafts and antiques at Laura Ingalls Wilder Memorial Park. For info: Pepin Visitor Information Center, PO Box 274, Pepin, WI 54759. Phone: (715) 442-3011. E-mail: pepinwis@nelson-tel.net. Web: www.pepinwisconsin.com.

MARIS, ROGER: BIRTH ANNIVERSARY. Sept 10, 1934. Baseball player, born Roger Eugene Maris, at Hibbing, MN. In 1961, Maris broke one of baseball's sacred records, hitting 61 home runs to surpass the mark set by Babe Ruth in 1927. This record wasn't broken until 1998 (and was broken again in 2001). He won the American League MVP award in 1960 and 1961 and finished his career with the St. Louis Cardinals. Died at Houston, TX, Dec 14, 1985.

BIRTHDAYS TODAY

Babette Cole, 56, author (*Dr. Dog, Princess Smartypants*), born Jersey, Channel Islands, UK, Sept 10, 1949.
Roy Doty, 83, cartoonist, author and illustrator (*Wonderful Circus Parade*), born Chicago, IL, Sept 10, 1922.
Matt Geiger, 36, basketball player, born Salem, MA, Sept 10, 1969.
Randy Johnson, 42, baseball player, born Walnut Creek, CA, Sept 10, 1963.
Joe Nieuwendyk, 39, hockey player, born Oshawa, ON, Canada, Sept 10, 1966.
John Sununu, 41, US Senator (R, New Hampshire), born Boston, MA, Sept 10, 1964.
Jay Williams, 24, basketball player, born Plainfield, NJ, Sept 10, 1981.

SEPTEMBER 11 — SUNDAY

Day 254 — 111 Remaining

ATTACK ON AMERICA: ANNIVERSARY. Sept 11, 2001. Terrorists hijacked four planes, piloting two of them into the World Trade Center's twin towers in New York City and one into the Pentagon in Washington. Passengers on the fourth plane appear to have attempted to overcome the hijackers, causing that plane to crash in western Pennsylvania instead of reaching its target in Washington. The twin towers at the WTC collapsed about an hour after being hit. Almost 3,000 people died as a result of the attack, including many police and firefighters. The terrorists were agents of Islamic extremist Osama bin Laden who was headquartered in Afghanistan. The US began bombing Afghanistan, attempting to force the ruling Taliban to turn over bin Laden. By the end of the year the Taliban was defeated and a new government was being established in Afghanistan.

BATTLE OF BRANDYWINE: ANNIVERSARY. Sept 11, 1777. The largest engagement of the American Revolution, between the Continental Army led by General George Washington and British forces led by General William Howe. Howe was marching to take Philadelphia when Washington chose an area on the Brandywine Creek near Chadds Ford, PA, to stop the advance. The American forces were defeated here and the British went on to take Philadelphia Sept 26. They spent the winter in the city while Washington's troops suffered in their encampment at Valley Forge, PA. For more info, visit the Independence Hall Association website at www.ushistory.org/brandywine/index.html.

ETHIOPIA: NEW YEAR'S DAY. Sept 11. Public holiday. This day in 2005 begins the year 1999 on the Ethiopian calendar. This is also the beginning of the year 1722 on the Coptic calendar.

MOON PHASE: FIRST QUARTER. Sept 11. Moon enters First Quarter phase at 7:37 AM, EDT.

NATIONAL GRANDPARENTS' DAY. Sept 11. To honor grandparents, to give grandparents an opportunity to show love for their children's children and to help children become aware of the strength, information and guidance older people can offer. Annually, the first Sunday after Labor Day. ***See Curriculum Connection.***

★**NATIONAL HISTORICALLY BLACK COLLEGES AND UNIVERSITIES WEEK.** Sept 11–17. Usually proclaimed for the second full week of September.

PAKISTAN: FOUNDER'S DEATH ANNIVERSARY. Sept 11. Pakistan observes the death anniversary in 1948 of Qaid-i-Azam Mohammed Ali Jinnah (founder of Pakistan) as a national holiday.

★**PATRIOT DAY.** Sept 11. On Dec 18, 2001, a joint resolution of Congress amended Title 36, Chapter 1, Sec 144 of the US Code to permit the President to declare Sept 11 of each year as Patriot Day—in commemoration of the terrorist attacks on the United States on Sept 11, 2001. The resolution requests that all state and local governments observe this day "with appropriate programs and activities," that the flag be displayed at half-staff from sunrise until sundown and that a moment of silence be observed in honor of those who lost their lives.

September 2005

S	M	T	W	T	F	S
				1	2	3
4	5	6	7	8	9	10
11	12	13	14	15	16	17
18	19	20	21	22	23	24
25	26	27	28	29	30	

SEPTEMBER 11
GRANDPARENTS AND ORAL HISTORY

Laptop computers, microwave ovens, digital cameras and cell phones are items many children believe have always existed, but 50 years ago many of them hadn't even been invented. Grandparents are just old enough to recall those days. Celebrate National Grandparents' Day by undertaking an oral history project in your classroom. This will give students a wonderful opportunity to discover the value of oral tradition, to connect on a different level with their grandparents, and will complement the history curriculum.

Preparing for an oral history project can be lots of fun. The class may want to brainstorm to create general categories for questions, for example, childhood memories, school memories, first-time voting, chores, holiday memories, etc. From there, the students can think up specific questions for each category. Work on developing questions that require more than "yes" or "no" as the answer. Primary students may only be able to handle one question per category and may need help with transcribing the answers. Older students should put together several questions per category as well as suggestions for follow-up questions.

The next step is preparing students to carry out their interviews. Some children will be able to interview their grandparents face-to-face. Others may opt for telephone, snail mail or even e-mail interviews. In all cases, students should be prepared with a list of questions that are clearly written on a piece of paper.

Here are some tips that will help students achieve a successful interview.

1. Give a copy of the questions to grandparents ahead of time. This way they have plenty of time to recall stories.
2. Have several pencils and plenty of paper ready at the start of the interview.
3. Don't be in a hurry to ask the next question. Give the grandparent enough time to answer a question.
4. Don't get worried if a grandparent cries a little bit. Both happy and sad times can cause tears.
5. Respect a grandparent's wish NOT to answer a specific question.
6. Correctly write down the grandparent's name and date on which the interview was held.

Depending on the resources available, students could tape-record their interviews with grandparents or simply write them. (If the oral history project is incorporated into the curriculum permanently, you might want to consider purchasing an inexpensive microcassette recorder. Try your school's PTA or PTO for the funds to buy one.) In either case, students should plan on producing a written record of their oral history experience, perhaps as part of the language arts curriculum.

If any grandparents live nearby, it would be nice to invite them to come to class. Each student could write down a question (preview them in advance), which would give everyone the chance to participate in a live interview. Middle school students and fun-loving grandparents might want to ham it up and create their own TV talk show format.

Like It Was: A Complete Guide to Writing Oral History by Cynthia Stokes Brown (Teachers & Writers Collaborative, 0-915-92412-9, $13.95 Young adult and adult), contains many helpful tips for teachers.

—Sally Walker

★ ★ ★

SPACE MILESTONE: *MARS GLOBAL SURVEYOR* (US). Sept 11, 1997. Launched Nov 7, 1996, this unmanned vehicle was put in orbit around Mars on this date. It is designed to compile global maps of Mars by taking high-resolution photos. This mission inaugurated a new series of Mars expeditions in which NASA will launch pairs of orbiters and landers to Mars every 26 months into the next decade. *Mars Global Surveyor* was paired with the lander *Mars Pathfinder*. More than 20,000 images of Mars taken by the spacecraft can be seen at www.msss.com/moc_gallery/index.html. See also: "Space Milestone: *Mars Pathfinder*" (July 4).

UNITED KINGDOM: BATTLE OF BRITAIN WEEK. Sept 11–17. Annually, the third week of September—the week containing Battle of Britain Day (Sept 15).

BIRTHDAYS TODAY

Daniel Akaka, 81, US Senator (D, Hawaii), born Honolulu, HI, Sept 11, 1924.

Philip Ardagh, 44, author (*A House Called Awful End, The Romans, The Aztecs*), born Kent, Sussex, England, Sept 11, 1961.

Anthony Browne, 59, author (*Voices in the Park*), born Sheffield, England, Sept 11, 1946.

Steven Lopez, 27, Olympic taekwondo champion, born New York, NY, Sept 11, 1978.

SEPTEMBER 12 — MONDAY

Day 255 — 110 Remaining

DEFENDERS DAY. Sept 12. Maryland. Public holiday. Annual reenactment of bombardment of Fort McHenry in 1814 which inspired Francis Scott Key to write the "Star-Spangled Banner."

OWENS, JESSE: BIRTH ANNIVERSARY. Sept 12, 1913. James Cleveland (Jesse) Owens, American athlete, winner of four gold medals at the 1936 Olympic Games at Berlin, Germany, was born at Oakville, AL. Owens set 11 world records in track and field. During one track meet, at Ann Arbor, MI, May 23, 1935, Owens, representing Ohio State University, broke five world records and tied a sixth in the space of 45 minutes. Died at Tucson, AZ, Mar 31, 1980. For more info: *Jesse Owens*, by Tom Streissguth (Lerner, 0-8225-4940-9, $25.26 Gr. 4–6).

SPACE MILESTONE: *LUNA 2* (USSR). Sept 12, 1959. First spacecraft to land on moon was launched.

SUBSTITUTE TEACHER APPRECIATION WEEK. Sept 12–16. Although substitute teachers get no sick days or respect, they teach when the regular teacher cannot and continually adjust to different classroom situations. Annually, the second week of September. For info: Dorothy Zjawin, 61 W Colfax Ave, Roselle Park, NJ 07204. Phone: (908) 241-6241.

VIDEO GAMES DAY. Sept 12. A day for kids who love video games to celebrate the fun they have playing them and to thank their parents for all the cartridges and quarters they have provided to indulge this hobby.

BIRTHDAYS TODAY

Sam Brownback, 49, US Senator (R, Kansas), born Garnett, KS, Sept 12, 1956.

Yao Ming, 25, basketball player, born Shanghai, China, Sept 12, 1980.

Ruben Studdard, 27, singer, born Christopher Ruben Studdard at Birmingham, AL, Sept 12, 1978.

Valerie Tripp, 54, author (the Molly, Felicity, Samantha and Josefina series in the American Girls collection), born Mount Kisco, NY, Sept 12, 1951.

SEPTEMBER 13 — TUESDAY

Day 256 — 109 Remaining

BARRY, JOHN: DEATH ANNIVERSARY. Sept 13, 1803. Revolutionary War hero John Barry, first American to hold the rank of commodore, died at Philadelphia, PA. He was born at Tacumshane, County Wexford, Ireland, in 1745. He has been called the "Father of the American Navy."

DAHL, ROALD: BIRTH ANNIVERSARY. Sept 13, 1916. Author (*Charlie and the Chocolate Factory, James and the Giant Peach, Matilda*), born at Llandaff, South Wales, Great Britain. Died Nov 23, 1990, at Oxford, England.

"THE MUPPET SHOW" TV PREMIERE: ANNIVERSARY. Sept 13, 1976. This comedy variety show was hosted by Kermit the Frog from "Sesame Street." Other Jim Henson puppet characters included Miss Piggy, Fozzie the Bear and The Great Gonzo. Many celebrities made guest appearances on the show, which was broadcast in more than 100 countries. "Muppet Babies" was a Saturday morning cartoon spin-off that aired from 1984 to 1992. *The Muppet Movie* (1979) was the first of many films based on "The Muppet Show."

REED, WALTER: BIRTH ANNIVERSARY. Sept 13, 1851. American army physician especially known for his yellow fever research. Born at Gloucester County, VA, he served as an army surgeon for more than 20 years and as a professor at the Army Medical College. He died at Washington, DC, Nov 22, 1902. The US Army's general hospital at Washington, DC, is named in his honor.

SCHUMANN, CLARA: BIRTH ANNIVERSARY. Sept 13, 1819. Pianist and composer, wife of composer Robert Schumann. Born at Leipzig, Germany, she died May 20, 1896, at Frankfurt, Germany. For info: *Clara Schumann: Piano Virtuoso*, by Susanna Reich (Clarion, 0-395-89119-1, $18 Gr. 5 & up) and *Her Piano Sang: A Story About Clara Schumann*, by Barbara Allman (Carolrhoda, 1-57505-012-9, $15.95 Gr. 3–6).

"SCOOBY-DOO, WHERE ARE YOU?" TV PREMIERE: ANNIVERSARY. Sept 13, 1969. One of the most enduring Saturday morning cartoons in the history of television, Scooby and the gang travel around in a van called The Mystery Machine and solve spooky (and often hilarious) mysteries. Fred, Daphne and Velma usually do the work, while Shaggy, originally voiced by radio personality Casey Kasem, and his lovable Great Dane Scooby-Doo look for something to eat. Over the years, the show has appeared on various networks and with various titles, and in the 1970s often featured "guest" characters, including the Harlem Globetrotters, Tim Conway, Dick Van Dyke, Don Knotts and Jonathan Winters. Scooby's relatives also have made appearances, including Scooby-Dum and the pesky Scrappy-Doo. A live-action feature film was released in 2002 starring Freddie Prinze, Sarah Michelle Gellar, Matthew Lillard, Linda Cardellini and a digital Scooby.

"STAR-SPANGLED BANNER" INSPIRED: ANNIVERSARY. Sept 13–14, 1814. During the War of 1812, on the night of Sept 13, Francis Scott Key was aboard a ship that was delayed in Baltimore harbor by the British attack there on Fort McHenry. Key had no choice but to anxiously watch the battle. That experience and seeing the American flag still flying over the fort the next morning inspired him to pen the verses that, coupled with the tune of a popular drinking song, became our official national anthem in 1931, 117 years after the words were written.

US CAPITAL ESTABLISHED AT NEW YORK CITY: ANNIVERSARY. Sept 13, 1789. Congress picked New York, NY, as the location of the new US government in place of Philadelphia, which had served as the capital up until this time. In 1790 the capital moved back to Philadelphia and in 1800 moved permanently to Washington, DC.

BIRTHDAYS TODAY

Else Holmelund Minarik, 85, author (the Little Bear series), born Aarhus, Denmark, Sept 13, 1920.

Ben Savage, 25, actor ("Boy Meets World"), born Chicago, IL, Sept 13, 1980.

Mildred Taylor, 62, author (*The Land, Let the Circle Be Unbroken*, Newbery for *Roll of Thunder, Hear My Cry*), born Jackson, MS, Sept 13, 1943.

SEPTEMBER 14 — WEDNESDAY

Day 257 — 108 Remaining

ARMSTRONG, WILLIAM H.: BIRTH ANNIVERSARY. Sept 14, 1914. Newbery Award–winning author (*Sounder*). Born at Lexington, VA, he died Apr 11, 1999, at Kent, CT.

SOLO TRANSATLANTIC BALLOON CROSSING: ANNIVERSARY. Sept 14–18, 1984. Joe W. Kittinger, 56-year-old balloonist, left Caribou, ME, in a 10-story-tall helium-filled balloon named *Rosie O'Grady's Balloon of Peace* on Sept 14, 1984, crossed the Atlantic Ocean and reached the French coast, above the town of Capbreton, in bad weather Sept 17. He crash-landed amid wind and rain near Savone, Italy, Sept 18. His nearly 84-hour flight, covering about 3,535 miles, was the first solo balloon crossing of the Atlantic Ocean.

WILSON, JAMES: BIRTH ANNIVERSARY. Sept 14, 1742. Signer of the Declaration of Independence and one of the first associate justices of the US Supreme Court. Born at Fifeshire, Scotland, he died Aug 21, 1798, at Edenton, NC.

BIRTHDAYS TODAY

Diane Goode, 56, author (*Diane Goode's Book of Scary Stories and Songs*), illustrator (*When I Was Young in the Mountains, Diane Goode's Book of Giants and Little People*), born Brooklyn, NY, Sept 14, 1949.

John Steptoe, 55, author and illustrator (*Mufaro's Beautiful Daughters: An African Tale, Story of Jumping Mouse*), born Brooklyn, NY, Sept 14, 1950.

Elizabeth Winthrop, 57, author (*The Castle in the Attic, The Battle for the Castle*), born Washington, DC, Sept 14, 1948.

★ ★ ★

September 2005

S	M	T	W	T	F	S
				1	2	3
4	5	6	7	8	9	10
11	12	13	14	15	16	17
18	19	20	21	22	23	24
25	26	27	28	29	30	

SEPTEMBER 15 — THURSDAY

Day 258 — 107 Remaining

COOPER, JAMES FENIMORE: BIRTH ANNIVERSARY. Sept 15, 1789. American novelist, historian and social critic, born at Burlington, NJ, Cooper was one of the earliest American writers to develop a native American literary tradition. His most popular works are the five novels comprising The Leatherstocking Tales, featuring the exploits of one of the truly unique American fictional characters, Natty Bumppo. These novels, *The Deerslayer, The Last of the Mohicans, The Pathfinder, The Pioneers* and *The Prairie*, chronicle Natty Bumppo's continuing flight away from the rapid settlement of America. Cooper died Sept 14, 1851, at Cooperstown, NY, the town founded by his father.

COSTA RICA: INDEPENDENCE DAY. Sept 15. National holiday. Gained independence from Spain in 1821.

EL SALVADOR: INDEPENDENCE DAY. Sept 15. National holiday. Gained independence from Spain in 1821.

FIRST NATIONAL CONVENTION FOR BLACKS: 175th ANNIVERSARY. Sept 15, 1830. The first national convention for blacks was held at Bethel Church, Philadelphia, PA. The convention was called to find ways to better the condition of black people and was attended by delegates from seven states. Bishop Richard Allen was elected as the first convention president.

GUATEMALA: INDEPENDENCE DAY. Sept 15. National holiday. Gained independence from Spain in 1821.

HONDURAS: INDEPENDENCE DAY. Sept 15. National holiday. Gained independence from Spain in 1821.

JAPAN: RESPECT FOR THE AGED DAY. Sept 15. National holiday to honor Japan's senior citizens—especially those who are centenarians.

JUMBO THE ELEPHANT: DEATH ANNIVERSARY. Sept 15, 1882. One of history's most beloved animals, Jumbo the elephant, died in a tragic railroad accident on this day at St. Thomas, ON, Canada. Jumbo, the star attraction of P.T. Barnum's circus, was caught crossing railroad tracks as an unscheduled locomotive was approaching. The impact derailed the train and Jumbo was killed. Legend has it that Jumbo pushed a smaller elephant out of the way before the crash. Barnum donated the skeleton to the American Museum of Natural History (where it still resides) and the one-ton hide to Tufts University in Massachusetts (where it was destroyed in a 1975 fire). For more on Jumbo, see also "Jumbo the Elephant Arrives in America: Anniversary" (Apr 9).

KIRSTEN, SAMANTHA AND MOLLY DEBUT: ANNIVERSARY. Sept 15, 1986. The first three American Girl dolls representing different historical periods debuted. They were joined in later years by Addy, Felicity, Josefina and Kit. More than 9 million dolls and 90 million books about them have been sold. For more info: www.americangirl.com.

"THE LONE RANGER" TV PREMIERE: ANNIVERSARY. Sept 15, 1949. This character was created for a radio serial in 1933 by George W. Trendle. The famous masked man was the alter ego of John Reid, a Texas Ranger who was the only survivor of an ambush. He was nursed back to health by his Native American friend, Tonto. Both men traveled around the West on their trusty steeds, Silver and Scout, fighting injustice. On TV Clayton Moore played the Lone Ranger/John Reid and Jay Silverheels costarred as Tonto. The theme music was Rossini's "William Tell Overture."

★ **NATIONAL HISPANIC HERITAGE MONTH.** Sept 15–Oct 15. Presidential Proclamation. Beginning in 1989, always issued for Sept 15–Oct 15 of each year (Public Law 100–402 of Aug 17, 1988). Previously issued each year for the week including Sept 15 and 16 since 1968 at request (Public Law 90–498 of Sept 17, 1968). For info: *The New York Public Library Amazing Hispanic American History: A Book of Answers for Kids*, by George Ochoa (Wiley, 0-471-19204-X, $12.95 Gr. 4 & up) and *Big Spanish Heritage Activity Book*, by Walter Yoder (Sunstone Press, 0-86534-239-3, $8.95 Gr. 3–9).

★**NATIONAL POW/MIA RECOGNITION DAY.** Sept 15. Annually, the third Thursday in September.

NICARAGUA: INDEPENDENCE DAY. Sept 15. National holiday. Gained independence from Spain in 1821.

OKLAHOMA STATE FAIR. Sept 15–25. State Fair Park, Oklahoma City, OK. One of the top 10 state fairs in North America includes six buildings of commercial exhibits, 10 barns for livestock and horse competitions, Disney on Ice, The State Fair Circus, PRCA championship rodeo, live entertainment and motor sports events. Est attendance: 1,000,000. For info: Oklahoma State Fair, PO Box 74943, Oklahoma City, OK 73147. Phone: (405) 948-6700. Fax: (405) 948-6828. E-mail: mail@oklahomastatefair.com. Web: www.oklahomastatefair.com.

PIPER, WATTY: BIRTH ANNIVERSARY. Sept 15, 1870. Born Mabel Caroline Bragg at Milford, MA. Piper is best known for her classic tale *The Little Engine That Could*. She died Apr 25, 1945.

TAFT, WILLIAM HOWARD: BIRTH ANNIVERSARY. Sept 15, 1857. The 27th president of the US was born at Cincinnati, OH. His term of office was Mar 4, 1909–Mar 3, 1913. Following his presidency he became a law professor at Yale University until his appointment as Chief Justice of the US Supreme Court in 1921. Died at Washington, DC, Mar 8, 1930, and was buried at Arlington National Cemetery. For info: www.ipl.org/ref/POTUS.

UNITED KINGDOM: BATTLE OF BRITAIN DAY. Sept 15. Commemorates end of biggest daylight bombing raid of Britain by German Luftwaffe, in 1940. Said to have been the turning point against Hitler's siege of Britain in WWII.

***USA TODAY* FIRST PUBLISHED: ANNIVERSARY.** Sept 15, 1982. "The Nation's Newspaper" hit the newsstands this day in 1982. It featured general interest articles for a national audience—a new approach among daily newspapers.

WHOOPING CRANE FALL MIGRATION. Sept 15–Nov 15 (approximate). The tallest birds in North America—the whooping cranes—leave their summer nesting grounds at Wood Buffalo National Park in the Northwest Territories and Alberta, Canada, and migrate 2,500 miles south to their wintering grounds at the Aransas National Wildlife Refuge on the Gulf Coast of Texas. Their 4-to-6-week trip takes them through Alberta, Saskatchewan, Montana, the Dakotas, Nebraska, Kansas, Oklahoma and Texas. These cranes are 5 feet tall with a 7-foot wingspan. Their name comes from their loud call, which can be heard 2 miles away. They are an endangered species in the US and Canada. See also: "Whooping Crane Spring Migration" (Mar 1) and "Longest Human-Led Migration: Anniversary" (Dec 3). For more info: The International Crane Foundation site at savingcranes.org or the Whooping Crane Eastern Partnership at www.bringbackthecranes.org.

BIRTHDAYS TODAY

Tomie dePaola, 71, illustrator and author (*Strega Nona; Nana Upstairs, Nana Downstairs*), born Thomas De Paola at Meriden, CT, Sept 15, 1934.

Mike Dunleavy, 25, basketball player, born Fort Worth, TX, Sept 15, 1980.

Prince Harry, 21, Henry Charles Albert David, son of Prince Charles and Princess Diana, born London, England, Sept 15, 1984.

Carlos Ruiz, 26, soccer player, born Guatemala City, Guatemala, Sept 15, 1979.

SEPTEMBER 16 — FRIDAY

Day 259 — 106 Remaining

ANNE BRADSTREET DAY. Sept 16. An official date proclaimed by the governor of the Commonwealth of Massachusetts to honor Anne Bradstreet, America's first poet who is also recognized as the first published woman poet in the English language. Anne Bradstreet was born in 1612 in England and came to America in 1630. Unbeknownst to Anne, her brother-in-law took some of her poetry back to England where it was published in 1630 as *The Tenth Muse Lately Sprung Up in America.* Subsequent editions were also published at Boston. She died at Andover, MA, Sept 16, 1672. For info: Sue Ellen Holmes, Dir, Stevens Memorial Library, PO Box 8, North Andover, MA 01845. Phone: (978) 688-9505. Fax: (978) 688-9507. E-mail: Sholmes@mailserv.mvlc.lib.ma.us.

THE BIG E. Sept 16–Oct 2. West Springfield, MA. New England's fall classic and one of the nation's largest fairs. Each September, The Big E features all free entertainment including top-name talent, a big-top circus and horse show. Also children's attractions, daily parade, historic village, Avenue of States, Better Living Center and much more. Annually, beginning the second Friday after Labor Day. Est attendance: 1,000,000. For info: Eastern States Exposition, 1305 Memorial Ave, West Springfield, MA 01089. Phone: (413) 737-2443. Fax: (413) 787-0127. E-mail: info@thebige.com. Web: www.thebige.com.

CHEROKEE STRIP DAY: ANNIVERSARY. Sept 16, 1893. Optional school holiday, Oklahoma. Greatest "run" for Oklahoma land in 1893.

GENERAL MOTORS FOUNDING: ANNIVERSARY. Sept 16, 1908. The giant automobile manufacturing company was founded by William Crapo "Billy" Durant, a Flint, MI, entrepreneur.

MAYFLOWER DAY: ANNIVERSARY. Sept 16, 1620. Anniversary of the departure of the *Mayflower* from Plymouth, England, with 102 passengers and a small crew. Vicious storms were encountered en route which caused serious doubt about the wisdom of continuing, but the ship reached Provincetown, MA, Nov 21, and discharged the Pilgrims at Plymouth, MA, Dec 26, 1620.

MEXICO: INDEPENDENCE DAY. Sept 16. National Day. The official celebration begins at 11 PM Sept 15 and continues through Sept 16. On the night of the 15th, the President of Mexico steps onto the balcony of the National Palace at Mexico City and voices the same "El Grito" (Cry for Freedom) that Father Hidalgo gave on the night of Sept 15, 1810, which began Mexico's rebellion from Spain.

NATIONAL PLAY-DOH® DAY. Sept 16. To commemorate the introduction of Play-Doh. Joe McVicker of Cincinnati sent some non-toxic wallpaper cleaner to his sister-in-law, a nursery school teacher. She found it to be an excellent replacement for modeling clay. In 1955, McVicker took the product to an educational convention and by 1956 Play-Doh was being sold commercially.

NATIVE AMERICAN DAY IN MASSACHUSETTS. Sept 16. Proclaimed annually by the governor for the third Friday in September.

OLD IRONSIDES SAVED BY POEM: ANNIVERSARY. Sept 16, 1830. Alarmed by a newspaper report that Congress was to have the USS *Constitution* (popularly known as "Old Ironsides") sent to a scrap yard, law student Oliver Wendell Holmes dashed off a poem in protest. The poem began "Ay, tear her tattered ensign down!/Long has it waved on high,/And many an eye has danced to see/That banner in the sky." "Old Ironsides," published anonymously this day in the *Boston Daily Advertisor*, was to stir up national outrage as newspaper after newspaper reprinted it. Congress instead appropriated money for the frigate's reconstruction, and Old Ironsides still floats today. (Some historians think that Holmes never actually saw the ship he saved.) See also: "Old Ironsides Launched: Anniversary" (Oct 21).

PAPUA NEW GUINEA: INDEPENDENCE DAY. Sept 16. National holiday. Commemorates independence from Australian administration in 1975.

REY, H.A.: BIRTH ANNIVERSARY. Sept 16, 1898. Born Hans Augusto Rey at Hamburg, Germany. Rey illustrated the Curious George series, while his wife, Margaret Rey, wrote the stories. He died at Cambridge, MA, Aug 26, 1977.

UNITED NATIONS: INTERNATIONAL DAY FOR THE PRESERVATION OF THE OZONE LAYER. Sept 16. On Dec 19, 1994, the General Assembly proclaimed this day to commemorate the date in 1987 on which Montreal Protocol on Substances that Deplete the Ozone Layer was signed (Res 49/114). States are invited to devote the Day to promote, at the national level, activities in accordance with the objectives of the Protocol. The ozone layer filters sunlight and prevents the adverse effects of ultraviolet radiation from reaching the Earth's surface, thereby preserving life on the planet. For info: United Nations, Dept of Public Info, Public Inquiries Unit, Rm GA-57, New York, NY 10017. Phone: (212) 963-4475. Fax: (212) 963-0071. E-mail: inquiries@un.org.

BIRTHDAYS TODAY

Kimberly Alexis Bledel, 24, actress ("The Gilmore Girls"), born Houston, TX, Sept 16, 1981.

David Copperfield, 49, magician, illusionist, born Metuchen, NJ, Sept 16, 1956.

Robin Yount, 50, Hall of Fame baseball player, born Danville, IL, Sept 16, 1955.

September 2005

S	M	T	W	T	F	S
				1	2	3
4	5	6	7	8	9	10
11	12	13	14	15	16	17
18	19	20	21	22	23	24
25	26	27	28	29	30	

SEPTEMBER 17 — SATURDAY

Day 260 — 105 Remaining

BATTLE OF ANTIETAM: ANNIVERSARY. Sept 17, 1862. This date has been called America's bloodiest day in recognition of the high casualties suffered in the Civil War battle between General Robert E. Lee's Confederate forces and General George McClellan's Union army. Estimates vary, but more than 25,000 Union and Confederate soldiers were killed or wounded in this battle on the banks of the Potomac River at Maryland.

BURGER, WARREN E.: BIRTH ANNIVERSARY. Sept 17, 1907. Former Chief Justice of the US, Warren E. Burger was born at St. Paul, MN. A conservative on criminal matters, but a progressive on social issues, he had the longest tenure (1969–86) of any chief justice in this century. Appointed by President Nixon, he voted in the majority on *Roe v Wade* (1973), which upheld a woman's right to an abortion, and on *US v Nixon* (1974), which forced Nixon to surrender audiotapes to the Watergate special prosecutor. He died June 25, 1995, at Washington, DC.

★ **CITIZENSHIP DAY.** Sept 17. Presidential Proclamation always issued for Sept 17 at request (Public Law 82–261 of Feb 29, 1952). Customarily issued as "Citizenship Day and Constitution Week." Replaces Constitution Day.

CONSTITUTION OF THE US: ANNIVERSARY. Sept 17, 1787. Delegations from 12 states at the Constitutional Convention at Philadelphia, PA, voted unanimously to approve the proposed document. Thirty-nine of the 42 delegates present signed it and the Convention adjourned, after drafting a letter of transmittal to the Congress. The proposed constitution stipulated that it would take effect when ratified by nine states. This day is a legal holiday in Arizona and Florida. For activities and lesson plans on the Constitution, visit the National Archives website at www.nara.gov/education/teaching/constitution/home.html.

★ **CONSTITUTION WEEK.** Sept 17–23. Presidential Proclamation always issued for the period of Sept 17–23 each year since 1955 (Public Law 84–915 of Aug 2, 1956).

FOSTER, ANDREW "RUBE": BIRTH ANNIVERSARY. Sept 17, 1879. Rube Foster's efforts in baseball earned him the title of "The Father of Negro Baseball." He was a manager and star pitcher, pitching 51 victories in one year. In 1919, he called a meeting of black baseball owners and organized the first black baseball league, the Negro National League. He served as its president until his death in 1930. Foster was born at Calvert, TX, the son of a minister. He died Dec 9, 1930, at Kankakee, IL.

HARVEST MOON. Sept 17. So called because the full moon nearest the autumnal equinox extends the hours of light into the evening and helps the harvester with his long day's work. Moon enters Full Moon phase at 10:01 PM, EDT.

HENDRICKS, THOMAS ANDREWS: BIRTH ANNIVERSARY. Sept 17, 1819. The 21st vice president of the US (1885), born at Muskingum County, OH. Died at Indianapolis, IN, Nov 25, 1885.

INTERNATIONAL COASTAL CLEANUP DAY. Sept 17. A million volunteers remove and tabulate 12 million pieces of trash on 21,000 miles of beaches as well as below the water. Takes place in over 100 countries. Annually, the third Saturday in September. For info: The Ocean Conservancy, 1725 DeSales St NW, Washington, DC 20036. Phone: (202) 429-5609. Fax: (202) 872-0619. E-mail: cleanup@oceanconservancyva.org. Web: www.oceanconservancy.org.

LAURA INGALLS WILDER FESTIVAL. Sept 17. Mansfield, MO. Laura Wilder lived in Mansfield on the farm she and her husband Almanzo built when she wrote the Little House series of books. The Laura Ingalls Wilder museum and home will be open for tours. There will be activities for the whole family—contests, parades, music, arts and crafts, food, games, an outdoor musical and more. Annually, on the third Saturday in September. For info: Laura Ingalls Wilder/Rose Wilder Lane Historic Home & Museum, 3068 Highway A, Mansfield, MO 65704. Phone: (417) 924-3526 or (877) 924-7126. Web: www.lauraingallswilderhome.com.

MOON PHASE: FULL MOON. Sept 17. Moon enters Full Moon phase at 10:01 PM, EDT.

NATIONAL CONSTITUTION CENTER CONSTITUTION WEEK. Sept 17–23. To celebrate and commemorate the signing of the US Constitution Sept 17, 1787, the National Constitution Center sponsors special events and activities. Annually, Sept 17–23. Est attendance: 150,000. For info: Natl Constitution Center, 525 Arch St, Independence Mall, Philadelphia, PA 19106. Phone: (215) 923-0004. Fax: (215) 923-1749. Web: www.constitutioncenter.org.

NATIONAL CONSTITUTION CENTER GROUNDBREAKING: 5th ANNIVERSARY. Sept 17, 2000. Established by an act of Congress, the National Constitution Center was constructed on Independence Mall at Philadelphia. It opened to the public on July 4, 2003. It was established to increase awareness and understanding of the US Constitution, its history and relevance to our daily lives. For more info, including teacher resources: www.constitutioncenter.org.

NATIONAL FOOTBALL LEAGUE FORMED: 85th ANNIVERSARY. Sept 17, 1920. The National Football League was formed at Canton, OH.

VON STEUBEN, BARON FRIEDRICH: 275th BIRTH ANNIVERSARY. Sept 17, 1730. Prussian-born general, born at Magdeburg, Prussia, who served in the American Revolution. He died at Remsen, NY, Nov 28, 1794.

BIRTHDAYS TODAY

Bjorn Berg, 82, illustrator (*Old Mrs Pepperpot*), born Munich, Germany, Sept 17, 1923.

Mark Brunell, 35, football player, born Los Angeles, CA, Sept 17, 1970.

Paul Goble, 72, author and illustrator (Caldecott for *The Girl Who Loved Wild Horses*), born Surrey, England, Sept 17, 1933.

Charles E. Grassley, 72, US Senator (R, Iowa), born New Hartford, IA, Sept 17, 1933.

Phil Jackson, 60, former basketball coach, former player, author (*Sacred Hoops*), born Deer Lodge, MT, Sept 17, 1945.

Gail Carson Levine, 58, author (*Ella Enchanted, The Fairy's Mistake, The Wish*), born New York, NY, Sept 17, 1947.

David H. Souter, 66, Associate Justice of the US Supreme Court, born Melrose, MA, Sept 17, 1939.

Rasheed Wallace, 31, basketball player, born Philadelphia, PA, Sept 17, 1974.

SEPTEMBER 18 — SUNDAY

Day 261 — 104 Remaining

CHILE: INDEPENDENCE DAY. Sept 18. National holiday. Gained independence from Spain in 1810. ***See Curriculum Connection.***

CHINA: MOON FESTIVAL or MID-AUTUMN FESTIVAL. Sept 18. According to folk legend this day is the birthday of the earth god T'u-ti Kung. The festival indicates the year's hard work in the fields will soon end with the harvest. People express gratitude to heaven as represented by the moon and to earth as symbolized by the earth god for all good things from the preceding year. Special harvest foods are eaten, especially "moon cakes." Observed on the 15th day of the eighth month of the Chinese lunar calendar, this festival is called by different names in different places, but is widely recognized throughout the Far East, including Taiwan, Korea, Singapore and Hong Kong. Date here is for China, date in other countries will differ.

COLUMBUS'S LAST VOYAGE TO THE NEW WORLD: ANNIVERSARY. Sept 18, 1502. Columbus landed at Costa Rica on his fourth and last voyage to the New World. He returned to Spain in 1504 and died there in 1506.

DEAF AWARENESS WEEK. Sept 18–24. Nationwide celebration to promote deaf culture, American Sign Language and deaf heritage. Activities include library displays, interpreted story hours, Open Houses in residential schools and mainstream programs, exhibit booths in shopping malls with "Five Minute Sign Language Lessons," material distribution. Annually, the last full week of September. For info: National Assn of the Deaf, 814 Thayer Ave, Silver Spring, MD 20910-4500. Fax: (301) 587-1791. E-mail: nadinfo@nad.org. Web: www.nad.org.

DIEFENBAKER, JOHN: BIRTH ANNIVERSARY. Sept 18, 1895. Canadian lawyer, statesman and Conservative prime minister (1957–63). Born at Normandy Township, Ontario, Canada, he died at Ottawa, Ontario, Aug 16, 1979. Diefenbaker was a member of the Canadian Parliament from 1940 until his death.

IRON HORSE OUTRACED BY HORSE: 175th ANNIVERSARY. Sept 18, 1830. In a widely celebrated race, the first locomotive built in America, the Tom Thumb, lost to a horse. Mechanical difficulties plagued the steam engine over the nine-mile course between Riley's Tavern and Baltimore, MD, and a boiler leak prevented the locomotive from finishing the race. In the early days of trains, engines were nicknamed "Iron Horses."

KOREA: CHUSOK. Sept 18. Gala celebration by Koreans everywhere. Autumn harvest thanksgiving moon festival. Observed on 15th day of eighth lunar month (eighth full moon of lunar calendar) each year. Koreans pay homage to ancestors and express gratitude to guarding spirits for another year of rich crops. A time to visit tombs, leave food and prepare for coming winter season. Traditional food is "moon cake," made on eve of Chusok, with rice, chestnuts and jujube fruits. Games, dancing and gift exchanges. Observed since Silla Dynasty (beginning of first millennium).

NATIONAL DOG WEEK. Sept 18–24. To promote the relationship of dogs to mankind and emphasize the need for the proper care and treatment of dogs. Annually, the last full week in Sep-

SEPTEMBER 18
CHILE, COUNTRY OF EXTREMES

Imagine the map of a country with volcanoes, deserts, shipwrecks, ancient writing, fjords, glaciers, fertile valleys, active plate tectonics, gigantic stone figures, deep-sea channels and more. There is magic and mystery in that map, and it is the map of the Republic of Chile, which celebrates its independence from Spain on this day in 1810. By integrating your unit of geography or geology with Chile, you can bring out the excitement of discovery and exploration.

Chile is a country of extremes. To begin with, it is more than ten times longer than it is wide, forming a long, thin strip along the west coast of South America. All along its spine runs a portion of the Andes Mountains, the world's longest mountain chain. In the north, the Atacama Desert scorches under the sun; it is one of the earth's driest ranges, as it sits in the rain shadow of the Andes. In between are what Chileans call the pampas, fertile valleys that support agriculture. In the south, glowing blue icebergs float and calve into the Pacific Ocean. A useful resource for grades 3–6 is *South America (Geography Mini Unit Series)* by Jo Ellen Moore (Evan-Moor Educational Publishers, 1-557-99711-X, $12.95).

The Andes Mountains are the handiwork of plate tectonics; they are a result of the huge-scale collision and subduction of tectonic plates. The Pacific sea floor is slowly spreading out from its central rift valley, expanding at the current rate of more than four centimeters (almost two inches) each year. As it creeps steadily outward, it meets with a less dense continental plate, the Nazca Plate, that forms South America. As a result, the denser basaltic ocean plate is driven under. When it dives into the earth's mantle, it causes the land above it to buckle and grow, thus forming the Andes. As the ocean plate is pushed even further into the earth's depths, it melts under the intense heat and becomes molten rock, or magma. The magma, under pressure, escapes through cracks and fissures in Chile's hundreds of volcanoes. Much of Chile's landscape and island formations are a result of volcanic activity as well, a testament to the strength and power of geologic processes.

At the southern tip of Chile lies an archipelago of volcanic islands called the Juan Fernandez Islands. The word "archipelago," so often reduced to a vocabulary word to memorize, gains depth when students learn that these were the islands made famous in 1719 with the publishing of *Robinson Crusoe,* by Daniel Defoe. His book is based on a true story of a sailor named Alexander Selkirk who spent four years alone on the Juan Fernandez Islands in the early 1700s. *Robinson Crusoe* is a classic story that brings to life the danger and excitement of exploring a part of the world when its maps had not yet been made. There is an excellent junior edition of *Robinson Crusoe* by Scholastic Junior Classics (0-439-23621-5, $4 Ages 9–12).

Easter Island, a small volcanic island about 2,000 miles off the coast from Chile, has plenty of mysteries to engage the minds and imaginations of your students. It was discovered by Europeans on Easter Day, 1722. From the water it is possible to see the giant stone figures staring intently over the coast. The island has 887 huge stone statues, the average height being 13 feet and the average weight 14 tons. The stone monoliths, called Moai by the Rapa Nui people who still live there, were long ago carved from the soft volcanic tuff comprising most of the island. Why were they carved? Why were they set up facing the ocean with their stern and solemn faces? How were they moved, sometimes to a distance of six miles, from the quarry site? Perhaps we would know more answers to the secrets of the island, had not so many of the island's inhabitants been enslaved or decimated by disease. The mysteries surrounding this island do not end with the Maoi. The ancestry of the Rapa Nui people is widely disputed, although current archaeological evidence points to a Polynesian emigration by boat around AD 400. Likewise, the mysterious script of wavy figures, Rongorongo, remains undeciphered. You can find out more about Easter Island by visiting PBS Nova at www.pbs.org/wgbb/nova/lostempires/easter. Books recommended include *The Enigmas of Easter Island: Island on the Edge* by Paul Bahn, John Flenley, Paul G. Bahn (Oxford University Press, 0-19-280340-9, $21 Adult). If you are interested in a comprehensive look at the history of Easter Island (both pre- and post-European) the Abrams Discoveries History Series has a book called *Discoveries: Easter Island* by Michel Orliac and Catherine Orliac (Harry N. Abrams, 0-810-92834-5, $10 Adult).

—Adrienne van den Beemt

tember. For info: Morris Raskin, Secy, Dogs on Stamps Study Unit (DOSSU), 202 A Newport Rd, Monroe Township, NJ 08831. Phone: (609) 655-7411. E-mail: mraskin@verizon.net.

NATIONAL FARM ANIMALS AWARENESS WEEK. Sept 18–24. A week to promote awareness of farm animals and their natural behaviors. This week is dedicated to learning about farm animals and appreciating their many interesting and unique qualities. Annually, the third full week in September. For info: Karen Graham, The Humane Society of the US, Farm Animal Section, 2100 L St NW, Washington, DC 20037. Phone: (301) 258-3110. E-mail: kgraham@hsus.org. Web: www.hsus.org.

★**NATIONAL FARM SAFETY AND HEALTH WEEK.** Sept 18–24. Presidential Proclamation issued since 1982 for the third week in September. Previously, from 1944, for one of the last two weeks in July.

September 2005

S	M	T	W	T	F	S
				1	2	3
4	5	6	7	8	9	10
11	12	13	14	15	16	17
18	19	20	21	22	23	24
25	26	27	28	29	30	

NATIONAL PUBLIC LANDS DAY. Sept 18. To involve citizen volunteers in cleaning and maintaining public lands. Each year, more than 70,000 volunteers take part in all 50 states, the District of Columbia, and Puerto Rico. For info: The National Environmental Education & Training Foundation. Web: www.npld.com.

READ, GEORGE: BIRTH ANNIVERSARY. Sept 18, 1733. Lawyer and signer of the Declaration of Independence, born at Cecil County, MD. Died Sept 21, 1798, at New Castle, DE.

STORY, JOSEPH: BIRTH ANNIVERSARY. Sept 18, 1779. Associate justice of the US Supreme Court (1811–45) was born at Marblehead, MA. "It is astonishing," he wrote a few months before his death, "how easily men satisfy themselves that the Constitution is exactly what they wish it to be." Story died Sept 10, 1845, at Cambridge, MA, having served 33 years on the Supreme Court bench.

US AIR FORCE ESTABLISHED: ANNIVERSARY. Sept 18, 1947. Although its heritage dates back to 1907 when the Army first established military aviation, the US Air Force became a separate military service on this date.

US CAPITOL CORNERSTONE LAID: ANNIVERSARY. Sept 18, 1793. President George Washington laid the Capitol cornerstone at Washington, DC, in a Masonic ceremony. That event was the first and last recorded occasion at which the stone with its engraved silver plate was seen. In 1958, during the extension of the east front of the Capitol, an unsuccessful effort was made to find it. For a virtual tour of the Capitol: www.senate.gov/vtour/welcome.htm.

BIRTHDAYS TODAY

Lance Armstrong, 34, cyclist, six-time winner of the Tour de France, born Plano, TX, Sept 18, 1971.

Robert F. Bennett, 72, US Senator (R, Utah), born Salt Lake City, UT, Sept 18, 1933.

Sara Hildebrand, 26, Olympic diver, born St. Paul, MN, Sept 18, 1979.

Ticha Penichiero, 31, basketball player, born Figueira da Foz, Portugal, Sept 18, 1974.

SEPTEMBER 19 — MONDAY

Day 262 — 103 Remaining

CARROLL, CHARLES: BIRTH ANNIVERSARY. Sept 19, 1737. American Revolutionary leader and signer of the Declaration of Independence, born at Annapolis, MD. The last surviving signer of the Declaration, he died Nov 14, 1832, at Baltimore, MD.

"ICEMAN" MUMMY DISCOVERED: ANNIVERSARY. Sept 19, 1991. At 10,531 feet in the Austrian-Italian Alps, two hikers discovered a 5,300-year-old frozen mummy. The late Neolithic man, nicknamed "Iceman" and "Ötzi" (for the Ötzal Alps), carried rough bow and arrows as well as a copper axe, and wore a grass cloak for warmth. His shoes were made from bearskin, deer hide and tree bark. Ötzi, who now rests as a frozen exhibit at the South Tyrol Museum of Archaeology at Bolzano, Italy, was gently thawed in September 2000 in order for scientists to conduct valuable DNA analysis and determine his last meal. For more info: *Ice Mummy: Discovery of a 5,000 Year Old Man* by M. & C. Dubowski (Random House, 0-679-85647-1, $3.99 Gr. 4 & up).

MEXICO CITY EARTHQUAKE: 20th ANNIVERSARY. Sept 19–20, 1985. Nearly 10,000 persons perished in the earthquakes (8.1 and 7.5 respectively, on the Richter scale) that devastated Mexico City. Damage to buildings was estimated at more than $1 billion, and 100,000 homes were destroyed or severely damaged. For more info go to the National Earthquake Information Center: wwwneic.cr.usgs.gov.

POWELL, LEWIS F., JR: BIRTH ANNIVERSARY. Sept 19, 1907. Former associate justice of the Supreme Court of the US, nominated by President Nixon Oct 21, 1971. (Took his seat Jan 7, 1972.) Justice Powell was born at Suffolk, VA. In 1987, he announced his retirement from the Court. He died Aug 25, 1998, at Richmond, VA. For more info: oyez.northwestern.edu/justices/justices.cgi.

RAIN OF FROG EGGS: ANNIVERSARY. Sept 19, 2003. In a remarkable phenomenon, a Connecticut resident discovered that the sky was raining down frog eggs on this date. Apparently, Hurricane Isabel had swept them up in North Carolina and released them farther north as the storm dissipated.

SAINT CHRISTOPHER (SAINT KITTS) AND NEVIS: INDEPENDENCE DAY. Sept 19. National holiday. Commemorates the independence of these Caribbean islands from Britain in 1983.

SAINT JANUARIUS (GENNARO): FEAST DAY. Sept 19. Fourth-century bishop of Benevento, martyred near Naples, Italy, whose relics in the Naples Cathedral are particularly famous because on his feast days the blood in a glass vial is said to liquefy in response to prayers of the faithful. This phenomenon is said to occur also on the first Saturday in May (May 6 in 2006).

TALK LIKE A PIRATE DAY. Sept 19. A day when people everywhere add a touch of larceny to their dialogue by talking like pirates: for example, "Arr, matey, it be a fine day." While it is inherently a guy thing, women have been known to enjoy the day, because they have to be addressed as "me beauty." Arr! Annually, Sept 19. For info: Mark Summers. E-mail: capnslappy@talklikeapirate.com. Web: www.talklikeapirate.com.

TYPOGRAPHIC SMILEY FACE: ANNIVERSARY. Sept 19, 1982. Seeking a way to avoid online misunderstandings, a Carnegie Mellon University computer scientist suggested tagging messages with a "smiley face" made up of a colon, minus sign and closing parentheses to be read sideways that would alert the recipient of a lighthearted tone. Dr. Scott E. Fahlman posted this symbol—now universally referred to as an emoticon—on a university electronic message board on this day in 1982.

BIRTHDAYS TODAY

James Haskins, 64, author (*Bayard Rustin: Behind the Scenes of the Civil Rights Movement*), born Montgomery, AL, Sept 19, 1941.

Nick Johnson, 27, baseball player, born Sacramento, CA, Sept 19, 1978.

SEPTEMBER 20 — TUESDAY

Day 263 — 102 Remaining

FIRST COMPLETE CIRCLE IN AN AIRPLANE: ANNIVERSARY. Sept 20, 1904. Orville Wright, flying a new plane, the *Wright Flyer II*, made the first complete circle in an airplane at Huffman Prairie, just outside Dayton, OH. As the Wright Brothers continued to experiment with flying, they used a catapult to help launch their flying machine in the air.

NETHERLANDS: PRINSJESDAG. Sept 20. Official opening of parliament at The Hague. The queen of the Netherlands, by tradition, rides in a golden coach to the Hall of Knights for the annual opening of parliament. Annually, on the third Tuesday in September.

BIRTHDAYS TODAY

Arthur Geisert, 64, author and illustrator (*Oink, The Giant Ball of String, Roman Numerals I to M*), born Dallas, TX, Sept 20, 1941.

Guy Lefleur, 54, Hall of Fame hockey player, born Thurso, QC, Canada, Sept 20, 1951.

Michael J. Rosen, 51, author (*Elijah's Angel, The Heart is Big Enough*), born Columbus, OH, Sept 20, 1954.

Tony Tallarico, 72, author, illustrator (*I Can Draw Everything, Drawing & Cartooning Sci-Fi*), born Brooklyn, NY, Sept 20, 1933.

★ ★ ★

SEPTEMBER 21 — WEDNESDAY

Day 264 — 101 Remaining

ARMENIA: INDEPENDENCE DAY. Sept 21. Public holiday. Commemorates independence from the Soviet Union in 1991.

BELIZE: INDEPENDENCE DAY. Sept 21. National holiday. Commemorates independence of the former British Honduras from Britain in 1981.

CHIEF JOSEPH: DEATH ANNIVERSARY. Sept 21, 1904. Nez Percé chief, whose Indian name was In-Mut-Too-Yah-Lat-Lat, was born about 1840 at Wallowa Valley, Oregon Territory, and died on the Colville Reservation at Washington State. Faced with war or resettlement to a reservation, Chief Joseph led a dramatic attempt to escape to Canada. After three months and more than 1,000 miles, he and his people were surrounded 40 miles from Canada and sent to a reservation at Oklahoma. Though the few survivors were later allowed to relocate to another reservation at Washington, they never regained their ancestral lands.

HOPKINSON, FRANCIS: BIRTH ANNIVERSARY. Sept 21, 1737. Signer of the Declaration of Independence. Born at Philadelphia, PA, he died there May 9, 1791.

HOUDINI PREMIERES HIS GREATEST ESCAPE: ANNIVERSARY. Sept 21, 1912. The master magician and escape artist Harry Houdini premiered his greatest escape act on this date at the Circus Busch in Berlin, Germany. It was his Water Torture Cell, which involved lowering Houdini into a glass-fronted, water-filled brass cell upside down—his ankles locked into clamps. The audience could see him briefly underwater, then a screen was placed in front so that Houdini could perform his secret escape—which he accomplished in two minutes or less. The act was a sensation. Only a handful of people knew the secret of the Water Torture Cell and they never divulged it. See also: "Houdini, Harry: Birth Anniversary" (Mar 24).

MALTA: INDEPENDENCE DAY. Sept 21. National Day. Commemorates independence from Britain in 1964.

NATIONAL YOUTH OF THE YEAR. Sept 21 (tentative). Washington, DC. Each year a Boys and Girls Club member is selected by a panel of judges from among five regional finalists to be the National Youth of the Year and spokesperson for Boys and Girls Clubs of America. This selection is open to Boys and Girls Club members only—ages 18 and under. Finalists are selected based on leadership qualities and service exhibited to home and family, spiritual values, service to community and Club, excellence in school and obstacles overcome. Winners are presented at a Congressional breakfast and to the president at the White House. Usually awarded the third Wednesday in September. For info: Kevin W. Davis, Dir of Program Services, Boys and Girls Clubs of America, 1230 W Peachtree St NW, Atlanta, GA 30309. Web: www.bgca.org.

TAYLOR, MARGARET SMITH: BIRTH ANNIVERSARY. Sept 21, 1788. Wife of Zachary Taylor, 12th president of the US, born at Calvert County, MD. Died Aug 18, 1852.

UNITED NATIONS: INTERNATIONAL DAY OF PEACE. Sept 21. The General Assembly, in resolution 55/282, of Sept 7, 2001, decided that, beginning in 2002, the International Day of Peace should be observed on Sept 21 each year. The Assembly declared that the Day be observed as a day of global ceasefire and non-violence, an invitation to all nations and people to honor a cessation of hostilities during the Day.

BIRTHDAYS TODAY

Stephen King, 58, author (*Pet Sematary, The Shining, Misery*), born Portland, ME, Sept 21, 1947.

Bill Murray, 55, comedian ("Saturday Night Live"), actor (*Ghostbusters, Groundhog Day*), born Evanston, IL, Sept 21, 1950.

Nicole Richie, 24, television personality ("The Simple Life"), born Berkeley, CA, Sept 21, 1981.

September 2005

S	M	T	W	T	F	S
				1	2	3
4	5	6	7	8	9	10
11	12	13	14	15	16	17
18	19	20	21	22	23	24
25	26	27	28	29	30	

SEPTEMBER 22 — THURSDAY

Day 265 — 100 Remaining

AUTUMN. Sept 22–Dec 21. In the Northern Hemisphere, autumn begins today with the autumnal equinox, at 6:23 PM, EDT. Note that in the Southern Hemisphere today is the beginning of spring. Everywhere on Earth (except near the poles) the sun rises due east and sets due west and daylight length is nearly identical—about 12 hours, 8 minutes.

ELEPHANT APPRECIATION DAY. Sept 22. Celebrate the earth's largest, most interesting and most noble endangered land animal. Free info kit from: Wayne Hepburn, Mission Media Inc, PO Box 50095, Sarasota, FL 34232. E-mail: elefunt@gte.net. Web: www.himandus.net/elephanteria.

EMANCIPATION PROCLAMATION: ANNIVERSARY. Sept 22, 1862. One of the most important presidential proclamations of American history, in which Abraham Lincoln freed the slaves in the rebelling states. (Four slave states had not seceded from the Union.) "That on . . . [Jan 1, 1863] . . . all persons held as slaves within any state or designated part of a state, the people whereof shall then be in rebellion against the United States, shall be then, thenceforward, and forever, free. . . ." For more info go to Ben's Guide to US Government for Kids: bensguide.gpo.gov. See also: "13th Amendment: Anniversary" (Dec 6) for abolition of slavery in all states.

ICE CREAM CONE: BIRTHDAY. Sept 22, 1903. Italo Marchiony emigrated from Italy in the late 1800s and soon thereafter went into business at New York, NY, with a pushcart dispensing lemon ice. Success soon led to a small fleet of pushcarts, and the inventive Marchiony was inspired to develop a cone, first made of paper, later of pastry, to hold the tasty delicacy. On Sept 22, 1903, his application for a patent for his new mold was filed, and US Patent No 746971 was issued to him Dec 15, 1903.

JAPAN: AUTUMNAL EQUINOX DAY. Sept 22. National holiday. When this day falls on a Sunday, it is celebrated on the following Monday.

MALI: INDEPENDENCE DAY. Sept 22. National holiday commemorating independence from France in 1960. Mali, in West Africa, was known as French Sudan while a colony.

SLOBODKINA, ESPHYR: BIRTH ANNIVERSARY. Sept 22, 1908. Author and illustrator of much-beloved children's books, she was born at Cheliabinsk, Siberia. She came to America at the age of 20 and met her mentor Margaret Wise Brown through a family friend. She illustrated several of Brown's titles (*The Little Fireman, Sleepy ABC*) but after Brown's death, decided to try her hand at writing as well as illustrating. Her most popular book is *Caps for Sale: A Tale of a Peddler, Some Monkeys and Their Monkey Business*, which has sold more than two million copies since its publication in 1938. Slobodkina died July 28, 2002, at Glen Head, NY.

STATE FAIR OF VIRGINIA. Sept 22–Oct 2. Richmond Raceway Complex, Richmond, VA. The pride of Virginia's industry of agriculture can be seen in more than 3,000 exhibitions, competitions and shows. Virginia's greatest annual educational and entertainment event. Est attendance: 350,000. For info: State Fair of Virginia, PO Box 26805, Richmond, VA 23261-6805. Phone: (804) 569-3200. Fax: (804) 569-3252. Web: www.statefair.com.

US POSTMASTER GENERAL ESTABLISHED: ANNIVERSARY. Sept 22, 1789. Congress established the office of postmaster general, following the departments of state, war and treasury.

BIRTHDAYS TODAY

Bonnie Hunt, 41, actress ("Life with Bonnie," *Beethoven, Jumanji*), born Chicago, IL, Sept 22, 1964.

Ronaldo, 29, Brazilian soccer player, born Ronaldo Luiz Nazario de Lima, Rio de Janeiro, Brazil, Sept 22, 1976.

SEPTEMBER 23 — FRIDAY

Day 266 — 99 Remaining

BALTIMORE BOOK FESTIVAL. Sept 23–25. Baltimore, MD. The mid-Atlantic's premier celebration of literary arts features authors, poetry readings, cookbook and home & garden demonstrations, and more than 125 exhibitors and booksellers. Many special programs for children. For info: Baltimore Book Festival, 7 Redwood St, Ste 500, Baltimore, MD 21202. Phone: (410) 752-8632. Fax: (410) 385-0361. Web: www.baltimoreevents.org/calendar/events/book_index.html.

CHARLES, RAY: BIRTH ANNIVERSARY. Sept 23, 1930. Born at Albany, GA, Ray Charles Robinson began losing his sight at age 5. He began formal music training at the St. Augustine School for the Deaf and Blind, and by age 15 was earning a living as a musician. He went on to become one of the most influential performers of all time. As a pianist, singer, songwriter, band leader and producer, he played country, jazz, rock, gospel and standards. His renditions of "Georgia On My Mind," "I Can't Stop Loving You" and "America the Beautiful" are considered true American classics. He died at Beverly Hills, CA, June 10, 2004.

"THE JETSONS" TV PREMIERE: ANNIVERSARY. Sept 23, 1962. "Meet George Jetson. His boy Elroy. Daughter Judy. Jane, his wife. . . . " These words introduced us to the Jetsons, a cartoon family living in the 21st century, the Flintstones of the Space Age. We followed the exploits of George and his family, as well as his unstable work relationship with his greedy, ruthless boss Cosmo Spacely. Voices were provided by George O'Hanlon as George, Penny Singleton as Jane, Janet Waldo as Judy, Daws Butler as Elroy, Don Messick as Astro, the family dog and Mel Blanc as Spacely. New episodes created in 1985 introduced a new pet, Orbity.

LIBRA, THE BALANCE. Sept 23–Oct 22. In the astronomical/astrological zodiac that divides the sun's apparent orbit into 12 segments, the period Sept 23–Oct 22 is identified traditionally as the sun sign of Libra, the Balance. The ruling planet is Venus.

"LITTLE ROCK NINE": ANNIVERSARY. Sept 23, 1957. Nine African-American students entered Central High School at Little Rock, AR. They had tried to begin school Sept 4 but were denied entrance by National Guard troops called out by Governor Orval Faubus to resist integration. President Dwight Eisenhower responded by sending federal troops to protect the students. Eight of the nine students completed the school year, showing America that black students could endure the hatred directed at them.

McGUFFEY, WILLIAM HOLMES: BIRTH ANNIVERSARY. Sept 23, 1800. American educator and author of the famous *McGuffey Readers*, born at Washington County, PA. Probably no other textbooks have had a greater influence on American life. More than 120 million copies were sold. McGuffey died at Charlottesville, VA, May 4, 1873.

PLANET NEPTUNE DISCOVERY: ANNIVERSARY. Sept 23, 1846. Neptune is 2,796,700,000 miles from the sun (about 30 times as far from the sun as Earth). Eighth planet from the sun, Neptune takes 164.8 years to revolve around the sun. Diameter is about 31,000 miles compared to Earth at 7,927 miles. Discovered by German astronomer Johann Galle. For more info: *Uranus, Neptune, and Pluto*, by Robin Kerrod (Lerner, 0-8225-3908-X, $21.27 Gr. 4–6) or go to Nine Planets: Multimedia Tour of the Solar System at www.seds.org/billa/tnp.

SAUDI ARABIA: ANNIVERSARY OF KINGDOM UNIFICATION. Sept 23. National holiday. Commemorates unification in 1932.

BIRTHDAYS TODAY

Bruce Brooks, 55, author (*What Hearts, The Moves Make the Man*), born Washington, DC, Sept 23, 1950.

Sila María Calderón, 63, Governor of Puerto Rico, born San Juan, PR, Sept 23, 1942.

Eric Scott Montross, 34, basketball player, born Indianapolis, IN, Sept 23, 1971.

SEPTEMBER 24 — SATURDAY

Day 267 — 98 Remaining

BANNED BOOKS WEEK—CELEBRATING THE FREEDOM TO READ. Sept 24–Oct 1. Brings to the attention of the general public the importance of the freedom to read and the harm censorship causes to our society. Sponsors: American Library Association, American Booksellers Association, American Booksellers Association for Free Expression, American Society of Journalists and Authors, Association of American Publishers, National Association of College Stores. For lists of frequently challenged books, visit the following websites: www.ala.org/bbooks/index.html and www.cs.cmu.edu/People/spok/most-banned.html. For info: Judith F. Krug, American Library Assn, Office for Intellectual Freedom, 50 E Huron St, Chicago, IL 60611. Phone: (312) 280-4223. Fax: (312) 280-4227. E-mail: oif@ala.org. Web: www.ala.org/bbooks.

BEHN, HARRY: BIRTH ANNIVERSARY. Sept 24, 1898. Author, best remembered for his children's books, *Trees* and *Crickets and Bullfrogs and Whispers of Thunder*. Born at McCabe, CT, Behn died Sept 5, 1973.

CAMBODIA: CONSTITUTIONAL DECLARATION DAY. Sept 24. National holiday. Commemorates the constitution of 1993.

GUINEA-BISSAU: INDEPENDENCE DAY: ANNIVERSARY. Sept 24. National holiday. Commemorates independence from Portugal in 1974.

HENSON, JIM: BIRTH ANNIVERSARY. Sept 24, 1936. Puppeteer, born at Greenville, MS. Jim Henson created a unique brand of puppetry known as the Muppets. Kermit the Frog, Big Bird, Rowlf, Bert and Ernie, Gonzo, Animal, Miss Piggy and Oscar the Grouch are a few of the puppets that captured the hearts of children and adults alike in television and film productions including "Sesame Street," "The Jimmy Dean Show," "The Muppet Show," *The Muppet Movie, The Muppets Take Manhattan, The Great Muppet Caper* and *The Dark Crystal.* Henson began his career in 1954 as producer of the TV show "Sam and Friends" at Washington, DC. He introduced the Muppets in 1956. His creativity was rewarded with 18 Emmy Awards, 7 Grammy Awards, 4 Peabody Awards and 5 ACE Awards from the National Cable Television Association. Henson died unexpectedly May 16, 1990, at New York, NY. For more info: *Jim Henson: Young Puppeteer*, by Leslie Gourse (Aladdin, 0-68-983398-9, $4.99 Gr. 4–7).

KIWANIS KIDS' DAY. Sept 24. To honor and assist youth—our greatest resource. Annually, the fourth Saturday in September. For info: Kiwanis Intl, Member Services, 3636 Woodview Trace, Indianapolis, IN 46268. E-mail: kiwanismail@kiwanis.org. Web: www.kiwanis.org.

MARSHALL, JOHN: 250th BIRTH ANNIVERSARY. Sept 24, 1755. Fourth Chief Justice of the Supreme Court, born at Germantown, VA. Served in House of Representatives and as secretary of state under John Adams. Appointed by President Adams to the position of chief justice in January 1801, he became known as "The Great Chief Justice." Marshall's court was largely responsible for defining the role of the Supreme Court and basic organizing principles of government in the early years after adoption of the Constitution in such cases as *Marbury v Madison, McCulloch v Maryland, Cohens v Virginia* and *Gibbons v Ogden.* He died at Philadelphia, PA, July 6, 1835. For more info: oyez.northwestern.edu/justices/justice.cgi.

MOZAMBIQUE: ARMED FORCES DAY. Sept 24. National holiday. Commemorates the beginning of the 1964 war for independence.

RAWLS, WILSON: BIRTH ANNIVERSARY. Sept 24, 1913. Author (*Where the Red Fern Grows*), born at Scraper, OK. Died Dec 16, 1984. For a study guide to *Where the Red Fern Grows*: glencoe.com/sec/literature/litlibrary.

SOUTH AFRICA: HERITAGE DAY. Sept 24. A celebration of South African nationhood, commemorating the multicultural heritage of this rainbow nation.

BIRTHDAYS TODAY

Jane Cutler, 69, author (*Darcy and Gran Don't Like Babies*), born the Bronx, NY, Sept 24, 1936.

Eddie George, 32, football player, born Philadelphia, PA, Sept 24, 1973.

Morgan Hamm, 23, Olympic gymnast, born Ashland, WI, Sept 24, 1982.

Paul Hamm, 23, Olympic gymnast, born Ashland, WI, Sept 24, 1982.

Kevin Sorbo, 47, actor ("Hercules"), born Mound, MN, Sept 24, 1958.

★ ★ ★

September 2005

S	M	T	W	T	F	S
				1	2	3
4	5	6	7	8	9	10
11	12	13	14	15	16	17
18	19	20	21	22	23	24
25	26	27	28	29	30	

SEPTEMBER 25 — SUNDAY

Day 268 — 97 Remaining

FIRST AMERICAN NEWSPAPER PUBLISHED: ANNIVERSARY. Sept 25, 1690. The first (and only) edition of *Publick Occurrences Both Foreign and Domestick* was published by Benjamin Harris, at the London-Coffee-House, Boston, MA. Authorities considered this first newspaper published in the US offensive and ordered immediate suppression.

FIRST WOMAN SUPREME COURT JUSTICE: ANNIVERSARY. Sept 25, 1981. Sandra Day O'Connor was sworn in as the first woman associate justice of the US Supreme Court on this date. She had been nominated by President Ronald Reagan in July 1981. For more info: oyez.northwestern.edu/justices/justices.cgi.

★**GOLD STAR MOTHER'S DAY.** Sept 25. Presidential Proclamation always for last Sunday of each September since 1936. Proclamation 2424 of Sept 14, 1940, covers all succeeding years.

GREENWICH MEAN TIME BEGINS: ANNIVERSARY. Sept 25, 1676. On this day two very accurate clocks were set in motion at the Royal Observatory at Greenwich, England. Greenwich Mean Time (now called Universal Time) became standard for England; in 1884 it became standard for the world.

MAJOR LEAGUE BASEBALL'S FIRST DOUBLEHEADER: ANNIVERSARY. Sept 25, 1882. The first major league baseball doubleheader was played between the Providence, RI and Worcester, MA teams.

MOON PHASE: LAST QUARTER. Sept 25. Moon enters Last Quarter phase at 2:41 AM, EDT.

PACIFIC OCEAN DISCOVERED: ANNIVERSARY. Sept 25, 1513. Vasco Núñez de Balboa, a Spanish conquistador, stood high atop a peak in the Darien, in present-day Panama, becoming the first European to look upon the Pacific Ocean, claiming it as the South Sea in the name of the King of Spain.

REEVE, CHRISTOPHER: BIRTH ANNIVERSARY. Sept 25, 1952. Born at New York, NY, this actor was best known for his portrayal of the title character in *Superman* (1978) and three sequels during the 1980s. After being paralyzed in a horseback riding accident, he was confined to a wheelchair and became an activist for spinal-cord research and awareness. He died at Mount Kisco, NY, Oct 10, 2004.

RWANDA: REPUBLIC DAY. Sept 25. National holiday. Commemorates the 1961 referendum that abolished the monarchy.

SEQUOIA AND KINGS CANYON NATIONAL PARKS ESTABLISHED: ANNIVERSARY. Sept 25, 1890. Area in central California established as a national park. For more info: www.nps.gov/sequ.

BIRTHDAYS TODAY

Cooper Edens, 60, author (*If You're Afraid of the Dark, Remember the Night Rainbow; Santa Cows*), born Washington, DC, Sept 25, 1945.

Jim Murphy, 58, author of nonfiction (*The Great Fire, The Boy's War, An American Plague*), born Newark, NJ, Sept 25, 1947.

Andrea Davis Pinkney, 42, author (*Dear Benjamin Banneker, I Smell Honey, Duke Ellington*), born Sept 25, 1963.

Scottie Pippen, 40, basketball player, born Hamburg, AR, Sept 25, 1965.

James Ransome, 44, illustrator (*Sweet Clara and the Freedom Quilt*), born Rich Square, NC, Sept 25, 1961.

Will Smith, 37, rapper, actor ("The Fresh Prince of Bel Air," *Men in Black*), born Philadelphia, PA, Sept 25, 1968.

Barbara Walters, 74, journalist, interviewer, TV host ("20/20"), born Boston, MA, Sept 25, 1931.

SEPTEMBER 26 — MONDAY

Day 269 — 96 Remaining

APPLESEED, JOHNNY: BIRTH ANNIVERSARY. Sept 26, 1774. John Chapman, better known as Johnny Appleseed, believed to have been born at Leominster, MA. Died at Allen County, IN, Mar 11, 1845. Planter of orchards and friend of wild animals, he was regarded as a great medicine man by the Indians. For more info: *Johnny Appleseed: The Story of a Legend*, by Will Moses (Philomel, 0-3992-3153-6, $16 Gr. K–3).

"THE BRADY BUNCH" TV PREMIERE: ANNIVERSARY. Sept 26, 1969. This enduring sitcom starred Robert Reed as widower Mike Brady, who has three sons and is married to Carol (played by Florence Henderson), who has three daughters. Nutty housekeeper Alice was played by Ann B. Davis. Sons Greg (Barry Williams), Peter (Christopher Knight) and Bobby (Mike Lookinland) and daughters Marcia (Maureen McCormick), Jan (Eve Plumb) and Cindy (Susan Olsen) experienced the typical crises of youth. The original series ended in 1974, but film spoofs, TV specials and short-lived series have followed since.

FIRST TELEVISED PRESIDENTIAL DEBATE: 45th ANNIVERSARY. Sept 26, 1960. The debate between presidential candidates John F. Kennedy and Richard Nixon was televised from a WBBM-TV, Chicago TV studio.

GERSHWIN, GEORGE: BIRTH ANNIVERSARY. Sept 26, 1898. American composer remembered for his many enduring songs and melodies, including "The Man I Love," "Strike Up the Band," "Funny Face," "I Got Rhythm" and the opera *Porgy and Bess*. Many of his works were in collaboration with his brother, Ira. Born at Brooklyn, NY, he died of a brain tumor at Beverly Hills, CA, July 11, 1937. See also: "Gershwin, Ira: Birth Anniversary" (Dec 6). For more info: *George Gershwin: American Composer*, by Catherine Reef (Morgan Reynolds, 1-883846-58-7, $19.95 Gr. 5–8). ***See Curriculum Connection.***

POPE PAUL VI: BIRTH ANNIVERSARY. Sept 26, 1897. Giovanni Battista Montini, 262nd pope of the Roman Catholic Church, born at Concesio, Italy. Elected pope June 21, 1963. Died at Castel Gandolfo, near Rome, Italy, Aug 6, 1978.

SHAMU'S 20th BIRTHDAY. Sept 26. Shamu was born at Sea World at Orlando, FL, Sept 26, 1985, and is the first killer whale born in captivity to survive. Shamu is now living at Sea World's Texas park. For more info: www.seaworld.org/killer_whale/killer whales.html.

BIRTHDAYS TODAY

Serena Williams, 24, tennis player, born Saginaw, MI, Sept 26, 1981.

SEPTEMBER 26
GEORGE GERSHWIN'S BIRTH ANNIVERSARY

George Gershwin was born Sept 26, 1898, in New York City. He learned to play piano as a young boy, and by his late teens was already writing songs and scrapping along in the bustling world of Tin Pan Alley and Broadway. It was a raucous environment teeming with creativity and competition, and the young composer had a vision. In 1919 he landed his first big hit when Al Jolson performed his song "Swanee." A vintage Jolson recording of "Swanee" that's full of fun, scratchy character can be found on *You Ain't Heard Nothin' Yet: Jolie's Finest Columbia Recordings* (Columbia, 1994).

Gershwin loved exploring music outside his work for Broadway and popular songwriting. Orchestral composition was particularly compelling, and his 1928 move to Paris was the inspiration for a sweeping work called "An American in Paris." With its gentle zigs and audacious zags, the nearly 20-minute piece expressed a typical American tourist's initial wide-eyed, roller-coaster reaction to the broad avenues and lively brasseries of the City of Light. At that time Paris was full of famous artists—from Pablo Picasso and Ernest Hemingway to Russian composer Igor Stravinsky—and Gershwin's piece was both steeped in and in awe of that vitality. A nice overview of the period is provided by Arlen J. Hansen's *Expatriate Paris: A Cultural and Literary Guide to Paris of the 1920s* (Arcade Publishing, 1-559-70018-1, $15 Adult).

Performed by a full orchestra—including strings, brass, wind and percussion—"An American in Paris" begins with a jaunty reading of its main melody, punctuated by big surges of strings and brass. The moments of halting tranquility are like a smile from a stranger or the lights along the River Seine, while the bold instrumental rushes suggest the overwhelming chaos of a busy downtown street. This grand introduction drifts to a quieter middle, where a trumpet sighs wistfully over clopping percussion and touches of wavering brass. Here, Gershwin illustrates the inevitable sadness of a traveler who's far from home. But the layered strings soon take a hopeful turn, and before Gershwin's mythical tourist knows it, the city's grace and romance greet him once more. Tremendous flourishes of cymbal and brass lead into jazzy stretches that evoke the exotic sights and exciting sounds of nighttime Paris, as well as the piece's eventual, heartwarming finale.

The instrumental dynamics of "An American in Paris" are clear and straightforward throughout, and students can identify the various sections of the piece as well as the distinct instruments used to create its different moods. Recordings and arrangements vary, but full orchestra recordings include *Essential Gershwin* (Decca, 2003); *Rhapsody in Blue/An American in Paris* (Point Classics/Eclipse Music Group, 1994); and *Bernstein Conducts Gershwin* (Sony, 2003), a New York Philharmonic performance. In addition, Gershwin's narrative for "An American in Paris" framed the Oscar-winning Gene Kelly film of the same name, released in 1951. Its most ambitious dance number is set to "An American in Paris"; Rhino's 1996 release is the definitive soundtrack. —Johnny Loftus

SEPTEMBER 27 — TUESDAY

Day 270 — 95 Remaining

ADAMS, SAMUEL: BIRTH ANNIVERSARY. Sept 27, 1722. Revolutionary leader and Massachusetts state politician Samuel Adams, cousin to President John Adams, was born at Boston. He died there Oct 2, 1803. As a delegate to the First and Second Continental Congresses, Adams urged a vigorous stand against England. He signed the Declaration of Independence and the Articles of Confederation and supported the war for independence. Adams served as lieutenant governor of Massachusetts under John Hancock from 1789 to 1793 and then as governor until 1797.

ANCESTOR APPRECIATION DAY. Sept 27. A day to learn about and appreciate one's forebears. For info: A.A.D. Assn, PO Box 3, Montague, MI 49437-0003.

ETHIOPIA: CROSS DAY. Sept 27. National holiday. Commemorates the finding of the true cross (*Maskal*). Also a holiday in Eritrea.

SAINT VINCENT DE PAUL: FEAST DAY. Sept 27. French priest, patron of charitable organizations and founder of the Vincentian Order and cofounder of the Sisters of Charity. Canonized 1737 (lived 1581?–1660).

BIRTHDAYS TODAY

Martin Handford, 49, author and illustrator (*Where's Waldo?*), born London, England, Sept 27, 1956.
Stephen Douglas (Steve) Kerr, 40, basketball player, born Beirut, Lebanon, Sept 27, 1965.
Mike Schmidt, 56, Hall of Fame baseball player, born Dayton, OH, Sept 27, 1949.
Gerhard Schroeder, 55, Chancellor of Germany, born Mossenberg, Germany, Sept 27, 1950.
Bernard Waber, 81, author (*Lyle, Lyle, Crocodile; The House on East 88th Street; Ira Sleeps Over*), born Philadelphia, PA, Sept 27, 1924.

SEPTEMBER 28 — WEDNESDAY

Day 271 — 94 Remaining

CABRILLO DAY: ANNIVERSARY OF DISCOVERY OF CALIFORNIA. Sept 28, 1542. California. Commemorates discovery of California by Portuguese navigator Juan Rodriguez Cabrillo who reached San Diego Bay. Cabrillo died at San Miguel Island, CA, Jan 3, 1543. His birth date is unknown. The Cabrillo National Monument marks his landfall and Cabrillo Day is still observed in California (in some areas on the Saturday nearest Sept 28—Sept 24 in 2005).

POKÉMON DEBUTS IN AMERICA: ANNIVERSARY. Sept 28, 1998. This wildly popular Game Boy game, featuring Mewtwo, Pikachu, Meowth and Snorlax, first debuted in Japan on Feb 27, 1996. The goal of the game is to find, capture and train the hundreds of different Pokémon (pocket monsters). Trading cards also proved immensely popular with US kids. The Pokémon animated TV show debuted in 1998 and *Pokémon the First Movie: Mewtwo Strikes Back* was released Nov 10, 1999. Several sequels followed, as well as numerous other video games, toys and other related merchandise.

September 2005

S	M	T	W	T	F	S
				1	2	3
4	5	6	7	8	9	10
11	12	13	14	15	16	17
18	19	20	21	22	23	24
25	26	27	28	29	30	

TAIWAN: CONFUCIUS'S BIRTHDAY AND TEACHERS' DAY. Sept 28. National holiday, designated as Teachers' Day. Confucius is the Latinized name of Kung-futzu, born at Shantung province on the 27th day of the tenth moon (lunar calendar) in the 22nd year of Kuke Hsiang of Lu (551 BC). He died at age 72, having spent some 40 years as a teacher. Teachers' Day is observed annually on Sept 28.

WIGGIN, KATE DOUGLAS: BIRTH ANNIVERSARY. Sept 28, 1856. Kate Wiggin was born Kate Douglas Smith at Philadelphia, PA. She helped organize the first free kindergarten on the West Coast in 1878 at San Francisco, and in 1880 she and her sister established the California Kindergarten Training School. After moving back to the East Coast, she devoted herself to writing, producing a number of children's books including *The Birds' Christmas Carol, Polly Oliver's Problem* and *Rebecca of Sunnybrook Farm*. She died at Harrow, England, Aug 24, 1923.

WILLARD, FRANCES ELIZABETH CAROLINE: BIRTH ANNIVERSARY. Sept 28, 1839. American educator and reformer, president of the Women's Christian Temperance Union, 1879–98 and women's suffrage leader, born at Churchville, NY. Died at New York, NY, Feb 18, 1898.

BIRTHDAYS TODAY

Grant Fuhr, 43, former hockey player, born Spruce Grove, AB, Canada, Sept 28, 1962.
Lenny Krayzelburg, 30, Olympic swimmer, born Odessa, Russia (now Ukraine), Sept 28, 1975.
Se Ri Pak, 28, golfer, born Daejeon, South Korea, Sept 28, 1977.
Gwyneth Paltrow, 32, actress (*Shakespeare in Love, Emma*), born Los Angeles, CA, Sept 28, 1973.
Brian Rafalski, 32, hockey player, born Dearborn, MI, Sept 28, 1973.

SEPTEMBER 29 — THURSDAY

Day 272 — 93 Remaining

ENGLAND: SCOTLAND YARD: ANNIVERSARY OF FIRST PUBLIC APPEARANCE. Sept 29, 1829. The first public appearance of Greater London's Metropolitan Police occurred amid jeering and abuse from disapproving political opponents. Public sentiment turned to confidence and respect in the ensuing years. The Metropolitan Police had been established by an act of Parliament in June 1829, at the request of Home Secretary Sir Robert Peel, after whom the London police officers became more affectionately known as "bobbies." Scotland Yard, the site of their first headquarters near Charing Cross, soon became the official name of the force.

FERMI, ENRICO: BIRTH ANNIVERSARY. Sept 29, 1901. Nuclear physicist, born at Rome, Italy. Played a prominent role in the splitting of the atom and in the construction of the first American nuclear reactor. Died at Chicago, IL, Nov 16, 1954.

MICHAELMAS. Sept 29. The feast of St. Michael and All Angels in the Greek and Roman Catholic Churches.

PARAGUAY: BOQUERÓN DAY. Sept 29. National holiday. Commemorates a battle during the Chaco War in 1932.

SPACE MILESTONE: *DISCOVERY* (US). Sept 29, 1988. Space Shuttle *Discovery*, after numerous reschedulings, launched from Kennedy Space Center, FL, with a five-member crew on board, and landed Oct 3 at Edwards Air Force Base, CA. It marked the first American manned flight since the *Challenger* tragedy in 1986. See also: "*Challenger* Space Shuttle Explosion: Anniversary" (Jan 28).

BIRTHDAYS TODAY

Stan Berenstain, 82, author and illustrator, with his wife Jan (the Berenstain Bears series), born Philadelphia, PA, Sept 29, 1923.

Mohini Bhardwaj, 27, Olympic gymnast, born Philadelphia, PA, Sept 29, 1978.

Bryant Gumbel, 57, TV host ("Today," "The Public Eye"), sportscaster, born New Orleans, LA, Sept 29, 1948.

Donald Hall, 77, poet and author (*The Ox-Cart Man, When Willard Met Babe Ruth*), born New Haven, CT, Sept 29, 1928.

Bill Nelson, 63, US Senator (D, Florida), born Miami, FL, Sept 29, 1942.

Lech Walesa, 62, Poland labor leader, Solidarity founder, born Popowo, Poland, Sept 29, 1943.

SEPTEMBER 30 — FRIDAY

Day 273 — 92 Remaining

ARCHAEOPTERYX FOSSIL DISCOVERY ANNOUNCED: ANNIVERSARY. Sept 30, 1861. German scientist Hermann von Meyer announced the discovery of an incredible fossil from Bavaria's Solnhofen limestone quarries in a scholarly journal on this date—exciting the world's scientific community. Although a fossilized feather had been discovered a month earlier, this find was a complete skeleton of a "feather-clad" animal that showed both avian and reptilian characteristics. The Jurassic period creature (some 150 million years old) was later named Archaeopteryx, or "ancient wing." It is considered the oldest known bird. It was the size of a pigeon and had teeth as well as grasping claws on its wings.

BABE RUTH SETS HOME RUN RECORD: ANNIVERSARY. Sept 30, 1927. George Herman "Babe" Ruth hit his 60th home run of the season off Tom Zachary of the Washington Senators. Ruth's record for the most homers in a single season stood for 34 years—until Roger Maris hit 61 in 1961. Maris's record was broken in 1998, first by Mark McGwire of the St. Louis Cardinals and then by Sammy Sosa of the Chicago Cubs. In 2001 the record was broken by Barry Bonds with 73 home runs.

BOTSWANA: INDEPENDENCE DAY. Sept 30. National holiday. The former Bechuanaland Protectorate (British Colony) became the independent Republic of Botswana in 1966.

D'AULAIRE, EDGAR PARIN: BIRTH ANNIVERSARY. Sept 30, 1898. Author, with his wife Ingri (*Norse Gods and Giants*), born at Munich, Germany. Died May 1, 1986.

FEAST OF SAINT JEROME. Sept 30. Patron saint of scholars and librarians.

"THE FLINTSTONES" TV PREMIERE: 45th ANNIVERSARY. Sept 30, 1960. This Hanna Barbera cartoon comedy was set in prehistoric times. Characters included two Stone Age families, Fred and Wilma Flintstone and their neighbors Barney and Betty Rubble. In 1994 *The Flintstones* film was released, starring John Goodman, Rick Moranis, Elizabeth Perkins and Rosie O'Donnell.

GUADALUPE MOUNTAINS NATIONAL PARK ESTABLISHED: ANNIVERSARY. Sept 30, 1972. Area in western Texas along Texas–New Mexico border, originally authorized Oct 15, 1966, was established as a national park. For more info: www.nps.gov/gumo/index.htm.

HALEAKALA NATIONAL PARK ESTABLISHED: 45th ANNIVERSARY. Sept 30, 1960. Summit of a volcano on Maui in the Hawaiian Islands was authorized as a part of Hawaii National Park on Aug 1, 1916. In 1960 Haleakala was established as a separate national park. The park was expanded in 1969 to include the Kipahulu Valley. For more info: www.nps.gov/hale/index.htm.

HONG KONG: BIRTHDAY OF CONFUCIUS. Sept 30. Observed on the 27th day of the eighth lunar month.

MEREDITH ENROLLS AT OLE MISS: ANNIVERSARY. Sept 30, 1962. Rioting broke out when James Meredith became the first black to enroll in the all-white University of Mississippi. President Kennedy sent US troops to the area to force compliance with the law. Three people died in the fighting and 50 were injured. On June 6, 1966, Meredith was shot while participating in a civil rights march at Mississippi. On June 25 Meredith, barely recovered, rejoined the marchers near Jackson, MS.

STATE FAIR OF TEXAS. Sept 30–Oct 23. Fair Park, Dallas, TX. Features a Broadway musical, college football games, new car show, concerts, livestock shows and traditional events and entertainment including exhibits, creative arts and parades. Est attendance: 3,000,000. For info: Public Relations, State Fair of Texas, PO Box 150009, Dallas, TX 75315. Phone: (214) 421-8716. Fax: (214) 421-8710. E-mail: pr@bigtex.com. Web: www.bigtex.com.

BIRTHDAYS TODAY

Martina Hingis, 25, tennis player, born Kosice, Slovakia, Sept 30, 1980.

Blanche Lambert Lincoln, 45, US Senator (D, Arkansas), born Helena, MT, Sept 30, 1960.

Dominique Moceanu, 24, gymnast, born Hollywood, CA, Sept 30, 1981.

OCTOBER 1 — SATURDAY

Day 274 — 91 Remaining

ADOPT-A-SHELTER DOG MONTH. Oct 1–31. To promote the adoption of dogs from local shelters, the ASPCA sponsors this important observance. "Make pet adoption your first option®" is a message the organization promotes throughout the year in an effort to end the euthanasia of all adoptable animals. For info: ASPCA Media Relations, 424 E 92nd St, New York, NY 10128. Phone: (212) 876-7700, ext. 4655. E-mail: press@aspca.org. Web: www.aspca.org.

BOOK IT! READING INCENTIVE PROGRAM. Oct 1, 2005–Mar 31, 2006. This is a six-month program for students in grades K–6 sponsored by Pizza Hut. Teachers set monthly reading goals for students. When a monthly reading goal is met, the child receives a certificate for a free pizza. If the whole class meets its goal, a pizza party is provided for the class. For info: Book It!, PO Box 2999, Wichita, KS 67201. Phone: (800) 4-BOOK IT. Fax: (316) 687-8937. Web: www.bookitprogram.com.

CARTER, JIMMY: BIRTHDAY. Oct 1, 1924. The 39th president (Jan 20, 1977–Jan 20, 1981) of the US, born James Earl Carter at Plains, GA. For more info: www.ipl.org/ref/POTUS.

CD PLAYER DEBUTS: ANNIVERSARY. Oct 1, 1982. The first compact disc player, jointly developed by Sony, Philips and Polygram, went on sale. It cost $625 (more than $1,000 in current dollars).

CHILDREN'S MAGAZINE MONTH. Oct 1–31. Nationwide literacy initiative to raise awareness and create interest in children's magazines. For info: Assn of Educational Publishers, 510 Heron Dr, Ste 309, Logan Township, NJ 08085. Web: www.childmagmonth.org.

CHINA: NATIONAL DAY. Oct 1. Commemorates the founding of the People's Republic of China in 1949.

CYPRUS: INDEPENDENCE DAY. Oct 1. National holiday. Commemorates independence from Britain in 1960.

DISNEY WORLD OPENED: ANNIVERSARY. Oct 1, 1971. Disney's second theme park opened at Orlando, FL. See also: "Disneyland Opened: Anniversary" (July 17).

October 2005

S	M	T	W	T	F	S
						1
2	3	4	5	6	7	8
9	10	11	12	13	14	15
16	17	18	19	20	21	22
23	24	25	26	27	28	29
30	31					

DIVERSITY AWARENESS MONTH. Oct 1–31. Celebrating, promoting and appreciating the diversity of our society. Also, a month to foster and further our understanding of the inherent value of all races, genders, nationalities, age groups, religions, sexual orientations, classes and disabilities. Annually, in October. For more info: *Our Family, Our Friends, Our World: An Annotated Guide to Significant Multicultural Books for Children and Teenagers*, by Lyn Miller-Lachmann (Bowker, 0-8352-3025-2, $49.95) and *This Land Is Our Land: A Guide to Multicultural Literature for Children and Young Adults*, by Althea K. Helbig and Agnes Regan Perkins (Greenwood, 0-313-28742-2, $49.95). For info: Carole Copeland Thomas, C. Thomas & Associates, 400 W Cummings Park, Ste 1725-154, Woburn, MA 01801. Phone: (800) 801-6599 or (508) 947-5755. Fax: (508) 947-3903. E-mail: Carole@TellCarole.com. Web: www.TellCarole.com.

DOMESTIC VIOLENCE AWARENESS MONTH. Oct 1–31. Commemorated since 1987, this month attempts to raise awareness of efforts to end violence against women and their children. The Domestic Violence Awareness Month Project is a collaborative effort of the National Resource Center on Domestic Violence, Family Violence Prevention Fund, National Coalition Against Domestic Violence, National Domestic Violence Hotline and the National Network to End Domestic Violence. For info: NCADV, PO Box 18749, Denver, CO 80218. Phone: (303) 839-1852. Web: www.ncadv.org.

EAT BETTER, EAT TOGETHER MONTH. Oct 1–31. Time to encourage families to eat together. Research indicates that children who eat with their families not only have better nutrition, but they do better in school and have fewer behavior problems. A tool kit has been created to show how family meals can be simple, easy and nutritious. Call for the top 10 ways to eat better, eat together. For info: Sue Butkus, Nutrition Education Network of Washington State, Cooperative Extension, Washington State Univ, 7612 Pioneer Way E, Puyallup, WA 98317-4989. Phone: (253) 445-4553. Web: nutrition.wsu.edu/eat.

FAMILY HEALTH MONTH. Oct 1–31. For info: American Academy of Family Physicians, 11400 Tomahawk Creek Pkwy, Leawood, KS 66211-2672. Phone: (800) 274-2237. Web: www.aafp.org.

FIREPUP'S BIRTHDAY. Oct 1. Firepup spends his time teaching fire safety awareness to children in a fun-filled and nonthreatening manner. The US Fire Administration's site at www.usfa.fema.gov/kids has materials to help kids learn fire safety. For info: National Fire Safety Council, Inc, PO Box 378, Michigan Center, MI 49254-0378. Phone: (517) 764-2811.

GERMAN-AMERICAN HERITAGE MONTH. Oct 1–31. A month celebrating America's German heritage. Numerous historical programs, museum and library exhibits, cultural events, genealogical workshops and more planned. For info: Dr. Don Heinrich Tolzmann, Dir, German-American Studies Program, 806 Blegen Library, Univ of Cincinnati, PO Box 210113, Cincinnati, OH 45221-0113. Phone: (513) 556-1955. Fax: (513) 556-2113. E-mail: don.tolzmann@uc.edu.

HARRISON, CAROLINE LAVINIA SCOTT: BIRTH ANNIVERSARY. Oct 1, 1832. First wife of Benjamin Harrison, 23rd president of the US, born at Oxford, OH. Died at Washington, DC, Oct 25, 1892. She was the second first lady to die in the White House.

INTERNATIONAL DINOSAUR MONTH. Oct 1–31. Devoted to the study of dinosaurs and the protection and preservation of their fossils. Also in appreciation of the contributions to human knowledge of paleontologists, dino-artists and dino-educators.

OCTOBER 1–31
KIDS LOVE A MYSTERY MONTH

Sometimes, the classics are the best. There have been so many new mystery series in the past few years, such as Lemony Snicket's "A Series of Unfortunate Events," maybe this month it's time to step back and make sure your students aren't missing the wonderful books that their parents read, too.

For the youngest chapter book readers, the classic series The Bobbsey Twins is back in print this year. Grosset & Dunlap has rolled out several volumes of the original series by Laura Lee Hope. These stories, while a little dated, offer an innocence and sense of wonder and discovery often missing in contemporary fiction. Not to be overlooked from the same publisher are the classic Nancy Drew and Hardy Boys mystery series; their style of chapters ending with cliffhangers makes them great choices to read aloud, a chapter a day. Any library should have a large assortment of those classics by Carolyn Keene and Franklin W. Dixon.

What do missing roller skates, eight stuffed penguins and a trapeze artist's inheritance have in common? All are elements in mysteries solved by Idaville's very own *Encyclopedia Brown, Boy Detective* (Skylark/Bantam, 0-553-15724-8, $4.99 Ages 9–12). All nineteen volumes of Donald Sobol's classic series follow the same pattern: collections of short, unrelated, brain-twister mysteries, with the solutions found at the back of the book. A perfect choice for the low-level, high-interest reader, as they won't need to finish the entire book to get to the satisfying conclusion. Or try reading one story aloud just before lunch—have your students come back from recess with the solution.

For girls who love horses and mysteries, the Trixie Belden series provides the perfect combination. Trixie and her friends have a secret club, ride horses, moan over household chores and homework and stumble across adventure and danger in their small town in upstate New York. Back in print this year using the classic illustrations from the 1950s, the series starts with *The Secret of the Mansion* (Random House, 0-375-82412-X, $6.99 Ages 8–12). Authors Julie Campbell and Kathryn Kenny originally wrote 38 stories; 12 are currently available with more to come.

Older readers will love trying to solve the puzzle of *The Westing Game* by Ellen Raskin (Penguin, 0-14-038664-5, $5.99 Ages 10 and up). Winner of the 1978 Newbery Medal, this whodunit is filled with quirky characters forced to play a "game," working both with and against each other to solve the murder of the eccentric millionaire Mr. Westing. But is he actually even dead?

Of course, for those voracious readers who need the newest and the best, don't overlook *Chasing Vermeer* by Blue Balliett (Scholastic, 0-439-37294-1, $16.95 Ages 9–12). The book is vibrantly illustrated by Brett Helquist, who is also responsible for the illustrations in A Series of Unfortunate Events. Set in Chicago, the story follows two sixth-grade classmates as they solve a puzzle involving museums, math and a valuable stolen painting. See if you can find all of the hidden clues!

—Kathryn Keil

INTERNATIONAL FRUGAL FUN DAY. Oct 1. A day to celebrate that having fun doesn't have to be costly. Do at least one fun thing for yourself and/or your family that is free of cost or under $5 a person: a concert or play, a hike, a meal out, a picnic, an art gallery or museum tour, a day trip, a boat ride. Annually, the first Saturday in October. For info: Shel Horowitz, PO Box 1164, Northampton, MA 01061-1164. Phone: (413) 586-2388. E-mail: shel@frugalfun.com. Web: www.frugalfun.com.

KIDS LOVE A MYSTERY MONTH. Oct 1–31. A month of celebration of mysteries for children. Kids who participate in this literary program may be eligible for a free certificate or even an autographed book! This event opens up a wonderful opportunity for everyone—authors, parents, teachers, librarians, and booksellers—to reach out to the children in their communities and give them the lifelong gift of reading. ***See Curriculum Connection.*** For info: Janet Riehecky, 657 Shenandoah Trail, Elgin, IL 60123. Phone: (847) 695-9781. E-mail: jr@janetriehecky.com. Web: www.mysterywriters.org. See also: www.kidsloveamystery.com.

LATINO BOOK & FAMILY FESTIVAL—HOUSTON. Oct 1–2. George R. Brown Convention Center, Houston, TX. Produced along with actor Edward James Olmos, this festival is a celebration of books, careers, culture, education, health, recreation, travel and more. It is the largest Latino consumer trade show in the US. Attendees will enjoy hundreds of booths and activities including book signings, storytelling, poetry readings, food, entertainment and workshops. For info: Latino Book & Family Festivals, 3980 Cazador St, Los Angeles, CA 90065. E-mail: kathy@latinobookfestival.com. Web: www.LBFF.us or www.openabook.org.

LIONS CLUBS INTERNATIONAL PEACE POSTER CONTEST. Oct 1. Contest for children ages 11–13. All entries must be sponsored by a local Lions Club. Today is the deadline to request contest kits from the International Headquarters. Posters due to sponsoring Lions Club by Nov 15, 2005. Finalist judging held on Feb 1, 2006. Dates are tentative, please call to verify. For info: Public Relations Dept, International Assn of Lions Clubs, 300 22nd St, Oak Brook, IL 60523-8842. Phone: (630) 571-5466. Web: www.lionsclub.org.

MARIS BREAKS HOME RUN RECORD: ANNIVERSARY. Oct 1, 1961. Roger Maris of the New York Yankees hit his 61st home run, breaking Babe Ruth's record for the most home runs in a season. Maris hit his homer against pitcher Tracy Stallard of the Boston Red Sox as the Yankees won, 1–0. Controversy over the record arose because the American League had adopted a 162-game schedule in 1961, and Maris played in 161 games. In 1927, when Ruth set his record, the schedule called for 154 games, and Ruth played in 151. On Sept 8, 1998, Mark McGwire of the St. Louis Cardinals hit his 62nd home run, breaking Maris's record, and a few days later, Sept 13, 1998, Sammy Sosa of the Chicago Cubs also hit his 62nd. On Oct 5, 2001, Barry Bonds of the San Francisco Giants broke the record, finishing the season with 73 homers.

MONTH OF THE YOUNG ADOLESCENT. Oct 1–31. Youth between the ages of 10–15 undergo more extensive physical, mental, social and emotional changes than at any other time of life, with the exception of infancy. Initiated by the National Middle School Association and endorsed by 29 other national organizations focusing on youth, this month is designed to bring attention to the importance of this age in a person's development. For info: National Middle School Assn, 4151 Executive Pkwy, Ste 300, Westerville, OH 43081. Phone: (800) 528-NMSA. E-mail: info@nmsa.org. Web: www.nmsa.org.

NATIONAL BOOK MONTH. Oct 1–31. When the world demands more and more of our time, National Book Month invites everyone in America to take time out to treat themselves to a unique pleasure: reading a good book. Readers participate in National Book Month annually through literary events held at schools, bookstores, libraries, community centers and arts organizations. The organization also sponsors the annual National Book Awards, which include an award for a children's book. For info: National Book Foundation, 95 Madison Ave, Ste 709, New York, NY 10016. Phone: (212) 685-0261. Fax: (212) 235-6570. E-mail: nationalbook@nationalbook.org. Web: www.nationalbook.org.

★**NATIONAL BREAST CANCER AWARENESS MONTH.** Oct 1–31.

NATIONAL CONSTRUCTION TOY MONTH. Oct 1–31. A celebration of the creativity and educational value children gain from building with construction toys. For info: K'nex Industries, 2990 Bergey Rd, Hatfield, PA 19440. Phone: (215) 996-4835. Fax: (215) 996-4222. E-mail: email@knex.com. Web: www.knex.com.

NATIONAL CRIME PREVENTION MONTH. Oct 1–31. During Crime Prevention Month, individuals can commit to working on at least one of three levels—family, neighborhood or community—to drive violence and drugs from our world. It is also a time to honor individuals who have accepted personal responsibility for their neighborhoods and groups who work for the community's common good. Annually, every October. For info: National Crime Prevention Council, 1000 Connecticut Ave NW, 13th Fl, Washington, DC 20036. Phone: (202) 466-6272. Fax: (202) 296-1356. Web: www.weprevent.org or www.ncpc.org.

NATIONAL DENTAL HYGIENE MONTH. Oct 1–31. To increase public awareness of the importance of preventive oral health care and the dental hygienist's role as the preventive professional. Annually, during the month of October. For info: Public Relations, American Dental Hygienists' Assn, 444 N Michigan Ave, Ste 3400, Chicago, IL 60611. Phone: (312) 440-8900. Web: www.adha.org.

★**NATIONAL DISABILITY EMPLOYMENT AWARENESS MONTH.** Oct 1–31. Presidential Proclamation issued for the month of October (PL100–630, Title III, Sec 301a of Nov 7, 1988). Previously issued as "National Employ the Handicapped Week" for the first week in October since 1945.

NATIONAL FAMILY SEXUALITY EDUCATION MONTH. Oct 1–31. A national coalition effort to support parents as the first and primary sexuality educators of their children by providing information for parents and young people. For info: Planned Parenthood Federation of America, Education Dept, 434 W 33rd St, New York, NY 10001. Phone: (212) 261-4628. Fax: (212) 247-6269. E-mail: education@ppfa.org. Web: www.plannedparenthood.org.

NATIONAL GEOGRAPHIC BEE 2006 REGISTRATION DEADLINE APPROACHING. Oct 1. Principals must register their schools to participate in the National Geographic Bee by October 15, 2005. For registration info go to www.nationalgeographic.com/geographicbee.

NATIONAL GO ON A FIELD TRIP MONTH. Oct 1–31. A month to highlight the importance of the field trip as a way to help children learn. Studies show that children learn 40–60 percent more outside the classroom. The field trip is a great way to teach valuable life skills and career education. For info: Field Trip Factory, 1735 N Paulina, #413, Chicago, IL 60622. Phone: (773) 342-9510. Web: fieldtripfactory.com.

October 2005

S	M	T	W	T	F	S
						1
2	3	4	5	6	7	8
9	10	11	12	13	14	15
16	17	18	19	20	21	22
23	24	25	26	27	28	29
30	31					

NATIONAL ORTHODONTIC HEALTH MONTH. Oct 1–31. A beautiful, healthy smile is only the most obvious benefit of orthodontic treatment. National Orthodontic Health Month spotlights the important role of orthodontic care in overall physical health and emotional well-being. The observance is sponsored by the American Association of Orthodontists (AAO), which supports research and education leading to quality patient care and promotes increased public awareness of the need for and benefits of orthodontic treatment. For info: Pam Paladin, American Assn of Orthodontists, 401 N Lindbergh St, St. Louis, MO 63141-7816. Phone: (314) 993-1700. Fax: (314) 997-1745. E-mail: ppaladin@aaortho.org. Web: www.braces.org.

NATIONAL POPCORN POPPIN' MONTH. Oct 1–31. To celebrate the wholesome, economical, natural food value of popcorn, America's native snack. For info: The Popcorn Board, 401 N Michigan Ave, Chicago, IL 60611-4267. Phone: (312) 644-6610. Web: www.popcorn.org.

NATIONAL READING GROUP MONTH. Oct 1–31. Reading group members celebrate the joy of a book shared and inspire individuals who do not belong to a reading group to join one or start their own. Organizations, bookstores and libraries are encouraged to sponsor reading group events during this month. Perhaps your students would like to form a themed group as an extracurricular activity. For info: Alice Dillon, 14511 Pfeifer Way, Lake Oswego, OR 97035. Phone: (503) 636-1242. Fax: (503) 635-5119. E-mail: NotesintheMargin@aol.com or Martha Burns, 41 Park Ln, Essex Fells, NJ 07021. E-mail: mlbwrite@aol.com.

NATIONAL ROLLER SKATING MONTH. Oct 1–31. A month-long celebration recognizing the health benefits and recreational enjoyment of this long-loved pastime. Also includes in-line skating and an emphasis on safe skating. For info: Roller Skating Assn, 6905 Corporate Dr, Indianapolis, IN 46278. Phone: (317) 347-2626. Fax: (317) 347-2636. E-mail: rsa@rollerskating.org. Web: www.rollerskating.com.

NATIONAL STAMP COLLECTING MONTH. Oct 1–31. Sponsored by the US Postal Service to introduce a new generation to the exciting world of stamp collecting. For info: Stamp Services, US Postal Service, 475 L'Enfant Plaza SW, Rm 5670, Washington, DC 20260-2437. Web: www.usps.gov.

NIGERIA: INDEPENDENCE DAY. Oct 1. National holiday. This West African nation became independent of Great Britain in 1960 and a republic in 1963.

POLISH AMERICAN HERITAGE MONTH. Oct 1–31. A national celebration of Polish history, culture and pride, in cooperation with the Polish American Congress and Polonia Across America. For info: Michael Blichasz, Chair, Polish American Cultural Center, National HQ, 308 Walnut St, Philadelphia, PA 19106. Phone: (215) 922-1700. Fax: (215) 922-1518. E-mail: mail@polishamericancenter.org. Web: www.polishamericancenter.org.

STOCKTON, RICHARD: 275th BIRTH ANNIVERSARY. Oct 1, 1730. Lawyer and signer of the Declaration of Independence, born at Princeton, NJ. Died there, Feb 8, 1781.

SUPER MARIO BROTHERS RELEASED: 20th ANNIVERSARY. Oct 1, 1985. In 1985 the Nintendo Entertainment System (NES) for home use was introduced and the popular game for the NES, Super Mario Brothers, was released on this date. In 1989 Nintendo introduced Game Boy, the first handheld game system with interchangeable game cartridges. For more info: www.nintendo.com.

TUVALU: NATIONAL HOLIDAY. Oct 1. Commemorates independence from Great Britain in 1978.

UNITED NATIONS: INTERNATIONAL DAY OF OLDER PERSONS. Oct 1. On Dec 14, 1990, the General Assembly designated Oct 1 as the International Day for the Elderly. It appealed for contributions to the Trust Fund for Aging (which supports projects in developing countries in implementation of the Vienna International Plan of Action on Aging adopted at the 1982 World Assembly on Aging) and endorsed an action program on aging for 1992 and beyond as outlined by the Secretary-General (Res 45/106). On Dec 21, 1995, the Assembly changed the name from "for the Elderly" to "of Older Persons" to conform with the 1991 UN Principles for Older Persons. For info: United Nations, Dept of Public Info, Rm GA-57, New York, NY 10017. Phone: (212) 963-4475. E-mail: inquiries@un.org. Web: www.un.org.

UNIVERSAL CHILDREN'S WEEK. Oct 1–7. To disseminate throughout the world info on the needs of children and to distribute copies of the Declaration of the Rights of the Child. For complete info, send $4 to cover expense of printing, handling and postage. Annually, the first seven days of October. For info: Dr. Stanley Drake, Pres, Intl Soc of Friendship and Good Will, 8592 Roswell Rd, Ste 251, Atlanta, GA 30350-1867. Phone: (678) 795-1362. Web: www.friendshipandgoodwill.org.

US 2006 FEDERAL FISCAL YEAR BEGINS. Oct 1, 2005–Sept 30, 2006.

VEGETARIAN MONTH. Oct 1–31. This educational event advances awareness of the many surprising ethical, environmental, economic, health, humanitarian and other benefits of the increasingly popular vegetarian lifestyle. Each year in the US about one million more people become vegetarians. This event promotes personal and planetary healing with respect for all life. For info: Vegetarian Awareness Network, Communications Center, PO Box 321, Knoxville, TN 37901-0321. Phone: (800) USA-VEGE.

VIRGINIA CHILDREN'S FESTIVAL. Oct 1. Town Point Park, Norfolk, VA. 17th annual. An all-day family program hosted by nationally famous children's entertainers, costumed characters and five stages of entertainment. Also, magic, giant puppets, creative dance and many other activities for a day of fantasy and fun. Est attendance: 45,000. For info: Norfolk Festevents, Ltd, 120 W Main St, Norfolk, VA 23510. Phone: (757) 441-2345. Fax: (757) 441-5198. Web: www.festeventsva.org.

WORLD VEGETARIAN DAY. Oct 1. Celebration of vegetarianism's benefits to humans, animals and our planet. In addition to individuals, participants include libraries, schools, colleges, restaurants, food services, health-care centers, health food stores, workplaces and many more. For info: North American Vegetarian Society, Box 72, Dolgeville, NY 13329. Phone: (518) 568-7970. Fax: (518) 568-7979. E-mail: navs@telenet.net. Web: navs-online .com.

YOSEMITE NATIONAL PARK ESTABLISHED: ANNIVERSARY. Oct 1, 1890. Yosemite Valley and Mariposa Big Tree Grove, granted to the State of California June 30, 1864, were combined and established as a national park. For more park info: Yosemite National Park, PO Box 577, Yosemite National Park, CA 95389. Web: www.nps.gov/yose.

BIRTHDAYS TODAY

Jimmy Carter, 81, 39th president of the US, Nobel Peace Prize recipient (2002), born James Earl Carter, Jr, at Plains, GA, Oct 1, 1924.

Stephen Collins, 58, actor ("7th Heaven"), born Des Moines, IA, Oct 1, 1947.

Julie Andrews Edwards, 70, actress (*The Sound of Music, Mary Poppins*), author (*Mandy, Dumpy the Dump Truck*), born Walton-on-Thames, Surrey, England, Oct 1, 1935.

Mark McGwire, 42, former baseball player, born Pomona, CA, Oct 1, 1963.

Ann Morris, 75, author (*Bread, Bread, Bread; Houses and Homes*), born New York, NY, Oct 1, 1930.

Elizabeth Partridge, 54, author (*Restless Spirit: The Life and Work of Dorothea Lange*), born Berkeley, CA, Oct 1, 1951.

William Hubbs Rehnquist, 81, Chief Justice of the US Supreme Court, born Milwaukee, WI, Oct 1, 1924.

OCTOBER 2 — SUNDAY

Day 275 — 90 Remaining

GANDHI, MOHANDAS KARAMCHAND (MAHATMA): BIRTH ANNIVERSARY. Oct 2, 1869. Indian political and spiritual leader who achieved world honor and fame for his advocacy of nonviolent resistance as a weapon against tyranny was born at Porbandar, India. He was assassinated in the garden of his home at New Delhi, Jan 30, 1948. On the anniversary of Gandhi's birth (Gandhi Jayanti) thousands gather at the park on the Jumna River at Delhi where Gandhi's body was cremated. Hymns are sung, verses from the Gita, the Koran and the Bible are recited and cotton thread is spun on small spinning wheels (one of Gandhi's favorite activities). Other observances held at his birthplace and throughout India on this public holiday. For more info: www.mahatma.org.in or *Gandhi*, by Demi (Simon & Schuster, 0-689-84149-3, $19.95 Gr. 3–6).

GUINEA: INDEPENDENCE DAY. Oct 2. National Day. Guinea gained independence from France in 1958.

JAPAN: NEWSPAPER WEEK. Oct 2–8. During this week newspapers make an extensive effort to acquaint the public with their functions and the role of a newspaper in a free society. Annually, the first week in October.

NATIONAL CUSTODIAL WORKERS DAY. Oct 2. A day to honor custodial workers—those who clean up after us. For info: Bette Tadajewski, Saint John the Baptist Church, 2425 Frederick, Alpena, MI 49707. Phone: (517) 354-3019.

NORTH CASCADES NATIONAL PARK ESTABLISHED: ANNIVERSARY. Oct 2, 1968. Located in the state of Washington. For more info: www.nps.gov/noca/index.htm.

"PEANUTS" DEBUTS: 55th ANNIVERSARY. Oct 2, 1950. This comic strip by Charles M. Schulz featured Charlie Brown, his sister Sally, Lucy, Linus and Charlie's dog Snoopy. The last daily "Peanuts" strip was published Jan 3, 2000, and the last new Sunday strip was published Feb 13, 2000. Schulz died the evening before the final strip appeared. Newspapers continue to run "Peanuts" in reruns, and it remains immensely popular.

REDWOOD NATIONAL PARK ESTABLISHED: ANNIVERSARY. Oct 2, 1968. California's Redwood National Park was established. For more info: www.nps.gov/redw/index.html. For more park info: Redwood National Park, 1111 Second St, Crescent City, CA 95531.

WORLD COMMUNION SUNDAY. Oct 2. Communion is celebrated by Christians all over the world. Annually, the first Sunday in October.

BIRTHDAYS TODAY

Jennifer Owings Dewey, 64, author (*Stories on Stone; Antarctic Journal: Four Months at the Bottom of the World*), born Chicago, IL, Oct 2, 1941.

OCTOBER 3 — MONDAY

Day 276 — 89 Remaining

"CAPTAIN KANGAROO" TV PREMIERE: 50th ANNIVERSARY. Oct 3, 1955. On the air until 1985, this was the longest-running children's TV show until it was surpassed by "Sesame Street." Starring Bob Keeshan as Captain Kangaroo, it was broadcast on CBS and PBS. Other characters included Mr Green Jeans, Grandfather Clock, Bunny Rabbit, Mr Moose and Dancing Bear. Keeshan was an advocate for excellence in children's programming and even supervised which commercials would appear on the program. In 1997 "The All New Captain Kangaroo" debuted, starring John McDonough.

★**CHILD HEALTH DAY.** Oct 3. Presidential Proclamation always issued for the first Monday of October. Proclamation has been issued since 1928. In 1959 Congress changed celebration day from May 1 to the present observance (Pub Res No. 46 of May 18, 1928, and Public Law 86–352 of Sept 22, 1959).

GERMAN REUNIFICATION: 15th ANNIVERSARY. Oct 3, 1990. After 45 years of division, East and West Germany reunited, just four days short of East Germany's 41st founding anniversary (Oct 7, 1949). The new united Germany took the name the Federal Republic of Germany, the formal name of the former West Germany and adopted the constitution of the former West Germany. Today is a national holiday in Germany.

HONDURAS: FRANCISCO MORAZAN HOLIDAY. Oct 3. Public holiday in honor of Francisco Morazan, national hero, who was born in 1799.

KOREA: NATIONAL FOUNDATION DAY. Oct 3. National holiday also called Tangun Day, as it commemorates the day when legendary founder of the Korean nation, Tangun, established his kingdom of Chosun in 2333 BC.

"MICKEY MOUSE CLUB" TV PREMIERE: 50th ANNIVERSARY. Oct 3, 1955. This afternoon show for children was on ABC. Among its young cast members were Mouseketeers Annette Funicello and Shelley Fabares. The show was revived in 1977 and 1989. Christina Aguilera, Keri Russell, Justin Timberlake and Britney Spears were cast members on the new edition.

MOON PHASE: NEW MOON. Oct 3. Moon enters New Moon phase at 6:28 AM, EDT.

ROBINSON NAMED BASEBALL'S FIRST BLACK MAJOR LEAGUE MANAGER: ANNIVERSARY. Oct 3, 1974. The only major league player selected most valuable player in both the American and National Leagues, Frank Robinson was hired by the Cleveland Indians as baseball's first black major league manager. During his playing career Robinson represented the American League in four World Series playing for the Baltimore Orioles, led the Cincinnati Reds to a National League pennant and hit 586 home runs in 21 years of play.

ROSH HASHANAH BEGINS AT SUNDOWN. Oct 3. Jewish New Year. See "Rosh Hashanah" (Oct 4).

SOLAR ECLIPSE. Oct 3. Annular eclipse of the sun. Visible in Atlantic Ocean, Spain and Portugal, Africa and Indian Ocean.

SUPREME COURT 2005–2006 TERM BEGINS. Oct 3. Traditionally, the Supreme Court's annual term begins on the first Monday in October and continues with seven two-week sessions of oral arguments. Between the sessions are six recesses during which the opinions are written by the justices. Ordinarily, all cases are decided by the following June or July. For a database of cases, biographies of the justices past and present and a virtual tour of the Supreme Court building on the Web: oyez.nwu.edu.

UNITED NATIONS: WORLD HABITAT DAY. Oct 3. The UN General Assembly, by a resolution of Dec 17, 1985, has designated the first Monday of October each year as World Habitat Day. The first observance of this day, Oct 5, 1986, marked the 10th anniversary of the first international conference on the subject. (Habitat: UN Conference on Human Settlements, Vancouver, Canada, 1976.) Info from: United Nations, Dept of Public Info, Public Inquiries Unit, Rm GA-57, New York, NY 10017. Phone: (212) 963-4475. Fax: (212) 963-0071. E-mail: inquiries@un.org. Web: www.un.org.

BIRTHDAYS TODAY

Jeff Bingaman, 62, US Senator (D, New Mexico), born El Paso, TX, Oct 3, 1943.

Molly Cone, 87, author (*Mishmash, The Story of Shabbat*), born Tacoma, WA, Oct 3, 1918.

Kevin Richardson, 33, singer (Backstreet Boys), born Lexington, KY, Oct 3, 1972.

Bob Riley, 61, Governor of Alabama (R), born Ashland, AL, Oct 3, 1944.

Gayle Ross, 54, author (*How Rabbit Tricked Otter*), born Texas, Oct 3, 1951.

Ashlee Simpson, 21, singer, actress ("7th Heaven"), born Dallas, TX, Oct 3, 1984.

OCTOBER 4 — TUESDAY

Day 277 — 88 Remaining

"DICK TRACY" COMIC STRIP DEBUTS: ANNIVERSARY. Oct 4, 1931. Chester Gould's new comic strip, "Plainclothes Tracy," first appeared on this date in the *Detroit Daily Mirror* and later was syndicated in nearly 1,000 newspapers under the revised title, "Dick Tracy." Tracy, a clean-cut, square-jawed detective, uses fancy gadgets to battle such foes as Pruneface, Flat Top, Mumbles and others. Creator Gould died May 11, 1985, but the strip continues today.

October 2005

S	M	T	W	T	F	S
						1
2	3	4	5	6	7	8
9	10	11	12	13	14	15
16	17	18	19	20	21	22
23	24	25	26	27	28	29
30	31					

GREGORIAN CALENDAR ADJUSTMENT: ANNIVERSARY. Oct 4, 1582. Pope Gregory XIII issued a bulletin that decreed that the day following Thursday, Oct 4, 1582, should be Friday, Oct 15, 1582, thus correcting the Julian Calendar, then 10 days out of date relative to the seasons. This reform was effective in most Catholic countries, though the Julian Calendar continued in use in Britain and the American colonies until 1752, in Japan until 1873, in China until 1912, in Russia until 1918, in Greece until 1923 and in Turkey until 1927. See also: "Gregorian Calendar Day: Anniversary" (Feb 24) and "Calendar Adjustment Day: Anniversary" (Sept 2).

HAYES, RUTHERFORD BIRCHARD: BIRTH ANNIVERSARY. Oct 4, 1822. The 19th president of the US (Mar 4, 1877–Mar 3, 1881), born at Delaware, OH. In his inaugural address, Hayes said: "He serves his party best who serves the country best." He died at Fremont, OH, Jan 17, 1893. For more info: www.ipl.org/ref/POTUS.

JOHNSON, ELIZA McCARDLE: BIRTH ANNIVERSARY. Oct 4, 1810. Wife of Andrew Johnson, 17th president of the US, born at Leesburg, TN. Died at Greeneville, TN, Jan 15, 1876.

LAWSON, ROBERT: BIRTH ANNIVERSARY. Oct 4, 1892. Author and illustrator, born at New York, NY. Lawson is the only children's writer to win both the Newbery Medal (for *Rabbit Hill* in 1945) and the Caldecott Medal (for *They Were Strong and Good* in 1941). He also wrote *Ben & Me* and *Mr. Revere and I* and illustrated such classics as *Mr. Popper's Penguins* and *Adam of the Road*. He died at Westport, CT, May 26, 1957.

LESOTHO: NATIONAL DAY. Oct 4. National holiday. Commemorates independence from Britain in 1966.

ROSH HASHANAH or JEWISH NEW YEAR. Oct 4. Jewish holy day; observed on following day (Oct 5) also. Hebrew calendar date: Tishri 1, 5766. Rosh Hashanah (literally "Head of the Year") is the beginning of 10 days of repentance and spiritual renewal. (Began at sundown of previous day.)

SAINT FRANCIS OF ASSISI: FEAST DAY. Oct 4. Giovanni Francesco Bernardone, religious leader, founder of the Friars Minor (Franciscan Order), born at Assisi, Umbria, Italy, in 1181. Died at Porziuncula, Oct 3, 1226. One of the best-loved saints of all time. For more info: *Brother Sun, Sister Moon: The Life and Stories of St. Francis*, by Margaret Mayo (Little, Brown, 0-316-56466-4, $16.95 Gr. 3–6).

SPACE MILESTONE: *SPUTNIK I* (USSR). Oct 4, 1957. Anniversary of launching of first successful man-made Earth satellite. *Sputnik I* ("satellite") weighing 184 lbs was fired into orbit from the USSR's Tyuratam launch site. Transmitted radio signal for 21 days, decayed Jan 4, 1958. The beginning of the Space Age and man's exploration beyond Earth. This first-in-space triumph by the Soviets resulted in a stepped-up emphasis on the teaching of science in American classrooms.

STRATEMEYER, EDWARD L.: BIRTH ANNIVERSARY. Oct 4, 1862. American author of children's books, Stratemeyer was born at Elizabeth, NJ. He created numerous series of popular children's books including The Bobbsey Twins, The Hardy Boys, Nancy Drew and Tom Swift. He and his Stratemeyer Syndicate, using 60 or more pen names, produced more than 800 books. More than four million copies were in print in 1987. Stratemeyer died at Newark, NJ, May 10, 1930.

UNITED NATIONS: WORLD SPACE WEEK. Oct 4–10. To celebrate the contributions of space science and technology to the betterment of the human condition. The dates recall the launch on Oct 4, 1957, of the first artificial satellite, *Sputnik I*, and the entry into force, on Oct 10, 1967, of the Treaty on Principles Governing the Activities of States in the Exploration and Use of Outer Space. For info: United Nations, Dept of Public Info, New York, NY 10017. Web: www.un.org.

BIRTHDAYS TODAY

Don Brown, 56, author (*Ruth Law Thrills a Nation*), born Rockville Center, NY, Oct 4, 1949.
Vicky Bullett, 38, basketball player, born Martinsburg, WV, Oct 4, 1967.
Rachael Leigh Cook, 26, actress (*She's All That, The Baby-Sitters Club*), born Minneapolis, MN, Oct 4, 1979.
Karen Cushman, 64, author (*Catherine, Called Birdy*; Newbery Medal for *The Midwife's Apprentice*), born Chicago, IL, Oct 4, 1941.
Chuck Hagel, 59, US Senator (R, Nebraska), born North Platte, NE, Oct 4, 1946.
Susan Meddaugh, 61, author, illustrator (*Martha Speaks, Hog-Eye*), born Montclair, NJ, Oct 4, 1944.
Alicia Silverstone, 29, actress (*Clueless, Batman & Robin*), born San Francisco, CA, Oct 4, 1976.
Donald Sobol, 81, author (the Encyclopedia Brown series), born New York, NY, Oct 4, 1924.

OCTOBER 5 — WEDNESDAY

Day 278 — 87 Remaining

ARTHUR, CHESTER ALAN: BIRTH ANNIVERSARY. Oct 5, 1829. The 21st president of the US, born at Fairfield, VT, succeeded to the presidency following the death of James A. Garfield. Term of office: Sept 20, 1881–Mar 3, 1885. Arthur was not successful in obtaining the Republican party's nomination for the following term. He died at New York, NY, Nov 18, 1886. For more info: www.ipl.org/ref/POTUS.

BALLOONS AROUND THE WORLD. Oct 5. Balloon twisting and sculpting artists donate an hour or more to a charity of their choice in their community. Annually, the first Wednesday in October. For info: Jeff Brown, 135 W Second St, Juneau, AK 99801. Phone: (907) 586-1670. E-mail: jbrown@alaska.net. Web: www.balloonsaroundtheworld.com.

BONDS BREAKS HOME RUN RECORD: ANNIVERSARY. Oct 5, 2001. Barry Bonds of the San Francisco Giants broke Mark McGwire's 1998 home run record when he hit his 71st homer of the season in a game against the Los Angeles Dodgers at Pacific Bell Park. Later in the game he hit another homer. The Dodgers beat the Giants, 11–10, eliminating them from the playoffs. On Oct 7 Bonds hit one more homer to finish the season with 73. He also broke Babe Ruth's slugging record of .847 with .863.

CHIEF JOSEPH SURRENDER: ANNIVERSARY. Oct 5, 1877. After a 1,700-mile retreat, Chief Joseph and the Nez Percé Indians surrendered to US cavalry troops at Bear's Paw near Chinook,

MT. Chief Joseph made his famous speech of surrender, "From where the sun now stands, I will fight no more forever."

FITZHUGH, LOUISE: BIRTH ANNIVERSARY. Oct 5, 1928. Author best known for her 1965 classic *Harriet the Spy*, Fitzhugh was born at Memphis, TN. Also an artist, she provided the illustrations for her own works, which included *The Long Secret, Sport* and *Nobody's Family is Going to Change*. She died at New Milford, CT, Nov 19, 1974.

GODDARD, ROBERT HUTCHINGS: BIRTH ANNIVERSARY. Oct 5, 1882. The "father of the Space Age," born at Worcester, MA. Largely ignored or ridiculed during his lifetime because of his dreams of rocket travel, including travel to other planets. Launched a liquid-fuel-powered rocket Mar 16, 1926, at Auburn, MA. Died Aug 10, 1945, at Baltimore, MD. See also: "Goddard Day" (Mar 16).

MISSISSIPPI STATE FAIR. Oct 5–16. Jackson, MS. Features nightly professional entertainment, livestock show, midway carnival, domestic art exhibits. Est attendance: 620,000. For info: Mississippi Fair Commission, PO Box 892, Jackson, MS 39205. Phone: (601) 961-4000. Fax: (601) 354-6545.

NATIONAL WALK OUR CHILDREN TO SCHOOL DAY. Oct 5. This day was established to encourage adults and children to walk together to raise awareness about three things: the exercise value of walking, the importance of teaching children safe walking behaviors and the need for more walkable communities. Sponsored by the Partnership for a Walkable America, a national alliance of public and private organizations committed to making walking safer, easier and more enjoyable. Annually, the Wednesday of the first full week in October. For info: Natl Walk Our Children to School Day, Natl Safety Council, 1121 Spring Lake Dr, Itasca, IL 60143-3201. Phone: (800) 621-7615, ext 2383. Fax: (630) 775-2185. E-mail: thompsoh@nsc.org. Web: www.walkto school-usa.org.

PORTUGAL: REPUBLIC DAY. Oct 5. National holiday. Commemorates the founding of the republic in 1910.

RAMADAN: THE ISLAMIC MONTH OF FASTING. Oct 5–Nov 3. Begins on Islamic lunar calendar date Ramadan 1, 1426, and observance starts at sunset on the previous day. Ramadan, the ninth month of the Islamic calendar, is holy because it was during this month that the Holy Qur'an [Koran] was revealed. All adults of sound body and mind fast from dawn (before sunrise) until sunset to achieve spiritual and physical purification and self-discipline, abstaining from food, drink and intimate relations. It is a time for feeling a common bond with the poor and needy, a time of piety and prayer. Different methods for "anticipating" the visibility of the new moon crescent at Mecca are used by different Muslim groups. US date may vary. Began at sunset the preceding day.

STONE, THOMAS: DEATH ANNIVERSARY. Oct 5, 1787. Signer of the Declaration of Independence, born 1743 (exact date unknown) at Charles County, MD. Died at Alexandria, VA.

TECUMSEH: DEATH ANNIVERSARY. Oct 5, 1813. Shawnee Indian chief and orator, born at Old Piqua near Springfield, OH, in March 1768. Tecumseh is regarded as one of the greatest Native American leaders. He came to prominence between the years 1799 and 1804 as a powerful orator, defending his people against whites. He denounced as invalid all treaties by which Indians ceded their lands and condemned the chieftains who had entered into such agreements. With his brother Tenskwatawa, the Prophet, he established a town on the Tippecanoe River near Lafayette, IN, and then embarked on a mission to organize an Indian confederation to stop white encroachment. Although he advocated peaceful methods and negotiation, he did not rule out war as a last resort as he visited tribes throughout the country. While he was away, William Henry Harrison defeated the Prophet at the Battle of Tippecanoe Nov 7, 1811, and burned the town. Tecumseh organized a large force of Indian warriors and assisted the British in the War of 1812. Tecumseh was defeated and killed at the Battle of the Thames, Oct 5, 1813.

UNITED NATIONS: WORLD TEACHERS' DAY. Oct 5. For info: United Nations, Dept of Public Info, Public Inquiries Unit, Rm GA-57, New York, NY 10017. Phone: (212) 963-4475. E-mail: inquiries@un.org. Web: www.un.org.

ZION, GENE: BIRTH ANNIVERSARY. Oct 5, 1913. Author, best known for *Harry the Dirty Dog*, born at New York, NY. Zion died in New York on Dec 5, 1975.

BIRTHDAYS TODAY

Clive Barker, 53, author (*Abarat, The Thief of Always*), born Liverpool, England, Oct 5, 1952.
Grant Hill, 33, basketball player, born Dallas, TX, Oct 5, 1972.
Bil Keane, 83, cartoonist ("Family Circus"), born Philadelphia, PA, Oct 5, 1922.
Mario Lemieux, 40, Hall of Fame hockey player, born Montreal, QC, Canada, Oct 5, 1965.
Patrick Roy, 40, former hockey player, born Quebec City, QC, Canada, Oct 5, 1965.
David Shannon, 46, author and illustrator (*No, David!*), born Washington, DC, Oct 5, 1959.
Kate Winslet, 30, actress (*Titanic*), born Reading, England, Oct 5, 1975.

OCTOBER 6 — THURSDAY

Day 279 — 86 Remaining

ARIZONA STATE FAIR. Oct 6–23. Phoenix, AZ. Festival, concerts, flea markets, entertainment and food. For info: Arizona State Fair, 1826 W McDowell Rd, Phoenix, AZ 85007. Phone: (602) 252-6771. Fax: (602) 495-1302. E-mail: info@azstatefair .com. Web: www.azstatefair.com.

FAST OF GEDALYA. Oct 6. Jewish holiday. Hebrew calendar date: Tishri 3, 5766. Tzom Gedalya begins at first light of day and commemorates the 6th-century BC assassination of Gedalya Ben Achikam.

★ **GERMAN-AMERICAN DAY.** Oct 6. Celebration of German heritage and contributions German Americans have made to the building of the nation. A Presidential Proclamation has been issued each year since 1987. Annually, Oct 6.

IG® NOBEL PRIZE CEREMONY. Oct 6 (tentative). Sanders Theatre, Harvard University, Cambridge, MA. The "Fifteenth 1st Annual." Honors scientific achievements that cannot or should not be reproduced, with prizes awarded by Nobel laureates. Sponsored by the science humor magazine *Annals of Improbable Research*. Annually, first Thursday in October pending theatre availability. For info: Marc Abrahams, *Annals of Improbable Research*, PO Box 380853, Cambridge, MA 02238. Phone: (617) 491-4437. E-mail: marca@chem2.harvard.edu. Web: www.improb able.com.

October 2005

S	M	T	W	T	F	S
						1
2	3	4	5	6	7	8
9	10	11	12	13	14	15
16	17	18	19	20	21	22
23	24	25	26	27	28	29
30	31					

MOODY, HELEN WILLS: 100th BIRTH ANNIVERSARY. Oct 6, 1905. One of the greatest tennis players of the 20th century was born at Centreville, CA. Moody, 1921's US national junior champion, had a phenomenal professional career: with a .919 winning average, she won 52 out of 92 tournaments between 1919 and 1938. She won Wimbledon eight out of nine tries, the US Open seven times and the French Open four times. Amazingly, from 1927 to 1932, she did not lose one single set in any singles competition. A 1924 Olympic gold-medal winner for singles and doubles, Moody also became in 1928 the first player to win a Grand Slam. "Little Miss Poker Face" (as she was nicknamed for her no-nonsense style) was inducted into the International Tennis Hall of Fame in 1969. She died Jan 1, 1998, at Carmel, CA.

SOUTH CAROLINA STATE FAIR. Oct 6–16. Columbia, SC. Conklin Shows, rides, musical entertainment, food booths and children's activities. Est attendance: 576,000. For info: South Carolina State Fair, PO Box 393, Columbia, SC 29202. Phone: (803) 799-3387. Fax: (803) 799-1760. E-mail: geninfo@scstatefair.org.

VINING, ELIZABETH GRAY: BIRTH ANNIVERSARY. Oct 6, 1902. Author of *Adam of the Road* under the name Elizabeth Gray, born at Philadelphia, PA. Won Newbery Medal (1943). Died Nov 27, 1999, at Kennett Square, PA.

YOM KIPPUR WAR: ANNIVERSARY. Oct 6–25, 1973. A surprise attack by Egypt and Syria pushed Israeli forces several miles behind the 1967 cease-fire lines. Israel was caught off guard, partly because the attack came on the holiest Jewish religious day. After 18 days of fighting, hostilities were halted by the UN Oct 25. Israel partially recovered from the initial setback but failed to regain all the land lost in the fighting.

BIRTHDAYS TODAY

Betsy Hearne, 63, author (*Seven Brave Women*), born Wilsonville, AL, Oct 6, 1942.

Rebecca Lobo, 32, former basketball player, born Southwick, MA, Oct 6, 1973.

Jeanette Winter, 66, author and illustrator (*My Name Is Georgia*), born Chicago, IL, Oct 6, 1939.

OCTOBER 7 — FRIDAY

Day 280 — 85 Remaining

ALABAMA NATIONAL FAIR. Oct 7–16. Garrett Coliseum/Fairgrounds, Montgomery, AL. A midway filled with exciting rides and games, arts and crafts, exhibits, livestock shows, racing pigs, a circus, a petting zoo, food and entertainment. Est attendance: 225,000. For info: Alabama National Fair, PO Box 3304, Montgomery, AL 36109-0304. Phone: (334) 272-6831. Fax: (334) 272-6835. Web: www.alnationalfair.org.

ARKANSAS STATE FAIR AND LIVESTOCK SHOW. Oct 7–16. Barton Coliseum and State Fairground, Little Rock, AR. Est attendance: 400,000. For info: Arkansas State Fair, 2600 Howard St, Little Rock, AR 72206. Phone: (501) 372-8341. Fax: (501) 372-4197. Web: www.arkfairgrounds.com.

"ARTHUR" TV PREMIERE: ANNIVERSARY. Oct 7, 1996. This animated show, based on Marc Brown's popular series of books, features the aardvark Arthur, his sister D.W. and a host of friends from their elementary school.

CABBAGE PATCH® KIDS DEBUTED: ANNIVERSARY. Oct 7, 1983. These popular dolls come with their own birth certificates and adoption papers. More than 3 million of the dolls were sold for the holiday season in 1983. Today, there are several varieties of Cabbage Patch® Kids.

GEORGIA NATIONAL FAIR. Oct 7–16. Georgia National Fairgrounds, Perry, GA. Traditional state agricultural fair features thousands of entries in horse, livestock, horticultural, youth, home and fine arts categories. Family entertainment, education and fun. Sponsored by the State of Georgia. Annually, beginning the fifth Friday after Labor Day. Est attendance: 366,000. For info: John P. Webb, Jr, CFE, Georgia National Fair, PO Box 1367, Perry, GA 31069. Phone: (478) 987-3247. E-mail: webb1@alltell.net. Web: www.gnfa.com.

NATIONAL STORYTELLING FESTIVAL. Oct 7–9. Jonesborough, TN. Tennessee's oldest town plays host to the most dynamic storytelling event dedicated to the oral tradition. This three-day celebration showcases storytellers, stories and traditions from across America and around the world. Annually, the first full weekend in October. Est attendance: 10,000. For info: Storytelling Center, 116 W Main, Jonesborough, TN 37659. Phone: (800) 952-8392. Fax: (423) 913-8219. E-mail: info@storytellingcenter.net. Web: www.storytellingfestival.net.

RODNEY, CAESAR: BIRTH ANNIVERSARY. Oct 7, 1728. Signer of the Declaration of Independence and Revolutionary War hero. He is remembered for his historic 80-mile ride from Delaware to Philadelphia in July of 1776 to cast the tie-breaking vote that assured unanimity among the colonies in declaring independence from Britain. Later, he served as president (governor) of Delaware and was speaker of the Assembly until his death. Born near Dover, DE, he died at Dover, June 29, 1784. He was honored by Delaware in 1999 by having his likeness engraved on the new state quarter.

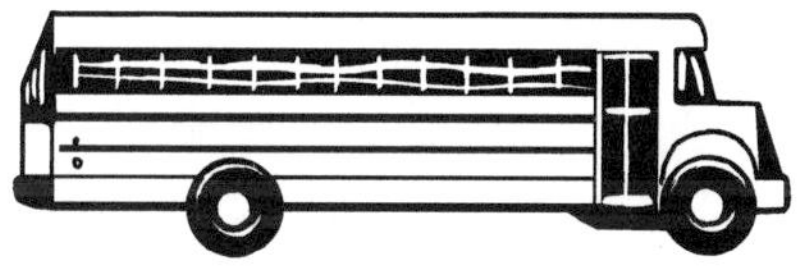

SOUTHERN FESTIVAL OF BOOKS: A CELEBRATION OF THE WRITTEN WORD. Oct 7–9. Nashville, TN. To promote reading, writing, the literary arts and a broader understanding of the language and culture of the South, this annual festival will feature readings, talks and panel discussions by more than 200 authors, exhibit booths of publishing companies and bookstores, autographing sessions, a comprehensive children's program and the Cafe Stage, which is a performance corner for authors, storytellers and musicians. Annually, the second weekend in October. Est attendance: 30,000. For info: Serenity Gerbman, Dir, Southern Festival of Books, Tennessee Humanities Council, 1003 18th Ave S, Nashville, TN 37212. Phone: (615) 320-7001, ext 15. Fax: (615) 321-4586. E-mail: serenity@tn-humanities.org. Web: www.tn-humanities.org.

WALLACE, HENRY AGARD: BIRTH ANNIVERSARY. Oct 7, 1888. The 33rd vice president of the US (1941–45), born at Adair County, IA. Died at Danbury, CT, Nov 18, 1965.

BIRTHDAYS TODAY

Diane Ackerman, 57, author (*The Moon by Whale Light*), born Waukegan, IL, Oct 7, 1948.

Priest Holmes, 32, football player, born Fort Smith, AR, Oct 7, 1973.

Vladimir Putin, 53, Russian president, born St. Petersburg, Russia, Oct 7, 1952.

Desmond Tutu, 74, South African archbishop, Nobel Peace Prize winner, born Klerksdrop, South Africa, Oct 7, 1931.

OCTOBER 8 — SATURDAY

Day 281 — 84 Remaining

GREAT CHICAGO FIRE: ANNIVERSARY. Oct 8, 1871. Chicago fire began, according to legend, when Mrs O'Leary's cow kicked over the lantern in her barn on DeKoven Street. The fire leveled 3½ sq miles, destroying 17,450 buildings and leaving 98,500 people homeless and about 250 people dead. Financially, the loss was $200 million. On the same day a fire destroyed the entire town of Peshtigo, WI, killing more than 1,100 people. For more info: *The Great Fire*, by Jim Murphy (Scholastic, 0-59-047267-4, $16.95 Gr. 3–7) or www.chicagohistory.org/fire.

PERU: DAY OF THE NAVY. Oct 8. Public holiday in Peru, commemorating Combat of Angamos.

PESHTIGO FOREST FIRE: ANNIVERSARY. Oct 8, 1871. One of the most disastrous forest fires in history began at Peshtigo, WI, the same day the Great Chicago Fire began. The Wisconsin fire burned across six counties, killing more than 1,100 persons.

BIRTHDAYS TODAY

Chevy Chase, 62, comedian, actor (*Caddyshack, National Lampoon's Vacation*), born Cornelius Crane, New York, NY, Oct 8, 1943.

Matt Damon, 35, actor (*Saving Private Ryan*), born Cambridge, MA, Oct 8, 1970.

Barthe DeClements, 85, author (*Nothing's Fair in Fifth Grade*), born Seattle, WA, Oct 8, 1920.

Bill Elliott, 50, race car driver, born Dawsonville, GA, Oct 8, 1955.

Jesse Jackson, 64, civil rights leader, international diplomat, founder of the Rainbow Coalition/Operation PUSH, born Greenville, NC, Oct 8, 1941.

Faith Ringgold, 75, artist, author (*Tar Beach, My Dream of Martin Luther King*), born New York, NY, Oct 8, 1930.

Rashaan Salaam, 31, former football player, born San Diego, CA, Oct 8, 1974.

R.L. Stine, 62, author (the Goosebumps series), born Columbus, OH, Oct 8, 1943.

OCTOBER 9 — SUNDAY

Day 282 — 83 Remaining

★**FIRE PREVENTION WEEK.** Oct 9–15. Presidential Proclamation issued annually for the first or second week in October since 1925. For many years prior to 1925, National Fire Prevention Day was observed in October. Annually, the Sunday through Saturday period during which Oct 9 falls.

FIRE PREVENTION WEEK. Oct 9–15. To increase awareness of the dangers of fire and to educate the public on how to stay safe from fire. For info: Public Affairs Office, National Fire Protection Assn, One Batterymarch Park, Quincy, MA 02269. Phone: (617) 770-3000. E-mail: public_affairs@nfpa.org. Web: www.nfpa.org.

GRANDMOTHER'S DAY IN FLORIDA AND KENTUCKY. Oct 9. A ceremonial day on the second Sunday in October.

"HEY ARNOLD!" TV PREMIERE: ANNIVERSARY. Oct 9, 1996. From Nickelodeon Studios, this animated show revolves around Arnold, a fourth-grader with a football-shaped head and an eccentric group of friends. He lives with his grandparents on the poor side of town, in a multiracial retirement home. His friends include Gerald, who is the coolest kid in the class, and nasty Helga, who torments him daily but actually harbors a huge crush.

ICELAND: LEIF ERIKSON DAY. Oct 9. Celebrates the discovery of North America in the year 1000 by the Norse explorer.

KOREA: ALPHABET DAY (HANGUL). Oct 9. Celebrates anniversary of promulgation of Hangul (24-letter phonetic alphabet) by King Sejong of the Yi Dynasty, in 1446. For more info: *The King's Secret: The Legend of King Sejong*, by Carol Farley (HarperCollins, 0-68-812776-2, $15.95 Gr. 1 & up).

★**LEIF ERIKSON DAY.** Oct 9. Presidential Proclamation always issued for Oct 9 since 1964 (Public Law 88-566 of Sept 2, 1964) at request. Honors the Norse explorer who is widely believed to have been the first European to visit the American continent.

NATIONAL METRIC WEEK. Oct 9–15. To maintain an awareness of the importance of the metric system as the primary system of measurement for the US. Annually, the week of the tenth month containing the tenth day of the month. For info: US Metric Assn, 10245 Andasol Ave, Northridge, CA 91325-1504. Phone: (818) 363-5606. Web: www.metric.org.

NATIONAL SCHOOL LUNCH WEEK. Oct 9–15. To celebrate good nutrition and healthy, safe school lunches. Annually, the second full week in October. For info: Service Center, American School Food Service Assn, 700 S Washington St, Ste 300, Alexandria, VA 22314-4287. Phone: (703) 739-3900. Web: www.asfsa.org.

★**NATIONAL SCHOOL LUNCH WEEK.** Oct 9–15. Presidential Proclamation issued for the week beginning with the second Sunday in October since 1962 (Public Law 87–780 of Oct 9, 1962). Note: Not issued in 1981.

PERU: DAY OF NATIONAL HONOR. Oct 9. National holiday. Commemorates the 1968 nationalization of the oil fields.

SAINT-SAËNS, CAMILLE: BIRTH ANNIVERSARY. Oct 9, 1835. Born at Paris, France, Camille Saint-Saëns was a classical composer best known for *Danse Macabre* and *The Carnival of the Animals.* Also a gifted pianist and organist, he was considered a child prodigy. He died at Algiers, France, on Dec 16, 1921.

SAMOA AND AMERICAN SAMOA: WHITE SUNDAY. Oct 9. The second Sunday in October. For the children of Samoa and American Samoa, this is the biggest day of the year. Traditional roles are reversed, as children lead church services, are served special foods and receive gifts of new church clothes and other special items. All the children dress in white. The following Monday is an official holiday.

UGANDA: INDEPENDENCE DAY: ANNIVERSARY. Oct 9. National holiday commemorating achievement of autonomy from Britain in 1962.

October 2005

S	M	T	W	T	F	S
						1
2	3	4	5	6	7	8
9	10	11	12	13	14	15
16	17	18	19	20	21	22
23	24	25	26	27	28	29
30	31					

UNITED NATIONS: WORLD POST DAY. Oct 9. An annual special observance of Postal Administrations of the Universal Postal Union (UPU). Annually, Oct 9. For info: United Nations, Dept of Public Info, Public Inquiries Unit, Rm GA-57, New York, NY 10017. Phone: (212) 963-4475. Fax: (212) 963-0071. E-mail: inquiries@un.org. Web: www.un.org.

"WISHBONE" TV PREMIERE: 10th ANNIVERSARY. Oct 9, 1995. The first episode of this popular series that retells classic stories with a dog named Wishbone who imagines himself as a character in signature scenes premiered on PBS. It was the first of a two-part series titled "Tail in Twain," based on Mark Twain's *The Adventures of Tom Sawyer*. Other episodes have been based on stories by Ovid, Goethe, Jane Austen, Washington Irving, Edgar Allan Poe and others. There were several related book series as well, including one that was adapted versions of the classics, and another in which Wishbone is a detective solving local whodunits. For more info: www.pbs.org/wishbone.

BIRTHDAYS TODAY

Zachery Ty Bryan, 24, actor ("Home Improvement"), born Aurora, CO, Oct 9, 1981.
Steven Burns, 32, former TV host ("Blue's Clues"), born Boyertown, PA, Oct 9, 1973.
Johanna Hurwitz, 68, author (*Busybody Nora, The Adventures of Ali Baba Bernstein*), born New York, NY, Oct 9, 1937.
Trent Lott, 64, US Senator (R, Mississippi), born Duck Hill, MS, Oct 9, 1941.
Mike Singletary, 47, Hall of Fame football player, born Houston, TX, Oct 9, 1958.
Annika Sorenstam, 35, golfer, born Stockholm, Sweden, Oct 9, 1970.

OCTOBER 10 — MONDAY

Day 283 — 82 Remaining

AMERICAN INDIAN HERITAGE DAY (ALABAMA). Oct 10. First declared in 2000, this state holiday will also be observed as Columbus Day in Alabama. Annually, the second Monday in October.

BONZA BOTTLER DAY™. Oct 10. To celebrate when the number of the day is the same as the number of the month. Bonza Bottler Day™ is an excuse to have a party at least once a month. For info: Gail M. Berger, 14 Fernwood Dr, Taylors, SC 29687. Phone: (864) 609-9874. E-mail: gberger5@aol.com.

CANADA: THANKSGIVING DAY. Oct 10. Observed on second Monday in October each year.

COLUMBUS DAY OBSERVANCE. Oct 10. Public Law 90–363 sets observance of Columbus Day on the second Monday in October. Applicable to federal employees and to the District of Columbia, but also observed in most states. Commemorates the landfall of Columbus in the New World, Oct 12, 1492. See also: "Columbus Day (Traditional)" (Oct 12).

★**COLUMBUS DAY.** Oct 10. Presidential Proclamation, always the second Monday in October. Observed Oct 12 from 1934 to 1970 (Pub Res No 21 of Apr 30, 1934). Public Law 90–363 of June 28, 1968, required that beginning in 1971 it would be observed on the second Monday in October.

CUBA: BEGINNING OF INDEPENDENCE WARS DAY. Oct 10. National holiday. Commemorates the beginning of the struggle against Spain in 1868.

★ ★ ★

DOUBLE TENTH DAY. Oct 10. Tenth day of 10th month, Double Tenth Day, is observed by many Chinese as the anniversary of the outbreak of the revolution against the imperial Manchu dynasty, Oct 10, 1911. Sun Yat-Sen and Huan Hsing were among the revolutionary leaders.

FIJI: INDEPENDENCE DAY. Oct 10. National holiday on the second Monday in October. Commemorates independence from Britain in 1970.

JAPAN: HEALTH-SPORTS DAY. Oct 10. National holiday to encourage physical activity for building sound body and mind. Created in 1966 to commemorate the day of the opening of the 18th Olympic Games at Tokyo, Oct 10, 1964. Celebrated on the second Monday in October.

MARSHALL, JAMES: BIRTH ANNIVERSARY. Oct 10, 1942. Illustrator, born at San Antonio, TX. Marshall is best known for his George and Martha series of books. He illustrated more than 70 children's books including *The Owl and the Pussycat*. Died at New York, NY, Oct 13, 1992.

MOON PHASE: FIRST QUARTER. Oct 10. Moon enters First Quarter phase at 3:01 PM, EDT.

NATIVE AMERICANS DAY IN SOUTH DAKOTA. Oct 10. Observed as a legal holiday, dedicated to the remembrance of the great Native American leaders who contributed so much to the history of South Dakota. Annually, the second Monday in October.

US NAVAL ACADEMY FOUNDED: ANNIVERSARY. Oct 10, 1845. A college to train officers for the navy was founded at Annapolis, MD. Women were admitted in 1976. The Academy's motto is "Honor, Courage, Commitment." For more info: www.usna.edu.

US VIRGIN ISLANDS–PUERTO RICO FRIENDSHIP DAY. Oct 10. Columbus Day (second Monday in October) also celebrates historical friendship between peoples of the Virgin Islands and Puerto Rico.

YORKTOWN VICTORY DAY. Oct 10. Observed as a holiday in Virginia. Annually, the second Monday in October. See also: "Yorktown Day: Anniversary" (Oct 19).

BIRTHDAYS TODAY

Bob Burnquist, 29, skateboarder, born Rio de Janeiro, Brazil, Oct 10, 1976.
Nancy Carlson, 52, author (*I Like Me!, Louanne Pig in the Talent Show, Arnie and the New Kid*), born Minneapolis, MN, Oct 10, 1953.
Dale Earnhardt, Jr, 31, race car driver, son of the late Dale Earnhardt, Sr, born Concord, NC, Oct 10, 1974.
Brett Favre, 36, football player, born Gulfport, MS, Oct 10, 1969.
Nina Jaffe, 53, author (*The Cow of No Color, The Way Meat Loves Salt*), born New York, NY, Oct 10, 1952.
Daniel San Souci, 57, author, illustrator (*The Ugly Duckling, Cendrillon: A Caribbean Cinderella*), born San Francisco, CA, Oct 10, 1948.
Robert D. San Souci, 59, author (*Short & Shivery, The Faithful Friend, Young Merlin*), born San Francisco, CA, Oct 10, 1946.

OCTOBER 11 — TUESDAY

Day 284 — 81 Remaining

CHINA: CHUNG YEUNG FESTIVAL. Oct 11. This festival relates to the old story of the Han Dynasty, when a soothsayer advised a man to take his family to a high place on the ninth day of the ninth moon for 24 hours in order to avoid disaster. The man obeyed and found, on returning home, that all living things had died a sudden death in his absence. Part of the celebration is climbing to high places. Date in other countries will differ from China's.

★**GENERAL PULASKI MEMORIAL DAY.** Oct 11. Presidential Proclamation always issued for Oct 11 since 1929. Requested by Congressional Resolution each year from 1929–46. (Since 1947 has been issued by custom.) Note: Proclamation 4869, of Oct 5, 1981, covers all succeeding years.

***MARY ROSE* WRECK RAISED: ANNIVERSARY.** Oct 11, 1982. King Henry VIII's favorite battleship, the *Mary Rose* (built in 1511), sank on July 19, 1545, off Portsmouth Sound, England. The wreck was discovered in 1966, and, in an amazing feat of engineering, in 1982 the hull was raised in a special steel "cradle" in a slow effort that took eight hours. More than 60 million people watched the process unfold on television. Some 20,000 artifacts were found at the wreck site, illuminating a 16th-century world. The *Mary Rose* can be now seen in its own museum in Portsmouth, England. For more info, www.maryrose.org.

NATIONAL COMING OUT DAY. Oct 11. A project of the Human Rights Campaign. An international day of visibility for the lesbian, gay, bisexual and transgender community since 1988. For info: National Coming Out Project, 640 Rhode Island Ave NW, Washington, DC 20036. Phone: (800) 866-6263. E-mail: ncop@hrc.org. Web: www.hrc.org.

ROBINSON, ROSCOE, JR: BIRTH ANNIVERSARY. Oct 11, 1928. The first black American to achieve the Army rank of four-star general. Born at St. Louis, MO, and died at Washington, DC, July 22, 1993.

ROOSEVELT, ANNA ELEANOR: BIRTH ANNIVERSARY. Oct 11, 1884. Wife of Franklin Delano Roosevelt, 32nd president of the US, was born at New York, NY. She led an active and independent life and was the first wife of a president to give her own news conference in the White House (1933). Widely known throughout the world, she was affectionately called "the first lady of the world." She served as US delegate to the United Nations General Assembly for a number of years before her death at New York, NY, Nov 7, 1962. A prolific writer, she wrote in *This Is My Story*, "No one can make you feel inferior without your consent." For more info: *Eleanor*, by Barbara Cooney (Viking, 0-670-86159-6, $15.99 Gr. K–3).

SPACE MILESTONE: *DISCOVERY STS-92*: 100th SHUTTLE FLIGHT: 5th ANNIVERSARY. Oct 11, 2000. The space shuttle *Discovery* was launched on its 28th flight. This marked the shuttle program's 100th mission. On this flight, *Discovery* was headed to the International Space Station, where it docked successfully on Oct 13. On earlier flights, the shuttles *Columbia, Challenger, Endeavour, Atlantis* and *Discovery* had launched the Hubble Space Telescope and Chandra X-Ray Observatory, docked with the *Mir* space station and supported scientific research. The first shuttle flight took place in 1981. Since the first mission, space shuttles have carried 261 individuals and nearly 3 million pounds of payload, and logged an estimated 350 million miles. See also: "Space Milestone: *Columbia STS-1*" (Apr 12). For more info: *The Space Shuttle*, by Allison Lassieur (Children's Press, 0-516-22003-9, $22 Gr. 2–4).

STONE, HARLAN FISKE: BIRTH ANNIVERSARY. Oct 11, 1872. Former associate justice and later chief justice of the US Supreme Court who wrote more than 600 opinions and dissents for that court, Stone was born at Chesterfield, NH. He served on the Supreme Court from 1925 until his death, at Washington, DC, Apr 22, 1946. For more info: oyez.northwestern.edu/justices/justices.cgi.

VATICAN COUNCIL II: ANNIVERSARY. Oct 11, 1962. The 21st ecumenical council of the Roman Catholic Church was convened by Pope John XXIII. It met in four annual sessions, concluding Dec 8, 1965. It dealt with the renewal of the Church and introduced sweeping changes, such as the use of the vernacular rather than Latin in the Mass.

BIRTHDAYS TODAY

Russell Freedman, 76, author (Newbery for *Lincoln: A Photobiography*), born San Francisco, CA, Oct 11, 1929.

Orlando Hernandez, 36, baseball player, known as "El Duque," born Villa Clara, Cuba, Oct 11, 1969.

Patty Murray, 55, US Senator (D, Washington), born Seattle, WA, Oct 11, 1950.

Michelle Trachtenberg, 20, actress ("Buffy the Vampire Slayer," *Harriet the Spy*), born New York, NY, Oct 11, 1985.

Jon Steven (Steve) Young, 44, former football player, born Salt Lake City, UT, Oct 11, 1961.

★ ★ ★

OCTOBER 12 — WEDNESDAY

Day 285 — 80 Remaining

BAHAMAS: DISCOVERY DAY. Oct 12. Commemorates the landing of Columbus in the Bahamas in 1492.

BELIZE: COLUMBUS DAY. Oct 12. Public holiday.

BOER WAR: ANNIVERSARY. Oct 12, 1899. The Boers of the Transvaal and Orange Free State in southern Africa declared war on the British. The Boer states were annexed by Britain in 1900 but guerrilla warfare on the part of the Boers caused the war to drag on. It was finally ended May 31, 1902, by the Treaty of Vereeniging.

COLUMBUS DAY (TRADITIONAL). Oct 12. Public holiday in most countries in the Americas and in most Spanish-speaking countries. Observed under different names (Dia de la Raza or Day of the Race) and on different dates (most often, as in US, on the second Monday in October). Anniversary of Christopher Columbus's arrival, Oct 12, 1492, after a dangerous voyage across "shoreless Seas," at the Bahamas (probably the island of Guanahani), which he renamed El Salvador and claimed in the name of the Spanish crown. In his *Journal*, he wrote: "As I saw that they (the natives) were friendly to us, and perceived that they could be much more easily converted to our holy faith by gentle means than by force, I presented them with some red caps, and strings of beads to wear upon the neck, and many other trifles of small value, wherewith they were much delighted, and becamed wonderfully attached to us." See also: "Columbus Day Observance" (Oct 10).

October 2005

S	M	T	W	T	F	S
						1
2	3	4	5	6	7	8
9	10	11	12	13	14	15
16	17	18	19	20	21	22
23	24	25	26	27	28	29
30	31					

DAY OF THE SIX BILLION: ANNIVERSARY. Oct 12, 1999. According to the United Nations, the population of the world reached six billion on this date. More than one-third of the world's people live in China and India. It wasn't until 1804 that the world's population reached one billion; now a billion people are added to the population about every 12 years. See also: "Day of the Five Billion: Anniversary" (July 11).

EQUATORIAL GUINEA: INDEPENDENCE DAY. Oct 12. National holiday. The former Spanish Guinea gained independence from Spain in 1968.

MEXICO: DIA DE LA RAZA. Oct 12. Columbus Day is observed as the "Day of the Race," a fiesta time to commemorate the discovery of America as well as the common interests and cultural heritage of the Spanish and Indian peoples and the Hispanic nations.

NATIONAL BRING YOUR TEDDY BEAR TO WORK AND SCHOOL DAY. Oct 12. A celebration and observation of the help, stress relief and joy that teddy bears bring into the lives of people of all ages and stages. Annually, the second Wednesday in October. For info: Susan E. Schwartz, Teddies Are the Answer, 454 26th Ave, San Mateo, CA 94403. Phone: (650) 349-3184. Fax: (650) 345-4944. E-mail: suwho2@rcn.com.

NATIONAL COUNCIL FOR GEOGRAPHIC EDUCATION MEETING. Oct 12–15. Birmingham, AL. For info: National Council for Geographic Education, 16A Leonard Hall, Indiana Univ of PA, Indiana, PA 15705. Phone: (412) 357-6290. Web: www.ncge.org.

SPAIN: NATIONAL HOLIDAY. Oct 12. Called Hispanity Day of the Day of Spanish Consciousness. Honors Christopher Columbus and the Spanish conquerors of Latin America.

UNITED NATIONS: INTERNATIONAL DAY FOR NATURAL DISASTER REDUCTION. Oct 12. The General Assembly made this designation for the second Wednesday of October each year as part of its efforts to foster international cooperation in reducing the loss of life, property damage and social and economic disruption caused by natural disasters. For info: United Nations, Dept of Public Info, New York, NY 10017.

YOM KIPPUR BEGINS AT SUNDOWN. Oct 12. Jewish Day of Atonement. See "Yom Kippur" (Oct 13).

BIRTHDAYS TODAY

Kirk Cameron, 35, actor ("Growing Pains"), born Panorama City, CA, Oct 12, 1970.

Alice Childress, 85, author (*A Hero Ain't Nothin' But a Sandwich*), born Charlestown, SC, Oct 12, 1920.

Dave Freudenthal, 55, Governor of Wyoming (D), born Thermopolis, WY, Oct 12, 1950.

Marion Jones, 30, track runner, born Los Angeles, CA, Oct 12, 1975.

OCTOBER 13 — THURSDAY

Day 286 — 79 Remaining

BROWN, JESSE LEROY: BIRTH ANNIVERSARY. Oct 13, 1926. Jesse Leroy Brown was the first black American naval aviator and also the first black naval officer to lose his life in combat when he was shot down over Korea, Dec 4, 1950. On Mar 18, 1972, USS *Jesse L. Brown* was launched as the first ship to be named in honor of a black naval officer. Brown was born at Hattiesburg, MS.

BURUNDI: ASSASSINATION OF THE HERO OF THE NATION DAY. Oct 13. National holiday. Commemorates assassination of Prince Louis Rwagasore in 1961.

PITCHER, MOLLY: BIRTH ANNIVERSARY. Oct 13, 1754. "Molly Pitcher," heroine of the American Revolution, was a water carrier at the Battle of Monmouth (Sunday, June 28, 1778) where she distinguished herself by loading and firing a cannon after her husband, John Hays, was wounded. Affectionately known as "Sergeant Molly" after General Washington issued her a warrant as a noncommissioned officer. Her real name was Mary Hays McCauley (née Ludwig). Born near Trenton, NJ, she died at Carlisle, PA, Jan 22, 1832.

RICHTER, CONRAD: BIRTH ANNIVERSARY. Oct 13, 1890. Author of books for children and adults, born at Pine Grove, PA. His book *The Light in the Forest* was made into a Disney film in 1958. *The Fields* won the Pulitzer Prize for fiction in 1951. Other works include *The Trees* and *The Town*. Richter died at Pottsville, PA, Oct 30, 1968.

US NAVY: AUTHORIZATION ANNIVERSARY. Oct 13, 1775. Commemorates legislation passed by Second Continental Congress authorizing the acquisition of ships and establishment of a navy.

WHITE HOUSE CORNERSTONE LAID: ANNIVERSARY. Oct 13, 1792. The cornerstone for the presidential residence at 1600 Pennsylvania Ave NW, Washington, DC, designed by James Hoban, was laid. The first presidential family to occupy it was that of John Adams, in November 1800. With three stories and more than 100 rooms, the White House is the oldest building at Washington. First described as the "presidential palace," it acquired the name "White House" about 10 years after construction was completed. Burned by British troops in 1814, it was reconstructed, refurbished and reoccupied by 1817. For more info: *The White House*, by Nathan Aaseng (Lucent, 1-56006-708-X, $19.96 Gr. 7–10). Take a virtual tour of the White House at www.whitehouse.gov. Young children can visit the White House for Kids site at www.whitehouse.gov/WH/kids/html/home.html.

YOM KIPPUR or DAY OF ATONEMENT. Oct 13. Holiest Jewish observance. A day for fasting, repentance and seeking forgiveness. Hebrew calendar date: Tishri 10, 5766.

BIRTHDAYS TODAY

Maria Cantwell, 47, US Senator (D, Washington), born Indianapolis, IN, Oct 13, 1958.

Paul Pierce, 28, basketball player, born Oakland, CA, Oct 13, 1977.

Jerry Rice, 43, football player, born Starkville, MS, Oct 13, 1962.

Summer Sanders, 33, Olympic gold medal swimmer, children's TV host ("Figure It Out"), born Roseville, CA, Oct 13, 1972.

Paul Simon, 64, singer/songwriter, born Newark, NJ, Oct 13, 1941.

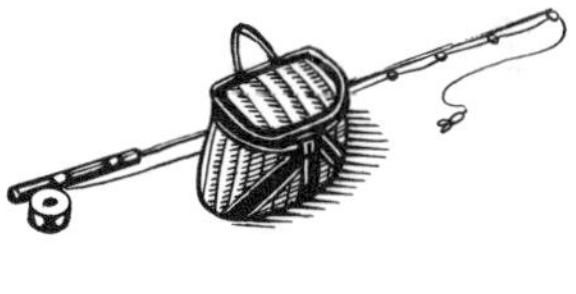

OCTOBER 14 — FRIDAY

Day 287 — 78 Remaining

EISENHOWER, DWIGHT DAVID: BIRTH ANNIVERSARY. Oct 14, 1890. The 34th president of the US, born at Denison, TX. Served two terms as president, Jan 20, 1953–Jan 20, 1961. Nicknamed "Ike," he held the rank of five-star general of the army (resigned in 1952, and restored by act of Congress in 1961). He served as supreme commander of the Allied forces in western Europe during WWII. In his Farewell Address (Jan 17, 1961), speaking about the "conjunction of an immense military establishment and a large arms industry," he warned: "In the councils of government, we must guard against the acquisition of unwarranted influence, whether sought or unsought, by the military-industrial complex. The potential of the disastrous rise of misplaced power exists and will persist." An American hero, Eisenhower died at Washington, DC, Mar 28, 1969. For more info: www.ipl.org/ref/POTUS.

KING WINS NOBEL PEACE PRIZE: ANNIVERSARY. Oct 14, 1964. Martin Luther King, Jr, became the youngest recipient of the Nobel Peace Prize when awarded the honor. Dr. King donated the entire $54,000 prize money to furthering the causes of the civil rights movement.

LEE, FRANCIS LIGHTFOOT: BIRTH ANNIVERSARY. Oct 14, 1734. Signer of the Declaration of Independence. Born at Westmoreland County, VA, he died Jan 11, 1797, at Richmond County, VA.

LENSKI, LOIS: BIRTH ANNIVERSARY. Oct 14, 1893. Children's author and illustrator, born at Springfield, OH. She wrote *Cotton In My Sack* and *Strawberry Girl*, which was awarded the Newbery Medal in 1946. Lenski died at Tarpon Springs, FL, Sept 11, 1974.

NORTH CAROLINA STATE FAIR. Oct 14–23. State Fairgrounds, Raleigh, NC. Agricultural fair with livestock, arts and crafts, home arts, entertainment and carnival. Est attendance: 750,000. For info: Wesley Wyatt, Mgr, North Carolina State Fair, 1025 Blue Ridge Blvd, Raleigh, NC 27607. Phone: (919) 821-7400. Fax: (919) 733-5079. Web: www.ncstatefair.org.

PENN, WILLIAM: BIRTH ANNIVERSARY. Oct 14, 1644. Founder of Pennsylvania, born at London, England. Penn died July 30, 1718, at Buckinghamshire, England. Presidential Proclamation 5284 of Nov 28, 1984, conferred honorary citizenship of the USA upon William Penn and his second wife, Hannah Callowhill Penn. They were the third and fourth persons to receive honorary US citizenship (following Winston Churchill and Raoul Wallenberg). For more info: *William Penn: Founder of Pennsylvania*, by Steven Kroll (Holiday, 0-8234-1439-6, $16.96 Gr. 3–5).

SOUND BARRIER BROKEN: ANNIVERSARY. Oct 14, 1947. Flying a Bell X-1 at Muroc Dry Lake Bed, CA, Air Force pilot Chuck Yeager flew faster than the speed of sound, ushering in the era of supersonic flight.

BIRTHDAYS TODAY

Elisa Kleven, 47, author (*The Paper Princess*), illustrator (*Abuela*), born Los Angeles, CA, Oct 14, 1958.

October 2005

S	M	T	W	T	F	S
						1
2	3	4	5	6	7	8
9	10	11	12	13	14	15
16	17	18	19	20	21	22
23	24	25	26	27	28	29
30	31					

OCTOBER 15 — SATURDAY

Day 288 — 77 Remaining

ABRAHAM LINCOLN URGED TO GROW WHISKERS: ANNIVERSARY. Oct 15, 1860. During the presidential campaign of 1860, 11-year-old Grace Bedell wrote to candidate Abraham Lincoln urging him to grow a beard. "[I]f you will let your whiskers grow . . . you would look a great deal better for your face is so thin." "Whiskers," Grace predicted, would bring more votes. Lincoln answered her in a letter dated Oct 19, 1860, in which he said growing whiskers might be viewed as a "silly affect[at]ion." Nonetheless, Lincoln did grow a beard not long after and was even able to meet little Bedell during an 1861 train stop on the way to his inauguration. For more info: *Mr. Lincoln's Whiskers* by Karen Winnick (Boyds Mills Press, 1-5639-7485-1, $15.95 Gr. K–4). ***See Curriculum Connection.***

CROW RESERVATION OPENED FOR SETTLEMENT: ANNIVERSARY. Oct 15, 1892. By Presidential Proclamation 1.8 million acres of Crow Indian reservation were opened to settlers. The government had induced the Crow to give up a portion of their land in the mountainous western area in the state of Montana, for which they received 50 cents per acre.

FIRST MANNED FLIGHT: ANNIVERSARY. Oct 15, 1783. Jean Francois Pilatre de Rozier and Francois Laurent, Marquis d'Arlandes, became the first people to fly when they ascended in a Montgolfier hot-air balloon at Paris, France, less than three months after the first public balloon flight demonstration (June 5, 1783), and only a year after the first experiments with small paper and fabric balloons by the Montgolfier brothers, Joseph and Jacques, in November 1782. The first manned free flight lasted about 4 minutes and carried the passengers at a height of about 84 feet. On Nov 21, 1783, they soared 3,000 feet over Paris for 25 minutes.

NATIONAL GROUCH DAY. Oct 15. Honor a grouch. All grouches deserve a day to be recognized. Annually, Oct 15. For info: Alan R. Miller, Carter Middle School, 300 Upland Dr, Room 207, Clio, MI 48420. Phone: (810) 591-0503.

ORIONIDS METEOR SHOWERS. Oct 15–29 (approximate). Annual meteor showers caused when orbiting earth passes through the trail of Halley's Comet. This happens two times a year (see "Eta Aquarids Meteor Showers" [Apr 21]). Dates are approximately the same every year, with the height of the showers coming around Oct 21. Named for their appearance near the Orion constellation. See also: "Last Perihelion of Halley's Comet" (Feb 9).

SPACE MILESTONE: *CASSINI* (US). Oct 15, 1997. This plutonium-powered spacecraft arrived at Saturn in 2004. It will orbit the planet, take pictures of its 18 known moons and dispatch a probe to Titan, the largest of these moons.

★ **WHITE CANE SAFETY DAY.** Oct 15. Presidential Proclamation always issued for Oct 15 since 1964 (Public Law 88–628 of Oct 6, 1964).

WILSON, EDITH BOLLING GALT: BIRTH ANNIVERSARY. Oct 15, 1872. Second wife of Woodrow Wilson, 28th president of the US, born at Wytheville, VA. She died at Washington, DC, Dec 28, 1961.

BIRTHDAYS TODAY

Barry Moser, 65, illustrator (*In the Beginning: Creation Stories from Around the World; Telling Time with Big Mama Cat*), born Chattanooga, TN, Oct 15, 1940.

OCTOBER 15
TALKING TO YOUR GOVERNMENT

After last year's presidential election, children are certainly aware that Americans vote for many of the people who serve in our government. Yet many students have no idea that they can communicate with our elected representatives. In fact, a letter written by one child had a direct effect on the appearance of one of our most famous presidents: Abraham Lincoln.

On Oct 15, 1860, 11-year-old Grace Bedell, who lived in Westfield, NY, wrote a letter to a then clean-shaven Abraham Lincoln, who was campaigning for president. She urged him to grow whiskers because his face was so thin. Lincoln responded to her suggestion, at first with a letter. Later, while en route to his inauguration in New York, Lincoln met Grace. According to Grace, he stepped down from the train platform and shook her hand. Then he stooped down and said, "You see, I let these whiskers grow for you, Grace."

Grace's original letter is part of the Burton Historical Collection of the Detroit Public Library. However, students can read the text of Grace's and Lincoln's letters at www.buffalohistoryworks.com/lincoln/whiskers.htm. *Mr. Lincoln's Whiskers,* by Karen Winnick (Boyds Mills Press, 1-56397-805-9, $8.95 Ages 5–9) is a picture book that recounts the story of the candidate and the little girl. The letters are reproduced in the author's notes.

On the anniversary of Grace's plucky letter, why not directly involve your class with our government? Identify and discuss several national, or even global, issues that concern your students. Ask each child to write a letter to a national representative and express her or his views on the issues. Your students can discover that their voices will be heard and that children CAN make a difference.

To write to your state's United States senators, address the letter to The Honorable [name of your senator], US Senate, Washington DC 20510. To write to your state's United States congressional representative, address mail to The Honorable [name of your representative], US House of Representatives, Washington DC 20515. At the national level, representatives are likely to respond with a form letter. Many senators and members of Congress maintain websites (a partial list can be found in the appendix). Your students might be interested in information found on them.

A personal response is often received when letters are sent to county or town representatives—a council member, for example. You can get their names and addresses in the government section of your local phone book, or by calling your town hall or county seat. Again, identify a local issue for students to write about. Some examples of topics could include how to petition for a stop sign; how the building site for a new school is determined; what are the taxes their parents pay used for.

Given enough notice, an alderperson might be available to visit your class. If so, have students prepare questions in advance. Some towns videotape council meetings or broadcast them on TV or radio. See if a copy would be available for showing in your classroom. Students might enjoy watching a portion of a meeting, especially if a vote is taken to enact a new municipal law.

—Sally Walker

OCTOBER 16 — SUNDAY

Day 289 — 76 Remaining

AMERICA'S FIRST DEPARTMENT STORE: ANNIVERSARY. Oct 16, 1868. Salt Lake City, UT. America's first department store, "ZCMI" (Zion's Co-Operative Mercantile Institution), is still operating at Salt Lake City. It was founded under the direction of Brigham Young. For info: Museum of Church History and Art, 45 North West Temple, Salt Lake City, UT 84150. Phone: (801) 240-4604.

AMERICA'S SAFE SCHOOLS WEEK. Oct 16–22. To motivate key education and law enforcement policymakers, as well as parents, students and community residents, to vigorously advocate schools that are safe and free of violence, weapons and drugs. Annually, the third full week in October, from Sunday–Saturday. For info: National School Safety Center, 141 Duesenberg Dr, Ste 11, Westlake Village, CA 91362. Phone: (805) 373-9977. Web: nssc1.org.

BEN-GURION, DAVID: BIRTH ANNIVERSARY. Oct 16, 1886. First prime minister of the state of Israel. Born at Plonsk, Poland, he died at Tel Aviv, Israel, Dec 1, 1973.

DICTIONARY DAY. Oct 16. The birthday of Noah Webster, American teacher and lexicographer, is occasion to encourage every person to acquire at least one dictionary—and to use it regularly.

DOUGLAS, WILLIAM ORVILLE: BIRTH ANNIVERSARY. Oct 16, 1898. American jurist, world traveler, conservationist, outdoorsman and author. Born at Maine, MN, he served as justice of the US Supreme Court longer than any other justice (36 years). Died at Washington, DC, Jan 19, 1980. For more info: oyez.northwestern.edu/justices/justices.cgi.

JOHN BROWN'S RAID: ANNIVERSARY. Oct 16, 1859. Abolitionist John Brown, with a band of about 20 men, seized the US Arsenal at Harpers Ferry, WV. Brown was captured and the insurrection put down by Oct 19. Brown was hanged at Charles Town, VA (now WV), Dec 2, 1859. For more info: *The John Brown Slavery Revolt,* by David Devillers (Enslow, 0-7660-1385-5, $20.95 Gr. 6 & up).

LATINO BOOK & FAMILY FESTIVAL—LOS ANGELES. Oct 16–17. Los Angeles, CA. Produced along with actor Edward James Olmos, this festival is a celebration of books, careers, culture, education, health, recreation, travel and more. It is the largest Latino consumer trade show in the US. Attendees will enjoy hundreds of booths and activities including book signings, storytelling, poetry readings, food, entertainment and workshops. For info: Latino Book & Family Festivals, 3980 Cazador St, Los Angeles, CA 90065. E-mail: kathy@latinobookfestival.com. Web: www.LBFF.us or www.openabook.org.

MILLION MAN MARCH: 10th ANNIVERSARY. Oct 16, 1995. Hundreds of thousands of black men met at Washington, DC, for a "holy day of atonement and reconciliation" organized by Louis Farrakhan, leader of the Nation of Islam. Marchers pledged to take responsibility for themselves, their families and their communities.

★**NATIONAL CHARACTER COUNTS WEEK.** Oct 16–22. One of the greatest building blocks of character is citizen service. The future belongs to those who have the strength of character to live a life of service to others.

★**NATIONAL FOREST PRODUCTS WEEK.** Oct 16–22. Presidential Proclamation always issued for the week beginning with the third Sunday in October since 1960 (Public Law 86–753 of Sept 13, 1960).

NATIONAL HIGH SCHOOL ACTIVITIES WEEK. Oct 16–22. Includes many activities: National Be A Sport Day, National Fine Arts Activities Day and National Community Service/Participation Day. Annually, the third week in October. For info: National Federation of State High School Assn, PO Box 690, Indianapolis, IN 46206. Phone: (317) 972-6900. Fax: (317) 822-5700. Web: www.nfhs.org.

NATIONAL SCHOOL BUS SAFETY WEEK. Oct 16–22. This week is set aside to focus attention on school bus safety—from the standpoint of the bus drivers, students and the motoring public. The theme for 2005 is "Flashing Red Means Stop Ahead!" Annually, the third full week of October, starting on Sunday. For info: National Assn for Pupil Transportation, 1850 Western Ave, Albany, NY 12203. Phone: (800) 989-6278. E-mail: sbsw@napt.org. Web: www.napt.org.

TEEN READ WEEK. Oct 16–22. The teen years are a time when many kids reject reading as being just another dreary assignment. The goal of Teen Read Week is to encourage young adults to read for sheer pleasure as well as learning. Also to remind parents, teachers and others that reading for fun is important for teens as well as young children and to increase awareness of the resources available at libraries. More than 1,400 schools and public libraries are registered to participate. For info: Young Adult Library Services Assn, American Library Assn, 50 E Huron St, Chicago, IL 60611. Phone: (800) 545-2433, ext 4390. E-mail: yalsa@ala.org. Web: www.ala.org/teenread.

UNITED NATIONS: WORLD FOOD DAY. Oct 16. Annual observance to heighten public awareness of the world food problem and to strengthen solidarity in the struggle against hunger, malnutrition and poverty. Date of observance is anniversary of founding of Food and Agriculture Organization (FAO), Oct 16, 1945, at Quebec, Canada. For info: United Nations, Dept of Public Info, New York, NY 10017. Web: www.un.org.

WEBSTER, NOAH: BIRTH ANNIVERSARY. Oct 16, 1758. American teacher and journalist whose name became synonymous with the word "dictionary" after his compilations of the earliest American dictionaries of the English language. Born at West Hartford, CT, he died at New Haven, CT, May 28, 1843.

WORLD FOOD DAY. Oct 16. To increase awareness, understanding and informed action on hunger. Annually, on the founding date of the UN Food and Agriculture Organization. For info: Patricia Young, US National Committee for World Food Day, 2175 K St NW, Washington, DC 20437. Phone: (202) 653-2404. Web: www.worldfooddayusa.org.

October 2005

S	M	T	W	T	F	S
						1
2	3	4	5	6	7	8
9	10	11	12	13	14	15
16	17	18	19	20	21	22
23	24	25	26	27	28	29
30	31					

YWCA WEEK WITHOUT VIOLENCE. Oct 16–22. Third full week in October. Some communities may sponsor celebrations on different dates. For info: YWCA of the USA, 1015 18th St NW, Ste 1100, Washington, DC 20036. Phone: (202) 467-0801. Web: www.ywca.org.

BIRTHDAYS TODAY

Joseph Bruchac, 63, author (*Thirteen Moons on Turtle's Back, The Boy Who Lived with Bears and Other Iroquois Stories*), born Saratoga Springs, NY, Oct 16, 1942.

Paul Kariya, 31, hockey player, born Vancouver, BC, Canada, Oct 16, 1974.

Kordell Stewart, 33, football player, born New Orleans, LA, Oct 16, 1972.

OCTOBER 17 — MONDAY

Day 290 — 75 Remaining

HAMMON, JUPITER: BIRTH ANNIVERSARY. Oct 17, 1711. America's first published black poet, whose birth anniversary is celebrated annually as Black Poetry Day, was born into slavery, probably at Long Island, NY. He was taught to read, however, and as a trusted servant was allowed to use his master's library. With the publication on Christmas Day, 1760, of the 88-line broadside poem "An Evening Thought," Jupiter Hammon, then 49, became the first black in America to publish poetry. Hammon died in 1790. The exact date and place of his death are unknown.

HUNTER'S MOON. Oct 17. The full moon following Harvest Moon. So called because the moon's light in the evening extends the day's length for hunters. Moon enters Full Moon phase at 8:14 AM, EDT.

INTERNATIONAL INFECTION CONTROL WEEK. Oct 17–23. To promote awareness of prevention and treatment of infection. Annually, the third week in October. For info: Assn for Professionals in Infection Control and Epidemiology, 1275 K St NW, Ste 1000, Washington, DC 20005-4006. Phone: (202) 789-1890. Fax: (202) 789-1899. E-mail: APICinfo@apic.org. Web: www.apic.org.

JAMAICA: NATIONAL HEROES DAY. Oct 17. National holiday established in 1969. Always observed on the third Monday in October.

JOHNSON, RICHARD MENTOR: 225th BIRTH ANNIVERSARY. Oct 17, 1780. The 9th vice president of the US (1837–41). Born at Floyd's Station, KY, he died at Frankfort, KY, Nov 19, 1850.

★ ★ ★

LUNAR ECLIPSE. Oct 17. Partial eclipse of the moon. Visible in North America, Asia, Australia and Pacific region.

MOON PHASE: FULL MOON. Oct 17. Moon enters Full Moon phase at 8:14 AM, EDT.

NATIONAL CHEMISTRY WEEK. Oct 17–21. To celebrate the contributions of chemistry to modern life and to help the public understand that chemistry affects every part of our lives. Activities include an array of outreach programs such as open houses, contests, workshops, exhibits and classroom visits. 10 million participants nationwide. The theme for 2005 is "The Joys of Toys." For info: Office of Community Activities, American Chemical Society, 1155 16th St NW, Washington, DC 20036. Phone: (202) 872-6078. Fax: (202) 872-4353. E-mail: ncw@acs.org. Web: www.chemistry.org/ncw.

NATIONAL HEALTH EDUCATION WEEK. Oct 17–23. Annually, the third week in October. For info: National Center for Health Education, 375 Hudson St, New York, NY 10014. Phone: (212) 463-4053. Web: www.nche.org.

POPE JOHN PAUL I: BIRTH ANNIVERSARY. Oct 17, 1912. Albino Luciani, 263rd pope of the Roman Catholic Church. Born at Forno di Canale, Italy, he was elected pope Aug 26, 1978. Died at Rome, 34 days after his election, Sept 28, 1978. Shortest papacy since Pope Leo XI (Apr 1–27, 1605).

SAN FRANCISCO 1989 EARTHQUAKE: ANNIVERSARY. Oct 17, 1989. The San Francisco Bay area was rocked by an earthquake registering 7.1 on the Richter scale at 5:04 PM, EDT, just as the nation's baseball fans settled in to watch the 1989 World Series. A large audience was tuned in to the pregame coverage when the quake hit and knocked the broadcast off the air. The quake caused damage estimated at $10 billion and killed 67 people, many of whom were caught in the collapse of the double-decked Interstate 80, at Oakland, CA. For more info: *The San Francisco Earthquake, 1989*, by Victoria Sherrow (Enslow, 0-7660-1060-0, $18.95 Gr. 4–8) or go to the National Earthquake Information Center: wwwneic.cr.usgs.gov.

SUKKOT BEGINS AT SUNDOWN. Oct 17. Jewish Feast of Tabernacles. See "Sukkot" (Oct 18).

UNITED NATIONS: INTERNATIONAL DAY FOR THE ERADICATION OF POVERTY. Oct 17. The General Assembly proclaimed this observance (Res 47/196) to promote public awareness of the need to eradicate poverty and destitution in all countries, particularly the developing nations. For more info, go to the UN's website for children at www.un.org/Pubs/CyberSchoolBus/. Annually, Oct 17.

US VIRGIN ISLANDS: HURRICANE THANKSGIVING DAY. Oct 17. Third Monday in October is a legal holiday celebrating the end of hurricane season.

BIRTHDAYS TODAY

Judith Caseley, 54, author (*Mama, Coming and Going; When Grandpa Came to Stay*), born Rahway, NJ, Oct 17, 1951.

Alan Garner, 71, author (*The Stone Book, Once Upon a Time*), born Congleton, England, Oct 17, 1934.

Mae Jemison, 49, scientist, astronaut, host ("Susan B. Anthony Slept Here"), born Decatur, AL, Oct 17, 1956.

Chris Kirkpatrick, 34, singer ('N Sync), born Pittsburgh, PA, Oct 17, 1971.

OCTOBER 18 — TUESDAY

Day 291 — 74 Remaining

ALASKA DAY. Oct 18. Alaska. Anniversary of transfer of Alaska from Russia to the US, which became official on Sitka's Castle Hill, Oct 18, 1867. This is a holiday in Alaska; when it falls on a weekend it is observed on the following Monday.

ASSOCIATION FOR EDUCATIONAL COMMUNICATIONS AND TECHNOLOGY ANNUAL CONVENTION. Oct 18–25. Orlando, FL. The theme for 2005's conference is "Exploring the Vision." For info: Assn for Educational Communications & Technology, 1800 N Stonelake Dr, Ste 2, Bloomington, IN 47404. Phone: (877) 677-AECT. Fax: (812) 335-7678. E-mail: aect@aect.org. Web: www.aect.org.

FIRST NEWSPAPER COMIC STRIP: ANNIVERSARY. Oct 18, 1896. Although cartoons had appeared in newspapers for many years, the comic strip—a narrative told in cartoons over several panels—took its main form with the appearance of "The Yellow Kid Takes a Hand at Golf" in the *New York Journal*'s weekly supplement *American Humorist*. The creator was Richard Fenton Outcault. In March 1897, the *Yellow Kid Magazine* gathered the strips and became the first published collection of a comic strip—setting the stage for the first comic books in the late 1920s. See also: "Outcault, Richard Fenton: Birth Anniversary" (Jan 14). ***See Curriculum Connection.***

LITERATURE FESTIVAL. Oct 18. University of Kansas Union, Lawrence, KS. 12th annual. Festival of children's literature. For info: The Writing Conference, Inc, PO Box 664, Ottawa, KS 66067. Fax: (785) 242-0407. E-mail: jbushman@writingconference.com. Web: www.writingconference.com.

SAINT LUKE: FEAST DAY. Oct 18. Patron saint of doctors and artists, himself a physician and painter, authorship of the third Gospel and Acts of the Apostles is attributed to him. Died about AD 68. Legend says that he painted portraits of Mary and Jesus.

SILVERSTEIN, SHEL: BIRTH ANNIVERSARY. Oct 18, 1932. Cartoonist and children's author, best remembered for his poetry that included *A Light in the Attic* and *The Giving Tree*. Silverstein won the Michigan Young Reader's Award for *Where The Sidewalk Ends*. Also a songwriter, he wrote "The Unicorn Song" and "A Boy Named Sue" for Johnny Cash. Born at Chicago, IL, he died at Key West, FL, May 9, 1999. For more info: *Meet Shel Silverstein*, by S. Ward (Rosen, 0-8239-5709-8, $18.75 Gr. K–4).

SUKKOT, SUCCOTH or FEAST OF TABERNACLES, FIRST DAY. Oct 18. Hebrew calendar date: Tishri 15, 5766, begins nine-day festival in commemoration of Jewish people's 40 years of wandering in the desert and thanksgiving for the fall harvest. This high holiday season closes with Shemini Atzeret (see entry on Oct 25) and Simchat Torah (see entry on Oct 26).

WATER POLLUTION CONTROL ACT: ANNIVERSARY. Oct 18, 1972. Overriding President Nixon's veto, Congress passed a $25 billion Water Pollution Control Act.

OCTOBER 18
COMICS IN THE CLASSROOM

Today, 109 years ago, a comic strip made its first appearance in an American newspaper. The strip, which was a narrative told in cartoons over several panels, featured the "Yellow Kid," a homely little fellow with an overlarge yellow shirt. The Yellow Kid's popularity spawned more newspaper strips, and the popularity of newspaper strips led to inexpensive pamphlet-size collections in the early 1930s. These collections were the early comic books, and soon Superman, Batman and other comic book heroes were thrilling children.

Although parents through the ages haven't always been partial to comic books and cartoons, kids love them. Luckily for everyone, there are masters of the art form who have created amazing characters and visuals. Sometimes a child who is slow to develop reading skills discovers a comic book that sparks his or her interest. Here is information on two masters of the comic book—one from the golden age of comics, the other working today—who might thrill your class.

Carl Barks (1901–2000) is the world-famous chronicler of Donald Duck, Scrooge McDuck and other classic characters in Walt Disney comic books from 1943 to 1967. Although he didn't create Donald Duck, Barks is credited with making his comic book incarnation more well-rounded, penning stories and visuals of high adventure and slapstick humor. Donald and his nephews went to the Wild West, to the high seas or inside a mummy's tomb. Barks studied such references as *National Geographic* magazine to make his cartoons as authentic as possible. (As authentic as having a duck hero will allow!) He created the miserly Scrooge McDuck, Donald's uncle, in 1947. Uncle Scrooge was so successful that he got his own comic book. Old copies of Barks' work are available in comic book shops, but Gladstone Publishing, Ltd., has collected classic Donald and Scrooge stories in paperback editions. Some examples include *Walt Disney's Donald Duck: The Terror of the River* (0-944599-01-X, $5.95 All ages) or *Walt Disney's Uncle Scrooge: The Mines of King Solomon* (0-944599-00-1, $5.95 All ages).

Jeff Smith created the internationally successful *Bone* comic books featuring lovable blobby creatures from the mythic land of Boneville. Although the comic book series has ended (it ran from 1991–2004), it has been collected into one mammoth volume of 1,300 pages (Cartoon Books, 1-888963-14-X, $39.95 All ages—also available in individual volumes). In this saga, Fone Bone and his cousins Phony and Smiley leave Boneville and find adventure in an Edenic valley that is populated by sneaky dragons and fearsome rat creatures. There's comedy as well as drama here, but the beautiful black and white drawings are an equal draw. The rat creatures are scary, but not enough to alarm younger readers. A great entrée to the world of *Bone* is through a prequel, *Stupid, Stupid Rat-tails,* featuring the irascible Big Johnson Bone, a frontier hero in the mold of Davey Crockett (Cartoon Books, 1-888963-06-9, $9.95 All ages). Smith's work has been acclaimed by the cartoon world as well as the American Library Association. —Holly McGuire

October 2005

S	M	T	W	T	F	S
						1
2	3	4	5	6	7	8
9	10	11	12	13	14	15
16	17	18	19	20	21	22
23	24	25	26	27	28	29
30	31					

BIRTHDAYS TODAY

Joyce Hansen, 63, author (*I Thought My Soul Would Rise and Fly: The Diary of Patsy, a Freed Girl*), born New York, NY, Oct 18, 1942.

Jesse Helms, 84, retired 5-term US Senator (R, North Carolina), born Monroe, NC, Oct 18, 1921.

Wynton Marsalis, 44, classical and jazz musician, born New Orleans, LA, Oct 18, 1961.

Jim Talent, 49, US Senator (R, Missouri), born Des Peres, MO, Oct 18, 1956.

OCTOBER 19 — WEDNESDAY

Day 292 — 73 Remaining

THE DAY OF NATIONAL CONCERN ABOUT YOUNG PEOPLE AND GUN VIOLENCE. Oct 19. Students are encouraged on this day to sign a pledge that they will never carry a gun to school or resolve a dispute with a gun and they will urge their friends to do the same. More than 1,000,000 middle and high school students have signed the Pledge Against Gun Violence. For info: Student Pledge Against Gun Violence, 112 Nevada St, Northfield, MN 55057. Phone: (507) 645-5378. Web: www.pledge.org.

FRENCH POLYNESIA: HAWAIKI NUI VA'A RACE. Oct 19. Spectacular, three-day, open water traditional outrigger canoe race. More than 2,000 racers in more than 100 canoes battle for 78 miles, traveling from Huahine to Raiatea to Tahaa to Bora Bora. *Va'a* is the Tahitian word for canoe. Held since 1992, the race begins the third Wednesday of October every year.

JEFFERSON, MARTHA WAYLES SKELTON: BIRTH ANNIVERSARY. Oct 19, 1748. Wife of Thomas Jefferson, third president of the US. Born at Charles City County, VA, she died at Monticello, VA, Sept 6, 1782.

MISSOURI DAY. Oct 19. Observed by teachers and pupils of schools with appropriate exercises throughout the state of Missouri. Annually, the third Wednesday of October.

YORKTOWN DAY: "AMERICA'S REAL INDEPENDENCE DAY." Oct 19. Yorktown, VA. Representatives of the US, France and other nations involved in the American Revolution gather to celebrate the anniversary of the victory (Oct 19, 1781) that assured American independence. Parade and commemorative ceremonies. Annually, Oct 19. Est attendance: 2,000. For info: Public Affairs Officer, Colonial National Historical Park, Box 210, Yorktown, VA 23690. Phone: (757) 898-2410. Web: www.nps.gov/colo.

YORKTOWN DAY: ANNIVERSARY. Oct 19, 1781. More than 7,000 English and Hessian troops, led by British General Lord Cornwallis, surrendered to General George Washington at Yorktown, VA, effectively ending the war between Britain and her American colonies. There were no more major battles, but the provisional treaty of peace was not signed until Nov 30, 1782, and the final Treaty of Paris, Sept 3, 1783.

BIRTHDAYS TODAY

Ed Emberley, 74, author, illustrator (*Go Away, Big Green Monster; Drummer Hoff*), born Malden, MA, Oct 19, 1931.

Dan Gutman, 50, author (*Honus and Me, The Kid Who Ran for President*), born New York, NY, Oct 19, 1955.

John Lithgow, 60, actor ("Third Rock from the Sun," *Shrek*), author (*The Remarkable Farkle McBride*), born Rochester, NY, Oct 19, 1945.

Bernard Lodge, 72, author (*There Was an Old Woman Who Lived in a Glove, Prince Ivan and the Firebird*), born Chalfont, St. Peter, Buckinghamshire, England, Oct 19, 1933.

Philip Pullman, 59, author (*The Golden Compass, The Subtle Knife*), born Norwich, England, Oct 19, 1946.

OCTOBER 20 — THURSDAY

Day 293 — 72 Remaining

BLACK POETRY DAY. Oct 20 (tentative). To recognize the contribution of black poets to American life and culture and to honor Jupiter Hammon, the first black in America to publish his own verse. Jupiter Hammon of Huntington, Long Island, NY, was born Oct 17, 1711. The celebration includes a poetry reading by an important black poet. For info: Black Poetry Day Committee, EOP Office, Algonquin Hall, SUNY-Plattsburgh, Plattsburgh, NY 12901-2681. Phone: (518) 564-2263. E-mail: marlenefields@plattsburgh.edu.

DEWEY, JOHN: BIRTH ANNIVERSARY. Oct 20, 1859. Philosopher of education, born near Burlington, VT. A professor at the University of Chicago and Columbia University, Dewey was committed to child-centered education, learning by doing and integrating schools with the outside world. He died at New York, NY, June 2, 1952.

GUATEMALA: REVOLUTION DAY. Oct 20. Public holiday in Guatemala.

JOHNSON, CROCKETT: BIRTH ANNIVERSARY. Oct 20, 1906. Author (*Harold and the Purple Crayon*), cartoonist, born David Leisk at New York, NY. Died July 11, 1975. For more info: www.ksu.edu/english/nelp/purple/index.html.

KENYA: KENYATTA DAY. Oct 20. Observed as a public holiday. Honors Jomo Kenyatta, first president of Kenya.

MacARTHUR RETURNS TO THE PHILIPPINES: ANNIVERSARY. Oct 20, 1944. In mid-September of 1944 American military leaders made the decision to begin the invasion of the Philippines on Leyte, a small island north of the Surigao Strait. With General Douglas MacArthur in overall command, US aircraft dropped hundreds of tons of bombs in the area of Dulag. Four divisions landed on the east coast, and after a few hours General MacArthur set foot on Philippine soil for the first time since he was ordered to Australia Mar 11, 1942, thus fulfilling his promise, "I shall return."

MANTLE, MICKEY: BIRTH ANNIVERSARY. Oct 20, 1931. Baseball Hall of Famer, born at Spavinaw, OK. Died Aug 13, 1995, at Dallas, TX.

BIRTHDAYS TODAY

Nikki Grimes, 55, poet and author (*Meet Danitra Brown*, Coretta Scott King Awards for *Bronx Masquerade* and *Talkin' About Bessie*), also writes as Naomi McMillen, born New York, NY, Oct 20, 1950.

Eddie Jones, 34, basketball player, born Pompano Beach, FL, Oct 20, 1971.

Viggo Mortensen, 47, actor (*The Lord of the Rings* trilogy), born New York, NY, Oct 20, 1958.

★ ★ ★

OCTOBER 21 — FRIDAY

Day 294 — 71 Remaining

FILLMORE, CAROLINE CARMICHAEL McINTOSH: BIRTH ANNIVERSARY. Oct 21, 1813. Second wife of Millard Fillmore, 13th president of the US, born at Morristown, NJ. Died at New York, NY, Aug 11, 1881.

INCANDESCENT LAMP DEMONSTRATED: ANNIVERSARY. Oct 21, 1879. Thomas A. Edison demonstrated the first incandescent lamp that could be used economically for domestic purposes. This prototype, developed at his Menlo Park, NJ, laboratory, could burn for 13½ hours.

NOBEL, ALFRED BERNHARD: BIRTH ANNIVERSARY. Oct 21, 1833. Swedish chemist and engineer who invented dynamite was born at Stockholm, Sweden, and died at San Remo, Italy, Dec 10, 1896. His will established the Nobel Prize. See also: "Nobel Prize Awards Ceremonies: Anniversary" (Dec 10). For more info: www.nobel.se.

OLD IRONSIDES LAUNCHED: ANNIVERSARY. Oct 21, 1797. The USS *Constitution* was launched and christened by Captain James Sever on this date at Boston, making this frigate the oldest commissioned warship afloat in the world. Congress had commissioned *Constitution* and five other ships in 1794. The *Constitution* earned its nickname and place in America's heart through valiant service in the War of 1812: in a fight with Britain's HMS *Guerriere* on Aug 19, 1812, sailors reported a British shot repelled by the side of the ship and cried that its sides were made of iron. No enemy ever boarded the warship in its days of active service. The ship now rests at Boston Harbor. See also: "Old Ironsides Saved by Poem: Anniversary" (Sept 16).

STATE FAIR OF LOUISIANA. Oct 21–Nov 6. Fairgrounds, Shreveport, LA. Educational, agricultural, commercial exhibits, entertainment. Est attendance: 250,000. For info: Sam Giordano, Pres/Genl Mgr, Louisiana State Fairgrounds, 3701 Hudson St, Shreveport, LA 71109. Phone: (318) 635-1361. Fax: (318) 631-4909.

TAIWAN: OVERSEAS CHINESE DAY. Oct 21. Thousands of overseas Chinese come to Taiwan for this and other occasions that make October a particularly memorable month.

UNITED KINGDOM: THE TRAFALGAR WEEKEND. Oct 21–23. A special weekend bringing together the peoples, families and communities of Britain, Northern Ireland and the Channel Islands in commemoration of the 200th anniversary of the Battle of Trafalgar. Events include Royal Navy celebrations at Portsmouth at the HMS *Victory*, a musical celebration of the sea and the Battle of Trafalgar at London's Albert Hall, parades, memorial services and more. For info: The Trafalgar Weekend, The Office, Sarunds House, Farnham, Blandford Forum, Dorset, United Kingdom DT11 8DE. Web: www.trafalgarweekend.co.uk.

BIRTHDAYS TODAY

Janet Ahlberg, 61, illustrator (*The Jolly Postman*), born Croydon, England, Oct 21, 1944.

Ann Cameron, 62, author (*The Most Beautiful Place in the World, The Stories Julian Tells*), born Rice Lake, WI, Oct 21, 1943.

Ursula K. Le Guin, 76, author (*Catwings, The Wizard of Earthsea, The Tombs of Atuan, The Left Hand of Darkness*), born Berkeley, CA, Oct 21, 1929.

Jeremy Miller, 29, actor ("Growing Pains"), born West Covina, CA, Oct 21, 1976.

Ellen Wittlinger, 57, author (*Hard Love*), born Belleville, IL, Oct 21, 1948.

OCTOBER 22 — SATURDAY

Day 295 — 70 Remaining

FOXX, JIMMIE: BIRTH ANNIVERSARY. Oct 22, 1907. Baseball Hall of Fame first baseman, born at Sudlersville, MD. Died at Miami, FL, July 21, 1967.

HOLY SEE: NATIONAL HOLIDAY. Oct 22. The state of Vatican City and the Holy See observe Oct 22 as a national holiday.

INTERNATIONAL STUTTERING AWARENESS DAY. Oct 22. For info: National Stuttering Assn, 119 W 40th St, New York, NY 10018. Phone: 800 WE STUTTER. Web: www.nsastutter.org or www.stutteringhomepage.com.

LISZT, FRANZ: BIRTH ANNIVERSARY. Oct 22, 1811. Hungarian pianist and composer (*Hungarian Rhapsodies*). Born at Raiding, Hungary, he died July 31, 1886, at Bayreuth, Germany.

MAKE A DIFFERENCE DAY. Oct 22. This national day of community service is sponsored by *USA WEEKEND.* Volunteer projects completed are judged by well-known celebrities. Selected projects receive $10,000 in charitable awards to further their good work. Key projects are honored in April during National Volunteer Week. More than two million people nationwide participate. For info: Make a Difference Day, *USA WEEKEND*, 7950 Jones Branch Dr, McLean, VA 22107. Phone: (800) 416-3824. Web: www.makeadifferenceday.com.

RANDOLPH, PEYTON: DEATH ANNIVERSARY. Oct 22, 1775. First president of the Continental Congress, died at Philadelphia, PA. Born about 1721 (exact date unknown), at Williamsburg, VA.

BIRTHDAYS TODAY

Haley Barbour, 58, Governor of Mississippi (R), born Yazoo County, MS, Oct 22, 1947.

Brian Anthony Boitano, 42, Olympic gold medal figure skater, born Mountain View, CA, Oct 22, 1963.

Jeff Goldblum, 53, actor (*Jurassic Park, Independence Day*), born Pittsburgh, PA, Oct 22, 1952.

Zachary Walker Hanson, 20, singer (Hanson), born Arlington, VA, Oct 22, 1985.

Jonathan Lipnicki, 15, actor (*Jerry Maguire, The Little Vampire, Stuart Little*), born Westlake Village, CA, Oct 22, 1990.

Bill Owens, 55, Governor of Colorado (R), born Fort Worth, TX, Oct 22, 1950.

Ichiro Suzuki, 32, baseball player, born Kasugai, Japan, Oct 22, 1973.

October 2005

S	M	T	W	T	F	S
						1
2	3	4	5	6	7	8
9	10	11	12	13	14	15
16	17	18	19	20	21	22
23	24	25	26	27	28	29
30	31					

OCTOBER 23 — SUNDAY

Day 296 — 69 Remaining

APPERT, NICOLAS: BIRTH ANNIVERSARY. Oct 23, 1752. Also known as "Canning Day," this is the anniversary of the birth of French chef, chemist, confectioner, inventor and author Nicolas Appert, at Chalons-Sur-Marne. Appert, who also invented the bouillon tablet, is best remembered for devising a system of heating foods and sealing them in airtight containers. Known as the "father of canning," Appert won a prize of 12,000 francs from the French government in 1809, and the title "Benefactor of Humanity" in 1812, for his inventions which revolutionized our previously seasonal diet. Appert died at Massy, France, June 3, 1841.

CAMBODIA: PEACE TREATY DAY. Oct 23. National holiday. Commemorates 1991 peace treaty.

EAGER, EDWARD: DEATH ANNIVERSARY. Oct 23, 1964. Born at Toledo, OH in 1911, Eager wrote children's fantasy novels in the style of his favorite author, E. Nesbit. Like Nesbit, he wrote about ordinary children caught up in magical adventures. Some of his more popular books are *Half Magic* and *Magic By the Lake*. He died in Connecticut.

EDERLE, GERTRUDE: 100th BIRTH ANNIVERSARY. Oct 23, 1905. Born at New York, NY, in 1905 (some sources say 1906), Gertrude Ederle was an Olympic gold medal–winning swimmer who set numerous world records. In 1926, President Woodrow Wilson called her "America's best girl" when she became the first woman to swim across the English Channel (see also entry on Aug 6). She died at Wyckoff, NJ, Nov 30, 2003. For more info: *America's Champion Swimmer: Gertrude Ederle*, by David A. Adler (Harcourt/Gulliver, 0-15-201969-3, $16 Gr. K–3).

HUNGARY: ANNIVERSARY OF 1956 REVOLUTION. Oct 23. National holiday.

HUNGARY DECLARED INDEPENDENT: ANNIVERSARY. Oct 23, 1989. Hungary declared itself an independent republic, 33 years after Russian troops crushed a popular revolt against Soviet rule. The announcement followed a weeklong purge by Parliament of the Stalinist elements from Hungary's 1949 constitution, which defined the country as a socialist people's republic. Acting head of state Matyas Szuros made the declaration in front of tens of thousands of Hungarians at Parliament Square, speaking from the same balcony from which Imre Nagy addressed rebels 33 years earlier. Nagy was hanged for treason after Soviet intervention. Free elections held in March 1990 removed the Communist party to the ranks of the opposition for the first time in four decades.

SCORPIO, THE SCORPION. Oct 23–Nov 22. In the astronomical/astrological zodiac that divides the sun's apparent orbit into 12 segments, the period Oct 23–Nov 22 is identified, traditionally, as the sun sign of Scorpio, the Scorpion. The ruling planet is Pluto or Mars.

STEVENSON, ADLAI EWING: BIRTH ANNIVERSARY. Oct 23, 1835. The 23rd vice president of the US (1893–97), born at Christian County, KY. Died at Chicago, IL, June 14, 1914. He was grandfather of Adlai E. Stevenson, the Democratic candidate for president in 1952 and 1956.

THAILAND: CHULALONGKORN DAY. Oct 23. Annual commemoration of the death of King Chulalongkorn the Great, who died Oct 23, 1910, after a 42-year reign. King Chulalongkorn abolished slavery in Thailand. Special ceremonies with floral tributes and incense at the foot of his equestrian statue in front of Bangkok's National Assembly Hall.

BIRTHDAYS TODAY

Laurie Halse Anderson, 44, author (*Speak; Catalyst; Fever, 1793*), born Potsdam, NY, Oct 23, 1961.

Jim Bunning, 74, US Senator (R, Kentucky), born Southgate, KY, Oct 23, 1931.

Gordon Korman, 42, author (*The Toilet Paper Tigers, The Twinkie Squad*), born Montreal, QC, Canada, Oct 23, 1963.

John Lackey, 27, baseball player, born Abilene, TX, Oct 23, 1978.

Melquiades (Mel) R. Martinez, 59, US Senator (R, Florida), former US Secretary of Housing and Urban Development (G.W. Bush administration), born Sagua la Grande, Cuba, Oct 23, 1946.

Pele, 65, former soccer player, born Edson Arantes do Nascimento, Tres Coracoes, Brazil, Oct 23, 1940.

Keith Van Horn, 30, basketball player, born Fullerton, CA, Oct 23, 1975.

"Weird Al" Yankovic, 46, singer, satirist ("The Weird Al Show"), born Lynwood, CA, Oct 23, 1959.

OCTOBER 24 — MONDAY

Day 297 — 68 Remaining

INTERNATIONAL SCHOOL LIBRARY DAY. Oct 24. Annually, the fourth Monday in October. For info: International Assn of School Librarians, Ste 300, PO Box 34069, Seattle, WA 98124-1069. Fax: (604) 925-0566. E-mail: iasl@rockland.com. Web: www.iasl-slo.org/isld.html.

MOON PHASE: LAST QUARTER. Oct 24. Moon enters Last Quarter phase at 9:17 PM, EDT.

NEW ZEALAND: LABOR DAY. Oct 24. National holiday. The fourth Monday in October.

SHERMAN, JAMES SCHOOLCRAFT: 150th BIRTH ANNIVERSARY. Oct 24, 1855. The 27th vice president of the US (1909–12), born at Utica, NY. Died there Oct 30, 1912.

★**UNITED NATIONS DAY.** Oct 24. Presidential Proclamation. Always issued for Oct 24 since 1948. (By unanimous request of the UN General Assembly.)

UNITED NATIONS DAY: 60th ANNIVERSARY OF FOUNDING. Oct 24, 1945. Official United Nations holiday commemorates founding of the United Nations and effective date of the United Nations Charter. In 1971 the General Assembly recommended this day be observed as a public holiday by UN member states (Res 2782/xxvi). For more info, visit the UN's website for children at www.un.org/Pubs/CyberSchoolBus.

UNITED NATIONS: DISARMAMENT WEEK. Oct 24–30. In 1978, the General Assembly called on member states to highlight the danger of the arms race, propagate the need for its cessation and increase public understanding of the urgent task of disarmament. Observed annually, beginning on the anniversary of the founding of the UN.

ZAMBIA: INDEPENDENCE DAY. Oct 24. National holiday commemorates independence of what was then Northern Rhodesia from Britain in 1964. Celebrations in all cities, but main parades of military, labor and youth organizations are at capital, Lusaka. The fourth Monday in October.

BIRTHDAYS TODAY

Corey Dillon, 31, football player, born Seattle, WA, Oct 24, 1974.

Rafael Furcal, 28, baseball player, born Loma de Cabrera, Dominican Republic, Oct 24, 1977.

Kweisi Mfume, 57, NAACP president, born Baltimore, MD, Oct 24, 1948.

Monica, 25, singer, born Monica Arnold, Atlanta, GA, Oct 24, 1980.

Mike Rounds, 51, Governor of South Dakota (R), born Huron, SD, Oct 24, 1954.

Catherine Sutherland, 31, actress (*Turbo: A Power Rangers Movie*, "Power Rangers Turbo"), born Sydney, Australia, Oct 24, 1974.

OCTOBER 25 — TUESDAY

Day 298 — 67 Remaining

KAZAKHSTAN: INDEPENDENCE DAY. Oct 25. National holiday. Commemorates 1991 declaration of independence from the USSR.

LAILAT UL QADR: THE NIGHT OF POWER. Oct 25 (approximate). "The Night of Power" falls on one of the last 10 days of Ramadan on an odd-numbered night (Islamic calendar dates: Ramadan 21, 23, 25, 27 or 29, 1426). It commemorates the night of the first revelation of the Holy Qur'an to Muhammad by the angel Gabriel. The Holy Qur'an states that praying on this night is better than praying 1,000 months. Since it is not known which day it is, Muslims feel it is best to pray on each of the possible nights. Different methods for "anticipating" the visibility of the new moon crescent at Mecca are used by different Muslim sects or groups. US date may vary.

OCTOBER 25
A THOUSAND CRANES: THE 50TH ANNIVERSARY OF SADAKO SASAKI'S DEATH

Sadako Sasaki was two years old when her home, Hiroshima, Japan, was destroyed by an atomic bomb in the closing days of WWII. In January 1955, dizziness was the first symptom of her survivor's legacy, leukemia. (So many Hiroshima residents were diagnosed with leukemia that it was called the "atom bomb disease.")

Inspired by a folktale in which the gods grant a wish to those who fold 1,000 origami cranes, Sadako began folding cranes in hopes of getting well. She completed 644 cranes before her death on Oct 25, 1955. Her classmates finished the 1,000 cranes in order that they be buried with her. Students across Japan, moved by her story, collected money to create a monument to her. A statue of Sadako was erected in 1958 at the Hiroshima Peace Park and visitors continue to place folded cranes there.

To mark the 50th anniversary of Sadako Sasaki's death, share her story with your class. There are a number of inspiring books, including the classic *Sadako and the Thousand Paper Cranes* by Eleanor Coerr (Puffin, 0-698-11802-2, $5.99 Ages 9–12). Coerr published an abridged version for ages 4–8 entitled *Sadako* (PaperStarBook, 0-698-11588-0, $6.99).

This story is also a great way to introduce your class to the art of folded paper—origami. A good book for children is John Montroll's *Easy Origami* (Dover, 0-486-27298-2, $3.95 All ages). To make paper cranes, go to www.monkey.org/~aidan/origami/crane to find detailed photo illustrations. The World Peace Project for Children operates a website on Sadako Sasaki and, besides giving information on her, offers instruction on making an origami crane. Some classrooms have made cranes to send to Sasaki's statue in Hiroshima—perhaps your class would like to tackle such a worthy project? —Holly McGuire

MARCELLINO, FRED: BIRTH ANNIVERSARY. Oct 25, 1936. Illustrator and author of children's books was born at Brooklyn, NY. Best known for his Caldecott Honor book *Puss in Boots*, he also wrote and illustrated *I, Crocodile*, and provided the art for new editions of E.B. White's classics *Stuart Little* and *The Trumpet of the Swan*. He died July 12, 2001, at New York, NY.

PICASSO, PABLO RUIZ: BIRTH ANNIVERSARY. Oct 25, 1881. Called by many the greatest artist of the 20th century, Pablo Picasso excelled as a painter, sculptor and engraver. He is said to have commented once: "I am only a public entertainer who has understood his time." Born at Malaga, Spain, he died Apr 8, 1973, at Mougins, France. For more info: *Picasso*, by Stefano Loria (Peter Bedrick, 0-87226-318-5, $22.50 Gr. 4–7).

SASAKI, SADAKO: 50th DEATH ANNIVERSARY. Oct 25, 1955. Born at Hiroshima, Japan, in 1943, Sadako Sasaki was two years old when her city was hit by an atomic bomb in the closing days of WWII. She was diagnosed with leukemia in January 1955, and, inspired by a folk tale in which the gods grant a wish to those who fold 1,000 paper cranes, began the task. She died on this date having folded 644 cranes, and her classmates finished the rest. Students across Japan, moved by her story, collected money to create a monument to her that was erected at Hiroshima Peace Park in 1958. Visitors continue to place folded cranes there. ***See Curriculum Connection.***

SHEMINI ATZERET. Oct 25. Hebrew calendar date: Tishri 22, 5766. The eighth day of Solemn Assembly, part of the Sukkot Festival (see entry on Oct 18), with memorial services and cycle of Biblical readings in the synagogue. (Began at sundown of previous day.)

SQUID BATTLES FISHERMEN: ANNIVERSARY. Oct 25, 1873. Although literature abounds with tales of giant squid battling humans, there has been only one reliably reported instance. As chronicled in Richard Ellis's *The Search for the Giant Squid*, two fishermen in Portugal Cove at Conception Bay, Newfoundland, encountered what they thought was flotsam floating near their skiff, but the "flotsam" started writhing and attacked the boat with 19-foot-long tentacles while displaying a beak "as big as a six-gallon keg." The men were able to hack off a tentacle with an ax, and the squid sank out of sight. The recovered tentacle provided scientists with the first opportunity to study an elusive animal often thought to be mythical.

STATE CONSTITUTION DAY IN MASSACHUSETTS. Oct 25. Proclaimed annually by the governor to commemorate the adoption of the state constitution in 1780.

TAIWAN: RETROCESSION DAY. Oct 25. Commemorates restoration of Taiwan to Chinese rule in 1945, after half a century of Japanese occupation.

BIRTHDAYS TODAY

Brad Gilchrist, 46, cartoonist ("Nancy"), works with his brother Guy Gilchrist, born Torrington, CT, Oct 25, 1959.
Pedro Martinez, 34, baseball player, born Manoguyabo, Dominican Republic, Oct 25, 1971.
Midori, 34, violinist, born Osaka, Japan, Oct 25, 1971.

October 2005

S	M	T	W	T	F	S
						1
2	3	4	5	6	7	8
9	10	11	12	13	14	15
16	17	18	19	20	21	22
23	24	25	26	27	28	29
30	31					

OCTOBER 26 — WEDNESDAY

Day 299 — 66 Remaining

AUSTRIA: NATIONAL DAY. Oct 26. National holiday. Commemorates the withdrawal of Soviet troops.

ERIE CANAL: ANNIVERSARY. Oct 26, 1825. The Erie Canal, first US major man-made waterway, was opened, providing a water route from Lake Erie to the Hudson River. Construction started July 4, 1817, and the canal cost $7,602,000. Cannons fired and celebrations were held all along the route for the opening. For more info: *The Amazing, Impossible Erie Canal*, by Cheryl Harness (Simon & Schuster, 0-02-742641-6, $16 Gr. 3–8) or the New York State Canal System's website at www.canals.state.ny.us.

MULE DAY. Oct 26. Anniversary of the first importation of Spanish jacks to the US, a gift from King Charles III of Spain. Mules are said to have been bred first in this country by George Washington from a pair delivered at Boston, Oct 26, 1785.

SIMCHAT TORAH. Oct 26. Hebrew calendar date: Tishri 23, 5766. Rejoicing in the Torah concludes the nine-day Sukkot Festival (see entry on Oct 18). Public reading of the Pentateuch is completed and begun again, symbolizing the need for ever-continuing study. (Began at sundown of previous day.)

TECHNOLOGY + LEARNING CONFERENCE. Oct 26–28. Denver, CO. The annual conference will bring together 3,000 K–12 educators to see what's new, share experiences and find out what's working in every area of education technology. Sponsored by the National School Boards Association and cosponsored by 25 education organizations. Workshops, roundtables, exhibits and more. For info: National School Boards Assn, 1680 Duke St, Alexandria, VA 22314. Phone: (703) 838-6722. E-mail: info@nsba.org. Web: www.nsba.org.

BIRTHDAYS TODAY

Hillary Rodham Clinton, 58, US Senator (D, New York), former First Lady, born Park Ridge, IL, Oct 26, 1947.
Sasha Cohen, 21, figure skater, born Westwood, CA, Oct 26, 1984.
Steven Kellogg, 64, author (*Paul Bunyan, The Mysterious Tadpole, Can I Keep Him?*), illustrator (*The Day Jimmy's Boa Ate the Wash, How Much is a Million?*), born Norwalk, CT, Oct 26, 1941.
Eric Rohmann, 48, author and illustrator (*Time Flies, The Cinder-Eyed Cats*, Caldecott Medal for *My Friend Rabbit*), born Riverside, IL, Oct 26, 1957.

OCTOBER 27 — THURSDAY

Day 300 — 65 Remaining

BAGNOLD, ENID: BIRTH ANNIVERSARY. Oct 27, 1889. Novelist and playwright (*National Velvet*), born at Rochester, Kent, England. She died at London, England, Mar 31, 1981.

CHICAGO INTERNATIONAL CHILDREN'S FILM FESTIVAL. Oct 27–Nov 6. Cannes for Kids! Children's films from around the world plus workshops with directors, animators and movie makeup artists. For info: Chicago International Children's Film Festival, Facets Multimedia, 1517 W Fullerton Ave, Chicago, IL 60614. Phone: (773) 281-9075. E-mail: kidsfest@facets.org.

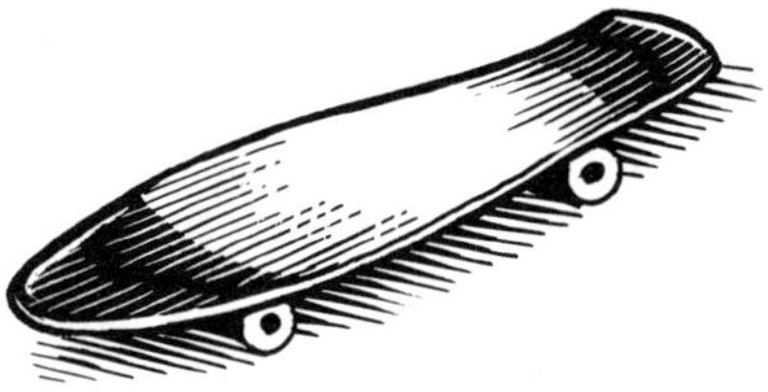

COOK, JAMES: BIRTH ANNIVERSARY. Oct 27, 1728. English sea captain and explorer who discovered the Hawaiian Islands and brought Australia and New Zealand into the British Empire. The US space shuttle *Endeavour* is named after his ship. Born at Marton-in-Cleveland, Yorkshire, England, and was killed Feb 14, 1779, at Hawaii.

HURRICANE MITCH: ANNIVERSARY. Oct 27, 1998. More than 6,000 people were killed in Honduras by flooding caused by Hurricane Mitch. Several thousand more were killed in other Central American countries, especially Nicaragua. For info about hurricanes: www.fema.gov/kids/hurr.htm.

NAVY DAY. Oct 27. Observed since 1922.

NEW YORK CITY SUBWAY: ANNIVERSARY. Oct 27, 1904. Running from City Hall to West 145th Street, the New York City subway began operation. It was privately operated by the Interborough Rapid Transit Company and later became part of the system operated by the New York City Transit Authority.

ROOSEVELT, THEODORE: BIRTH ANNIVERSARY. Oct 27, 1858. The 26th president of the US, succeeded to the presidency on the assassination of William McKinley. He was the youngest man to have ever served as president of the US. His term of office: Sept 14, 1901–Mar 3, 1909. Roosevelt was the first president to ride in an automobile (1902), to submerge in a submarine (1905) and to fly in an airplane (1910). Although his best remembered quote is, "Speak softly and carry a big stick," he also said, "The first requisite of a good citizen in this Republic of ours is that he shall be able and willing to pull his weight." Born at New York, NY, Roosevelt died at Oyster Bay, NY, Jan 6, 1919. For more info: *Bully for You, Teddy Roosevelt!*, by Jean Fritz (Putnam, 0-399-21769-X, $15.99 Gr. 7–9) and *Young Teddy Roosevelt*, by Cheryl Harness (National Geographic, 0-7922-7094-0, $17.95 Gr. 2–5) or www.ipl.org/ref/POTUS.

SAINT VINCENT AND THE GRENADINES: INDEPENDENCE DAY. Oct 27. National Day commemorating independence from Britian in 1979.

TURKMENISTAN: INDEPENDENCE DAY. Oct 27. National holiday. Commemorates independence from the Soviet Union in 1991.

"THE WONDERFUL WORLD OF DISNEY" TV PREMIERE: ANNIVERSARY. Oct 27, 1954. This highly successful and long-running show has appeared on different networks under different names but has always been essentially the same show. It was the first prime-time anthology series for kids and was originally titled "Disneyland" to promote the park and upcoming Disney releases. Presentations include Disney feature films as well as original productions. During the early era, the popular Davy Crockett segments were considered to be the first TV miniseries. The show ran on ABC until 1961, when it moved to NBC and ran for another 20 years, until 1981. It appeared on several different networks throughout the 1980s, but was finally cancelled by NBC in 1991. It was revived once again by ABC in 1997 as "The Wonderful World of Disney," and continues to air in its traditional weekend time slot.

BIRTHDAYS TODAY

Brad Radke, 33, baseball player, born Eau Claire, WI, Oct 27, 1972.

OCTOBER 28 — FRIDAY

Day 301 — 64 Remaining

CZECH REPUBLIC: FOUNDATION OF THE REPUBLIC. Oct 28, 1918. National Day, anniversary of the bloodless revolution in Prague, after which the Czechs and Slovaks united to form Czechoslovakia (a union they dissolved without bloodshed in 1993).

GREECE: "OCHI DAY." Oct 28. National holiday commemorating Greek resistance and refusal to open its borders when Mussolini's Italian troops attacked Greece in 1940. "Ochi" means no! Celebrated with military parades, especially at Athens and Thessaloniki.

SAINT JUDE'S DAY. Oct 28. St. Jude, the saint of hopeless causes, was martyred along with St. Simon at Persia, and their feast is celebrated jointly. St. Jude was supposedly the brother of Jesus, and, like his brother, a carpenter by trade. He is most popular with those who attempt the impossible and with students, who often ask for his help on exams.

SALK, JONAS: BIRTH ANNIVERSARY. Oct 28, 1914. Dr. Jonas Salk, developer of the Salk polio vaccine, was born at New York, NY. Salk announced his development of a successful vaccine in 1953, the year after a polio epidemic claimed some 3,300 lives in the US. Polio deaths were reduced by 95 percent after the introduction of the vaccine. Salk spent the last 10 years of his life doing AIDS research. He died June 23, 1995, at La Jolla, CA.

SPACE MILESTONE: INTERNATIONAL SPACE RESCUE AGREEMENT: 35th ANNIVERSARY. Oct 28, 1970. US and USSR officials agreed upon space rescue cooperation.

STATUE OF LIBERTY: DEDICATION ANNIVERSARY. Oct 28, 1886. Frederic Auguste Bartholdi's famous sculpture, the statue of *Liberty Enlightening the World*, on Bedloe's Island at New York Harbor, was dedicated. Ground breaking for the structure was in April 1883. A sonnet by Emma Lazarus, inside the pedestal of the statue, contains the words: "Give me your tired, your poor, your huddled masses yearning to breathe free, the wretched refuse of your teeming shore. Send these, the homeless, tempest-tost to me, I lift my lamp beside the golden door!" For more info: *Liberty*, by Lynn Curlee (Atheneum, 0-68-982823-3, $18 Gr. 2–7) or visit the National Parks Service website at www.nps.gov/stli/index.htm. The September 2001 issue of *Appleseeds* magazine (for Gr. 2–4) is devoted to the Statue of Liberty.

★ ★ ★

TEXAS BOOK FESTIVAL. Oct 28–30. State Capitol and Capitol Extension, Austin, TX. 10th annual fair benefiting the public libraries of Texas. More than 150 authors will give readings, participate in panel discussions and sign books. Outdoor book fair with displays by publishers and booksellers. Free. Est attendance: 30,000. For info: Texas Book Festival, 610 Brazos St, Ste 200, Austin, TX 78701. Phone: (512) 477-4055. Fax: (512) 322-0722.

BIRTHDAYS TODAY

Carolyn Coman, 54, author (*What Jamie Saw, Many Stones*), born Evanston, IL, Oct 28, 1951.

Terrell Davis, 33, football player, born San Diego, CA, Oct 28, 1972.

Bill Gates, 50, computer software executive (Microsoft), born Seattle, WA, Oct 28, 1955.

Julia Roberts, 38, actress (Oscar for *Erin Brockovich; My Best Friend's Wedding*), born Smyrna, GA, Oct 28, 1967.

OCTOBER 29 — SATURDAY

Day 302 — 63 Remaining

CANADIAN CHILDREN'S BOOK WEEK. Oct 29–Nov 5 (tentative). Every fall, thousands of children and adults participate in Book Week activities held across Canada: in schools, in public libraries, in bookstores, in community centers—anywhere there are people who care about children and the books they read. Sponsored by the Canadian Children's Book Centre, information about programs and about author appearances can be found on its website. For info: Canadian Children's Book Centre, Ste 101, 40 Orchard View Blvd, Canada. Phone: (416) 975-0010. Fax: (416) 975-8970. E-mail: info@bookcentre.ca. Web: www.bookweek.ca or www.bookcentre.ca.

CHILDREN'S LITERATURE FESTIVAL. Oct 29. Keene State College, Keene, NH. 29th anniversary in 2005. To promote the reading, studying and use of children's literature. Speakers for the festival have included Tomie dePaola, Trina Schart Hyman, Jane Yolen, Patricia and Fredrick McKissack, Patricia MacLachlan and David Shannon. For info: Dr. David E. White, Festival Dir, Keene State College, 229 Main St, Keene, NH 03435. Phone: (603) 358-2302. E-mail: dwhite@keene.edu. Web: www.keene.edu/clf.

EMMETT, DANIEL DECATUR: BIRTH ANNIVERSARY. Oct 29, 1815. Creator of words and music for the song "Dixie," which became a fighting song for Confederate troops and the unofficial "national anthem" of the South. Emmett was born at Mount Vernon, OH, and died there June 28, 1904.

INTERNET CREATED: ANNIVERSARY. Oct 29, 1969. The first connection on what would become the Internet was made on this day when bits of data flowed between computers at UCLA and the Stanford Research Institute. This was the beginning of Arpanet, the precurser to the Internet developed by the Department of Defense. By the end of 1969, four sites were connected: UCLA, the Stanford Research Institute, the University of California, Santa Barbara and the University of Utah. By the next year there were 10 sites and soon there were applications like e-mail and file transfer utilities. The @ symbol was adopted in 1972 and a year later 75 percent of Arpanet traffic was e-mail. Arpanet was decommissioned in 1990 and the National Science Foundation's NSFnet took over the role of backbone of the Internet.

October 2005

S	M	T	W	T	F	S
						1
2	3	4	5	6	7	8
9	10	11	12	13	14	15
16	17	18	19	20	21	22
23	24	25	26	27	28	29
30	31					

RALEIGH, SIR WALTER: DEATH ANNIVERSARY. Oct 29, 1618. Soldier, colonizer and writer, born about 1552 at Hayes Barton, South Devon, England. After 1581 he spelled his name Ralegh. A favorite of Queen Elizabeth I, he sent colonists to North Carolina who brought back tobacco and the potato, which he popularized in Britain. In 1595 and 1617, he went to South America and gathered stories about gold mines. He fell out of favor with Elizabeth's successor, James I, and was beheaded in 1618. For more info: *Sir Walter Ralegh and the Quest for El Dorado*, by Marc Aronson (Houghton Mifflin, 0-395-84827-X, $20 Gr. 7 & up).

SPACE MILESTONE: *DISCOVERY* (US): OLDEST MAN IN SPACE. Oct 29, 1998. Former astronaut and senator John Glenn became the oldest man in space when he traveled on the shuttle *Discovery* at the age of 77. In 1962 on *Friendship 7* he had been the first American to orbit Earth. See also: "Space Milestone: *Friendship 7*" (Feb 20). For more info: *John Glenn's Return to Space*, by Greg Vogt (Twenty-First Century, 0-7613-1614-0, $22.90 Gr. 4–7).

STOCK MARKET CRASH: ANNIVERSARY. Oct 29, 1929. Prices on the New York Stock Exchange plummeted and virtually collapsed four days after President Herbert Hoover had declared, "The fundamental business of the country . . . is on a sound and prosperous basis." More than 16 million shares were dumped and billions of dollars were lost. The boom was over and the nation faced nearly a decade of depression. Some analysts had warned that the buying spree, with prices 15 to 150 times above earnings, had to stop at some point. Frightened investors ordered their brokers to sell at whatever price. The resulting Great Depression, which lasted till about 1939, involved North America, Europe and other industrialized countries. In 1932 one out of four US workers was unemployed. For more info: *Black Tuesday: The Stock Market Crash of 1929*, by Barbara Silberdick Feinberg (Millbrook, 1-5629-4574-2, $24.90 Gr. 4–7).

TURKEY: REPUBLIC DAY. Oct 29. Anniversary of the founding of the republic in 1923.

BIRTHDAYS TODAY

Amanda Beard, 24, Olympic swimmer, born Irvine, CA, Oct 29, 1981.

Rhonda Gowler Greene, 50, author (*Barnyard Song*), born Salem, IL, Oct 29, 1955.

Dirk Kempthorne, 54, Governor of Idaho (R), born San Diego, CA, Oct 29, 1951.

Denis Potvin, 52, Hall of Fame hockey player, born Ottawa, ON, Canada, Oct 29, 1953.

OCTOBER 30 — SUNDAY

Day 303 — 62 Remaining

ADAMS, JOHN: BIRTH ANNIVERSARY. Oct 30, 1735. First vice president and second president of the US (Mar 4, 1797–Mar 3, 1801), born at Braintree, MA. Adams had been George Washington's vice president. He once wrote in a letter to Thomas Jefferson: "You and I ought not to die before we have explained ourselves to each other." John Adams and Thomas Jefferson died on the same day, July 4, 1826, the 50th anniversary of adoption of the Declaration of Independence. Adams's last words: "Thomas Jefferson still survives." Jefferson's last words: "Is it the fourth?" Adams was the father of John Quincy Adams (sixth president of the US). For more info: www.ipl.org/ref/POTUS.

DAYLIGHT SAVING TIME ENDS; STANDARD TIME RESUMES. Oct 30–Apr 2, 2006. Standard Time resumes at 2 AM on the last Sunday in October in each time zone, as provided by the Uniform Time Act of 1966 (as amended in 1986 by Public Law 99–359). Many use the popular rule: "spring forward, fall back" to remember which way to turn their clocks.

DEVIL'S NIGHT. Oct 30. Formerly a "Mischief Night" on the evening before Halloween and an occasion for harmless pranks, chiefly observed by children. However, in some areas of the US, the destruction of property and endangering of lives has led to the imposition of dusk-to-dawn curfews during the last two or three days of October. Not to be confused with "Trick or Treat" or "Beggar's Night," usually observed on Halloween. See also: "Hallowe'en" (Oct 31).

DOLPHINS SHIELD SWIMMERS FROM GREAT WHITE SHARK: ANNIVERSARY. Oct 30, 2004. As four people swam in the ocean off Whangarei, New Zealand, a pod of seven dolphins began aggressively herding them into a tight group. The swimmers discovered that a 10-foot great white shark was about 6 feet away and that the dolphins were protecting them—going so far as to slap the water with their tails to keep the humans within the protective ring. A report in Whangarei's *Northern Advocate* said that the humans stayed in the ring for 40 minutes before the danger was gone.

NATIONAL STORYTELLER OF THE YEAR CONTEST. Oct 30. Millersport, OH. Official Storyteller of the Year named at this event. Sponsored by the Creative Arts Institute, Inc and the Columbus Storytelling Guild. Est attendance: 2,000. For info: Donna Foster, Creative Arts, 8021 Kennedy Rd, Blacklick, OH 43004. Phone: (614) 759-9407. Fax: (614) 759-8480. E-mail: curtcain@ohiohills.com.

POST, EMILY: BIRTH ANNIVERSARY. Oct 30, 1872. Emily Post was born at Baltimore, MD. Published in 1922, her book *Etiquette: The Blue Book of Social Usage* instantly became the American bible of manners and social behavior and established Post as the household name in matters of etiquette. It was in its 10th edition at the time of her death Sept 25, 1960, at New York, NY. *Etiquette* inspired a great many letters asking Post for advice on manners in specific situations. She used these letters as the basis for her radio show and for her syndicated newspaper column, which eventually appeared in more than 200 papers.

BIRTHDAYS TODAY

Eric A. Kimmel, 59, author (*Hershel and the Hanukkah Goblins, Anansi and the Talking Melon*), born Brooklyn, NY, Oct 30, 1946.

Diego Maradona, 45, former soccer player, born Lanus, Argentina, Oct 30, 1960.

OCTOBER 31 — MONDAY

Day 304 — 61 Remaining

FIRST BLACK PLAYS IN NBA GAME: 55th ANNIVERSARY. Oct 31, 1950. Earl Lloyd became the first black ever to play in an NBA game when he took the floor for the Washington Capitols at Rochester, NY. Lloyd was actually one of three blacks to become NBA players in the 1950 season, the others being Nat "Sweetwater" Clifton, who was signed by the New York Knicks, and Chuck Cooper, who was drafted by the Boston Celtics (and debuted the night after Lloyd).

HALLOWE'EN or ALL HALLOW'S EVE. Oct 31. An ancient celebration combining Druid autumn festival and Christian customs. Hallowe'en (All Hallow's Eve) is the beginning of Hallowtide, a season that embraces the Feast of All Saints (Nov 1) and the Feast of All Souls (Nov 2). The observance, dating from the sixth or seventh centuries, has long been associated with

OCTOBER 31
GREAT HALLOWEEN READ-ALOUDS!

Are you ready to turn your classroom into a spooky storytelling center? Play with the lighting in your classroom—how dark can you make it while still being able to see the text (and keep things safe for your students)? Can you use flashlights to add to the spookiness? Tissue paper around a flashlight in the middle of your classroom rug can become a pretend campfire, around which to tell spine-tingling tales of Halloween night!

Of course, there will always be the weak-of-heart amongst your students, so consider starting with the tamest of titles. *Halloween Bugs* by David Carter (Simon & Schuster, 0-689-85916-3, $10.95 Ages 3–7) is a classic pop-up book with a different surprise on each page. As you open each door, a different creepy-crawly comes out. Also try Jack Prelutsky's poetry collection *It's Halloween,* illustrated by Marilyn Hafner (William Morrow, 0-688-14733-X, $5.95 Ages 5–8). Perfect for beginning readers and not too scary.

If you need to explore the theme of cooperation in your class, *Big Pumpkin* by Erica Silverman, illustrated by S.D. Schindler (Simon & Schuster, 0-689-80129-7, $6.99 Ages 4–7), might help. Maybe your students can help figure out the best way for the witch to get her pumpkin made into a pie before the bat does.

Some silly titles will help keep the mood from getting too scary too soon; *Shake Dem Halloween Bones* by W. Nikola-Lisa, illustrated by Mike Reed (Houghton Mifflin, 0-618-07034-6, $6.95 Ages 4–8), will have your students stomping and giggling as the fairy tale characters arrive for the hip-hop Halloween ball.

Moving into slightly spooky realm, *The Little Old Lady Who Was Not Afraid of Anything* by Linda Williams, illustrated by Megan Lloyd (HarperCollins, 0-06-443183-5, $5.99 Ages 4–7), will have your students chanting along with the "CLOMP, CLOMPS" and "WIGGLE WIGGLES," and *Scary, Scary Halloween* by Eve Bunting, illustrated by Jan Brett (Houghton Mifflin, 0-8991-9799-X, $5.95 Ages 5–8), will have them whispering, "It must be Halloween . . . ."

Now if you're ready to REALLY scare some kids, Alvin Schwartz's classic *Scary Stories To Tell in the Dark* and two sequels are packaged together in a three-volume set (HarperCollins, 0-06-440465-X, $17.97 Ages 9–12). These collections of short stories, poems and songs are among some of the best ghost stories every collected for kids. How much creepiness can your class take? —Kathryn Keil thoughts of the dead, spirits, witches, ghosts and devils. In fact, the ancient Celtic Feast of Samhain, the festival that marked the beginning of winter and of the New Year, was observed Nov 1. See also: "Trick or Treat or Beggar's Night" (Oct 31). For more info: *Halloween Program Sourcebook*, edited by Sue Ellen Thompson (Omnigraphics, 0-7808-0388-4, $48 All ages). ***See Curriculum Connection.***

LOW, JULIET GORDON: BIRTH ANNIVERSARY. Oct 31, 1860. Founded Girl Scouts of the USA Mar 12, 1912, at Savannah, GA. Born at Savannah, she died there Jan 17, 1927.

MOUNT RUSHMORE COMPLETION: ANNIVERSARY. Oct 31, 1941. The Mount Rushmore National Memorial was completed after 14 years of work. First suggested by Jonah Robinson of the South Dakota State Historical Society, the memorial was dedicated in 1925, and work began in 1927. The memorial contains sculptures of the heads of Presidents George Washington, Thomas Jefferson, Abraham Lincoln and Theodore Roosevelt. The 60-foot-tall sculptures represent, respectively, the nation's founding, political philosophy, preservation, and expansion and conservation. For more info: www.nps.gov/moru.

NATIONAL MAGIC DAY. Oct 31. Traditionally observed on the anniversary of the death of Harry Houdini in 1926.

NEVADA: ADMISSION DAY: ANNIVERSARY. Oct 31. Became 36th state in 1864. Observed as a holiday in Nevada.

PACA, WILLIAM: BIRTH ANNIVERSARY. Oct 31, 1740. Signer of the Declaration of Independence. Born at Abingdon, MD, he died Oct 13, 1799, at Talbot County, MD.

REFORMATION DAY: ANNIVERSARY. Oct 31, 1517. Anniversary of the day on which Martin Luther nailed his 95 theses to the door of Wittenberg's Palace church, denouncing the selling of papal indulgences—the beginning of the Reformation in Germany. Observed by many Protestant churches as Reformation Sunday, on this day if it is a Sunday or on the Sunday before Oct 31 if it is not.

TAIWAN: CHIANG KAI-SHEK DAY. Oct 31. National holiday to honor memory of Generalissimo Chiang Kai-Shek, the first constitutional president of the Republic of China, born on this day in 1887.

TAYLOR, SYDNEY: BIRTH ANNIVERSARY. Oct 31, 1904. Born at New York, NY, Sydney Taylor was an actress and professional dancer with the Martha Graham Dance Company. She also wrote, choreographed and directed original plays in addition to writing books for children. Her beloved *All-of-a-Kind Family* (1951) was based on her own experiences growing up on the Lower East Side of Manhattan in the early 1900s. This unique book about a loving Jewish family was honored by the Jewish Book Council and the Association of Jewish Libraries. Sequels included *All-of-a-Kind Family Downtown* and *Ella of All-of-a-Kind Family*. She died Feb 12, 1978, at Queens, NY.

TRICK OR TREAT or BEGGAR'S NIGHT. Oct 31. A popular custom on Hallowe'en, in which children wearing costumes visit neighbors' homes, calling out "Trick or Treat" and "begging" for candies or gifts to place in their beggars' bags. Some children Trick or Treat for UNICEF, collecting money for this organization. For more info, go to www.unicef.org. In recent years there has been increased participation by adults, often parading in elaborate or outrageous costumes and also requesting candy.

BIRTHDAYS TODAY

Katherine Paterson, 73, author (Newbery for *The Bridge to Terabithia, Jacob Have I Loved*), born Qing Jiang, China, Oct 31, 1932.

Jane Pauley, 55, TV journalist ("Dateline"), born Indianapolis, IN, Oct 31, 1950.

Dan Rather, 74, journalist, anchor ("CBS Evening News"), born Wharton, TX, Oct 31, 1931.

Adrienne Richard, 84, author (*Pistol*), born Evanston, IL, Oct 31, 1921.

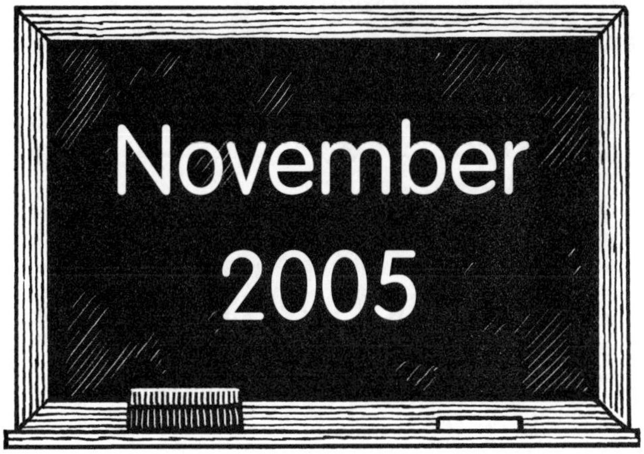

NOVEMBER 1 — TUESDAY

Day 305 — 60 Remaining

ALGERIA: REVOLUTION ANNIVERSARY. Nov 1. National holiday commemorating the revolution against France in 1954.

ALL HALLOWS or ALL SAINTS' DAY. Nov 1. Roman Catholic Holy Day of Obligation. Commemorates the blessed, especially those who have no special feast days. Observed Nov 1 since Pope Gregory IV set the date of recognition in 835. All Saints' Day is a legal holiday in Louisiana. Halloween is the evening before All Hallows Day.

ANTIGUA AND BARBUDA: NATIONAL HOLIDAY. Nov 1. Commemorates independence from Britain in 1981.

AVIATION HISTORY MONTH. Nov 1–30. Anniversary of aeronautical experiments in November 1782 (exact dates unknown), by Joseph Michel Montgolfier and Jacques Etienne Montgolfier, brothers living at Annonay, France. Inspired by Joseph Priestley's book *Experiments Relating to the Different Kinds of Air*, the brothers experimented with filling paper and fabric bags with smoke and hot air, leading to the invention of the hot-air balloon, man's first flight and the entire science of aviation and flight.

GUATEMALA: KITE FESTIVAL OF SANTIAGO SACATEPEQUEZ. Nov 1. Long ago, when evil spirits disturbed the good spirits in the local cemetery, a magician told the townspeople a secret way to get rid of the evil spirits—by flying kites (because the evil spirits were frightened by the noise of wind against paper). Since then, the kite festival has been held at the cemetery each year Nov 1, and it is said that "to this day no one knows of bad spirits roaming the streets or the cemetery of Santiago Sacatepequez," a village about 20 miles from Guatemala City. Nowadays, the youth of the village work for many weeks to make the elaborate and giant kites to fly on All Saints' Day (Nov 1) or All Souls' Day (Nov 2).

HOCKEY MASK INVENTED: ANNIVERSARY. Nov 1, 1959. Tired of stopping hockey pucks with his face, Montreal Canadiens goalie Jacques Plante, having received another wound, reemerged from the locker room with seven new stitches—and a plastic face mask he had made from fiberglass and resin. Although Cliff Benedict had tried a leather mask back in the '20s, the idea didn't catch on, but after Plante wore his, goalies throughout the NHL began wearing protective plastic face shields.

INDIA: DIWALI (DEEPAVALI). Nov 1. Diwali (or Divali), the five-day festival of lights, is the prettiest of all Indian festivals. It celebrates the victory of Lord Rama over the demon king Ravana. Thousands of flickering lights illuminate houses and transform urban landscapes while fireworks add color and noise. The goddess of wealth, Lakshmi, is worshipped in Hindu homes on Diwali. Houses are whitewashed and cleaned and elaborate designs drawn on thresholds with colored powder to welcome the fastidious goddess. Because there is no one universally accepted Hindu calendar, this holiday may be celebrated on a different date in some parts of India but it always falls in the months of October or November. For more info: *Divali*, by Dilip Kadodwala (Raintree, 0-8172-4616-9, $22.11 Gr. 4–6).

INTERNATIONAL DRUM MONTH. Nov 1–30. 14th annual celebration of the worldwide popularity of all types of drums. Annually, the month of November. For info: Percussion Mktg Council, PO Box 33252, Cleveland, OH 44133. Phone: (440) 582-7006. E-mail: kbdustman@aol.com. Web: www.playdrums.com.

MEDICAL SCHOOL FOR WOMEN OPENED AT BOSTON: ANNIVERSARY. Nov 1, 1848. Founded by Samuel Gregory, a pioneer in medical education for women, the Boston Female Medical School opened as the first medical school exclusively for women. The original enrollment was 12 students. In 1874, the school merged with the Boston University School of Medicine and formed one of the first coed medical schools in the world.

MERLIN'S SNUG HUGS FOR KIDS. Nov 1–Dec 17. Each community is encouraged to provide new winter outerwear for foster and needy children. Event runs for six weeks and includes the Crochet and Knit-A-Thon, and on the final day (Dec 17), Merlin's caravan collects the new winter clothes and delivers them to Children's Home & Aid Society of Illinois. Sponsor: Merlin's Muffler & Brake. Annually, the first week of November through the third week of December. For info: Kathleen Quinn, ProQuest/2020, PO Box 2373, Glenview, IL 60025-2373. Phone: (847) 998-9950. Fax: (847) 998-9945. Web: www.merlins.com.

MEXICO: DAY OF THE DEAD. Nov 1–2. Observance begins during last days of October when "Dead Men's Bread" is sold in bakeries—round loaves, decorated with sugar skulls. Departed souls are remembered not with mourning but with a spirit of friendliness and good humor. Cemeteries are visited and graves are decorated. ***See Curriculum Connection.***

MOON PHASE: NEW MOON. Nov 1. Moon enters New Moon phase at 8:24 PM, EST.

★**NATIONAL ADOPTION MONTH.** Nov 1–30.

★**NATIONAL ALZHEIMER'S DISEASE MONTH.** Nov 1–30. To increase awareness of Alzheimer's disease and what is being done to advance research and help patients, their families and their caregivers.

★**NATIONAL AMERICAN INDIAN HERITAGE MONTH.** Nov 1–30.

NATIONAL AUTHORS' DAY. Nov 1. This observance was adopted by the General Federation of Women's Clubs in 1929 and in 1949 was given a place on the list of special days, weeks and months prepared by the US Dept of Commerce. The resolution states: "by celebrating an Authors' Day as a nation, we would not only show patriotism, loyalty, and appreciation of the men and women who have made American literature possible, but would also encourage and inspire others to give of themselves in making a better America. . . ." It was also resolved "that we commemorate an Authors' Day to be observed on November First each year."

★**NATIONAL DIABETES MONTH.** Nov 1–30.

★**NATIONAL FAMILY CAREGIVERS MONTH.** Nov 1–30. To honor family members who care for aging relatives or those with disabilities.

NATIONAL FAMILY LITERACY DAY®. Nov 1. Celebrated all over the country with special activities and events that showcase the importance of family literacy programs. These programs bring parents and children together in the classroom to learn and support each other in efforts to further their education and improve their life skills. Sponsored by the National Center for Family Literacy and Toyota. Annually, Nov 1. For info: National Center for Family Literacy, 325 W Main St, Ste 300, Louisville, KY 40202. Phone: (502) 584-1133 or (877) FAMLIT 1. Fax: (502) 584-0172. E-mail: ncfl@famlit.org. Web: www.famlit.org.

NATIONAL YOUTH MONTH. Nov 1–30. A monthlong effort to increase public awareness about the problems of birth defects and infant mortality. For info: March of Dimes, 1275 Mamaroneck Ave, White Plains, NY 10605. Phone: (914) 997-4600. Web: www.marchofdimes.com.

PEANUT BUTTER LOVERS' MONTH. Nov 1–30. Celebration of America's favorite food and #1 sandwich. For info: Peanut Advisory Board, 1025 Sugar Pike Way, Canton, GA 30115. Web: www.peanutbutterlovers.com.

PRESIDENT FIRST OCCUPIES THE WHITE HOUSE: ANNIVERSARY. Nov 1, 1800. The federal government had been located at Philadelphia from 1790 until 1800. On Nov 1, 1800, President John Adams and his family moved into the newly completed White House at Washington, DC, the nation's new capital. To take a virtual tour of the White House, go to: www.whitehouse.gov.

PRIME MERIDIAN SET: ANNIVERSARY. Nov 1, 1884. Delegates from 25 nations met in October 1884, at Washington, DC, at the International Meridian Conference to set up time zones for the world. On this day the treaty adopted by the Conference took effect, making Greenwich, England, the Prime Meridian (i.e., zero longitude) and setting the International Date Line at 180° longitude in the Pacific. Every 15° of longitude equals one hour and there are 24 meridians. While some countries do not strictly observe this system (for example, while China stretches over five time zones, it is the same time everywhere in China), it has brought predictability and logic to time throughout the world.

US VIRGIN ISLANDS: LIBERTY DAY. Nov 1. Officially "D. Hamilton Jackson Memorial Day," commemorating establishment of the first press in the Virgin Islands in 1915.

WORLD COMMUNICATION WEEK. Nov 1–7. To stress the importance of communication among the more than five billion human beings in the world who speak more than 3,000 languages and to promote communication by means of the international language Esperanto. For complete info, send $5 to cover expense of printing, handling and postage. Annually, the first seven days of November. For info: Dr. Stanley Drake, Pres, Intl Society of Friendship and Goodwill, 8592 Roswell Rd, Ste 251, Atlanta, GA 30350-1867. Phone: (678) 795-1362. Web: www.friendshipandgoodwill.org.

November 2005

S	M	T	W	T	F	S
		1	2	3	4	5
6	7	8	9	10	11	12
13	14	15	16	17	18	19
20	21	22	23	24	25	26
27	28	29	30			

BIRTHDAYS TODAY

Hilary Knight, 79, illustrator (Eloise series), born Hempstead, Long Island, NY, Nov 1, 1926.

Nicholasa Mohr, 67, author (*The Magic Shell/El Regalo Mágico, Nilda*), born New York, NY, Nov 1, 1938.

Tim Pawlenty, 45, Governor of Minnesota (R), born St. Paul, MN, Nov 1, 1960.

Fernando Anguamea Valenzuela, 45, former baseball player, born Navojoa, Sonora, Mexico, Nov 1, 1960.

NOVEMBER 2 — WEDNESDAY

Day 306 — 59 Remaining

ALL SOULS' DAY. Nov 2. Commemorates the faithful departed. Catholic observance.

BOONE, DANIEL: BIRTH ANNIVERSARY. Nov 2, 1734. American frontiersman, explorer and militia officer, born at Berks County, near Reading, PA. In February 1778, he was captured at Blue Licks, KY, by Shawnee Indians, under Chief Blackfish, who adopted Boone when he was inducted into the tribe as "Big Turtle." Boone escaped after five months, and in 1781 was captured briefly by the British. He experienced a series of personal and financial disasters during his life but continued a rugged existence, hunting until his 80s. Boone died at St. Charles County, MO, Sept 26, 1820. The bodies of Daniel Boone and his wife, Rebecca, were moved to Frankfort, KY, in 1845.

FIRST SCHEDULED RADIO BROADCAST: 85th ANNIVERSARY. Nov 2, 1920. Station KDKA at Pittsburgh, PA, broadcast the results of the presidential election. The station received its license to broadcast Nov 7, 1921. By 1922 there were about 400 licensed radio stations in the US.

HARDING, WARREN GAMALIEL: BIRTH ANNIVERSARY. Nov 2, 1865. The 29th president of the US was born at Corsica, OH. His term of office: Mar 4, 1921–Aug 2, 1923 (died in office). His undistinguished administration was tainted by the Teapot Dome scandal. He died suddenly while on a western speaking tour at San Francisco, CA, Aug 2, 1923. For more info: www.ipl.org/ref/POTUS.

NORTH DAKOTA: ADMISSION DAY: ANNIVERSARY. Nov 2. Became 39th state in 1889.

POLK, JAMES KNOX: BIRTH ANNIVERSARY. Nov 2, 1795. The 11th president of the US (Mar 4, 1845–Mar 3, 1849) was born at Mecklenburg County, NC. A compromise candidate at the 1844 Democratic Party convention, Polk was awarded the nomination on the ninth ballot. He declined to be a candidate for a second term and declared himself to be "exceedingly relieved" at the completion of his presidency. He died shortly thereafter at Nashville, TN, June 15, 1849. For more info: www.ipl.org/ref/POTUS.

SOUTH DAKOTA: ADMISSION DAY: ANNIVERSARY. Nov 2. Became 40th state in 1889.

SPACE MILESTONE: INTERNATIONAL SPACE STATION INHABITED: 5th ANNIVERSARY. Nov 2, 2000. On Oct 31, 2000, a *Soyuz* shuttle left with the first crew to live in the International Space Station, American commander Bill Shepherd and two Russians, Yuri Gidzenko and Sergei Krikalev. The flight left from the same site in Central Asia where *Sputnik* was launched in 1957, beginning the Space Age, and arrived at the International Space Station (ISS) on Nov 2. The astronauts stayed on board the ISS until March 2001, when they were replaced by a crew that arrived on the shuttle *Discovery*. The ISS has no formal name but has been nicknamed *Alpha* by its crew. It orbits the Earth every 90 minutes at an altitude of 230 miles. Sixteen nations are par-

NOVEMBER 2
DAY OF THE DEAD

Cultures around the world have traditional remembrances of loved ones, but nowhere is the celebration so colorful and festive as during the Mexican holiday Día de los Muertos, or Day of the Dead. Mexicans are not afraid about getting close up and personal with death. La Muerte, Death, is also commonly known by several teasing and endearing nicknames: La Catrina (Fancy Lady), La Flaca (Skinny), La Huesuda (Boney) and La Pelona (Baldie). The celebration is not morbid or scary like the manner in which many Americans celebrate Halloween around the same time of the year. The Day of the Dead is a joyful remembrance of the dead and a celebration of the continuity of life.

Before the conquest of Mexico in the 16th century, the native people honored children and the departed during the Aztec month of Miccailhuitontli, which was presided over by one of the Aztec gods, Mictecacihuatl, the Lady of the Dead. While the Aztec celebration fell in July or August, after the conquest, Spanish priests moved the holiday so that it coincided with the Catholic holidays of All Saints' Day (Nov 1) and All Souls' Day (Nov 2). In present-day Mexico, the first day of remembrance is for children who have died—Día de los Angelitos, or Day of the Little Angels (Nov 1). The second day—Day of the Dead—is for honoring deceased adults.

During the celebration of Day of the Dead, Mexicans first welcome the dead back into their homes by making altars decorated with big colorful flowers, photos, candles and offerings of special foods, especially the favorite food and drinks of departed loved ones. Then the families visit the graves of relatives, cutting weeds and painting the tombs bright colors. They decorate the burial sites with candles, wreaths and colorful flowers like marigolds. On the Day of the Dead, families spend time in the cemeteries, which become the sites of lively reunions, picnics, socializing and story telling about loved ones. A great story book with beautiful illustrations is *Day of the Dead* by Tony Johnson (Voyager Books, 0-15-202446-8, $6 Ages 5–9).

Like any traditional celebration, there are specific foods and decorations associated with the Day of the Dead. The most common is pan de los muertos (bread of the dead), which is a delicious, sweet, egg-batter bread. It is often shaped into the form of a bone, or a small plastic skeleton is baked inside, giving luck to the person who receives that piece. Special chocolates and sugar candies are also made to resemble skeletons and bones. Typical recipes can be found online at http://yumfood.net/articles/diadelosmuertos.html.

A common decoration during the Day of the Dead are handmade banners fashioned from intricately cut tissue paper. This art is called *papel picado* (punched paper), and has roots in the Aztec culture. The tissue paper is folded and then cut, like the process of making paper snowflakes. Designs include flowers, angels, crosses, birds and skeletons. The paper designs are then glued side by side and strung like streamers. Colors traditionally used for the Day of the Dead festivities are vibrant pink, orange and purple. For simple step-by-step instructions, visit www.dltk-kids.com/world/mexico/mpapel_picado.htm. A fascinating book that features interviews with artisans is *The Skeleton at the Feast: The Day of the Dead in Mexico,* by Elizabeth Carmichael and Chloe Sayer (University of Texas Press, 0-292-77658-6, $34.95 Adult).

While it is enjoyable for children to learn the foods and crafts of this Mexican holiday, perhaps the activity most in the true spirit of the Day of the Dead would be for students to learn about a departed family member. They could research an oral history project, asking a grandmother or grandfather about their great-grandparents, for example. This is the core of the celebration: listening to stories, visiting resting sites, learning about family and heritage, remembering the past and finding links to the present. —Adrienne van den Beemt

ticipating in the ISS project. The construction of the station will be completed in 2006. See also: "Space Milestone: International Space Station Launch" (Dec 4).

BIRTHDAYS TODAY

Jeannie Baker, 55, author and illustrator (*Where the Forest Meets the Sea*), born Nov 2, 1950.

Danny Cooksey, 30, actor ("Pepper Ann," *The Little Mermaid*), born Moore, OK, Nov 2, 1975.

Natalie Kinsey-Warnock, 49, author (*The Canada Geese Quilt, The Night the Bells Rang*), born Vermont, Nov 2, 1956.

Fran Manushkin, 63, author (*Miriam's Cup*), born Chicago, IL, Nov 2, 1942.

NOVEMBER 3 — THURSDAY

Day 307 — 58 Remaining

AUSTIN, STEPHEN FULLER: BIRTH ANNIVERSARY. Nov 3, 1793. A principal founder of Texas, for whom its capital city was named, Austin was born at Wythe County, VA. He first visited Texas in 1821 and established a settlement there the following year, continuing a colonization project started by his father, Moses Austin. Thrown in prison when he advocated formation of a separate state (Texas still belonged to Mexico), he was freed in 1835, lost a campaign for the presidency (of the Republic of Texas) to Sam Houston in 1836, and died (while serving as Texas secretary of state) at Austin, TX, Dec 27, 1836.

DAVID McCORD CHILDREN'S LITERATURE FESTIVAL. Nov 3. Framingham State College, Framingham, MA. For info: Joan Claflin, 121 Mechanic St, Upton, MA 01568. Phone: (508) 529-3367.

DOMINICA: NATIONAL DAY. Nov 3. National holiday. Commemorates the independence of this Caribbean island from Britain on this day in 1978.

JAPAN: CULTURE DAY. Nov 3. National holiday.

LIBERIA: THANKSGIVING DAY. Nov 3. National holiday on the first Thursday in November.

MICRONESIA: INDEPENDENCE DAY. Nov 3. National holiday commemorating independence from the US in 1986.

NATIONAL MIDDLE SCHOOL ASSOCIATION ANNUAL CONFERENCE. Nov 3–5. Philadelphia, PA. For info: National

Middle School Assn, 4151 Executive Pkway, Ste 300, Westerville, OH 43081. Phone: (614) 895-4730 or (800) 528-NMSA. Web: www.nmsa.org.

PANAMA: INDEPENDENCE DAY: ANNIVERSARY. Nov 3. Panama declared itself independent of Colombia in 1903.

PUBLIC TELEVISION DEBUTS: ANNIVERSARY. Nov 3, 1969. A string of local educational TV channels united on this day under the Public Broadcasting System banner. Today there are 348 PBS stations.

SANDWICH DAY: BIRTH ANNIVERSARY OF JOHN MONTAGUE. Nov 3, 1718. A day to recognize the inventor of the sandwich, John Montague, Fourth Earl of Sandwich, born at London, England. He was England's first lord of the admiralty, secretary of state for the northern department, postmaster general and the man after whom Captain Cook named the Sandwich Islands in 1778. A rake and a gambler, he is said to have invented the sandwich as a time-saving nourishment while engaged in a 24-hour-long gambling session in 1762. He died at London, England, Apr 30, 1792.

SPACE MILESTONE: *SPUTNIK 2* (USSR). Nov 3, 1957. A dog named Laika became the first animal sent into space. Total weight of craft and dog was 1,121 lbs. The satellite was not capable of returning the dog to Earth and she died when her air supply was gone. Nicknamed "Muttnik" by the American press.

WHITE, EDWARD DOUGLASS: BIRTH ANNIVERSARY. Nov 3, 1845. Ninth Chief Justice of the Supreme Court, born at La Fourche Parish, LA. During the Civil War, he served in the Confederate Army after which he returned to New Orleans to practice law. Elected to the US Senate in 1891, he was appointed to the Supreme Court by Grover Cleveland in 1894. He became Chief Justice under President William Taft in 1910 and served until 1921. He died at Washington, DC, May 19, 1921. For more info: oyez .northwestern.edu/justices/justices.cgi.

BIRTHDAYS TODAY

Brent Ashabranner, 84, author (*Our Beckoning Borders: Illegal Immigration to America*), born Shawnee, OK, Nov 3, 1921.

Janell Cannon, 48, author, illustrator (*Stellaluna, Crickwing*), born St. Paul, MN, Nov 3, 1957.

Evgeny Plushenko, 23, Olympic gold medal figure skater, born Vologograd, Russia, Nov 3, 1982.

Roseanne, 52, comedienne, actress ("Roseanne," *She-Devil*), born Roseanne Barr, Salt Lake City, UT, Nov 3, 1953.

November 2005

S	M	T	W	T	F	S
		1	2	3	4	5
6	7	8	9	10	11	12
13	14	15	16	17	18	19
20	21	22	23	24	25	26
27	28	29	30			

NOVEMBER 4 — FRIDAY

Day 308 — 57 Remaining

EID-AL-FITR: CELEBRATING THE FAST. Nov 4. Islamic calendar date: Shawwal 1, 1426. Begins at sunset on the previous day. This feast/festival celebrates having completed the Ramadan fasting (which began Oct 16) and usually lasts for several days. Everyone wears new clothes; children receive gifts from parents and relatives; games, folktales, plays, puppet shows, trips to amusement parks; children are allowed to stay up late. Different methods for "anticipating" the visibility of the new moon crescent at Mecca are used by different Muslim groups. US date may vary. For more info: *Id-ul-Fitr*, by Kerena Marchant (Millbrook, 0-7613-0963-2, $20.90 Gr. K–3). ***See Curriculum Connection.***

ITALY: VICTORY DAY. Nov 4. Commemorates the signing of a WWI treaty by Austria in 1918 which resulted in the transfer of Trentino and Trieste from Austria to Italy.

KING TUT TOMB DISCOVERY: ANNIVERSARY. Nov 4, 1922. One of the most important archaeological discoveries of modern times occurred at Luxor, Egypt, in 1922. It was the tomb of Egypt's child-king, Tutankhamen, who became pharaoh at the age of nine and died, probably in the year 1352 BC, when he was 19. Perhaps the only ancient Egyptian royal tomb to have escaped plundering by grave robbers, it was discovered more than 3,000 years after Tutankhamen's death by English archaeologist Howard Carter, leader of an expedition financed by Lord Carnarvon. The entrance to the tomb was found on this day but the tomb was not entered until later in the month. The priceless relics yielded by King Tut's tomb were placed in Egypt's National Museum at Cairo. For more info: *Illustrated Encyclopedia of Ancient Egypt* by Geraldine Harris and Delia Pemberton (McGraw-Hill, 0-8722-6606-0, $29.95, Gr. 3 & up).

MISCHIEF NIGHT. Nov 4. Observed in England, Australia and New Zealand. Nov 4, the eve of Guy Fawkes Day, is occasion for bonfires and firecrackers to commemorate failure of the plot to blow up the Houses of Parliament Nov 5, 1605. See also: "England: Guy Fawkes Day" (Nov 5).

NORTH, STERLING: BIRTH ANNIVERSARY. Nov 4, 1906. Born at Edgerton, WI, Sterling North graduated from the University of Chicago and had a successful career as a journalist. His novel, *So Dear to My Heart*, published in 1947, was an enormous success and was made into a feature film by Walt Disney in 1949. *Rascal*, an autobiographical story about raising a pet raccoon, was a Newbery Honor Book in 1964 and was also made into a Disney film in 1969. North died Dec 21, 1974, at Morristown, NJ.

PANAMA: FLAG DAY. Nov 4. Public holiday.

UNESCO: ANNIVERSARY. Nov 4, 1946. The United Nations Educational, Scientific and Cultural Organization was formed. For more info: www.unesco.org.

BIRTHDAYS TODAY

Laura Bush, 59, First Lady, wife of George W. Bush, 43rd president of the US, born Laura Welch, Midland, TX, Nov 4, 1946.

Carlos Gutierrez, 52, US Secretary of Commerce, born Havana, Cuba, Nov 4, 1953.

Gail E. Haley, 66, author and illustrator (Caldecott for *A Story, A Story*), born Charlotte, NC, Nov 4, 1939.

Ralph Macchio, 43, actor (*The Karate Kid, The Outsiders*), born Huntington, NY, Nov 4, 1962.

Andrea McArdle, 42, singer, actress (Broadway's original *Annie*), born Philadelphia, PA, Nov 4, 1963.

NOVEMBER 4
EID MUBARAK! BLESSED CELEBRATION!

Eid-al-Fitr is one of the most joyous celebrations in the Muslim year. Observed by about one billion Muslims worldwide, Eid-al-Fitr is a time to celebrate good things, the bounty of God (or Allah, in Arabic) and friends and family. Share this beautiful holiday with your students and help promote understanding and connections among people of all faiths.

Eid-al-Fitr is celebrated for three days following Ramadan, which is a month of daily fasting; adults go without food or drink from dawn till dusk. Ramadan is a time of worship, prayer, reflection and reading from the Qur'an. The 27th night of Ramadan is Lailat ul-Qadr ("The Night of Power"), which commemorates the time that the first verses of the Qur'an were revealed to the prophet Mohammed.

The Muslim calendar is a lunar calendar, and a new month begins with the first sighting of the new crescent moon. Because of the uncertainty related to when the moon will first be spotted, it is not generally known when exactly the celebration will begin. Children especially watch the sky with great anticipation, scanning the heavens for a sliver of moon that will end the month of fasting.

When the crescent moon is finally sighted, it starts off a flurry of action. Callers ascend the minarets of mosques in every neighborhood to spread the word. News spreads through radio, television and cell phones as friends and family call one another to say that the "Night of the Moon" has begun. The shops will be open all night, selling sweets, decorations and clothing. It is a custom that every Muslim wears entirely new clothing on Eid-al-Fitr, and so throngs of people pour into the streets, shopping for festive new clothing, bangles and henna for hand designs.

Any family that does not have the resources to provide new clothing for its members will be looked after and provided for by the community. In fact, during Ramadan, most families pay a small "tax" in food or money so that their less fortunate neighbors can celebrate as well. This tax is not enforced by law, but nearly everyone who can contribute does so in order to share the joy of Eid-al-Fitr.

Eid-al-Fitr lasts for the first three days of the month of Shawwal. On the first morning before dawn, men and boys are called to mosques to pray. So many of them turn out that the prayers need to be held in large, public places like soccer stadiums to accommodate them all. They then return to their homes for the first breakfast since the month before. Eid-al-Fitr means "Festival of Fast-Breaking," and indeed the fast is broken with the biggest meal of the next three days. After a month of fasting, people are so appreciative and thankful for the food provided by God and family.

As the day continues, friends and family visit one another in all their new clothes. Children do not receive gifts; rather, they are given small amounts of money from each and every adult who visits. Special sweets made from milk, sugar and cardamom are sold on the streets, and neighborhoods feel like festivals with people walking from house to house.

There are many wonderful and beautifully illustrated children's books that you can share with your students. *Fasting and Dates: A Ramadan and Eid-ul-Fitr Story* by Jonny Zucker, is written so that first and second graders could read it on their own (Barron's Educational Series, 0-764-12671-7, $6.95). *Magid Fasts for Ramadan* by Mary Matthews, is set in present-day Egypt and follows the story of Magid, a boy who wants to fast even though he isn't old enough (Clarion Books, 0-618-04035-8, $6.95 Ages 4–8). A beautiful photo essay that is perfect for the classroom, *Celebrating Ramadan* by Diane Hoyt-Goldsmith and Lawrence Migdale, follows an American fourth grader through Ramadan (Holiday House, 0-8234-1581-3, $17.95 Ages 9–12). Lastly, to get a feel of the festivals of Ramadan, Eid-al-Fitr, and Eid-al-Adha, read *Three Muslim Festivals* by Ibrahim Ali Aminah and A. Ghazi (Iqar International Educational Foundation, 1-563-16308-X, $8.95). —Adrienne van den Beemt

NOVEMBER 5 — SATURDAY

Day 309 — 56 Remaining

EL SALVADOR: DAY OF THE FIRST SHOUT FOR INDEPENDENCE. Nov 5. National holiday. Commemorates the first Central American battle for independence from Spain in 1811.

ENGLAND: GUY FAWKES DAY. Nov 5. Anniversary of the "Gunpowder Plot." Conspirators planned to blow up the Houses of Parliament and King James I in 1605. Twenty barrels of gunpowder, which they had secreted in a cellar under Parliament, were discovered on the night of Nov 4, the very eve of the intended explosion, and the conspirators were arrested. They were tried and convicted, and Jan 31, 1606, eight (including Guy Fawkes) were beheaded and their heads displayed on pikes at London Bridge. Though there were at least 11 conspirators, Guy Fawkes is most remembered. In 1606, the Parliament, which was to have been annihilated, enacted a law establishing Nov 5 as a day of public thanksgiving. It is still observed, and on the night of Nov 5, the whole country lights up with bonfires and celebration. "Guys" are burned in effigy and the old verses repeated: "Remember, remember the fifth of November/Gunpowder treason and plot;/I see no reason why Gunpowder Treason/Should ever be forgot."

GEORGE W. BUSH AND LAURA BUSH WEDDING: ANNIVERSARY. Nov 5, 1977. George W. Bush and Laura Welch were married at Midland, TX. They have twin daughters, Barbara Pierce Bush and Jenna Welch Bush, born in 1981.

★ ★ ★

MULTICULTURAL CHILDREN'S BOOK FESTIVAL. Nov 5. John F. Kennedy Center for the Performing Arts, Washington, DC. 10th annual. Books come to life in this daylong series of free 30-minute readings celebrating the lives, cultures and stories of the African, African American, Asian, Caribbean, Latino and Native American peoples. Many authors and illustrators will be present and there will be books for sale. For info: John F. Kennedy Center for the Performing Arts, 2700 F St NW, Washington, DC 20566. Phone: (202) 416-8838 or (800) 444-1324. Web: www.kennedy-center.org/programs/specialevents/bookfestival.

SADIE HAWKINS DAY. Nov 5. Widely observed in US, usually on the first Saturday in November. Tradition established in "Li'l Abner" comic strip in 1930s by cartoonist Al Capp. A popular occasion when women and girls are encouraged to take the initiative in inviting the man or boy of their choice for a date. A similar tradition is associated with Feb 29 in leap years.

BIRTHDAYS TODAY

Raymond Bial, 57, author, illustrator (*Amish Home, One-Room School*), born Danville, IL, Nov 5, 1948.

Larry Dane Brimner, 56, author (*A Migrant Family, Snowboarding*), born St. Petersburg, FL, Nov 5, 1949.

Ted Kulongoski, 65, Governor of Oregon (D), born rural Missouri, Nov 5, 1940.

Marcia Sewall, 70, author (*The Pilgrims of Plimoth*), born Providence, RI, Nov 5, 1935.

Jerry Stackhouse, 31, basketball player, born Kinston, NC, Nov 5, 1974.

NOVEMBER 6 — SUNDAY

Day 310 — 55 Remaining

"GOOD MORNING AMERICA" TV PREMIERE: 30th ANNIVERSARY. Nov 6, 1975. This ABC morning program is a mixture of news reports, features and interviews with newsmakers and people of interest. It was the first program to compete with NBC's "Today" show and initially aired as "A.M. America." Hosts have included David Hartman, Nancy Dussault, Sandy Hill, Charles Gibson, Joan Lunden, Lisa McRee, Kevin Newman and Diane Sawyer.

NAISMITH, JAMES: BIRTH ANNIVERSARY. Nov 6, 1861. Inventor of the game of basketball was born at Almonte, ON, Canada. Died at Lawrence, KS, Nov 28, 1939. Basketball became an Olympic sport in 1936.

SAXOPHONE DAY (ADOLPHE SAX BIRTH ANNIVERSARY). Nov 6. A day to recognize the birth anniversary of Adolphe Sax, Belgian musician and inventor of the saxophone and the saxotromba. Born at Dinant, Belgium in 1814, Antoine Joseph Sax, later known as Adolphe, was the eldest of 11 children of a musical instrument builder. Sax contributed an entire family of brass wind instruments for band and orchestra use. He was accorded fame and great wealth, but business misfortunes led to bankruptcy. Sax died in poverty at Paris, Feb 7, 1894.

SOUSA, JOHN PHILIP: BIRTH ANNIVERSARY. Nov 6, 1854. American composer and band conductor, remembered for stirring marches such as "The Stars and Stripes Forever," "Semper Fidelis" and "El Capitan," born at Washington, DC. Died at Reading, PA, Mar 6, 1932. See also: "The Stars and Stripes Forever Day: Anniversary" (May 14).

SWEDEN: GUSTAVUS ADOLPHUS DAY. Nov 6. Honors Sweden's king and military leader killed in 1632.

BIRTHDAYS TODAY

Sally Field, 59, actress (Oscars for *Norma Rae, Places in the Heart*; *Mrs Doubtfire*), born Pasadena, CA, Nov 6, 1946.

Maria Shriver, 50, former broadcast journalist ("Dateline"), author (*What's Heaven?*), born Chicago, IL, Nov 6, 1955.

November 2005

S	M	T	W	T	F	S
		1	2	3	4	5
6	7	8	9	10	11	12
13	14	15	16	17	18	19
20	21	22	23	24	25	26
27	28	29	30			

NOVEMBER 7 — MONDAY

Day 311 — 54 Remaining

BANGLADESH: SOLIDARITY DAY. Nov 7. National holiday. Commemorates a 1975 coup.

CANADIAN PACIFIC RAILWAY: TRANSCONTINENTAL COMPLETION ANNIVERSARY. Nov 7, 1885. At 9:30 AM the last spike was driven at Craigellachie, BC, completing the Canadian Pacific Railway's 2,980-mile transcontinental railroad track between Montreal, QC, in the east and Port Moody, BC, in the west.

CURIE, MARIE SKLODOWSKA: BIRTH ANNIVERSARY. Nov 7, 1867. Polish chemist and physicist, born at Warsaw, Poland. In 1903 she was awarded, with her husband Pierre, the Nobel Prize for physics for their discovery of the element radium. Died near Sallanches, France, July 4, 1934. For more info: *Marie Curie*, by Leonard Everett Fisher (Macmillan, 0-02-735375-3, $14.95 Gr. 3–6).

FIRST BLACK GOVERNOR ELECTED: ANNIVERSARY. Nov 7, 1989. L. Douglas Wilder was elected governor of Virginia, becoming the first elected black governor in US history. Wilder had previously served as lieutenant governor of Virginia.

KEY CLUB INTERNATIONAL WEEK. Nov 7–13. To recognize service projects of more than 180,000 school members. Annually, the first full week of November. For info: Key Club International, 3636 Woodview Trace, Indianapolis, IN 46268-3196. Phone: (317) 875-8755. Fax: (317) 879-0204. E-mail: keyclub@kiwanis.org. Web: www.keyclub.org.

KIDS' GOAL SETTING WEEK. Nov 7–11. Encourage parents to foster goal-setting habits in their children's lives so that their children can make their dreams come true. For info: Gary Ryan Blair, The GoalsGuy, 36181 E Lake Rd, Ste 139, Palm Harbor, FL 34685. Phone: (877) GOALSGUY. Fax: (800) 731-GOAL. E-mail: info@goalsguy.com. Web: www.goalsguy.com.

REPUBLICAN SYMBOL: ANNIVERSARY. Nov 7, 1874. Thomas Nast used an elephant to represent the Republican Party in a satirical cartoon in *Harper's Weekly*. Today the elephant is still a well-recognized symbol for the Republican Party in political cartoons.

ROOSEVELT ELECTED TO FOURTH TERM: ANNIVERSARY. Nov 7, 1944. Defeating Thomas Dewey, Franklin D. Roosevelt became the first, and only, person elected to four terms as President of the US. Roosevelt was inaugurated the following Jan 20 but died in office Apr 12, 1945, serving only 53 days of the fourth term.

RUSSIA: GREAT OCTOBER SOCIALIST REVOLUTION: ANNIVERSARY. Nov 7, 1917. This holiday in the old Soviet Union was observed for two days with parades, military displays and appearances by Soviet leaders. According to the old Russian calendar, the revolution took place Oct 25, 1917. Soviet calendar reform causes observance to fall Nov 7 (Gregorian). The Bolshevik Revolution began at Petrograd, Russia, on the evening of Nov 6 (Gregorian), 1917. A new government headed by Nikolai Lenin took office the following day under the name Council of People's Commissars. Leon Trotsky was commissar for foreign affairs and Josef Stalin became commissar of national minorities. In the mid-1990s, President Yeltsin issued a decree renaming this holiday the "Day of National Reconciliation and Agreement."

BIRTHDAYS TODAY

Anthony Thomas, 28, football player, born Winnfield, LA, Nov 7, 1977.

Mary Travers, 68, composer, singer (Peter, Paul and Mary, "Puff, the Magic Dragon"), born Louisville, KY, Nov 7, 1937.

NOVEMBER 8 — TUESDAY

Day 312 — 53 Remaining

CORTÉS CONQUERS MEXICO: ANNIVERSARY. Nov 8, 1519. After landing on the Yucatan peninsula in April, Spaniard Hernan Cortés and his troops marched into the interior of Mexico to the Aztec capital and took the Aztec emperor Montezuma hostage.

ELECTION DAY. Nov 8. Annually, the first Tuesday after the first Monday in November. Many state and local government elections are held on this day, as well as presidential and congressional elections. All US House seats and one-third of US Senate seats are up for election in even-numbered years. Presidential elections are held in even-numbered years that can be divided by four. This day is a holiday in 12 states.

HALLEY, EDMUND: BIRTH ANNIVERSARY. Nov 8, 1656. Astronomer and mathematician, born at London, England. Astronomer Royal, 1721–42. Died at Greenwich, England, Jan 14, 1742. He observed the great comet of 1682 (now named for him), first conceived its periodicity and wrote in his *Synopsis of Comet Astronomy*: " . . . I may venture to foretell that this Comet will return again in the year 1758." It did, and Edmund Halley's memory is kept alive by the once-every-generation appearance of Halley's Comet. There have been 28 recorded appearances of this comet since 240 BC. Average time between appearances is 76 years. Halley's Comet is next expected to be visible in 2061.

HOPE DIAMOND MAILED TO SMITHSONIAN: ANNIVERSARY. Nov 8, 1958. The world's most famous blue diamond (at 45.52 carats, the largest dark blue diamond) was donated to the Smithsonian Institution by famed New York jeweler Harry Winston on this date. The priceless gem was sent via registered mail (postage $2.44, but insurance more than $140) after one of

NOVEMBER 8
HOPE DIAMOND MAILED TO SMITHSONIAN

Few people can resist a sparkling diamond. When turned in the light, a cut diamond's faceted sides reflect all colors of the rainbow. While there are many spectacular diamonds, the Hope Diamond leaps to the forefront as one of the world's most famous. Believe it or not, the Hope Diamond was mailed by its donor to the Smithsonian Institution in Washington DC. (See entry under Nov 8 for more details on this unusual mailing.)

The Hope Diamond was found in the 1600s in India. Gem experts believe that it is more than a billion years old. Like many famous gemstones, the Hope Diamond has passed through many hands and been owned by many illustrious people, among them King Louis XV, of France, and possibly England's King George IV.

Diamonds are composed of carbon, the same element that makes up graphite, the substance often called pencil lead. Both form solid crystals and are minerals, but the similarities end there. While steel-gray-colored graphite is so soft you can write with it, diamonds are the hardest mineral known on Earth. Because no other mineral can scratch a diamond, only diamonds can be used to cut other diamonds. The reason why a diamond is so hard is because the carbon atoms in a diamond crystal are all bonded to one another. That forms a structure that is highly resistant to flaking or breaking apart. Most diamond crystals are octahedral, or eight-sided. Crystal colors range from colorless, to red, to black. The Hope diamond is a blue diamond.

Diamonds form deep beneath Earth's crust under the high-pressure, high-temperature conditions found in the upper part of the Earth's mantle. Volcanic activity moves magma from Earth's depths toward the surface, sometimes in pipelike structures called kimberlites. Many of the world's diamonds are mined, or dug, from kimberlites. Diamonds can also be found in sand and gravel deposits of certain streambeds. The largest quantities of natural diamonds are found in Australia, Russia and the African continent.

Diamonds are measured in weight units called carats; one carat is equal to .02 gram or 200 milligrams. The Hope Diamond weighs 45.52 carats. Although large, it is not the world's largest. The Cullinan Diamond, found in South Africa, weighed 3,106 carats when it was first discovered. It was later cut into a number of smaller stones with the largest of them, called the Star of Africa, weighing 530 carats.

Only a small percentage of the world's diamonds are sufficiently flawless to be used in jewelry. Flawed diamonds are widely used for industrial purposes. Their hardness makes them perfect for the precision cutting and drilling of materials such as metal and rock. Students can readily find examples of diamond saws and diamond drill bits in hardware stores.

For fun with diamonds, younger students might enjoy learning about birthstones. Each month has a different birthstone, or gem, that is associated with it. The diamond, for example, is the gem for April. Supposedly, a birthstone brings luck when worn by a person born in that month. Students could research information about their birthstones and share their findings with the class in writing or orally. A birthstone list is included in most encyclopedias or can be easily found on the Internet. Students could present legends and stories of famous birthstones.

Another writing project would be for students to create their own legendary gemstone and a provenance to go with it. Descriptions of the geologic conditions that lead to the stone's formation could be supplied, as well as the stone's weight, color, size and jewelry setting, if any. (The jewelry setting of the imaginary stone would make a fun art project.)

Junior high students might find it instructive to read about the social and working conditions that occur in certain countries where diamond mines exist. Read about the "conflict" or "blood" diamonds from Sierra Leone (see *National Geographic*, March 2002, "Diamonds: The Real Story" or search newspaper websites). Compare and contrast the information they find with the working conditions and lives of miners of other materials—coal, for example.

Books for young readers include *Gems*, by Stuart A. Kallen (Kidhaven Press, 0-7377-1028-4, $23.70 Ages 7–12); *Gems*, by Holly Cefrey (PowerKids Press, 0-823-96467-1, $17.25 Ages 7–12); and for reading about the legends associated with famous gemstones, *The Deadly Diamonds*, by Laurence and Irene Swinburne (Steck-Vaughn, 0-8114-6856-9, $6.30 Ages 8–12).

—Sally Walker

Winston's employees rode to the post office with it on the New York subway. The postal carrier delivered it to the Smithsonian on Nov 10 amid great fanfare. The Hope was rumored to be cursed, as it may have originally been part of a diamond stolen during the bloody French Revolution, but the curse has been debunked for the most part. For more info: Encyclopedia Smithsonian online page at www.si.edu/resource/faq/nmnh/hope.htm. For more info on gemstones: *Gemstones* (Smithsonian Handbooks/DK, 0-789-48985-6, $20 All ages). ***See Curriculum Connection.***

MONTANA: ADMISSION DAY: ANNIVERSARY. Nov 8. Became 41st state in 1889.

MOON PHASE: FIRST QUARTER. Nov 8. Moon enters First Quarter phase at 8:57 PM, EST.

NATIONAL PARENTS AS TEACHERS DAY. Nov 8. To pay tribute to the more than 3,000 Parents as Teachers programs located in 50 states and other countries. These programs give all parents, regardless of social or economic circumstance, the support and guidance necessary to be their children's best first teacher in the critical early years. National PAT Day is celebrated on Nov 8, the birthday of Mildred Winter, PAT Founding Director. For info: Parents as Teachers National Center, 2228 Ball St, St. Louis, MO 63146. Phone: (800) PAT-4YOU. Fax: (314) 432-8963. E-mail: info@patnc.org. Web: www.patnc.org.

NATIONAL YOUNG READER'S DAY. Nov 8. Pizza Hut and the Center for the Book in the Library of Congress established National Young Reader's Day to remind Americans of the joys and importance of reading for young people. Schools, libraries, families and communities nationwide use this day to celebrate youth reading in a variety of creative and educational ways. Ideas on ways you can celebrate this special day are available. Annually, on the second Tuesday in November. For info: Shelley Morehead, The BOOK IT! Program, PO Box 2999, Wichita, KS 67201. Phone: (800) 426-6548 or (316) 687-8236. Fax: (316) 685-0977. E-mail: read@bookitprogram.com. Web: www.bookitprogram.com.

X-RAY DISCOVERY DAY: ANNIVERSARY. Nov 8, 1895. Physicist Wilhelm Conrad Röntgen discovered X-rays, beginning a new era in physics and medicine. Although X-rays had been observed previously, it was Röntgen, a professor at the University of Würzburg (Germany), who successfully repeated X-ray experimentation and who is credited with the discovery. For more info: *The Mysterious Rays of Dr. Röntgen*, by Beverly Gherman (Atheneum, 0-689-31839-1, $14.95 Gr. 2–5) or *The Head Bone's Connected to the Neck Bone: The Weird, Wacky, and Wonderful X-Ray*, by Carla Killough McClafferty (Farrar, Straus, 0-374-32908-7, $17 Gr. 5–8).

November 2005

S	M	T	W	T	F	S
		1	2	3	4	5
6	7	8	9	10	11	12
13	14	15	16	17	18	19
20	21	22	23	24	25	26
27	28	29	30			

BIRTHDAYS TODAY

Alfre Woodard, 52, actress (*Cross Creek, Miss Evers' Boys*), born Tulsa, OK, Nov 8, 1953.

NOVEMBER 9 — WEDNESDAY

Day 313 — 52 Remaining

AGNEW, SPIRO THEODORE: BIRTH ANNIVERSARY. Nov 9, 1918. The 39th vice president of the US, born at Baltimore, MD. Twice elected vice president (1968 and 1972), Agnew became the second person to resign that office, on Oct 10, 1973. Agnew entered a plea of no contest to a charge of income tax evasion (on contract kickbacks received while he was governor of Maryland and after he became vice president). He died Sept 17, 1996, at Berlin, MD. See also: "Calhoun, John Caldwell: Birth Anniversary" (Mar 18).

BANNEKER, BENJAMIN: BIRTH ANNIVERSARY. Nov 9, 1731. American astronomer, mathematician, clockmaker, surveyor and almanac author, called "first black man of science." Took part in original survey of city of Washington. Banneker's *Almanac* was published 1792–97. Born at Elliott's Mills, MD, he died at Baltimore, MD, Oct 9, 1806. A fire that started during his funeral destroyed his home, library, notebooks, almanac calculations, clocks and virtually all belongings and documents related to his life. For more info: *Dear Benjamin Banneker*, by Andrea Davis Pinkney (Harcourt, 0-15-200417-3, $14.95 Gr. 2–4) or *Benjamin Banneker: American Mathematician and Astronomer*, by Bonnie Hinman (Chelsea House, 0-7910-5348-2, $16.95 Gr. 3–6).

BERLIN WALL OPENED: ANNIVERSARY. Nov 9, 1989. After 28 years as a symbol of the Cold War, the Berlin Wall was opened. East Germany opened checkpoints along its border with West Germany after a troubled month that saw many citizens flee to the West through other countries. Coming amidst the celebration of East Germany's 40-year anniversary, the pro-democracy demonstrations led to the resignation of Erich Honecker, East Germany's head of state and party chief, who had supervised the construction of the wall. He was replaced by Egon Krenz, who promised open political debate and a lessening of restrictions on travel in attempts to stem the flow of East Germans to the West. By opening the Berlin Wall, East Germany began a course that led to the de facto reunification of the two Germanys by summer 1990. The Berlin Wall was constructed Aug 13, 1961. Berlin was at the center of a superpower crisis as US President Kennedy increased troop strength in response to the blockade of West Berlin by the Soviets. Honecker started construction, with Soviet leader Krushchev's blessing, of the 27.9-mile wall across the city. Many attempts to scale or breech the wall ensued throughout the years. But on the evening of Nov 9, 1989, citizens of both sides walked freely through the barrier as others danced atop the structure to celebrate the end of an era.

CAMBODIA: INDEPENDENCE DAY. Nov 9. National Day. Commemorates independence from France in 1949.

EAST COAST BLACKOUT: 40th ANNIVERSARY. Nov 9, 1965. Massive electric power failure starting in western New York state at 5:16 PM, cut electric power to much of northeastern US and Ontario and Quebec in Canada. More than 30 million persons in an area of 80,000 square miles were affected. The experience provoked studies of the vulnerability of 20th-century technology.

KRISTALLNACHT (CRYSTAL NIGHT): ANNIVERSARY. Nov 9–10, 1938. During the evening of Nov 9 and into the morning of Nov 10, 1938, mobs in Germany destroyed thousands of shops and homes carrying out a pogrom against Jews. Synagogues were burned down or demolished. There were bonfires in every Jewish neighborhood, fueled by Jewish prayer books, Torah scrolls and volumes of philosophy, history and poetry. More than 30,000 Jews were arrested and 91 killed. The night got its name from the smashing of glass store windows. For more info on the Holocaust: www.ushmm.org/outreach.

NATIONAL ASSOCIATION FOR GIFTED CHILDREN CONVENTION. Nov 9–13. Kentucky International Convention Center, Louisville, KY. Educational sessions for administrators, counselors, coordinators, teachers and parents. Est attendance: 4,000. For info: National Assn for Gifted Children, 1707 L St NW, Ste 550, Washington, DC 20036. Phone: (202) 785-4268.

NATIONAL CHILD SAFETY COUNCIL FOUNDING: 50th ANNIVERSARY. Nov 9, 1955. National Child Safety Council (NCSC) at Jackson, MI. NCSC is the oldest and largest nonprofit organization in the US dedicated solely to the personal safety and well-being of young children. Distributes comprehensive safety education materials to children and adults through local law enforcement and the Council's mascot, SafetyPup®. For info: Barbara Handley Huggett, Dir Research and Development, NCSC, Box 1368, Jackson, MI 49204-1368. Phone: (517) 764-6070. E-mail: bhuggett@nfcd.org.

THOMPSON, KAY: BIRTH ANNIVERSARY. Nov 9, 1908. Born at St. Louis, MO, Thompson wrote the Eloise series of children's books. Eloise was a spoiled, mischievous six-year-old who lives in New York's Plaza Hotel. Books include *Eloise in Paris, Eloise in Moscow* and *Eloise at Christmastime*. In 1999, Simon and Schuster released a new version called *The Absolutely Essential Eloise*. Thompson died at New York, NY, July 2, 1998.

BIRTHDAYS TODAY

Pat Cummings, 55, author (*Talking with Adventurers*), born Chicago, IL, Nov 9, 1950.

Adam Dunn, 26, baseball player, born Houston, TX, Nov 9, 1979.

Lois Ehlert, 71, author and illustrator (*Planting a Rainbow, Eating the Alphabet*), born Beaver Dam, WI, Nov 9, 1934.

Lynn Hall, 68, author (the Dragon series), born Lombard, IL, Nov 9, 1937.

Nick Lachey, 32, singer (98 Degrees), television personality ("Newlyweds: Nick & Jessica"), born Harlan, KY, Nov 9, 1973.

NOVEMBER 10 — THURSDAY

Day 314 — 51 Remaining

AREA CODES INTRODUCED: ANNIVERSARY. Nov 10, 1951. The North American Numbering Plan which provided area codes for Canada, the US and many Caribbean nations was devised in 1947 by AT&T and Bell Labs. However, all long-distance calls were operator-assisted. On this date, the mayor of Englewood, NJ (area code 201) direct-dialed the mayor of Alameda, CA, using his area code. By 1960 all telephone customers could dial long-distance calls. Because of the proliferation of faxes, modems and cell phones, the US could run out of area codes as early as 2007.

BADLANDS NATIONAL PARK ESTABLISHED: ANNIVERSARY. Nov 10, 1978. South Dakota's Badlands National Monument, authorized Mar 4, 1929, was established as a national park and preserve. For more info: www.nps.gov/badl/index.htm.

***EDMUND FITZGERALD* SINKING: 30th ANNIVERSARY.** Nov 10, 1975. The ore carrier *Edmund Fitzgerald* broke in two during a heavy storm in Lake Superior (near Whitefish Point). There were no survivors of this, the worst Great Lakes ship disaster of the decade, which took the lives of 29 crew members.

MARINE CORPS BIRTHDAY: ANNIVERSARY. Nov 10. Commemorates the Marine Corps' establishment in 1775. Originally part of the Navy, it became a separate unit July 11, 1789.

MICROSOFT RELEASES WINDOWS: ANNIVERSARY. Nov 10, 1983. In 1980, Microsoft signed a contract with IBM to design an operating system, MS-DOS, for a personal computer that IBM was developing. On this date Microsoft released Windows, an extension of MS-DOS with a graphical user interface.

PANAMA: FIRST SHOUT OF INDEPENDENCE. Nov 10. National holiday. Commemorates Panama's first battle for independence from Spain in 1821.

"SESAME STREET" TV PREMIERE: ANNIVERSARY. Nov 10, 1969. An important, successful long-running children's show, "Sesame Street" educates children while they have fun. It takes place along a city street, featuring a diverse cast of humans and puppets. Through singing, puppetry, film clips and skits, kids are taught letters, numbers, concepts and other lessons. Human cast members have included Loretta Long, Matt Robinson, Roscoe Orman, Bob McGrath, Linda Bove, Buffy Sainte-Marie, Ruth Buzzi, Will Lee, Northern J. Calloway, Emilio Delgado and Sonia Manzano. Favorite Jim Henson muppets include Ernie, Bert, Grover, Oscar the Grouch, Kermit the Frog, Cookie Monster, life-sized Big Bird and Mr Snuffleupagus. Variations on "Sesame Street" are aired in 78 countries. For more info: www.pbs.org/kids/sesame.

SPACE MILESTONE: *LUNA 17* (USSR): 35th ANNIVERSARY. Nov 10, 1970. This unmanned spacecraft landed and released *Lunakhod 1* (8-wheel, radio-controlled vehicle) on Moon's Sea of Rains Nov 17, which explored the lunar surface, sending data back to Earth.

BIRTHDAYS TODAY

Sal Barracca, 58, author, with wife Debra (*The Adventures of Taxi Dog*), born Brooklyn, NY, Nov 10, 1947.

Isaac Bruce, 33, football player, born Fort Lauderdale, FL, Nov 10, 1972.

Saxby Chambliss, 62, US Senator (R, Georgia), born Warrenton, NC, Nov 10, 1943.

Neil Gaiman, 45, author (*Coraline*, the Sandman series), born Porchester, England, Nov 10, 1960.

Kenny Rogers, 41, baseball player, born Savannah, GA, Nov 10, 1964.

Sinbad, 49, actor (*Unnecessary Roughness*, "A Different World"), born David Adkins, Benton Harbor, MI, Nov 10, 1956.

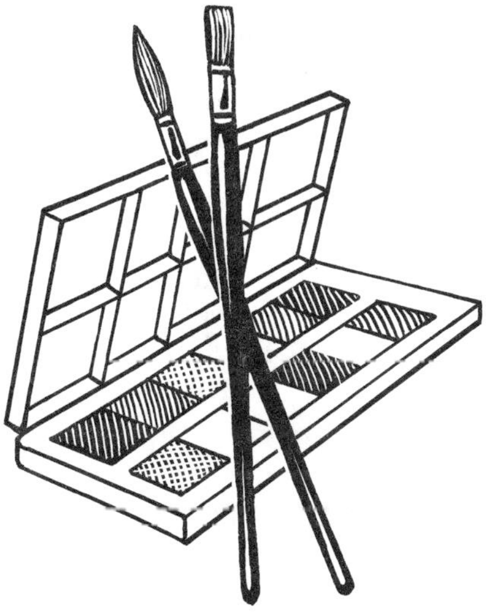

NOVEMBER 11

REMEMBERING OUR ARMED FORCES—PART ONE

There are five branches of the United States Armed Forces: Army, Navy, Air Force, Marine Corps and Coast Guard. Though duties vary by technical distinction and governmental mandate, it is the collective goal of the armed services to protect the nation and project strength, both at home and around the globe. Veterans Day is an excellent day to learn about these branches.

United States Army

The United States Army was born in the heat of battle, established by the Second Continental Congress in June 1775 to protect the burgeoning nation from the advancing forces of England. Over the years the Army has adapted in both role and size to America's own changes. During the 19th century, it was primarily a force for internal and border security, barring of course the tumultuous years of the Civil War (1861–65). Expansionist policies of the early 1900s landed Army forces in far-flung places but also facilitated great advances, for example, the work of Army doctors to eradicate yellow fever (1903). The two World Wars galvanized the US Army into a professional fighting force—by 1945, there were 17 Regular Army divisions (10,000 to 16,000 troops). Today the Army continues to be America's principal means of national defense, as well as offering public support in areas such as engineering, public safety and job training.

Resources include the Army's own website at www.army.mil, as well as *The Army* by Harold Nelson, et al (Hugh Lauter Levin Associates; 0-883-63101-6 Adult), *Revolutionary Soldier: 1775–1783*, by C. Keith Wilbur (Globe Pequot, 1-5644-0166-9; $14.95 Ages 4–8), *You Wouldn't Want to Be a Civil War Soldier: A War You'd Rather Not Fight*, by Thomas Ratliff, David Antram and David Salariya (Franklin Watts, 0-531-16393-8; $9.95 Ages 9–12) and *US Army Physical Fitness Guide: Strength, Endurance, Nutrition*, by the US Army (Hatherleigh Press, 1-5782-6131-7; $19.95 Adult).

United States Navy

Congress followed its establishment of an Army with the October 1775 authorization of the Continental Navy, which fought the British during the war. Upon independence the Continental Navy became the US Navy, which continued the mandate to defend America and project strength both in port and at sea. (The frigate *Constitution* survives from the late 1790s.) The US Navy's role and use fluctuated over the course of the 19th and early 20th centuries. But as it did with the Army, WWII forced the Navy to grow up fast. Today the Navy operates 289 ships, including nine carriers and six attack submarines, and more than 4,000 aircraft. According to www.Navy.mil, its stated mission is "to maintain, train and equip combat-ready Naval forces" for the protection of America and the high seas.

Resources include *US Navy: A Complete History* by M. Hill Goodspeed (Hugh Lauter Levin Associates, 0-8836-3112-1, $75 Adult), *The Old Navy* by Harry Baehr and Christopher B. Price (Authorhouse, 0-7596-9133-9, $15.50 Adult), *The Incredible Story of Aircraft Carriers (Kid's Guide to Incredible Technology)* by Greg Roza, Leonello Calvetti and Lorenzo Cecchi (PowerKids Press, 0-823-96701-X, $19.95 Ages 4–8). —Johnny Loftus

NOVEMBER 11 — FRIDAY

Day 315 — 50 Remaining

ANGOLA: INDEPENDENCE DAY. Nov 11. National holiday. The West African state of Angola gained its independence from Portugal in 1975.

BONZA BOTTLER DAY™. Nov 11. To celebrate when the number of the day is the same as the number of the month. Bonza Bottler Day™ is an excuse to have a party at least once a month. For info: Gail M. Berger, 14 Fernwood Dr, Taylors, SC 29687. Phone: (864) 609-9874. E-mail: gberger5@aol.com.

CANADA: REMEMBRANCE DAY. Nov 11. Honors those who died in WWI and WWII. Public holiday.

COLOMBIA: CARTAGENA INDEPENDENCE DAY. Nov 11. National holiday. Commemorates the declaration of independence of the city in 1811.

FRENCH WEST INDIES: CONCORDIA DAY. Nov 11. St. Martin/Sint Maarten. Public holiday. Parades and joint ceremony by French and Dutch officials at the obelisk Border Monument commemorating the long-standing peaceful coexistence of both countries on this island.

"GOD BLESS AMERICA" FIRST PERFORMED: ANNIVERSARY. Nov 11, 1938. Irving Berlin wrote this song especially for Kate Smith. She first sang it during her regular radio broadcast. It quickly became a great patriotic favorite of the nation and one of Smith's most requested songs.

November 2005

S	M	T	W	T	F	S
		1	2	3	4	5
6	7	8	9	10	11	12
13	14	15	16	17	18	19
20	21	22	23	24	25	26
27	28	29	30			

MARTINMAS. Nov 11. The Feast Day of St. Martin of Tours, who lived about AD 316–397. A bishop, he became one of the most popular saints of the Middle Ages. The period of warm weather often occurring about the time of his feast day is sometimes called St. Martin's Summer (especially in England).

POLAND: INDEPENDENCE DAY. Nov 11. Poland regained independence in 1918, after having been partitioned among Austria, Prussia and Russia for more than 120 years.

SPACE MILESTONE: *GEMINI 12* (US). Nov 11, 1966. Last Project Gemini manned Earth orbit launched. Buzz Aldrin spent five hours on a space walk, setting a new record.

SWEDEN: SAINT MARTIN'S DAY. Nov 11. Originally in memory of St. Martin of Tours; also associated with Martin Luther, who is celebrated the day before. Marks the end of the autumn's work and the beginning of winter activities.

VETERANS DAY. Nov 11. Veterans Day was observed Nov 11 from 1919 through 1970. Public Law 90–363, the "Monday Holiday Law," provided that, beginning in 1971, Veterans Day would be observed on "the fourth Monday in October." This movable observance date, which separated Veterans Day from the Nov 11 anniversary of WWI Armistice, proved unpopular. State after state moved its observance back to the traditional Nov 11 date, and finally Public Law 94–97 of Sept 18, 1975, required that, effective Jan 1, 1978, the observance of Veterans Day revert to Nov 11. For more info about Veterans Day, go to the website of the US Department of Veterans Affairs at www.va.gov/pubaff/vetsday or the Veterans of Foreign Wars at www.vfw.org/amesm/origins .shtml. ***See Curriculum Connection.***

★ ★ ★

NOVEMBER 11
REMEMBERING OUR ARMED FORCES—PART TWO

After the Army and Navy, there are three more branches of US armed forces: Marine Corps, Air Force and Coast Guard.

United States Marine Corps

Since its inception during the Revolutionary War (November 1775), the Corps has been important as a quick-response force that—unlike other branches of the military—utilizes and integrates land, sea and air elements into its combat role. Another key difference is the emphasis on rifle training for each Marine, not just the infantry. In other words, every Marine is an infantryman, from firemen and cooks to pilots and officers. After playing a significant role in the early 20th-century expansion of American influence throughout the globe, the Marines saw major action in both World Wars I and II as well as Korea and Vietnam. The Marine Corps exists today as the second smallest (just over 175,000 on active duty), but quite possibly the proudest, of the US armed forces, rich in history and ready at a moment's notice. "Semper Fidelis," the Marines' Latin motto, translates as "Always Faithful."

Resources include the USMC's official website at www.usmc.mil, as well as *Marine Book: A Portrait of America's Military Elite* by Chuck Lawliss (Thames & Hudson, 0-500-27665-X, $19.95 Adult), *Life in the Marines* by Robert C. Kennedy (Children's Press, 0-516-23548-6, $6.95 Ages 9–12) and *Navajo Code Talkers* by Andrew Santella (Compass Point, 0-756-50611-5, $22.60 Ages 9–12), an interesting history of the USMC's use of native Navajo speakers as message senders during its battle for the Pacific in WWII.

United States Air Force

The US Air Force was part of the Army's Signal Corps in the early 1900s, operating balloons on the field of battle. Still part of the Army during WWII, in 1947 the Air Force was established as a separate military service. In addition to protecting America's skies and its troops on the ground (with both fighter aircraft and bombers), the USAF is responsible for all the satellites the military operates in outer space as well as the country's missile defense.

Resources include the Air Force's official website at www.af.mil, as well as *The US Air Force* by Sandra Donovan (Lerner Publications, 0-8225-1436-2, $26.60 Ages 9–12), *Life as an Air Force Fighter Pilot*, by Robert C. Kennedy (Children's Press, 0-516-23345-9, $22 Ages 9–12) and—for a more personalized look at the branch—*Belly Gunner* by Carol Edgemon Hipperson (21st Century Books, 0-7613-1873-9, $27.90 Young adult).

United States Coast Guard

Though its roots go back to the late 18th century, the United States Coast Guard wasn't officially formed until 1915, when Congress created it as a service dedicated to maritime law enforcement and lifesaving at sea. Other areas under USCG jurisdiction include port security, international vessel inspection and operation of the nation's lighthouses. While the Coast Guard operates under the authority of the Department of Homeland Security, it can be mobilized as part of the US Navy in time of war. The Coast Guard currently includes about 7,000 officers and 30,000 enlisted men; it operates more than 1,000 boats of various types as well as 200-plus aircraft, including helicopters and planes.

Visit the United States Coast Guard online at www.uscg.mil; other resources include *The US Coast Guard* by Dennis L. Noble (Gareth Street, 0-836-85681-3, $30.00 Ages 9–12), *Always Ready: Today's US Coast Guard* by Kit Bonner and Carolyn Bonner (Motorbooks International, 0-760-31727-5, $17.95 All ages) and *Mayday! Mayday! The Most Exciting Missions of Rescue, Interdiction and Combat in the 200-Year Annals of the US Coast Guard* by Samuel Schreiner (Donald I Fine, 1-5561-1195-9 Young adult and adult).

—Johnny Loftus

★**VETERANS DAY.** Nov 11. Presidential Proclamation. Formerly called "Armistice Day" and proclaimed each year since 1926 for Nov 11. Public Law 83–380 of June 1, 1954, changed the name to "Veterans Day."

WASHINGTON: ADMISSION DAY: ANNIVERSARY. Nov 11. Became 42nd state in 1889.

WORLD WAR I ARMISTICE: ANNIVERSARY. Nov 11, 1918. Anniversary of armistice between Allied and Central Powers ending WWI, signed at 5 AM, Nov 11, 1918, in Marshal Foch's railway car in the Forest of Compiegne, France. Hostilities ceased at 11 AM. Recognized in many countries as Armistice Day, Remembrance Day, Veterans Day, Victory Day or World War I Memorial Day. Many places observe a silent memorial at the 11th hour of the 11th day of the 11th month each year. See also: "Veterans Day" (Nov 11). For more info: *World War I*, by Simon Adams (DK, 0-7894-7939-7, $15.95 Gr. 6–12).

BIRTHDAYS TODAY

Barbara Boxer, 65, US Senator (D, California), born Brooklyn, NY, Nov 11, 1940.

Leonardo DiCaprio, 31, actor (*Titanic, Catch Me If You Can*), born Hollywood, CA, Nov 11, 1974.

Peg Kehret, 69, author (*Horror at the Haunted House*), born LaCrosse, WI, Nov 11, 1936.

Kurt Vonnegut, Jr, 83, novelist (*Slaughterhouse Five, Cat's Cradle*), born Indianapolis, IN, Nov 11, 1922.

NOVEMBER 12 — SATURDAY

Day 316 — 49 Remaining

ARCHES NATIONAL PARK ESTABLISHED: ANNIVERSARY. Nov 12, 1971. Area of natural wind-eroded formations in eastern Utah, originally proclaimed a national monument Apr 12, 1929, was established as a national park. For more info: www.nps.gov/arch/index.htm.

BLACKMUN, HARRY A.: BIRTH ANNIVERSARY. Nov 12, 1908. Former associate justice of the Supreme Court of the US, nominated by President Nixon Apr 14, 1970. Justice Blackmun was born at Nashville, IL, Nov 12, 1908. He retired from the Court Aug 3, 1994, and died Mar 4, 1999, at Arlington, VA.

LATINO BOOK & FAMILY FESTIVAL—CHICAGO. Nov 12–13. Unity School, Chicago, IL. Produced along with actor Edward James Olmos, this festival is a celebration of books, careers, culture, education, health, recreation, travel and more. It is the largest Latino consumer trade show in the US. Attendees will enjoy hundreds of booths and activities including book signings, storytelling, poetry readings, food, entertainment and workshops. For info: Latino Book & Family Festivals, 3980 Cazador St, Los Angeles, CA 90065. E-mail: kathy@latinobookfestival.com. Web: www.LBFF.us or www.openabook.org.

STANTON, ELIZABETH CADY: BIRTH ANNIVERSARY. Nov 12, 1815. American suffragette and reformer, Elizabeth Cady Stanton was born at Johnstown, NY. "We hold these truths to be self-evident," she said at the first Women's Rights Convention, in 1848, "that all men and women are created equal." She died at New York, NY, Oct 26, 1902. For more info: *You Want Women to Vote, Lizzie Stanton?*, by Jean Fritz (Putnam, 0-399-22786-5, $16.99 Gr. 5–9) or *Elizabeth Cady Stanton: The Right Is Ours*, by Harriet Sigerman (Oxford, 0-19-511969-X, $24 Gr. 6–10). The March 2000 issue of *Cobblestone* magazine is devoted to Stanton.

SUN YAT-SEN: BIRTH ANNIVERSARY (TRADITIONAL). Nov 12. Although his actual birth date in 1866 is not known, Dr. Sun Yat-Sen's traditional birthday commemoration is held Nov 12. Heroic leader of China's 1911 revolution, he died at Peking, Mar 12, 1925. The death anniversary is also widely observed. See also: "Sun Yat-Sen: Death Anniversary" (Mar 12).

TYLER, LETITIA CHRISTIAN: BIRTH ANNIVERSARY. Nov 12, 1790. First wife of John Tyler, 10th president of the US, born at New Kent County, VA. Died at Washington, DC, Sept 10, 1842.

BIRTHDAYS TODAY

Ernie Fletcher, 53, Governor of Kentucky (R), born Mount Sterling, KY, Nov 12, 1952.

Norman Mineta, 74, US Secretary of Transportation (George W. Bush administration), former Commerce secretary (Clinton administration), born San Jose, CA, Nov 12, 1931.

Jack Reed, 56, US Senator (D, Rhode Island), born Providence, RI, Nov 12, 1949.

Marjorie Weinman Sharmat, 77, author (*Nate the Great* and sequels), born Portland, ME, Nov 12, 1928.

Sammy Sosa, 37, baseball player, born San Pedro de Macoris, Dominican Republic, Nov 12, 1968.

NOVEMBER 13 — SUNDAY

Day 317 — 48 Remaining

★**AMERICAN EDUCATION WEEK.** Nov 13–19. Presidential Proclamation 5403, of Oct 30, 1985, covers all succeeding years. Always the first full week preceding the fourth Thursday in November. Issued from 1921–25 and in 1936, sometimes for a week in December and sometimes as National Education Week. After an absence of a number of years, this proclamation was issued each year from 1955–82 (issued in 1955 as a prelude to the White House Conference on Education). Previously, Proclamation 4967, of Sept 13, 1982, covered all succeeding years as the second week in November.

AMERICAN EDUCATION WEEK. Nov 13–19. Focuses attention on the importance of education and all that it stands for. Annually, the week preceding the week of Thanksgiving. For info: National Education Assn (NEA), 1201 16th St NW, Washington, DC 20036. Phone: (202) 833-4000. Web: www.nea.org.

BRANDEIS, LOUIS DEMBITZ: BIRTH ANNIVERSARY. Nov 13, 1856. American jurist, associate justice of US Supreme Court (1916–39), born at Louisville, KY. Died at Washington, DC, Oct 5, 1941.

GERMANY: VOLKSTRAUERTAG. Nov 13. Memorial Day and national day of mourning in all German states. Observed on the Sunday before Totensonntag.

November 2005

S	M	T	W	T	F	S
		1	2	3	4	5
6	7	8	9	10	11	12
13	14	15	16	17	18	19
20	21	22	23	24	25	26
27	28	29	30			

***JOBARIA* EXHIBITED: ANNIVERSARY.** Nov 13, 1999. The dinosaur *Jobaria tiguidensis* was first exhibited at the National Geographic Society at Washington, DC, on this date. The 135-million-year-old sauropod was discovered in the African country of Niger in 1997. It is 15 feet high at the hip and 70 feet long. A mold of the plant-eating dinosaur is being exhibited since the actual skeleton is too heavy. The original skeleton was returned to Niger. For more info: www.projectexploration.org.

NATIONAL GEOGRAPHY AWARENESS WEEK. Nov 13–19. To focus public awareness on the importance of the knowledge of geography. The theme for the 2005 GAW is "Migrations." GAW will look at the changing face of community. Annually, the third week in November. For info: Natl Geographic Society, Education and Children's Programs, 1145 17th St NW, Washington, DC 20036. Web: www.nationalgeographic.com/geographyaction.

STEVENSON, ROBERT LOUIS: BIRTH ANNIVERSARY. Nov 13, 1850. Scottish author, born at Edinburgh, Scotland, known for his *Child's Garden of Verses* and novels such as *Treasure Island* and *Kidnapped*. Died at Samoa, Dec 3, 1894.

STOKES BECOMES FIRST BLACK MAYOR IN US: ANNIVERSARY. Nov 13, 1967. Carl Burton Stokes became the first black in the US elected mayor when he won the Cleveland, OH, mayoral election. Died Apr 3, 1996.

BIRTHDAYS TODAY

Jez Alborough, 46, author and illustrator (*Where's My Teddy?*), born Surrey, England, Nov 13, 1959.

Whoopi Goldberg, 56, comedienne, actress (*Ghost, Sister Act, The Color Purple*), born New York, NY, Nov 13, 1949 (some sources say 1950 or 1955).

Vincent (Vinny) Testaverde, 42, football player, born New York, NY, Nov 13, 1963.

NOVEMBER 14 — MONDAY

Day 318 — 47 Remaining

CHILDREN'S BOOK WEEK. Nov 14–20. An annual event, sponsored by the Children's Book Council, to encourage the enjoyment of reading for young people. For info: The Children's Book Council, Inc, 12 W 37th St, 2nd Flr, New York, NY 10018-2073. E-mail: marketing@cbcbooks.org. Web: www.cbcbooks.org.

COPLAND, AARON: BIRTH ANNIVERSARY. Nov 14, 1900. American composer, born at Brooklyn, NY. Incorporating American folk music, he strove to create an American music style that was both popular and artistic. He composed ballets, film scores and orchestral works, including *Fanfare for the Common Man* (1942), *Appalachian Spring* (1944) (for which he won the Pulitzer Prize) and the score for *The Heiress* (1948) (for which he won an Oscar). He died Dec 2, 1990, at North Tarrytown, NY.

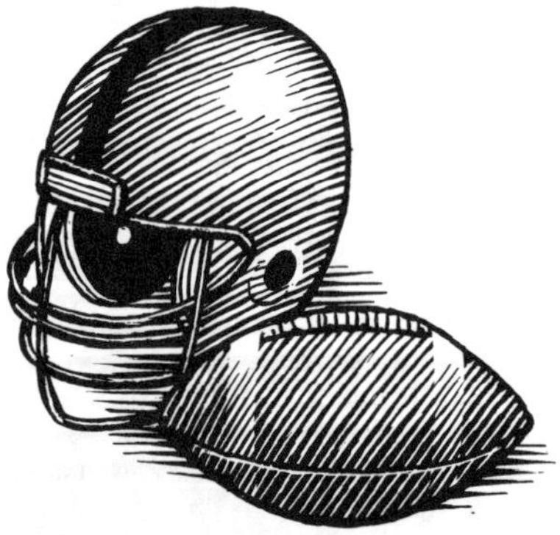

EISENHOWER, MAMIE DOUD: BIRTH ANNIVERSARY. Nov 14, 1896. Wife of Dwight David Eisenhower, 34th president of the US, born at Boone, IA. Died Nov 1, 1979, at Gettysburg, PA.

GUINEA-BISSAU: READJUSTMENT MOVEMENT'S DAY. Nov 14. National holiday.

INDIA: CHILDREN'S DAY. Nov 14. Holiday observed throughout India.

JORDAN: KING HUSSEIN: BIRTH ANNIVERSARY. Nov 14. H.M. King Hussein is honored each year on the anniversary of his birth in 1935 at Amman, Jordan. He died there Feb 7, 1999.

LINDGREN, ASTRID: BIRTH ANNIVERSARY. Nov 14, 1907. World famous children's author, born at Vimmerby, Sweden. Lindgren wrote 88 books and plays, many of which have been made into films, television programs, radio shows and cartoons. Her most popular title was 1945's *Pippi Longstocking*, which has been translated into at least 80 languages. In addition to several sequels about Pippi, she was also known for *The Tomten, The Children of the Noisy Village* and *Ronia, the Robber's Daughter*. She died at Stockholm, Sweden, on Jan 28, 2002.

MILES, MISKA: BIRTH ANNIVERSARY. Nov 14, 1899. Author (*Annie and the Old One*), whose real name was Patricia Miles Martin, born at Cherokee, KS. Died Jan 1, 1986, at San Mateo, CA.

MONET, CLAUDE: BIRTH ANNIVERSARY. Nov 14, 1840. French Impressionist painter (*Water Lillies*), born at Paris. Died at Giverny, France, Dec 5, 1926.

NATIONAL AMERICAN TEDDY BEAR DAY. Nov 14. The Vermont Teddy Bear Company® celebrates the birth of America's most beloved companion, the Teddy bear, annually on Nov 14. The legend goes that President Theodore Roosevelt spared the life of a bear while on a big game hunt in Mississippi in 1902. Clifford Berryman, political cartoonist, recorded the incident. Thus America's love affair with the Teddy bear began. For info: The Vermont Teddy Bear Company®, 6655 Shelburne Rd, Shelburne, VT 05482. Web: VermontTeddyBear.com.

NATIONAL GEOGRAPHIC BEE 2006, SCHOOL LEVEL. Nov 14–Jan 13, 2006. Principals must register their schools by Oct 15, 2005 for the 2006 National Geographic Bee. School competitions begin in mid-November and end the second week in January. Nationwide contest involving millions of students at the school level. The Bee is designed to encourage the teaching and study of geography. There are three levels of competition. A student must win a school-level Bee in order to win the right to take a written exam. The written test determines the top 100 students in each state who are eligible to go on to the state level. National Geographic brings the state winner and his/her teacher to Washington for the national level in May. Alex Trebek moderates the national level. For info: National Geographic Bee, National Geographic Society, 1145 17th St NW, Washington, DC 20036. Web: www.nationalgeographic.com/geographicbee.

NEHRU, JAWAHARLAL: BIRTH ANNIVERSARY. Nov 14, 1889. Indian leader and first prime minister after independence. Born at Allahabad, India, he died May 27, 1964, at New Delhi.

STEIG, WILLIAM: BIRTH ANNIVERSARY. Nov 14, 1907. Prolific cartoonist, satirist and illustrator, William Steig was born at Brooklyn, NY. *The New Yorker* published more than 1,600 of his drawings, including 117 covers, and he wrote more than 25 books for children. He won the Caldecott Medal in 1970 for *Sylvester and the Magic Pebble,* and received two Newbery Honors, for *Abel's Island* and *Dr. De Soto.* Other favorites include *The Amazing Bone, Brave Irene, CDB* and *Shrek,* the basis for the 2001 animated film featuring Mike Myers. Steig died at Boston, MA, Oct 3, 2003.

YOUTH APPRECIATION WEEK. Nov 14–20. Annually, the second full week of November, Monday–Sunday. For info: Optimist International, 4494 Lindell Blvd, St. Louis, MO 63108. Phone: (314) 371-6000. Web: www.optimist.org.

BIRTHDAYS TODAY

Prince Charles, 57, Prince of Wales, heir to the British throne, born London, England, Nov 14, 1948.

Condoleezza Rice, 51, US Secretary of State, former National Security Adviser (George W. Bush administration), born Birmingham, AL, Nov 14, 1954.

Curt Schilling, 39, baseball player, born Anchorage, AK, Nov 14, 1966.

Nancy Tafuri, 59, author, illustrator (*Have You Seen My Duckling?*), born Brooklyn, NY, Nov 14, 1946.

NOVEMBER 15 — TUESDAY

Day 319 — 46 Remaining

AMERICA RECYCLES DAY. Nov 15. To promote recycling and recycled products. More than 40 states participate. For info: National Program Mgr, America Recycles Day, 1325 G St NW, Ste 1025, Washington, DC 20005. Phone: (202) 347-0450. Web: www.americarecyclesday.org.

★ **AMERICA RECYCLES DAY.** Nov 15. To promote recycling and recycled products. Annually, every Nov 15.

BRAZIL: REPUBLIC DAY. Nov 15. Commemorates the Proclamation of the Republic in 1889.

JAPAN: SHICHI-GO-SAN. Nov 15. Annual children's festival. The *Shichi-Go-San* (Seven-Five-Three) rite, observed Nov 15, is "the most picturesque event in the autumn season." Parents take their three-year-old children of either sex, five-year-old boys and seven-year-old girls to the parish shrines dressed in their best clothes. There the guardian spirits are thanked for the healthy growth of the children and prayers are offered for their further development.

LEONID METEOR SHOWER. Nov 15–17 (approximate). Annual mid-November meteor shower as Earth passes through the dust trail of Comet Tempel-Tuttle. Meteor shower occurs in the sky of the Leo constellation. Tempel-Tuttle orbits the sun every 33 years, and it was last closest to the Earth in 1998. As a result of this orbit, the Leonid meteor showers are more spectacular every 33 years.

MOON PHASE: FULL MOON. Nov 15. Moon enters Full Moon phase at 7:57 PM, EST.

★ ★ ★

NATIONAL COMMUNITY EDUCATION DAY. Nov 15. To recognize and promote strong relationships between public schools and the communities they serve and to help schools develop new relationships with parents, community members, local organizations and agencies. Annually, the Tuesday of American Education Week. For info: National Community Education Assn, 3929 Old Lee Hwy, Ste 91-A, Fairfax, VA 22030-2401. Phone: (703) 359-8973. Fax: (703) 359-0972. E-mail: ncea@ncea.com. Web: www.ncea.com.

O'KEEFFE, GEORGIA: BIRTH ANNIVERSARY. Nov 15, 1887. Described as one of the greatest American artists of the 20th century, O'Keeffe painted desert landscapes and flower studies. Born at Sun Prairie, WI, she was married to the famous photographer Alfred Stieglitz. She died at Santa Fe, NM, Mar 6, 1986. For more info: *My Name Is Georgia: A Portrait*, by Jeanette Winter (Harcourt, 0-15-201649-X, $16 Gr. 2–4).

BIRTHDAYS TODAY

Daniel Manus Pinkwater, 64, author (*Lizard Music, Snarkout Boys and the Avocado of Death*), born Memphis, TN, Nov 15, 1941.

Bill Richardson, 58, Governor of New Mexico (D), former Secretary of Energy (Clinton Administration), born Pasadena, CA, Nov 15, 1947.

NOVEMBER 16 — WEDNESDAY

Day 320 — 45 Remaining

ESTONIA: DAY OF NATIONAL REBIRTH. Nov 16. National holiday. Commemorates the 1988 Declaration of Sovereignty.

GERMANY: BUSS UND BETTAG. Nov 16. Buss und Bettag (Repentance Day) is observed on the Wednesday before the last Sunday of the church year. A legal public holiday in all German states except Bavaria (where it is observed only in communities with predominantly Protestant populations).

LEWIS AND CLARK EXPEDITION REACHES PACIFIC OCEAN: 200th ANNIVERSARY. Nov 16, 1805. Lewis and Clark's Corps of Discovery reached the Pacific Ocean on this date. They had glimpsed it on Nov 7, moving Clark to write in his journal: "Great joy in camp! We are in view of the Ocean, this great Pacific Ocean which we have been so anxious to see. And the roaring or noise of the waves breaking on the rocky shores . . . may be heard distinctly." ***See Curriculum Connection.***

November 2005

S	M	T	W	T	F	S
		1	2	3	4	5
6	7	8	9	10	11	12
13	14	15	16	17	18	19
20	21	22	23	24	25	26
27	28	29	30			

NATIONAL EDUCATIONAL SUPPORT PERSONNEL DAY. Nov 16. A mandate of the delegates to the 1987 National Education Association Representative Assembly called for a special day during American Education Week to honor the contributions of school support employees. Local associations and school districts salute support staff on this 18th annual observance, the Wednesday of American Education Week. For info: Communications, National Education Assn (NEA), 1201 16th St NW, Washington, DC 20036. Phone: (202) 822-7200. Fax: (202) 822-7292. Web: www.nea.org.

OKLAHOMA: ADMISSION DAY: ANNIVERSARY. Nov 16. Became 46th state in 1907.

RIEL, LOUIS: HANGING ANNIVERSARY. Nov 16, 1885. Born at St. Boniface, MB, Canada, Oct 23, 1844, Louis Riel, leader of the Metis (French/Indian mixed ancestry), was elected to Canada's House of Commons in 1873 and 1874, but never seated. Confined to asylums for madness (feigned or falsely charged, some said), Riel became a US citizen in 1883. In 1885 he returned to western Canada to lead the North West Rebellion. Defeated, he surrendered and was tried for treason, convicted and hanged, at Regina, NWT, Canada. Seen as a patriot and protector of French culture in Canada, Riel's life and death became a legend and a symbol of the problems between French and English Canadians.

ROMAN CATHOLICS ISSUE NEW CATECHISM: ANNIVERSARY. Nov 16, 1992. For the first time since 1563, the Roman Catholic Church issued a new universal catechism, which addressed modern-day issues.

SAINT EUSTATIUS, WEST INDIES: STATIA AND AMERICA DAY. Nov 16. St. Eustatius, Leeward Islands. To commemorate the first salute to an American flag by a foreign government, from Fort Oranje in 1776. Festivities include sports events and dancing. During the American Revolution St. Eustatius was an important trading center and a supply base for the colonies.

SPACE MILESTONE: *VENERA 3* (USSR): 40th ANNIVERSARY. Nov 16, 1965. This unmanned space probe crashed into Venus, Mar 1, 1966. First man-made object on another planet.

UNITED NATIONS: INTERNATIONAL DAY FOR TOLERANCE. Nov 16. On Dec 12, 1996, the General Assembly established the International Day for Tolerance, to commemorate the adoption by UNESCO member states of the Declaration of Principles on Tolerance on Nov 16, 1995. For info: United Nations, Dept of Public Info, New York, NY 10017. Web: www.un.org.

BIRTHDAYS TODAY

Oksana Baiul, 28, Olympic figure skater, born Dniepropetrovsk, Ukraine, Nov 16, 1977.

Victoria Chess, 66, illustrator (*King Long Shanks*), born Chicago, IL, Nov 16, 1939.

Jean Fritz, 90, author (Laura Ingalls Wilder Medal for *The Cabin Faced West;* Newbery Honor for *Homesick: My Own Story*), born Hankow, China, Nov 16, 1915.

Dwight Eugene Gooden, 41, former baseball player, born Tampa, FL, Nov 16, 1964.

Robin McKinley, 53, author (Newbery for *The Hero and the Crown*), born Jennifer Carolyn Robin McKinley, Warren, OH, Nov 16, 1952.

Angela Shelf Medearis, 49, author (*Poppa's New Pants*), born Hampton, VA, Nov 16, 1956.

Carolyn Reeder, 68, author (*Shades of Gray*), born Washington, DC, Nov 16, 1937.

★ ★ ★

NOVEMBER 16
FLORA AND FAUNA OF THE LEWIS AND CLARK EXPEDITION

When Thomas Jefferson commissioned Meriwether Lewis and William Clark to find a route to the Pacific, they could only imagine the wonders they would see. As they departed St. Louis on May 14, 1806, with a company of 33 men, they were prepared to take note of many new things, including flora, fauna, native peoples and geological formations. Today marks the 200th anniversary of when the expedition reached the Pacific and it's a great time to discuss the flora and fauna that they discovered on their journey.

Fauna, including insects, provided some of the expedition's most interesting and frustrating events. Mosquitoes and fleas were a constant—and itchy—trial. The 300 pounds of buffalo grease purchased from a trader came in handy: as a skin lotion to prevent bites and as cooking grease. Bear (the Corps came across a grizzly for the first time), elk, birds and fish were varied and plentiful. Clark's field notes record many discoveries, classifications and measurements. A science extension activity would be for your class to locate those areas where Clark observed the various animals and plants during the expedition. Can those animals be found in those places today? If not, why? Are any of the animals or plants endangered today? If so, what led to their endangerment?

The expedition botanists were intrigued by the many new plants they encountered. By talking with indigenous peoples, they learned ways that plants could be used for medicinal purposes as well as food sources. Collecting specimens was an important part of the expedition. Students could catalog, map and draw a vegetation map of the area outside your school. They can measure leaf lengths and tree trunk circumferences and diameters. Leaf specimens can be collected and mounted in the classroom.

Use a road atlas to generate some math fun with regard to the Lewis and Clark Expedition. (Rand McNally's *The Road Atlas*, updated yearly, is an excellent, affordable choice. It's also a great resource tool to have on hand in the classroom.) Ask students to chart Lewis and Clark's route in two ways: the first using interstate highways to create a fast, direct route from St. Louis, the second on small secondary roads that closely follow the riverbeds and overland routes used by the expedition. How long would it take a car to drive each route? How do the two mileages compare?

Two well-written books, both by Dorothy Hinshaw Patent, deal specifically with the fauna and flora found during the expedition. *Animals on the Trail with Lewis and Clark* (Clarion, 0-395-91415-9, $18 Ages 8 & up) and *Plants on the Trail with Lewis and Clark* (Clarion, 0-618-06776-0, $18 Ages 8 & up). They contain lists and detailed information about animals and plants.

Many general books about Lewis and Clark's journey are available for young readers. Recently, attention has been focused on Native American Sacagawea's and African-American York's roles in the expedition. General books on the expedition and specific books on them include *How We Crossed the West: The Adventures of Lewis & Clark*, Rosalyn Schanzer (National Geographic, 0-7922-3738-2, $18 Ages 7–11); *Sacagawea*, Lise Erdrich (Carolrhoda Books, 0-876-14646-9, $16.95 Ages 7 & up); *On the Trail of Sacagawea*, Peter Lourie (Boyds Mills, 1-56397-840-7, $18.95 Ages 8–11); *A Picture Book of Lewis and Clark*, David Adler (Holiday House, 0-8234-1735-2, $6.95 Ages 5–9); *On the Trail of Lewis and Clark*, Peter Lourie (Boyds Mills, 1-59078-268-2, $11.95 Ages 8–11); *York's Adventures with Lewis and Clark*, Rhoda Blumberg (HarperCollins, 0-06-009111-8, $17.99 Ages 8 & up).

The PBS website www.pbs.org/lewisandclark provides a wealth of material about the expedition, as well as interactive student activities and classroom projects.

—Sally Walker

NOVEMBER 17 — THURSDAY

Day 321 — 44 Remaining

GREAT AMERICAN SMOKEOUT. Nov 17. A day observed to celebrate smoke-free environments. Annually, the third Thursday in November. For info: PR Dept, American Cancer Society, 1599 Clifton Rd NE, Atlanta, GA 30329. Phone: (800) 227-2345. Web: www.cancer.org.

LARGEST PRIME NUMBER FOUND: ANNIVERSARY. Nov 17, 2003. As part of the Great Internet Mersenne Prime Search effort in which volunteers donated the time of more than 200,000 computers to make calculations, college student Michael Shafer's computer found the largest prime number: 2 to the 20,996,011th power minus 1. This prime number is 6,320,430 digits long.

NATIONAL COUNCIL OF TEACHERS OF ENGLISH ANNUAL CONVENTION. Nov 17–20. Pittsburgh, PA. For info: National Council of Teachers of English, 1111 W Kenyon Rd, Urbana, IL 61801-1096. Phone: (800) 369-6283 or (217) 328-3870. Web: www.ncte.org.

NATIONAL COUNCIL FOR THE SOCIAL STUDIES ANNUAL MEETING. Nov 17–20. Kansas City, MO. 85th annual meeting. For info: National Council for the Social Studies, 8555 16th St, Ste 500, Silver Spring, MD 20910. Phone: (301) 588-1800. Web: www.socialstudies.org.

BIRTHDAYS TODAY

Justin Cooper, 17, actor (*Liar, Liar,* "Brother's Keeper"), born Los Angeles, CA, Nov 17, 1988.

Danny DeVito, 61, actor (*Twins, Matilda*), born Asbury Park, NJ, Nov 17, 1944.

(Clarke) Isaac Hanson, 25, singer (Hanson), born Tulsa, OK, Nov 17, 1980.

James M. Inhofe, 71, US Senator (R, Oklahoma), born Des Moines, IA, Nov 17, 1934.

NOVEMBER 18 — FRIDAY

Day 322 — 43 Remaining

AMERICAN COUNCIL ON THE TEACHING OF FOREIGN LANGUAGES ANNUAL CONFERENCE. Nov 18–20. Hyatt Regency & Baltimore Convention Center, Baltimore, MD. 39th annual meeting. For info: American Council on the Teaching of Foreign Languages, 6 Executive Plaza, Yonkers, NY 10701-6801. Phone: (914) 963-8830. Web: www.actfl.org.

DAGUERRE, LOUIS JACQUES MANDE: BIRTH ANNIVERSARY. Nov 18, 1789. French tax collector, theater scene-painter, physicist and inventor, was born at Cormeilles-en-Parisis, France. He is remembered for his invention of the daguerreotype photographic process—one of the earliest to permit a photographic image to be chemically fixed to provide a permanent picture. The process was presented to the French Academy of Science Jan 7, 1839. Daguerre died near Paris, France, July 10, 1851.

LATVIA: INDEPENDENCE DAY. Nov 18. National holiday. Commemorates the declaration of an independent Latvia in 1918.

MICKEY MOUSE'S BIRTHDAY. Nov 18. The comical activities of squeaky-voiced Mickey Mouse first appeared in 1928, on the screen of the Colony Theatre at New York City. The film, Walt Disney's *Steamboat Willie,* was the first animated cartoon talking picture. For more info: disney.go.com.

★**NATIONAL FARM-CITY WEEK.** Nov 18–24. Presidential Proclamation issued for a week in November since 1956, customarily for the week ending with Thanksgiving Day. Requested by congressional resolutions from 1956–58; since 1959 issued annually without request.

OMAN: NATIONAL HOLIDAY. Nov 18. Sultanate of Oman celebrates its national day.

"POWERPUFF GIRLS" TV PREMIERE: ANNIVERSARY. Nov 18, 1998. The city of Townsville is constantly overrun with monsters, usually led by evil villain/monkey Mojo Jo Jo. Luckily, there are three little girls who, as a result of a scientific experiment gone wrong, have superpowers to combat this evil. Feisty redhead Blossom, blonde sweetheart Bubbles and ready-to-fight brunette Buttercup use their flying, karate-chops, heat vision and extraordinary strength to save the world each night. This tongue-in-cheek program on Cartoon Network is just as popular with teenagers and adults as it is with younger kids; the feature film *The Powerpuff Girls Movie,* released in 2002, was extremely successful.

SHEPARD, ALAN: BIRTH ANNIVERSARY. Nov 18, 1923. Astronaut, born at East Derry, NH. Shepard was the first American in space when he flew *Freedom 7* in 1961, just 23 days after Russian Yuri Gargarin was the first person in space. Shepard died July 21, 1998, near Monterey, CA.

SOUTH AFRICA ADOPTS NEW CONSTITUTION: ANNIVERSARY. Nov 18, 1993. After more than 300 years of white majority rule, basic civil rights were finally granted to blacks in South Africa. The constitution providing such rights was approved by representatives of the ruling party, as well as members of 20 other political parties.

TEDDY BEAR: ANNIVERSARY. Nov 18, 1902. The *Washington Evening Star* published a cartoon on this day showing President Teddy Roosevelt while he was on a hunting trip in Mississippi refusing to shoot a mother bear. Candy store operator Morris Michtom and his wife of Brooklyn, NY, obtained the president's permission to use his name on their brown plush toy bear. While stuffed bears had been available for many years, this was the first to be called a teddy bear. For more info: *The Legend of the Teddy Bear,* by Frank Murphy (Sleeping Bear Press, 1-58536-013-9, $16.95 Gr. 2–4).

US UNIFORM TIME ZONE PLAN: ANNIVERSARY. Nov 18, 1883. Charles Ferdinand Dowd, a Connecticut schoolteacher and one of the early advocates of uniform time, proposed a time zone plan of the US (four zones of 15 degrees), which he and others persuaded the railroads to adopt and place in operation. Info from National Bureau of Standards Monograph 155. See also: "US Standard Time Act: Anniversary" (Mar 19).

BIRTHDAYS TODAY

Dante Bichette, 42, former baseball player, born West Palm Beach, FL, Nov 18, 1963.

Raghib (Rocket) Ismail, 36, former football player, born Elizabeth, NJ, Nov 18, 1969.

Wilma Mankiller, 60, Chief of the Cherokee Nation 1985–95, born Tahlequah, OK, Nov 18, 1945.

Warren Moon, 49, former football player, born Los Angeles, CA, Nov 18, 1956.

Ted Stevens, 82, US Senator (R, Alaska), born Indianapolis, IN, Nov 18, 1923.

Nancy Van Laan, 66, author (*So Say the Little Monkeys*), born Baton Rouge, LA, Nov 18, 1939.

NOVEMBER 19 — SATURDAY

Day 323 — 42 Remaining

BELIZE: GARIFUNA DAY. Nov 19. Public holiday celebrating the first arrival of Black Caribs from St. Vincent and Rotan to southern Belize in 1823.

CAMPANELLA, ROY: BIRTH ANNIVERSARY. Nov 19, 1921. Baseball Hall of Fame catcher, born at Philadelphia, PA. Died at Woodland Hills, CA, June 26, 1993.

COLD WAR FORMALLY ENDED: 15th ANNIVERSARY. Nov 19–21, 1990. A summit was held at Paris with the leaders of the Conference on Security and Cooperation in Europe (CSCE). The highlight of the summit was the signing of a treaty to dramatically reduce conventional weapons in Europe, thereby ending the Cold War.

FIRST AUTOMATIC TOLL COLLECTION MACHINE: ANNIVERSARY. Nov 19, 1954. At the Union Toll Plaza on New Jersey's Garden State Parkway motorists dropped 25¢ into a wire mesh hopper and a green light flashed. The first modern toll road was the Pennsylvania Turnpike, which opened in 1940, but tolls were collected by an attendant.

GARFIELD, JAMES ABRAM: BIRTH ANNIVERSARY. Nov 19, 1831. The 20th president of the US was born at Orange, OH, and was the first left-handed president. Term of office: Mar 4–Sept 19, 1881. While walking into the Washington, DC, railway station on the morning of July 2, 1881, Garfield was shot by disappointed office seeker Charles J. Guiteau. He survived, in very weak condition, until Sept 19, 1881, when he succumbed to blood poisoning at Elberon, NJ (where he had been taken for recuperation). Guiteau was tried, convicted and hanged at the jail at Washington, June 30, 1882. For more info: www.ipl.org/ref/POTUS.

LINCOLN'S GETTYSBURG ADDRESS: ANNIVERSARY. Nov 19, 1863. Seventeen acres of the Civil War battlefield at Gettysburg, PA, were dedicated as a national cemetery. Noted orator Edward Everett spoke for two hours; the address that Lincoln delivered in less than two minutes was later recognized as one of

November 2005

S	M	T	W	T	F	S
		1	2	3	4	5
6	7	8	9	10	11	12
13	14	15	16	17	18	19
20	21	22	23	24	25	26
27	28	29	30			

the most eloquent of the English language. Five manuscript copies in Lincoln's hand survive, including the rough draft begun in ink at the executive mansion at Washington and concluded in pencil at Gettysburg on the morning of the dedication (kept at the Library of Congress). For more info: *The Gettysburg Address* (Houghton Mifflin, 0-395-69824-3, $14.95 Gr. 3–5), *Abraham Lincoln's Gettysburg Address: Four Score and More*, by Barbara Silberdick Feinberg (Twenty First Century, 0-7613-1610-8, $24.40 Gr. 4–8) or go to Ben's Guide to US Government for Kids: bensguide .gpo.gov.

MONACO: NATIONAL HOLIDAY. Nov 19.

PELÉ SCORES 1,000th GOAL: ANNIVERSARY. Nov 19, 1969. Playing for the Santos team, legendary Brazilian soccer player Pelé scored his 1,000th goal in competition on a penalty kick against the team Vasco de Gama. Pelé dedicated this emotional and tremendous feat to Brazil's poor children and its elderly and suffering. By the time Pelé retired in 1977, he had scored an astounding 1,281 goals in 1,363 matches—a world record that still stands.

PUERTO RICO: DISCOVERY DAY. Nov 19. Public holiday. Columbus discovered Puerto Rico in 1493 on his second voyage to the New World.

RETIRED TEACHER'S DAY IN FLORIDA. Nov 19. A ceremonial day to honor the retired teachers of the state.

"ROCKY AND HIS FRIENDS" TV PREMIERE: ANNIVERSARY. Nov 19, 1959. This popular cartoon featured the adventures of a talking squirrel, Rocky (Rocket J. Squirrel), and his friend Bullwinkle, a flaky moose. The tongue-in-cheek dialogue contrasted with the simple plots in which Rocky and Bullwinkle tangled with Russian bad guys Boris Badenov and Natasha (who worked for Mr Big). Other popular segments on the show included the adventures of Sherman and Mr Peabody (an intelligent talking dog). In 1961 the show was renamed "The Bullwinkle Show," but the cast of characters remained the same.

SCHAEFER, JACK: BIRTH ANNIVERSARY. Nov 19, 1907. Author of the bestseller *Shane*, which was later made into an award-winning film. Born at Cleveland, OH, Schaefer died Jan 24, 1991, at Santa Fe, NM.

THAILAND: ELEPHANT ROUND-UP AT SURIN. Nov 19. Elephant demonstrations in morning, elephant races and tug-of-war between 100 men and one elephant. Observed since 1961 on third Saturday in November. Special trains from Bangkok on previous day.

ZION NATIONAL PARK ESTABLISHED: ANNIVERSARY. Nov 19, 1919. Utah's Mukuntuweap National Monument, proclaimed July 31, 1909, and later incorporated in Zion National Monument by proclamation Mar 18, 1918, was established as Zion National Park in 1919. For more park info: Zion National Park, Springdale, UT 84767-1099. Web: www.nps.gov/zion.

BIRTHDAYS TODAY

Eileen Collins, 49, first female shuttle commander, Lieutenant Colonel USAF, born Elmira, NY, Nov 19, 1956.

Gail Devers, 39, Olympic gold medal sprinter, born Seattle, WA, Nov 19, 1966.

Jodie Foster, 43, actress (*Little Man Tate, Nell*), director (*Home for the Holidays*), born Los Angeles, CA, Nov 19, 1962.

Thomas R. Harkin, 66, US Senator (D, Iowa), born Cumming, IA, Nov 19, 1939.

Ahmad Rashad, 56, sportscaster, former football player, born Bobby Moore, Portland, OR, Nov 19, 1949.

Meg Ryan, 44, actress (*Sleepless in Seattle, You've Got Mail*), born Fairfield, CT, Nov 19, 1961.

Kerri Strug, 28, Olympic gymnast, born Tucson, AZ, Nov 19, 1977.

Ted Turner, 67, baseball, basketball and cable TV executive, born Cincinnati, OH, Nov 19, 1938.

NOVEMBER 20 — SUNDAY

Day 324 — 41 Remaining

BILL OF RIGHTS: ANNIVERSARY OF FIRST STATE RATIFICATION. Nov 20, 1789. New Jersey became the first state to ratify 10 of the 12 amendments to the US Constitution proposed by Congress Sept 25. These 10 amendments came to be known as the Bill of Rights.

GERMANY: TOTENSONNTAG. Nov 20. The Protestant population's day of remembrance of the dead. Observed on the last Sunday of the church year (the Sunday before Advent).

KENNEDY, ROBERT FRANCIS: BIRTH ANNIVERSARY. Nov 20, 1925. US Senator and younger brother of John F. Kennedy (35th president), born at Brookline, MA. An assassin shot him at Los Angeles, CA, June 5, 1968, while he was campaigning for the presidential nomination. He died the next day. Sirhan Sirhan was convicted of his murder.

LAURIER, SIR WILFRED: BIRTH ANNIVERSARY. Nov 20, 1841. Canadian statesman (premier, 1896–1911), born at St. Lin, QC, Canada. Died Feb 17, 1919, at Ottawa, ON, Canada.

MEXICO: REVOLUTION DAY. Nov 20. Anniversary of the social revolution launched by Francisco I. Madero in 1910. National holiday.

MOTHER GOOSE PARADE. Nov 20. El Cajon, CA. "A celebration of children." Floats depict Mother Goose rhymes and fairy tales. Bands, equestrians and clowns. Traditionally, the Sunday before Thanksgiving. Est attendance: 450,000. For info: Mother Goose Parade Assn, 480 N Magnolia Ave, Ste 106, El Cajon, CA 92020. Phone: (619) 444-8712. Fax: (619) 444-3971. E-mail: mothergooseparade@att.net. Web: www.mothergooseparade .com.

NATIONAL ADOPTION WEEK. Nov 20–26. To commemorate the success of three kinds of adoption—infant, special needs and intercountry—through a variety of special events. Annually, the week of Thanksgiving. Est attendance: 15,000. For info: National Council for Adoption, 225 N Washington St, Alexandria, VA 22314-2520. Phone: (703) 299-6633. Fax: (703) 299-6004. Web: www.adoptioncouncil.org.

NATIONAL BIBLE WEEK. Nov 20–27. An interfaith campaign to promote reading and study of the Bible. Resource packets available. Governors and mayors across the country proclaim National Bible Week observance in their constituencies. Annually, from the Sunday preceding Thanksgiving to the following Sunday. For info:

Thomas R. May, Pres, National Bible Assn, 1865 Broadway, 7th Fl, New York, NY 10023. Phone: (212) 408-1390. E-mail: tmay@nationalbible.org. Web: www.nationalbible.org.

★**NATIONAL FAMILY WEEK.** Nov 20–26. Annually, the week containing Thanksgiving.

NATIONAL GAME AND PUZZLE WEEK. Nov 20–26. 11th annual event to increase appreciation of board games and puzzles while preserving the tradition of investing time with family and friends. Part of The Million Minute Family Challenge™, conducted Sept 1–Dec 31. Special teacher material and media information available, including press kits, interviews, etc. Annually, the Sunday through Saturday of Thanksgiving week. For info: Frank Beres, National Game and Puzzle Week, PO Box 268, Beloit, WI 53512-0268. Phone: (800) 524-4263. Fax: (608) 362-8178. E-mail: patch@patchproducts.com. Web: www.millionminute.com.

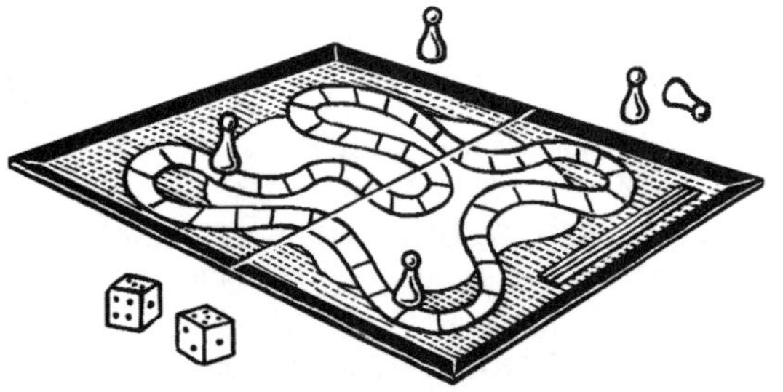

PASADENA DOO DAH PARADE. Nov 20. Pasadena, CA. No theme, no judging, no prizes, no order of march, no motorized vehicles and no animals. Annually, the Sunday before Thanksgiving. For info: Light Bringer Project, 64 N Raymond Ave, Pasadena, CA 91103. Phone: (626) 440-7379. Web: www.pasadenadoodahparade.com.

UNITED NATIONS: UNIVERSAL CHILDREN'S DAY. Nov 20. Designated by the UN General Assembly as Universal Children's Day. First observance was in 1953. A time to honor children with special ceremonies and festivals and to make children's needs known to governments. Observed on different days in more than 120 nations; Nov 20 marks the day in 1959 when the General Assembly adopted the Declaration of the Rights of the Child.

WOLCOTT, OLIVER: BIRTH ANNIVERSARY. Nov 20, 1726. Signer of the Declaration of Independence, Governor of Connecticut, born at Windsor, CT. Died Dec 1, 1797, at Litchfield, CT.

BIRTHDAYS TODAY

Marion Dane Bauer, 67, author (*On My Honor*), born Oglesby, IL, Nov 20, 1938.

Joseph R. Biden, Jr, 63, US Senator (D, Delaware), born Scranton, PA, Nov 20, 1942.

Matt Blunt, 35, Governor of Missouri (R), born Strafford, MO, Nov 20, 1970.

Robert C. Byrd, 88, US Senator (D, West Virginia), born North Wilkesboro, NC, Nov 20, 1917.

November 2005

S	M	T	W	T	F	S
		1	2	3	4	5
6	7	8	9	10	11	12
13	14	15	16	17	18	19
20	21	22	23	24	25	26
27	28	29	30			

NOVEMBER 21 — MONDAY

Day 325 — 40 Remaining

CONGRESS FIRST MEETS IN WASHINGTON: ANNIVERSARY. Nov 21, 1800. Congress met at Philadelphia from 1790 to 1800, when the north wing of the new Capitol at Washington, DC, was completed. The House and Senate were scheduled to meet in the new building Nov 17, 1800, but a quorum wasn't achieved until Nov 21. To take a virtual tour of the Capitol, go to: www.senate.gov/vtour.

NORTH CAROLINA RATIFIES CONSTITUTION: ANNIVERSARY. Nov 21. Became 12th state to ratify Constitution in 1789.

SPEARE, ELIZABETH GEORGE: BIRTH ANNIVERSARY. Nov 21, 1908. Author (Newbery for *The Bronze Bow, The Witch of Blackbird Pond*), born at Melrose, MA. Died at Tucson, AZ, Nov 15, 1994. For a study guide to *The Witch of Blackbird Pond*: glencoe.com/sec/literature/litlibrary.

UNITED NATIONS: WORLD TELEVISION DAY. Nov 21. On Dec 17, 1996, the General Assembly proclaimed this day as World Television Day, commemorating the date in 1996 on which the first World Television Forum was held at the UN. Info from: United Nations, Dept of Public Info, New York, NY 10017.

WORLD HELLO DAY. Nov 21. Everyone who participates greets 10 people. People in 180 countries have participated in this annual activity for advancing peace through personal communication. Heads of state of 114 countries have expressed approval of the event. 33rd annual observance. For info: Michael McCormack, The McCormack Brothers, PO Box 15592, Beverly Hills, CA 90209. Web: www.worldhelloday.org.

BIRTHDAYS TODAY

Troy Aikman, 39, former football player, born West Covina, CA, Nov 21, 1966.

Mary Jane Auch, 67, author, illustrator (*I Was a Third Grade Science Project, The Nutquacker*), born Mineola, NY, Nov 21, 1938.

Phil Bredesen, 62, Governor of Tennessee (D), born Shortsville, NY, Nov 21, 1943.

Richard J. Durbin, 61, US Senator (D, Illinois), born East St. Louis, IL, Nov 21, 1944.

George Kenneth (Ken) Griffey, Jr, 36, baseball player, born Donora, PA, Nov 21, 1969.

Stanley (Stan the Man) Musial, 85, Hall of Fame baseball player, born Donora, PA, Nov 21, 1920.

Tasha Schwikert, 21, gymnast, born Las Vegas, NV, Nov 21, 1984.

Marlo Thomas, 67, actress ("That Girl"), author (*Free to Be . . . You and Me*), born Detroit, MI, Nov 21, 1938.

Megan Whalen Turner, 40, author (*The Thief*), born Fort Sill, OK, Nov 21, 1965.

NOVEMBER 22 — TUESDAY

Day 326 — 39 Remaining

ADAMS, ABIGAIL SMITH: BIRTH ANNIVERSARY. Nov 22, 1744. Wife of John Adams, second president of the US, born at Weymouth, MA. Died Oct 28, 1818, at Quincy, MA. For more info: *Abigail Adams*, by Alexandra Wallner (Holiday, 0-8234-1442-6, $16.95 Gr. K–3) or *John & Abigail Adams: An American Love Story*, by Judith St. George (Holiday, 0-8234-1571-6, $22.95 Gr. 6–9).

GARNER, JOHN NANCE: BIRTH ANNIVERSARY. Nov 22, 1868. The 32nd vice president of US (1933–41), born at Red River County, TX. Died at Uvalde, TX, Nov 7, 1967.

★ ★ ★

KENNEDY, JOHN F., ASSASSINATION: ANNIVERSARY. Nov 22, 1963. President John F. Kennedy was slain by a sniper while riding in an open automobile at Dallas, TX. Accused assassin Lee Harvey Oswald was killed in police custody while awaiting trial.

LEBANON: INDEPENDENCE DAY. Nov 22. National Day. Gained independence from France in 1943.

NATIONAL STOP THE VIOLENCE DAY. Nov 22. Radio and television stations across the nation are encouraged to promote "Peace on the Streets" and help put an end to gang (and other) violence through Stop the Violence Day. Participating stations unite to call for a one-day cease fire, the idea being, "If we can stop the violence for one day, we can stop the violence everyday, one day at a time." Stations also encourage listeners/viewers to wear and display white ribbons that day and drive with their headlights on as a show of peace. Many stations hold peace rallies with local community leaders and also conduct a moment of silence on the air in honor of the year's victims of violence. Begun in 1990. Annually, on the anniversary of President John F. Kennedy's assassination. For info: Cliff Berkowitz, Pres, Lost Coast Communications, Inc, PO Box 25, Ferndale, CA 95536. Phone: (707) 786-5104. Fax: (707) 786-5100.

SAGITTARIUS, THE ARCHER. Nov 22–Dec 21. In the astronomical/astrological zodiac that divides the sun's apparent orbit into 12 segments, the period Nov 22–Dec 21 is identified, traditionally, as the sun sign of Sagittarius, the Archer. The ruling planet is Jupiter.

TEACH, EDWARD "BLACKBEARD": DEATH ANNIVERSARY. Nov 22, 1718. The English pirate of the Caribbean and American Atlantic met his end at Ocracoke Island, NC, in hand-to-hand combat with British naval forces defending coastal cities. Born around 1680 at Bristol, England, Teach had a notorious reputation in a pirate career that lasted from 1716–18 aboard his ship *Queen Anne's Revenge*. Teach grew his hair and beard to long lengths and plaited them, and set lighted cords about his head to create evil-looking smoke around him. For more info: www.ocracoke-nc.com/blackbeard/ or *Eyewitness: Pirate* by Richard Platt (DK Publishing, 0-789-46608-2, $19.99 Ages 9–12).

BIRTHDAYS TODAY

Boris Becker, 38, former tennis player, born Leimen, Germany, Nov 22, 1967.

Guion S. Bluford, Jr, 63, first black astronaut in space, born Philadelphia, PA, Nov 22, 1942.

Jamie Lee Curtis, 47, actress, author (*Today I Feel Silly and Other Moods That Make My Day*), born Los Angeles, CA, Nov 22, 1958.

NOVEMBER 23 — WEDNESDAY

Day 327 — 38 Remaining

JAPAN: LABOR THANKSGIVING DAY. Nov 23. National holiday.

MOON PHASE: LAST QUARTER. Nov 23. Moon enters Last Quarter phase at 5:11 PM, EST.

PIERCE, FRANKLIN: BIRTH ANNIVERSARY. Nov 23, 1804. The 14th president of the US (Mar 4, 1853–Mar 3, 1857) was born at Hillsboro, NH. Not nominated until the 49th ballot at the Democratic party convention in 1852, he was refused his party's nomination in 1856 for a second term. Pierce died at Concord, NH, Oct 8, 1869. For more info: www.ipl.org/ref/POTUS.

RUTLEDGE, EDWARD: BIRTH ANNIVERSARY. Nov 23, 1749. Signer of the Declaration of Independence, governor of South Carolina, born at Charleston, SC. Died there Jan 23, 1800.

"WHAT DO YOU LOVE ABOUT AMERICA" DAY. Nov 23. One day to talk about what's great about our country and its people. In the midst of cynicism, let's talk to each other about what we love. Annually, the day before Thanksgiving. For info: Chuck Sutherland, 6906 Waggoner Pl, Dallas, TX 75230. Phone: (214) 696-9214. Fax: (214) 722-1266. E-mail: sutherla@swbell.net.

BIRTHDAYS TODAY

Vin Baker, 34, basketball player, born Lake Wales, FL, Nov 23, 1971.

Jim Doyle, 60, Governor of Wisconsin (D), born Madison, WI, Nov 23, 1945.

Mary L. Landrieu, 50, US Senator (D, Louisiana), born Arlington, VA, Nov 23, 1955.

Charles E. Schumer, 55, US Senator (D, New York), born Brooklyn, NY, Nov 23, 1950.

Gloria Whelan, 82, author (National Book Award for *Homeless Bird*; *Once on This Island*, *The Indian School*), born Detroit, MI, Nov 23, 1923.

NOVEMBER 24 — THURSDAY

Day 328 — 37 Remaining

AMERICA'S THANKSGIVING PARADE. Nov 24. Woodward Ave, Detroit, MI. The annual parade kicks off the holiday season with more than 25 floats, 15 huge balloons and 1,000 costumed marchers. Annually, on Thanksgiving morning since 1924. Est attendance: 1,300,000. For info: Dennis Carnovale, The Parade Co, 9600 Mt Elliott, Detroit, MI 48211. Phone: (313) 923-7400. Fax: (313) 923-2920. Web: www.theparade.org.

BARKLEY, ALBEN WILLIAM: BIRTH ANNIVERSARY. Nov 24, 1877. The 35th vice president of the US (1949–53), born at Graves County, KY. Died at Lexington, VA, Apr 30, 1956.

BURNETT, FRANCES HODGSON: BIRTH ANNIVERSARY. Nov 24, 1849. Children's author, noted for the classics *Little Lord Fauntleroy*, *The Secret Garden* and *A Little Princess*. Born at Manchester, England, she died at Long Island, NY, Oct 29, 1924.

MACY'S THANKSGIVING DAY PARADE. Nov 24. New York, NY. 79th annual. Starts at 9 AM, EST, in Central Park West. A part of everyone's Thanksgiving, the parade grows bigger and better each year. Featuring floats, giant balloons, marching bands and famous stars, the parade is televised for the whole country. For info: New York CVB, 810 Seventh Ave, 3rd Fl, New York, NY 10019. Phone: (212) 484-1222. Web: www.nycvisit.com.

TAYLOR, ZACHARY: BIRTH ANNIVERSARY. Nov 24, 1784. The soldier who became 12th president of the US (Mar 4, 1849–July 9, 1850) was born at Orange County, VA. He was nominated at the Whig party convention in 1848, but, the story goes, he did not accept the letter notifying him of his nomination because it had postage due. He cast his first vote in 1846, when he was 62 years old. Becoming ill July 4, 1850, he died at the White House, July 9. For more info: www.ipl.org/ref/POTUS.

★**THANKSGIVING DAY.** Nov 24. Presidential Proclamation. Always issued for the fourth Thursday in November. See also: "First US Holiday by Presidential Proclamation: Anniversary" (Nov 26).

THANKSGIVING DAY. Nov 24. Legal public holiday (Public Law 90–363 sets Thanksgiving Day on the fourth Thursday in November). Observed in all states. In most states, the Friday after Thanksgiving is also a holiday; in Nevada it is called Family Day. For more info: *Let's Celebrate Thanksgiving*, by Peter and Connie Roop (Millbrook, 0-7613-0973-X, $19.90 Gr. PreK–3).

UCHIDA, YOSHIKO: BIRTH ANNIVERSARY. Nov 24, 1921. Author (*Journey to Topaz: A Story of the Japanese-American Evacuation*), born at Alameda, CA. Died in 1992. For a study guide to her book *Picture Bride*: glencoe.com/sec/literature/litlibrary.

BIRTHDAYS TODAY

Sylvia Louise Engdahl, 72, author (*Enchantress from the Stars*), born Los Angeles, CA, Nov 24, 1933.

Mordicai Gerstein, 70, author (*The Wild Boy*, Caldecott Medal for *The Man Who Walked Between the Towers*), born Los Angeles, CA, Nov 24, 1935.

Meredith Henderson, 22, actress ("The Adventures of Shirley Holmes: Detective"), born Ottawa, ON, Canada, Nov 24, 1983.

Keith Primeau, 34, hockey player, born Toronto, ON, Canada, Nov 24, 1971.

Ruth Sanderson, 54, author, illustrator (*The Twelve Dancing Princesses*, *Papa Gatto*), born Ware, MA, Nov 24, 1951.

NOVEMBER 25 — FRIDAY

Day 329 — 36 Remaining

AUTOMOBILE SPEED REDUCTION: ANNIVERSARY. Nov 25, 1973. Anniversary of the presidential order requiring a cutback from the 70 MPH speed limit due to the energy crisis. The 55 MPH National Maximum Speed Limit (NMSL) was established by Congress in January 1974. The National Highway Traffic Administration reported that "the 55 MPH NMSL forestalled 48,310 fatalities through 1980. There were also reductions in crash-related injuries and property damage." Motor fuel savings were estimated at 2.4 billion gallons per year. Notwithstanding, in 1987 Congress permitted states to increase speed limits on rural interstate highways to 65 MPH.

BOSNIA AND HERZEGOVINA: NATIONAL DAY. Nov 25. National holiday. Commemorates the 1943 declaration of statehood within the Yugoslav Federation.

BUY NOTHING DAY. Nov 25. A 24-hour moratorium on consumer spending, a celebration of simplicity, about getting our runaway consumer culture back onto a sustainable path. Annually, on the first shopping day after Thanksgiving. For info: The Media Foundation, 1243 W 7th Ave, Vancouver, BC, Canada V6H 1B7. Phone: (800) 663-1243 or (604) 736-9401. Fax: (604) 737-6021. E-mail: buynothingday@adbusters.org. Web: www.adbusters.org/campaigns.

CARNEGIE, ANDREW: BIRTH ANNIVERSARY. Nov 25, 1835. American financier, philanthropist and benefactor of more than 2,500 libraries, was born at Dunfermline, Scotland. Carnegie Hall, Carnegie Foundation and the Carnegie Endowment for International Peace are among his gifts. Carnegie died at his summer estate, "Shadowbrook," MA, Aug 11, 1919. For more info: www.pbs.org/wgbh/amex/carnegie.

DEPARTMENT OF HOMELAND SECURITY CREATED: ANNIVERSARY. Nov 25, 2002. In the aftermath of the Sept 11, 2001, terrorist attacks on the United States, the Department of Homeland Security was created for the purpose of monitoring safety and threats within and against the United States. Signed into law on this date, the Homeland Security Act of 2002 restructured sections of 22 different federal agencies, including the CIA, FBI and Secret Service, in the most significant governmental reorganization since 1947 when Harry S Truman reorganized the Armed Forces and created the Department of Defense. A new cabinet position was created and former Pennsylvania Governor Tom Ridge was confirmed by the Senate as the first Secretary on Jan 24, 2003.

DiMAGGIO, JOSEPH PAUL (JOE): BIRTH ANNIVERSARY. Nov 25, 1914. Baseball Hall of Fame outfielder, born at Martinez, CA. In 1941 he was on "the streak," getting a hit in 56 consecutive games. He was the American League MVP for three years, was the batting champion in 1939 and led the league in RBIs in both 1941 and 1948. DiMaggio died at Harbour Island, FL, Mar 8, 1999. For more info: www.pbs.org/wgbh/amex/dimaggio.

EASTMAN, P.D.: BIRTH ANNIVERSARY. Nov 25, 1909. Philip Dey Eastman was born at Amherst, MA. His *Are You My Mother?* and *Go, Dog, Go!* rank among the bestselling children's books of all time. He died Jan 7, 1986.

FAMILY DAY IN NEVADA. Nov 25. Observed annually on the Friday following the fourth Thursday in November.

POPE JOHN XXIII: BIRTH ANNIVERSARY. Nov 25, 1881. Angelo Roncalli, 261st pope of the Roman Catholic Church, born at Sotte il Monte, Italy. Elected pope, Oct 28, 1958. Died June 3, 1963, at Rome, Italy.

SHOPPING REMINDER DAY. Nov 25. One month before Christmas, a reminder to shoppers that there are only 28 more shopping days (excluding Christmas Eve) after today until Christmas.

SURINAME: INDEPENDENCE DAY. Nov 25. Holiday. Gained independence from the Netherlands in 1975.

UNITED NATIONS: INTERNATIONAL DAY FOR THE ELIMINATION OF VIOLENCE AGAINST WOMEN. Nov 25. Observed by the United Nations since 1993 on the anniversary of the 1960 murder of the Mirabal sisters in the Dominican Republic. In 2004, UN Secretary-General Kofi Annan said, "Let us be encouraged that there is a growing understanding of the problem. But let us also pledge to do our utmost to protect women, banish such violence and build a world in which women enjoy their rights and freedoms on an equal basis with men. Annually, Nov 25. For more info: www.un.org.

November 2005

S	M	T	W	T	F	S
		1	2	3	4	5
6	7	8	9	10	11	12
13	14	15	16	17	18	19
20	21	22	23	24	25	26
27	28	29	30			

BIRTHDAYS TODAY

Marc Brown, 59, author and illustrator (the Arthur series), born Erie, PA, Nov 25, 1946.
Cris Carter, 40, former football player, born Troy, OH, Nov 25, 1965.
Shirley Climo, 77, author (*The Egyptian Cinderella, The Irish Cinderlad*), born Cleveland, OH, Nov 25, 1928.
Crescent Dragonwagon, 53, author (*Half a Moon and One Whole Star*), born Ellen Zolotow, New York, NY, Nov 25, 1952.
Robert Ehrlich, Jr, 48, Governor of Maryland (R), born Baltimore, MD, Nov 25, 1957.
John Lynch, 53, Governor of New Hampshire (D), born Waltham, MA, Nov 25, 1952.
Clint Mathis, 29, soccer player, born Conyers, GA, Nov 25, 1976.
Donovan McNabb, 29, football player, born Dolton, IL, Nov 25, 1976.
Andrea Stinson, 38, basketball player, born Mooresville, NC, Nov 25, 1967.

NOVEMBER 26 — SATURDAY

Day 330 — 35 Remaining

***ALICE IN WONDERLAND* PUBLISHED: ANNIVERSARY.** Nov 26, 1865. Lewis Carroll's novel was published on this date. *Through the Looking Glass* followed in 1871.

CUSTER BATTLEFIELD BECOMES LITTLE BIGHORN BATTLEFIELD: ANNIVERSARY. Nov 26, 1991. The US Congress approved a bill renaming Custer Battlefield National Monument as Little Bighorn Battlefield National Monument. The bill also authorized the construction of a memorial to the Native Americans who fought and died at the battle known as Custer's Last Stand. Introduced by then Representative Ben Nighthorse Campbell, the only Native American in Congress, the bill was signed into law by President George Bush. For more info: www.nps.gov/libi/index.htm.

FIRST US HOLIDAY BY PRESIDENTIAL PROCLAMATION: ANNIVERSARY. Nov 26, 1789. President George Washington proclaimed Nov 26, 1789, to be Thanksgiving Day. Both Houses of Congress, by their joint committee, had requested him to recommend "a day of public thanksgiving and prayer, to be observed by acknowledging with grateful hearts the many and signal favors of Almighty God, especially by affording them an opportunity to peaceably establish a form of government for their safety and happiness." Proclamation issued Oct 3, 1789.

MEXICO: GUADALAJARA INTERNATIONAL BOOK FAIR. Nov 26–Dec 4. Latin America's largest book fair with exhibitors from all over the Spanish-speaking world. Est attendance: 425,000. For info: David Unger, Guadalajara Book Fair–US Office, Div of Hum, NAC 5225, City College, New York, NY 10031. Phone: (212) 650-7925. Fax: (212) 650-7912. E-mail: filny@aol.com.

MONGOLIA: REPUBLIC DAY. Nov 26. National day. Commemorates declaration of the republic in 1924.

SCHULZ, CHARLES: BIRTH ANNIVERSARY. Nov 26, 1922. Cartoonist, born at Minneapolis, MN. Created the "Peanuts" comic strip that debuted on Oct 2, 1950. The strip included Charlie Brown, his sister Sally, his dog Snoopy, friends Linus and Lucy and a variety of other characters. Stricken with colon cancer, Schulz's last daily strip was published Jan 3, 2000, and his last Sunday strip was published Feb 13, 2000, the day after he died. The strip ran in more than 2,500 newspapers in many different countries. Schulz won the Reuben Award in both 1955 and 1964 and was named International Cartoonist of the Year in 1978. Several TV specials were spin-offs of the strip including "It's the Great Pumpkin Charlie Brown" and "You're a Good Man Charlie Brown." Schulz died at Santa Rosa, CA, Feb 12, 2000. See also: "Peanuts Debuts: Anniversary" (Oct 2).

SLINKY® INTRODUCED: 60th ANNIVERSARY. Nov 26, 1945. In 1943 engineer Richard James was working in a Philadelphia shipyard trying to find a way to stabilize a piece of equipment on a ship in heavy seas. One idea was to suspend it on springs. One day a spring tumbled off his desk, giving him the idea for a toy. The accidental plaything was introduced by James and his wife in a Philadelphia department store during the 1945 Christmas season. Today more than 250,000,000 Slinkys have been sold. For more info: www.slinkytoys.com.

TRUTH, SOJOURNER: DEATH ANNIVERSARY. Nov 26, 1883. A former slave who had been sold four different times, Sojourner Truth became an evangelist who argued for abolition and women's rights. After a troubled early life, she began her evangelical career in 1843, traveling through New England until she discovered the utopian colony called the Northampton Association of Education and Industry. It was there she was exposed to, and became an advocate for, the cause of abolition, working with Frederick Douglass, Wendell Phillips, William Lloyd Garrison and others. In 1850 she befriended Lucretia Mott, Elizabeth Cady Stanton and other feminist leaders and actively began supporting calls for women's rights. In 1870 she attempted to petition Congress to create a "Negro State" on public lands in the West. Born at Ulster County, NY, about 1790, with the name Isabella Van Wagener, she died Nov 26, 1883, at Battle Creek, MI. For more info: *Sojourner Truth: A Voice for Freedom*, by Patricia and Fredrick McKissack (Enslow, 0-8949-0313-6, $14.95 Gr. K–3), *Only Passing Through: The Story of Sojourner Truth*, by Anne Rockwell (Random House, 0-679-99186-7, $16.95 Gr. 2–5), *Sojourner Truth: Ain't I a Woman?* by Patricia and Fredrick McKissack (Scholastic, 0-59-044691-6, $4.50 Gr. 3–7) or www.sojournertruth.org.

BIRTHDAYS TODAY

Samuel Bodman, 67, US Secretary of Energy, born Chicago, IL, Nov 26, 1938.
Jessica Bowman, 25, actress ("Dr. Quinn, Medicine Woman"), born Walnut Creek, CA, Nov 26, 1980.
Shannon Dunn, 33, Olympic snowboarder, born Arlington Heights, IL, Nov 26, 1972.
Dale Jarrett, 49, race car driver, born Conover, NC, Nov 26, 1956.
Shawn Kemp, 36, basketball player, born Elkhart, IN, Nov 26, 1969.
Chris Osgood, 33, hockey player, born Peace River, AB, Canada, Nov 26, 1972.
Laurence Pringle, 70, science writer (*An Extraordinary Life: The Story of a Monarch Butterfly*), born Rochester, NY, Nov 26, 1935.

NOVEMBER 27 — SUNDAY

Day 331 — 34 Remaining

ADVENT, FIRST SUNDAY. Nov 27. Advent includes the four Sundays before Christmas: Nov 27, Dec 4, Dec 11 and Dec 18 in 2005.

JOHN F. KENNEDY DAY IN MASSACHUSETTS. Nov 27. Proclaimed annually by the governor for the last Sunday in November.

LIVINGSTON, ROBERT R.: BIRTH ANNIVERSARY. Nov 27, 1746. Member of the Continental Congress, farmer, diplomat and jurist, born at New York, NY. It was Livingston who administered the oath of office to President George Washington in 1789. He died at Clermont, NY, Feb 26, 1813.

WEIZMANN, CHAIM: BIRTH ANNIVERSARY. Nov 27, 1874. Israeli statesman, born near Pinsk, Byelorussia. He played an important role in bringing about the British government's Balfour Declaration, calling for the establishment of a national home for Jews at Palestine. He died at Tel Aviv, Israel, Nov 9, 1952.

BIRTHDAYS TODAY

Richard Codey, 59, Acting Governor of New Jersey (D), born Orange, NJ, Nov 27, 1946.

Hilary Hahn, 26, violinist, born Lexington, VA, Nov 27, 1979.

Kevin Henkes, 45, author and illustrator (Caldecott for *Kitten's First Full Moon*, Newbery Honor for *Olive's Ocean*), born Racine, WI, Nov 27, 1960.

Bill Nye, 50, host ("Bill Nye, the Science Guy"), born Washington, DC, Nov 27, 1955.

Jimmy Rollins, 27, baseball player, born Oakland, CA, Nov 27, 1978.

Nick Van Exel, 34, basketball player, born Kenosha, WI, Nov 27, 1971.

Jaleel White, 29, actor ("Family Matters"), born Pasadena, CA, Nov 27, 1976.

NOVEMBER 28 — MONDAY

Day 332 — 33 Remaining

ALBANIA: INDEPENDENCE DAY: ANNIVERSARY. Nov 28. National holiday. Commemorates independence from the Ottoman Empire in 1912.

CHAD: REPUBLIC DAY. Nov 28. National holiday. Commemorates the proclamation of the republic in 1958.

MAURITANIA: INDEPENDENCE DAY. Nov 28. National holiday. This country in the northwest part of Africa attained sovereignty from France on this day in 1960.

PANAMA: INDEPENDENCE FROM SPAIN. Nov 28. Public holiday. Commemorates the independence of Panama (which at the time was part of Colombia) from Spain in 1821.

November 2005

S	M	T	W	T	F	S
		1	2	3	4	5
6	7	8	9	10	11	12
13	14	15	16	17	18	19
20	21	22	23	24	25	26
27	28	29	30			

BIRTHDAYS TODAY

Stephanie Calmenson, 53, author (*Dinner at the Panda Palace, The Gator Girls*), born Brooklyn, NY, Nov 28, 1952.

Ed Harris, 55, actor (*The Right Stuff*), born Englewood, NJ, Nov 28, 1950.

Mary Lyons, 58, author of biographies (*Catching the Fire: Philip Simmons, Blacksmith*), born Macon, GA, Nov 28, 1947.

Ed Young, 74, author and illustrator (Caldecott for *Lon Po Po: A Red Riding Hood Story from China*), born Tientsin, China, Nov 28, 1931.

NOVEMBER 29 — TUESDAY

Day 333 — 32 Remaining

ALCOTT, LOUISA MAY: BIRTH ANNIVERSARY. Nov 29, 1832. American author, born at Philadelphia, PA. Died at Boston, MA, Mar 6, 1888. Her most famous novel was *Little Women*, the classic story of Meg, Jo, Beth and Amy. For more info: www.alcottweb.com or www.louisamayalcott.org.

CHRISTMAS TREE AT ROCKEFELLER CENTER: ANNUAL LIGHTING. Nov 29 (tentative). New York, NY. Lighting of the huge Christmas tree in Rockefeller Plaza signals the opening of the holiday season at New York City. More than 30,000 lights are strung on 5 miles of electric wire. In 1933, the first formal tree lighting ceremony took place with 700 lights. Date is usually a weekday during the week after Thanksgiving.

CZECHOSLOVAKIA ENDS COMMUNIST RULE: ANNIVERSARY. Nov 29, 1989. Czechoslovakia ended 41 years of one-party communist rule when the Czechoslovak parliament voted unanimously to repeal the constitutional clauses giving the Communist Party a guaranteed leading role in the country and promoting Marxism-Leninism as the state ideology. The vote came at the end of a 12-day revolution sparked by the beating of protestors Nov 17. Although the Communist Party remained in power, the tide of reform led to its ouster by the Civic Forum, headed by playwright Vaclav Havel. The Civic Forum demanded free elections with equal rights for all parties, a mixed economy and support for foreign investment. In the first free elections in Czechoslovakia since WWII, Vaclav Havel was elected president.

LEWIS, C.S. (CLIVE STAPLES): BIRTH ANNIVERSARY. Nov 29, 1898. British scholar, novelist and author (*The Screwtape Letters, Chronicles of Narnia*), born at Belfast, Ireland. In 1950, he published *The Lion, the Witch and the Wardrobe*, the first of the immensely popular seven-volume Chronicles of Narnia series. Died at Oxford, England, Nov 22, 1963.

WAITE, MORRISON R.: BIRTH ANNIVERSARY. Nov 29, 1816. Seventh Chief Justice of the Supreme Court, born at Lyme, CT. Appointed Chief Justice by President Ulysses S. Grant Jan 19, 1874. The Waite Court is remembered for its controversial rulings that did much to rehabilitate the idea of states' rights after the Civil War and early Reconstruction years. Waite died at Washington, DC, Mar 23, 1888. For more info: oyez.northwestern.edu/justices/justices.cgi.

BIRTHDAYS TODAY

Helga Aichinger, 68, illustrator (*The Shepherd*), born Traun, Austria, Nov 29, 1937.

Eric Beddows, 54, illustrator (*Joyful Noise*), born Woodstock, ON, Canada, Nov 29, 1951.

Jacques Rene Chirac, 73, President of France, born Paris, France, Nov 29, 1932.

Madeleine L'Engle, 87, author (*A Ring of Endless Light, A Swiftly Tilting Planet*, Newbery for *A Wrinkle in Time*), born New York, NY, Nov 29, 1918.

Janet Napolitano, 48, Governor of Arizona (D), born Pittsburgh, PA, Nov 29, 1957.

Mariano Rivera, 36, baseball player, born Panama City, Panama, Nov 29, 1969.

Adam Zolotin, 22, actor (*Jack*), born Long Island, NY, Nov 29, 1983.

NOVEMBER 30 — WEDNESDAY

Day 334 — 31 Remaining

BARBADOS: INDEPENDENCE DAY. Nov 30. National holiday. Gained independence from Great Britain in 1966.

CHISHOLM, SHIRLEY: BIRTH ANNIVERSARY. Nov 30, 1924. Born at Brooklyn, NY, Shirley St. Hill Chisholm was an educator, author and politician who was the first African-American woman elected to the United States House of Representatives. A liberal Democrat, she was known for her strong opinions and outspoken nature as she represented the Bedford-Stuyvesant neighborhood of New York City in Congress from 1974–1982. She fought against poverty and discrimination, and ran for the 1972 Democratic nomination for President just to prove that she could. She retired from politics in the 1980s, and died at Ormond Beach, FL, Jan 1, 2005.

MONTGOMERY, LUCY MAUD: BIRTH ANNIVERSARY. Nov 30, 1874. Author, known for her classic Anne of Green Gables series of books. Her first, *Anne of Green Gables*, was published in 1908. Born at New London, Prince Edward Island, Canada, Montgomery died at Toronto, Canada, Apr 24, 1952.

PHILIPPINES: BONIFACIO DAY. Nov 30. Also known as National Heroes' Day. Commemorates birth in 1863 of Andres Bonifacio, leader of the 1896 revolt against Spain.

SAINT ANDREW'S DAY. Nov 30. Feast day of the apostle and martyr, Andrew, who died about AD 60. Patron saint of Scotland.

TWAIN, MARK: BIRTH ANNIVERSARY. Nov 30, 1835. Celebrated American author, born Samuel Langhorne Clemens, whose books include *The Adventures of Tom Sawyer*, *The Adventures of Huckleberry Finn* and *The Prince and the Pauper*. Born at Florida, MO, Twain is quoted as saying, "I came in with Halley's Comet in 1835. It is coming again next year, and I expect to go out with it." He did. Twain died at Redding, CT, Apr 21, 1910 (just one day after Halley's Comet's perihelion).

ZEMACH, MARGOT: BIRTH ANNIVERSARY. Nov 30, 1931. Illustrator (Caldecott for *Duffy and the Devil*), born at Los Angeles, CA. Died May 21, 1989, at Berkeley, CA.

BIRTHDAYS TODAY

Clay Aiken, 27, singer, born Clayton Harris Grissom at Raleigh, NC, Nov 30, 1978.

Richard Burr, 50, US Senator (R, North Carolina), born Charlottesville, VA, Nov 30, 1955.

Joan Ganz Cooney, 76, founder of the Children's Television Workshop and creator of "Sesame Street," born Nov 30, 1929.

Ivan Rodriguez, 34, baseball player, born Vega Baja, Puerto Rico, Nov 30, 1971.

Margaret Spellings, 48, US Secretary of Education, born in Michigan, Nov 30, 1957.

Paul Stookey, 68, singer, songwriter (Peter, Paul and Mary), born Baltimore, MD, Nov 30, 1937.

Natalie Williams, 35, basketball player, born Long Beach, CA, Nov 30, 1970.

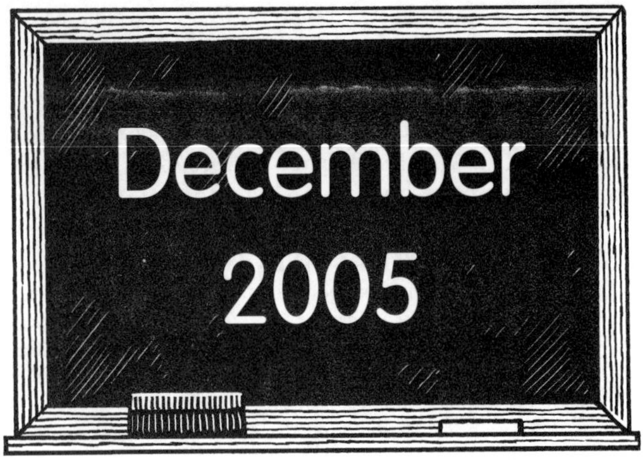

DECEMBER 1 — THURSDAY

Day 335 — 30 Remaining

ANTARCTICA MADE A SCIENTIFIC PRESERVE: ANNIVERSARY. Dec 1, 1959. Representatives of 12 nations, including the US and the Soviet Union, signed a treaty at Washington, DC, setting aside Antarctica as a scientific preserve, free from military activity. Antarctica is equal in area to the US and Europe combined. For more info: quest.arc.nasa.gov/antarctica2/main/s_index.html or www.glacier.rice.edu.

BASKETBALL CREATED: ANNIVERSARY. Dec 1, 1891. James Naismith was a teacher of physical education at the International YMCA Training College at Springfield, MA. In order to create an indoor sport that could be played during the winter months, he nailed up peach baskets at opposite ends of the gym and gave students soccer balls to toss into them. Thus was born the game of basketball.

BINGO'S BIRTHDAY MONTH. Dec 1–31. To celebrate the innovation and manufacture of the game of Bingo in 1929 by Edwin S. Lowe. Bingo has grown into a five-billion-dollar-a-year charitable fund-raiser. For info: Tara Snowden, Pres, Bingo Bugle, Inc, Box 527, Vashon, WA 98070. Phone: (800) 327-6437 or (206) 463-5656. E-mail: tara@bingobugle.com.

MOON PHASE: NEW MOON. Dec 1. Moon enters New Moon phase at 10:01 AM, EST.

PORTUGAL: INDEPENDENCE DAY. Dec 1. Public holiday. Became independent of Spain in 1640.

ROMANIA: NATIONAL DAY. Dec 1. National holiday. Commemorates unification of Romania and Transylvania in 1918.

ROSA PARKS DAY: 50th ANNIVERSARY OF ARREST. Dec 1, 1955. Anniversary of the arrest of Rosa Parks, at Montgomery, AL, for refusing to give up her seat and move to the back of a municipal bus. Her arrest triggered a yearlong boycott of the city bus system and led to legal actions which ended racial segregation on municipal buses throughout the southern US. The event has been called the birth of the modern civil rights movement. Rosa McCauley Parks was born at Tuskegee, AL, Feb 4, 1913. For more info: *If a Bus Could Talk: The Story of Rosa Parks*, by Faith Ringgold (Simon & Schuster, 0-68-981892-0, $16 Gr. K–3). ***See Curriculum Connection.***

SAFE TOYS AND GIFTS MONTH. Dec 1–31. What toys are dangerous to children's eyesight? Tips on how to choose age-appropriate toys will be distributed. For info: Prevent Blindness America®, 500 E Remington Rd, Schaumburg, IL 60173. Phone: (800) 331-2020. Fax: (847) 843-8458. Web: www.preventblindness.org.

UNITED NATIONS: WORLD AIDS DAY. Dec 1. In 1988 the World Health Organization of the United Nations declared Dec 1 as World AIDS Day, an international day of awareness and education about AIDS. The WHO is the leader in global direction and coordination of AIDS prevention, control, research and education. A program called UN-AIDS was created to bring together the skills and expertise of the World Bank, UNDP, UNESCO, UNICEF, UNFPA and the WHO to strengthen and expand national capacities to respond to the pandemic.

UNIVERSAL HUMAN RIGHTS MONTH. Dec 1–31. To disseminate throughout the world information about human rights and distribute copies of the Universal Declaration of Human Rights in English and other languages. Please send $5 to cover expense of printing, handling and postage. Annually, the month of December. For info: Dr. Stanley Drake, Pres, Intl Soc of Friendship & Good Will, 8592 Roswell Rd, Ste 251, Atlanta, GA 30350-1867. Phone: (678) 795-1362. Web: www.friendshipandgoodwill.org.

★**WORLD AIDS DAY.** Dec 1.

BIRTHDAYS TODAY

Jan Brett, 56, author and illustrator (*Trouble with Trolls, The Mitten*), born Hingham, MA, Dec 1, 1949.

Larry Walker, 39, baseball player, born Maple Ridge, BC, Canada, Dec 1, 1966.

Tisha Waller, 35, track and field athlete, born Atlanta, GA, Dec 1, 1970.

DECEMBER 2 — FRIDAY

Day 336 — 29 Remaining

ARTIFICIAL HEART TRANSPLANT: ANNIVERSARY. Dec 2, 1982. Barney C. Clark, 61, became the first recipient of a permanent artificial heart. The operation was performed at the University of Utah Medical Center at Salt Lake City. Near death at the time of the operation, Clark survived almost 112 days after the implantation. He died Mar 23, 1983.

FIRST SELF-SUSTAINING NUCLEAR CHAIN REACTION: ANNIVERSARY. Dec 2, 1942. Physicist Enrico Fermi led a team of scientists at the University of Chicago in producing the first controlled, self-sustaining nuclear chain reaction. As part of the "Manhattan Project," their first simple nuclear reactor was built under the stands of the University's football stadium. This work led to the development of the atomic bomb, first tested on July 16, 1945, at Alamogordo, NM.

LAOS: NATIONAL DAY. Dec 2. National holiday commemorating proclamation of Lao People's Democratic Republic in 1975.

MONROE DOCTRINE: ANNIVERSARY. Dec 2, 1823. President James Monroe, in his annual message to Congress, enunciated the doctrine that bears his name and that was long hailed as a statement of US policy. "... In the wars of the European powers in matters relating to themselves we have never taken any part ... we should consider any attempt on their part to extend their system to any portion of this hemi-sphere as dangerous to our peace and safety...."

December 2005

S	M	T	W	T	F	S
				1	2	3
4	5	6	7	8	9	10
11	12	13	14	15	16	17
18	19	20	21	22	23	24
25	26	27	28	29	30	31

DECEMBER 1
ROSA PARKS AND THE MONTGOMERY BUS BOYCOTT—THE 50TH ANNIVERSARY

During the 1800s, a group of segregation laws legalized the separation of races. Under these laws, referred to as Jim Crow laws, blacks were not allowed to use the same facilities as white people. Blacks had to use separate bathrooms, drinking fountains, public swimming pools, restaurants and hotels. They were only permitted to sit in certain areas in places such as movie theaters. Children attended separate schools. Some states justified these laws by declaring that the facilities were "separate but equal."

The 1954 Supreme Court ruling in the case of *Brown v Board of Education of Topeka* struck down segregation as permissible in public schools. From that point, challenges to Jim Crow laws became more frequent and support began building for the social changes that led to the Civil Rights Acts of 1964 and 1968.

Rosa Parks, an African-American woman, lived in Montgomery, AL, in 1955. Interested in civil rights, she was an active member of the National Association for the Advancement of Colored People and served as the chapter's secretary for several years. On Dec 1, tired from a long day working as a seamstress in a department store, Rosa Parks boarded a bus as she headed homeward. She sat in the area designated as "colored seating." When the front of the bus, reserved for whites only, became overcrowded, the bus driver ordered Parks and three other African Americans to move farther back. The others moved, but Parks refused. She was forced off the bus and arrested.

In support of Parks's action, Dr. Martin Luther King, Jr., headed a boycott of the Montgomery bus system. Beginning on Dec 5, 1955, the African-American community stopped using buses. The boycott continued for 382 days, only ending on Dec 20, 1956, when the US Supreme Court ruled that segregated buses were unconstitutional.

The successful boycott required the agreement and support of several thousand people. Those who participated subjected themselves to many inconveniences. But their goal—equality—was worth it.

One way to help students relate to the difficulties and sacrifices people made is to ask them how their lives would change if they had to make alternative arrangements for all their transportation needs for a certain time period, perhaps two weeks or a month. Since public transportation is not available in many suburban communities, some students would have to imagine how they would get around if their family's car(s) were taken away. Children who ride a bus to school could be asked to restructure their days as if the school bus were no longer available and they had no family car. How would their schedule change? How far would they have to walk to school or to stores? Would they have to get up a lot earlier to accommodate the schedule change? Would they have to eliminate sport practices or music lessons?

Children's literature offers many informational books about Parks and the Montgomery Bus Boycott. *I am Rosa Parks* by Rosa Parks and Jim Haskins (Penguin, 0-8037-1206-5, $13.99 Ages 7–9), is an easy reader version of *Rosa Parks: My Story* by Parks and Haskins (Puffin, 0-14-130120-1, $6.99 Ages 10 & up), which is Parks's autobiography. Parks later published *Dear Mrs. Parks: A Dialogue with Today's Youth* (Lee & Low, 1-8800-0061-X, $9.95 Ages 8 & up), which contains a collection of letters written to her and her response to them. *Rosa Parks* by Eloise Greenfield (HarperCollins, 0-06-442025-6, $4.25 Ages 7–10) and *Rosa Parks* by Maryann Weidt (Lerner, 0-8225-4673-6, $25.26 Ages 8–10) are illustrated biographies. Picture books include *A Picture Book of Rosa Parks* by David Adler (Holiday House, 0-8234-1177-X, $6.95 Ages 4–7).

—Sally Walker

NATIONAL PARKS ESTABLISHED IN ALASKA: 25th ANNIVERSARY. Dec 2, 1980. Eight national parks were established in Alaska on this date. Mount McKinley National Park, which was established Feb 26, 1917, and Denali National Monument, which was proclaimed Dec 1, 1978, were combined as Denali National Park and Preserve. Gates of the Arctic National Monument, proclaimed Dec 1, 1978; Glacier Bay National Monument, proclaimed Feb 25, 1925; and Katmai National Monument, proclaimed Sept 24, 1918, were established as national parks and preserves. Kenai Fjords National Monument, proclaimed Dec 1, 1978, and Kobuk Valley National Monument, proclaimed Dec 1, 1978, were established as national parks. Lake Clark National Monument, proclaimed Dec 1, 1978, and Wrangell–St. Elias National Monument, proclaimed Dec 1, 1978, were established as national parks and preserves. For info: www.nps.gov.

SEURAT, GEORGES: BIRTH ANNIVERSARY. Dec 2, 1859. French Neo-Impressionist painter, born at Paris, France. Died there Mar 29, 1891. Seurat is known for his style of painting with small dots of color called "pointillism."

UNITED ARAB EMIRATES: INDEPENDENCE DAY. Dec 2. Anniversary of the day in 1971 when a federation of seven sheikdoms known as the Trucial States declared independence from the UK and became known as the United Arab Emirates.

BIRTHDAYS TODAY

Wayne Allard, 62, US Senator (R, Colorado), born Fort Collins, CO, Dec 2, 1943.

Randy Gardner, 47, former figure skater, born Marina del Rey, CA, Dec 2, 1958.

David Macaulay, 59, illustrator and author (*The New Way Things Work*, Caldecott for *Black and White*), born Burton-on-Trent, England, Dec 2, 1946.

Stone Phillips, 51, anchor ("Dateline"), born Texas City, TX, Dec 2, 1954.

Harry Reid, 66, US Senator (D, Nevada), born Searchlight, NV, Dec 2, 1939.

Monica Seles, 32, tennis player, born Novi Sad, Yugoslavia, Dec 2, 1973.

Britney Spears, 24, singer, born Kentwood, LA, Dec 2, 1981.

William Wegman, 62, artist/photographer (of dogs), born Holyoke, MA, Dec 2, 1943.

DECEMBER 3 — SATURDAY

Day 337 — 28 Remaining

ILLINOIS: ADMISSION DAY: ANNIVERSARY. Dec 3. Became 21st state in 1818.

LONGEST HUMAN-LED MIGRATION: ANNIVERSARY. Dec 3, 2001. An ultralight aircraft leading young whooping cranes on a new migration route completed the 1,200-mile journey on this date. The migration began at Necedah National Wildlife Refuge in Wisconsin and ended in Florida, where humans dressed as cranes led the birds to the Chassahowitzka National Wildlife Refuge. This effort was made to reintroduce the endangered bird into eastern North America. This migration was in addition to the Canada-Texas migration of a wild flock. See also: "Whooping Crane Fall Migration" (Sept 15) and "Whooping Crane Spring Migration" (Mar 1). For more info: Whooping Crane Eastern Partnership at www.bringbackthecranes.org.

UNITED NATIONS: INTERNATIONAL DAY OF DISABLED PERSONS. Dec 3. On Oct 14, 1992 (Res 47/3), at the end of the Decade of Disabled Persons, the General Assembly proclaimed Dec 3 to be an annual observance to promote the continuation of integrating the disabled into general society.

BIRTHDAYS TODAY

Francesca Lia Block, 43, author (*Weetzie Bat, Violet & Claire*), born Los Angeles, CA, Dec 3, 1962.

Brian Bonsall, 24, actor (*Blank Check*, "Family Ties"), born Torrance, CA, Dec 3, 1981.

Anna Chlumsky, 25, actress (*My Girl, My Girl 2*), born Chicago, IL, Dec 3, 1980.

Sheree Fitch, 49, author (*Toes in My Nose, Sleeping Dragons All Around*), born Ottawa, ON, Canada, Dec 3, 1956.

Brendan Fraser, 37, actor (*George of the Jungle, The Mummy*), born Indianapolis, IN, Dec 3, 1968.

Bucky Lasek, 33, skateboarder, born Baltimore, MD, Dec 3, 1972.

Julianne Moore, 45, actress (*The Lost World: Jurassic Park II*), born Fayetteville, NC, Dec 3, 1960.

Katarina Witt, 40, Olympic figure skater, born Karl-Marx-Stadt, East Germany, Dec 3, 1965.

December 2005

S	M	T	W	T	F	S
				1	2	3
4	5	6	7	8	9	10
11	12	13	14	15	16	17
18	19	20	21	22	23	24
25	26	27	28	29	30	31

DECEMBER 4 — SUNDAY

Day 338 — 27 Remaining

CLERC-GALLAUDET WEEK. Dec 4–10. Week in which to celebrate the birth anniversaries of Laurent Clerc (Dec 26, 1785) and Thomas Hopkins Gallaudet (Dec 10, 1787). Clerc and Gallaudet pioneered education for the deaf in the US. Library activities will include a lecture on Clerc and Gallaudet and their contemporaries, storytelling for all ages and a display of books, videotapes, magazines, newspapers and posters. For info: Library for Deaf Action, 2930 Craiglawn Rd, Silver Spring, MD 20904-1816. Phone: (301) 572-5168 (TTY). Fax: (301) 572-4134. E-mail: alicehagemeyer @aol.com.

LEAF, MUNRO: 100th BIRTH ANNIVERSARY. Dec 4, 1905. Born at Hamilton, MD. Leaf authored and illustrated the children's book *The Story of Ferdinand*. He died at Garrett Park, MD, Dec 21, 1976.

SPACE MILESTONE: INTERNATIONAL SPACE STATION LAUNCH (US). Dec 4, 1998. The shuttle *Endeavour* took a US component of the space station named *Unity* into orbit 220 miles from Earth where spacewalking astronauts fastened it to a component launched by the Russians on Nov 20, 1998. Soon to be completed, it will be 356 feet across and 290 feet long and will support a crew of up to seven. For more info: *The International Space Station*, by Franklyn M. Branley (HarperCollins, 0-06-028702-0, $16.89 Gr. K–3). See also: "Space Milestone: International Space Station Inhabited" (Nov 2).

BIRTHDAYS TODAY

George Ancona, 76, author (*Pablo Remembers: The Fiesta of the Day of the Dead*), born New York, NY, Dec 4, 1929.

Jeff Blake, 35, football player, born Sanford, FL, Dec 4, 1970.

DECEMBER 5 — MONDAY

Day 339 — 26 Remaining

AFL-CIO FOUNDED: 50th ANNIVERSARY. Dec 5. The American Federation of Labor and the Congress of Industrial Organizations joined together in 1955, following 20 years of rivalry, to become the nation's leading advocate for trade unions.

AUSTRIA: KRAMPUSLAUF. Dec 5. Salzburg region. On the eve of St. Nicholas Day, Austrians celebrate the Krampuslauf (Krampus Run). In folklore, the Krampus is a devilish companion of St. Nicholas who punishes bad children just as St. Nicholas rewards good ones. The Krampus, represented by costumed revelers, is usually depicted as a dark, hairy, cloven-hooved beast with red horns, a leering mouth, chains and a switch. Children are invited to throw snowballs at the Krampus. Also known as Krampus Day.

CENTRAL AFRICAN REPUBLIC: NATIONAL DAY OBSERVED. Dec 5. Commemorates Proclamation of the Republic Dec 1, 1958. On this date, the country called Ubangi-Shari changed its name to Central African Republic. In 1960 it gained its independence from France. Usually observed on the first Monday in December.

DISNEY, WALT: BIRTH ANNIVERSARY. Dec 5, 1901. Animator, filmmaker, born at Chicago, IL. Disney died at Los Angeles, CA, Dec 15, 1966. For more info: *The Man Behind the Magic: The Story of Walt Disney*, by Katherine Greene and Richard Greene (Viking, 0-67-088476-6, $14.99 Gr. 4–7).

★ ★ ★

HAITI: DISCOVERY DAY. Dec 5. Commemorates the discovery of Haiti by Christopher Columbus in 1492. Public holiday.

MONTGOMERY BUS BOYCOTT BEGINS: 50th ANNIVERSARY. Dec 5, 1955. Rosa Parks was arrested at Montgomery, AL, Dec 1, 1955, for refusing to give up her seat on a bus to a white man. In support of Parks, and to protest the arrest, the black community of Montgomery organized a boycott of the bus system. The boycott lasted from Dec 5, 1955, to Dec 20, 1956, when a US Supreme Court ruling was implemented at Montgomery, integrating the public transportation system. ***See Curriculum Connection.***

NETHERLANDS: SINTERKLAAS. Dec 5. Traditionally on the eve of St. Nicholas Day (Dec 6), Sinterklaas brings gifts to Dutch children, accompanied by his Moorish helper, "Black Pete." However, the number of people celebrating this holiday has dropped, as more Dutch families exchange gifts on Dec 25 instead.

PICKETT, BILL: BIRTH ANNIVERSARY. Dec 5, 1870. African-American cowboy, born at Jenks-Branch, TX. A star rodeo performer, Pickett died Apr 2, 1932, at Ponca City, OK.

THAILAND: KING'S BIRTHDAY AND NATIONAL DAY. Dec 5. Celebrated throughout the kingdom with colorful pageantry. Stores and houses decorated with spectacular illuminations at night. Public holiday.

TOGO: SLED DOG HERO: DEATH ANNIVERSARY. Dec 5, 1929. When Nome, AK, was threatened by a diphtheria epidemic in late January 1925, a dog sled relay team delivered lifesaving serum in a 674-mile journey. Togo, a 10-year-old Siberian Husky, was the lead dog for the first 350 miles of the journey—which took place in temperatures almost 50 degrees below zero. His efforts left him lame, and after the trip he retired to Maine, where he died on this date. His preserved body is now at Wasilla, AK. See also: "Sled Dogs Save Nome: Anniversary" (Feb 2) and "Balto: Sled Dog Hero: Death Anniversary" (Mar 14). For more info: *Togo* by Robert Blake (Philomel Books, 0-399-23381-4, $16.99 Ages 4–8).

TWENTY-FIRST AMENDMENT TO US CONSTITUTION RATIFIED: ANNIVERSARY. Dec 5, 1933. Prohibition ended with the repeal of the Eighteenth Amendment by the Twenty-First Amendment.

UNITED NATIONS: INTERNATIONAL VOLUNTEER DAY FOR ECONOMIC AND SOCIAL DEVELOPMENT. Dec 5. In a resolution of Dec 17, 1985, the UN General Assembly recognized the desirability of encouraging the work of all volunteers. It invited governments to observe, annually Dec 5, the "International Volunteer Day for Economic and Social Development, urging them to take measures to heighten awareness of the important contribution of volunteer service." A day commemorating the establishment in December 1970 of the UN Volunteers program and inviting world recognition of volunteerism in the international development movement. For info: United Nations, Dept of Public Info, Public Inquiries Unit, Rm GA-57, New York, NY 10017. Phone: (212) 963-4475. Fax: (212) 963-0071. E-mail: inquiries@un.org. Web: www.un.org.

VAN BUREN, MARTIN: BIRTH ANNIVERSARY. Dec 5, 1782. The eighth president of the US (Mar 4, 1837–Mar 3, 1841), Van Buren was the first to have been born a citizen of the US. He had served as vice president under Andrew Jackson. He was a widower for nearly two decades before he entered the White House. His daughter-in-law, Angelica, served as White House hostess during an administration troubled by bank and business failures, depression and unemployment. Van Buren was born at Kinderhook, NY, and died there July 24, 1862. For info: www.ipl.org/ref/POTUS.

WHEATLEY, PHILLIS: DEATH ANNIVERSARY. Dec 5, 1784. Born at Senegal, West Africa, about 1754, Phillis Wheatley was brought to the US in 1761 and purchased as a slave by a Boston tailor named John Wheatley. She was allotted unusual privileges for a slave, including being allowed to learn to read and write. She wrote her first poetry at age 14, and her first work was published in 1770. Wheatley's fame as a poet spread throughout Europe as well as the US after her *Poems on Various Subjects, Religious and Moral* was published at England in 1773. She was invited to visit George Washington's army headquarters after he read a poem she had written about him in 1776. Phillis Wheatley died at about age 30 at Boston, MA. For more info: *Hang a Thousand Trees with Ribbons: The Story of Phillis Wheatley*, by Ann Rinaldi (Harcourt, 0-15-200876-4, $12 Gr. 4–9).

BIRTHDAYS TODAY

Frankie Muniz, 20, actor ("Malcolm in the Middle," *My Dog Skip*), born Ridgewood, NJ, Dec 5, 1985.

DECEMBER 6 — TUESDAY

Day 340 — 25 Remaining

ECUADOR: DAY OF QUITO. Dec 6. Commemorates founding of city of Quito by Spaniards in 1534.

EVERGLADES NATIONAL PARK ESTABLISHED: ANNIVERSARY. Dec 6, 1947. Part of vast marshland area on the southern Florida peninsula, originally authorized May 30, 1934, was established as a national park. For more info: www.nps.gov/ever/index.htm.

FINLAND: INDEPENDENCE DAY: ANNIVERSARY. Dec 6. National holiday. Declaration of independence from Russia in 1917.

GERALD FORD SWORN IN AS VICE PRESIDENT: ANNIVERSARY. Dec 6, 1973. Gerald Ford was sworn in as vice president under Richard Nixon, following the resignation of Spiro Agnew who pled no contest to a charge of income tax evasion. On Aug 9, 1974, Ford was sworn in as president of the United States, after Nixon's resignation. See also: "Agnew, Spiro Theodore: Birth Anniversary" (Nov 9).

GERSHWIN, IRA: BIRTH ANNIVERSARY. Dec 6, 1896. Pulitzer Prize–winning American lyricist and author who collaborated with his brother, George, and with many other composers. Among his Broadway successes: *Lady Be Good, Funny Face, Strike Up the Band* and such songs as "The Man I Love," "Someone to Watch Over Me," "I Got Rhythm" and hundreds of others. Born at New York, NY, he died at Beverly Hills, CA, Aug 17, 1983. See also: "Gershwin, George: Birth Anniversary" (Sept 26).

HALIFAX, NOVA SCOTIA, DESTROYED: ANNIVERSARY. Dec 6, 1917. More than 1,650 people were killed at Halifax when the Norwegian ship *Imo* plowed into the French munitions ship *Mont Blanc*. *Mont Blanc* was loaded with 4,000 tons of TNT, 2,300 tons of picric acid, 61 tons of other explosives and a deck of highly flammable benzene, which ignited and touched off an explosion. In addition to those killed, 1,028 were injured. A tidal wave, caused by the explosion, washed much of the city out to sea.

MISSOURI EARTHQUAKES: ANNIVERSARY. Dec 6, 1811. The most violent and prolonged series of earthquakes in US history occurred not in California, but in the Midwest at New Madrid, MO. They lasted until Feb 12, 1812. There were few deaths because of the sparse population. For more info go to the National Earthquake Information Center: wwwneic.cr.usgs.gov.

ROBERT-HOUDIN, JEAN EUGÈNE: 200th BIRTH ANNIVERSARY. Dec 6, 1805. The founder of modern magic who was the first to use electricity in his illusions. Robert-Houdin also popularized wearing evening attire (instead of wizard's robes) on stage. He inspired scores of younger magicians, including Harry Houdini, whose stage name saluted Robert-Houdin's name. Born at Blois, France, Robert-Houdin died at St. Gervais, France, on June 13, 1871.

SAINT NICHOLAS DAY. Dec 6. One of the most venerated saints of both eastern and western Christian churches, of whose life little is known, except that he was Bishop of Myra in what is now Turkey in the fourth century, and that from early times he has been one of the most often pictured saints, especially noted for his charity. Santa Claus and the presentation of gifts is said to derive from Saint Nicholas. For more info: *Saint Nicholas*, by Ann Tompert (Boyds Mills Press, 1-56397-844-X, $15.95 Gr. 1 & up).

SPAIN: CONSTITUTION DAY. Dec 6. National holiday. Commemorates the approval of the new constitution in 1978.

THIRTEENTH AMENDMENT TO US CONSTITUTION RATIFIED: ANNIVERSARY. Dec 6, 1865. The Thirteenth Amendment to the Constitution was ratified, abolishing slavery in the US. "Neither slavery nor involuntary servitude, save as a punishment for crime whereof the party shall have been duly convicted, shall exist within the United States, or any place subject to their jurisdiction." This amendment was proclaimed Dec 18, 1865. The Thirteenth, Fourteenth and Fifteenth amendments are considered the Civil War Amendments. See also: "Emancipation Proclamation: Anniversary" (Sept 22) for Lincoln's proclamation freeing slaves in the rebelling states.

YATES, ELIZABETH: 100th BIRTH ANNIVERSARY. Dec 6, 1905. Author of novels and biographies for children, she was born at Buffalo, NY. She published her first book in 1938 and wrote more than 50 others. Her most famous title, *Amos Fortune, Free Man,* won the Newbery Medal in 1951. It told the true story of an African prince who is sold into slavery and brought to America, who eventually is able to purchase his own freedom. It remains in print today. Yates died July 29, 2001, at Concord, NH.

December 2005

S	M	T	W	T	F	S
				1	2	3
4	5	6	7	8	9	10
11	12	13	14	15	16	17
18	19	20	21	22	23	24
25	26	27	28	29	30	31

BIRTHDAYS TODAY

John Reynolds Gardiner, 61, author (*Stone Fox, Top Secret*), born Los Angeles, CA, Dec 6, 1944.

DECEMBER 7 — WEDNESDAY

Day 341 — 24 Remaining

DELAWARE RATIFIES CONSTITUTION: ANNIVERSARY. Dec 7, 1787. Delaware became the first state to ratify the proposed Constitution. It did so by unanimous vote.

★**NATIONAL PEARL HARBOR REMEMBRANCE DAY.** Dec 7.

NATIONAL ASSOCIATION FOR THE EDUCATION OF YOUNG CHILDREN CONFERENCE. Dec 7–10. Washington, DC. For info: National Assn for the Education of Young Children, 1509 16th St NW, Washington, DC 20036. Phone: (202) 232-8777. Fax: (202) 328-1846. E-mail: naeyc@naeyc.org. Web: www.naeyc.org.

PEARL HARBOR DAY: ANNIVERSARY. Dec 7, 1941. At 7:55 AM (local time), "a date that will live in infamy," nearly 200 Japanese aircraft attacked Pearl Harbor, HI, long considered the US "Gibraltar of the Pacific." The raid, which lasted little more than one hour, left nearly 3,000 dead. Nearly the entire US Pacific Fleet was at anchor there, and few ships escaped damage. Several were sunk or disabled, while 200 US aircraft on the ground were destroyed. The attack on Pearl Harbor brought about immediate US entry into WWII, a Declaration of War being requested by President Franklin D. Roosevelt and approved by the Congress Dec 8, 1941. For info: *Pearl Harbor*, by Stephen Krensky (Aladdin, 0-68-984213-9, $15 Gr. K–3).

SPACE MILESTONE: *GALILEO* (US): 10th ANNIVERSARY. Dec 7, 1995. Launched Oct 18, 1989, by the space shuttle *Atlantis*, the spacecraft *Galileo* entered the orbit of Jupiter on this date after a six-year journey. It orbited Jupiter for two years, sending out probes to study three of its moons. Organic compounds, the ingredients of life, were found on them. For more info: galileo.jpl.nasa.gov.

TUNIS, JOHN: BIRTH ANNIVERSARY. Dec 7, 1889. Author of sports books (*The Kid Comes Back, Iron Duke*), born at Boston, MA. Died Feb 4, 1975.

UNITED NATIONS: INTERNATIONAL CIVIL AVIATION DAY. Dec 7. On Dec 6, 1996, the General Assembly proclaimed Dec 7 as International Civil Aviation Day. On Dec 7, 1944, the convention on International Civil Aviation, which established the International Civil Aviation Organization, was signed. Info from: United Nations, Dept of Public Info, New York, NY 10017.

BIRTHDAYS TODAY

Larry Bird, 49, basketball coach, former player, born West Baden, IN, Dec 7, 1956.

Aaron Carter, 18, singer ("Shake It"), born Tampa, FL, Dec 7, 1987.

Eric Chavez, 28, baseball player, born Los Angeles, CA, Dec 7, 1977.

Thad Cochran, 68, US Senator (R, Mississippi), born Pontotoc, MS, Dec 7, 1937.

Susan M. Collins, 53, US Senator (R, Maine), born Caribou, ME, Dec 7, 1952.

Anne Fine, 58, author (*The Tulip Touch, Alias Madame Doubtfire*), born County Durham, England, Dec 7, 1947.

Terrell Owens, 32, football player, born Alexander City, AL, Dec 7, 1973.

Steve Parker, 53, author (*The Body Atlas, Brain Surgery for Beginners*), born Warrington, England, Dec 7, 1952.

DECEMBER 8 — THURSDAY

Day 342 — 23 Remaining

AMERICAN FEDERATION OF LABOR (AFL) FOUNDED: ANNIVERSARY. Dec 8, 1886. Originally founded at Pittsburgh, PA, as the Federation of Organized Trades and Labor Unions of the United States and Canada in 1881, the union was reorganized in 1886 under the name American Federation of Labor (AFL). The AFL was dissolved as a separate entity in 1955 when it merged with the Congress of Industrial Organizations to form the AFL-CIO. See also: "AFL-CIO Founded: Anniversary (Dec 5)."

CHINESE NATIONALISTS MOVE TO TAIWAN: ANNIVERSARY. Dec 8, 1949. The government of Chiang Kai-Shek moved to Taiwan (Formosa) after being driven out of mainland China by the communists led by Mao Tse-Tung.

FEAST OF THE IMMACULATE CONCEPTION. Dec 8. Roman Catholic Holy Day of Obligation.

FIRST STEP TOWARD A NUCLEAR-FREE WORLD: ANNIVERSARY. Dec 8, 1987. The Soviet Union and the US signed a treaty at Washington eliminating medium-range and shorter-range missiles. This was the first treaty completely doing away with two entire classes of nuclear arms. These missiles, with a range of 500 to 5,500 kilometers, were to be scrapped under strict supervision within three years of the signing.

GUAM: LADY OF CAMARIN DAY HOLIDAY. Dec 8. Declared a legal holiday by Guam legislature, Mar 2, 1971.

MOON PHASE: FIRST QUARTER. Dec 8. Moon enters First Quarter phase at 4:36 AM, EST.

NAFTA SIGNED: ANNIVERSARY. Dec 8, 1993. President Clinton signed the North American Free Trade Agreement which cut tariffs and eliminated other trade barriers between the US, Canada and Mexico. The Agreement went into effect Jan 1, 1994.

SEGAR, ELZIE CRISLER: BIRTH ANNIVERSARY. Dec 8, 1894. Creator of "Thimble Theater," the comic strip that came to be known as "Popeye." Centered on the Oyl family, especially daughter Olive, the strip introduced a new central character in 1929. A one-eyed sailor with bulging muscles, Popeye became the strip's star attraction almost immediately. Popeye made it to the silver screen in animated form and in 1980 became a movie with Robin Williams playing the lead. Segar was born at Chester, IL. He died Oct 13, 1938, at Santa Monica, CA.

SOVIET UNION DISSOLVED: ANNIVERSARY. Dec 8, 1991. The Union of Soviet Socialist Republics ceased to exist, as the republics of Russia, Byelorussia and Ukraine signed an agreement at Minsk, Byelorussia, creating the Commonwealth of Independent States. The remaining republics, with the exception of Georgia, joined in the new Commonwealth as it began the slow and arduous process of removing the yoke of communism and dealing with strong separatist and nationalistic movements within the various republics.

THURBER, JAMES: BIRTH ANNIVERSARY. Dec 8, 1894. Author for adults and children (*The Thirteen Clocks*), born at Columbus, OH. Died at New York, NY, Nov 2, 1961.

BIRTHDAYS TODAY

Mary Azarian, 65, illustrator (Caldecott for *Snowflake Bentley*), born Washington, DC, Dec 8, 1940.

Teri Hatcher, 41, actress ("Lois & Clark"), born Sunnyvale, CA, Dec 8, 1964.

Dominic Monaghan, 29, actor (*The Lord of the Rings* trilogy, "Lost"), born Berlin, Germany, Dec 8, 1976.

Mike Mussina, 37, baseball player, born Williamsport, PA, Dec 8, 1968.

Teresa Weatherspoon, 40, basketball player, US Olympic Basketball Team, born Jasper, TX, Dec 8, 1965.

DECEMBER 9 — FRIDAY

Day 343 — 22 Remaining

BIRDSEYE, CLARENCE: BIRTH ANNIVERSARY. Dec 9, 1886. American industrialist who developed a way of deep-freezing foods. He was marketing frozen fish by 1925 and was one of the founders of General Foods Corporation. Born at Brooklyn, NY, he died at New York, NY, Oct 7, 1956.

BRUNHOFF, JEAN DE: BIRTH ANNIVERSARY. Dec 9, 1899. Author and illustrator of *The Story of Babar* and *The Little Elephant*. Born at Paris, France, Brunhoff died at Switzerland, Oct 16, 1937. In later years, the Babar series was continued by his son Laurent.

COMPUTER MOUSE DEVELOPED: ANNIVERSARY. Dec 9, 1968. Designed as a pointing device to help users interact with their computers, the mouse was first developed in 1968 but its use didn't become widespread until 1984 when Apple attached it to its Macintosh computer.

HARRIS, JOEL CHANDLER: BIRTH ANNIVERSARY. Dec 9, 1848. American author, creator of the Uncle Remus stories, born at Eatonton, GA. Died July 3, 1908, at Atlanta, GA.

McGRAW, ELOISE JARVIS: BIRTH ANNIVERSARY. Dec 9, 1915. Award-winning author of fantasy and historical novels for children, she was born at Houston, TX. She received the Newbery Honor Award three times, in 1953 for *Moccasin Trail*, in 1962 for *The Golden Goblet* and in 1997 for *The Moorchild*. She died at Portland, OR, Nov 30, 2000.

PETRIFIED FOREST NATIONAL PARK ESTABLISHED: ANNIVERSARY. Dec 9, 1962. Arizona's Petrified Forest National Monument, proclaimed Dec 8, 1906, was established as a national park. For more info: www.nps.gov/pefo/index.htm.

TANZANIA: INDEPENDENCE AND REPUBLIC DAY. Dec 9. Tanganyika became independent of Britain on this day in 1961. The republics of Tanganyika and Zanzibar joined to become one state (Apr 27, 1964) renamed (Oct 29, 1964) the United Republic of Tanzania.

BIRTHDAYS TODAY

Joan W. Blos, 77, author (Newbery for *A Gathering of Days: A New England Girl's Journal, 1830–1832*), born New York, NY, Dec 9, 1928.

Thomas Daschle, 58, former US Senator (D, South Dakota), born Aberdeen, SD, Dec 9, 1947.

Mary Downing Hahn, 68, author (*Time for Andrew, The Doll in the Garden*), born Washington, DC, Dec 9, 1937.

Donny Osmond, 48, actor, singer ("Donny and Marie"; stage: *Joseph and the Amazing Technicolor Dreamcoat*), born Ogden, UT, Dec 9, 1957.

DECEMBER 10 — SATURDAY

Day 344 — 21 Remaining

DEWEY, MELVIL: BIRTH ANNIVERSARY. Dec 10, 1851. American librarian and inventor of the Dewey decimal book classification system was born at Adams Center, NY. Born Melville Louis Kossuth Dewey, he was an advocate of spelling reform, urged use of the metric system and was interested in many other education reforms. Dewey died at Highlands County, FL, Dec 26, 1931.

DICKINSON, EMILY: 175th BIRTH ANNIVERSARY. Dec 10, 1830. One of America's greatest poets, Emily Dickinson was born at Amherst, MA. She was reclusive and frail in health. She died May 15, 1886, at Amherst. Seven of her poems were published during her life, but after her death her sister, Lavinia, discovered almost 2,000 more poems locked in her bureau. They were published gradually, over 50 years, beginning in 1890. The little-known Emily Dickinson who was born, lived and died at Amherst is now recognized as one of the most original poets of the English-speaking world. ***See Curriculum Connection.***

FIRST US SCIENTIST RECEIVES NOBEL PRIZE: ANNIVERSARY. Dec 10, 1907. University of Chicago professor Albert Michelson, eminent physicist known for his research on the speed of light and optics, became the first US scientist to receive the Nobel Prize.

GALLAUDET, THOMAS HOPKINS: BIRTH ANNIVERSARY. Dec 10, 1787. A hearing educator who, with Laurent Clerc, founded the first public school for deaf people, Connecticut Asylum for the Education and Instruction of Deaf and Dumb Persons (now the American School for the Deaf), at Hartford, CT, Apr 15, 1817. Gallaudet was born at Philadelphia, PA, and died Sept 9, 1851, at Hartford, CT.

GODDEN, RUMER: BIRTH ANNIVERSARY. Dec 10, 1907. Author of the popular children's tales *The Doll's House, Miss Happiness and Miss Flower* and *The Story of Holly & Ivy*. Born at Sussex, England, Godden died at Thornhill, Scotland, Nov 8, 1998.

★**HUMAN RIGHTS DAY.** Dec 10. Presidential Proclamation 2866, of Dec 6, 1949, covers all succeeding years. Customarily issued as "Bill of Rights Day, Human Rights Day and Week."

December 2005

S	M	T	W	T	F	S
				1	2	3
4	5	6	7	8	9	10
11	12	13	14	15	16	17
18	19	20	21	22	23	24
25	26	27	28	29	30	31

★**HUMAN RIGHTS WEEK.** Dec 10–16. Presidential Proclamation issued since 1958 for the week of Dec 10–16, except in 1986. See also: "Human Rights Day" (Dec 10) and "Bill of Rights Day" (Dec 15).

INTERNATIONAL SHAREWARE DAY. Dec 10. A day to take the time to reward the efforts of thousands of computer programmers who trust that if we try their programs and like them, we will pay for them. Unfortunately, very few payments are received, thus stifling the programmers' efforts. This observance is meant to prompt each of us to inventory our PCs and Macs, see if we are using any shareware, and then take the time in the holiday spirit to write payment checks to the authors. Hopefully this will keep shareware coming. Annually, the second Saturday in December. For info: David Lawrence, Online Today, Net Music Countdown, 145 S Glenoaks Blvd, Ste 336, Burbank, CA 91501. Phone: (818) 563-3123. E-mail: david@onlinetonight.net. Web: www.onlinetonight.net.

"THE MIGHTY MOUSE PLAYHOUSE" TV PREMIERE: 50th ANNIVERSARY. Dec 10, 1955. An all-time favorite of the Saturday-morning crowd (including adults). CBS had a hit with their pint-sized cartoon character Mighty Mouse, who was a tongue-in-cheek version of Superman. The show had other feature cartoons such as "The Adventures of Gandy Goose" and "Heckle and Jeckle."

MISSISSIPPI: ADMISSION DAY: ANNIVERSARY. Dec 10. Became 20th state in 1817.

NOBEL PRIZE AWARDS CEREMONIES: ANNIVERSARY. Dec 10. Oslo, Norway and Stockholm, Sweden. Alfred Nobel, Swedish chemist and inventor of dynamite, who died in 1896, provided in his will that income from his $9 million estate should be used for annual prizes to be awarded to people who are judged to have made the most valuable contributions to the good of humanity. The Nobel Peace Prize is awarded by a committee of the Norwegian parliament and the presentation is made at the Oslo City Hall. Five other prizes, for physics, chemistry, medicine, literature and economics, are presented in a ceremony at Stockholm, Sweden. Both ceremonies traditionally are held on the anniversary of the death of Alfred Nobel. First awarded in 1901, the current value of each prize is about $1,000,000. See also: "Nobel, Alfred Bernhard: Birth Anniversary" (Oct 21). For more info: www.nobel.se.

NORTON, MARY: BIRTH ANNIVERSARY. Dec 10, 1903. British children's writer known for The Borrowers series, for which she received the Carnegie Medal. Her book *Bed-Knob and Broomstick* was made into a movie by Disney in 1971. Born at London, England, she died at Hartland, Devon, England, Aug 29, 1992.

RALPH BUNCHE AWARDED NOBEL PEACE PRIZE: 55th ANNIVERSARY. Dec 10, 1950. Dr. Ralph Johnson Bunche became the first black man awarded the Nobel Peace Prize. Bunche was awarded the prize for his efforts in mediation between Israel and neighboring Arab states in 1949.

RED CLOUD: DEATH ANNIVERSARY. Dec 10, 1909. Sioux Indian chief Red Cloud was born in 1822 (exact date unknown), near North Platte, NE. A courageous leader and defender of Indian rights, Red Cloud was the son of Lone Man and Walks as She Thinks. His unrelenting determination caused US abandonment of the Bozeman trail and of three forts that interfered with Indian hunting grounds. Red Cloud died at Pine Ridge, SD.

THAILAND: CONSTITUTION DAY. Dec 10. A public holiday throughout Thailand.

TREATY OF PARIS ENDS SPANISH-AMERICAN WAR: ANNIVERSARY. Dec 10, 1898. Following the conclusion of the

DECEMBER 10
EMILY DICKINSON'S 175TH BIRTHDAY

Emily Dickinson is recognized as one of America's most important poets. She was born on this day in 1830 at Amherst, MA, where she spent her whole life. Dickinson is often portrayed as an eccentric recluse who spent most of her life in her room. In reality, she was sociable and enjoyed the company of her friends. It was only in the last fifteen years of her life that she became reclusive.

Dickinson, who began to write poetry as a teenager, was extremely private about her work. Of the nearly 2,000 poems she wrote, only about ten were published during her lifetime. Dickinson carried on correspondence with family and friends her whole life, and she often included poems in these letters. Dickinson asked her sister Lavinia to destroy her work after she died, but Lavinia organized and published many of the poems.

Dickinson's work, condensed but often fragmented, anticipated modernist poetry. While her early writing shows conventional forms, she experimented more in her later poetry. Some of her innovations included dashes, random capitalization, imperfect rhymes, the poem's physical appearance on the page and uncommon word choices and metaphors. Her poems span a range of themes; one of her most famous poems is about hope:

Hope is the thing with feathers
That perches in the soul,
And sings the tune without the words,
And never stops at all,

And sweetest in the gale is heard
And sore must be the storm
That could abash the little bird
That kept so many warm.

I've heard it in the chillest land,
And on the strangest sea;
Yet, never, in extremity,
It asked a crumb of me.

In this poem, Dickinson uses the symbol of a bird to discuss hope without explicitly describing it. Older students will probably be able to explain how Dickinson uses this symbol by exploring the language of the poem itself. Younger students may want to approach the comparison from the other direction, describing what hope feels like and comparing this feeling to a bird.

One good strategy when discussing symbolism is to have students brainstorm the characteristics they associate with the symbol (a bird), then examine each of these associations to see how it may be used to describe the abstraction (hope). Because Dickinson describes the bird, students can use her words to relate the image she creates back to the emotion of hope. For example, Dickinson says of the bird that she "heard it in the chillest land." Reminding students that the poem is about emotions may help them understand what "the chillest land" represents.

There are lots of books about Emily Dickinson intended for young readers. Elizabeth Spires' *The Mouse of Amherst* (Farrar Straus and Giroux, 0-374-45411-6, $4.95), for ages 9–12, is told from the point of view of a mouse living in Emily's house. Another book for similar ages is Michael Bedard's *Emily*, illustrated by Caldecott winner Barbara Cooney (Random House, 0-385-30697-0, $16.95). A beautiful picture book about a young girl who lives across the street from the Dickinsons, this biography is moving and unique.

There are two beautifully illustrated collections of Dickinson's poetry intended specifically for young audiences; Karen Ackerman has edited the collection *A Brighter Garden*, all nature-themed poems brought vividly to life by Tasha Tudor (Philomel Books, 0-399-21490-9, $19.99 Ages 8–12). Tudor's exquisite watercolors capture the mood of the poetry perfectly. Sterling Publishing's series Poetry for Young People brings us *Emily Dickinson* edited by Frances S. Bolin (0-8069-0635-9, $14.95 Ages 9–12). Chi Chung illustrates 35 of Dickinson's best loved poems in this charming collection that also includes a brief biography and index.

—Elizabeth Van Buren

Spanish-American War in 1898, American and Spanish ambassadors met at Paris, France, to negotiate a treaty. Under the terms of this treaty, Spain granted the US the Philippine Islands and the islands of Guam and Puerto Rico, and agreed to withdraw from Cuba. Senatorial debate over the treaty centered on the US's move toward imperialism by acquiring the Philippines. A vote was taken Feb 6, 1899, and the treaty passed by a one-vote margin. President William McKinley signed the treaty Feb 10, 1899. For more info: *The Spanish-American War*, by Edward F. Dolan (Millbrook, 0 7613 1453 9, $28.90 Gr. 5 8).

UNITED NATIONS: HUMAN RIGHTS DAY. Dec 10. Official UN observance day. Date is the anniversary of adoption of the "Universal Declaration of Human Rights" in 1948. The Declaration sets forth basic rights and fundamental freedoms to which all men and women everywhere in the world are entitled. For more info, go to the UN's website for children at www.un.org/Pubs/CyberSchoolBus.

UZBEKISTAN: CONSTITUTION DAY. Dec 10. National holiday. Commemorates the constitution of 1991.

BIRTHDAYS TODAY

Rod Blagojevich, 49, Governor of Illinois (D), born Chicago, IL, Dec 10, 1956.

Raven Symone, 20, actress ("The Cosby Show," *Dr. Dolittle*), born Atlanta, GA, Dec 10, 1985.

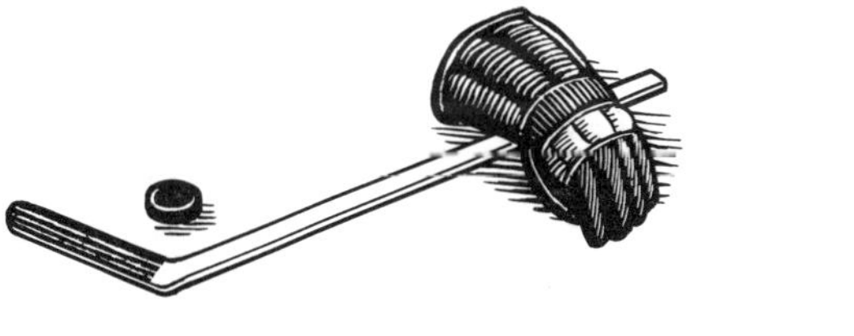

DECEMBER 11 — SUNDAY

Day 345 — 20 Remaining

BURKINA FASO: NATIONAL DAY. Dec 11. Gained independence within the French community, 1958.

INDIANA: ADMISSION DAY: ANNIVERSARY. Dec 11. Became 19th state in 1816.

INTERNATIONAL CHILDREN'S DAY OF BROADCASTING. Dec 11. A celebration of the enormous energy and creative potential of children. More than 2,000 broadcasters around the world produce special programs for and about children. Annually, the second Sunday in December. For more info: UNICEF, United Nations, New York, NY 10017. Web: www.unicef.org/icdb.

NATIONAL CHILDREN'S MEMORIAL DAY. Dec 11. A day to remember the more than 79,000 young people who die in the US every year. Annually, the second Sunday in December. For info: The Compassionate Friends, Inc, PO Box 3696, Oak Brook, IL 60522-3696. Phone: (877) 969-0010. E-mail: nationaloffice@compassionatefriends.org. Web: www.compassionatefriends.org.

SPACE MILESTONE: *MARS CLIMATE ORBITER* (US). Dec 11, 1998. This unmanned rocket was to track the movement of water vapor over Mars, which it was scheduled to reach in September 1999. However, it flew too close to Mars and is presumed destroyed. On Jan 3, 1999, *Mars Polar Lander* was launched. It was to burrow into the ground and analyze the soil of Mars. However, on Dec 3, 1999, as it was landing, communications with the robot craft were lost.

UNITED NATIONS: UNICEF: ANNIVERSARY. Dec 11, 1946. Anniversary of the establishment by the UN General Assembly of the United Nations International Children's Emergency Fund (UNICEF). For info: United Nations, Dept of Public Info, New York, NY 10017. Web: www.unicef.org.

$$\begin{array}{r} 105 \\ \times\ 3 \\ \hline 315 \end{array}$$

BIRTHDAYS TODAY

Max Baucus, 64, US Senator (D, Montana), born Helena, MT, Dec 11, 1941.

Jermaine Jackson, 51, singer, musician (Jackson 5, "Daddy's Home," "Let's Get Serious"), born Gary, IN, Dec 11, 1954.

William Joyce, 48, author and illustrator (*Dinosaur Bob, Rolie Polie Olie*), born Shreveport, LA, Dec 11, 1957.

John F. Kerry, 62, US Senator (D, Massachusetts), born Denver, CO, Dec 11, 1943.

Rider Strong, 26, actor ("Boy Meets World"), born San Francisco, CA, Dec 11, 1979.

December 2005

S	M	T	W	T	F	S
				1	2	3
4	5	6	7	8	9	10
11	12	13	14	15	16	17
18	19	20	21	22	23	24
25	26	27	28	29	30	31

DECEMBER 12 — MONDAY

Day 346 — 19 Remaining

BONZA BOTTLER DAY™. Dec 12. To celebrate when the number of the day is the same as the number of the month. Bonza Bottler Day™ is an excuse to have a party at least once a month. For info: Gail M. Berger, 14 Fernwood Dr, Taylors, SC 29687. Phone: (864) 609-9874. E-mail: gberger5@aol.com.

DAY OF OUR LADY OF GUADALUPE. Dec 12. The legend of Guadalupe tells how in December 1531, an Indian, Juan Diego, saw the Virgin Mother on a hill near Mexico City, who instructed him to go to the bishop and have him build a shrine to her on the site of the vision. After his request was initially rebuffed, the Virgin Mother appeared to Juan Diego three days later. She instructed him to pick roses growing on a stony and barren hill-

DECEMBER 12
POINSETTIA DAY

In the US, the poinsettia plant (scientific name *Euphorbia pulcherrima*, which means "very beautiful") is a widely popular Christmas decoration. The fiery red, pink or white bracts are offset by large green leaves, but surprisingly, these showy bracts are not the poinsettia's flowers. Bracts are special leaves that grow at the base of the poinsettia's flowers. The small, yellow, bowl-shaped clusters located in the center of the bracts are the actual flowers. They bloom in November and December. Poinsettias are a tropical plant, native to Central America and Mexico. In the US, they grow outdoors only in warm, southern areas. Wild and in the garden, poinsettias can grow as tall as 15 feet; potted plants grow up to 4 feet tall.

The ancient Aztecs used poinsettias (named *cuetlayochitl*) to make dye for coloring cloth and cosmetics. Poinsettias were introduced in the US in the late 1820s by botanist Joel R. Poinsett, who served as the first US ambassador to Mexico. He sent plants back to his plantation in South Carolina. The plant's common name in the US honors Poinsett's contribution. Today, poinsettias are the bestselling potted plant in the US, with most sales occurring during the weeks approaching Christmas. There are more than 100 varieties available.

In Mexico, a charming legend is told about the poinsettia. On Christmas Eve, a poor girl is dismayed because she has no money to buy a gift for the infant Jesus. A relative assures her that a humble gift, given with love, is more important than any other kind of gift. She picks a handful of poinsettias and brings them as her offering.

Two books for young readers lovingly retell the story: *The Miracle of the First Poinsettia: A Mexican Christmas Story* by Joanne Oppenheim (Barefoot Books, 1-8414-8245-5, $16.99 All ages) and *The Legend of the Poinsettia* by Tomie de Paola (Putnam, 0-399-21692-8, $16.99 All ages).

A fun extension of these stories would be to read and compare other legendary flower stories. The Native American tale *Peboan and Seegwun* by Charles Larry (Farrar, Straus and Giroux, 0-374-45750-6, Out of print All ages) is a beautifully illustrated story about the flowers known as spring beauties. The narcissus is another popular spring flower. It has its roots in Greek mythology and retellings are widely available in books that contain collections of Greek myths.

Poinsettias are not edible plants, but contrary to popular belief, they are not poisonous. If ingested in large quantities, the leaves and bracts can make a child ill. For this reason, keep poinsettias out of the reach of small children. —Sally Walker side nearby and take them to the bishop as proof. Although flowers do not normally bloom in December, Juan Diego found the roses and took them to the bishop. As he opened his mantle to drop the roses on the floor, an image of the Virgin Mary appeared among them. The bishop built the sanctuary as instructed. Our Lady of Guadalupe became the patroness of Mexico City and by 1746 was the patron saint of all New Spain and by 1910 of all Latin America.

FIRST BLACK SERVES IN US HOUSE OF REPRESENTATIVES: ANNIVERSARY. Dec 12, 1870. Joseph Hayne Rainey of Georgetown, SC, was sworn in as the first black to serve in the US House of Representatives. Rainey filled the seat of Benjamin Franklin Whittemore, which had been declared vacant by the House. He served until Mar 3, 1879.

JAY, JOHN: BIRTH ANNIVERSARY. Dec 12, 1745. American statesman, diplomat and first chief justice of the US Supreme Court (1789–95), coauthor (with Alexander Hamilton and James Madison) of the influential *Federalist* papers, was born at New York, NY. Jay died at Bedford, NY, May 17, 1829.

KENYA: JAMHURI DAY. Dec 12. Jamhuri Day (Independence Day) is Kenya's official National Day, commemorating proclamation of the republic and independence from the UK in 1963.

MEXICO: GUADALUPE DAY. Dec 12. One of Mexico's major celebrations. Honors the "Dark Virgin of Guadalupe," the republic's patron saint. Parties and pilgrimages, with special ceremonies at the Shrine of Our Lady of Guadalupe, at Mexico City.

PENNSYLVANIA RATIFIES CONSTITUTION: ANNIVERSARY. Dec 12, 1787. Pennsylvania became the second state to ratify the US Constitution, by a vote of 46 to 23.

POINSETTIA DAY (JOEL ROBERTS POINSETT: DEATH ANNIVERSARY). Dec 12. A day to enjoy poinsettias and to honor Dr. Joel Roberts Poinsett, the American diplomat who introduced the Central American plant that is named for him into the US. Poinsett was born at Charleston, SC, Mar 2, 1799. He also served as a member of Congress and as secretary of war. He died near Statesburg, SC, Dec 12, 1851. The poinsettia has become a favorite Christmas season plant. ***See Curriculum Connection.***

RUSSIA: CONSTITUTION DAY. Dec 12. National holiday commemorating the adoption of the new constitution in 1993.

SUPREME COURT RULES FOR BUSH: 5th ANNIVERSARY. Dec 12, 2000. The Supreme Court ruled by a vote of 5 to 4 that there could be no further counting of Florida's disputed votes in the 2000 presidential election. After five weeks of conflict over the vote count in Florida, Democratic candidate Al Gore conceded the election to George W. Bush.

TURKMENISTAN: NEUTRALITY DAY. Dec 12. National holiday. Commemorates the UN's recognition of neutrality in 1995.

BIRTHDAYS TODAY

Tracy Austin, 43, former tennis player, born Rolling Hills Estates, CA, Dec 12, 1962.

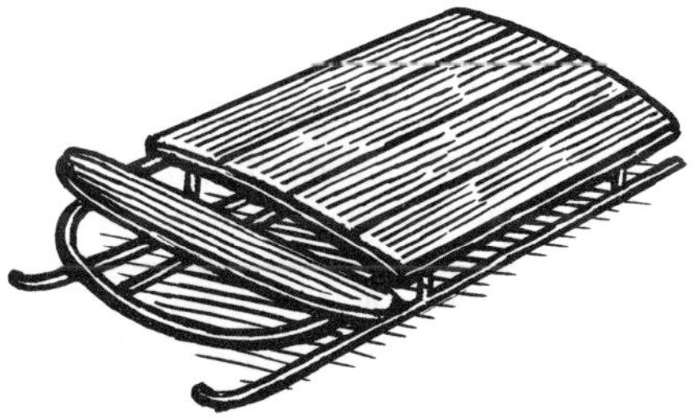

DECEMBER 13 — TUESDAY

Day 347 — 18 Remaining

LINCOLN, MARY TODD: BIRTH ANNIVERSARY. Dec 13, 1818. Wife of Abraham Lincoln, 16th president of the US, born at Lexington, KY. Died at Springfield, IL, July 16, 1882.

MALTA: REPUBLIC DAY. Dec 13. National holiday. Malta became a republic in 1974.

NEW ZEALAND FIRST SIGHTED BY EUROPEANS: ANNIVERSARY. Dec 13, 1642. Captain Abel Tasman of the Dutch East India Company first sighted New Zealand but was kept from landing by Maori warriors. In 1769 Captain James Cook landed and claimed formal possession for Great Britain.

NORTH AND SOUTH KOREA END WAR: ANNIVERSARY. Dec 13, 1991. North and South Korea signed a treaty of reconciliation and nonaggression, formally ending the Korean War—38 years after fighting ceased in 1953. This agreement was not hailed as a peace treaty, and the armistice that was signed July 27, 1953, between the UN and North Korea, was to remain in effect until it could be transformed into a formal peace.

SWEDEN: SANTA LUCIA DAY. Dec 13. Nationwide celebration of festival of light, honoring St. Lucia. Many hotels have their own Lucia, a young girl attired in a long, flowing white gown with a wreath of candles in her hair, who serves guests coffee and lussekatter (saffron buns) in the early morning.

BIRTHDAYS TODAY

Sergei Fedorov, 36, hockey player, born Pskov, Russia, Dec 13, 1969.
Tamora Pierce, 51, author (*In the Realms of the Gods,* the Magic Circle series), born Connellsville, PA, Dec 13, 1954.
Johan Reinhard, 62, anthropologist, mountaineer, author (*Discovering the Inca Ice Maiden*), born Joliet, IL, Dec 13, 1943.
Dick Van Dyke, 80, actor, comedian (*Mary Poppins*, "The Dick Van Dyke Show"), born West Plains, MO, Dec 13, 1925.
Tom Vilsack, 55, Governor of Iowa (D), born Pittsburgh, PA, Dec 13, 1950.

DECEMBER 14 — WEDNESDAY

Day 348 — 17 Remaining

ALABAMA: ADMISSION DAY: ANNIVERSARY. Dec 14. Became the 22nd state in 1819.

HALCYON DAYS. Dec 14–28. Traditionally, the seven days before and the seven days after the winter solstice. To the ancients a time when a fabled bird called the halcyon (pronounced HAL-cee-on) calmed the wind and waves—a time of calm and tranquility.

SOUTH POLE DISCOVERY: ANNIVERSARY. Dec 14, 1911. The elusive object of many expeditions dating from the 7th century, the South Pole was located and visited by Roald Amundsen with four companions and 52 sled dogs. All five men and 12 of the dogs returned to base camp safely. Next to visit the South Pole, Jan 17, 1912, was a party of five led by Captain Robert F. Scott, all of whom perished during the return trip. A search party found their frozen bodies 11 months later. See also: "Amundsen, Roald: Birth Anniversary" (July 16).

SUTCLIFFE, ROSEMARY: BIRTH ANNIVERSARY. Dec 14, 1920. Author of historical novels for children (*The Lantern Bearers, Eagle of the Ninth*), born at East Clanden, England. Died July 23, 1992.

★ ★ ★

BIRTHDAYS TODAY

Craig Biggio, 40, baseball player, born Smithtown, NY, Dec 14, 1965.
Rhoda Blumberg, 88, author (*Full Steam Ahead: The Race to Build a Transcontinental Railroad*), born New York, NY, Dec 14, 1917.
Patty Duke, 59, actress (Oscar for *The Miracle Worker*; Emmy for *My Sweet Charlie*), born Elmhurst, NY, Dec 14, 1946.
John Neufeld, 67, author (*Lisa, Bright and Dark; Edgar Allan*), born Chicago, IL, Dec 14, 1938.
Michael Owen, 26, soccer player, born Chester, England, Dec 14, 1979.

DECEMBER 15 — THURSDAY

Day 349 — 16 Remaining

★**BILL OF RIGHTS DAY.** Dec 15. Presidential Proclamation. Has been proclaimed each year since 1962, but was omitted in 1967 and 1968. (Issued in 1941 and 1946 at Congressional request and in 1947 without request.) Since 1968 has been included in Human Rights Day and Week Proclamation.

BILL OF RIGHTS: ANNIVERSARY. Dec 15, 1791. The first 10 amendments to the US Constitution, known as the Bill of Rights, became effective following ratification by Virginia. The anniversary of ratification and of effect is observed as Bill of Rights Day and is proclaimed annually by the President. For more info: *A Kids' Guide to America's Bill of Rights: Curfews, Censorship, and the 100-Pound Giant* by Kathleen Krull (Avon/Camelot, 0-380-97497-5, $16 Gr. 5–8), *The Bill of Rights: How We Got It and What It Means* by Milton Meltzer (out of print, but available in library collections), or go to Ben's Guide to US Government for Kids: bensguide.gpo.gov.

CURAÇAO: KINGDOM DAY AND ANTILLEAN FLAG DAY. Dec 15. This day commemorates the Charter of Kingdom, signed at the Knight's Hall at The Hague in 1954, granting the Netherlands Antilles complete autonomy. The Antillean Flag was hoisted for the first time Dec 15, 1959.

EIFFEL, ALEXANDRE GUSTAVE: BIRTH ANNIVERSARY. Dec 15, 1832. Eiffel, the French engineer who designed the 1,000 ft-high, million-dollar, open-lattice wrought iron Eiffel Tower, and who participated in designing the Statue of Liberty, was born at Dijon, France. The Eiffel Tower, weighing more than 7,000 tons, was built for the Paris International Exposition of 1889. Eiffel died at Paris, France, Dec 23, 1923.

MOON PHASE: FULL MOON. Dec 15. Moon enters Full Moon phase at 11:15 AM, EST.

PUERTO RICO: NAVIDADES. Dec 15–Jan 6. Traditional Christmas season begins mid-December and ends on Three Kings Day. Elaborate nativity scenes, carolers, special Christmas foods and trees from Canada and US. Gifts on Christmas Day and on Three Kings Day.

SITTING BULL: DEATH ANNIVERSARY. Dec 15, 1890. Famous Sioux Indian leader, medicine man and warrior of the Hunkpapa Teton band. Known also by his native name, Tatanka-yatanka, Sitting Bull was born on the Grand River, SD. He first accompanied his father on the warpath at the age of 14 against the Crow and thereafter rapidly gained influence within his tribe. In 1886 he led a raid on Fort Buford. His steadfast refusal to go to a reservation led General Phillip Sheridan to initiate a campaign against him which led to the massacre of Lieutenant Colonel George Custer's men at Little Bighorn, after which Sitting Bull fled to Canada, remaining there until 1881. Although many in his tribe surrendered on their return, Sitting Bull remained hostile until his death in a skirmish with the US soldiers along the Grand River. For more info: *Sitting Bull and His World*, by Albert Marrin (Dutton, 0-525-45944-8, $25 Gr. 6–12).

December 2005

S	M	T	W	T	F	S
				1	2	3
4	5	6	7	8	9	10
11	12	13	14	15	16	17
18	19	20	21	22	23	24
25	26	27	28	29	30	31

SMITH, BETTY: BIRTH ANNIVERSARY. Dec 15, 1904. Author, born at New York, NY. Her books include *A Tree Grows in Brooklyn*, *Tomorrow Will Be Better* and *Joy in the Morning*. Smith died at Shelton, CT, Jan 17, 1972.

BIRTHDAYS TODAY

Kathleen Babineaux Blanco, 63, Governor of Louisiana (D), born Iberia Parish, LA, Dec 15, 1942.
Alexandra Stevenson, 25, tennis player, born San Diego, CA, Dec 15, 1980.
Garrett Wang, 37, actor ("Star Trek: Voyager"), born Riverside, CA, Dec 15, 1968.
Mark Warner, 51, Governor of Virginia (D), born Indianapolis, IN, Dec 15, 1954.

DECEMBER 16 — FRIDAY

Day 350 — 15 Remaining

BAHRAIN: INDEPENDENCE DAY. Dec 16. National holiday. Commemorates independence from British protection in 1971.

BANGLADESH: VICTORY DAY. Dec 16. National holiday. Commemorates victory over Pakistan in 1971. The former East Pakistan became Bangladesh.

BATTLE OF THE BULGE: ANNIVERSARY. Dec 16, 1944. By late 1944 the German Army was in retreat and Allied forces were on German soil. But a surprise German offensive was launched in the Belgian Ardennes Forest on this date. The Nazi commanders, hoping to minimize any aerial counterattack by the Allies, chose a time when foggy, rainy weather prevailed and the initial attack by eight armored divisions along a 75-mile front took the Allies by surprise, the 5th Panzer Army penetrating to within 20 miles of crossings on the Meuse River. US troops were able to hold fast at bottlenecks in the Ardennes, but by the end of December the German push had penetrated 65 miles into the Allied lines (though their line had narrowed from the initial 75 miles to 20 miles). By that time the Allies began to respond and the Germans were stopped by Montgomery on the Meuse and by Patton at Bastogne. The weather cleared and Allied aircraft began to bomb the German forces and supply lines by Dec 26. The German Army withdrew from the Ardennes, Jan 21, 1945, having lost 120,000 men.

BEETHOVEN, LUDWIG VAN: BIRTH ANNIVERSARY. Dec 16, 1770. Regarded by many as the greatest orchestral composer of all time, Ludwig van Beethoven was born at Bonn, Germany. Impairment of his hearing began before he was 30, but even total deafness did not halt his composing and conducting. His last appearance on the concert stage was to conduct the premiere of his *Ninth Symphony*, at Vienna, May 7, 1824. He was unable to hear either the orchestra or the applause. Of a stormy temperament, he is said to have died during a violent thunderstorm Mar 26, 1827, at Vienna.

BOSTON TEA PARTY: ANNIVERSARY. Dec 16, 1773. Anniversary of Boston patriots' boarding of British vessel at anchor at Boston Harbor. Contents of nearly 350 chests of tea were dumped into the harbor to protest the British monopoly on tea imports. This was one of several events leading to the American Revolution. For info: *The Boston Tea Party*, by Laurie O'Neill (Millbrook, 0-761-30006-6, $23.90 Gr. 3–6) or *Boston Tea Party*, by Pamela Duncan Edwards (Putnam, 0-399-23357-1, $15.99 Gr. 1–3).

KAZAKHSTAN: REPUBLIC DAY. Dec 16. National Day. Commemorates independence from the Soviet Union in 1991.

MEXICO: POSADAS. Dec 16–24. A nine-day annual celebration throughout Mexico. Processions of "pilgrims" knock at doors asking for posada (shelter), commemorating the search by Joseph and Mary for a shelter in which the infant Jesus might be born. Pilgrims are invited inside, and fun and merrymaking ensue with blindfolded guests trying to break a "piñata" (papier mâché decorated earthenware utensil filled with gifts and goodies) suspended from the ceiling. Once the piñata is broken, the gifts are distributed and celebration continues. For info: *Las Posadas: A Hispanic Christmas Celebration*, by Diane Hoyt-Goldsmith (Holiday, 0-8234-1449-3, $16.95 Gr. 4–6).

PHILIPPINES: SIMBANG GABI. Dec 16–25. Nationwide. A nine-day novena of predawn masses, also called "Misa de Gallo." One of the traditional Filipino celebrations of the holiday season.

SOUTH AFRICA: RECONCILIATION DAY. Dec 16. National holiday. Celebrates the spirit of reconciliation, national unity and peace amongst all citizens.

UNDERDOG DAY. Dec 16. To salute, before the year's end, all of the underdogs and unsung heroes—the Number Two people who contribute so much to the Number One people we read about. (Sherlock Holmes's Dr. Watson and Robinson Crusoe's Friday are examples.) Observed annually on the third Friday in December since its founding in 1976 by the late Peter Moeller, THE Chief Underdog. For info: A. Moeller, Underdogs Intl, Box 71, Clio, MI 48420-0071.

BIRTHDAYS TODAY

Bill Brittain, 75, author (*The Wish Giver: Three Tales of Coven Tree*), born Rochester, NY, Dec 16, 1930.

Donald Carcieri, 63, Governor of Rhode Island (R), born East Greenwich, RI, Dec 16, 1942.

Peter Dickinson, 78, author (*The Lion Tamer's Daughter: And Other Stories*), born Livingston, Zambia, Dec 16, 1927.

DECEMBER 17 — SATURDAY

Day 351 — 14 Remaining

AZTEC CALENDAR STONE DISCOVERY: ANNIVERSARY. Dec 17, 1790. One of the wonders of the western hemisphere—the Aztec Calendar or Solar Stone—was found beneath the ground by workmen repairing Mexico City's Central Plaza. The intricately carved stone, 11 feet, 8 inches in diameter and weighing nearly 25 tons, proved to be a highly developed calendar monument to the sun. Believed to have been carved in the year 1479, this extraordinary time-counting basalt tablet originally stood in the Great Temple of the Aztecs. Buried along with other Aztec idols, soon after the Spanish conquest in 1521, it remained hidden until 1790. Its 52-year cycle had regulated many Aztec ceremonies, including human sacrifices to save the world from destruction by the gods.

CLEAN AIR ACT PASSED BY CONGRESS: ANNIVERSARY. Dec 17, 1967. A sweeping set of laws to protect us from air pollution was passed this day. This was the first legislation to place pollution controls on the automobile industry.

FLOYD, WILLIAM: BIRTH ANNIVERSARY. Dec 17, 1734. Signer of the Declaration of Independence, member of Congress, born at Brookhaven, NY. Died at Westernville, NY, Aug 4, 1821.

KING, W.L. MACKENZIE: BIRTH ANNIVERSARY. Dec 17, 1874. Former Canadian prime minister, born at Berlin, Ontario. Served 21 years, the longest term of any prime minister in the English-speaking world. Died at Kingsmere, Canada, July 22, 1950.

"THE SIMPSONS" TV PREMIERE: ANNIVERSARY. Dec 17, 1989. FOX TV's hottest animated family, "The Simpsons," premiered as a half-hour weekly sitcom. The originator of Homer, Marge, Bart, Lisa and Maggie is cartoonist Matt Groening. Voices are provided by Nancy Cartwright, Dan Castellaneta, Julie Kavner, Hank Azaria, Harry Shearer and Yeardley Smith. The show's 300th episode, "Barting Over," aired Feb 16, 2003.

★**WRIGHT BROTHERS DAY.** Dec 17. Presidential Proclamation always issued for Dec 17 since 1963 (PL88–209 of Dec 17, 1963). Issued twice earlier at Congressional request in 1959 and 1961.

WRIGHT BROTHERS' FIRST POWERED FLIGHT: ANNIVERSARY. Dec 17, 1903. Orville and Wilbur Wright, brothers, bicycle shop operators, inventors and aviation pioneers, after three years of experimentation with kites and gliders, achieved the first documented successful powered and controlled flights of an airplane. The flights, near Kitty Hawk, NC, piloted first by Orville then by Wilbur Wright, were sustained for less than one minute but represented man's first powered airplane flight and the beginning of a new form of transportation. Orville Wright was born at Dayton, OH, Aug 19, 1871, and died there Jan 30, 1948. Wilbur Wright was born at Millville, IN, Apr 16, 1867, and died at Dayton, OH, May 30, 1912. For more info: *The Wright Brothers: How They Invented the Airplane*, by Russell Freedman (Holiday, 0-8234-0875-2, $18.95 Gr. 4–6).

BIRTHDAYS TODAY

David Kherdian, 74, author (*The Road from Home: The Story of an Armenian Girl*), born Racine, WI, Dec 17, 1931.

DECEMBER 18 — SUNDAY

Day 352 — 13 Remaining

CAPITOL REEF NATIONAL PARK ESTABLISHED: ANNIVERSARY. Dec 18, 1971. Area of outstanding geological features, colorful canyons, prehistoric Fremont petroglyphs and Mormon historic fruit orchards and buildings in south central Utah, originally proclaimed a national monument Aug 2, 1937, was established as a national park. For more info: www.nps.gov/care/index.htm.

COBB, TY: BIRTH ANNIVERSARY. Dec 18, 1886. Tyrus (Ty) Cobb, Baseball Hall of Fame outfielder, born at Narrows, GA. He played 24 years and got more hits than any other player, until Pete Rose. Inducted into the Hall of Fame in 1936. Died at Atlanta, GA, July 17, 1961. For more info: www.cmgww.com/baseball/cobb/index.html.

NEW JERSEY RATIFIES CONSTITUTION: ANNIVERSARY. Dec 18, 1787. New Jersey became the third state to ratify the Constitution (following Delaware and Pennsylvania). It did so unanimously.

NIGER: REPUBLIC DAY. Dec 18. National holiday. This West African nation gained autonomy within the French community on this day in 1958.

UNITED NATIONS: INTERNATIONAL MIGRANTS DAY. Dec 18. Recognizes the contributions that millions of migrant workers make to the global economy, and seeks to draw attention to the precarious state of their rights. For info: United Nations, Dept of Public Info, New York, NY 10017. Web: www.un.org.

BIRTHDAYS TODAY

Christina Aguilera, 25, singer, born Staten Island, NY, Dec 18, 1980.
Katie Holmes, 27, actress ("Dawson's Creek"), born Toledo, OH, Dec 18, 1978.
Brad Pitt, 42, actor (*A River Runs Through It, Ocean's Eleven*), born Shawnee, OK, Dec 18, 1963.
Marilyn Sachs, 78, author (the Veronica Ganz series), born the Bronx, NY, Dec 18, 1927.
Steven Spielberg, 59, producer, director (*E.T.: The Extra-Terrestrial*, the Indiana Jones series, *Schindler's List*), born Cincinnati, OH, Dec 18, 1946.

December 2005

S	M	T	W	T	F	S
				1	2	3
4	5	6	7	8	9	10
11	12	13	14	15	16	17
18	19	20	21	22	23	24
25	26	27	28	29	30	31

DECEMBER 19 — MONDAY

Day 353 — 12 Remaining

LA FARGE, OLIVER: BIRTH ANNIVERSARY. Dec 19, 1901. American author and anthropologist, born at New York, NY. La Farge wrote the children's book *Laughing Boy*. He died at Albuquerque, NM, Aug 2, 1963.

SPACE MILESTONE: FIRST RADIO BROADCAST FROM SPACE. Dec 19, 1958. At 3:15 PM, EST, the US Earth satellite *Atlas* transmitted the first radio voice broadcast from space, a 58-word recorded Christmas greeting from President Dwight D. Eisenhower: "to all mankind America's wish for peace on earth and good will toward men everywhere." The satellite had been launched from Cape Canaveral Dec 18.

WOODSON, CARTER GODWIN: BIRTH ANNIVERSARY. Dec 19, 1875. Historian who introduced black studies to colleges and universities, born at New Canton, VA. His scholarly works included *The Negro in Our History, The Education of the Negro Prior to 1861*. Known as the father of black history, he inaugurated Negro History Week. Woodson was working on a six-volume *Encyclopaedia Africana* when he died at Washington, DC, Apr 3, 1950. For more info: *Carter G. Woodson: The Man Who Put "Black" in American History*, by Jim Haskins and Kathleen Benson (Millbrook, 0-7613-1264-1, $24.90 Gr. 4–6).

BIRTHDAYS TODAY

Eve Bunting, 77, author (*Sixth-Grade Sleepover, Smoky Night*), born Anne Evelyn Bolton, Maghera, Ireland, Dec 19, 1928.
Alyssa Milano, 33, actress ("Charmed," "Who's the Boss?"), born Brooklyn, NY, Dec 19, 1972.
Jake Plummer, 31, football player, born Boise, ID, Dec 19, 1974.
Warren Sapp, 33, football player, born Plymouth, FL, Dec 19, 1972.
Reggie White, 44, former football player, born Chattanooga, TN, Dec 19, 1961.

DECEMBER 20 — TUESDAY

Day 354 — 11 Remaining

AMERICAN POET LAUREATE ESTABLISHMENT: 20th ANNIVERSARY. Dec 20, 1985. A bill empowering the Librarian of Congress to annually name a Poet Laureate/Consultant in Poetry was signed into law by President Ronald Reagan. In return for a $10,000 stipend as Poet Laureate and a salary (about $35,000) as the Consultant in Poetry, the person named will present at least one major work of poetry and will appear at selected national ceremonies. The first Poet Laureate of the US was Robert Penn Warren, appointed to that position by the Librarian of Congress, Feb 26, 1986.

CLINTON IMPEACHMENT PROCEEDINGS: ANNIVERSARY. Dec 20, 1998. President Bill Clinton was impeached by a House of Representatives that was divided along party lines. He was charged with perjury and obstruction of justice stemming from a relationship with a White House intern. He was then tried by the Senate in January 1999. On Feb 12, 1999, he was acquitted on both charges. Clinton was only the second US president to undergo impeachment proceedings. Andrew Johnson was impeached by the House in 1867 but the Senate voted against impeachment and he finished his term of office. See also: "Johnson Impeachment Proceedings: Anniversary" (Feb 24). For more info: *The Impeachment of Bill Clinton*, by Nathan Aaseng (Lucent, 1-56006-651-2, $18.96 Gr. 6–9).

LOUISIANA PURCHASE DAY: ANNIVERSARY. Dec 20, 1803. One of the greatest real estate deals in history, when more than a million square miles of the Louisiana Territory were turned over to the US by France on this date. The treaty had been signed on Apr 30, 1803, giving the US the land for a price of about $20 per square mile. It nearly doubled the size of the country, extending the western border to the Rocky Mountains. For more info: *The Louisiana Purchase*, by James A. Corrick (Lucent, 1-56006-637-7, $19.96 Gr. 7–10).

MACAU REVERTS TO CHINESE CONTROL: ANNIVERSARY. Dec 20, 1999. Macau, a tiny province on the southeast coast of China, reverted to Chinese rule on this day. It had been a Portuguese colony since 1557. With the return of Hong Kong in 1997 and the return of Macau, no part of mainland China is occupied by a foreign power.

SACAGAWEA: DEATH ANNIVERSARY. Dec 20, 1812. As a young Shoshone Indian woman, Sacagawea in 1805 (with her two-month-old boy strapped to her back) traveled with the Lewis and Clark Expedition, serving as an interpreter. It is said that the expedition could not have succeeded without her aid. She was born about 1787 and died at Fort Manuel on the Missouri River. Few other women have been so often honored. There are statues, fountains and memorials of her, and her name has been given to a mountain peak. In 2000 the US Mint issued a $1 coin with Sacagawea's picture on it. For more info: *A Picture Book of Sacagawea*, by David A. Adler (Holiday House, 0-823-41485-X, $16.95 All ages); *Girl of the Shining Mountains: Sacagawea's Story*, by Peter Roop and Connie Roop (Hyperion, 0-786-80492-0, $14.99 Gr. 5–8).

SAMUEL SLATER DAY IN MASSACHUSETTS. Dec 20. Proclaimed annually by the governor, this day commemorates Samuel Slater, the founder of the American factory system. He came to America from England and built a cotton mill at Rhode Island in 1790. He directed many New England mills until his death in 1835.

SOUTH CAROLINA: SECESSION ANNIVERSARY. Dec 20, 1860. South Carolina's legislature voted to secede from the US, the first state to do so. Within six weeks, five more states seceded. On Feb 4, 1861, representatives from the six states met at Montgomery, AL, to establish a government and on Feb 9, Jefferson Davis was elected president of the Confederate States of America. Eventually, 11 states made up the Confederacy: Alabama, Arkansas, Florida, Georgia, Louisiana, Mississippi, North Carolina, South Carolina, Tennessee, Texas and Virginia.

VIRGINIA COMPANY EXPEDITION TO AMERICA: ANNIVERSARY. Dec 20, 1606. Three small ships, the *Susan Constant*, the *Godspeed* and the *Discovery*, commanded by Captain Christopher Newport, departed London, England, bound for America, where the royally chartered Virginia Company's approximately 120 persons established the first permanent English settlement in what is now the US at Jamestown, VA, May 14, 1607.

BIRTHDAYS TODAY

Michael J. Caduto, 50, author (*Keepers of the Earth, Earth Tales from Around the World*), born Providence, RI, Dec 20, 1955.

Lulu Delacre, 48, author (*Arroz Con Leche: Popular Songs and Rhymes from Latin America*), born Rio Piedras, Puerto Rico, Dec 20, 1957.

Rich Gannon, 40, football player, born Philadelphia, PA, Dec 20, 1965.

Uri Geller, 59, psychic, clairvoyant, born Tel Aviv, Israel, Dec 20, 1946.

M.B. Goffstein, 65, author and illustrator (*Fish for Supper*), born St. Paul, MN, Dec 20, 1940.

Sonny Perdue, 59, Governor of Georgia (R), born Perry, GA, Dec 20, 1946.

DECEMBER 21 — WEDNESDAY

Day 355 — 10 Remaining

FIRST CROSSWORD PUZZLE: ANNIVERSARY. Dec 21, 1913. The first crossword puzzle was compiled by Arthur Wynne and published in a supplement to the *New York World*.

GIBSON, JOSH: BIRTH ANNIVERSARY. Dec 21, 1912. Joshua (Josh) Gibson, Baseball Hall of Fame catcher born at Buena Vista, GA, is regarded as the greatest slugger to play in the Negro Leagues and perhaps the greatest ballplayer ever. Gibson starred with the Pittsburgh Crawfords. His long home runs are the stuff of legend. Inducted into the Hall of Fame in 1972. Died at Pittsburgh, PA, Jan 20, 1947.

HUMBUG DAY. Dec 21. Allows all those preparing for Christmas to vent their frustrations. Twelve "humbugs" allowed. [©2002 by WH.] For info: Thomas & Ruth Roy, Wellcat Holidays, 2418 Long Lane, Lebanon, PA 17046. Phone: (717) 279-0184. E-mail: info@wellcat.com. Web: www.wellcat.com.

IRAN: YALDA. Dec 21. Yalda, the longest night of the year, is celebrated by Iranians. The ceremony has an Indo-Iranian origin, where Light and Good were considered to struggle against Darkness and Evil. With fires burning and lights lit, family and friends gather to stay up through the night helping the sun in its battle against darkness. They recite poetry, tell stories and eat special fruits and nuts until the sun, triumphant, reappears in the morning.

PILGRIM LANDING: ANNIVERSARY. Dec 21, 1620. According to Governor William Bradford's *History of Plymouth Plantation*, "On Munday," [Dec 21, 1620, New Style] the Pilgrims, aboard the *Mayflower*, reached Plymouth, MA, "sounded ye harbor, and founde it fitt for shipping; and marched into ye land, & founde diverse cornfields, and ye best they could find, and ye season & their presente necessitie made them glad to accepte of it. . . . And after wards tooke better view of ye place, and resolved wher to pitch their dwelling; and them and their goods." Plymouth Rock, the legendary place of landing since it first was "identified" in 1769, nearly 150 years after the landing, has been a historic shrine since. The landing anniversary is observed in much of New England as Forefathers' Day.

SPACE MILESTONE: *APOLLO 8* (US). Dec 21, 1968. First moon voyage launched, manned by Colonel Frank Borman, Captain James A. Lovell, Jr and Major William A. Anders. Orbited moon Dec 24, returned to Earth Dec 27. First men to orbit the moon and see the side of the moon away from Earth. For more info: *Project Apollo*, by Diane M. Sipiera and Paul P. Sipiera (Children's Press, 0-516-20435-1, $21 Gr. K–3).

WINTER. Dec 21–Mar 20, 2006. In the Northern Hemisphere winter begins today with the winter solstice, at 1:35 PM, EST. Note that in the Southern Hemisphere today is the beginning of summer. Between the Equator and Arctic Circle the sunrise and sunset points on the horizon are farthest south for the year and daylight length is minimum (ranging from 12 hours, 8 minutes, at the equator to zero at the Arctic Circle). For more info: *The Winter Solstice*, by Ellen Jackson (Millbrook, 0-7613-0297-2, $7.95 Gr. PreK–3).

BIRTHDAYS TODAY

Chris Evert Lloyd, 51, broadcaster and former tennis player, born Fort Lauderdale, FL, Dec 21, 1954.

Kiefer Sutherland, 39, actor (*Flatliners*, "24"), born London, England, Dec 21, 1966.

DECEMBER 22 — THURSDAY

Day 356 — 9 Remaining

CAPRICORN, THE GOAT. Dec 22–Jan 19. In the astronomical and astrological zodiac that divides the sun's apparent orbit into 12 segments, the period Dec 22–Jan 19 is identified, traditionally, as the sun sign of Capricorn, the Goat. The ruling planet is Saturn.

COELACANTH DISCOVERED: ANNIVERSARY. Dec 22, 1938. Scientists in South Africa identified a huge fish called a coelacanth which up until this time had been thought to be extinct. Since then other coelacanths have been found in the ocean.

FIRST GORILLA BORN IN CAPTIVITY: BIRTH ANNIVERSARY. Dec 22, 1956. "Colo" was born at the Columbus, OH, zoo, weighing in at 3¼ pounds, the first gorilla born in captivity.

OGLETHORPE, JAMES EDWARD: BIRTH ANNIVERSARY. Dec 22, 1696. English general, author and colonizer of Georgia. Founder of the city of Savannah. Oglethorpe was born at London. He died June 30, 1785, at Cranham Hall, Essex, England.

BIRTHDAYS TODAY

Mick Inkpen, 53, author, illustrator (the Kipper series, the Wibbly Pig series), born Romford, England, Dec 22, 1952.

Claudia Alta (Lady Bird) Johnson, 93, former First Lady, widow of Lyndon Johnson, the 36th president of the US, born Karnack, TX, Dec 22, 1912.

Jerry Pinkney, 66, illustrator (*John Henry*), born Philadelphia, PA, Dec 22, 1939.

Bonnie Pryor, 63, author (*The Dream Jar*), born California, Dec 22, 1942.

Diane K. Sawyer, 59, journalist ("Prime Time Live," "Good Morning America"), born Glasgow, KY, Dec 22, 1946.

December 2005

S	M	T	W	T	F	S
				1	2	3
4	5	6	7	8	9	10
11	12	13	14	15	16	17
18	19	20	21	22	23	24
25	26	27	28	29	30	31

DECEMBER 23 — FRIDAY

Day 357 — 8 Remaining

FIRST NONSTOP FLIGHT AROUND THE WORLD WITHOUT REFUELING: ANNIVERSARY. Dec 23, 1987. Dick Rutan and Jeana Yeager set a new world record of 216 hours of continuous flight, breaking their own record of 111 hours set July 15, 1986. The aircraft *Voyager* departed from Edwards Air Force Base at California, Dec 14, 1987, and landed Dec 23, 1987. The journey covered 24,986 miles at an official speed of 115 MPH.

JAPAN: BIRTHDAY OF THE EMPEROR. Dec 23. National Day. Holiday honoring Emperor Akihito, born in 1933.

METRIC CONVERSION ACT: 30th ANNIVERSARY. Dec 23, 1975. The Congress of the US passed Public Law 94–168, known as the Metric Conversion Act of 1975. This act declares that the SI (International System of Units) will be this country's basic system of measurement and establishes the US Metric Board, which is responsible for the planning, coordination and implementation of the nation's voluntary conversion to SI. (Congress had authorized the metric system as a legal system of measurement in the US by an act passed July 28, 1866. In 1875, the US became one of the original signers of the Treaty of the Metre, which established an international metric system.)

MEXICO: FEAST OF THE RADISHES. Dec 23. Oaxaca. Figurines of people and animals cleverly carved out of radishes are sold during festivities.

MOON PHASE: LAST QUARTER. Dec 23. Moon enters Last Quarter phase at 2:36 PM, EST.

TRANSISTOR INVENTED: ANNIVERSARY. Dec 23, 1947. John Bardeen, Walter Brattain and William Shockley of Bell Laboratories shared the Nobel Prize for their invention of the transistor, which led to a revolution in communications and electronics.

WALKER, SARAH BREEDLOVE (MADAME C.J.): BIRTH ANNIVERSARY. Dec 23, 1867. Born at Delta, LA, Madame Walker built a successful hair care business with products for African Americans and was one of the first women in the US to become a millionaire in her own right. She died May 3, 1919, at Irvington, NY. For more info: *Vision of Beauty: The Story of Sarah Breedlove Walker*, by Kathryn Lasky (Candlewick, 0-7636-0253-1, $16.99 Gr. 3–5).

BIRTHDAYS TODAY

Akihito, 72, Emperor of Japan, born Tokyo, Japan, Dec 23, 1933.

Avi, 68, author (Newbery Medal for *Crispin: The Cross of Lead;* Newbery Honors for *The True Confessions of Charlotte Doyle, Nothing But the Truth*), born Avi Wortis, New York, NY, Dec 23, 1937.

Scott Gomez, 26, hockey player, born Anchorage, AK, Dec 23, 1979.

Corey Haim, 34, actor (*Lucas, The Lost Boys*), born Toronto, ON, Canada, Dec 23, 1971.

Martin Kratt, 40, zoologist, cohost with his brother Chris ("Kratts' Creatures," "Zoboomafoo"), born Summit, NJ, Dec 23, 1965.

DECEMBER 24 — SATURDAY

Day 358 — 7 Remaining

AUSTRIA: "SILENT NIGHT, HOLY NIGHT" CELEBRATIONS. Dec 24. Oberndorf, Hallein and Wagrain, Salzburg, Austria. Commemorating the creation of the Christmas carol here in 1818.

CARSON, CHRISTOPHER "KIT": BIRTH ANNIVERSARY. Dec 24, 1809. American frontiersman, soldier, trapper, guide and Indian agent best known as Kit Carson. Born at Madison County, KY, he died at Fort Lyon, CO, May 23, 1868.

CHRISTMAS EVE. Dec 24. Family gift-giving occasion in many Christian countries.

GRUELLE, JOHNNY: 125th BIRTH ANNIVERSARY. Dec 24, 1880. Author of the Raggedy Ann and Raggedy Andy books, born at Arcola, IL. Died at Miami Beach, FL, Jan 9, 1938.

LIBYA: INDEPENDENCE DAY. Dec 24. Libya gained its independence from Italy in 1951.

BIRTHDAYS TODAY

Debra Barracca, 52, author, with husband Sal (*The Adventures of Taxi Dog*), born New York, NY, Dec 24, 1953.

Lynn Munsinger, 54, illustrator (*Tacky the Penguin, Howliday Inn*), born Greenfield, MA, Dec 24, 1951.

Eddie Pope, 32, soccer player, born Greensboro, NC, Dec 24, 1973.

Jeff Sessions, 59, US Senator (R, Alabama), born Hybart, AL, Dec 24, 1946.

DECEMBER 25 — SUNDAY

Day 359 — 6 Remaining

BARTON, CLARA: BIRTH ANNIVERSARY. Dec 25, 1821. Clarissa Harlowe Barton, American nurse and philanthropist, founder of the American Red Cross, was born at Oxford, MA. In 1881, she became first president of the American Red Cross (founded May 21, 1881). She died at Glen Echo, MD, Apr 12, 1912.

CHRISTMAS. Dec 25. Christian festival commemorating the birth of Jesus of Nazareth. Most popular of Christian observances, Christmas as a Feast of the Nativity dates from the 4th century. Although Jesus's birth date is not known, the Western church selected Dec 25 for the feast, possibly to counteract the non-Christian festivals of that approximate date. Many customs from non-Christian festivals (Roman Saturnalia, Mithraic sun's birthday, Teutonic yule, Druidic and other winter solstice rites) have been adopted as part of the Christmas celebration (lights, mistletoe, holly and ivy, holiday tree, wassailing and gift giving, for example). Some Orthodox Churches celebrate Christmas Jan 7 based on the "old calendar" (Julian). Theophany (recognition of the divinity of Jesus) is observed Dec 25 and also Jan 6, especially by the Eastern Orthodox Church.

PAKISTAN: BIRTHDAY OF QAID-I-AZAM. Dec 25. Commemorates the birth in 1876 at Karachi, then part of India, of Mohammed Ali Jinnah, the founder of the Islamic Republic of Pakistan. When Pakistan became independent of India in 1947, he became the first governor general. That year he was given the title Qaid-i-Azam (Great Leader). He died at Karachi, Sept 11, 1948. This day is a holiday in Pakistan.

TAIWAN: CONSTITUTION DAY. Dec 25. National holiday. Commemorates the constitution of 1946.

WASHINGTON CROSSES THE DELAWARE: ANNIVERSARY. Dec 25, 1776. One of the most famous events of the American Revolution happened on a bleak Christmas night, during driving snow. General George Washington led 2,400 men across the Delaware River at McConkey's Ferry, Bucks County, PA, to conduct a surprise attack on Hessian troops at Trenton, NJ. Local fishermen conducted the troops across the river, finally assembling at 3:00 AM on the other side. Washington achieved victory at the Battle of Trenton, a key battle which changed the course of the war to the rebelling colonists' favor. For more info: *When Washington Crossed the Delaware* by Lynne Cheney (Simon & Schuster, 0-689-87043-4, $16.95 All ages).

BIRTHDAYS TODAY

Rickey Henderson, 47, former baseball player, born Chicago, IL, Dec 25, 1958.

Mary Elizabeth (Sissy) Spacek, 56, actress (Oscar for *Coal Miner's Daughter; Missing*), born Quitman, TX, Dec 25, 1949.

DECEMBER 26 — MONDAY

Day 360 — 5 Remaining

BAHAMAS: JUNKANOO. Dec 26. Kaleidoscope of sound and spectacle combining a bit of Mardi Gras, mummer's parade and ancient African tribal rituals. Revelers in colorful costumes parade through the streets to sounds of cowbells, goat skin drums and many other homemade instruments. Annually, on Boxing Day.

BOXING DAY. Dec 26. Ordinarily observed on the first day after Christmas. A legal holiday in Canada, the United Kingdom and many other countries. Formerly a day when Christmas gift boxes were expected by a postman, the lamplighter, the trash man and others who render services to the public at large. When Boxing Day falls on a Saturday or Sunday, the Monday or Tuesday immediately following may be proclaimed or observed as a bank or public holiday.

CHANUKAH. Dec 26–Jan 2, 2006. Feast of Lights or Feast of Dedication. This festival lasting eight days commemorates the victory of Maccabees over Syrians (165 BC) and rededication of the Temple of Jerusalem. Begins on Hebrew calendar date Kislev 25, 5766. (Began at sundown of previous day.) For more info: *A Hanukkah Treasury*, edited by Eric A. Kimmel (Holt, 0-8050-5293-3, $19.95 All ages).

CHRISTMAS AT THE TOP MUSEUM. Dec 26, 28, 29. Spinning Top Museum, Burlington, WI. Enjoy the traditional, universal toys of tops and top games, well-loved Christmas gifts around the world in the 2-hour museum program: 35 hands-on games and experiments, two videos, view the exhibit of 2,000 items, plus a live show by top collector. Reservations required. For info: Spinning Top Museum, 533 Milwaukee Ave (Hwy 36), Burlington, WI 53105. Phone: (262) 763-3946.

CLERC, LAURENT: BIRTH ANNIVERSARY. Dec 26, 1785. The first deaf teacher in America, Laurent Clerc assisted Thomas Hopkins Gallaudet in establishing the first public school for the deaf, Connecticut Asylum for the Education and Instruction of Deaf and Dumb Persons (now the American School for the Deaf), at Hartford, CT, in 1817. For 41 years Clerc trained new teachers in the use of sign language and in methods of teaching the deaf. Clerc was born at LaBalme, France, and died July 18, 1869.

KIDS AFTER CHRISTMAS. Dec 26–Jan 1, 2006. Mystic, CT. Everyone pays the youth admission and enjoys a full day of crafts, entertainment and the lore of the sea. Est attendance: 3,000. For info: Mystic Seaport, 75 Greenmanville Ave, Box 6000, Mystic, CT 06355. Phone: (860) 572-5315 or (888) 9SEAPORT. Web: www.visitmysticseaport.org.

KWANZAA. Dec 26–Jan 1, 2006. American black family observance created in 1966 by Dr. Maulana Karenga in recognition of traditional African harvest festivals. This seven-day festival stresses self-reliance and unity of the black family, with a harvest feast (karamu) on the next to the last day and a day of meditation on the final one. Each day is dedicated to a principle that African Americans should live by— Day 1: Unity; Day 2: Self-determination; Day 3: Collective work and responsibility; Day 4: Cooperative economics; Day 5: Purpose; Day 6: Creativity; Day 7: Faith. Kwanzaa means "first fruit" in Swahili. For more info: *The Children's Book of Kwanzaa: A Guide to Celebrating the Holiday*, by Dolores Johnson (Atheneum, 0-68-980864-X, $16 Gr. 4–6).

MAO TSE-TUNG: BIRTH ANNIVERSARY. Dec 26, 1893. Chinese librarian, teacher, communist revolutionist and "founding father" of the People's Republic of China, born at Hunan Province, China. Died at Beijing, Sept 9, 1976.

NATIONAL WHINER'S DAY™. Dec 26. A day dedicated to whiners, especially those who return Christmas gifts and need lots of attention. People are encouraged to be happy about what they do have, rather than unhappy about what they don't have. The most famous whiner(s) of the year will be announced. Nominations accepted through Dec 15. For more info, please send SASE to: Rev. Kevin C. Zaborney, 2023 Vickory Rd, Caro, MI 48723. Phone: (989) 673-6696. E-mail: revkev@avci.net. Web: www.geocities.com/hugging_whining.

NELSON, THOMAS: BIRTH ANNIVERSARY. Dec 26, 1738. Merchant and signer of the Declaration of Independence, born at Yorktown, VA. Died at Hanover County, VA, Jan 4, 1789.

RADIUM DISCOVERED: ANNIVERSARY. Dec 26, 1898. French scientists Pierre and Marie Curie discovered the element radium, for which they later won the Nobel Prize for Physics.

SAINT STEPHEN'S DAY. Dec 26. One of the seven deacons named by the apostles to distribute alms. Died during 1st century. Feast Day is observed as a public holiday in Austria.

SECOND DAY OF CHRISTMAS. Dec 26. Observed as holiday in many countries.

SHENANDOAH NATIONAL PARK ESTABLISHED: 70th ANNIVERSARY. Dec 26, 1935. Area of Blue Ridge Mountains of Virginia, originally authorized May 22, 1926, was established as a national park. For more info: www.nps.gov/shen/index.html. For more park info: Shenandoah National Park, Rte 4, Box 348, Luray, VA 22835. Web: www.nps.gov/shen.

SLOVENIA: INDEPENDENCE DAY. Dec 26. National holiday. Commemorates the day in 1990 when the results of an election on separation from the Yugoslav Union were announced.

SOUTH AFRICA: DAY OF GOODWILL. Dec 26. National holiday. Replaces Boxing Day.

December 2005

S	M	T	W	T	F	S
				1	2	3
4	5	6	7	8	9	10
11	12	13	14	15	16	17
18	19	20	21	22	23	24
25	26	27	28	29	30	31

BIRTHDAYS TODAY

Evan Bayh, 50, US Senator (D, Indiana), born Shirkieville, IN, Dec 26, 1955.

Susan Butcher, 51, sled dog racer, born Cambridge, MA, Dec 26, 1954.

Carlton Fisk, 58, Hall of Fame baseball player, born Bellows Falls, VT, Dec 26, 1947.

Jean Van Leuween, 68, author (the Oliver & Amanda Pig series, *Going Home*) , born Glen Ridge, NJ, Dec 26, 1937.

DECEMBER 27 — TUESDAY

Day 361 — 4 Remaining

D'AULAIRE, INGRI: BIRTH ANNIVERSARY. Dec 27, 1904. Author, with her husband Edgar (*Norse Gods and Giants*), born at Kongsberg, Norway. Died Oct 24, 1980.

"HOWDY DOODY" TV PREMIERE: ANNIVERSARY. Dec 27, 1947. The first popular children's show was brought to TV by Bob Smith and was one of the first regular NBC shows to be shown in color. The show was set in the circus town of Doodyville, populated by people and puppets. Children sat in the bleachers' "Peanut Gallery" and participated in activities such as songs and stories. Human characters were Buffalo Bob (Bob Smith), the silent clown Clarabell (Bob Keeshan, Bobby Nicholson and Lew Anderson), storekeeper Cornelius Cobb (Nicholson), Chief Thunderthud (Bill LeCornec), Princess Summerfall Winterspring (Judy Tyler and Linda Marsh), Bison Bill (Ted Brown) and wrestler Ugly Sam (Dayton Allen). Puppet costars included Howdy Doody, Phineas T. Bluster, Dilly Dally, Flub-a-Dub, Captain Scuttlebutt, Double Doody and Heidi Doody. The filmed adventures of Gumby were also featured. In the final episode, Clarabell broke his long silence to say, "Goodbye, kids."

PASTEUR, LOUIS: BIRTH ANNIVERSARY. Dec 27, 1822. French chemist-bacteriologist born at Dole, Jura, France. Died at Villeneuve l'Etang, France, Sept 28, 1895. Among his contributions to the germ theory of disease, he was the discoverer of prophylactic inoculation against rabies. He also proved that the spoilage of perishable food products could be prevented by the technique of heat treatment. This process, pasteurization, was named for him.

SAINT JOHN, APOSTLE-EVANGELIST: FEAST DAY. Dec 27. Son of Zebedee, Galilean fisherman, and Salome. Died about AD 100. Roman Rite Feast Day is Dec 27. (Observed May 8 by Byzantine Rite.)

BIRTHDAYS TODAY

Aidan Chambers, 71, author (Michael L. Printz Award for *Postcards from No Man's Land*), born Chester-le-Street, Durham, England, Dec 27, 1934.

Lisa Jakub, 27, actress (*Mrs Doubtfire, A Pig's Tale*), born Toronto, ON, Canada, Dec 27, 1978.

Deuce McAllister, 27, football player, born Dulymus Jenod McAllister, Lena, MS, Dec 27, 1978.

Diane Stanley, 62, author and illustrator (*Peter the Great*), born Abilene, TX, Dec 27, 1943.

DECEMBER 28 — WEDNESDAY

Day 362 — 3 Remaining

AUSTRALIA: PROCLAMATION DAY. Dec 28. Observed in South Australia.

BRINK, CAROL RYRIE: BIRTH ANNIVERSARY. Dec 28, 1895. Author of novels for middle school children, born at Moscow, ID. She won the 1936 Newbery Medal for *Caddie Woodlawn,* the story of her own grandmother's pioneer childhood. Other favorites include *Baby Island* and *The Pink Motel.* She died at La Jolla, CA, Aug 15, 1981.

ENDANGERED SPECIES ACT: ANNIVERSARY. Dec 28, 1973. President Richard Nixon signed the Endangered Species Act into law.

HOLY INNOCENTS DAY (CHILDERMAS). Dec 28. Commemoration of the massacre of children at Bethlehem, ordered by King Herod who wanted to destroy, among them, the infant Savior. Early and medieval accounts claimed as many as 144,000 victims, but more recent writers, noting that Bethlehem was a very small town, have revised the estimates of the number of children killed to between six and 20.

IOWA: ADMISSION DAY: ANNIVERSARY. Dec 28. Became 29th state in 1846.

PLEDGE OF ALLEGIANCE RECOGNIZED: 60th ANNIVERSARY. Dec 28, 1945. The US Congress officially recognized the Pledge of Allegiance and urged its frequent recitation in America's schools. The pledge was composed in 1892 by Francis Bellamy, a Baptist minister. At the time, Bellamy was chairman of a committee of state school superintendents of education, and several public schools adopted his pledge as part of the Columbus Day quadricentennial celebration that year. In 1954, the Knights of Columbus persuaded Congress to add the words "under God" to the pledge.

***POOR RICHARD'S ALMANACK*: ANNIVERSARY.** Dec 28, 1732. The *Pennsylvania Gazette* carried the first known advertisement for the first issue of *Poor Richard's Almanack* by Richard Saunders (Benjamin Franklin) for the year 1733. The advertisement promised "many pleasant and witty verses, jests and sayings . . ." America's most famous almanac, *Poor Richard's* was published through the year 1758 and has been imitated many times since. From *The Autobiography of Benjamin Franklin*: "In 1732 I first publish'd my Almanack, under the name of *Richard Saunders*; it was continu'd by me about twenty-five years, commonly call'd *Poor Richard's Almanack.* I endeavor'd to make it both entertaining and useful, and it accordingly came to be in such demand, that I reap'd considerable profit from it, vending annually near ten thousand. And observing that it was generally read, scarce any neighborhood in the province being without it, I consider'd it as a proper vehicle for conveying instruction among the common people, who bought scarcely any other books; I therefore filled all the little spaces that occurr'd between the remarkable days in the calendar with proverbial sentences, chiefly such as inculcated industry and frugality, as the means of procuring wealth, and thereby securing virtue; it being more difficult for a man in want, to act always honestly, as, to use here one of those proverbs, *it is hard for an empty sack to stand upright.*"

WILSON, WOODROW: BIRTH ANNIVERSARY. Dec 28, 1856. The 28th president of the US was born Thomas Woodrow Wilson at Staunton, VA. Twice elected president (1912 and 1916), it was Wilson who said, "The world must be made safe for democracy," as he asked the Congress to declare war on Germany, Apr 2, 1917. His first wife, Ellen, died Aug 6, 1914, and he married Edith Bolling Galt, Dec 18, 1915. He suffered a paralytic stroke Sept 16, 1919, never regaining his health. There were many speculations about who (possibly Mrs Wilson?) was running the government during his illness. His second term of office ended Mar 3, 1921, and he died at Washington, DC, Feb 3, 1924. For info: www.ipl.org/ref/POTUS.

BIRTHDAYS TODAY

Ray Bourque, 45, former hockey player, born Montreal, QC, Canada, Dec 28, 1960.

Cynthia DeFelice, 54, author (*The Apprenticeship of Lucas Whitaker*), born Philadelphia, PA, Dec 28, 1951.

Elizabeth Fitzgerald Howard, 78, author (*Aunt Flossie's Hats, Chita's Christmas Tree*), born Boston, MA, Dec 28, 1927.

Johnny Isakson, 61, US Senator (R, Georgia), born Atlanta, GA, Dec 28, 1944.

Tim Johnson, 59, US Senator (D, South Dakota), born Canton, SD, Dec 28, 1946.

Nancy Luenn, 51, author (*Nessa's Fish, Squish! A Wetland Walk*), born Pasadena, CA, Dec 28, 1954.

Patrick Rafter, 33, tennis player, born Mount Isa, Queensland, Australia, Dec 28, 1972.

Todd Richards, 36, Olympic snowboarder, born Worcester, MA, Dec 28, 1969.

MacKenzie Rosman, 16, actress ("7th Heaven"), born Charleston, SC, Dec 28, 1989.

Denzel Washington, 51, actor (*Glory, Remember the Titans, Training Day*), director, born Mount Vernon, NY, Dec 28, 1954.

DECEMBER 29 — THURSDAY

Day 363 — 2 Remaining

ATWATER, RICHARD: BIRTH ANNIVERSARY. Dec 29, 1892. Author, with his wife Florence, of the Newbery Award winner *Mr. Popper's Penguins*. Born at Chicago, IL, he died Aug 21, 1948, at Downey, WI.

JOHNSON, ANDREW: BIRTH ANNIVERSARY. Dec 29, 1808. The 17th president of the US (Apr 15, 1865–Mar 3, 1869), Andrew Johnson was born at Raleigh, NC. Upon Abraham Lincoln's assassination Johnson became president. He was the first US president to be impeached, and he was acquitted Mar 26, 1868. After his term as president he made several unsuccessful attempts to win public office. Finally he was elected to the US Senate from Tennessee and served in the Senate from Mar 4, 1875, until his death, at Carter's Station, TN, July 31, 1875. For info: www.ipl.org/ref/POTUS.

TEXAS: ADMISSION DAY: ANNIVERSARY. Dec 29. Became 28th state in 1845.

WOUNDED KNEE MASSACRE: ANNIVERSARY. Dec 29, 1890. Anniversary of the massacre of more than 200 Native American men, women and children by the US 7th Cavalry at Wounded Knee Creek, SD. Government efforts to suppress a ceremonial religious practice, the Ghost Dance (which called for a messiah who would restore the bison to the plains, make the white men disappear and bring back the old Native American way of life), had resulted in the death of Sitting Bull Dec 15, 1890, which further inflamed the disgruntled Native Americans and culminated in the slaughter at Wounded Knee Dec 29. For more info: *Wounded Knee 1890: The End of the Plains Indian Wars*, by Tom Streissguth (Facts on File, 0-8160-3600-4, $19.95 Gr. 7–12).

YMCA ORGANIZED: ANNIVERSARY. Dec 29, 1851. The first US branch of the Young Men's Christian Association was organized at Boston. It was modeled on an organization begun at London in 1844. For more info: www.ymca.net.

BIRTHDAYS TODAY

Molly Garrett Bang, 62, author and illustrator (*The Paper Crane; Ten, Nine, Eight*), born Princeton, NJ, Dec 29, 1943.

Irene Brady, 62, author and illustrator (*Wild Mouse*), born Ontario, OR, Dec 29, 1943.

Laveranues Coles, 28, football player, born Jacksonville, FL, Dec 29, 1977.

Jay Fiedler, 34, football player, born Oceanside, NY, Dec 29, 1971.

Jan Greenberg, 63, author (*Chuck Close, Up Close*), born St. Louis, MO, Dec 29, 1942.

Jason Kreis, 33, soccer player, born Omaha, NE, Dec 29, 1972.

DECEMBER 30 — FRIDAY

Day 364 — 1 Remaining

KIPLING, RUDYARD: BIRTH ANNIVERSARY. Dec 30, 1865. English poet, novelist and short story writer, and Nobel prize laureate, Kipling was born at Bombay, India. After working as a journalist at India, he traveled around the world. He married an American and lived at Vermont for several years. Kipling is best known for his children's stories, such as *Jungle Book* and *Just So Stories* and poems such as "The Ballad of East and West" and "If." He died at London, England, Jan 18, 1936.

MADAGASCAR: NATIONAL HOLIDAY. Dec 30. Anniversary of the change of the name Malagasy Republic to the Democratic Republic of Madagascar in 1975.

MOON PHASE: NEW MOON. Dec 30. Moon enters New Moon phase at 10:12 PM, EST.

PHILIPPINES: RIZAL DAY. Dec 30. Commemorates martyrdom of Dr. Jose Rizal in 1896.

BIRTHDAYS TODAY

Kerry Collins, 33, football player, born Lebanon, PA, Dec 30, 1972.

Kristin Kreuk, 23, actress ("Smallville"), born Vancouver, BC, Canada, Dec 30, 1982.

Jane Langton, 83, author (*The Fledgling*), born Boston, MA, Dec 30, 1922.

Matt Lauer, 48, news anchor ("Today"), born New York, NY, Dec 30, 1957.

Kenyon Martin, 28, basketball player, born Saginaw, MI, Dec 30, 1977.

Mercer Mayer, 62, author and illustrator (*East of the Sun, West of the Moon*), born Little Rock, AR, Dec 30, 1943.

Eldrick (Tiger) Woods, 30, golfer, born Cypress, CA, Dec 30, 1975.

December 2005

S	M	T	W	T	F	S
				1	2	3
4	5	6	7	8	9	10
11	12	13	14	15	16	17
18	19	20	21	22	23	24
25	26	27	28	29	30	31

DECEMBER 31 — SATURDAY

Day 365 — 0 Remaining

FIRST BANK OPENS IN US: ANNIVERSARY. Dec 31, 1781. The first modern bank in the US, the Bank of North America, was organized by Robert Morris and received its charter from the Confederation Congress in 1781. It began operations Jan 7, 1782, at Philadelphia.

DECEMBER 31
HENRI MATISSE'S BIRTH ANNIVERSARY

Henri Matisse, French painter, sculptor and cultural personality, was one of the greatest artists of the 20th century. He was always interested in color, and early on in his career Matisse poured that fascination into a wild and woolly artistic movement called Fauvism. He and his fellow Fauvist painters filled canvases with panels of color that depicted our world—people, places, faces and shapes—in bold outlines and stunning chromatic shifts. The art was impressionistic and emotional, but also very daring for its time, and eventually its participants moved on to other inspirations. *Joy of Life* (1905) is an example from Matisse's Fauvist period. *The Fauve Landscape* by Judi Freeman, et al (Los Angeles County Museum of Art, 0-8758-7151-8, $24.95 All ages) and *Fauvism* by Sarah Whitfield (Thames & Hudson, 0-50-020227-3, $14.95 All ages) both provide overviews of the movement, complete with color panels.

Matisse's own work continued to explore emotion through color and strong strokes. While he could often be abstract, there was usually an almost whimsical quality that kept his pieces human and, of course, very vibrant. (An example would be *Lady in Blue* from 1937; www.abcgallery.com/index.html has a nice selection of full-color images.)

Later in life a crippling illness prevented Matisse from painting; however, it didn't stop him from making art. Using scissors, brightly colored pieces of paper, an opaque type of paint called gouache and his own still vital imagination, Matisse created spectacular pieces from paper cutouts that had been fashioned into both organic and geometric shapes. Examples of these works include *Flowing Hair* (1952) and *Creole Dancer* (1950). *Henri Matisse 1869–1954: Master of Colour* by Volkmar Essers (Taschen, 3-8228-5977-X, $7.99 All ages) provides both a history of Matisse and reproductions of his paintings. Younger children will enjoy *A Magical Day with Matisse* by Julie Merberg and Suzanne Bober (Chronicle Books, 0-8118-3414-X, $6.95 Ages baby–preschool).

It's fun and easy for students to re-create Matisse's cutouts. Students can make shapes out of construction paper or tissue paper and glue them to larger panels in designs of their own choosing. Stars are always a good starter shape, as are flowers, odd-sized triangles or even more free-form shapes like an imaginary mess of fern leaves. All of these components were apparent in Matisse's work at various points, as were the basic principles of color, like primary (red, yellow, blue), secondary (green, violet, orange) and tertiary (red-orange, yellow-green, blue-violet). *Jazz* is Henri Matisse's own famous book on cutouts and color; it's available from George Braziller Publishers (0-807-61291-X, $15.95). *Henri Matisse: Drawing with Scissors (Smart About Art)* by Jane O'Connor and Jessie Hartland (Grosset & Dunlap, 0-448-42519-X, $5.99 Ages 4–8) is a further resource on introducing Matisse cutout activities to the classroom.

—Johnny Loftus

LEAP SECOND ADJUSTMENT TIME. Dec 31. One of the times that have been favored for the addition or subtraction of a second from clock time (to coordinate atomic and astronomical time). The determination to adjust is made by the Central Bureau of the International Earth Rotation Service at Paris.

MATISSE, HENRI: BIRTH ANNIVERSARY. Dec 31, 1869. Painter, born at Le Cateau, France. Matisse also designed textiles and stained glass windows. Died at Nice, France, Nov 3, 1954. For more info: *Matisse from A to Z*, by Marie Sellier (Peter Bedrick, 0-87226-475-0, $14.95 All ages). ***See Curriculum Connection.***

NEW YEAR'S EVE. Dec 31. The last evening of the Gregorian calendar year, traditionally a night for merrymaking to welcome in the new year.

PANAMA: ASSUMES CONTROL OF CANAL: ANNIVERSARY. Dec 31, 1999. With the expiration of the Panama Canal Treaty of 1979 at noon, the Republic of Panama assumed full responsibility for the canal and the US Panama Canal Commission ceased to exist.

SCOTLAND: HOGMANAY. Dec 31. The Scottish New Year celebrations date from ancient pagan times. Hogmanay (no one is sure the origin of the name) traditions include fireworks and torch-lit processions in the cities and bonfires in the rural areas. "First footing" is still observed: it is believed to be good luck for the first foot over the threshold to be that of a dark-haired stranger bearing a piece of coal, shortbread or whiskey. After the midnight chimes, everyone sings "Auld Lang Syne."

BIRTHDAYS TODAY

Val Kilmer, 46, actor (*Batman Forever*), born Los Angeles, CA, Dec 31, 1959.

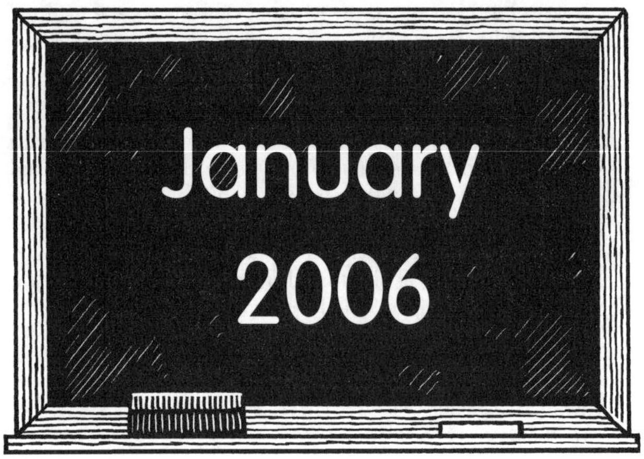

JANUARY 1 — SUNDAY

Day 1 — 364 Remaining

SUNDAY, JANUARY ONE, 2006. Jan 1. First day of the first month of the Gregorian calendar year, Anno Domini 2006, a Common Year, and (until July 4th) the 230th year of American independence. New Year's Day is a public holiday in the US and in many other countries. Traditionally, it is a time for personal stocktaking and for making resolutions for the coming year. Financial accounting begins anew for businesses and individuals whose fiscal year is the calendar year. Jan 1 has been observed as the beginning of the year in most English-speaking countries since the British Calendar Act of 1751, prior to which the New Year began Mar 25 (approximating the vernal equinox). Earth begins another orbit of the sun, during which it, and we, will travel some 583,416,000 miles in 365.24219 days. New Year's Day has been called "Everyman's Birthday," and in some countries a year is added to everyone's age Jan 1 rather than on the anniversary of each person's birth.

AUSTRALIA: COMMONWEALTH FORMED: ANNIVERSARY. Jan 1, 1901. The six colonies of Victoria, New South Wales, Queensland, South Australia, Western Australia and Northern Territory were united into one nation. The British Parliament had passed the Commonwealth Constitution Bill in the spring of 1900 and Queen Victoria signed the document Sept 17, 1900.

BEANIE BABIES® INTRODUCED: ANNIVERSARY. Jan 1, 1994. During this month the first nine Beanie Babies were introduced. Since then, hundreds of different models of the plush animals have been released. For more info: www.ty.com.

BONZA BOTTLER DAY™. Jan 1. To celebrate when the number of the day is the same as the number of the month. Bonza Bottler Day™ is an excuse to have a party at least once a month. For info: Gail M. Berger, Bonza Bottler Day, 14 Fernwood Dr, Taylors, SC 29687. Phone: (864) 609-9874. E-mail: gberger5@aol.com.

CUBA: ANNIVERSARY OF THE REVOLUTION. Jan 1. National holiday celebrating the overthrow of the government of Fulgencio Batista in 1959 by the revolutionary forces of Fidel Castro, which had begun a civil war in 1956.

January 2006

S	M	T	W	T	F	S
1	2	3	4	5	6	7
8	9	10	11	12	13	14
15	16	17	18	19	20	21
22	23	24	25	26	27	28
29	30	31				

CUBA: LIBERATION DAY. Jan 1. A national holiday that celebrates the end of Spanish rule in 1899. Cuba, the largest island of the West Indies, was a Spanish possession from its discovery by Columbus (Oct 27, 1492) until 1899. Under US military control 1899–1902 and 1906–09, a republican government took over Jan 28, 1909, and controlled the island until overthrown Jan 1, 1959, by Fidel Castro's revolutionary movement.

CZECH-SLOVAK DIVORCE: ANNIVERSARY. Jan 1, 1993. As Dec 31, 1992, gave way to Jan 1, 1993, the 74-year-old state of Czechoslovakia separated into two nations—Slovakia and the Czech Republic. The Slovaks held a celebration through the night in the streets of Bratislava amid fireworks, bell ringing, singing of the new country's national anthem and the raising of the Slovak flag. In the new Czech Republic no official festivities took place, but later in the day the Czechs celebrated with a solemn oath by their parliament. The nation of Czechoslovakia ended peacefully though polls showed that most Slovaks and Czechs would have preferred that Czechoslovakia survive. Before the split Czech Prime Minister Vaclav Klaus and Slovak Prime Minister Vladimir Meciar reached an agreement on dividing everything from army troops and gold reserves to the art on government building walls.

ELLIS ISLAND OPENED: ANNIVERSARY. Jan 1, 1892. Ellis Island was opened on New Year's Day in 1892. Over the years more than 20 million individuals were processed through the immigration station. The island was used as a point of deportation as well; in 1932 alone, 20,000 people were deported from Ellis Island. When the US entered WWII in 1941, Ellis Island became a Coast Guard Station. It closed Nov 12, 1954, and was declared a national park in 1956. After years of disuse it was restored and was reopened as a museum in 1990. For more info: www.nps.gov/stli/serv02.htm.

EURO INTRODUCED: ANNIVERSARY. Jan 1, 1999. The euro, the common currency of 12 members of the European Union, was introduced for use by banks. The value of the currencies of Austria, Belgium, Finland, France, Germany, Greece, Ireland, Italy, Luxembourg, the Netherlands, Portugal and Spain were locked in at a permanent conversion rate to the euro. On Jan 1, 2002, euro bills and coins began circulating; other currencies were phased out as of February 2002. For more info: europa.eu.int.

HAITI: INDEPENDENCE DAY. Jan 1. A national holiday commemorating the proclamation of independence in 1804. Haiti, occupying the western third of the island Hispaniola (second largest of the West Indies), was a Spanish colony from the time of its discovery by Columbus in 1492 until 1697, then a French colony until the proclamation of independence in 1804.

JAPANESE ERA NEW YEAR. Jan 1–3. Celebration of the beginning of the year Heisei Eighteen, the 18th year of Emperor Akihito's reign.

KLIBAN, B(ERNARD): BIRTH ANNIVERSARY. Jan 1, 1935. Cartoonist B. Kliban was born at Norwalk, CT. He was known for his satirical drawings of cats engaged in human pursuits, which appeared in the books *Cat* (1975), *Never Eat Anything Bigger than Your Head & Other Drawings* (1976) and *Whack Your Porcupine* (1977). His drawings appeared on T-shirts, greeting cards, calendars, bedsheets and other merchandise, creating a $50 million industry before his death at San Francisco, CA, Aug 12, 1990.

MEXICO: ZAPATISTA REBELLION: ANNIVERSARY. Jan 1, 1994. Declaring war against the government of President Carlos Salinas de Gortari, the Zapatista National Liberation Army seized four towns in the state of Chiapas in southern Mexico. The rebel group, which took its name from the early 20th-century Mexican revolutionary Emiliano Zapata, issued a declaration stating that they were protesting discrimination against the Indian population of the region and against their severe poverty.

MUMMERS PARADE. Jan 1. Philadelphia, PA. World famous New Year's Day parade of 20,000 spectacularly costumed Mummers in a colorful parade that goes on all day. Has taken place since the 1700s. Est attendance: 100,000. For info: Mummers Parade, 1100 S 2nd St, Philadelphia, PA 19147. Phone: (215) 636-1666. E-mail: parade@mummers.com. Web: www.mummers.com.

NATIONAL ENVIRONMENTAL POLICY ACT: ANNIVERSARY. Jan 1, 1970. The National Environmental Policy Act of 1969 established the Council on Environmental Quality and made it federal government policy to protect the environment.

NATIONAL MENTORING MONTH. Jan 1–30. Since 2002, National Mentoring Month seeks to focus national attention on the need for mentors as well as on how each of us can work together to increase the number of mentors and assure brighter futures for our young people. Annually, the month of January. For info: MENTOR/The National Mentoring Partnership, 1600 Duke St, Ste 300, Alexandria, VA 22314. Phone: (703) 224-2200. Web: www.mentoring.org.

NEW YEAR'S DAY. Jan 1. Legal holiday in all states and territories of the US and in most other countries. The world's most widely celebrated holiday. For more info: *Happy New Year, Everywhere!*, by Arlene Erlbach (Millbrook, 0-7613-1707-4, $23.90 Gr. 2–5).

NEW YEAR'S DISHONOR LIST. Jan 1. Since 1976, America's dishonor list of words banished from the Queen's English. Overworked words and phrases (e.g., *bling bling, ripped from the headlines, must-see TV*). Send nominations to the following address: For info: PR Office, Lake Superior State Univ, Sault Ste Marie, MI 49783. Phone: (906) 635-2315. Fax: (906) 635-2623. Web: www.lssu.edu/banished.

OATMEAL MONTH. Jan 1–31. Celebrate oatmeal, a low-fat, sodium-free whole grain that when eaten daily as a part of a diet that's low in saturated fat and cholesterol may help reduce the risk of heart disease. Delicious recipes, helpful hints and tips from Quaker® Oats, The Oat Expert, will make enjoying the heart health benefits oatmeal has to offer easy, convenient and, above all, delicious. For info: The Oat Expert. Phone: (312) 629-1234. E-mail: oatexpert@aol.com.

REVERE, PAUL: BIRTH ANNIVERSARY. Jan 1, 1735. American patriot, silversmith and engraver, maker of false teeth, eyeglasses, picture frames and surgical instruments. Best remembered for his famous ride Apr 18, 1775, to warn patriots that the British were coming, celebrated in Longfellow's poem, "The Midnight Ride of Paul Revere." Born at Boston, MA, died there May 10, 1818. For more info: *In Their Own Words: Paul Revere*, by George Sullivan (Scholastic, 0-439-14748-4, $15.95 Gr. 3–6) and *The Midnight Ride of Paul Revere*, by Henry Wadsworth Longfellow (Handprint, 1-9297-6613-0, $17.95 Gr. 3 & up). See also: "Paul Revere's Ride: Anniversary" (Apr 18).

ROSE BOWL GAME PRESENTED BY ATT. Jan 1. Pasadena, CA. Football conference champions from Big Ten and Pac-10 meet in the Rose Bowl game. The Tournament of Roses has been an annual New Year's Day event since 1890. In 1902 a football game was added: Michigan defeated Stanford 49–0 in what was the first postseason football game. Called the Rose Bowl since 1923, it is preceded each year by the Tournament of Roses Parade. Est attendance: 100,000. For info: Program Coord, Tournament of Roses, 391 S Orange Grove Blvd, Pasadena, CA 91184. Phone: (626) 449-4100. Fax: (626) 449-9066. Web: www.tournamentofroses.com.

ROSS, BETSY: BIRTH ANNIVERSARY. Jan 1, 1752. According to legend based largely on her grandson's revelations in 1870, needleworker Betsy Ross created the first Stars and Stripes flag in 1775, under instructions from George Washington. Her sewing and flag-making skills were well known, but there is little corroborative evidence of her role in making the first Stars and Stripes. The account is generally accepted, however, in the absence of any documented claims to the contrary. She was born Elizabeth Griscom at Philadelphia, PA, and died there Jan 30, 1836. For more info: *Betsy Ross: The American Flag and Life in Young America*, by Ryan Randolph (Rosen, 0-8239-5730-6, $23.95 Gr. 4–8).

RUSSIA: NEW YEAR'S DAY OBSERVANCE. Jan 1–2. National holiday. Modern tradition calls for setting up New Year's trees in homes, halls, clubs, palaces of culture and the hall of the Kremlin Palace. Children's parties with Granddad Frost and his granddaughter, Snow Girl. Games, songs, dancing, special foods, family gatherings and exchanges of gifts and New Year's cards.

SAINT BASIL'S DAY. Jan 1. St. Basil's or St. Vasily's feast day observed by Eastern Orthodox churches. Special traditions for the day include serving St. Basil cakes, each of which contains a coin. Feast day observed Jan 14 by those churches using the Julian calendar.

SOLEMNITY OF MARY, MOTHER OF GOD. Jan 1. Holy Day of Obligation in Roman Catholic Church since calendar reorganization of 1969, replacing the Feast of the Circumcision, which had been recognized for more than 14 centuries.

SUDAN: INDEPENDENCE DAY. Jan 1. National holiday. Sudan was proclaimed a sovereign independent republic Jan 1, 1956, ending its status as an Anglo-Egyptian condominium (since 1899).

TAIWAN: FOUNDATION DAY. Jan 1. National holiday. Commemorates the founding of the Republic of China in 1912.

TOURNAMENT OF ROSES PARADE. Jan 1. Pasadena, CA. 117th annual parade. Includes flower-bedecked floats, bands and equestrians. Starts 8 AM, EST. Est attendance: 1,000,000. For info: Pasadena Tournament of Roses Assn, 391 S Orange Grove Blvd, Pasadena, CA 91184. Phone: (626) 449-4100. Fax: (626) 449-9066. Web: www.tournamentofroses.com.

WALK YOUR PET MONTH. Jan 1–31. New Year's resolutions aren't just for humans. Most of our four-legged furry friends need to watch their weight and begin an exercise program, too. Grab that leash and walk! For info: Laurie Teague, PO Box 9315, Chico, CA 95927. Phone: (530) 342-1380. Fax: (530) 342-3870. E-mail: info@petcpr.com. Web: www.petcpr.com.

WAYNE, "MAD ANTHONY": BIRTH ANNIVERSARY. Jan 1, 1745. American Revolutionary War general whose daring, sometimes reckless, conduct earned him the nickname "Mad Anthony" Wayne. His courage and shrewdness as a soldier made him a key figure in the capture of Stony Point, NY (1779), preventing Benedict Arnold's delivery of West Point to the British, and in subduing hostile Indians of the Northwest Territory (1794). He was born at Waynesboro, PA, and died at Presque Isle, PA, Dec 15, 1796.

Z DAY. Jan 1. To give recognition on the first day of the year to all persons and places whose names begin with the letter "Z" and who are always listed or thought of last in any alphabetized list. For info: Tom Zager, 4545 Kirkwood Dr, Sterling Heights, MI 48310. E-mail: tee_zee@excite.com.

BIRTHDAYS TODAY

Joe Cannon, 31, soccer player, born Los Altos Hills, CA, Jan 1, 1975.

Jon Corzine, 59, US Senator (D, New Jersey), born Taylorville, IL, Jan 1, 1947.

JANUARY 2 — MONDAY

Day 2 — 363 Remaining

ASIMOV, ISAAC: BIRTH ANNIVERSARY. Jan 2, 1920. Although Isaac Asimov was one of the world's best-known writers of science fiction, his almost 500 books deal with subjects as diverse as the Bible, works for preschoolers, college textbooks, mysteries, chemistry, biology, limericks, Shakespeare, Gilbert and Sullivan and modern history. During his prolific career he helped to elevate science fiction from pulp magazines to a more intellectual level. Some of his works include the *Foundation Trilogy, The Robots of Dawn, Robots and Empire, Nemesis, Murder at the A.B.A.* (in which he himself was a character), *The Gods Themselves* and *I, Robot*, in which he posited the famous Three Laws of Robotics. *The Clock We Live On* is a book for children on the origins of calendars. Asimov was born near Smolensk, Russia, and died at New York, NY, Apr 6, 1992.

55-MPH SPEED LIMIT: ANNIVERSARY. Jan 2, 1974. President Richard Nixon signed a bill requiring states to limit highway speeds to a maximum of 55 MPH. This measure was meant to conserve energy during the crisis precipitated by the embargo imposed by the Arab oil-producing countries. A plan, used by some states, limited sale of gasoline on odd-numbered days for cars whose plates ended in odd numbers and even-numbered days for even-numbered plates. Some states limited purchases to $2–$3 per auto and lines as long as six miles resulted in some locations. See also: "Arab Oil Embargo Lifted: Anniversary" (Mar 13).

GEORGIA RATIFIES CONSTITUTION: ANNIVERSARY. Jan 2, 1788. By unanimous vote, Georgia became the fourth state to ratify the Constitution.

HAITI: ANCESTORS' DAY. Jan 2. Commemoration of the ancestors. Also known as Hero's Day. Public holiday.

JAPAN: KAKIZOME. Jan 2. Traditional Japanese festival gets under way when the first strokes of the year are made on paper with the traditional brushes.

RUSSIA: PASSPORT PRESENTATION. Jan 2. A ceremony for 16-year-olds, who are recognized as citizens of the country. Always on the first working day of the New Year.

January 2006

S	M	T	W	T	F	S
1	2	3	4	5	6	7
8	9	10	11	12	13	14
15	16	17	18	19	20	21
22	23	24	25	26	27	28
29	30	31				

SPACE MILESTONE: *LUNA 1* (USSR). Jan 2, 1959. Launch of robotic moon probe that missed the moon and became the first spacecraft from Earth to orbit the sun.

SPAIN CAPTURES GRANADA: ANNIVERSARY. Jan 2, 1492. Spaniards took the city of Granada from the Moors, ending seven centuries of Muslim rule in Spain.

SWITZERLAND: BERCHTOLDSTAG. Jan 2. Holiday in many cantons. Commemorates Duke Berchtold V, who founded the city of Berne in the 12th century. Now mainly a children's holiday.

TAFT, HELEN HERRON: BIRTH ANNIVERSARY. Jan 2, 1861. Wife of William Howard Taft, 27th president of the US, born at Cincinnati, OH. Died at Washington, DC, May 22, 1943.

WOLFE, JAMES: BIRTH ANNIVERSARY. Jan 2, 1727. English general who commanded the British army's victory over Montcalm's French forces on the Plains of Abraham at Quebec City in 1759. As a result, France surrendered Canada to England. Wolfe was born at Westerham, Kent, England. He died at the Plains of Abraham of battle wounds, Sept 13, 1759.

BIRTHDAYS TODAY

Brian Boucher, 29, hockey player, born Woonsocket, RI, Jan 2, 1977.

David Cone, 43, former baseball player, born Kansas City, MO, Jan 2, 1963.

Dennis Hastert, 64, Speaker of the House of Representatives (R), born Aurora, IL, Jan 2, 1942.

JANUARY 3 — TUESDAY

Day 3 — 362 Remaining

ALASKA: ADMISSION DAY. Jan 3. Alaska, which had been purchased from Russia in 1867, became the 49th state in 1959. The area of Alaska is nearly one-fifth the size of the rest of the US.

BURKINA FASO: ANNIVERSARY OF THE 1966 UPHEAVAL. Jan 3. National holiday. Commemorates the change in government leadership.

CONGRESS ASSEMBLES. Jan 3. The Constitution provides that "the Congress shall assemble at least once in every year. . . ." and the 20th Amendment specifies "and such meeting shall begin at noon on the 3rd day of January, unless they shall by law appoint a different day."

COOLIDGE, GRACE ANNA GOODHUE: BIRTH ANNIVERSARY. Jan 3, 1879. Wife of Calvin Coolidge, 30th president of the US, born at Burlington, VT. Died at Northampton, MA, July 8, 1957.

DRINKING STRAW PATENTED: ANNIVERSARY. Jan 3, 1888. A drinking straw made out of paraffin-covered paper was patented by Marvin Stone of Washington, DC. It replaced natural rye straws.

KIDFILM® FESTIVAL. Jan 3–16 (tentative). Dallas, TX. 21st annual. Oldest and largest-attended international children's film festival in the world. 50 shorts and features shown with filmmakers in attendance. Each year, a major figure in media (for all ages) is honored. Est attendance: 24,000. For info: USA Film Festival, 6116 N Central Expressway, Suite 105, Dallas, TX 75206. Phone: (214) 821-6300 or (214) 821-FILM (for 24-hour updates of film programming). Fax: (214) 821-6364. E-mail: info@usafilmfestival.com. Web: www.usafilmfestival.com.

MOTT, LUCRETIA (COFFIN): BIRTH ANNIVERSARY. Jan 3, 1793. American teacher, minister, antislavery leader and (with Elizabeth Cady Stanton) one of the founders of the women's rights movement in the US. Born at Nantucket, MA, she died near Philadelphia, PA, Nov 11, 1880.

SPACE MILESTONE: *MARS EXPLORATION ROVER SPIRIT*. Jan 3, 2004. After traveling 302.6 million miles from its June 10, 2003, launch at Cape Canaveral Air Force Station, FL, the *Mars Exploration Rover Spirit* landed at Gusev Crater on Mars. The robotic rover's mission was to examine the soil and environment of the red planet. By Jan 6, *Spirit* had taken the sharpest color photograph of Mars ever achieved. *Spirit*'s twin rover, *Opportunity*, landed Jan 24, 2004. NASA's website for children about *Spirit* and *Opportunity* can be found at http://marsprogram.jpl.nasa.gov/funzone_flash.html.

TOLKIEN, J.R.R. (JOHN RONALD REUEL): BIRTH ANNIVERSARY. Jan 3, 1892. Author of *The Hobbit* (1937) and *The Lord of the Rings*. Though best known for his fantasies, Tolkien was also a serious philologist. Born at Bloemfontein, South Africa, he died at Bournemouth, England, Sept 2, 1973.

WIND CAVE NATIONAL PARK ESTABLISHED: ANNIVERSARY. Jan 3, 1903. President Theodore Roosevelt signed a bill on this date establishing South Dakota's Wind Cave a national park and preserve. It was the first national park established for the preservation of a cave. For more info: www.nps.gov/wica/index.htm.

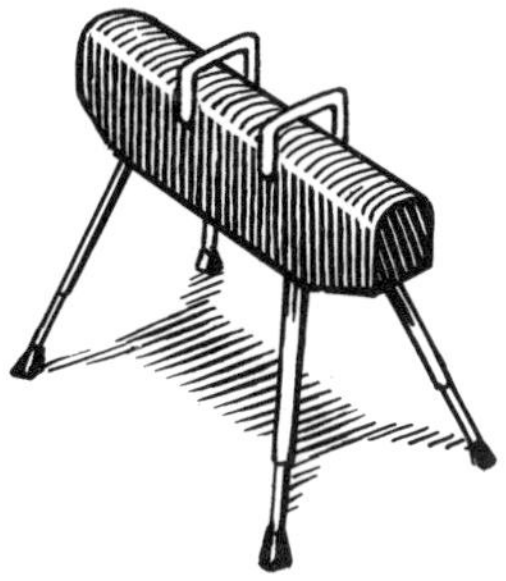

BIRTHDAYS TODAY

Alma Flor Ada, 68, author (*Yours Truly, Goldilocks*), born Camaguey, Cuba, Jan 3, 1938.
Joan Walsh Anglund, 80, author and illustrator (*Crocus in the Snow, Bedtime Book*), born Hinsdale, IL, Jan 3, 1926.
Mel Gibson, 50, actor (*Lethal Weapon*, voice of John Smith in *Pocahontas*), born New York, NY, Jan 3, 1956.
Bobby Hull, 67, Hall of Fame hockey player, born Point Anne, ON, Canada, Jan 3, 1939.
Alex Linz, 17, actor (*Home Alone 3*), born Santa Barbara, CA, Jan 3, 1989.

JANUARY 4 — WEDNESDAY

Day 4 — 361 Remaining

BRAILLE, LOUIS: BIRTH ANNIVERSARY. Jan 4, 1809. The inventor of a widely used touch system of reading and writing for the blind was born at Coupvray, France. Permanently blinded at the age of three by a leatherworking awl in his father's saddle-making shop, Braille developed a system of writing that used, ironically, an awl-like stylus to punch marks in paper that could be felt and interpreted by the blind. The system was largely ignored until after Braille died in poverty, suffering from tuberculosis, at Paris, Jan 6, 1852. For info: *Louis Braille: The Blind Boy Who Wanted to Read*, by Dennis Fradin (Silver Burdett, 0-614-29054-6, $6.95 Gr. K–5) and *Out of Darkness: The Story of Louis Braille*, by Russell Freedman (Houghton Mifflin, 0-395-77516-7, $15.95 Gr. 5 & up).

EARTH AT PERIHELION. Jan 4. At approximately 10 AM, EST, planet Earth will reach Perihelion, that point in its orbit when it is closest to the sun (about 91,400,000 miles). The Earth's mean distance from the sun (mean radius of its orbit) is reached early in the months of April and October. Note that Earth is closest to the sun during Northern Hemisphere winter. See also: "Earth at Aphelion" (July 3).

GENERAL TOM THUMB: BIRTH ANNIVERSARY. Jan 4, 1838. Charles Sherwood Stratton, perhaps the most famous midget in history, was born at Bridgeport, CT. His growth almost stopped during his first year, but he eventually reached a height of three feet, four inches and a weight of 70 pounds. "Discovered" by P.T. Barnum in 1842, Stratton, as "General Tom Thumb," became an internationally known entertainer and on tour performed before Queen Victoria and other heads of state. On Feb 10, 1863, he married another midget, Lavinia Warren. Stratton died at Middleborough, MA, July 15, 1883.

GRIMM, JACOB: BIRTH ANNIVERSARY. Jan 4, 1785. Librarian, mythologist and philologist, born at Hanau, Germany. Most remembered for *Grimm's Fairy Tales* (in collaboration with his brother Wilhelm). Died at Berlin, Germany, Sept 20, 1863. See also: "Grimm, Wilhelm Carl: Birth Anniversary" (Feb 24). For more info: *The Brothers Grimm: Two Lives, One Legacy*, by Donald R. Hettinga (Clarion, 0-6180-5599-1, $22 Gr. 5 & up).

MYANMAR: INDEPENDENCE DAY: ANNIVERSARY. Jan 4, 1948. National Day. The British controlled the country from 1826 until 1948 when it was granted independence. Formerly Burma, the country's name was changed to the Union of Myanmar in 1989 to reflect that the population is made up not just of the Burmese but of many other ethnic groups as well.

NEWTON, SIR ISAAC: BIRTH ANNIVERSARY. Jan 4, 1643. Sir Isaac Newton was the chief figure of the scientific revolution of the 17th century, a physicist and mathematician who laid the foundations of calculus, studied the mechanics of planetary motion and discovered the law of gravitation. Born at Woolsthorpe, England, he died at London, England, Mar 20, 1727. Newton was born before Great Britain adopted the Gregorian calendar. His Julian (Old Style) birth date is Dec 25, 1642. For more info: *Isaac Newton: Discovering Laws That Govern the Universe*, by Michael White (Blackbirch, 1-56711-326-5, $19.95 Gr. 4–7).

POLISH AMERICAN IN THE HOUSE: ANNIVERSARY. Jan 4, 1977. Maryland Democrat Barbara Mikulski took her seat in the US House of Representatives, the first Polish American ever to do so. An able voice for female as well as working-class Baltimore constituents of the 3rd District, Mikulski went on to be elected to the US Senate.

POP MUSIC CHART INTRODUCED: 70th ANNIVERSARY. Jan 4, 1936. *Billboard* magazine published the first list of bestselling pop records, covering the week that ended Dec 30, 1935. On the list were recordings by the Tommy Dorsey and the Ozzie Nelson orchestras.

TRIVIA DAY. Jan 4. In celebration of those who know all sorts of facts and/or have doctorates in uselessology. For info: Robert L. Birch, Puns Corps, Box 2364, Falls Church, VA 22042-0364.

UTAH: ADMISSION DAY: ANNIVERSARY. Jan 4. Became the 45th state in 1896.

BIRTHDAYS TODAY

Robert Burleigh, 70, poet (*Hoops*), born Chicago, IL, Jan 4, 1936.
Etienne Delessert, 65, author and illustrator (*How the Mouse Was Hit on the Head With a Stone and So Discovered the World*), born Lausanne, Switzerland, Jan 4, 1941.
Phyllis Reynolds Naylor, 73, author (Newbery for *Shiloh*), born Anderson, IN, Jan 4, 1933.

JANUARY 5 — THURSDAY

Day 5 — 360 Remaining

AILEY, ALVIN: BIRTH ANNIVERSARY. Jan 5, 1931. Born at Rogers, TX, Alvin Ailey began his career as a choreographer in the late 1950s after a successful career as a dancer. He founded the Alvin Ailey American Dance Theater, drawing from classical ballet, jazz, Afro-Caribbean and modern dance idioms to create the 79 ballets of the company's repertoire. He and his work played a central part in establishing a role for blacks in the world of modern dance. Ailey died Dec 1, 1989, at New York, NY.

CARVER, GEORGE WASHINGTON: DEATH ANNIVERSARY. Jan 5, 1943. Black American agricultural scientist, author, inventor and teacher. Born into slavery at Diamond Grove, MO, probably in 1864. His research led to the creation of synthetic products made from peanuts, potatoes and wood. Carver died at Tuskegee, AL. His birthplace became a national monument in 1953. For more info: *George Washington Carver: Nature's Trailblazer*, by Teresa Rogers (Twenty-First Century, 0-8050-2115-9, $14.95 Gr. 5–7).

DECATUR, STEPHEN: BIRTH ANNIVERSARY. Jan 5, 1779. American naval officer (whose father and grandfather, both also named Stephen Decatur, were also seafaring men), born at Sinepuxent, MD. In a toast at a dinner in Norfolk in 1815, Decatur spoke his most famous words: "Our country! In her intercourse with foreign nations may she always be in the right; but our country, right or wrong." Mortally wounded in a duel with Commodore James Barron, at Bladensburg, MD, on the morning of Mar 22, 1820, Decatur was carried to his home at Washington where he died a few hours later.

ITALY: EPIPHANY FAIR. Jan 5. Piazza Navona, Rome, Italy. On the eve of Epiphany a fair of toys, sweets and presents takes place among the beautiful Bernini Fountains.

MONDALE, WALTER F.: BIRTHDAY. Jan 5, 1928. The 42nd vice president (1977–81) of the US, born at Ceylon, MN.

PICCARD, JEANNETTE RIDLON: BIRTH ANNIVERSARY. Jan 5, 1895. First American woman to qualify as a free balloon pilot (1934). One of the first women to be ordained an Episcopal priest (1976). Pilot for record-setting balloon ascent into stratosphere (57,579 ft) from Dearborn, MI, Oct 23, 1934, with her husband, Jean Felix Piccard. She was an identical twin married to an identical twin. Born at Chicago, IL, she died at Minneapolis, MN, May 17, 1981. See also: "Piccard, Jean Felix: Birth Anniversary" (Jan 28) and "Piccard, Auguste: Birth Anniversary" (Jan 28).

TWELFTH NIGHT. Jan 5. Evening before Epiphany. Twelfth Night marks the end of medieval Christmas festivities and the end of Twelfthtide (the 12-day season after Christmas ending with Epiphany). Also called Twelfth Day Eve. ***See Curriculum Connection.***

WYOMING INAUGURATES FIRST WOMAN GOVERNOR IN US: ANNIVERSARY. Jan 5, 1925. Nellie Tayloe (Mrs William B.) Ross became the first woman to serve as governor upon her inauguration as governor of Wyoming. She had previously finished out the term of her husband, who had died in office. In 1974 Ella Grasso of Connecticut became the first woman to be elected governor in her own right.

January 2006

S	M	T	W	T	F	S
1	2	3	4	5	6	7
8	9	10	11	12	13	14
15	16	17	18	19	20	21
22	23	24	25	26	27	28
29	30	31				

JANUARY 5
TWELFTH NIGHT

Twelfth Night marks the end of 12 days of Christmas festivities. It is the evening before Epiphany, which is celebrated by Christians as the time when the magi visited baby Jesus, when Jesus was baptized and when the miracle at Cana occurred. In New Orleans, it marks the beginning of the Carnival season, which culminates in Mardi Gras, as well as the end of Christmas.

Twelfth Night is an event with rich cultural traditions in Christian homes throughout the world. The roots of Twelfth Night celebrations can be traced to England and France where popular masquerading parties were and continue to be the main form of entertainment. Practical jokes and tricks are often played at these parties and there is plenty of dancing and eating. Costumes are prominently featured in Twelfth Night festivities; men dress as women, women dress as men and partygoers wear clothes inside out, among other acts of revelry.

An enduring and widespread Twelfth Night tradition is the crowning of the King and/or Queen. A bean, or in some countries a ceramic baby, is baked into a cake (often called the King's cake) and the person whose piece of cake contains the bean is crowned the King or Queen. This means that everyone must do as he or she says and they may have their every whim indulged. Some claim this tradition dates back to 12th-century France when a coin was hidden within the cake to symbolize the gifts of the wise men to Jesus. Others say that it originated in ancient Rome and the bean was a symbol of good luck.

The composition of the cake varies from country to country. In England, it is a dense fruitcake; in Spain, the doughnut-shaped cake is flavored with orange-flower water; in France, the cake is shaped like a crown and decorated with sugarcoated fruit; in Louisiana, the cake is a cinnamon-flavored oval braid. No matter what the cake's flavor or shape, it is a treat that is highly anticipated by all Twelfth Night celebrants.

In some parts of the world—particularly Spain, Mexico and other Hispanic countries—Twelfth Night day (Jan 6) is a day when gifts are exchanged, another symbol of the gifts the wise men brought to the infant Jesus. Children leave their shoes by their beds or their bedroom doors while they sleep and awake to find them filled with tasty treats and sweets. In many homes, this is the day when Christmas decorations are taken down, formally signaling the end of the Christmas season.

William Shakespeare's comedy *Twelfth Night* appears to draw inspiration from this holiday. References to Christmas, a tune sung by one character that resembles "The Twelve Days of Christmas" and characters that carry out acts of mischief and merriment all nod to Twelfth Night traditions. It is unclear, however, whether or not Shakespeare intended for his play to be performed on or around the Twelfth Night.

—Denise Frank

BIRTHDAYS TODAY

Lynne Cherry, 54, author (*The Great Kapok Tree, A River Ran Wild*), born Philadelphia, PA, Jan 5, 1952.

Mike DeWine, 59, US Senator (R, Ohio), born Springfield, OH, Jan 5, 1947.

Warrick Dunn, 31, football player, born Baton Rouge, LA, Jan 5, 1975.

Walter Frederick Mondale, 78, 42nd vice president of the US and candidate for president in 1984, born Ceylon, MN, Jan 5, 1928.

Ed Rendell, 62, Governor of Pennsylvania (D), born New York, NY, Jan 5, 1944.

JANUARY 6 — FRIDAY

Day 6 — 359 Remaining

ARMENIAN CHRISTMAS. Jan 6. Christmas is observed in the Armenian Church, the oldest national Christian church.

CARNIVAL SEASON. Jan 6–Feb 28. A secular festival preceding Lent. A time of merrymaking and feasting before the austere days of Lenten fasting and penitence (40 weekdays between Ash Wednesday and Easter Sunday). The word *carnival* probably is derived from the Latin *carnem levare,* meaning "to remove meat." Depending on local custom, the carnival season may start any time between Nov 11 and Shrove Tuesday. Conclusion of the season is much less variable, being the close of Shrove Tuesday in most places. Celebrations vary considerably, but the festival often includes many theatrical aspects (masks, costumes and songs) and has given its name (in the US) to traveling amusement shows that may be seen throughout the year. Observed traditionally in Roman Catholic countries from Epiphany through Shrove Tuesday. For more info: *Carnival,* by Clare Chandler (Millbrook, 0-7613-0373-1, $20.90 Gr. K–3).

EPIPHANY or TWELFTH DAY. Jan 6. Known also as Old Christmas Day and Twelfthtide. On the twelfth day after Christmas, Christians celebrate the visit of the Magi or Wise Men to the baby Jesus. In many countries, this is the day children receive gifts, rather than Christmas day. Epiphany of Our Lord, one of the oldest Christian feasts, is observed in Roman Catholic churches in the US on a Sunday between Jan 2 and 8. Theophany of the Eastern Orthodox Church is observed on this day in churches using the Gregorian calendar and Jan 19 in those churches using the Julian calendar and celebrates the manifestation of the divinity of Jesus at the time of his baptism in the Jordan River by John the Baptist.

ITALY: LA BEFANA. Jan 6. Epiphany festival in which the "Befana," a kindly witch, bestows gifts on children—toys and candy for those who have been good, but a lump of coal or a pebble for those who have been naughty. The festival begins on the night of Jan 5 with much noise and merrymaking (when the Befana is supposed to come down the chimneys on her broom, leaving gifts in children's stockings) and continues with fairs, parades and other activities.

JOAN OF ARC: BIRTH ANNIVERSARY. Jan 6, 1412. Born at the village of Domremy, in the Meuse River valley of France. At this time there was civil war in France, with one faction being aided by the English. As a teenager, Joan led an army to drive the English out of northern France. Captured, she was burned at the stake as a witch and a heretic on May 30, 1431. Her martyrdom inspired the unification of the French people, who drove the English out of France. Joan was made a saint in 1920. For more info: *Joan of Arc,* by Diane Stanley (Morrow, 0-688-14330-X, $15.95 Gr. 4–8). See also: "Saint Joan of Arc: Feast Day" (May 30).

MOON PHASE: FIRST QUARTER. Jan 6. Moon enters First Quarter phase at 1:56 PM, EST.

NATIONAL SMITH DAY. Jan 6. The commonest surname in the English-speaking world is Smith. There are an estimated 2,382,500 Smiths in the US. This special day honors the birthday in 1580 of Captain John Smith, the leader of the English colonists who settled at Jamestown, VA, in 1607, thus making him one of the first American Smiths. On this special day, all derivatives, such as Goldsmith, are invited to participate. Please send $10 for each request for Eventological Literature. For info: Adrienne Sioux Koopersmith, 1437 W Rosemont, 1W, Chicago, IL 60660-1319. E-mail: askoopersmith@hotmail.com.

NEW MEXICO: ADMISSION DAY: ANNIVERSARY. Jan 6. Became 47th state in 1912.

PAN AM CIRCLES EARTH: ANNIVERSARY. Jan 6, 1942. A Pan American Airways plane arrived in New York to complete the first around-the-world trip by a commercial aircraft.

SANDBURG, CARL: BIRTH ANNIVERSARY. Jan 6, 1878. American poet ("Fog," "Chicago"), biographer of Lincoln, historian and folklorist, born at Galesburg, IL. Died at Flat Rock, NC, July 22, 1967. For more info: *Carl Sandburg: A Biography,* by Milton Meltzer (Millbrook, 0-7613-1364-8, $29.90 Gr. 5–10).

SMITH, JEDEDIAH STRONG: BIRTH ANNIVERSARY. Jan 6, 1799. Mountain man, fur trader and one of the first explorers of the American West, Smith helped develop the Oregon Trail. He was the first American to reach California by land and first to travel by land from San Diego, up the West Coast to the Canadian border. Smith was born at Jericho (now Bainbridge), NY, and was killed by Comanche Indians along the Santa Fe Trail in what is now Kansas, May 27, 1831.

SPACE MILESTONE: *LUNAR EXPLORER* (US). Jan 6, 1998. NASA headed back to the moon for the first time since the *Apollo 17* flight 25 years before. This unmanned probe searches for evidence of frozen water on the moon.

THREE KINGS DAY. Jan 6. Major festival of Christian Church observed in many parts of the world with gifts, feasting, last lighting of Christmas lights and burning of Christmas greens. In many European countries children get their Christmas presents on Three Kings Day. Twelfth and last day of the Feast of the Nativity. Commemorates visit of the Three Wise Men (Kings or Magi) to Bethlehem.

BIRTHDAYS TODAY

Vera Cleaver, 87, children's author, with her husband Bill (*Where the Lilies Bloom*), born Ridgewood, NJ, Jan 6, 1919.

Ina R. Friedman, 80, author (*How My Parents Learned to Eat*), born Chester, PA, Jan 6, 1926.

Gabrielle Reece, 36, pro volleyball player, born La Jolla, CA, Jan 6, 1970.

JANUARY 7 — SATURDAY

Day 7 — 358 Remaining

FILLMORE, MILLARD: BIRTH ANNIVERSARY. Jan 7, 1800. The 13th president of the US (July 10, 1850–Mar 3, 1853), Fillmore succeeded to the presidency upon the death of Zachary Taylor, but he did not get the hoped-for nomination from his party in 1852. He ran for president unsuccessfully in 1856 as candidate of the "Know-Nothing Party," whose platform demanded, among other things, that every government employee (federal, state and local) should be a native-born citizen. Fillmore was born at Locke, NY, and died at Buffalo, NY, Mar 8, 1874. For more info: www.ipl.org/ref/POTUS.

FIRST BALLOON FLIGHT ACROSS ENGLISH CHANNEL: ANNIVERSARY. Jan 7, 1785. Dr. John Jeffries, a Boston physician, and Jean-Pierre Blanchard, French aeronaut, crossed the English Channel from Dover, England, to Calais, France, landing in a forest after being forced to throw overboard all ballast, equipment and even most of their clothing to avoid a forced landing in the icy waters of the English Channel. Blanchard's trousers are said to have been the last article thrown overboard.

GERMANY: MUNICH FASCHING CARNIVAL. Jan 7–Feb 28. Munich. From Jan 7 through Shrove Tuesday is Munich's famous carnival season. Costume balls are popular throughout carnival. High points on Fasching Sunday (Feb 26) and Shrove Tuesday

(Feb 28) with great carnival outside at the Viktualienmarkt and on Pedestrian Mall.

JAPAN: NANAKUSA. Jan 7. Festival dates back to the 7th century and recalls the seven plants served to the emperor that are believed to have great medicinal value—shepherd's purse, chickweed, parsley, cottonweed, radish, hotoke-no-za and aona.

MONTGOLFIER, JACQUES ETIENNE: BIRTH ANNIVERSARY. Jan 7, 1745. Merchant and inventor born at Annonay, France. With his older brother, Joseph Michel, in November 1782, conducted experiments with paper and fabric bags filled with smoke and hot air, which led to invention of the hot-air balloon and humankind's first flight. Died at Serrieres, France, Aug 2, 1799. See also: "First Balloon Flight: Anniversary" (June 5); "Montgolfier, Joseph Michel: Birth Anniversary" (Aug 26) and "Aviation History Month" (Nov 1).

NATIONAL JOYGERM DAY. Jan 7. When Joygerms unfurled all over the world invite crusty curmudgeons, cagey killjoys, the pale and peaked with a penchant for peevishness, the tired, tense and timid. . . to mingle with a myriad of merry mirthmakers, happy huggers, gallant gigglers and grinners and soothing, sunny smilers. Free Joygerm membership cards available singly or in quantity. For info: Joygerm Junkie Joan E. White, Founder, Joygerms Unlimited, PO Box 555, Eastwood Station, Syracuse, NY 13206-0555. Phone: (315) 472-2779.

RUSSIA: CHRISTMAS OBSERVANCE. Jan 7. National holiday.

TRANSATLANTIC PHONING: ANNIVERSARY. Jan 7, 1927. Commercial transatlantic telephone service between New York and London was inaugurated. There were 31 calls made the first day.

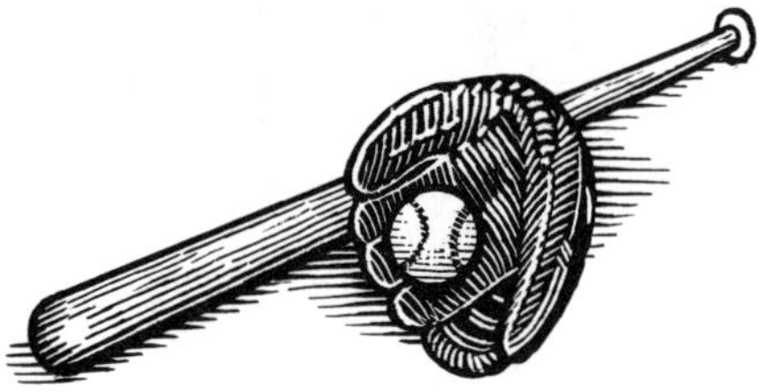

BIRTHDAYS TODAY

Donald Brashear, 34, hockey player, born Bedford, IN, Jan 7, 1972.
Kay Chorao, 69, author and illustrator (*The Baby's Bedtime Book, Pig and Crow*), born Elkhart, IN, Jan 7, 1937.
Katie Couric, 49, cohost ("Today Show"), born Arlington, VA, Jan 7, 1957.
Eric Gagne, 30, baseball player, born Montreal, QC, Canada, Jan 7, 1976.
Minfong Ho, 55, author (*Hush!: A Thai Lullaby*), born Rangoon, Burma, Jan 7, 1951.
Francisco Rodriguez, 24, baseball player, born Caracas, Venezuela, Jan 7, 1982.
Alfonso Soriano, 30, baseball player, born San Pedro de Macoris, Dominican Republic, Jan 7, 1976.
John R. Thune, 45, US Senator (R, South Dakota), born Pierre, SD, Jan 7, 1961.

January 2006

S	M	T	W	T	F	S
1	2	3	4	5	6	7
8	9	10	11	12	13	14
15	16	17	18	19	20	21
22	23	24	25	26	27	28
29	30	31				

JANUARY 8 — SUNDAY

Day 8 — 357 Remaining

AT&T DIVESTITURE: ANNIVERSARY. Jan 8, 1982. In the most significant antitrust suit since the breakup of Standard Oil in 1911, American Telephone and Telegraph agreed to give up its 22 local Bell System companies ("Baby Bells"). These companies represented 80 percent of AT&T's assets. This ended the corporation's virtual monopoly of US telephone service.

BATTLE OF NEW ORLEANS: ANNIVERSARY. Jan 8, 1815. British forces suffered crushing losses (more than 2,000 casualties) in an attack on New Orleans, LA. Defending US troops were led by General Andrew Jackson, who became a popular hero as a result of the victory. Neither side knew that the War of 1812 had

JANUARY 8
EARTH'S ROTATION PROVED

Jean Foucault, a French physicist, first demonstrated to the world the Earth's rotation on its axis on this day in 1851. He did so using a pendulum he set up in the Pantheon in Paris. Foucault's pendulum consisted of a 61-pound, extra-large ball of lead that was suspended from a 220-foot wire. The wire was attached to a ball-and-socket-type clasp so that it was free to rotate in any direction. Inertia made the pendulum swing out and gravity pulled it back. The heavy weight of the ball or "bob" was necessary to ensure that air and wind currents didn't influence the bob's movements. Foucault initially set the pendulum to swing from north to south. Over time, as a result of the Earth's rotation, the pendulum began to swing in a clockwise direction. From there, it moved northeast-southwest, east-west, southeast-northwest and finally north-south once again.

The movement of a pendulum is a kind of optical illusion. While it appears that the pendulum is changing direction ever so slightly, it is, in fact, the earth that is rotating under the pendulum. The bob's degree of movement is directly related to where on the planet the pendulum is set up. At the North Pole, for example, it swings 360 degrees in 24 hours; in Washington DC, it swings 226 degrees; and at the equator, it is 0 degrees.

The California Academy of Sciences has an excellent website that presents an informative and accessible description of Foucault's pendulum and the earth's rotation. It is especially good for those who have a computerized classroom as the simple language and fun drawings and diagrams are sure to interest students. The website is www.calacademy.org/products/pendulum/index.html.

The American Association for the Advancement of Science (www.aaas.org) runs a wonderful website called Science NetLinks that gives K–12 teachers helpful suggestions for presenting various science lessons, including one on Foucault's pendulum. It offers information about the science behind pendulums, what students should know before engaging in a more complex discussion and instructions for creating a pendulum in the classroom. Go to www.sciencenetlinks.com and type "Foucault's Pendulum" into the search engine.

Finally, the PBS Kids website is the perfect place to recommend youngsters go to learn about Foucault's pendulum on their own. It is a lively website with fun graphics. Not only does it present facts about and the basic science behind pendulums, but it also provides students with directions for making their own pendulums. The direct link is http://pbskids.org/zoom/games/pendulum/index.html. —Denise Frank ended two weeks previously with the signing of the Treaty of Ghent, Dec 24, 1814. Battle of New Orleans Day is observed in Louisiana.

CHOU EN-LAI: 30th DEATH ANNIVERSARY. Jan 8, 1976. Anniversary of the death of Chou En-Lai, premier of the State Council of the People's Republic of China. He was born in 1898 (exact date unknown).

EARTH'S ROTATION PROVED: ANNIVERSARY. Jan 8, 1851. Using a device now known as Foucault's pendulum in his Paris home, physicist Jean Foucault demonstrated that the Earth rotates on its axis. ***See Curriculum Connection.***

GREECE: MIDWIFE'S DAY or WOMEN'S DAY. Jan 8. Midwife's Day or Women's Day is celebrated Jan 8 each year to honor midwives and all women. "On this day women stop their housework and spend their time in cafés, while the men do all the housework chores and look after the children." In some villages, men caught outside "will be stripped . . . and drenched with cold water."

MARCO POLO: DEATH ANNIVERSARY. Jan 8, 1324. Merchant famous for his travel to China, where he worked for Kublai Khan. Born around 1254 in Venice, he died there after writing a book about his travels in Asia.

PRESLEY, ELVIS AARON: BIRTH ANNIVERSARY. Jan 8, 1935. Popular American rock singer, born at Tupelo, MS. Although his middle name was spelled incorrectly as "Aron" on his birth certificate, Elvis had it legally changed to "Aaron," which is how it is spelled on his gravestone. Died at Memphis, TN, Aug 16, 1977. For more info: *All Shook Up: The Life and Death of Elvis Presley*, by Barry Denenberg (Scholastic, 0-439-09504-2, $16.95 Gr. 4–7).

SWITZERLAND: MEITLISUNNTIG. Jan 8. On Meitlisunntig, the second Sunday in January, the girls of Meisterschwanden and Fahrwangen, in the Seetal district of Aargau, Switzerland, stage a procession in historical uniforms and a military parade before a female General Staff. According to tradition, the custom dates from the Villmergen War of 1712, when the women of both communes gave vital help that led to victory. Popular festival follows the procession.

UNIVERSAL LETTER-WRITING WEEK. Jan 8–14. The purpose of this week is for people all over the world to get the new year off to a good start by sending letters and cards to friends and acquaintances not only in their own country but to people throughout the world. For complete information and suggestions about writing good letters, send $5 to cover expense of printing, handling and postage. For info: Dr. Stanley Drake, Intl Society of Friendship and Goodwill, 8592 Roswell Rd, Ste 251, Atlanta, GA 30350 1867. Phone: (678) 795-1362. Web: www.friendshipand goodwill.org.

WAR ON POVERTY: ANNIVERSARY. Jan 8, 1964. President Lyndon Johnson declared a War on Poverty in his State of the Union address. He stressed improved education as one of the cornerstones of the program. The following Aug 20, he signed a $947.5 million antipoverty bill designed to assist more than 30 million citizens.

BIRTHDAYS TODAY

Nancy Bond, 61, author (*A String on the Harp*), born Bethesda, MD, Jan 8, 1945.
Mike Cameron, 33, baseball player, born LaGrange, GA, Jan 8, 1973.
Floyd Cooper, 50, author, illustrator (*Coming Home: From the Life of Langston Hughes; Meet Danitra Brown*), born Tulsa, OK, Jan 8, 1956.
Stephen Manes, 57, author (*Be a Perfect Person in Just Three Days*), born Pittsburgh, PA, Jan 8, 1949.
Marjorie Priceman, 48, illustrator (*Zin! Zin! Zin! A Violin; What Zeesie Saw on Delancy Street*), born Long Island, NY, Jan 8, 1958.
Bob Taft, 64, Governor of Ohio (R), born Boston, MA, Jan 8, 1942.

JANUARY 9 — MONDAY

Day 9 — 356 Remaining

AVIATION IN AMERICA: ANNIVERSARY. Jan 9, 1793. A Frenchman, Jean-Pierre Francois Blanchard, made the first manned free-balloon flight in America's history at Philadelphia, PA. The event was watched by President George Washington and many other high government officials. The hydrogen-filled balloon rose to a height of about 5,800 feet, traveled some 15 miles and landed 46 minutes later in New Jersey. Reportedly Blanchard had one passenger on the flight—a little black dog.

BROOKS, WALTER R.: BIRTH ANNIVERSARY. Jan 9, 1886. Children's author (Freddy the Pig series), born at Rome, NY. Died Aug 17, 1958.

CATT, CARRIE LANE CHAPMAN: BIRTH ANNIVERSARY. Jan 9, 1859. American women's rights leader, founder (in 1919) of the National League of Women Voters. Born at Ripon, WI, she died at New Rochelle, NY, Mar 9, 1947.

CONNECTICUT RATIFIES CONSTITUTION: ANNIVERSARY. Jan 9, 1788. By a vote of 128 to 40, Connecticut became the fifth state to ratify the Constitution.

ENGLAND: PLOUGH MONDAY. Jan 9. Always the Monday after Twelfth Day. Work on the farm is resumed after the festivities of the 12 days of Christmas. On preceding Sunday ploughs may be blessed in churches. Celebrated with dances and plays.

JAPAN: COMING-OF-AGE DAY. Jan 9. National holiday for youth of the country who have reached adulthood (20 years of age) during the preceding year. Annually, the second Monday in January.

NATIONAL CLEAN-OFF-YOUR-DESK DAY. Jan 9. To provide one day early each year for every desk worker to see the top of the desk and prepare for the following year's paperwork. Annually, the second Monday in January. For info: A.C. Moeller, Box 71, Clio, MI 48420-1042.

NATIONAL THANK GOD IT'S MONDAY! DAY. Jan 9. Besides holidays, such as Presidents' Day, being celebrated on Mondays, people everywhere start new jobs, have birthdays, celebrate promotions and begin vacations on Mondays. A day in recognition of this first day of the week. Annually, the second Monday in January. For info: Dorothy Zjawin, 61 W Colfax Ave, Roselle Park, NJ 07204. Phone: (908) 241-6241.

NIXON, RICHARD MILHOUS: BIRTH ANNIVERSARY. Jan 9, 1913. Richard Nixon served as the 36th vice president of the US (under President Dwight D. Eisenhower) Jan 20, 1953 to Jan 20, 1961. He was the 37th president of the US, serving Jan 20, 1969 to Aug 9, 1974, when he resigned the presidency while under threat of impeachment. First US president to resign that office. He was born at Yorba Linda, CA, and died at New York, NY, Apr 22, 1994. For more info: www.ipl.org/ref/POTUS.

PANAMA: MARTYRS' DAY. Jan 9. Public holiday.

PHILIPPINES: FEAST OF THE BLACK NAZARENE. Jan 9. Culmination of a nine-day fiesta. Manila's largest procession takes place in the afternoon of Jan 9, in honor of the Black Nazarene, whose shrine is at the Quiapo Church.

YAWM ARAFAT: THE STANDING AT ARAFAT. Jan 9. Islamic calendar date: Dhu-Hijjah 9, 1426. The day when people on the Hajj (pilgrimage to Mecca) assemble for "the Standing" at the plain of Arafat at Mina, Saudi Arabia, near Mecca. This gathering is a foreshadowing of the Day of Judgment. Different methods for "anticipating" the visibility of the new moon crescent at Mecca are used by different Muslim groups. US date may vary. Began at sunset the preceding day.

BIRTHDAYS TODAY

Clyde Robert Bulla, 92, author (*The Chalk Box Kid*), born King City, MO, Jan 9, 1914.

Sergio Garcia, 26, golfer, born Borriol, Spain, Jan 9, 1980.

Mat Hoffman, 34, BMX bike racer, born Oklahoma City, OK, Jan 9, 1972.

A.J. McLean, 28, singer (Backstreet Boys), born West Palm Beach, FL, Jan 9, 1978.

Joely Richardson, 41, actress (*101 Dalmatians*), born London, England, Jan 9, 1965.

JANUARY 10 — TUESDAY

Day 10 — 355 Remaining

EID-AL-ADHA: FEAST OF THE SACRIFICE. Jan 10. Islamic calendar date: Dhu-Hijjah 10, 1426. Commemorates Abraham's willingness to sacrifice his son Ishmael in obedience to God. It is part of the Hajj (pilgrimage to Mecca). The day begins with the sacrifice of an animal in remembrance of the Angel Gabriel's substitution of a lamb as Abraham's offering. One-third of the meat is given to the poor and the rest is shared with friends and family. Celebrated with gifts and general merrymaking, the festival usually continues for several days. It is celebrated as Tabaski in Benin, Burkina Faso, Guinea, Guinea-Bissau, Ivory Coast, Mali, Niger and Senegal and as Kurban Bayram in Turkey and Bosnia. Different methods for "anticipating" the visibility of the moon crescent at Mecca are used by different Muslim groups. US date may vary. Began at sunset the preceding day.

LEAGUE OF NATIONS: FOUNDING ANNIVERSARY. Jan 10, 1920. Through the Treaty of Versailles, the League of Nations came into existence. Fifty nations entered into a covenant designed to avoid war. The US never joined the League of Nations, which was dissolved Apr 18, 1946.

PLASTIC DUCKY FLEET SAILS THE PACIFIC: ANNIVERSARY. Jan 10, 1992. During a storm in the North Pacific Ocean, at 44.7°N, 178.1°E, a ship lost several cargo containers containing almost 30,000 bathtub toys—including more than 7,000 plastic yellow duckies. Scientists seized on this unique opportunity to use the duckies to monitor the four currents that make up the North Pacific Gyre. Duckies showed up first in November 1992 on the Alaskan coast. The last recorded ducky appeared in 1995. Speculation that the remaining duckies would be swept into Arctic waters to reappear in the Atlantic in 2003 or later has not been confirmed. For ducky alerts visit www.beachcombers.org. It is estimated that 10,000 cargo containers wash into the world's oceans every year, releasing untold amounts of objects. ***See Curriculum Connection.***

UNITED NATIONS GENERAL ASSEMBLY: 60th ANNIVERSARY. Jan 10, 1946. On the 26th anniversary of the establishment of the unsuccessful League of Nations, delegates from 51 nations met at London, England, for the first meeting of the UN General Assembly.

WOMEN'S SUFFRAGE AMENDMENT INTRODUCED IN CONGRESS: ANNIVERSARY. Jan 10, 1878. Senator A.A. Sargent of California, a close friend of Susan B. Anthony, introduced into the US Senate a women's suffrage amendment known as the Susan B. Anthony Amendment. It wasn't until Aug 26, 1920, 42 years later, that the amendment was signed into law, becoming the 19th Amendment to the United States Constitution.

JANUARY 10
LITTLE DUCKIES AND OCEAN CURRENTS

On this day in 1992, a container filled with 29,000 plastic toys, including yellow ducks, red beavers, blue turtles and green frogs, was swept off a cargo vessel during a terrible storm in the North Pacific. Ever since then, scientists have been tracking the toys as they wash ashore in order to study ocean currents. Telling the hardy ducks' story and mapping their travels is an excellent way to engage your class in learning about ocean currents and environmental concerns.

Initially, the ducks traveled around the Pacific gyre, a huge circular ocean current. Surface currents such as this one are influenced by deeper ocean current patterns and wind variations. According to Curt Ebbesmeyer and James Ingraham, oceanographers and experts on the ducks, these little plastic toys can trek up to 15 miles a day across the ocean's surface. Their speed is nearly two times as fast as the upper ocean currents because of wind propulsion.

Within the first two years after they fell overboard, about 400 ducks were found sunning themselves on the shores of Washington, Alaska and Canada. Others broke off from the Pacific gyre and traveled through the Bering Sea to the Arctic Ocean. Scientist believe that, after hitching a ride on icebergs past Greenland, the ducks would find themselves, once again, on an oceanic merry-go-round, only this time it would be the Atlantic gyre. Scientists are waiting to see if the ducks will start washing up on northeastern state shores.

While the story of the duckies' travels is charming, it prompts reflection upon ecological issues. Nearly 10,000 of 100 million containers shipped annually fall overboard. Scientists have taken advantage of these accidents to study ocean currents. The National Oceanic and Atmospheric Administration (www.noaa.gov), for example, has studied spills of 80,000 Nike shoes, 34,000 hockey gloves and 1,100 logs of timber in addition to the plastic toys. Unfortunately, plastic refuse, after years of environmental exposure, is transformed into tiny floating fragments that absorb industrial pollutants and are then ingested by sea life. Because of currents, the earth's oceans are not confined; the water in the Pacific Ocean will eventually find its way into the Atlantic Ocean. The duckies' journeys show us, in part, that the natural recycling of the earth's water can have widespread global effects if the water is polluted.

For more information, see www.seabean.com/ThingsThatFloat/duckies/index.htm and www.agu.org/sci_soc/ducks.html.

—Denise Frank

January 2006

S	M	T	W	T	F	S
1	2	3	4	5	6	7
8	9	10	11	12	13	14
15	16	17	18	19	20	21
22	23	24	25	26	27	28
29	30	31				

BIRTHDAYS TODAY

Lloyd Bloom, 59, illustrator (*Like Jake and Me*), born New York, NY, Jan 10, 1947.

Remy Charlip, 77, author and illustrator (*Fortunately; Why I Will Never Ever Ever Ever Have Enough Time to Read This Book; Hooray for Me!*), born Jan 10, 1929.

Sook Nyul Choi, 69, author (*The Year of Impossible Goodbyes*), born Pyongyang, Korea, Jan 10, 1937.

Adam Kennedy, 30, baseball player, born Riverside, CA, Jan 10, 1976.

Mark Pryor, 43, US Senator (D, Arkansas), born Fayetteville, AR, Jan 10, 1963.

Glenn Robinson, 33, basketball player, born Gary, IN, Jan 10, 1973.

JANUARY 11 — WEDNESDAY

Day 11 — 354 Remaining

CUCKOO DANCING WEEK. Jan 11–17. To honor the memory of Laurel and Hardy, whose theme, "The Dancing Cuckoos," shall be heard throughout the land as their movies are seen and their antics greeted by laughter by old and new fans of these unique masters of comedy. [Originated by the late William T. Rabe of Sault Ste. Marie, MI.]

"DESIGNATED HITTER" RULE ADOPTED: ANNIVERSARY. Jan 11, 1973. American League adopted the "designated hitter" rule, whereby an additional player is used to bat for the pitcher.

HAMILTON, ALEXANDER: BIRTH ANNIVERSARY. Jan 11, 1755. American statesman, one of the authors of *The Federalist* papers and first secretary of the treasury, Hamilton was born in the British West Indies. Engaged in a duel with Aaron Burr at Weehawken, NJ, on July 11, 1804, he was mortally wounded and died the next day. For more info: *More Perfect Union: The Story of Alexander Hamilton*, by Nancy Whitelaw (Morgan Reynolds, 1-8838-4620-X, $19.95 Gr. 4–7).

HOSTOS, EUGENIO MARIA: BIRTH ANNIVERSARY. Jan 11, 1839. Puerto Rican patriot, scholar and author of more than 50 books. Born at Rio Canas, Puerto Rico, he died at Santo Domingo, Dominican Republic, Aug 11, 1903.

INTERNATIONAL THANK YOU DAYS. Jan 11–18. An eight-day period in which to thank someone from your past or present who did something nice for you. Write, call, fax or e-mail him or her and say thank you. [©1994] For info: Adrienne Sioux Koopersmith, 1437 W Rosemont, #1W, Chicago, IL 60660-1319. E-mail: askoopersmith@hotmail.com.

LEOPOLD, ALDO: BIRTH ANNIVERSARY. Jan 11, 1887. Naturalist and author who made a profound contribution to the American environmental movement. Best known for his book *A Sand County Almanac*. Born at Burlington, IA, he died Apr 21, 1948, at Sauk County, WI.

MacDONALD, JOHN A.: BIRTH ANNIVERSARY. Jan 11, 1815. Canadian statesman, first prime minister of Canada. Born at Glasgow, Scotland, he died June 6, 1891, at Ottawa, Canada.

NEPAL: NATIONAL UNITY DAY. Jan 11. Celebration paying homage to King Prithvinarayan Shah (1723–75), founder of the present house of rulers of Nepal and creator of the unified Nepal of today.

O'BRIEN, ROBERT C.: BIRTH ANNIVERSARY. Jan 11, 1918. Author (Newbery for *Mrs Frisby and the Rats of NIMH*), born Robert Conly at Brooklyn, NY. Died at Washington, DC, Mar 5, 1973.

★ ★ ★

US SURGEON GENERAL DECLARES CIGARETTES HAZARDOUS: ANNIVERSARY. Jan 11, 1964. US Surgeon General Luther Terry issued the first government report saying that smoking may be hazardous to one's health.

BIRTHDAYS TODAY

Jean Chretien, 72, 20th prime minister of Canada, born Shawinigan, QC, Canada, Jan 11, 1934.

Steven Otfinoski, 57, author (*Triumph and Terror: The French Revolution*), born Queens, NY, Jan 11, 1949.

JANUARY 12 — THURSDAY

Day 12 — 353 Remaining

FIRST ELECTED WOMAN SENATOR: ANNIVERSARY. Jan 12, 1932. Hattie W. Caraway, a Democrat from Arkansas, was the first woman elected to the US Senate. Born in 1878, Caraway was appointed to the Senate on Nov 13, 1931, to fill out the term of her husband, Senator Thaddeus Caraway, who had died a few days earlier. On Jan 12, 1932, she won a special election to fill the remaining months of his term. Subsequently elected to two more terms, she served in the Senate until January 1945. She was an adept and tireless legislator (once introducing 43 bills on the same day) who worked for women's rights (once cosponsoring an equal rights amendment) and supported New Deal policies. She died Dec 21, 1950, at Falls Church, VA. The first woman to be elected to the Senate without having been appointed first was Margaret Chase Smith of Maine, who had served first in the House. She was elected to the Senate in 1948.

HAYES, IRA HAMILTON: BIRTH ANNIVERSARY. Jan 12, 1922. Ira Hayes was one of six US Marines who raised the American flag on Iwo Jima's Mount Suribachi, Feb 23, 1945, following a US assault on the Japanese stronghold. The event was immortalized by AP photographer Joe Rosenthal's famous photo and later by a Marine War Memorial monument at Arlington, VA. Hayes was born on a Pima Indian Reservation at Arizona. He returned home after WWII a much celebrated hero but Hayes was unable to cope with fame. He was found dead on the Sacaton Indian Reservation at Arizona, Jan 24, 1955.

LONDON, JACK: BIRTH ANNIVERSARY. Jan 12, 1876. American author of short stories, novels and travel stories of the sea and the far north, many marked by brutal realism. His most widely known work is *The Call of the Wild*, the great dog story published in 1903. London was born at San Francisco, CA. He died Nov 22, 1916, near Santa Rosa, CA. For a study guide to *The Call of the Wild*: glencoe.com/sec/literature/litlibrary.

PERRAULT, CHARLES: BIRTH ANNIVERSARY. Jan 12, 1628. Born at Paris, France, Charles Perrault was a lawyer and writer who is best remembered for his collection of fairy tales, *Contes de ma mere l'oie*, which he adapted from local folklore. This was the first story collection to use the phrase "Mother Goose Tales," and included the first publication of such stories as "Cinderella," "Sleeping Beauty" and "Little Red Riding Hood." He died May 15, 1703, at Paris.

PESTALOZZI, JOHANN HEINRICH: BIRTH ANNIVERSARY. Jan 12, 1746. Swiss educational reformer, born at Zurich. His theories laid the groundwork for modern elementary education. He died Feb 17, 1827, at Brugg, Switzerland.

TANZANIA: ZANZIBAR REVOLUTION DAY. Jan 12. National day. Zanzibar became independent in December 1963, under a sultan.

BIRTHDAYS TODAY

Marian Hossa, 27, hockey player, born Stara Lubovna, Czechoslovakia, Jan 12, 1979.

Andrew Lawrence, 18, actor ("Brotherly Love," "Oliver Beene," *Prince for a Day*), born Philadelphia, PA, Jan 12, 1988.

Iza Trapini, 52, author, illustrator (*The Itsy Bitsy Spider, I'm a Little Teapot*), born Warsaw, Poland, Jan 12, 1954.

JANUARY 13 — FRIDAY

Day 13 — 352 Remaining

ALGER, HORATIO, JR: BIRTH ANNIVERSARY. Jan 13, 1834. American clergyman and author of more than 100 popular books for boys (some 20 million copies sold). Honesty, frugality and hard work assured that the heroes of his books would find success, wealth and fame. Born at Revere, MA, he died at Natick, MA, July 18, 1899.

FRIDAY THE THIRTEENTH. Jan 13. Variously believed to be a lucky or unlucky day. Every year has at least one Friday the 13th, but never more than three. There are two Fridays the 13th in 2006. Fear of the number 13 is known as triskaidekaphobia.

FRISBEE INTRODUCED: ANNIVERSARY. Jan 13, 1957. Legend has it that in the 1920s New England college students tossed pie tins from the Frisbie Baking Company of Bridgeport, CT. The first plastic flying disc was released by the Wham-O Company on this date as the Pluto Platter, for its resemblance to a UFO. In 1958 it was renamed the Frisbee. More than 100 million Frisbees have been sold and there are numerous Frisbee tournaments across America every year.

LEE-JACKSON DAY IN VIRGINIA. Jan 13. Annually, the Friday preceding the third Monday in January. Honoring Robert E. Lee and Thomas (Stonewall) Jackson.

RADIO BROADCASTING: ANNIVERSARY. Jan 13, 1910. Radio pioneer and electron tube inventor Lee De Forest arranged the world's first radio broadcast to the public at New York, NY. He succeeded in broadcasting the voice of Enrico Caruso along with other stars of the Metropolitan Opera to several receiving locations in the city where listeners with earphones marveled at wireless music from the air. Though only a few were equipped to listen, it was the first broadcast to reach the public and the beginning of a new era in which wireless radio communication became almost universal. See also: "First Scheduled Radio Broadcast: Anniversary" (Nov 2).

★ **STEPHEN FOSTER MEMORIAL DAY.** Jan 13. Presidential Proclamation 2957 of Dec 13, 1951 (designating Jan 13, 1952), covers all succeeding years. (Public Law 82–225 of Oct 27, 1951.) Observed on the anniversary of Foster's death, Jan 13, 1864, at New York, NY. See also: "Foster, Stephen: Birth Anniversary" (July 4).

SWEDEN: SAINT KNUT'S DAY. Jan 13. "The 20th day of Knut" is the traditional end of the Christmas season. In Norway, this day is known as Tyvendedagen or "20th Day."

TOGO: LIBERATION DAY: ANNIVERSARY. Jan 13. National holiday. Commemorates 1963 uprising.

BIRTHDAYS TODAY

Orlando Bloom, 29, actor (*The Lord of the Rings* trilogy, *Pirates of the Caribbean*), born Canterbury, Kent, England, Jan 13, 1977.

Michael Bond, 80, author (*A Bear Called Paddington, Paddington At Work*), born Newbury, Berkshire, England, Jan 13, 1926.

JANUARY 14 — SATURDAY

Day 14 — 351 Remaining

ARNOLD, BENEDICT: BIRTH ANNIVERSARY. Jan 14, 1741. American officer who deserted to the British during the Revolutionary War and whose name has since become synonymous with treachery. Born at Norwich, CT, he died June 14, 1801, at London, England. For more info: *Benedict Arnold and the American Revolution*, by David C. King (Blackbirch, 1-56711-221-8, $19.95 Gr. 5 & up).

LOFTING, HUGH: BIRTH ANNIVERSARY. Jan 14, 1886. Author and illustrator, known for the Doctor Dolittle series. In his books the famous Dr. Dolittle has the ability to talk with animals. *The Voyages of Dr. Dolittle* won the Newbery Medal in 1923. Born at Maidenhead, England, Lofting died at Santa Monica, CA, Sept 26, 1947.

MINORITY SCIENTISTS SHOWCASE. Jan 14–16. St. Louis, MO. Open new doors to future science careers and interests during Martin Luther King, Jr, weekend with hands-on activities and information available as part of a free program. Meet and talk with African Americans working in science-related fields throughout the St. Louis area. Annually, Martin Luther King, Jr, weekend. Est attendance: 2,000. For info: St. Louis Science Center, 5050 Oakland Ave, St. Louis, MO 63110. Phone: (800) 456-SLSC. Web: www.slsc.org.

MOON PHASE: FULL MOON. Jan 14. Moon enters Full Moon phase at 4:48 AM, EST.

OUTCAULT, RICHARD FENTON: BIRTH ANNIVERSARY. Jan 14, 1863. When R.F. Outcault was asked by the *New York World*'s Sunday editor to submit drawings for use with their new color printing process, the "funny papers" were born. Outcault's first effort, titled "Origin of a New Species," was published Nov 18, 1894. The first regular color cartoon, "Hogan's Alley," drawn by Outcault, began appearing with its main character's blustery comments written across his yellow nightshirt—making him the "Yellow Kid." The term "yellow journalism" was coined for news-

January 2006

S	M	T	W	T	F	S
1	2	3	4	5	6	7
8	9	10	11	12	13	14
15	16	17	18	19	20	21
22	23	24	25	26	27	28
29	30	31				

papers featuring the Kid. Outcault's strip "Buster Brown" brought him celebrity and fortune. Outcault was born at Lancaster, OH, and died Sept 25, 1928, at Flushing, NY. See also "First Newspaper Comic Strip" (Oct 18).

RATIFICATION DAY. Jan 14, 1784. Anniversary of the act that officially ended the American Revolution and established the US as a sovereign power. On Jan 14, 1784, the Continental Congress, meeting at Annapolis, MD, ratified the Treaty of Paris, thus fulfilling the Declaration of Independence of July 4, 1776.

SPACE MILESTONE: *SOYUZ 4* (USSR). Jan 14, 1969. First docking of two manned spacecraft (with *Soyuz 5*) and first interchange of spaceship personnel in orbit by means of space walks.

WHIPPLE, WILLIAM: BIRTH ANNIVERSARY. Jan 14, 1730. American patriot and signer of the Declaration of Independence. Born at Kittery, ME, he died at Portsmouth, NH, Nov 10, 1785.

BIRTHDAYS TODAY

Shannon Lucid, 63, astronaut, holds the record for longest stay in space by a woman and by an American, born Shanghai, China, Jan 14, 1943.

JANUARY 15 — SUNDAY

Day 15 — 350 Remaining

INTERNATIONAL PRINTING WEEK. Jan 15–21. To develop public awareness of the printing/graphic arts industry. Annually, the week including Ben Franklin's birthday, Jan 17. For info: Kevin P. Keane, Exec Dir, International Assn of Printing House Craftsmen, 7042 Brooklyn Blvd, Minneapolis, MN 55429-1370. Phone: (800) 466-4274. Web: www.iaphc.org.

KING, MARTIN LUTHER, JR: BIRTH ANNIVERSARY. Jan 15, 1929. Black civil rights leader, minister, advocate of nonviolence and recipient of the Nobel Peace Prize (1964). Born at Atlanta, GA, he was assassinated at Memphis, TN, Apr 4, 1968. After his death many states and territories observed his birthday as a holiday. In 1983 the Congress approved HR 3706, "A bill to amend Title 5, United States Code, to make the birthday of Martin Luther King, Jr, a legal public holiday." Signed by the president on Nov 2, 1983, it became Public Law 98–144. The law sets the third Monday in January for observance of King's birthday. First observance was Jan 20, 1986. For more info: *Martin Luther King*, by Rosemary Bray (Greenwillow, 0-688-13131-X, $16 Gr 2–4) and *Dear Dr. King: Letters from Today's Children to Dr. Martin Luther King, Jr*, by Jan Colbert and Ann McMillan Harms (Hyperion, 0-7868-1462-4, $6.99 Gr 3–8) and *Martin's Big Words: The Life of Dr. Martin Luther King, Jr*, by Doreen Rappaport (Hyperion, 0-7868-0714-8, $15.99 All Ages). See also: "King, Martin Luther, Jr: Birthday Observed" (Jan 16).

LIVINGSTON, PHILIP: BIRTH ANNIVERSARY. Jan 15, 1716. Merchant and signer of the Declaration of Independence, born at Albany, NY. Died at York, PA, June 12, 1778.

WORLD RELIGION DAY. Jan 15. To proclaim the oneness of religion and the belief that world religion will unify the peoples of the earth. Baha'i-sponsored observance established in 1950. Annually, the third Sunday in January. For info: Baha'is of the US, Office of Public Information, 1320 19th St NW, Suite 350, Washington, DC 20036. Phone: (202) 466-9870. Fax: (202) 466-9873. E-mail: opi@usbnc.org. Web: www.us.bahai.org.

BIRTHDAYS TODAY

Drew Brees, 27, football player, born Austin, TX, Jan 15, 1979.

Andrea Martin, 59, actress (*Jimmy Neutron, Boy Genius; Anastasia*), born Portland, ME, Jan 15, 1947.

JANUARY 16 — MONDAY

Day 16 — 349 Remaining

APPRECIATE A DRAGON DAY. Jan 16. In school and public libraries everywhere, children will have the opportunity to choose dragons from popular literature and participate in activities to share their enthusiasm for the dragon of their choice. For info: Donita Tompkins, 5031 Stillwater Dr, Colorado Springs, CO 80918. Phone: (719) 635-3940. E-mail: dtompkins@peoplepc.com. Web: www.dragonspell.us.

DEAN, DIZZY: BIRTH ANNIVERSARY. Jan 16, 1911. Jay Hanna "Dizzy" Dean, major league pitcher (St. Louis Cardinals) and Baseball Hall of Fame member was born at Lucas, AR. Following his baseball career, Dean established himself as a radio and TV sports announcer and commentator, becoming famous for his innovative delivery. "He slud into third," reported Dizzy, who on another occasion explained that "Me and Paul [baseball player brother Paul "Daffy" Dean] . . . didn't get much education." Died at Reno, NV, July 17, 1974.

EIGHTEENTH AMENDMENT TO US CONSTITUTION RATIFIED: ANNIVERSARY. Jan 16, 1919. Nebraska became the 36th state to ratify the prohibition amendment on this date, and the 18th Amendment became part of the US Constitution. One year later, Jan 16, 1920, the 18th Amendment took effect and the sale of alcoholic beverages became illegal in the US with the Volstead Act providing for enforcement. This was the first time that an amendment to the Constitution dealt with a social issue. The 21st Amendment, repealing the 18th, went into effect Dec 6, 1933.

EL SALVADOR: NATIONAL DAY OF PEACE. Jan 16. Public holiday. Anniversary of the end of 12 years of civil war with the signing of a peace treaty on Jan 16, 1992.

JAPAN: HARU-NO-YABUIRI. Jan 16. Employees and servants who have been working over the holidays are given a day off.

KING, MARTIN LUTHER, JR: BIRTHDAY OBSERVED. Jan 16. Public Law 98–144 designates the third Monday in January as an annual legal public holiday observing the birth of Martin Luther King, Jr. First observed in 1986. In New Hampshire, this day is designated Civil Rights Day. See also: "King, Martin Luther, Jr: Birth Anniversary" (Jan 15).

MALAWI: JOHN CHILEMBWE DAY. Jan 16. National holiday. Commemorates an early martyr for independence who died in 1915.

★ **MARTIN LUTHER KING, JR, FEDERAL HOLIDAY.** Jan 16. Presidential Proclamation has been issued without request each year for the third Monday in January since 1986.

NATIONAL NOTHING DAY. Jan 16. Anniversary of National Nothing Day, an event created by newspaperman Harold Pullman Coffin and first observed in 1973 "to provide Americans with one national day when they can just sit without celebrating, observing or honoring anything." Since 1975, though many other events have been listed on this day, lighthearted traditional observance of Coffin's idea has continued. Coffin, a native of Reno, NV, died at Capitola, CA, Sept 12, 1981.

NO NAME-CALLING WEEK. Jan 16–20 (tentative). An annual week of educational activities aimed at ending name-calling of all kinds. The No Name-Calling Coalition will provide schools with the tools and inspiration needed to launch an ongoing dialogue about ways to eliminate bullying in their communities. A resource kit for educators is available. Annually, the third week in January.

★ ★ ★

For info: The No Name-Calling Coalition. E-mail: info@nonamecallingweek.org. Web: www.nonamecallingweek.org.

PERSIAN GULF WAR BEGINS: 15th ANNIVERSARY. Jan 16, 1991. Allied forces launched a major air offensive against Iraq to begin the Gulf War. The strike was designed to destroy Iraqi air defenses, command, control and communication centers. As Desert Shield became Desert Storm, the world was able to see and hear for the first time an initial engagement of war as CNN broadcasters, stationed at Baghdad, broadcast the attack live.

RELIGIOUS FREEDOM DAY. Jan 16, 1786. The legislature of Virginia adopted a religious freedom statute that protected Virginians against any requirement to attend or support any church and against discrimination. This statute, which had been drafted by Thomas Jefferson and introduced by James Madison, later was the model for the First Amendment to the US Constitution.

★ **RELIGIOUS FREEDOM DAY.** Jan 16. On the day of the adoption in 1786 of a religious freedom statute by the Virginia legislature.

BIRTHDAYS TODAY

Joe Horn, 34, football player, born Tupelo, MS, Jan 16, 1972.
Kate McMullan, 59, author (the Dragon Slayers' Academy Series), born St. Louis, MO, Jan 16, 1947.
Albert Pujols, 26, baseball player, born Santo Domingo, Dominican Republic, Jan 16, 1980.
Martha Weston, 59, author and illustrator (*Bad Baby Brother*), born Asheville, NC, Jan 16, 1947.

JANUARY 17 — TUESDAY

Day 17 — 348 Remaining

BELLAIRS, JOHN: BIRTH ANNIVERSARY. Jan 17, 1938. Author of mystery and horror novels for children, born at Marshall, MI. Some of his best-known books are *The House With a Clock in Its Walls* and *The Figure in the Shadows*, part of a series featuring the orphan Lewis Barnaveldt and his uncle, who is a witch. Another popular series features the character Johnny Dixon (*The Eyes of the Killer Robot*). Bellairs died at Haverhill, MA, Mar 8, 1991. After his death, many of his partial manuscripts were completed and published by writer Brad Strickland.

COIN FLIP FOR BENJAMIN FRANKLIN'S 300th BIRTHDAY. Jan 17. On this day—Benjamin Franklin's 300th birthday—students around the world can commemorate this milestone event by participating in a common scientific enterprise. Students are invited to flip a coin ten times and then enter their data at The Franklin Institute Online. There, their data will merge with the aggregated results from coin flips in classrooms and homes around the world. In this way, students will see how science is a distributed, shared pursuit of knowledge by curious thinkers, a lesson that honors the legacy of Benjamin Franklin. Students should pick the smallest valued coin of their country's coinage (keeping in mind Franklin's famous adage: "A penny saved is a penny earned"). For more info: The Franklin Institute Online. Web: sln.fi.edu/flip.

★ ★ ★

January 2006

S	M	T	W	T	F	S
1	2	3	4	5	6	7
8	9	10	11	12	13	14
15	16	17	18	19	20	21
22	23	24	25	26	27	28
29	30	31				

JANUARY 17
BENJAMIN FRANKLIN'S 300TH BIRTHDAY

If Ben Franklin were still alive, he'd be 300 years old today. He was an inventor and scientist, printer, author, diplomat and American Founding Father who was one of the drafters and signers of the Declaration of Independence. To list his accomplishments would take more room that this brief sidebar allows, but here are some fun facts to dazzle your students with:

Franklin founded America's first subscription library.

He published America's first political cartoon.

He founded the University of Pennsylvania.

He invented the bifocals, the lightning rod and the Franklin stove.

His experiments with electricity (yes, the kite and key) gained him the prestigious Copley Medal.

Hard work was the hallmark of his long life. His beginnings were humble and harsh: he was the 15th child of 17 children and began working six days a week for twelve hours at a stretch at the age of 10 years. But he blossomed into a Renaissance man. When Franklin died on Apr 17, 1790, at the age of 84, the world mourned and 20,000 people thronged to his funeral.

His 300th birthday will be a national and international celebration of museum exhibits, special events and even a commissioned symphony (to premiere at Philadelphia, PA, in November 2005). Your class can even take part in the special events: today is the "Coin Flip for Benjamin Franklin's 300th Birthday," sponsored by the Franklin Institute Online. See the event description for more details.

Sometimes Franklin's accomplishments overshadow the man himself. Franklin's sense of humor is legendary. When he was 22 years old, he wrote an epitaph, which he wanted inscribed on his tombstone. Read this epitaph (which was not used) and discuss how it showed his sense of wit and humor and why it is actually appropriate to Franklin's life. Candace Fleming's biography of Franklin (see below) contains a reproduction and transcription of the epitaph on page 104.

For books about Benjamin Franklin see *The Hatmaker's Sign: A Story by Benjamin Franklin,* retold by Candace Fleming (Scholastic, 0-531-07174-X, $6.99 Ages 5 & up); *Ben Franklin's Almanac: Being a True Account of the Good Gentleman's Life*, by Candace Fleming (Atheneum, 0-689-83549-3, $19.95 Ages 9 & up); *Who Was Benjamin Franklin?* by Dennis Fradin (Grosset & Dunlap, 0-448-42495-9, $4.99 Ages 8–10); and *How Ben Franklin Stole the Lightning*, by Rosalyn Schanzer (HarperCollins, 0-688-16993-7, $16.99 Ages 7–10).

The Electric Ben Franklin, at www.ushistory.org/Franklin, has oodles of information about all aspects of Franklin's life. Check out Ben Franklin 300 at www.benfranklin300.com for updates on tercentenary (have the class dissect that word!) events in 2006—including the traveling exhibition, "Benjamin Franklin: In Search of a Better World," that will land in five US cities before going to Paris, France, in November 2007. This site will also offer teachers interactive resources and lesson plans. The Quotable Ben Franklin, at www.ushistory.org/franklin/quotable/index.htm, offers the best of his wit and wisdom. (See also the Curriculum Connections on his proverbs and on his armonica [March].)

—Sally Walker

JANUARY 17
THE WIT AND WISDOM OF BEN FRANKLIN

As you celebrate Benjamin Franklin's 300th birthday year, remind your students of his fame as a wit and sage. Franklin produced *Poor Richard's Almanack* off and on from 1733 to 1758, with Franklin taking the guise of fictitious, crotchety Richard Saunders, who wrote to provide the "publick good." The almanac was filled with moon phases, agricultural advice and what is usual to the genre, but wherever there were empty spaces, Franklin filled them with "proverbial sentences, chiefly such as inculcated industry and frugality as the means of procuring wealth and thereby securing virtue." Facsimiles and selections of Franklin's proverbs are easily available (one is the Modern Library edition, 0-679-64038-X, $10.95 All ages).

Writing a "Franklin Proverb" or "Franklin Thought for the Day" on the blackboard each school day during the month of January is a great way to call attention to Ben's musings and to commemorate his birthday. Take a class vote to discover which adage or quotation is the class favorite, then discuss why.

Here are a few to get you started:

Fish and visitors stink after three days.

All would live long, but none would be old.

Tongue double, brings trouble.

Eat to live, and not live to eat.

Great talkers, little doers.

One Today is worth two Tomorrows.

Nothing dries sooner than a Tear.

Tell me my Faults, and mend your own.

He that sows Thorns should never go barefoot.

A false Friend and a Shadow attend only while the Sun shines.

—Sally Walker

CORMIER, ROBERT: BIRTH ANNIVERSARY. Jan 17, 1925. Author of 18 critically acclaimed books for young adults, born at Leominster, MA. Among his most significant works are *The Chocolate War, We All Fall Down* and *Tunes for Bears to Dance To*. He was known for many years to accept telephone calls from his young readers who felt lonely or distraught. In fact, he published his home phone number in his 1977 novel *I Am the Cheese*. He died Nov 2, 2000, at Leominster, MA.

FIRST NUCLEAR-POWERED SUBMARINE VOYAGE: ANNIVERSARY. Jan 17, 1955. The world's first nuclear-powered submarine, the *Nautilus*, now forms part of the *Nautilus* Memorial Submarine Force Library and Museum at the Naval Submarine Base New London at Groton, CT. At 11 AM, EST, the commanding officer, Commander Eugene P. Wilkerson, ordered all lines cast off and sent the historic message: "Under way on nuclear power." Highlights of the *Nautilus*: keel laid by President Harry S Truman June 14, 1952; christened and launched by Mrs Dwight D. Eisenhower Jan 21, 1954; commissioned to the US Navy Sept 30, 1954.

FRANKLIN, BENJAMIN: 300th BIRTH ANNIVERSARY. Jan 17, 1706. "Elder statesman of the American Revolution," oldest signer of both the Declaration of Independence and the Constitution, scientist, diplomat, author, printer, publisher, philosopher, philanthropist and self-made, self-educated man. Author, printer and publisher of *Poor Richard's Almanack* (1733–58). Born at Boston, MA, Franklin died at Philadelphia, PA, Apr 17, 1790. In 1728 Franklin wrote a premature epitaph for himself. It first appeared in print in Ames's 1771 almanac: "The Body of BENJAMIN FRANKLIN/Printer/Like a Covering of an old Book/Its contents torn out/And stript of its Lettering and Gilding,/Lies here, Food for Worms;/But the work shall not be lost,/It will (as he believ'd) appear once more/In a New and more beautiful Edition/Corrected and amended/By the Author." For more info: *The Amazing Life of Benjamin Franklin*, by James Cross Giblin (Scholastic, 0-590-48534-2, $17.95 Gr. 4–6). ***See Curriculum Connections.***

JAPAN SUFFERS MAJOR EARTHQUAKE: ANNIVERSARY. Jan 17, 1995. Japan suffered its second most deadly earthquake in the 20th century when a 20-second temblor left 5,500 dead and more than 21,600 people injured. The epicenter was six miles beneath Awaji Island at Osaka Bay. This was just 20 miles west of Kobe, Japan's sixth-largest city and a major port that accounted for 12 percent of the country's exports. Measuring 7.2 on the Richter scale, the quake collapsed or badly damaged more than 30,400 buildings and left 275,000 people homeless. For more info go to the National Earthquake Information Center: wwwneic.cr.usgs.gov.

LEWIS, SHARI: BIRTH ANNIVERSARY. Jan 17, 1934. Puppeteer Shari Lewis, creator of Lamb Chop and Charlie Horse, was born Shari Hurwitz at New York, NY. She won 12 Emmys for her children's television programs, which included "The Shari Lewis Show" (1960–63) and "Lamb Chop's Play-Along," first airing in 1992. Her characters inspired dozens of books, videos and toys, as well as computer software. She died Aug 3, 1998, at Los Angeles, CA.

MEXICO: BLESSING OF THE ANIMALS AT THE CATHEDRAL. Jan 17. Church of San Antonio at Mexico City or Xochimilco provide best sights of chickens, cows and household pets gaily decorated with flowers. (Saint's day for San Antonio Abad, patron saint of domestic animals.)

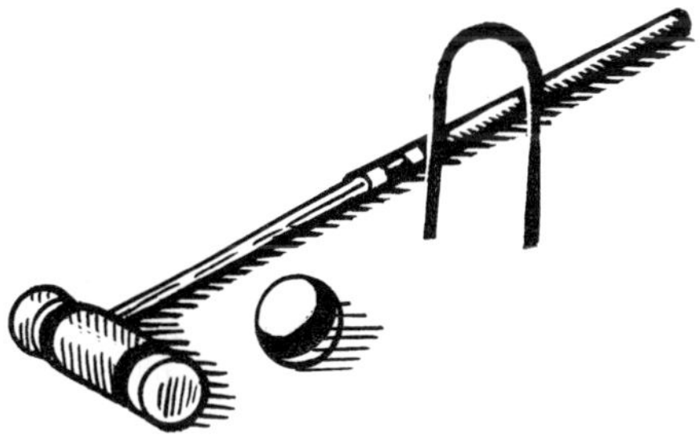

SOUTHERN CALIFORNIA EARTHQUAKE: ANNIVERSARY. Jan 17, 1994. An earthquake measuring 6.6 on the Richter scale struck the Los Angeles area about 4:20 AM. The epicenter was at Northridge in the San Fernando Valley, about 20 miles northwest of downtown Los Angeles. The death toll was 51, 16 of whom were killed in the collapse of one apartment building. More than 25,000 people were made homeless by the quake. Many buildings were destroyed and others made uninhabitable due to structural damage. A section of the Santa Monica Freeway, part of the Simi Valley Freeway and three major overpasses collapsed. Hundreds of aftershocks occurred in the following several weeks. Costs to repair the damages were estimated at 15–30 billion dollars. For more info go to the National Earthquake Information Center: wwwneic.cr.usgs.gov.

BIRTHDAYS TODAY

Muhammad Ali, 64, former heavyweight champion boxer who changed his name after converting to Islam, born Cassius Marcellus Clay, Jr, Louisville, KY, Jan 17, 1942.

Jim Carrey, 44, actor (*Lemony Snicket's A Series of Unfortunate Events, Ace Ventura, How the Grinch Stole Christmas*), born Newmarket, ON, Canada, Jan 17, 1962.

Ruth Ann Minner, 71, Governor of Delaware (D), born Milford, DE, Jan 17, 1935.

JANUARY 18 — WEDNESDAY

Day 18 — 347 Remaining

FIRST BLACK US CABINET MEMBER: 40th ANNIVERSARY. Jan 18, 1966. Robert Clifton Weaver was sworn in as Secretary of Housing and Urban Development, becoming the first black cabinet member in US history. He was nominated by President Lyndon Johnson. Born Dec 29, 1907, at Washington, DC, Weaver died at New York, NY, July 17, 1997.

POOH DAY: A.A. MILNE: BIRTH ANNIVERSARY. Jan 18, 1882. Anniversary of the birth of A(lan) A(lexander) Milne, English author, especially remembered for his children's stories: *Winnie the Pooh* and *The House at Pooh Corner*. Also the author of *Mr Pim Passes By, When We Were Very Young* and *Now We Are Six*. Born at London, England, he died at Hartfield, England, Jan 31, 1956. For more info: *Meet A.A. Milne*, by S. Ward (Rosen, 0-8239-5708-X, $18.75 Gr. K–4) or go to www.kirjasto.sci.fi/aamilne.htm.

RANSOME, ARTHUR: BIRTH ANNIVERSARY. Jan 18, 1884. Author, born at Leeds, Yorkshire, England. His children's books were based on his childhood explorations in the Lake Country and featured children whose parents could indulge them in long vacations. His works include *We Didn't Mean to Go to Sea, Secret Water* and *Swallows and Amazons*. He won the Carnegie Medal in 1936 for *The Pigeon Post*. Ransome died June 3, 1967, at Manchester, England.

ROGET, PETER MARK: BIRTH ANNIVERSARY. Jan 18, 1779. English physician, best known as author of Roget's *Thesaurus of English Words and Phrases*, first published in 1852. Roget was also the inventor of the "log-log" slide rule. Born at London, England, Roget died at West Malvern, Worcestershire, England, Sept 12, 1869.

BIRTHDAYS TODAY

Mark Messier, 45, hockey player, born Edmonton, AB, Canada, Jan 18, 1961.

Alan Schroeder, 45, author of biographies (*Ragtime Tumpie*), born Alameda, CA, Jan 18, 1961.

January 2006

S	M	T	W	T	F	S
1	2	3	4	5	6	7
8	9	10	11	12	13	14
15	16	17	18	19	20	21
22	23	24	25	26	27	28
29	30	31				

JANUARY 19 — THURSDAY

Day 19 — 346 Remaining

CÉZANNE, PAUL: BIRTH ANNIVERSARY. Jan 19, 1839. French post-Impressionist painter known for his landscapes, born at Aix-en-Provence, France. He died at Aix, Oct 22, 1906. For more info: *Cézanne from A to Z*, by Marie Sellier (Peter Bedrick, 0-87226-476-9, $14.95 All ages).

CONFEDERATE HEROES DAY. Jan 19. Observed on anniversary of Robert E. Lee's birthday. Official holiday in Texas, also called Confederate Memorial Day.

ETHIOPIA: TIMKET. Jan 19. National holiday. Epiphany in the Coptic and Ethiopian Orthodox churches. The festival lasts through Jan 20 or 21. Also a holiday in Eritrea.

LEE, ROBERT E.: BIRTH ANNIVERSARY. Jan 19, 1807. Greatest military leader of the Confederacy, son of Revolutionary War general Henry (Light Horse Harry) Lee. His surrender Apr 9, 1865, to Union General Ulysses S. Grant brought an end to the Civil War. Born at Westmoreland County, VA, he died at Lexington, VA, Oct 12, 1870. His birthday is observed in Florida, Kentucky, Louisiana, South Carolina and Tennessee. Observed on third Monday in January in Alabama, Arkansas and Mississippi (Jan 16 in 2006).

"LIZZIE MCGUIRE" TV PREMIERE: 5th ANNIVERSARY. Jan 19, 2001. Popular with girls ages 9 to 14, "Lizzie McGuire" is a live-action program appearing on the Disney Channel. Hilary Duff appears as the main character of Lizzie, a seventh grader learning to cope with boys, curfews and parents.The show features its own website (www.disney.go.com/disneychannel/lizziemcguire) where fans can find out more about the show, read Lizzie's journal and chat online with other kids.

POE, EDGAR ALLAN: BIRTH ANNIVERSARY. Jan 19, 1809. American poet and story writer, called "America's most famous man of letters." Born at Boston, MA, he was orphaned in dire poverty in 1811 and was raised by Virginia merchant John Allan. A magazine editor of note, he is best remembered for his poetry (especially "The Raven") and for his tales of suspense. Died at Baltimore, MD, Oct 7, 1849.

TIN CAN PATENT: ANNIVERSARY. Jan 19, 1825. Ezra Daggett and Thomas Kensett obtained a patent for a process for storing food in tin cans.

BIRTHDAYS TODAY

Nina Bawden, 81, author (*Carrie's War*), born London, England, Jan 19, 1925.

Pat Mora, 64, author (*Tomás and the Library Lady*), born El Paso, TX, Jan 19, 1942.

Junior Seau, 37, football player, born Tiaina Seau, Jr, San Diego, CA, Jan 19, 1969.

Will Weaver, 56, author (*Farm Team, Striking Out*), born Park Rapids, MN, Jan 19, 1950.

JANUARY 20 — FRIDAY

Day 20 — 345 Remaining

AMERICAN LIBRARY ASSOCIATION MIDWINTER MEETING. Jan 20–25. San Antonio, TX. For info: American Library Assn, 50 E Huron St, Chicago, IL 60611. Phone: (800) 545-2433. Web: www.ala.org.

AQUARIUS, THE WATER CARRIER. Jan 20–Feb 19. In the astronomical/astrological zodiac, which divides the sun's apparent orbit into 12 segments, the period Jan 20–Feb 19 is identified, traditionally, as the sun sign of Aquarius, the Water Carrier. The ruling planet is Uranus or Saturn.

ARBOR DAY IN FLORIDA. Jan 20. A ceremonial day on the third Friday in January.

AZERBAIJAN: DAY OF THE MARTYRS. Jan 20. National holiday. Commemorates Azeri civilians killed by Soviets in fight for independence in 1990.

CAMCORDER DEVELOPED: ANNIVERSARY. Jan 20, 1982. Five companies (Hitachi, JVC, Philips, Matsushita and Sony) agreed to cooperate on the construction of a camera with a built-in videocassette recorder.

GUINEA-BISSAU: NATIONAL HEROES DAY. Jan 20. National holiday.

LEE, RICHARD HENRY: BIRTH ANNIVERSARY. Jan 20, 1732. Signer of the Declaration of Independence. Born at Westmoreland County, VA, he died June 19, 1794, at his birthplace.

US REVOLUTIONARY WAR: CESSATION OF HOSTILITIES: ANNIVERSARY. Jan 20, 1783. The British and US Commissioners signed a preliminary "Cessation of Hostilities," which was ratified by England's King George III Feb 14 and led to the Treaties of Paris and Versailles, Sept 3, 1783, ending the war.

BIRTHDAYS TODAY

Edwin (Buzz) Aldrin, 76, former astronaut, one of first three men on moon, born Montclair, NJ, Jan 20, 1930.

JANUARY 21 — SATURDAY

Day 21 — 344 Remaining

ALLEN, ETHAN: BIRTH ANNIVERSARY. Jan 21, 1738. Revolutionary War hero and leader of the Vermont "Green Mountain Boys." Born at Litchfield, CT, he died at Burlington, VT, Feb 12, 1789. For more info: *Ethan Allen: The Green Mountain Boys and Vermont's Path to Statehood*, by Jacqueline Ching (Rosen, 0-8239-5723-3, $23.95 Gr. 4–8).

BRECKINRIDGE, JOHN CABELL: BIRTH ANNIVERSARY. Jan 21, 1821. The 14th vice president of the US (1857–61), serving under President James Buchanan. Born at Lexington, KY, he died there May 17, 1875.

FIRST CONCORDE FLIGHT: 30th ANNIVERSARY. Jan 21, 1976. The supersonic Concorde airplane was put into service by Britain and France. Concorde service ended Oct 24, 2003.

JACKSON, THOMAS JONATHAN "STONEWALL": BIRTH ANNIVERSARY. Jan 21, 1824. Confederate general and one of the most famous soldiers of the American Civil War, best known as "Stonewall" Jackson. Born at Clarksburg, VA (now WV), Jackson died of wounds received in battle near Chancellorsville, VA, May 10, 1863. For more info: *Standing Like a Stone Wall: The Life of General Thomas J. Jackson*, by James I. Robertson (Simon & Schuster, 0-689-82419-X, $22 Gr. 5–8).

★ ★ ★

PHILIPPINES: ATI-ATIHAN FESTIVAL. Jan 21–22. Kalibo, Aklan. One of the most colorful celebrations in the Philippines, the Ati-Atihan Festival commemorates the peace pact between the Ati of Panay (pygmies) and the Malays, who were early migrants in the islands. The townspeople blacken their bodies with soot, don colorful and bizarre costumes and sing and dance in the streets. The festival also celebrates the Feast Day of Santo Niño (the infant Jesus). Annually, the third weekend in January.

BIRTHDAYS TODAY

Hakeem Abdul Olajuwon, 43, former basketball player, born Lagos, Nigeria, Jan 21, 1963.

JANUARY 22 — SUNDAY

Day 22 — 343 Remaining

ANSWER YOUR CAT'S QUESTION DAY. Jan 22. If you will stop what you are doing and take a look at your cat, you will observe that the cat is looking at you with a serious question. Meditate upon it, then answer the question! Annually, Jan 22. [©2002 by WH.] For info: Thomas & Ruth Roy, Wellcat Holidays, 2418 Long Ln, Lebanon, PA 17046. Phone: (717) 279-0184. E-mail: info@wellcat.com. Web: www.wellcat.com.

FIRST WILD ANIMAL WITH ARTIFICIAL LENSES: ANNIVERSARY. Jan 22, 2004. During two hours of surgery, veterinarians removed the cataracts from a young great horned owl's eyes and implanted new artificial lenses in the first such recorded operation. Minerva, as she was named by rescuers, was found starving on a fence—her cataracts prevented her from hunting for food. After the operation at the University of Wisconsin-Madison Veterinary School, Minerva underwent a recuperation time and then was released back into the wild on Apr 30, 2004.

MOON PHASE: LAST QUARTER. Jan 22. Moon enters Last Quarter phase at 10:14 AM, EST.

UKRAINE: UKRAINIAN DAY. Jan 22. National holiday. Commemorates 1918 proclamation of the republic.

VINSON, FRED M.: BIRTH ANNIVERSARY. Jan 22, 1890. The 13th Chief Justice of the US Supreme Court, born at Louisa, KY. Served in the House of Representatives, appointed Director of War Mobilization during WWII and Secretary of the Treasury under President Harry Truman. Nominated by Truman to succeed Harlan F. Stone as Chief Justice. Died at Washington, DC, Sept 8, 1953. For more info: oyez.northwestern.edu/justices/justices.cgi.

BIRTHDAYS TODAY

Sheila Gordon, 79, author (*Waiting for the Rain*), born Johannesburg, South Africa, Jan 22, 1927.

Blair Lent, 76, author and illustrator (*Tikki Tikki Tembo*), born Boston, MA, Jan 22, 1930.

Rafe Martin, 60, author (*The Boy Who Lived with the Seals*), born Rochester, NY, Jan 22, 1946.

Beverley Mitchell, 25, actress (*Mother of the Bride*, "7th Heaven"), born Arcadia, CA, Jan 22, 1981.

JANUARY 23 — MONDAY

Day 23 — 342 Remaining

BLACKWELL, ELIZABETH, AWARDED MD: ANNIVERSARY. Jan 23, 1849. Dr. Elizabeth Blackwell became the first woman to receive an MD degree. The native of Bristol, England, was awarded her degree by the Medical Institution of Geneva, NY. For more info: *Elizabeth Blackwell: The First Woman Doctor,* by Ira Peck (Millbrook, 0-7613-1854-2, $21.90 Gr. 4–7).

HANCOCK, JOHN: BIRTH ANNIVERSARY. Jan 23, 1737. American patriot and statesman, first signer of the Declaration of Independence. Born at Braintree, MA, he died at Quincy, MA, Oct 8, 1793. Because of his conspicuous signature on the Declaration of Independence, Hancock's name has become part of the American language, referring to any handwritten signature, as in "Put your John Hancock on that!" (Some sources cite Hancock's Old Style birth date of Jan 12, 1736/7.)

HEWES, JOSEPH: BIRTH ANNIVERSARY. Jan 23, 1730. Signer of the Declaration of Independence. Born at Princeton, NJ, he died Nov 10, 1779, at Philadelphia, PA.

MANET, ÉDOUARD: BIRTH ANNIVERSARY. Jan 23, 1832. French artist (*Déjeuner sur l'herbe, Olympia*), born at Paris, France. He died at Paris, Apr 30, 1883.

NATIONAL HANDWRITING DAY. Jan 23. Popularly observed on the birthday of John Hancock to encourage more legible handwriting. (Some sources cite Hancock's Old Style birth date of Jan 12, 1736/7.)

STEWART, POTTER: BIRTH ANNIVERSARY. Jan 23, 1915. Associate Justice of the Supreme Court of the US, nominated by President Eisenhower, Jan 17, 1959. (Oath of office, May 15, 1959.) Born at Jackson, MI, he retired in July 1981 and died Dec 7, 1985, at Putney, VT. Buried at Arlington National Cemetery. For more info: oyez.northwestern.edu/justices/justices.cgi.

TWENTIETH AMENDMENT TO US CONSTITUTION RATIFIED: ANNIVERSARY. Jan 23, 1933. The 20th Amendment was ratified, fixing the date of the presidential inauguration at the current Jan 20 instead of the previous Mar 4. It also specified that were the president-elect to die before taking office, the vice president-elect would succeed to the presidency. In addition, it set Jan 3 as the official opening date of Congress each year.

TWENTY-FOURTH AMENDMENT TO US CONSTITUTION RATIFIED: ANNIVERSARY. Jan 23, 1964. Poll taxes and other taxes were eliminated as a prerequisite for voting in all federal elections by the 24th Amendment.

BIRTHDAYS TODAY

Tom Carper, 59, US Senator (D, Delaware), born Beckley, WV, Jan 23, 1947.

Katherine Holabird, 58, author (the Angelina Ballerina series), born Cambridge, MA, Jan 23, 1948.

Frank Lautenberg, 82, US Senator (D, New Jersey), born Paterson, NJ, Jan 23, 1924.

★ ★ ★

January 2006

S	M	T	W	T	F	S
1	2	3	4	5	6	7
8	9	10	11	12	13	14
15	16	17	18	19	20	21
22	23	24	25	26	27	28
29	30	31				

JANUARY 24 — TUESDAY

Day 24 — 341 Remaining

CALIFORNIA GOLD DISCOVERY: ANNIVERSARY. Jan 24, 1848. James W. Marshal, an employee of John Sutter, accidentally discovered gold while building a sawmill near Coloma, CA. Efforts to keep the discovery secret failed, and the gold rush got under way in 1849. Had the gold rush not occurred, it might have taken California years to reach the population of 60,000 necessary for statehood, but the 49ers increased the population beyond that figure in one year and in 1850 California became a state. For more info: *The Wells Fargo Book of the Gold Rush,* by Margaret Rau (Atheneum, 0-689-83019-X, $18 Gr. 6–10).

BIRTHDAYS TODAY

Tatyana M. Ali, 27, actress ("Sesame Street," "The Fresh Prince of Bel Air"), born Long Island, NY, Jan 24, 1979.

Mary Lou Retton, 38, Olympic gold medal gymnast, born Fairmont, WV, Jan 24, 1968.

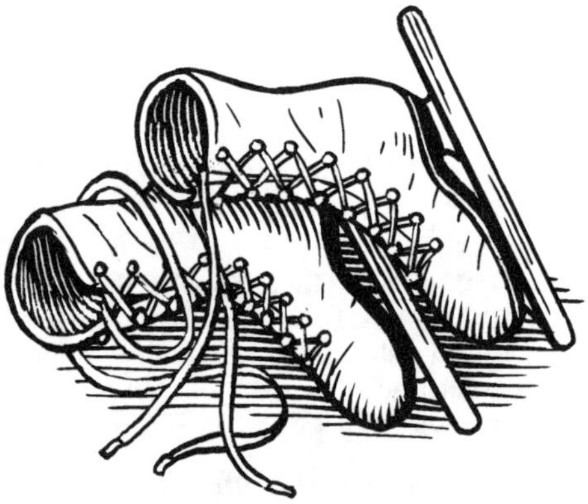

JANUARY 25 — WEDNESDAY

Day 25 — 340 Remaining

AROUND THE WORLD IN 72 DAYS: ANNIVERSARY. Jan 25, 1890. Newspaper reporter Nellie Bly (pen name used by Elizabeth Cochrane Seaman) set off from Hoboken, NJ, on Nov 14, 1889, to attempt to break Jules Verne's imaginary hero Phileas Fogg's record of voyaging around the world in 80 days. She did beat Fogg's record, taking 72 days, 6 hours, 11 minutes and 14 seconds to make the trip. She traveled by train, boat and even rickshaw on her adventure, arriving back in New Jersey on Jan 25, 1890.

CURTIS, CHARLES: BIRTH ANNIVERSARY. Jan 25, 1860. The 31st vice president of the US (1929–33). Born at Topeka, KS, he died at Washington, DC, Feb 8, 1936.

FIRST SCHEDULED TRANSCONTINENTAL FLIGHT: ANNIVERSARY. Jan 25, 1959. American Airlines opened the jet age in the US with the first scheduled transcontinental flight on a Boeing 707 nonstop from California to New York.

FIRST WINTER OLYMPICS: ANNIVERSARY. Jan 25, 1924. The First Winter Olympics took place at Chamonix, France, with 16 nations participating. The ski jump, previously unknown, thrilled spectators. The Olympics offered a boost to skiing, which would become much more popular during the next decade.

MACINTOSH COMPUTER RELEASED: ANNIVERSARY. Jan 25, 1984. Apple Computer released its new Macintosh model on this day, which eventually replaced the Apple II. The new computer sold for $2,495.

MARJAN, THE LION OF KABUL: DEATH ANNIVERSARY. Jan 25, 2002. Born around 1976, Marjan the Lion became a symbol for the hardiness of Afghanistan and a beloved mascot of Kabul through decades of war. A German zoo gave the 2-year-old male lion to the Kabul Zoo in 1978. After the Russians invaded Afghanistan in 1979 and then when the Taliban controlled the country, the zoo fell on hard times and the animals lacked basic necessities—despite the heroic care of their unpaid caretakers. Marjan lost an eye and his hearing when a Taliban soldier hurled a grenade at him. Still, the lion persevered and died of old age a few months after Afghanistan was liberated from the Taliban regime.

NATIONAL COMPLIMENT DAY. Jan 25. This day is set aside to compliment at least five people. Not only are compliments appreciated by the receiver, they lift the spirit of the giver. Compliments provide a quick and easy way to connect positively with those you come in contact with. Giving compliments forges bonds, dispels loneliness and just plain feels good. Annually, the fourth Wednesday in January. For info: Debby Hoffman, Positive Results Seminars, PO Box 3478, Concord, NH 03303-3478. Phone: (603) 783-4446. E-mail: Debby@DebbyHoffman.com. Or Kathy Chamberlin, Respectful Communication, 724 Park Ave, Contoocook, NH 03229-3089. Phone: (603) 746-6227. E-mail: KathyChamberlin@aol.com. Web: www.complimentday.com.

"ROBOT" ENTERS WORLD LEXICON: 85th ANNIVERSARY. Jan 25, 1921. Today, the play *R.U.R.* premiered at the National Theater in Prague, Czechoslovakia. "R.U.R." stood for "Rossum's Universal Robots," and the play concerned artificial human workers who rebel against their human masters. Czech dramatist Karel Capek and his brother, Josef Capek, derived "robot" from the Czech noun *robota*, which means "labor" and "servitude." As the play became a hit worldwide (with an English translation published in 1923), the concept of the robot took hold. Capek's robots were chemically created; today's real and fictional robots are metallic machines.

BIRTHDAYS TODAY

Conrad Burns, 71, US Senator (R, Montana), born Gallatin, MO, Jan 25, 1935.
Chris Chelios, 44, hockey player, born Chicago, IL, Jan 25, 1962.
Debbi Chocolate, 52, author (*A Very Special Kwanzaa, Kente Colors*), born Chicago, IL, Jan 25, 1954.

JANUARY 26 — THURSDAY

Day 26 — 339 Remaining

AUSTRALIA: AUSTRALIA DAY—FIRST BRITISH SETTLEMENT. Jan 26, 1788. A shipload of convicts arrived briefly at Botany Bay (which proved to be unsuitable) and then at Port Jackson (later the site of the city of Sydney). Establishment of an Australian prison colony was to relieve crowding of British prisons. Australia Day, formerly known as Foundation Day or Anniversary Day, has been observed since about 1817 and has been a public holiday since 1838.

COLEMAN, BESSIE: BIRTH ANNIVERSARY. Jan 26, 1893. The first African American to receive a pilot's license, Coleman had to go to France to study flying, since she was denied admission to aviation schools in the US because of her race and sex. She took part in acrobatic air exhibitions where her stunt-flying and figure eights won her many admirers. Born at Atlanta, TX, she died in a plane crash at Jacksonville, FL, Apr 30, 1926. For more info: *Fly, Bessie, Fly*, by Lynn Joseph (Simon & Schuster, 0-689-81339-2, $16 Gr. 1–4).

DENTAL DRILL PATENT: ANNIVERSARY. Jan 26, 1875. George F. Green, of Kalamazoo, MI, patented the electric dental drill.

DODGE, MARY MAPES: BIRTH ANNIVERSARY. Jan 26, 1831. Children's author, known for her book *Hans Brinker or, The Silver Skates*. Born at New York, NY, she died at Ontenora Park, NY, Aug 21, 1905.

DOMINICAN REPUBLIC: NATIONAL HOLIDAY. Jan 26. An official public holiday celebrates the birth anniversary of Juan Pablo Duarte, one of the fathers of the republic.

FRANKLIN PREFERS TURKEY: ANNIVERSARY. Jan 26, 1784. In a letter to his daughter, Benjamin Franklin expressed his unhappiness over the choice of the eagle as the symbol of America. He preferred the turkey. "I wish the bald eagle had not been chosen as the representative of our country; he is a bird of bad moral character; like those among men who live by sharping and robbing; he is generally poor, and often very lousy. The turkey is a much more respectable bird, and withal a true original native of America."

GRANT, JULIA DENT: BIRTH ANNIVERSARY. Jan 26, 1826. Wife of Ulysses Simpson Grant, 18th president of the US. Born at St. Louis, MO, she died at Washington, DC, Dec 14, 1902.

INDIA: REPUBLIC DAY. Jan 26. National holiday. Anniversary of Proclamation of the Republic, Basant Panchmi. In 1929, Indian National Congress resolved to work for establishment of a sovereign republic, a goal that was realized Jan 26, 1950, when India became a democratic republic.

INDIAN EARTHQUAKE: 5th ANNIVERSARY. Jan 26, 2001. An earthquake that struck the state of Gujarat in India left more than 25,000 dead. The quake was estimated to be 7.7 on the Richter scale. India's largest port at Kandla suffered severe damage.

MICHIGAN: ADMISSION DAY: ANNIVERSARY. Jan 26. Michigan became 26th state in 1837.

ROCKY MOUNTAIN NATIONAL PARK ESTABLISHED: ANNIVERSARY. Jan 26, 1915. Under President Woodrow Wilson, the area covering more than 1,000 square miles in Colorado became a national park. For more info: www.nps.gov/romo/index.htm.

BIRTHDAYS TODAY

Vince Carter, 29, basketball player, born Daytona Beach, FL, Jan 26, 1977.

Mark Dayton, 59, US Senator (D, Minnesota), born Minneapolis, MN, Jan 26, 1947.

Jules Feiffer, 77, author (*The Man in the Ceiling; Bark, George*), illustrator (*The Phantom Tollbooth*), born the Bronx, NY, Jan 26, 1929.

Wayne Gretzky, 45, Hall of Fame hockey player, born Brantford, ON, Canada, Jan 26, 1961.

JANUARY 27 — FRIDAY

Day 27 — 338 Remaining

APOLLO I **: SPACECRAFT FIRE: ANNIVERSARY.** Jan 27, 1967. Three American astronauts, Virgil I. Grissom, Edward H. White and Roger B. Chaffee, died when fire suddenly broke out at 6:31 PM in *Apollo I* during a launching simulation test, as it stood on the ground at Cape Kennedy, FL, Jan 27, 1967. First launching in the Apollo program had been scheduled for Feb 27, 1967.

AUSCHWITZ LIBERATED BY SOVIETS: ANNIVERSARY. Jan 27, 1945. The Soviet army liberated about 6,000 prisoners of the Nazi concentration camp Auschwitz. It is estimated that 1.5 million inmates were killed at Auschwitz between 1941 and liberation—95 percent of those were Jewish.

CARROLL, LEWIS: BIRTH ANNIVERSARY. Jan 27, 1832. Pseudonym of English mathematician and author, born Charles Lutwidge Dodgson, at Cheshire, England. Best known for his children's classic, *Alice's Adventures in Wonderland. Alice* was written for Alice Liddell, daughter of a friend, and first published in 1886. *Through the Looking-Glass*, a sequel, and *The Hunting of the Snark* followed. Carroll's books for children proved equally enjoyable to adults, and they overshadowed his serious works on mathematics. He died at Guildford, Surrey, England, Jan 14, 1898. For more info: www.lewiscarroll.org/k12.html.

GERMANY: DAY OF REMEMBRANCE FOR VICTIMS OF NAZISM. Jan 27. Since 1996, commemorated on this day, the date in 1945 that Soviet soldiers liberated the Auschwitz concentration camp.

MOZART, WOLFGANG AMADEUS: 250th BIRTH ANNIVERSARY. Jan 27, 1756. One of the world's greatest composers. Born at Salzburg, Austria, into a gifted musical family, Mozart began performing at age three and composing at age five. Some of the best known of his more than 600 compositions include the operas *Marriage of Figaro, Don Giovanni, Cosi fan tutte* and *The Magic Flute*, his unfinished Requiem Mass, his C Major Symphony known as the *Jupiter* and many quartets and piano concertos. He died at Vienna, Dec 5, 1791.

January 2006

S	M	T	W	T	F	S
1	2	3	4	5	6	7
8	9	10	11	12	13	14
15	16	17	18	19	20	21
22	23	24	25	26	27	28
29	30	31				

UNITED KINGDOM: HOLOCAUST MEMORIAL DAY. Jan 27. Commemorated since 2001 on the day in 1945 that the Auschwitz concentration camp was liberated. For more info: www.holocaustmemorialday.gov.uk.

VIETNAM PEACE AGREEMENT SIGNED: ANNIVERSARY. Jan 27, 1973. US and North Vietnam, along with South Vietnam and the Viet Cong, signed an "Agreement on ending the war and restoring peace in Vietnam." Signed at Paris, France, to take effect Jan 28 at 8 AM Saigon time, thus ending US combat role in a war that had involved American personnel stationed in Vietnam since defeated French forces had departed under terms of the Geneva Accords in 1954. This was the longest war in US history with more than one million combat deaths (US deaths: 47,366). However, within weeks of the departure of American troops the war between North and South Vietnam resumed. For the Vietnamese, the war didn't end until Apr 30, 1975, when Saigon fell to Communist forces.

BIRTHDAYS TODAY

Harry Allard, 78, author, with James Marshall (*Miss Nelson Is Missing!*), born Evanston, IL, Jan 27, 1928.

James M. Deem, 56, author (*Bodies from the Bog*), born Wheeling, WV, Jan 27, 1950.

Julie Foudy, 35, retired soccer player, born San Diego, CA, Jan 27, 1971.

Laura McGee Kvasnosky, 55, author (*Zelda and Ivy*), born Sacramento, CA, Jan 27, 1951.

Julius B. Lester, 67, author (*To Be a Slave, Black Folktales*), born St. Louis, MO, Jan 27, 1939.

Fred Taylor, 30, football player, born Pahokee, FL, Jan 27, 1976.

Janice VanCleave, 64, author (*Guide to the Best Science Fair Projects; 200 Gooey, Slippery, Slimy, Weird and Fun Experiments; Biology for Every Kid*), born Houston, TX, Jan 27, 1942.

JANUARY 28 — SATURDAY

Day 28 — 337 Remaining

CHALLENGER **SPACE SHUTTLE EXPLOSION: 20th ANNIVERSARY.** Jan 28, 1986. At 11:39 AM, EST, the space shuttle *Challenger STS-51L* exploded, 74 seconds into its flight and about 10 miles above the earth. Hundreds of millions around the world watched television replays of the horrifying event that killed seven people, destroyed the billion-dollar craft, suspended all shuttle flights and halted, at least temporarily, much of the US manned space flight program. Killed were teacher Christa McAuliffe (who was to have been the first ordinary citizen in space) and six crew members: Francis R. Scobee, Michael J. Smith, Judith A. Resnik, Ellison S. Onizuka, Ronald E. McNair and Gregory B. Jarvis. For more info: *Space Disasters*, by Elaine Landau (Watts, 0-5311-6431-4, $8.95 Gr. 4–7).

MacKENZIE, ALEXANDER: BIRTH ANNIVERSARY. Jan 28, 1822. The man who became the first Liberal prime minister of Canada (1873–78) was born at Logierait, Perth, Scotland. He died at Toronto, Apr 17, 1892.

MARTÍ, JOSÉ JULIAN: BIRTH ANNIVERSARY. Jan 28, 1853. Cuban patriot and author, born at Havana, Cuba. Martí was exiled to Spain several times for his political beliefs, and there he studied law before coming to the US in the 1880s. In New York, he helped organize the Cuban Revolutionary Party, which planned an 1895 invasion to secure Cuban independence from Spain. Marti was killed in battle at Dos Rios, Cuba, May 19, 1895.

PICCARD, AUGUSTE: BIRTH ANNIVERSARY. Jan 28, 1884. Scientist and explorer, born at Basel, Switzerland. Record-setting balloon ascents into stratosphere and ocean depth descents and explorations. Twin brother of Jean Felix Piccard. Died at Lausanne, Switzerland, Mar 24, 1962. See also: "Piccard, Jeannette Ridlon: Birth Anniversary" (Jan 5) and "Piccard, Jean Felix: Birth Anniversary" (Jan 28).

PICCARD, JEAN FELIX: BIRTH ANNIVERSARY. Jan 28, 1884. Scientist, engineer, explorer, born at Basel, Switzerland. Noted for cosmic-ray research and record-setting balloon ascensions into stratosphere. Reached 57,579 ft in sealed gondola piloted by his wife, Jeannette, in 1934. Twin brother of Auguste Piccard. Died at Minneapolis, MN, Jan 28, 1963. See also: "Piccard, Jeannette Ridlon: Birth Anniversary" (Jan 5) and "Piccard, Auguste: Birth Anniversary" (Jan 28).

BIRTHDAYS TODAY

Nick Carter, 26, singer (Backstreet Boys), born Jamestown, NY, Jan 28, 1980.
Daunte Culpepper, 29, football player, born Ocala, FL, Jan 28, 1977.
Joey Fatone, 29, singer ('N Sync), born Brooklyn, NY, Jan 28, 1977.
Vera B. Williams, 79, author and illustrator (*A Chair for My Mother*), born Hollywood, CA, Jan 28, 1927.
Elijah Wood, 25, actor (*Flipper, The Lord of the Rings*), born Cedar Rapids, IA, Jan 28, 1981.

JANUARY 29 — SUNDAY

Day 29 — 336 Remaining

CATHOLIC SCHOOLS WEEK. Jan 29–Feb 4. Jointly sponsored by the National Catholic Educational Association and the US Catholic Conference. Annually, beginning on the last Sunday in January. For info: National Catholic Educational Assn, 1077 30th St NW, Ste 100, Washington, DC 20007-3852. Phone: (202) 337-6232. E-mail: nceaadmin@ncea.org. Web: www.ncea.org.

CHINESE NEW YEAR. Jan 29. Traditional Chinese lunar year begins at sunset on the day of second New Moon following the winter solstice. Outside China, the date of the New Year may differ by a day. The New Year can begin any time from Jan 21 through Feb 21. Begins the Year of the Dog. Generally celebrated until the Lantern Festival 15 days later, but merchants usually reopen their stores and places of business on the fifth day of the first lunar month (Feb 2). This holiday is celebrated as Tet in Vietnam. See also: "China: Lantern Festival" (Feb 12). For more info: *Celebrating Chinese New Year,* by Diane Hoyt-Goldsmith (Holiday House, 0-8234-1393-4, $16.95 Gr. 3–5) or *Chinese New Year,* by Sarah Moyse (Millbrook, 0-7613-0374-X, $20.90 Gr. K–3).

KANSAS: ADMISSION DAY: ANNIVERSARY. Jan 29. Became the 34th state in 1861.

McKINLEY, WILLIAM: BIRTH ANNIVERSARY. Jan 29, 1843. The 25th president (Mar 4, 1897–Sept 14, 1901) of the US, born at Niles, OH. Died in office, at Buffalo, NY, Sept 14, 1901, as the result of a gunshot wound by an anarchist assassin Sept 6, 1901, while he was attending the Pan-American Exposition. For more info: www.ipl.org/ref/POTUS.

MOON PHASE: NEW MOON. Jan 29. Moon enters New Moon phase at 9:15 AM, EST.

PERIGEAN SPRING TIDES. Jan 29. Spring tides, the highest possible tides, occur when New Moon or Full Moon takes place within 24 hours of the moment the Moon is nearest Earth (perigee) in its monthly orbit. The word *spring* refers not to the season but comes from the German word *springen*, "to rise up."

"THE RAVEN" PUBLISHED: ANNIVERSARY. Jan 29, 1845. One of the most famous poems in American literature—containing the classic lines: "Once upon a midnight dreary . . ." and "Quoth the Raven, 'Nevermore'"—was published on this date in New York's *Evening Mirror* newspaper. The author was anonymous, but the poem was such a sensation that soon the author was revealed as literary critic and author Edgar Allan Poe. Despite the celebrity status Poe enjoyed as a result of "The Raven," it did not relieve his poverty: Poe received $15 for the poem.

THE SEEING EYE CREATED IN AMERICA: ANNIVERSARY. Jan 29, 1929. Dorothy Eustis incorporated The Seeing Eye on this date. The Nashville, TN, school was the first in America to train dogs to aid the seeing impaired. Classes began in February of that year and included Buddy, the first dog trained to aid the blind.

BIRTHDAYS TODAY

Christopher Collier, 76, author of historical fiction, with his brother James Lincoln Collier (*My Brother Sam Is Dead*), born New York, NY, Jan 29, 1930.
Dominik Hasek, 41, hockey player, born Pardubice, Czechoslovakia, Jan 29, 1965.
Andrew Keegan, 27, actor ("Party of Five"), born Shadow Hills, CA, Jan 29, 1979.
Ronald Stacey King, 39, former basketball player, born Lawton, OK, Jan 29, 1967.
Jason James Richter, 26, actor (*Free Willy*), born Medford, OR, Jan 29, 1980.
Rosemary Wells, 63, author and illustrator (*Noisy Nora, Benjamin and Tulip*, the Max and Ruby series), born New York, NY, Jan 29, 1943.
Oprah Winfrey, 52, TV talk show hostess (Emmys for "The Oprah Winfrey Show"), actress (*Beloved*), born Kosciusko, MS, Jan 29, 1954.

JANUARY 30 — MONDAY

Day 30 — 335 Remaining

GANDHI, MOHANDAS: ASSASSINATION ANNIVERSARY. Jan 30, 1948. The Indian leader who advocated nonviolent resistance against tyranny was assassinated in his garden at New Delhi on this date. See also: "Gandhi, Mohandas Karamchand (Mahatma): Birth Anniversary" (Oct 2).

JORDAN: KING'S BIRTHDAY. Jan 30. National holiday. Commemorates the birth of King Abdullah II in 1962.

NATIONAL INANE ANSWERING MESSAGE DAY. Jan 30. Annually, the day set aside to change, shorten, replace or delete those ridiculous and/or annoying answering machine messages that waste the time of anyone who must listen to them. [©2002 by WH.] For info: Thomas & Ruth Roy, Wellcat Holidays, 2418 Long Ln, Lebanon, PA 17046. Phone: (717) 279-0184. E-mail: info@wellcat.com. Web: www.wellcat.com.

OSCEOLA: DEATH ANNIVERSARY. Jan 30, 1838. Native American leader during the Second Seminole War (1835–42), he led the fight against the removal of the Florida Seminoles to Indian territory. He was captured under a flag of truce in 1837 and imprisoned at Fort Marion in St. Augustine. He was moved to Fort Moultrie at Charleston Harbor, SC, where he died. He was born near present-day Tuskegee, AL, ca. 1804.

ROOSEVELT, FRANKLIN DELANO: BIRTH ANNIVERSARY. Jan 30, 1882. The 32nd president of the US, Roosevelt was the only president to serve more than two terms—FDR was elected four times. Term of office: Mar 4, 1933–Apr 12, 1945. He supported the Allies in WWII before the US entered the struggle by supplying them with war materials through the Lend-Lease Act; he became deeply involved in broad decision making after the Japanese attack on Pearl Harbor Dec 7, 1941. Born at Hyde Park, NY, he died a few months into his fourth term at Warm Springs, GA, Apr 12, 1945. For more info: www.ipl.org/ref/POTUS.

BIRTHDAYS TODAY

Lloyd Alexander, 82, author (*The Black Cauldron*, Newbery for *The High King*), born Philadelphia, PA, Jan 30, 1924.

John Baldacci, 51, Governor of Maine (D), born Bangor, ME, Jan 30, 1955.

Richard (Dick) Cheney, 65, 46th vice president of the US, born Lincoln, NE, Jan 30, 1941.

Allan W. Eckert, 75, author (*Incident at Hawk's Hill*), born Buffalo, NY, Jan 30, 1931.

Guy Gilchrist, 49, author, illustrator, cartoonist (*Mudpie, Tiny Dinos*), with his brother Brad Gilchrist, born Winsted, CT, Jan 30, 1957.

Polly Horvath, 49, author (*The Trolls*), born Kalamazoo, MI, Jan 30, 1957.

Tony Johnston, 64, author (*The Magic Maguey*), born Los Angeles, CA, Jan 30, 1942.

Jalen Rose, 33, basketball player, born Detroit, MI, Jan 30, 1973.

Adam Luke Springfield, 23, actor ("Wishbone"), born Baltimore, MD, Jan 30, 1983.

JANUARY 31 — TUESDAY

Day 31 — 334 Remaining

ISLAMIC NEW YEAR. Jan 31. Islamic calendar date: Muharram 1, 1427. The first day of the first month of the Islamic calendar. Different methods for "anticipating" the visibility of the new moon crescent at Mecca are used by different groups. US date may vary. Began at sunset the preceding day.

McDONALD'S OPENS FIRST RESTAURANT IN THE SOVIET UNION: ANNIVERSARY. Jan 31, 1990. McDonald's Corporation opened its first fast-food restaurant in the Soviet Union.

MORRIS, ROBERT: BIRTH ANNIVERSARY. Jan 31, 1734. Signer of the Declaration of Independence, the Articles of Confederation and the Constitution. One of only two men to sign all three documents. Born at Liverpool, England, he died May 7, 1806, at Philadelphia, PA.

NAURU: NATIONAL HOLIDAY. Jan 31. Republic of Nauru. Commemorates independence in 1968 from a UN trusteeship administered by Australia, New Zealand and the UK.

ROBINSON, JACKIE: BIRTH ANNIVERSARY. Jan 31, 1919. Jack Roosevelt Robinson, athlete and business executive, first black to enter professional major league baseball (Brooklyn Dodgers, 1947–56). Voted National League's Most Valuable Player in 1949 and elected to the Baseball Hall of Fame in 1962. Born at Cairo, GA, Robinson died at Stamford, CT, Oct 24, 1972. For more info: *Jackie Robinson: Overcoming Adversity*, by Gina DeAngelis (Chelsea House, 0-7910-5897-2, $19.95 Gr. 5–8).

SCOTLAND: UP HELLY AA. Jan 31. Lerwick, Shetland Islands. Norse galley burned in impressive ceremony symbolizing sacrifice to the sun. Old Viking custom. Annually, the last Tuesday in January. Tourist Information Centre, Market Cross, Lerwick, Shetland, Scotland ZE1 0LU. Phone: (44) (595) 693-434. Fax: (44) (595) 695-807. Web: www.visitshetland.com.

SPACE MILESTONE: *EXPLORER 1* (US). Jan 31, 1958. The first successful US satellite. Although launched four months later than the Soviet Union's *Sputnik, Explorer* reached a higher altitude and detected a zone of intense radiation inside Earth's magnetic field. This was later named the Van Allen radiation belts. More than 65 subsequent *Explorer* satellites were launched through 1984.

SPACE MILESTONE: PROJECT MERCURY TEST (US): 45th ANNIVERSARY. Jan 31, 1961. A test of Project Mercury spacecraft accomplished the first US recovery of a large animal from space. Ham, the chimpanzee, successfully performed simple tasks in space.

BIRTHDAYS TODAY

Queen Beatrix, 68, Queen of the Netherlands, born Sostdijk, Netherlands, Jan 31, 1938.

Denise Fleming, 56, author (*In the Small, Small Pond*), born Toledo, OH, Jan 31, 1950.

Gerald McDermott, 65, illustrator and author (Caldecott for *Arrow to the Sun*), born Detroit, MI, Jan 31, 1941.

Nolan Ryan, 59, Hall of Fame baseball player, born Lynn Nolan Ryan, Refugio, TX, Jan 31, 1947.

Justin Timberlake, 25, singer ('N Sync), born Memphis, TN, Jan 31, 1981.

FEBRUARY 1 — WEDNESDAY

Day 32 — 333 Remaining

★ **AMERICAN HEART MONTH.** Feb 1–28. Presidential Proclamation issued each year for February since 1964. (Public Law 88–254 of Dec 30, 1963.)

AMERICAN HEART MONTH. Feb 1–28. Volunteers across the country spend one to four weeks canvassing neighborhoods and providing educational information about heart disease and stroke. For info: American Heart Assn, 7272 Greenville Ave, Dallas, TX 75231. Phone: (888) MY-HEART. Fax: (214) 369-3685. Web: www.americanheart.org.

BLACK MARIA STUDIO: ANNIVERSARY. Feb 1, 1893. The first moving picture studio was completed, built on Thomas Edison's laboratory compound at West Orange, NJ, at a cost of less than $700. The wooden structure of irregular oblong shape was covered with black tar paper. It had a sharply sloping roof hinged at one edge so that half of it could be raised to admit sunlight. Fifty feet in length, it was mounted on a pivot enabling it to be swung around to follow the changing position of the sun. There was a stage draped in black at one end of the single room. Though the structure was officially called a Kinetographic Theater, it was nicknamed the "Black Maria" because it resembled an old-fashioned police wagon. It was described as "hot and cramped" by "Gentleman" Jim Corbett, the pugilistic idol who was the subject of an early movie made in the studio.

CAR INSURANCE FIRST ISSUED: ANNIVERSARY. Feb 1, 1898. Travelers Insurance Company issued the first car insurance against accidents with horses.

***COLUMBIA* SPACE SHUTTLE DISASTER: ANNIVERSARY.** Feb 1, 2003. Minutes before space shuttle *Columbia* was due to land after a successful 16-day scientific mission, it disintegrated 40 miles above the state of Texas, killing its seven-member crew. Commander Rick Husband, pilot William McCool, Michael Anderson, David Brown, Kalpana Chawla (first woman astronaut from India), Laurel Clark and Ilan Ramon (first Israeli astronaut) lost their lives and were mourned worldwide. *Columbia* was the first shuttle to fly in space (1981).

EASY-BAKE® OVEN DEBUTS: ANNIVERSARY. Feb 1, 1964. This toy was officially introduced this month at the American Toy Fair. Later Easy-Bake brand snack mixes to be used with the ovens were introduced. More than 16 million ovens and more than 100 million mix sets have been sold.

FIRST SESSION OF THE SUPREME COURT: ANNIVERSARY. Feb 1, 1790. The Supreme Court of the United States met for the first time at New York City with Chief Justice John Jay presiding.

FREEDOM DAY: ANNIVERSARY. Feb 1. Anniversary of President Abraham Lincoln's approval, Feb 1, 1865, of the 13th Amendment to the US Constitution (abolishing slavery): "1. Neither slavery nor involuntary servitude, except as a punishment for crime whereof the party shall have been duly convicted, shall exist within the United States or any place subject to their jurisdiction. 2. Congress shall have power to enforce this article by appropriate legislation." The amendment had been proposed by the Congress Jan 31, 1865; ratification was completed Dec 18, 1865.

G.I. JOE INTRODUCED: ANNIVERSARY. Feb 1, 1964. This toy action figure was introduced by Hasbro and sold for $2.49. It was the first mass-market doll intended for boys and was a great success.

GREENSBORO SIT-IN: ANNIVERSARY. Feb 1, 1960. Commercial discrimination against blacks and other minorities provoked a nonviolent protest. At Greensboro, NC, four students from the Agricultural and Technical College at Greensboro (Ezell Blair, Jr, Franklin McCain, Joseph McNeill and David Richmond) sat down at a Woolworths store lunch counter and ordered coffee. Refused service, they remained all day. The following days similar sit-ins took place at the Woolworths lunch counter. Before the week was over they were joined by a few white students. The protest spread rapidly, especially in southern states. More than 1,600 persons were arrested before the year was over for participating in sit-ins. Civil rights for all became a cause for thousands of students and activists. In response, equal accommodation regardless of race became the rule at lunch counters, hotels and business establishments in thousands of places.

HUGHES, LANGSTON: BIRTH ANNIVERSARY. Feb 1, 1902. African-American poet and author, born at Joplin, MO. Among his works are the poetry collection *Montage of a Dream Deferred*, plays, a novel, memoirs and short stories. Hughes died May 22, 1967, at New York, NY. For more info: *Langston Hughes: American Poet*, by Alice Walker (HarperCollins, rev. ed., 0-06-021518-6, $16.95 Gr. 2–6) or *Visiting Langston*, by Willie Perdomo (Henry Holt, 0-8050-6744-2, $15.95 Gr. K–3). ***See Curriculum Connection.***

LIBRARY LOVERS' MONTH. Feb 1–28. A monthlong celebration of school, public and private libraries of all types. This is a time for everyone, especially library support groups, to recognize the value of libraries and to work to ensure that the nation's libraries will continue to serve. For info: Stephanie Stokes, Friends and Foundations of California Libraries, 11045 Wrightwood Pl, Studio City, CA 91604-3961. Phone: (818) 980-7476. E-mail: librarylovers@librarysupport.net. Web: www.librarysupport.net/librarylovers.

★ **NATIONAL AFRICAN AMERICAN HISTORY MONTH.** Feb 1–28.

NATIONAL BIRD FEEDING MONTH. Feb 1–28. To recognize that February is one of the most difficult winter months in much of the US for birds to survive in the wild and to encourage people to provide food, water and shelter to supplement the wild birds' natural diet of weed seeds and harmful insects. For info: National Bird Feeding Month, 7370 MacArthur Blvd, Glen Echo, MD 20812. Web: www.birdfeeding.org.

NATIONAL BLACK HISTORY MONTH. Feb 1–28. Traditionally the month containing Abraham Lincoln's birthday (Feb 12) and Frederick Douglass's presumed birthday (Feb 14). Observance of a special period to recognize achievements and contributions by African Americans dates from February 1926, when it was

FEBRUARY 1
NATIONAL BLACK HISTORY MONTH: LANGSTON HUGHES

Carter G. Woodson's proposed celebration of the contributions made by African Americans originally began as Negro History Week in 1926, and was renamed Black History Week in the 1970s. Since 1976, February has been designated as National Black History Month. While many African Americans have enriched American culture, the words of poet Langston Hughes, particularly, speak to the hearts of millions of people. James Langston Hughes, called the "Poet Laureate of the Negro Race," was born Feb 1, 1902, at Joplin, MO. It seems fitting that his birth date should begin National Black History Month.

Hughes, raised by his mother and later his grandmother, wrote one of his most famous poems, "The Negro Speaks of Rivers," at the age of 18, after visiting his long-absent father in Mexico. Robert Burleigh's picture book *Langston's Train Ride* (Scholastic, 0-439-35239-8, $16.95 Ages 7 & up) focuses on the moment when a poet first gives voice to his/her words, and he includes Hughes' poem "The Negro Speaks of Rivers." For this reason, it's great to use this book with junior high and older students. Ask them to think and write about moments in their own lives that sparked a creative response and if it changed them in any way.

In her book, *My Soul Looks Back, 'Less I Forget: A Collection of Quotations by People of Color* (HarperCollins), Dorothy Winbush Riley quotes Langston Hughes as follows, "There are many barriers people try to break down. I try to do it with poetry." This quotation is a marvelous springboard for a writing activity for middle school and older students. First, ask students what kinds of barriers they have experienced in their lives. Remember, barriers may be physical, mental, social and emotional. Next, ask students what strategies they use to combat their barriers. (Perhaps a school guidance counselor would be willing to present some ideas.) Encourage students to write a poem—in whatever poetry form they are comfortable with—that calls the reader's attention to one of the barriers that the student seeks to overcome.

Two poems well suited for discussion in junior high and high school classes are "Let America Be American Again" and "A Dream Deferred." The first is an extremely thought-provoking poem about America and the themes of freedom and equality. The second is a short poem, filled with images, asking what happens to unfulfilled dreams and aspirations. This poem is especially suited to high school students, as they look toward their future.

Hughes wrote a series of short sketches about a man named Simple. A witty and intelligent, yet uneducated, black man, Simple expressed his opinions about current social issues in language that was understandable to the common man. High school students can read selections from *The Best of Simple* (Hill and Wang, 0-374-52133-6, $13 Adult), a collection of Hughes' favorite Simple essays. The topics, which include social injustice, are still relevant. Creative writers might be encouraged to try their hand at penning a modern-day equivalent of Simple. What issues would he/she tackle? And what might his/her commonsense offerings about them be?

While he also wrote prose and plays, Hughes is best known for his poetry. Langston Hughes died May 22, 1967.

There are many books for young readers that contain information about Langston Hughes. Picture book readers will enjoy *Visiting Langston* by Willie Perdomo, illustrated by Bryan Collier (Holt, 0-8050-6744-2, $15.95 Gr. K & up). Biographies for young readers include *Langston Hughes* by Milton Meltzer (Millbrook Press, 0-7613-0327-8, $20.95 Gr. 3 & up), *Langston Hughes*, by Philip S. Bryant (Raintree, 1-4109-0037-1, $8.95 Gr. 3 & up), *Langston Hughes: Great American Poet* by Patricia and Fredrick McKissack (Enslow Publishers, 0-89490-315-2, $14.95 Gr. K–3). Junior high and high school readers can be introduced to adult books, collections of Hughes' poems and recordings of Hughes reading his work. Several excellent sources are *The Big Sea: An Autobiography* by Langston Hughes, introduction by Arnold Rampersad (Hill and Wang, 0-809-01549-8, $15); *The Collected Poems of Langston Hughes*, edited by Arnold Rampersad (Knopf, 0-679-42631-0) and *Langston Hughes Reads* (sound recording, Caedmon Audio, 0694522732, # CF 1640).

I, Too, Sing America: Three Centuries of African American Poetry, by Catherine Clinton (Houghton Mifflin, 0-395-89599-5, $21 All ages), is a collection of poems by prominent African-American poets.

—Sally Walker

launched by Dr. Carter G. Woodson and others. Variously designated Negro History, Black History, Afro-American History, African-American History, Black Heritage and Black Expressions, the observance period was initially one week but since 1976 has been the entire month of February. Visit the website of the Association for the Study of African-American Life and History for the current year's theme and information on a theme-related kit you can purchase. *Black History Month Resource Book* (2nd ed, Gale, 0-7876-1755-X, $47) includes both programmatic ideas and lists of resources in all media for all ages. ***See Curriculum Connection.*** For info: Assn for the Study of African-American Life and History, Howard University, C.B. Powell Building, 525 Bryant St, Ste C142, Washington, DC 20059. Phone: (202) 865-0053. E-mail: asalh@earthlink.net. Web: www.asalh.org.

NATIONAL CHERRY MONTH. Feb 1–28. To publicize the colorful red tart cherry. Recipes, posters and table tents available. For info: Cherry Marketing Institute, PO Box 30285, Lansing, MI 48909-7785. E-mail: info@cherrymkt.org. Web: www.usacherries.com.

February 2006

S	M	T	W	T	F	S
			1	2	3	4
5	6	7	8	9	10	11
12	13	14	15	16	17	18
19	20	21	22	23	24	25
26	27	28				

NATIONAL CHILDREN'S DENTAL HEALTH MONTH. Feb 1–28. To increase dental awareness and stress the importance of regular dental care. For info: American Dental Assn, 211 E Chicago Ave, Chicago, IL 60611. Web: www.ada.org.

NATIONAL EDUCATION GOALS: ANNIVERSARY. Feb 1, 1990. In September 1989, President George H.W. Bush and 50 governors met at a historic Education Summit to draft goals for American K–12 schools for the year 2000. In February 1990, the National Education Goals were announced by the president and adopted by the governors. In July 1990, the National Education Goals Panel was formed to assess and report state and national progress toward the goals. For more info: www.negp.gov.

NATIONAL HOT BREAKFAST MONTH. Feb 1–28. Take time out this month to start your day with a good hot breakfast. Sponsored by Jimmy Dean Foods. For info: Travis Green, Sara Lee Foods, 10151 Carver Rd, Cincinnati, OH 45242-4719. Phone: (513) 936-2665. E-mail: travis.green@saralee.com. Web: www.jimmydean.com.

NATIONAL SIGN UP FOR SUMMER CAMP MONTH. Feb 1–28. Every year more than ten million children continue a national tradition by attending day or resident camps. Building self-confidence, learning new skills and making memories that last a lifetime are just a few examples of what makes camp special and why camp does children a world of good. To find the right program, parents begin looking at summer camps during this month—and sign their children up while there are still vacancies. For info: Public Relations, American Camping Assn, 5000 State Rd 67N, Martinsville, IN 46151. Phone: (765) 342-8456. E-mail: pr@aca-camps.org. Web: www.ACAcamps.org.

NORTH CAROLINA SWEETPOTATO MONTH. Feb 1–28. To educate the public about the nutritional benefits and versatility of sweet potatoes. North Carolina farmers want America to know that sweet potatoes aren't just for turkeys anymore. Available year-round, sweet potatoes are loaded with beta carotene and vitamin C. They can be boiled, baked, microwaved, grilled, broiled, fried, mashed, sauteed, candied or served raw. North Carolina produces more sweet potatoes than any other state. For info: Sue Johnson-Langdon, North Carolina SweetPotato Commission, 1327 N Brightleaf Blvd, Ste H, Smithfield, NC 27577. Phone: (919) 989-7323. Fax: (919) 989-3015. E-mail: ncsweetsue@aol.com. Web: www.ncsweetpotatoes.com.

RETURN SHOPPING CARTS TO THE SUPERMARKET MONTH. Feb 1–28. A monthlong opportunity to return stolen shopping carts, milk crates, bread trays and ice cream baskets to supermarkets and to avoid the increased food prices that these thefts cause. Annually, the month of February. Sponsor: Illinois Food Retailers Association. For info: Anthony A. Dinolfo, Grocer-"Retired," 163 Fairfield Dr, New Lenox, IL 60451-3523. Phone: (815) 463-9136.

ROBINSON CRUSOE DAY. Feb 1. Anniversary of the rescue, Feb 1, 1709, of Alexander Selkirk, Scottish sailor who had been put ashore (in September 1704) on the uninhabited island, Juan Fernandez, at his own request after a quarrel with his captain. His adventures formed the basis for Daniel Defoe's book *Robinson Crusoe*. A day to be adventurous and self-reliant.

ST. LAURENT, LOUIS STEPHEN: BIRTH ANNIVERSARY. Feb 1, 1882. Canadian lawyer and prime minister, born at Compton, Quebec. Died at Quebec City, July 25, 1973.

BIRTHDAYS TODAY

Michael B. Enzi, 62, US Senator (R, Wyoming), born Bremerton, WA, Feb 1, 1944.

Jerry Spinelli, 65, author (*Wringer*, Newbery for *Maniac Magee*), born Norristown, PA, Feb 1, 1941.

Boris Yeltsin, 75, former Russian president, born Sverdlovsk, Russia, Feb 1, 1931.

FEBRUARY 2 — THURSDAY

Day 33 — 332 Remaining

BASEBALL HALL OF FAME CHARTER MEMBERS ELECTED: 70th ANNIVERSARY. Feb 2, 1936. The five charter members of the brand-new Baseball Hall of Fame at Cooperstown, NY, were announced. Of 226 ballots cast, Ty Cobb was named on 222, Babe Ruth on 215, Honus Wagner on 215, Christy Mathewson on 205 and Walter Johnson on 189. A total of 170 votes were necessary to be elected to the Hall of Fame.

BONZA BOTTLER DAY™. Feb 2. To celebrate when the number of the day is the same as the number of the month. Bonza Bottler Day™ is an excuse to have a party at least once a month. For info: Gail M. Berger, 14 Fernwood Dr, Taylors, SC 29687. Phone: (864) 609-9874. E-mail: gberger5@aol.com.

CANDLEMAS DAY or PRESENTATION OF THE LORD. Feb 2. Observed in Roman Catholic and Eastern Orthodox churches. Commemorates presentation of Jesus in the temple and the purification of Mary 40 days after his birth. Candles have been blessed since the 11th century. Formerly called the Feast of Purification of the Blessed Virgin Mary. Old Scottish couplet proclaims: "If Candlemas is fair and clear/There'll be two winters in the year."

GROUNDHOG DAY. Feb 2. Old belief that if the sun shines on Candlemas Day, or if the groundhog sees his shadow when he emerges on this day, six weeks of winter will ensue.

GROUNDHOG DAY IN PUNXSUTAWNEY, PENNSYLVANIA. Feb 2. Widely observed traditional annual Candlemas Day event at which "Punxsutawney Phil, king of the weather prophets," is the object of a search. Tradition is said to have been established by early German settlers. The official trek (which began in 1887) is followed by a weather prediction for the next six weeks. Phil made his dramatic film debut with Bill Murray in *Groundhog Day*.

MEXICO: DIA DE LA CANDELARIA. Feb 2. All Mexico celebrates Candlemas Day with dances, processions and bullfights.

***THE RECORD OF A SNEEZE*: ANNIVERSARY.** Feb 2, 1893. One day after Thomas Edison's "Black Maria" studio was completed at West Orange, NJ, a studio cameraman took the first "close-up" in film history. *The Record of a Sneeze*, starring Edison's assistant Fred P. Ott, was also the first motion picture to receive a copyright (1894). See also: "Black Maria Studio: Anniversary" (Feb 1).

SLED DOGS SAVE NOME: ANNIVERSARY. Feb 2, 1925. When a diphtheria outbreak was diagnosed in Nome, AK (population 1,500), on Jan 21, the nearest large amount of antitoxin serum was in Anchorage. Bitter winter temperatures made air delivery impossible, so a heroic dog sled relay was set up. 300,000 units of serum were delivered by train to Nenana, AK, and on Jan 27—in temperatures of 40–50° below zero—20 mushers drove scores of dogs on a 674-mile journey to Nome in 127 hours. Togo was the lead dog for the first 350 miles, and Balto was the lead dog on the final 53 miles. The frozen serum arrived at 5:30 AM, and once thawed and administered, there were no more diphtheria deaths. Balto became a national hero, and a statue was erected in his honor in New York City's Central Park. See also: "Togo: Sled Dog Hero: Death Anniversary" (Dec 5) and "Balto: Sled Dog Hero: Death Anniversary" (Mar 14). For more info: *The Great Serum Race: Blazing the Iditarod Trail* by Debbie S. Miller (Walker & Co., 0-8027-8811-4, $17.95 Gr. 3–6).

TREATY OF GUADALUPE HIDALGO: ANNIVERSARY. Feb 2, 1848. The war between Mexico and the US formally ended with the signing of the Treaty of Guadalupe Hidalgo, signed in the village for which it was named. The treaty provided for Mexico's cession to the US of the territory that became the states of California, Nevada, Utah, most of Arizona and parts of New Mexico, Colorado and Wyoming, in exchange for $15 million from the US. In addition, Mexico relinquished all rights to Texas north of the Rio Grande. The Senate ratified the treaty Mar 10, 1848.

WALTON, GEORGE: DEATH ANNIVERSARY. Feb 2, 1804. Signer of the Declaration of Independence. Born at Prince Edward County, VA, 1749 (exact date unknown). Died at Augusta, GA.

BIRTHDAYS TODAY

John Cornyn, 54, US Senator (R, Texas), born Houston, TX, Feb 2, 1952.

Judith Viorst, 75, author (*The Tenth Good Thing About Barney; Alexander and the Terrible, Horrible, No Good, Very Bad Day*), born Newark, NJ, Feb 2, 1931.

FEBRUARY 3 — FRIDAY

Day 34 — 331 Remaining

FIFTEENTH AMENDMENT TO US CONSTITUTION RATIFIED: ANNIVERSARY. Feb 3, 1870. The 15th Amendment granted that the right of citizens to vote shall not be denied on account of race, color or previous condition of servitude.

INCOME TAX BIRTHDAY: SIXTEENTH AMENDMENT TO US CONSTITUTION: RATIFICATION ANNIVERSARY. Feb 3, 1913. The 16th Amendment granted Congress the authority to levy taxes on income. (Church bells did not ring throughout the land and no dancing in the streets was reported.)

JAPAN: BEAN-THROWING FESTIVAL (SETSUBUN). Feb 3. Setsubun marks the last day of winter according to the lunar calendar. Throngs at temple grounds throw beans to drive away imaginary devils.

MOZAMBIQUE: HEROES' DAY. Feb 3. National holiday. Commemorates all heroic citizens, especially Eduardo Mondlane, assassinated on this date in 1969.

NORTH AMERICA'S COLDEST RECORDED TEMPERATURE: ANNIVERSARY. Feb 3, 1947. At Snag, in Canada's Yukon Territory, a temperature of 81 degrees below zero (Fahrenheit) was recorded on this date, a record low for all of North America.

SPACE MILESTONE: *CHALLENGER STS-10* (US). Feb 3, 1984. Shuttle *Challenger* launched from Kennedy Space Center, FL, with a crew of five (Vance Brand, Robert Gibson, Ronald McNair, Bruce McCandless and Robert Stewart). On Feb 7 two astronauts became the first to fly freely in space (propelled by their backpack jets), untethered to any craft. Landed at Cape Canaveral, FL, Feb 11.

VIETNAM: ANNIVERSARY OF THE FOUNDING OF THE COMMUNIST PARTY. Feb 3. National holiday. Vietnamese Communist Party founded in 1930.

February 2006

S	M	T	W	T	F	S
			1	2	3	4
5	6	7	8	9	10	11
12	13	14	15	16	17	18
19	20	21	22	23	24	25
26	27	28				

BIRTHDAYS TODAY

Vlade Divac, 38, basketball player, born Prijepolje, Yugoslavia, Feb 3, 1968.

Paul S. Sarbanes, 73, US Senator (D, Maryland), born Salisbury, MD, Feb 3, 1933.

FEBRUARY 4 — SATURDAY

Day 35 — 330 Remaining

ANGOLA: BEGINNING OF THE ARMED STRUGGLE DAY. Feb 4. National holiday. Commemorates the beginning of the war of independence against the Portuguese in 1961.

APACHE WARS BEGAN: ANNIVERSARY. Feb 4, 1861. The period of conflict known as the Apache Wars began at Apache Pass, AZ, when Army Lieutenant George Bascom arrested Apache Chief Cochise for raiding a ranch. Cochise escaped and declared war. The wars lasted 25 years under the leadership of Cochise and, later, Geronimo.

LAURA INGALLS WILDER GINGERBREAD SOCIABLE. Feb 4. Pomona, CA. The 39th annual event commemorates the birthday (Feb 7, 1867) of the renowned author of the Little House books. The library has on permanent display the handwritten manuscript of *Little Town on the Prairie* and other Wilder memorabilia. Entertainment by fiddlers, craft displays, apple cider and gingerbread. Annually, the first Saturday in February. Est attendance: 200. For info: Marguerite F. Raybould, Friends of the Pomona Public Library, 625 S Garey Ave, Pomona, CA 91766. Phone: (909) 620-2043. Fax: (909) 620-3713. Web: www.youseemore.com/pomona/about.asp.

LINDBERGH, CHARLES AUGUSTUS: BIRTH ANNIVERSARY. Feb 4, 1902. American aviator Charles "Lucky Lindy" Lindbergh was the first to fly solo and nonstop over the Atlantic Ocean, New York to Paris, May 20–21, 1927. Born at Detroit, MI, he died at Kipahula, Maui, HI, Aug 27, 1974. For more info: *Flight: The Journey of Charles Lindbergh*, by Robert Burleigh (Philomel Books, 0-3992-2272-3, $16.99 Gr. K–3) and *Charles A. Lindbergh: A Human Hero*, by James Giblin (Clarion, 0-395-63389-3, $18 Gr. 4–7) and www.pbs.org/wgbh/amex/lindbergh. See also: "Lindbergh Flight: Anniversary" (May 20).

QUAYLE, J. DANFORTH: BIRTHDAY. Feb 4, 1947. The 44th vice president (1989–93) of the US, born at Indianapolis, IN.

SRI LANKA: INDEPENDENCE DAY: ANNIVERSARY. Feb 4. Democratic Socialist Republic of Sri Lanka observes National Day. On Feb 4, 1948, Ceylon (as it was then known) obtained independence from Great Britain. The name Sri Lanka was adopted in 1972.

BIRTHDAYS TODAY

Russell Hoban, 81, author of books illustrated by his wife Lillian (*Bedtime for Frances*), born Lansdale, PA, Feb 4, 1925.

Rosa Lee Parks, 93, civil rights leader who refused to give up her seat on the bus, born Tuskegee, AL, Feb 4, 1913.

Carly Patterson, 18, Olympic gymnast, born Baton Rouge, LA, Feb 4, 1988.

Denis Savard, 45, Hall of Fame hockey player, born Point Gatineau, QC, Canada, Feb 4, 1961.

FEBRUARY 5 — SUNDAY

Day 36 — 329 Remaining

AFRICAN AMERICAN READ-IN. Feb 5–6. Schools, libraries and community organizations are urged to make literacy a significant part of Black History Month by hosting Read-Ins in their communities. Report your results by submitting the 2006 African American Read-In Chain Report Card. This 17th national Read-In is sponsored by the Black Caucus of the National Council of Teachers of English. Annually, the first Sunday in February for communities and the first Monday in February for schools. For an African American Read-In Packet: Dr. Sandra E. Gibbs, African American Read-In, NCTE, 1111 W Kenyon Rd, Urbana, IL 61801-1096. Phone: (800) 369-6283. E-mail: sgibbs@ncte.org. Web: www.ncte.org/prog.

BOY SCOUTS OF AMERICA ANNIVERSARY WEEK. Feb 5–11. Commemorating the founding of the organization Feb 8, 1910. Annually, the week (Sunday through Saturday) including the founding day, Feb 8. For info: Boy Scouts of America, 1325 W Walnut Hill Ln, Irving, TX 75015-2079. Web: www.scouting.org.

FAMILY-LEAVE BILL: ANNIVERSARY. Feb 5, 1993. President Bill Clinton signed legislation requiring companies with 50 or more employees (and all government agencies) to allow employees to take up to 12 weeks unpaid leave in a 12-month period to deal with the birth or adoption of a child or to care for a relative with a serious health problem. The bill became effective Aug 5, 1993.

MEXICO: CONSTITUTION DAY. Feb 5. The present constitution, embracing major social reforms, was adopted in 1917. National holiday.

MOON PHASE: FIRST QUARTER. Feb 5. Moon enters First Quarter phase at 1:29 AM, EST.

★ **NATIONAL CONSUMER PROTECTION WEEK.** Feb 5–11 (tentative). Usually proclaimed in early February, although the date varies.

STUBBY JOINS WWI FRONT LINES: ANNIVERSARY. Feb 5, 1918. Stubby, the bull terrier mascot of the US 102nd Infantry, 26th Division, entered the French trenches on this day in 1918. He showed himself a brave dog by alerting soldiers to mustard gas attacks and once snagging a German spy. Stubby spent 18 months in France and participated in 17 battles. He returned home a hero, was given the honorary rank of sergeant, met presidents Wilson, Harding and Coolidge, and was awarded numerous medals—including a gold one given by General John "Black Jack" Pershing. Stubby was born in 1917 and died in 1926.

SUPER BOWL XL. Feb 5. Ford Field, Detroit, MI. The battle between the NFC and AFC champions. For info: PR Dept, The National Football League, 410 Park Ave, New York, NY 10022. Web: www.superbowl.com.

SWITZERLAND: HOMSTROM. Feb 5. Scuol. Burning of straw men on poles as a symbol of winter's imminent departure. Annually, the first Sunday in February.

WEATHERMAN'S [WEATHERPERSON'S] DAY. Feb 5. Commemorates the birth of one of America's first weathermen, John Jeffries, a Boston physician who kept detailed records of weather conditions, 1774–1816. Born at Boston, Feb 5, 1744, and died there Sept 16, 1819. See also: "First Balloon Flight Across English Channel: Anniversary" (Jan 7).

WITHERSPOON, JOHN: BIRTH ANNIVERSARY. Feb 5, 1723. Clergyman, signer of the Declaration of Independence and reputed coiner of the word *Americanism* (in 1781). Born near Edinburgh, Scotland. Died at Princeton, NJ, Nov 15, 1794.

BIRTHDAYS TODAY

Henry Louis (Hank) Aaron, 72, baseball executive, Baseball Hall of Fame outfielder, all-time home run leader, born Mobile, AL, Feb 5, 1934.

Roberto Alomar, 38, baseball player, born Ponce, Puerto Rico, Feb 5, 1968.

Jennifer Granholm, 47, Governor of Michigan (D), born Vancouver, BC, Canada, Feb 5, 1959.

Patricia Lauber, 82, author (the Let's Read and Find Out science series, *Volcano: The Eruption and Healing of Mount St. Helens*), born New York, NY, Feb 5, 1924.

David Wiesner, 49, author and illustrator (Caldecott for *Tuesday*), born Bridgewater, NJ, Feb 5, 1957.

FEBRUARY 6 — MONDAY

Day 37 — 328 Remaining

ACCESSION OF QUEEN ELIZABETH II: ANNIVERSARY. Feb 6, 1952. Princess Elizabeth Alexandra Mary succeeded to the British throne (becoming Elizabeth II, Queen of the United Kingdom of Great Britain and Northern Ireland and Head of the Commonwealth) upon the death of her father, King George VI, Feb 6, 1952. Her coronation took place June 2, 1953, at Westminster Abbey at London. For info: www.royal.gov.uk/output/page218.asp.

BURR, AARON: 250th BIRTH ANNIVERSARY. Feb 6, 1756. Third vice president of the US (Mar 4, 1801–Mar 3, 1805). While vice president, Burr challenged political enemy Alexander Hamilton to a duel and mortally wounded him July 11, 1804, at Weehawken, NJ. Indicted for the challenge and for murder, he returned to Washington to complete his term of office (during which he presided over the impeachment trial of Supreme Court Justice Samuel Chase). In 1807 Burr was arrested, tried for treason (in an alleged scheme to invade Mexico and set up a new nation in the West) and acquitted. Born at Newark, NJ, he died at Staten Island, NY, Sept 14, 1836.

MASSACHUSETTS RATIFIES CONSTITUTION: ANNIVERSARY. Feb 6, 1788. By a vote of 187 to 168, Massachusetts became the sixth state to ratify the Constitution.

NATIONAL SCHOOL COUNSELING WEEK. Feb 6–10. Promotes counseling in the school and community. Annually, first full week in February. Kits are available for purchase online to help your school plan their celebration. For info: American School Counselor Assn, 1101 King St, Ste 625, Alexandria, VA 22314. Phone: (800) 306-4722. Fax: (703) 683-1619. E-mail: asca@schoolcounselor.org. Web: www.schoolcounselor.org.

NEW ZEALAND: WAITANGI DAY. Feb 6. National Day. Commemorates signing of the Treaty of Waitangi in 1840 (at Waitangi, Chatham Islands, New Zealand). The treaty, between the native Maori and the European peoples, provided for development of New Zealand under the British Crown.

100 BILLIONTH CRAYOLA CRAYON® PRODUCED: ANNIVERSARY. Feb 6, 1996. On this date, the 100 billionth crayola was produced by Binney & Smith, Inc, in New York. The first box of eight crayons was introduced in 1903 in the popular yellow and green box. Since 1903, crayons have come in boxes of 24, 48, 64 and 96. The word *crayola* means oily chalk.

REAGAN, RONALD WILSON: BIRTH ANNIVERSARY. Feb 6, 1911. 40th president of the US (1981–89). Former sportscaster, motion picture actor, governor of California (1967–74); he was the oldest and the first divorced person to become president. Born at Tampico, IL. Married actress Jane Wyman in 1940 (divorced in 1948); married actress Nancy Davis, Mar 4, 1952. The "Great Communicator" ushered in a decade of conservative policies upon his election in 1980 and was an indefatigable critic of communist states: he famously challenged Soviet president Gorbachev to "tear down this wall!" at the Berlin Wall in 1987. He died at his Los Angeles, CA, home on June 5, 2004. For more info: www.ipl.org /ref/POTUS.

RUTH, "BABE": BIRTH ANNIVERSARY. Feb 6, 1895. One of baseball's greatest heroes, George Herman "Babe" Ruth was born at Baltimore, MD. The left-handed pitcher—"the Sultan of Swat"—hit 714 home runs in 22 major league seasons of play and played in 10 World Series. Died at New York, NY, Aug 16, 1948.

BIRTHDAYS TODAY

Tom Brokaw, 66, TV journalist, author (*The Greatest Generation*), born Yankton, SD, Feb 6, 1940.

Betsy Duffey, 53, author (*How to Be Cool in the Third Grade*), born Anderson, SC, Feb 6, 1953.

Jim Nicholson, 68, US Secretary of Veteran's Affairs, born Struble, IA, Feb 6, 1938.

FEBRUARY 7 — TUESDAY

Day 38 — 327 Remaining

BALLET INTRODUCED TO THE US: ANNIVERSARY. Feb 7, 1827. Renowned French danseuse Madame Francisquy Hutin introduced ballet to the US with a performance of *The Deserter*, staged at the Bowery Theater, New York, NY. A minor scandal erupted when the ladies in the lower boxes left the theater upon viewing the light and scanty attire of Madame Hutin and her troupe.

DICKENS, CHARLES: BIRTH ANNIVERSARY. Feb 7, 1812. English social critic and novelist, born at Portsmouth, England. Among his most successful books: *Oliver Twist, The Posthumous Papers of the Pickwick Club, David Copperfield* and *A Christmas Carol.* Died at Gad's Hill, England, June 9, 1870, and was buried at Westminster Abbey. For more info: *Charles Dickens: The Man Who Had Great Expectations* by Diane Stanley and Peter Vennema (Morrow, 0-688-09111-3, $14.93 Gr. 4–8).

ELEVENTH AMENDMENT TO US CONSTITUTION (SOVEREIGNTY OF THE STATES): RATIFICATION ANNIVERSARY. Feb 7, 1795. The 11th Amendment to the Constitution was ratified, curbing the powers of the federal judiciary in relation to the states. The amendment reaffirmed the sovereignty of the states by prohibiting suits against them.

GIPSON, FRED: BIRTH ANNIVERSARY. Feb 7, 1908. Born near Mason, TX. Gipson is known for such works as *Old Yeller, Savage Sam* and *Little Arliss*. In 1959 he won the William Allen White Children's Book Award and the First Sequoyah Award. Gipson died at Mason County, TX, Aug 17, 1973.

GRENADA: INDEPENDENCE DAY. Feb 7. National Day. Commemorates independence from Great Britain in 1974.

100th DAY OF SCHOOL. Feb 7 (approximate). Use your own school calendar to compute this date for your students. This day can help you teach lower elementary students the concept of 100. For activities that will facilitate this, visit users.aol.com/a100th day/ideas.html. The following books will also be helpful: *100 Days of School*, by Trudy Harris (Millbrook, 0-7613-1271-4, $21.90 Gr. K–2); *The 100th Day of School*, by Angela Shelf Medearis (Scholastic, 0-590-25944-X, $3.99 Gr. K–2) and *100th Day of*

FEBRUARY 7
THE WORLD OF LAURA INGALLS WILDER

Laura Ingalls Wilder was born on this day in 1867. She is famous for her novels, based on her own life, about growing up on the American frontier. Laura lived in Wisconsin, Kansas, Minnesota, Iowa and the Dakota Territory (now South Dakota) as her parents moved from place to place looking for work and open land to farm.

When Laura was growing up, the federal government granted large pieces of western land to settlers at a low cost. To keep the land, they had to build a house on it and remain there for five years. Laura's father, Charles Ingalls, tried to acquire land this way in Kansas, but the land belonged to Native Americans. He had to move away, and he tried again in Minnesota. Laura wrote about living there in a dugout house in her book *On the Banks of Plum Creek* (Harper Trophy, 0-06-440004-2, $6.99).

In addition to the hardships caused by moving from place to place so frequently, Laura's family faced challenges common to settlers on the prairie. Two years in a row, their crops were destroyed by swarms of grasshoppers. One winter, recounted in *The Long Winter* (Harper Trophy, 0-06-440006-9, $6.99), the people in Laura's town nearly died of starvation.

Meanwhile, Laura was going to school and discovering that she loved to read and write. When she was still a teenager, she became a schoolteacher. She also got married at 18 to Almanzo Wilder, whom she nicknamed "Manly." Although Laura later called the novel with the story of her marriage to Almanzo *These Happy Golden Years* (HarperCollins, 0-06-440008-5, $6.99), life could still be challenging for the frontier couple. The strength Laura developed during her childhood served her well as she continued her life in the Midwest with her husband. Despite some misfortunes, they eventually settled happily on a farm in Missouri.

It was there that Laura began to write steadily, publishing articles about farming. However, she didn't start writing stories from her own life until she was in her 60s. What started as a single autobiography turned into a series of books for children, which her daughter Rose helped her edit. The first was *Little House in the Big Woods* (Harper Trophy, 0-06-440001-8), based on Laura's childhood in the Big Woods of Wisconsin. Published in 1932, it became a huge hit. Laura followed with the whole series of Little House books.

Laura didn't just write because she wanted to tell her story to the public. She also wanted to share with a younger generation how the country came to be. Older students might like to investigate how Wilder adjusts her real-life experiences to craft a fictional story meant to represent the abstract experience of life on the American frontier in the late 19th century.

Some books to explore are Wilder's novels themselves, including *Little House on the Prairie* (Harper Trophy, 0-06-440007-7, $6.99) and *By the Shores of Silver Lake* (Harper Trophy, 0-06-440005-0, $6.99), as well as William Anderson's *Laura Ingalls Wilder: A Biography* (Harper Trophy, 0-06-446103-3, $6.99 Ages 8–12). —Elizabeth Van Buren

February 2006

S	M	T	W	T	F	S
			1	2	3	4
5	6	7	8	9	10	11
12	13	14	15	16	17	18
19	20	21	22	23	24	25
26	27	28				

School Activities, by Hope Blecher-Sass (Teacher Created Materials, 1-57690-199-8, $2.95). Also see the November 1999 issue of *Book Links* for "Celebrating the One Hundredth Day of School."

SPACE MILESTONE: *STARDUST* (US). Feb 7, 1999. *Stardust* began its three billion-mile journey to collect comet dust on this date. The unmanned mission was to meet up with Comet Wild-2 in January 2004 and the comet samples will reach Earth in January 2006. This is the first US mission devoted solely to a comet. NASA plans three more over a four-year period. You can track its progress at http://stardust.jpl.nasa.gov.

WILDER, LAURA INGALLS: BIRTH ANNIVERSARY. Feb 7, 1867. Author of *The Little House on the Prairie* and its sequels. Born at Pepin, WI, Wilder died Feb 10, 1957, at Mansfield, MO. For more info: *Laura Ingalls Wilder*, by S. Ward (Rosen, 0-8239-5712-8, $18.75 Gr. K–4). ***See Curriculum Connection.***

BIRTHDAYS TODAY

Garth Brooks, 44, singer, born Tulsa, OK, Feb 7, 1962.
Juwan Howard, 33, basketball player, born Chicago, IL, Feb 7, 1973.
Herb Kohl, 71, US Senator (D, Wisconsin), born Milwaukee, WI, Feb 7, 1935.
Ashton Kutcher, 28, actor ("That 70s Show," *Dude, Where's My Car?*), born Cedar Rapids, IA, Feb 7, 1978.

FEBRUARY 8 — WEDNESDAY

Day 39 — 326 Remaining

BOY SCOUTS OF AMERICA FOUNDED: ANNIVERSARY. Feb 8, 1910. The Boy Scouts of America was founded at Washington, DC, by William Boyce, based on the work of Sir Robert Baden-Powell with the British Boy Scout Association. For more info: www.scouting.org.

JAPAN: HA-RI-KU-YO (NEEDLE MASS). Feb 8. Ha-Ri-Ku-Yo, a Needle Mass, may be observed on either Feb 8 or Dec 8. Girls do no needlework; instead they gather old and broken needles, which they dedicate to the Awashima Shrine at Wakayama. Girls pray to Awashima Myozin (their protecting deity) that their needlework, symbolic of love and marriage, will be good. Participation in the Needle Mass hopefully leads to a happy marriage.

JAPAN: SNOW FESTIVAL. Feb 8–12. Sapporo, Hokkaido. Huge, elaborate snow and ice sculptures are erected on the Odori-Koen Promenade.

OPERA DEBUT IN THE COLONIES: ANNIVERSARY. Feb 8, 1735. The first opera produced in the colonies was performed at the Courtroom, at Charleston, SC. The opera was *Flora; or the Hob in the Well*, written by Colley Cibber.

SHERMAN, WILLIAM TECUMSEH: BIRTH ANNIVERSARY. Feb 8, 1820. Born at Lancaster, OH, General Sherman is especially remembered for his devastating march through Georgia during the Civil War and his statement "War is hell." Died at New York, NY, Feb 14, 1891.

SLOVENIA: PRESEREN DAY. Feb 8. National holiday. Commemorates France Preseren, Slovenia's national poet, who died on this day in 1849.

SPACE MILESTONE: *ARABSAT-1*. Feb 8, 1985. League of Arab States communications satellite launched into geosynchronous orbit from Kourou, French Guiana, by European Space Agency.

VERNE, JULES: BIRTH ANNIVERSARY. Feb 8, 1828. French writer, sometimes called "the father of science fiction," born at Nantes, France. Author of *Around the World in Eighty Days, Twenty Thousand Leagues Under the Sea* and many other novels. Died at Amiens, France, Mar 24, 1905.

BIRTHDAYS TODAY

Ted Koppel, 66, TV journalist ("Nightline"), born Lancashire, England, Feb 8, 1940.
Alonzo Mourning, 36, basketball player, born Chesapeake, VA, Feb 8, 1970.
Anne Rockwell, 72, author (*Apples and Pumpkins, Things That Go, Sweet Potato Pie*), born Memphis, TN, Feb 8, 1934.

FEBRUARY 9 — THURSDAY

Day 40 — 325 Remaining

ASHURA: TENTH DAY. Feb 9. Islamic calendar date: Muharram 10, 1427. Commemorates death of Muhammad's grandson and the Battle of Karbala. A time of fasting, reflection and meditation. Jews of Medina fasted on the tenth day in remembrance of their salvation from Pharoah. Different methods for "anticipating" the visibility of the new moon crescent at Mecca are used by different groups. US date may vary. Began at sunset the preceding day.

FLORIDA STATE FAIR. Feb 9–20. Florida State Fair Grounds, Tampa, FL. The fair features the best arts, crafts, competitive exhibits, equestrian shows, livestock, entertainment and food found in Florida. Also not to be missed is "Cracker Country," where cultural and architectural history has been preserved. Annually, in February. Est attendance: 500,000. For info: Sherry Powell, Mktg & Advertising Mgr, Florida State Fair, PO Box 11766, Tampa, FL 33680. Phone: (813) 621-7821 or (813) 622-PARK. Web: www.floridastatefair.com.

HARRISON, WILLIAM HENRY: BIRTH ANNIVERSARY. Feb 9, 1773. Ninth president of the US (Mar 4–Apr 4, 1841). His term of office was the shortest in our nation's history—32 days. He was the first president to die in office (of pneumonia contracted during inaugural ceremonies). Born at Berkeley, VA, he died at Washington, DC, Apr 4, 1841. His grandson Benjamin Harrison was the 23rd president of the US. For more info: www.ipl.org/ref/POTUS.

LAST PERIHELION OF HALLEY'S COMET: 20th ANNIVERSARY. Feb 9, 1986. This date marks the last time Halley's Comet was at its closest point to the sun (perihelion)—about 55 million miles away. During this period, the comet came closest to Earth on Nov 27, 1985 (inbound), and Apr 11, 1986 (outbound). The next perihelion will be in 2061. The comet is named for English astronomer Edmund Halley, who calculated its roughly 76-year orbit in the eighteenth century. It has a nucleus of 10 × 5 × 5 miles. One of the highlights of Halley's Comet's 1986 arrival was the launch of a multinational squad of spacecraft to get the first close-up photographs. The last (and most distant) image of this comet was taken on Jan 11, 1994, by the European South Observatory when it was near the orbit of Uranus. See also: "Eta Aquarids Meteor Showers" (Apr 21) and "Orionids Meteor Showers" (Oct 15).

NATIONAL GIRLS AND WOMEN IN SPORTS DAY. Feb 9. Celebrates and honors all girls and women participating in sports. Recognizes the passage of Title IX in 1972, the law that guarantees gender equity in federally funded school programs, including athletics. Sponsored by Girls Inc, the Girl Scouts, the National Association for Girls and Women in Sports, the Women's Sports Foundation and the YWCA. For info: Women's Sports Foundation, Eisenhower Park, East Meadow, NY 11554. Phone: (516) 542-4700.

BIRTHDAYS TODAY

David Gallagher, 21, actor ("7th Heaven"), born College Point, NY, Feb 9, 1985.

Joe Pesci, 63, actor (*Home Alone, Home Alone 2*), born Newark, NJ, Feb 9, 1943.

Jimmy Smith, 37, football player, born Detroit, MI, Feb 9, 1969.

FEBRUARY 10 — FRIDAY

Day 41 — 324 Remaining

FIRST COMPUTER CHESS VICTORY OVER HUMAN: 10th ANNIVERSARY. Feb 10, 1996. IBM's Deep Blue computer defeated world champion Garry Kasparov in 34 moves on this date in Philadelphia, PA—the first such victory by a computer in tournament conditions. Kasparov, however, went on to win the tournament, defeating the computer three times (the other two matches were draws). In May 1997, in a six-game rematch, Deep Blue emerged the overall victor. Deep Blue, an RS/6000 supercomputer, can evaluate 200 million chess positions a second, but is not capable of using artificial intelligence to "learn." Kasparov was reigning World Chess Champion from 1985 to 2000. For more info: www.research.ibm.com/deepblue.

FRENCH AND INDIAN WAR ENDS: ANNIVERSARY. Feb 10, 1763. The Treaty of Paris was signed, ending the French and Indian War in North America. Known in Europe as the Seven Years War, this conflict ranged from North America to India, with many European nations involved. In North America French expansion in the Ohio River Valley in the 1750s led to conflict with Great Britain. Some Indians fought alongside the French; a young George Washington fought for the British. As a result of the signing of the Treaty of Paris, France lost all claims to Canada and had to cede Louisiana to Spain. Fifteen years later French bitterness over the loss of its North American colonies to Britain contributed to France's supporting the colonists in the American Revolution. For info: *Struggle for a Continent: The French and Indian Wars*, by Betsy Maestro (HarperCollins, 0-688-1345505, $15.89 Gr. 3–6).

MALTA: FEAST OF ST. PAUL'S SHIPWRECK. Feb 10. Valletta. Holy day of obligation. Commemorates shipwreck of St. Paul on the north coast of Malta in AD 60.

TWENTY-FIFTH AMENDMENT TO US CONSTITUTION RATIFIED (PRESIDENTIAL SUCCESSION, DISABILITY): ANNIVERSARY. Feb 10, 1967. Procedures for presidential succession were further clarified by the 25th Amendment, along with provisions for continuity of power in the event of a disability or illness of the president.

February 2006

S	M	T	W	T	F	S
			1	2	3	4
5	6	7	8	9	10	11
12	13	14	15	16	17	18
19	20	21	22	23	24	25
26	27	28				

BIRTHDAYS TODAY

Lucy Cousins, 42, author, illustrator (the Maisy books, *ZaZa's Baby Brother, Katy Cat and Beaky Boo*), born Reading, England, Feb 10, 1964.

E.L. Konigsburg, 76, author (Newbery for *The View From Saturday, From the Mixed-up Files of Mrs Basil E. Frankweiler*), born Elaine Lobl, New York, NY, Feb 10, 1930.

Mark Teague, 43, author (*The Secret Shortcut*), illustrator (the Poppleton series, *Flying Dragon Room*), born La Mesa, CA, Feb 10, 1963.

Tina Thompson, 31, basketball player, born Los Angeles, CA, Feb 10, 1975.

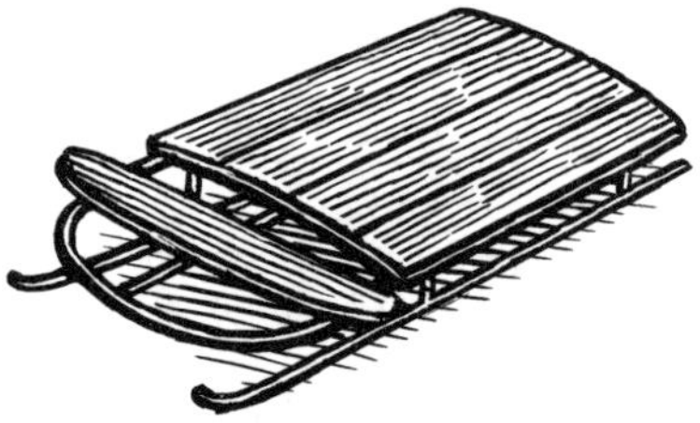

FEBRUARY 11 — SATURDAY

Day 42 — 323 Remaining

CAMEROON: YOUTH DAY. Feb 11. Public holiday.

EDISON, THOMAS ALVA: BIRTH ANNIVERSARY. Feb 11, 1847. American inventive genius and holder of more than 1,200 patents (including the incandescent electric lamp, phonograph, electric dynamo and key parts of many now-familiar devices such as the movie camera, telephone transmitter, etc). Edison said, "Genius is 1 percent inspiration and 99 percent perspiration." His birthday is now widely observed as Inventor's Day. Born at Milan, OH, and died at Menlo Park, NJ, Oct 18, 1931. For more info: *Thomas Edison*, by Anna Sproule (Blackbirch, 1-56711-331-1, $19.95 Gr. 5–7).

FULLER, MELVILLE WESTON: BIRTH ANNIVERSARY. Feb 11, 1833. Eighth chief justice of the US Supreme Court. Born at Augusta, ME, he died at Sorrento, ME, July 4, 1910. For more info: oyez.northwestern.edu/justices/justices.cgi.

IRAN: NATIONAL DAY. Feb 11. National holiday. Commemorates revolution in 1979 that overthrew the Shah and let to the founding of the republic.

JAPAN: NATIONAL FOUNDATION DAY. Feb 11. Marks the founding of the Japanese nation. In 1872 the government officially set Feb 11, 660 BC, as the date of accession to the throne of the Emperor Jimmu (said to be Japan's first emperor) and designated the day a national holiday by the name of Empire Day. The holiday was abolished after WWII, but was revived as National Foundation Day in 1966. Ceremonies are held with Their Imperial Majesties the Emperor and Empress, the Prime Minister and other dignitaries attending.

MANDELA, NELSON: PRISON RELEASE: ANNIVERSARY. Feb 11, 1990. After serving more than 27½ years of a life sentence (convicted, with eight others, of sabotage and conspiracy to overthrow the government), South Africa's Nelson Mandela, 71 years old, walked away from the Victor Verster prison farm at Paarl, South Africa, a free man. He had survived the governmental system of apartheid. Mandela greeted a cheering throng of well-wishers, along with hundreds of millions of television viewers worldwide, with demands for an intensification of the struggle for equality for blacks, who make up nearly 75 percent of South Africa's population. For more info: www.anc.org.za/people/mandela.html or *Nelson Mandela*, by Reggie Finlayson (Lerner, 0-8225-4936-0, $25.26 Gr. 4–7) or *Nelson Mandela and Apartheid in World History*, by Ann Graham Gaines (Enslow, 0-7660-1463-0, $20.95 Gr. 5–9).

SPACE MILESTONE: *ENDEAVOUR* MAPPING MISSION (US). Feb 11, 2000. This manned flight spent 9 days in space creating a 3-D map of more than 75 percent of the Earth's surface. Once compiled and finished, it will be the most accurate and complete topographic map of the Earth ever produced.

SPACE MILESTONE: *OSUMI* (JAPAN). Feb 11, 1970. First Japanese satellite launched. Japan became fourth nation to send a satellite into space.

VATICAN CITY: INDEPENDENCE ANNIVERSARY. Feb 11, 1929. The Lateran Treaty, signed by Pietro Cardinal Gasparri and Benito Mussolini, guaranteed the independence of the State of Vatican City and recognized the sovereignty of the Holy See over it. Area is about 109 acres.

BIRTHDAYS TODAY

Brandy, 27, singer, actress ("Cinderella," "Moesha"), born Brandy Norwood, Macomb, MS, Feb 11, 1979.

Jeb Bush, 53, Governor of Florida (R), born Midland, TX, Feb 11, 1953.

Matthew Lawrence, 26, actor ("Brotherly Love," "Boy Meets World"), born Abington, PA, Feb 11, 1980.

Mike Leavitt, 55, US Secretary of Health and Human Services, born Cedar City, UT, Feb 11, 1951.

Jane Yolen, 67, author (*Owl Moon, The Devil's Arithmetic, Briar Rose, Sleeping Ugly*), born New York, NY, Feb 11, 1939.

FEBRUARY 12 — SUNDAY

Day 43 — 322 Remaining

ADAMS, LOUISA CATHERINE JOHNSON: BIRTH ANNIVERSARY. Feb 12, 1775. Wife of John Quincy Adams, sixth president of the US. Born at London, England, she died at Washington, DC, May 14, 1852.

CHINA: LANTERN FESTIVAL. Feb 12. Traditional Chinese festival falls on 15th day of first month of Chinese lunar calendar year. Lantern processions mark end of the Chinese New Year holiday season. Also celebrated in Taiwan and Korea. See also: "Chinese New Year" (Jan 29). Date in other countries will differ from China's by up to one day.

DARWIN, CHARLES ROBERT: BIRTH ANNIVERSARY. Feb 12, 1809. Author and naturalist, born at Shrewsbury, England. Best remembered for his books *On the Origin of Species by Means of Natural Selection, or the Preservation of Favoured Races in the Struggle for Life* and *The Descent of Man and Selection in Relation to Sex*. Died at Down, Kent, England, Apr 19, 1882. For more info: *Charles Darwin: Revolutionary Biologist*, by J. Edward Evans (Lerner, 0-8225-4914-X, $21.50 Gr. 6–9).

KOSCIUSKO, THADDEUS: BIRTH ANNIVERSARY. Feb 12, 1746. Polish patriot and American Revolutionary War figure. Born at Lithuania, he died at Solothurn, Switzerland, Oct 15, 1817. The governor of Massachusetts proclaims the first Sunday in February as Kosciusko Day (Feb 5 in 2006).

LINCOLN, ABRAHAM: BIRTH ANNIVERSARY. Feb 12, 1809. The 16th president of the US (Mar 4, 1861–Apr 15, 1865) and the first to be assassinated (on Good Friday, Apr 14, 1865, at Ford's Theatre at Washington, DC). His presidency encompassed the tragic Civil War. Especially remembered are his Emancipation Proclamation (Jan 1, 1863) and his Gettysburg Address (Nov 19, 1863). Born at Hardin County, KY, he died at Washington, DC, Apr 15, 1865. Lincoln's birthday is observed as part of Presidents' Day in most states, but is a legal holiday in Florida, Illinois and Kentucky and an optional bank holiday in Iowa, Maryland, Michigan, Pennsylvania, Washington and West Virginia. See also: "Presidents' Day" (Feb 20). For more info: *Lincoln: A Photobiography*, by Russell Freedman (Houghton Mifflin, 0-89-919380-3, $17 Gr. 4–6) and *Lincoln: In His Own Words*, edited by Milton Meltzer (Harcourt Brace, 0-15-245437-3, $22.95 Gr. 6–8). For links to Lincoln sites on the Web, go to www.ipl.org/ref/POTUS.

FEBRUARY 12
LOST PENNY DAY

Consider the lowly penny: bumping around at the bottom of purses, lying unwanted on dirty sidewalks, collecting in lint trays of dryers. One penny doesn't buy anything anymore. Yet, the sage Benjamin Franklin declaimed, "A penny saved is a penny earned." It's his most famous proverb.

Today, Abraham Lincoln's birthday, is also Lost Penny Day, an unusual holiday that celebrates Lincoln by advising us to put those unloved pennies featuring our 16th president to work. It's a fun holiday to share with your class.

Start a class project: Have your students, starting today, begin collecting those lost pennies they see lying around. Put a big jar in your classroom to store them in or have your students collect them at home. At the end of the school year, make a field trip to your local bank with all the pennies for counting. The bank personnel might even let your students have a look at the machine that sorts all the change. The end amount may not be much, but it may strike home the value of saving and being patient. The sponsor of Lost Penny Day asks that gathered pennies be donated to a good cause. And that's always a good message. Perhaps your class can pick a worthy clause to donate these lost pennies. —Holly McGuire

LOST PENNY DAY. Feb 12. Today is set aside to put all of those pennies stashed in candy dishes, bowls and jars back in circulation. Take those pennies and give them to a shelter or agency that assists the homeless or your local Humane Society. Annually, on President Abraham Lincoln's birthday, the man depicted on the copper penny. [©1995] For info: Adrienne Sioux Koopersmith, 1437 W Rosemont, #1W, Chicago, IL 60660-1319. E-mail: askoopersmith@hotmail.com. ***See Curriculum Connection.***

MOON PHASE: FULL MOON. Feb 12. Moon enters Full Moon phase at 11:44 PM, EST.

MYANMAR: UNION DAY. Feb 12. National holiday. Commemorates the formation of the Union of Burma on this date in 1947. Later the country's name was changed to Myanmar.

NAACP FOUNDED: ANNIVERSARY. Feb 12, 1909. The National Association for the Advancement of Colored People was founded by W.E.B. Dubois and Ida Wells-Barnett, among others, to wage a militant campaign against lynching and other forms of racial oppression. Its legal wing brought many lawsuits that successfully challenged segregation in the 1950s and '60s. For more info: www.naacp.org. The February 2001 issue of *Cobblestone* magazine was devoted to the NAACP.

SAFETYPUP'S® BIRTHDAY. Feb 12. Safetypup®, created by the National Child Safety Council, joyously celebrates his birthday by bringing safety awareness/education messages to children in a positive, nonthreatening manner. Safetypup® has achieved a wonderful balance of safety sense, caution and childlike enthusiasm about life and helping kids "Stay Safe and Sound." For info: Barbara Handley Huggett, Dir, NCSC, Research and Development, Box 1368, Jackson, MI 49204-1368. Phone: (517) 764-6070.

BIRTHDAYS TODAY

Ann Atwood, 93, author and illustrator (*Haiku: The Mood of Earth*), born California, Feb 12, 1913.

Judy Blume, 68, author (*Are You There God? It's Me, Margaret; Tales of a Fourth Grade Nothing; Superfudge*), born Elizabeth, NJ, Feb 12, 1938.

Joanna Kerns, 53, actress ("Growing Pains"), born San Francisco, CA, Feb 12, 1953.

Josephine Poole, 73, author (*Joan of Arc*), born London, England, Feb 12, 1933.

Christina Ricci, 26, actress (*Sleepy Hollow, Addams Family Values*), born Santa Monica, CA, Feb 12, 1980.

David Small, 61, illustrator (*The Library*, Caldecott Medal for *So You Want to Be President?*), Caldecott Honor for *The Gardener*, author (*Imogene's Antlers*), born Detroit, MI, Feb 12, 1945.

Arlen Specter, 76, US Senator (R, Pennsylvania), born Wichita, KS, Feb 12, 1930.

Jacqueline Woodson, 42, author (*I Hadn't Meant to Tell You This*, Coretta Scott King Award for *Miracle's Boys*), born Columbus, OH, Feb 12, 1964.

FEBRUARY 13 — MONDAY

Day 44 — 321 Remaining

FIRST MAGAZINE PUBLISHED IN AMERICA: ANNIVERSARY. Feb 13, 1741. Andrew Bradford published *The American Magazine* just three days ahead of Benjamin Franklin's *General Magazine*.

GET A DIFFERENT NAME DAY. Feb 13. If you dislike your name, or merely find it boring, today is the day to adopt the moniker of your choice. [©2002 by WH.] For info: Thomas & Ruth Roy, Wellcat Holidays, 2418 Long Ln, Lebanon, PA 17046. Phone: (717) 279-0184. E-mail: info@wellcat.com. Web: www.wellcat.com.

LAST *PEANUTS* STRIP: ANNIVERSARY. Feb 13, 2000. A beloved cultural institution ended on this day: the last new *Peanuts* Sunday strip was published Feb 13, 2000 (the last daily *Peanuts* strip was published Jan 3, 2000). Creator Charles M. Schulz died the evening before the final strip appeared.

TRUMAN, BESS (ELIZABETH) VIRGINIA WALLACE: BIRTH ANNIVERSARY. Feb 13, 1885. Wife of Harry S Truman, 33rd president of the US. Born at Independence, MO, and died there Oct 18, 1982.

TU B'SHVAT. Feb 13. Hebrew calendar date: Shebat 15, 5766. The 15th day of the month of Shebat in the Hebrew calendar year is set aside as Hamishah Asar (New Year of the Trees or Jewish Arbor Day), a time to show respect and appreciation for trees and plants. (Began at sundown of previous day.)

WOOD, GRANT: BIRTH ANNIVERSARY. Feb 13, 1892. American artist, especially noted for his powerful realism and satirical paintings of the American scene, was born near Anamosa, IA. He was a printer, sculptor, woodworker and high school and college teacher. Among his best-remembered works are *American Gothic, Fall Plowing* and *Stone City*. Died at Iowa City, IA, Feb 12, 1942.

BIRTHDAYS TODAY

Charlie Garner, 34, football player, born Fairfax, VA, Feb 13, 1972.

Janet Taylor Lisle, 59, author (*Afternoon of the Elves, The Art of Keeping Cool*), born Englewood, NJ, Feb 13, 1947.

Randy Moss, 29, football player, born Rand, WV, Feb 13, 1977.

Ouida Sebestyen, 82, author (*Words by Heart*), born Vernon, TX, Feb 13, 1924.

William Sleator, 61, author (*Interstellar Pig, House of Stairs*), born Havre de Grace, MD, Feb 13, 1945.

Simms Taback, 74, author and illustrator (Caldecott Medal for *Joseph Had a Little Overcoat;* Caldecott Honor for *There Was an Old Lady Who Swallowed a Fly*), born New York, NY, Feb 13, 1932.

Chuck Yeager, 83, pilot who broke the sound barrier, born Myra, WV, Feb 13, 1923.

FEBRUARY 14 — TUESDAY

Day 45 — 320 Remaining

ARIZONA: ADMISSION DAY. Feb 14. Arizona became the 48th state in 1912.

ENIAC COMPUTER INTRODUCED: 60th ANNIVERSARY. Feb 14, 1946. J. Presper Eckert and John W. Mauchly demonstrated the Electronic Numerical Integrator and Computer (ENIAC) for the first time at the University of Pennsylvania. The huge computer occupied a 1,500-square-foot room and contained nearly 18,000 vacuum tubes. The Army commissioned the computer to speed the calculation of firing tables for artillery. By the time the computer was ready, World War II was over. However, ENIAC prepared the way for future generations of computers.

FERRIS WHEEL DAY. Feb 14, 1859. Anniversary of the birth of George Washington Gale Ferris, American engineer and inventor, at Galesburg, IL. Among his many accomplishments as a civil engineer, Ferris is best remembered as the inventor of the Ferris wheel, which he developed for the World's Columbian Exposition at Chicago, IL, in 1893. Built on the Midway Plaisance, the 250-feet-in-diameter Ferris wheel (with 36 coaches, each capable of carrying 40 passengers), proved one of the greatest attractions of the fair. It was America's answer to the Eiffel Tower of the Paris International Exposition of 1889. Ferris died at Pittsburgh, PA, Nov 22, 1896.

FIRST PRESIDENTIAL PHOTOGRAPH: ANNIVERSARY. Feb 14, 1849. President James Polk became the first US president to be photographed while in office. The photographer was Mathew B. Brady, who would become famous for his photography during the American Civil War.

February 2006

S	M	T	W	T	F	S
			1	2	3	4
5	6	7	8	9	10	11
12	13	14	15	16	17	18
19	20	21	22	23	24	25
26	27	28				

OREGON: ADMISSION DAY. Feb 14. Became 33rd state in 1859.

RACE RELATIONS DAY. Feb 14. A day designated by some churches to recognize the importance of interracial relations. Formerly was observed on Abraham Lincoln's birthday or on the Sunday preceding it. Since 1970 observance has generally been Feb 14.

SPACE MILESTONE: *NEAR* ORBITS ASTEROID. Feb 14, 2000. The robot spacecraft *Near Earth Asteroid Rendezvous* (now called *NEAR* Shoemaker) finished circling the asteroid Eros on this day. Eros is called a near-Earth asteroid because its orbit crosses that of Earth and poses a potential collision danger. *NEAR* continued orbiting the asteroid for a year, moving closer to the surface to make more precise measurements and take thousands of pictures. In October 2000, it passed within three miles of Eros. Though it was never designed for landing, on Feb 12, 2001, *NEAR* touched down on Eros, history's first landing of an object on an asteroid. *NEAR* was launched from Cape Canaveral, FL, Feb 17, 1996.

SPACE MILESTONE: 100th SPACEWALK: 5th ANNIVERSARY. Feb 14, 2001. The two astronauts from the space shuttle *Atlantis* took the 100th spacewalk; the first had been taken by American Edward White in 1965. On their excursion Thomas Jones and Robert Curbeam, Jr, put the finishing touches on the International Space Station's new science lab *Destiny*. See also: "Space Milestone: *Gemini* 4" (June 3).

VALENTINE'S DAY. Feb 14. St. Valentine's Day celebrates the feasts of two Christian martyrs of this name. One, a priest and physician, was beheaded at Rome, Italy, Feb 14, AD 269, during the reign of Emperor Claudius II. Another Valentine, the Bishop of Terni, is said to have been beheaded, also at Rome, Feb 14 (possibly in a later year). Both history and legend are vague and contradictory about details of the Valentines and some say that Feb 14 was selected for the celebration of Christian martyrs as a diversion from the ancient pagan observance of Lupercalia. An old legend has it that birds choose their mates on Valentine's Day. Now it is one of the most widely observed unofficial holidays. It is an occasion for the exchange of gifts (usually books, flowers or sweets) and greeting cards with affectionate or humorous messages. ***See Curriculum Connection.*** For more info: *Heart, Cupids, and Red Roses: The Story of the Valentine Symbols*, by Edna Barth (Clarion, 0-618-06789-2, $16 Gr. 3–6) or *Let's Celebrate Valentine's Day*, by Peter Roop (Millbrook, 0-7613-0972-1, $19.90 Gr. PreK–3).

BIRTHDAYS TODAY

Drew Bledsoe, 34, football player, born Ellensburg, WA, Feb 14, 1972.

Michael Bloomberg, 64, Mayor of New York City (R), born Brighton, MA, Feb 14, 1942.

Odds Bodkin, 53, storyteller, author (*The Crane Wife*), born New York, NY, Feb 14, 1953.

Judd Gregg, 59, US Senator (R, New Hampshire), born Nashua, NH, Feb 14, 1947.

Milan Hejduk, 30, hockey player, born Usti-nad-Labem, Czechoslovakia, Feb 14, 1976.

Steve McNair, 33, football player, born Mount Olive, MS, Feb 14, 1973.

Phyllis Root, 57, author (*What Baby Wants*), born Fort Wayne, IN, Feb 14, 1949.

Paul O. Zelinsky, 53, illustrator (Caldecott for *Rapunzel*, *Rumpelstiltskin*), born Evanston, IL, Feb 14, 1953.

FEBRUARY 14
ODD COUPLES

Romeo and Juliet, Tom Sawyer and Becky Thatcher, Snow White and Prince Charming—these are just a few of the famous romantic couples of literature. But today, on Valentine's Day, why not introduce your class to some of the *odd* couples of love and friendship? Maybe they've already seen a Muppet film with Kermit the Frog pursued by the glamorous Miss Piggy? Celebrating unusual couples can open the door to discussions of tolerance and being open-minded.

One of the first odd couples of literature was Edward Lear's Owl and Pussy-cat from the poem of the same name (written in 1867 and first published in Boston in 1870). Lear is the English Victorian poet of nonsense verse in which he sang of the incongruous and unexpected—all with a sense of fun. "The Owl and the Pussy-cat" is a delightful three-stanza poem (easily found anthologized) that makes for a fun read-aloud today. The fowl and cat go to sea in a "pea-green boat" and plan their wedding—officiated over by the "Turkey who lives on the hill." The Owl and Pussy-cat walk to the "edge of the sand" where they dance "by the light of the moon."

In Tor Seidler's enchanting classic *The Wainscott Weasel* (Harper Trophy, 0-06-205911-4, $11.95 All ages), illustrated by Fred Marcellino, the enterprising hero-weasel, Bagley Brown Jr., finds himself in love with the beautiful silvery fish Bridget. He collects bugs for her to eat and spends his evenings rapturously watching her flicker underwater in the moonlight. Bridget is practical about all this ("Fish are meant for fish," she gently explains) and lets him down with care. It's a beautiful tale that makes this interspecies love story believable.

Odd couples don't have to be in love, of course. There's Charlotte the spider and Wilbur the pig in E.B. White's unforgettable tale of friendship, *Charlotte's Web*. Find your favorite odd-couple stories and share them with your class. Ask them what makes your example an odd couple? Is it a believable friendship or romance? Ask your students if they've ever had a special friendship that the world around them couldn't understand. (See also the Curriculum Connection about Edward Lear on May 12.) —Holly McGuire

FEBRUARY 15 — WEDNESDAY

Day 46 — 319 Remaining

ANTHONY, SUSAN BROWNELL: BIRTH ANNIVERSARY. Feb 15, 1820. American reformer and advocate of women's suffrage. She was the first American woman to have her likeness on coinage (1979, Susan B. Anthony dollar). Born at Adams, MA, she died at Rochester, NY, Mar 13, 1906.

CANADA: MAPLE LEAF FLAG ADOPTED: ANNIVERSARY. Feb 15, 1965. The new Canadian national flag was raised in Ottawa, Canada's capital, on this day. The red-and-white flag with a red maple leaf in the center replaced the Red Ensign flag, which had the British Union Jack in the upper left-hand corner. Commemorated as National Flag of Canada Day.

CLARK, ABRAHAM: BIRTH ANNIVERSARY. Feb 15, 1726. Signer of the Declaration of Independence, farmer and lawyer. Born at Elizabethtown, NJ, and died there Sept 15, 1794.

GALILEI, GALILEO: BIRTH ANNIVERSARY. Feb 15, 1564. Physicist and astronomer who helped overthrow medieval concepts of the world, born at Pisa, Italy. He proved the theory that all bodies, large and small, descend at equal speed and gathered evidence to support Copernicus's theory that the Earth and other planets revolve around the sun. Galileo died at Florence, Italy, Jan 8, 1642. For more info: *Starry Messenger*, by Peter Sis (Farrar, Straus, 0-374-37191-1, $16 Gr. 2–6) or *Galileo Galilei: Inventor,*

Astronomer, and Rebel, by Michael White (Blackbirch, 1-56711-325-7, $18.95 Gr. 5–8).

RIVER OF WORDS ENVIRONMENTAL POETRY AND ART CONTEST. Feb 15. Deadline for submissions for this annual poetry and art contest on the theme of watersheds. Open to students K–12. Teacher's Guide and teacher training workshops available. For entry form, contact: River of Words Project, 2547 Eighth St, 13B, Berkeley, CA 94710. Phone: (510) 548-POEM. Fax: (510) 548-2095. E-mail: info@riverofwords.org. Web: www.riverofwords.org.

SUTTER, JOHN AUGUSTUS: BIRTH ANNIVERSARY. Feb 15, 1803. Born at Kandern, Germany, Sutter established the first white settlement on the site of Sacramento, CA, in 1839, and owned a large tract of land there, which he named New Helvetia. The first great gold strike in the US was on his property, at Sutter's Mill, Jan 24, 1848. His land was soon overrun by gold seekers who, he claimed, slaughtered his cattle and stole or destroyed his property. Sutter was bankrupt by 1852. Died at Washington, DC, June 18, 1880.

BIRTHDAYS TODAY

Norman Bridwell, 78, author and illustrator (*Clifford, the Big Red Dog*), born Kokomo, IN, Feb 15, 1928.
Jan Spivey Gilchrist, 57, illustrator, author (*Nathaniel Talking, Lift Ev'ry Voice and Sing*), born Chicago, IL, Feb 15, 1949.
Matt Groening, 52, cartoonist ("The Simpsons"), born Portland, OR, Feb 15, 1954.
Jaromir Jagr, 34, hockey player, born Kladno, Czechoslovakia, Feb 15, 1972.
Doris Orgel, 77, author (*The Devil in Vienna*), born Vienna, Austria, Feb 15, 1929.

FEBRUARY 16 — THURSDAY

Day 47 — 318 Remaining

LITHUANIA: INDEPENDENCE DAY: ANNIVERSARY. Feb 16. National Day. The anniversary of Lithuania's declaration of independence in 1918 is observed as the Baltic state's Independence Day. In 1940 Lithuania became a part of the Soviet Union under an agreement between Joseph Stalin and Adolf Hitler. On Mar 11, 1990, Lithuania declared its independence from the Soviet Union, the first of the Soviet republics to do so. After demanding independence, Lithuania set up a border police force and aided young men in efforts to avoid the Soviet military draft, prompting then Soviet leader Mikhail Gorbachev to send tanks into the capital of Vilnius and impose oil and gas embargoes. In the wake of the failed coup attempt in Moscow, Aug 19, 1991, Lithuanian independence finally was recognized.

LONGEST TRAFFIC JAM IN HISTORY: ANNIVERSARY. Feb 16, 1980. Travelers traveling north from Lyon, France, got snarled in the longest continuous traffic jam in history on this date: the cars stretched from Lyon to Paris—more than 109 miles.

WILSON, HENRY: BIRTH ANNIVERSARY. Feb 16, 1812. The 18th vice president of the US (1873–75). Born at Farmington, NH, he died at Washington, DC, Nov 22, 1875.

February 2006

S	M	T	W	T	F	S
			1	2	3	4
5	6	7	8	9	10	11
12	13	14	15	16	17	18
19	20	21	22	23	24	25
26	27	28				

BIRTHDAYS TODAY

Jerome Bettis, 34, football player, born Detroit, MI, Feb 16, 1972.
LeVar Burton, 49, actor, host ("Reading Rainbow"), born Landsthul, Germany, Feb 16, 1957.
Ahman Green, 29, football player, born Omaha, NE, Feb 16, 1977.

FEBRUARY 17 — FRIDAY

Day 48 — 317 Remaining

GERONIMO: DEATH ANNIVERSARY. Feb 17, 1909. American Indian of the Chiricahua (Apache) tribe was born about 1829 in Arizona. He was the leader of a small band of warriors whose devastating raids in Arizona, New Mexico and Mexico caused the US Army to send 5,000 men to recapture him after his first escape. He was confined at Fort Sill, OK, where he died after dictating, for publication, the story of his life.

NATIONAL PTA FOUNDERS' DAY: ANNIVERSARY. Feb 17, 1897. Celebrates the PTA's founding by Phoebe Apperson Hearst and Alice McLellan Birney. For info: National PTA, 330 N Wabash, Ste 2100, Chicago, IL 60611. Phone: (312) 670-6782. Fax: (312) 670-6783. E-mail: info@pta.org. Web: www.pta.org.

BIRTHDAYS TODAY

Vanessa Atler, 24, gymnast, born Valencia, CA, Feb 17, 1982.
Joseph Gordon-Levitt, 25, actor ("3rd Rock from the Sun," *Halloween H20*), born Los Angeles, CA, Feb 17, 1981.
Paris Hilton, 25, socialite, television personality ("The Simple Life"), born New York, NY, Feb 17, 1981.
Michael Jordan, 43, former basketball player, former minor league baseball player, born Brooklyn, NY, Feb 17, 1963.
Robert Newton Peck, 78, author (the Soup series, *A Day No Pigs Would Die*), born Vermont, Feb 17, 1928.
Craig Thomas, 73, US Senator (R, Wyoming), born Cody, WY, Feb 17, 1933.

FEBRUARY 18 — SATURDAY

Day 49 — 316 Remaining

COW MILKED WHILE FLYING IN AN AIRPLANE: ANNIVERSARY. Feb 18, 1930. Elm Farm Ollie became the first cow to fly in an airplane. During the flight, which was attended by reporters, she was milked and the milk was sealed in paper containers and parachuted over St. Louis, MO.

DAVIS, JEFFERSON: INAUGURATION ANNIVERSARY. Feb 18, 1861. In the years before the Civil War, Jefferson Davis was the acknowledged leader of the Southern bloc in the US Senate and a champion of states' rights, but he had little to do with the secessionist movement until after his home state of Mississippi joined the Confederacy Jan 9, 1861. Davis withdrew from the Senate that same day. He was unanimously chosen as president of the Confederacy's provisional government and inaugurated at Montgomery, AL, Feb 18. Within the next year he was elected to a six-year term by popular vote and was inaugurated a second time Feb 22, 1862, at Richmond, VA.

GAMBIA: INDEPENDENCE DAY. Feb 18. National holiday. Independence from Britain granted on this day in 1965. Referendum in April 1970 established Gambia as a republic within the Commonwealth.

PLANET PLUTO DISCOVERY: ANNIVERSARY. Feb 18, 1930. Pluto, the ninth planet, was discovered by astronomer Clyde Tombaugh at the Lowell Observatory at Flagstaff, AZ. It was given the name of the Roman god of the underworld. Some astronomers do not believe that Pluto is a planet. For more info: *Uranus, Neptune, and Pluto*, by Robin Kerrod (Lerner, 0-8225-3908-X, $21.27 Gr. 4–6) or go to Nine Planets: Multimedia Tour of the Solar System at www.seds.org/billa/tnp.

BIRTHDAYS TODAY

Barbara Joosse, 57, author (*Mama, Do You Love Me?, Ghost Trap: A Wild Willie Mystery*), born Grafton, WI, Feb 18, 1949.

John Warner, 79, US Senator (R, Virginia), born Washington, DC, Feb 18, 1927.

FEBRUARY 19 — SUNDAY

Day 50 — 315 Remaining

COPERNICUS, NICOLAUS: BIRTH ANNIVERSARY. Feb 19, 1473. Polish astronomer and priest who revolutionized scientific thought with what came to be called the Copernican theory, that placed the sun instead of the Earth at the center of our planetary system. Born at Torun, Poland, he died at East Prussia, May 24, 1543.

JAPANESE INTERNMENT: ANNIVERSARY. Feb 19, 1942. As a result of President Franklin Roosevelt's Executive Order 9066, some 110,000 Japanese-Americans living in coastal Pacific areas were placed in concentration camps in remote areas of Arizona, Arkansas, inland California, Colorado, Idaho, Utah and Wyoming. The interned Japanese-Americans (two-thirds were US citizens) lost an estimated $400 million in property. They were allowed to return to their homes Jan 2, 1945. For more info: *Life in a Japanese American Internment Camp*, by Diane Yancey (Lucent, 1-56006-345-9, $17.96 Gr. 6–12).

NATIONAL ENGINEERS WEEK. Feb 19–25. This 55th annual observance, cosponsored by 140 national engineering societies and many major national corporations, will feature classroom programs in elementary and secondary schools throughout the US, shopping mall exhibits, engineering workplace tours and other events. ***See Curriculum Connection.*** For more info: National Engineers Week Headquarters, 1420 King St, Alexandria, VA 22314. Phone: (703) 684-2852. E-mail: eweek@nspe.org. Web: www.eweek.org.

BIRTHDAYS TODAY

Jeff Daniels, 51, actor (*101 Dalmatians, Fly Away Home*), born Athens, GA, Feb 19, 1955.

Jill Krementz, 66, author and photographer (*A Very Young Dancer*, the How It Feels series), born New York, NY, Feb 19, 1940.

FEBRUARY 19–25
NATIONAL ENGINEER'S WEEK

Engineering is one of the fastest-growing professions in the US. This week's celebration marks a great opportunity for you to point out the vast opportunities for both the boys and girls in your class. By studying engineering, they will see the ultimate uses for the math problems and physics skills that they work so hard on every day. Engineers design roller coasters, computer software, space ship components and NASCAR vehicles. There are limitless opportunities for the child who is interested.

The American Society for Engineering Education (ASEE) has set up a wonderful website for teachers and students to learn as much as they can about this exciting field. At www.engineeringk12.org, the ASEE EngineeringK12 Center has gathered all sorts of resources suitable for use in any classroom in the K–12 community. From profiles of "cool" engineers to lesson plans to plans for science fair projects to links related to engineering education, almost anything you would need to celebrate this "week" can be found on this wonderful site.

Of course, the sponsors of the event have great information on their own website as well. The National Engineers Week Foundation, a group funded by many corporate sponsors, is able to offer teachers in-service planning, contests, curriculum materials and all sorts of other great resources. Check them out at www.eweek.org, and be sure to look at their product catalog featuring posters, buttons, stickers, certificates and more. They've set up a special website for older students (grades 6–9) at www.discoveringengineering.org with all sorts of games and downloads.

Also check out the PBS program "Zoom" and its website, www.pbskids.org/zoom, where they have worked in conjunction with the Foundation to set up some interesting activities, experiments and projects that might be suitable for your younger students. The "ZOOM Into Engineering" video and teacher resource "toolkit," featuring experiments like the egg bungee jump and construction of a puff mobile, can be ordered from the Foundation for minimal costs. —Kathryn Keil

FEBRUARY 20 — MONDAY

Day 51 — 314 Remaining

ADAMS, ANSEL: BIRTH ANNIVERSARY. Feb 20, 1902. American photographer, known for his photographs of Yosemite National Park, born at San Francisco, CA. Adams died at Monterey, CA, Apr 22, 1984. For info: *Eye on the World: A Story About Ansel Adams*, by Julie Dunlap (Carolrhoda, 0-876-14966-2, $5.95 Gr. K–3).

CLOSEST APPROACH OF A COMET TO EARTH: ANNIVERSARY. Feb 20, 1491. The closest approach of a comet to earth apparently happened on this date in 1491, when an unnamed comet came within 860,000 miles (.0094 AU). By comparison, the closest approach that Halley's Comet made to earth was on Apr 10, 837 AD, at 3 million miles.

DOUGLASS, FREDERICK: DEATH ANNIVERSARY. Feb 20, 1895. American journalist, orator and antislavery leader. Born at Tuckahoe, MD, probably in February 1817. Died at Anacostia Heights, Washington, DC. His original name before his escape from slavery was Frederick Augustus Washington Bailey. For more info: *Frederick Douglass in His Own Words*, edited by Milton Meltzer (Harcourt, 0-15-229492-9, $22 Gr. 7 & up) or *Frederick Douglass: Leader Against Slavery*, by Patricia McKissack and Fredrick McKissack (Enslow, 0-8949-0306-3, $14.95 Gr. K–3). See also: "Douglass Escapes to Freedom: Anniversary" (Sept 3).

NORTHERN HEMISPHERE HOODIE-HOO DAY. Feb 20. At high noon (local time) citizens are asked to go outdoors and yell "Hoodie-Hoo" to chase away winter and make ready for spring, one month away. [©2002 by WH.] For info: Thomas & Ruth Roy, Wellcat Holidays, 2418 Long Ln, Lebanon, PA 17046. Phone: (717) 279-0184. E-mail: info@wellcat.com. Web: www.wellcat.com.

PISCES, THE FISH. Feb 20–Mar 20. In the astronomical/astrological zodiac, which divides the sun's apparent orbit into 12 segments, the period Feb 20–Mar 20 is identified, traditionally, as the sun sign of Pisces, the Fish. The ruling planet is Neptune.

PRESIDENTS' DAY. Feb 20. Presidents' Day observes the birthdays of George Washington (Feb 22) and Abraham Lincoln (Feb 12). With the adoption of the Monday Holiday Law (which moved the observance of George Washington's birthday from Feb 22 each year to the third Monday in February), some of the specific significance of the event was lost and added impetus was given to the popular description of that holiday as Presidents' Day. Present usage often regards Presidents' Day as a day to honor all former presidents of the US. While the federal holiday still is George Washington's birthday, many states now declare Presidents' Day to be a holiday. Annually, the third Monday in February.

SPACE MILESTONE: *FRIENDSHIP 7* (US): FIRST AMERICAN TO ORBIT EARTH: ANNIVERSARY. Feb 20, 1962. John Herschel Glenn, Jr, became the first American, and the third man, to orbit Earth. Aboard the capsule *Friendship 7,* he made three orbits of Earth. Spacecraft was *Mercury-Atlas 6*. In 1998 the 77-year-old Glenn went into space once again on the space shuttle *Discovery* to study the effects of aging.

SPACE MILESTONE: *MIR* SPACE STATION (USSR): 20th ANNIVERSARY. Feb 20, 1986. A "third-generation" orbiting space station, *Mir* (Peace), was launched without crew from the Baikonur space center at Leninsk, Kazakhstan. It was 40 feet long, weighed 47 tons and had six docking ports. Russian and American crews used the station for 15 years. Russia took *Mir* out of service in March 2001.

WASHINGTON, GEORGE: BIRTHDAY OBSERVANCE (LEGAL HOLIDAY). Feb 20. Legal public holiday (Public Law 90–363 sets Washington's birthday observance on the third Monday in February each year—applicable to federal employees and to the District of Columbia). Observed on this day in all states. See also: "Washington, George: Birth Anniversary" (Feb 22).

BIRTHDAYS TODAY

Charles Barkley, 43, former basketball player, born Leeds, AL, Feb 20, 1963.

Phil Esposito, 64, Hall of Fame hockey player, born Sault Ste Marie, ON, Canada, Feb 20, 1942.

Rosemary Harris, 83, author (*The Moon in the Cloud*), born London, England, Feb 20, 1923.

Brian Littrell, 31, singer (Backstreet Boys), born Lexington, KY, Feb 20, 1975.

Stephon Marbury, 29, basketball player, born Brooklyn, NY, Feb 20, 1977.

Mitch McConnell, 64, US Senator (R, Kentucky), born Colbert County, AL, Feb 20, 1942.

February 2006

S	M	T	W	T	F	S
			1	2	3	4
5	6	7	8	9	10	11
12	13	14	15	16	17	18
19	20	21	22	23	24	25
26	27	28				

FEBRUARY 21 — TUESDAY

Day 52 — 313 Remaining

BANGLADESH: MARTYRS' DAY. Feb 21. National mourning day or Shaheed Day in memory of martyrs of the Bengali Language Movement in 1952.

BATTLE OF VERDUN: 90th ANNIVERSARY. Feb 21–Dec 18, 1916. The German High Command launched an offensive on the Western Front at Verdun, France, which became WWI's single longest battle. An estimated one million men were killed, decimating both the German and French armies.

FIRST WOMAN TO GRADUATE FROM DENTAL SCHOOL: ANNIVERSARY. Feb 21, 1866. Lucy Hobbs became the first woman to graduate from a dental school at Cincinnati, OH.

MOON PHASE: LAST QUARTER. Feb 21. Moon enters Last Quarter phase at 2:17 AM, EST.

UNITED NATIONS: INTERNATIONAL MOTHER LANGUAGE DAY. Feb 21. To help raise awareness among all peoples of the distinct and enduring value of their languages. Info from: United Nations, Dept of Public Info, New York, NY 10017. Web: www.un.org.

WASHINGTON MONUMENT DEDICATED: ANNIVERSARY. Feb 21, 1885. Monument to the first president was dedicated at Washington, DC. For more info: www.nps.gov/wash/index.htm.

BIRTHDAYS TODAY

Jim Aylesworth, 63, author (*The Gingerbread Man*), born Jacksonville, FL, Feb 21, 1943.

Charlotte Church, 20, singer (*Voice of an Angel*), born Wales, Feb 21, 1986.

Steve Francis, 29, basketball player, born Silver Springs, MD, Feb 21, 1977.

Patricia Hermes, 70, author (*When Snow Lay Soft on the Mountain*), born Brooklyn, NY, Feb 21, 1936.

Jennifer Love Hewitt, 27, actress (*I Know What You Did Last Summer*, "Party of Five"), born Waco, TX, Feb 21, 1979.

Victor Martinez, 52, author (National Book Award for *Parrot in the Oven: Mi Vida*), born Fresno, CA, Feb 21, 1954.

Olympia J. Snowe, 59, US Senator (R, Maine), born Augusta, ME, Feb 21, 1947.

FEBRUARY 22 — WEDNESDAY

Day 53 — 312 Remaining

BADEN-POWELL, ROBERT: BIRTH ANNIVERSARY. Feb 22, 1857. British army officer who founded the Boy Scouts and Girl Guides. Born at London, England, he died at Kenya, Africa, Jan 8, 1941.

MONTGOMERY BOYCOTT ARRESTS: 50th ANNIVERSARY. Feb 22, 1956. On Feb 20 white city leaders of Montgomery, AL, issued an ultimatum to black organizers of the three-month-old Montgomery bus boycott. They said if the boycott ended immediately there would be "no retaliation whatsoever." If it did not end, it was made clear they would begin arresting black leaders. Two days later, 80 well-known boycotters, including Rosa Parks, Martin Luther King, Jr, and E.D. Nixon, marched to the sheriff's office in the county courthouse, where they gave themselves up for arrest. They were booked, fingerprinted and photographed. The next day the story was carried by newspapers all over the world.

PUERTO RICO: CARNIVAL DE PONCE. Feb 22–28. Ponce. Carnival, artisans fair, parade with floats and papier-mâché masks. Annually, the week before Ash Wednesday. Est attendance: 100,000. For info: Tourism Dir, Municipality of Ponce, PO Box 331709, Ponce, Puerto Rico 00733. Phone: (787) 841-8044. E-mail: munponce@coqui.net. Web: www.ponceweb.org.

SAINT LUCIA: INDEPENDENCE DAY: ANNIVERSARY. Feb 22. National holiday. Commemorates independence from Britain in 1979.

WADLOW, ROBERT PERSHING: BIRTH ANNIVERSARY. Feb 22, 1918. Tallest man in recorded history, born at Alton, IL. Though only 9 lbs at birth, by age 10 Wadlow already stood more than 6 feet tall and weighed 210 lbs. When Wadlow died at age 22, he was a remarkable 8 feet 11.1 inches tall, 490 lbs. His gentle, friendly manner in the face of constant public attention earned him the name "Gentle Giant." Wadlow died July 15, 1940, at Manistee, MI, of complications resulting from a foot infection.

WASHINGTON, GEORGE: BIRTH ANNIVERSARY. Feb 22, 1732. First president of the US ("First in war, first in peace and first in the hearts of his countrymen" in the words of Henry "Light-Horse Harry" Lee). Born at Westmoreland County, VA, Feb 22, 1732 (New Style). When he was born the colonies were still using the Julian (Old Style) calendar and the year began in March, so the date on the calendar when he was born was Feb 11, 1731. He died at Mount Vernon, VA, Dec 14, 1799. See also: "Washington, George: Birthday Observance (Legal Holiday)" (Feb 20 in 2006). For more info: *George Washington & the Founding of a Nation*, by Albert Marrin (Dutton, 0-525-46481-6, $25 Gr. 7 & up) or www.ipl.org/ref/POTUS.

WOOLWORTHS FIRST OPENED: ANNIVERSARY. Feb 22, 1879. The first chain store, Woolworths, opened at Utica, NY. In 1997, the closing of the chain was announced.

BIRTHDAYS TODAY

Drew Barrymore, 31, actress (*E.T.: The Extra Terrestrial, The Wedding Singer, Charlie's Angels*), born Culver City, CA, Feb 22, 1975.

Michael Te Pei Chang, 34, tennis player, born Hoboken, NJ, Feb 22, 1972.

Lisa Fernandez, 35, softball player, born Long Beach, CA, Feb 22, 1971.

William Frist, 54, US Senator (R, Tennessee), born Nashville, TN, Feb 22, 1952.

Steve Irwin, 44, naturalist, television personality ("The Crocodile Hunter"), born Victoria, Australia, Feb 22, 1962.

Edward Moore (Ted) Kennedy, 74, US Senator (D, Massachusetts), born Boston, MA, Feb 22, 1932.

Kazuhiro Sasaki, 38, baseball player, born Sendai, Japan, Feb 22, 1968.

FEBRUARY 23 — THURSDAY

Day 54 — 311 Remaining

DU BOIS, W.E.B.: BIRTH ANNIVERSARY. Feb 23, 1868. William Edward Burghardt Du Bois, American educator and leader of the movement for black equality. Born at Great Barrington, MA, he died at Accra, Ghana, Aug 27, 1963. "The cost of liberty," he wrote in 1909, "is less than the price of repression." The February 2000 issue of *Cobblestone* magazine was devoted to Du Bois.

FIRST CLONING OF AN ADULT ANIMAL: ANNIVERSARY. Feb 23, 1997. Researchers in Scotland announced the first cloning of an adult animal, a lamb they named Dolly with a genetic makeup identical to that of her mother. This led to worldwide speculation about the possibility of human cloning. On Mar 4, President Clinton imposed a ban on the federal funding of human cloning research.

GUYANA: ANNIVERSARY OF REPUBLIC. Feb 23, 1970. National holiday. Located in South America, Guyana became a republic within the British Commonwealth Feb 23, 1970.

HANDEL, GEORGE FREDERICK: BIRTH ANNIVERSARY. Feb 23, 1685. Born at Halle, Saxony, Germany, Handel and Bach, born the same year, were perhaps the greatest masters of Baroque music. Handel's most frequently performed work is the oratorio *Messiah*, which was first heard in 1742. He died at London, England, Apr 14, 1759. See also: "Bach, Johann Sebastian: Birth Anniversary" (Mar 21).

INTRODUCE A GIRL TO ENGINEERING DAY. Feb 23. 7th annual. During National Engineers Week, the engineering community is asked to mobilize women and men engineers to reach more than 1 million girls and encourage them to pursue the fields that lead to engineering careers. Website includes links for teachers. For info: National Engineers Week Headquarters, 1420 King St, Alexandria, VA 22314. Phone: (703) 684-2852. E-mail: eweek@nspe.org. Web: www.eweek.org/site/News/Eweek/girlsday.shtml.

IWO JIMA DAY: ANNIVERSARY. Feb 23, 1945. The American flag was raised on the Pacific island of Iwo Jima by US marines after the World War II battle.

THE NATIONAL CONFERENCE ON EDUCATION. Feb 23–26. San Diego, CA. 138th annual conference. For info: American Assn of School Administrators, 801 N Quincy St, Ste 700, Arlington, VA 22203-1730. Phone: (703) 528-0700. Fax: (703) 841-1543. Web: www.aasa.org.

TAYLOR, GEORGE: 225th DEATH ANNIVERSARY. Feb 23, 1781. Signer of the Declaration of Independence. Born 1716 at British Isles (exact date unknown). Died at Easton, PA.

BIRTHDAYS TODAY

Laura Geringer, 58, author (the Myth Men series), born New York, NY, Feb 23, 1948.

Patricia Richardson, 55, actress ("Home Improvement"), born Bethesda, MD, Feb 23, 1951.

Walter Wick, 53, illustrator, photographer (the I Spy series, *A Drop of Water*), born Hartford, CT, Feb 23, 1953.

FEBRUARY 24 — FRIDAY

Day 55 — 310 Remaining

COURTENAY-LATIMER, MARJORIE: BIRTH ANNIVERSARY. Feb 24, 1907. Born in South Africa, this naturalist discovered in 1938 that the species coelacanth, a bony, four-finned fish, was not extinct, as had been previously presumed. The species is much studied by scientists as a link in the evolutionary chain. Self-taught, she also studied natural history and wildflowers. Courtenay-Latimer died at East London, South Africa, May 17, 2004.

ESTONIA: INDEPENDENCE DAY. Feb 24, 1918. National holiday. Commemorates declaration of independence from decades of Danish, Swedish, German and Russian rule. Estonia was forcibly incorporated into the USSR in 1940, but gained back its independence in 1991.

GREGORIAN CALENDAR DAY: ANNIVERSARY. Feb 24, 1582. Pope Gregory XIII, enlisting the expertise of distinguished astronomers and mathematicians, issued a bull correcting the Julian calendar that was then 10 days in error. The new calendar named for him, the Gregorian calendar, became effective Oct 4, 1582, in most Catholic countries, in 1752 in Britain and the American colonies, in 1918 in Russia and in 1923 in Greece. It is the most widely used calendar in the world today. See also: "Calendar Adjustment Day: Anniversary" (Sept 2) and "Gregorian Calendar Adjustment: Anniversary" (Oct 4).

GRIMM, WILHELM CARL: BIRTH ANNIVERSARY. Feb 24, 1786. Mythologist and author, born at Hanau, Germany. Best remembered for *Grimm's Fairy Tales*, in collaboration with his brother, Jacob. Died at Berlin, Germany, Dec 16, 1859. See also: "Grimm, Jacob: Birth Anniversary" (Jan 4). For more info: *The Brothers Grimm: Two Lives, One Legacy*, by Donald R. Hettinga (Clarion, 0-6180-5599-1, $22 Gr. 5 & up).

JOHNSON IMPEACHMENT PROCEEDINGS: ANNIVERSARY. Feb 24, 1867. In a showdown over Reconstruction policy following the Civil War, the House of Representatives voted to impeach President Andrew Johnson. During the two years following the end of the war, the Republican-controlled Congress had sought to severely punish the South. Congress passed the Reconstruction Act that divided the South into five military districts headed by officers who were to take their orders from General Grant, the head of the army, instead of from President Johnson. In addition, Congress passed the Tenure of Office Act, which required Senate approval before Johnson could remove any official whose appointment was originally approved by the Senate. Johnson vetoed this act but the veto was overridden by Congress. To test the constitutionality of the act, Johnson dismissed Secretary of War Edwin Stanton, triggering the impeachment vote. On Mar 5, 1868, the Senate convened as a court to hear the charges against President Johnson. The Senate vote of 35–19 fell one vote short of the two-thirds majority necessary for impeachment. For more info: www.law.umkc.edu/faculty/projects/ftrials/ftrials.htm.

MEXICO: FLAG DAY. Feb 24. *El Día de la Bandera.* National holiday honoring the Mexican flag, which was created in 1821 after Mexico achieved independence.

February 2006

S	M	T	W	T	F	S
			1	2	3	4
5	6	7	8	9	10	11
12	13	14	15	16	17	18
19	20	21	22	23	24	25
26	27	28				

WAGNER, HONUS: BIRTH ANNIVERSARY. Feb 24, 1874. American baseball great, born John Peter Wagner, at Carnegie, PA. Nicknamed the "Flying Dutchman," Wagner was among the first five players elected to the Baseball Hall of Fame in 1936. Died at Carnegie, Dec 6, 1955.

BIRTHDAYS TODAY

Beth Broderick, 47, actress ("Sabrina, the Teenage Witch"), born Falmouth, KY, Feb 24, 1959.

Jeff Garcia, 36, football player, born Gilroy, CA, Feb 24, 1970.

Lleyton Hewitt, 25, tennis player, born Adelaide, Australia, Feb 24, 1981.

Steven Jobs, 51, cofounder of Apple computer company, born Los Altos, CA, Feb 24, 1955.

Joseph I. Lieberman, 64, US Senator (D, Connecticut), born Stamford, CT, Feb 24, 1942.

Uri Orlev, 75, author (*Lydia, Queen of Palestine; The Man from the Other Side*), born Warsaw, Poland, Feb 24, 1931.

FEBRUARY 25 — SATURDAY

Day 56 — 309 Remaining

BRAZIL: CARNIVAL. Feb 25–28. Especially in Rio de Janeiro, this carnival is one of the great folk festivals and the big annual event in the life of Brazilians. Begins on Saturday night before Ash Wednesday and continues through Shrove Tuesday.

CLAY BECOMES HEAVYWEIGHT CHAMP: ANNIVERSARY. Feb 25, 1964. Twenty-two-year-old Cassius Clay (later Muhammad Ali) became world heavyweight boxing champion by defeating Sonny Liston. At the height of his athletic career Ali was well known for both his fighting ability and personal style. His most famous saying was "I am the greatest!" In 1967 he was convicted of violating the Selective Service Act and was stripped of his title for refusing to be inducted into the armed services during the Vietnam War. Ali cited religious convictions as his reason for refusal. In 1971 the Supreme Court reversed the conviction. Ali is the only fighter to win the heavyweight title three separate times. He defended that title nine times. For more info: *The Greatest: Muhammad Ali*, by Walter Dean Myers (Scholastic, 0-590-54342-3, $16.95 Gr. 5 & up).

KUWAIT: NATIONAL DAY. Feb 25. National holiday.

MALTA: CARNIVAL. Feb 25–28. Valletta. Festival dates from 1535 when Knights of St. John of Jerusalem introduced Carnival at Malta. Dancing (featuring the sword dance, or "Parata," and other national dances), bands, decorated trucks and grotesque masks. Annually, the Saturday through Tuesday before Ash Wednesday.

NATIONAL BANK CHARTERED BY CONGRESS: ANNIVERSARY. Feb 25, 1791. The First Bank of the US at Philadelphia, PA, was chartered. Proposed as a national (or central) bank by Alexander Hamilton, it lost its charter in 1811. The Second Bank of the US received a charter in 1816, which expired in 1836. Since that time, the US has had no central bank. Central banking functions are carried out by the Federal Reserve System, established in 1913.

RENOIR, PIERRE AUGUSTE: BIRTH ANNIVERSARY. Feb 25, 1841. Impressionist painter, born at Limoges, France. Renoir's paintings are known for their joy and sensuousness as well as their use of light. In his later years he was crippled by arthritis and would paint with the brush strapped to his hand. He died at Cagnes-sur-Mer, Provence, France, Dec 17, 1919.

BIRTHDAYS TODAY

Sean Astin, 35, actor (*The Goonies, The Lord of the Rings*), born Santa Monica, CA, Feb 25, 1971.

Cynthia Voigt, 64, author (Newbery for *Homecoming; Dicey's Song*), born Boston, MA, Feb 25, 1942.

Josh Wolff, 29, soccer player, born Stone Mountain, GA, Feb 25, 1977.

FEBRUARY 26 — SUNDAY

Day 57 — 308 Remaining

CODY, WILLIAM FREDERIC "BUFFALO BILL": BIRTH ANNIVERSARY. Feb 26, 1846. American frontiersman who claimed to have killed more than 4,000 buffalos, born at Scott County, IA. Subject of many heroic yarns, Cody became successful as a showman, taking his Wild West Show across the US and to Europe. Died Jan 10, 1917, at Denver, CO.

FASCHING SUNDAY. Feb 26. Germany and Austria. The last Sunday before Lent.

FEDERAL COMMUNICATIONS COMMISSION CREATED: ANNIVERSARY. Feb 26, 1934. President Franklin D. Roosevelt ordered the creation of a Communications Commission, which became the FCC. It was created by Congress June 19, 1934, to oversee communication by radio, wire or cable. TV and satellite communication later became part of its charge.

GRAND CANYON NATIONAL PARK ESTABLISHED: ANNIVERSARY. Feb 26, 1919. By an act of Congress, Grand Canyon National Park was established. An immense gorge cut through the high plateaus of northwest Arizona by the raging Colorado River and covering 1,218,375 acres, Grand Canyon National Park is considered one of the most spectacular natural phenomena in the world. For more info: www.nps.gov/grca.

ITALY: CARNIVAL WEEK. Feb 26–Mar 4. Milan. Carnival week is held according to local tradition, with shows and festive events for children on Tuesday and Thursday. Parades of floats, figures in the costume of local folk characters Meneghin and Cecca, parties and more traditional events are held on Saturday. Annually, the Sunday–Saturday of Ash Wednesday week.

KUWAIT: LIBERATION DAY. Feb 26. National holiday. Commemorates the liberation of Kuwait City from Iraqi troops on this day in 1991.

SHROVETIDE. Feb 26–28. The three days before Ash Wednesday: Shrove Sunday, Monday and Tuesday—a time for confession and for festivity before the beginning of Lent.

STRAUSS, LEVI: BIRTH ANNIVERSARY. Feb 26, 1829. Bavarian immigrant Levi Strauss created the world's first pair of jeans—Levi's 501 jeans—for California's gold miners in 1850. Born at Buttenheim, Bavaria, Germany, he died in 1902.

BIRTHDAYS TODAY

Sarah Ezer, 24, actress ("The Adventures of Shirley Holmes: Detective"), born Vancouver, BC, Canada, Feb 26, 1982.

Marshall Faulk, 33, football player, born New Orleans, LA, Feb 26, 1973.

Sharon Bell Mathis, 69, author (*The Hundred Penny Box*), born Atlantic City, NJ, Feb 26, 1937.

J.T. Snow, 38, baseball player, born Long Beach, CA, Feb 26, 1968.

Jenny Thompson, 33, Olympic swimmer, born Dover, NH, Feb 26, 1973.

Bernard Wolf, 76, author (*HIV Positive*), born New York, NY, Feb 26, 1930.

FEBRUARY 27 — MONDAY

Day 58 — 307 Remaining

CARNIVAL. Feb 27–28. Period of festivities, feasts, foolishness and gaiety immediately before Lent begins on Ash Wednesday. Ordinarily Carnival includes only Fasching (the Feast of Fools), being the Monday and Tuesday immediately preceding Ash Wednesday. The period of Carnival may also be extended to include longer periods in some areas. See also: "Carnival Season" (Jan 6).

DOMINICAN REPUBLIC: INDEPENDENCE DAY. Feb 27. National Day. Independence gained in 1844 with the withdrawal of Haitians, who had controlled the area for 22 years.

FASCHING. Feb 27–28. In Germany and Austria, Fasching, also called Fasnacht, Fasnet or Feast of Fools, is a Shrovetide festival with processions of masked figures, both beautiful and grotesque. Always the two days (Rose Monday and Shrove Tuesday) between Fasching Sunday and Ash Wednesday.

ICELAND: BUN DAY. Feb 27. Children invade homes in the morning with colorful sticks and receive gifts of whipped cream buns (on Shrove Monday).

KUWAIT LIBERATED AND 100-HOUR WAR ENDS: 15th ANNIVERSARY. Feb 27, 1991. Allied troops entered Kuwait City, Kuwait, four days after launching a ground offensive. President George Bush declared Kuwait to be liberated and ceased all offensive military operations in the Gulf War. The end of military operations at midnight EST came 100 hours after the beginning of the land attack.

LONGFELLOW, HENRY WADSWORTH: BIRTH ANNIVERSARY. Feb 27, 1807. American poet and writer, born at Portland, ME. He is best remembered for his classic narrative poems, such as *The Song of Hiawatha, Paul Revere's Ride* and *The Wreck of the Hesperus*. Died at Cambridge, MA, Mar 24, 1882. For more info: *Henry Wadsworth Longfellow: America's Beloved Poet*, by Bonnie Lukes (Morgan Reynolds, 1-883846-31-5, $19.95 Gr. 6–12).

MOON PHASE: NEW MOON. Feb 27. Moon enters New Moon phase at 7:31 PM, EST.

PERIGEAN SPRING TIDES. Feb 27. Spring tides, the highest possible tides, which occur when New Moon or Full Moon takes place within 24 hours of the moment the Moon is nearest Earth (perigee) in its monthly orbit. The word *spring* refers not to the season but comes from the German word *springen*, "to rise up."

SHROVE MONDAY. Feb 27. The Monday before Ash Wednesday. In Germany and Austria, this is called Rose Monday.

TRINIDAD AND TOBAGO: CARNIVAL. Feb 27–28. Port of Spain. Called by islanders "the mother of all carnivals," a special tradition that brings together people from all over the world in an incredible colorful setting that includes the world's most celebrated calypsonians, steel band players, costume designers and masqueraders. Annually, the two days before Ash Wednesday. For info: National Carnival Commission, Tourism and Industrial Development Co, Administration Bldg, Queen Park Savannah, Port of Spain, Trinidad and Tobago, West Indies. Phone: (809) 623-1932. Fax: (809) 623-3848.

TWENTY-SECOND AMENDMENT TO US CONSTITUTION (TWO-TERM LIMIT): RATIFICATION ANNIVERSARY. Feb 27, 1950. After the four successive presidential terms of Franklin Roosevelt, the 22nd Amendment limited the tenure of presidential office to two terms.

BIRTHDAYS TODAY

Tony Gonzales, 30, football player, born Torrance, CA, Feb 27, 1976.

Uri Shulevitz, 71, author and illustrator (*The Treasure*), born Warsaw, Poland, Feb 27, 1935.

FEBRUARY 28 — TUESDAY

Day 59 — 306 Remaining

ICELAND: BURSTING DAY. Feb 28. Shrove Tuesday feasts with salted mutton and thick pea soup.

MARDI GRAS. Feb 28. Celebrated especially at New Orleans, LA, Mobile, AL, and certain Mississippi and Florida cities. Last feast before Lent. Although Mardi Gras ("Fat Tuesday," literally) is properly limited to Shrove Tuesday, it has come to be popularly applied to the preceding two weeks of celebration.

SHROVE TUESDAY. Feb 28. Always the day before Ash Wednesday. Sometimes called Pancake Tuesday. A legal holiday in certain counties in Florida.

TAIWAN: TWO-TWENTY-EIGHT DAY. Feb 28. National holiday. Commemorates the thousands of Taiwanese killed in 1947 following the transfer of control from the Japanese to the Nationalists.

TENNIEL, JOHN: BIRTH ANNIVERSARY. Feb 28, 1820. Illustrator and cartoonist, born at London, England. Best remembered for his illustrations for Lewis Carroll's *Alice's Adventures in Wonderland*. Died at London, Feb 25, 1914.

BIRTHDAYS TODAY

Eric Lindros, 33, hockey player, born London, ON, Canada, Feb 28, 1973.

Megan McDonald, 47, author (the Judy Moody series), born Pittsburgh, PA, Feb 28, 1959.

Donna Jo Napoli, 58, author (*The Prince of the Pond, Stones in Water*), born Miami, FL, Feb 28, 1948.

Dean Smith, 75, basketball coach, born Emporia, KS, Feb 28, 1931.

Jamaal Tinsley, 28, basketball player, born Brooklyn, NY, Feb 28, 1978.

MARCH 1 — WEDNESDAY

Day 60 — 305 Remaining

★**AMERICAN RED CROSS MONTH.** Mar 1–31. Presidential Proclamation for Red Cross Month issued each year for March since 1943. Issued as American Red Cross Month since 1987.

THE ARRIVAL OF MARTIN PINZON: ANNIVERSARY. Mar 1, 1493. Martin Alonzo Pinzon (1440–1493), Spanish shipbuilder and navigator (and co-owner of the *Niña* and the *Pinta*), accompanied Christopher Columbus on his first voyage, as commander of the *Pinta*. Storms separated the ships on their return voyage, and the *Pinta* first touched land at Bayona, Spain, where Pinzon gave Europe its first news of the discovery of the New World before Columbus's landing at Palos. Pinzon's brother, Vicente Yanez Pinzon, was commander of the third caravel of the expedition, the *Niña*.

ARTICLES OF CONFEDERATION RATIFIED: 225th ANNIVERSARY. Mar 1, 1781. This compact made among the original 13 states had been adopted by the Continental Congress Nov 15, 1777, and submitted to the states for ratification Nov 17, 1777. Maryland was the last state to approve, Feb 27, 1781, but Congress named Mar 1, 1781, as the day of formal ratification. The Articles of Confederation remained the supreme law of the nation until Mar 4, 1789, when Congress first met under the Constitution.

ASH WEDNESDAY. Mar 1. Marks the beginning of Lent. Forty weekdays and six Sundays (Saturday considered a weekday) remain until Easter Sunday. Named for use of ashes in ceremonial penance.

ASSOCIATION FOR SUPERVISION AND CURRICULUM DEVELOPMENT CONFERENCE. Mar 1–3. Chicago, IL. For info: Assn for Supervision and Curriculum Development, 1703 N Beauregard St, Alexandria, VA 22311-1714. Phone: (703) 578-9600. Fax: (703) 575-5400. Web: www.ascd.org.

BOSNIA AND HERZEGOVINA: INDEPENDENCE DAY. Mar 1. Commemorates independence in 1991.

★**IRISH-AMERICAN HERITAGE MONTH.** Mar 1–31. Presidential Proclamation called for by House Joint Resolution 401 (PL 103–379).

JAPAN: OMIZUTORI (WATER-DRAWING FESTIVAL). Mar 1–14. Todaiji, Nara. At midnight, a solemn rite is performed in the flickering light of pine torches. People rush for sparks from the torches, which are believed to have magic power against evil. Most spectacular on the night of Mar 12. The ceremony of drawing water is observed at 2 AM Mar 13, to the accompaniment of ancient Japanese music.

WOMEN'S HISTORY MONTH
MARCH 1–31

Instead of focusing on any one particular famous woman this year, why not make sure that your classroom library has plenty of collections on the shelf celebrating the accomplishments of women from all walks of life? Here are some recommended selections.

Older students will embrace this first collection of fascinating stories about women who have made America great. *33 Things Every Girl Should Know About Women's History: From Suffragettes to Skirt Lengths to the ERA* (Crown Books, 0-375-81122-2, $12.95 Ages 12 & up) is edited by Tonya Bolden and features excerpts from various essays, poetry, historical diaries and fiction. Historic photographs and timelines help round out this wonderful collection.

For grades 4–7, two books offer inspiration to girls who love math, science or engineering. *Sky's the Limit: Stories of Discovery by Women and Girls* (Houghton Mifflin, 0-618-49489-8, $7.95) features accounts of women who made their mark in scientific fields. Author Catherine Thimmensh includes stories of women who made discoveries in the fields of paleontology, anthropology, astronomy and biology, all brought to life by Melissa Sweet's detailed illustrations. The same author team also brings us *Girls Think of Everything: Stories of Ingenious Inventions By Women* (Houghton Mifflin, 0-318-19563-7, $6.95). Did you know correction fluid, disposable diapers and chocolate chip cookies all came to be through female ingenuity?

Second Lady Lynne Cheney has put together a wonderful collection for younger children called *A Is for Abigail: An Almanac of Amazing American Women* (Simon & Schuster, 0-689-85819-1, $16.95). Through each letter of the alphabet we are introduced to women who made a difference in America, complete with quotations, background information and brilliant illustrations by Robin Preiss Glasser. First Ladies from Martha Washington to Laura Bush are highlighted, as is poet Emily Dickinson and singer Mahalia Jackson. There's a role model for every student in these pages.

With an assortment of books like this on your shelf, you'll have wonderful examples of women's history right at your fingertips, not just this month but all year long.

—Kathryn Keil

KOREA: SAMILJOL or INDEPENDENCE MOVEMENT DAY. Mar 1. Koreans observe the anniversary of the independence movement against Japanese colonial rule in 1919.

LENT. Mar 1–Apr 15. Most Christian churches observe period of fasting and penitence (40 weekdays and six Sundays—Saturday considered a weekday) beginning on Ash Wednesday and ending on the Saturday before Easter.

MENTAL RETARDATION AWARENESS MONTH. Mar 1–31. To educate the public about the needs of this nation's more than seven million citizens with mental retardation and about ways to prevent retardation. The Arc is a national organization on mental retardation, formerly the Association for Retarded Citizens. For info: The Arc, 1010 Wayne Ave, Ste 650, Silver Spring, MD 20910. Phone: (301) 565-3842. Fax: (301) 565-3542. Web: www.thearc.org.

MUSIC IN OUR SCHOOLS MONTH. Mar 1–31. To increase public awareness of the importance of music education as part of a balanced curriculum. Additional information and awareness items are available from MENC. For info: Music Educators

Natlional Conference, 1806 Robert Fulton Dr, Reston, VA 20191. Phone: (800) 336-3768. Web: www.menc.org. ***See Curriculum Connection.***

NATIONAL CRAFT MONTH. Mar 1–31. Promoting the fun and creativity of hobbies and crafts. For info: Hobby Industry Assn, National Craft Month, PO Box 348, Elmwood Park, NJ 07407. Phone: (201) 794-1133. Fax: (201) 797-0657. E-mail: hia@hobby.org. Web: www.hobby.org.

NATIONAL FROZEN FOOD MONTH. Mar 1–31. Promotes a national awareness of the economical and nutritional benefits of frozen foods. Annually, the month of March. For info: Julie Henderson, VP Communications, National Frozen and Refrigerated Food Assn, 4755 Linglestown Rd, Ste 300, Harrisburg, PA 17112. Phone: (717) 657-8601. Fax: (717) 657-9862. E-mail: info@nfraweb.org. Web: www.nfraweb.org.

NATIONAL MIDDLE LEVEL EDUCATION MONTH. Mar 1–31. To encourage middle level schools to schedule local events focusing on the educational needs of early adolescents. For info: Dir of Middle Level Services, National Assn of Secondary School Principals, 1904 Association Dr, Reston, VA 20190. Phone: (703) 860-7263. Web: www.principals.org/schoolimprove/middlelevel_home.cfm.

NATIONAL NUTRITION MONTH®. Mar 1–31. To educate consumers about the importance of good nutrition by providing the latest practical information on how simple it can be to eat healthfully. For info: The American Dietetic Assn, 120 S Riverside Plaza, Ste 2000, Chicago, IL 60606-6995. Phone: (312) 899-0040. Fax: (312) 899-4739. E-mail: knowledge@eatright.org. Web: www.eatright.org.

NATIONAL PIG DAY. Mar 1. To accord to the pig its rightful, though generally unrecognized, place as one of man's most intelligent and useful domesticated animals. Annually, Mar 1. For more info send SASE to: Ellen Stanley, 7006 Miami, Lubbock, TX 79413.

NATIONAL TALK WITH YOUR TEEN ABOUT SEX MONTH. Mar 1–31. The importance of frank talk with teenagers about sex is emphasized. Parents are encouraged to provide their teenage children with current, accurate information and open lines for communication, as well as support their self-esteem, reduce misinformation and guide teenagers toward making responsible decisions regarding sex. Annually, the month of March. For info send SASE to: Teresa Langston, Dir, Parenting Without Pressure (PWOP), 1330 Boyer St, Longwood, FL 32750-6311. Phone: (407) 767-2524. Web: www.parentingwithoutpressure.com.

NATIONAL UMBRELLA MONTH. Mar 1–31. In honor of one of the most versatile and underrated inventions of the human race, this month is dedicated to the purchase, use of and conversation about umbrellas. Annually, the month of March. For info: Thomas Edward Knibb, 1654 Colonial Way, Frederick, MD 21702-3919. Phone: (301) 695-7351. E-mail: tomknibb@juno.com.

NATIONAL WOMEN'S HISTORY MONTH. Mar 1–31. A time for reexamining and celebrating the wide range of women's contributions and achievements that are too often overlooked in the telling of US history. A theme kit on Women's History Month for grades 5–12 is available each year from the National Women's History Project. ***See Curriculum Connection.*** For info: National Women's History Project, 3343 Industrial Dr, Ste 4, Santa Rosa, CA 95403. Phone: (707) 636-2288. Fax: (707) 636-2909. E-mail: nwhp@aol.com. Web: www.nwhp.org.

March 2006

S	M	T	W	T	F	S
			1	2	3	4
5	6	7	8	9	10	11
12	13	14	15	16	17	18
19	20	21	22	23	24	25
26	27	28	29	30	31	

MARCH 1–31
BENJAMIN FRANKLIN'S ARMONICA

March is Music in Our Schools Month. Why not celebrate it and Benjamin Franklin's 300th birthday year with a little music of a unique sort? Franklin loved music and invented a musical instrument called the glass armonica. This unusual instrument contained 37 different-sized glass jars that were set on an iron spindle. Arranged from largest to smallest, the instrument was played by holding a wet finger against a spinning jar rim. This produced a humming sound. Large jars created low musical tones, while high-pitched tones were made with small jars.

Celebrate Ben's ingenuity by making an imitation glass armonica in your classroom. You will need eight open-necked jars of varying sizes to create a one-octave scale. Arrange the jars from large to small. The empty largest jar will serve as the lowest note in your octave. Tune the other seven jars to create a musical scale. The individual notes can be 'tuned' by adding water to each jar. This raises the tone. (If you need help, ask the music teacher to lend a hand.)

To produce the glass armonica tone, a student must first thoroughly wet his/her fingertip. When a wet fingertip is rubbed around the jar's rim, a note will be produced. (Primary students may find this difficult. If so, they can create a musical tone by tapping the side of the jars with a spoon instead.) Encourage students to experiment and see if they can use their glass armonica to play the song "Happy Birthday" in Ben's honor. What other songs can they play—or even compose—with the jars? This is a fun musical activity and it also complements science curriculum units on sound and physics.

Go to www.glassarmonica.com for the history of the glass armonica, as well as information about William Wilde Zeitler, a contemporary musician who plays modern versions of Franklin's instrument. —Sally Walker

NEBRASKA: ADMISSION DAY: ANNIVERSARY. Mar 1. Nebraska became the 37th state in 1867.

NEWSCURRENTS STUDENT EDITORIAL CARTOON CONTEST DEADLINE. Mar 1. Students in grades K–12 can win US Savings Bonds and get their work published in a national book by entering the annual Newscurrents Student Editorial Cartoon Contest. Participants must submit original cartoons on any subject of nationwide interest by this date. Complete rules available. For info: Jeff Robbins, Knowledge Unlimited, PO Box 52, Madison, WI 53701. Phone: (800) 356-2303. Fax: (800) 618-1570. Web: www.newscurrents.com.

OHIO: ADMISSION DAY: ANNIVERSARY. Mar 1. Ohio became the 17th state in 1803.

OPTIMISM MONTH. Mar 1–31. To encourage people to boost their optimism. Research proves optimists achieve more health, prosperity and happiness than pessimists. Use this monthlong celebration to practice optimism and turn optimism into a delightful, permanent habit. Free "Tip Sheets" available. For info: Dr. Michael Mercer & Dr. Maryann Troiani, The Mercer Group, Inc, 25597 Drake Rd, Barrington, IL 60010. Phone: (847) 382-0690. Email: drmercer@mercersystems.com.

PARAGUAY: NATIONAL HEROES' DAY. Mar 1. National holiday. Honors all who have died for the country.

PEACE CORPS FOUNDED: 45th ANNIVERSARY. Mar 1, 1961. Official establishment of the Peace Corps by President John F. Kennedy's signing of executive order. The Peace Corps has sent more than 170,000 volunteers to 136 developing countries to help people help themselves. The volunteers assist in projects such as health, education, water sanitation, agriculture, nutrition and forestry. For info: Peace Corps, 1111 20th St NW, Washington, DC 20526. Web: www.peacecorps.gov.

PLAY-THE-RECORDER MONTH. Mar 1–31. American Recorder Society members all over the continent will celebrate the organization's annual Play-the-Recorder Month by performing in public places such as libraries, bookstores, museums and shopping malls. Some will offer workshops on playing the recorder or demonstrations in schools. Founded in 1939, the ARS is the membership organization for all recorder players, including amateurs to leading professionals. Annually, the month of March. For info: American Recorder Society, PO Box 631, Littleton, CO 80160-0631. Phone: (303) 347-1120. Web: www.american recorder.org.

RED CROSS MONTH. Mar 1–31. To make the public aware of American Red Cross service in the community. There are some 1,300 Red Cross offices nationwide; each local office plans its own activities. For info on activities in your area, contact your local Red Cross office. For info: American Red Cross National HQ, Office of Public Inquiry, 431 18th St NW, Washington, DC 20006. Phone: (202) 639-3520. E-mail: info@usa.redcross.org. Web: www .redcross.org.

RETURN THE BORROWED BOOKS WEEK. Mar 1–7. To remind you to make room for those precious old volumes that will be returned to you, by cleaning out all that worthless trash that your friends are waiting for. Annually, the first seven days of March. For info: Inter-Global Society for Prevention of Cruelty to Cartoonists, Al Kaelin, Secy, 3119 Chadwick Dr, Los Angeles, CA 90032. Phone: (323) 221-7909.

SALEM WITCH HYSTERIA BEGINS: ANNIVERSARY. Mar 1, 1692. The Massachusetts Bay Colony village of Salem had experienced a strange February in which several teenaged girls exhibited bizarre behavior and attributed their ailments to witches. Three women were then arrested on Feb 29, 1692. One of the accused, Tituba, a West Indian slave, broke down under questioning on Mar 1 and admitted to being a witch. Soon the teenaged girls accused four other residents, and by the end of April, 19 women had been accused of witchcraft and were languishing in jail—including a four-year-old child. Massachusetts governor Sir William Phips, seeking to control the growing terror, ordered trials held. In October, the special court was dissolved after growing protests of the trials' unjust proceedings. By then, 19 people had been hung, 5 had died in jail, 1 had been tortured to death and more than 150 had been imprisoned. Two dogs were also executed. On Jan 14, 1697, Judge Samuel Sewall publicly apologized and a court-ordered day of atonement began. In 1711, all those accused of witchcraft were pardoned by the colony's legislature.

SAVE YOUR VISION MONTH. Mar 1–31. To remind Americans that vision is one of the most vital of all human needs and its protection is of great significance to the health and welfare of every individual. For info: American Optometric Assn, 243 N Lindbergh Blvd, St. Louis, MO 63141. Phone: (314) 991-4100. Fax: (314) 991-4101. E-mail: slthomas@aoa.org. Web: www.aoa.org.

SILLY PUTTY® DEBUTS: ANNIVERSARY. Mar 1, 1950. Sometime this month, Silly Putty was launched in Connecticut by Peter Hodgson. It had been discovered six years earlier by an engineer at General Electric who was trying to develop a synthetic rubber. He combined boric acid and silicone oil and got bouncing putty. No one at GE could figure out anything practical to do with it. Hodgson bought a batch of the stuff, put it in plastic eggs and it went on to become a very popular toy. More than 300 million eggs have been sold. Silly Putty even went to the moon in 1968 with the *Apollo* 8 astronauts. In the late 1970s, Silly Putty was bought by Binney & Smith Inc, the company that makes Crayola crayons. For more info: www.sillyputty.com.

SLAYTON, DONALD "DEKE" K.: BIRTH ANNIVERSARY. Mar 1, 1924. "Deke" Slayton, longtime chief of flight operations at the Johnson Space Center, was born at Sparta, WI. Slayton was a member of Mercury Seven, the original group of young military aviators chosen to inaugurate America's sojourn into space. Unfortunately, a heart problem prevented him from participating in any of the Mercury flights. When in 1971 the heart condition mysteriously went away, Slayton flew on the last Apollo Mission. The July 1975 flight, involving a docking with a Soviet Soyuz spacecraft, symbolized a momentary thaw in relations between the two nations. During his years as chief of flight operations, Slayton directed astronaut training and selected the crews for nearly all missions. He died June 13, 1993, at League City, TX.

SWITZERLAND: CHALANDRA MARZ. Mar 1. Engadine. Springtime traditional event when costumed young people, ringing bells and cracking whips, drive away the demons of winter.

WALES: SAINT DAVID'S DAY. Mar 1. Celebrates patron saint of Wales. Welsh tradition calls for the wearing of a leek on this day.

WHOOPING CRANE SPRING MIGRATION. Mar 1–May 7 (approximate). The endangered whooping crane leaves its overwintering refuge at Aransas National Wildlife Refuge in Texas for its summer nesting grounds at Wood Buffalo National Park in the Northwest Territories and Alberta, Canada, around this date. See also: "Whooping Crane Fall Migration" (Sept 15) and "Longest Human-Led Migration: Anniversary" (Dec 3). For more info: The International Crane Foundation site at http://savingcranes.org or the Whooping Crane Eastern Partnership at www.bringbackthe cranes.org.

★**WOMEN'S HISTORY MONTH.** Mar 1–31.

YELLOWSTONE NATIONAL PARK ESTABLISHED: ANNIVERSARY. Mar 1, 1872. The first area in the world to be designated a national park, most of Yellowstone is in Wyoming, with small sections in Montana and Idaho. It was established by an act of Congress. For more info: www.nps.gov/yell.

YOUTH ART MONTH. Mar 1–31. To emphasize the value and importance of participation in art activities and education for all children and youth. For info: Council for Art Education, Inc, 1280 Main St, PO Box 479, Hanson, MA 02341. Phone: (781) 293-4100. Fax: (781) 294-0808. Web: acminet.org/youthartmonth.

BIRTHDAYS TODAY

Barbara Helen Berger, 61, author (*A Lot of Otters*), born Lancaster, CA, Mar 1, 1945.

Stephen Davis, 32, football player, born Spartanburg, SC, Mar 1, 1974.

Ron Francis, 43, hockey player, born Sault Ste Marie, ON, Canada, Mar 1, 1963.

Yolanda Griffith, 36, former basketball player, born Chicago, IL, Mar 1, 1970.

Ron Howard, 52, actor ("Happy Days," "Andy Griffith Show"), producer, director (*Parenthood, Far and Away*), born Duncan, OK, Mar 1, 1954.

Chris Webber, 33, basketball player, born Detroit, MI, Mar 1, 1973.

MARCH 2 — THURSDAY

Day 61 — 304 Remaining

ETHIOPIA: ADWA DAY. Mar 2, 1896. Ethiopian forces under Menelik II inflicted a crushing defeat on the invading Italians at Adwa.

GEISEL, THEODOR "DR. SEUSS": BIRTH ANNIVERSARY. Mar 2, 1904. Theodor Seuss Geisel, the creator of *The Cat in the Hat* and *How the Grinch Stole Christmas*, was born at Springfield, MA. Known to children and parents as Dr. Seuss, his books have sold more than 200 million copies and have been translated into 20 languages. His career began with *And to Think That I Saw It on Mulberry Street*, which was turned down by 27 publishing houses before being published by Vanguard Press. His books included many messages, from environmental consciousness in *The Lorax* to the dangers of pacifism in *Horton Hatches the Egg* and *Yertle the Turtle*'s thinly veiled references to Hitler as the title character. He was awarded a Pulitzer Prize in 1984 "for his contribution over nearly half a century to the education and enjoyment of America's children and their parents." He died Sept 24, 1991, at La Jolla, CA.

HIGHWAY NUMBERS INTRODUCED: ANNIVERSARY. Mar 2, 1925. A joint board of state and federal highway officials created the first system of interstate highway numbering in the US. Standardized road signs identifying the routes were also introduced. Later the system would be improved with the use of odd and even numbers that distinguish between north-south and east-west routes respectively.

HOUSTON, SAM: BIRTH ANNIVERSARY. Mar 2, 1793. American soldier and politician, born at Rockbridge County, VA, is remembered for his role in Texas history. Houston was a congressman (1823–27) and governor (1827–29) of Tennessee. He resigned his office as governor in 1829 and rejoined the Cherokee Indians (with whom he had lived for several years as a teenage runaway), who accepted him as a member of their tribe. Houston went to Texas in 1832 and became commander of the Texan army in the War for Texan Independence, which was secured when Houston routed the much larger Mexican forces led by Santa Ana, Apr 21, 1836, at the Battle of San Jacinto. After Texas's admission to the Union, Houston served as US senator and later as governor of the state. He was deposed in 1861 when he refused to swear allegiance to the Confederacy. Houston, the only person to have been elected governor of two different states, failed to serve his full term of office in either. The city of Houston, TX, was named for him. He died July 26, 1863, at Huntsville, TX.

March 2006

S	M	T	W	T	F	S
			1	2	3	4
5	6	7	8	9	10	11
12	13	14	15	16	17	18
19	20	21	22	23	24	25
26	27	28	29	30	31	

MOUNT RAINIER NATIONAL PARK ESTABLISHED: ANNIVERSARY. Mar 2, 1899. Located in the Cascade Range in north-central Washington state, this is the fourth oldest park in the national park system. For more info: www.nps.gov/mora.

NSSEA ED EXPO AND SCHOOL EQUIPMENT SHOW. Mar 2–5. Orlando, FL. Find new products for back to school at this conference sponsored by the National School Supply & Equipment Association. The Ed Expo runs Mar 2–4 and the School Equipment Show is Mar 3–5, 2006. For info: Shari Levine or Monique Ferguson, National School Supply & Equipment Association, 8300 Colesville Rd., Ste. 250, Silver Spring, MD 20910. Phone: (301) 495-0240 or (800)395-5550. Fax: (301) 495-3330. Web: www.nssea.org.

READ ACROSS AMERICA DAY. Mar 2. A national reading campaign that advocates that all children read a book on Mar 2. Celebrated in honor of Dr. Seuss's birthday. For info: National Education Assn, 1201 16th St NW, Washington, DC, 20036. Phone: (202) 822-7830. Web: www.nea.org/readacross.

SPACE MILESTONE: *PIONEER 10* (US). Mar 2, 1972. This unmanned probe began a journey on which it passed and photographed Jupiter and its moons, 620 million miles from Earth, in December 1973. It crossed the orbit of Pluto, and then in 1983 become the first known Earth object to leave our solar system. On Sept 22, 1987, *Pioneer 10* reached another space milestone at 4:19 PM, when it reached a distance 50 times farther from the sun than the sun is from Earth.

SPACE MILESTONE: *SOYUZ 28* (USSR). Mar 2, 1978. Cosmonauts Alexi Gubarev and Vladimir Remek linked with *Salyut 6* space station Mar 3, visiting crew of *Soyuz 26*. Returned to Earth Mar 10. Remek, from Czechoslovakia, was the first person in space from a country other than the US or USSR. Launched Mar 2, 1978.

TEXAS INDEPENDENCE DAY. Mar 2, 1836. Texas adopted Declaration of Independence from Mexico.

BIRTHDAYS TODAY

Leo Dillon, 73, illustrator, with his wife Diane Dillon (Caldecotts for *Why Mosquitoes Buzz in People's Ears, Ashanti to Zulu: African Traditions*), born Brooklyn, NY, Mar 2, 1933.

Russell D. Feingold, 53, US Senator (D, Wisconsin), born Janesville, WI, Mar 2, 1953.

Anne Isaacs, 57, author (*Swamp Angel, Treehouse Tales*), born Buffalo, NY, Mar 2, 1949.

Ken Salazar, 51, US Senator (D, Colorado), born San Luis Valley, CO, Mar 2, 1955.

MARCH 3 — FRIDAY

Day 62 — 303 Remaining

BELL, ALEXANDER GRAHAM: BIRTH ANNIVERSARY. Mar 3, 1847. Inventor of the telephone, born at Edinburgh, Scotland, Alexander Graham Bell acquired his interest in the transmission of sound from his father, Melville Bell, a teacher of the deaf. His employment of visual devices to teach articulation to the deaf contributed to the theory from which he derived the principle of the vibrating membrane used in the telephone. On Mar 10, 1876, Bell spoke the first electrically transmitted sentence to his assistant in the next room, "Mr Watson, come here, I want you." The Bell Telephone Company was formed by Bell and two backers in July 1877. He died near Baddeck, Nova Scotia, Canada, Aug 2, 1922. For more info: *Always Inventing: A Photobiography of Alexander Graham Bell* by Tom L. Matthews (National Geographic, 0-7922-7391-5, $16.95 Gr. 4–7).

BONZA BOTTLER DAY™. Mar 3. To celebrate when the number of the day is the same as the number of the month. Bonza Bottler Day™ is an excuse to have a party at least once a month. For info: Gail M. Berger, 14 Fernwood Dr, Taylors, SC 29687. Phone: (864) 609-9874. E-mail: gberger5@aol.com.

BULGARIA: LIBERATION DAY. Mar 3. Grateful tribute to the Russian, Romanian and Finnish soldiers and Bulgarian volunteers who, in the Russo-Turkish War, 1877–78, liberated Bulgaria from five centuries of Ottoman rule.

FLORIDA: ADMISSION DAY: ANNIVERSARY. Mar 3. Became 27th state in 1845.

I WANT YOU TO BE HAPPY DAY. Mar 3. A day dedicated to reminding people to be thoughtful of others by showing love and care and concern, even if things are not going well for them. For info: Harriette W. Grimes, Grandmother, PO Box 545, Winter Garden, FL 34777-0545. Fax: (407) 656-2790. Email: lgrimes@cybr.net.

JAPAN: HINAMATSURI (DOLL FESTIVAL). Mar 3. This special festival for girls is observed throughout Japan. Annually, Mar 3.

MALAWI: MARTYR'S DAY. Mar 3. Public holiday in Malawi.

MISSOURI COMPROMISE: ANNIVERSARY. Mar 3, 1820. In February 1819, a bill was introduced into Congress that would admit Missouri to the Union as a state that prohibited slavery. At the time there were 11 free states and 10 slave states. Southern congressmen feared this would upset the balance of power between North and South. As a compromise, on this date Missouri was admitted as a slave state but slavery was forever prohibited in the northern part of the Louisiana Purchase. In 1854 this act was repealed when Kansas and Nebraska were allowed to decide on slave or free status by popular vote.

NATIONAL ANTHEM DAY: 75th ANNIVERSARY. Mar 3, 1931. The bill designating "The Star-Spangled Banner" as our national anthem was adopted by the US Senate and went to President Herbert Hoover for signature. The president signed it the same day. ***See Curriculum Connection.***

***TIME* MAGAZINE FIRST PUBLISHED: ANNIVERSARY.** Mar 3, 1923. The first issue of *Time* bore this date. The magazine was founded by Henry Luce and Briton Hadden. In 1996 *Time for Kids* was launched. For more info: www.timeforkids.com.

WORLD DAY OF PRAYER. Mar 3. An ecumenical event that reinforces bonds between peoples of the world as they join in a global circle of prayer. Annually, the first Friday in March. Sponsor: International Committee for World Day of Prayer. Church Women United is the National World Day of Prayer Committee for the US. For info: Church Women United, 475 Riverside Dr, Ste 1626, New York, NY 10115. Phone: (212) 870-3339 or (800) 298-5551. Fax: (212) 870-2338. Web: www.churchwomen.org.

MARCH 3
75th ANNIVERSARY OF THE NATIONAL ANTHEM

Today marks the anniversary of the adoption of the song *The Star-Spangled Banner* as the national anthem of the United States. This song was written as a poem by Francis Scott Key during the War of 1812 as he watched a British attack on Fort Henry in Maryland. The assault continued through the night, and when the air suddenly became silent, no one knew who had won the battle. It was not until daybreak of Sept 14, 1814, that Key could see the American flag still flying over Fort Henry. The British had retreated.

Key wrote his poem on the back of a letter, and first had it published in Baltimore under the title "Defence of Fort McHenry." It was picked up by newspapers and it was soon set to music—that of an old English pub tune called "Anacreon in Heaven." In October 1814, a Baltimore actor sang Key's new song in a public performance and called it "The Star-Spangled Banner." More than 100 years later, Congress finally passed a bill making the song our official national anthem, and President Herbert Hoover signed the bill making it law on Mar 3, 1931.

There are several great books that tell the story not only of Francis Scott Key but also the War of 1812, considered by many historians to be the "forgotten" war in American history. Peter Spier's picture book *The Star-Spangled Banne*r (Bantam, 0-440-40697-8, $10.95 Ages 4–10) has very detailed artwork showing the dramatic battle at Fort Henry, and it also includes the sheet music and lyrics for the beloved song. *The Star-Spangled Banner* by Catherine A. Welch and Carrie Warwick (Lerner Publishing, 1-575-05697-6, $5.95 Ages 7–10) and other titles also dramatically illustrate the "bombs bursting in air" and "rockets' red glare."

The National Association for Music Education (MENC) is presenting a yearlong campaign to encourage all Americans to learn the words to the anthem and to take great pride in singing it. Visit their website at http://thenationalanthemproject.org for more information, including the lyrics, sheet music and helpful advice on getting all your students to hit the high notes! There is also fascinating information about the "rules" governing when, where and how the national anthem may be performed in public.

The Smithsonian website also has lots of great information about the anthem; visit their website at www.si.edu/resource/faq/nmah/starflag.htm. The Smithsonian's National Museum of American History in Washington, DC, has the original flag that flew above Fort Henry in their collection, and students can also see the flag on The Smithsonian's website.

—Kathryn Keil

BIRTHDAYS TODAY

Jessica Biel, 24, actress ("7th Heaven"), born Ely, MN, Mar 3, 1982.

Erik Blegvad, 83, illustrator (*The Tenth Good Thing About Barney*, *Diamond in the Window*), born Copenhagen, Denmark, Mar 3, 1923.

Jacqueline Joyner-Kersee, 44, Olympic gold medal heptathlete, born East St. Louis, IL, Mar 3, 1962.

Patricia MacLachlan, 68, author (Newbery for *Sarah, Plain and Tall*), born Cheyenne, WY, Mar 3, 1938.

★ ★ ★

MARCH 4 — SATURDAY

Day 63 — 302 Remaining

ADAMS, JOHN QUINCY: RETURN TO CONGRESS: ANNIVERSARY. Mar 4, 1830. John Quincy Adams returned to the House of Representatives to represent the district of Plymouth, MA. He was the first former president to do so and served for eight consecutive terms.

CONGRESS: ANNIVERSARY OF FIRST MEETING UNDER CONSTITUTION. Mar 4, 1789. The first Congress met at New York, NY. A quorum was obtained in the House on Apr 1, in the Senate Apr 5 and the first Congress was formally organized Apr 6. Electoral votes were counted, and George Washington was declared president (69 votes) and John Adams vice president (34 votes).

GROVER CLEVELAND'S SECOND PRESIDENTIAL INAUGURATION: ANNIVERSARY. Mar 4, 1893. Grover Cleveland was inaugurated for a second but nonconsecutive term as president. In 1885 he had become 22nd president of the US and in 1893 the 24th. Originally a source of some controversy, the Congressional Directory for some time listed him only as the 22nd president. The directory now lists him as both the 22nd and 24th presidents, though some historians continue to argue that one person cannot be both. Benjamin Harrison served during the intervening term, defeating Cleveland in electoral votes, though not in the popular vote.

HOT SPRINGS NATIONAL PARK ESTABLISHED: 85th ANNIVERSARY. Mar 4, 1921. To protect the hot springs of Arkansas the government set aside Hot Springs Reservation on Apr 20, 1832. In 1921 the area became a national park. For more info: www.nps.gov/hots/index.htm.

NATIONAL ART EDUCATION ASSOCIATION ANNUAL CONVENTION. Mar 4–8. Boston, MA. For info: National Art Education Assn, 1916 Association Dr, Reston, VA 20191-1590. Phone: (703) 860-8000. Web: www.naea-reston.org.

OLD INAUGURATION DAY. Mar 4. Anniversary of the date set for beginning the US presidential term of office, 1789–1933. Although the Continental Congress had set the first Wednesday of March 1789 as the date for the new government to convene, a quorum was not present to count the electoral votes until Apr 6. Though George Washington's term of office began Mar 4, he did not take the oath of office until Apr 30, 1789. All subsequent presidential terms (except successions following the death of an incumbent), until Franklin D. Roosevelt's second term, began Mar 4. The 20th Amendment (ratified Jan 23, 1933) provided that "the terms of the President and Vice President shall end at noon on the 20th day of January . . . and the terms of their successors shall then begin."

PENNSYLVANIA DEEDED TO WILLIAM PENN: 325th ANNIVERSARY. Mar 4, 1681. To satisfy a debt of £16,000, King Charles II of England granted a royal charter, deed and governorship of Pennsylvania to William Penn.

***PEOPLE* MAGAZINE: ANNIVERSARY.** Mar 4, 1974. This popular magazine highlighting celebrities was officially launched with the Mar 4, 1974, issue featuring a cover photo of Mia Farrow.

March 2006

S	M	T	W	T	F	S
			1	2	3	4
5	6	7	8	9	10	11
12	13	14	15	16	17	18
19	20	21	22	23	24	25
26	27	28	29	30	31	

PULASKI, CASIMIR: BIRTH ANNIVERSARY. Mar 4, 1747. American Revolutionary War hero, General Kazimierz (Casimir) Pulaski, born at Winiary, Mazovia, Poland, the son of a count. He was a patriot and military leader in Poland's fight against Russia of 1770–71 and went into exile at the partition of Poland in 1772. He went to America in 1777 to join the Revolution, fighting with General Washington at Brandywine and also serving at Germantown and Valley Forge. He organized the Pulaski Legion to wage guerrilla warfare against the British. Mortally wounded in a heroic charge at the siege of Savannah, GA, he died aboard the warship *Wasp* Oct 11, 1779. Pulaski Day is celebrated Oct 11 in Nebraska schools and in Massachusetts and on the first Monday of March in Illinois and Indiana (Mar 6 in 2006). It is a day of special school observance in Wisconsin on Mar 4.

ROCKNE, KNUTE: BIRTH ANNIVERSARY. Mar 4, 1888. Legendary Notre Dame football coach, born at Voss, Norway. Known for such sayings as "Win one for the Gipper," he died at Cottonwood Falls, KS, Mar 31, 1931.

VERMONT: ADMISSION DAY: ANNIVERSARY. Mar 4. Vermont became the 14th state in 1791.

BIRTHDAYS TODAY

David A. Carter, 49, author, illustrator (*Jingle Bugs, Alpha Bugs, How Many Bugs in a Box?*), born Salt Lake City, UT, Mar 4, 1957.
Landon Donovan, 24, soccer player, born Redlands, CA, Mar 4, 1982.
Peyton Manning, 30, football player, born New Orleans, LA, Mar 4, 1976.
Rick Perry, 56, Governor of Texas (R), born Haskell, TX, Mar 4, 1950.
Dav Pilkey, 40, author and illustrator (the Dumb Bunnies series, the Captain Underpants series, *The Paperboy*), also known as Sue Denim, born Cleveland, OH, Mar 4, 1966.
Peggy Rathmann, 53, author and illustrator (Caldecott for *Officer Buckle and Gloria*), born St. Paul, MN, Mar 4, 1953.

MARCH 5 — SUNDAY

Day 64 — 301 Remaining

BOSTON MASSACRE: ANNIVERSARY. Mar 5, 1770. A skirmish between British troops and a crowd at Boston, MA, became widely publicized and contributed to the unpopularity of the British regime in America before the American Revolution. Five men were killed and six more were injured by British troops commanded by Captain Thomas Preston.

CHANNEL ISLANDS NATIONAL PARK ESTABLISHED: ANNIVERSARY. Mar 5, 1980. California's Channel Islands Monument, authorized in 1938 by President Franklin D. Roosevelt, consisted of the islands of Anacapa and Santa Barbara. In 1980 President Jimmy Carter signed a bill establishing the Channel Islands National Park consisting of the islands Anacapa, San Miguel, Santa Barbara, Santa Cruz and Santa Rosa. For more info: www.nps.gov/chis.index.htm.

CHILDREN'S LITERATURE FESTIVAL. Mar 5–7. James C. Kirkpatrick Library, Central Missouri State University, Warrensburg, MO. 38th annual. For children in grades 4–8. Est attendance: 7,000. For info: Children's Literature Festival, Central Missouri State Univ, Warrensburg, MO 64093. Phone: (660) 543-4306. Fax: (660) 543-8001. Web: library.cmsu.edu/children.htm.

CRISPUS ATTUCKS DAY: DEATH ANNIVERSARY. Mar 5, 1770. Honors Crispus Attucks, possibly a runaway slave, who was the first to die in the Boston Massacre.

LUXEMBOURG: BÜRGSONNDEG. Mar 5. Young people build a huge bonfire on a hill to celebrate the victorious sun, marking the end of winter. A tradition dating to pre-Christian times. The Sunday after Ash Wednesday.

MERCATOR, GERHARDUS: BIRTH ANNIVERSARY. Mar 5, 1512. Cartographer-geographer Mercator was born at Rupelmonde, Belgium. His Mercator projection for maps provided an accurate ratio of latitude to longitude (though it distorts the relative size of land masses) and is still used today. He also introduced the term "atlas" for a collection of maps. He died at Duisberg, Germany, Dec 2, 1594.

PYLE, HOWARD: BIRTH ANNIVERSARY. Mar 5, 1853. Illustrator and author, known for the children's books *Bearskin* and *The Merry Adventures of Robin Hood*. Born at Wilmington, DE, Pyle died at Florence, Italy, Nov 9, 1911.

SAINT PIRAN'S DAY. Mar 5. Celebrates the birthday of St. Piran, the patron saint of Cornish tinners. Cornish worldwide celebrate this day.

★ **SAVE YOUR VISION WEEK.** Mar 5–11. Presidential Proclamation issued for the first full week of March since 1964, except 1971 and 1982 when issued for the second week of March. (Public Law 88–1942, of Dec 30, 1963.)

BIRTHDAYS TODAY

Merrion Frances (Mem) Fox, 60, author (*Possum Magic, Koala Lou*), born Australia, Mar 5, 1946.

Jake Lloyd, 17, actor (*Star Wars: The Phantom Menace*), born Fort Collins, CO, Mar 5, 1989.

MARCH 6 — MONDAY

Day 65 — 300 Remaining

BROWNING, ELIZABETH BARRETT: 200th BIRTH ANNIVERSARY. Mar 6, 1806. English poet, author of *Sonnets from the Portuguese*, wife of poet Robert Browning and subject of the play *The Barretts of Wimpole Street*, was born near Durham, England. She died at Florence, Italy, June 29, 1861.

CLEAN MONDAY. Mar 6. Clean, or Green, Monday is the first Monday of Lent on the Orthodox calendar.

FALL OF THE ALAMO: ANNIVERSARY. Mar 6, 1836. Anniversary of the fall of the Texan fort, the Alamo, in what is now San Antonio, TX. The siege, led by Mexican general Santa Ana, began Feb 23 and reached its climax Mar 6, when the last of the defenders was slain. Texans, under General Sam Houston, rallied with the war cry "Remember the Alamo" and, at the Battle of San Jacinto, Apr 21, defeated and captured Santa Ana, who signed a treaty recognizing Texas's independence. For more info: *Voices of the Alamo* by Sherry Garland (Scholastic, 0-590-98833-6, $16.95 Gr. 3–6) or www.thealamo.org.

GHANA: INDEPENDENCE DAY. Mar 6. National holiday. Gained independence from Great Britain in 1957.

GUAM: DISCOVERY DAY or MAGELLAN DAY. Mar 6. Commemorates discovery of Guam in 1521. Annually, the first Monday in March.

MICHELANGELO: BIRTH ANNIVERSARY. Mar 6, 1475. Michelangelo Buonarroti, a prolific Renaissance painter, sculptor, architect and poet who had a profound effect on Western art, born at Caprese, Italy. Michelangelo's fresco painting on the ceiling of the Sistine Chapel at the Vatican in Rome and his statues *David* and *The Pieta* are among his best-known achievements. Appointed architect of St. Peter's in 1542, a post he held until his death Feb 18, 1564, at Rome. For more info: *Michelangelo* by Gabriella Di Cagno (Peter Bedrick, 0-87226-319-3, $22.50 Gr. 4–7) or *Michelangelo* by Diane Stanley (HarperCollins, 0-688-15086-1, $15.98 Gr. 5–8).

MOON PHASE: FIRST QUARTER. Mar 6. Moon enters First Quarter phase at 3:16 PM, EST.

NATIONAL SCHOOL BREAKFAST WEEK. Mar 6–10. To focus on the importance of a nutritious breakfast served in the schools, giving children a good start to their day. Annually, the first full week in March (weekdays). For info: American School Food Service Assn, 700 S Washington St, Ste 300, Alexandria, VA 22314. Phone: (703) 739-3900. E-mail: asfsa@asfsa.org. Web: www.asfsa.org.

NEWSPAPER IN EDUCATION WEEK. Mar 6–10. A weeklong celebration using newspapers in the classroom as living textbooks. Each year, more than 700 newspapers in the US and Canada participate in this event. Annually, the first full week in March (weekdays). For info: Mgr Education Programs, Newspaper Assn of America Foundation, 1921 Gallows Rd, Ste 600, Vienna, VA 22182-3900. Phone: (703) 902-1730. E-mail: abboj@naa.org. Web: www.naa.org.

ORTHODOX LENT. Mar 6–Apr 22. Great Lent or Easter Lent, observed by Eastern Orthodox Churches, lasts until Holy Week begins on Orthodox Palm Sunday (Apr 16). The first day of Lent is known as Clean Monday as the Great Fast begins. Orthodox Christians abstain from eating meat, dairy and fish.

BIRTHDAYS TODAY

Christopher S. Bond, 67, US Senator (R, Missouri), born St. Louis, MO, Mar 6, 1939.

Michael Finley, 33, basketball player, born Melrose Park, IL, Mar 6, 1973.

Alan Greenspan, 80, economist, Chairman of the Federal Reserve Board, born New York, NY, Mar 6, 1926.

Thatcher Hurd, 57, author, illustrator (*Zoom City, Blackberry Ramble*), born Burlington, VT, Mar 6, 1949.

Ryan Nyquist, 27, BMX bike racer, born Los Gatos, CA, Mar 6, 1979.

Shaquille Rashan O'Neal, 34, basketball player, born Newark, NJ, Mar 6, 1972.

Chris Raschka, 47, author, illustrator (Caldecott honor for *Yo! Yes?; Charlie Parker Played Be-Bop*), born Huntington, PA, Mar 6, 1959.

MARCH 7 — TUESDAY

Day 66 — 299 Remaining

ANTARCTIC ICE SHELF COLLAPSES: ANNIVERSARY. Mar 7, 2002. During the period from Jan 31 to Mar 7, 2002, the Larsen B segment of the Larsen Ice Shelf collapsed, disintegrated and sent thousands of icebergs into the Weddell Sea off the Antarctic Peninsula. Larsen B was 650 feet thick and 1,300 square miles—slightly larger than the state of Rhode Island—and it contained 750 billion tons of ice. Despite the volume of ice, the sea level wasn't affected because the ice shelf was already floating. The Larsen Ice Shelf is estimated to be 12,000 years old. About 40% of it remains (Larsen A collapsed in 1995). The Peninsula has seen 50 years of warming temperatures.

BURBANK, LUTHER: BIRTH ANNIVERSARY. Mar 7, 1849. American naturalist and author, creator and developer of many new varieties of flowers, fruits, vegetables and trees. Luther Burbank's birthday is observed by some as Bird and Arbor Day. Born at Lancaster, MA, he died at Santa Rosa, CA, Apr 11, 1926.

HOPKINS, STEPHEN: BIRTH ANNIVERSARY. Mar 7, 1707. Colonial governor (Rhode Island) and signer of the Declaration of Independence. Born at Providence, RI, and died there July 13, 1785.

MONOPOLY INVENTED: ANNIVERSARY. Mar 7, 1933. While unemployed during the Depression, Charles Darrow devised this game. He sold it himself for two years; Monopoly was mass marketed by Parker Brothers beginning in 1935. Darrow died a millionaire in 1967.

TOWN MEETING DAY IN VERMONT. Mar 7. The first Tuesday in March is an official state holiday in Vermont. Nearly every town elects officers, approves budget items and deals with a multitude of other items in a daylong public meeting of the voters.

BIRTHDAYS TODAY

Michael Eisner, 64, Disney executive, born Mount Kisco, NY, Mar 7, 1942.

MARCH 8 — WEDNESDAY

Day 67 — 298 Remaining

FIRST US INCOME TAX: ANNIVERSARY. Mar 8, 1913. The Internal Revenue Service began to levy and collect income taxes.

GRAHAME, KENNETH: BIRTH ANNIVERSARY. Mar 8, 1859. Scottish author, born at Edinburgh. His children's book, *The Wind in the Willows*, has as its main characters a mole, a rat, a badger and a toad. He died July 6, 1932, at Pangbourne, Berkshire.

INTERNATIONAL (WORKING) WOMEN'S DAY. Mar 8. A day to honor women, especially working women. Said to commemorate an 1857 march and demonstration at New York, NY, by female garment and textile workers. Believed to have been first proclaimed for this date at an international conference of women held at Helsinki, Finland, in 1910, "that henceforth Mar 8 should be declared International Women's Day." The 50th anniversary observance, at Peking, China, in 1960, cited Clara Zetkin (1857–1933) as "initiator of Women's Day on Mar 8." This is perhaps the most widely observed holiday of recent origin and is unusual among holidays originating in the US in having been widely adopted and observed in other nations, including socialist countries. In Russia it is a national holiday, and flowers or gifts are presented to women workers.

RUSSIA: INTERNATIONAL WOMEN'S DAY. Mar 8. National holiday.

SYRIAN ARAB REPUBLIC: REVOLUTION DAY: ANNIVERSARY. Mar 8, 1963. Official public holiday commemorating assumption of power by Revolutionary National Council.

THOMPSON, LAMARCUS A.: BIRTH ANNIVERSARY. Mar 8, 1848. Thompson built the world's first roller coaster, the "Gravity Pleasure Switchback Railway," which opened at Coney Island, Brooklyn, NY, on June 13, 1884. There had been primitive railed pleasure rides before (as early as the 15th century in Russia), but Thompson was the first to fully take advantage of advances in engineering so that cars did roll and coast with the assistance of gravity. The success of his coaster spawned an amusement park ride industry. By 1888 he had created 50 roller coasters worldwide. Born at Jersey, OH, the "Father of Gravity" died May 8, 1919. See also: "First Roller Coaster Opens: Anniversary" (June 13).

UNITED NATIONS: DAY FOR WOMEN'S RIGHTS AND INTERNATIONAL PEACE. Mar 8. An international day observed by the organizations of the United Nations system. (Also known as International Women's Day.) For more info, visit the UN's website for children at www.un.org/Pubs/CyberSchoolBus/.

VAN BUREN, HANNAH HOES: BIRTH ANNIVERSARY. Mar 8, 1783. Wife of Martin Van Buren, 8th president of the US. Born at Kinderhook, NY, she died at Albany, NY, Feb 5, 1819.

BIRTHDAYS TODAY

George Allen, 54, US Senator (R, Virginia), born Whittier, CA, Mar 8, 1952.

Marcia Newby, 18, gymnast, born Virginia Beach, VA, Mar 8, 1988.

Freddie Prinze, Jr, 30, actor (*Scooby-Doo; I Know What You Did Last Summer*), born Los Angeles, CA, Mar 8, 1976.

Peter Roop, 55, author, with his wife Connie (*I, Columbus; Keep the Lights Burning, Abbie*), born Winchester, MA, Mar 8, 1951.

Robert Sabuda, 41, illustrator (*The Christmas Alphabet, The Paper Dragon*), born Pinckney, MI, Mar 8, 1965.

James Van Der Beek, 29, actor ("Dawson's Creek"), born Cheshire, CT, Mar 8, 1977.

March 2006

S	M	T	W	T	F	S
			1	2	3	4
5	6	7	8	9	10	11
12	13	14	15	16	17	18
19	20	21	22	23	24	25
26	27	28	29	30	31	

MARCH 9 — THURSDAY

Day 68 — 297 Remaining

BARBIE DEBUTS: ANNIVERSARY. Mar 9, 1959. The popular doll debuted in stores. More than 800 million dolls have been sold. For more info: www.barbie.com.

BELIZE: BARON BLISS DAY. Mar 9. Official public holiday. Celebrated in honor of Sir Henry Edward Ernest Victor Bliss, a great benefactor of Belize.

GRANT COMMISSIONED COMMANDER OF ALL UNION ARMIES: ANNIVERSARY. Mar 9, 1864. In Washington, DC, Ulysses S. Grant accepted his commission as Lieutenant General, becoming the commander of all the Union armies. In October 1863 he had been put in charge of the Army of the Mississippi.

PANIC DAY. Mar 9. Run around all day in a panic, telling others you can't handle it anymore. [©2002 by WH.] For info: Thomas & Ruth Roy, Wellcat Holidays, 2418 Long Ln, Lebanon, PA 17046. Phone: (717) 279-0184. E-mail: info@wellcat.com. Web: www.wellcat.com.

VESPUCCI, AMERIGO: BIRTH ANNIVERSARY. Mar 9, 1451. Italian navigator, merchant and explorer for whom the Americas were named. Born at Florence, Italy. He participated in at least two expeditions between 1499 and 1502 that took him to the coast of South America, where he discovered the Amazon and Plata rivers. Vespucci's expeditions were of great importance because he believed that he had discovered a new continent, not just a new route to the Orient. Neither Vespucci nor his exploits achieved the fame of Columbus, but the New World was to be named for Amerigo Vespucci, by an obscure German geographer and mapmaker, Martin Waldseemuller. Ironically, in his work as an outfitter of ships, Vespucci had been personally acquainted with Christopher Columbus. Vespucci died at Seville, Spain, Feb 22, 1512. See also: "Waldseemuller, Martin: Remembrance Day" (Apr 25).

BIRTHDAYS TODAY

Margot Apple, 60, illustrator (*Sheep in a Jeep*), born Detroit, MI, Mar 9, 1946.

MARCH 10 — FRIDAY

Day 69 — 296 Remaining

SALVATION ARMY IN THE US: ANNIVERSARY. Mar 10, 1880. Commissioner George Scott Railton and seven women officers landed at New York to officially begin the work of the Salvation Army in the US. For more info: www.salvationarmyusa.org.

TELEPHONE INVENTION: ANNIVERSARY. Mar 10, 1876. Alexander Graham Bell transmitted the first telephone message to his assistant in the next room: "Mr Watson, come here, I want you," at Cambridge, MA. See also: "Bell, Alexander Graham: Birth Anniversary" (Mar 3).

TUBMAN, HARRIET: DEATH ANNIVERSARY. Mar 10, 1913. American abolitionist, Underground Railroad leader, born a slave at Bucktown, Dorchester County, MD, about 1820 or 1821. She escaped from a Maryland plantation in 1849 and later helped more than 300 slaves reach freedom. Died at Auburn, NY. For more info: *Minty: A Story of Young Harriet Tubman* by Alan Schroeder (Dial, 0-8037-1889-6, $16.99 Gr. K–3). For more info on the Underground Railroad, visit www.undergroundrailroad.com or www.nationalgeographic.com/features/99/railroad.

★ ★ ★

US PAPER MONEY ISSUED: ANNIVERSARY. Mar 10, 1862. The first paper money was issued in the US on this date. The denominations were $5 (Hamilton), $10 (Lincoln) and $20 (Liberty). They were not legal tender when first issued but became so by an act on Mar 17, 1862.

BIRTHDAYS TODAY

Kwame Brown, 24, basketball player, born Charleston, SC, Mar 10, 1982.

Kim Campbell, 59, first woman prime minister of Canada (1993), born Vancouver Island, BC, Canada, Mar 10, 1947.

Shannon Miller, 29, Olympic gold medal gymnast, born Rolla, MO, Mar 10, 1977.

MARCH 11 — SATURDAY

Day 70 — 295 Remaining

BUREAU OF INDIAN AFFAIRS ESTABLISHED: ANNIVERSARY. Mar 11, 1824. The US War Department created the Bureau of Indian Affairs.

FLU PANDEMIC OF 1918 HITS US: ANNIVERSARY. Mar 11, 1918. The first cases of the "Spanish" influenza were reported in the US when 107 soldiers became sick at Fort Riley, KS. By the end of 1920 nearly 25 percent of the US population had had it. As many as 500,000 civilians died from the virus, exceeding the number of US troops killed abroad in WWI. Worldwide, more than 1 percent of the global population, or 22 million people, had died by 1920. The origin of the virus was never determined absolutely, though it was probably somewhere in Asia. The name "Spanish" influenza came from the relatively high number of cases in that country early in the epidemic. Due to the panic, cancellation of public events was common and many public service workers wore masks on the job. Emergency tent hospitals were set up in some locations due to overcrowding.

GAG, WANDA: BIRTH ANNIVERSARY. Mar 11, 1893. Author and illustrator (*Millions of Cats*), born at New Ulm, MN. Died at Milford, NJ, June 27, 1946. For more info: www.ortakales.com/illustrators.

JOHNNY APPLESEED DAY (JOHN CHAPMAN DEATH ANNIVERSARY). Mar 11, 1845. Anniversary of the death of John Chapman, better known as Johnny Appleseed, believed to have been born at Leominster, MA, Sept 26, 1774. The planter of orchards and friend of wild animals was regarded by the Indians as a great medicine man. He died at Allen County, IN. See also: "Appleseed, Johnny: Birth Anniversary" (Sept 26).

KEATS, EZRA JACK: BIRTH ANNIVERSARY. Mar 11, 1916. Author and illustrator born at Brooklyn, NY, Keats was one of the first successful picture book illustrators to use African-American and Hispanic children as his central characters. Born to impoverished Jewish immigrants from Poland, he changed his name from Jacob Ezra Katz as a result of anti-Semitic prejudices in the 1940s. He authored and/or illustrated more than 85 books for children, including such classics as *Peter's Chair, Over in the Meadow* and *Whistle for Willie.* He won the Caldecott Medal in 1963 for *The Snowy Day*, and *Goggles!* was a Caldecott Honor Book in 1970. He died May 6, 1983, at New York, NY.

PAINE, ROBERT TREAT: BIRTH ANNIVERSARY. Mar 11, 1731. Jurist and signer of the Declaration of Independence. Born at Boston, MA, he died there May 11, 1814.

BIRTHDAYS TODAY

Elton Brand, 27, basketball player, born Peekskill, NY, Mar 11, 1979.

Curtis Brown, Jr, 50, astronaut, commander of the 1998 shuttle *Discovery*, born Elizabethtown, NC, Mar 11, 1956.

Jonathan London, 59, author (the Froggy series), born Brooklyn, NY, Mar 11, 1947.

Gale Norton, 52, US Secretary of the Interior (George W. Bush administration), born Wichita, KS, Mar 11, 1954.

Antonin Scalia, 70, Associate Justice of the US Supreme Court, born Trenton, NJ, Mar 11, 1936.

MARCH 12 — SUNDAY

Day 71 — 294 Remaining

BOYCOTT, CHARLES CUNNINGHAM: BIRTH ANNIVERSARY. Mar 12, 1832. Charles Cunningham Boycott, born at Norfolk, England, has been immortalized by having his name become part of the English language. In County Mayo, Ireland, the Tenants' "Land League" in 1880 asked Boycott, an estate agent, to reduce rents (because of poor harvest and dire economic conditions). Boycott responded by serving eviction notices on the tenants, who retaliated by refusing to have any dealings with him. Charles Stewart Parnell, then president of the National Land League and agrarian agitator, retaliated against Boycott by formulating and implementing the method of economic and social ostracism that came to be called a "boycott." Boycott died at Suffolk, England, June 19, 1897.

GIRL SCOUT WEEK. Mar 12–18. To observe the anniversary of the founding of the Girl Scouts of the USA, the largest voluntary organization for girls and women in the world, which began Mar 12, 1912. For info: Media Services, Girl Scouts of the USA, 420 Fifth Ave, New York, NY 10018. Phone: (212) 852-8000. Fax: (212) 852-6514. Web: www.girlscouts.org.

GIRL SCOUTS OF THE USA FOUNDING: ANNIVERSARY. Mar 12, 1912. Juliette Low founded the Girl Scouts of the USA at Savannah, GA. For more info: www.girlscouts.org.

GREAT BLIZZARD OF '88: ANNIVERSARY. Mar 12, 1888. One of the most devastating blizzards to hit the northeastern US began in the early hours of Monday, Mar 12, 1888. A snowfall of 40–50 inches, accompanied by gale-force winds, left drifts as high as 30–40 feet. More than 400 people died in the storm (200 at New York City alone). For more info: *Blizzard: The Storm That Changed America* by Jim Murphy (Scholastic, 0-59-067309-2, $18.95 Gr. 3–7).

HAMILTON, VIRGINIA: BIRTH ANNIVERSARY. Mar 12, 1936. Children's author known for books on the African-American experience, born at Yellow Springs, OH. She won both the National Book Award and the Newbery Medal for 1975's *M.C. Higgins, the Great*, and was the first children's author ever to receive the MacArthur Foundation's "genius" grant. Among her other honors were numerous Newbery Honor Awards, an Edgar Allan Poe Award, a Coretta Scott King Award and several King Honors, as well as the Hans Christian Andersen Medal. She is best remembered for her titles *The People Could Fly: American Black Folktales*, *Zeely*, *Many Thousand Gone* and *Her Stories*. She died Feb 19, 2002, at Yellow Springs.

LESOTHO: MOSHOESHOE'S DAY. Mar 12. National holiday. Commemorates the great leader, Chief Moshoeshoe I, who unified the Basotho people, beginning in 1820.

MAURITIUS: INDEPENDENCE DAY: ANNIVERSARY. Mar 12, 1968. National holiday commemorates attainment of independent nationhood (within the British Commonwealth) by this island state in the western Indian Ocean on this day in 1968.

PIERCE, JANE MEANS APPLETON: 200th BIRTH ANNIVERSARY. Mar 12, 1806. Wife of Franklin Pierce, 14th president of the US. Born at Hampton, NH, she died at Concord, NH, Dec 2, 1863.

SUN YAT-SEN: DEATH ANNIVERSARY. Mar 12, 1925. The heroic leader of China's 1911 revolution is remembered on the anniversary of his death at Peking, China. Observed as Arbor Day in Taiwan.

BIRTHDAYS TODAY

Kent Conrad, 58, US Senator (D, North Dakota), born Bismarck, ND, Mar 12, 1948.

Carl Hiaasen, 53, author (*Hoot*), born Fort Lauderdale, FL, Mar 12, 1953.

Naomi Shihab Nye, 54, author (*Habibi, This Same Sky*), born St. Louis, MO, Mar 12, 1952.

Mitt Romney, 59, Governor of Massachusetts (R), born Detroit, MI, Mar 12, 1947.

Darryl Strawberry, 44, former baseball player, born Los Angeles, CA, Mar 12, 1962.

MARCH 13 — MONDAY

Day 72 — 293 Remaining

ARAB OIL EMBARGO LIFTED: ANNIVERSARY. Mar 13, 1974. The oil-producing Arab countries agreed to lift their five-month embargo on petroleum sales to the US. During the embargo, prices went up 300 percent and a ban was imposed on Sunday gasoline sales. The embargo was in retaliation for US support of Israel during the October 1973 Middle-East War.

CAMP FIRE USA BIRTHDAY WEEK. Mar 13–19. To celebrate the anniversary of Camp Fire USA (founded on Mar 17, 1910, as Camp Fire Girls). For info: Camp Fire USA, 4601 Madison Ave, Kansas City, MO 64112. Phone: (816) 756-1950. Fax: (816) 756-2650. E-mail: info@campfireusa.org. Web: www.campfireusa.org.

DEAF HISTORY MONTH. Mar 13–Apr 15. Observance of three of the most important anniversaries for deaf Americans: Apr 15,

March 2006

S	M	T	W	T	F	S
			1	2	3	4
5	6	7	8	9	10	11
12	13	14	15	16	17	18
19	20	21	22	23	24	25
26	27	28	29	30	31	

MARCH 13–19
INTERNATIONAL BRAIN AWARENESS WEEK

Instead of saying your heart is broken it is more accurate to say that your brain is broken, since the brain is where emotions such as love are felt. Kids learn from an early age that the brain is the seat of all knowledge. They also learn that the brain is a fragile object, one that they must protect through the use of safety helmets and nourish by eating healthy foods. The brain is also a complex organ and one that may seem daunting to teach younger children about. This need not be the case given the numerous resources available to you both online and in print.

There are a variety of excellent websites dedicated to helping educators inspire students to learn about the brain. At www.dana.org, you can find information on activities and events throughout the United States dedicated to increasing awareness of the latest advances in understanding the function of the brain and brain disorders. This can be found under the "Brain Awareness Week" link. Under the same link, through the "Education Resources" section, the Dana Alliance for Brain Initiatives offers an extensive list of recommended books about the brain, categorized by age appropriateness and including descriptions of each book. The folks at Dana also run "Brainy Kids" at www.dana.org/kids. Brainy Kids offers both students and teachers a wealth of information, including activities.

Neuroscience for Kids is a fun site that offers information appropriate for sharing with children of all ages, including activities, experiments, games, book recommendations, quotes and even a sample lesson plan. All this can be found at http://faculty.washington.edu/chudler/neurok.html.

Another great resource is the kid-friendly http://kidshealth.org. Type "brain" into the search engine to find information that will appeal to children.

The brain's functions are many and varied. Ask students to describe some of them. While they are likely to list things like thinking and feeling, they may be surprised to learn that the brain controls many of the body's vital functions, including the senses and the regulation of internal organs.

Who couldn't use extra help memorizing spelling words? Explain to students that memory is something that can be enhanced through a few simple techniques. In order to function properly, it's necessary for the brain to be well nourished. Eating healthy foods regularly helps you be more aware and alert as well as think more clearly. Also, people remember things that they relate to better, and they tend to remember things they've heard more than once. When students meet someone new for the first time, they should repeat the person's name and connect the name to either someone they know with the same name or a rhyme, such as "This is Ann, who has a great tan."

—Denise Frank

1817, establishment of the first public school for the deaf in America, later known as The American School for the Deaf; Apr 8, 1864, charter signed by President Lincoln authorizing the board of directors of the Columbia Institution (now Gallaudet University) to grant college degrees to deaf students; Mar 13, 1988, the victory of the Deaf President Now movement at Gallaudet.

EARMUFFS PATENTED: ANNIVERSARY. Mar 13, 1887. Chester Greenwood of Maine received a patent for earmuffs.

FILLMORE, ABIGAIL POWERS: BIRTH ANNIVERSARY. Mar 13, 1798. First wife of Millard Fillmore, 13th president of the US. Born at Stillwater, NY. It is said that the White House was without any books until Abigail Fillmore, formerly a teacher, made a room on the second floor into a library. Within a year, Congress appropriated $250 for the president to spend on books for the White House. Died at Washington, DC, Mar 30, 1853.

INTERNATIONAL BRAIN AWARENESS WEEK. Mar 13–19. International effort to advance public awareness about the progress, promise and benefits of brain research. ***See Curriculum Connection.*** For info: Dana Alliance for Brain Initiatives, 745 Fifth Ave, Ste 900, New York, NY 10151. E-mail: bawinfo@dana.org. Web: www.dana.org/brainweek.

NATIONAL OPEN AN UMBRELLA INDOORS DAY. Mar 13. The purpose of this day is for people to open umbrellas indoors and note whether they have any bad luck. Annually, Mar 13. For info: Thomas Edward Knibb, 1624 Colonial Way, Frederick, MD 21702-3919. E-mail: tomknibb@juno.com.

PLANET URANUS DISCOVERY: 225th ANNIVERSARY. Mar 13, 1781. German-born English astronomer Sir William Herschel discovered the seventh planet from the sun, Uranus. For more info: *Uranus, Neptune, and Pluto* by Robin Kerrod (Lerner, 0-8225-3908-X, $21.27 Gr. 4–6) or go to Nine Planets: Multimedia Tour of the Solar System at www.seds.org/billa/tnp.

PRIESTLY, JOSEPH: BIRTH ANNIVERSARY. Mar 13, 1733. English clergyman and scientist, discoverer of oxygen, born at Fieldhead, England. He and his family narrowly escaped an angry mob attacking their home because of his religious and political views. They moved to the US in 1794. Died at Northumberland, PA, Feb 6, 1804.

SAINT AUBIN, HELEN "CALLAGHAN": BIRTH ANNIVERSARY. Mar 13, 1929. Helen Candaele St. Aubin, known as Helen Callaghan during her baseball days, was born at Vancouver, British Columbia, Canada. Saint Aubin and her sister, Margaret Maxwell, were recruited for the All-American Girls Professional Baseball League, which flourished in the 1940s when many major league players were off fighting WWII. She first played at age 15 for the Minneapolis Millerettes, an expansion team that moved to Indiana and became the Fort Wayne Daisies. For the 1945 season the left-handed outfielder led the league with a .299 average and 24 extra base hits. In 1946 she stole 114 bases in 111 games. Her son Kelly Candaele's documentary on the women's baseball league inspired the film *A League of Their Own*. Saint Aubin, who was known as the "Ted Williams of women's baseball," died Dec 8, 1992, at Santa Barbara, CA.

TA'ANIT ESTHER (FAST OF ESTHER). Mar 13. Hebrew calendar date: Adar 13, 5766. Commemorates Queen Esther's fast, in the 6th century BC, to save the Jews of ancient Persia. (Began at sundown of previous day.) Ordinarily observed Adar 13, the Fast of Esther is observed on the previous Thursday (Adar 11) when Adar 13 is a Sabbath.

UNITED KINGDOM: COMMONWEALTH DAY. Mar 13. Replaces Empire Day observance recognized until 1958. Observed on second Monday in March. Also observed in the British Virgin Islands, Gibraltar and Newfoundland, Canada.

BIRTHDAYS TODAY

Diane Dillon, 73, illustrator, with her husband Leo Dillon (Caldecotts for *Why Mosquitoes Buzz in People's Ears, Ashanti to Zulu: African Traditions*), born Glendale, CA, Mar 13, 1933.

John Hoeven, 49, Governor of North Dakota (R), born Bismarck, ND, Mar 13, 1957.

Ellen Raskin, 78, author (Newbery for *The Westing Game*), born Milwaukee, WI, Mar 13, 1928 (some sources say 1925).

MARCH 14 — TUESDAY

Day 73 — 292 Remaining

BALTO: SLED DOG HERO: DEATH ANNIVERSARY. Mar 14, 1933. Balto, a young husky, was the lead dog on the final 53-mile leg of the epic diphtheria serum run from Nenana to Nome, AK, in 1925. He became a national hero, and on Dec 17, 1925, a statue of Balto was unveiled in New York's Central Park. For the next two years, Balto and his dog team were exhibited in cheap stage acts under unhealthy conditions, but were rescued in 1927 and brought to Cleveland where they were the pampered stars of the city zoo. After his death on this day in 1933, Balto's preserved body was displayed at the Cleveland Museum of Natural History, where it remains. See also: "Sled Dogs Save Nome: Anniversary" (Feb 2) and "Togo: Sled Dog Hero: Death Anniversary" (Dec 5). For more info: *The Bravest Dog Ever: The True Story of Balto* by Natalie Standiford (Random House, 0-3948-9695-5, $3.99 Ages 4–8).

DE ANGELI, MARGUERITE: BIRTH ANNIVERSARY. Mar 14, 1889. Author and illustrator, born at Lampeer, MI. She won the Newbery Medal in 1950 for her classic *The Door in the Wall.* Her first book was *Ted & Nina Go to the Grocery Store* in 1935. She died at Detroit, MI, June 16, 1987. For more info: www.deangeli.lapeer.org.

EINSTEIN, ALBERT: BIRTH ANNIVERSARY. Mar 14, 1879. Theoretical physicist best known for his theory of relativity. Born at Ulm, Germany, he won the Nobel Prize in 1921. Died at Princeton, NJ, Apr 18, 1955. For more info: *Einstein, Visionary Scientist* by John B. Severance (Clarion, 0-395-93100-2, $15 Gr. 5–8).

JONES, CASEY: BIRTH ANNIVERSARY. Mar 14, 1864. Railroad engineer and hero of ballad, whose real name was John Luther Jones. Born near Cayce, KY, he died in a railroad wreck near Vaughn, MS, Apr 30, 1900. For more info: *Casey Jones* by Allan Drummond (Farrar, Straus, 0-374-31175-7, $16 Gr. K & up).

LUNAR ECLIPSE. Mar 14. Penumbral eclipse of the Moon. Visible in North America, Central America, South America, Europe, Africa, Asia.

MARSHALL, THOMAS RILEY: BIRTH ANNIVERSARY. Mar 14, 1854. The 28th vice president of the US (1913–21). Born at North Manchester, IN, he died at Washington, DC, June 1, 1925.

MOON PHASE: FULL MOON. Mar 14. Moon enters Full Moon phase at 6:35 PM, EST.

NATIONAL CHILDREN'S CRAFT DAY. Mar 14. To encourage children's creativity through crafts. Celebrate by painting, sculpting or creating arts and crafts projects. Annually, Mar 14 in National Craft Month. For info: S&S Worldwide Arts & Crafts, 75 Mill St, Colchester, CT 06415. Phone: (800) 243-9232. Web: www.ssww.com.

PURIM. Mar 14. Hebrew calendar date: Adar 14, 5766. Feasts, gifts, charity and the reading of the Book of Esther mark this joyous commemoration of Queen Esther's intervention, in the 6th century BC, to save the Jews of ancient Persia. Haman's plot to exterminate the Jews was thwarted, and he was hanged on the very day he had set for the execution of the Jews. (Began at sundown of previous day.)

March 2006

S	M	T	W	T	F	S
			1	2	3	4
5	6	7	8	9	10	11
12	13	14	15	16	17	18
19	20	21	22	23	24	25
26	27	28	29	30	31	

TAYLOR, LUCY HOBBS: BIRTH ANNIVERSARY. Mar 14, 1833. Lucy Beaman Hobbs, first woman in America to receive a degree in dentistry (Ohio College of Dental Surgery, 1866) and to be admitted to membership in a state dental association. Born at Franklin County, NY. In 1867 she married James M. Taylor, who also became a dentist (after she instructed him in the essentials). Active women's rights advocate. Died at Lawrence, KS, Oct 3, 1910.

BIRTHDAYS TODAY

Michael Caine, 73, actor (*Dirty Rotten Scoundrels, The Muppet Christmas Carol*), born Bermondsey, London, England, Mar 14, 1933.

Tom Coburn, 58, US Senator (R, Oklahoma), born Casper, WY, Mar 14, 1948.

Billy Crystal, 59, actor (*Monsters, Inc; The Princess Bride; City Slickers*), born Long Beach, NY, Mar 14, 1947.

Jordan Taylor Hanson, 23, singer (Hanson), born Jenks, OK, Mar 14, 1983.

MARCH 15 — WEDNESDAY

Day 74 — 291 Remaining

BELARUS: CONSTITUTION DAY. Mar 15. National holiday. Commemorates the constitution adopted in 1994.

IDES OF MARCH. Mar 15. On the Roman calendar, days were not numbered sequentially through a month. Instead, each month had three division days: kalends, nones and ides. Days were then numbered around these divisions: e.g., III Kalends or IV Nones. The ides occurred on the 15th of the month (or on the 13th in months with fewer than 31 days). Julius Caesar was assassinated on this day in 44 BC. This system continued to be used in Europe through the Middle Ages. When Shakespeare wrote "Beware the ides of March" in his play *Julius Caesar,* his audience understood what this meant.

JACKSON, ANDREW: BIRTH ANNIVERSARY. Mar 15, 1767. Seventh president of the US (Mar 4, 1829–Mar 3, 1837) was born in a log cabin at Waxhaw, SC. Jackson was the first president since George Washington who had not attended college. He was a military hero in the War of 1812. His presidency reflected his democratic and egalitarian values. Died at Nashville, TN, June 8, 1845. His birthday is observed as a holiday in Tennessee. For more info: www.ipl.org/ref/POTUS.

LIBERIA: J.J. ROBERTS DAY. Mar 15. National holiday. Commemorates the birth in 1809 of the country's first president.

MAINE: ADMISSION DAY: ANNIVERSARY. Mar 15. Became 23rd state in 1820. Prior to this date, Maine had been part of Massachusetts.

TESOL ANNUAL CONFERENCE. Mar 15–19. Tampa Bay, FL. Annual meeting of Teachers of English to Speakers of Other Languages. For info: TESOL, 700 S Washington St, Ste 200, Alexandria, VA 22314. Phone: (703) 836-0774. E-mail: conv@tesol.edu. Web: www.tesol.org.

WASHINGTON'S ADDRESS TO CONTINENTAL ARMY OFFICERS: ANNIVERSARY. Mar 15, 1783. George Washington addressed a meeting at Newburgh, NY, of Continental Army officers who were dissatisfied and rebellious for want of back pay, food, clothing and pensions. General Washington called for patience, opening his speech with the words: "I have grown grey in your service. . . ." Congress later acted to satisfy most of the demands.

★ ★ ★

BIRTHDAYS TODAY

Ruth Bader Ginsburg, 73, Associate Justice of the US Supreme Court, born Brooklyn, NY, Mar 15, 1933.

Ruth White, 64, author (*Belle Prater's Boy*), born Whitewood, VA, Mar 15, 1942.

MARCH 16 — THURSDAY

Day 75 — 290 Remaining

ABSOLUTELY INCREDIBLE KID DAY. Mar 16. Camp Fire USA, one of the nation's oldest and largest youth development organizations, holds this annual event to encourage adults to write a letter to a child in their life to tell children how special they are and how much they mean to them. Annually, the third Thursday in March. For info: Camp Fire USA, 4601 Madison Ave, Kansas City, MO 64112. Phone: (816) 756-1950. E-mail: kidday@campfireusa.org. Web: www.campfireusa.org.

BLACK PRESS DAY: ANNIVERSARY OF THE FIRST BLACK NEWSPAPER. Mar 16, 1827. Anniversary of the founding of the first black newspaper in the US, *Freedom's Journal*, on Varick Street at New York, NY.

CLYMER, GEORGE: BIRTH ANNIVERSARY. Mar 16, 1739. Signer of the Declaration of Independence and of the US Constitution. Born at Philadelphia, PA, and died there Jan 24, 1813.

GODDARD DAY: 80th ANNIVERSARY. Mar 16, 1926. Commemorates first liquid-fuel-powered rocket flight, devised by Robert Hutchings Goddard (1882–1945) at Auburn, MA.

MADISON, JAMES: BIRTH ANNIVERSARY. Mar 16, 1751. Fourth president of the US (Mar 4, 1809–Mar 3, 1817), born at Port Conway, VA. He was president when British forces invaded Washington, DC, requiring Madison and other high officials to flee while the British burned the Capitol, the president's residence and most other public buildings (Aug 24–25, 1814). Died at Montpelier, VA, June 28, 1836. For more info: *The Great Little Madison* by Jean Fritz (Putnam, 0-399-21768-1, $15.99 Gr. 7–9) or www.ipl.org/ref/POTUS.

NIXON, THELMA CATHERINE PATRICIA RYAN: BIRTH ANNIVERSARY. Mar 16, 1912. Wife of Richard Milhous Nixon, 37th president of the US. Born at Ely, NV, she died at Park Ridge, NJ, June 22, 1993.

US MILITARY ACADEMY FOUNDED: ANNIVERSARY. Mar 16, 1802. President Thomas Jefferson signed legislation establishing the United States Military Academy to train officers for the army. The Academy opened on July 4, 1802. The college is located at West Point, NY, on the site of the oldest continuously occupied military post in America. Women were admitted to West Point in 1976. The Academy's motto is "Duty, Honor, Country." For more info: www.usma.edu.

BIRTHDAYS TODAY

Mary Chalmers, 79, author and illustrator (*Come for a Walk With Me*), born Camden, NJ, Mar 16, 1927.

Sid Fleischman, 86, author (Newbery for *The Whipping Boy*), born Albert Sidney Fleischman, Brooklyn, NY, Mar 16, 1920.

William Mayne, 78, author (*Lady Muck*), born Kingston-upon-Hull, England, Mar 16, 1928.

MARCH 17 — FRIDAY

Day 76 — 289 Remaining

CAMP FIRE USA: ANNIVERSARY. Mar 17, 1910. To commemorate the anniversary of the founding of Camp Fire USA and the service given to children and youth across the nation. Founded in 1910 as Camp Fire Girls. For info: Camp Fire USA, 4601 Madison Ave, Kansas City, MO 64112. Phone: (816) 756-1950. Fax: (816) 756-2650. E-mail: info@campfireusa.org. Web: www.campfireusa.org.

EVACUATION DAY IN MASSACHUSETTS. Mar 17. Proclaimed annually by the governor, Evacuation Day commemorates the anniversary of the evacuation from Boston of British troops in 1776.

IRELAND: NATIONAL DAY. Mar 17. St. Patrick's Day is observed in the Republic of Ireland as a legal national holiday.

NORTHERN IRELAND: SAINT PATRICK'S DAY HOLIDAY. Mar 17. National Holiday.

RUSTIN, BAYARD: BIRTH ANNIVERSARY. Mar 17, 1910. Black pacifist and civil rights leader, Bayard Rustin was an organizer and participant in many of the great social protest marches—for jobs, freedom and nuclear disarmament. He was arrested and imprisoned more than 20 times for his civil rights and pacifist activities. Born at West Chester, PA, Rustin died at New York, NY, Aug 24, 1987.

SAINT PATRICK'S DAY. Mar 17. Commemorates the patron saint of Ireland, Bishop Patrick (AD 389–461) who, about AD 432, left his home in the Severn Valley, England, and introduced Christianity into Ireland. Feast Day in the Roman Catholic Church. A national holiday in Ireland and Northern Ireland. For more info: *Patrick: Patron Saint of Ireland* by Tomie de Paola (Holiday, 0-8234-0924-4, $16.95 Gr. K–3) or *Saint Patrick* by Ann Tompert (Boyds Mills, 1-56397-659-5, $15.95 Gr. 2–4).

SAINT PATRICK'S DAY PARADE. Mar 17. Fifth Avenue, New York, NY. Held since 1762, the parade of 200,000 begins the two-mile march at 11:00 AM and lasts about six hours. Starts on 44th Street and 5th Avenue and ends at 86th Street and First Avenue. Est attendance: 1,000,000. For info: NY CVB, 810 Seventh Ave, New York, NY 10019. Phone: (800) NYC-VISIT or (212) 484-1222.

SOUTH AFRICAN WHITES VOTE TO END MINORITY RULE: ANNIVERSARY. Mar 17, 1992. A referendum proposing ending white minority rule through negotiations was supported by a whites-only ballot. The vote of 1,924,186 (68.6 percent) whites in support of President F.W. de Klerk's reform policies was greater than expected.

TANEY, ROGER B.: BIRTH ANNIVERSARY. Mar 17, 1777. Fifth Chief Justice of the Supreme Court, born at Calvert County, MD. Served as Attorney General under President Andrew Jackson. Nominated as Secretary of the Treasury, he became the first presidential nominee to be rejected by the Senate because of his strong stance against the Bank of the United States as a central bank. A year later, he was nominated to the Supreme Court as an associate justice by Jackson, but his nomination was stalled until the death of Chief Justice John Marshall July 6, 1835. Taney was nominated to fill Marshall's place on the bench and after much resistance he was sworn in as Chief Justice in March 1836. His tenure on the Supreme Court is most remembered for the Dred Scott decision. He died at Washington, DC, Oct 12, 1864. For more info: oyez.northwestern.edu/justices/justices.cgi.

BIRTHDAYS TODAY

Keith Baker, 53, author (*Big Fat Hen, Hide and Snake*), born LaGrande, OR, Mar 17, 1953.

Penelope Lively, 73, author (*Moon Tiger*), born Cairo, Egypt, Mar 17, 1933.

MARCH 18 — SATURDAY

Day 77 — 288 Remaining

ARUBA: FLAG DAY. Mar 18. Aruba national holiday. Display of flags, national music and folkloric events.

CALHOUN, JOHN CALDWELL: BIRTH ANNIVERSARY. Mar 18, 1782. American statesman and first vice president of the US to resign that office (Dec 28, 1832). Born at Abbeville District, SC, he died at Washington, DC, Mar 31, 1850.

CLEVELAND, GROVER: BIRTH ANNIVERSARY. Mar 18, 1837. The 22nd (Mar 4, 1885–Mar 3, 1889) and 24th (Mar 4, 1893–Mar 3, 1897) president of the US was born Stephen Grover Cleveland at Caldwell, NJ. He ran for president for the intervening term and received a plurality of votes cast but failed to win electoral college victory for that term. Only president to serve two nonconsecutive terms. Also the only president to be married in the White House. He married 21-year-old Frances Folsom, his ward. Their daughter, Esther, was the first child of a president to be born in the White House. Died at Princeton, NJ, June 24, 1908. For more info: www.ipl.org/ref/POTUS.

INDIA: HOLI. Mar 18. In this spring Hindu festival people run through the streets sprinkling each other with colored water and tossing brightly hued powders. This is observed by Hindus without regard to caste. Huge bonfires are built on the eve of Holi. Because there is no universally accepted Hindu calendar, this holiday may be celebrated on a different date in some parts of India but it always falls in February or March.

SAVE THE FLORIDA PANTHER DAY. Mar 18. A ceremonial day on the third Saturday in March.

SPACE MILESTONE: *VOSKHOD 2* (USSR). Mar 18, 1965. Colonel Leonov stepped out of the capsule for 20 minutes in a special space suit, the first man to leave a spaceship. It was two months prior to the first US space walk. See also: "Space Milestone: *Gemini 4* (US)" (June 3).

March 2006

S	M	T	W	T	F	S
			1	2	3	4
5	6	7	8	9	10	11
12	13	14	15	16	17	18
19	20	21	22	23	24	25
26	27	28	29	30	31	

BIRTHDAYS TODAY

Bonnie Blair, 42, former Olympic gold medal speed skater, born Cornwall, NY, Mar 18, 1964.

Douglas Florian, 56, poet, illustrator (*Beast Feast, Insectlopedia, Mammalabilia*), born New York, NY, Mar 18, 1950.

Brian Griese, 31, football player, born Miami, FL, Mar 18, 1975.

Queen Latifah, 36, singer, actress (*Chicago*, "Living Single"), born Dana Owens, East Orange, NJ, Mar 18, 1970.

Alexei Yagudin, 26, Olympic gold medal figure skater, born Leningrad, Russia, Mar 18, 1980.

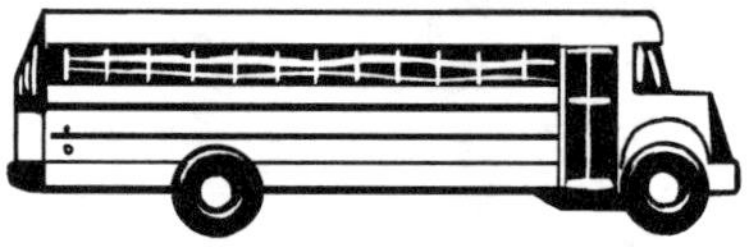

MARCH 19 — SUNDAY

Day 78 — 287 Remaining

ANONYMOUS GIVING WEEK. Mar 19–25. A time to celebrate the true spirit of giving. Experience the joy in random acts of kindness. Leave a legacy of anonymous contribution. Perfect for a one-time or all-week adventure designed to share time, talent and treasure. Annually, the week containing the first day of spring. For info: Janna Krammer, Legacy Institute, Inc, 42747 Blackhawk Rd, Harris, MN 55032. Phone: (877) 646-9100. E-mail: info@anonymousgivingweek.com. Web: www.anonymousgiving week.com.

BRADFORD, WILLIAM: BIRTH ANNIVERSARY. Mar 19, 1589. Pilgrim father, governor of Plymouth Colony, born at Yorkshire, England, and baptized Mar 19, 1589. Sailed from Southampton, England, on the *Mayflower* in 1620. Died at Plymouth, MA, May 9, 1657. For more info: *William Bradford: Rock of Plymouth* by Kieran Doherty (Twenty-First Century, 0-7613-1304-4, $22.90 Gr. 6–10).

EARP, WYATT: BIRTH ANNIVERSARY. Mar 19, 1848. Born at Monmouth, IL, and died Jan 13, 1929, at Los Angeles, CA. A legendary figure of the Old West, Earp worked as a railroad hand, saloonkeeper, gambler, lawman, gunslinger, miner and real estate investor at various times. Best known for his involvement in the gunfight at the OK Corral Oct 26, 1881, at Tombstone, AZ.

IRAN: NATIONAL DAY OF OIL: ANNIVERSARY. Mar 19. National holiday. Commemorates nationalization of oil fields in 1963.

McKEAN, THOMAS: BIRTH ANNIVERSARY. Mar 19, 1734. Signer of the Declaration of Independence. Born at Chester County, PA, he died June 24, 1817.

NATIONAL AGRICULTURE WEEK. Mar 19–25. To honor America's providers of food and fiber and to educate the general public about the US agricultural system. Annually, the week that includes the first day of spring. For info: Agriculture Council of America, 11020 King St, Ste 205, Overland Park, KS 66210. Phone: (913) 491-1895. Fax: (913) 491-6502. E-mail: info@agday.org. Web: www.agday.org.

★**NATIONAL POISON PREVENTION WEEK.** Mar 19–25. Presidential Proclamation issued each year for the third full week of March since 1962. (Public Law 87–319 of Sept 26, 1961.)

NATIONAL POISON PREVENTION WEEK. Mar 19–25. To aid in encouraging the American people to learn of the dangers of accidental poisoning and to take preventive measures against it. Annually, the third full week in March. For info: Ken Giles, Secy, Poison Prevention Week Council, Box 1543, Washington, DC 20013. E-mail: kgiles@cpsc.gov. Web: www.cpsc.gov.

OPERATION IRAQI FREEDOM: ANNIVERSARY. Mar 19, 2003. At 9:30 PM, EST, two hours past a deadline for Iraqi dictator Saddam Hussein to step down from power, US and British forces began air strikes against his regime. A ground campaign (adding Australian forces) followed quickly, and by Apr 9 Baghdad was in allied control and Hussein had disappeared. On May 1 President George W. Bush announced the end of major military operations in Iraq, although a peacekeeping force remained to battle insurgents. Hussein was captured by US forces on Dec 13, 2003.

SWALLOWS RETURN TO SAN JUAN CAPISTRANO. Mar 19. Traditional date (St. Joseph's Day), since 1776, for swallows to return to old mission of San Juan Capistrano, CA.

US STANDARD TIME ACT: ANNIVERSARY. Mar 19, 1918. Anniversary of passage by the Congress of the Standard Time Act, which authorized the Interstate Commerce Commission to establish standard time zones for the US. The act also established Daylight Saving Time, to save fuel and to promote other economies in a country at war. Daylight Saving Time first went into operation on Easter Sunday, Mar 31, 1918. The Uniform Time Act of 1966, as amended in 1986, by Public Law 99–359, now governs standard time in the US. See also: "Daylight Saving Time Begins" (Apr 2).

WARREN, EARL: BIRTH ANNIVERSARY. Mar 19, 1891. American jurist, 14th Chief Justice of the US Supreme Court. Born at Los Angeles, CA, Warren was a former California governor who was appointed to the bench by President Eisenhower. He presided over the Supreme Court during the Civil Rights era, and is best remembered for his decision in *Brown* v. *Board of Ed.*, a landmark segregation case. He retired from the bench in 1969, and died at Washington, DC, July 9, 1974. For more info: oyez.northwestern.edu/justices/justices.cgi.

BIRTHDAYS TODAY

Glenn Close, 59, actress (*101 Dalmatians*), born Greenwich, CT, Mar 19, 1947.

Hazel Dodge, 47, author (*The Ancient Life: Life in Classical Athens & Rome*), born Feltham, England, Mar 19, 1959.

Andre Miller, 30, basketball player, born Los Angeles, CA, Mar 19, 1976.

Hedo Turkoglu, 27, basketball player, born Hidayet Turkoglu, at Istanbul, Turkey, Mar 19, 1979.

Bruce Willis, 51, actor (*Die Hard, The Sixth Sense*), born Penn's Grove, NJ, Mar 19, 1955.

MARCH 20 — MONDAY

Day 79 — 286 Remaining

AUSTRALIA: CANBERRA DAY. Mar 20. Australian Capital Territory. Public holiday the third Monday in March.

JAPAN: VERNAL EQUINOX DAY. Mar 20. A national holiday in Japan. When Mar 20 falls on a Sunday, it is celebrated on the following Monday.

LEGOLAND OPENS: ANNIVERSARY. Mar 20, 1999. The Legoland theme park for children ages 2–12 opened on this day at Carlsbad, CA. It is the third Legoland park; the others are in Denmark and England. More than 30 million Lego pieces went into the construction of 40 rides and attractions. Since its beginnings in the 1950s, the Danish maker has manufactured more than 189 billion Lego blocks. Legos were introduced in the US in 1962. For info: Legoland, One Lego Dr, Carlsbad, CA 92008. Phone: (760) 918-LEGO. Web: www.lego.com.

MARTIN, BILL JR.: BIRTH ANNIVERSARY. Mar 20, 1916. Children's book author born at Hiawatha, KS, Martin did not learn to read until he was in college. He went on to earn a doctorate in early childhood education and author dozens of highly-regarded titles, including his series of picture books with illustrator Eric Carle that includes *Brown Bear, Brown Bear, What Do You See?* and *Polar Bear, Polar Bear, What Do You Hear?*. *Knots on a Counting Rope* and *Chicka Chicka Boom Boom* are also perennial favorites. He died Aug 11, 2004, at Commerce, TX.

NATIONAL AGRICULTURE DAY. Mar 20. A day when producers, agricultural associations, corporations, universities, government agencies and countless others across America gather to recognize and celebrate the abundance provided by agriculture. Annually, the first day of spring. Week of celebration: Mar 19–25. For info: Agriculture Council of America, 11020 King St, Ste 205, Overland Park, KS 66210. Phone: (913) 491-1895. Fax: (913) 491-6502. E-mail: info@agday.com. Web: www.agday.org.

NATIONAL ENERGY EDUCATION WEEK. Mar 20–24. To make energy education part of the school curriculum. Monday through Friday, where Friday is the second to the last Friday in March. For info: National Energy Education Development Project, PO Box 2518, Reston, VA 20195. Phone: (800) 875-5029. Web: www.need.org.

SPRING. Mar 20–June 21. In the Northern Hemisphere spring begins today with the vernal equinox, at 1:26 PM, EST. Note that in the Southern Hemisphere today is the beginning of autumn. Sun rises due east and sets due west everywhere on Earth (except near poles) and the daylight length (interval between sunrise and sunset) is virtually the same everywhere today: 12 hours, 8 minutes.

TUNISIA: INDEPENDENCE DAY. Mar 20. Commemorates treaty in 1956 by which France recognized Tunisian autonomy.

WARMEST US WINTER ON RECORD: ANNIVERSARY. Mar 20, 2000. The warmest winter in US history ended on this date. The National Climatic Data Center later declared the winter of 1999–2000 the warmest US winter in the 103 years that the Federal Government had been keeping record of climatic conditions.

BIRTHDAYS TODAY

Mitsumasa Anno, 80, author and illustrator (*Topsy-Turvies, Anno's Alphabet*), born Tsuwano, Japan, Mar 20, 1926.

Ellen Conford, 64, author (*Hail, Hail Camp Timberwood*), born New York, NY, Mar 20, 1942.

Lois Lowry, 69, author (Newbery for *Number the Stars, The Giver*), born Honolulu, HI, Mar 20, 1937.

Bobby Orr, 58, Hall of Fame hockey player, born Parry Sound, ON, Canada, Mar 20, 1948.

Pat Riley, 61, basketball coach and former player, born Schenectady, NY, Mar 20, 1945.

Louis Sachar, 52, author (Newbery and National Book Award for *Holes*), born East Meadow, NY, Mar 20, 1954.

MARCH 21 — TUESDAY

Day 80 — 285 Remaining

ARIES, THE RAM. Mar 21–Apr 19. In the astronomical/astrological zodiac, which divides the sun's apparent orbit into 12 segments, the period Mar 21–Apr 19 is identified, traditionally, as the sun sign of Aries, the Ram. The ruling planet is Mars.

BACH, JOHANN SEBASTIAN: BIRTH ANNIVERSARY. Mar 21, 1685. Organist and composer, one of the most influential composers in musical history. Born at Eisenach, Germany, he died at Leipzig, Germany, July 28, 1750. For more info: *Sebastian: A Book about Bach* by Jeanette Winter (Harcourt, 0-15-200629-X, $16 Gr. 2–4).

FIRST ROUND-THE-WORLD BALLOON FLIGHT: ANNIVERSARY. Mar 21, 1999. Swiss psychiatrist Bertrand Piccard and British copilot Brian Jones landed in the Egyptian desert on this date, having flown 29,056 miles nonstop around the world in a hot-air balloon, the *Breitling Orbiter 3*. Leaving from Chateau d'Oex in the Swiss Alps on Mar 1, the trip took 19 days, 21 hours and 55 minutes. Piccard is the grandson of balloonist Auguste Piccard, who was the first to ascend into the stratosphere in a balloon. See also: "Piccard, Auguste: Birth Anniversary" (Jan 28).

IRANIAN NEW YEAR: NORUZ. Mar 21. National celebration for all Iranians, this is the traditional Persian New Year. (In Iran spring comes Mar 21.) It is a celebration of nature's rebirth. Every household spreads a special cover with symbols for the seven good angels on it. These symbols are sprouts, wheat germ, apples, hyacinth, fruit of the jujube, garlic and sumac heralding life, rebirth, health, happiness, prosperity, joy and beauty. A fish bowl is also customary, representing the end of the astrological year, and wild rue is burned to drive away evil and bring about a happy New Year. This pre-Islamic holiday, a legacy of Zoroastrianism, is also celebrated as Navruz, Nau-Roz or Noo Roz in Afghanistan, Albania, Azerbaijan, Kazakhstan, Kyrgyzstan, Tajikistan, Turkmenistan and Uzbekistan. For info: Mahvash Tafreshi, Librarian, Farmingdale Public Library, 116 Merritts Rd, Farmingdale, NY 11735. Phone: (516) 249-9090. Fax: (516) 694-9697. Or Yassaman Djalali, Librarian, West Valley Branch Library, 1243 San Tomas Aquino Rd, San Jose, CA 95117. Phone: (408) 244-4766.

JUAREZ, BENITO: 200th BIRTH ANNIVERSARY. Mar 21, 1806. A full-blooded Zapotec Indian, Benito Pablo Juarez was born at Oaxaca, Mexico in 1806, and learned Spanish at age 12. Juarez became judge of the civil court in Oaxaca in 1842, a member of congress in 1846 and governor in 1847. In 1858, following a rebellion against the constitution, he became president. He died at Mexico City, July 18, 1872. A symbol of liberation and of Mexican resistance to foreign intervention, his birthday is a public holiday in Mexico.

March 2006

S	M	T	W	T	F	S
			1	2	3	4
5	6	7	8	9	10	11
12	13	14	15	16	17	18
19	20	21	22	23	24	25
26	27	28	29	30	31	

LEWIS, FRANCIS: BIRTH ANNIVERSARY. Mar 21, 1713. Signer of the Declaration of Independence, born at Wales. Died Dec 31, 1802, at Long Island, NY.

NAMIBIA: INDEPENDENCE DAY: ANNIVERSARY. Mar 21. National Day. Commemorates independence from South Africa in 1990.

NAW-RUZ. Mar 21. Baha'i New Year's Day. Astronomically fixed to commence the year. One of the nine days of the year when Baha'is suspend work. For info: Baha'is of the US, Office of Public Info, 1320 Nineteenth St NW, Ste 350, Washington, DC 20036. Phone: (202) 466-9870. Fax: (202) 466-9873. E-mail: opi@usbnc.org. Web: www.us.bahai.org.

POCAHONTAS (REBECCA ROLFE): DEATH ANNIVERSARY. Mar 21, 1617. Pocahontas, daughter of Powhatan, born about 1595, near Jamestown, VA, leader of the Indian union of Algonquin nations, helped to foster good will between the colonists of the Jamestown settlement and her people. Pocahontas converted to Christianity, was baptized with the name Rebecca and married John Rolfe Apr 5, 1614. In 1616 she accompanied Rolfe on a trip to his native England, where she was regarded as an overseas "ambassador." Pocahontas's stay in England drew so much attention to the Virginia Company's Jamestown settlement that lotteries were held to help support the colony. Shortly before she was scheduled to return to Jamestown, Pocahontas died at Gravesend, Kent, England, of either smallpox or pneumonia. For more info: *Pocahontas: An American Princess* by Joyce Milton (Penguin Putnam, 0-448-42298-0, $13.89 Gr. 2–3).

PUBLIC LIBRARY ASSOCIATION CONFERENCE. Mar 21–25. Boston, MA. For info: Public Library Assn/ALA, 50 E Huron St, Chicago, IL 60611. Phone: (800) 545-2433. Web: www.pla.org.

SOUTH AFRICA: HUMAN RIGHTS DAY. Mar 21. National holiday. Commemorates the massacre in 1960 at Sharpeville and all those who lost their lives in the struggle for equal rights as citizens of South Africa.

UNITED NATIONS: INTERNATIONAL DAY FOR THE ELIMINATION OF RACIAL DISCRIMINATION. Mar 21. Initiated by the United Nations General Assembly in 1966 to be observed annually Mar 21, the anniversary of the killing of 69 African demonstrators at Sharpeville, South Africa, in 1960, as a day to remember "the victims of Sharpeville and those countless others in different parts of the world who have fallen victim to racial injustice" and to promote efforts to eradicate racial discrimination worldwide. Info from: United Nations, Dept of Public Info, New York, NY 10017.

WISNIEWSKI, DAVID: BIRTH ANNIVERSARY. Mar 21, 1953. Born at Middlesex, England, David Wisniewski spent his childhood all over Europe and the US (his father served in the Air Force). After one semester of college, he dropped out to attend Ringling Brothers and Barnum & Bailey Circus Clown College. He worked for many years as a circus clown and a shadow puppeteer. When his children were born, he stopped touring and used his shadow-puppet skill to create layered cut-paper illustrations that were used in children's books. His book *Golem* was awarded the 1997 Caldecott Medal. Also popular are his books *Tough Cookie* and *The Secret Knowledge of Grownups*. He died Sept 11, 2002, at Alexandria, VA.

BIRTHDAYS TODAY

Matthew Broderick, 44, actor (*Ferris Bueller's Day Off, Inspector Gadget*; stage: *The Producers*), born New York, NY, Mar 21, 1962.

Peter Catalanotto, 47, author and illustrator (*Dylan's Day Out*), born Long Island, NY, Mar 21, 1959.

Lisa Desimini, 42, author and illustrator (*My House*), born Brooklyn, NY, Mar 21, 1964.

Michael Foreman, 68, author and illustrator (*Seal Surfer*), born Pakefield, Suffolk, England, Mar 21, 1938.

Margaret Mahy, 70, author (*The Rattlebang Picnic*), born Whakatane, New Zealand, Mar 21, 1936.

Rosie O'Donnell, 44, talk show host, actress (*A League of Their Own, The Flintstones*), born Commack, NY, Mar 21, 1962.

MARCH 22 — WEDNESDAY

Day 81 — 284 Remaining

CALDECOTT, RANDOLPH: BIRTH ANNIVERSARY. Mar 22, 1846. Illustrator who brought greater beauty to children's books, born at Chester, England. He died at St. Augustine, FL, Feb 12, 1886. The Caldecott Medal given annually by the American Library Association for the most distinguished American picture book for children is named in his honor. For info: *Randolph Caldecott: The Children's Illustrator* by Marguerite Lewis (Highsmith, 0-913853-22-4, $10.95 Gr. 2–7).

EQUAL RIGHTS AMENDMENT SENT TO STATES FOR RATIFICATION: ANNIVERSARY. Mar 22, 1972. The Senate passed the 27th Amendment, prohibiting discrimination on the basis of sex, sending it to the states for ratification. Hawaii led the way as the first state to ratify and by the end of the year 22 of the required states had ratified it. On Oct 6, 1978, the deadline for ratification was extended to June 30, 1982, by Congress. The amendment still lacked three of the required 38 states for ratification. This was the first extension granted since Congress set seven years as the limit for ratification. The amendment failed to achieve ratification as the deadline came and passed and no additional states ratified the measure.

FIRST WOMEN'S COLLEGIATE BASKETBALL GAME: ANNIVERSARY. Mar 22, 1893. The first women's collegiate basketball game was played at Smith College at Northampton, MA. Senda Berenson, then Smith's director of physical education and "mother of women's basketball," supervised the game, in which Smith's sophomore team beat the freshman team 5–4. For info: Dir of Media Relations, Smith College, Office of College Relations, Northampton, MA 01063. Phone: (413) 585-2190. Fax: (413) 585-2174. Web: www.smith.edu.

INTERNATIONAL GOOF-OFF DAY. Mar 22. A day of relaxation and a time to be oneself; a day for some good-humored fun and some good-natured silliness. Everyone needs one special day each year to goof off.

LASER PATENTED: ANNIVERSARY. Mar 22, 1960. The first patent for a laser (Light Amplification by Stimulated Emission of Radiation) was granted to Arthur Schawlow and Charles Townes.

MOON PHASE: LAST QUARTER. Mar 22. Moon enters Last Quarter phase at 2:10 PM, EST.

PUERTO RICO: EMANCIPATION DAY. Mar 22. Holiday commemorating the end of slavery in 1873.

SPACE MILESTONE: RECORD TIME IN SPACE. Mar 22, 1995. Russian cosmonaut Valery Polyakov returned to Earth after setting a record of 438 days in space aboard *Mir*. Previous records include three Soviet cosmonauts who spent 237 days in space at *Salyut 7* space station in 1984, a Soviet cosmonaut who spent 326 days aboard *Mir* in 1987 and two Soviets who spent 366 days aboard *Mir* in 1988. The US space endurance record was set by Carl Walz and Daniel Bursch, who stayed 196 days in space aboard *Endeavor*, completing their mission on June 19, 2002. US astronaut Shannon Lucid set the record for women in space with her 188-day stay on *Mir* in 1996.

TUSKEGEE AIRMEN ACTIVATED: 65th ANNIVERSARY. Mar 22, 1941. This pioneering and highly decorated WWII African-American aviator unit gained their name during training at the US Army airfield near Tuskegee, AL. They were activated as the 99th Pursuit Squadron and later formed the 332nd Fighter Group (with the 100th, 301st and 302nd squadrons). 992 black pilots emerged from training to fly P-39, P-40, P-47 and P-51 aircraft in more than 15,000 sorties in North Africa, Sicily and Europe. On escort missions, they were the only unit that never lost a US bomber. They shot down 111 enemy planes and destroyed 273 planes on the ground.

UNITED NATIONS: WORLD DAY FOR WATER. Mar 22. The General Assembly declared this observance (Res 47/193) to promote public awareness of how water resource development contributes to economic productivity and social well-being.

BIRTHDAYS TODAY

Shawn Bradley, 34, basketball player, born Landstuhl, West Germany, Mar 22, 1972.

Marcus Camby, 32, basketball player, born Hartford, CT, Mar 22, 1974.

Robert Quinlan (Bob) Costas, 54, sportscaster, born New York, NY, Mar 22, 1952.

Orrin Grant Hatch, 72, US Senator (R, Utah), born Pittsburgh, PA, Mar 22, 1934.

Cristen Powell, 27, race car driver, born Portland, OR, Mar 22, 1979.

William Shatner, 75, actor ("Star Trek"; "TJ Hooker"), author (Tek novels), born Montreal, QC, Canada, Mar 22, 1931.

Elvis Stojko, 34, figure skater, born Newmarket, ON, Canada, Mar 22, 1972.

Karen Lynn Williams, 54, author (*Painted Dreams, One Thing I'm Good At*), born Hamden, CT, Mar 22, 1952.

MARCH 23 — THURSDAY

Day 82 — 283 Remaining

COLFAX, SCHUYLER: BIRTH ANNIVERSARY. Mar 23, 1823. The 17th vice president of the US (1869–73). Born at New York, NY. Died Jan 13, 1885, at Mankato, MN.

LIBERTY DAY: ANNIVERSARY. Mar 23, 1775. Anniversary of Patrick Henry's speech for arming the Virginia militia at St. John's Church, Richmond, VA. "I know not what course others may take, but as for me, give me liberty or give me death."

NEAR MISS DAY: ANNIVERSARY. Mar 23, 1989. A mountain-sized asteroid passed within 500,000 miles of Earth, a very close call according to NASA. Impact would have equaled the strength of 40,000 hydrogen bombs, created a crater the size of the District of Columbia and devastated everything for 100 miles in all directions.

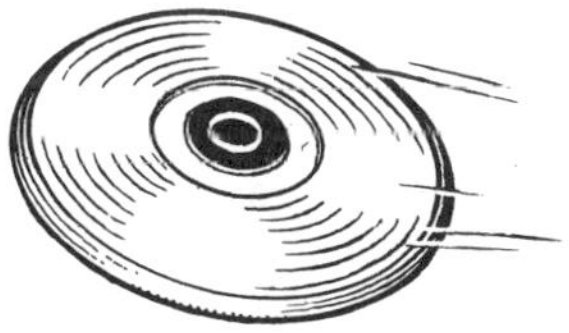

NEW ZEALAND: OTAGO AND SOUTHLAND PROVINCIAL ANNIVERSARY. Mar 23. In addition to the statutory public holidays of New Zealand, there is in each provincial district a holiday for the provincial anniversary. This is observed in Otago and Southland.

"O.K." FIRST APPEARANCE IN PRINT: ANNIVERSARY. Mar 23, 1839. *The Boston Morning Post* printed the first known "o.k." on this day in 1839. It derived from a jovial misspelling of "all correct"—"oll korrect." Etymologist Allen Read doggedly tracked down the word's origin in the 1960s. "O.K." is now used in most languages.

PAKISTAN: REPUBLIC DAY. Mar 23. National holiday. The All-India-Muslim League adopted a resolution calling for a Muslim homeland in 1940. On the same day in 1956 Pakistan declared itself a republic.

SPACE MILESTONE: *MIR* ABANDONED (RUSSIA). Mar 23, 2001. The 140-ton *Mir* space station, launched in 1986, was brought down into the South Pacific near Fiji, about 1,800 miles east of New Zealand, just before 1 AM EST. Two-thirds of the station burned up during its controlled descent. *Mir's* core component had been aloft for more than 15 years and orbited Earth 86,330 times. Nearly 100 people, 7 of them American, had spent some time on *Mir*. See also: "Space Milestone: *Mir* Space Station (USSR)" (Feb 20).

UNITED NATIONS: WORLD METEOROLOGICAL DAY. Mar 23. An international day observed by meteorological services throughout the world and by the organizations of the UN system. For info: United Nations, Dept of Public Info, New York, NY 10017.

BIRTHDAYS TODAY

Mike Easley, 56, Governor of North Carolina (D), born Nash County, NC, Mar 23, 1950.

Jason Kidd, 33, basketball player, born San Francisco, CA, Mar 23, 1973.

Moses Eugene Malone, 52, former basketball player, born Petersburg, VA, Mar 23, 1954.

MARCH 24 — FRIDAY

Day 83 — 282 Remaining

CLEAVER, BILL: BIRTH ANNIVERSARY. Mar 24, 1920. Children's author, with his wife, Vera, of *Where the Lilies Bloom*, among other books. Born at Seattle, WA. Died Aug 20, 1981.

***EXXON VALDEZ* OIL SPILL: ANNIVERSARY.** Mar 24, 1989. The tanker *Exxon Valdez* ran aground at Prince William Sound, leaking 11 million gallons of oil into one of nature's richest habitats. For more info: *The Exxon Valdez* by Victoria Sherrow (Enslow, 0-7660-1058-9, $18.85 Gr. 4–8).

HOUDINI, HARRY: BIRTH ANNIVERSARY. Mar 24, 1874. Magician and escape artist, born at Budapest, Hungary. Lecturer, athlete, author, expert on history of magic, exposer of fraudulent mediums and motion picture actor. Was best known for his ability to escape from locked restraints (handcuffs, straitjackets, coffins, boxes and milk cans). He died at Detroit, MI, Oct 31, 1926. Anniversary of his death (Halloween) has been the occasion for meetings of magicians and attempts at communication by mediums. For more info: *Spellbinder: The Life of Harry Houdini* by Tom Lalicki (Holiday, 0-8234-1499-X, $18.95 Gr. 3–7).

March 2006

S	M	T	W	T	F	S
			1	2	3	4
5	6	7	8	9	10	11
12	13	14	15	16	17	18
19	20	21	22	23	24	25
26	27	28	29	30	31	

PHILIPPINE INDEPENDENCE: ANNIVERSARY. Mar 24, 1934. President Franklin Roosevelt signed a bill granting independence to the Philippines. The bill, which took effect July 4, 1946, brought to a close almost half a century of US control of the islands.

POWELL, JOHN WESLEY: BIRTH ANNIVERSARY. Mar 24, 1834. American geologist and explorer, born at Mount Morris, NY. Powell is best known for his explorations of the Grand Canyon by boat on the Colorado River. He died at Haven, ME, Sept 23, 1902. For more info: *Exploring the Earth with John Wesley Powell* by Michael Elsohn Ross (Carolrhoda, 1-5750-5254-7, $19.94 Gr. 5–6).

RHODE ISLAND VOTERS REJECT CONSTITUTION: ANNIVERSARY. Mar 24, 1788. In a popular referendum, Rhode Island rejected the new Constitution by a vote of 2,708 to 237. The state later (May 29, 1790) ratified the Constitution and ratified the Bill of Rights, June 7, 1790.

TB BACILLUS DISCOVERED: ANNIVERSARY. Mar 24, 1882. The tuberculosis bacillus was discovered by German scientist Robert Koch.

BIRTHDAYS TODAY

Dr. Roger Bannister, 77, distance runner, broke the 4-minute-mile record in 1954, born Harrow, Middlesex, England, Mar 24, 1929.

Aaron Brooks, 30, football player, born Newport News, VA, Mar 24, 1976.

Christine Gregoire, 59, Governor of Washington (D), born Adrian, MI, Mar 24, 1947.

MARCH 25 — SATURDAY

Day 84 — 281 Remaining

BORGLUM, GUTZON: BIRTH ANNIVERSARY. Mar 25, 1871. American sculptor who created the huge sculpture of four American presidents (Washington, Jefferson, Lincoln and Theodore Roosevelt) at Mount Rushmore National Memorial in the Black Hills of South Dakota. Born John Gutzon de la Mothe Borglum at Bear Lake, ID, the son of Mormon pioneers, he worked the last 14 years of his life on the Mount Rushmore sculpture. He died at Chicago, IL, Mar 6, 1941.

FEAST OF ANNUNCIATION. Mar 25. Celebrated in the Roman Catholic Church in commemoration of the message of the Angel Gabriel to Mary that she was to be the Mother of Christ.

GREECE: INDEPENDENCE DAY. Mar 25. National holiday. Celebrates the beginning of the Greek revolt for independence from the Ottoman Empire on Mar 25, 1821 (OS). Greece attained independence in 1829.

★**GREEK INDEPENDENCE DAY: A NATIONAL DAY OF CELEBRATION OF GREEK AND AMERICAN DEMOCRACY.** Mar 25.

MARYLAND DAY. Mar 25. Commemorates arrival of Lord Baltimore's first settlers in Maryland in 1634.

NATO ATTACKS YUGOSLAVIA: ANNIVERSARY. Mar 25, 1999. After many weeks of unsuccessful negotiations with Yugoslav leader Slobodan Milosevic over the treatment of ethnic Albanians in the Kosovo Province by Serb forces, NATO forces began bombing Serbia and Kosovo. In retaliation, hundreds of thousands of Kosovo Albanians were driven from their homes into Albania, Macedonia and Montenegro. Peace talks began in June 1999.

PECAN DAY: ANNIVERSARY. Mar 25, 1775. Anniversary of the planting by George Washington of pecan trees (some of which still survive) at Mount Vernon. The trees were a gift to Washington from Thomas Jefferson, who had planted a few pecan trees from the southern US at Monticello, VA. The pecan, native to southern North America, is sometimes called "America's own nut." First cultivated by American Indians, it has been transplanted to other continents but has failed to achieve wide use or popularity outside the US.

TRIANGLE SHIRTWAIST FIRE: 95th ANNIVERSARY. Mar 25, 1911. At about 4:30 PM, fire broke out at the Triangle Shirtwaist Company at New York, NY, minutes before the seamstresses were to go home. Some workers were fatally burned while others leaped to their deaths from the windows of the 10-story building. The fire lasted only 18 minutes but left 146 workers dead, most of them young immigrant women. It was found that some of the deaths were a direct result of workers being trapped on the ninth floor by a locked door. Labor law forbade locking factory doors while employees were at work, and owners of the company were indicted on charges of first- and second-degree manslaughter. The tragic fire became a turning point in labor history, bringing about reforms in health and safety laws. For more info: *The Triangle Shirtwaist Company Fire of 1911* by Gina De Angelis (Chelsea House, 0-7910-5267-2, $19.95 Gr. 7–12).

BIRTHDAYS TODAY

John Ensign, 48, US Senator (R, Nevada), born Roseville, CA, Mar 25, 1958.

Tom Glavine, 40, baseball player, born Concord, MA, Mar 25, 1966.

Cammi Granato, 35, Olympic ice hockey player, born Maywood, IL, Mar 25, 1971.

Elton John, 59, singer, songwriter (*The Lion King* soundtrack), born Reginald Kenneth Dwight, Pinner, England, Mar 25, 1947.

Avery Johnson, 41, basketball player, born New Orleans, LA, Mar 25, 1965.

MARCH 26 — SUNDAY

Day 85 — 280 Remaining

BANGLADESH: INDEPENDENCE DAY. Mar 26. Commemorates East Pakistan's independence in 1971 as the state of Bangladesh. Celebrated with parades, youth festivals and symposia.

CAMP DAVID ACCORD SIGNED: ANNIVERSARY. Mar 26, 1979. Israeli Prime Minister Menachem Begin and Egyptian President Anwar Sadat signed the Camp David peace treaty, ending 30 years of war between their two countries. The agreement was fostered by President Jimmy Carter.

FROST, ROBERT LEE: BIRTH ANNIVERSARY. Mar 26, 1874. American poet who tried his hand at farming, teaching, shoemaking and editing before winning acclaim as a poet. Pulitzer Prize winner. Born at San Francisco, CA, he died at Boston, MA, Jan 29, 1963.

MacDONALD, BETTY: BIRTH ANNIVERSARY. Mar 26, 1908. Born Anne Elizabeth Bard at Boulder, CO. She was the author of the Mrs Piggle-Wiggle series, books featuring a character parents turned to when their children's behavior was out of control. Mrs Piggle-Wiggle was famous for her "Won't-Pick-Up-the-Toys Cure" and her "Answer-Backers Cure." Titles in the series include *Mrs Piggle-Wiggle* and *Hello, Mrs Piggle-Wiggle*. MacDonald died at Carmel Valley, CA, Feb 7, 1958.

MAKE UP YOUR OWN HOLIDAY DAY. Mar 26. This day is a day you may name for whatever you wish. Reach for the stars! Make up a holiday! Annually, Mar 26. [©2002 by WH.] For info: Thomas & Ruth Roy, Wellcat Holidays, 2418 Long Ln, Lebanon, PA 17046. Phone: (717) 279-0184. E-mail: info@wellcat.com. Web: www.wellcat.com.

PRINCE JONAH KUHIO KALANIANOLE DAY. Mar 26. Hawaii. Commemorates the man who, as Hawaii's delegate to the US Congress, introduced the first bill for statehood in 1919. Not until 1959 did Hawaii become a state.

SOVIET COSMONAUT RETURNS TO NEW COUNTRY: ANNIVERSARY. Mar 26, 1992. After spending 313 days in space in the Soviet *Mir* space station, cosmonaut Serge Krikalev returned to Earth and to what was for him a new country. He left Earth May 18, 1991, a citizen of the Soviet Union, but during his stay aboard the space station, the Soviet Union crumbled and became the Commonwealth of Independent States. Originally scheduled to return in October 1991, Krikalev's return was delayed by five months due to his country's disintegration and the ensuing monetary problems.

BIRTHDAYS TODAY

Marcus Allen, 46, former football player, born San Diego, CA, Mar 26, 1960.

Thomas A. (T.A.) Barron, 54, author (*The Lost Years of Merlin, The Fires of Merlin, The Ancient One*), born in Colorado, Mar 26, 1952.

Lincoln Chafee, 53, US Senator (R, Rhode Island), born Warwick, RI, Mar 26, 1953.

Elaine Lan Chao, 53, US Secretary of Labor (George W. Bush administration), born Taipei, Taiwan, Mar 26, 1953.

Jon Huntsman, Jr, 46, Governor of Utah (R), born Palo Alto, CA, Mar 26, 1960.

Sandra Day O'Connor, 76, Associate Justice of the US Supreme Court, born El Paso, TX, Mar 26, 1930.

John Houston Stockton, 44, former basketball player, born Spokane, WA, Mar 26, 1962.

MARCH 27 — MONDAY

Day 86 — 279 Remaining

EARTHQUAKE STRIKES ALASKA: ANNIVERSARY. Mar 27, 1964. The strongest earthquake in North American history (8.4 on the Richter scale) struck Alaska, east of Anchorage, killing 117 people. This was the second worst earthquake of the 20th century in terms of magnitude. For more info go to the National Earthquake Information Center: wwwneic.cr.usgs.gov.

FUNKY WINKERBEAN: ANNIVERSARY. Mar 27, 1972. Anniversary of the nationally syndicated comic strip. For info: Tom Batiuk, Creator, 2750 Substation Rd, Medina, OH 44256. Phone: (330) 722-8755.

KITE FLYING DAY. Mar 27. One of the favorite rites of spring is flying kites in the March winds. It has provided fun for families for years. For info: Lindsay Benson, 13116 Frog Hollow Ct, Oak Hill, VA 20171. Phone: (703) 471-5784. E-mail: winniontoe@aol.com.

MYANMAR: RESISTANCE DAY. Mar 27. National holiday. Commemorates the day in 1945 when Burma (later Myanmar) joined the Allies in World War II.

NATIONAL SLEEP AWARENESS WEEK. Mar 27–Apr 2. All Americans are urged to recognize the dangers of untreated sleep disorders and the importance of proper sleep to their health, safety and productivity. "8ZZZs, please!" For info: National Sleep Foundation, 1522 K St NW, Ste 500, Washington, DC 20005. Phone: (888) NSF-SLEEP. Web: www.sleepfoundation.org.

RÖNTGEN, WILHELM CONRAD: BIRTH ANNIVERSARY. Mar 27, 1845. German scientist who discovered X-rays (1895) and won a Nobel Prize in 1901. Born at Lennep, Prussia, he died at Munich, Germany, Feb 10, 1923. See also: "X-Ray Discovery Day: Anniversary" (Nov 8).

SEWARD'S DAY: ANNIVERSARY OF THE ACQUISITION OF ALASKA. Mar 27. Observed in Alaska near anniversary of its acquisition from Russia in 1867. The treaty of purchase was signed between the Russians and the Americans Mar 30, 1867, and ratified by the Senate May 28, 1867. The territory was formally transferred Oct 18, 1867. Annually, the last Monday in March.

BIRTHDAYS TODAY

Mariah Carey, 36, singer, born New York, NY, Mar 27, 1970.

Randall Cunningham, 43, former football player, born Santa Barbara, CA, Mar 27, 1963.

Dick King-Smith, 84, author (*Babe: The Gallant Pig, A Mouse Called Wolf, The Cuckoo Child*), born Bitton, Gloucestershire, England, Mar 27, 1922.

Patricia Wrede, 53, author (*Dealing with Dragons, Talking to Dragons*), born Chicago, IL, Mar 27, 1953.

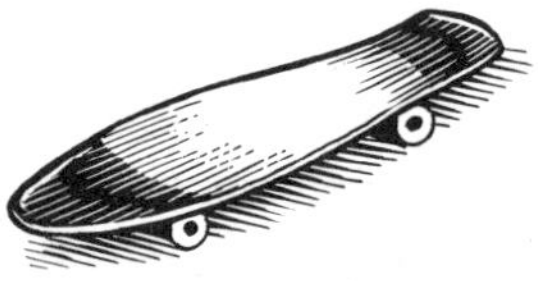

March 2006

S	M	T	W	T	F	S
			1	2	3	4
5	6	7	8	9	10	11
12	13	14	15	16	17	18
19	20	21	22	23	24	25
26	27	28	29	30	31	

MARCH 28 — TUESDAY

Day 87 — 278 Remaining

AMERICAN DIABETES ASSOCIATION ALERT DAY. Mar 28. A one-day "wake-up call" for those eight million Americans who have diabetes and don't even know it. During the Alert, local ADA affiliates use the diabetes risk test—a simple paper-and-pencil quiz—to communicate the risk factors and symptoms of the disease. Annually, the fourth Tuesday in March. For more info, call 1-800-DIABETES (342-2383), or go to www.diabetes.org.

CZECH REPUBLIC: TEACHERS' DAY. Mar 28. Celebrates birth on this day of Jan Amos Komensky (Comenius), Moravian educational reformer (1592–1671).

"GREATEST SHOW ON EARTH" FORMED: 125th ANNIVERSARY. Mar 28, 1881. P.T. Barnum and James A. Bailey merged their circuses to form the "Greatest Show on Earth." For more info: www.ringling.com/history.

LIBYA: BRITISH BASES EVACUATION DAY. Mar 28. National holiday. Commemorates the day in 1970 when British bases in Libya were closed.

SPACE MILESTONE: *NOAA-8* (US). Mar 28, 1983. Search and Rescue Satellite (SARSAT) launched from Vandenburg Air Force Base, CA, to aid in locating ships and aircraft in distress. *Kosmos 1383*, launched July 1, 1982, by the USSR, in a cooperative rescue effort, is credited with saving more than 20 lives.

THREE MILE ISLAND NUCLEAR POWER PLANT ACCIDENT: ANNIVERSARY. Mar 28, 1979. A series of accidents beginning at 4 AM, EST, at Three Mile Island on the Susquehanna River about 10 miles southeast of Harrisburg, PA, was responsible for extensive reevaluation of the safety of existing nuclear power generating operations. Equipment and other failures reportedly brought Three Mile Island close to a meltdown of the uranium core, threatening extensive radiation contamination. For more info: www.pbs.org/wgbh/amex/world and *Meltdown: A Race Against Nuclear Disaster at Three Mile Island* by Wilborn Hampton (Candlewick, 0-7636-0715-0, $19.99 Gr. 5 & up).

BIRTHDAYS TODAY

Byrd Baylor, 82, author (*I'm In Charge of Celebrations*), born San Antonio, TX, Mar 28, 1924.

Frank Hughes Murkowski, 73, Governor of Alaska (R), former US Senator, born Seattle, WA, Mar 28, 1933.

Earnie Stewart, 37, soccer player, born Veghal, Holland, Mar 28, 1969.

Keith Tkachuk, 34, hockey player, born Melrose, MA, Mar 28, 1972.

MARCH 29 — WEDNESDAY

Day 88 — 277 Remaining

CANADA: BRITISH NORTH AMERICA ACT: ANNIVERSARY. Mar 29, 1867. This act of the British Parliament established the Dominion of Canada, uniting Ontario, Quebec, Nova Scotia and New Brunswick. Union was proclaimed July 1, 1867. The remaining colonies in Canada were still ruled directly by Great Britain until Manitoba joined the Dominion in 1870, British Columbia in 1871, Prince Edward Island in 1873, Alberta and Saskatchewan in 1905 and Newfoundland in 1949. See also: "Canada: Canada Day" (July 1).

CENTRAL AFRICAN REPUBLIC: BOGANDA DAY. Mar 29. National holiday. Commemorates the death in 1959 of the first president, Barthelemy Boganda.

HOOVER, LOU HENRY: BIRTH ANNIVERSARY. Mar 29, 1875. Wife of Herbert Clark Hoover, 31st president of the US. Born at Waterloo, IA, she died at Palo Alto, CA, Jan 7, 1944.

MOON PHASE: NEW MOON. Mar 29. Moon enters New Moon phase at 5:15 AM, EST.

NIAGARA FALLS RUNS DRY: ANNIVERSARY. Mar 29, 1848. A massive assemblage of ice blocks formed upstream of Niagara Falls late on Mar 29, 1848, and by midnight had stopped water flow over the Falls (which are actually three falls: the American, the Horseshoe [or Canadian] and the Bridal Veil). The ice jam held until Apr 1, when the waters of Lake Erie punched through and things got back to normal. Until that happened, hundreds of the curious swarmed into the now-waterless gorge to hunt for 1812 war relics and geological souvenirs while thousands of spectators watched from above. Although the American Falls has stopped flowing before, this Mar 29, 1848 stoppage was the first and only time the entire falls was affected. For info on Niagara Falls: www.infoniagara.com.

SOLAR ECLIPSE. Mar 29. Total eclipse of the sun. Visible in Brazil, Atlantic Ocean, northern Africa and central Asia (especially Mongolia).

TAIWAN: YOUTH DAY. Mar 29.

TEXAS LOVE THE CHILDREN DAY. Mar 29. A day recognizing every child's right and need to be loved. Promoting the hope that one day all children will live in loving, safe environments and will be given proper health care and equal learning opportunities. Precedes the start of National Child Abuse Prevention Month (April). For info: Patty Murphy, 1101 Lynda Lane, Arlington, TX 76013. Phone: (817) 980-9591. E-mail: MURPH0@swbell.net.

TWENTY-THIRD AMENDMENT TO US CONSTITUTION RATIFIED: 45th ANNIVERSARY. Mar 29, 1961. District of Columbia residents were given the right to vote in presidential elections under the 23rd Amendment.

TYLER, JOHN: BIRTH ANNIVERSARY. Mar 29, 1790. The 10th president of the US (Apr 6, 1841–Mar 3, 1845). Born at Greenway, VA, Tyler succeeded to the presidency upon the death of William Henry Harrison. Tyler's first wife died while he was president, and he remarried before the end of his term of office, becoming the first president to marry while in office. Fifteen children were born of the two marriages. In 1861 he was elected to the Congress of the Confederate States but died at Richmond, VA, Jan 18, 1862, before being seated. His death received no official tribute from the US government. For more info: www.ipl.org/ref/POTUS.

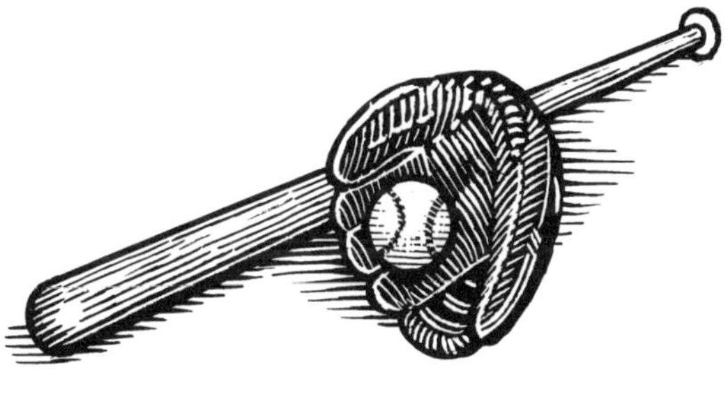

YOUNG, DENTON TRUE (CY): BIRTH ANNIVERSARY. Mar 29, 1867. Baseball Hall of Fame pitcher, born at Gilmore, OH. Young is baseball's all-time winningest pitcher, having accumulated 511 victories in his 22-year career. The Cy Young Award is given each year in his honor to major league's best pitcher. Inducted into the Hall of Fame in 1937. Died at Peoli, OH, Nov 4, 1955.

BIRTHDAYS TODAY

Jennifer Capriati, 30, tennis player, born New York, NY, Mar 29, 1976.

Lucy Lawless, 38, actress ("Xena"), born Mount Albert, Auckland, New Zealand, Mar 29, 1968.

MARCH 30 — THURSDAY

Day 89 — 276 Remaining

ANESTHETIC FIRST USED IN SURGERY: ANNIVERSARY. Mar 30, 1842. Dr. Crawford W. Long, having seen the use of nitrous oxide and sulfuric ether at "laughing gas" parties, observed that individuals under their influences felt no pain. On this date, he removed a tumor from the neck of a man who was under the influence of ether.

DOCTORS' DAY. Mar 30. Traditional annual observance since 1933 to honor America's physicians on anniversary of occasion when Dr. Crawford W. Long became the first physician to use ether as an anesthetic agent in a surgical technique, Mar 30, 1842. The red carnation has been designated the official flower of Doctors' Day.

PENCIL PATENTED: ANNIVERSARY. Mar 30, 1858. First pencil with the eraser top was patented by Hyman Lipman.

SEWELL, ANNA: BIRTH ANNIVERSARY. Mar 30, 1820. Born at Yarmouth, England, Anna Sewell is best known for her book *Black Beauty*. Published in 1877, her tale centers around the abuses and injustices to horses she saw while growing up. She died at Old Catton, Norfolk, England, Apr 25, 1878.

TRINIDAD AND TOBAGO: SPIRITUAL BAPTIST LIBERATION SHOUTER DAY. Mar 30. Public Holiday.

VAN GOGH, VINCENT: BIRTH ANNIVERSARY. Mar 30, 1853. Dutch post-Impressionist painter, especially known for his bold and powerful use of color (*Sunflowers, The Starry Night*). Born at Groot Zundert, Netherlands, he died at Auvers-sur-Oise, France, July 29, 1890. For more info: *Vincent Van Gogh* by Enrica Crispino (Peter Bedrick, 0-87226-525-0, $22.50 Gr. 4–7) or *Vincent Van Gogh: Portrait of an Artist*,by Jan Greenberg and Sandra Jordan (Delacorte, 0-385-32806-0, $14.95 Ages 10 & up).

BIRTHDAYS TODAY

Robbie Coltrane, 56, actor (*Harry Potter and the Sorcerer's Stone*), born Rutherglen, Scotland, Mar 30, 1950 (some sources say Mar 31).

MARCH 31 — FRIDAY

Day 90 — 275 Remaining

CHAVEZ, CESAR ESTRADA: BIRTH ANNIVERSARY. Mar 31, 1927. Labor leader who organized migrant farm workers in support of better working conditions. Chavez initiated the National Farm Workers Association in 1962, attracting attention to the migrant farm workers' plight by organizing boycotts of products including grapes and lettuce. He was born at Yuma, AZ, and died Apr 23, 1993, at San Luis, AZ. His birthday is a holiday in California. For more info: *Cesar Chavez: Leader for Migrant Farm Workers* by Doreen Gonzales (Enslow, 0-89490-760-3, $19.95 Gr. 5–8).

CHESNUT, MARY BOYKIN MILLER: BIRTH ANNIVERSARY. Mar 31, 1823. Born at Pleasant Hill, SC, and died Nov 22, 1886, at Camden, SC. During the Civil War Chesnut accompanied her husband, a Confederate staff officer, on military missions. She kept a journal of her experiences and observations, which was published posthumously as *A Diary from Dixie*, a perceptive portrait of Confederate military and political leaders and an insightful view of Southern life during the Civil War.

EIFFEL TOWER: ANNIVERSARY. Mar 31, 1889. Built for the Paris Exhibition of 1889, the tower was named for its architect, Alexandre Gustave Eiffel, and is one of the world's best-known landmarks. For more info: *The Eiffel Tower* by Meg Greene (Lucent, 1-56006-826-4, $19.96 Gr. 7–10).

GORE, ALBERT, JR: BIRTHDAY. Mar 31, 1948. The 45th vice president (1993–2001) of the US, born at Washington, DC.

HAYDN, FRANZ JOSEPH: BIRTH ANNIVERSARY. Mar 31, 1732. Composer of symphonies, oratorios and masses, born at Rohrau, Austria. Haydn was a friend of Mozart and Beethoven. He died May 31, 1809, at Vienna, Austria.

JOHNSON, JOHN (JACK): BIRTH ANNIVERSARY. Mar 31, 1878. In 1908 Jack Johnson became the first African American to win the heavyweight boxing championship when he defeated Tommy Burns at Sydney, Australia. Unable to accept a black's triumph, the boxing world tried to find a white challenger. Jim Jeffries, former heavyweight title holder, was badgered out of retirement. On July 4, 1919, at Reno, NV, the "battle of the century" proved to be a farce when Johnson handily defeated Jeffries. Race riots swept the US and plans to exhibit the film of the fight were canceled. Johnson was born at Galveston, TX, and died in an automobile accident June 10, 1946, at Raleigh, NC. He was inducted into the Boxing Hall of Fame in 1990. The film *The Great White Hope* is based on his life.

NATIONAL GEOGRAPHIC BEE 2006, STATE LEVEL. Mar 31. Site is different in each state—many are in state capitals. Winners of school-level competitions who scored in the top 100 in their state on a written test compete in the State Geographic Bees. The winner of each state bee will go to Washington, DC, for the national level in May. For info: National Geographic Bee, National Geographic Society, 1145 17th St NW, Washington, DC 20036. Web: www.nationalgeographic.com/geographicbee.

RABI'I: THE MONTH OF THE MIGRATION. Mar 31. Begins on Islamic calendar date Rabi'I 1, 1427. The month of the migration or Hegira of the Prophet Muhammad from Mecca to Medina in AD 622, the event that was used as the starting year of the Islamic era. Different methods for "anticipating" the visibility of the new moon crescent at Mecca are used by different Muslim groups. US date may vary. Began at sunset the preceding day.

US VIRGIN ISLANDS: TRANSFER DAY. Mar 31. Commemorates transfer resulting from purchase of the Virgin Islands by the US from Denmark, Mar 31, 1917, for $25 million.

BIRTHDAYS TODAY

Pavel Bure, 35, hockey player, born Moscow, USSR, Mar 31, 1971.

Gordie Howe, 78, Hall of Fame hockey player, born Floral, SK, Canada, Mar 31, 1928.

Steve Jenkins, 54, author and illustrator (*Big and Little, The Top of the World: Climbing Mount Everest*), born Hickory, NC, Mar 31, 1952.

Patrick J. Leahy, 66, US Senator (D, Vermont), born Montpelier, VT, Mar 31, 1940.

Rhea Perlman, 58, actress (*Matilda*), born Brooklyn, NY, Mar 31, 1948.

Steve Smith, 37, basketball player, born Highland Park, MI, Mar 31, 1969.

APRIL 1 — SATURDAY

Day 91 — 274 Remaining

ALCOHOL AWARENESS MONTH. Apr 1–30. To help raise awareness among community prevention leaders and citizens about the problem of underage drinking. Concentrates on community grassroots activities. For info: Public Info Dept, National Council on Alcoholism and Drug Dependence, Inc, 20 Exchange Pl, New York, NY 10005. Phone: (212) 269-7797. Fax: (212) 269-7510. E-mail: national@ncadd.org. Web: www.ncadd.org.

APRIL FOOLS' or ALL FOOLS' DAY. Apr 1. April Fools' Day seems to have begun in France in 1564. Apr 1 used to be New Year's Day but the New Year was changed to Jan 1 that year. People who insisted on celebrating the "old" New Year became known as April fools. The general concept of a feast of fools, however, is an old one. The Romans had such a day and medieval monasteries had days when the abbot or bishop was replaced for a day by a common monk, who would order his superiors to do the most menial or ridiculous tasks. According to Brady's *Clavis Calendaria* (1812): "The joke of the day is to deceive persons by sending them upon frivolous and nonsensical errands; to pretend they are wanted when they are not, or, in fact, any way to betray them into some supposed ludicrous situation, so as to enable you to call them 'An April Fool.'"

BE KIND TO ANIMALS KIDS CONTEST DEADLINE. Apr 1. Application deadline for this contest. The national winner will receive a $5,000 scholarship. For info: American Humane Assn, 63 Inverness Dr East, Englewood, CO 80112. Phone: (303) 792-9900. Web: www.americanhumane.org.

BULGARIA: SAINT LASARUS DAY. Apr 1. Ancient Slavic holiday of young girls, in honor of the goddess of spring and love.

CANADA: NUNAVUT INDEPENDENCE: ANNIVERSARY. Apr 1, 1999. Nunavut became Canada's third independent territory. This self-governing territory with an Inuit majority was created from the eastern half of the Northwest Territories. In 1992 Canada's Inuit people accepted a federal land-claim package granting them control over the new territory. ***See Curriculum Connection.***

★CANCER CONTROL MONTH. Apr 1–30.

GOLDEN RULE WEEK. Apr 1–7. The purpose of this week is to remind everyone of the importance of the Golden Rule in making this a better world in which we all may live. For a copy of the Golden Rule of 10 religions, send $5 to cover printing and postage. For info: Dr. Stanley J. Drake, Pres, Intl Society of Friendship and Goodwill, 8592 Roswell Rd, Ste 251, Atlanta, GA 30350-1867. Phone: (678) 795-1362. Web: www.friendshipandgoodwill.org.

APRIL 1–30
NATIONAL POETRY MONTH

The Sept 26 Curriculum Connection on George Gershwin spoke of how his composition "An American in Paris" invoked the sounds of the city through music. During National Poetry Month, discover how the rhythm of words can conjure an urban landscape.

The last few years have brought several delightful children's poetry books that focus on the city. *A City Is* is a collection of New York poetry for ages 4 to 8 by the late poet and playwright Norman Rosten (Henry Holt, 0-8050-6793-0, $16.95). Rosten, who was the first poet laureate of Brooklyn, captures the city in wonderful details—fire trucks, sirens, "great towers of stone"—and an exuberant tone. Melanie Hope Greenberg provides the beautiful, almost folkloric, artwork.

For children ages 9 to 12, introduce them to *Sidewalk Chalk: Poems of the City* by Carole Boston Weatherford (Boyds Mills Press, 1-563-970848, $15.95). Weatherford depicts the city through the eyes of a child and records typical neighborhood activities and sights: rope-jumping, playing hoops, shopping in the local market, hanging out in the city pool. *Hey You! C'Mere: A Poetry Slam* by Elizabeth Swados (Arthur A. Levine Books, 0-439-09257-4, $16.95) also provides city poetry for the 6 to 12 age group. In this colorful book, illustrated by Joe Cepeda, seven neighborhood kids create their own poetry slam out of the texture of the city.

A great anthology to have in the classroom is *Sky Scape/City Scape: Poems of City Life*, collected by Jane Yolen (Boyds Mills Press, 1-563-97179-8, $15.95 Ages 6–10). Among the poets featured are Langston Hughes, Carl Sandburg, Rachel Field, Ann Turner and more. Beautiful chalk and pastel pictures by Ken Condon accompany the 25 poems—almost like sidewalk chalk art.

Create your own poetry of the city: ask your class which sights and sounds—banging trash cans in the night, honking horns, laughing kids in parks, water dripping from a fire hydrant—they most associate with urban life. Jot them on the chalkboard to create free verse in the style of Norman Rosten.

—Holly McGuire

HARVEY, WILLIAM: BIRTH ANNIVERSARY. Apr 1, 1578. Physician, born at Folkestone, England. The first to discover the mechanics of the circulation of the blood. Died at Roehampton, England, June 3, 1657.

MONTH OF THE YOUNG CHILD®. Apr 1–30. Michigan. To promote awareness of the importance of young children and their specific needs in today's society. Many communities celebrate with special events for children and families. For info: Michigan Assn for the Education of Young Children, Beacon Pl, Ste 1-D, 4572 S Hagadorn Rd, East Lansing, MI 48823-5385. Phone: (800) 336-6424 or (517) 336-9700. Fax: (517) 336-9790. E-mail: moyc@miaeyc.com. Web: www.miaeyc.com.

NATIONAL ASSOCIATION OF ELEMENTARY SCHOOL PRINCIPALS ANNUAL CONFERENCE. Apr 1–4. San Antonio, TX. 85th annual. For info: National Assn of Elementary School Principals, 1615 Duke St, Alexandria, VA 22314. Phone: (703) 684-3345 or (800) 38-NAESP. Fax: (800) 39-NAESP. E-mail: naesp@naesp.org. Web: www.naesp.org.

NATIONAL AUTISM AWARENESS MONTH. Apr 1–30. A month filled with events such as conferences, presentations, dis-

APRIL 1
MEETING THE INUIT

Today is a great time to introduce your class to the people who live in the snowy reaches of North America and Greenland—the Inuit. Ask your class what they think of when they hear the name Inuit. Perhaps they conjure up igloos, dogsleds, rubbing noses instead of kissing and so forth. All these images are accurate today, but the Inuit live in two worlds, and other images should be houses made of modern materials, snowmobiles and western-style handshakes. Your class might mention the name Eskimo, which was given the Inuit by the Athabaskan people and means "raw meat eaters." Arriving Europeans soon adopted the insulting term. Inuit means "the people" and is the preferred term today.

This is an exciting time to be Inuit. On Apr 1, 1999, the government of Canada and the people of the large areas to the west and north of Hudson Bay finally signed an agreement making Nunavut (which means "our land") a native-controlled territory of approximately 250,000 square miles. The people of Nunavut will be able to make important decisions on how this land is administered and will have more opportunity to rediscover their heritage. (The government of Nunavut has an informative website at www.gov.nu.ca.) Greenland released the Inuit in its country to home rule in 1979, after which point the Inuit withdrew from the European Union.

Who are these people? The ancestors of today's Inuit have been hunting and fishing the icy reaches of the Arctic for thousands of years. They divided eventually into two main groups: the Yupik, who live in Siberia and western Alaska; and the Inupiaq who occupy eastern Alaska, Greenland and parts of Canada. The rest of the world and the dwellers of the far north had little contact until the landing of Erik the Red, a Viking, on Greenland in AD 983. Other early explorers also visited in the 16th century but did not stay. The Inuit continued in their traditional ways, following game and fishing until quite recently. Caribou, whale, seal, walrus, birds, fish and berries all played important roles in the native diet.

Contact in the last 150 years or more with European explorers, missionaries and settlers caused many problems for the Inuit. New diseases and foods ill suited to the climate decimated some populations. Missionaries converted them to different religions (sometimes at gunpoint), thus destroying the traditions of song, dance and story that carried the history of the people. Also lost were the ways of doing important tasks like hunting, building shelters and relating to others. Recently, pollution from city populations far away has spread into the formerly clean Arctic, making some animals and fish toxic to eat. Despite all of this, the Inuit continue and many are working to be sure the coming generations learn the important languages, songs and skills that will help them thrive well into the future.

Inuit people live in a part of the world where it is difficult just to stay alive. They are hardworking people but also love to play games, socialize with friends and family, make music and have fun. Have you ever seen a picture of an Inuit blanket toss game? Sort of like a trampoline except your friends toss you up in the air on a leather blanket. Some old games have changed little in thousands of years and are easy to play in a classroom. Here is a variety of Inuit games to get your class having fun.

Many games are a test of strength and skill and some of them are really tough. Leg wrestling is a lot like arm wrestling except the contestants lay on the ground head to toe, side by side. They hook legs and see who can pull the other person's leg to the floor.

Another test of skill that is always good for a laugh often involves husband-and-wife couples, but can be played with any team. Traditionally, men would stand a certain number of paces away from the women who would be holding up sewing needles. Each man has a piece of thread. He races to his wife and tries to thread her needle. Much merriment ensues as the men tend to have a pretty hard time with a task the women would be handy with. The first man to thread the needle wins.

For this next game you will need a sawed-off broom handle about 12 inches in length. Students should stand close to one other, each child on a piece of tape marking where their feet are to stay. Two students each grab an end of the handle and pull or push trying to make the other contestant lose his or her balance and step off the mark or release the stick. The winner should have the stick at the end but not have left the foot marker.

Inuit people sometimes play string games. Do any of your children know the one we often call "witch's broom"? It is very close to one *ajarraaq* (string puzzle) that they know as the "tent."

—Luisa Gerasimo

plays and media attention. Contact the NJ Center for Outreach and Services for the Autism Community for information on how you can become an "Autism Awareness Ambassador." This is a national celebration. Annually, the month of April. For info: Courtney Knox, COSAC, 1450 Parkside Ave, Ste 22, Ewing, NJ 08638. Phone: (609) 883-8100. Fax: (609) 883-5509. E-mail: information@njcosac.org. Web: www.njcosac.org.

★**NATIONAL CHILD ABUSE PREVENTION MONTH.** Apr 1–30.

NATIONAL CHILD ABUSE PREVENTION MONTH. Apr 1–30. For info: Prevent Child Abuse America, 200 S Michigan Ave, 17th Fl, Chicago, IL 60604. Phone: (312) 663-3520. Web: www.preventchildabuse.org.

April 2006

S	M	T	W	T	F	S
						1
2	3	4	5	6	7	8
9	10	11	12	13	14	15
16	17	18	19	20	21	22
23	24	25	26	27	28	29
30						

★**NATIONAL DONATE LIFE MONTH.** Apr 1–30. To encourage Americans to consider organ and tissue donation and to sign donor cards when getting a driver's license. Annually, the month of April. Previously proclaimed as National Organ and Tissue Donor Awareness Week. For info: US Dept of Health and Human Service, 200 Independence Ave SW, Washington, DC 20201. Phone: (202) 619-0257 or (877) 696-6775. Web: www.organdonor.gov.

NATIONAL HUMOR MONTH. Apr 1–30. Focuses on the joy and therapeutic value of laughter and how it can reduce stress, improve job performance and enrich the quality of life. For info: send SASE (68¢) to: Larry Wilde, Dir, The Carmel Institute of Humor, 25470 Canada Dr, Carmel, CA 93923-8926. Web: www.larrywilde.com.

NATIONAL KNUCKLES DOWN MONTH. Apr 1–30. To recognize and revive the American tradition of playing and collecting marbles and keep it rolling along. Please send self-addressed, stamped envelope with inquiries. For info: Cathy C. Runyan-Svacina, The Marble Lady, 7812 NW Hampton Rd, Kansas City, MO 64152. Phone/fax: (816) 587-8687. Web: www.themarblelady.com.

NATIONAL POETRY MONTH. Apr 1–30. Annual observance to pay tribute to the great legacy and ongoing achievement of American poets and the vital place of poetry in American culture. In a proclamation issued in honor of the first observance, President Bill Clinton called it "a welcome opportunity to celebrate not only the unsurpassed body of literature produced by our poets in the past, but also the vitality and diversity of voices reflected in the works of today's American poets . . . . Their creativity and wealth of language enrich our culture and inspire a new generation of Americans to learn the power of reading and writing at its best." Spearheaded by the Academy of American Poets, this is the largest and most extensive celebration of poetry in American history. ***See Curriculum Connection.*** For info: Academy of American Poets, 588 Broadway, Ste 604, New York, NY 10012-3210. Phone: (212) 274-0343. Web: www.poets.org.

NATIONAL YOUTH SPORTS SAFETY MONTH. Apr 1–30. Bringing public attention to the prevalent problem of injuries in youth sports. This event promotes safety in sports activities and is supported by more than 60 national sports and medical organizations. For info: National Youth Sports Safety Foundation, One Beacon St, Ste 3333, Boston, MA 02108. Phone: (617) 367-6677. Fax: (617) 722-9999. E-mail: NYSSF@aol.com. Web: www.nyssf.org.

PREVENTION OF ANIMAL CRUELTY MONTH. Apr 1–30. The ASPCA sponsors this crucial month, which is designed to prevent cruelty to animals by focusing on public awareness, advocacy and public education campaigns. For info: ASPCA Public Affairs Dept, 424 E 92nd St, New York, NY 10128. Phone: (212) 876-7700. E-mail: press@aspca.org. Web: www.aspca.org.

SCHOOL LIBRARY MEDIA MONTH. Apr 1–30. Celebrates the work of school library media specialists in our nation's elementary and secondary schools. For info: American Assn of School Librarians, American Library Assn, 50 E Huron St, Chicago, IL 60611. Phone: (800) 545-2433. E-mail: AASL@ala.org. Web: www.ala.org/aasl.

US AIR FORCE ACADEMY ESTABLISHED: ANNIVERSARY. Apr 1, 1954. The US Air Force Academy was established at Colorado Springs, CO, to train officers for the Air Force. Women were first admitted in 1976. For more info: www.usafa.af.mil.

US HOUSE OF REPRESENTATIVES ACHIEVES A QUORUM: ANNIVERSARY. Apr 1, 1789. First session of Congress was held Mar 4, 1789, but not enough representatives arrived to achieve a quorum until Apr 1.

YMCA HEALTHY KIDS DAY. Apr 1. To promote the health of children nationwide. Contact your local YMCA for events in your area. Annually, on the first Saturday in April. For info: YMCA of the USA, 101 N Wacker Dr, Chicago, IL 60606. Phone: (312) 977-0031.

BIRTHDAYS TODAY

Anne McCaffrey, 80, author (*The Dragonriders of Pern*), born Cambridge, MA, Apr 1, 1926.

Karen Wallace, 55, author (*Imagine You Are a Crocodile*), born Ottawa, ON, Canada, Apr 1, 1951.

APRIL 2 — SUNDAY

Day 92 — 273 Remaining

ANDERSEN, HANS CHRISTIAN: BIRTH ANNIVERSARY. Apr 2, 1805. Author chiefly remembered for his more than 150 fairy tales, many of which are regarded as classics of children's literature. Among his tales are "The Princess and the Pea," "The Snow Queen" and "The Ugly Duckling." Andersen was born at Odense, Denmark, and died at Copenhagen, Denmark, Aug 4, 1875.

BARTHOLDI, FREDERIC AUGUSTE: BIRTH ANNIVERSARY. Apr 2, 1834. French sculptor who created *Liberty Enlightening the World* (better known as the Statue of Liberty), which stands in New York Harbor. Also remembered for the *Lion of Belfort* at Belfort, France. Born at Colman, Alsace, France, he died at Paris, France, Oct 4, 1904.

CHECK YOUR BATTERIES DAY. Apr 2. A day set aside for checking the batteries in your smoke detector, carbon monoxide detector, HVAC thermostat, audio/visual remote controls and other electronic devices. This could save your life! Annually, the first Sunday in April.

DAYLIGHT SAVING TIME BEGINS. Apr 2–Oct 29. Daylight Saving Time begins at 2 AM. The Uniform Time Act of 1966 (as amended in 1986 by Public Law 99–359), administered by the US Dept of Transportation, provides that Standard Time in each zone be advanced one hour from 2 AM on the first Sunday in April until 2 AM on the last Sunday in October (except where state legislatures provide exemption, as in Hawaii and parts of Arizona and Indiana). Many use the popular rule "spring forward, fall back" to remember which way to turn their clocks.

FIRST WHITE HOUSE EASTER EGG ROLL: ANNIVERSARY. Apr 2, 1877. The first White House Easter Egg Roll took place during the administration of Rutherford B. Hayes. The traditional event was discontinued by President Franklin D. Roosevelt in 1942 and reinstated Apr 6, 1953, by President Dwight D. Eisenhower.

HELLER, RUTH: BIRTH ANNIVERSARY. Apr 2, 1923. Author, illustrator and designer, Ruth Heller was known for her picture books that taught grammer lessons in imaginative ways. Titles like *Many Luscious Lollipops: A Book About Adjectives* and *Merry-Go-Round: A Book About Nouns* explained the parts of speech using creative language and bold illustration. She also designed a series of maze and coloring books enjoyed by both children and adults. Born at Winnipeg, MB, Canada, she died at San Francisco, CA, on July 1, 2004.

INTERNATIONAL CHILDREN'S BOOK DAY. Apr 2. Commemorates the international aspects of children's literature and observes Hans Christian Andersen's birthday. 2006 theme: The Destiny of Books Is Written in the Stars. Sponsor: International Board on Books for Young People, Nonnenweg 12, Postfach, CH-4003 Basel, Switzerland. For info: USBBY Secretariat, Box 8139, Newark, DE 19714-8139. Phone: (302) 731-1600. E-mail: usbby@reading.org.

NATIONAL LIBRARY WEEK. Apr 2–8. A nationwide observance sponsored by the American Library Association. Celebrates libraries and librarians, the pleasures and importance of reading and invites library use and support. For programming ideas, see: *Library Celebrations* by Cyndy Dingwall (Highsmith, 1-5795-0027-7, $16.95). Call the American Library Association at 1-800-545-2433 for a catalog of NLW materials. For info: American Library Assn, Public Info Office, 50 E Huron St, Chicago, IL 60611. Phone: (312) 280-5044. Fax: (312) 944-8520. E-mail: pio@ala.org. Web: www.ala.org.

NATIONAL WEEK OF THE OCEAN. Apr 2–8. A week focusing on humanity's interdependence with the ocean, asking each of us to appreciate, protect and use the ocean wisely. Annually, the first full week in April. For info: *The Oceans Atlas* by Anita Ganeri (DK, 1-56458-475-5, $19.95 Gr. 3–8). For info and teacher's packet: Pres/Cofounder, Cynthia Hancock, National Week of the Ocean, Inc, PO Box 179, Ft Lauderdale, FL 33302. Phone: (954) 462-5573. Web: www.national-week-of-the-ocean.org.

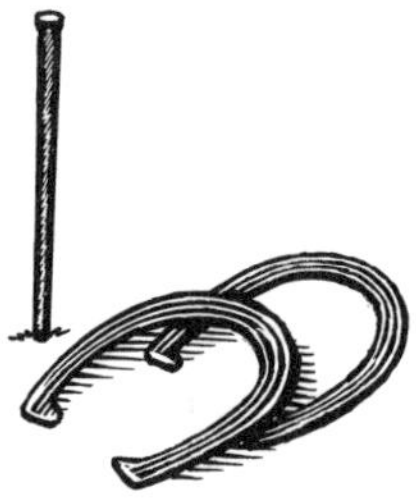

NICKELODEON CHANNEL TV PREMIERE: ANNIVERSARY. Apr 2, 1979. Nickelodeon, the cable TV network for kids owned by MTV Networks, premiered. In 1985 Nick at Nite began offering classic TV programs in the evening hours. For more info: teachers.nick.com or www.nickjr.com.

PASCUA FLORIDA DAY. Apr 2. Also known as Florida State Day, this holiday commemorates the sighting of Florida by Ponce de León in 1513. He named the land Pascua Florida because of its discovery at Easter, the "Feast of the Flowers." Florida also commemorates Pascua Florida Week, Mar 27–Apr 2. When Apr 2 falls on a weekend, the governor may declare the preceding Friday or the following Monday as State Day.

PASSION WEEK. Apr 2–8. The week beginning on the fifth Sunday in Lent; the week before Holy Week.

PASSIONTIDE. Apr 2–15. The last two weeks of Lent (Passion Week and Holy Week), beginning with the fifth Sunday of Lent (Passion Sunday) and continuing through the day before Easter (Holy Saturday).

PONCE DE LEÓN DISCOVERS FLORIDA: ANNIVERSARY. Apr 2, 1513. Juan Ponce de León discovered Florida, landing at the site that became the city of St. Augustine. He claimed the land for the king of Spain.

US MINT: ANNIVERSARY. Apr 2, 1792. The first US Mint was established at Philadelphia, PA, as authorized by an act of Congress. For more info: www.usmint.gov/kids.

WEEK OF THE YOUNG CHILD. Apr 2–8. To focus on the importance of quality early childhood education. For info: Pat Spahr, Dir of Info Development, National Assn for the Education of Young Children, 1509 16th St NW, Washington, DC 20036. Phone: (800) 424-2460. Fax: (202) 328-1846. E-mail: naeyc@naeyc.org. Web: www.naeyc.org.

BIRTHDAYS TODAY

Dave Ross, 57, author (*A Book of Kisses*), born Scotia, NY, Apr 2, 1949.

Doug Wechsler, 55, author (*Bizarre Bugs*), born New York, NY, Apr 2, 1951.

April 2006

S	M	T	W	T	F	S
						1
2	3	4	5	6	7	8
9	10	11	12	13	14	15
16	17	18	19	20	21	22
23	24	25	26	27	28	29
30						

APRIL 3 — MONDAY

Day 93 — 272 Remaining

"BETWEEN THE LIONS" TV PREMIERE: ANNIVERSARY. Apr 3, 2000. This animated PBS show is designed to help children ages 4–7 learn to read. The lions Theo, Cleo, Lionel and Leona run a magical library. For more info: www.pbs.org/wgbh/lions.

BLACKS RULED ELIGIBLE TO VOTE: ANNIVERSARY. Apr 3, 1944. The US Supreme Court, in an 8–1 ruling, declared that blacks could not be barred from voting in the Texas Democratic primaries. The high court repudiated the contention that political parties are private associations and held that discrimination against blacks violated the 15th Amendment.

BOSTON PUBLIC LIBRARY: ANNIVERSARY. Apr 3, 1848. The Massachusetts legislature passed legislation enabling Boston to levy a tax for a public library. This created the funding model for public libraries in the US. The Boston Public Library opened its doors in 1854. For more info: www.bpl.org.

IRVING, WASHINGTON: BIRTH ANNIVERSARY. Apr 3, 1783. American author, attorney and one-time US Minister to Spain, Irving was born at New York, NY. Creator of "Rip Van Winkle" and "The Legend of Sleepy Hollow," he was also the author of many historical and biographical works, including *A History of the Life and Voyages of Christopher Columbus* and the *Life of Washington*. Died at Tarrytown, NY, Nov 28, 1859.

ISLE ROYALE NATIONAL PARK ESTABLISHED: ANNIVERSARY. Apr 3, 1940. Isle Royale is the largest of a group of more than 200 islands that make up this national park preserve. To preserve upper Michigan's flora and fauna, Congress authorized a national park in 1931 and it was established in 1940. For more info: www.nps.gov/isro/index.htm.

MARSHALL PLAN: ANNIVERSARY. Apr 3, 1948. Suggested by Secretary of State George C. Marshall in a speech at Harvard, June 5, 1947, the legislation for the European Recovery Program, popularly known as the Marshall Plan, was signed by President Truman on Apr 3, 1948. After distributing more than $12 billion in war-torn Europe, the program ended in 1952.

NATIONAL BLUE RIBBON WEEK. Apr 3–9. Wear a blue ribbon to show your concern about and objection to child abuse. Nationwide public awareness effort. Annually, the first full week in April, beginning on Monday. For info: The National Exchange Club, 3050 Central Ave, Toledo, OH 43606-1700. Phone: (419) 535-3232 or (800) 924-2643. E-mail: info@preventchildabuse.com. Web: www.preventchildabuse.com.

WOMAN PRESIDES OVER US SUPREME COURT: ANNIVERSARY. Apr 3, 1995. Supreme Court Justice Sandra Day O'Connor became the first woman to preside over the US high court when she sat in for Chief Justice William H. Rehnquist and second in seniority Justice John Paul Stevens when both were out of town.

BIRTHDAYS TODAY

Amanda Bynes, 20, actress ("All That," "The Amanda Show," *Big Fat Liar*), born Thousand Oaks, CA, Apr 3, 1986.

Jane Goodall, 72, biologist, author (*The Chimpanzee Family Book, The Chimpanzees I Love*), born London, England, Apr 3, 1934.

Eddie Murphy, 45, comedian, actor (*Dr. Dolittle, Shrek*), born Brooklyn, NY, Apr 3, 1961.

Bernie Parent, 61, Hall of Fame hockey player, born Montreal, QC, Canada, Apr 3, 1945.

Picabo Street, 35, Olympic skier, born Triumph, ID, Apr 3, 1971.

APRIL 4 — TUESDAY

Day 94 — 271 Remaining

BONZA BOTTLER DAY™. Apr 4. To celebrate when the number of the day is the same as the number of the month. Bonza Bottler Day™ is an excuse to have a party at least once a month. For info: Gail M. Berger, 14 Fernwood Dr, Taylors, SC 29687. Phone: (864) 609-9874. E-mail: gberger5@aol.com.

DIX, DOROTHEA LYNDE: BIRTH ANNIVERSARY. Apr 4, 1802. American social reformer and author, born at Hampden, ME. She left home at age 10, was teaching at age 14 and founded a home for girls at Boston while still in her teens. In spite of frail health, she was a vigorous crusader for humane conditions in insane asylums, jails and almshouses and for the establishment of state-supported institutions to serve those needs. Named superintendent of women nurses during the Civil War. Died at Trenton, NJ, July 17, 1887.

FLAG ACT OF 1818: ANNIVERSARY. Apr 4, 1818. Congress approved the first flag of the US.

KING, MARTIN LUTHER, JR: ASSASSINATION ANNIVERSARY. Apr 4, 1968. The Reverend Dr. Martin Luther King, Jr, was shot at Memphis, TN. James Earl Ray was serving a 99-year sentence for the crime at the time of his death in 1998. See also: "King, Martin Luther, Jr: Birth Anniversary" (Jan 15).

KING OPPOSES VIETNAM WAR: ANNIVERSARY. Apr 4, 1967. Speaking before the Overseas Press Club at New York City, Reverend Dr. Martin Luther King, Jr, announced his opposition to the Vietnam War. That same day at the Riverside Church, King suggested that those who saw the war as dishonorable and unjust should avoid military service. He proposed that the US take new initiatives to conclude the war.

NORTH ATLANTIC TREATY RATIFIED: ANNIVERSARY. Apr 4, 1949. The North Atlantic Treaty Organization was created by this treaty, which was signed by 12 nations, including the US. (Other countries joined later.) The NATO member nations are united for common defense.

SALTER ELECTED FIRST WOMAN MAYOR IN US: ANNIVERSARY. Apr 4, 1887. The first woman elected mayor in the US was Susanna Medora Salter, who was elected mayor of Argonia, KS. Her name had been submitted for election without her knowledge by the Women's Christian Temperance Union, and she did not know she was a candidate until she went to the polls to vote. She received a two-thirds majority vote and served one year for the salary of $1.

SENEGAL: INDEPENDENCE DAY. Apr 4. National holiday. Commemorates independence from France in 1960.

VITAMIN C ISOLATED: ANNIVERSARY. Apr 4, 1932. Vitamin C was first isolated by C.C. King at the University of Pittsburgh.

BIRTHDAYS TODAY

Maya Angelou, 78, poet, author (*My Painted House, My Friendly Chicken, and Me; Life Doesn't Frighten Me*), born St. Louis, MO, Apr 4, 1928.

Richard G. Lugar, 74, US Senator (R, Indiana), born Indianapolis, IN, Apr 4, 1932.

Dave Mirra, 34, BMX bike racer, born Syracuse, NY, Apr 4, 1972.

Johanna Reiss, 74, author (*The Upstairs Room*), born Winterswijk, Netherlands, Apr 4, 1932.

Scott Rolen, 31, baseball player, born Jasper, IN, Apr 4, 1975.

APRIL 5 — WEDNESDAY

Day 95 — 270 Remaining

CHINA: QING MING FESTIVAL. Apr 5. This Confucian festival was traditionally celebrated on the fourth or fifth day of the third month but is now on either Apr 4 or 5 in China. It is observed by the maintenance of ancestral graves, the presentation of food, wine and flowers as offerings and the burning of paper money at gravesides to help ancestors in the afterworld. People also picnic and gather for family meals. Also observed in Taiwan.

COUNCIL FOR EXCEPTIONAL CHILDREN ANNUAL CONVENTION. Apr 5–9. Salt Lake City, UT. For info: Council for Exceptional Children, 1110 N Glebe Rd, Ste 300, Arlington, VA 22201-5704. Phone: (888) CEC-SPED or (703) 620-3660. Fax: (703) 264-9494. Web: www.cec.sped.org.

LISTER, JOSEPH: BIRTH ANNIVERSARY. Apr 5, 1827. English physician who was the founder of aseptic surgery, born at Upton, Essex, England. Died at Walmer, England, Feb 10, 1912.

MOON PHASE: FIRST QUARTER. Apr 5. Moon enters First Quarter phase at 8:01 AM, EDT.

PARAPROFESSIONAL APPRECIATION DAY. Apr 5. Established several years ago by the Governor of Missouri, this holiday honors the contributions of paraprofessionals, especially in education. Annually, the first Wednesday in April. For info: Valerie Pennington, McQuerry Elementary School, 607 S Third St, Odessa, MO 64076. Phone: (816) 230-5334.

RESNIK, JUDITH A.: BIRTH ANNIVERSARY. Apr 5, 1949. Dr. Judith A. Resnik, the second American woman in space (1984), was born at Akron, OH. The 36-year-old electrical engineer was the mission specialist on the Space Shuttle *Challenger*. She perished with all others aboard when *Challenger* exploded Jan 28, 1986. See also: "*Challenger* Space Shuttle Explosion: Anniversary" (Jan 28).

TAIWAN: NATIONAL TOMB-SWEEPING DAY. Apr 5. National holiday since 1972. According to Chinese custom, the tombs of ancestors are swept "clear and bright" and rites honoring ancestors are held. Tomb-Sweeping Day is observed Apr 5, which is also the anniversary of the death of Chiang Kai-Shek.

THANK YOU, SCHOOL LIBRARIAN DAY. Apr 5. Recognizes the unique contribution made by school librarians who are resource people extraordinaire, supporting the myriad educational needs of faculty, staff, students and parents *all year long*! Three cheers to all the public, private and parochial school infomaniacs whose true love of reading and lifelong learning makes them great role models for kids of all ages. To help celebrate, take your school librarian to lunch, donate a book in his/her honor to the library, tell your librarian what a difference he/she has made

APRIL 5

BOOKER T. WASHINGTON TURNS 150!

Booker T. Washington was a respected educator, orator and civil rights crusader at a point in the nation's history when opportunities for blacks were few and far between. His self-made rise from slave to teacher, thinker and consultant to presidents tapped into the bootstraps cultural climate of turn-of-the-century America and helped make Washington an important figure in the continuing story of our country. See *Up From Slavery* (W.W. Norton, 0-393-96725-5, $12.80 Adult), Washington's autobiography, first published in 1901.

Booker T. Washington was born on this day in 1856, in a settlement outside Roanoke, VA. After the early years of slavery and President Lincoln's 1862 Emancipation Proclamation, he moved with his family to West Virginia, where they labored in the mines. Despite the backbreaking work and his young age, Washington still found time for studying and eventually made his way—on foot, it's often said—to the Hampton Institute, a preparatory school located hundreds of miles away in Virginia. (See *Educating the Disenfranchised and Disinherited: Samuel Chapman Armstrong and Hampton Institute, 1839–1893* by Robert Francis Engs [University of Tennessee Press, 1-572-33051-1, $32.50 Adult].)

Washington studied at Hampton from 1872 to 1875, when he left for work as a schoolteacher in West Virginia. By now having begun to make a name for himself, Washington was eventually asked to head his own school, which he did in 1881. Under his watchful eye the Tuskegee Institute in Alabama became one of the era's leading African-American educational institutions.

The tenets of a Tuskegee education were also the basis for Washington's thinking on the plight of the black man in the postslavery era of the late 19th and early 20th centuries. First, Tuskegee urged students to become educators so that they might spread knowledge throughout the ranks of the disenfranchised. But there was also an emphasis on the trades and farming as well as Washington's insistence on cleanliness and moral character. The main idea was to help many African Americans quickly with finding employment and gaining character, instead of pushing immediately for higher education as Washington's critics (notably W.E.B. Du Bois) tended to suggest. "The opportunity to earn a dollar in a factory just now," Washington said in 1895 in his landmark, mission-setting "Atlanta Compromise" speech, "is worth infinitely more than the opportunity to spend a dollar in an opera house." (Read a full transcript of the speech at www.pbs.org/greatspeeches/timeline.)

Though his theories and opinions could be contentious, Washington remained a thoughtful and passionate civil rights advocate as well as a role model for African Americans struggling to find their voice and footing amidst the racial antagonism of the time. His Tuskegee Institute became a leading black college and supported the important work of people like renowned agricultural scientist George Washington Carver (see *George Washington Carver: Peanut Wizard* by Laura Driscoll [Grossett & Dunlap, 0-448-43243-9, $5.99 Ages 4–8]). Washington's work also contributed to the ideas and methods of the civil rights movement that would take hold and change minds in the 1950s and 1960s.

Further resources include *Booker T. Washington: The Making of a Black Leader, 1856–1901* by Louis R. Harlan (Oxford University Press, 0-195-01915-6, $21.50 Adult) and its companion volume *Booker T. Washington: The Wizard of Tuskegee, 1901–1915*, again by Harlan (Oxford University Press, 0-195-04229-8, $24.95 Adult).

—Johnny Loftus

in your life. Sponsor: "Carpe Libris" (Seize the Book), a loosely knit group of underappreciated librarians. Annually, the Wednesday of National Library Week. For info: Judyth Lessee, Organizer, Carpe Libris, 3645 E Pima St, Tucson, AZ 85716. Phone: (520) 232-8424. E-mail: judyth.lessee@tusd.k12.az.us.

WASHINGTON, BOOKER TALLAFERRO: 150th BIRTH ANNIVERSARY. Apr 5, 1856. Black educator and leader, born at Franklin County, VA. "No race can prosper," he wrote in *Up from Slavery*, "till it learns that there is as much dignity in tilling a field as in writing a poem." Died at Tuskegee, AL, Nov 14, 1915. For more info: *More Than Anything Else* by Marie Bradby (Orchard, 0-5310-9464-2, $15.95 Gr. K–3) or *The Story of Booker T. Washington* by Patricia McKissack and Fredrick McKissack (Children's Press, 0-5160-4758-2, $20.50 Gr. 3–7). ***See Curriculum Connection.***

BIRTHDAYS TODAY

Richard Peck, 72, author (Newbery Medal for *A Year Down Yonder*, Newbery Honor for *A Long Way from Chicago*), born Decatur, IL, Apr 5, 1934.

Colin Powell, 69, former US Secretary of State (George W. Bush administration), former Chairman US Joint Chiefs of Staff, born New York, NY, Apr 5, 1937.

April 2006

S	M	T	W	T	F	S
						1
2	3	4	5	6	7	8
9	10	11	12	13	14	15
16	17	18	19	20	21	22
23	24	25	26	27	28	29
30						

APRIL 6 — THURSDAY

Day 96 — 269 Remaining

"BARNEY & FRIENDS" TV PREMIERE: ANNIVERSARY. Apr 6, 1992. Although most adults find it saccharine, this PBS show is enormously popular with preschoolers. Purple dinosaur Barney, his dinosaur pals Baby Bop and B.J., and a multi-ethnic group of children sing, play games and learn simple lessons about getting along with one another. "Bedtime with Barney" was a 1994 prime-time special. For more info: www.pbs.org/barney.

FIRST MODERN OLYMPICS: ANNIVERSARY. Apr 6, 1896. The first modern Olympics formally opened at Athens, Greece, after a 1,500-year hiatus. For more info: www.olympic.org.

GANDHI MAKES SALT: ANNIVERSARY. Apr 6, 1930. Mohandas Gandhi, frustrated by British indifference to Indian civil rights demands, planned a symbolic, peaceful protest by conducting a 241-mile march from Sabarmati Ashram to the coast at Dandi. Leaving on Mar 12, Gandhi and his followers arrived at Dandi on Apr 5, and on Apr 6, he made salt by boiling sea water—a violation of the salt law, which granted royal monopoly in its manufacture and levied heavy taxes on its purchasers. His peaceful act and the two-mile-long procession that accompanied it gained worldwide headlines. Besides Gandhi, thousands of Indians were arrested as they, too, made salt in protest.

NATIONAL SCIENCE TEACHERS ASSOCIATION NATIONAL CONVENTION. Apr 6–9. Anaheim, CA. Offering the latest in science content, teaching strategy and research, all presented by science educators. Features speakers, educational field trips, short courses, exciting social events and the largest exhibition of science materials around. For info: National Science Teachers Assn, 1840 Wilson Blvd, Arlington, VA 22201-3000. Phone: (703) 243-7100. Web: www.nsta.org.

NORTH POLE DISCOVERED: ANNIVERSARY. Apr 6, 1909. Robert E. Peary reached the North Pole after several failed attempts. The team consisted of Peary, leader of the expedition; Matthew A. Henson, a black man who had served with Peary since 1886 as ship's cook, carpenter and blacksmith, and then as Peary's co-explorer and valuable assistant; and four Eskimo guides—Coquesh, Ootah, Eginwah and Seegloo. They sailed July 17, 1908, on the ship *Roosevelt*, wintering on Ellesmere Island. After a grueling trek with dwindling food supplies, Henson and two of the Eskimos were first to reach the Pole. An exhausted Peary arrived 45 minutes later and confirmed their location. Dr. Frederick A. Cook, surgeon on an earlier expedition with Peary, claimed to have reached the Pole first, but that could not be substantiated and the National Geographic Society credited the Peary expedition.

TEFLON INVENTED: ANNIVERSARY. Apr 6, 1938. Polytetrafluoroethylene resin was invented by Roy J. Plunkett while he was employed by E.I. Du Pont de Nemours & Co. Commonly known as Teflon, it revolutionized the cookware industry. This substance or something similar coated three-quarters of the pots and pans in America at the time of Plunkett's death in 1994.

THAILAND: CHAKRI DAY. Apr 6. Commemorates foundation of present dynasty by King Rama I (1782–1809), who also established Bangkok as capital.

US ENTERS WORLD WAR I: ANNIVERSARY. Apr 6, 1917. After Congress approved a declaration of war against Germany, the US entered WWI, which had begun in 1914.

US SENATE ACHIEVES A QUORUM: ANNIVERSARY. Apr 6, 1789. The US Senate was formally organized after achieving a quorum.

VIRGINIA HAMILTON CONFERENCE. Apr 6–7. Kent State Univ, Kent, OH. 22nd annual conference on multicultural literature for children and young adults. For info: College of Continuing Studies, Kent State University, PO Box 5190, Kent, OH 44242-0001. Phone: (800) 672-KSU2. E-mail: amanna@slis.kent.edu. Web: dept.kent.edu/virginiahamiltonconf/.

BIRTHDAYS TODAY

Alice Bach, 64, author (*The Meat in the Sandwich*), born New York, NY, Apr 6, 1942.

Graeme Base, 48, author and illustrator (*The Worst Band in the Universe, Animalia, The Eleventh Hour*), born Amersham, England, Apr 6, 1958.

Bret Boone, 37, baseball player, born El Cajon, CA, Apr 6, 1969.

Candace Cameron Bure, 30, actress ("Full House"), born Panorama City, CA, Apr 6, 1976.

APRIL 7 — FRIDAY

Day 97 — 268 Remaining

KING, WILLIAM RUFUS DEVANE: BIRTH ANNIVERSARY. Apr 7, 1786. The 13th vice president of the US who died on the 46th day after taking the Oath of Office, of tuberculosis, at Cahaba, AL, Apr 18, 1853. The Oath of Office had been administered to King Mar 4, 1853, at Havana, Cuba, as authorized by a special act of Congress (the only presidential or vice presidential oath to be administered outside the US). Born at Sampson County, NY, King was the only vice president of the US who had served in both the House of Representatives and the Senate.

METRIC SYSTEM: ANNIVERSARY. Apr 7, 1795. The metric system was adopted at France, where it had been developed.

NO HOUSEWORK DAY. Apr 7. No trash. No dishes. No making of beds or washing of laundry. And no guilt. Give it a rest. [©2002 by WH.] For info: Thomas & Ruth Roy, Wellcat Holidays, 2418 Long Ln, Lebanon, PA 17046. Phone: (717) 279-0184. E-mail: info@wellcat.com. Web: www.wellcat.com.

RWANDA: GENOCIDE'S REMEMBRANCE DAY. Apr 7. National holiday. Memorial to the massacres of 1994.

SPACE MILESTONE: *MARS ODYSSEY* (US): 5th ANNIVERSARY. Apr 7, 2001. *Odyssey* was launched on this day and successfully entered Mars's orbit on Oct 24, 2001. The one-way trip is 286 million miles. The two-and-one-half year mission will monitor space radiation, seek out underground water and identify minerals on the Red Planet.

STUDENT GOVERNMENT DAY IN MASSACHUSETTS. Apr 7. Proclaimed annually by the governor for the first Friday in April.

UNITED NATIONS: WORLD HEALTH DAY. Apr 7. A United Nations observance commemorating the establishment of the World Health Organization in 1948. For more information, visit the UN's website for children at www.un.org/Pubs/CyberSchoolBus.

WORLD HEALTH ORGANIZATION: ANNIVERSARY. Apr 7, 1948. This agency of the UN was founded to coordinate international health systems. It is headquartered at Geneva. Among its achievements is the elimination of smallpox.

BIRTHDAYS TODAY

Tiki Barber, 31, football player, born Roanoke, VA, Apr 7, 1975.

Alan R. Carter, 59, author (*Up Country*), born Eau Claire, WI, Apr 7, 1947.

Jackie Chan, 52, actor, martial arts star, born Hong Kong, Apr 7, 1954.

Mitchell Daniels, 57, Governor of Indiana (R), born Monongahela, PA, Apr 7, 1949.

APRIL 8 — SATURDAY

Day 98 — 267 Remaining

BIRTHDAY OF THE BUDDHA: BIRTH ANNIVERSARY. Apr 8. Among Buddhist holidays, this is the most important as it commemorates the birthday of the Buddha. It is known as the Day of Vesak. The founder of Buddhism had the given name Siddhartha, the family name Gautama and the clan name Shaka. He is commonly called the Buddha, meaning in Sanskrit "the enlightened one." He is thought to have lived in India from c. 563 BC to 483 BC. Because it is often observed on the lunar calendar, this holiday can occur in April or May. It is a holiday in Indonesia, Korea, Thailand and Singapore.

BLACK SENATE PAGE APPOINTED: ANNIVERSARY. Apr 8, 1965. Sixteen-year-old Lawrence Bradford of New York City was the first black page appointed to the US Senate.

CAREER HOME RUN RECORD SET BY HANK AARON: ANNIVERSARY. Apr 8, 1974. Henry ("Hammerin' Hank") Aaron hit the 715th home run of his career, breaking the record set by Babe Ruth in 1935. Playing for the Atlanta Braves, Aaron broke the record at Atlanta in a game against the Los Angeles Dodgers. He finished his career in 1976 with a total of 755 home runs. This record remains unbroken. At the time of his retirement, Aaron also held records for first in RBIs, second in at-bats and runs scored and third in base hits.

JAPAN: FLOWER FESTIVAL (HANA MATSURI). Apr 8. Commemorates Buddha's birthday. Ceremonies in all temples.

MORRIS, LEWIS: BIRTH ANNIVERSARY. Apr 8, 1726. Signer of the Declaration of Independence, born at Westchester County, NY. Died Jan 22, 1798, at the Morrisania manor at NY.

NATIONAL SCHOOL BOARDS ASSOCIATION ANNUAL CONFERENCE. Apr 8–11. New Orleans, LA. 66th annual. For info: National School Boards Assn, 1680 Duke St, Alexandria, VA 22314. Phone: (703) 838-6722. Fax: (703) 683-7590. E-mail: info@nsba.org. Web: www.nsba.org.

SEVENTEENTH AMENDMENT TO US CONSTITUTION RATIFIED: ANNIVERSARY. Apr 8, 1913. Prior to the 17th Amendment, members of the Senate were elected by each state's respective legislature. The advent and popularity of primary elections during the last decade of the 19th century and the early 20th century and a string of senatorial scandals, most notably a scandal involving William Lorimer, an Illinois political boss in 1909, forced the Senate to end its resistance to a constitutional amendment requiring direct popular election of senators.

TUTOR APPRECIATION DAY. Apr 8. A day to express appreciation for the volunteer and paid tutors who help us all be better students and wiser people. Annually, the first Saturday of April, with the exception of Apr 1. For info: Sharon Huntington, 3321 S 7700 W, Magna, UT 84044. Phone/fax: (801) 250-6574. E-mail: SHuntington@helpuwrite.com. Web: www.helpuwrite.com.

VOYAGEURS NATIONAL PARK ESTABLISHED: ANNIVERSARY. Apr 8, 1975. Minnesota's Voyageurs area was preserved by Congress on Jan 8, 1971. Four years later, it became the 36th US national park. For more info: www.nps.gov/voya/index.htm.

April 2006

S	M	T	W	T	F	S
						1
2	3	4	5	6	7	8
9	10	11	12	13	14	15
16	17	18	19	20	21	22
23	24	25	26	27	28	29
30						

WILLIAMS, WILLIAM: 275th BIRTH ANNIVERSARY. Apr 8, 1731. Signer of the Declaration of Independence, born at Lebanon, CT. Died there Aug 2, 1811.

BIRTHDAYS TODAY

Kofi Annan, 68, UN Secretary General, born Kumasi, Ghana, Apr 8, 1938.

Susan Bonners, 59, author and illustrator (*A Penguin Year*), born Chicago, IL, Apr 8, 1947.

Ruth Chew, 86, author and illustrator (*The Wednesday Witch*), born Minneapolis, MN, Apr 8, 1920.

Elizabeth (Betty) Ford, 88, former First Lady, wife of Gerald Ford, 38th president of the US, born Chicago, IL, Apr 8, 1918.

Trina Schart Hyman, 67, illustrator (Caldecott Medal for *Saint George and the Dragon*, Caldecott Honors for *Hershel and the Hanukkah Goblins, Little Red Riding Hood, A Child's Calendar*), born Philadelphia, PA, Apr 8, 1939.

APRIL 9 — SUNDAY

Day 99 — 266 Remaining

BLACK PAGE APPOINTED TO US HOUSE OF REPRESENTATIVES: ANNIVERSARY. Apr 9, 1965. Fifteen-year-old Frank Mitchell of Springfield, IL, was the first black appointed a page to the US House of Representatives.

CIVIL RIGHTS BILL OF 1866: ANNIVERSARY. Apr 9, 1866. The Civil Rights Bill of 1866, passed by Congress over the veto of President Andrew Johnson, granted blacks the rights and privileges of American citizenship and formed the basis for the Fourteenth Amendment to the US Constitution.

CIVIL WAR ENDING: ANNIVERSARY. Apr 9, 1865. At 1:30 PM, General Robert E. Lee, commander of the Army of Northern Virginia, surrendered to General Ulysses S. Grant, commander-in-chief of the Union Army, ending four years of civil war. The meeting took place in the house of Wilmer McLean at the village of Appomattox Court House, VA. Confederate soldiers were permitted to keep their horses and go free to their homes, while Confederate officers were allowed to retain their swords and side arms as well. Grant wrote the terms of surrender. Formal surrender took place at the Courthouse Apr 12. Death toll for the Civil War is estimated at 500,000 men.

ECKERT, J(OHN) PRESPER, JR: BIRTH ANNIVERSARY. Apr 9, 1919. Coinventor with John W. Mauchly of ENIAC (Electronic Numerical Integrator and Computer), which was first demonstrated at the Moore School of Electrical Engineering at the University of Pennsylvania at Philadelphia, Feb 14, 1946 (generally considered the birth of the computer age). Originally designed to process artillery calculations for the Army, ENIAC was also used in the Manhattan Project. Eckert and Mauchly formed Electronic Control Company, which later became Unisys Corporation. Eckert was born at Philadelphia and died at Bryn Mawr, PA, June 3, 1995.

GREECE: DUMB WEEK. Apr 9–15. The week preceding Holy Week on the Orthodox calendar is known as Dumb Week, as no services are held in churches throughout this period except on Friday, eve of the Saturday of Lazarus.

HOLY WEEK. Apr 9–15. Christian observance dating from the fourth century, known also as Great Week. The seven days beginning on the sixth and final Sunday in Lent (Palm Sunday), consisting of: Palm Sunday, Monday of Holy Week, Tuesday of Holy

★ ★ ★

Week, Spy Wednesday (or Wednesday of Holy Week), Maundy Thursday, Good Friday and Holy Saturday (or Great Sabbath or Easter Even). A time of solemn devotion to and memorializing of the suffering (passion), death and burial of Christ. Formerly a time of strict fasting.

JUMBO THE ELEPHANT ARRIVES IN AMERICA: ANNIVERSARY. Apr 9, 1882. The most famous elephant in history was captured as a calf near Lake Chad, Africa, in 1861. He became part of the London Zoo in 1865, where he gained the name Jumbo (from a West African word for elephant) and grew to 11½ feet tall and seven tons. Tremendously popular, he gave London children rides until 1882, when American circus impresario P.T. Barnum bought him for $10,000. The British public was enraged while the waiting American public was thrilled. Jumbo arrived at Manhattan, NY, on Easter Sunday. In an amazing spectacle, Jumbo paraded up Broadway in a crate pulled by 16 horses. Jumbo was just as popular in the US as he was in Britain, and his name entered the English language to describe anything oversized. See also: "Jumbo the Elephant: Death Anniversary" (Sept 15).

KRUMGOLD, JOSEPH: BIRTH ANNIVERSARY. Apr 9, 1908. Author (Newbery for *Onion John* and *. . . And Now Miguel*), born at Jersey City, NJ. Died July 10, 1980.

PALM SUNDAY. Apr 9. Commemorates Christ's last entry into Jerusalem, when His way was covered with palms by the multitudes. Beginning of Holy (or Great) Week in Western Christian churches.

★ **PAN AMERICAN WEEK.** Apr 9–15. Presidential Proclamation customarily issued as "Pan American Day and Pan American Week." Always issued for the week including Apr 14, except in 1965, from 1946 through 1948, 1955 through 1977, and 1979.

PHILIPPINES: BATAAN DAY. Apr 9, 1942. Araw Ng Kagitingan, national observance to commemorate the fall of Bataan. The infamous "Death March" is reenacted at the Mount Samat Shrine, the Dambana ng Kagitingan.

ROBESON, PAUL BUSTILL: BIRTH ANNIVERSARY. Apr 9, 1898. Paul Robeson, born at Princeton, NJ, was an All-American football player at Rutgers University and received his law degree from Columbia University in 1923. After being seen by Eugene O'Neill in an amateur stage production, he was offered a part in O'Neill's play *The Emperor Jones*. His performance in that play with the Provincetown Players established him as an actor. Without ever having taken a voice lesson, he also became a popular singer. His stage credits include *Show Boat, Porgy and Bess, The Hairy Ape* and *Othello*, which enjoyed the longest Broadway run of a Shakespearean play. In 1950 he was denied a passport by the US for refusing to sign an affidavit stating whether he was or ever had been a member of the Communist Party. The action was overturned by the Supreme Court in 1958. His film credits include *Emperor Jones, Show Boat* and *Song of Freedom*. Robeson died at Philadelphia, PA, Jan 23, 1976. For more info: *Paul Robeson: A Voice to Remember* by Patricia McKissack and Fredrick McKissack (Enslow, 0-8949-0310-1, $14.95 Gr. K–3).

TUNISIA: MARTYRS' DAY. Apr 9.

WINSTON CHURCHILL DAY. Apr 9. Anniversary of enactment of legislation in 1963 that made the late British statesman an honorary citizen of the US.

BIRTHDAYS TODAY

Margaret Peterson Haddix, 42, author (*Running Out of Time, Among the Hidden*), born Washington Court House, OH, Apr 9, 1964.

Jacques Villeneuve, 35, auto racer, born St. Jean d'Iberville, QC, Canada, Apr 9, 1971.

APRIL 10 — MONDAY

Day 100 — 265 Remaining

COMMODORE PERRY DAY. Apr 10, 1794. Matthew Calbraith Perry, commodore in the US Navy, negotiator of first treaty between US and Japan (Mar 31, 1854). Born at South Kingston, RI, he died Mar 4, 1858, at New York, NY.

PULITZER, JOSEPH: BIRTH ANNIVERSARY. Apr 10, 1847. American journalist and newspaper publisher, born at Budapest, Hungary. Died at Charleston, SC, Oct 29, 1911. In his will, he left an endowment that created the Columbia School of Journalism and the Pulitzer Prizes, awards for journalism, letters, drama and education that have been awarded annually since 1917.

ROBERT GRAY BECOMES FIRST AMERICAN TO CIRCUMNAVIGATE THE EARTH: ANNIVERSARY. Apr 10, 1790. When Robert Gray docked the *Columbia* at Boston Harbor, he became the first American to circumnavigate the earth. He sailed from Boston, MA, in September 1787, to trade with Indians of the Pacific Northwest. From there he sailed to China and then continued around the world. His 42,000-mile journey opened trade between New England and the Pacific Northwest and helped the US establish claims to the Oregon Territory.

SAFETY PIN PATENTED: ANNIVERSARY. Apr 10, 1849. Walter Hunt of New York patented the first safety pin.

SALVATION ARMY FOUNDER'S DAY. Apr 10, 1829. Birth anniversary of William Booth, a Methodist minister who began an evangelical ministry in the East End of London in 1865 and established mission stations to feed and house the poor. In 1878 he changed the name of the organization to the Salvation Army. Booth was born at Nottingham, England; he died at London, Aug 20, 1912.

YOUNG PEOPLE'S POETRY WEEK. Apr 10–16. Annually, during National Poetry Month. Sponsored by The Children's Book Council, this event highlights poetry for children and young adults and encourages everyone to celebrate poetry—read it, enjoy it, write it—in their homes, childcare centers, classrooms, libraries and bookstores. The CBC is coordinating its promotional efforts with the Academy of American Poets, the sponsor of National Poetry Month in April, and The Center for the Book in the Library of Congress. For info: Children's Book Council, PO Box 2640, JAF Station, New York, NY 10016-2640. Phone: (212) 966-1990. Fax: (888) 807-9355. E-mail: staff@cbcbooks.org. Web: www.cbcbooks.org.

BIRTHDAYS TODAY

David A. Adler, 59, author (the Cam Jansen mystery series), born New York, NY, Apr 10, 1947.

Haley Joel Osment, 18, actor (*The Sixth Sense, Bogus*), born Los Angeles, CA, Apr 10, 1988.

Martin Waddell, 65, author (*Can't You Sleep, Little Bear?; Owl Babies*), born Belfast, Northern Ireland, Apr 10, 1941.

APRIL 11 — TUESDAY

Day 101 — 264 Remaining

CHILDREN'S DAY IN FLORIDA. Apr 11. A legal holiday on the second Tuesday in April.

CIVIL RIGHTS ACT OF 1968: ANNIVERSARY. Apr 11, 1968. Exactly one week after the assassination of Martin Luther King, Jr, the Civil Rights Act of 1968 (protecting civil rights workers, expanding the rights of Native Americans and providing antidiscrimination measures in housing) was signed into law by President Lyndon B. Johnson, who said: " . . . the proudest moments of my presidency have been times such as this when I have signed into law the promises of a century."

EVERETT, EDWARD: BIRTH ANNIVERSARY. Apr 11, 1794. American statesman and orator, born at Dorcester, MA. It was Edward Everett who delivered the main address at the dedication of Gettysburg National Cemetery, Nov 19, 1863. President Abraham Lincoln also spoke at the dedication, and his brief speech (less than two minutes) is remembered while Everett's is not. Once a candidate for vice president of the US (1860), Everett died at Boston, MA, Jan 15, 1865.

HUGHES, CHARLES EVANS: BIRTH ANNIVERSARY. Apr 11, 1862. The 11th chief justice of the US Supreme Court. Born at Glens Falls, NY, he died at Osterville, MA, Aug 27, 1948. For more info: oyez.northwestern.edu/justices/justices.cgi.

LIBERATION OF BUCHENWALD CONCENTRATION CAMP: ANNIVERSARY. Apr 11, 1945. Buchenwald, north of Weimar, Germany, was entered by Allied troops. It was the first of the Nazi concentration camps to be liberated. It had been established in 1937 and about 56,000 people died there. For more info: www.ushmm.org/outreach.

MAWLID AL NABI: THE BIRTHDAY OF THE PROPHET MUHAMMAD. Apr 11. Mawlid al-Nabi (Birth of the Prophet Muhammad) is observed on Muslim calendar date Rabi al-Awal 12, 1427. Different methods for calculating the visibility of the new moon crescent at Mecca are used by different Muslim groups. US date may vary. Began at sunset the preceding day.

SPACE MILESTONE: *APOLLO 13* (US). Apr 11, 1970. Astronauts Jim Lovell, Fred Haise and Jack Swigert were endangered when an oxygen tank ruptured. The planned moon landing was cancelled. Details of the accident were made public and the world shared concern for the crew who splashed down successfully in the Pacific Apr 17. The film *Apollo 13*, starring Tom Hanks, accurately told this story.

UGANDA: LIBERATION DAY: ANNIVERSARY. Apr 11. Republic of Uganda celebrates anniversary of overthrow of Idi Amin's dictatorship in 1979.

BIRTHDAYS TODAY

Josh Server, 27, actor (Nickelodeon's "All That"), born Highland Park, IL, Apr 11, 1979.

April 2006

S	M	T	W	T	F	S
						1
2	3	4	5	6	7	8
9	10	11	12	13	14	15
16	17	18	19	20	21	22
23	24	25	26	27	28	29
30						

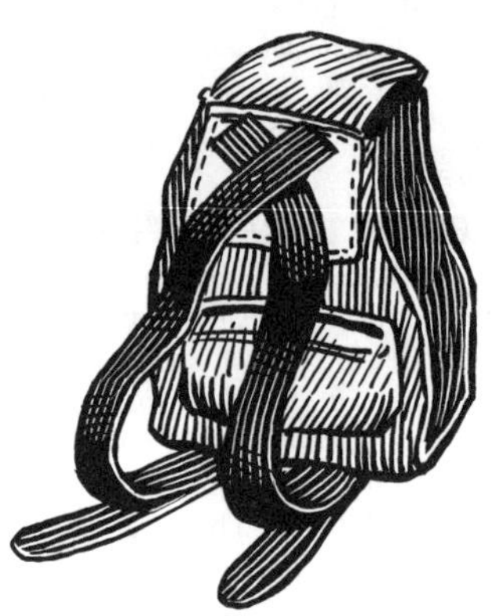

APRIL 12 — WEDNESDAY

Day 102 — 263 Remaining

THE BIG WIND: ANNIVERSARY. Apr 12, 1934. The highest-velocity natural wind ever recorded occurred in the morning at the Mount Washington, NH, Observatory. Three weather observers, Wendell Stephenson, Alexander McKenzie and Salvatore Pagliuca, observed and recorded the phenomenon in which gusts reached 231 miles per hour—"the strongest natural wind ever recorded on the earth's surface."

CLAY, HENRY: BIRTH ANNIVERSARY. Apr 12, 1777. Statesman, born at Hanover County, VA. Was the Speaker of the House of Representatives and later became the leader of the new Whig party. He was defeated for the presidency three times. Clay died at Washington, DC, June 29, 1852.

PASSOVER BEGINS AT SUNDOWN. Apr 12. See "Pesach" (Apr 13).

POLIO VACCINE: ANNIVERSARY. Apr 12, 1955. Anniversary of announcement that the polio vaccine developed by American physician Dr. Jonas E. Salk was "safe, potent and effective." Incidence of the dreaded infantile paralysis, or poliomyelitis, declined by 95 percent following introduction of preventive vaccines. The first mass innoculation of children against polio began at Pittsburgh, PA, Feb 23, 1954.

ROOSEVELT, FRANKLIN DELANO: DEATH ANNIVERSARY. Apr 12, 1945. With the end of WWII only months away, the nation and the world were stunned by the sudden death of the president shortly into his fourth term of office. He was stricken with a cerebral hemorrhage and died at Warm Springs, GA. Roosevelt, the 32nd president of the US (Mar 4, 1933–Apr 12, 1945), was the only president to serve more than two terms—he was elected to four consecutive terms. See also: "Roosevelt, Franklin Delano: Birth Anniversary" (Jan 30).

SPACE MILESTONE: *COLUMBIA STS-1* (US) FIRST SHUTTLE FLIGHT: 25th ANNIVERSARY. Apr 12, 1981. First flight of Shuttle *Columbia*. Two astronauts (John Young and Robert Crippen), on first manned US space mission since *Apollo-Soyuz* in July 1976, spent 54 hours in space (36 orbits of Earth) before landing at Edwards Air Force Base, CA, Apr 14.

SPACE MILESTONE: *VOSTOK I*, FIRST MAN IN SPACE: 45th ANNIVERSARY. Apr 12, 1961. Yuri Gagarin became the first man in space when he made a 108-minute voyage, orbiting Earth in a 10,395-lb vehicle, *Vostok I*, launched by the USSR.

TRUANCY LAW: ANNIVERSARY. Apr 12, 1853. The first truancy law was enacted at New York. A $50 fine was charged against parents whose children between the ages of five and 15 were absent from school.

BIRTHDAYS TODAY

Nicholas Brendon, 35, actor ("Buffy the Vampire Slayer"), born Los Angeles, CA, Apr 12, 1971.

Beverly Cleary, 90, author (the Henry/Ribsy and Ramona series; Newbery Medal for *Dear Mr Henshaw*, 2003 National Medal of Arts), born McMinnville, OR, Apr 12, 1916.

Gary Soto, 54, poet, author (*Neighborhood Odes, Too Many Tamales*), born Fresno, CA, Apr 12, 1952.

APRIL 13 — THURSDAY

Day 103 — 262 Remaining

BUTTS, ALFRED M.: BIRTH ANNIVERSARY. Apr 13, 1899. Alfred Butts was a jobless architect in the Depression when he invented the board game Scrabble. The game was just a fad for Butts's friends until a Macy's executive saw the game being played at a resort in 1952, and the world's largest store began carrying it. Manufacturing of the game was turned over to Selchow & Righter when 35 workers were producing 6,000 sets a week. Butts received three cents per set for years. He said, "One-third went to taxes. I gave one-third away, and the other third enabled me to have an enjoyable life." Butts was born at Poughkeepsie, NY. He died Apr 4, 1993, at Rhinebeck, NY.

HENRY, MARGUERITE: BIRTH ANNIVERSARY. Apr 13, 1902. Born at Milwaukee, WI, Henry received the Newbery Medal in 1949 for her book *The King of the Wind*. She also authored *Misty of Chincoteague, Brighty of Grand Canyon* and other books about horses. Henry died at Rancho Santa Fe, CA, Nov 26, 1997.

INDIA: BAISAKHI. Apr 13. Sikh holiday that commemorates the founding of the brotherhood of Khalsa in 1699. A large fair is held at the Golden Temple at Amritsar, the central shrine of Sikhism.

JEFFERSON, THOMAS: BIRTH ANNIVERSARY. Apr 13, 1743. Third president of the US (Mar 4, 1801–Mar 3, 1809), born at Shadwell, VA. He had previously served as vice president under John Adams. Jefferson, who died at Charlottesville, VA, July 4, 1826, wrote his own epitaph: "Here was buried Thomas Jefferson, author of the Declaration of American Independence, of the statute of Virginia for religious freedom, and father of the University of Virginia." A holiday in Alabama and Oklahoma. For info: www.ipl.org/ref/POTUS or *Thomas Jefferson: A Picture Book Biography* by James Cross Giblin (Scholastic, 0-590-44838-2, $16.95 Gr. 4–6).

MAUNDY THURSDAY or HOLY THURSDAY. Apr 13. The Thursday before Easter, originally "dies mandate," celebrates Christ's injunction to love one another, "Mandatus novum do vobis. . . ." ("A new commandment I give to you. . . .")

MOON PHASE: FULL MOON. Apr 13. Moon enters Full Moon phase at 12:40 PM, EDT.

★**NATIONAL D.A.R.E. DAY.** Apr 13. The Drug Abuse Resistance Education (D.A.R.E.) program helps children in grades K–12 learn the skills they need to avoid involvement in drugs, gangs and violence.

PESACH or PASSOVER. Apr 13–20. Hebrew calendar dates: Nisan 15–22, 5766. Apr 13, the first day of Passover, begins an eight-day celebration of the delivery of the Jews from slavery in Egypt. Unleavened bread (matzoh) is eaten at this time. (Began at sundown of previous day.)

***SILENT SPRING* PUBLICATION: ANNIVERSARY.** Apr 13, 1962. Rachel Carson's *Silent Spring* warned humankind that for the first time in history every person is subjected to contact with dangerous chemicals from conception until death. Carson painted a vivid picture of how chemicals—used in many ways but particularly in pesticides—have upset the balance of nature, undermining the survival of countless species. This enormously popular and influential book was a soft-spoken battle cry to protect our natural surroundings. Its publication signaled the beginning of the environmental movement.

SRI LANKA: SINHALA AND TAMIL NEW YEAR. April 13–14. This New Year festival includes traditional games, the wearing of new clothes in auspicious colors and special foods. Public holiday.

THAILAND: SONGKRAN FESTIVAL. Apr 13–15. Public holiday. Thai water festival. To welcome the new year the image of Buddha is bathed with holy or fragrant water and lustral water is sprinkled on celebrants. Joyous event, especially observed at Thai Buddhist temples.

BIRTHDAYS TODAY

Baron Davis, 27, basketball player, born Los Angeles, CA, Apr 13, 1979.

Erik Christian Haugaard, 83, author (*The Rider and His Horse*), born Frederiksberg, Denmark, Apr 13, 1923.

Lee Bennett Hopkins, 68, poet (*Blast Off!: Poems about Space*), born Scranton, PA, Apr 13, 1938.

Garry Kasparov, 43, International Grandmaster chess player, born Baku, Azerbaijan, Apr 13, 1963.

APRIL 14 — FRIDAY

Day 104 — 261 Remaining

CHILDREN WITH ALOPECIA DAY. Apr 14. If you are a child (or have a child) who is losing your hair because of the disease alopecia, today is your day to stand up and be proud of not having hair. For info: Madison Grace Woytovich, 130 Park Rd South, Wyomissing, PA 19610. Phone: (610) 375-3453. E-mail: betsywoytovich@yahoo.com.

FIRST AMERICAN ABOLITION SOCIETY FOUNDED: ANNIVERSARY. Apr 14, 1775. The first abolition organization formed in the US was The Society for the Relief of Free Negroes Unlawfully Held in Bondage, founded at Philadelphia, PA.

FIRST DICTIONARY OF AMERICAN ENGLISH PUBLISHED: ANNIVERSARY. Apr 14, 1828. Noah Webster published his *American Dictionary of the English Language*.

GOOD FRIDAY. Apr 14. Observed in commemoration of the crucifixion. Oldest Christian celebration. Possible corruption of "God's Friday." Observed in some manner by most Christian sects and as a public holiday or part holiday in Delaware, Florida, Hawaii, Illinois, Indiana, Kentucky, New Jersey, North Carolina, Pennsylvania and Tennessee.

HONDURAS: DIA DE LAS AMERICAS. Apr 14. Honduras. Pan-American Day, a national holiday.

INTERNATIONAL MOMENT OF LAUGHTER DAY. Apr 14. Laughter is a potent and powerful way to deal with the difficulties of modern living. Since the physical, emotional and spiritual benefits of laughter are widely accepted, this day is set aside for everyone to take the necessary time to experience the power of laughter. For info: Izzy Gesell, Head Honcho of Wide Angle Humor, PO Box 962, Northampton, MA 01061. Phone: (413) 586-2634. E-mail: izzy@izzyg.com. Web: www.izzyg.com.

LINCOLN, ABRAHAM: ASSASSINATION ANNIVERSARY. Apr 14, 1865. President Abraham Lincoln was shot while watching a performance of *Our American Cousin* at Ford's Theatre, Washington, DC. He died the following day. Assassin was John Wilkes Booth, a young actor.

★**PAN-AMERICAN DAY.** Apr 14. Presidential Proclamation 1912, of May 28, 1930, covers every Apr 14 (required by Governing Board of Pan-American Union). Proclamation issued each year since 1948.

PAN-AMERICAN DAY IN FLORIDA. Apr 14. A holiday to be observed in the public schools of Florida honoring the republics of Latin America. If Apr 14 should fall on a day that is not a school day, then Pan-American Day should be observed on the preceding school day.

SULLIVAN, ANNE: BIRTH ANNIVERSARY. Apr 14, 1866. Anne Sullivan, born at Feeding Hills, MA, became well known for "working miracles" with Helen Keller, who was blind and deaf. Nearly blind herself, Sullivan used a manual alphabet communicated by the sense of touch to teach Keller to read, write and speak and then to help her go on to higher education. Anne Sullivan died Oct 20, 1936, at Forest Hills, NY.

BIRTHDAYS TODAY

Brad Ausmus, 37, baseball player, born New Haven, CT, Apr 14, 1969.
Cynthia Cooper, 43, basketball player, born Chicago, IL, Apr 14, 1963.
Sarah Michelle Gellar, 29, actress (*Scooby-Doo*, "Buffy the Vampire Slayer"), born New York, NY, Apr 14, 1977.
Greg Maddux, 40, baseball player, born San Angelo, TX, Apr 14, 1966.
Pete Rose, 65, former baseball manager and player, born Cincinnati, OH, Apr 14, 1941.

APRIL 15 — SATURDAY

Day 105 — 260 Remaining

EASTER EVEN. Apr 15. The Saturday before Easter. Last day of Holy Week and of Lent.

FIRST MCDONALD'S OPENS: ANNIVERSARY. Apr 15, 1955. The first franchised McDonald's was opened at Des Plaines, IL, by Ray Kroc, who had gotten the idea from a hamburger joint at San Bernardino, CA, run by the McDonald brothers. By the mid-1990s, there were more than 15,000 McDonald's in 70 countries.

FIRST SCHOOL FOR DEAF FOUNDED: ANNIVERSARY. Apr 15, 1817. Thomas Hopkins Gallaudet and Laurent Clerc founded the first US public school for the deaf, Connecticut Asylum for the Education and Instruction of Deaf and Dumb Persons (now the American School for the Deaf), at Hartford, CT.

INCOME TAX PAY DAY. Apr 15. A day all Americans need to know—the day by which taxpayers are supposed to make their accounting of the previous year and pay their share of the cost of government. The US Internal Revenue Service provides free forms.

PEALE, CHARLES WILLSON: BIRTH ANNIVERSARY. Apr 15, 1741. American portrait painter (best known for his many portraits of colonial and American Revolutionary War figures) was born at Queen Anne County, MD. His children Raphaelle, Rembrandt, Titian, Rubens and his niece Sarah were also artists. Died at Philadelphia, PA, Feb 22, 1827.

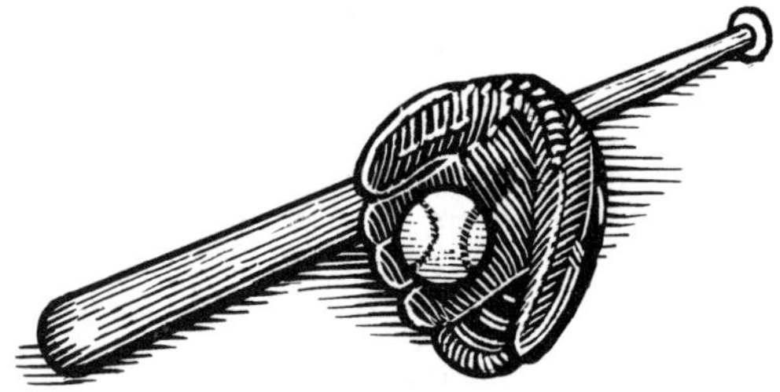

ROBINSON BREAKS MAJOR LEAGUE BASEBALL COLOR BARRIER: ANNIVERSARY. Apr 15, 1947. On this date, Jackie Robinson played his first game with the Brooklyn Dodgers against the Boston Braves to become the first African American to break into Major League Baseball. He was later voted Rookie of the Year.

SINKING OF THE *TITANIC*: ANNIVERSARY. Apr 15, 1912. The "unsinkable" luxury liner *Titanic* on its maiden voyage from Southampton, England, to New York, NY, struck an iceberg just before midnight Apr 14, and sank at 2:27 AM, Apr 15. The *Titanic* had 2,227 persons aboard. Of these, 1,522 lives were lost. About 705 people were rescued from the icy waters off Newfoundland by the liner *Carpathia*, which reached the scene about two hours after the *Titanic* went down. For more info: *The Story of the Titanic*, by Eric Kently (DK, 0-7894-7943-5, $17.95 Gr. 4–8). See also: "*Titanic* Discovered: Anniversary" (Sept 1).

BIRTHDAYS TODAY

Evelyn Ashford, 49, Olympic gold medal track athlete, born Shreveport, LA, Apr 15, 1957.
Jacqueline Briggs Martin, 61, author (*Snowflake Bentley*), born Lewiston, ME, Apr 15, 1945.
Jason Sehorn, 35, football player, born Sacramento, CA, Apr 15, 1971.
Emma Watson, 16, actress (*Harry Potter and the Sorcerer's Stone*), born Oxford, England, Apr 15, 1990.

APRIL 16 — SUNDAY

Day 106 — 259 Remaining

DENMARK: QUEEN MARGRETHE'S BIRTHDAY. Apr 16. Thousands of children gather to cheer the queen at Amalienborg Palace and the Royal Guard wears scarlet gala uniforms.

DIEGO, JOSE de: BIRTH ANNIVERSARY. Apr 16, 1866. Puerto Rican patriot and political leader, Jose de Diego was born at Aguadilla, Puerto Rico. His birthday is a holiday in Puerto Rico. He died July 16, 1918, at New York, NY.

EASTER SUNDAY. Apr 16. Commemorates the Resurrection of Christ. Most joyous festival of the Christian year. The date of

★ ★ ★

April 2006

S	M	T	W	T	F	S
						1
2	3	4	5	6	7	8
9	10	11	12	13	14	15
16	17	18	19	20	21	22
23	24	25	26	27	28	29
30						

Easter, a movable feast, is derived from the lunar calendar: the first Sunday following the first ecclesiastical full moon on or after Mar 21—always between Mar 22 and Apr 25. The Council of Nicaea (AD 325) prescribed that Easter be celebrated on the Sunday after Passover, as that feast's date had been established in Jesus' time. Orthodox Christians continue to use the Julian calendar, so that Easter can sometimes be as much as five weeks apart in the Western and Eastern churches. Easter in 2007 will be Apr 8; in 2008 it will be Mar 23. Many other dates in the Christian year are derived from the date of Easter. See also: "Orthodox Easter Sunday or Pascha" (Apr 23).

EGG SALAD WEEK. Apr 16–22. Dedicated to the many delicious uses for all of the Easter eggs that have been cooked, colored, hidden and found. Annually, the full week after Easter. For info: Linda Braun, Consumer Serv Dir, American Egg Board, 1460 Renaissance Dr, Park Ridge, IL 60068. E-mail: aeb@aeb.org. Web: www.aeb.org.

NATIONAL COIN WEEK. Apr 16–22. 83rd annual. To promote the history and lore of numismatics and the hobby of coin collecting. Annually, the third full week of April, Sunday through Saturday. For info: Gail Baker, Dir of Educ, American Numismatic Assn, 818 N Cascade Ave, Colorado Springs, CO 80903. Phone: (719) 632-2646 or (800) 367-9723. Fax: (719) 634-4085. Web: www.money.org.

★ **NATIONAL PARK WEEK.** Apr 16–23.

NATIONAL PTA EARTH WEEK. Apr 16–22. In 1990 the National PTA recognized the importance of the environment to the health and safety of our children and designated the week in which Earth Day falls (Apr 22) as Earth Week. During Earth Week, PTA members and others work to improve the environment in their homes, schools and communities. For info: National PTA Environmental Awareness Program, 330 N Wabash Ave, Ste 2100, Chicago, IL 60611-3690. Phone: (312) 670-6782. Fax: (312) 670-6783. E-mail: info@pta.org. Web: www.pta.org.

NATIONAL WILDLIFE WEEK. Apr 16–22. In 1938 the National Wildlife Federation created National Wildlife Week, a celebration to alert the public to the needs of wildlife and NWF's efforts to preserve wildlife and their habitats. NWF educates students, families and adults about wildlife conservation issues and encourages them to become environmental stewards. For info: National Wildlife Federation, 8925 Leesburg Pike, Vienna, VA 22184. Phone: (703) 790-4000. E-mail: wildlife@nwf.org. Web: www.nwf.org.

ORTHODOX PALM SUNDAY. Apr 16. Celebration of Christ's entry into Jerusalem, when his way was covered with palms by the multitudes. Beginning of Holy Week in the Orthodox Church.

WILLIAMS, GARTH: BIRTH ANNIVERSARY. Apr 16, 1912. One of the most beloved and prolific children's illustrators of all time. Born at New York, NY, he tried to become a cartoonist, but instead found success as the illustrator of E.B. White's *Stuart Little*, published in 1945. He soon turned to illustrating full-time, creating illustrations for all nine of Laura Ingalls Wilder's "Little House" books, as well as White's *Charlotte's Web* and George Selden's *The Cricket in Times Square*. He also illustrated books by Margaret Wise Brown, Randall Jarrell and Russell Hoban, among others. In 1958 he became a subject of controversy with his publication of *The Rabbit's Wedding*, a book that he both wrote and illustrated, that told the story of a marriage between a black rabbit and a white rabbit. He died on May 8, 1996, at his home at Marfil, Guanajuato, Mexico.

WRIGHT, WILBUR: BIRTH ANNIVERSARY. Apr 16, 1867. Aviation pioneer (with his brother Orville), born at Millville, IN. Died at Dayton, OH, May 30, 1912.

BIRTHDAYS TODAY

Kareem Abdul-Jabbar, 59, Hall of Fame basketball player, born Lewis Ferdinand Alcindor, Jr, New York, NY, Apr 16, 1947.

Eleanor E. Tate, 58, author (*The Secret of Gumbo Grove*), born Canton, MO, Apr 16, 1948.

Fernando Vina, 37, baseball player, born Sacramento, CA, Apr 16, 1969.

APRIL 17 — MONDAY

Day 107 — 258 Remaining

AMERICAN SAMOA: FLAG DAY. Apr 17. National holiday commemorating first raising of American flag in what was formerly Eastern Samoa in 1900. Public holiday with singing, dancing, costumes and parades.

EASTER MONDAY. Apr 17. Holiday or bank holiday in many places, including England, Northern Ireland, Wales, Canada and North Carolina in the US.

ELLIS ISLAND FAMILY HISTORY DAY. Apr 17. Ellis Island, New York, NY. By official proclamation of our nation's governors, Apr 17 has been designated as "Ellis Island Family History Day." Sponsored by The Statue of Liberty–Ellis Island Foundation, Inc, and the National Genealogical Society, this annual day recognizes the achievements and contributions made to America by Ellis Island immigrants and their descendants. Historically, Apr 17 marks the day in 1907 when more immigrants were processed through the island than on any other day in its colorful history: 11,747 people. In addition, the Foundation has established the "Ellis Island Family Heritage Awards," which are given annually to a select number of Ellis Island immigrants or their descendants who have made a significant contribution to the American experience. For info: Maria Antenorcruz, Statue of Liberty–Ellis Island Foundation, Inc, 292 Madison Ave, 14th Fl, New York, NY 10017. Phone: (212) 561-4542. Fax: (212) 779-1990. E-mail: mantenorcruz@ellisisland.org. Web: www.ellisisland.org.

NEW JERSEY DAY. Apr 17. The governor issues annually a proclamation designating Apr 17 as New Jersey Day, commemorating the anniversary of the beginning of unified government in the state.

PATRIOT'S DAY IN MASSACHUSETTS AND MAINE. Apr 17. Commemorates Battles of Lexington and Concord, 1775. Annually, the third Monday in April.

SOUTH AFRICA: FAMILY DAY. Apr 17. National holiday. Annually, Easter Monday.

SPACE MILESTONE: *COLUMBIA NEUROLAB* (US). Apr 17, 1998. Seven astronauts and scientists were launched with 2,000 animals (crickets, mice, snails and fish) to study the nervous system in space.

SYRIAN ARAB REPUBLIC: INDEPENDENCE DAY. Apr 17. Official holiday. Proclaimed independence from France in 1946.

VERRAZANO DAY: ANNIVERSARY. Apr 17, 1524. Celebrates discovery of New York harbor by Giovanni Verrazano, Florentine navigator, 1485–1527.

WHITE HOUSE EASTER EGG ROLL. Apr 17. Traditionally held on the south lawn of the executive mansion on Easter Monday. Custom is said to have started at the Capitol grounds about 1810. It was transferred to the White House Lawn in the 1870s.

BIRTHDAYS TODAY

Jane Kurtz, 54, author (*Pulling the Lion's Tale*), born Portland, OR, Apr 17, 1952.

APRIL 18 — TUESDAY

Day 108 — 257 Remaining

CANADA: CONSTITUTION ACT OF 1982: ANNIVERSARY. Apr 18, 1982. Replacing the British North America Act of 1867, the Canadian Constitution Act of 1982 provides Canada with a new set of fundamental laws and civil rights. Signed by Queen Elizabeth II, at Parliament Hill, Ottawa, Canada, it went into effect at 12:01 AM, Sunday, Apr 19, 1982.

MENC: THE NATIONAL ASSOCIATION FOR MUSIC EDUCATION NATIONAL CONFERENCE. Apr 18–22. Salt Lake City, UT. For info: Music Educators National Conference, 1806 Robert Fulton Dr, Reston, VA 22091. Phone: (703) 860-4000. Web: www.menc.org.

NATIONAL CATHOLIC EDUCATIONAL ASSOCIATION CONVENTION AND EXPOSITION. Apr 18–21. New Orleans, LA. Annual meeting for NCEA members and anyone working in, or interested in, the welfare of Catholic education. Est attendance: 11,000. For info: National Catholic Educational Assn, 1077 30th St NW, Ste 100, Washington, DC 20007. Phone: (202) 337-6232. Fax: (202) 333-6706. E-mail: nceaadmin@ncea.org. Web: www.ncea.org.

PAUL REVERE'S RIDE: ANNIVERSARY. Apr 18, 1775. The "Midnight Ride" of Paul Revere and William Dawes started at about 10 PM, to warn American patriots between Boston, MA, and Concord, MA, of the approaching British. For more info: *The Midnight Ride of Paul Revere* by Henry Wadsworth Longfellow (National Geographic, 0-7922-7674-4, $16.95 Gr. K–3).

PET OWNERS INDEPENDENCE DAY. Apr 18. Dog and cat owners take day off from work and the pets go to work in their place, since most pets are jobless, sleep all day and do not even take out the trash. [©2002 by WH.] For info: Thomas & Ruth Roy, Wellcat Holidays, 2418 Long Ln, Lebanon, PA 17046. Phone: (717) 279-0184. E-mail: info@wellcat.com. Web: www.wellcat.com.

April 2006

S	M	T	W	T	F	S
						1
2	3	4	5	6	7	8
9	10	11	12	13	14	15
16	17	18	19	20	21	22
23	24	25	26	27	28	29
30						

APRIL 18
100th ANNIVERSARY OF THE SAN FRANCISCO EARTHQUAKE

Shortly after five o'clock on the morning of Apr 18, 1906, residents of San Francisco and nearby areas experienced one of Earth's most frightening forces: an earthquake. Buildings crumbled, roads buckled and gas pipes snapped apart as the ground shook. Fires, the result of leaking gas, consumed the city. For three days, smoke-filled air and additional ground tremors kept the people in a constant state of fear. In fact, more people were injured and more property was damaged by the fires and the quake's aftershocks than were harmed by the initial earthquake.

California's geographic position makes it particularly earthquake prone. According to the Theory of Plate Tectonics, Earth's lithosphere, or brittle rocky surface, is composed of about 10 large moving "plates" of rock (there are a number of smaller plates too).

The plates shift on Earth's surface, slowly bending and twisting in response to Earth's physical dynamics. Among these are the convection forces found in one of Earth's layers called the mantle. Unlike rock in the lithosphere, rock in the mantle is hot and soft. Plates that compose the lithosphere float on top of the mantle rock. As they move, plate edges drift apart, bump into and scrape against each other. These movements cause stress to build up inside the rock in much the same way that pulling an elastic band stresses the rubber. And like an elastic band, when rock is stressed too much, it breaks. That's what causes an earthquake!

California's long coastline follows along the edges of two large plates: the Pacific Plate and the North American Plate. If you were to look at a geological map that pinpoints areas where earthquakes most frequently occur, you would quickly notice that the majority of quakes occur along plate edges.

The San Francisco earthquake is fascinating to research. There are microfilm/microfiche newspaper accounts that are readily available in public libraries. A number of websites contain fascinating information about earthquakes in general. One of them—geared toward students—is maintained by the Federal Emergency Management Agency (FEMA) and can be found at www.fema.gov/kids/quake.htm.

Shelley Tanaka's *A Day that Changed America: Earthquake!* (Hyperion, 0-7868-1882-4, $16.99 Ages 8–12) tells the story of the quake through the eyes of several young people who experienced it. The book is a mixture of fictionalized text with sidebars and double-page spreads that contain earthquake facts. Tanaka also includes a list of websites and archival sources.

For a scientific explanation of earthquakes see *Earthquakes* by Sally M. Walker (Carolrhoda Books, 0-8761-4888-7, $21.27 Ages 10 & up) and *Earthquake Games* by Matthys Levy and Mario Salvadori (McElderry, 0-6898-1367-8, Out of print, Ages 8 & up), which contains a number of easy-to-do earthquake experiments. For younger readers, see Franklyn Branley's *Earthquakes* (HarperTrophy, 0-06-445135-6, $4.99 Ages 4–8), part of the Let's Read and Find Out series, and *Earthquakes* by Ellen J. Prager (National Geographic, 0-7922-8202-7, $16.95 Ages 5–8). Adults seeking information, without being overwhelmed by scientific jargon, will enjoy *Earthshaking Science* by Susan Elizabeth Hough (Princeton University Press, 0-6911-1819-1, $17.95).

There are many novels about the San Francisco earthquake. The popular Magic Tree House series, by Mary Pope Osborne, offers *Earthquake in the Early Morning* (Random House, 0-679-89070-X, $3.99 Ages 4–8). Middle school and junior high readers will find *Earthquake at Dawn* by Kristiana Gregory (Gulliver Books, 0-1520-4681-X, $5.99 Ages 10 & up) an engaging read.

—Sally Walker

SAN FRANCISCO 1906 EARTHQUAKE: 100th ANNIVERSARY. Apr 18, 1906. The business section of San Francisco, approximately 10,000 acres, was destroyed by earthquake. The first quake registered at 5:13 AM, followed by fire. Nearly 4,000 lives were lost during the quake. For more info: *The San Francisco Earthquake of 1906* by Lisa A. Chippendale (Chelsea, 0-7910-5270-2, $19.95 Gr. 7–12). ***See Curriculum Connection.***

"THIRD WORLD" DAY: ANNIVERSARY. Apr 18, 1955. Anniversary of the first use of the phrase "third world," which was used by Indonesia's President Sukarno in his opening speech at the Bandung Conference. Representatives of nearly 30 African and Asian countries (2,000 attendees) heard Sukarno praise the American war of independence, "the first successful anticolonial war in history." More than half the world's population, he said, was represented at this "first intercontinental conference of the so-called colored peoples, in the history of mankind." The phrase and the idea of a "third world" rapidly gained currency, generally signifying the aggregate of nonaligned peoples and nations—the nonwhite and underdeveloped portion of the world.

YANKEE STADIUM OPENS: ANNIVERSARY. Apr 18, 1923. More than 74,000 fans attended Opening Day festivities as the New York Yankees inaugurated their new stadium. Babe Ruth christened it with a game-winning three-run homer into the right-field bleachers. In his coverage of the game for the *New York Evening Telegram* sportswriter Fred Lieb described Yankee Stadium as "The House That Ruth Built," and the name stuck.

ZIMBABWE: INDEPENDENCE DAY. Apr 18. National holiday commemorates the recognition by Great Britain of Zimbabwean independence in 1980. Prior to this, the country had been the British colony of Southern Rhodesia.

BIRTHDAYS TODAY

Melissa Joan Hart, 30, actress ("Sabrina, the Teenage Witch"), born Long Island, NY, Apr 18, 1976.

Rick Moranis, 52, actor (*Honey, I Shrunk the Kids; Honey, We Shrunk Ourselves*), born Toronto, ON, Canada, Apr 18, 1954.

APRIL 19 — WEDNESDAY

Day 109 — 256 Remaining

BATTLE OF LEXINGTON AND CONCORD: ANNIVERSARY. Apr 19, 1775. Massachusetts. Start of the American Revolution as the British fired the "shot heard 'round the world." For more info: *The Shot Heard Round the World: The Battles of Lexington and Concord* by Nancy Whitelaw (Morgan Reynolds, 1-883846-75-7, $20.95 Gr. 5–8).

GARFIELD, LUCRETIA RUDOLPH: BIRTH ANNIVERSARY. Apr 19, 1832. Wife of James Abram Garfield, the 20th president of the US, born at Hiram, OH. Died at Pasadena, CA, Mar 14, 1918.

OKLAHOMA CITY BOMBING: ANNIVERSARY. Apr 19, 1995. A car bomb exploded outside the Alfred P. Murrah Federal Building at Oklahoma City, OK, killing 168 people, 19 of them children at a day-care center; a nurse died of head injuries sustained while helping in rescue efforts. The blast ripped off the north face of the nine-story building, leaving a 20-foot-wide crater and debris two stories high. Structurally unsound and dangerous, the bombed building was razed May 23. Timothy J. McVeigh, a decorated Gulf War army vet who is alleged to have been deeply angered by the Bureau of Alcohol, Tobacco and Firearms attack on the Branch Davidian compound at Waco, TX, exactly two years before, was convicted of the bombing and was executed June 11, 2001. For more info: *One April Morning: Children Remember the Oklahoma City Bombing* by Nancy Lamb (Lothrop, 0-6881-4666-X, $16 Gr. K–3).

PATRIOT'S DAY IN FLORIDA. Apr 19. A ceremonial day commemorating the first blood shed in the American Revolution at Lexington and Concord in 1775.

SHERMAN, ROGER: BIRTH ANNIVERSARY. Apr 19, 1721. American statesman, member of the Continental Congress (1774–81 and 1783–84), signer of the Declaration of Independence and of the Constitution, was born at Newton, MA. He also calculated astronomical and calendar information for an almanac. Sherman died at New Haven, CT, July 23, 1793.

SIERRA LEONE: NATIONAL HOLIDAY. Apr 19. Sierra Leone became a republic in 1971.

SPACE MILESTONE: *SALYUT* (USSR): 35th ANNIVERSARY. Apr 19, 1971. The Soviet Union launched *Salyut*, the first manned orbiting space laboratory. It was replaced in 1986 by *Mir*, a manned space station and laboratory.

APRIL 20 — THURSDAY

Day 110 — 255 Remaining

FIRST LADIES TAKE FLIGHT: ANNIVERSARY. Apr 20, 1933. During a White House dinner, the First Lady of the US, Eleanor Roosevelt, and America's first lady of flight, Amelia Earhart, left for a spontaneous night flight over Washington, DC, in an Eastern Air Transport plane. Earhart, the first woman to fly solo over the Atlantic, did fly the plane a short bit, and Roosevelt, who had a student pilot license, was allowed to view the cockpit. The flight was newsworthy at a time when air travel was still young and viewed as dangerous. For more info: a fictionalized version of the flight is in the lovely picture book *Amelia and Eleanor Go For A Ride* by Pam Muñoz Ryan and illustrated by Brian Selznick (Scholastic, 0-590-96075-X, $16.96 Gr. 1–4 and Read Aloud).

HITLER, ADOLF: BIRTH ANNIVERSARY. Apr 20, 1889. German dictator, obsessed with superiority of the "Aryan race." Hitler was born at Braunau am Inn, Austria. He rose in politics quickly (despite a brief time in prison during which he wrote *Mein Kampf*) as leader of the Nazis, feeding on German anger over the economy and WWI defeat. He also fanned violent anti-Semitism, which later resulted in millions of Jewish deaths in concentration camps. A German plebiscite vested sole executive power in Führer Adolf Hitler Aug 19, 1934. In seeking to increase German power, he started WWII in 1939. Facing certain defeat by the Allied Forces, he shot himself Apr 30, 1945, in a Berlin bunker where he had been hiding for more than three months.

ICELAND: "FIRST DAY OF SUMMER." Apr 20. A national public holiday, *Sumardagurinn fyrsti*, with general festivities, processions and much street dancing, especially at Reykjavik, greets the coming of summer. Flags are flown on this day. Annually, the Thursday between Apr 19 and 25.

MOON PHASE: LAST QUARTER. Apr 20. Moon enters Last Quarter phase at 11:28 PM, EDT.

TAURUS, THE BULL. Apr 20–May 20. In the astronomical/astrological zodiac that divides the sun's apparent orbit into 12 segments, the period Apr 20–May 20 is identified, traditionally, as the sun sign of Taurus, the Bull. The ruling planet is Venus.

BIRTHDAYS TODAY

Mary Hoffman, 61, author (*Amazing Grace*), born Eastleigh, Hampshire, England, Apr 20, 1945.
Joey Lawrence, 30, actor ("Brotherly Love," "Blossom"), born Philadelphia, PA, Apr 20, 1976.
Pat Roberts, 70, US Senator (R, Kansas), born Topeka, KS, Apr 20, 1936.
John Paul Stevens, 86, Associate Justice of the US Supreme Court, born Chicago, IL, Apr 20, 1920.

APRIL 21 — FRIDAY

Day 111 — 254 Remaining

BRAZIL: TIRADENTES DAY. Apr 21. National holiday commemorating execution of national hero, dentist Jose da Silva Xavier, nicknamed Tiradentes (tooth-puller), a conspirator in revolt against the Portuguese in 1789.

ETA AQUARIDS METEOR SHOWER. Apr 21–May 12 (approximate). Annual meteor shower caused when orbiting earth passes through the trail of Halley's Comet. Dates are approximately the same every year, with the height of the showers coming around May 5. See also: "Last Perihelion of Halley's Comet" (Feb 9) and "Orionids Meteor Showers" (Oct 15).

FROEBEL, FRIEDRICH: BIRTH ANNIVERSARY. Apr 21, 1782. German educator and author Friedrich Froebel, who believed that play is an important part of a child's education, was born at Oberwiessbach, Thuringia. Froebel invented the kindergarten, founding the first one at Blankenburg, Germany, in 1837. Froebel also invented a series of toys which he intended to stimulate learning. (The American architect Frank Lloyd Wright as a child received these toys [maplewood blocks] from his mother and spoke throughout his life of their value.) Froebel's ideas about the role of directed play, toys and music in children's education had a profound influence in England and the US, where the nursery school became a further extension of his ideas. Froebel died at Marienthal, Germany, June 21, 1852.

INDONESIA: KARTINI DAY. Apr 21. Republic of Indonesia. Honors Raden Adjeng Kartini, pioneer in the emancipation of the women of Indonesia.

ITALY: BIRTHDAY OF ROME. Apr 21. Celebration of the founding of Rome, traditionally thought to be in 753 BC.

KINDERGARTEN DAY. Apr 21. A day to recognize the importance of play, games and "creative self-activity" in children's education and to note the history of the kindergarten. Observed on the anniversary of the birth of Friedrich Froebel (Apr 21, 1782) who established the first kindergarten in 1837. German immigrants brought Froebel's ideas to the US in the 1840s. The first kindergarten in a public school in the US was started in 1873, at St. Louis, MO.

★ ★ ★

April 2006

S	M	T	W	T	F	S
						1
2	3	4	5	6	7	8
9	10	11	12	13	14	15
16	17	18	19	20	21	22
23	24	25	26	27	28	29
30						

SAN JACINTO DAY. Apr 21. Texas. Commemorates Battle of San Jacinto in which Texas won independence from Mexico in 1836. A 570-foot monument, dedicated on the 101st anniversary of the battle, marks the site on the banks of the San Jacinto River, about 20 miles from the present city of Houston, TX, where General Sam Houston's Texans decisively defeated the Mexican forces led by Santa Ana in the final battle between Texas and Mexico.

BIRTHDAYS TODAY

Ed Belfour, 41, hockey player, born Carman, MB, Canada, Apr 21, 1965.
Queen Elizabeth II, 80, Queen of the United Kingdom, born London, England, Apr 21, 1926.
Barbara Park, 59, author (the Junie B. Jones series), born Mount Holly, NJ, Apr 21, 1947.

APRIL 22 — SATURDAY

Day 112 — 253 Remaining

BRAZIL: DISCOVERY OF BRAZIL DAY. Apr 22. Commemorates discovery by Pedro Alvarez Cabral in 1500.

COINS STAMPED "IN GOD WE TRUST": ANNIVERSARY. Apr 22, 1864. By Act of Congress, the phrase "In God We Trust" began to be stamped on all US coins.

EARTH DAY. Apr 22. Earth Day, first observed Apr 22, 1970, with the message "Give Earth a Chance" and attention to reclaiming the purity of the air, water and living environment. Earth Day 1990 was a global event with more than 200 million participating in 142 countries. Note: Earth Day activities are held by many groups on various dates, often on the weekend closest to Apr 22. The vernal equinox (i.e., the first day of spring) has been chosen by some for this observance. For more info: *Let's Celebrate Earth Day* by Connie Roop and Peter Roop (Millbrook, 0-7613-1812-7, $21.90 Gr. 1–3). For info: Earth Day Network, 1616 P St NW, Ste 200, Washington, DC 20036. Phone: (202) 518-0044. Web: www.earthday.net.

FIRST SOLO TRIP TO NORTH POLE: ANNIVERSARY. Apr 22, 1994. Norwegian explorer Borge Ousland became the first person to make the trip to the North Pole alone. The trip took 52 days, during which he pulled a 265-pound sled. Departing from Cape Atkticheskiy at Siberia Mar 2, he averaged about 18½ miles per day over the 630-mile journey. Ousland had traveled to the Pole on skis with Erling Kagge in 1990.

GIRL SCOUT LEADER'S DAY. Apr 22. To recognize the people who make Girl Scouting possible. An opportunity for girls involved in Girl Scouting to honor their troop leaders. Annually, Apr 22. For info: Media Services, Girl Scouts of the USA, 420 Fifth Ave, New York, NY 10018. Phone: (212) 852-8000. Fax: (212) 852-6514. Web: www.girlscouts.org.

OKLAHOMA DAY. Apr 22. Oklahoma.

OKLAHOMA LAND RUSH: ANNIVERSARY. Apr 22, 1889. At noon a gun shot signaled the start of the Oklahoma land rush as thousands of settlers rushed into the territory to claim land. Under pressure from cattlemen, the federal government opened 1,900,000 acres of central Oklahoma that had been bought from the Creek and Seminole tribes.

BIRTHDAYS TODAY

Eileen Christelow, 63, author (*Five Little Monkeys Jumping on the Bed, Don't Wake Up Mama!*), born Washington, DC, Apr 22, 1943.

Paula Fox, 83, author (Newbery for *The Slave Dancer*), born New York, NY, Apr 22, 1923.

S.E. Hinton, 57, author (*The Outsiders, Tex*), born New York, NY, Apr 22, 1949.

APRIL 23 — SUNDAY

Day 113 — 252 Remaining

BERMUDA: PEPPERCORN CEREMONY. Apr 23. St. George. Commemorates the payment of one peppercorn in 1816 to the governor of Bermuda for rental of Old State House by the Masonic Lodge.

BUCHANAN, JAMES: BIRTH ANNIVERSARY. Apr 23, 1791. The 15th president of the US, born near Mercersburg, PA, was the only president who never married. He served one term in office, Mar 4, 1857–Mar 3, 1861, and died at Lancaster, PA, June 1, 1868. For info: www.ipl.org/ref/POTUS.

FIRST MOVIE THEATER OPENS: ANNIVERSARY. Apr 23, 1896. The first movie theater opened in Koster and Bial's Music Hall at New York City. Up until this time, people viewed movies individually by looking into a Kinetoscope, a box-like "peep show." The first Kinetoscope parlor opened at New York in 1894. But in 1896 Thomas Edison introduced the Vitascope which projected films on a screen. This was the first time in the US that an audience sat in a theater and viewed a movie together.

FIRST PUBLIC SCHOOL IN AMERICA: ANNIVERSARY. Apr 23, 1635. The Boston Latin School opened and is America's oldest public school. This is the Gregorian calendar date; the school was actually founded Apr 13 on the Julian calendar. For more info: bls.org.

GRANGE WEEK. Apr 23–29. State and local recognition for Grange's contribution to rural/urban America. Celebrated at National Headquarters at Washington, DC, and in all states with local, county and state Granges. Begun in 1867, the National Grange is the oldest US rural community service, family-oriented organization with a special interest in agriculture. Annually, the last full week in April. For info: Kermit W. Richardson, National Master, The National Grange, 1616 H St NW, Washington, DC 20006. Phone: (202) 628-3507 or (888) 4-GRANGE. Fax: (202) 347-1091. Web: www.grange.org.

NATIONAL VOLUNTEER WEEK. Apr 23–29. National Volunteer Week honors those who reach out to others through volunteer community service and calls attention to the need for more community services for individuals, groups and families to help solve serious social problems that affect our communities. For info: Customer Information Center, Points of Light Foundation, 1400 I St NW, Ste 800, Washington, DC 20005. Phone: (202) 729-8000. Fax: (202) 223-9256. E-mail: info@pointsoflight.org. Web: www.pointsoflight.org.

★**NATIONAL VOLUNTEER WEEK.** Apr 23–29.

NATIONAL YWCA WEEK. Apr 23–29. To promote the YWCA of the USA nationally. Annually, the last full week in April. For info: YWCA of the USA, Empire State Bldg, Ste 301, 350 Fifth Ave, New York, NY 10118. Phone: (212) 273-7800. Web: www.ywca.org.

ORTHODOX EASTER SUNDAY OR PASCHA. Apr 23. Observed by Eastern Orthodox Churches. See also: "Easter Sunday" (Apr 16).

PEARSON, LESTER B.: BIRTH ANNIVERSARY. Apr 23, 1897. The 14th prime minister of Canada, born at Toronto, Canada. He was Canada's chief delegate at the San Francisco conference where the UN charter was drawn up and later served as president of the General Assembly. He wrote the proposal that resulted in the formation of the North Atlantic Treaty Organization (NATO). He was awarded the Nobel Peace Prize. Died at Rockcliffe, Canada, Dec 27, 1972. For more info: www.uwc.ca/pearson/library/lester/lester.htm.

PHYSICISTS DISCOVER TOP QUARK: ANNIVERSARY. Apr 23, 1994. Physicists at the Department of Energy's Fermi National Accelerator Laboratory found evidence for the existence of the subatomic particle called the top quark, the last undiscovered quark of the six predicted to exist by current scientific theory. The discovery provides strong support for the quark theory of the structure of matter. Quarks are subatomic particles that make up protons and neutrons found in the nuclei of atoms. The five other quark types that had already been proven to exist are the up quark, down quark, strange quark, charm quark and bottom quark. Further experimentation over many months confirmed the discovery, and it was publicly announced Mar 2, 1995.

SAINT GEORGE FEAST DAY. Apr 23. Martyr and patron saint of England, who died Apr 23, AD 303. Hero of the George and the dragon legend. The story says that his faith helped him slay a vicious dragon that demanded daily sacrifice after the king's daughter became the intended victim.

SHAKESPEARE, WILLIAM: BIRTH AND DEATH ANNIVERSARY. Apr 23. England's most famous and most revered poet and playwright. He was born at Stratford-on-Avon, England, Apr 23, 1564 (Old Style), baptized there three days later and died there on his birthday, Apr 23, 1616 (Old Style). Author of at least 36 plays and 154 sonnets, Shakespeare created the most influential and lasting body of work in the English language, an extraordinary exploration of human nature. His epitaph: "Good frend for Jesus sake forbeare, To digg the dust enclosed heare. Blese be ye man that spares thes stones, And curst be he that moves my bones." For more info: *Shakespeare: His Work and His World* by Michael Rosen (Candlewick, 0-7636-1568-4, $19.99 Gr. 5–9).

SKY AWARENESS WEEK. Apr 23–29. 16th annual. A celebration of the sky and an opportunity to appreciate its natural beauty, to understand sky and weather processes and to work together to protect the sky as a natural resource (it's the only one we have). Events are held at schools, nature centers, etc, all across the US. For info: Mike Mogil, How The Weatherworks, 301 Creek Valley Ln, Rockville, MD 20850-5604. Phone: (800) 8CLOUD9 or (301) 527-9339. E-mail: skyweek@weatherworks.com. Web: www.weatherworks.com.

SPAIN: BOOK DAY AND LOVER'S DAY. Apr 23. Barcelona. Saint George's Day and the anniversary of the death of Spanish writer Miguel de Cervantes have been observed with special ceremonies in the Palacio de la Disputacion and throughout the city since 1714. Book stands are set up in the plazas and on street corners. This is Spain's equivalent of Valentine's Day. Women give books to men; men give roses to women.

TURKEY: NATIONAL SOVEREIGNTY AND CHILDREN'S DAY: ANNIVERSARY. Apr 23. Commemorates Grand National Assembly's inauguration in 1923.

UNITED NATIONS: WORLD BOOK AND COPYRIGHT DAY. Apr 23. Observed throughout the United Nations system.

BIRTHDAYS TODAY

Tony Esposito, 63, Hall of Fame hockey player, born Sault Ste Marie, ON, Canada, Apr 23, 1943.

Andruw Jones, 29, baseball player, born Willemstad, Curacao, Netherlands Antilles, Apr 23, 1977.

APRIL 24 — MONDAY

Day 114 — 251 Remaining

ARMENIA: ARMENIAN MARTYRS DAY. Apr 24. Commemorates the massacre of Armenians under the Ottoman Turks in 1915 and the date deportations from Turkey began. Also called Armenian Genocide Memorial Day. Adolf Hitler, in a speech at Obersalzberg Aug 22, 1939, is reported to have said, "Who today remembers the Armenian extermination?" in an apparent justification of the Nazis' use of genocide.

CANADA: NEWFOUNDLAND: SAINT GEORGE'S DAY. Apr 24. Holiday observed in Newfoundland on Monday nearest Feast Day (Apr 23) of Saint George.

CONFEDERATE MEMORIAL DAY IN ALABAMA. Apr 24. State holiday on the fourth Monday in April. Other Southern states observe Confederate Memorial Day on different dates; see entries on Jan 19, Apr 26, May 10 and June 3.

CONFEDERATE MEMORIAL DAY IN MISSISSIPPI. Apr 24. Annually, last Monday in April. Observed on other days in other Southern states.

IRELAND: EASTER RISING: 90th ANNIVERSARY. Apr 24, 1916. Irish nationalists seized key buildings in Dublin and proclaimed an Irish republic. The rebellion collapsed, however, and it wasn't until 1922 that the Irish Free State, the predecessor of the Republic of Ireland, was established.

LIBRARY OF CONGRESS: ANNIVERSARY. Apr 24, 1800. Congress approved an act providing "for the purchase of such books as may be necessary for the use of Congress . . . and for fitting up a suitable apartment for containing them." Thus began one of the world's greatest libraries. Originally housed in the Capitol, it moved to its own quarters in 1897. For more information about the library, visit its website at lcweb.loc.gov.

April 2006

S	M	T	W	T	F	S
						1
2	3	4	5	6	7	8
9	10	11	12	13	14	15
16	17	18	19	20	21	22
23	24	25	26	27	28	29
30						

NATIONAL PLAYGROUND SAFETY WEEK. Apr 24–28. An opportunity for families, community parks, schools and childcare facilities to focus on preventing public playground-related injuries. Sponsored by the National Program for Playground Safety (NPPS), this event helps educate the public about the more than 200,000 children (that's one child every 2½ minutes) who require emergency room treatment for playground-related injuries each year. Annually, last full week in April, from Monday to Friday. For info: National Program for Playground Safety, School of HPELS, WRC 205, University of Northern Iowa, Cedar Falls, IA 50614-0618. Phone: (800) 554-PLAY. Fax: (319) 273-7308. Web: www.playgroundsafety.org.

NATIONAL TV-TURNOFF WEEK. Apr 24–30. For the 12th annual event, more than 7 million Americans will go without TV for 7 days. For info: TV-Turnoff Network, 1200 29th St NW, Lower Level #1, Washington, DC 20007. Phone: (202) 333-9220. Fax: (202) 333-9221. Web: www.tvturnoff.org.

NESS, EVALINE: BIRTH ANNIVERSARY. Apr 24, 1911. Author and illustrator (Caldecott for *Sam, Bangs & Moonshine*), born at Union City, OH. Died Aug 12, 1986, at Kingston, NY.

BIRTHDAYS TODAY

A. Paul Cellucci, 58, US ambassador to Canada, former Governor of Massachusetts (R), born Hudson, MA, Apr 24, 1948.

Kelly Clarkson, 24, singer, born Burleson, TX, Apr 24, 1982.

Larry (Chipper) Jones, 34, baseball player, born DeLand, FL, Apr 24, 1972.

Eric Snow, 33, basketball player, born Canton, OH, Apr 24, 1973.

Omar Vizquel, 39, baseball player, born Caracas, Venezuela, Apr 24, 1967.

APRIL 25 — TUESDAY

Day 115 — 250 Remaining

AMERICAN ALLIANCE FOR HEALTH, PHYSICAL EDUCATION, RECREATION AND DANCE NATIONAL CONVENTION & EXPOSITION. Apr 25–29. Salt Lake City, UT. For info: American Alliance for Health, Physical Education, Recreation & Dance, 1900 Association Dr, Reston, VA 20191-1598. Phone: (800) 213-7193. Web: www.aahperd.org.

ANZAC DAY. Apr 25. Australia, New Zealand and Samoa. Memorial day and veterans' observance, especially to mark WWI Anzac landing at Gallipoli, Turkey, in 1915 (ANZAC: Australia and New Zealand Army Corps).

EGYPT: SINAI DAY. Apr 25. National holiday celebrating the liberation of Sinai in 1982 after the peace treaty between Egypt and Israel.

FIRST LICENSE PLATES: ANNIVERSARY. Apr 25, 1901. New York began requiring license plates on automobiles, the first state to do so.

ISRAEL: HOLOCAUST DAY (YOM HASHOAH). Apr 25. Hebrew calendar date: Nisan 27, 5766. A day established by Israel's Knesset as a memorial to the Jewish dead of WWII. Anniversary in Jewish calendar of Nisan 27, 5705 (corresponding to Apr 10, 1945, in the Gregorian calendar), the day on which Allied troops liberated the first Nazi concentration camp, Buchenwald, north of Weimar, Germany, where about 56,000 prisoners, many of them Jewish, perished.

ITALY: LIBERATION DAY: ANNIVERSARY. Apr 25. National holiday. Commemorates the liberation of Italy from German troops in 1945.

LOVELACE, MAUD HART: BIRTH ANNIVERSARY. Apr 25, 1892. Author of the Betsy-Tacy books, born at Mankato, MN. Died at California, Mar 11, 1980.

MARCONI, GUGLIELMO: BIRTH ANNIVERSARY. Apr 25, 1874. Inventor of wireless telegraphy (1895) born at Bologna, Italy. Died at Rome, Italy, July 20, 1937.

NATIONAL TEACH CHILDREN TO SAVE DAY. Apr 25. Contact your local bank for materials for grades K–12. For info: American Bankers Assn Education Foundation, 1120 Connecticut Ave NW, Washington, DC 20036. Phone: (800) BANKERS. E-mail: edufoun@aba.com. Web: www.aba.com.

PORTUGAL: LIBERTY DAY. Apr 25. Public holiday. Anniversary of the 1974 revolution.

SPACE MILESTONE: HUBBLE SPACE TELESCOPE DEPLOYED (US). Apr 25, 1990. Deployed by *Discovery*, this telescope is the largest on-orbit observatory to date and is capable of imaging objects up to 14 billion light-years away. The resolution of images was expected to be seven to 10 times greater than images from Earth-based telescopes, since the Hubble Space Telescope is not hampered by Earth's atmospheric distortion. Launched Apr 12, 1990, from Kennedy Space Center, FL. Unfortunately, the telescope's lenses were defective so that the anticipated high quality of imaging was not possible. In 1993, however, the world watched as a shuttle crew successfully retrieved the Hubble from orbit, executed the needed repair and replacement work and released it into orbit once more. In December 1999, the space shuttle *Discovery* was launched to do major repairs on the telescope.

SWAZILAND: NATIONAL FLAG DAY. Apr 25. National holiday.

THEODORE ROOSEVELT NATIONAL PARK ESTABLISHED: ANNIVERSARY. Apr 25, 1947. Located in North Dakota, the Theodore Roosevelt National Park includes two sections of the Badlands on the Missouri River as well as Theodore Roosevelt's Elkhorn Ranch. For more info: www.nps.gov/thro/index.htm.

WALDSEEMULLER, MARTIN: REMEMBRANCE DAY. Apr 25, 1507. Little is known about the obscure scholar now called the "godfather of America," the German geographer and mapmaker Martin Waldseemuller, who gave America its name. In a book titled *Cosmographiae Introductio*, published Apr 25, 1507, Waldseemuller wrote: "Inasmuch as both Europe and Asia received their names from women, I see no reason why any one should justly object to calling this part Amerige, i.e., the land of Amerigo, or America, after Amerigo, its discoverer, a man of great ability." Believing it was the Italian navigator and merchant Amerigo Vespucci who had discovered the new continent, Waldseemuller sought to honor Vespucci by placing his name on his map of the world, published in 1507. First applied only to the South American continent, it soon was used for both the American continents. Waldseemuller did not learn about the voyage of Christopher Columbus until several years later. Of the thousand copies of his map that were printed, only one is known to have survived. Waldseemuller probably was born at Radolfzell, Germany, about 1470. He died at St. Die, France, about 1517–20. See also: "Vespucci, Amerigo: Birth Anniversary" (Mar 9).

BIRTHDAYS TODAY

Tim Duncan, 30, basketball player, born St. Croix, US Virgin Islands, Apr 25, 1976.

Jon Kyl, 64, US Senator (R, Arizona), born Oakland, NE, Apr 25, 1942.

George Ella Lyon, 57, author (*Come a Tide, Dreamplace*), born Harlan, KY, Apr 25, 1949.

APRIL 26 — WEDNESDAY

Day 116 — 249 Remaining

AUDUBON, JOHN JAMES: BIRTH ANNIVERSARY. Apr 26, 1785. American artist and naturalist, best known for his *Birds of America*, born at Haiti. Died Jan 27, 1851, at New York, NY. For more info: *Capturing Nature: The Writings and Art of John James Audubon*, edited by Peter Roop and Connie Roop (Walker, 0-8027-8205-1, $17.85 Gr. 4–6).

CHERNOBYL NUCLEAR REACTOR DISASTER: 20th ANNIVERSARY. Apr 26, 1986. At 1:23 AM, local time, an explosion occurred at the Chernobyl atomic power station at Pripyat in the Ukraine. The resulting fire burned for days, sending radioactive material into the atmosphere. More than 100,000 persons were evacuated from a 300-square-mile area around the plant. Three months later 31 people were reported to have died and thousands exposed to dangerous levels of radiation. Estimates projected an additional 1,000 cancer cases in nations downwind of the radioactive discharge. The plant was encased in a concrete tomb in an effort to prevent the still-hot reactor from overheating again and to minimize further release of radiation.

CONFEDERATE MEMORIAL DAY IN FLORIDA AND GEORGIA. Apr 26. Observed on the anniversary of the date in 1865 that Confederate General Joseph E. Johnston surrendered to General William T. Sherman in Durham, NC. Other southern states observe Confederate Memorial Day on different dates; see entries for Jan 19, Apr 24, May 10 and June 3.

"DRAGONBALL Z" TV PREMIERE: ANNIVERSARY. Apr 26, 1989. This popular anime program debuted on Japanese television on this date. The continuing saga of Goku, his son Gohan, friends Krillen, Piccolo and Vegeta battling evil in futuristic Japan proved to be an enormous hit when it was dubbed for American television and began airing on the Cartoon Network. Other related series include "Dragonball" and "Dragonball GT," although those are less commonly seen in the US. Action figures, models, trading cards and video games have all been licensed.

NATIONAL COUNCIL OF TEACHERS OF MATHEMATICS ANNUAL MEETING. Apr 26–29. St. Louis, MO. For info: National Council of Teachers of Mathematics, 1906 Association Dr, Reston, VA 20191-1593. Phone: (703) 620-9840. Fax: (703) 476-2970. E-mail: infocentral@nctm.org. Web: www.nctm.org.

RICHTER SCALE DAY. Apr 26. A day to recognize the importance of Charles Francis Richter's research and his work in development of the earthquake magnitude scale that is known as the

Richter scale. Richter, an American author, physicist and seismologist, was born Apr 26, 1900, near Hamilton, OH. An Earthquake Awareness Week was observed in recognition of his work. Richter died at Pasadena, CA, Sept 30, 1985.

SOUTH AFRICAN MULTIRACIAL ELECTIONS: ANNIVERSARY. Apr 26–29, 1994. For the first time in the history of South Africa, the nation's approximately 18 million blacks voted in multiparty elections. This event marked the definitive end of apartheid, the system of racial separation that had kept blacks and other minorities out of the political process. The election resulted in Nelson Mandela of the African National Congress being elected president and F.W. de Klerk (incumbent president) of the National Party vice president.

TANZANIA: UNION DAY. Apr 26. Celebrates the 1964 union between mainland Tanzania (formerly Tanganyika) and the islands of Zanzibar and Pemba.

BIRTHDAYS TODAY

Patricia Reilly Giff, 71, author (*Lily's Crossing, Pictures of Hollis Woods*, the Polk Street School series), born Brooklyn, NY, Apr 26, 1935.

Tom Welling, 29, actor ("Smallville"), born New York, NY, Apr 26, 1977.

APRIL 27 — THURSDAY

Day 117 — 248 Remaining

BABE RUTH DAY: ANNIVERSARY. Apr 27, 1947. Babe Ruth Day was celebrated in every ballpark in organized baseball in the US as well as Japan. Mortally ill with throat cancer, Ruth appeared at Yankee Stadium to thank his former club for the honor.

BEMELMANS, LUDWIG: BIRTH ANNIVERSARY. Apr 27, 1898. Author, illustrator and artist, born at Austria. Ludwig Bemelmans created the Madeline series, including *Mad About Madeline: The Complete Series*. In 1998 a Madeline film was released. Bemelmans died at New York, NY, Oct 1, 1962. For more info: *Bemelmans: The Life & Art of Madeline's Creator* by John Bemelmans Marciano (Viking, 0-670-88460-X, $40).

GRANT, ULYSSES SIMPSON: BIRTH ANNIVERSARY. Apr 27, 1822. The 18th president of the US (Mar 4, 1869–Mar 3, 1877), born Hiram Ulysses Grant at Point Pleasant, OH. He graduated from the US Military Academy in 1843. President Lincoln promoted Grant to lieutenant general in command of all the Union armies Mar 9, 1864. On Apr 9, 1865, Grant received General Robert E. Lee's surrender, at Appomattox Court House, VA, which he announced to the Secretary of War as follows: "General Lee surrendered the Army of Northern Virginia this afternoon on terms proposed by myself. The accompanying additional correspondence will show the conditions fully." Nicknamed "Unconditional Surrender Grant," he died at Mount McGregor, NY, July 23, 1885, just four days after completing his memoirs. He was buried at Riverside Park, New York, NY, where Grant's Tomb was dedicated in 1897. For info: www.ipl.org/ref/POTUS.

LANTZ, WALTER: BIRTH ANNIVERSARY. Apr 27, 1900. Originator of Universal Studios' animated opening sequence for their first major musical film, *The King of Jazz*. Walter Lantz is best remembered as the creator of Woody Woodpecker, the bird with the wacky laugh and the taunting ways. Lantz received a lifetime achievement Academy Award for his animation in 1979. He was born at New Rochelle, NY, and died Mar 22, 1994, at Burbank, CA.

April 2006

S	M	T	W	T	F	S
						1
2	3	4	5	6	7	8
9	10	11	12	13	14	15
16	17	18	19	20	21	22
23	24	25	26	27	28	29
30						

MAGELLAN, FERDINAND: DEATH ANNIVERSARY. Apr 27, 1521. Portuguese explorer Ferdinand Magellan was probably born near Oporto, Portugal, about 1480, but neither the place nor the date is certain. Usually thought of as the first man to circumnavigate the earth, he died before completing the voyage; thus his co-leader, Basque navigator Juan Sebastian de Elcano, became the world's first circumnavigator. The westward, 'round-the-world expedition began Sept 20, 1519, with five ships and about 250 men. Magellan was killed by natives of the Philippine island of Mactan.

MOON PHASE: NEW MOON. Apr 27. Moon enters New Moon phase at 3:44 PM, EDT.

MORSE, SAMUEL FINLEY BREESE: BIRTH ANNIVERSARY. Apr 27, 1791. American artist and inventor, after whom the Morse code is named, was born at Charlestown, MA, and died at New York, NY, Apr 2, 1872. Graduating from Yale University in 1810, he went to the Royal Academy of London to study painting. After returning to America he achieved success as a portraitist. Morse conceived the idea of an electromagnetic telegraph while on shipboard, returning from art instruction in Europe in 1832, and he proceeded to develop his idea. With financial assistance approved by Congress, the first telegraph line in the US was constructed, between Washington, DC, and Baltimore, MD. The first message tapped out by Morse from the Supreme Court Chamber at the US Capitol building May 24, 1844, was: "What hath God wrought?"

NATIONAL PLAYGROUND SAFETY DAY. Apr 27. An opportunity for families, community parks, schools and childcare facilities to focus on preventing public playground-related injuries. Sponsored by the National Program for Playground Safety (NPPS), this event helps educate the public about the more than 200,000 children (that's one child every 2½ minutes) who require emergency room treatment for playground-related injuries each year. Annually, the last Thursday in April. For info: National Program for Playground Safety, School of HPELS, WRC 205, University of Northern Iowa, Cedar Falls, IA 50614-0618. Phone: (800) 554-PLAY. Fax: (319) 273-7308. Web: www.playgroundsafety.org.

SCHOOL PRINCIPALS' RECOGNITION DAY IN MASSACHUSETTS. Apr 27. Proclaimed annually by the governor.

SIERRA LEONE: INDEPENDENCE DAY. Apr 27. National Day. Commemorates independence from Britain in 1961.

SLOVENIA: INSURRECTION DAY. Apr 27. National holiday. Commemorates the founding of the resistance against Axis troops in 1941.

SOUTH AFRICA: FREEDOM DAY. Apr 27. National holiday. Commemorates the day in 1994 when, for the first time, all South Africans had the opportunity to vote.

TAKE OUR DAUGHTERS AND SONS TO WORK DAY. Apr 27. A national public education campaign sponsored by the Ms Foundation for Women in which children aged 9–15 go to work with adult hosts—parents, grandparents, cousins, aunts, uncles, friends. Annually, the fourth Thursday in April. For info: Take Our Daughters and Sons to Work Day, Ms Foundation for Women, 120 Wall St, 33rd Floor, New York, NY 10005. Phone: (800) 676-7780 or (212) 742-2300. Fax: (212) 742-1531. E-mail: tods@ms.foundation.org. Web: www.DaughtersandSonstoWork.org.

TOGO: INDEPENDENCE DAY. Apr 27. National holiday. Gained independence from France in 1960.

BIRTHDAYS TODAY

John Burningham, 70, author (*Hey! Get Off Our Train; Cloudland*), born Farnham, Surrey, England, Apr 27, 1936.

Coretta Scott King, 79, lecturer, writer, widow of Dr. Martin Luther King, Jr, born Marion, AL, Apr 27, 1927.

Nancy Shaw, 60, author (*Sheep in a Jeep, Sheep in a Shop*), born Pittsburgh, PA, Apr 27, 1946.

APRIL 28 — FRIDAY

Day 118 — 247 Remaining

AFGHANISTAN: ISLAMIC STATE'S VICTORY DAY. Apr 28. National holiday. Commemorates the Mujaheddin capture of Kabul in 1992.

BIOLOGICAL CLOCK GENE DISCOVERED: ANNIVERSARY. Apr 28, 1994. Northwestern University announced that the so-called biological clock, that gene governing the daily cycle of waking and sleeping called the circadian rhythm, had been found in mice. Never before pinpointed in a mammal, the biological clock gene was found on mouse chromosome #5.

CONNECTICUT STORYTELLING FESTIVAL. Apr 28–30. Connecticut College, New London, CT. Annual festival features performances for families and adults, plus workshops and story-sharing by Connecticut and nationally renowned storytellers. Annually, the last full weekend in April. Est attendance: 300. For info: Annie Burnham, Adm, Connecticut Storytelling Center, Connecticut College Box 5295, 270 Mohegan Ave, New London, CT 06320. Phone: (860) 439-2764. Fax: (860) 439-2895. E-mail: csc@conncoll.edu.

MARYLAND RATIFIES CONSTITUTION: ANNIVERSARY. Apr 28, 1788. Maryland became the seventh state to ratify the Constitution, by a vote of 63 to 11.

MONROE, JAMES: BIRTH ANNIVERSARY. Apr 28, 1758. The fifth president of the US was born at Westmoreland County, VA, and served two terms in that office (Mar 4, 1817–Mar 3, 1825). Monrovia, the capital city of Liberia, is named after him, as is the Monroe Doctrine, which he enunciated at Washington, DC, Dec 2, 1823. Last of three presidents to die on US Independence Day, Monroe died at New York, NY, July 4, 1831. For info: www.ipl.org/ref/POTUS.

MUTINY ON THE *BOUNTY*: ANNIVERSARY. Apr 28, 1789. The most famous of all naval mutinies occurred on board HMS *Bounty*. Captain of the *Bounty* was Lieutenant William Bligh, a mean-tempered disciplinarian. The ship, with a load of breadfruit tree plants from Tahiti, was bound for Jamaica. Fletcher Christian, leader of the mutiny, put Bligh and 18 of his loyal followers adrift in a 23-foot open boat. Miraculously Bligh and all of his supporters survived a 47-day voyage of more than 3,600 miles, before landing on the island of Timor, June 14, 1789. In the meantime, Christian had put all of the remaining crew (excepting eight men and himself) ashore at Tahiti where he picked up 18 Tahitians (six men and 12 women) and set sail again. Landing at Pitcairn Island in 1790 (probably uninhabited at the time), they burned the *Bounty* and remained undiscovered for 18 years, when an American whaler, the *Topaz*, called at the island (1808) and found only one member of the mutinous crew surviving. However, the little colony had thrived and, when counted by the British in 1856, numbered 194 persons.

NATIONAL ARBOR DAY. Apr 28. Since 1872, a day to honor and plant trees. Observed the last Friday in April (although some states have different dates), which is generally a good planting date throughout the country. First observance of Arbor Day was in Nebraska, Apr 10, 1872, where it is still a state holiday. For info: National Arbor Day Foundation, 100 Arbor Ave, Nebraska City, NE 68410. Web: www.arborday.org.

SPACE MILESTONE: FIRST TOURIST IN SPACE. Apr 28, 2001. Millionaire US businessman Dennis Tito reportedly paid the Russian space agency $20 million to accompany *Soyuz TM* to the International Space Station. The rocket with Tito and two Russian cosmonauts was launched this day from the Baikonur launch in Kazakhstan and arrived at the ISS on Apr 30, 2001. The crew returned to Earth a week later. NASA initially objected to the inclusion of the 60-year-old tycoon on the mission but dropped its opposition.

BIRTHDAYS TODAY

Jessica Alba, 25, actress ("Dark Angel"), born Pomona, CA, Apr 28, 1981.

Lois Duncan, 72, author (*The Circus Comes Home, I Know What You Did Last Summer*), born Philadelphia, PA, Apr 28, 1934.

Amy Hest, 56, author (*In the Rain with Baby Duck, When Jessie Came Across the Sea*), born New York, NY, Apr 28, 1950.

Virginia Kroll, 58, author (*Beginnings: How Families Came to Be; Masai and I; Jaha and Jamil Went Down the Hill*), born Buffalo, NY, Apr 28, 1948.

Harper Lee, 80, author (*To Kill A Mockingbird*), 1961 Pulitzer Prize for fiction, born Monroeville, AL, Apr 28, 1926.

Jay Leno, 56, TV talk show host ("Tonight Show"), comedian, born New Rochelle, NY, Apr 28, 1950.

Catherine Reef, 55, writer of history and biography (*John Steinbeck*), born New York, NY, Apr 28, 1951.

Nate Richert, 28, actor ("Sabrina, the Teenage Witch"), born St. Paul, MN, Apr 28, 1978.

APRIL 29 — SATURDAY

Day 119 — 246 Remaining

ELLINGTON, "DUKE" (EDWARD KENNEDY): BIRTH ANNIVERSARY. Apr 29, 1899. "Duke" Ellington, one of the most influential individuals in jazz history, was born at Washington, DC. By 1923 he was leading a small group of musicians at the Kentucky Club at New York City who became the core of his big band. Ellington is credited with being one of the founders of big band jazz. He used his band as an instrument for composition and orchestration to create big band pieces, film scores, operas, ballets, Broadway shows and religious music. Ellington was responsible for more than 1,000 musical pieces. He drew together instruments from different sections of the orchestra to develop unique and haunting sounds such as that of his famous "Mood Indigo." "Duke" Ellington died May 24, 1974, at New York City. For more info: *Duke Ellington: The Piano Prince and His Orchestra* by Andrea Davis Pinkney (Hyperion, 0-7868-2150-7, $16.49 Gr. K–3).

ELLSWORTH, OLIVER: BIRTH ANNIVERSARY. Apr 29, 1745. Third chief justice of the US Supreme Court, born at Windsor, CT. Died there on Nov 26, 1807. For more info: oyez.northwestern.edu/justices/justices.cgi.

HIROHITO MICHI-NO-MIYA, EMPEROR: BIRTH ANNIVERSARY. Apr 29, 1901. Former Emperor of Japan, born at Tokyo. Hirohito's death Jan 27, 1989, ended the reign of the world's longest ruling monarch. He became the 124th in a line of monarchs when he ascended to the Chrysanthemum Throne in 1926. Hirohito presided over perhaps the most eventful years in the 2,500 years of recorded Japanese history, including the attempted military conquest of Asia, the attack on the US that brought that country into WWII, leading to Japan's ultimate defeat after the US dropped atomic bombs on Hiroshima and Nagasaki, and the amazing economic restoration following the war that led Japan to a preeminent position of economic strength.

JAPAN: GREENERY DAY. Apr 29. National holiday.

NATIONAL SAFE KIDS WEEK. Apr 29–May 6 (tentative). For info: National SAFE KIDS Campaign, 111 Michigan Ave NW, Washington, DC 20010-2970. Phone: (202) 662-0600. Web: www.safekids.org.

TAIWAN: CHENG CHENG KUNG LANDING DAY. Apr 29. Commemorates landing in Taiwan in 1661 of Ming Dynasty loyalist Cheng Cheng Kung (Koxinga), who ousted Dutch colonists who had occupied Taiwan for 37 years. Main ceremonies held at Tainan, in south Taiwan, where Dutch had their headquarters and where Cheng is buried.

ZIPPER PATENTED: ANNIVERSARY. Apr 29, 1913. Gideon Sundbach of Hoboken, NJ, received a patent for the zipper.

BIRTHDAYS TODAY

Andre Agassi, 36, tennis player, born Las Vegas, NV, Apr 29, 1970.
Curtis Joseph, 39, hockey player, born Keswick, ON, Canada, Apr 29, 1967.
Kate Mulgrew, 51, actress ("Star Trek: Voyager"), born Dubuque, IA, Apr 29, 1955.
Jill Paton Walsh, 69, author (*Fireweed*), born London, England, Apr 29, 1937.
Debbie Stabenow, 56, US Senator (D, Michigan), born Clare, MI, Apr 29, 1950.

April 2006

S	M	T	W	T	F	S
						1
2	3	4	5	6	7	8
9	10	11	12	13	14	15
16	17	18	19	20	21	22
23	24	25	26	27	28	29
30						

APRIL 30 — SUNDAY

Day 120 — 245 Remaining

BUGS BUNNY'S DEBUT: ANNIVERSARY. Apr 30, 1938. Warner Bros.' "wascally wabbit" first appeared on screen in the theatrical short "Porky's Hare Hunt," directed by Ben "Bugs" Hardaway and released on this date. Chuck Jones and Tex Avery further developed him into the character we know now—in such cartoons as "A Wild Hare" (1940), in which Bugs asks "What's up, Doc?" for the first time and first kisses perennial foe Elmer Fudd. The rabbit's noisy carrot munching was based on Clark Gable's carrot chewing in the film *It Happened One Night* (1934).

FIRST PRESIDENTIAL TELECAST: ANNIVERSARY. Apr 30, 1939. Franklin D. Roosevelt was the first president to appear on television in a telecast from the New York World's Fair. However, since scheduled programming had yet to begin, he was beamed to only 200 TV sets in a 40-mile radius. See also: "Regular TV Broadcasts Begin: Anniversary" (July 1).

HARRISON, MARY SCOTT LORD DIMMICK: BIRTH ANNIVERSARY. Apr 30, 1858. Second wife of Benjamin Harrison, 23rd president of the US, born at Honesdale, PA. Died at New York, NY, Jan 5, 1948.

INTERNATIONAL READING ASSOCIATION ANNUAL CONVENTION. Apr 30–May 4. Chicago, IL 51st annual. For info: International Reading Assn, 800 Barksdale Rd, PO Box 8139, Newark, DE 19714-8139. Phone: (302) 731-1600. E-mail: conferences@reading.org. Web: www.reading.org.

INTERNATIONAL SCHOOL SPIRIT SEASON. Apr 30–Sept 30. To recognize everyone who has helped to make school spirit better and to provide time to plan improved spirit ideas for the coming school year. For info: Jim Hawkins, Chairman, Pepsters, Committee for More School Spirit, PO Box 122652, San Diego, CA 92112. Phone: (619) 280-0999.

★**JEWISH HERITAGE WEEK.** Apr 30–May 7 (tentative). The week that contains Israeli Independence Day, which is May 3 in 2006.

LOUISIANA: ADMISSION DAY: ANNIVERSARY. Apr 30. Became 18th state in 1812.

MOTHER, FATHER DEAF DAY. Apr 30. A day to honor deaf parents and recognize the gifts of culture and language they give to their hearing children. Annually, the last Sunday of April. Sponsored by Children of Deaf Adults International, Inc (CODA). For info: T. Teske, Deaf Awareness Events, CODA. E-mail: tteske2724@aol.com. Web: www.coda-international.org.

NATIONAL HONESTY DAY (WITH HONEST ABE AWARDS). Apr 30. To celebrate honesty and those who are honest and honorable in their dealings with others. Nominations accepted for most honest people and companies. Winners to be awarded "Honest Abe" awards and given "Abies" on National Honesty Day. Annually, Apr 30. For info: M. Hirsh Goldberg, Author of *The Book of Lies*, 3103 Szold Dr, Baltimore, MD 21208. Phone: (410) 486-4150.

NETHERLANDS: QUEEN'S BIRTHDAY. Apr 30. A public holiday in celebration of the Queen's birthday and the Dutch National Day. The whole country parties as young and old participate in festivities such as markets, theater, music and games.

ORGANIZATION OF AMERICAN STATES FOUNDED: ANNIVERSARY. Apr 30, 1948. This regional alliance was founded by 21 nations of the Americas at Bogota, Colombia. Its purpose is to further economic development and integration among nations of the Western hemisphere, to promote representative democracy and to help overcome poverty. The Pan-American Union, with offices at Washington, DC, serves as the General Secretariat for the OAS. For more info: www.oas.org.

SPANK OUT DAY USA. Apr 30. A day on which all caretakers of children—parents, teachers and daycare workers—are asked not to use corporal punishment as discipline and to become acquainted with positive, effective disciplinary alternatives. For info: Nadine Block, EPOCH-USA, 155 W Main St, Ste 1603, Columbus, OH 43215. Phone: (614) 221-8829. E-mail: nblock@infinet.com. Web: www.stophitting.com.

SWEDEN: FEAST OF VALBORG. Apr 30. An evening celebration in which Sweden "sings in the spring" by listening to traditional hymns to the spring, often around community bonfires. Also known as Walpurgis Night, the Feast of Valborg occurs annually, Apr 30.

SWITZERLAND: LANDSGEMEINDE. Apr 30. In one of the last examples of direct democracy, the citizens of Switzerland's smallest canton, Appenzell Inner Rhoden, gather annually on the last Sunday of April to vote. As part of the tradition, which dates back to the 14th century, men wear swords. Uniquely, they don't cast secret ballots but raise their arms in full view of their neighbors. About 2,000 to 3,000 voters of 18 years and older come to the square of the canton capital, Appenzell, after attending a morning church service. Once affairs of the canton are voted on, festivities begin.

THEATER IN NORTH AMERICA FIRST PERFORMANCE: ANNIVERSARY. Apr 30, 1598. On the banks of the Rio Grande, near present-day El Paso, TX, the first North American theatrical performance was acted. The play was a Spanish commedia featuring an expedition of soldiers. On July 10 of the same year, the same group produced *Moros y Los Cristianos* (Moors and Christians), an anonymous play.

VIETNAM: LIBERATION DAY. Apr 30. National holiday. Commemorates the fall of Saigon in 1975, ending the Vietnam War.

WASHINGTON, GEORGE: PRESIDENTIAL INAUGURATION ANNIVERSARY. Apr 30, 1789. George Washington was inaugurated as the first president of the US under the new Constitution at New York, NY. Robert R. Livingston administered the oath of office to Washington on the balcony of Federal Hall, at the corner of Wall and Broad Streets.

BIRTHDAYS TODAY

Dorothy Hinshaw Patent, 66, author (*Bold and Bright Black-and-White Animals*), born Rochester, MN, Apr 30, 1940.

Isiah Thomas, 45, basketball coach, Hall of Fame basketball player, born Chicago, IL, Apr 30, 1961.

MAY 1 — MONDAY

Day 121 — 244 Remaining

★**ASIAN PACIFIC AMERICAN HERITAGE MONTH.** May 1–31. Presidential Proclamation issued honoring Asian Pacific Americans each year since 1979. Public Law 102-450 of Oct 28, 1992, designated the observance for the month of May each year.

ASTRONOMY WEEK. May 1–7. To take astronomy to the people. Astronomy Week is observed during the calendar week in which Astronomy Day falls, beginning on Monday and continuing through Sunday. See also: "Astronomy Day" (May 6).

BETTER HEARING AND SPEECH MONTH. May 1–31. A nationwide public information campaign held each May to inform the 41 million Americans with hearing and speech problems that help is available. Annually, the month of May. For info: American Speech-Language-Hearing Assn, 10801 Rockville Pike, Rockville, MD 20852-3279. Phone: (301) 897-5700. Web: www.professional.asha.org.

"FREEDOM RIDERS": 45th ANNIVERSARY. May 1, 1961. Militant students joined James Farmer of the Congress of Racial Equality (CORE) to conduct "freedom rides" on public transportation from Washington, DC, across the deep South to New Orleans. The trips were intended to test Supreme Court decisions and Interstate Commerce Commission regulations prohibiting discrimination in interstate travel. In several places riders were brutally beaten by local people and policemen. The rides were patterned after a similar challenge to segregation, the 1947 Journey of Reconciliation, which tested the US Supreme Court's June 3, 1946, ban against segregation in interstate bus travel. For more info: *Freedom Rides: Journey for Justice* by James Haskins (Hyperion, 0-7868-0048-8, $14.95 Gr. 6–8).

FREEDOM SHRINE MONTH. May 1–31. To bring America's heritage of freedom to public attention through presentations or rededications of Freedom Shrine displays of historic American documents by Exchange Clubs. For info: The National Exchange Club, 3050 Central Ave, Toledo, OH 43606-1700. Phone: (800) 924-2643. E-mail: nechq@aol.com. Web: www.nationalexchangeclub.com.

May 2006

S	M	T	W	T	F	S
	1	2	3	4	5	6
7	8	9	10	11	12	13
14	15	16	17	18	19	20
21	22	23	24	25	26	27
28	29	30	31			

GET CAUGHT READING MONTH. May 1–31. Celebrities appear in ads appealing to young people to remind them of the joys of reading. For info: Assn of American Publishers, 71 Fifth Ave, New York, NY 10003. Phone: (212) 255-0200. Web: www.publishers.org or www.getcaughtreading.org.

GREAT BRITAIN FORMED: ANNIVERSARY. May 1, 1707. A union between England and Scotland resulted in the formation of Great Britain. (Wales had been part of England since the 1500s.) Today's United Kingdom consists of Great Britain and Northern Ireland.

KEEP MASSACHUSETTS BEAUTIFUL MONTH. May 1–31. Proclaimed annually by the governor.

LABOR DAY. May 1. In 76 countries, May 1 is observed as a workers' holiday. When it falls on a Saturday or Sunday, the following Monday is observed as a holiday. Bermuda, Canada and the US are the only countries that observe Labor Day in September.

★**LAW DAY.** May 1. Presidential Proclamation issued each year for May 1 since 1958 at request. (Public Law 87–20 of Apr 7, 1961.)

LEI DAY. May 1. Hawaii. On this special day—the Hawaiian version of May Day—leis are made, worn, given, displayed and entered in lei-making contests. One of the most popular Lei Day celebrations takes place in Honolulu at Kapiolani Park at Waikiki. Includes the state's largest lei contest, the crowning of the Lei Day Queen, Hawaiian music, hula and flowers galore.

★**LOYALTY DAY.** May 1. Presidential Proclamation issued annually for May 1 since 1959 at request. (Public Law 85–529 of July 18, 1958.) Note that an earlier proclamation was issued in 1955.

MARSHALL ISLANDS: CONSTITUTION DAY. May 1. National holiday.

MAY DAY. May 1. The first day of May has been observed as a holiday since ancient times. Spring festivals, maypoles and May baskets are still common, but the political importance of May Day has grown since the 1880s, when it became a workers' day. Now widely observed as a workers' holiday or as Labor Day. In most European countries, when May Day falls on Saturday or Sunday, the Monday following is observed as a holiday, with bank and store closings, parades and other festivities.

MOTHER GOOSE DAY. May 1. To re-appreciate the old nursery rhymes. Motto is "Either alone or in sharing, read childhood nursery favorites and feel the warmth of Mother Goose's embrace." Annually, May 1. For info: Gloria T. Delamar, Founder, Mother Goose Society. Phone: (215) 782-1059. E-mail: mother.goose.society@juno.com. Web: www.delamar.org/mothergoosesociety. ***See Curriculum Connection.***

NATIONAL ALLERGY/ASTHMA AWARENESS MONTH. May 1–31. Kit of materials available for $15 from this nonprofit organization. For info: Frederick S. Mayer, Pres, Pharmacist Planning Services, Inc, c/o Allergy Council of America (ACA), 101 Lucas Valley Rd, #210, San Rafael, CA 94903. Phone: (415) 479-8628. Fax: (415) 479-8608. E-mail: ppsi@aol.com. Web: www.ppsinc.org.

NATIONAL BARBECUE MONTH. May 1–31. To encourage people to start enjoying barbecuing early in the season when Daylight Saving Time lengthens the day. Annually, the month of May. Sponsor: Hearth, Patio, and Barbecue Association. For info: NBM, DHM Group, Inc, 9 Professional Circle, Ste 101, Colts Neck, NJ 07722. Fax: (732) 866-4466.

NATIONAL BIKE MONTH. May 1–31. 50th annual celebration of bicycling for recreation and transportation. Local activities sponsored by bicycling organizations, environmental groups,

PTAs, police departments, health organizations and civic groups. About five million participants nationwide. Annually, the month of May. For info: Patrick McCormick, Comm Dir, League of American Bicyclists, 1612 K St, Ste 800, Washington, DC 20006. Phone: (202) 822-1333. Fax: (202) 822-1334. E-mail: bikeleague@bikeleague.org. Web: www.bikeleague.org.

NATIONAL EGG MONTH. May 1–31. Dedicated to the versatility, convenience, economy and good nutrition of "the incredible edible egg." Annually, the month of May. For info: Linda Braun, Consumer Serv Dir, American Egg Board, 1460 Renaissance Dr, Park Ridge, IL 60068. E-mail: aeb@aeb.org. Web: www.aeb.org.

NATIONAL HAMBURGER MONTH. May 1–31. Sponsored by White Castle, the original fast-food hamburger chain, founded in 1921, to pay tribute to one of America's favorite foods. With or without condiments, on or off a bun or bread, hamburgers have grown in popularity since the early 1920s and are now an American meal mainstay. For info: White Castle Mgnt Co, Mktg Dept, 555 W Goodale St, Columbus, OH 43215-1171. Phone: (614) 228-5781. Fax: (614) 228-8841. Web: www.whitecastle.com.

NATIONAL MENTAL HEALTH MONTH. May 1–31. For info: National Mental Health Assn, 2001 Beauregard St, 12th Fl, Alexandria, VA 22311. Phone: (800) 969-6642 or (703) 684-7722. E-mail: infoctr@nmha.org. Web: www.nmha.org.

NATIONAL MOVING MONTH. May 1–31. Recognizing America's mobile roots and kicking off the busiest moving season of the year. Each year more than 21 million Americans move between Memorial Day and Labor Day, with the average American moving every seven years. During this month moving experts will be educating Americans on how to plan a successful move, to pack efficiently and handle the uncertainties and questions that moving children may have. For info: Allied Van Lines. Web: www.alliedvan.com.

NATIONAL PHYSICAL FITNESS AND SPORTS MONTH. May 1–31. Encourages individuals and organizations to promote fitness activities and programs. For info: President's Council on Physical Fitness and Sports, HHH Building, 200 Independence Ave SW, Room 738H, Washington, DC 20201-0004. Phone: (202) 690-9000. Fax: (202) 690-5211. Web: www.fitness.gov.

NATIONAL PTA TEACHER APPRECIATION WEEK. May 1–7. PTAs across the country conduct activities to strengthen respect and support for teachers and the teaching profession. Annually, the first full week in May. For info: National PTA, 330 N Wabash Ave, Ste 2100, Chicago, IL 60611. Phone: (312) 670-6782. Fax: (312) 670-6783. E-mail: info@pta.org. Web: www.pta.org.

NATIONAL SALSA MONTH. May 1–31. Recognizing salsa as America's favorite condiment, used more often than even ketchup as a topping, dip, marinade and to spice up countless recipes. National Salsa Month celebrates more than 50 years of picante sauce, a salsa created in 1947, and celebrates Cinco de Mayo, a Mexican holiday now recognized across North America. For info: Pace Foods, c/o Dublin & Associates, 1017 N Main St, Ste 201, San Antonio, TX 78212. Phone: (210) 227-0221. Web: www.pacefoods.com.

★**OLDER AMERICANS MONTH.** May 1–31. Presidential Proclamation; from 1963 through 1973 this was called "Senior Citizens Month." In May 1974 it became Older Americans Month. In 1980 the title included Senior Citizens Day, which was observed May 8, 1980. Has been issued since 1963.

PEN-FRIENDS WEEK INTERNATIONAL. May 1–7. To encourage everyone to have one or more pen-friends not only in their own country but in other countries. For complete information on how to become a good pen-friend and information about how to write good letters, send $5 to cover expense of printing, handling and postage. Annually, May 1–7. For info: Dr. Stanley J. Drake, Pres, Intl Society of Friendship and Good Will, 8592 Roswell Rd, Ste 251, Atlanta, GA 30350 1867. Phone: (678) 795-1362. Web: www.frienshipandgoodwill.org.

PRESERVATION MONTH. May 1–31. Formerly National Historic Preservation Week, this campaign draws public attention to

MAY 1
MOTHER GOOSE DAY

Today is Mother Goose Day, a day to celebrate old nursery rhymes and perhaps rediscover Mother Goose if you've not thought of her in a while. The Mother Goose Society sponsors this special day annually on May 1, and their website at www.librarysupport.net/mothergoosesociety offers history, rhymes and "goose links" for fans. "Mother Goose" as a figure has a murky history—the character can't be found in history until the 17th century. Charles Perrault's 1697 collection of fairy tales mentions her and from there she grew into a figure associated with nursery literature in many European and later American traditions.

For young classes, this can be a day of looking at the fun rhymes—"Peter, Peter, Pumpkin Eater," "Little Bo-Peep," "Hickory, Dickory, Dock" and many more. One of the more famous rhymes associated with Mother Goose is "Hey Diddle, Diddle":

Hey! diddle, diddle,
The cat and the fiddle,
The cow jumped over the moon;
The little dog laughed
To see such sport,
And the dish ran away with the spoon.

Like the poetry of Edward Lear (see the May 12 Curriculum Connection), these nursery rhymes are simple and nonsensical. In fact, having a session on both Lear and Mother Goose could make for a fun afternoon.

One of the most popular Mother Goose editions is that from 1916 by Blanche Fisher Wright (facsimile edition, Scholastic, 0-590-22517-0, $9.95 Ages 4–8), complete with quaint Victorian-style color illustrations. It's probably the edition your students' grandmothers and great-grandmothers grew up with. *Tomie dePaola's Mother Goose* (Putnam, 0-399-21258-2, $21.99 Ages 4–8) is a great version for today's kids, featuring 200 rhymes arranged thematically.

Some of the Mother Goose rhymes, growing as they did from centuries-old folk tales and traditions, have darker undercurrents: after all, Humpty-Dumpty did have a great fall. One author/illustrator who created his own dark version of Mother Goose was famed *New Yorker* columnist Charles Addams, whose 1967 collection was recently re-released (*The Charles Addams' Mother Goose*, Simon & Schuster, 0-689-84874-9, $19.95 Ages 4–8). Addams uses macabre illustrations for the rhymes—depicting witches, goblins and other spooky sorts—some terrifying but some playful (the fallen Humpty hatches into a dinosaur!). It may be a little scary for tots, but for students who find most Mother Gooses too sweet, it's the perfect antidote. —Holly McGuire historic preservation including neighborhoods, districts, landmark buildings, open space and maritime heritage. Annually, the month of May. For info: Gary Kozel, National Trust for Historic Preservation, 1785 Massachusetts Ave NW, Washington, DC 20036. Phone: (202) 588-6000. Fax: (202) 588-6299. E-mail: pr@nthp.org. Web: www.nationaltrust.org.

RUSSIA: INTERNATIONAL LABOR DAY. May 1–2. Public holiday in Russian Federation. "Official May Day demonstrations of working people."

SAVE THE RHINO DAY. May 1. May day! May day! Rhinos still in danger! Help save the world's remaining rhinos on the verge of extinction! Get involved with local, national and international conservation efforts to stop the senseless slaughter of these gentle pachyderms. Call your local zoo or write Really, Rhinos! For info: Judyth Lessee, Founder, Really, Rhinos!, PO Box 40503, Tucson, AZ 85717-0503. Phone: (520) 327-9048. E-mail: rinophyl@dakotacom.net.

SCHOOL PRINCIPALS' DAY. May 1. A day of recognition for all elementary, middle and high school principals for their leadership and dedication to providing the best education possible for their students. Annually, May 1. For info: Janet Dellaria, 202 N Bennett St, Geneva, IL 60134. Phone: (630) 232-0425.

VEGETARIAN RESOURCE GROUP'S ESSAY CONTEST FOR KIDS. May 1. Children ages 18 and under are encouraged to submit a two- to three-page essay on topics related to vegetarianism. Essays accepted up to May 1. Winners announced Sept 15 and will receive a $50 savings bond. For info: The Vegetarian Resource Group, PO Box 1463, Baltimore, MD 21203. Phone: (410) 366-8343. E-mail: vrg@vrg.org. Web: www.vrg.org.

WILLIAMS, ARCHIE: BIRTH ANNIVERSARY. May 1, 1915. Archie Williams, along with Jesse Owens and others, debunked Hitler's theory of the superiority of Aryan athletes at the 1936 Berlin Olympics. As a black member of the US team, Williams won a gold medal by running the 400-meter in 46.5 seconds (.4 second slower than his own record of earlier that year). Williams, who was born at Oakland, CA, earned a degree in mechanical engineering from the University of California–Berkeley in 1939 but had to dig ditches for a time because they weren't hiring black engineers. In time Williams became an airplane pilot and for 22 years he trained Tuskegee Institute pilots including the black air corps of WWII. He joined the Army Air Corps in 1942. When asked during a 1981 interview about his treatment by the Nazis during the 1936 Olympics, he replied, "Well, over there at least we didn't have to ride in the back of the bus." Archie Williams died June 24, 1993, at Fairfax, CA.

YOUNG ACHIEVERS MONTH. May 1–31. International Leadership Network's Young Achievers Program recognizes and encourages leaders of tomorrow. Motivates positive behavior, leadership and accomplishment. Community recognition events honor student leaders in grades 5–10. Annually, the month of May. For info: Barbara Eichhorst, International Leadership Network, 1750 S Brentwood Blvd, Ste 502, St Louis, MO 63144. Phone: (314) 961-5978. Fax: (312) 961-8716. E-mail: inleadnet@aol.com. Web: www.YoungAchievers.us.

★ ★ ★

May 2006

S	M	T	W	T	F	S
	1	2	3	4	5	6
7	8	9	10	11	12	13
14	15	16	17	18	19	20
21	22	23	24	25	26	27
28	29	30	31			

BIRTHDAYS TODAY

Daniel Kirk, 54, author, illustrator (*Bigger, Breakfast at the Liberty Diner*), born Elyria, OH, May 1, 1952.

Curtis Martin, 33, football player, born Pittsburgh, PA, May 1, 1973.

Elizabeth Marie Pope, 89, author (*The Perilous Gard*), born Washington, DC, May 1, 1917.

MAY 2 — TUESDAY

Day 122 — 243 Remaining

CHILDHOOD DEPRESSION AWARENESS DAY. May 2. Also known as Green Ribbon Day. Annually, the first Tuesday in the first full week in May. For info: National Mental Heath Assn, 2001 Beauregard St, 12th Fl, Alexandria, VA 22311. Phone: (800) 969-6642 or (703) 684-7722. Web: www.nmha.org.

ISRAEL: YOM HA'ZIKKARON (REMEMBRANCE DAY). May 2. Hebrew date: Iyar 4, 5766. Honors the more than 20,000 Israeli soldiers killed in battle since the start of the nation's war for independence in 1947. Always the day before Israeli Independence Day. (Began at sundown of previous day.)

KING JAMES BIBLE PUBLISHED: ANNIVERSARY. May 2, 1611. King James I had appointed a committee of learned men to produce a new translation of the Bible in English which was published this day. This version, popularly called the King James Version, is known in England as the Authorized Version.

LEONARDO DA VINCI: DEATH ANNIVERSARY. May 2, 1519. Italian artist, scientist and inventor. Painter of the famed *Last Supper*, perhaps the first painting of the High Renaissance, and of the *Mona Lisa*. Inventor of the first parachute. Born at Vinci, Italy, in 1452 (exact date unknown), he died at Amboise, France. For more info: *Leonardo Da Vinci*, by Diane Stanley (Morrow, 0-688-10438-X, $15.93 Gr. K–3) or www.mos.org/sln/Leonardo/LeoHomePage.html.

ROBERT'S RULES DAY. May 2, 1837. Anniversary of the birth of Henry M. Robert (General, US Army), author of *Robert's Rules of Order*, a standard parliamentary guide. Born at Robertville, SC, he died at Hornell, NY, May 11, 1923.

SPOCK, BENJAMIN: BIRTH ANNIVERSARY. May 2, 1903. Pediatrician and author, born at New Haven, CT. His book on child-rearing, *Common Sense Book of Baby and Child Care* later called *Baby and Child Care*, has sold more than 30 million copies. In 1955 he became professor of child development at Western Reserve University at Cleveland, OH. He resigned from this position in 1967 to devote his time to the pacifism movement. Spock died at San Diego, CA, Mar 15, 1998.

BIRTHDAYS TODAY

David Beckham, 31, soccer player, born Leytonstone, London, England, May 2, 1975.

MAY 3 — WEDNESDAY

Day 123 — 242 Remaining

"CBS EVENING NEWS" TV PREMIERE: ANNIVERSARY. May 3, 1948. This news program began as a 15-minute telecast with Douglas Edwards as anchor. Walter Cronkite succeeded him in 1962 and expanded the show to 30 minutes; Eric Sevareid served as commentator. Dan Rather anchored the newscasts upon Cronkite's retirement in 1981 until March 2005.

ISRAEL: YOM HA'ATZMA'UT (INDEPENDENCE DAY). May 3. Hebrew calendar date: Iyar 5, 5766. Celebrates proclamation of independence from British mandatory rule by Palestinian Jews and establishment of the state of Israel and the provisional government May 14, 1948 (Hebrew calendar date: Iyar 5, 5708). Dates in the Hebrew calendar vary from their Gregorian equivalents from year to year, so, while Iyar 5 in 1948 was May 14, in 2005 it was May 14 and in 2006 it is May 3. (Began at sundown of previous day.)

JAPAN: CONSTITUTION MEMORIAL DAY. May 3. National holiday commemorating constitution of 1947.

MEXICO: DAY OF THE HOLY CROSS. May 3. Celebrated especially by construction workers and miners, a festive day during which anyone who is building must give a party for the workers. A flower-decorated cross is placed on every piece of new construction in the country.

NATIONAL PUBLIC RADIO FIRST BROADCAST: 35th ANNIVERSARY. May 3, 1971. National noncommercial radio network, financed by Corporation for Public Broadcasting, began programming.

POLAND: CONSTITUTION DAY (SWIETO TRZECIEGO MAJO). May 3. National Day. Celebrates ratification of Poland's first constitution, 1791.

PROJECT ACES DAY. May 3. 18th annual celebration of fitness when All Children Exercise Simultaneously. "The World's Largest Exercise Class" takes place the first Wednesday in May as schools in all 50 states and 50 different countries hold fitness classes, assemblies and other fitness education events involving millions of children, parents and teachers. Conducted in cooperation with the President's Council of Physical Fitness and Sports during National Physical Fitness and Sports Month. For info send SASE to: Dept C, Youth Fitness Coalition, PO Box 6452, Jersey City, NJ 07306-0452. Phone: (201) 433-8993. E-mail: yfcprojectaces@yahoo.com. Web: projectaces.com.

UNITED NATIONS: WORLD PRESS FREEDOM DAY. May 3. A day to recognize that a free, pluralistic and independent press is an essential component of any democratic society and to promote press freedom in the world.

BIRTHDAYS TODAY

Michael Cadnum, 57, author (*Heat, The Book of the Lion*), born Orange, CA, May 3, 1949.

Mavis Jukes, 59, author (*Like Jake and Me*), born Nyack, NY, May 3, 1947.

Pete Seeger, 87, folksinger, author (*Abiyoyo*), born New York, NY, May 3, 1919.

David Vitter, 45, US Senator (R, Louisiana), born New Orleans, LA, May 3, 1961.

Ron Wyden, 57, US Senator (D, Oregon), born Wichita, KS, May 3, 1949.

MAY 4 — THURSDAY

Day 124 — 241 Remaining

CHINA: YOUTH DAY. May 4. Annual public holiday "recalls the demonstration on May 4, 1919, by thousands of patriotic students in Beijing's Tiananmen Square to protest imperialist aggression in China."

CURAÇAO: MEMORIAL DAY. May 4. Victims of WWII are honored on this day. Military ceremonies at the War Monument. Not an official public holiday.

DISCOVERY OF JAMAICA BY CHRISTOPHER COLUMBUS: ANNIVERSARY. May 4, 1494. Christopher Columbus discovered Jamaica. The Arawak Indians were its first inhabitants.

JAPAN: GOLDEN WEEK HOLIDAY. May 4. National holiday.

MANN, HORACE: BIRTH ANNIVERSARY. May 4, 1796. American educator, author, public servant, known as the "father of public education in the US," was born at Franklin, MA. Founder of Westfield (MA) State College, president of Antioch College and editor of the influential *Common School Journal*. Mann died at Yellow Springs, OH, Aug 2, 1859.

★ **NATIONAL DAY OF PRAYER.** May 4. Presidential Proclamation always issued for the first Thursday in May since 1981. (Public Law 100–307 of May 5, 1988.) From 1957 to 1981, a day in October was designated, except in 1972 and 1975 through 1977.

SPACE DAY. May 4. Previous Space Days have included a live broadcast over the Web in which astronauts and scientists answered questions from kids worldwide, a live satellite broadcast about space exploration and local events in schools and communities. The Space Day website contains lesson plans for teachers and games and puzzles for kids. Annually, the first Thursday in May. For info: www.spaceday.com.

SPACE MILESTONE: *ATLANTIS* (US). May 4, 1989. First American planetary expedition in 11 years. Space shuttle *Atlantis* was launched, its major objective to deploy the *Magellan* spacecraft on its way to Venus to map the planet's surface. The shuttle was on its 65th orbit when it landed May 8, mission accomplished.

TYLER, JULIA GARDINER: BIRTH ANNIVERSARY. May 4, 1820. Second wife of John Tyler, 10th president of the US, born at Gardiners Island, NY. Died at Richmond, VA, July 10, 1889.

WHALE AWARENESS DAY IN MASSACHUSETTS. May 4. Proclaimed annually by the governor for the first Thursday in May.

BIRTHDAYS TODAY

Lance Bass, 27, musician ('N Sync), born Laurel, MS, May 4, 1979.

Ben Grieve, 30, baseball player, 1998 American League Rookie of the Year, born Arlington, TX, May 4, 1976.

Dawn Staley, 36, basketball player, born Philadelphia, PA, May 4, 1970.

Don Wood, 61, illustrator (*King Bidgood's in the Bathtub, The Napping House*), born Atwater, CA, May 4, 1945.

MAY 5 — FRIDAY

Day 125 — 240 Remaining

BLY, NELLIE: BIRTH ANNIVERSARY. May 5, 1867. Born at Cochran's Mills, PA, Nellie Bly was the pseudonym used by pioneering American journalist Elizabeth Cochrane Seaman. Like her namesake in a Stephen Foster song, Nellie Bly was a social reformer and human rights advocate. As a journalist, she is best known for her exposé of conditions in what were then known as insane asylums, where she posed as an inmate. As an adventurer, she is best known for her 1889–90 tour around-the-world in 72 days, in which she bettered the time of Jules Verne's fictional character Phileas Fogg by eight days. She died at New York, NY, Jan 27, 1922. For more info: www.pbs.org/wgbh/amex/world.

BONZA BOTTLER DAY™. May 5. To celebrate when the number of the day is the same as the number of the month. Bonza Bottler Day™ is an excuse to have a party at least once a month. For info: Gail M. Berger, 14 Fernwood Dr, Taylors, SC 29687. Phone: (864) 609-9874. E-mail: gberger5@aol.com.

CHINA: BIRTHDAY OF LORD BUDDHA. May 5. Religious observances are held in Buddhist temples and Buddha's statue is bathed. Annually, the eighth day of fourth lunar month. Date in other countries will differ from China's.

ETHIOPIA: PATRIOTS VICTORY DAY. May 5. National holiday. Commemorates the 1941 liberation of Addis Ababa.

JAPAN: CHILDREN'S DAY. May 5. National holiday. Observed on the fifth day of the fifth month each year. For more info: *Japanese Children's Day and the Obon Festival* by Dianne M. MacMillan (Enslow, 0-8949-0818-9, $18.95 Gr. PreK–3).

KOREA: CHILDREN'S DAY. May 5. A time for families to take their children on excursions. Parks and children's centers throughout the country are packed with excited and colorfully dressed children. A national holiday since 1975.

LIONNI, LEO: BIRTH ANNIVERSARY. May 5, 1910. Author and illustrator, born at Amsterdam, Netherlands. Lionni wrote his first children's book, *Little Blue and Little Yellow*, in 1959. He wrote and illustrated more than 30 children's books including *Frederick* and *Swimmy*. He died at Chianti, Italy, Oct 11, 1999.

May 2006

S	M	T	W	T	F	S
	1	2	3	4	5	6
7	8	9	10	11	12	13
14	15	16	17	18	19	20
21	22	23	24	25	26	27
28	29	30	31			

MEXICO: CINCO DE MAYO. May 5. Mexican national holiday recognizing the anniversary of the Battle of Puebla, May 5, 1862, in which Mexican troops under General Ignacio Zaragoza, outnumbered three to one, defeated invading French forces of Napoleon III. Anniversary is observed by Mexicans everywhere with parades, festivals, dances and speeches.

MOON PHASE: FIRST QUARTER. May 5. Moon enters First Quarter phase at 1:13 AM, EDT.

NETHERLANDS: LIBERATION DAY. May 5. National holiday. Marks liberation of the Netherlands from Nazi Germany in 1945.

SPACE MILESTONE: *FREEDOM 7* (US): 45th ANNIVERSARY. May 5, 1961. First US astronaut in space, second man in space, Alan Shepard, Jr, projected 115 miles into space in suborbital flight reaching a speed of more than 5,000 MPH. This was the first piloted Mercury mission.

THAILAND: CORONATION DAY. May 5. Thailand.

MAY 6 — SATURDAY

Day 126 — 239 Remaining

ASTRONOMY DAY. May 6. To take astronomy to the people. International Astronomy Day is observed on a Saturday near the first quarter moon between mid-April and mid-May. Cosponsored by 15 astronomical organizations. See also: "Astronomy Week" (May 1–7). Web: www.astroleague.org.

***HINDENBURG* DISASTER: ANNIVERSARY.** May 6, 1937. The dirigible *Hindenburg* exploded as it approached the mooring mast at Lakehurst, NJ, after a transatlantic voyage. Of its 97 passengers and crew, 36 died in the accident, which ended the dream of mass transportation via dirigible. For more info: *The Hindenburg* by Patrick O'Brien (Henry Holt, 0-8050-6415-X, $17 Gr. 2–5).

JARRELL, RANDALL: BIRTH ANNIVERSARY. May 6, 1915. Poet, born at Nashville, TN. Jarrell also wrote books for children, including *The Animal Family* and *The Gingerbread Rabbit*. He died Oct 14, 1965, at Chapel Hill, NC.

KENTUCKY DERBY. May 6. Churchill Downs, Louisville, KY. The running of America's premier thoroughbred horse race, inaugurated in 1875. First jewel in the "Triple Crown," traditionally followed by the Preakness (the second Saturday after Derby) and the Belmont Stakes (the fifth Saturday after Derby). Annually, the first Saturday in May.

NATIONAL NURSES DAY AND WEEK. May 6–12. A week to honor the outstanding efforts of nurses everywhere to strengthen the health of the nation. Annually, beginning May 6, National Nurses Day, and ending May 12, Florence Nightingale's birthday. Call or write for a free catalog. For info: American Nurses Assn, 600 Maryland Ave SW, Ste 100W, Washington, DC 20024. Phone: (800) 274-4262. Fax: (202) 651-7003. E-mail: dpope@ana.org. Web: www.nursingworld.org.

NO HOMEWORK DAY. May 6. Millions of kids, all of them overloaded with homework, get a much-needed night off tonight. Teachers, give 'em a break tonight, don't give homework! [©2002 by WH.] For info: Thomas & Ruth Roy, Wellcat Holidays, 2418 Long Ln, Lebanon, PA 17046. Phone: (717) 279-0184. E-mail: info@wellcat.com. Web: www.wellcat.com.

PEARY, ROBERT E.: 150th BIRTH ANNIVERSARY. May 6, 1856. Born at Cresson, PA. Peary served as a cartographic draftsman in the US Coast and Geodetic Survey for two years, then joined the US Navy's Corps of Civil Engineers in 1881. He first

MAY 6
POLAR EXPLORATION

Voyages to the North and South Poles are fraught with dangers that sometime prove fatal. Frigid temperatures, treacherous ice and snow, and fierce winds are only three of the perils encountered by intrepid explorers and scientists. Yet people still go. Why? What do they hope to find?

Some seek adventure and, perhaps, the distinction of being "the first." Admiral Robert Peary, born May 6, 1856, at Cresson, PA, was one of the men who sought this honor. After 18 years of Arctic polar exploration, he achieved his goal when he reached the North Pole, Apr 6, 1909. Matthew Henson, also an American explorer, made the journey with him. Henson later said he trekked ahead of Peary and claimed to have reached the Pole first. (The Pole's exact location can only be measured with instrumentation, by lines of latitude and longitude. There's no visible land form that expresses it. In fact, the North Pole is under the frozen Arctic Sea.) Both men wrote about their voyage: Peary published *The North Pole*, his account of the expedition; Henson wrote *A Negro Explorer at the North Pole*.

Today, scientists journey to the Poles seeking the answers to questions about Earth's past. Pollen, plant remains and fossils that are locked in the polar ice contain clues to Earth's ancient climates and land forms. In the Arctic, scientists study the flora, fauna and the peoples who live there. They learned why polar bears, the intriguing white bears found only in the Arctic, have black skin and tongues. And on Devon Island, the site of a huge meteor crater, they even conduct experiments to determine the best way to grow plants in a harsh environment as part of a plan for the exploration of Mars!

In the Antarctic, scientists study how land and sea animals have adapted to life in a frigid climate. They sample air bubbles frozen deep inside ice as they search for information about past atmospheric conditions. On some of Antarctica's remotest mountains, paleontologists have discovered dinosaur bones—proof that the climate has changed and that land masses have moved.

For science curricula, global warming is a hot news topic. Archival searches at newspaper websites, for example, *The New York Times*, *Washington Post* and *Chicago Tribune*, will yield oodles of articles about the subject. In addition to "global warming," helpful search keywords include Ross Ice Shelf, icebergs, Arctic and/or Antarctic ice sheet and Kyoto Accord. A classroom debate on the topic of global warming could be a very informative discussion. For fun, compare the real scientific information that student investigators discover about global warming with the blockbuster movie *The Day After Tomorrow*. (The "science" is iffy, but the movie is lots of fun. And it gets people thinking about the subject.)

Also for science units, comparing and contrasting Arctic and Antarctic flora and fauna, past and present, is a highly fascinating way for students to explore polar similarities and differences. For example, why do penguins only live in the Southern hemisphere? The topics of Earth's magnetic forces and the aurora borealis and the aurora australis (northern and southern lights) can be part of polar study units. See Elaine Scott's *Poles Apart: Why Penguins and Polar Bears Will Never Be Neighbors* (Viking, 0-670-05925-0, $17.99 Ages 10 & up) which explores all these topics in an entertaining manner. *Under the Ice*, by Kathy Conlan (Kids Can Press, 1-553-37001-5, $16.95 Ages 8–12), recounts one scientist's experiences in Antarctica.

Another exciting topic is comparing and contrasting the historical experiences of polar explorers. Students can investigate the difficulties of travel, plus the kinds of equipment needed, past and present, to navigate the unique challenges presented by these two environments. *Shipwreck at the Bottom of the World*, by Jennifer Armstrong (Crown, 0-375-81049-8, $12.95 Ages 10 & up), is the story of Ernest Shackelton's 1914 doomed Antarctic expedition. It is a captivating survival story and adventure writing at its best. For a lyrical picture book about early Antarctic exploration see Robert Burleigh's *Black Whiteness: Admiral Byrd Alone in Antarctica* (Atheneum, 0-689-81299-X, $17.95 Ages 5 & up), which would be a good inclusion in poetry units. Patricia Calvert's *Robert E. Peary: To the Top of the World* (Benchmark Books, 0-761-41242-5, $29.93 Ages 10 & up) is a biography of Peary and his expeditions.

Websites that have information and pictures about polar research include Arctic Theme Page at www.arctic.noaa.gov and Virtual Tour: Antarctica at http://astro.uchicago.edu/cara/vtour/.

—Sally Walker

worked as an explorer in tropical climates as he served as subchief of the Inter-Ocean Canal Survey in Nicaragua. After reading of the inland ice of Greenland, Peary became attracted to the Arctic. He organized and led eight Arctic expeditions and is credited with the verification of Greenland's island formation, proving that the polar ice cap extended beyond 82° north latitude and discovering the Melville meteorite on Melville Bay, in addition to his famous discovery of the North Pole, Apr 6, 1909. Peary died Feb 20, 1920, at Washington, DC. ***See Curriculum Connection.***

PENN, JOHN: BIRTH ANNIVERSARY. May 6, 1740. Signer of the Declaration of Independence, born at Caroline County, VA. Died Sept 14, 1788.

BIRTHDAYS TODAY

Tony Blair, 53, British prime minister, born Edinburgh, Scotland, May 6, 1953.

Martin Brodeur, 34, hockey player, born Montreal, QC, Canada, May 6, 1972.

George Clooney, 45, actor ("ER," *Batman and Robin*), born Augusta, KY, May 6, 1961.

Kristine O'Connell George, 52, author (*The Great Frog Race And Other Poems*), born Denver, CO, May 6, 1954.

Ted Lewin, 71, author and illustrator (*The Storytellers*), born Buffalo, NY, May 6, 1935.

Willie Mays, 75, Hall of Fame baseball player, born Westfield, AL, May 6, 1931.

Barbara McClintock, 51, author and illustrator (*The Fantastic Drawings of Danielle*), born Flemington, NJ, May 6, 1955.

Richard C. Shelby, 72, US Senator (R, Alabama), born Birmingham, AL, May 6, 1934.

MAY 7 — SUNDAY

Day 127 — 238 Remaining

BARRIER AWARENESS DAY IN KENTUCKY. May 7.

BE KIND TO ANIMALS WEEK®. May 7–13. To promote kindness and humane care toward animals. Annually, the first full week of May. Features "Be Kind to Animals Kid Contest." For info: Joyce Briggs, American Humane Assn, 63 Inverness Dr E, Englewood, CO 80112. Phone: (800) 227-4645 or (303) 792-9900. Fax: (303) 792-5333. E-mail: info@americanhumane.org. Web: www.americanhumane.org.

BEAUFORT SCALE DAY (FRANCIS BEAUFORT BIRTH ANNIVERSARY). May 7, 1774. A day to honor the British naval officer Sir Francis Beaufort, who devised in 1805 a scale of wind force from 0 (calm) to 12 (hurricane) that was based on observation, not requiring any special instruments. The scale was adopted for international use in 1874 and has since been enlarged and refined. Beaufort was born at Flower Hill, Meath, Ireland, and died at Brighton, England, Dec 17, 1857.

BEETHOVEN'S *NINTH SYMPHONY* PREMIERE: ANNIVERSARY. May 7, 1824. Beethoven's *Ninth Symphony in D Minor* was performed for the first time at Vienna, Austria. Known as the *Choral* because of his use of voices in symphonic form for the first time, the Ninth was his musical interpretation of Schiller's *Ode to Joy*. Beethoven was completely deaf when he composed it, and it was said a soloist had to tug on his sleeve when the performance was over to get him to turn around and see the enthusiastic response he could not hear.

BRAHMS, JOHANNES: BIRTH ANNIVERSARY. May 7, 1833. Regarded as one of the greatest composers of 19th-century music, Johannes Brahms was born at Hamburg, Germany. His works were firmly rooted in traditional classical principles and truly Romantic in spirit. Brahms completed his most important work, *Ein Deutsches Requiem* (*The German Requiem*, 1857–68), after his mother's death in 1865. It is considered to be one of the best examples of 19th-century choral music and was presented with great success throughout Germany. Brahms died at Vienna, Austria, Apr 3, 1897.

BROWNING, ROBERT: BIRTH ANNIVERSARY. May 7, 1812. English poet and husband of poet Elizabeth Barrett Browning, born at Camberwell, near London. Known for his dramatic monologues. Died at Venice, Italy, Dec 12, 1889.

DIEN BIEN PHU FALLS: ANNIVERSARY. May 7, 1954. Vietnam's victory over France at Dien Bien Phu ended the Indochina War. This battle is considered one of the greatest victories won by a former colony over a colonial power.

EL SALVADOR: DAY OF THE SOLDIER. May 7. National holiday. Commemorates the founding of the armed forces in 1824.

GERMANY'S FIRST SURRENDER: ANNIVERSARY. May 7, 1945. Russian, American, British and French ranking officers crowded into a second-floor recreation room of a small redbrick schoolhouse (which served as Eisenhower's headquarters) at Reims, Germany. Representing Germany, Field Marshall Alfred Jodl signed an unconditional surrender of all German fighting forces. After a signing that took almost 40 minutes, Jodl was ushered into Eisenhower's presence. The American general asked the German if he fully understood what he had signed and informed Jodl that he would be held personally responsible for any deviation from the terms of the surrender, including the requirement that German commanders sign a formal surrender to the USSR at a time and place determined by that government.

NATIONAL FAMILY WEEK. May 7–13. Traditionally the first Sunday and the first full week in May are observed as National Family Week in many Christian churches.

NATIONAL PET WEEK. May 7–13. To promote public awareness of veterinary medical service for animal health and care. Annually, the first full week in May. For info: The American Veterinary Medical Assn, 1931 N Meacham Rd, Schaumburg, IL 60173. Phone: (847) 285-6667. Web: www.avma.org.

TCHAIKOVSKY, PETER ILICH: BIRTH ANNIVERSARY. May 7, 1840. Ranked among the outstanding composers of all time, Peter Ilich Tchaikovsky was born at Vatkinsk, Russia. His musical talent was not encouraged and he embarked upon a career in law, not studying music seriously until 1861. Among his famous works are the three-act ballet *Sleeping Beauty*, two-act ballet *The Nutcracker* and the symphony *Pathetique*. He died at St. Petersburg, Nov 6, 1893.

BIRTHDAYS TODAY

Pete V. Domenici, 74, US Senator (R, New Mexico), born Albuquerque, NM, May 7, 1932.

Nonny Hogrogian, 74, author and illustrator (Caldecott for *One Fine Day*), born New York, NY, May 7, 1932.

MAY 8 — MONDAY

Day 128 — 237 Remaining

CZECH REPUBLIC: LIBERATION DAY: ANNIVERSARY. May 8. Commemorates the liberation of Czechoslovakia from the Germans in 1945.

DUNANT, JEAN HENRI: BIRTH ANNIVERSARY. May 8, 1828. Author and philanthropist, founder of the Red Cross Society, was born at Geneva, Switzerland. Nobel prize winner in 1901. Died at Heiden, Switzerland, Oct 30, 1910.

FRANCE: ARMISTICE DAY. May 8. Commemorates the surrender of Germany to Allied forces and the cessation of hostilities in 1945.

GERMANY'S SECOND SURRENDER: ANNIVERSARY. May 8, 1945. Stalin refused to recognize the document of unconditional surrender signed at Reims the previous day, so a second signing was held at Berlin. The event was turned into an elaborate formal ceremony by the Soviets who had lost some 20 million lives during WWII. As in the Reims document, the end of hostilities was set for 12:01 AM local time on May 9.

May 2006

S	M	T	W	T	F	S
	1	2	3	4	5	6
7	8	9	10	11	12	13
14	15	16	17	18	19	20
21	22	23	24	25	26	27
28	29	30	31			

LAVOISIER, ANTOINE LAURENT: EXECUTION ANNIVERSARY. May 8, 1794. French chemist and the "father of modern chemistry." Especially noted for having first explained the real nature of combustion and for showing that matter is not destroyed in chemical reactions. Born at Paris, France, Aug 26, 1743, Lavoisier was guillotined at the Place de la Revolution for his former position as a tax collector. The Revolutionary Tribunal is reported to have responded to a plea to spare his life with the statement: "We need no more scientists in France."

MOUNT PELÉE ERUPTION: ANNIVERSARY. May 8, 1902. In the worst volcanic disaster of the 20th century, Mount Pelée erupted on the tiny French Caribbean island of Martinique. In minutes, a cloud of ashes, gases and rocks destroyed the thriving port city of Saint-Pierre, killing all but one of its 30,000 inhabitants.

NO SOCKS DAY. May 8. If we give up wearing socks for one day, it will mean a little less laundry, thereby contributing to the betterment of the environment. Besides, we will all feel a bit freer, at least for one day. Annually, May 8. [©2002 by WH.] For info: Thomas & Ruth Roy, Wellcat Holidays, 2418 Long Ln, Lebanon, PA 17046. Phone: (717) 279-0184. E-mail: info@wellcat.com. Web: www.wellcat.com.

TRUMAN, HARRY S: BIRTH ANNIVERSARY. May 8, 1884. The 33rd president of the US, succeeded to that office upon the death of Franklin D. Roosevelt, Apr 12, 1945, and served until Jan 20, 1953. Born at Lamar, MO, Truman was the last of nine US presidents who did not attend college. Affectionately nicknamed "Give 'em Hell Harry" by admirers. Truman died at Kansas City, MO, Dec 26, 1972. His birthday is a holiday in Missouri. For info: www.ipl.org/ref/POTUS.

V-E DAY: ANNIVERSARY. May 8, 1945. Victory in Europe Day commemorates the unconditional surrender of Germany to Allied Forces, ending WWII in Europe. The surrender document was signed by German representatives at General Dwight D. Eisenhower's headquarters at Reims to become effective, and hostilities to end, at one minute past midnight on May 9, 1945, which was 9:01 PM, EDT, on May 8 in the US. President Harry S Truman on May 8 declared May 9, 1945, to be "V-E Day," but it later came to be observed on May 8 in the US. A separate German surrender to the USSR was signed at Karlshorst, near Berlin, May 8. See also: "Russia: Victory Day" (May 9).

WORLD RED CROSS DAY. May 8. A day for commemorating the birth of Jean Henry Dunant, the Swiss founder of the International Red Cross Movement in 1863, and for recognizing the humanitarian work of the Red Cross around the world. For info on activities in your area, contact your local Red Cross chapter. For info: American Red Cross National Headquarters, 2025 E St NW, Washington, DC 20006. Web: www.redcross.org.

BIRTHDAYS TODAY

Peter Connolly, 71, author (*The Ancient City: Life in Classical Athens & Rome*), born Surrey, England, May 8, 1935.

Bobby Labonte, 42, race car driver, born Corpus Christi, TX, May 8, 1964.

Milton Meltzer, 91, author (*Langston Hughes: A Biography; Brother, Can You Spare a Dime: The Great Depression*), born Worcester, MA, May 8, 1915.

MAY 9 — TUESDAY

Day 129 — 236 Remaining

BARRIE, J.M.: BIRTH ANNIVERSARY. May 9, 1860. Author, born at Kirriemuir, Scotland. Wrote the popular children's tale *Peter Pan*, which first became a movie in 1924. Barrie died at London, England, June 19, 1937.

BROWN, JOHN: BIRTH ANNIVERSARY. May 9, 1800. Abolitionist leader, born at Torrington, CT, and hanged Dec 2, 1859, at Charles Town, WV. Leader of attack on Harpers Ferry, Oct 16, 1859, which was intended to give impetus to movement for escape and freedom for slaves. His aim was frustrated and in fact resulted in increased polarization and sectional animosity. Legendary martyr of the abolitionist movement. For more info: *Fiery Vision: The Life and Death of John Brown* by Clinton Cox (Scholastic, 0-590-47574-6, $15.95 Gr. 5–8).

DU BOIS, WILLIAM PENE: BIRTH ANNIVERSARY. May 9, 1916. Illustrator and author of children's books, born at Nutley, NJ. Du Bois was the recipient of the Newbery Medal in 1948 for his book *The Twenty-One Balloons*. He died at Nice, France, Feb 5, 1993.

ESTES, ELEANOR: 100th BIRTH ANNIVERSARY. May 9, 1906. Author, born at West Haven, CT. Known for her book *The Hundred Dresses*, Estes won a Newbery Medal in 1952 for her children's book *Ginger Pye*. Died at Hamden, CT, July 15, 1988.

EUROPEAN UNION: ANNIVERSARY OBSERVANCE. May 9, 1950. Member countries of the European Union commemorate the announcement by French statesman Robert Schuman of the "Schuman Plan" for establishing a single authority for production of coal, iron and steel in France and Germany. This organization was a forerunner of the European Economic Community, founded in 1957, which later became the European Union.

GOODMAN, BENNY: BIRTH ANNIVERSARY. May 9, 1909. Jazz clarinetist and bandleader, born Benjamin David Goodman at Chicago, IL. His band was the first to play jazz at New York's Carnegie Hall. He died June 13, 1986, at New York, NY. For more info: *Once Upon a Time in Chicago: The Story of Benny Goodman* by Jonah Winter (Hyperion, 0-7868-0462-9, $14.99 All ages).

NATIONAL TEACHER DAY. May 9. To pay tribute to American educators, sponsored by the National Education Association, Teacher Day falls during the National PTA's Teacher Appreciation Week. Local communities and organizations are encouraged to use this opportunity to honor those who influence and inspire the next generation through their work. Annually, the Tuesday of the first full week in May. For info: National Education Assn (NEA), 1201 16th St NW, Washington, DC 20036. Phone: (202) 833-4000. Web: www.nea.org.

RUSSIA: VICTORY DAY. May 9. National holiday observed annually to commemorate the 1945 Allied Forces defeat of Nazi Germany in WWII and to honor the 20 million Soviet people who died in that war. Hostilities ceased and the German surrender became effective at one minute after midnight May 9, 1945. See also: "V-E Day: Anniversary" (May 8).

"VAST WASTELAND" SPEECH: 45th ANNIVERSARY. May 9, 1961. Speaking before the bigwigs of network TV at the annual convention of the National Association of Broadcasters, Newton Minow, the new chairman of the Federal Communications Commission, exhorted those executives to sit through an entire day of their own programming. He suggested that they "will observe a vast wasteland." Further, he urged them to try for "imagination in programming, not sterility; creativity, not imitation; experimentation, not conformity; excellence, not mediocrity."

BIRTHDAYS TODAY

Richard Adams, 86, author (*Watership Down*), born Newbury, England, May 9, 1920.

Candice Bergen, 60, actress ("Murphy Brown"), daughter of ventriloquist Edgar Bergen, born Beverly Hills, CA, May 9, 1946.

Tony Gwynn, 46, former baseball player, born Los Angeles, CA, May 9, 1960.

Steve Yzerman, 41, hockey player, born Cranbrook, BC, Canada, May 9, 1965.

MAY 10 — WEDNESDAY

Day 130 — 235 Remaining

CONFEDERATE MEMORIAL DAY IN NORTH AND SOUTH CAROLINA. May 10. Observed on the anniversary of the date of the capture of Jefferson Davis by Union troops. Other southern states observe Confederate Memorial Day on other dates; see listings on Jan 19, Apr 24, Apr 26 and June 3 for more info.

THE DAY OF THE TEACHER (EL DIA DEL MAESTRO). May 10. California honors its teachers every year on the Day of the Teacher. Patterned after "El Dia Del Maestro" celebrated in Mexico, the Day of the Teacher was originated by the Association of Mexican-American Educators and the California Teachers Association and designated by the California legislature. A tribute to all teachers and their lasting influence on children's lives. Annually, the second Wednesday of May. For info: California Teachers Assn, PO Box 921, Burlingame, CA 94011. Phone: (650) 697-1400. Fax: (650) 552-5002. Web: www.cta.org.

GOLDEN SPIKE DRIVING: ANNIVERSARY. May 10, 1869. Anniversary of the meeting of Union Pacific and Central Pacific railways, at Promontory Point, UT. On that day a golden spike was driven by Leland Stanford, president of the Central Pacific, to celebrate the linkage. The golden spike was promptly removed for preservation. Long called the final link in the ocean-to-ocean railroad, this event cannot be accurately described as completing the transcontinental railroad, but it did complete continuous rail tracks between Omaha and Sacramento. See also: "Transcontinental US Railway Completion: Anniversary" (Aug 15).

JEFFERSON DAVIS CAPTURED: ANNIVERSARY. May 10, 1865. Confederate President Jefferson Davis, his wife and cabinet officials were captured at Irwinville, GA, by the 4th Michigan Cavalry. The prisoners were taken to Nashville, TN, and later sent to Richmond, VA.

NATIONAL SCHOOL NURSE DAY. May 10. A day to honor and recognize the school nurse, School Nurse Day has been established to foster a better understanding of the role of school nurses in the educational setting. Annually, the Wednesday during National Nurses Week (May 6–12). For info: Sharon Conley, Naional Assn of School Nurses, Inc, 1416 Park St, Ste A, Castle Rock, CO 80109. Phone: (207) 883-2117. Fax: (207) 883-2683. Web: www.nasn.org.

ROSS, GEORGE: BIRTH ANNIVERSARY. May 10, 1730. Lawyer and signer of the Declaration of Independence, born at New Castle, DE. Died at Philadelphia, PA, July 14, 1779.

May 2006

S	M	T	W	T	F	S
	1	2	3	4	5	6
7	8	9	10	11	12	13
14	15	16	17	18	19	20
21	22	23	24	25	26	27
28	29	30	31			

SINGAPORE: VESAK DAY. May 10. Public holiday. Monks commemorate their Lord Buddha's entry into Nirvana by chanting holy sutras and freeing captive birds.

TRUST YOUR INTUITION DAY. May 10. Today is the day we pay homage to the wonderful gift of sixth sense, "gut" feelings or that still small voice that is sometimes the only clue we have to go on in this ever-changing world. [©1994] For info: Adrienne Sioux Koopersmith, 1437 W Rosemont, #1W, Chicago, IL 60660-1319. Phone: (773) 743-5341. Fax: (773) 743-5395. E-mail: la_koop@yahoo.com.

BIRTHDAYS TODAY

Caroline B. Cooney, 59, author (*The Face on the Milk Carton, Driver's Ed, Whatever Happened to Janie?*), born Geneva, NY, May 10, 1947.

Christopher Paul Curtis, 52, author (Newbery for *Bud, Not Buddy;* Newbery Honor for *The Watsons Go to Birmingham—1963*), born Flint, MI, May 10, 1954.

Bruce McMillan, 59, author and illustrator (*Jelly Beans for Sale*), born Boston, MA, May 10, 1947.

Rick Santorum, 48, US Senator (R, Pennsylvania), born Winchester, VA, May 10, 1958.

Kenan Thompson, 28, actor ("All That," "Kenan & Kel"), born Atlanta, GA, May 10, 1978.

MAY 11 — THURSDAY

Day 131 — 234 Remaining

EAT WHAT YOU WANT DAY. May 11. Here's a day you may actually enjoy yourself. Ignore all those on-again/off-again warnings. [©2002 by WH.] For info: Thomas & Ruth Roy, Wellcat Holidays, 2418 Long Ln, Lebanon, PA 17046. Phone: (717) 279-0184. E-mail: info@wellcat.com. Web: www.wellcat.com.

FAIRBANKS, CHARLES WARREN: BIRTH ANNIVERSARY. May 11, 1852. The 26th vice president of the US (1905–09), born at Unionville Center, OH. Died at Indianapolis, IN, June 4, 1918.

GLACIER NATIONAL PARK ESTABLISHED: ANNIVERSARY. May 11, 1910. This national park is located in northwest Montana, on the Canadian border. In 1932 Glacier and Waterton Lakes National Park in Alberta were joined together by the governments of the US and Canada as Waterton-Glacier International Peace Park. For more info: www.nps.gov/glac.

GRAHAM, MARTHA: BIRTH ANNIVERSARY. May 11, 1894. Martha Graham was born at Allegheny, PA, and became one of the giants of the modern dance movement in the US. She began her dance career at the comparatively late age of 22 and joined the Greenwich Village Follies in 1923. Her new ideas began to surface in the late '20s and '30s, and by the mid-1930s she was incorporating the rituals of the southwestern American Indians in her work. She is credited with bringing a new psychological depth to modern dance by exploring primal emotions and ancient rituals in her work. She performed until the age of 75, and premiered in her 180th ballet, *The Maple Leaf Rag,* in the fall of 1990. Died Apr 1, 1991, at New York, NY. For more info: *Martha Graham: A Dancer's Life* by Russell Freedman (Clarion, 0-395-74655-8, $18 Gr. 7–12).

HART, JOHN: DEATH ANNIVERSARY. May 11, 1779. Signer of the Declaration of Independence, farmer and legislator, born about 1711 (exact date unknown), at Stonington, CT, died at Hopewell, NJ.

★ ★ ★

JAPAN: CORMORANT FISHING FESTIVAL. May 11–Oct 15. Cormorant fishing on the Nagara River, Gifu. "This ancient method of catching Ayu, a troutlike fish, with trained cormorants, takes place nightly under the light of blazing torches."

MINNESOTA: ADMISSION DAY: ANNIVERSARY. May 11. Became 32nd state in 1858.

SUTTON HOO SHIP BURIAL DISCOVERED: ANNIVERSARY. May 11, 1939. In 1938 in rural Suffolk, England, archaeologist Basil Brown began excavating 18 mounds on the property of Mrs. Edith Pretty. On this date, in the largest mound, Brown discovered a series of rusted ship rivets and realized that he had found an undisturbed royal Anglo-Saxon ship burial. The ship—the largest such ever found—was 90 feet long and 14 feet wide (the wood had rotted away, leaving only an outline). Also discovered were gold, bronze, silver and gemmed artifacts and weapons. World War II interrupted the excavations, but in the late 20th century, more was discovered in the other mounds, including a rider buried next to his horse. The ship burial at Sutton Hoo is believed to be that of the pagan East Anglian King Raedwald, who ruled in the early 600s AD.

BIRTHDAYS TODAY

Sheila Burnford, 88, author (*The Incredible Journey*), born Scotland, May 11, 1918.

James Jeffords, 72, US Senator (I, Vermont), born Rutland, VT, May 11, 1934.

Austin O'Brien, 25, actor ("The Baby-Sitters Club," *My Girl 2*), born Eugene, OR, May 11, 1981.

Natasha Richardson, 43, actress (*The Parent Trap*), born London, England, May 11, 1963.

Peter Sis, 57, illustrator and author (*The Starry Messenger*), born Prague, Czechoslovakia, May 11, 1949.

Zilpha Keatley Snyder, 79, author (*The Witches of Worm, The Headless Cupid*), born Lemoore, CA, May 11, 1927.

MAY 12 — FRIDAY

Day 132 — 233 Remaining

DENMARK: COMMON PRAYER DAY. May 12. Public holiday. The fourth Friday after Easter, known as "Store Bededag," is a day for prayer and festivity.

LEAR, EDWARD: BIRTH ANNIVERSARY. May 12, 1812. English artist and author, remembered for his children's poem *The Owl and the Pussycat*. Also the writer of limericks (see below). Born at Highgate, England, Lear died at San Remo, Italy, Jan 29, 1888. ***See Curriculum Connection.***

LIMERICK DAY. May 12. Observed on the birthday of one of its champions, Edward Lear, who was born in 1812. The limerick, which dates from the early 18th century, has been described as the "only fixed verse form indigenous to the English language." It gained its greatest popularity following the publication of Edward Lear's *Book of Nonsense* (and its sequels). Write a limerick today! Example: There was a young poet named Lear/Who said, it is just as I fear/Five lines are enough/For this kind of stuff/Make a limerick each day of the year.

NATIVE AMERICAN RIGHTS RECOGNIZED: ANNIVERSARY. May 12, 1879. When the United States tried to forcibly remove the Poncas from their homeland in Nebraska to an Oklahoma reservation, their chief, Standing Bear, brought suit to prevent it. The Unites States claimed that Standing Bear could not bring suit because as a Native American he had no legal standing in US law. In *Standing Bear v George Crook* at US District Court, Judge J. Dundy ruled on this day that "an Indian is a PERSON within the meaning of the laws of the United States." This landmark decision was appealed by the US to the Supreme Court, who dismissed it. Standing Bear was not forced to move his tribe, but other Native Americans were not able to use the decision to their advantage in other disputes with the US.

NIGHTINGALE, FLORENCE: BIRTH ANNIVERSARY. May 12, 1820. English nurse and public health activist who contributed perhaps more than any other single person to the development

MAY 12
THERE ONCE WAS A MAN NAMED LEAR

If your class is ready for a little nonsense, then May 12 is the best day for it! The English artist and poet Edward Lear was born this day in 1812, and in honor of his popularizing the limerick, May 12 has been dubbed Limerick Day.

Lear, born to a family of 21 children, strove to overcome illness and bleak prospects. He had epilepsy in a time when hardly anything was understood about it. Lear kept it a secret and used it as a personal challenge: he traveled the world and refused to let his illness be an obstacle. A talented artist and painter (he catalogued tropical birds from life), his ambition was to be a landscape artist, but he was destined to be better known for his books of nonsense that were filled with simple poems called limericks that children (and adults) loved. Here are some classic examples:

There was a Young Lady whose nose,
Was so long that it reached to her toes;
So she hired an Old Lady,
Whose conduct was steady,
To carry that wonderful nose.

There was an Old Man with a beard,
Who said, "It is just as I feared!—
Two Owls and a Hen,
Four Larks and a Wren,
Have all built their nests in my beard!

The rhyme scheme is constant—aabba—with usually the last word in line 1 repeated in line 5. (Lear's limericks have four lines—lines three and four are combined.) Nothing is too serious in a limerick, and Lear made sure it was pleasantly silly. The children he knew clamored for more.

Lear is also the famous author of the poems "The Owl and the Pussy-cat" (see the Feb 14 Curriculum Connection on odd couples), "The Jumblies" and many more, plus many delightful alphabets ("E was a little Egg/Upon the breakfast table . . ."). Lear died Jan 26, 1888, not long after his *Book of Nonsense* had been named one of the top books of that century.

The definitive edition of Lear's works is *Edward Lear: The Complete Verse and Other Nonsense*, edited by Vivien Noakes (Penguin, 0-14-200227-5, $16 All ages). Although Lear illustrated his own work with priceless line art drawings, many modern illustrators have contributed fun picture books perfect for the classroom. Among them are *Nonsense!*, illustrated by Valorie Fisher (Atheneum, 0-689-863-3802, $16.95 Ages 4–8); *The Pelican Chorus: And Other Nonsense*, illustrated by the late Fred Marcellino (Harper Trophy, 0-06-057571-9, $6.99 Ages 4–8); and *A Was Once an Apple Pie*, illustrated by Julie Lacome (Candlewick Press, 0-763-60103-9, Ages 4–8). And Jan Brett, Hilary Knight and Michael Hague are just a few of the great illustrators who have brought "The Owl and the Pussy-cat" to life.

—Holly McGuire

of modern nursing procedures and the dignity of nursing as a profession. During the Crimean War, she supervised nursing care in the British hospital at Scutari, Turkey, where she reduced the death rate dramatically. Returning to England, she reorganized the army medical service. She was the founder of the Nightingale training school for nurses and author of *Notes on Nursing*. Born at Florence, Italy, she died at London, England, Aug 13, 1910. For more info: *Heart and Soul: The Story of Florence Nightingale* by Gena K. Gorrell (Tundra, 0-88776-494-0, $18.95 Gr. 5–9).

BIRTHDAYS TODAY

Jennifer Armstrong, 45, author (*Steal Away, Shipwreck at the Bottom of the World*), born Waltham, MA, May 12, 1961.

Yogi Berra, 81, former baseball manager and Hall of Fame baseball player, born Lawrence Peter Berra, St. Louis, MO, May 12, 1925.

Tony Hawk, 37, skateboarder, born Carlsbad, CA, May 12, 1969.

Dave Heineman, 57, Governor of Nebraska (R), born Falls City, NE, May 12, 1948.

Farley Mowat, 85, author (*Owls in the Family*), born Belleville, ON, Canada, May 12, 1921.

MAY 13 — SATURDAY

Day 133 — 232 Remaining

MOON PHASE: FULL MOON. May 13. Moon enters Full Moon phase at 2:51 AM, EDT.

NATIONAL BABYSITTERS DAY. May 13. To give babysitters across the nation appreciation and special recognition for their quality child care. Annually, the Saturday before Mother's Day. For info: Barbara Baldwin, Safety Whys, PO Box 1177, Helotes, TX 78023-1177. Phone: (210) 695-9838. Fax: (210) 695-5673. Web: www.safetywhys.com.

NATIONAL TOURISM WEEK. May 13–21. To promote and enhance awareness of travel and tourism's importance to the economic, social and cultural well-being of the US. For info: Travel Industry Assn of America, 1100 New York Ave NW, Ste 450, Washington, DC 20005-3934. Phone: (202) 408-8422. E-mail: dminic@tia.org. Web: www.tia.org.

NETHERLANDS: NATIONAL WINDMILL DAY. May 13. About 950 windmills still survive and some 300 still are used occasionally and have been designated national monuments by the government. As many windmills as possible are in operation on National Windmill Day for the benefit of tourists. Annually, the second Saturday in May.

SPACE MILESTONE: *ENDEAVOUR* (US). May 13, 1992. Three astronauts from the shuttle *Endeavour* simultaneously walked in space for the first time.

BIRTHDAYS TODAY

Mike Bibby, 28, basketball player, born Cherry Hill, NJ, May 13, 1978.

Francine Pascal, 68, author (the Sweet Valley High series), born New York, NY, May 13, 1938.

Stevie Wonder, 55, singer, musician (16 Grammy Awards; "I Just Called to Say I Love You"), born Steveland Morris Hardaway, Saginaw, MI, May 13, 1951.

May 2006

S	M	T	W	T	F	S
	1	2	3	4	5	6
7	8	9	10	11	12	13
14	15	16	17	18	19	20
21	22	23	24	25	26	27
28	29	30	31			

MAY 14 — SUNDAY

Day 134 — 231 Remaining

CARLSBAD CAVERNS NATIONAL PARK ESTABLISHED: ANNIVERSARY. May 14, 1930. Located in southwestern New Mexico, Carlsbad Caverns was proclaimed a national monument, Oct 25, 1923, and later established as national park and preserve. For more info: www.nps.gov/carl/index.htm. ***See Curriculum Connection.***

FAHRENHEIT, GABRIEL DANIEL: BIRTH ANNIVERSARY. May 14, 1686. German physicist whose name is attached to one of the major temperature measurement scales. He introduced the use of mercury in thermometers and greatly improved their accuracy. Born at Danzig, Germany, he died at Amsterdam, Holland, Sept 16, 1736.

FIRST FEMALE HOUSE PAGE APPOINTMENT: ANNIVERSARY. May 14, 1973. The House of Representatives received formal approval of the appointment of female pages in 1972. In the 93rd Congress, Felda Looper was appointed as the first female page with a regular term. Gene Cox had served as a female page for three hours 34 years earlier.

GIRLS INC GIRLS' RIGHTS WEEK. May 14–20. To focus national and local attention on the goals of Girls Incorporated as an organization for the rights and needs of girls. Begins the second Sunday in May. For info: Girls Inc, 120 Wall St, 3rd Fl, New York, NY 10005. Phone: (212) 509-2000. Web: www.girlsinc.org.

JAMESTOWN, VIRGINIA: FOUNDING ANNIVERSARY. May 14, 1607. The first permanent English settlement in what is now the US took place at Jamestown, VA (named for England's King James I), on this date. Captains John Smith and Christopher Newport were among the leaders of the group of royally chartered Virginia Company settlers who had traveled from Plymouth, England, in three small ships: *Susan Constant*, *Godspeed* and *Discovery*. For more info: *James Towne: Struggle for Survival* by Marcia Sewall (Simon & Schuster, 0-689-81814-9, $16 Gr. 3–5).

LEWIS AND CLARK EXPEDITION SETS OUT: ANNIVERSARY. May 14, 1804. Charged by President Thomas Jefferson with finding a route to the Pacific, Captain Meriwether Lewis and Lieutenant William Clark left St. Louis with a 33-member group skilled in botany, zoology, outdoor survival and other scientific skills. They arrived at the Pacific coast of Oregon in November 1805 and returned to St. Louis, Sept 23, 1806. For more info: *In Their Own Words: Lewis and Clark* by George Sullivan (Scholastic, 0-439-14749-2, $15.95 Gr. 3–6) and www.pbs.org/lewisandclark.

MAY 14
STALACTITES AND STALAGMITES

Today marks the anniversary of the 1930 establishment of Carlsbad Caverns National Park. Located in New Mexico's Chihuahua Desert, the Carlsbad cave systems are among the most spectacular in the world. In fact, the park was named a World Heritage Site. The park is comprised of more than 100 caves, including Lechuguilla Cave—the nation's deepest limestone cave (1,567 feet). The "Big Room" in Carlsbad Cavern is 25 stories high. Carlsbad is a feast of otherworldly sights and colors. It is also home to one million Mexican free-tailed bats, which leave the caverns at sunset in an amazing mass.

A visit to Carlsbad is probably not on your field trip list, but you can visit it online. The Carlsbad Caverns National Park official web page, www.carlsbad.caverns.national-park.com, has historical, geological, biological and other information besides photos and visitation information. The National Park Service's site, www.npa.gov/cave, has historical information as well as ideas for classroom instruction.

Perhaps instead of a visit, you can try for your own mini-classroom cavern formations. In a simple experiment from *The McGraw-Hill Big Book of Science Activities* by Robert W. Wood (McGraw-Hill, 0-07-071873-3, $15.95 Ages 8–12), you can "grow" stalagmites and stalactites. If you have difficulty remembering the difference between stalagmites (which form from the ground of a cave) and stalactites (which form from the ceiling), just remember the "g" in stalagmite means "ground" and the "c" in stalactite means ceiling. The formations in Carlsbad took 500,000 years to develop, but all you need are a few days.

Your class will need:

2 large glass jars
heavy cotton string
cardboard
Epsom salts
water
a tablespoon

Fill your jars about two-thirds full of water and place them a few inches apart on the cardboard. Stir several tablespoons of Epsom salts into each jar. Take the string and lower one end into one jar and the other end into the other jar—letting the part of the string between the jars sag to form a small "v."

After a few days, you and your class will see an "icicle" falling from the string and a cone mounding up on the cardboard base. These are your stalactites (from the string) and stalagmites (on the ground). This process mimics the conditions in a limestone cave, where drops of water containing dissolved limestone fall to the floor. Limestone is made of calcium carbonate, which dissolves in the water that flows over limestone rocks. Year after year, the calcium carbonate builds up when the water evaporates to create wonderful cave formations. In your classroom experiment, the salt solution in the jar travels up the string and is deposited where the water drips. The salt remains after the water evaporates, creating stalactites and stalagmites.

And if all this cave talk has your class excited, and if you enjoyed the Curriculum Connection in August about adopting animals, then you might want to investigate the Adopt-a-Bat program at Carlsbad Caverns (www.ccgma.org/adoptabat.html). For only $6, your class can have a pretty unique classroom "pet."

—Holly McGuire

MILLION MOM MARCH: ANNIVERSARY. May 14, 2000. Women rallied at Washington, DC, and 60 other cities to urge Congress to "get serious about common sense gun legislation." For info: Million Mom March, 1225 Eye St NW, Ste 1100, Washington, DC 20005. Phone: (888) 989-MOMS. Web: www.millionmommarch.com.

★**MOTHER'S DAY.** May 14. Presidential Proclamation always issued for the second Sunday in May. (Pub Res No. 2 of May 8, 1914.)

MOTHER'S DAY. May 14. Observed first in 1907 at the request of Anna Jarvis of Philadelphia, PA, who asked her church to hold a service in memory of all mothers on the anniversary of her mother's death. Annually, the second Sunday in May.

NATIONAL FAMILY MONTH®. May 14–June 18. A monthlong national observance to celebrate and promote strong, supportive families. Sponsored by KidsPeace®, a private, not-for-profit organization that has been helping kids overcome crisis since 1982. Annually, Mother's Day through Father's Day. For info: KidsPeace, 5300 KidsPeace Dr, Orefield, PA 18069. Phone: (800) 25P-EACE. Web: www.familymonth.net.

NATIONAL POLICE WEEK. May 14–20. See also: "Peace Officer Memorial Day" (May 15). For info: American Police Hall of Fame and Museum, 3801 Biscayne Blvd, Miami, FL 33137. Phone: (305) 573-0070. Web: www.aphf.org.

NATIONAL STUTTERING AWARENESS WEEK. May 14–20. Since 1988, a special nationwide commitment to educate the public about this complex disorder. Seeks to work toward the prevention of stuttering in children and to let adults know that help is available. Annually, the second full week in May. For info: Stuttering Foundation of America, 3100 Walnut Grove Rd, Ste 603, Memphis, TN 38111-0749. Phone: (800) 992-9392 or (901) 452-7343. Web: www.stutteringhelp.org.

★**NATIONAL TRANSPORTATION WEEK.** May 14–20. Presidential Proclamation issued for week including third Friday in May since 1960. (Public Law 86–475 of May 20, 1960, first requested; Public Law 87–449 of May 14, 1962, requested an annual proclamation.)

NORWAY: MIDNIGHT SUN AT NORTH CAPE. May 14–July 30. In the "Land of the Midnight Sun," this is the first day of the season with around-the-clock sunshine. At North Cape and parts of Russia, Alaska, Canada and Greenland surrounding the Arctic Ocean, the sun never dips below the horizon from May 14 to July 30, but the night is bright long before and after these dates. At the equator, on the other hand, the length of day and night never varies.

★**POLICE WEEK.** May 14–20. Presidential Proclamation 3537 of May 4, 1963, covers all succeeding years. (Public Law 87–726 of Oct 1, 1962.) Always the week including May 15 since 1962.

READING IS FUN WEEK. May 14–20. To highlight the importance and fun of reading. For info: Reading Is Fundamental, Inc, 1825 Connecticut Ave NW, Ste 400, Washington, DC 20009. Phone: (877) RIF-READ. Fax: (202) 287-3196. E-mail: contactus@rif.org. Web: www.rif.org.

SELDEN, GEORGE: BIRTH ANNIVERSARY. May 14, 1929. Born at Hartford, CT, author of beloved classic novels about animal characters from his native town. *The Cricket in Times Square* describes the adventures of a Connecticut cricket who, by chance, travels to the Times Square Subway Station in New York. Sequels include *Chester Cricket's New Home, Harry Cat's Pet Puppy* and *Tucker's Countryside*. He died at New York, NY, Dec 5, 1989.

SMALLPOX VACCINE DISCOVERED: ANNIVERSARY. May 14, 1796. In the 18th century, smallpox was a widespread and often fatal disease. Edward Jenner, a physician in rural England, heard reports of dairy farmers who apparently became immune to smallpox as a result of exposure to cowpox, a related but milder disease. After two decades of studying the phenomenon, Jenner injected cowpox into a healthy eight-year-old boy, who subsequently developed cowpox. Six weeks later, Jenner inoculated the boy with smallpox. He remained healthy. Jenner called this new procedure *vaccination*, from *vaccinia*, another term for cowpox. Within 18 months, 12,000 people in England had been vaccinated and the number of smallpox deaths dropped by two-thirds.

SPACE MILESTONE: *SKYLAB* (US). May 14, 1973. The US launched *Skylab*, its first manned orbiting laboratory.

"THE STARS AND STRIPES FOREVER" DAY: ANNIVERSARY. May 14, 1897. Anniversary of the first public performance of John Philip Sousa's march "The Stars and Stripes Forever" at Philadelphia, PA. The occasion was the unveiling of a statue of George Washington. President William McKinley was present.

WAAC: ANNIVERSARY. May 14, 1942. During WWII women became eligible to enlist for noncombat duties in the Women's Auxiliary Army Corps (WAAC) by an act of Congress. Women also served as Women Appointed for Voluntary Emergency Service (WAVES), Women's Auxiliary Ferrying Squadron (WAFS) and Coast Guard or Semper Paratus Always Ready Service (SPARS), the Women's Reserve of the Marine Corps.

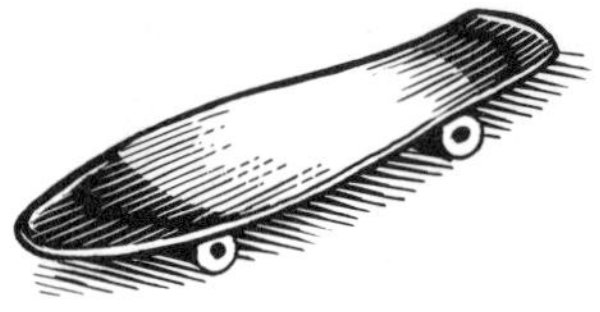

BIRTHDAYS TODAY

Eoin Colfer, 41, author (*Artemis Fowl; Artemis Fowl: The Arctic Incident*), born Wexford, Ireland, May 14, 1965.

Byron L. Dorgan, 64, US Senator (D, North Dakota), born Dickinson, ND, May 14, 1942.

George Lucas, 62, filmmaker (*The Empire Strikes Back, Star Wars*), born Modesto, CA, May 14, 1944.

Tony Perez, 64, Hall of Fame baseball player and former manager, born Camaguey, Cuba, May 14, 1942.

Valerie Still, 45, basketball player, born Lexington, KY, May 14, 1961.

May 2006

S	M	T	W	T	F	S
	1	2	3	4	5	6
7	8	9	10	11	12	13
14	15	16	17	18	19	20
21	22	23	24	25	26	27
28	29	30	31			

MAY 15 — MONDAY

Day 135 — 230 Remaining

BAUM, L(YMAN) FRANK: 150th BIRTH ANNIVERSARY. May 15, 1856. The American newspaperman who wrote the Wizard of Oz stories was born at Chittenango, NY. Although *The Wonderful Wizard of Oz* is the most famous, Baum also wrote many other books for children, including more than a dozen about Oz. He died at Hollywood, CA, May 6, 1919.

FIRST FLIGHT ATTENDANT: ANNIVERSARY. May 15, 1930. Ellen Church became the first airline stewardess (today's flight attendant), flying on a United Airlines flight from San Francisco to Cheyenne, WY.

JAPAN: AOI MATSURI (HOLLYHOCK FESTIVAL). May 15. Kyoto. The festival features a pageant reproducing imperial processions of ancient times that paid homage to the shrine of Shimogamo and Kamigamo.

MEXICO: SAN ISIDRO DAY. May 15. Day of San Isidro Labrador celebrated widely in farming regions to honor St. Isidore, the Plowman. Livestock is gaily decorated with flowers. Celebrations usually begin about May 13 and continue for about a week.

NYLON STOCKINGS: ANNIVERSARY. May 15, 1940. Nylon hose went on sale at stores throughout the country. Competing producers bought their nylon yarn from E.J. Du Pont de Nemours. W.H. Carothers of Du Pont developed nylon, called "Polymer 66," in 1935. It was the first totally man-made fiber and over time substituted for other materials and came to have widespread application.

PARAGUAY: INDEPENDENCE DAY. May 15. Commemorates independence from Spain, attained 1811.

★**PEACE OFFICER MEMORIAL DAY.** May 15. Presidential Proclamation 3537, of May 4, 1963, covers all succeeding years. (Public Law 87–726 of Oct 1, 1962.) Always May 15 of each year since 1963; however, first issued in 1962 for May 14.

PEACE OFFICER MEMORIAL DAY. May 15. An event honored by some 21,000 police departments nationwide. Memorial ceremonies at 10 AM in American Police Hall of Fame and Museum, Miami, FL. See also: "National Police Week" (May 14–20). Sponsor: National Association of Chiefs of Police. Est attendance: 1,000. For info: American Police Hall of Fame and Museum, 3801 Biscayne Blvd, Miami, FL 33137. Phone: (305) 573-0070. Web: www.aphf.org.

SEATTLE INTERNATIONAL CHILDREN'S FESTIVAL. May 15–22. Seattle, WA. The largest performing arts festival for families in the US. Artists from Europe, Asia, Africa, Australia and the Americas present theater, dance, music, puppets and acrobatics. This organization is also active throughout the year providing resources to teachers; see the "Curriculum Support" section of their website for more information. Est attendance: 51,000. For info: Seattle International Children's Festival, 305 Harrison, Seattle, WA 98109-3944. Phone: (206) 684-7338. E-mail: kidsfest@seattleinternational.org. Web: www.seattleinternational.org.

UNITED NATIONS: INTERNATIONAL DAY OF FAMILIES. May 15. The general assembly (Res 47/237) Sept 20, 1993, voted this as an annual observance beginning in 1994.

WILSON, ELLEN LOUISE AXSON: BIRTH ANNIVERSARY. May 15, 1860. First wife of Woodrow Wilson, 28th president of the US, born at Savannah, GA. She died at Washington, DC, Aug 6, 1914.

BIRTHDAYS TODAY

David Almond, 55, author (*Skellig*, Michael L. Printz Award for *Kit's Wilderness*), born Newcastle-upon-Tyne, England, May 15, 1951.

George Brett, 53, Hall of Fame baseball player, born Glen Dale, WV, May 15, 1953.

Nancy Garden, 68, author (*Dove and Sword, Annie on My Mind*), born Boston, MA, May 15, 1938.

Norma Fox Mazer, 75, author (*A Figure of Speech*), born New York, NY, May 15, 1931.

Leigh Ann Orsi, 25, actress ("Home Improvement," *Pet Shop*), born Los Angeles, CA, May 15, 1981.

Kathleen Sibelius, 58, Governor of Kansas (D), born Cincinnati, OH, May 15, 1948.

Emmitt Smith, 37, football player, born Escambia, FL, May 15, 1969.

MAY 16 — TUESDAY

Day 136 — 229 Remaining

BIOGRAPHERS DAY. May 16, 1763. Anniversary of the meeting, at London, England, of James Boswell and Samuel Johnson, beginning history's most famous biographer-biographee relationship. Boswell's *Journal of a Tour to the Hebrides* (1785) and his *Life of Samuel Johnson* (1791) are regarded as models of biographical writing. Thus, this day is recommended as one on which to start reading or writing a biography.

FIRST ACADEMY AWARDS: ANNIVERSARY. May 16, 1929. About 270 people attended a dinner at the Hollywood Roosevelt Hotel at which the first Academy Awards were given in 12 categories for films made in 1927–1928. The silent film *Wings* won Best Picture. A committee of only 20 members selected the winners that year. By the third year, the entire membership of the Academy voted. More information can be found at www.oscar.com.

FIRST WOMAN TO CLIMB MOUNT EVEREST: ANNIVERSARY. May 16, 1975. Japanese climber Junko Tabei, leading an all-woman expedition to Mount Everest, became the first woman to reach the summit on this date in 1975. Taking the South-East Ridge route, Tabei was delayed by an avalanche before her last leg up the mountain. "Even after reaching the peak," she later recalled, "instead of shouting with excitement I was simply happy that I didn't have to go any higher!"

GWINNETT, BUTTON: DEATH ANNIVERSARY. May 16, 1777. Signer of the Declaration of Independence, born at Down Hatherley, Gloucestershire, England, about 1735 (exact date unknown). Died following a duel at St. Catherine's Island, off of Savannah, GA.

LAG B'OMER. May 16. Hebrew calendar date: Iyar 18, 5766. Literally, the 33rd day of the omer (harvest time), the 33rd day after the beginning of Passover. Traditionally a joyous day for weddings, picnics and outdoor activities. (Began at sundown of previous day.)

MORTON, LEVI PARSONS: BIRTH ANNIVERSARY. May 16, 1824. The 22nd vice president of the US (1889–93), born at Shoreham, VT. Died at Rhinebeck, NY, May 16, 1920.

REY, MARGARET: 100th BIRTH ANNIVERSARY. May 16, 1906. Children's author, born at Hamburg, Germany. Together with her illustrator husband, H.A. Rey, she produced the Curious George series. Rey died at Cambridge, MA, Dec 21, 1996.

SEWARD, WILLIAM HENRY: BIRTH ANNIVERSARY. May 16, 1801. American statesman, secretary of state under Lincoln and Andrew Johnson. Seward negotiated the purchase of Alaska from Russia for $7,200,000. At the time some felt the price was too high and referred to the purchase as "Seward's Folly." Seward was governor of New York, 1839–43, and a member of the US Senate, 1848–1860. On the evening of Lincoln's assassination, Apr 14, 1865, Seward was stabbed in the throat by Lewis Posell, a fellow conspirator of John Wilkes Booth. Seward recovered and maintained his cabinet position under President Andrew Johnson until 1869. Born at Florida, NY, he died at Auburn, NY, Oct 10, 1872.

BIRTHDAYS TODAY

Caroline Arnold, 62, author (*Trapped in Tar*), born Minneapolis, MN, May 16, 1944.

David Boreanaz, 37, actor ("Angel," "Buffy the Vampire Slayer"), born Buffalo, NY, May 16, 1969 (some sources say 1971).

Bruce Coville, 56, author (*Jeremy Thatcher, Dragon Catcher; Aliens Ate My Homework*), born Syracuse, NY, May 16, 1950.

Gabriela Sabatini, 36, former tennis player, born Buenos Aires, Argentina, May 16, 1970.

Joan Benoit Samuelson, 49, Olympic gold medal runner, born Cape Elizabeth, ME, May 16, 1957.

MAY 17 — WEDNESDAY

Day 137 — 228 Remaining

***BROWN v BOARD OF EDUCATION OF TOPEKA* DECISION: ANNIVERSARY.** May 17, 1954. The US Supreme Court ruled unanimously that segregation of public schools "solely on the basis of race" denied black children "equal educational opportunity" even though "physical facilities and other 'tangible' factors may have been equal. Separate educational facilities are inherently unequal." The case was argued before the Court by Thurgood Marshall, who would go on to become the first black appointed to the Supreme Court. For more info: www.yale.edu/ynhti/pubs/A5/wolff.html.

JENNER, EDWARD: BIRTH ANNIVERSARY. May 17, 1749. English physician, born at Berkeley, England. He was the first to establish a scientific basis for vaccination with his work on smallpox. Jenner died at Berkeley, England, Jan 26, 1823.

NEW YORK STOCK EXCHANGE ESTABLISHED: ANNIVERSARY. May 17, 1792. Some two dozen merchants and brokers agreed to establish what is now known as the New York Stock Exchange. In fair weather they operated under a buttonwood tree on Wall Street, at New York, NY. In bad weather they moved to the shelter of a coffeehouse to conduct their business. For more info: www.nyse.com.

NORWAY: CONSTITUTION DAY OR INDEPENDENCE DAY. May 17. National holiday. The constitution was signed in 1814. Parades and children's festivities.

SUE EXHIBITED: ANNIVERSARY. May 17, 2000. Sue, the largest and most complete *Tyrannosaurus rex* ever discovered, went on exhibition this day at the Field Museum in Chicago. Sue's skeleton was discovered in South Dakota in 1990. It is 90 percent complete and is 41 feet long and 13 feet tall at the hips. The meat-eating dinosaur is 67 million years old and would have weighed 7 tons when it was alive. Sue is named after Susan Hendrickson, the fossil hunter who discovered the dinosaur. The Field Museum spent more than $8 million to purchase Sue in 1997. A life-size cast of Sue will be exhibited at Disney World. For info: Field Museum, Roosevelt Road at Lake Shore Drive, Chicago, IL 60605-2496. Phone: (312) 322-8859. Web: www.fmnh.org/Sue. For more info: *A Dinosaur Named Sue: The Story of the Colossal Fossil* by Pat Relf (Scholastic, 0-439-09985-4, $15.95 Gr. 1–5).

UNITED NATIONS: WORLD TELECOMMUNICATION DAY. May 17. A day to draw attention to the necessity and importance of further development of telecommunications in the global community. For more information, visit the UN's website for children at www.un.org/Pubs/CyberSchoolBus/.

BIRTHDAYS TODAY

Eloise Greenfield, 77, author (*Night on Neighborhood Street*), born Parmalee, NC, May 17, 1929.

Mia Hamm, 34, former soccer player, born Selma, AL, May 17, 1972.

Ben Nelson, 65, US Senator (D, Nebraska), born McCook, NE, May 17, 1941.

Tony Parker, 24, basketball player, born Bruges, Belgium, May 17, 1982.

Gary Paulsen, 67, author (Newbery Honors for *The Hatchet, Dogsong, The Winter Room*), born Minneapolis, MN, May 17, 1939.

Bob Saget, 50, actor ("Full House"), born Philadelphia, PA, May 17, 1956.

MAY 18 — THURSDAY

Day 138 — 227 Remaining

FONTEYN, MARGOT: BIRTH ANNIVERSARY. May 18, 1919. Born Margaret Hookman at Reigate, Surrey, England, Margot Fonteyn was a famed ballet dancer during the '30s and '40s. She died at Panama City, Panama, Feb 21, 1991.

HAITI: FLAG AND UNIVERSITY DAY. May 18. Public holiday.

HOBAN, LILLIAN: BIRTH ANNIVERSARY. May 18, 1925. Illustrator (*Best Friends for Frances, Bread and Jam for Frances*) and author (*Joe and Betsy the Dinosaur, Arthur's Loose Tooth*) born at Philadelphia, PA, May 18, 1925. Died at New York, NY, July 17, 1998.

INTERNATIONAL MUSEUM DAY. May 18. To pay tribute to museums of the world. "Museums are an important means of cultural exchange, enrichment of cultures and development of mutual understanding, cooperation and peace among people." Annually, May 18. Sponsor: International Council of Museums, Paris, France. For info: AAM/ICOM, 1575 Eye St NW, 4th Floor, Washington, DC 20005. Phone: (202) 289-9115. Fax: (202) 289-6578. Web: icom.museum/imd.html.

MOUNT SAINT HELENS ERUPTION: ANNIVERSARY. May 18, 1980. A major eruption of Mount St. Helens volcano, in southwestern Washington, blew steam and ash more than 11 miles into the sky. This was the first major eruption of Mount St. Helens since 1857, though Mar 26, 1980, there had been a warning eruption of smaller magnitude. For more info, visit Volcano World: volcano.und.nodak.edu.

May 2006

S	M	T	W	T	F	S
	1	2	3	4	5	6
7	8	9	10	11	12	13
14	15	16	17	18	19	20
21	22	23	24	25	26	27
28	29	30	31			

POPE JOHN PAUL II: BIRTH ANNIVERSARY. May 18, 1920. Karol Wojtyla, 264th pope of the Roman Catholic Church, born at Wadowice, Poland. Elected pope Oct 16, 1978. He was the first non-Italian to be elected pope in 456 years (since the election of Pope Adrian VI, in 1522) and the first Polish pope.

TURKMENISTAN: REVIVAL AND UNITY DAY. May 18. National holiday. Commemorates the 1992 constitution.

URUGUAY: BATTLE OF LAS PIEDRAS DAY. May 18. National holiday. Commemorates an 1811 battle fought for independence from Spain.

VISIT YOUR RELATIVES DAY. May 18. A day to renew family ties and joys by visiting often-thought-of-seldom-seen relatives. Annually, May 18. For info: A.C. Moeller, Box 71, Clio, MI 48420-1042.

BIRTHDAYS TODAY

Karyn Bye, 35, Olympic ice hockey player, born River Falls, WI, May 18, 1971.

Debbie Dadey, 47, author, with Marcia Thornton Jones (the Bailey School Kids series), born Morganfield, KY, May 18, 1959.

Brad Friedel, 35, soccer player, born Lakewood, OH, May 18, 1971.

Ron Hirschi, 58, author (*Spring, People of Salmon and Cedar*), born Bremerton, WA, May 18, 1948.

Reggie Jackson, 60, Hall of Fame baseball player, born Reginald Martinez Jackson, Wyncote, PA, May 18, 1946.

Jari Kurri, 46, Hall of Fame hockey player, born Helsinki, Finland, May 18, 1960.

Donyell Marshall, 33, basketball player, born Reading, PA, May 18, 1973.

Colin McNaughton, 55, author and illustrator (*Making Friends with Frankenstein*), born Wallsend-upon-Tyne, England, May 18, 1951.

Ken Mochizuki, 52, author (*Baseball Saved Us*), born Seattle, WA, May 18, 1954.

MAY 19 — FRIDAY

Day 139 — 226 Remaining

BOYS' CLUBS FOUNDED: 100th ANNIVERSARY. May 19, 1906. The Federated Boys' Clubs, which later became the Boys' and Girls' Clubs of America, was founded. For more info: www.bgca.org.

MALCOLM X: BIRTH ANNIVERSARY. May 19, 1925. Black nationalist and civil rights activist Malcolm X was born Malcolm Little at Omaha, NE. While serving a prison term he resolved to transform his life. On his release in 1952 he changed his name to Malcolm X and worked for the Nation of Islam until he was suspended by Black Muslim leader Elijah Muhammed Dec 4, 1963. Malcolm X later made the pilgrimage to Mecca and became an orthodox Muslim. He was assassinated as he spoke to a meeting at the Audubon Ballroom at New York, NY, Feb 21, 1965. For more info: *Malcolm X: By Any Means Necessary* by Walter Dean Myers (Scholastic, 0-590-46484-1, $10.75 Gr. 6–9) or *Malcolm X: A Fire Burning Brightly* by Walter Dean Myers (HarperCollins, 0-06-027708-4, $15.95 Gr. 3–6).

NATIONAL BIKE TO WORK DAY. May 19. At the state or local level, Bike to Work events are conducted by small and large businesses, city governments, bicycle clubs and environmental groups. About two million participants nationwide. Annually, the third Friday in May. For info: Patrick McCormick, Comm Dir, League of American Bicyclists, 1612 K St NW, Ste 401, Washington, DC 20006. Phone: (202) 822-1333. Fax: (202) 822-1334. E-mail: bikeleague@bikeleague.org. Web: www.bikeleague.org.

★**NATIONAL SAFE BOATING WEEK.** May 19–26. Presidential Proclamation during May since 1995. From 1958 through 1977, issued for a week including July 4 (Public Law 85–445 of June 4, 1958). From 1981 through 1994, issued for the first week in June (Public Law 96–376 of Oct 3, 1980). From 1995, issued for a seven-day period ending on the Friday before Memorial Day. Not issued from 1978 through 1980.

SCIENCE OLYMPIAD NATIONAL TOURNAMENT. May 19–20. Indiana University, Bloomington, IN. For grades 6–12, a rigorous academic interscholastic competition consisting of a series of individual and team events following the format of popular board games, TV shows and athletic games. These challenging and motivational events are well balanced between the various science disciplines of biology, earth science, chemistry, physics, computers and technology. There is also a balance between events requiring knowledge of science facts, concepts, processes, skills and science applications. For info: Science Olympiad, 5955 Little Pine Ln, Rochester, MI 48306. Phone: (248) 651-4013. Fax: (248) 651-7835. Web: www.soinc.org.

TEACHER'S DAY IN FLORIDA. May 19. A ceremonial day on the third Friday in May.

TURKEY: YOUTH AND SPORTS DAY. May 19. Public holiday commemorating the beginning of a national movement for independence in 1919, led by Mustafa Kemal Ataturk.

TWENTY-SEVENTH AMENDMENT TO US CONSTITUTION RATIFIED: ANNIVERSARY. May 19, 1992. The 27th amendment to the Constitution was ratified, prohibiting Congress from giving itself immediate pay raises.

VIETNAM: HO CHI MINH'S BIRTHDAY. May 19. National holiday. Leader of wars against France and the US; born May 19, 1890. Died Sept 2, 1969.

BIRTHDAYS TODAY

Arthur Dorros, 56, author (*Abuela, La Isla*), born Washington, DC, May 19, 1950.

Sarah Ellis, 54, author (*Back of Beyond: Stories of the Supernatural*), born Vancouver, BC, Canada, May 19, 1952.

Tom Feelings, 73, author (*Soul Looks Back in Wonder; The Middle Passage: White Ships, Black Cargo*), born Brooklyn, NY, May 19, 1933.

Kevin Garnett, 30, basketball player, born Mauldin, SC, May 19, 1976.

Eric Lloyd, 20, actor (*Dunston Checks In, The Santa Clause*), born Glendale, CA, May 19, 1986.

MAY 20 — SATURDAY

Day 140 — 225 Remaining

★**ARMED FORCES DAY.** May 20. Presidential Proclamation 5983, of May 17, 1989, covers the third Saturday in May in all succeeding years. Originally proclaimed as "Army Day" for Apr 6, beginning in 1936 (S. Con. Res. 30 of Apr 2, 1936). S. Con. Res. 5 of Mar 16, 1937, requested annual Apr 6 issuance, which was done through 1949. Always the third Saturday in May since 1950. Traditionally issued once by each Administration.

CAMEROON: NATIONAL HOLIDAY. May 20. Republic of Cameroon. Commemorates declaration of the United Republic of Cameroon May 20, 1972. Prior to this, the country had been a federal republic with two states, Eastern Cameroon and Western Cameroon.

COUNCIL OF NICAEA I: ANNIVERSARY. May 20–Aug 25, 325. The first ecumenical council of Christian Church, called by Constantine I, first Christian emperor of the Roman Empire. Nearly 300 bishops are said to have attended this first of 21 ecumenical councils (latest, Vatican II, began Sept 11, 1962), which was held at Nicaea, in Asia Minor (today's Turkey). The council condemned Arianism (which denied the divinity of Christ), formulated the Nicene Creed and fixed the day of Easter—always on a Sunday.

EAST TIMOR: INDEPENDENCE: ANNIVERSARY. May 20, 2002. East Timor became fully independent from Indonesia on this day. Indonesia had controlled the tiny nation since 1975. East Timor had previously been a colony of Portugal for 450 years.

ELIZA DOOLITTLE DAY. May 20. To honor Miss Doolittle (heroine of Bernard Shaw's *Pygmalion*) for demonstrating the importance and the advantage of speaking one's native language properly. For info: H.M. Chase, Doolittle Day Committee, 2460 Devonshire Rd, Ann Arbor, MI 48104-2706.

HOMESTEAD ACT: ANNIVERSARY. May 20, 1862. President Lincoln signed the Homestead Act, opening millions of acres of government-owned land in the West to settlers or "homesteaders," who had to reside on the land and cultivate it for five years.

LINDBERGH FLIGHT: ANNIVERSARY. May 20–21, 1927. Anniversary of the first solo trans-Atlantic flight. Captain Charles Augustus Lindbergh, 25-year-old aviator, departed from muddy Roosevelt Field, Long Island, NY, alone at 7:52 AM, May 20, 1927, in a Ryan monoplane named *Spirit of St. Louis*. He landed at Le Bourget airfield, Paris, at 10:24 PM Paris time (5:24 PM, NY time), May 21, winning a $25,000 prize offered by Raymond Orteig for the first nonstop flight between New York City and Paris, France (3,600 miles). The "flying fool" as he had been dubbed by some doubters became "Lucky Lindy," an instant world hero. See also: "Lindbergh, Charles Augustus: Birth Anniversary" (Feb 4).

MADISON, DOLLY (DOROTHEA) DANDRIDGE PAYNE TODD: BIRTH ANNIVERSARY. May 20, 1768. Wife of James Madison, 4th president of the US, born at Guilford County, NC. Died at Washington, DC, July 12, 1849.

MOON PHASE: LAST QUARTER. May 20. Moon enters Last Quarter phase at 5:20 AM, EDT.

NATIONAL SAFE BOATING WEEK. May 20–26. Brings boating safety to the public's attention, decreases the number of boating fatalities and makes the waterways safer for all boaters. Sponsors: National Safe Boating Council and US Coast Guard. For info: National Safe Boating Council. E-mail: nsbcdirect@safeboatingcouncil.org. Web: www.safeboatingcouncil.org.

★ ★ ★

WEIGHTS AND MEASURES DAY: ANNIVERSARY. May 20. Anniversary of international treaty, signed May 20, 1875, providing for the establishment of an International Bureau of Weights and Measures. The bureau was founded on international territory at Sevres, France.

BIRTHDAYS TODAY

Caralyn Buehner, 43, author (*The Escape of Marvin the Ape; It's a Spoon, Not a Shovel*), born St. George, UT, May 20, 1963.

Michael Crapo, 55, US Senator (R, Idaho), born Idaho Falls, ID, May 20, 1951.

Stan Mikita, 66, Hall of Fame hockey player, born Sokolce, Czechoslovakia, May 20, 1940.

Mary Pope Osborne, 57, author (the Magic Tree House series, *One World, Many Religions*), born Fort Sill, OK, May 20, 1949.

David Wells, 43, baseball player, born Torrance, CA, May 20, 1963.

MAY 21 — SUNDAY

Day 141 — 224 Remaining

AMERICAN RED CROSS: 125th FOUNDING ANNIVERSARY. May 21, 1881. Commemorates the founding of the American Red Cross by Clara Barton, its first president. The Red Cross had been founded in Switzerland in 1864 by representatives from 16 European nations. The organization is a voluntary, not-for-profit organization governed and directed by volunteers and provides disaster relief at home and abroad. 1.1 million volunteers are involved in community services such as collecting and distributing donated blood and blood products, teaching health and safety classes and acting as a medium for emergency communication between Americans and their armed forces.

FITZGERALD, JOHN D.: DEATH ANNIVERSARY. May 21, 1988. Born in either 1906 or 1907 at Price, UT, Fitzgerald was the author of eight semi-autobiographical novels about growing up in a small Mormon community. *The Great Brain* chronicles the exploits of his older brother Tom, a 12-year-old swindler with a "money-loving heart." John, who narrates the stories, both admires and is disgusted by his brother's antics. Sequels include *The Great Brain at the Academy* and *Me and My Little Brain*. Fitzgerald died at Titus, FL.

GEMINI, THE TWINS. May 21–June 20. In the astronomical/astrological zodiac, which divides the sun's apparent orbit into 12 segments, the period May 21–June 20 is traditionally identified as the sun sign period of Gemini, the Twins. The ruling planet is Mercury.

NATIONAL EDUCATIONAL BOSSES WEEK. May 21–27. A special week to honor bosses in the field of education such as principals and school superintendents. Annually, the third full week in May. For info: National Assn of Educational Office Professionals, PO Box 12619, Wichita, KS 67277. Phone: (316) 942-4822. Fax: (316) 942-7100. E-mail: naeop@naeop.org. Web: www.naeop.org.

NATIONAL ETIQUETTE WEEK. May 21–27. A national recognition of proper etiquette in all areas of American life (business, social, dining, international, wedding, computer, etc.). A self-assessment on the current status of civility in the US. Annually, the third week in May starting on Sunday. For info: Sandra Morisset, Protocol Training Services, PO Box 4981, New York, NY 10185. Phone: (212) 802-9098. Web: www.zyworld.com/etiquette.

SCHOOL SUPPORT STAFF WEEK. May 21–27. One way to show appreciation to instructional aides/assistants, custodial staff, maintenance workers and others who are many times overlooked for the jobs they do. They are vital to the running of the school and seldom get any recognition for a job well done. All employees of a school system who come in contact with our children are important. They all have lessons to teach our children, whether it is cleaning the school, making repairs or giving a child the extra help they need to succeed in school. Annually, the fourth week in May.

★ **WORLD TRADE WEEK.** May 21–27. Presidential Proclamation has been issued each year since 1948 for the third full week of May with three exceptions: 1949, 1955 and 1966.

BIRTHDAYS TODAY

Ricky Williams, 29, former football player, born San Diego, CA, May 21, 1977.

MAY 22 — MONDAY

Day 142 — 223 Remaining

BUCKLE UP AMERICA! WEEK. May 22–29. An observance to remind Americans of the importance of wearing seat belts. For info: Office of Occupant Protection, National Highway Traffic Safety Administration, 400 Seventh St SW, Washington, DC 20590. Phone: (202) 366-9550. Web: www.buckleupamerica.org or www.nhtsa.dot.gov.

CANADA: VICTORIA DAY. May 22. Commemorates the birth of Queen Victoria, May 24, 1819. Observed annually on the first Monday preceding May 25.

CRATER LAKE NATIONAL PARK ESTABLISHED: ANNIVERSARY. May 22, 1902. One of the world's deepest lakes, Crater Lake was first discovered in 1853. In 1885 William Gladstone Steele saw the Oregon lake and made it his personal goal to establish the lake and surrounding areas as a national park. His goal was attained 17 years later. For more info: www.nps.gov/crla/index.htm.

LOBEL, ARNOLD: BIRTH ANNIVERSARY. May 22, 1933. Illustrator and author (the Frog and Toad series, Caldecott for *Fables*), born at Los Angeles, CA. Died Dec 4, 1987, at New York, NY.

"MISTER ROGERS' NEIGHBORHOOD" TV PREMIERE: ANNIVERSARY. May 22, 1967. Presbyterian minister Fred Rogers hosted this long-running PBS children's program. Puppets and human characters interacted in the neighborhood of make-believe. Rogers played the voices of many of the puppets and educated young viewers on a variety of important subjects. The human cast members included: Betty Aberlin, Joe Negri, David Newell, Don Brockett, Francois Clemmons, Audrey Roth, Elsie Neal and Yoshi Ito. In 2001 the last episode was filmed. Amost 1,000 half-hour episodes of the program have aired.

May 2006

S	M	T	W	T	F	S
	1	2	3	4	5	6
7	8	9	10	11	12	13
14	15	16	17	18	19	20
21	22	23	24	25	26	27
28	29	30	31			

MOST POWERFUL EARTHQUAKE OF THE 20th CENTURY: ANNIVERSARY. May 22, 1960. An earthquake of a magnitude 9.5 struck southern Chile, killing 2,000 people and leaving 2,000,000 homeless. The earthquake also caused damage in Hawaii, Japan and the Philippines. While 20th-century earthquakes in Mexico City, Japan and Turkey resulted in far more deaths, this earthquake in Chile was of the highest magnitude on the Richter scale. For more info: wwwneic.cr.usgs.gov/neis/eqlists/10maps_world.html.

NATIONAL BACKYARD GAMES WEEK. May 22–29. Observance to celebrate the unofficial start of summer by fostering social interaction and family togetherness through backyard games. Get outside and be both physically and mentally stimulated, playing classic games of the past while discovering and creating new ways to be active and interact with neighbors and friends. For info: Frank Beres, Patch Products, PO Box 268, Beloit, WI 53511. Phone: (608) 362-6896. Fax: (608) 362-8178. E-mail: patch@patchproducts.com. Web: www.patchproducts.com.

NATIONAL MARITIME DAY. May 22. Anniversary of departure for first steamship crossing of the Atlantic from Savannah, GA, to Liverpool, England, by the steamship *Savannah* in 1819.

★**NATIONAL MARITIME DAY.** May 22. Presidential Proclamation always issued for May 22 since 1933. (Pub Res No. 7 of May 20, 1933.)

SRI LANKA: NATIONAL HEROES DAY. May 22. Commemorates the struggle of the leaders of the National Independence Movement to liberate the country from colonial rule. Public holiday.

SWITZERLAND: PACING THE BOUNDS. May 22. Liestal. Citizens set off at 8 AM and march along boundaries to the beating of drums and firing of pistols and muskets. Occasion for fetes. Annually, the Monday before Ascension Day.

UNITED NATIONS: INTERNATIONAL DAY FOR BIOLOGICAL DIVERSITY. May 22. A day to increase understanding and awareness of biodiversity issues. Originally observed on Dec 29, it was changed to May 22 to commemorate the adoption of the text of the Convention of Biological Diversity by the UN General Assembly. UN Secretary-General Kofi Annan said in 2003: "Biological diversity is essential for human existence and has a crucial role to play in sustainable development and the eradication of poverty. Biodiversity provides millions of people with livelihoods, helps to ensure food security, and is a rich source of both traditional medicines and modern pharmaceuticals." The consequences of ecosystem destabilization—floods, crop failure, loss of genetic resources and more—more often affect the world's poor. For info: United Nations, Dept of Public Info, New York, NY 10017.

YEMEN: NATIONAL DAY: ANNIVERSARY. May 22. Public holiday. Commemorates the reunification of Yemen in 1990.

BIRTHDAYS TODAY

Ann Cusack, 45, actress (*A League of Their Own*, "The Jeff Foxworthy Show"), born Brooklyn, NY, May 22, 1961.

Lisa Murkowski, 49, US Senator (R, Alaska), born Ketchikan, AK, May 22, 1957.

MAY 23 — TUESDAY

Day 143 — 222 Remaining

BROWN, MARGARET WISE: BIRTH ANNIVERSARY. May 23, 1910. Children's author, born at Brooklyn, NY. Brown wrote *Goodnight Moon* and *The Runaway Bunny*. She died at Nice, France, Nov 13, 1952.

CANADA: CALGARY INTERNATIONAL CHILDREN'S FESTIVAL. May 23–27. Calgary, AB. One of the largest children's festivals in North America, this event boasts the best in international theater, music, puppetry, dance, storytelling, mime, spectacle and more. For info: Calgary International Children's Festival, 205 8 Ave SE, Calgary, AB Canada T2G. Phone: (403) 294-7414. E-mail: admin@calgarychildfest.org. Web: www.calgarychildfest.org.

DEBORAH SAMSON DAY IN MASSACHUSETTS. May 23. Proclaimed annually by the governor to commemorate Deborah Samson, a Massachusetts schoolteacher who outfitted herself in men's clothing and fought in the American Revolution.

MESMER, FRIEDRICH ANTON: BIRTH ANNIVERSARY. May 23, 1734. German physician after whom Mesmerism was named. Magnetism and hypnotism were used by him in treating disease. Born at Iznang, Swabia, Germany, he died Mar 5, 1815, at Meersburg, Swabia, Germany.

NATIONAL GEOGRAPHIC BEE 2006: NATIONAL FINALS. May 23–24. National Geographic Society Headquarters, Washington, DC. The first-place winner from each state-level competition, Mar 31, advances to the national level. Alex Trebek of "Jeopardy!" fame moderates the finals which are televised on PBS stations. Students compete for scholarships and prizes totaling more than $50,000. For info: National Geographic Bee, National Geographic Society, 1145 17th St NW, Washington, DC 20036. Web: www.nationalgeographic.com/geographicbee.

NEW YORK PUBLIC LIBRARY: ANNIVERSARY. May 23, 1895. New York's then-governor Samuel J. Tilden was the driving force that resulted in the combining of the private Astor and Lenox libraries with a $2 million endowment and 15,000 volumes from the Tilden Trust to become the New York Public Library. For more info: www.nypl.org.

O'DELL, SCOTT: BIRTH ANNIVERSARY. May 23, 1898. Born at Los Angeles, CA. Scott O'Dell won the Newbery Medal in 1961 for his book *Island of the Blue Dolphins*. He published more than 26 children's books, including *The Black Pearl*. In 1972, O'Dell was awarded the Hans Christian Andersen International Award for lifetime achievement. He died at Santa Monica, CA, Oct 15, 1989. For a study guide to *Island of the Blue Dolphins*, see the website www.glencoe.com/sec/literature/litlibrary.

SOUTH CAROLINA RATIFIES CONSTITUTION: ANNIVERSARY. May 23, 1788. By a vote of 149 to 73, South Carolina became the eighth state to ratify the Constitution.

SWEDEN: LINNAEUS DAY. May 23. Stenbrohult. Commemorates the birth in 1707, of Carolus Linnaeus (Carl von Linne), Swedish naturalist who died at Uppsala, Sweden, Jan 10, 1778.

WORLD TURTLE DAY. May 23. An observance sponsored by American Tortoise Rescue to help people celebrate and protect turtles and tortoises, as well as their habitat around the world. For info: Susan Tellem, American Tortoise Rescue, 23852 Pacific Coast Highway, Malibu, CA 90265. Phone: (800) 938-3553. E-mail: turtleresq@aol.com. Web: www.tortoise.com or www.hsus.org/wildlife.

BIRTHDAYS TODAY

Susan Cooper, 71, author (Newbery for *The Grey King*), born Buckinghamshire, England, May 23, 1935.

Jewel, 32, singer, born Jewel Kilcher, Payson, UT, May 23, 1974.

MAY 24 — WEDNESDAY

Day 144 — 221 Remaining

BASEBALL FIRST PLAYED UNDER LIGHTS: ANNIVERSARY. May 24, 1935. The Cincinnati Reds defeated the Philadelphia Phillies by a score of 2–1, as more than 20,000 fans enjoyed the first night baseball game in the major leagues. The game was played at Crosley Field, Cincinnati, OH.

BELIZE: COMMONWEALTH DAY. May 24. Public holiday.

BERMUDA: BERMUDA DAY. May 24. National holiday celebrating the island's heritage. When the 24th falls on a Saturday, the holiday is observed the following Monday.

BROOKLYN BRIDGE OPENED: ANNIVERSARY. May 24, 1883. Nearly 14 years in construction, the $16 million Brooklyn Bridge over the East River connecting Manhattan and Brooklyn opened. Designed by John A. Roebling, the steel suspension bridge has a span of 1,595 feet. For more info: *The Brooklyn Bridge* by Elaine Pascoe (Blackbirch, 1-56711-173-4, $17.95 Gr. 4–6) or *Brooklyn Bridge* by Lynn Curlee (Simon & Schuster, 0-689-83183-8, $18 Gr. 3–6).

BULGARIA: ENLIGHTENMENT AND CULTURE DAY. May 24. National holiday celebrated by schoolchildren, students, people of science and art.

ECUADOR: BATTLE OF PICHINCHA DAY. May 24. National holiday. Commemorates the 1822 battle that marked the final defeat of Spain in Ecuador.

ERITREA: INDEPENDENCE DAY: ANNIVERSARY. May 24. National Day. Gained independence from Ethiopia in 1993 after 30-year civil war.

LEUTZE, EMANUEL: BIRTH ANNIVERSARY. May 24, 1816. Itinerant painter, born at Wurttemberg, Germany, who came to the US when he was nine years old and began painting by age 15. He painted some of the most famous of American works, such as *Washington Crossing the Delaware* (which is in the Metropolitan Museum of Art in New York), *Washington Rallying the Troops at Monmouth* and *Columbus Before the Queen*. Died July 18, 1868, at Washington, DC.

MORSE OPENS FIRST US TELEGRAPH LINE: ANNIVERSARY. May 24, 1844. The first US telegraph line was formally opened between Baltimore, MD, and Washington, DC. Samuel F.B. Morse sent the first officially telegraphed words "What hath God wrought?" from the Capitol building to Baltimore. Earlier messages had been sent along the historic line during testing, and one, sent May 1, contained the news that Henry Clay had been nominated as president by the Whig party, from a meeting at Baltimore. This message reached Washington one hour prior to a train carrying the same news.

May 2006

S	M	T	W	T	F	S
	1	2	3	4	5	6
7	8	9	10	11	12	13
14	15	16	17	18	19	20
21	22	23	24	25	26	27
28	29	30	31			

BIRTHDAYS TODAY

DaMarcus Beasley, 24, soccer player, born Fort Wayne, IN, May 24, 1982.

Diane DeGroat, 59, illustrator and author (*Happy Birthday to You, You Belong in the Zoo*), born Newton, NJ, May 24, 1947.

Tracy McGrady, 27, basketball player, born Bartow, FL, May 24, 1979.

MAY 25 — THURSDAY

Day 145 — 220 Remaining

AFRICAN FREEDOM DAY. May 25. Public holiday in Chad, Zambia, Zimbabwe and some other African states. Members of the Organization for African Unity (formed May 25, 1963) commemorate their independence from colonial rule with sports contests, political rallies and tribal dances.

ARGENTINA: REVOLUTION DAY. May 25. Commemoration of the revolt against Spanish rule and the declaration of independence of Argentina in 1810.

ARTHUR: ANNIVERSARY. May 25, 1976. Celebrate the anniversary of the first publication of Arthur—the star of one of the most successful children's books series and the Emmy Award-winning television show. Created by children's author and illustrator Marc Brown, the Arthur series of 75 books has sold more than 30 million copies. For ideas and materials: Web: www.pbskids.org/arthur.

ASCENSION DAY. May 25. Commemorates Christ's ascension into heaven. Observed since AD 68. Ascension Day is the 40th day after the Resurrection, counting Easter as the first day.

CONSTITUTIONAL CONVENTION: ANNIVERSARY. May 25, 1787. At Philadelphia, PA, the delegates from seven states, forming a quorum, opened the Constitutional Convention, which had been proposed by the Annapolis Convention, Sept 11–14, 1786. Among those who were in attendance: George Washington, Benjamin Franklin, James Madison, Alexander Hamilton and Elbridge Gerry. For more info: *A More Perfect Union: The Story of Our Constitution* by Betsy Maestro (Econo-Clad, 0-8335-6055-7, $15.80 Gr. 3–5).

GREATEST DAY IN TRACK AND FIELD: JESSE OWENS' REMARKABLE RECORDS: ANNIVERSARY. May 25, 1935. During the Big Ten Championships at the University of Michigan at Ann Arbor, MI, Jesse Owens, representing Ohio State University, broke three world records and tied a fourth in the space of 45 minutes—from 3:15 PM to 4:00 PM. The "Buckeye Bullet" (who was suffering from an injured back) set records in the running broad jump, the 220-yard dash, the 220-yard hurdles, and tied the record for the 100-yard dash. See also: "Owens, Jesse: Birth Anniversary" (Sept 12).

JORDAN: INDEPENDENCE DAY. May 25. National holiday. Commemorates treaty in 1946, proclaiming autonomy (from Britain) and establishing monarchy.

NATIONAL MISSING CHILDREN'S DAY. May 25. To promote awareness of the problem of missing children, to offer a forum for change and to offer safety information for children in schools and communities. Annually, May 25. For info: Child Find of America, Inc, PO Box 277, New Paltz, NY 12561-0277. Phone: (845) 255-1848 or (800) I-AM-LOST. Web: www.childfindofamerica.org.

NATIONAL TAP DANCE DAY. May 25. To celebrate this unique American art form that represents a fusion of African and European cultures and to transmit tap to succeeding generations through documentation and archival and performance support. Held on the anniversary of the birth of Bill "Bojangles" Robinson to honor his outstanding contribution to the art of tap dancing on stage and in films through the unification of diverse stylistic and racial elements.

POETRY DAY IN FLORIDA. May 25. In 1947 the Legislature decreed this day to be Poetry Day in all the public schools of Florida.

ROBINSON, BILL "BOJANGLES": BIRTH ANNIVERSARY. May 25, 1878. Considered one of the greatest tap dancers ever, Robinson was born at Richmond, VA, the grandson of a slave. Starting out in vaudeville, Robinson became a successful night-club performer and movie actor, appearing in several films with Shirley Temple and starring in *Stormy Weather* in 1943. He was the inspiration of many later Hollywood dancers, and his birthday is now National Tap Dance Day. He died at New York, NY, Nov 25, 1949.

***STAR WARS* RELEASED: ANNIVERSARY.** May 25, 1977. "May the Force be with you" entered the modern lexicon as a new kind of science fiction film opened at 32 theaters. George Lucas's space epic, starring Mark Hamill as Luke Skywalker, Harrison Ford as Han Solo and Carrie Fisher as Princess Leia, featured stunning special effects and was a smash hit worldwide. It went on to win six Academy Awards out of ten nominations—plus an additional special Academy Award for sound effects. The film was part of a larger saga, and in later years was retitled *Star Wars—Episode IV: A New Hope* as prequels were released.

BIRTHDAYS TODAY

Martha Alexander, 86, author and illustrator (*Nobody Asked Me If I Wanted a Baby Sister*), born Augusta, GA, May 25, 1920.

Carlos Bocanegra, 27, soccer player, born Upland, CA, May 25, 1979.

Ann McGovern, 76, author (*Too Much Noise*), born New York, NY, May 25, 1930.

Mike Myers, 43, actor (*Shrek, Wayne's World,* the Austin Powers series), born Scarsborough, ON, Canada, May 25, 1963.

Gordon Smith, 54, US Senator (R, Oregon), born Pendleton, OR, May 25, 1952.

Sheryl Swoopes, 35, basketball player, US Olympic basketball player, born Brownfield, TX, May 25, 1971.

Miguel Tejada, 30, baseball player, born Bani, Dominican Republic, May 25, 1976.

Joyce Carol Thomas, 68, author (*Marked by Fire, Brown Honey in Broomwheat Tea*), born Ponca City, OK, May 25, 1938.

Brian Urlacher, 28, football player, born Lovington, MI, May 25, 1978.

MAY 26 — FRIDAY

Day 146 — 219 Remaining

AUSTRALIA: SORRY DAY. May 26. A day to express sorrow for the forced removal of Aboriginal children from their families. For info: www.acn.net.au/articles/sorry.

GEORGIA: INDEPENDENCE RESTORATION DAY. May 26. National Day. Commemorates declaration of independence from Russia in 1918. The country was absorbed into the USSR in 1922, but declared their independence from the Soviets in 1991.

ISRAEL: YOM YERUSHALAYIM (JERUSALEM DAY). May 26. Hebrew calendar date: Iyar 28, 5766. Commemorates the liberation of the old city, June 7, 1967. (Began at sundown of previous day.)

BIRTHDAYS TODAY

Brent Musburger, 67, sportscaster, born Portland, OR, May 26, 1939.

Sally Kristen Ride, 55, one of the first seven women in the US astronaut program and the first American woman in space, born Encino, CA, May 26, 1951.

Lisbeth Zwerger, 52, illustrator (*Alice in Wonderland, The Wizard of Oz*), born Vienna, Austria, May 26, 1954.

MAY 27 — SATURDAY

Day 147 — 218 Remaining

BLOOMER, AMELIA JENKS: BIRTH ANNIVERSARY. May 27, 1818. American social reformer and women's rights advocate, born at Homer, NY. Her name is remembered especially because of her work for more sensible dress for women and her recommendation of a costume that had been introduced about 1849 by Elizabeth Smith Miller but came to be known as the "Bloomer Costume" or "Bloomers." Amelia Bloomer died at Council Bluffs, IA, Dec 30, 1894. For more info: *You Forgot Your Skirt, Amelia Bloomer* by Shana Corey (Scholastic, 0-439-07819-9, $16.95 Gr. K–3).

CARSON, RACHEL (LOUISE): BIRTH ANNIVERSARY. May 27, 1907. American scientist and author, born at Springdale, PA. She was the author of *The Sea Around Us* and *Silent Spring* (1962), a book that provoked widespread controversy over the use of pesticides and contributed to the beginning of the environmental movement. She died Apr 14, 1964, at Silver Spring, MD. For more info: *Rachel Carson: The Wonder of Nature* by Catherine Reef (Twenty-First Century, 0-941477-38-X, $14.95 Gr. 2–5).

CELLOPHANE TAPE PATENTED: ANNIVERSARY. May 27, 1930. Richard Gurley Drew received a patent for his adhesive tape, later manufactured by 3M as Scotch tape.

DUNCAN, ISADORA: BIRTH ANNIVERSARY. May 27, 1878. American-born interpretive dancer who revolutionized the entire concept of dance. Bare-footed, freedom-loving, liberated woman and rebel against tradition, she experienced worldwide professional success and profound personal tragedy (her two children drowned, her marriage failed and she met a bizarre death when the long scarf she was wearing caught in a wheel of the open car in which she was riding, strangling her). Born at San Francisco, CA, she died at Nice, France, Sept 14, 1927.

GOLDEN GATE BRIDGE OPENED: ANNIVERSARY. May 27, 1937. More than 200,000 people crossed San Francisco's Golden Gate Bridge on its first day.

HUMPHREY, HUBERT HORATIO: BIRTH ANNIVERSARY. May 27, 1911. Born at Wallace, SD, he served as 38th vice president of the US and ran for president in 1968 but lost narrowly to Richard Nixon. Humphrey died at Waverly, MN, Jan 13, 1978.

INTERNATIONAL JAZZ DAY. May 27. Jazz lovers worldwide celebrate jazz every May, on the Saturday of the Memorial Day weekend. Originated by the New Jersey Jazz Society, and sanctioned by the American Federation of Jazz Societies, the United Nations Jazz Society and the Sacramento Traditional Jazz Society. For info: Web: www.geocities.com/BourbonStreet/4270.

MOON PHASE: NEW MOON. May 27. Moon enters New Moon phase at 1:26 AM, EDT.

BIRTHDAYS TODAY

Christopher J. Dodd, 62, US Senator (D, Connecticut), born Willimantic, CT, May 27, 1944.

Antonio Freeman, 34, former football player, born Baltimore, MD, May 27, 1972.

Lynn Sweat, 72, illustrator (the Amelia Bedelia books), born Alexandria, LA, May 27, 1934.

Frank Thomas, 38, baseball player, born Columbus, GA, May 27, 1968.

MAY 28 — SUNDAY

Day 148 — 217 Remaining

AZERBAIJAN: DAY OF THE REPUBLIC: ANNIVERSARY. May 28. Public holiday. Commemorates the declaration of the Azerbaijan Democratic Republic in 1918.

FLEMING, IAN: BIRTH ANNIVERSARY. May 28, 1908. Author of *Chitty Chitty Bang Bang*, which was made into a popular movie for children, as well as the James Bond series of books. Born at London, England, he died at Canterbury, England, Aug 12, 1964.

ITALY: PALIO DEI BALESTRIERI. May 28. Gubbio. The last Sunday in May is set aside for a medieval crossbow contest between Gubbio and Sansepolcro; medieval costumes, arms.

ITALY: WEDDING OF THE SEA. May 28. Venice. The feast of the Ascension is the occasion of the ceremony recalling the "Wedding of the Sea" performed by Venice's Doge, who cast his ring into the sea from the ceremonial ship known as the *Bucintoro*, to symbolize eternal dominion. Annually, on the Sunday following Ascension.

SIERRA CLUB FOUNDED: ANNIVERSARY. May 28, 1892. Founded by famed naturalist John Muir, the Sierra Club promotes conservation of the natural environment by influencing public policy. It has been especially important in the founding of and protection of our national parks. For info: Sierra Club, 85 Second St, 2nd Floor, San Francisco, CA 94105-3441. Phone: (415) 977-5500. Web: www.sierraclub.org.

THORPE, JAMES FRANCIS (JIM): BIRTH ANNIVERSARY. May 28, 1888. This distinguished Native American athlete was the winner of pentathlon and decathlon events at the 1912 Olympic Games and a professional baseball and football player. Born near Prague, OK, he died at Lomita, CA, Mar 28, 1953.

BIRTHDAYS TODAY

Rudolph Giuliani, 62, former Mayor of New York City, born Brooklyn, NY, May 28, 1944.
Glen Rice, 39, basketball player, born Flint, MI, May 28, 1967.
Mark Sanford, 46, Governor of South Carolina (R), born Fort Lauderdale, FL, May 28, 1960.

MAY 29 — MONDAY

Day 149 — 216 Remaining

AMNESTY ISSUED FOR SOUTHERN REBELS: ANNIVERSARY. May 29, 1865. President Andrew Johnson issued a proclamation giving a general amnesty to all who participated in the rebellion against the US. High-ranking members of the Confederate government and military and those who owned more than $20,000 worth of property were excepted and had to apply individually to the President for a pardon. Once an oath of allegiance was taken, all former property rights, except those in slaves, were returned to the former owners.

May 2006

S	M	T	W	T	F	S
	1	2	3	4	5	6
7	8	9	10	11	12	13
14	15	16	17	18	19	20
21	22	23	24	25	26	27
28	29	30	31			

CONSTANTINOPLE FALLS TO THE TURKS: ANNIVERSARY. May 29, 1453. The city of Constantinople was captured by the Turks, who renamed it Istanbul (although the name wasn't officially changed until 1930). This conquest marked the end of the Byzantine Empire; the city became the capital of the Ottoman Empire.

HENRY, PATRICK: BIRTH ANNIVERSARY. May 29, 1736. American revolutionary leader and orator, born at Studley, VA, and died near Brookneal, VA, June 6, 1799. Especially remembered for his speech (Mar 23, 1775) for arming the Virginia militia, at St. John's Church, Richmond, VA, when he declared: "I know not what course others may take, but as for me, give me liberty or give me death." For more info: *Patrick Henry: Voice of the People* by Jon Kukla and Amy Kukla (Rosen, 0-8239-5725-X, $23.95 Gr. 4–8).

KENNEDY, JOHN FITZGERALD: BIRTH ANNIVERSARY. May 29, 1917. The 35th president of the US, born at Brookline, MA. Kennedy was the youngest man ever elected to the presidency, the first Roman Catholic and the first president to have served in the US Navy. He was assassinated while riding in an open automobile, at Dallas, TX, Nov 22, 1963. (Accused assassin Lee Harvey Oswald was killed at the Dallas police station by a gunman, Jack Ruby, two days later.) He was the fourth US president to be killed by an assassin, and the second to be buried at Arlington National Cemetery (the first was William Howard Taft). For more info: www.ipl.org/ref/POTUS or www.cs.umb.edu/jfk library/index.htm.

MEMORIAL DAY. May 29. Legal public holiday. (Public Law 90-363 sets Memorial Day on the last Monday in May. Applicable to federal employees and District of Columbia.) Also known as Decoration Day because of the tradition of decorating the graves of servicepeople. An occasion for honoring those who have died in battle. Observance dates from Civil War years in US: first documented observance at Waterloo, NY, May 5, 1865. See also: "Confederate Memorial Day" (Apr 24, Apr 26, May 10 and June 3).

★**MEMORIAL DAY, PRAYER FOR PEACE.** May 29. Presidential Proclamation issued each year since 1948. Public Law 81–512 of May 11, 1950, asks the president to proclaim annually this day as a day of prayer for permanent peace. Public Law 90–363 of June 28, 1968, requires that beginning in 1971 it will be observed the last Monday in May. Often titled "Prayer for Peace Memorial Day," and traditionally requests the flying of the flag at half-staff "for the customary forenoon period."

MOUNT EVEREST SUMMIT REACHED: ANNIVERSARY. May 29, 1953. New Zealand explorer Sir Edmund Hillary and Tensing Norgay, a Sherpa guide, became the first team to reach the summit of Mount Everest, the world's highest mountain.

RHODE ISLAND RATIFIES CONSTITUTION: ANNIVERSARY. May 29. Became the 13th state to ratify the Constitution in 1790.

VIRGINIA PLAN PROPOSED: ANNIVERSARY. May 29, 1787. Just five days after the Constitutional Convention met at Philadelphia, PA, the "Virginia Plan" was proposed. It called for establishment of a government consisting of a legislature with two houses, an executive (chosen by the legislature) and a judicial branch.

WISCONSIN: ADMISSION DAY: ANNIVERSARY. May 29, 1848. Became 30th state in 1848.

BIRTHDAYS TODAY

Andrew Clements, 57, author (*Frindle, Big Al*), born Camden, NJ, May 29, 1949.

Brock Cole, 68, author and illustrator (*Buttons, The Facts Speak for Themselves, The Goats*), born Charlotte, MI, May 29, 1938.

Rupert Everett, 47, actor (*Inspector Gadget, The Wild Thornberries Movie* [voice]), born Norfolk, England, May 29, 1959.

MAY 30 — TUESDAY

Day 150 — 215 Remaining

CROATIA: NATIONAL DAY: ANNIVERSARY. May 30. Public holiday commemorating statehood in 1990.

FIRST AMERICAN DAILY NEWSPAPER PUBLISHED: ANNIVERSARY. May 30, 1783. *The Pennsylvania Evening Post* became the first daily newspaper published in the US. The paper was published at Philadelphia, PA, by Benjamin Towne.

LINCOLN MEMORIAL DEDICATION: ANNIVERSARY. May 30, 1922. The memorial is made of marble from Colorado and Tennessee and limestone from Indiana. It stands in West Potomac Park at Washington, DC. The outside columns are Doric, the inside, Ionic. The Memorial was designed by architect Henry Bacon and its cornerstone was laid in 1915. A skylight lets light into the interiors where the compelling statue "Seated Lincoln," by sculptor Daniel Chester French, is situated. For more info: www.nps.gov/linc/index.htm.

SAINT JOAN OF ARC: FEAST DAY. May 30. French heroine and martyr, known as the Maid of Orleans, led the French against the English invading army. She was captured, found guilty of heresy and burned at the stake in 1431 (at age 19). Her innocence was declared in 1456 and she was canonized in 1920.

SPACE MILESTONE: *MARINER 9* (US): 35th ANNIVERSARY. May 30, 1971. Unmanned spacecraft was launched, entering Martian orbit the following Nov 13. The craft relayed temperature and gravitational fields and sent back spectacular photographs of both the surface of Mars and of her two moons. It was the first spacecraft to orbit another planet.

TRINIDAD: INDIAN ARRIVAL DAY. May 30. Port of Spain. Public holiday. About 40 percent of Trinidad's population is descended from immigrants who were brought from India by the British in the 1840s.

BIRTHDAYS TODAY

Blake Bashoff, 25, actor (*The New Swiss Family Robinson*), born Philadelphia, PA, May 30, 1981.

Trey Parker, 34, director, creator ("South Park"), born Auburn, AL, May 30, 1972.

Manny Ramirez, 34, baseball player, born Santo Domingo, Dominican Republic, May 30, 1972.

MAY 31 — WEDNESDAY

Day 151 — 214 Remaining

CHINA: DRAGON BOAT FESTIVAL. May 31. An important Chinese observance, the Dragon Boat Festival commemorates a hero of ancient China, poet Qu Yuan, who drowned himself in protest against injustice and corruption. It is said that rice dumplings were cast into the water to lure fish away from the body of the martyr, and this is remembered by the eating of zhong zi, glutenous rice dumplings filled with meat and wrapped in bamboo leaves. Dragon boat races are held on rivers. The Dragon Boat Festival is observed in many countries by their Chinese populations (date will differ: in North America will be May 30). Also called Fifth Month Festival or Summer Festival. Annually, the fifth day of the fifth lunar month.

COPYRIGHT LAW PASSED: ANNIVERSARY. May 31, 1790. President George Washington signed the first US copyright law. It gave protection for 14 years to books written by US citizens. In 1891 the law was extended to cover books by foreign authors as well.

GREAT AMERICAN GRUMP OUT. May 31. Kalamazoo, MI. We are asking America to go 24 hours without being grumpy or crabby. Can YOU meet the challenge? Kalamazoo school children, parents, businesses and the community will be involved in promoting peace, harmony and light-hearted humor on this day. For info: Janice Hathy, Smile Mania. Phone: (616) 349-7761. E-mail: grumpout@smilemania.com. Web: www.smilemania.com.

JOHNSTOWN FLOOD: ANNIVERSARY. May 31, 1889. Heavy rains caused the Connemaugh River Dam to burst. At nearby Johnstown, PA, the resulting flood killed more than 2,300 persons and destroyed the homes of thousands more. Nearly 800 unidentified drowning victims were buried in a common grave at Johnstown's Grandview Cemetery. So devastating was the flood and so widespread the sorrow for its victims that "Johnstown Flood" entered the language as a phrase to describe a disastrous event. The valley city of Johnstown, in the Allegheny Mountains, has been damaged repeatedly by floods. Floods in 1936 (25 deaths) and 1977 (85 deaths) were the next most destructive.

KOREA: TANO DAY. May 31. Fifth day of fifth lunar month. Summer food offered at the household shrine of the ancestors. Also known as Swing Day, since girls, dressed in their prettiest clothes, often compete in swinging matches. The Tano Festival usually lasts from the third through eighth day of the fifth lunar month.

NATIONAL SPELLING BEE FINALS. May 31–June 1. Washington, DC. 79th annual. Newspapers and other sponsors across the country send 245–255 youngsters to the finals at Washington, DC. Annually, Wednesday and Thursday of Memorial Day week. Est attendance: 1,000. For info: Scripps-Howard National Spelling Bee, 312 Walnut St, 28th Fl, Cincinnati, OH 45202. Phone: (513) 977-3040. Fax: (513) 977-3090. E-mail: bee@scripps.com. Web: www.spellingbee.com.

WHITMAN, WALT: BIRTH ANNIVERSARY. May 31, 1819. Poet and journalist, born at West Hills, Long Island, NY. Whitman's best known work, *Leaves of Grass* (1855), is a classic of American poetry. His poems celebrated all of modern life, including subjects that were considered taboo at the time. He died Mar 26, 1892, at Camden, NJ.

"WITH ALL DELIBERATE SPEED": ANNIVERSARY. May 31, 1955. In an instruction one year after its *Brown v Board of Education of Topeka* decision, the US Supreme Court ordered recalcitrant states to begin school integration "with all deliberate speed."

BIRTHDAYS TODAY

Kenny Lofton, 39, baseball player, born East Chicago, IN, May 31, 1967.

Harry Mazer, 81, author (*The Wild Kid*), born New York, NY, May 31, 1925.

JUNE 1 — THURSDAY

Day 152 — 213 Remaining

ADOPT-A-SHELTER CAT MONTH. June 1–30. To promote the adoption of cats from local shelters, the ASPCA sponsors this important observance. "Make pet adoption your first option®" is a message the organization promotes throughout the year in an effort to end the euthanasia of all adoptable animals. For info: ASPCA Public Affairs Dept, 424 E 92nd St, New York, NY 10128. Phone: (212) 876-7700, ext 4655. E-mail: press@aspca.org. Web: www.aspca.org.

ATLANTIC, CARIBBEAN AND GULF HURRICANE SEASON. June 1–Nov 30. For info: US Dept of Commerce, National Oceanic and Atmospheric Administration, Rockville, MD 20852. Web: www.nws.noaa.gov.

CANCER FROM THE SUN MONTH. June 1–30. To promote education and awareness of the dangers of skin cancer from too much exposure to the sun. Kit of materials available for $15 from this nonprofit organization. For info: Frederick Mayer, Pres, Pharmacy Council on Dermatology (PCD), 101 Lucas Valley Rd, #210, San Rafael, CA 94903. Phone: (415) 479-8628. Fax: (415) 479-8608. E-mail: ppsi@aol.com. Web: www.ppsinc.org.

CHILD VISION AWARENESS MONTH. June 1–30. To better educate and counsel the public on children's vision problems and detection of eye diseases in infants and children, to increase the number of school-aged children who have an eye exam by an eye doctor and to increase the number of children with learning disabilities having a developmental vision exam to rule out vision problems. There is a $15 charge for kit materials. For info: PPSI, 101 Lucas Valley Rd, Ste 210, San Rafael, CA 94903. Phone: (415) 479-8628. Fax: (415) 479-8608. E-mail: ppsi@aol.com. Web: www.ppsinc.org.

CHINA: INTERNATIONAL CHILDREN'S DAY. June 1.

CNN DEBUTED: ANNIVERSARY. June 1, 1980. The Cable News Network, TV's first all-news service, went on the air.

FIREWORKS SAFETY MONTHS. June 1–July 31. Activities during these months are designed to warn and educate parents and children about the dangers of playing with fireworks. Prevent Blindness America will offer suggestions for safer ways to cele-

June 2006

S	M	T	W	T	F	S
				1	2	3
4	5	6	7	8	9	10
11	12	13	14	15	16	17
18	19	20	21	22	23	24
25	26	27	28	29	30	

JUNE 1–30
NATIONAL SOUL FOOD MONTH

The term "comfort food" conjures up different images in the minds of different people depending on your family's ethnic and cultural origins. For many African Americans and those who grew up in the South, comfort food is synonymous with "soul food," the term used to describe cuisine developed by African slaves. These industrious and persevering people created hearty, energy-providing foods from meager means, usually from the meats and vegetables left over or thrown away from the slave owners' tables. In the traditional black kitchen, nothing was ever wasted.

A variety of green, leafy plants and weeds native to the southern states made up the staple of the black diet. Collards, kale, watercress, mustard greens and pokeweed were often steamed or panfried with lard (pig fat) for flavor. Cornmeal was used to make corn bread or corn pone, hush puppies (fried balls of cornmeal, onion and leftover fish) and cobblers. Meat staples consisted of mostly leftover parts of the pig, including pig's feet and ears, ham hocks, jowls, chitterlings or pig intestines and tripe or the muscular lining of the stomach. Dishes were flavored using a variety of vegetables and spices such as onions, garlic, thyme and bay leaves.

Eventually, the traditional slave diet and white southern food staples, as well as influences from a variety of immigrant cultures, combined to form the soul food most of us are familiar with today. Fried chicken, grits, watermelon, black-eyed peas, macaroni and cheese, and sweet potatoes are foods that grace the tables of many people in the United States, both black and white, and those from the north and south as well as all people and places in between.

The origins of the term "soul food" vary from source to source. Some say that it originated during the days of slavery while others say that it corresponded with the Civil Rights movement in the 1960s. The latter is a bit more likely, if only because this was a time when African Americans identified with the word "soul" relative to their culture—music, food, style of dress and outlook.

Write the term soul food on the board and ask students to define it and identify foods they consider soul food. You may also have students take the following simple soul food recipe home and ask their parents or guardians to help them make it. This activity fosters family togetherness and children will learn important food preparation skills.

Spoonbread
(Adapted from *Spoonbread & Strawberry Wine: Recipes and Reminiscences of a Family* by Norma Jean and Carole Darden [Harlem Moon, 0-3854-7270-6, $18.95].)

1 cup yellow cornmeal
2 cups boiling water in medium to large saucepan
3 tablespoons butter
1 teaspoon salt
3 large eggs, beaten
1 cup milk

Preheat oven to 375°. Slowly add cornmeal to the boiling water, stirring constantly until thick and smooth. Add butter and salt and cool to lukewarm. Add eggs and milk. Beat for 2 minutes, then pour into greased casserole dish and bake for 35 minutes or until golden brown. Spoon out while hot and smother in butter, molasses or honey. Makes 8 servings.

—Denise Frank

brate the Fourth of July. Materials that can easily be posted or distributed to the community will be provided. For info: Prevent Blindness America®, 500 E Remington Rd, Schaumburg, IL 60173. Phone: (800) 331-2020. Fax: (847) 843-8458. Web: www.prevent blindness.org.

GAY AND LESBIAN PRIDE MONTH. June 1–30. Observed this month because on June 28, 1969, the clientele of a gay bar at New York City rioted after the club was raided by the police. President Clinton issued a presidential proclamation for this month in 1999 and 2000.

INTERNATIONAL ACCORDION AWARENESS MONTH. June 1–30. To increase public awareness of this multicultural instrument and its influence and popularity in today's music. For info: All Things Accordion, PO Box 475136, San Francisco, CA 94147-5136. Phone: (415) 440-0800. E-mail: bellows@ladyofspain .com. Web: www.ladyofspain.com.

JUNE DAIRY MONTH. June 1–30. Since 1937 the dairy industry has set aside June as a time to pay tribute to the vital role milk and dairy products play in the American diet and the outstanding contribution of America's dairy farmers.

JUNE IS TURKEY LOVERS' MONTH. June 1–30. A monthlong campaign to promote awareness and increase turkey consumption at a nonholiday time. Annually, the month of June. For info: National Turkey Federation, 1225 New York Ave NW, Ste 400, Washington, DC 20005. Phone: (202) 898-0100. Fax: (202) 898-0203. E-mail: info@turkeyfed.org. Web: www.eatturkey.com.

KENTUCKY: ADMISSION DAY: ANNIVERSARY. June 1. Became 15th state in 1792.

KENYA: MADARAKA DAY. June 1. Madaraka Day (Self-Rule Day) is observed as a national public holiday.

MARQUETTE, JACQUES: BIRTH ANNIVERSARY. June 1, 1637. Father Jacques Marquette (Père Marquette), Jesuit missionary-explorer of the Great Lakes region. Born at Laon, France, he died at Ludington, MI, May 18, 1675.

NATIONAL RIVERS MONTH. June 1–30. Commemorated by local groups in many states.

NATIONAL ROSE MONTH. June 1–30. To recognize American-grown roses, our national floral emblem. America's favorite flower is grown in all 50 states and more than 1.2 billion fresh cut roses are sold at retail each year. For info: International Cut Flower Growers Assn. Web: www.rosesinc.org.

NATIONAL SAFETY MONTH. June 1–30. For info: National Safety Council, 1121 Spring Lake Dr, Itasca, IL 60143-3201. Phone: (800) 621-7615. Web: www.nsc.org.

NATIONAL SOUL FOOD MONTH. June 1–30. A month to recognize, educate and celebrate the heritage and history of the foods and foodways of African Americans and peoples from the African diaspora. The culinary contributions of this group have had an indelible impact on the menu of the American table and on mainstream American life and culture. ***See Curriculum Connection.*** For info: Culinary Historians of Chicago, PO Box 805987, Chicago, IL 60680. E-mail: saridgeway0622@yahoo.com. Web: www .culinaryhistorians.org.

ORTHODOX ASCENSION DAY. June 1. Observed by Eastern Orthodox Churches.

SAMOA: INDEPENDENCE DAY. June 1. Holiday commemorating independence from New Zealand in 1962. Name changed from Western Samoa in 1997.

STAND FOR CHILDREN DAY. June 1. Stand for Children is a national organization that encourages individuals to improve children's lives. Its mission is to identify, train and connect local children's activists engaging in advocacy, awareness-raising and service initiatives as part of Children's Action Teams. Annually, June 1. On this day each year a special issue, such as quality child care, is highlighted. For more info: *Stand for Children* by Marian Wright Edelman (Hyperion, 0-7868-0365-7, $15.95 Gr. 5–8). For info: Stand for Children, 516 SE Morrison St, Ste 206, Portland, OR 97214. Phone: (800) 663-4032. E-mail: stand@stand.org. Web: www.stand.org.

TENNESSEE: ADMISSION DAY: ANNIVERSARY. June 1. Became 16th state in 1796. Observed as a holiday in Tennessee.

BIRTHDAYS TODAY

Paul Coffey, 45, former hockey player, born Weston, ON, Canada, June 1, 1961.

Justine Henin-Hardenne, 24, tennis player, born Liege, Belgium, June 1, 1982.

Leah Komaiko, 52, author (*Annie Bananie, I Like the Music*), born Chicago, IL, June 1, 1954.

Alexi Lalas, 36, soccer player, born Detroit, MI, June 1, 1970.

JUNE 2 — FRIDAY

Day 153 — 212 Remaining

BAHAMAS: LABOR DAY. June 2. Public holiday. First Friday in June celebrated with parades, displays and picnics.

BHUTAN: CORONATION DAY. June 2. National holiday. Anniversary of the coronation of the 4th king in 1974.

BULGARIA: HRISTO BOTEV DAY. June 2. Poet and national hero Hristo Botev fell fighting Turks, 1876.

ITALY: REPUBLIC DAY. June 2. National holiday. Commemorates referendum in 1946 in which republic status was selected instead of return to monarchy.

SHAVUOT or FEAST OF WEEKS. June 2. Jewish Pentecost holy day. Hebrew date, Sivan 6, 5766. Celebrates giving of Torah (the Law) to Moses on Mount Sinai. (Began at sundown of previous day.)

UNITED KINGDOM: CORONATION DAY: ANNIVERSARY. June 2. Commemorates the crowning of Queen Elizabeth II in 1953.

YELL "FUDGE" AT THE COBRAS IN NORTH AMERICA DAY. June 2. Anywhere north of the Panama Canal. In order to keep poisonous cobra snakes out of North America, all citizens are asked to go outdoors at noon, local time, and yell "Fudge." Fudge makes cobras gag and the mere mention of it makes them skedaddle. Annually, June 2. [© 1999 by WH] For info: Thomas or Ruth Roy, Wellcat Holidays, 2418 Long Ln, Lebanon, PA 17046. Phone: (717) 279-0184. E-mail: info@wellcat.com. Web: www.well cat.com.

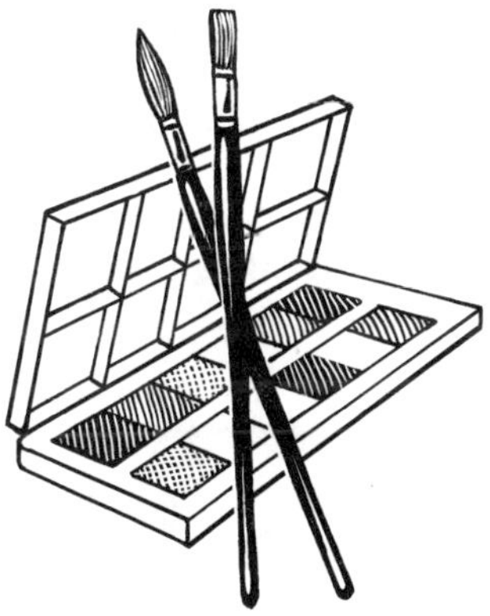

BIRTHDAYS TODAY

Freddy Adu, 17, soccer player, born Tema, Ghana, June 2, 1989.

Dana Carvey, 51, comedian, actor (*Wayne's World*, "Saturday Night Live"), born Missoula, MT, June 2, 1955.

Paul Galdone, 92, author (*The Little Red Hen*), born Budapest, June 2, 1914.

Norton Juster, 77, author (*The Phantom Tollbooth*), born Brooklyn, NY, June 2, 1929.

Helen Oxenbury, 68, author, illustrator (the Tom & Pippo series, *Clap Hands, Tickle Tickle*), born Suffolk, England, June 2, 1938.

Larry Robinson, 55, Hall of Fame hockey player, born Winchester, ON, Canada, June 2, 1951.

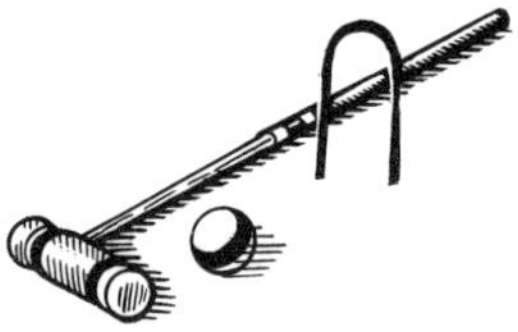

JUNE 3 — SATURDAY

Day 154 — 211 Remaining

CONFEDERATE MEMORIAL DAY/JEFFERSON DAVIS DAY. June 3. A holiday in Kentucky, Louisiana and Tennessee. Commemorated on the birthday of Jefferson Davis.

DAVIS, JEFFERSON: BIRTH ANNIVERSARY. June 3, 1808. American statesman, US senator, only president of the Confederate States of America. Imprisoned May 10, 1865–May 13, 1867, but never brought to trial, deprived of rights of citizenship after the Civil War. Davis was born at Todd County, KY, and died at New Orleans, LA, Dec 6, 1889. His citizenship was restored, posthumously, Oct 17, 1978, when President Carter signed an Amnesty Bill. This bill, he said, "officially completes the long process of reconciliation that has reunited our people following the tragic conflict between the states." Davis's birth anniversary is observed in Florida, Kentucky and South Carolina on this day, in Alabama on the first Monday in June and in Mississippi on the last Monday in May. Davis's birth anniversary is observed as Confederate Memorial Day in Kentucky and Tennessee. For more info: *Jefferson Davis: Confederate President* by Joey Frazier (Chelsea House, 0-7910-6006-3, $18.95 Gr. 3–5).

DREW, CHARLES RICHARD: BIRTH ANNIVERSARY. June 3, 1904. African-American physician who discovered how to store blood plasma and who organized the blood bank system in the US and UK during WWII. Born at Washington, DC, he was killed in an automobile accident near Burlington, NC, Apr 1, 1950. For more info: *Charles Drew: A Life-Saving Scientist* by Miles Shapiro (Raintree, 0-8172-4403-4, $18.98 Gr. 5–12).

FIRST WOMAN RABBI IN US: ANNIVERSARY. June 3, 1972. Sally Jan Priesand was ordained the first woman rabbi in the US. She became assistant rabbi at the Stephen Wise Free Synagogue, New York City, Aug 1, 1972.

HOBART, GARRET AUGUSTUS: BIRTH ANNIVERSARY. June 3, 1844. The 24th vice president of the US (1897–99), born at Long Branch, NJ. Died at Paterson, NJ, Nov 21, 1899.

MOON PHASE: FIRST QUARTER. June 3. Moon enters First Quarter phase at 7:06 PM, EDT.

June 2006

S	M	T	W	T	F	S
				1	2	3
4	5	6	7	8	9	10
11	12	13	14	15	16	17
18	19	20	21	22	23	24
25	26	27	28	29	30	

SPACE MILESTONE: *GEMINI 4* (US). June 3, 1965. James McDivitt and Edward White made 66 orbits of Earth. White took the first space walk by an American and maneuvered 20 minutes outside the capsule.

BIRTHDAYS TODAY

Margaret Cosgrove, 80, author and illustrator (*Wonders of the Tree World*), born Sylvania, OH, June 3, 1926.

Jan-Michael Gambill, 29, tennis player, born Spokane, WA, June 3, 1977.

Anita Lobel, 72, author and illustrator (*Away From Home; One Lighthouse, One Moon*), born Krakow, Poland, June 3, 1934.

JUNE 4 — SUNDAY

Day 155 — 210 Remaining

CHINA: TIANANMEN SQUARE MASSACRE: ANNIVERSARY. June 4, 1989. After almost a month and a half of student demonstrations for democracy, the Chinese government ordered its troops to open fire on the unarmed protestors at Tiananmen Square at Beijing. The demonstrations began Apr 18 as several thousand students marched to mourn the death of Hu Yaobang, a pro-reform leader within the Chinese government. A ban was imposed on such demonstrations; Apr 22, 100,000 gathered in Tiananmen Square in defiance of the ban. On May 13, 2,000 of the students began a hunger strike and May 20, the government imposed martial law and began to bring in troops. On June 2, the demonstrators turned back an advance of unarmed troops in the first clash with the People's Army. Under the cover of darkness, early June 4, troops opened fire on the assembled crowds and armored personnel carriers rolled into the square crushing many of the students as they lay sleeping in their tents. Although the government claimed that few died in the attack, estimates range from several hundred to several thousand casualties. In the following months thousands of demonstrators were rounded up and jailed.

FINLAND: FLAG DAY. June 4. Finland's armed forces honor the birth anniversary of Carl Gustaf Mannerheim, born in 1867.

GHANA: REVOLUTION DAY. June 4. National holiday.

JAPAN: DAY OF THE RICE GOD. June 4. Chiyoda. Annual rice-transplanting festival observed on first Sunday in June. Centuries-old rural folk ritual revived in 1930s and celebrated with colorful costumes, parades, music, dancing and prayers to the Shinto rice god Wbai-sama.

PENTECOST. June 4. The Christian feast of Pentecost commemorates descent of the Holy Spirit unto the Apostles, 50 days after Easter. Observed on the seventh Sunday after Easter. Recognized since the third century. See also: "Whitsunday" (below).

TEACHER'S DAY IN MASSACHUSETTS. June 4. Proclaimed annually by the governor for the first Sunday in June.

TONGA: EMANCIPATION DAY: ANNIVERSARY. June 4. National holiday. Commemorates independence from Britain in 1970.

UNITED NATIONS: INTERNATIONAL DAY OF INNOCENT CHILDREN VICTIMS OF AGGRESSION. June 4. On Aug 19, 1982, the General Assembly decided to commemorate June 4 of each year as the International Day of Innocent Children Victims of Aggression.

WHITSUNDAY. June 4. Whitsunday, the seventh Sunday after Easter, is a popular time for baptism. "White Sunday" is named for the white garments formerly worn by the candidates for baptism and occurs at the Christian feast of Pentecost. See also: "Pentecost" (above).

BIRTHDAYS TODAY

Darin Erstad, 32, baseball player, born Jamestown, ND, June 4, 1974.
Andrea Jaeger, 41, former tennis player, born Chicago, IL, June 4, 1965.
Linda Lingle, 53, Governor of Hawaii (R), born St. Louis, MO, June 4, 1953.
Scott Wolf, 38, actor ("Party of Five"), born Boston, MA, June 4, 1968.

JUNE 5 — MONDAY

Day 156 — 209 Remaining

AIDS FIRST NOTED: 25th ANNIVERSARY. June 5, 1981. A new disease was first described in a Centers for Disease Control newsletter on this date. On July 27, 1982, the CDC adopted Acquired Immune Deficiency Syndrome as the official name for the disease. The virus that causes AIDS was identified in 1983 and in May 1985 was named Human Immunodeficiency Virus (HIV) by the International Committee on the Taxonomy of Viruses. The first death from this disease in the developed world occurred in 1959. More than 420,000 Americans have died of AIDS. Worldwide, more than 22 million people have died of AIDS. About 40 million people worldwide are living with HIV/AIDS.

APPLE II COMPUTER RELEASED: ANNIVERSARY. June 5, 1977. The Apple II computer, with 4K of memory, went on sale for $1,298. Its predecessor, the Apple I, was sold largely to electronic hobbyists the previous year. Apple released the Macintosh computer Jan 24, 1984.

DENMARK: CONSTITUTION DAY. June 5. National holiday. Commemorates Denmark's becoming a constitutional monarchy in 1849.

FIRST BALLOON FLIGHT: ANNIVERSARY. June 5, 1783. The first public demonstration of a hot-air balloon flight took place at Annonay, France, where coinventor brothers Joseph and Jacques Montgolfier succeeded in launching their unmanned 33-foot-diameter *globe aerostatique*. It rose an estimated 1,500 feet and traveled, windborne, about 7,500 feet before landing after the 10-minute flight—the first sustained flight of any object achieved by man. The first manned flight was three months later. See also: "First Manned Flight: Anniversary" (Oct 15).

IRAN: FIFTEENTH OF KHORDAD. June 5. National holiday. Commemorates the deaths of clerics in 1963 in a clash with the shah's forces.

SCARRY, RICHARD McCLURE: BIRTH ANNIVERSARY. June 5, 1919. Author and illustrator of children's books was born at Boston, MA. Two widely known books of the more than 250 Scarry authored are *Richard Scarry's Best Word Book Ever* (1965) and *Richard Scarry's Please & Thank You* (1973). The pages are crowded with small animal characters who live like humans. More than 100 million copies of his books sold worldwide. Died Apr 30, 1994, at Gstaad, Switzerland.

UNITED NATIONS: WORLD ENVIRONMENT DAY. June 5. Observed annually on the anniversary of the opening of the UN Conference on the Human Environment held in Stockholm in 1972, which led to establishment of UN Environment Programme, based at Nairobi. The General Assembly has urged marking the day with activities reaffirming concern for the preservation and enhancement of the environment. For more info, visit the UN's website for children at www.un.org/Pubs/CyberSchoolBus/.

WHITMONDAY. June 5. The day after Whitsunday is observed as a public holiday in many European countries.

BIRTHDAYS TODAY

Allan Ahlberg, 68, author (*The Jolly Postman*), born Croydon, England, June 5, 1938.
Joe Clark, 67, Canada's 16th prime minister (1979–80), born High River, AB, Canada, June 5, 1939.
Torry Holt, 30, football player, born Greensboro, NC, June 5, 1976.
Bob Probert, 41, former hockey player, born Windsor, ON, Canada, June 5, 1965.
Mark Wahlberg, 35, actor (*Planet of the Apes*), singer (Marky Mark and the Funky Bunch), born Dorchester, MA, June 5, 1971.

JUNE 6 — TUESDAY

Day 157 — 208 Remaining

AARDEMA, VERNA: BIRTH ANNIVERSARY. June 6, 1911. Author (*Why Mosquitoes Buzz in People's Ears*), born at New Era, MI. Died May 11, 2000.

BONZA BOTTLER DAY™. June 6. To celebrate when the number of the day is the same as the number of the month. Bonza Bottler Day™ is an excuse to have a party at least once a month. For info: Gail M. Berger, 14 Fernwood Dr, Taylors, SC 29687. Phone: (864) 609-9874. E-mail: gberger5@aol.com.

D-DAY: ANNIVERSARY. June 6, 1944. In the early-morning hours Allied forces landed in Normandy on the north coast of France. In an operation that took months of planning, a fleet of 2,727 ships of every description converged from British ports from Wales to the North Sea. Operation Overlord involved 2,000,000 tons of war materials, including more than 50,000 tanks, armored cars, jeeps, trucks and half-tracks. The US alone sent 1,700,000 fighting men. The Germans believed the invasion would not take place under the adverse weather conditions of this early June day. But as the sun came up the village of Saint Mère Eglise was liberated by American parachutists and by nightfall the landing of 155,000 Allies attested to the success of D-Day. The long-awaited second front of WWII had at last materialized.

HALE, NATHAN: BIRTH ANNIVERSARY. June 6, 1755. American patriot Nathan Hale was born at Coventry, CT. During the battles for New York in the American Revolution, he volunteered to seek military intelligence behind enemy lines and was captured on the night of Sept 21, 1776. In an audience before General William Howe, Hale admitted he was an American officer and was ordered hanged the following morning. Although some question them, his dying words, "I only regret that I have but one life to lose for my country," have become a symbol of American patriotism. He was hanged Sept 22, 1776, at Manhattan, NY. For more info: *Nathan Hale: Voice of the People* by L.J. Krizner and Lisa Sita (Rosen, 0-8239-5724-1, $23.95 Gr. 4–8).

KOREA: MEMORIAL DAY. June 6. Nation pays tribute to the war dead and memorial services are held at the National Cemetery at Seoul. Legally recognized Korean holiday.

SPACE MILESTONE: *SOYUZ 11* (USSR): 35th ANNIVERSARY. June 6, 1971. Launched with cosmonauts G.T. Dobrovolsky, V.N. Volkov and V.I. Patsayev, who died during the return landing June 30, 1971, after a 24-day space flight. *Soyuz 11* had docked at *Salyut* orbital space station June 7–29; the cosmonauts entered the space station for the first time and conducted scientific experiments. First humans to die in space.

SUSAN B. ANTHONY FINED FOR VOTING: ANNIVERSARY. June 6, 1872. Seeking to test for women the citizenship and voting rights extended to black males under the 14th and 15th Amendments, Susan B. Anthony led a group of women who registered and voted at a Rochester, NY, election. She was arrested, tried and sentenced to pay a fine. She refused to do so and was allowed to go free by a judge who feared she would appeal to a higher court.

SWEDEN: FLAG DAY. June 6. Commemorates the day upon which Gustavus I (Gustavus Vasa) ascended the throne of Sweden in 1523.

BIRTHDAYS TODAY

Dalai Lama, 71, Tibet's spiritual leader and Nobel Peace Prize winner, born Taktser, China, June 6, 1935.

Marian Wright Edelman, 67, president of Children's Defense Fund, civil rights activist, born Bennettsville, SC, June 6, 1939.

Staci Keanan, 31, actress ("Step By Step"), born Devon, PA, June 6, 1975.

Cynthia Rylant, 52, author (*Dog Heaven, The Relatives Came*, the Henry & Mudge series, Newbery Medal for *Missing May*), born Hopewell, VA, June 6, 1954.

Peter Spier, 79, illustrator and author (*People*, Caldecott for *Noah's Ark*), born Amsterdam, Netherlands, June 6, 1927.

JUNE 7 — WEDNESDAY

Day 158 — 207 Remaining

APGAR, VIRGINIA: BIRTH ANNIVERSARY. June 7, 1909. Dr. Apgar developed the simple assessment method that permits doctors and nurses to evaluate newborns while they are still in the delivery room to identify those in need of immediate medical care. The Apgar score was first published in 1953 and the Perinatal Section of the American Academy of Pediatrics is named for Dr. Apgar. Born at Westfield, NJ, Apgar died Aug 7, 1974, at New York, NY.

BROOKS, GWENDOLYN: BIRTH ANNIVERSARY. June 7, 1917. Born at Topeka, KS, she was a poet who wrote about the struggles of African Americans, particularly women. Some of her most significant works include the poetry collections *Family Pictures* and *Blacks*, and the children's book *The Tiger Who Wore White Gloves*. In 1950 she became the first black writer to win the Pulitzer Prize, for her work "Annie Allen." She died at Chicago, IL, Dec 3, 2000.

GAUGUIN, PAUL: BIRTH ANNIVERSARY. June 7, 1848. French painter, born at Paris. He became a painter in middle age and renounced his life at Paris and moved to Tahiti. He is remembered for his broad, flat tones and use of color. He died on the island of Hiva Oa in the Marquesas, May 8, 1903.

VCR INTRODUCED: ANNIVERSARY. June 7, 1975. The Sony Corporation released its videocassette recorder, the Betamax, which sold for $995. Eventually, another VCR format, VHS, proved more successful and Sony stopped making the Betamax.

June 2006

S	M	T	W	T	F	S
				1	2	3
4	5	6	7	8	9	10
11	12	13	14	15	16	17
18	19	20	21	22	23	24
25	26	27	28	29	30	

JUNE
A GAGGLE OF GEESE; A CLUTTER OF CATS

As school winds down for the year and your students begin to get antsy for summer release, you might have a little fun with language—and pique their curiosity into obscure word meanings.

You and your students are no doubt familiar with nouns of multitudes, or group terms—although you may not have heard of these terms. "A pride of lions," "a pack of dogs" or "a school of fish" —"pride," "pack" and "school" are nouns of multitudes, a convenient and often colorful way of describing large groups of things, especially animals. English as a language is somewhat unique in having these terms: the terms aren't really necessary in that we could simply pluralize the items in question. But, long ago, as English expanded in the Middle Ages, it became an intellectual fad to come up with such terms, and they remain with us today—some more used than others.

James Lipton, best known as cable TV's interviewer of actors, compiled a fun book of these group terms titled *An Exaltation of Larks* (Penguin, 0-14-017096, $14.95 All Ages). It should be easily available in any library. In it, pick out some of the unique terms he has researched and write them on the chalkboard. Ask your students why the term is appropriate to the item in question. Or see if groups can look up obscure terms in the dictionary and then report why it's appropriate for the use. Here are some examples to have fun with:

a parliament of owls
a murder of crows
a knot of toads
a crash of rhinoceroses
a leap of leopards
a rafter of turkeys
an exaltation of larks
a skulk of foxes
a smack of jellyfish
a troop of kangaroo
a pod of seals
a gaggle of geese

As Lipton points out in his book, all of these terms are authentic and to be found in English literature of the past several centuries—most are still in use today.

After introducing students to nouns of multitude, perhaps they'd like to try coming up with their own? Broaden the discussion beyond animals to cover professions and groups of people and see what you or they come up with! Here are a few ideas to start with:

a __________ of jugglers
a __________ of surfers
a __________ of dog catchers
a __________ of mayors
a __________ of skydivers
a __________ of teachers
a __________ of coaches
a __________ of cheerleaders
a __________ of cooks
a __________ of sheriffs
a of doctors
a __________ of snowboarders

And, last of all, ask them what they'd call themselves: a __________ of students. —Holly McGuire

BIRTHDAYS TODAY

Louise Erdrich, 52, author (*The Birchbark House, Tracks*), born Little Falls, MN, June 7, 1954.
Nikki Giovanni, 63, author (*Spin a Soft Black Song*), born Knoxville, TN, June 7, 1943.
Allen Iverson, 31, basketball player, born Hampton, VA, June 7, 1975.
Anna Kournikova, 25, tennis player, born Moscow, Russia, June 7, 1981.
Mike Modano, 36, hockey player, born Livonia, MI, June 7, 1970.
Larisa Oleynik, 25, actress ("The Secret World of Alex Mack"), born San Francisco, CA, June 7, 1981.

JUNE 8 — THURSDAY

Day 159 — 206 Remaining

BILL OF RIGHTS PROPOSED: ANNIVERSARY. June 8, 1789. The Bill of Rights, which led to the first 10 amendments to the US Constitution, was first proposed by James Madison.

COCHISE: DEATH ANNIVERSARY. June 8, 1874. Born around 1810 in the Chiricahua Mountains of Arizona, Cochise became a fierce and courageous leader of the Apache. After his arrest in 1861, he escaped and launched the Apache Wars, which lasted for 25 years. He died 13 years later near his stronghold in southeastern Arizona.

McKINLEY, IDA SAXTON: BIRTH ANNIVERSARY. June 8, 1847. Wife of William McKinley, 25th president of the US, born at Canton, OH. Died at Canton, May 26, 1907.

WHITE, BYRON RAYMOND: BIRTH ANNIVERSARY. June 8, 1917. One of the longest serving justices of the Supreme Court of the US, Byron White was born at Fort Collins, CO. He was a football star in college (College Football Hall of Fame) and in the National Football League, as well as an academic standout: he was a Rhodes Scholar among other honors. A graduate of Yale Law School, White was a successful lawyer and director of the Justice Department before being nominated by President Kennedy for the highest court on Apr 3, 1962. White took the oath of office, Apr 16, 1962, and served 31 years before retiring in 1993. He died on Apr 15, 2002, at Denver, CO. For more info: oyez.northwestern.edu/justices/justices.cgi.

WRIGHT, FRANK LLOYD: BIRTH ANNIVERSARY. June 8, 1867. American architect, born at Richland Center, WI. In his autobiography Wright wrote: "No house should ever be *on* any hill or on anything. It should be *of* the hill, belonging to it, so hill and house could live together each the happier for the other." Wright died at Phoenix, AZ, Apr 9, 1959.

WYTHE, GEORGE: 200th DEATH ANNIVERSARY. June 8, 1806. Signer of the Declaration of Independence. Born at Elizabeth County, VA, about 1726 (exact date unknown). Died at Richmond, VA.

BIRTHDAYS TODAY

Tim Berners-Lee, 51, inventor of the World Wide Web, born London, England, June 8, 1955.
Barbara Pierce Bush, 81, former First Lady, wife of George H.W. Bush, 41st president of the US, born Rye, NY, June 8, 1925.
Kim Clijsters, 23, tennis player, born Bilzen, Belgium, June 8, 1983.
Lindsay Davenport, 30, tennis player, born Palos Verdes, CA, June 8, 1976.
Carolyn Meyer, 71, children's author (*Mary, Bloody Mary*), born Lewistown, PA, June 8, 1935.
Judy Sierra, 61, author (*Nursery Tales Around the World, Counting Crocodiles*), born Washington, DC, June 8, 1945.

JUNE 9 — FRIDAY

Day 160 — 205 Remaining

DONALD DUCK: BIRTHDAY. June 9, 1934. Donald Duck was "born," introduced in the Disney short *Orphans' Benefit*.

HOORAY FOR YEAR-ROUND SCHOOL DAY. June 9. To promote the benefits of a year-round school calendar which makes learning a continuous process and better suits the demanding educational needs of today's world. Annually, the second Friday in June. For more info, send 9½″ SASE to: Hooray for Year-Round School Day, Horace Mann Choice School, 3530-38th Ave, Rock Island, IL 61201.

JORDAN: ACCESSION DAY: ANNIVERSARY. June 9. National holiday. Commemorates the accession to the throne of King Abdullah II in 1999.

BIRTHDAYS TODAY

Michael J. Fox, 45, actor ("Family Ties," *Back to the Future* films), born Edmonton, AB, Canada, June 9, 1961.
Gregory Maguire, 52, author (*Seven Spiders Spinning*), born Albany, NY, June 9, 1954.
Natalie Portman, 25, actress (*Star Wars—Episodes I, II* and *III, Garden State*), born Natalie Herschlag, Jerusalem, Israel, June 9, 1981.
Ashley Postell, 20, gymnast, born Cheverly, MD, June 9, 1986.
Peja Stojakovic, 29, basketball player, born Predrag Stojakovic, Belgrade, Yugoslavia, June 9, 1977.

JUNE 10 — SATURDAY

Day 161 — 204 Remaining

BALLPOINT PEN PATENTED: ANNIVERSARY. June 10, 1943. Hungarian Laszlo Biro patented the ballpoint pen, which he had been developing since the 1930s. He was living at Argentina, where he had gone to escape the Nazis. In many languages, the word for ballpoint pen is "biro."

CONGO (BRAZZAVILLE): DAY OF NATIONAL RECONCILIATION. June 10. National holiday in Congo (Brazzaville).

FIRST FULL-SIZE DINOSAUR REPLICAS: ANNIVERSARY. June 10, 1854. When Crystal Palace was reopened to the public in Sydenham Park, London, on this day in 1854, among the attractions were the first full-size replicas of dinosaurs ever created. Sculptor Benjamin Waterhouse Hawkins, directed by Sir Richard Owen (who coined the term "dinosaur" in 1842), made iguanodons, pterodactyls, plesiosaurs, and other prehistoric creatures out of concrete, bricks and iron hoops. Since no complete dinosaur skeletons had been found at that point, the dinosaurs were created out of conjecture, but gave the public a way to imagine the "terrible lizards." For more info: *The Dinosaurs of Waterhouse Hawkins* by Barbara Kerley (Scholastic, 0-439-11494-2, $16.95 Ages 6 & up).

JORDAN: GREAT ARAB REVOLT AND ARMY DAY. June 10. Commemorates the beginning of the Great Arab Revolt in 1916. National holiday.

PORTUGAL: DAY OF PORTUGAL. June 10. National holiday. Anniversary of the death in 1580 of Portugal's national poet, Luis

Vas de Camoes (Camoens), born in 1524 (exact date unknown) at either Lisbon or possibly Coimbra. Died at Lisbon, Portugal.

UNITED KINGDOM: TROOPING THE COLOUR—QUEEN'S OFFICIAL BIRTHDAY PARADE. June 10 (tentative). National holiday in the United Kingdom. Horse Guards Parade, Whitehall, London. Colorful ceremony with music and pageantry during which Her Majesty The Queen takes the salute from her Household Division. Observance dates from 1805 in the reign of King George III. Starts at 11 AM. When requesting info, send SASE. Trooping the Colour is always the second or third Saturday in June; the Queen's actual birthday is Apr 21. Est attendance: 10,000. For info: The Ticket Office, HQ Household Division, 1 Chelsea Barracks, London, England SW1H 8RF. Web: www.army.mod.uk/ceremonialandheritage/.

BIRTHDAYS TODAY

Nat Hentoff, 81, author (*The Day They Came to Arrest the Book*), born Boston, MA, June 10, 1925.

Charlotte Herman, 69, author (*The House on Walenska Street, Millie Cooper 3B*), born Chicago, IL, June 10, 1937.

Tara Lipinski, 24, figure skater, born Philadelphia, PA, June 10, 1982.

Maurice Sendak, 78, author, illustrator (*Chicken Soup with Rice*, Caldecott Medal for *Where the Wild Things Are*), born Brooklyn, NY, June 10, 1928.

Leelee Sobieski, 24, actress (*Deep Impact*), born Liliane Sobieski, New York, NY, June 10, 1982.

JUNE 11 — SUNDAY

Day 162 — 203 Remaining

CHILDREN'S DAY IN MASSACHUSETTS. June 11. Annually, the second Sunday in June. The governor proclaims this day each year.

CHILDREN'S SUNDAY. June 11. Traditionally the second Sunday in June is observed as Children's Sunday in many Christian churches.

COUSTEAU, JACQUES: BIRTH ANNIVERSARY. June 11, 1910. French undersea explorer, writer and filmmaker, born at St. Andre-de-Cubzac, France. He invented the Aqualung, which allowed him and his colleagues to produce more than 80 documentary films about undersea life, two of which won Oscars. This scientist and explorer was awarded the French Legion of Honor for his work in the Resistance in WWII. He died at Paris, France, June 25, 1997. For more info: *Jacques Cousteau* by Lesley A. Dutemple (Lerner, 0-8225-4979-4, $25.26 Gr. 6–10).

KING KAMEHAMEHA I DAY. June 11. Designated state holiday in Hawaii honors memory of Hawaiian monarch (1737–1819). Governor appoints state commission to plan annual celebration.

June 2006

S	M	T	W	T	F	S
				1	2	3
4	5	6	7	8	9	10
11	12	13	14	15	16	17
18	19	20	21	22	23	24
25	26	27	28	29	30	

LIBYA: AMERICAN BASES EVACUATION DAY. June 11. National holiday. Commemorates the closing of an American military base in 1970.

MOON PHASE: FULL MOON. June 11. Moon enters Full Moon phase at 2:03 PM, EDT.

MOUNT PINATUBO ERUPTS IN PHILIPPINES: 15th ANNIVERSARY. June 11, 1991. Long-dormant volcano Mount Pinatubo erupted with a violent explosion, spewing ash and gases that could be seen for more than 60 miles, into the air. The surrounding areas were covered with ash and mud created by rainstorms. US military bases Clark and Subic Bay were also damaged. On July 6, 1992, Ellsworth Dutton of the National Oceanic and Atmospheric Administration's Climate Monitoring and Diagnostics Laboratory announced that a layer of sulfuric acid droplets released into the Earth's atmosphere by the eruption had cooled the planet's average temperature by about 1 degree Fahrenheit. The greatest difference was noted in the Northern Hemisphere with a drop of 1.5 degrees. Although the temperature drop was temporary, the climate trend made determining the effect of greenhouse warming on the Earth more difficult. For more info visit Volcano World: volcano.und.nodak.edu.

★**NATIONAL FLAG WEEK.** June 11–17. Presidential Proclamation issued each year since 1966 for the week including June 14. (Public Law 89–443 of June 9, 1966.) In addition, the president often calls upon the American people to participate in public ceremonies in which the Pledge of Allegiance is recited. For info: www.usflag.org.

ORTHODOX PENTECOST. June 11. Observed by Eastern Orthodox churches.

RACE UNITY DAY. June 11. Baha'i-sponsored observance promoting racial harmony and understanding and the essential unity of humanity. Annually, the second Sunday in June. For info: Office of Public Information, Baha'is of the US, 866 UN Plaza, Ste 120, New York, NY 10017-1822. Phone: (212) 803-2500. Fax: (212) 803-2573. E-mail: usopi-ny@bic.org. Web: www.us.bahai.org.

RANKIN, JEANNETTE: BIRTH ANNIVERSARY. June 11, 1880. First woman elected to the US Congress, a reformer, feminist and pacifist, was born at Missoula, MT. She was the only member of Congress to vote against a declaration of war against Japan in December 1941. Died May 18, 1973, at Carmel, CA.

ROYALL, ANNE: BIRTH ANNIVERSARY. June 11, 1769. America's first woman journalist was born Anne Newport in New Baltimore, MD. Widowed by the death of her husband, William Royall, Anne Royall turned to journalism to support herself. She became a Washington, DC–based reporter and editor who exposed the abuses of government first in *Paul Pry* (1831–1836; a newspaper typeset by orphans) and then *The Huntress* (1836–1854). Her criticism won her many enemies, and in 1829 she was prosecuted successfully as a "common scold"—the first woman in America to earn that legal description. Royall died at Washington, DC, on Oct 1, 1854.

TRINITY SUNDAY. June 11. Christian Holy Day on the Sunday after Pentecost commemorates the Holy Trinity, the three divine persons—Father, Son and Holy Spirit—in one God. See also: "Pentecost" (June 4).

BIRTHDAYS TODAY

Joe Montana, 50, former sportscaster and football player, born New Eagle, PA, June 11, 1956.

Robert Munsch, 61, author (*Thomas' Snowsuit*), born Pittsburgh, PA, June 11, 1945.

Gene Wilder, 73, actor (*Willy Wonka & the Chocolate Factory*), born Milwaukee, WI, June 11, 1933 (some sources say 1935).

JUNE 12 — MONDAY

Day 163 — 202 Remaining

BUSH, GEORGE H.W.: BIRTHDAY. June 12, 1924. The 41st president (Jan 20, 1989–Jan 20, 1993) of the US, born at Milton, MA. Bush had served as the 43rd vice president under Ronald Reagan. Bush's son, George W. Bush, was elected the 43rd president in 2000 and re-elected in 2004. For more info: www.ipl.org /ref/POTUS.

FRANK, ANNE: BIRTH ANNIVERSARY. June 12, 1929. Born at Frankfurt, Germany. Anne Frank moved with her family to Amsterdam to escape the Nazis but after Holland was invaded by Germany, they had to go into hiding. In 1942 Anne began to keep a diary. She died at Bergen-Belsen concentration camp in 1945. After the war, her father published her diary, on which a stage play and movie were later based. See also: "Diary of Anne Frank: The Last Entry: Anniversary" (Aug 1). For more info: *Anne Frank: A Hidden Life*,by Mirjam Pressler (Dutton, 0-525-46330-5, $15.99 Gr. 5–12) or www.annefrank.com.

NATIONAL BASEBALL HALL OF FAME: ANNIVERSARY. June 12, 1939. The National Baseball Hall of Fame and Museum, Inc, was dedicated at Cooperstown, NY. More than 200 individuals have been honored for their contributions to the game of baseball by induction into the Baseball Hall of Fame. The first players chosen for membership (1936) were Ty Cobb, Honus Wagner, Babe Ruth, Christy Mathewson and Walter Johnson. Relics and memorabilia from the history of baseball are housed at this shrine of America's national sport.

PHILIPPINES: INDEPENDENCE DAY. June 12. National holiday. Declared independence from Spain in 1898.

QUEEN ELIZABETH II'S OFFICIAL BIRTHDAY. June 12. A holiday in Australia, Belize, Cayman Islands, Fiji and Papua New Guinea on the second Monday in June. In New Zealand and Tuvalu it is commemorated on the first Monday in June. Queen Elizabeth's actual birthday is Apr 21.

RUSSIA: INDEPENDENCE DAY. June 12. National holiday. Commemorates the election in 1991 of the first popularly elected leader (Yeltsin) in the 1,000-year history of the Russian state.

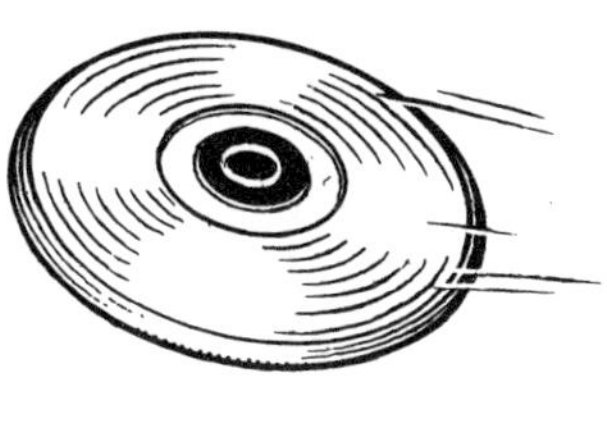

BIRTHDAYS TODAY

George Herbert Walker Bush, 82, 41st president of the US (1989–93), born Milton, MA, June 12, 1924.

Antawn Jamison, 30, basketball player, born Shreveport, LA, June 12, 1976.

Helen Lester, 70, author (*Hooway for Wodney Wat*), born Evanston, IL, June 12, 1936.

Hillary McKay, 47, author (*The Amber Cat*), born the Midlands, England, June 12, 1959.

JUNE 13 — TUESDAY

Day 164 — 201 Remaining

FIRST ROLLER COASTER OPENS: ANNIVERSARY. June 13, 1884. The world's first roller coaster opened today in 1884 at Coney Island, Brooklyn, NY. Built and later patented by LaMarcus Thompson, the "Gravity Pleasure Switchback Railway" boasted two parallel 600–foot tracks that descended from 50 feet. The cars traveled at six miles per hour. Riders paid five cents for their ride. The roller coaster was a sensation and soon amusement parks all over the US and the world featured them. See also: "Thompson, LaMarcus A.: Birth Anniversary" (Mar 8).

***MIRANDA* DECISION: 40th ANNIVERSARY.** June 13, 1966. The US Supreme Court rendered a 5–4 decision in the case of *Miranda v Arizona*, holding that the Fifth Amendment of the Constitution "required warnings before valid statements could be taken by police." The decision has been described as "providing basic legal protections to persons who might otherwise not be aware of their rights." Ernesto Miranda, the 23-year-old whose name became nationally known, was retried after the Miranda Decision, convicted and sent back to prison. Miranda was stabbed to death in a card game dispute at Phoenix, AZ, in 1976. A suspect in the killing was released by police after he had been read his "Miranda rights." Police procedures now routinely require the reading of a prisoner's constitutional rights ("Miranda") before questioning.

SCOTT, WINFIELD: BIRTH ANNIVERSARY. June 13, 1786. American army general, negotiator of peace treaties with the Indians and twice nominated for president (1848 and 1852). Leader of brilliant military campaign in Mexican War in 1847. Scott was born at Petersburg, VA, and died at West Point, NY, May 29, 1866.

BIRTHDAYS TODAY

Tim Allen, 53, comedian, actor (*The Santa Clause*, "Home Improvement"), born Denver, CO, June 13, 1953.

Jennifer Gillom, 42, basketball player, born Abbeville, MS, June 13, 1964.

Ashley Olsen, 20, actress ("Full House," "Two of a Kind"), born Sherman Oaks, CA, June 13, 1986.

Mary-Kate Olsen, 20, actress ("Full House," "Two of a Kind"), born Sherman Oaks, CA, June 13, 1986.

JUNE 14 — WEDNESDAY

Day 165 — 200 Remaining

ARMY ESTABLISHED BY CONGRESS: ANNIVERSARY. June 14, 1775. Anniversary of Resolution of the Continental Congress establishing the army as the first US military service.

BARTLETT, JOHN: BIRTH ANNIVERSARY. June 14, 1820. American editor and compiler of Bartlett's *Familiar Quotations* [1855] was born at Plymouth, MA. Though he had little formal education, he created one of the most-used reference works of the English language. No quotation of his own is among the more than 22,000 listed today, but in the preface to the first edition he wrote that the object of this work was to show "the obligation our language owes to various authors for numerous phrases and familiar quotations which have become 'household words.'" Bartlett died at Cambridge, MA, Dec 3, 1905. His book remains in print today in the 17th edition.

FIRST NONSTOP TRANSATLANTIC FLIGHT: ANNIVERSARY. June 14–15, 1919. Captain John Alcock and Lieutenant Arthur W. Brown flew a Vickers Vimy bomber 1,900 miles nonstop from St. Johns, Newfoundland, to Clifden, County Galway, Ireland. In spite of their crash landing in an Irish peat bog, their flight inspired public interest in aviation. See also: "Lindbergh Flight: Anniversary" (May 20).

★**FLAG DAY.** June 14. Presidential Proclamation issued each year for June 14. Proclamation 1335, of May 30, 1916, covers all succeeding years. Has been issued annually since 1941. (Public Law 81–203 of Aug 3, 1949.) Customarily issued as "Flag Day and National Flag Week," as in 1986; the president usually mentions "a time to honor America," Flag Day to Independence Day (89 Stat. 211). See also: "National Flag Day USA: Pause for the Pledge" (this date).

FLAG DAY: ANNIVERSARY OF THE STARS AND STRIPES. June 14, 1777. John Adams introduced the following resolution before the Continental Congress, meeting at Philadelphia, PA: "Resolved, That the flag of the thirteen United States shall be thirteen stripes, alternate red and white; that the union be thirteen stars, white on a blue field, representing a new constellation." Legal holiday in Pennsylvania. For more info: www.flagday.org.

JAPAN: RICE PLANTING FESTIVAL. June 14. Osaka. Ceremonial transplanting of rice seedlings in paddy field at Sumiyashi Shrine, Osaka.

MALAWI: FREEDOM DAY. June 14. National holiday. Commemorates free elections of 1994.

NATIONAL FLAG DAY USA: PAUSE FOR THE PLEDGE. June 14. Held simultaneously across the country at 7 PM, EDT. Public law 99–54 recognizes the Pause for the Pledge as part of National Flag Day ceremonies. The concept of the Pause for the Pledge of Allegiance was conceived as a way for all citizens to share a patriotic moment. National ceremony at Fort McHenry National Monument and Historic Shrine.

STOWE, HARRIET BEECHER: BIRTH ANNIVERSARY. June 14, 1811. American writer Harriet Beecher Stowe, daughter of the Reverend Lyman Beecher and sister of Henry Ward Beecher. Author of *Uncle Tom's Cabin*, an antislavery novel that provoked a storm of protest and resulted in fame for its author. Two characters in the novel attained such importance that their names became part of the English language—the Negro slave, Uncle Tom, and the villainous slaveowner, Simon Legree. The reaction to *Uncle Tom's Cabin* and its profound political impact are without parallel in American literature. It is said that during the Civil War, when Harriet Beecher Stowe was introduced to President Abraham Lincoln, his words to her were, "So you're the little woman who wrote the book that made this great war." Stowe was born at Litchfield, CT, and died at Hartford, CT, July 1, 1896. For more info: *Harriet Beecher Stowe and the Beecher Preachers* by Jean Fritz (Putnam, 0-399-22666-4, $15.99 Gr. 7–9).

June 2006

S	M	T	W	T	F	S
				1	2	3
4	5	6	7	8	9	10
11	12	13	14	15	16	17
18	19	20	21	22	23	24
25	26	27	28	29	30	

UNIVAC COMPUTER: 55th ANNIVERSARY. June 14, 1951. Univac 1, the world's first commercial computer, designed for the US Bureau of the Census, was unveiled, demonstrated and dedicated at Philadelphia, PA. Though this milestone of the computer age was the first commercial electronic computer, it had been preceded by ENIAC (Electronic Numeric Integrator and Computer), completed under the supervision of J. Presper Eckert, Jr, and John W. Mauchly, at the University of Pennsylvania, in 1946.

WARREN G. HARDING IS FIRST PRESIDENT TO BROADCAST ON RADIO: ANNIVERSARY. June 14, 1922. Warren G. Harding was the first president to broadcast a message over the radio. The event was the dedication of the Francis Scott Key Memorial at Baltimore, MD. The first official government message was broadcast Dec 6, 1923.

BIRTHDAYS TODAY

Bruce Degen, 61, author and illustrator (*Jamberry*), born Brooklyn, NY, June 14, 1945.

Steffi Graf, 37, former tennis player, born Bruhl, West Germany, June 14, 1969.

James Gurney, 48, author and illustrator (*Dinotopia*), born Glendale, CA, June 14, 1958.

Annia Hatch, 28, gymnast, born Guantanamo, Cuba, June 14, 1978.

Amy MacDonald, 55, author (*Little Beaver and the Echo*), born Beverly, MA, June 14, 1951.

Michael O. Tunnell, 56, author (*Mailing May, The Children of Topaz*), born in Texas, June 14, 1950.

Laurence Yep, 58, author (*Dragon's Gate, The Rainbow's People*), born San Francisco, CA, June 14, 1948.

JUNE 15 — THURSDAY

Day 166 — 199 Remaining

ARKANSAS: ADMISSION DAY: ANNIVERSARY. June 15. Became the 25th state in 1836.

JACKSON, RACHEL DONELSON ROBARDS: BIRTH ANNIVERSARY. June 15, 1767. Wife of Andrew Jackson, 7th president of the US, born at Halifax County, NC. Died at Nashville, TN, Dec 22, 1828.

MAGNA CARTA DAY: ANNIVERSARY. June 15, 1215. Anniversary of King John's sealing of the Magna Carta "in the meadow called Ronimed between Windsor and Staines on the fifteenth day of June in the seventeenth year of our reign." This document is regarded as the first charter of English liberties and one of the most important documents in the history of political and human freedom. Four original copies of the 1215 charter survive. The April 2000 issue of *Calliope* magazine was devoted to the Magna Carta.

MAYAN TOMB OF PACAL DISCOVERED: ANNIVERSARY. June 15, 1952. Since 1949, when he discovered the jungle-hidden Temple of Inscriptions at Palenque, Mexico, Mexican archeologist Dr. Alberto Ruz Lhuillier and his team had labored in a hidden stairway within the pyramid. On this day in 1952, they finished excavations and found the royal tomb of Mayan ruler Pacal (or "Shield")—undisturbed since his death in 683 AD. Covered by an ornately carved 11.5 × 6.5 foot sarcophagus lid, the tomb revealed Pacal's remains covered in jade and mother-of-pearl ornaments, and his face covered by a jade mosaic mask. This discovery marked the first time a tomb had been found within a Mayan pyramid.

NATIVE AMERICANS GAIN CITIZENSHIP: ANNIVERSARY. June 15, 1924. The US Congress passed a law on this day recognizing the citizenship of Native Americans.

TWELFTH AMENDMENT TO US CONSTITUTION RATIFIED: ANNIVERSARY. June 15, 1804. The 12th Amendment to the Constitution changed the method of electing the president and vice president after a tie in the electoral college during the election of 1800. Rather than each elector voting for two candidates with the candidate receiving the most votes elected president and the second-place candidate elected vice president, each elector was now required to designate his choice for president and vice president, respectively.

BIRTHDAYS TODAY

Courteney Cox Arquette, 42, actress ("Friends," "Family Ties"), born Birmingham, AL, June 15, 1964.

Wade Boggs, 48, Hall of Fame baseball player, born Omaha, NE, June 15, 1958.

Christopher Castile, 26, actor ("Step By Step," *Beethoven*), born Los Alamitos, CA, June 15, 1980.

Brian Jacques, 67, author (the Redwall series), born Liverpool, England, June 15, 1939.

Justin Leonard, 34, golfer, born Dallas, TX, June 15, 1972.

Betty Ren Wright, 79, author (*The Dollhouse Murders*), born Wakefield, MI, June 15, 1927.

JUNE 16 — FRIDAY

Day 167 — 198 Remaining

SOUTH AFRICA: YOUTH DAY. June 16. National holiday. Commemorates a student uprising in 1976 in Soweto against "Bantu Education" and the enforced teaching of the Afrikaans language.

SPACE MILESTONE: FIRST WOMAN IN SPACE, *VOSTOK 6* (USSR). June 16, 1963. Valentina Tereshkova, 26, former cotton-mill worker, born on a collective farm near Yaroslavl, USSR, became the first woman in space when her spacecraft, *Vostok 6*, took off from the Tyuratam launch site. She manually controlled *Vostok 6* during the 70.8-hour flight through 48 orbits of Earth and landed by parachute (separate from her cabin) June 19, 1963. In November 1963 she married cosmonaut Andrian Nikolayev, who had piloted *Vostok 3* through 64 earth orbits, Aug 11–15, 1962. Their child Yelena (1964) was the first born to space-traveler parents.

BIRTHDAYS TODAY

Kalli Dakos, 56, author, poet (*Mrs Cole on an Onion Roll; If You're Not Here, Please Raise Your Hand*), born Ottawa, ON, Canada, June 16, 1950.

Cobi Jones, 36, soccer player, born Westlake Village, CA, June 16, 1970.

M. Jodi Rell, 60, Governor of Connecticut (R), born Norfolk, VA, June 16, 1946.

Kerry Wood, 29, baseball player, born Irving, TX, June 16, 1977.

JUNE 17 — SATURDAY

Day 168 — 197 Remaining

BRANSCUM, ROBBIE: BIRTH ANNIVERSARY. June 17, 1937. Author best known for *The Adventures of Johnny May* and *Cameo Rose*. She won the Friends of American Writers Award in 1977 and the Edgar Allan Poe Award in 1983. Born near Big Flat, AR, Branscum died at Harrisonburg, VA, May 24, 1997.

BUNKER HILL DAY IN MASSACHUSETTS. June 17. Legal holiday in the county in commemoration of the Battle of Bunker Hill that took place in 1775. Proclaimed annually by the governor.

HOOPER, WILLIAM: BIRTH ANNIVERSARY. June 17, 1742. Signer of the Declaration of Independence, born at Boston, MA. Died Oct 14, 1790, at Hillsboro, NC.

ICELAND: INDEPENDENCE DAY. June 17. Anniversary of founding of republic in 1944 and independence from Denmark is major festival, especially in Reykjavik. Parades, competitions, street dancing.

SOUTH AFRICA REPEALS LAST APARTHEID LAW: 15th ANNIVERSARY. June 17, 1991. The Parliament of South Africa repealed the Population Registration Act, removing the law that was the foundation of apartheid. The law, first enacted in 1950, required the classification by race of all South Africans at birth. It established four compulsory racial categories: white, mixed race, Asian and black. Although this marked the removal of the last of the apartheid laws, blacks in South Africa still could not vote.

UNITED NATIONS: WORLD DAY TO COMBAT DESERTIFICATION AND DROUGHT. June 17. Proclaimed by the General Assembly Dec 19, 1994 (Res 49/115). States were invited to devote the World Day to promoting public awareness of the need for international cooperation to combat desertification and the effects of drought and on the implementation of the UN Convention to Combat Desertification. For info: United Nations, Dept of Public Info, New York, NY 10017.

WORLD JUGGLING DAY. June 17. Juggling clubs all over the world hold local festivals to demonstrate, teach and celebrate their art. Annually, the Saturday on or closest to June 17. For info: International Jugglers' Assn, PO Box 112550, Carrollton, TX 75011-2550. Web: www.juggle.org.

BIRTHDAYS TODAY

Leslie Baker, 57, author and illustrator (*The Third-Story Cat*), born Baltimore, MD, June 17, 1949.

Liza Ketchum, 60, author (*Orphan Journey Home, The Gold Rush*), born Albany, NY, June 17, 1946.

Venus Williams, 26, tennis player, born Lynwood, CA, June 17, 1980.

JUNE 18 — SUNDAY

Day 169 — 196 Remaining

CORPUS CHRISTI (US OBSERVANCE). June 18. A movable Roman Catholic celebration commemorating the institution of the Holy Eucharist. The solemnity has been observed on the Thursday following Trinity Sunday since 1246 (June 11 in 2006), except in the US, where it is observed on the Sunday following Trinity Sunday.

★ **FATHER'S DAY.** June 18. Presidential Proclamation issued for third Sunday in June in 1966 and annually since 1971. (Public Law 92–278 of Apr 24, 1972.)

FATHER'S DAY. June 18. Recognition of the third Sunday in June as Father's Day occurred first at the request of Mrs John B. Dodd of Spokane, WA, June 19, 1910. It was proclaimed for that date by the mayor of Spokane and recognized by the governor of Washington. The idea was publicly supported by President Calvin Coolidge in 1924, but not presidentially proclaimed until 1966. It was assured of annual recognition by Public Law 92–278 of April 1972.

MOON PHASE: LAST QUARTER. June 18. Moon enters Last Quarter phase at 10:08 AM, EDT.

NATIONAL SPLURGE DAY. June 18. Today is the day to go out and do something indulgent. Have fun! [©1994.] For info: Adrienne Sioux Koopersmith, 1437 W Rosemont, #1W, Chicago, IL 60660-1319. Phone: (773) 743-5341. Fax: (773) 743-5395. E-mail: askoopersmith@hotmail.com.

ORTHODOX FESTIVAL OF ALL SAINTS. June 18. Observed by Eastern Orthodox churches on the Sunday following Orthodox Pentecost (June 11 in 2006). Marks the end of the 18-week Triodion cycle.

SEYCHELLES: CONSTITUTION DAY. June 18. National holiday commemorating 1993 constitution.

SPACE MILESTONE: *CHALLENGER STS-7* (US): FIRST AMERICAN WOMAN IN SPACE: ANNIVERSARY. June 18, 1983. Shuttle *Challenger*, launched from Kennedy Space Center, FL, with crew of five, including Sally K. Ride (first American woman in space), Robert Crippen, Norman Thagard, John Fabian and Frederick Houck. Landed at Edwards Air Force Base, CA, June 24, after a near-perfect six-day mission.

WAR OF 1812: DECLARATION ANNIVERSARY. June 18, 1812. After much debate in Congress between "hawks" such as Henry Clay and John Calhoun and "doves" such as John Randolph, Congress issued a declaration of war on Great Britain. The action was prompted primarily by Britain's violation of America's rights on the high seas and British incitement of Indian warfare on the frontier. War was seen by some as a way to acquire Florida and Canada. The hostilities ended with the signing of the Treaty of Ghent, Dec 24, 1814, at Ghent, Belgium. For more info: *The War of 1812* by Andrew Santella (Children's Press, 0-516-21597-3, $20.50 Gr. 4–6).

BIRTHDAYS TODAY

Pat Hutchins, 64, author and illustrator (*Changes, Changes, The Wind Blew*), born Yorkshire, England, June 18, 1942.

Angela Johnson, 45, author (*Heaven*), born Tuskegee, AL, June 18, 1961.

Paul McCartney, 64, singer, songwriter (The Beatles), born Liverpool, England, June 18, 1942.

John D. (Jay) Rockefeller IV, 69, US Senator (D, West Virginia), born New York, NY, June 18, 1937.

Connie Roop, 55, author, with her husband Peter (*I, Columbus; Keep the Lights Burning, Abbie*), born Elkhorn, WI, June 18, 1951.

Chris Van Allsburg, 57, illustrator and author (Caldecott Medals for *The Polar Express* and *Jumanji*), born Grand Rapids, MI, June 18, 1949.

June 2006

S	M	T	W	T	F	S
				1	2	3
4	5	6	7	8	9	10
11	12	13	14	15	16	17
18	19	20	21	22	23	24
25	26	27	28	29	30	

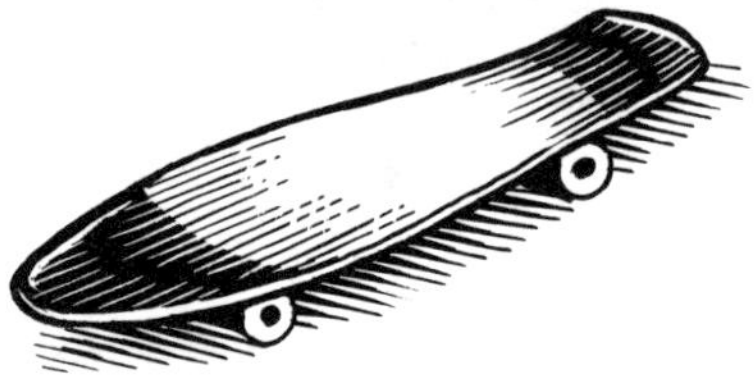

JUNE 19 — MONDAY

Day 170 — 195 Remaining

EMANCIPATION DAY IN TEXAS. June 19, 1865. In honor of the emancipation of the slaves in Texas.

FORTAS, ABE: BIRTH ANNIVERSARY. June 19, 1910. Abe Fortas was born at Memphis, TN. He was appointed to the Supreme Court by President Lyndon Johnson in 1965. Prior to his appointment he was known as a civil libertarian, having argued cases for government employees and other individuals accused by Senator Joe McCarthy of having communist affiliations. He argued the 1963 landmark Supreme Court case of *Gideon v Wainwright*, which established the right of indigent defendants to free legal aid in criminal prosecutions. In 1968 he was nominated by Johnson to succeed Chief Justice Earl Warren, but his nomination was withdrawn after much conservative opposition in the Senate. In 1969 Fortas became the first Supreme Court Justice to be forced to resign after revelations about questionable financial dealings were made public. He died Apr 5, 1982, at Washington, DC.

GARFIELD: BIRTHDAY. June 19, 1978. America's favorite lasagna-loving cat celebrates his birthday. *Garfield*, a modern classic comic strip created by Jim Davis, first appeared in 1978, and has brought laughter to millions. For info: Paws, Inc, Kim Campbell, 5440 E Co Rd 450 N, Albany, IN 47320. Web: www.garfield.com.

GEHRIG, LOU: BIRTH ANNIVERSARY. June 19, 1903. Henry Louis Gehrig, Baseball Hall of Fame first baseman, born Ludwig Heinrich Gehrig, at New York, NY. Gehrig, known as the "Iron Horse," played in 2,130 consecutive games, a record not surpassed until Cal Ripken did in 1995. He played 17 years with the Yankees, hit .340 and slugged 493 home runs, 23 of them grand slams. Gehrig retired in 1939 and was diagnosed with the degenerative muscle disease amyotrophic lateral sclerosis, later known as Lou Gehrig's disease. Died at New York, NY, June 2, 1941. For more info: *Lou Gehrig: The Luckiest Man* by David A. Adler (Harcourt, 0-15-202483-2, $6 Gr. 1–4).

JUNETEENTH. June 19. Celebrated in Texas to commemorate the day when Union General Granger proclaimed the slaves of Texas free. This is also a ceremonial holiday in Florida, commemorating the day slaves in Florida were notified of the Emancipation Proclamation. Juneteenth has become a day for commemoration by African Americans in many parts of the US.

URUGUAY: ARTIGAS DAY. June 19. National holiday. Commemorates the father of Uruguayan independence, General José Gervasio Artigas, born on this day in 1764.

US VIRGIN ISLANDS: ORGANIC ACT DAY. June 19. Commemorates the enactment by the US Congress, July 22, 1954, of the Revised Organic Act, under which the government of the Virgin Islands is organized. Observed annually on the third Monday in June.

BIRTHDAYS TODAY

Andrew Lauer, 41, actor (*I'll Be Home for Christmas*), born Santa Monica, CA, June 19, 1965.

Brian McBride, 34, soccer player, born Arlington Heights, IL, June 19, 1972.

Doug Mientkiewicz, 32, baseball player, born Toledo, OH, June 19, 1974.

Dirk Nowitzki, 28, basketball player, born Wurzburg, West Germany, June 19, 1978.

Elvira Woodruff, 55, author (*Ghosts Don't Get Goose Bumps*), born in New Jersey, June 19, 1951.

JUNE 20 — TUESDAY

Day 171 — 194 Remaining

ARGENTINA: FLAG DAY. June 20. National holiday.

CHESNUTT, CHARLES W.: BIRTH ANNIVERSARY. June 20, 1858. Born at Cleveland, OH, Chesnutt was considered by many as the first important black novelist. His collections of short stories included *The Conjure Woman* (1899) and *The Wife of His Youth and Other Stories of the Color Line* (1899). *The Colonel's Dream* (1905) dealt with the struggles of the freed slave. His work has been compared to later writers such as William Faulkner, Richard Wright and James Baldwin. He died Nov 15, 1932, at Cleveland.

UNITED NATIONS: WORLD REFUGEE DAY. June 20.

WEST VIRGINIA: ADMISSION DAY: ANNIVERSARY. June 20. Became 35th state in 1863. Observed as a holiday in West Virginia. The state of West Virginia is a product of the Civil War. Originally part of Virginia, West Virginia became a separate state when Virginia seceded from the Union.

BIRTHDAYS TODAY

LaVar Arrington, 28, football player, born Pittsburgh, PA, June 20, 1978.

John Goodman, 54, actor (*Arachnophobia, The Flintstones, Monsters, Inc*), born St. Louis, MO, June 20, 1952.

Nicole Kidman, 39, actress (Oscar for *The Hours; The Others, Moulin Rouge*), born Honolulu, HI, June 20, 1967.

Annette Curtis Klause, 53, author (*Blood and Chocolate*), born Bristol, England, June 20, 1953.

JUNE 21 — WEDNESDAY

Day 172 — 193 Remaining

CANCER, THE CRAB. June 21–July 22. In the astronomical/astrological zodiac, which divides the sun's apparent orbit into 12 segments, the period June 21–July 22 is identified, traditionally, as the sun sign of Cancer, the Crab. The ruling planet is the moon.

KRAUS, ROBERT: BIRTH ANNIVERSARY. June 21, 1925. Children's author and illustrator, Robert Kraus was born at Milwaukee, WI. He wrote, illustrated and edited more than 100 children's books from 1955 to the late 1990s. He was also a very successful cartoonist, drawing 21 *New Yorker* covers and about 450 cartoons for that magazine. His most beloved book is *Leo the Late Bloomer*, about a young tiger who can't quite keep up with his tiger friends. Other great Kraus titles include *Where are You Going, Little Mouse?; Milton, the Early Riser;* and *Herman the Helper.* Kraus died Aug 7, 2001, at Kent, CT.

NEW HAMPSHIRE RATIFIES CONSTITUTION: ANNIVERSARY. June 21, 1788. By a vote of 57 to 47, New Hampshire became the ninth state to ratify the Constitution.

SPACE MILESTONE: FIRST MANNED PRIVATE SPACEFLIGHT: ANNIVERSARY. June 21, 2004. Michael Melvill, flying the privately financed SpaceShipOne, flew 62 miles in altitude on this date, leaving the Earth's atmosphere. The spacecraft was designed by Burt Rutan and was financed by Paul Allen, philanthropist and Microsoft cofounder. SpaceShipOne made the flight from Mojave Airport at Mojave, CA.

SUMMER. June 21–Sept 23. In the Northern Hemisphere summer begins today with the summer solstice, at 8:26 AM, EDT. Note that in the Southern Hemisphere today is the beginning of winter. Anywhere between the Equator and Arctic Circle, the sun rises and sets farthest north on the horizon for the year and length of daylight is maximum (12 hours, 8 minutes at equator, increasing to 24 hours at Arctic Circle).

TOMPKINS, DANIEL D.: BIRTH ANNIVERSARY. June 21, 1774. Sixth vice president of the US (1817–25), born at Fox Meadows, NY. Died at Staten Island, NY, June 11, 1825.

WASHINGTON, MARTHA DANDRIDGE CUSTIS: BIRTH ANNIVERSARY. June 21, 1731. Wife of George Washington, first president of the US, born at New Kent County, VA. Died at Mount Vernon, VA, May 22, 1802.

BIRTHDAYS TODAY

Berkeley Breathed, 49, cartoonist ("Bloom County"), born Croatia, June 21, 1957.

James Douglas, 55, Governor of Vermont (R), born Springfield, MA, June 21, 1951.

Prince William, 24, son of Prince Charles and Princess Diana, born London, England, June 21, 1982.

JUNE 22 — THURSDAY

Day 173 — 192 Remaining

AMERICAN LIBRARY ASSOCIATION ANNUAL CONFERENCE. June 22–28. New Orleans, LA. Est attendance: 20,000. For info: Public Information Office, American Library Assn, 50 E Huron St, Chicago, IL 60611. Phone: (312) 280-5044. Fax: (312) 944-8520. E-mail: pio@ala.org. Web: www.ala.org.

CROATIA: ANTIFASCIST STRUGGLE COMMEMORATION DAY. June 22. National holiday. Anniversary of uprising against German invaders in 1941.

SWITZERLAND: MORAT BATTLE ANNIVERSARY. June 22, 1476. The little, walled town of Morat played a decisive part in Swiss history. There, the Confederates were victorious over Charles the Bold of Burgundy, laying the basis for French-speaking areas to become Swiss. Now an annual children's festival.

US DEPARTMENT OF JUSTICE: ANNIVERSARY. June 22, 1870. Established by an act of Congress, the Department of Justice is headed by the attorney general. Prior to 1870, the attorney general (whose office had been created Sept 24, 1789) had been a member of the president's cabinet but had not been the head of a department.

BIRTHDAYS TODAY

Dianne Feinstein, 73, US Senator (D, California), born San Francisco, CA, June 22, 1933.

Kurt Warner, 35, football player, born Burlington, IA, June 22, 1971.

JUNE 23 — FRIDAY

Day 174 — 191 Remaining

DENMARK: MIDSUMMER EVE. June 23. Celebrated all over the country with bonfires and merrymaking.

ESTONIA: VICTORY DAY. June 23. National holiday. Commemorates a battle against the Germans in 1919, during the War of Independence.

FIRST TYPEWRITER: ANNIVERSARY. June 23, 1868. First US typewriter was patented by Luther Sholes.

LUXEMBOURG: NATIONAL HOLIDAY. June 23. Commemorating birth of His Royal Highness Grand Duke Jean in 1921. Luxembourg's independence is also celebrated.

MIDSUMMER DAY/EVE CELEBRATIONS. June 23. Celebrates the beginning of summer with maypoles, music, dancing and bonfires. Observed mainly in northern Europe, including Finland, Latvia and Sweden. Day of observance is sometimes St. John's Day (June 24), with celebration on St. John's Eve (June 23) as well, or June 19. Time approximates the summer solstice. See also: "Summer" (June 21).

BIRTHDAYS TODAY

Felix Potvin, 35, hockey player, born Anjou, QC, Canada, June 23, 1971.

Theodore Taylor, 85, author (*The Cay, The Trouble with Tuck*), born Statesville, NC, June 23, 1921.

Clarence Thomas, 58, Associate Justice of the US Supreme Court, born Pinpoint, GA, June 23, 1948.

LaDainian Tomlinson, 27, football player, born Rosebud, TX, June 23, 1979.

JUNE 24 — SATURDAY

Day 175 — 190 Remaining

BERLIN AIRLIFT: ANNIVERSARY. June 24, 1948. In the early days of the Cold War the Soviet Union challenged the West's right of access to Berlin. The Soviets created a blockade, and an airlift to supply some 2,250,000 people at West Berlin resulted. The airlift lasted a total of 321 days and brought into Berlin 1,592,787 tons of supplies. Joseph Stalin finally backed down and the blockade ended May 12, 1949.

CANADA: QUEBEC FÊTE NATIONALE. June 24. Saint Jean Baptiste Day.

CIARDI, JOHN: BIRTH ANNIVERSARY. June 24, 1916. Poet for adults and children (*You Read to Me, I'll Read to You*), born at Boston, MA. Died Mar 30, 1986, at Edison, NJ.

LATVIA: JOHN'S DAY (MIDSUMMER NIGHT DAY). June 24. The festival of Jani, which commemorates the summer solstice and the name day of (Janis) John, is one of Latvia's most ancient as well as joyous rituals. This festival is traditionally celebrated in the countryside, as it emphasizes fertility and the beginning of summer. Festivities begin June 23.

NATIONAL PTA CONVENTION. June 24–26. Phoenix, AZ. Each year, the National PTA Convention and Exhibition serves as an important meeting ground where child advocates convene to work, learn and share. Attending the convention can put you in touch with the information, ideas and materials you need to help make your dreams for children happen! National PTA, 330 N. Wabash Ave, Ste 2100, Chicago IL, 60611. Phone: (800) 307-4PTA (4782). E-mail: info@pta.org. Web: www.pta.org.

PSFCA EAST WEST ALL-STAR GAME. June 24. Mansion Park, Altoona, PA. All-star football game featuring the finest college-bound athletes in Pennsylvania. Come see the "Beasts of the East" take on the "Best of the West" in a must-see, action-packed game. Annually, the last Saturday in June. Est attendance: 10,000. For info: Cheryl Ebersole, Allegheny Mountains CVB, One Convention Center Dr, Altoona, PA 16602. Phone: (814) 943-4183. Fax: (814) 943-8094. E-mail: info@amcvb.com. Web: www.eastwestgame.com.

SCOTLAND: BANNOCKBURN DAY. June 24. Anniversary of the Battle of Bannockburn in 1314 when Robert the Bruce defeated the English, winning Scottish independence.

THORNTON, MATTHEW: DEATH ANNIVERSARY. June 24, 1803. Signer of the Declaration of Independence. Born at Ireland about 1714, he died at Newburyport, MA.

VENEZUELA: BATTLE OF CARABOBO DAY. June 24. National holiday. Commemorates a victory in 1821 that assured independence from Spain.

BIRTHDAYS TODAY

Leonard Everett Fisher, 82, illustrator and author (*Great Wall of China*), born New York, NY, June 24, 1924.

Kathryn Lasky, 62, author (*Sugaring Time*), born Indianapolis, IN, June 24, 1944.

Jean Marzollo, 64, author (*Happy Birthday, Martin Luther King*), born Manchester, CT, June 24, 1942.

George Pataki, 61, Governor of New York (R), born Peekskill, NY, June 24, 1945.

Preki Radosavljevic, 43, soccer player, born Predrag Radosavljevic at Belgrade, Yugoslavia, June 24, 1963.

JUNE 25 — SUNDAY

Day 176 — 189 Remaining

BATTLE OF LITTLE BIGHORN: ANNIVERSARY. June 25, 1876. Lieutenant Colonel George Armstrong Custer, leading military forces of more than 200 men, attacked an encampment of Sioux Indians led by Chiefs Sitting Bull and Crazy Horse near Little Bighorn River, MT. Custer and all men in his immediate command were killed in the brief battle (about two hours) of Little Bighorn. For more info: *It Is a Good Day to Die: Indian Eyewitnesses Tell the Story of the Battle of Little Bighorn* by Herman Viola (Crown, 0-517-70913-9, $19.99 Gr. 5–8).

CBS SENDS FIRST COLOR TV BROADCAST OVER THE AIR: 55th ANNIVERSARY. June 25, 1951. Columbia Broadcasting System broadcast the first color television program. The four-hour program was carried by stations in New York City, Baltimore, Philadelphia, Boston and Washington, DC, although no color sets were owned by the public. At the time CBS, itself, owned fewer than 40 color receivers.

CIVIL WAR IN YUGOSLAVIA: 15th ANNIVERSARY. June 25, 1991. In an Eastern Europe freed from the iron rule of communism and the USSR, separatist and nationalist tensions sup-

June 2006

S	M	T	W	T	F	S
				1	2	3
4	5	6	7	8	9	10
11	12	13	14	15	16	17
18	19	20	21	22	23	24
25	26	27	28	29	30	

pressed for decades rose to a violent boiling point. The republics of Croatia and Slovenia declared their independence, sparking a fractious and bitter war that spread throughout what was formerly Yugoslavia. Ethnic rivalries between Serbians and Croatians began the military conflicts that spread to Slovenia, and in 1992 fighting began in Bosnia-Herzegovina between Serbians and ethnic Muslims. Although the new republics were recognized by the UN and sanctions passed to stop the fighting, it raged on through 1995 despite the efforts of UN peacekeeping forces.

FIRST WOMAN CANADIAN PRIME MINISTER SWORN IN: ANNIVERSARY. June 25, 1993. After winning the June 13 election to the leadership of the ruling Progressive-Conservative Party, Kim Campbell became Canada's 19th prime minister and its first woman prime minister. However, in the general election held Oct 25, 1993, the Liberal Party routed the Progressive-Conservatives in the worst defeat for a governing political party in Canada's 126-year history, reducing the former government's seats in the House of Commons from 154 to 2. Campbell was among those who lost their seats.

JOHN CARVER DAY IN MASSACHUSETTS. June 25. Proclaimed annually by the governor on the fourth Sunday in June to commemorate the first governor of the Plymouth Colony, John Carver, who served from 1620 to 1621.

KOREAN WAR BEGAN: ANNIVERSARY. June 25, 1950. Forces from northern Korea invaded southern Korea, beginning a civil war. US ground forces entered the conflict June 30. An armistice was signed at Panmunjom July 27, 1953, formally dividing the country in two—North Korea and South Korea. For more info: korea50.army.mil/teachers.html or www.koreanwar.go.kr. The Fall 1999 issue of *Cobblestone* (for students ages 9–14) was devoted to the Korean War.

LAST GREAT BUFFALO HUNT: ANNIVERSARY. June 25–27, 1882. By 1882 most of the estimated 60–75 million buffalo had been killed by white hide hunters, the meat left to rot. Buffalo numbered only about 50,000 when "The Last Great Buffalo Hunt" took place on Indian reservation lands near Hettinger, ND. Some 2,000 Teton Sioux Indians in full hunting regalia killed about 5,000 buffalo. The occasion is also referred to as "The Last Stand of the American Buffalo" as within 16 months the last of the free-ranging buffalo were gone. For more info: *Buffalo Hunt* by Russell Freedman (Holiday House, 0-8234-0702-0, $19.95 Gr. 3–7). For info: Wendy Hehn, Dir Community Promotions, Box 1323, Hettinger, ND 58639. Phone: (701) 567-2531. Fax: (701) 567-2690. E-mail: adamsdv@hettinger.ctctel.com. Web: www.hettingernd.com.

MONTSERRAT: VOLCANO ERUPTS: ANNIVERSARY. June 25, 1997. After lying dormant for 400 years, the Soufriere Hills volcano began to come to life in July 1995. It erupted in 1997, covering Plymouth, Montserrat's capital city, and two-thirds of the rest of the lush Caribbean island with a heavy layer of ash. Two-thirds of the population relocated to other islands or to Great Britain. For more info, visit Volcano World: volcano.und.nodak.edu.

MOON PHASE: NEW MOON. June 25. Moon enters New Moon phase at 12:05 PM, EDT.

MOZAMBIQUE: INDEPENDENCE DAY. June 25. National holiday. Commemorates independence from Portugal in 1975.

SLOVENIA: NATIONAL DAY. June 25. Public holiday. Commemorates independence from the former Yugoslavia in 1991.

SUPREME COURT BANS SCHOOL PRAYER: ANNIVERSARY. June 25, 1962. The US Supreme Court ruled that a prayer read aloud in public schools violated the 1st Amendment's separation of church and state. The court again struck down a law pertaining to the First Amendment when it disallowed an Alabama law that permitted a daily one-minute period of silent meditation or prayer in public schools June 1, 1985. (Vote 6–3.)

TWO YUGOSLAV REPUBLICS DECLARE INDEPENDENCE: 15th ANNIVERSARY. June 25, 1991. The republics of Slovenia and Croatia formally declared independence from Yugoslavia. The two northwestern republics did not, however, secede outright.

VIRGINIA RATIFIES CONSTITUTION: ANNIVERSARY. June 25. Became the 10th state to ratify the Constitution in 1788.

BIRTHDAYS TODAY

Eric Carle, 77, author (*The Very Hungry Caterpillar, The Very Busy Spider, The Grouchy Ladybug*), born Syracuse, NY, June 25, 1929.

Tololwa M. Mollel, 54, author (*The Orphan Boy: A Maasai Story*), born Tanzania, June 25, 1952.

Dikembe Mutombo, 40, basketball player, born Kinshasa, Zaire, June 25, 1966.

JUNE 26 — MONDAY

Day 177 — 188 Remaining

BAR CODE INTRODUCED: ANNIVERSARY. June 26, 1974. A committee formed in 1970 by US grocers and food manufacturers recommended in 1973 a Universal Product Code (i.e., a bar code) for supermarket items that would allow electronic scanning of prices. On this day in 1974 a pack of Wrigley's gum was swiped across the first checkout scanner at a supermarket at Troy, OH. Today bar codes are used to keep track of everything from freight cars to cattle.

BORDEN, SIR ROBERT LAIRD: BIRTH ANNIVERSARY. June 26, 1854. Canadian statesman and prime minister, born at Grand Pre, Nova Scotia. Died at Ottawa, June 10, 1937.

BUCK, PEARL S.: BIRTH ANNIVERSARY. June 26, 1892. Author (*The Big Wave*), noted authority on China and humanitarian. Nobel Prize winner. Born at Hillsboro, WV. Died Mar 6, 1973, at Danby, VT.

CANADA: NEWFOUNDLAND DISCOVERY DAY. June 26. Commemorates the discovery of Newfoundland by John Cabot in 1497. Observed on the Monday nearest June 24.

CN TOWER OPENING: 30th ANNIVERSARY. June 26, 1976. Birthday of the world's tallest freestanding structure, the CN Tower, 1,815 feet, 5 inches high, at Toronto, Ontario, Canada. For info: CN Tower, 301 Front St W, Toronto, ON, Canada M5V 2T6. Phone: (416) 360-8500. Fax: (416) 601-4713.

FARLEY, WALTER: BIRTH ANNIVERSARY. June 26, 1922. Children's author, born at New York, NY. He wrote the tale of the famous horse, *The Black Stallion* (1941), and later wrote the prequel, *The Young Black Stallion*, with his son in 1989. Farley died at Sarasota, FL, Oct 16, 1989.

FLAG AMENDMENT DEFEATED: ANNIVERSARY. June 26, 1990. The Senate rejected a proposed constitutional amendment that would have permitted states to prosecute those who destroyed or desecrated American flags. Similar legislation continues to be considered by Congress.

MADAGASCAR: INDEPENDENCE DAY. June 26. National holiday. Commemorates independence from France in 1960.

MIDDLETON, ARTHUR: BIRTH ANNIVERSARY. June 26, 1742. American Revolutionary leader and signer of the Declaration of Independence, born near Charleston, SC. Died at Goose Creek, SC, Jan 1, 1787.

PIZARRO, FRANCISCO: DEATH ANNIVERSARY. June 26, 1541. Spanish conqueror of Peru, born at Extremadura, Spain, ca. 1471. Pizarro died at Lima, Peru.

SAINT LAWRENCE SEAWAY DEDICATION: ANNIVERSARY. June 26, 1959. President Dwight D. Eisenhower and Queen Elizabeth II jointly dedicated the St. Lawrence Seaway in formal ceremonies held at St. Lambert, Quebec, Canada. A project undertaken jointly by Canada and the US, the waterway (which provides access between the Atlantic Ocean and the Great Lakes) had been opened to traffic Apr 25, 1959.

UNITED NATIONS CHARTER SIGNED: ANNIVERSARY. June 26, 1945. The UN Charter was signed at San Francisco, CA, by 50 nations.

UNITED NATIONS: INTERNATIONAL DAY AGAINST DRUG ABUSE AND ILLICIT TRAFFICKING. June 26. Following a recommendation of the 1987 International Conference on Drug Abuse and Illicit Trafficking, the United Nations General Assembly (Res 42/112) expressed its determination to strengthen action and cooperation for an international society free of drug abuse and proclaimed June 26 as an annual observance to raise public awareness. For info: UN, Dept of Public Info, Public Inquiries Unit, RM GA-57, New York, NY 10017. Phone: (212) 963-4475. Fax: (212) 963-0071. E-mail: inquiries@un.org.

ZAHARIAS, MILDRED "BABE" DIDRIKSON: BIRTH ANNIVERSARY. June 26, 1914. Born Mildred Ella Didrikson at Port Arthur, TX, the great athlete was nicknamed "Babe" after legendary baseball player Babe Ruth. She was named to the women's All-America basketball team when she was 16. At the 1932 Olympic Games, she won two gold medals and also set world records in the javelin throw and the 80-meter high hurdles; only a technicality prevented her from obtaining the gold in the high jump. Didrikson married professional wrestler George Zaharias in 1938, six years after she began playing golf casually. In 1946 Babe won the US Women's Amateur tournament, and in 1947 she won 17 straight golf championships and became the first American winner of the British Ladies' Amateur Tournament. Turning professional in 1948, she won the US Women's Open in 1950 and 1954, the same year she won the All-American Open. Babe also excelled in softball, baseball, swimming, figure skating, billiards—even football. In a 1950 Associated Press poll she was named the woman athlete of the first half of the 20th century. She died of cancer, Sept 27, 1956, at Galveston, TX. For more info: *Babe Didrikson Zaharias: The Making of a Champion* by Russell Freedman (Clarion, 0-395-63367-2, $18 Gr. 5 & up).

BIRTHDAYS TODAY

Robert Burch, 81, author (*Christmas with Ida Early*), born Inman, GA, June 26, 1925.

Derek Jeter, 32, baseball player, born Pequannock, NJ, June 26, 1974.

Chris O'Donnell, 36, actor (*Batman & Robin, Batman Forever*), born Winnetka, IL, June 26, 1970.

Michael Vick, 26, football player, born Newport News, VA, June 26, 1980.

Nancy Willard, 70, author (Newbery for *A Visit to William Blake's Inn: Poems for Innocent and Experienced Travelers*), born Ann Arbor, MI, June 26, 1936.

Charlotte Zolotow, 91, author (*Mr Rabbit and the Lovely Present, William's Doll, The Unfriendly Book*), born Norfolk, VA, June 26, 1915.

JUNE 27 — TUESDAY

Day 178 — 187 Remaining

DJIBOUTI: INDEPENDENCE DAY. June 27. National day. Commemorates independence from France in 1977.

HAPPY BIRTHDAY TO "HAPPY BIRTHDAY TO YOU." June 27, 1859. The melody of probably the most often sung song in the world, "Happy Birthday to You," was composed by Mildred J. Hill, a schoolteacher, born at Louisville, KY on this date. Her younger sister, Patty Smith Hill, was the author of the lyrics which were first published in 1893 as "Good Morning to All," a classroom greeting published in the book *Song Stories for the Sunday School*. The lyrics were amended in 1924 to include a stanza beginning "Happy Birthday to You." Now it is sung somewhere in the world every minute of the day. Although the authors are believed to have earned very little from the song, reportedly it later generated about $1 million a year for its copyright owner. The song is expected to enter public domain upon expiration of copyright in 2010. Mildred Hill died at Chicago, IL, June 5, 1916, without knowing that her melody would become the world's most popular song. Patty Hill, born Mar 27, 1868, at Louisville, KY, died at New York, NY, May 25, 1946.

KEESHAN, BOB: BIRTH ANNIVERSARY. June 27, 1927. Beloved by generations of American children as "Captain Kangaroo," Robert J. Keeshan was born at Lynbrook, NJ. He made his acting debut at age 21 as the original Clarabell, the ever-silent clown, sidekick to Buffalo Bob Smith on "The Howdy Doody Show." He was eventually fired from the show but his future as a children's entertainer was secure; on Oct 3, 1955, "Captain Kangaroo" premiered on CBS and it remained on the air for 38 years. Along with characters Mr. Green Jeans, Grandfather Clock, Bunny Rabbit and Mr. Moose, the gentle, patient Captain entertained and educated millions of children over the years. Keeshan died in Vermont on Jan 23, 2004.

KELLER, HELEN: BIRTH ANNIVERSARY. June 27, 1880. Born at Tuscumbia, AL, Helen Keller was left deaf and blind by a disease she contracted at 18 months of age. With the help of her teacher, Anne Sullivan, she graduated from college and had a career as an author and lecturer. She died June 1, 1968, at Westport, CT. For more info: *A Girl Named Helen Keller* by Margo Lundell (Scholastic, 0-590-47963-6, $3.99 Gr. 1–3), *Helen Keller* by Johanna Hurwitz (Random House, 0-679-87705-3, $3.99 Gr. 2–4) or *The World at Her Fingertips: The Story of Helen Keller* by Joan Dash (Scholastic, 0-590-90715-8, $15.95 Gr. 4–7).

BIRTHDAYS TODAY

Lucille Clifton, 70, author (*Everett Anderson's Goodbye*), born Depew, NY, June 27, 1936.

James Lincoln Collier, 78, author of historical fiction, with his brother Christopher Collier (*My Brother Sam Is Dead*), born New York, NY, June 27, 1928.

Jim Edmonds, 36, baseball player, born Fullerton, CA, June 27, 1970.

June 2006

S	M	T	W	T	F	S
				1	2	3
4	5	6	7	8	9	10
11	12	13	14	15	16	17
18	19	20	21	22	23	24
25	26	27	28	29	30	

JUNE 28 — WEDNESDAY

Day 179 — 186 Remaining

BISCAYNE NATIONAL PARK ESTABLISHED. June 28, 1980. Including the coral reefs and waters of Biscayne Bay and the area of the Atlantic Ocean which surrounds the northernmost Florida Keys, Biscayne National Monument was authorized Oct 18, 1968. It became a national park in 1980. For more info: www.nps.gov/bisc/index.htm.

FORBES, ESTHER: BIRTH ANNIVERSARY. June 28, 1891. Author and illustrator, born at Westborough, MA. She won the Pulitzer Prize for history in 1943 for her book *Paul Revere and the World He Lived In*. Her children's book, *Johnny Tremain*, was awarded the 1944 Newbery Medal. Forbes died at Worcester, MA, Aug 12, 1967. For a study guide to *Johnny Tremain* see the website glencoe.com/sec/literature/litlibrary.

MONDAY HOLIDAY LAW: ANNIVERSARY. June 28, 1968. President Lyndon B. Johnson approved Public Law 90–363, which amended section 6103(a) of title 5, United States Code, establishing Monday observance of Washington's Birthday, Memorial Day, Labor Day, Columbus Day and Veterans Day. The new holiday law took effect Jan 1, 1971. Veterans Day observance subsequently reverted to its former observance date, Nov 11. See individual holidays for more details.

TREATY OF VERSAILLES: ANNIVERSARY. June 28, 1919. The signing of the Treaty of Versailles at Versailles, France, formally ended World War I.

BIRTHDAYS TODAY

John Elway, 46, former football player, born Port Angeles, WA, June 28, 1960.

Mark Grace, 42, former baseball player, born Winston-Salem, NC, June 28, 1964.

Bette Greene, 72, author (*Philip Hall Likes Me, I Reckon Maybe*), born Memphis, TN, June 28, 1934.

Carl Levin, 72, US Senator (D, Michigan), born Detroit, MI, June 28, 1934.

JUNE 29 — THURSDAY

Day 180 — 185 Remaining

KEPES, JULIET A.: BIRTH ANNIVERSARY. June 29, 1919. Author and illustrator (Caldecott for *Five Little Monkeys*), born at London, England. Died Mar 11, 1999, at Cambridge, MA.

LATHROP, JULIA C.: BIRTH ANNIVERSARY. June 29, 1858. A pioneer in the battle to establish child-labor laws, Julia C. Lathrop was the first woman member of the Illinois State Board of Charities and in 1900 was instrumental in establishing the first juvenile court in the US. In 1912 President Taft named Lathrop chief of the newly created Children's Bureau, then part of the US Department of Commerce and Labor. In 1925 she became a member of the Child Welfare Committee of the League of Nations. Born at Rockford, IL, she died there, Apr 15, 1932.

MESA VERDE NATIONAL PARK ESTABLISHED: 100th ANNIVERSARY. June 29, 1906. Area of southwest Colorado established as a national park. For more info: www.nps.gov/meve/index.htm.

PETER AND PAUL DAY. June 29. Feast day for Saint Peter and Saint Paul. Commemorates dual martyrdom of Christian apostles Peter (by crucifixion) and Paul (by beheading) during persecution by Roman Emperor Nero. Observed since third century.

SAINT-EXUPERY, ANTOINE DE: BIRTH ANNIVERSARY. June 29, 1900. French aviator and children's author, born at Lyons, France. Saint-Exupery is best known for *The Little Prince*. Other books include *Wind, Sand and Stars* and *Night Flight*. Saint-Exupery died in a plane crash at sea, July 31, 1944.

SPACE MILESTONE: *ATLANTIS* DOCKS WITH *MIR*. June 29, 1995. An American space shuttle docked with a Russian space station for the first time, creating the biggest craft ever assembled in space. This linkup was the first step toward the creation of an International Space Station.

BIRTHDAYS TODAY

Theo Fleury, 38, former hockey player, born Oxbow, SK, Canada, June 29, 1968.

JUNE 30 — FRIDAY

Day 181 — 184 Remaining

CHARLES BLONDIN'S CONQUEST OF NIAGARA FALLS: ANNIVERSARY. June 30, 1859. Charles Blondin, a French acrobat and aerialist (whose real name was Jean François Gravelet), in view of a crowd estimated at more than 25,000 persons, walked across Niagara Falls on a tightrope. The walk required only about five minutes. On separate occasions he crossed blindfolded, pushing a wheelbarrow, carrying a man on his back and even on stilts. Blondin was born Feb 28, 1824, at St. Omer, France, and died at London, England, Feb 19, 1897.

CONGO (KINSHASA): INDEPENDENCE DAY. June 30. National holiday. The Democratic Republic of Congo was previously known as Zaire. Commemorates independence from Belgium in 1960.

A GIRAFFE'S INCREDIBLE JOURNEY: ANNIVERSARY. June 30, 1827. On this date a giraffe—the gift of the Viceroy of Egypt to the King of France and the first giraffe ever in France—arrived in Paris after a two-year, four-thousand-mile trip. The giraffe sailed across the Mediterranean Sea to Marseilles in the hold of a boat with her head peaking out from below deck in the hold. From Marseilles she walked 550 miles to Paris. All the while she was accompanied by faithful keepers who climbed a ladder every night to comb her head (she was more than 12 feet tall). The beloved giraffe—who influenced French fashion and culture—died on Jan 12, 1845, at Paris. For more info: *Zarafa* by Michael Allin (Walker, 0-8027-1339-4, $22 Adults, but accessible to middle-school readers). ***See Curriculum Connection.***

GUATEMALA: ARMED FORCES DAY. June 30. Guatemala observes public holiday.

LAST HURRAH FOR BRITISH HONG KONG: ANNIVERSARY. June 30, 1997. The crested flag of the British Crown Colony was officially lowered at midnight and replaced by a new flag (marked by the bauhinia flower) representing China's sovereignty over Hong Kong and the official transfer of power. Though Britain owned Hong Kong in perpetuity, the land areas surrounding the city were leased from China and the lease expired July 1, 1997. Rather than renegotiate a new lease, Britain ceded its claim to Hong Kong.

LEAP SECOND ADJUSTMENT TIME. June 30. June 30 is one of the times that has been favored for the addition or subtraction of a second from our clock time (to coordinate atomic and astronomical time). The determination to adjust is made by the Central Bureau of the International Earth Rotation Service, at Paris, France.

JUNE 30
ALL ABOUT GIRAFFES

Today is the anniversary of when the first giraffe to step on French soil arrived in Paris after an arduous journey. Use this occasion to learn about a magnificent creature.

In addition to the elephant, giraffes may be the animal that people most often envision when they think of African wildlife. The image of giraffes running is standard fare in many nature shows, and children giggle with delight when they watch a giraffe forage in tall treetops. Giraffes live south of the Sahara on grassy plains called savannas and in open woodland areas. They travel in herds and can live up to 25 years.

Giraffes are the tallest living land animal. Males can grow as tall as 18 feet. Although a giraffe's neck is much longer than a human neck, it contains the same number of cervical vertebrae: seven. Each giraffe vertebra is much longer than the corresponding vertebra found in a human's neck. Giraffes eat shrubs and fruit, but acacia trees are their favorite. The giraffe's prehensile tongue makes grasping leaves easy. Reaching tall treetops presents no problem for a fully grown giraffe. Drinking water is more difficult. In order to take a sip, a giraffe must spread its long spindly legs so its head can get close enough to the water. A giraffe usually drinks every two to three days.

A giraffe's coat has a tawny pattern whose mosaic-like, mottled appearance is perfect for blending in among sun-spotted leaves. Each giraffe's coat has its own pattern of markings.

In language arts, try writing stories on long, skinny "giraffe neck" paper. Also, students could write their own "Just So" stories, patterned after Rudyard Kipling's tales, to explain how the giraffe came to have its long neck (or legs, or tongue, or eyelashes).

Students can have science fun by comparing and contrasting the following giraffe facts with those of other animals, for example, an anteater's tongue with a giraffe's.

Giraffe Fun Facts:

- an adult giraffe's tongue is 21 inches long
- the legs of a fully grown giraffe are 6 feet long—the height of a tall man
- a giraffe can go many weeks without water
- a giraffe can close its nostrils to keep out blowing sand
- giraffes have the longest eyelashes of any animal

Photos and additional information about these fascinating animals can be found at Giraffes Online, www.giraffes.org.

Informational literature includes *Giraffes, the Sentinels of the Savannas*, by Helen Roney Sattler (Morrow, 0-688-08285-8, Ages 8–12); *Giraffes*, by Barbara K. Parker (Carolrhoda Books, 1-5750-5346-2, $24.26 Ages 8–12); *Giraffes*, by Emilie Lepthien (Children's Press, 0-516-26098-7, $6.95 Ages 7–11); and *A Giraffe Calf Grows Up*, by Joan Hewett (Carolrhoda Books, 1-5750-5197-4, $21.27 Ages 5–8).

Young listeners and readers will enjoy two picture books about giraffes. *Giraffes Can't Dance* by Giles Andreae (Scholastic, 0-439-28719-7, $16.95 Ages 3–6) is a picture book about a giraffe who wants to dance. He must create a dance that accommodates his unusual height and long legs. This book is a reassuring story that lets young listeners know that everyone can be wonderful in her/his own right. H.A. Rey, author of *Curious George*, tells the story of *Cecily G. and the Nine Monkeys* (Houghton Mifflin, 0-395-18430-4, $17 Ages 4-8), a lonely giraffe who befriends a group of monkeys.

—Sally Walker

MONROE, ELIZABETH KORTRIGHT: BIRTH ANNIVERSARY. June 30, 1768. Wife of James Monroe, fifth president of the US, born at New York, NY. Died at their Oak Hill estate at Loudon County, VA, Sept 23, 1830.

NATIONAL EDUCATION ASSOCIATION MEETING. June 30–July 5. Orlando, FL. Delegates from the local and state level debate issues and set NEA policy at the Representative Assembly. Est attendance: 10,000. For info: National Education Assn, 1201 16th St NW, Washington, DC 20036-3290. Phone: (202) 822-7769. Web: www.nea.org.

NOW FOUNDED: 40th ANNIVERSARY. June 30, 1966. The National Organization for Women was founded at Washington, DC, by people attending the Third National Conference on the Commission on the Status of Women. NOW's purpose is to take action to take women into full partnership in the mainstream of American society, exercising all privileges and responsibilities in equal partnership with men. For info: National Organization for Women, 733 15th St NW, Washington, DC 20005. Phone: (202) 628-8NOW. Web: www.now.org.

TWENTY-SIXTH AMENDMENT TO US CONSTITUTION RATIFIED: 35th ANNIVERSARY. June 30, 1971. The 26th Amendment to the Constitution granted the right to vote in all federal, state and local elections to all persons 18 years or older. On the date of ratification the US gained an additional 11 million potential voters. Up until this time, the minimum voting age was set by the states; in most states it was 21.

WHEELER, WILLIAM ALMON: BIRTH ANNIVERSARY. June 30, 1819. The 19th vice president of the US (1877–81), born at Malone, NY. Died there, June 4, 1887.

BIRTHDAYS TODAY

Dr. Robert Ballard, 64, explorer, oceanographer, author (*Exploring the Titanic, Ghost Liners*), born Wichita, KS, June 30, 1942.

Mollie Hunter, 84, author (*A Sound of Chariots*), born Longniddry, Scotland, June 30, 1922.

David McPhail, 66, author and illustrator (*Mole Music; Pigs Aplenty, Pigs Galore!*), born Newburyport, MA, June 30, 1940.

Michael Phelps, 21, Olympic swimmer, born Towson, MD, June 30, 1985.

Mitchell (Mitch) Richmond, 41, former basketball player, born Fort Lauderdale, FL, June 30, 1965.

JULY 1 — SATURDAY

Day 182 — 183 Remaining

BATTLE OF GETTYSBURG: ANNIVERSARY. July 1, 1863. After the Southern success at Chancellorsville, VA, Confederate General Robert E. Lee led his forces on an invasion of the North, initially targeting Harrisburg, PA. As Union forces moved to counter the invasion, the battle lines were eventually formed at Gettysburg, PA, in one of the Civil War's most crucial battles, beginning July 1, 1863. On the climactic third day of the battle (July 3), Lee ordered an attack on the center of the Union line, later to be known as Pickett's Charge. The 15,000 rebels were repulsed, ending the Battle of Gettysburg. After the defeat, Lee's forces retreated back to Virginia, listing more than one-third of the troops as casualties in the failed invasion. Union General George Meade initially failed to pursue the retreating rebels, allowing Lee's army to escape across the rain-swollen Potomac River. This battle had the highest casualties of any in the Civil War.

BOTSWANA: SIR SERETSE KHAMA DAY. July 1. National holiday. Commemorates birth in 1921 of first president.

BRITISH VIRGIN ISLANDS: TERRITORY DAY. July 1. National holiday.

BURUNDI: INDEPENDENCE DAY. July 1. National holiday. Anniversary of establishment of independence in 1962. Had been under Belgian administration as part of Ruanda-Urundi.

CANADA: CANADA DAY. July 1. National holiday. Canada's national day, formerly known as Dominion Day. Observed on following day when July 1 is a Sunday. Commemorates the confederation of Upper and Lower Canada and some of the Maritime Provinces into the Dominion of Canada in 1867.

DIANA, PRINCESS OF WALES: BIRTH ANNIVERSARY. July 1, 1961. Former wife of Charles, Prince of Wales, and mother of Prince William and Prince Harry. Born Lady Diana Spencer at Sandringham, England, she died in an automobile accident at Paris, France, Aug 31, 1997.

DORSEY, THOMAS A.: BIRTH ANNIVERSARY. July 1, 1899. Thomas A. Dorsey, the father of gospel music, was born at Villa Rica, GA. Originally a blues composer, Dorsey eventually combined blues and sacred music to develop gospel music. It was Dorsey's composition "Take My Hand, Precious Lord" that Reverend Dr. Martin Luther King, Jr, had asked to have performed just moments before his assassination. Dorsey, who composed more than 1,000 gospel songs and hundreds of blues songs in his lifetime, died Jan 23, 1993, at Chicago, IL.

JULY 1
A CLASS ZOO

Today marks the anniversary of the opening of America's first zoo, the Philadelphia Zoo. The zoo had originally been chartered in 1859, but the Civil War delayed its creation until 1874. The Philadelphia Zoo is still thriving today: more than a million visitors a year visit its special habitats featuring 1,600 animals, including the first giant otters ever exhibited in the US. A state-of-the-art animal hospital, adopt-an-animal program and children's zoo are added attractions. (See www.phillyzoo.org for more information.)

Your class may have "adopted" a wild animal (see the Curriculum Connection in August on this subject) or been excited to hear about giraffes last month, but today is a day that they could make their own "zoo." The project below aims to re-create the kind of worlds wild animals live in. Today, most leading zoos have dispensed with the animal-in-the-cage display system and instead allow human visitors to peek into the animal world.

Divide your students into groups and have each group research different habitats in terms of the animals to be found there. Examples of habitats include rain forest, wetlands, savannahs, tundra and many more (don't forget underwater habitats). Ask each group to consider questions about their habitats: What animals are found in the habitat they've selected? What are the living challenges like—do animals have to hibernate in the winter? How do desert animals cope with intense heat? What plants flourish in that habitat? Is camouflage of any importance in the habitat they're researching? What do animals eat? And who is an enemy of whom?

Each group then uses their information to create a diorama or shadowbox. In a large shoe box or other such container, each group needs to depict the appropriate look of their desert or forest or whatever along with the animals there. If the artistic aspects of this are too daunting for your class, bring some old nature magazines in (*National Geographic* is a great choice) so that students can cut out animal photographs and then paste to scrap cardboard to make stiff displays.

Once each shadowbox is finished, each group should present it to the class, sharing the answers to the questions they've been asked. It will be the next best thing to going to a zoo! And perhaps visiting a zoo is among the treats awaiting your students during summer break. —Holly McGuire

FIRST ADHESIVE US POSTAGE STAMPS ISSUED: ANNIVERSARY. July 1, 1847. The first adhesive US postage stamps were issued by the US Postal Service.

FIRST PHOTOGRAPHS USED IN A NEWSPAPER REPORT: ANNIVERSARY. July 1, 1848. The first instance of photojournalism occurred during the Paris Riots of 1848, when an enterprising French photographer known only as Thibault scrambled to a rooftop to chronicle the events. He took images on June 25 and 26. Wood engravings were made of the resulting two daguerreotypes, and on July 1 the images appeared in the weekly newspaper *L'Illustration Journal Universel*. More than 3,000 Parisians lost their lives during the June revolt.

FIRST US ZOO: ANNIVERSARY. July 1, 1874. The Philadelphia Zoological Society, the first US zoo, opened. Three thousand visitors traveled by foot, horse and carriage, and steamboat to visit the exhibits. Price of admission was 25 cents for adults and 10 cents for children. There were 1,000 animals in the zoo on opening day. For more info: www.phillyzoo.org. ***See Curriculum Connection.***

GHANA: REPUBLIC DAY. July 1. National holiday. Commemorates the inauguration of the Republic in 1960.

NATIONAL BAKED BEAN MONTH. July 1–31. To pay tribute to one of America's favorite and most healthful and nutritious foods, baked beans, made with dry or canned beans. For info: Bean Education & Awareness Network, 303 E Wacker Dr, Ste 418, Chicago, IL 60601. Phone: (312) 861-5200. Fax: (312) 861-5252. Web: www.americanbean.org.

NATIONAL BLUEBERRIES MONTH. July 1–31. To make the public aware that this is the peak month for fresh blueberries. For info: North American Blueberry Council, PO Box 1036, Folsom, CA 95763. Web: www.blueberry.org.

NATIONAL HOT DOG MONTH. July 1–31. Celebrates one of America's favorite hand-held foods with fun facts and new topping ideas. More than 16 billion hot dogs per year are sold in the US. For info: National Hot Dog & Sausage Council, 1700 N Moore St, Ste 1600, Arlington, VA 22209. Phone: (703) 841-2400. Web: www.hotdog.org.

NATIONAL RECREATION AND PARKS MONTH. July 1–31. To showcase and invite community participation in quality leisure activities for all segments of the population. For info: National Recreation and Parks Assn, 22377 Belmont Ridge Rd, Ashburn, VA 20148. Phone: (703) 858-2162. Fax: (703) 858-0794. E-mail: programs@nrpa.org. Web: www.nrpa.org.

NATIONAL TOM SAWYER DAYS (WITH FENCE PAINTING CONTEST). July 1–4 (tentative). Hannibal, MO. Frog jumping, mud volleyball, Tom and Becky Contest, parade, Tomboy Sawyer Contest, 10K run, arts & crafts show and fireworks launched from the banks of the Mississippi River. Highlight is the National Fence Painting Contest. Sponsor: Hannibal Jaycees. Est attendance: 100,000. For info: Hannibal Visitors Bureau, 505 N 3rd St, Hannibal, MO 63401. Phone: (573) 221-2477. Web: www.hannibaljaycees.org.

NICK AT NITE TV PREMIERE: ANNIVERSARY. July 1, 1985. The first broadcast of Nick at Nite, the creation of the kids' network Nickelodeon. Owned and operated by MTV Networks, Nick at Nite presents many of the old classic television series, such as "Happy Days," "The Brady Bunch" and "My Three Sons." For more info: www.nick-at-nite.com.

"READING RAINBOW" TV PREMIERE: ANNIVERSARY. July 1, 1983. Hosted by LeVar Burton, "Reading Rainbow" is a critically-acclaimed, award-winning program on PBS that encourages children to learn to read. Aimed at 4-to-8 year olds, the show features celebrities reading popular children's books, both fiction and nonfiction, and also has animated segments, music videos, "kid-on-the-street" interviews and information about social issues. The show has received many Emmy Awards, Parent's Choice Awards, many international awards and a prestigious Peabody. Many parents and teachers use the show as a guide to finding high-quality books for children.

REGULAR TV BROADCASTS BEGIN: 65th ANNIVERSARY. July 1, 1941. The Federal Communications Commission allowed 18 television stations to begin broadcasting this day. However, only two were ready: the New York stations owned by NBC and CBS.

RWANDA: INDEPENDENCE DAY. July 1. National holiday. Commemorates independence from Belgium in 1962.

SPACE MILESTONE: *KOSMOS 1383* (USSR). July 1, 1982. First search-and-rescue satellite—equipped to hear distress calls from aircraft and ships—launched in cooperative project with the US and France.

UNITED NATIONS: INTERNATIONAL DAY OF COOPERATIVES. July 1. On Dec 16, 1992, the General Assembly proclaimed this observance for the first Saturday of July 1995 (Res 47/60). On Dec 23, 1994, recognizing that cooperatives are becoming an indispensable factor of economic and social development, the Assembly invited governments, international organizations, specialized agencies and national and international cooperative organizations to observe this day annually on the first Saturday of July (Res 49/155). For info: United Nations, Dept of Public Info, New York, NY 10017.

ZIP CODES INAUGURATED: ANNIVERSARY. July 1, 1963. The US Postal Service introduced the five-digit zip code on this day. Some large cities had had two-digit zone codes prior to this date. For example, a neighborhood in New York City with a zone code of 16 now had a zip code of 10016.

BIRTHDAYS TODAY

Diane Hoyt-Goldsmith, 56, author (*Buffalo Days*), born Peoria, IL, July 1, 1950.

Carl Lewis, 45, Olympic gold medal sprinter and long jumper, born Birmingham, AL, July 1, 1961.

Emily Arnold McCully, 67, author and illustrator (Caldecott for *Mirette on the High Wire*), born Galesburg, IL, July 1, 1939.

JULY 2 — SUNDAY

Day 183 — 182 Remaining

AMELIA EARHART DISAPPEARS: ANNIVERSARY. July 2, 1937. In 1937 aviatrix Amelia Earhart planned an around-the-world trip via the equatorial route that would be the longest ever made. Having completed 22,000 miles of her journey, Earhart, accompanied by navigator Fred Noonan, took off on this date from Lae, New Guinea, for the final 7,000 miles over the Pacific. About 800 miles into their flight to tiny Howland Island, radio contact was lost with her craft. Despite a massive search by the US Navy and US Coast Guard, Earhart, Noonan and their plane were never found.

CIVIL RIGHTS ACT OF 1964: ANNIVERSARY. July 2, 1964. President Lyndon Johnson signed the Voting Rights Act of 1964 into law, prohibiting discrimination on the basis of race in public accommodations, in publicly owned or operated facilities, in employment and union membership and in the registration of voters. The bill included Title VI, which allowed for the cutoff of federal funding in areas where discrimination persisted.

July 2006

S	M	T	W	T	F	S
						1
2	3	4	5	6	7	8
9	10	11	12	13	14	15
16	17	18	19	20	21	22
23	24	25	26	27	28	29
30	31					

CONSTITUTION OF THE US TAKES EFFECT: ANNIVERSARY. July 2, 1788. Cyrus Griffin of Virginia, the president of the Congress, announced that the Constitution had been ratified by the required nine states (the ninth being New Hampshire, June 21, 1788), and a committee was appointed to make preparations for the change of government.

DECLARATION OF INDEPENDENCE RESOLUTION: ANNIVERSARY. July 2, 1776. Anniversary of adoption by the Continental Congress, Philadelphia, PA, of a resolution introduced June 7, 1776, by Richard Henry Lee of Virginia: "Resolved, That these United Colonies are, and of right ought to be, free and independent States, that they are absolved from all allegiance to the British Crown, and that all political connection between them and the State of Great Britain is, and ought to be, totally dissolved. That it is expedient forthwith to take the most effectual measures for forming foreign Alliances. That a plan of confederation be prepared and transmitted to the respective Colonies for their consideration and approbation." This resolution prepared the way for adoption, July 4, 1776, of the Declaration of Independence. See also: "Declaration of Independence Approval and Signing: Anniversary" (July 4).

HALFWAY POINT OF 2006. July 2. On July 2, 2006, 182½ days of the year will have elapsed and 182½ will remain before Jan 1, 2007.

MARSHALL, THURGOOD: BIRTH ANNIVERSARY. July 2, 1908. Thurgood Marshall, the first African American on the US Supreme Court, was born at Baltimore, MD. For more than 20 years, he served as director-counsel of the NAACP Legal Defense and Educational Fund. He experienced his greatest legal victory May 17, 1954, when the Supreme Court decision on *Brown v Board of Education* declared an end to the "separate but equal" system of racial segregation in public schools in 21 states. Marshall argued 32 cases before the Supreme Court, winning 29 of them, before becoming a member of the high court himself. Nominated by President Lyndon Johnson, he began his 24-year career on the high court Oct 2, 1967, becoming a voice of dissent in an increasingly conservative court. Marshall announced his retirement June 27, 1991, and he died Jan 24, 1993, at Washington, DC.

VESEY, DENMARK: DEATH ANNIVERSARY. July 2, 1822. Planner of what would have been the biggest slave revolt in US history, Denmark Vesey was executed at Charleston, SC. He had been born around 1767, probably in the West Indies, where he was sold at around age 14 to Joseph Vesey, captain of a slave ship. He purchased his freedom in 1800. In 1818 Vesey and others began to plot an uprising; he held secret meetings, collected disguises and firearms and chose a date in June 1822. But authorities were warned, and police and the military were out in full force. Over the next two months 130 blacks were taken into custody; 35, including Vesey, were hanged and 31 were exiled. As a result of the plot Southern legislatures passed more rigorous slave codes.

BIRTHDAYS TODAY

Kendrell Bell, 26, football player, born Augusta, GA, July 2, 1980.
Jose Canseco, Jr, 42, former baseball player, born Havana, Cuba, July 2, 1964.
Marguerite W. Davol, 78, author (*The Paper Dragon, Batwings*), born East Peoria, IL, July 2, 1928.
Vicente Fox Quesada, 64, president of Mexico, born Mexico City, Mexico, July 2, 1942.
Jack Gantos, 55, author (*Joey Pigza Swallowed the Key*, the Rotten Ralph series), born Mount Pleasant, PA, July 2, 1951.
Rita Golden Gelman, 69, author (*More Spaghetti, I Say!*), born Bridgeport, CT, July 2, 1937.
Jean Craighead George, 87, author (Newbery Medal for *Julie of the Wolves*, Newbery Honor for *My Side of the Mountain*), born Washington, DC, July 2, 1919.
Lindsay Lohan, 20, actress (*The Parent Trap*), born New York, NY, July 2, 1986.
Chris Lynch, 44, author (*Slot Machine, Iceman, Freewill*), born Boston, MA, July 2, 1962.
Richard Petty, 69, race car driver, born Level Cross, NC, July 2, 1937.

JULY 3 — MONDAY

Day 184 — 181 Remaining

AIR CONDITIONING APPRECIATION DAYS. July 3–Aug 15. Northern Hemisphere. During Dog Days, the hottest time of the year in the Northern Hemisphere, to acknowledge the contribution of air conditioning to a better way of life. Annually, July 3–Aug 15. For info: Air-Conditioning and Refrigeration Institute, 4100 N Fairfax Dr, Ste 200, Arlington, VA 22203. Phone: (703) 524-8800. Fax: (703) 528-3816. E-mail: ari@ari.org. Web: www.ari.org.

BELARUS: INDEPENDENCE DAY. July 3. National holiday commemorating the liberation of Minsk from German forces in 1944 during WWII. A former republic of the Soviet Union, it became independent in 1991.

BENNETT, RICHARD BEDFORD: BIRTH ANNIVERSARY. July 3, 1870. Former Canadian prime minister, born at Hopewell Hill, New Brunswick, Canada. Died at Mickelham, England, June 26, 1947.

CANADA: NEWFOUNDLAND MEMORIAL DAY. July 3.

CARIBBEAN OR CARICOM DAY. July 3. The anniversary of the treaty establishing the Caribbean Community (also called the Treaty of Chaguaramas), signed by the prime ministers of Barbados, Guyana, Jamaica and Trinidad and Tobago, July 4, 1973. Observed as a public holiday in Guyana and St. Vincent. Annually, the first Monday in July.

DOG DAYS. July 3–Aug 15. Hottest days of the year in Northern Hemisphere. Usually about 40 days, but variously reckoned at 30–54 days. Popularly believed to be an evil time "when the sea boiled, wine turned sour, dogs grew mad, and all creatures became languid, causing to man burning fevers, hysterics and phrensies" (from Brady's *Clavis Calendarium*, 1813). Originally the days when Sirius, the Dog Star, rose just before or at about the same time as sunrise (no longer true owing to precession of the equinoxes). Ancients sacrificed a brown dog at beginning of Dog Days to appease the rage of Sirius, believing that star was the cause of the hot, sultry weather.

EARTH AT APHELION. July 3. At approximately 7 PM, EDT, planet Earth will reach aphelion, that point in its orbit when it is farthest from the sun (about 94,510,000 miles). The Earth's mean distance from the sun (mean radius of its orbit) is reached early in the months of April and October. Note that Earth is farthest from the sun during Northern Hemisphere summer. See also: "Earth at Perihelion" (Jan 4).

HUNTINGTON, SAMUEL: BIRTH ANNIVERSARY. July 3, 1731. President of the Continental Congress, Governor of Connecticut, signer of the Declaration of Independence, born at Windham, CT, died at Norwich, CT, Jan 5, 1796.

IDAHO: ADMISSION DAY: ANNIVERSARY. July 3. Became 43rd state in 1890.

MOON PHASE: FIRST QUARTER. July 3. Moon enters First Quarter phase at 12:37 PM, EDT.

STAY OUT OF THE SUN DAY. July 3. For health's sake, give your skin a break today. [©2002 by WH.] For info: Thomas & Ruth Roy, Wellcat Holidays, 2418 Long Ln, Lebanon, PA 17046. Phone: (717) 279-0184. E-mail: info@wellcat.com. Web: www.wellcat.com.

US VIRGIN ISLANDS: DANISH WEST INDIES EMANCIPATION DAY. July 3, 1848. Commemorates freeing of slaves in the Danish West Indies. Ceremony at Frederiksted, St. Croix, where actual proclamation was first read by Governor-General Peter Von Scholten.

ZAMBIA: HEROES DAY. July 3. First Monday in July is Zambian national holiday—memorial day for Zambians who died in the struggle for independence.

BIRTHDAYS TODAY

Moises Alou, 40, baseball player, born Atlanta, GA, July 3, 1966.
Dave Barry, 59, humorist, author (*Peter and the Starcatchers*), born Brooklyn, NY, July 3, 1947.
Franny Billingsley, 52, author (*Well Wished, The Folk Keeper*), born Chicago, IL, July 3, 1954.
Tom Cruise, 44, actor (*Rain Man; Mission: Impossible; Minority Report*), born Syracuse, NY, July 3, 1962.
Teemu Selanne, 36, hockey player, born Helsinki, Finland, July 3, 1970.

JULY 4 — TUESDAY

Day 185 — 180 Remaining

"AMERICA THE BEAUTIFUL" PUBLISHED: ANNIVERSARY. July 4, 1895. The poem "America the Beautiful" by Katharine Lee Bates, a Wellesley College professor, was first published in the *Congregationalist*, a church publication. Later it was set to music. For more info: *Purple Mountain Majesties: The Story of Katharine Lee Bates and "America the Beautiful"* by Barbara Younger (Dutton, 0-525-45653-8, $15.99 Gr. 3–5). In *America the Beautiful*, 16 landscape paintings by Neil Waldman help bring the lyrics alive for children (Atheneum, 0-689-31861-8, $16 All ages).

COOLIDGE, CALVIN: BIRTH ANNIVERSARY. July 4, 1872. The 30th president of the US was born John Calvin Coolidge at Plymouth, VT. He succeeded to the presidency Aug 3, 1923, fol-

July 2006

S	M	T	W	T	F	S
						1
2	3	4	5	6	7	8
9	10	11	12	13	14	15
16	17	18	19	20	21	22
23	24	25	26	27	28	29
30	31					

JULY 4
KOKO THE GORILLA AND ANIMAL COMMUNICATION

Koko was born on July 4, 1971. She achieved world fame as a result of her participation in the longest running interspecies communication studies ever conducted. Today, Koko has an American Sign Language (ASL) vocabulary of approximately 1,000 words and she can understand even more spoken words! Koko isn't the only gorilla to learn sign language. Ndume (en-doo-may, means "male" in Swahili) and the late Michael also learned to communicate through hand signs, although not nearly to the same extent as Koko.

Kids of all ages love learning about Koko. Free teaching materials are available from Koko's official website at http://koko.org/kidsclub/teachers. These materials focus on conservation and learning about gorillas in general and communicating gorillas in particular.

Students may also enjoy learning how to "speak" like Koko using hand signs. Teach them a few simple ASL hand signs, such as "thank you" and "I love you." Thank you is a sign wherein the student uses a flat hand, puts her fingertips to her lips and moves her hand away from her face downward in an arching motion so that her palm ends up facing upwards. "I love you" is the simultaneous formation of the letters I, L and Y. Using either hand, have students spread their fingers apart and then put down the middle two fingers, leaving the pointer, thumb and pinky up. In order to send their message, students should direct the gesture with the palm toward the person they're speaking to. For visual demonstrations of these signs, simply type the keywords "American Sign Language" and "thank you" or "I love you" into an Internet browser. Encourage students to take these signs home to their families and practice them with their friends.

Mammals, reptiles and insects have their own unique means of communicating with one another and they do so for a variety of reasons. They use communication to warn of danger, find a mate and identify food sources. The way bees dart and dance, for example, indicates the direction and distance of food or a new hive location. Humpback whales have more complex, structured songs than dolphins; both use their sounds for navigation, locating food and breeding. By rubbing their wings together, male crickets make familiar chirping sounds. These sounds are essentially calls of courtship which the female crickets "hear" using eardrums located on their legs! Beavers slap their broad flat tails on the surface of the water and white-tailed deer flash the underside of their tails as a warning to others that danger is coming.

Play your students recordings of whales, dolphins, birds and frogs. If you have a computerized classroom, you can find samples of these recordings on the Internet using the keywords "recordings" and "animals." Be animal specific to help narrow your search. The world's largest archive of animal sounds can be found at the Cornell Lab of Ornithology's Macaulay Library's website at www.birds.cornell.edu/macaulaylibrary. *The Diversity of Animal Sounds* CD by the Macaulay Library of Natural Sounds ($19.95) is available from the American Birding Association at (800) 634-7736. If you happen to live in or have access to a fairly rural place, you could make your own tapes of birds, crickets and frogs.

—Denise Frank

AaBbCcDdEe

lowing the death of Warren G. Harding. Coolidge was elected president once, in 1924, but did "not choose to run for president in 1928." Nicknamed Silent Cal, he is reported to have said, "If you don't say anything, you won't be called on to repeat it." Coolidge died at Northampton, MA, Jan 5, 1933. For more info: www.ipl.org/ref/POTUS.

DECLARATION OF INDEPENDENCE APPROVAL AND SIGNING: ANNIVERSARY. July 4, 1776. The Declaration of Independence was approved by the Continental Congress: "Signed by Order and in Behalf of the Congress, John Hancock, President, Attest, Charles Thomson, Secretary." The official signing occurred Aug 2, 1776. For more info: *Give Me Liberty! The Story of the Declaration of Independence* by Russell Freedman (Holiday House, 0-8234-1448-5, $24.95 Gr. 5–8) or go to Ben's Guide to US Government for Kids: bensguide.gpo.gov. See also: "Declaration of Independence: Official Signing: Anniversary" (Aug 2).

FOSTER, STEPHEN: BIRTH ANNIVERSARY. July 4, 1826. Stephen Collins Foster, one of America's most famous and best-loved songwriters, was born at Lawrenceville, PA. Among his nearly 200 songs: "Oh! Susanna," "Camptown Races," "Old Folks at Home" ("Swanee River"), "Jeanie with the Light Brown Hair," "Old Black Joe" and "Beautiful Dreamer." Foster died in poverty at Bellevue Hospital at New York, NY, Jan 13, 1864. The anniversary of his death has been observed as Stephen Foster Memorial Day by Presidential Proclamation since 1952.

INDEPENDENCE DAY (FOURTH OF JULY). July 4, 1776. The US commemorates adoption of the Declaration of Independence by the Continental Congress. The nation's birthday. Legal holiday in all states and territories.

KOKO THE GORILLA: 35th BIRTHDAY. July 4, 1971. Koko, a lowland gorilla (full name: Hanabi-Ko, or "Fireworks Child" in Japanese), was born this day at the San Francisco Zoo. She is probably the most famous gorilla in the world due to her participation in the longest continuous experiment to teach language to animals. She was taught sign language beginning when she was about a year old, and she currently has a vocabulary of 1,000 signs. She has also had pets of her own: check out the book *Koko's Kitten* by Dr. Francine Patterson to learn more (Scholastic, 0-590-44425-5, $4.99, Ages 4–10). For more info: The Gorilla Foundation/Koko.org, 1733 Woodside Rd, Ste 330, Redwood City, CA 94061. Email: education@koko.org. Web: www.koko.org. ***See Curriculum Connection.***

PHILIPPINES: FIL-AMERICAN FRIENDSHIP DAY. July 4. Formerly National Independence Day, when the Philippines were a colony of the US, now celebrated as Fil-American Friendship Day.

SPACE MILESTONE: *MARS PATHFINDER* (US). July 4, 1997. Unmanned spacecraft landed on Mars after a seven-month flight. Carried *Sojourner*, a roving robotic explorer that sent back photographs of the landscape. One of its missions was to find if life ever existed on Mars. See also: "Space Milestone: *Mars Global Surveyor*" (Sept 11). For more info: *The Adventures of Sojourner: The Mission to Mars that Thrilled the World* by Susi Trautmann Wunsch (Firefly, 0-9650493-5-3, $22.95 Gr. 4–7).

ZAMBIA: UNITY DAY. July 4. Memorial day for Zambians who died in the struggle for independence. Political rallies stressing solidarity throughout country. Annually, the first Tuesday in July.

BIRTHDAYS TODAY

Horace Grant, 41, basketball player, born Augusta, GA, July 4, 1965.

JULY 5 — WEDNESDAY

Day 186 — 179 Remaining

ALGERIA: INDEPENDENCE DAY. July 5. National holiday. Commemorates the day in 1962 when Algeria gained independence from France, after more than 100 years as a colony.

BARNUM, PHINEAS TAYLOR: BIRTH ANNIVERSARY. July 5, 1810. Promoter of the bizarre and unusual. Barnum's American Museum opened in 1842, promoting unusual acts including the Feejee Mermaid, Chang and Eng (the original Siamese Twins) and General Tom Thumb. In 1850 he began his promotion of Jenny Lind, "The Swedish Nightingale," and parlayed her singing talents into a major financial success. Barnum also cultivated a keen interest in politics. As a founder of the newspaper *Herald of Freedom*, he wrote outspoken editorials that resulted not only in lawsuits but also in at least one jail sentence. In 1852 he declined the Democratic nomination for governor of Connecticut but did serve two terms in the Connecticut legislature beginning in 1865. He was defeated in a bid for US Congress in 1866 but served as mayor of Bridgeport, CT, from 1875 to 1876. In 1871 "The Greatest Show on Earth" opened at Brooklyn, NY; Barnum merged with his rival J.A. Bailey in 1881 to form the Barnum and Bailey Circus. P.T. Barnum was born at Bethel, CT, and died at Bridgeport, CT, Apr 7, 1891. For more info: *P.T. Barnum: Genius of the Three-Ring Circus* by Karen Clemens Warrick (Enslow, 0-7660-1447-9, $20.95 Gr. 5–8).

CAPE VERDE: NATIONAL DAY. July 5. Commemorates independence from Portugal in 1975.

ISLE OF MAN: TYNWALD DAY. July 5. For more than 1,000 years, the people of the Isle of Man have gathered at Tynwald Hill at St. John's to hear new laws read out, to present petitions and to swear in the island's four coroners. Tynwald (a word of Norse extraction) is the name of the Manx parliament, which is the world's oldest continually held parliament. Held annually on July 5, unless that date falls on a weekend, in which case the event occurs on the following Monday. For more info: www.gov.im/isleofman/tynwaldday.xml.

SLOVAKIA: SAINT CYRIL AND METHODIUS DAY. July 5. This day is dedicated to the Greek priests and scholars from Thessaloniki, who were invited by Prince Rastislav of Great Moravia to introduce Christianity and the first Slavic alphabet to the pagan people of the kingdom in AD 863.

VENEZUELA: INDEPENDENCE DAY. July 5. National holiday. Commemorates Proclamation of Independence from Spain in 1811. Independence was not actually achieved until 1821.

★ ★ ★

BIRTHDAYS TODAY

Janice Del Negro, 51, author (*Lucy Dove*), born the Bronx, NY, July 5, 1955.

Meredith Ann Pierce, 48, fantasy author (*The Darkangel*), born Seattle, WA, July 5, 1958.

JULY 6 — THURSDAY

Day 187 — 178 Remaining

BUSH, GEORGE W.: 60th BIRTHDAY. July 6, 1946. The 43rd president of the US (2001–), born at New Haven, CT. His father, George H.W. Bush, served as the 41st president. Bush is the second president whose father was also president; John Quincy Adams was the first.

COMOROS: INDEPENDENCE DAY: ANNIVERSARY. July 6. Federal and Islamic Republic of Comoros commemorates Declaration of Independence from France in 1975.

CZECH REPUBLIC: COMMEMORATION DAY OF BURNING OF JOHN HUS. July 6. In honor of Bohemian religious reformer John Hus, who was condemned as a heretic and burned at the stake on this date in 1415.

FIRST SUCCESSFUL ANTIRABIES INOCULATION: ANNIVERSARY. July 6, 1885. Louis Pasteur gave the first successful antirabies inoculation to a boy who had been bitten by an infected dog.

GERMANY: CAPITAL RETURNS TO BERLIN: ANNIVERSARY. July 6, 1999. The monthlong process of moving the German government from Bonn to Berlin began, eight years after Parliament had voted to return to its pre-WWII seat. Berlin officially became the capital of Germany on Sept 1, 1999, and Parliament reconvened at the newly restored Reichstag on Sept 7, 1999.

LITHUANIA: DAY OF STATEHOOD. July 6. National holiday. Commemorates the 1252 crowning of Mindaugas, who united Lithuania.

LUXEMBOURG: ETTELBRUCK REMEMBRANCE DAY. July 6. In honor of US General George Patton, Jr, WWII liberator of the Grand-Duchy of Luxembourg in 1945, who is buried at the American Military Cemetery at Hamm, Germany, among 5,100 soldiers of his famous Third Army.

MAJOR LEAGUE BASEBALL HOLDS FIRST ALL-STAR GAME: ANNIVERSARY. July 6, 1933. The first midsummer All-Star Game was held at Comiskey Park, Chicago, IL. Babe Ruth led the American League with a home run, as they defeated the National League 4–2. Prior to the summer of 1933, All-Star contests consisted of pre- and postseason exhibitions that often found teams made up of a few stars playing beside journeymen and even minor leaguers.

MALAWI: REPUBLIC DAY. July 6. National holiday. Commemorates independence of the former Nyasaland from Britain in 1964 and Malawi's becoming a republic in 1966.

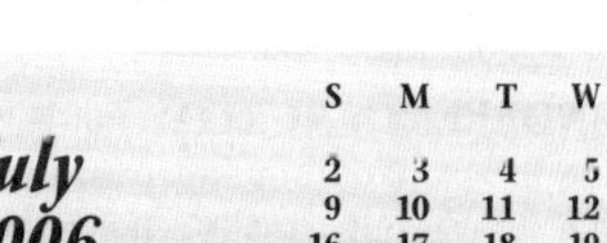

July 2006

S	M	T	W	T	F	S
						1
2	3	4	5	6	7	8
9	10	11	12	13	14	15
16	17	18	19	20	21	22
23	24	25	26	27	28	29
30	31					

BIRTHDAYS TODAY

George W. Bush, 60, 43rd president of the US (2001–), former Governor of Texas (R), born New Haven, CT, July 6, 1946.

Pau Gasol, 26, basketball player, born Barcelona, Spain, July 6, 1980.

Cheryl Harness, 55, author and illustrator (*The Amazing Impossible Erie Canal*), born California, July 6, 1951.

Nancy Davis Reagan, 85, former First Lady, wife of Ronald Reagan, 40th president of the US, born New York, NY, July 6, 1921.

JULY 7 — FRIDAY

Day 188 — 177 Remaining

BONZA BOTTLER DAY™. July 7. To celebrate when the number of the day is the same as the number of the month. Bonza Bottler Day™ is an excuse to have a party at least once a month. For info: Gail M. Berger, 14 Fernwood Dr, Taylors, SC 29687. Phone: (864) 609-9874. E-mail: gberger5@aol.com.

FATHER-DAUGHTER TAKE A WALK TOGETHER DAY. July 7. A special time in the summer for fathers and daughters of all ages to spend time together in the beautiful weather. Annually, July 7. For info: Janet Dellaria, 202 N Bennett St, Geneva, IL 60134. Phone: (630) 232-0425.

HAWAII ANNEXED BY US: ANNIVERSARY. July 7, 1898. President William McKinley signed a resolution annexing Hawaii. No change in government took place until 1900, when Congress passed an act making Hawaii an "incorporated" territory of the US. This act remained in effect until Hawaii became a state in 1959.

JAPAN: TANABATA (STAR FESTIVAL). July 7. As an offering to the stars, children set up bamboo branches to which colorful strips of paper bearing poems are tied.

LAURA INGALLS WILDER PAGEANT. July 7–9 (also July 14–16 and 21–23). Walnut Grove, MN. Performed the second, third and fourth weekends in July, the pageant attempts to catch the spirit of pioneer life as told in *On the Banks of Plum Creek* by Laura Ingalls Wilder. The live production tells the story of the Charles Ingalls family at Walnut Grove in the 1870s. For info: Wilder Pageant Committee, Box 385, Walnut Grove, MN 56180. Phone: (507) 859-2114.

LAURA INGALLS WILDER PAGEANT. July 7–9 (also July 14–16 and 21–23). De Smet, SD. An outdoor pageant on the natural prairie stage depicting "Medley of Memories," historically based on Laura Ingalls Wilder's life. Est attendance: 10,000. For info: The Laura Ingalls Wilder Pageant, PO Box 154, De Smet, SD 57231. Phone: (605) 692-2108 or (800) 880-3383. Web: www.desmetpageant.org.

PAIGE, LEROY ROBERT (SATCHEL): 100th BIRTH ANNIVERSARY. July 7, 1906. Baseball Hall of Fame pitcher, born at Mobile, AL. Paige was one of the most popular players in the Negro Leagues and was also, at age 42, the first black pitcher in the American League. Inducted into the Hall of Fame in 1971. Died at Kansas City, MO, June 8, 1982. For more info: *Satchel Paige* by Lesa Cline-Ransome (Simon & Schuster, 0-689-81151-9, $16 Gr. 2–4).

SOLOMON ISLANDS: INDEPENDENCE DAY: ANNIVERSARY. July 7. National holiday. Commemorates independence from Britain in 1978.

TANZANIA: SABA SABA DAY. July 7. Tanzania's mainland ruling party, TANU, was formed in 1954.

BIRTHDAYS TODAY

Michelle Kwan, 26, figure skater, born Torrance, CA, July 7, 1980.
Lisa Leslie, 34, basketball player, US Olympic Basketball Team, born Gardena, CA, July 7, 1972.
Joe Sakic, 37, hockey player, born Burnaby, BC, Canada, July 7, 1969.
Harriet Ziefert, 65, author (*My Tooth Is Loose, Where's Nicky?*), born Maplewood, NJ, July 7, 1941.

JULY 8 — SATURDAY

Day 189 — 176 Remaining

DECLARATION OF INDEPENDENCE FIRST PUBLIC READING: ANNIVERSARY. July 8, 1776. Colonel John Nixon read the Declaration of Independence to the assembled residents at Philadelphia's Independence Square.

ROCKEFELLER, NELSON ALDRICH: BIRTH ANNIVERSARY. July 8, 1908. The 41st vice president of the US (1974–77), born at Bar Harbor, ME. Rockefeller was nominated for vice president by President Ford when Ford assumed the presidency after the resignation of Richard Nixon. Rockefeller was the second person to have become vice president without being elected (Gerald Ford was the first). Rockefeller also served as governor of New York. He died Jan 26, 1979, at New York, NY.

BIRTHDAYS TODAY

Raffi Cavoukian, 58, children's singer and songwriter, born Cairo, Egypt, July 8, 1948.
James Cross Giblin, 73, author (*Chimney Sweep*), born Cleveland, OH, July 8, 1933.

JULY 9 — SUNDAY

Day 190 — 175 Remaining

ARGENTINA: INDEPENDENCE DAY. July 9. Anniversary of establishment of independent republic, with the declaration of independence from Spain in 1816.

FOURTEENTH AMENDMENT TO US CONSTITUTION RATIFIED: ANNIVERSARY. July 9, 1868. The 14th Amendment defined US citizenship and provided that no State shall have the right to abridge the rights of any citizen without due process and equal protection under the law. Coming three years after the Civil War, the 14th Amendment also included provisions for barring individuals who assisted in any rebellion or insurrection against the US from holding public office and releasing federal and state governments from any financial liability incurred in the assistance of rebellion or insurrection against the US.

HIGHEST TSUNAMI IN RECORDED HISTORY: ANNIVERSARY. July 9, 1958. An earthquake registering at 8.3 on the Richter Scale caused a massive landslide at the head of Lituya Bay, AK, which in turn created a tsunami of 1,700 feet—higher than the Sears Tower in Chicago (which is 1,450 feet). A 300-foot wave immediately followed, scouring bare about 4 to 5 square miles of land on both sides of the bay. Of 3 boats anchored at this remote spot, 1 was sunk with the loss of 2 lives; miraculously, the other 2 boats with their passengers survived the powerful waves.

MOROCCO: YOUTH DAY. July 9. National holiday. On the birthdate in 1929 of the former King Hassan II, who died in 1999.

BIRTHDAYS TODAY

Nancy Farmer, 65, author (*A Girl Named Disaster; The Ear, the Eye and the Arm; The House of the Scorpion*), born Phoenix, AZ, July 9, 1941.
Lindsey Graham, 51, US Senator (R, South Carolina), born Pickens County, SC, July 9, 1955.
Trent Green, 36, football player, born St. Louis, MO, July 9, 1970.
Tom Hanks, 50, actor (*Big, The Polar Express*; voice of Woody in *Toy Story*, Oscars for *Philadelphia, Forrest Gump*), born Concord, CA, July 9, 1956.
Donald Rumsfeld, 74, US Secretary of Defense (Ford and George W. Bush administrations), born Evanston, IL, July 9, 1932.
Fred Savage, 30, actor ("The Wonder Years," *The Princess Bride*), born Highland Park, IL, July 9, 1976.

JULY 10 — MONDAY

Day 191 — 174 Remaining

ASHE, ARTHUR: BIRTH ANNIVERSARY. July 10, 1943. Born at Richmond, VA, Arthur Ashe became a legend for his list of firsts as a black tennis player. He was chosen for the US Davis Cup team in 1963 and became captain in 1980. He won the US men's singles championship and US Open in 1968 and in 1975 the men's singles at Wimbledon. Ashe won a total of 33 career titles. In 1985 he was inducted into the International Tennis Hall of Fame. A social activist, Ashe worked to eliminate racism and stereotyping. He helped create inner-city tennis programs for youth and wrote the three-volume *A Hard Road to Glory: A History of the African-American Athlete*. Aware that *USA Today* intended to publish an article revealing that he was infected with the AIDS virus, Ashe announced Apr 8, 1992, that he probably contracted HIV through a transfusion during bypass surgery in 1983. He began a $5 million fund-raising effort on behalf of the Arthur Ashe Foundation for the Defeat of AIDS and during his last year campaigned for public awareness of the AIDS epidemic. He died at New York, NY, Feb 6, 1993.

BAHAMAS: INDEPENDENCE DAY: ANNIVERSARY. July 10. Public holiday. On this date in 1973, the Bahamas gained their independence after 250 years as a British Crown Colony.

BENSON, MILDRED WIRT: BIRTH ANNIVERSARY. July 10, 1905. Children's author and journalist, born at Ladora, IA. She started writing stories when she was in high school and was the first person to earn a master's degree in journalism from the University of Iowa, in 1927. She worked for several newspapers, and wrote more than 130 books for a publishing syndicate of children's books, most under pen names. Her most famous pen name was Carolyn Keene, and she wrote 23 of the 30 original Nancy Drew Mystery Stories under that name. The Nancy Drew series is still in print, has sold more than 200 million books and has been translated into 17 languages. Benson also wrote various volumes of the Penny Parker, Dana Girls and Ruth Fielding series, among others. She was still working as a columnist for the *Toledo Blade* at Toledo, OH, at the time of her death on May 29, 2002 at age 96.

BORIS YELTSIN INAUGURATED AS RUSSIAN PRESIDENT: 15th ANNIVERSARY. July 10, 1991. Boris Yeltsin took the oath of office as the first popularly elected president in Russia's 1,000-year history. He defeated the Communist Party candidate resoundingly, establishing himself as a powerful political counterpoint to Mikhail Gorbachev, the president of the Soviet Union, of which Russia was the largest republic. Yeltsin had been dismissed from the Politburo in 1987 and resigned from the Communist Party in 1989. His popularity forced Gorbachev to make concessions to the republics in the new union treaty forming the Confederation of Independent States. Suffering from poor health, Yeltsin resigned as president at the end of 1999.

CLERIHEW DAY. July 10. A day recognized in remembrance of Edmund Clerihew Bentley, journalist and author of the celebrated detective thriller *Trent's Last Case* (1912), but perhaps best known for his invention of a popular humorous verse form, the clerihew, consisting of two rhymed couplets of unequal length:"Edmund's middle name was Clerihew/A name possessed by very few,/But verses by Mr Bentley/Succeeded eminently." Bentley was born at London, July 10, 1875, and died there, Mar 30, 1956.

DALLAS, GEORGE MIFFLIN: BIRTH ANNIVERSARY. July 10, 1792. The 11th vice president of the US (1845–49), born at Philadelphia, PA. Died there, Dec 31, 1864.

DON'T STEP ON A BEE DAY. July 10. Wellcat Holidays reminds kids and grown-ups that now is the time of year when going barefoot can mean getting stung by a bee. If you get stung tell Mom. [©2002 by WH.] For info: Thomas & Ruth Roy, Wellcat Holidays, 2418 Long Ln, Lebanon, PA 17046. Phone: (717) 279-0184. E-mail: info@wellcat.com. Web: www.wellcat.com.

MOON PHASE: FULL MOON. July 10. Moon enters Full Moon phase at 11:02 PM, EDT.

O'HARA, MARY: BIRTH ANNIVERSARY. July 10, 1885. Born at Cape May, NJ, Mary O'Hara Alsop wrote the children's horse tale *My Friend Flicka*. She died at Chevy Chase, MD, Oct 15, 1980.

SPACE MILESTONE: *TELSTAR* (US). July 10, 1962. First privately owned satellite (American Telephone and Telegraph Company) and first satellite to relay live TV pictures across the Atlantic was launched.

US LIFTS SANCTIONS AGAINST SOUTH AFRICA: 15th ANNIVERSARY. July 10, 1991. President George Bush lifted US trade and investment sanctions against South Africa. The sanctions had been imposed through the Comprehensive Anti-Apartheid Act of 1986, which Congress had passed to punish South Africa for policies of racial separation.

WHITE CLOUD BIRTHDAY. July 10, 1996. A female albino buffalo was born this day at a farm near Michigan, ND. Albino buffalos are extremely rare: the odds of one being born are one in one billion. Native American tribes revere albino buffalos as mystical symbols of rebirth. The owners of the albino calf named her "White Cloud," and today she resides at the National Buffalo Museum at Jamestown, ND. (Amazingly, another albino buffalo, Mystical, was born on May 5, 2003, at Granville, ND, and is also thriving.) For more info, see White Cloud's web page at www.jamestownnd.com/promotiontourism/whitecloud.htm.

WYOMING: ADMISSION DAY: ANNIVERSARY. July 10. Became 44th state in 1890.

July 2006

S	M	T	W	T	F	S
						1
2	3	4	5	6	7	8
9	10	11	12	13	14	15
16	17	18	19	20	21	22
23	24	25	26	27	28	29
30	31					

BIRTHDAYS TODAY

Adam Foote, 35, hockey player, born Toronto, ON, Canada, July 10, 1971.

Brad Henry, 43, Governor of Oklahoma (D), born Shawnee, OK, July 10, 1963.

Anne Sibley O'Brien, 54, author and illustrator (*The Princess and the Beggar*), born Chicago, IL, July 10, 1952.

Candice F. Ransom, 54, author (*The Big Green Pocketbook*), born Washington, DC, July 10, 1952.

Jessica Simpson, 26, singer, television personality ("Newlyweds: Nick & Jessica"), born Abilene, TX, July 10, 1980.

JULY 11 — TUESDAY

Day 192 — 173 Remaining

ADAMS, JOHN QUINCY: BIRTH ANNIVERSARY. July 11, 1767. Sixth president of the US and the son of the second president, John Quincy Adams was born at Braintree, MA. After his single term as president, he served 17 years as a member of Congress from Plymouth, MA. He died Feb 23, 1848, at the House of Representatives (in the same room in which he had taken the presidential Oath of Office Mar 4, 1825). For more info: www.ipl.org/ref/POTUS.

BURR-HAMILTON DUEL: ANNIVERSARY. July 11, 1804. US Vice President Aaron Burr shot and mortally wounded former Secretary of the Treasury (and primary author of *The Federalist Papers*) Alexander Hamilton in a duel at Weehawken, NJ, on this date. Hamilton had insulted Burr and refused to make a public apology. Hamilton died the next day. Burr's political career thus ended.

DAY OF THE FIVE BILLION: ANNIVERSARY. July 11, 1987. An eight-pound baby boy, Matej Gaspar, born at 1:35 AM, EST, at Zagreb, Yugoslavia, was proclaimed the five billionth inhabitant of Earth. The United Nations Fund for Population Activities, hoping to draw attention to population growth, proclaimed July 11 as "Day of the Five Billion," noting that 150 babies are born each minute. See also: "Day of the Six Billion: Anniversary" (Oct 12).

MONGOLIA: NAADAM NATIONAL HOLIDAY. July 11. Public holiday. Commemorates overthrow of the feudal monarch in 1921.

NIAGARA MOVEMENT FOUNDED: ANNIVERSARY. July 11, 1905. Led by W.E.B. DuBois, 29 black intellectuals and activists founded the Niagara Movement at Niagara Falls, ON, Canada. The name of their movement alluded both to the location of their founding and to the "mighty current" of protest they hoped to undam. The movement disbanded in 1910, and the NAACP took over its goals.

SMITH, JAMES: 200th DEATH ANNIVERSARY. July 11, 1806. Signer of the Declaration of Independence, born at Ireland about 1719 (exact date unknown). Died at York, PA.

SPACE MILESTONE: *SKYLAB* (US): FALLS TO EARTH. July 11, 1979. The 82-ton spacecraft launched May 14, 1973, re-entered Earth's atmosphere. Expectation was that 20–25 tons probably would survive to hit Earth, including one piece of about 5,000 pounds. This generated intense international public interest in where it would fall. The chance that some person would be hit by a piece of *Skylab* was calculated at one in 152. Targets were drawn and *Skylab* parties were held but *Skylab* broke up and fell to Earth in a shower of pieces over the Indian Ocean and Australia, with no known casualties.

UNITED NATIONS: WORLD POPULATION DAY. July 11. In June 1989, the Governing Council of the United Nations Development Programme recommended that July 11 be observed by the international community as World Population Day. An outgrowth of the Day of Five Billion (July 11, 1987), the Day seeks to focus public attention on the urgency and importance of population issues, particularly in the context of overall development plans and programs and the need to create solutions to these problems. For info: United Nations, Dept of Public Info, Public Inquiries Unit, RM GA-57, New York, NY 10017. Phone: (212) 963-4475. Fax: (212) 963-0071. E-mail: inquiries@un.org.

WHITE, E.B.: BIRTH ANNIVERSARY. July 11, 1899. Author of books for adults and children (*Charlotte's Web, Trumpet of the Swan, Stuart Little*) and *New Yorker* editor. Born at Mount Vernon, NY, White died at North Brooklyn, ME, Oct 1, 1985. For more info: *E.B. White* by S. Ward (Rosen, 0-8239-5713-6, $18.75 Gr. K–4).

BIRTHDAYS TODAY

Helen Cresswell, 72, author (*The Night Watchmen*), born Nottinghamshire, England, July 11, 1934.
Jane Gardam, 78, author (*A Long Way from Verona*), born Coatham, England, July 11, 1928.
Patricia Polacco, 62, author (*Chicken Sunday, Pink and Say*), born Lansing, MI, July 11, 1944.
Michael Rosenbaum, 34, actor ("Smallville," *Sweet November*), born Oceanside, NY, July 11, 1972.
James Stevenson, 77, author and illustrator (*I Meant to Tell You*), born New York, NY, July 11, 1929.

JULY 12 — WEDNESDAY

Day 193 — 172 Remaining

ETCH-A-SKETCH INTRODUCED: ANNIVERSARY. July 12, 1960. In 1958 a French garage mechanic named Arthur Granjean developed a drawing toy he called The Magic Screen. In 1959 he exhibited his toy at a toy fair at Nuremberg, West Germany, where it was seen by a representative of the Ohio Art Company, a toy company at Bryan, OH. The rights were purchased and the product was renamed and released in 1960. More than 100 million have been sold.

KIRIBATI: INDEPENDENCE DAY. July 12. Republic of Kiribati attained independence from Britain in 1979. Formerly known as the Gilbert Islands.

NORTHERN IRELAND: ORANGEMEN'S DAY. July 12. National holiday commemorates Battle of Boyne, July 1 (Old Style), 1690, in which the forces of King William III of England, Prince of Orange, defeated those of James II, at Boyne River in Ireland. Ordinarily observed July 12. If July 12 is a Saturday or a Sunday the holiday observance is on the following Monday.

SAO TOME AND PRINCIPE: NATIONAL DAY: ANNIVERSARY. July 12. National holiday observed. Commemorates independence from Portugal in 1975.

SPYRI, JOHANNA: BIRTH ANNIVERSARY. July 12, 1827. Children's author, born at Hirzel, Switzerland. Her book *Heidi* is the story of an orphan girl who goes to live with her grandfather in the mountains. One of the most successful books of all time, *Heidi* has been translated into 50 languages. *Heidi* was made into a movie starring Shirley Temple in 1937. Spyri died at Zurich, Switzerland, July 7, 1901.

THOREAU, HENRY DAVID: BIRTH ANNIVERSARY. July 12, 1817. American author and philosopher, born at Concord, MA. Died there May 6, 1862. In *Walden* he wrote, "I frequently tramped eight or ten miles through the deepest snow to keep an appointment with a beechtree, or a yellow birch, or an old acquaintance among the pines."

BIRTHDAYS TODAY

Joan Bauer, 55, author (*Sticks, Rules of the Road*), born River Forest, IL, July 12, 1951.
Bill Cosby, 68, comedian, actor (Emmys for "I Spy," "The Cosby Show"), born Philadelphia, PA, July 12, 1938.
Kristi Yamaguchi, 35, Olympic gold medal figure skater, born Hayward, CA, July 12, 1971.

JULY 13 — THURSDAY

Day 194 — 171 Remaining

FAST OF TAMMUZ. July 13. Jewish holiday. Hebrew calendar date: Tammuz 17, 5766. Shiva Asar B'Tammuz begins at first light of day and commemorates the first-century Roman siege that breached the walls of Jerusalem. Begins a three-week time of mourning.

JAPAN: BON FESTIVAL (FEAST OF LANTERNS). July 13–15. Religious rites throughout Japan in memory of the dead, who, according to Buddhist belief, revisit Earth during this period. Lanterns are lighted for the souls. Spectacular bonfires in the shape of the character *dai* are burned on hillsides on the last day of the Bon or O-Bon Festival, bidding farewell to the spirits of the dead.

NORTHWEST ORDINANCE: ANNIVERSARY. July 13, 1787. The Northwest Ordinance, providing for government of the territory north of the Ohio River, became law. The ordinance guaranteed freedom of worship and the right to trial by jury, and it prohibited slavery.

WORLD CUP INAUGURATED: ANNIVERSARY. July 13, 1930. The first World Cup soccer competition was held at Montevideo, Uruguay, with 14 countries participating. The host country had the winning team.

BIRTHDAYS TODAY

Tom Birdseye, 55, author (*Under Our Skin: Kids Talk about Race*), born Durham, NC, July 13, 1951.

Marcia Brown, 88, illustrator and author (Caldecott Medals for *Shadow, Once a Mouse, Cinderella*), born Rochester, NY, July 13, 1918.

Ashley Bryan, 83, author and illustrator (*Lion and the Ostrich: And Other African Folk Tales*), born the Bronx, NY, July 13, 1923.

Harrison Ford, 64, actor (*The Fugitive*; the *Star Wars* and *Indiana Jones* films), born Chicago, IL, July 13, 1942.

Patrick Stewart, 66, actor ("Star Trek: The Next Generation," *Excalibur, LA Story*), born Mirfield, England, July 13, 1940.

JULY 14 — FRIDAY

Day 195 — 170 Remaining

CHILDREN'S PARTY AT GREEN ANIMALS. July 14. Green Animals Topiary Garden, Portsmouth, RI. Annual party for children and adults at Green Animals, a delightful topiary garden and children's toy museum. Party includes pony rides, merry-go-round, games, clowns, refreshments, hot dogs, hamburgers and more. Annually, July 14. Est attendance: 800. For info: The Preservation Society of Newport County, 424 Bellevue Ave, Newport, RI 02840. Phone: (401) 847-1000. Fax: (401) 847-1361. Web: www.NewportMansions.org.

FORD, GERALD R.: BIRTHDAY. July 14, 1913. The 38th president (1974–77) of the US. He was born Leslie King at Omaha, NE. He was named the 41st vice president in 1973 on the resignation of Spiro Agnew and became president on Aug 9, 1974, after the resignation of Richard M. Nixon. He was the only nonelected vice president and president of the US. For more info: www.ipl.org/ref/POTUS.

FRANCE: BASTILLE DAY OR FÊTE NATIONAL. July 14. Public holiday commemorating the fall of the Bastille at the beginning of the French Revolution in 1789. Also celebrated or observed in many other countries.

GARFIELD, LEON: BIRTH ANNIVERSARY. July 14, 1921. Author of children's books (*Smith, Shakespeare's Stories I* and *II*), born at Brighton, England. Died at London, England, June 2, 1996.

GUTHRIE, WOODY: BIRTH ANNIVERSARY. July 14, 1912. Singer famous for the song "This Land Is Your Land." Guthrie wrote more than 1,000 folk songs, ballads and children's songs. Born at Okemah, OK, Guthrie died at New York, NY, Oct 3, 1967. For more info: *Woody Guthrie: Poet of the People* by Bonnie Christensen (Knopf, 0-375-81113-3, $16.95 All Ages) and *This Land Is Your Land* by Woody Guthrie (Little, Brown, 0-31-639215-4, $15.95 Gr. K–3).

PARISH, PEGGY: BIRTH ANNIVERSARY. July 14, 1927. Author of the Amelia Bedelia series about the maid who takes things too literally. Titles include *Amelia Bedelia and the Surprise Shower; Thank You, Amelia Bedelia* and *Play Ball, Amelia Bedelia!* Parish was born at Manning, SC, and died there on Nov 19, 1988.

SCHWAN'S USA CUP. July 14–22 (tentative). Blaine, MN. The 21st annual youth soccer tournament for boys and girls ages 11 and up will include teams from 25 countries. For info: Schwan's USA Cup, National Sports Center, 1700 105th Ave NE, Blaine, MN 55449-4500. Phone: (763) 785-5656. E-mail: registrar@usacup.com. Web: www.usacup.com.

SINGER, ISAAC BASHEVIS: BIRTH ANNIVERSARY. July 14, 1904. Author who wrote in Yiddish and won the Nobel Prize for literature in 1978. His books for children include *The Fearsome Inn, When Shlemiel Went to Warsaw and Other Stories* and *Zlateh the Goat and Other Stories*. Born at Radzymin, Poland, I.B. Singer died at Surfside, FL, July 24, 1991.

BIRTHDAYS TODAY

Gerald Rudolph Ford, 93, 38th president of the US, born Leslie King, Omaha, NE, July 14, 1913.

Matthew Fox, 40, actor ("Lost," "Party of Five"), born Crowheart, WY, July 14, 1966.

Laura Joffe Numeroff, 53, author (*If You Give a Mouse a Cookie*), born Brooklyn, NY, July 14, 1953.

Harriette Gillem Robinet, 75, author (*Forty Acres and Maybe a Mule*), born Washington, DC, July 14, 1931.

JULY 15 — SATURDAY

Day 196 — 169 Remaining

BATTLE OF THE MARNE: ANNIVERSARY. July 15, 1918. General Erich Ludendorff launched Germany's fifth, and last, offensive to break through the Château-Thierry salient during WWI. This all-out effort involved three armies branching out from Rheims to cross the Marne River. The Germans were successful in crossing the Marne near Château-Thierry before American, British and Italian divisions stopped their progress. On July 18 General Foch, Commander-in-Chief of the Allied troops, launched a massive counteroffensive that resulted in a German retreat that continued for four months until they sued for peace in November.

MAXWELL, GAVIN: BIRTH ANNIVERSARY. July 15, 1914. Born at Elrig, Scotland. Children's author and illustrator, known for *Ring of Bright Water* and *The Rocks Remain*. Maxwell died at Inverness, Scotland, Sept 6, 1969.

MOORE, CLEMENT CLARKE: BIRTH ANNIVERSARY. July 15, 1779. American author and teacher, best remembered for his popular verse, "A Visit from Saint Nicholas" ("'Twas the Night Before Christmas"), which was first published anonymously and without Moore's knowledge in a newspaper, Dec 23, 1823. Moore was born at New York, NY, and died at Newport, RI, July 10, 1863. (In recent years, Moore's authorship of the poem has been challenged, with Henry Livingston, Jr, offered as the creator.)

NATIONAL RABBIT WEEK. July 15–21. To pay tribute to the rabbit for being a great companion to humans as a house pet. Recognition should also be given to any rabbit that has done something special to help mankind (e.g., saved someone's life, visited patients at a hospital, etc). The public should be informed during this week on the proper care of rabbits and the problems with buying an "Easter" rabbit. For info: Melvin Rabbit, CP 157, Place du Parc, Montreal, QC, H2X 4A4, Canada.

July 2006

S	M	T	W	T	F	S
						1
2	3	4	5	6	7	8
9	10	11	12	13	14	15
16	17	18	19	20	21	22
23	24	25	26	27	28	29
30	31					

REMBRANDT: 400th BIRTH ANNIVERSARY. July 15, 1606. Dutch painter and etcher, born Rembrant van Rijn at Leiden, Holland. Known for *The Night Watch* and many portraits and self-portraits, he died at Amsterdam, Holland, Oct 4, 1669. For more info: *Rembrandt and 17th-Century Holland* by Claudio Pescio (Peter Bedrick, 0-87226-317-7, $22.50 Gr. 4–7).

SAINT FRANCES XAVIER CABRINI: BIRTH ANNIVERSARY. July 15, 1850. First American saint, she founded schools, orphanages, convents and hospitals. Born at Lombardy, Italy, she died of malaria at Chicago, IL, Dec 22, 1917. Canonized July 7, 1946.

SAINT SWITHIN'S DAY. July 15. Swithun (Swithin), Bishop of Winchester (AD 852–862), died July 2, 862. Little is known of his life, but his relics were transferred into Winchester Cathedral July 15, 971, a day on which there was a heavy rainfall. According to old English belief, it will rain for 40 days thereafter when it rains on this day. "St. Swithin's Day, if thou dost rain, for 40 days it will remain; St. Swithin's Day, if thou be fair, for 40 days, 'will rain nea mair."

BIRTHDAYS TODAY

Marcia Thornton Jones, 48, author, with Debbie Dadey (the Bailey School Kids series), born Joliet, IL, July 15, 1958.

Jesse Ventura, 55, former professional wrestler, former Governor of Minnesota (I), born Minneapolis, MN, July 15, 1951.

George V. Voinovich, 70, US Senator (R, Ohio), born Cleveland, OH, July 15, 1936.

JULY 16 — SUNDAY

Day 197 — 168 Remaining

AMUNDSEN, ROALD: BIRTH ANNIVERSARY. July 16, 1872. Norwegian explorer, born near Oslo, Roald Amundsen was the first man to sail from the Atlantic to the Pacific Ocean via the Northwest Passage (1903–05). He discovered the South Pole (Dec 14, 1911) and flew over the North Pole in a dirigible in 1926. He flew, with five companions, from Norway, June 18, 1928, in a daring effort to rescue survivors of an Italian Arctic expedition. No trace of the rescue party or the airplane was ever located. See also: "South Pole Discovery: Anniversary" (Dec 14).

ATOMIC BOMB TESTED: ANNIVERSARY. July 16, 1945. In the New Mexican desert at Alamogordo Air Base, 125 miles southeast of Albuquerque, the experimental atomic bomb was set off at 5:30 AM. Dubbed "Fat Boy" by its creator, the plutonium bomb vaporized the steel scaffolding holding it as the immense fireball rose 8,000 feet in a fraction of a second—ultimately creating a mushroom cloud to a height of 41,000 feet. At ground zero the bomb emitted heat three times the temperature of the interior of the sun. All plant and animal life for a mile around ceased to exist. When informed by President Truman at Potsdam of the successful experiment, Winston Churchill responded, "It's the Second Coming in wrath!"

COMET CRASHES INTO JUPITER: ANNIVERSARY. July 16, 1994. The first fragment of the comet Shoemaker-Levy crashed into the planet Jupiter, beginning a series of spectacular collisions, each unleashing more energy than the combined effect of an explosion of all our world's nuclear arsenal. Video imagery from earthbound telescopes as well as the Hubble telescope provided vivid records of the explosions and their aftereffects. In 1993 the comet had shattered into a series of about a dozen large chunks that resembled "pearls on a string" after its orbit brought it within the gravitational effects of our solar system's largest planet. For more info: *Discovering Jupiter: The Amazing Collision in Space* by Melvin Berger (Scholastic, 0-5904-8824-4, $4.95 Gr. K–3).

DISTRICT OF COLUMBIA: ESTABLISHING LEGISLATION ANNIVERSARY. July 16, 1790. George Washington signed legislation that selected the District of Columbia as the permanent capital of the US. Boundaries of the district were established in 1792. Plans called for the government to remain housed at Philadelphia, PA, until 1800, when the new national capital would be ready for occupancy.

NATIONAL ICE CREAM DAY. July 16. To promote America's favorite dessert, ice cream, on "Sundae Sunday." Annually, the third Sunday in July.

SPACE MILESTONE: *APOLLO 11* (US): MAN SENT TO THE MOON. July 16, 1969. This launch resulted in man's first moon landing, the first landing on any extraterrestrial body. See also: "Space Milestone: Moon Day" (July 20).

WELLS, IDA B.: BIRTH ANNIVERSARY. July 16, 1862. African American journalist and anti-lynching crusader Ida B. Wells was born the daughter of slaves at Holly Springs, MS, and grew up as Jim Crow and lynching were becoming prevalent. Wells argued that lynchings occurred not to defend white women but because of whites' fear of economic competition from blacks. She traveled extensively, founding anti-lynching societies and black women's clubs. Wells's *Red Record* (1895) was one of the first accounts of lynchings in the South. She died Mar 25, 1931, at Chicago, IL. For more info: *Ida B. Wells: Mother of the Civil Rights Movement* by Dennis Brindell Fradin and Judith Bloom Fradin (Clarion, 0-395-89898-6, $18 Gr. 5 & up) or *Ida B. Wells-Barnett: A Voice Against Violence* by Patricia McKissack and Fredrick McKissack (Enslow, 0-8949-0301-2, $14.95 Gr. K–3).

BIRTHDAYS TODAY

Arnold Adoff, 71, poet (*Black Is Brown Is Tan*), born the Bronx, NY, July 16, 1935.

Richard Egielski, 54, author (*The Gingerbread Boy*), born New York, NY, July 16, 1952.

Barry Sanders, 38, former football player, born Wichita, KS, July 16, 1968.

Eve Titus, 84, author (*Basil of Baker Street*, the Anatole series), born New York, NY, July 16, 1922.

JULY 17 — MONDAY

Day 198 — 167 Remaining

BOTSWANA: PRESIDENTS DAY. July 17. National holiday. The third Monday in July.

DISNEYLAND OPENED: ANNIVERSARY. July 17, 1955. Disneyland, America's first theme park, opened at Anaheim, CA.

GERRY, ELBRIDGE: BIRTH ANNIVERSARY. July 17, 1744. Fifth vice president of the US (1813–14), born at Marblehead, MA. Died at Washington, DC, Nov 23, 1814. His name became part of the language (gerrymander) after he signed a redistricting bill while governor of Massachusetts in 1812.

KOREA: CONSTITUTION DAY: ANNIVERSARY. July 17. Legal national holiday. Commemorates the proclamation of the constitution of the republic of Korea in 1948. Ceremonies at Seoul's capitol plaza and all major cities.

MOON PHASE: LAST QUARTER. July 17. Moon enters Last Quarter phase at 3:12 PM, EDT.

★ ★ ★

PUERTO RICO: MUÑOZ-RIVERA DAY. July 17. Public holiday on the anniversary of the birth of Luis Muñoz-Rivera. The Puerto Rican patriot, poet and journalist was born at Barranquitas, Puerto Rico, in 1859. He died at Santurce, a suburb of San Juan, Puerto Rico, Nov 15, 1916.

SPACE MILESTONE: *APOLLO-SOYUZ* LINKUP (US, USSR). July 17, 1975. After three years of planning, negotiation and preparation, the first US–USSR joint space project reached fruition with the linkup in space of *Apollo 18* (crew: T. Stafford, V. Brand, D. Slayton; landed in Pacific Ocean July 24, during 136th orbit) and *Soyuz 19* (crew: A.A. Leonov, V.N. Kubasov; landed July 21, after 96 orbits). *Apollo 18* and *Soyuz 19* were linked for 47 hours (July 17–19) while joint experiments and transfer of personnel and materials back and forth between craft took place. Launch date was July 15, 1975.

SPACE MILESTONE: FIRST WOMAN WALKS IN SPACE. July 17, 1984. *Soyuz T-12*: USSR cosmonaut Svetlana Savitskaya became the first woman to walk in space (July 25) and the first woman to make more than one space voyage. With cosmonauts V. Dzhanibekov and I. Volk. Docked at *Salyut 7* July 18 and returned to Earth July 29.

"SPONGEBOB SQUAREPANTS" TV PREMIERE: ANNIVERSARY. July 17, 1999. Initially aimed at older children and adults, this animated program from Nickelodeon Studios is equally popular with the preschool set. The ever-cheerful SpongeBob is a sponge who lives on the bottom of the ocean, in a two-story pineapple, and works flipping crabby patties at the local hangout, The Krusty Krab. His best friend is a pink starfish named Patrick, and he also has a grumpy neighbor named Squidward Tentacles. Sales of products based on the show and its characters, including bandages, macaroni & cheese, underwear, bowling balls and neckties, exceeded $700 million in 2002.

US GIRLS' JUNIOR (GOLF) CHAMPIONSHIP. July 17–22. Carmel Country Club, Charlotte, NC. For girls under the age of 18. For info: US Golf Assn, Golf House, Championship Dept, Far Hills, NJ 07931. Phone: (908) 234-2300. Fax: (908) 234-9687. Web: www.usga.org.

BIRTHDAYS TODAY

Chris Crutcher, 60, author (*Staying Fat for Sarah Byrnes, Athletic Shorts*), born Cascade, ID, July 17, 1946.

Jason Jennings, 28, baseball player, born Dallas, TX, July 17, 1978.

Karla Kuskin, 74, author and illustrator (*The Philharmonic Gets Dressed, City Dog*), born New York, NY, July 17, 1932.

July 2006

S	M	T	W	T	F	S
						1
2	3	4	5	6	7	8
9	10	11	12	13	14	15
16	17	18	19	20	21	22
23	24	25	26	27	28	29
30	31					

JULY 18 — TUESDAY

Day 199 — 166 Remaining

AMERICAN FEDERATION OF TEACHERS CONVENTION. July 18–22. San Francisco, CA. For info: American Federation of Teachers, 555 New Jersey Ave NW, Washington, DC 20001. Phone: (202) 879-4587. Web: www.aft.org.

FIRST PERFECT SCORE IN OLYMPIC HISTORY: 30th ANNIVERSARY. July 18, 1976. At the Montreal Olympics, Romanian gymnast Nadia Comaneci scored the first "10" in Olympic history with her flawless performance of the compulsory exercise on the uneven bars. The scoreboard displayed a "1.00" because it couldn't go up to "10." Comaneci had seven total perfect scores and won five medals, including the gold for all-around performance. Four months previous to the Olympics, Comaneci had scored the first perfect score in international gymnastic competition history.

PRESIDENTIAL SUCCESSION ACT: ANNIVERSARY. July 18, 1947. President Harry S Truman signed an Executive Order determining the line of succession should the president be temporarily incapacitated or die in office. The speaker of the house and president pro tem of the senate are next in succession after the vice president. This line of succession became the 25th Amendment to the Constitution, which was ratified Feb 10, 1967.

RUTLEDGE, JOHN: DEATH ANNIVERSARY. July 18, 1800. American statesman, associate justice on the Supreme Court, born at Charleston, SC, in September 1739. Nominated second Chief Justice of the Supreme Court to succeed John Jay and served as Acting Chief Justice until his confirmation was denied because of his opposition to the Jay Treaty. He died at Charleston, SC.

URUGUAY: CONSTITUTION DAY. July 18. National holiday. Commemorates the country's first constitution, adopted on this day in 1830.

BIRTHDAYS TODAY

Felicia Bond, 52, illustrator (*If You Give a Mouse a Cookie, Tumble Bumble*), born Yokohama, Japan, July 18, 1954.

John Glenn, 85, astronaut, first American to orbit Earth, former US Senator (D, Ohio), born Cambridge, OH, July 18, 1921.

Anfernee (Penny) Hardaway, 34, basketball player, born Memphis, TN, July 18, 1972.

Torii Hunter, 31, baseball player, born Pine Bluff, AR, July 18, 1975.

Nelson Mandela, 88, former president of South Africa, born Transkei, South Africa, July 18, 1918.

Jerry Stanley, 65, author (*Hurry Freedom!; Children of the Dust Bowl*), born Highland Park, MI, July 18, 1941.

JULY 19 — WEDNESDAY

Day 200 — 165 Remaining

DEGAS, EDGAR: BIRTH ANNIVERSARY. July 19, 1834. French Impressionist painter, especially noted for his paintings of ballet dancers and horse races, was born at Paris, France. He died at Paris, Sept 26, 1917. For more info: *Edgar Degas* by Mike Venezia (Children's Press, 0-516-21593-0, $23 Gr. 2–4).

MERRIAM, EVE: BIRTH ANNIVERSARY. July 19, 1916. Poet, known for her children's books *You Be Good and I'll Be Night* and *A Gaggle of Geese*. Born at Philadelphia, PA, Merriam died Apr 11, 1992.

NEWBERY, JOHN: BIRTH ANNIVERSARY. July 19, 1713. The first bookseller and publisher to make a specialty of children's books. Born at Waltham St. Lawrence, England, he died Dec 22, 1767, at London, England. The American Library Association awards the Newbery Medal annually for the most distinguished contribution to American literature for children.

NICARAGUA: NATIONAL LIBERATION DAY. July 19. Following the National Day of Joy (July 17—anniversary of date in 1979 when dictator Anastasio Somoza Debayle fled Nicaragua) is annual July 19 observance of National Liberation Day, anniversary of day the National Liberation Army claimed victory over the Somoza dictatorship.

WOMEN'S RIGHTS CONVENTION AT SENECA FALLS: ANNIVERSARY. July 19, 1848. A convention concerning the rights of women, called by Lucretia Mott and Elizabeth Cady Stanton, was held at Seneca Falls, NY, July 19–20, 1848. The issues discussed included voting, property rights and divorce. The convention drafted a "Declaration of Sentiments" that paraphrased the Declaration of Independence, addressing man instead of King George, and called for women's "immediate admission to all the rights and privileges which belong to them as citizens of the United States." This convention was the beginning of an organized women's rights movement in the US. The most controversial issue was Stanton's demand for women's right to vote.

BIRTHDAYS TODAY

Teresa Edwards, 42, basketball player, born Cairo, GA, July 19, 1964.

Topher Grace, 28, actor ("That '70s Show"), born New York, NY, July 19, 1978.

Chris Kratt, 37, biologist, cohost with his brother Martin ("Kratts' Creatures," "Zoboomafoo"), born Summit, NJ, July 19, 1969.

JULY 20 — THURSDAY

Day 201 — 164 Remaining

COLOMBIA: INDEPENDENCE DAY. July 20. National holiday. Commemorates the beginning of the independence movement with an uprising against Spanish officials in 1810 at Bogota. Colombia gained independence from Spain in 1819 when Simon Bolivar decisively defeated the Spanish.

DELAWARE STATE FAIR. July 20–29. Harrington, DE. Fireworks, country, gospel and pop talent, rodeos, demolition derby, amusement rides and harness racing. Plenty of food and entertainment. Starts annually the third Thursday of July. Est attendance: 216,000. For info: Delaware State Fair, PO Box 28, Harrington, DE 19952. Phone: (302) 398-3269. Fax: (302) 398-5030. Web: www.delawarestatefair.com.

FIRST SPECIAL OLYMPICS: ANNIVERSARY. July 20, 1968. One thousand mentally retarded athletes from the US and Canada competed in the first Special Olympics at Soldier Field, Chicago, IL. Today more than one million athletes from 146 countries compete in local, national and international games.

JAPAN: MARINE DAY. July 20. National holiday.

LOCUST PLAGUE OF 1874: ANNIVERSARY. July 20–30, 1874. The Rocky Mountain locust, long a pest in the American Midwest, became an even bigger threat in the summer of 1874. Beginning in late July, the largest recorded swarm of this insect descended on the Great Plains. It is estimated that 124 billion insects formed a swarm 1,800 miles long and 110 miles wide that ranged from Canada and the Dakotas down to Texas. Contemporary accounts said that the locusts blocked out the sun and devastated farms in mere minutes. The swarms continued in smaller size for the next several years and caused an estimated $200 million in crop destruction.

★ ★ ★

PROVENSEN, MARTIN: BIRTH ANNIVERSARY. July 20, 1916. Author and illustrator, with his wife Alice (Caldecott for *The Glorious Flight: Across the Channel with Louis Bleriot*), born at Chicago, IL. Died Mar 27, 1987, at New York, NY.

SPACE MILESTONE: MOON DAY. July 20, 1969. Anniversary of man's first landing on moon. Two US astronauts (Neil Alden Armstrong and Edwin Eugene Aldrin, Jr) landed lunar module *Eagle* at 4:17 PM, EDT, and remained on lunar surface 21 hours, 36 minutes and 16 seconds. The landing was made from the *Apollo XI*'s orbiting command and service module, code named *Columbia*, whose pilot, Michael Collins, remained aboard. Armstrong was first to set foot on the moon. Armstrong and Aldrin were outside the spacecraft, walking on the moon's surface, approximately 2¼ hours. The astronauts returned to Earth July 24, bringing photographs and rock samples. For more info: *One Giant Leap: The Story of Neil Armstrong* by Don Brown (Houghton Mifflin, 0-395-88401-2, $16 Gr. 2–4).

BIRTHDAYS TODAY

Mark Buehner, 47, illustrator (*Harvey Potter's Balloon Farm, The Adventures of Taxi Dog, The Escape of Marvin the Ape*), born Salt Lake City, UT, July 20, 1959.

Larry E. Craig, 61, US Senator (R, Idaho), born Council, ID, July 20, 1945.

Peter Forsberg, 33, hockey player, born Ornskoldsvik, Sweden, July 20, 1973.

Sir Edmund Hillary, 87, explorer, with Tenzing Norgay first to ascend Mount Everest, born Auckland, New Zealand, July 20, 1919.

Charles Johnson, Jr, 35, baseball player, born Fort Pierce, FL, July 20, 1971.

Barbara Ann Mikulski, 70, US Senator (D, Maryland), born Baltimore, MD, July 20, 1936.

Bengie Molina, 32, baseball player, born Rio Piedras, Puerto Rico, July 20, 1974.

Claudio Reyna, 33, soccer player, born Livingston, NJ, July 20, 1973.

JULY 21 — FRIDAY

Day 202 — 163 Remaining

BELGIUM: NATIONAL HOLIDAY. July 21. Marks accession of first Belgian king, Leopold I, in 1831 after independence from the Netherlands.

CLEVELAND, FRANCES FOLSOM: BIRTH ANNIVERSARY. July 21, 1864. Wife of Grover Cleveland, 22nd and 24th president of the US, born at Buffalo, NY. She was the youngest First Lady at age 22, and the first to marry a president in the White House. Died at Princeton, NJ, Oct 29, 1947.

GUAM: LIBERATION DAY. July 21. US forces returned to Guam on this day in 1944.

NORTH DAKOTA STATE FAIR. July 21–29. Minot, ND. For nine days the State Fair features the best in big-name entertainment, farm and home exhibits, displays, the Midway and NPRA rodeo. Est attendance: 250,000. For info: North Dakota State Fair, Box 1796, Minot, ND 58702. Phone: (701) 857-7620. Fax: (701) 857-7622. E-mail: ndsf@minot.com. Web: www.ndstatefair.com.

BIRTHDAYS TODAY

Brandi Chastain, 38, soccer player, born San Jose, CA, July 21, 1968.
Hatty Jones, 18, actress (*Madeline*), born London, England, July 21, 1988.
Janet Reno, 68, former US Attorney General (Clinton administration), born Miami, FL, July 21, 1938.
C.C. Sabathia, 26, baseball player, born Vallejo, CA, July 21, 1980.
Robin Williams, 55, actor (*Hook, Mrs Doubtfire*, the voice of the Genie in *Aladdin*), born Chicago, IL, July 21, 1951.

JULY 22 — SATURDAY

Day 203 — 162 Remaining

BIANCO, MARGERY WILLIAMS: 225th BIRTH ANNIVERSARY. July 22, 1881. Author of children's books (*The Velveteen Rabbit*, written under the name Margery Williams). Born at London, England, she died at New York, NY, Sept 4, 1944.

CALDER, ALEXANDER: BIRTH ANNIVERSARY. July 22, 1898. Internationally acclaimed American abstract artist who invented the mobile. Born at Lawnton, PA, Calder took a degree in mechanical engineering, but was drawn into art. By the 1930s, he was the most famous American artist in the world. Calder created the mobile, a delicate hanging kinetic sculpture whose form changed continuously due to air currents or motors. His stationary abstract sculptures were termed "stabiles," and they influenced many generations of artists to turn to industrial materials and monumental scope for expression as he had (with works like *Flamingo* [1974]). His whimsical miniature circus crafted out of wire and cork has delighted viewers of all ages since its creation in the 1930s. Calder died Nov 11, 1976, at New York, NY. For more info: *American Masters: Alexander Calder* (Winstar/PBS video, B00000IRDW, $19.98 All ages).

PIED PIPER OF HAMELIN: ANNIVERSARY—MAYBE. July 22, 1376. According to legend, the German town of Hamelin, plagued with rats, bargained with a piper who promised to, and did, pipe the rats out of town and into the Weser River. Refused payment for his work, the piper then piped the children out of town and into a hole in a hill, never to be seen again. More recent historians suggest that the event occurred in 1284 when young men of Hamelin left the city on colonizing adventures.

SPOONER'S DAY *(WILLIAM SPOONER BIRTH ANNIVERSARY)*. July 22. A day named for the Reverend William Archibald Spooner (born at London, England, July 22, 1844), whose frequent slips of the tongue led to coinage of the term *spoonerism* to describe them. A day to remember the scholarly man whose accidental transpositions gave us blushing crow (for crushing blow), tons of soil (for sons of toil), queer old dean (for dear old queen), swell foop (for fell swoop) and half-warmed fish (for half-formed wish). Warden of New College, Oxford, 1903–24, Spooner died at Oxford, England, Aug 29, 1930.

BIRTHDAYS TODAY

Tim Brown, 40, football player, born Dallas, TX, July 22, 1966.
Kay Bailey Hutchison, 63, US Senator (R, Texas), born Galveston, TX, July 22, 1943.
Keyshawn Johnson, 34, football player, born Los Angeles, CA, July 22, 1972.

July 2006

S	M	T	W	T	F	S
						1
2	3	4	5	6	7	8
9	10	11	12	13	14	15
16	17	18	19	20	21	22
23	24	25	26	27	28	29
30	31					

JULY 23 — SUNDAY

Day 204 — 161 Remaining

CANADA: NATIONAL DROWNING PREVENTION DAY. July 23. Drowning is the third leading cause of unintentional death for Canadians under the age of 60. The majority of deaths caused by drowning are preventable. While out enjoying water activities this summer, the Lifesaving Society urges everyone to please remember the following precautions: always wear a lifejacket while in or near water, keep a close eye on children near and in water, do not consume alcohol while boating and learn rescue skills. For info: The Lifesaving Society, 287 McArthur Ave, Ottawa, ON, K1L 6P3, Canada. Phone: (613) 746-5694. E-mail: experts@lifesaving.ca. Web: www.lifesaving.ca.

EGYPT: REVOLUTION DAY. July 23, 1952. Anniversary of the Revolution in 1952, which was launched by army officers and changed Egypt from a monarchy to a republic.

FIRST US SWIMMING SCHOOL: ANNIVERSARY. July 23, 1827. The first swimming school in the US opened at Boston, MA. Its pupils included John Quincy Adams and James Audubon.

LEO, THE LION. July 23–Aug 22. In the astronomical/astrological zodiac, which divides the sun's apparent orbit into 12 segments, the period July 23–Aug 22 is identified, traditionally, as the sun sign of Leo, the Lion. The ruling planet is the sun.

SPACE MILESTONE: *COLUMBIA*: FIRST FEMALE COMMANDER. July 23, 1999. Colonel Eileen Collins led a shuttle mission to deploy a $1.5 billion X-ray telescope, the Chandra Observatory, into space. It is a sister satellite to the Hubble Space Telescope. It is named after Nobel Prize winner Subrahmanyar Chandrasekhan.

SPACE MILESTONE: *SOYUZ 37* (USSR). July 23, 1980. Cosmonauts Viktor Gorbatko and Lieutenant Colonel Pham Tuan (Vietnam), the first non-Caucasian in space, docked at *Salyut 6* July 24. Returned to Earth July 31.

BIRTHDAYS TODAY

Anthony M. Kennedy, 70, Associate Justice of the US Supreme Court, born Sacramento, CA, July 23, 1936.
Gary Payton, 38, basketball player, born Oakland, CA, July 23, 1968.
Robert Quackenbush, 77, author (the Miss Mallard series), born Hollywood, CA, July 23, 1929.
Daniel Radcliffe, 17, actor (*Harry Potter and the Sorcerer's Stone*), born London, England, July 23, 1989 (some sources say July 31).

JULY 24 — MONDAY

Day 205 — 160 Remaining

BOLIVAR, SIMON: BIRTH ANNIVERSARY. July 24, 1783. "The Liberator," born at Caracas, Venezuela. Commemorated in Venezuela and other Latin American countries. Died Dec 17, 1830, at Santa Marta, Colombia. Bolivia is named after him.

EARHART, AMELIA: BIRTH ANNIVERSARY. July 24, 1897. Aviator, born at Atchison, KS. First woman to cross the Atlantic solo and fly solo across the Pacific from Hawaii to California. Lost in the Pacific Ocean on flight from New Guinea to Howland Island, July 2, 1937. For more info: *Lost Star: The Story of Amelia Earhart* by Patricia Lauber (Scholastic, 0-590-41159-4, $4.50 Gr. 4–7) and *Amelia and Eleanor Go For a Ride* by Pam Muñoz Ryan (Scholastic, 0-590-96075-X, $16.95 Gr. 1–4).

PIONEER DAY: ANNIVERSARY. July 24. Utah. Commemorates the first settlement in the Salt Lake Valley in 1847 by Brigham Young.

US VIRGIN ISLANDS: HURRICANE SUPPLICATION DAY. July 24. Legal holiday. Population attends churches to pray for protection from hurricanes. Annually, the fourth Monday in July.

BIRTHDAYS TODAY

Barry Bonds, 42, baseball player, born Riverside, CA, July 24, 1964.
Karl Malone, 43, basketball player, born Summerfield, LA, July 24, 1963.
Albert Marrin, 70, author of military history (*Commander in Chief Abraham Lincoln and the Civil War*), born New York, NY, July 24, 1936.
Anna Paquin, 24, actress (*Fly Away Home*), born Winnipeg, MB, Canada, July 24, 1982.
Mara Wilson, 19, actress (*Mrs Doubtfire, Matilda*), born Burbank, CA, July 24, 1987.

JULY 25 — TUESDAY

Day 206 — 159 Remaining

COSTA RICA: GUANACASTE DAY. July 25. National holiday. Commemorates the transfer of the region of Guanacaste from Nicaragua to Costa Rica which was confirmed by a referendum on this day in 1825.

HARRISON, ANNA SYMMES: BIRTH ANNIVERSARY. July 25, 1775. Wife of William Henry Harrison, ninth president of the US, born at Morristown, NJ. Died at North Bend, IN, Feb 25, 1864.

MOON PHASE: NEW MOON. July 25. Moon enters New Moon phase at 12:31 AM, EDT.

PUERTO RICO: CONSTITUTION DAY. July 25. Also called Commonwealth Day or Occupation Day. Commemorates proclamation of constitution in 1952.

TUNISIA: REPUBLIC DAY. July 25. National holiday. Commemorates the proclamation of the republic in 1957.

BIRTHDAYS TODAY

Ron Barrett, 69, illustrator (*Cloudy with a Chance of Meatballs*), born the Bronx, NY, July 25, 1937.
Evgeni Nabokov, 31, hockey player, born Kamenogorsk, USSR, July 25, 1975.
Clyde Watson, 59, author (*Applebet: An ABC*), born New York, NY, July 25, 1947.

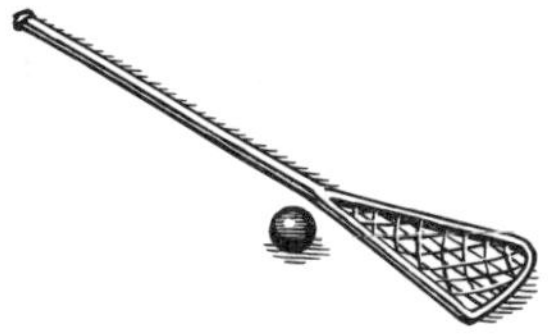

JULY 26 — WEDNESDAY

Day 207 — 158 Remaining

AMERICANS WITH DISABILITIES ACT SIGNED: ANNIVERSARY. July 26, 1990. President Bush signed the Americans with Disabilities Act, which went into effect two years later. It required that public facilities be made accessible to the disabled.

CATLIN, GEORGE: BIRTH ANNIVERSARY. July 26, 1796. American artist known for his paintings of Native American life, born at Wilkes-Barre, PA. He toured the West, painting more than 500 portraits. He died Dec 23, 1872, at Jersey City, NJ.

CHINCOTEAGUE PONY PENNING. July 26–27. Chincoteague Island, VA. To round up the 150 wild ponies living on Assateague Island and swim them across the inlet to Chincoteague, where about 80–90 of them are sold. Annually, the last Wednesday and Thursday of July. Marguerite Henry's *Misty of Chincoteague* is an account of this event. Est attendance: 50,000. For info: Jacklyn Russell, Chamber of Commerce, Box 258, Chincoteague, VA 23336. Phone: (757) 336-6161. Fax: (757) 336-1242. E-mail: pony@intercom.net. Web: www.chincoteaguechamber.com.

CLINTON, GEORGE: BIRTH ANNIVERSARY. July 26, 1739. Fourth vice president of the US (1805–12), born at Little Britain, NY. Died at Washington, DC, Apr 20, 1812.

CUBA: NATIONAL HOLIDAY: ANNIVERSARY OF REVOLUTION. July 26. Anniversary of 1953 beginning of Fidel Castro's revolutionary "26th of July Movement."

CURAÇAO: CURAÇAO DAY. July 26. "Although not officially recognized by the government as a holiday, various social entities commemorate the fact that on this day Alonso de Ojeda, a companion of Christopher Columbus, discovered the Island of Curaçao in 1499, sailing into Santa Ana Bay, the entrance of the harbor of Willemstad."

FIRST US TRANSCONTINENTAL CAR TRIP: ANNIVERSARY. July 26, 1903. The first transcontinental car trip across the US was completed when Horatio Nelson, along with his mechanic and a dog, arrived in New York, NY. It had taken 63 days for him to complete the drive (in a Winton automobile) that began in San Francisco, CA. The car had to be pulled by horses after breakdowns more than once in the trip.

LIBERIA: INDEPENDENCE DAY. July 26. National holiday. Became republic in 1847, under aegis of the US Societies for Repatriating Former Slaves in Africa.

MALDIVES: INDEPENDENCE DAY: ANNIVERSARY. July 26. National holiday. Commemorates the independence of this group of 200 islands in the Indian Ocean from Britain in 1965.

NEW YORK RATIFIES CONSTITUTION: ANNIVERSARY. July 26. Became 11th state to ratify the Constitution in 1788.

US ARMY FIRST DESEGREGATED: ANNIVERSARY. July 26, 1944. During WWII the US Army ordered desegregation of its training camp facilities. Later the same year black platoons were assigned to white companies in a tentative step toward integration of the battlefield. However, it was not until after the War —July 26, 1948—that President Harry Truman signed an order officially integrating the armed forces.

US DEPARTMENT OF DEFENSE CREATED: ANNIVERSARY. July 26, 1947. President Truman signed legislation unifying the War Department (Army) and the Navy in the Department of Defense. The Air Force was made independent of the Army at the same time. Truman nominated James Forrestal to be the first Secretary of Defense. The legislation also provided for the National Security Council, the Central Intelligence Agency and the Joint Chiefs of Staff.

BIRTHDAYS TODAY

Jan Berenstain, 83, author and illustrator, with her husband Stan (the Berenstain Bears series), born Philadelphia, PA, July 26, 1923.

JULY 27 — THURSDAY

Day 208 — 157 Remaining

BARBOSA, JOSÉ CELSO: BIRTH ANNIVERSARY. July 27, 1857. Puerto Rican physician and patriot, born at Bayamon, Puerto Rico. His birthday is a holiday in Puerto Rico. He died at San Juan, Puerto Rico, Sept 21, 1921.

INSULIN FIRST ISOLATED: 85th ANNIVERSARY. July 27, 1921. Dr. Frederick Banting and his assistant at the University of Toronto Medical School, Charles Best, gave insulin to a dog whose pancreas had been removed. In 1922 insulin was first administered to a diabetic, a 14-year-old boy.

KOREAN WAR ARMISTICE: ANNIVERSARY. July 27, 1953. Armistice agreement ending war that had lasted three years and 32 days was signed at Panmunjom, Korea (July 26, US time), by US and North Korean delegates. Both sides claimed victory at conclusion of two years, 17 days of truce negotiations. For more info: korea50.army.mil/teachers/index.shtml or www.koreanwar.go.kr. The Fall 1999 issue of *Cobblestone* (for ages 9–14) was devoted to the Korean War.

US DEPARTMENT OF STATE FOUNDED: ANNIVERSARY. July 27, 1789. The first presidential cabinet department, called the Department of Foreign Affairs, was established by the Congress. Later the name was changed to the Department of State.

WALK ON STILTS DAY. July 27. A day to walk on stilts, providing a chance to develop self-confidence through mastery of balance and coordination! A chance to enjoy the challenge of childhood no matter your age. A celebration of daring accomplishments at homes, circuses and theme parks everywhere. For info: Bill "Stretch" Coleman, Stiltwalker.com, 930 S. Decatur St, Denver, CO 80219. Phone: (303) 922-4655. E-mail: stretch@stiltwalker.com. Web: www.stiltwalker.com.

BIRTHDAYS TODAY

Christina Björk, 68, author (*Linnea in Monet's Garden*), born Stockholm, Sweden, July 27, 1938.
Jessie Haas, 47, author (*Beware the Mare, Unbroken*), born Westminster, VT, July 27, 1959.
Paul Janeczko, 61, poet (*Home on the Range: Cowboy Poetry*), born Passaic, NJ, July 27, 1945.
Courtney Kupets, 20, gymnast, born Bedford, TX, July 27, 1986.
Alex Rodriguez, 31, baseball player, born New York, NY, July 27, 1975.

★ ★ ★

July 2006

S	M	T	W	T	F	S
						1
2	3	4	5	6	7	8
9	10	11	12	13	14	15
16	17	18	19	20	21	22
23	24	25	26	27	28	29
30	31					

JULY 28 — FRIDAY

Day 209 — 156 Remaining

BANGOR STATE FAIR. July 28–Aug 6. Auditorium Civic Center State Fairgrounds, Bangor, ME. For info: Bangor State Fair, 100 Dutton St, Bangor, ME 04401. Phone: (207) 947-5555. Fax: (207) 947-5105. E-mail: info@bangorstatefair.com. Web: www.bangorstatefair.com.

HEYWARD, THOMAS: BIRTH ANNIVERSARY. July 28, 1746. American Revolutionary soldier, signer of the Declaration of Independence. Died Mar 6, 1809.

IOWA STORYTELLING FESTIVAL. July 28–29. City Park, Clear Lake, IA. This annual storytelling event is held in a scenic lakeside setting. Friday evening "Stories After Dark." Two performances Saturday plus story exchange for novice tellers. Annually, the last Friday and Saturday in July. Est attendance: 800. For info: Jean Casey, Dir, Clear Lake Public Library, 200 N 4th St, Clear Lake, IA 50428. Phone: (641) 357-6133. Fax: (641) 357-4645.

MONTANA STATE FAIR. July 28–Aug 5. Great Falls, MT. Horse racing, petting zoo, carnival, discount days, nightly entertainment and plenty of food. Est attendance: 200,000. For info: Kelly Michel, State Fair, Box 1888, Great Falls, MT 59403. Phone: (406) 727-8900. Fax: (406) 452-8955. Web: www.mtexpopark.com.

ONASSIS, JACQUELINE LEE BOUVIER KENNEDY: BIRTH ANNIVERSARY. July 28, 1929. Editor, widow of John Fitzgerald Kennedy (35th president of the US), born at Southampton, NY. Later married (Oct 20, 1968) Greek shipping magnate Aristotle Socrates Onassis, who died Mar 15, 1975. The widely admired and respected former First Lady died May 19, 1994, at New York, NY.

PERU: INDEPENDENCE DAY. July 28. San Martin declared independence in 1821. After the final defeat of Spanish troops by Simon Bolivar in 1824, Spanish rule ended.

POTTER, (HELEN) BEATRIX: BIRTH ANNIVERSARY. July 28, 1866. Author and illustrator of the Peter Rabbit stories for children, born at London, England. Died at Sawrey, Lancashire, Dec 22, 1943. For more info: *Beatrix Potter* by Alexandra Wallner (Holiday House, 0-8234-1181-8, $15.95 Gr. K–2) or the Peter Rabbit Homepage at www.peterrabbit.co.uk.

SPIDERS IN SPACE: ANNIVERSARY. July 28, 1973. Two common cross spiders, Arabella and Anita, were launched into space with other critters for experiments on NASA's *Skylab 3*. They were part of experiments to see whether spiders could spin webs in a weightless environment. Astronaut Arabella went on to spin the first web in space, and Anita contributed a web, too.

WORLD WAR I BEGINS: ANNIVERSARY. July 28, 1914. Archduke Francis Ferdinand of Austria-Hungary and his wife were assassinated at Sarajevo, Bosnia, by a Serbian nationalist, touching off the conflict that became WWI. Austria-Hungary declared war on Serbia July 28, the formal beginning of the war. Within weeks, Germany entered the war on the side of Austria-Hungary and Russia, France and Great Britain on the side of Serbia.

BIRTHDAYS TODAY

Natalie Babbitt, 74, author and illustrator (*Tuck Everlasting*), born Dayton, OH, July 28, 1932.

Jim Davis, 61, creator ("Garfield"), born Marion, IN, July 28, 1945.

JULY 29 — SATURDAY

Day 210 — 155 Remaining

ALL-AMERICAN SOAP BOX DERBY. July 29 (tentative). Akron, OH. Boys and girls, ages 9–16, build their own cars and race them down Derby Downs. This is the 68th annual race. Est attendance: 20,000. For info: International Soap Box Derby, PO Box 7225, Derby Downs, Akron, OH 44306. Phone: (330) 733-9723. E-mail: soapbox@aasbd.org. Web: aasbd.org.

***LORD OF THE RINGS*: FIRST PART PUBLISHED: ANNIVERSARY.** July 29, 1954. *The Fellowship of the Ring*, the first part of J.R.R. Tolkien's epic, *The Lord of the Rings*, was published on this date in London, England by George Allen and Unwin. The publishers chose to publish the book in three parts because it was so long. *The Two Towers* was published on Nov 11, 1954, and *The Return of the King* was published on Oct 20, 1955.

NASA ESTABLISHED: ANNIVERSARY. July 29, 1958. President Eisenhower signed a bill creating the National Aeronautics and Space Administration to direct US space policy. For more info: www.nasa.gov.

NORFOLK PUBLIC LIBRARY LITERATURE FESTIVAL. July 29. Johnny Carson Theatre, Norfolk, NE. Presentations by award-winning, nationally known authors, book reviews, book displays and sales and autograph sessions. The last Saturday in July. Est attendance: 300. For info: Karen Drevo, Youth Services Librarian, Norfolk Public Library, 308 Prospect Ave, Norfolk, NE 68701. Phone: (402) 844-2100. E-mail: kdrevo@ci.norfolk.ne.us.

ROOSEVELT, ALICE HATHAWAY LEE: BIRTH ANNIVERSARY. July 29, 1861. First wife of Theodore Roosevelt, 26th President of the US, whom she married in 1880. Born at Chestnut Hill, MA, she died at New York, NY, Feb 14, 1884.

BIRTHDAYS TODAY

Debbie Black, 40, basketball player, born Philadelphia, PA, July 29, 1966.

Sharon Creech, 61, author (Newbery for *Walk Two Moons*), born Cleveland, OH, July 29, 1945.

Elizabeth Hanford Dole, 70, US Senator (R, North Carolina), former president of American Red Cross, former US Secretary of Transportation and US Secretary of Labor, wife of former Senator Bob Dole, born Salisbury, NC, July 29, 1936.

Peter Jennings, 68, journalist (anchorman for "ABC Evening News"), born Toronto, ON, Canada, July 29, 1938.

Kathleen Krull, 54, author (*Wilma Unlimited: How Wilma Rudolph Became the World's Fastest Woman*), born Fort Leonard Wood, MO, July 29, 1952.

Connie Porter, 47, author (*Meet Addy, Addy Learns a Lesson*), born Lackawanna, NY, July 29, 1959.

JULY 30 — SUNDAY

Day 211 — 154 Remaining

PAPERBACK BOOKS INTRODUCED: ANNIVERSARY. July 30, 1935. Although books bound in soft covers were first introduced in 1841 at Leipzig, Germany, by Christian Bernhard Tauchnitz, the modern paperback revolution dates to the publication of the first Penguin paperback by Sir Allen Lane at London in 1935. Penguin Number 1 was *Ariel: The Life of Shelley*, by Andre Maurois.

VANUATU: INDEPENDENCE DAY: ANNIVERSARY. July 30. Vanuatu became an independent republic in 1980, breaking ties with France and the UK. National holiday.

BIRTHDAYS TODAY

Lamar Alexander, 66, US Senator (R, Tennessee), born Maryville, TN, July 30, 1940.

Irene Ng, 32, actress ("Mystery Files of Shelby Woo"), born Malaysia, July 30, 1974.

Marcus Pfister, 46, author, illustrator (*The Rainbow Fish, Dazzle the Dinosaur*), born Bern, Switzerland, July 30, 1960.

Arnold Schwarzenegger, 59, Governor of California (R), actor (*The Terminator, Twins, True Lies*), former bodybuilder, born Graz, Austria, July 30, 1947.

JULY 31 — MONDAY

Day 212 — 153 Remaining

HARRY POTTER: BIRTHDAY. July 31. Author J.K. Rowling gave her fictional character Harry Potter the same birthday as her own. He is 11 years old in the first book, *Harry Potter and the Sorcerer's Stone*. Harry made his film debut in 2001. For more info: www.scholastic.com/harrypotter/home.asp.

PRESIDENT'S ENVIRONMENTAL YOUTH AWARD NATIONAL COMPETITION DEADLINE. July 31. Young people in all 50 states are invited to participate in the President's Environmental Youth Award program, which offers them, individually and collectively, an opportunity to be recognized for environmental efforts in their community. The program encourages individuals, school classes, schools, summer camps and youth organizations to promote local environmental awareness and positive community involvement. For info: Office of Environmental Education, US Environmental Protection Agency, 1200 Pennsylvania Ave NW (MC 1704A), Washington, DC 20460. Phone: (202) 564-0443. Fax: (202) 564-2754. Web: www.epa.gov/enviroed.

US PATENT OFFICE OPENS: ANNIVERSARY. July 31, 1790. The first US Patent Office opened its doors and the first US patent was issued to Samuel Hopkins of Vermont for a new method of making pearlash and potash. The patent was signed by George Washington and Thomas Jefferson.

BIRTHDAYS TODAY

Lynne Reid Banks, 77, author (*The Indian in the Cupboard*), born London, England, July 31, 1929.

Marty Booker, 30, football player, born Marrero, LA, July 31, 1976.

Dean Cain, 40, actor ("Lois & Clark"), born Mt Clemens, MI, July 31, 1966.

Tim Couch, 29, football player, born Hyden, KY, July 31, 1977.

Jonathan Ogden, 32, football player, born Washington, DC, July 31, 1974.

J.K. Rowling, 41, author (the Harry Potter series), born Joanne Rowling, Bristol, England, July 31, 1965.

RESOURCES

PROFESSIONAL READING

Financial Tips for Teachers, by Alan Jay Weiss and Larry Strauss. 7th edition. Contemporary Books, 0-7373-0302-6, $13.95.

Unbelievably Good Deals That You Absolutely Can't Get Unless You're a Teacher, by Barry Harrington and Beth Christensen. 2nd edition. Contemporary Books, 0-8092-2877-7, $12.95.

BIBLIOGRAPHIES

Exploring Science in the Library: Resources and Activities for Young People, edited by Maria Sosa and Tracy Gath. American Library Association, 0-8389-0768-7, $32. Hands-on supplemental activities for science instruction in the library with an annotated bibliography of science trade books.

Literature Connection to American History, K-6: Resources to Enhance and Entice, by Lynda G. Adamson. Libraries Unlimited, 1-56308-502-X, $33.50. A similar volume by Adamson covers books appropriate for grades 7-12.

Great Books for African American Children, by Pamela Toussaint. Plume, 0-45-228044-3, $12.95.

Once Upon a Heroine: 450 Books for Girls to Love, by Alison Cooper-Mullin and Jennifer Marmaduke Coye. Contemporary Books, 0-8092-3020-8, $16.95.

ACTIVITY BOOKS

Library Celebrations, by Cyndy Dingwall. Highsmith, 1-5795-0027-7, $16.95. Creative programs for Children's Book Week, National Library Week, author visits and other events that celebrate books and libraries.

HOLIDAY BOOKS

The Latino Holiday Book: From Cinco de Mayo to Dia de los Muertos: The Celebrations and Traditions of Hispanic-Americans, by Valerie Menard. Marlowe, 1-5692- 4646-7, $15.95.

The Encyclopedia of Easter, Carnival & Lent, by Tanya Gulevich. Omnigraphics, 0-7808-0432-5, $48.

Halloween Program Sourcebook, edited by Sue Ellen Thompson. Omnigraphics, 0-7808-0388-4, $48.

Thanksgiving Program Sourcebook, edited by Sue Ellen Thompson. Omnigraphics, 0-7808-0403-1, $48.

PERIODICALS

These publications suggest books or websites related to specific themes for grades K–8.

Book Links: Connecting Books, Libraries, and Classrooms. 6/year at $27.95. American Library Association, 50 E Huron St, Chicago, IL 60611. Web: www.ala.org/BookLinks.

Web Feet K–8: Subject Guide to Web Sites & Additional Resources. 9/year at $75. Rock Hill Communications, 14 Rock Hill Rd, Bala Cynwyd, PA 19004. Web: www.webfeetguides.com.

WEBSITES

• Ben's Guide to US Government for Kids: bensguide.gpo.gov

Information about the branches of government, the election process and more for grades K–2, 3–5, 6–8 and 9–12. Also links to other government websites for children.

• US Government site: www.firstgov.gov

Serves as an index to hundreds of government websites.

• CIA World Factbook: www.odci.gov/cia/publications/factbook/index.html.

Detailed information about every country of the world.

• United Nations Infonation: www.un.org/Pubs/CyberSchoolBus/infonation/e_infonation.htm.

Statistical information on 185 nations.

• Fifty States and Capitals: www.50states.com

Information on US states and territories, plus many relevant links.

• Consumer Information Center: www.pueblo.gsa.gov.

Many helpful government pamphlets available online.

• Libraries: sunsite.berkeley.edu/Libweb.

Links to the catalogs of more than 6,600 libraries in 115 countries can be found here.

• The American Memory Project at the Library of Congress: memory.loc.gov.

Thousands of photographs and the text of documents and pamphlets suitable for upper elementary and middle school students.

• The Educator's Reference Desk: www.eduref.org.

Formerly known as AskERIC, this site features over 2,000 lesson plans that you can browse by subject, and links to more than 3,000 other educational, reference and library websites.

• Oyate Native American site: www.oyate.org.

This site features evaluations of books and other materials for children that provide honest portrayals of Native Americans.

• Center for the Study of Books in Spanish for Children and Adolescents site: www.csusm.edu/csb.

Evaluations of more than 5,000 books in Spanish for youth.

• Literature Study Guides: glencoe.com/sec/literature/litlibrary

Study guides for more than 50 novels for middle schoolers and up.

• PBS site: www.pbs.org.

This site has information on kids' favorite TV shows, such as "Arthur" and "Clifford." "Reading Rainbow" is also found here. Bill Nye, the Science Guy, has his own website at www.billnye.com.

• CBC site: www.cbc4kids.ca

This site from the Canadian Broadcasting Corporation has stuff for kids on both sides of the border.

• How Stuff Works site: www.howstuffworks.com

Simple explanations of how airplanes fly or refrigerators work.

• MathStories: www.mathstories.com

More than 4,000 math word problems for grades 1–8. Subscription site.

• NASA sites: www.nasa.gov and kids.msfc.nasa.gov

The National Aeronautics and Space Administration features sites for both adults and kids keeping us up to date on our latest efforts to explore the moon, stars, Mars and beyond. A site specifically for teachers can be found at edspace.nasa.gov.

AUTHOR SITES

Many children's authors and illustrators have websites. Dav Pikey, Virginia Hamilton and Jan Brett, for example, have interesting ones. For links to these sites, go to:

• Children's Literature Web Guide at www.acs.ucalgary.ca/~dkbrown/authors.html

• Kay Vandergrift's Learning about the Author and Illustrator Pages at www.scils.rutgers.edu/~kvander/AuthorSite.

For scheduled chats with authors, go to Scholastic's Authors Online site: www2.scholastic.com/teachers/authorsandbooks/authorstudies/authorstudies.jhtml.

SOME FACTS ABOUT THE UNITED STATES

State	Capital	Popular name	Area (sq. mi.)	State bird	State flower	State tree	Admitted to the Union	Order of Admission
Alabama	Montgomery	Cotton or Yellowhammer State; or Heart of Dixie	51,609	Yellowhammer	Camellia	Southern pine (Longleaf pine)	1819	22
Alaska	Juneau	Last Frontier	591,004	Willow ptarmigan	Forget-me-not	Sitka spruce	1959	49
Arizona	Phoenix	Grand Canyon State	114,000	Cactus wren	Saguaro (giant cactus)	Palo Verde	1912	48
Arkansas	Little Rock	The Natural State	53,187	Mockingbird	Apple blossom	Pine	1836	25
California	Sacramento	Golden State	158,706	California valley quail	Golden poppy	California redwood	1850	31
Colorado	Denver	Centennial State	104,091	Lark bunting	Rocky Mountain columbine	Blue spruce	1876	38
Connecticut	Hartford	Constitution State	5,018	Robin	Mountain laurel	White oak	1788	5
Delaware	Dover	First State	2,044	Blue hen chicken	Peach blossom	American holly	1787	1
Florida	Tallahassee	Sunshine State	58,664	Mockingbird	Orange blossom	Cabbage (sabal) palm	1845	27
Georgia	Atlanta	Empire State of the South	58,910	Brown thrasher	Cherokee rose	Live oak	1788	4
Hawaii	Honolulu	Aloha State	6,471	Nene (Hawaiian goose)	Hibiscus	Kukui	1959	50
Idaho	Boise	Gem State	83,564	Mountain bluebird	Syringa (mock orange)	Western white pine	1890	43
Illinois	Springfield	Prairie State	56,345	Cardinal	Native violet	White oak	1818	21
Indiana	Indianapolis	Hoosier State	36,185	Cardinal	Peony	Tulip tree or yellow poplar	1816	19
Iowa	Des Moines	Hawkeye State	56,275	Eastern goldfinch	Wild rose	Oak	1846	29
Kansas	Topeka	Sunflower State	82,277	Western meadowlark	Sunflower	Cottonwood	1861	34
Kentucky	Frankfort	Bluegrass State	40,409	Kentucky cardinal	Goldenrod	Kentucky coffeetree	1792	15
Louisiana	Baton Rouge	Pelican State	47,752	Pelican	Magnolia	Bald cypress	1812	18
Maine	Augusta	Pine Tree State	33,265	Chickadee	White pine cone and tassel	White pine	1820	23
Maryland	Annapolis	Old Line State	10,577	Baltimore oriole	Black-eyed Susan	White oak	1788	7
Massachusetts	Boston	Bay State	8,284	Chickadee	Mayflower	American elm	1788	6
Michigan	Lansing	Wolverine State	58,527	Robin	Apple blossom	White pine	1837	26
Minnesota	St. Paul	North Star State	84,402	Common loon	Pink and white lady's-slipper	Norway, or red, pine	1858	32
Mississippi	Jackson	Magnolia State	47,689	Mockingbird	Magnolia	Magnolia	1817	20
Missouri	Jefferson City	Show Me State	69,697	Bluebird	Hawthorn	Flowering dogwood	1821	24
Montana	Helena	Treasure State	147,046	Western meadowlark	Bitterroot	Ponderosa pine	1889	41
Nebraska	Lincoln	Cornhusker State	77,355	Western meadowlark	Goldenrod	Cottonwood	1867	37
Nevada	Carson City	Silver State	110,540	Mountain bluebird	Sagebrush	Single-leaf piñon	1864	36
New Hampshire	Concord	Granite State	9,304	Purple finch	Purple lilac	White birch	1788	9

State	Capital	Popular name	Area (sq. mi.)	State bird	State flower	State tree	Admitted to the Union	Order of Admission
New Jersey	Trenton	Garden State	7,787	Eastern goldfinch	Purple violet	Red oak	1787	3
New Mexico	Santa Fe	Land of Enchantment	121,593	Roadrunner	Yucca flower	Piñon, or nut pine	1912	47
New York	Albany	Empire State	49,108	Bluebird	Rose	Sugar maple	1788	11
North Carolina	Raleigh	Tar Heel State or Old North State	52,669	Cardinal	Dogwood	Pine	1789	12
North Dakota	Bismarck	Peace Garden State	70,702	Western meadowlark	Wild prairie rose	American elm	1889	39
Ohio	Columbus	Buckeye State	41,330	Cardinal	Scarlet carnation	Buckeye	1803	17
Oklahoma	Oklahoma City	Sooner State	69,956	Scissortail flycatcher	Mistletoe	Redbud	1907	46
Oregon	Salem	Beaver State	97,073	Western meadowlark	Oregon grape	Douglas fir	1859	33
Pennsylvania	Harrisburg	Keystone State	45,308	Ruffed grouse	Mountain laurel	Hemlock	1787	2
Rhode Island	Providence	Ocean State	1,212	Rhode Island Red	Violet	Red maple	1790	13
South Carolina	Columbia	Palmetto State	31,113	Carolina wren	Carolina jessamine	Palmetto	1788	8
South Dakota	Pierre	Sunshine State	77,116	Ring-necked pheasant	American pasqueflower	Black Hills spruce	1889	40
Tennessee	Nashville	Volunteer State	42,114	Mockingbird	Iris	Tulip poplar	1796	16
Texas	Austin	Lone Star State	266,807	Mockingbird	Bluebonnet	Pecan	1845	28
Utah	Salt Lake City	Beehive State	84,899	Sea Gull	Sego lily	Blue spruce	1896	45
Vermont	Montpelier	Green Mountain State	9,614	Hermit thrush	Red clover	Sugar maple	1791	14
Virginia	Richmond	Old Dominion	40,767	Cardinal	Dogwood	Dogwood	1788	10
Washington	Olympia	Evergreen State	68,139	Willow goldfinch	Coast rhododendron	Western hemlock	1889	42
West Virginia	Charleston	Mountain State	24,231	Cardinal	Rhododendron	Sugar maple	1863	35
Wisconsin	Madison	Badger State	56,153	Robin	Wood violet	Sugar maple	1848	30
Wyoming	Cheyenne	Equality State	97,809	Meadowlark	Indian paintbrush	Cottonwood	1890	44

STATE & TERRITORY ABBREVIATIONS: UNITED STATES

Alabama . . . . AL
Alaska . . . . AK
Arizona . . . . AZ
Arkansas . . . . AR
American Samoa . . . . AS
California . . . . CA
Colorado . . . . CO
Connecticut . . . . CT
Delaware . . . . DE
District of Columbia . . . . DC
Florida . . . . FL
Georgia . . . . GA
Guam . . . . GU
Hawaii . . . . HI
Idaho . . . . ID
Illinois IL
Indiana . . . . IN
Iowa . . . . IA
Kansas . . . . KS
Kentucky . . . . KY
Louisiana . . . . LA
Maine . . . . ME
Maryland . . . . MD
Massachusetts . . . . MA
Michigan . . . . MI
Minnesota . . . . MN
Mississippi . . . . MS
Missouri . . . . MO
Montana . . . . MT
Nebraska . . . . NE
Nevada . . . . NV
New Hampshire . . . . NH
New Jersey . . . . NJ
New Mexico . . . . NM
New York . . . . NY
North Carolina . . . . NC
North Dakota . . . . ND
Ohio . . . . OH
Oklahoma . . . . OK
Oregon . . . . OR
Pennsylvania . . . . PA
Puerto Rico . . . . PR
Rhode Island . . . . RI
South Carolina . . . . SC
South Dakota . . . . SD
Tennessee . . . . TN
Texas . . . . TX
Utah . . . . UT
Vermont . . . . VT
Virginia . . . . VA
Virgin Islands VI
Washington . . . . WA
West Virginia . . . . WV
Wisconsin . . . . WI
Wyoming . . . . WY

SOME FACTS ABOUT THE PRESIDENTS

	Name	Birthdate, Place	Party	Tenure	Died	First Lady	Vice President
1.	George Washington	2/22/1732, Westmoreland Cnty, VA	Federalist	1789–1797	12/14/1799	Martha Dandridge Custis	John Adams
2.	John Adams	10/30/1735, Braintree (Quincy), MA	Federalist	1797–1801	7/4/1826	Abigail Smith	Thomas Jefferson
3.	Thomas Jefferson	4/13/1743, Shadwell, VA	Democratic-Republican	1801–1809	7/4/1826	Martha Wayles Skelton	Aaron Burr, 1801–05 George Clinton, 1805–09
4.	James Madison	3/16/1751, Port Conway, VA	Democratic-Republican	1809–1817	6/28/1836	Dolley Payne Todd	George Clinton, 1809–12 Elbridge Gerry, 1813–14
5.	James Monroe	4/28/1758, Westmoreland Cnty, VA	Democratic-Republican	1817–1825	7/4/1831	Elizabeth Kortright	Daniel D. Tompkins
6.	John Q. Adams	7/11/1767, Braintree (Quincy), MA	Democratic-Republican	1825–1829	2/23/1848	Louisa Catherine Johnson	John C. Calhoun
7.	Andrew Jackson	3/15/1767, Waxhaw Settlement, SC	Democrat	1829–1837	6/8/1845	Mrs. Rachel Donelson Robards	John C. Calhoun, 1829–32 Martin Van Buren, 1833–37
8.	Martin Van Buren	12/5/1782, Kinderhook, NY	Democrat	1837–1841	7/24/1862	Hannah Hoes	Richard M. Johnson
9.	William H. Harrison	2/9/1773, Charles City Cnty, VA	Whig	1841	4/4/1841†	Anna Symmes	John Tyler
10.	John Tyler	3/29/1790, Charles City Cnty, VA	Whig	1841–1845	1/18/1862	Letitia Christian Julia Gardiner	
11.	James K. Polk	11/2/1795, near Pineville, NC	Democrat	1845–1849	6/15/1849	Sarah Childress	George M. Dallas
12.	Zachary Taylor	11/24/1784, Barboursville, VA	Whig	1849–1850	7/9/1850†	Margaret Mackall Smith	Millard Fillmore
13.	Millard Fillmore	1/7/1800, Locke, NY	Whig	1850–1853	3/8/1874	Abigail Powers Mrs. Caroline Carmichael McIntosh	
14.	Franklin Pierce	11/23/1804, Hillsboro, NH	Democrat	1853–1857	10/8/1869	Jane Means Appleton	William R. D. King
15.	James Buchanan	4/23/1791, near Mercersburg, PA	Democrat	1857–1861	6/1/1868		John C. Breckinridge
16.	Abraham Lincoln	2/12/1809, near Hodgenville, KY	Republican	1861–1865	4/15/1865*	Mary Todd	Hannibal Hamlin, 1861–65 Andrew Johnson, 1865
17.	Andrew Johnson	12/29/1808, Raleigh, NC	Democrat	1865–1869	7/31/1875	Eliza McCardle	
18.	Ulysses S. Grant	4/27/1822, Point Pleasant, OH	Republican	1869–1877	7/23/1885	Julia Boggs Dent	Schuyler Colfax, 1869–73 Henry Wilson, 1873–75
19.	Rutherford B. Hayes	10/4/1822, Delaware, OH	Republican	1877–1881	1/17/1893	Lucy Ware Webb	William A. Wheeler
20.	James A. Garfield	11/19/1831, Orange, OH	Republican	1881	9/19/1881*	Lucretia Rudolph	Chester A. Arthur
21.	Chester A. Arthur	10/5/1829, Fairfield, VT	Republican	1881–1885	11/18/1886	Ellen Lewis Herndon	
22.	Grover Cleveland	3/18/1837, Caldwell, NJ	Democrat	1885–1889	6/24/1908	Frances Folsom	Thomas A. Hendricks, 1885
23.	Benjamin Harrison	8/20/1833, North Bend, OH	Republican	1889–1893	3/13/1901	Caroline Lavinia Scott Mrs. Mary Dimmick	Levi P. Morton
24.	Grover Cleveland	3/18/1837, Caldwell, NJ	Democrat	1893–1897	6/24/1908	Frances Folsom	Adlai Stevenson, 1893–97

☆ The Teacher's Calendar, 2005–2006 ☆

	Name	Birthdate, Place	Party	Tenure	Died	First Lady	Vice President
25.	William McKinley	1/29/1843, Niles, OH	Republican	1897–1901	9/14/1901*	Ida Saxton	Garret A. Hobart, 1897–99 Theodore Roosevelt, 1901
26.	Theodore Roosevelt	10/27/1858, New York, NY	Republican	1901–1909	1/6/1919	Alice Hathaway Lee Edith Kermit Carow	Charles W. Fairbanks
27.	William H. Taft	9/15/1857, Cincinnati, OH	Republican	1909–1913	3/8/1930	Helen Herron	James S. Sherman
28.	Woodrow Wilson	12/28/1856, Staunton, VA	Democrat	1913–1921	2/3/1924	Ellen Louise Axson Edith Bolling Galt	Thomas R. Marshall
29.	Warren G. Harding	11/2/1865, near Corsica, OH	Republican	1921–1923	8/2/1923†	Florence Kling DeWolfe	Calvin Coolidge
30.	Calvin Coolidge	7/4/1872, Plymouth Notch, VT	Republican	1923–1929	1/5/1933	Grace Anna Goodhue	Charles G. Dawes
31.	Herbert C. Hoover	8/10/1874, West Branch, IA	Republican	1929–1933	10/20/1964	Lou Henry	Charles Curtis
32.	Franklin D. Roosevelt	1/30/1882, Hyde Park, NY	Democrat	1933–1945	4/12/1945†	Eleanor Roosevelt	John N. Garner, 1933–41 Henry A. Wallace, 1941–45 Harry S Truman, 1945
33.	Harry S Truman	5/8/1884, Lamar, MO	Democrat	1945–1953	12/26/1972	Elizabeth Virginia (Bess) Wallace	Alben W. Barkley
34.	Dwight D. Eisenhower	10/14/1890, Denison, TX	Republican	1953–1961	3/28/1969	Mamie Geneva Doud	Richard M. Nixon
35.	John F. Kennedy	5/29/1917, Brookline, MA	Democrat	1961–1963	11/22/1963*	Jacqueline Lee Bouvier	Lyndon B. Johnson
36.	Lyndon B. Johnson	8/27/1908, near Stonewall, TX	Democrat	1963–1969	1/22/1973	Claudia Alta (Lady Bird) Taylor	Hubert H. Humphrey
37.	Richard M. Nixon	1/9/1913, Yorba Linda, CA	Republican	1969–1974**	4/22/1994	Thelma Catherine (Pat) Ryan	Spiro T. Agnew, 1969–73 Gerald R. Ford, 1973–74
38.	Gerald R. Ford	7/14/1913, Omaha, NE	Republican	1974–1977		Elizabeth (Betty) Bloomer	Nelson A. Rockefeller
39.	James E. Carter, Jr	10/1/1924, Plains, GA	Democrat	1977–1981		Rosalynn Smith	Walter F. Mondale
40.	Ronald W. Reagan	2/6/1911, Tampico, IL	Republican	1981–1989	6/5/2004	Nancy Davis	George H. W. Bush
41.	George H. W. Bush	6/12/1924, Milton, MA	Republican	1989–1993		Barbara Pierce	J. Danforth Quayle
42.	William J. Clinton	8/19/1946, Hope, AR	Democrat	1993–2001		Hillary Rodham	Albert Gore, Jr.
43.	George W. Bush	7/6/1946, New Haven, CT	Republican	2001–		Laura Welch	Richard Cheney

*assassinated while in office
**resigned Aug 9, 1974
† died while in office—nonviolently

STATE GOVERNORS/US SENATORS

Know who your elected officials are! Below are the mailing addresses, phone numbers and either a website or e-mail address for the governors and US senators for all 50 states. Contact information was current as of February 2005. If you need more information, go to your state's webpage or to www.senate.gov. Information on US representatives can be found at www.house.gov.

ALABAMA

Governor Bob Riley (R)
State Capitol
600 Dexter Avenue, Room N-104
Montgomery, AL 36130
334-242-7100
www.governor.state.al.us

Senator Jeff Sessions (R)
United States Senate
Washington, DC 20510
(202) 224-4124
senator@sessions.senate.gov

Senator Richard C. Shelby (R)
United States Senate
Washington, DC 20510
(202) 224-5744
senator@shelby.senate.gov

ALASKA

Governor Frank Murkowski (R)
PO Box 110001
Juneau, AK 99811-0001
(907) 465-3500
www.gov.state.ak.us

Senator Ted Stevens (R)
United States Senate
Washington, DC 20510
(202) 224-3004
stevens.senate.gov/webform.htm

Senator Lisa Murkowski (R)
United States Senate
Washington, DC 20510
(202) 224-6665
murkowski.senate.gov/contact.html

ARIZONA

Governor Janet Napolitano (D)
1700 West Washington
Phoenix, Arizona 85007
(602) 542-4331
www.governor.state.az.us

Senator Jon Kyl (R)
United States Senate
Washington, DC 20510
(202) 224-4521
kyl.senate.gov/contact.cfm

Senator John McCain (R)
United States Senate
Washington, DC 20510
(202) 224-2235
mccain.senate.gov/index.cfm

ARKANSAS

Governor Mike Huckabee (R)
State Capital, Room 250
Little Rock, AR 72201
(501) 682-2345
www.state.ar.us/governor/governor.html

Senator Blanche Lambert Lincoln (D)
United States Senate
Washington, DC 20510
(202) 224-4843
lincoln.senate.gov/webform.html

Senator Mark Pryor (D)
United States Senate
Washington, DC 20510
(202) 224-2353
pryor.senate.gov/email_webform.htm

CALIFORNIA

Governor Arnold Schwarzenegger (R)
State Capitol Building
Sacramento, CA 95814
(916) 445-2841
governor@governor.ca.gov

Senator Barbara Boxer (D)
United States Senate
Washington, DC 20510
(202) 224-3553
boxer.senate.gov/contact

Senator Dianne Feinstein (D)
United States Senate
Washington, DC 20510
(202) 224-3841
feinstein.senate.gov/email.html

COLORADO

Governor Bill Owens (R)
136 State Capitol
Denver, CO 80203
(303) 866-2471
governorowens@state.co.us

Senator Wayne Allard (R)
United States Senate
Washington, DC 20510
(202) 224-5941
allard.senate.gov/contactme

Senator Ken Salazar (D)
United States Senate
Washington, DC 20510
(202) 224-5852
salazar.senate.gov/contactus.cfm

CONNECTICUT

Governor John Rowland (R)
State Capitol, 210 Capitol Ave
Hartford, CT 06106
(860) 566-4840
Governor.Rowland@po.state.ct.us

Senator Christopher Dodd (D)
United States Senate
Washington, DC 20510
(202) 224-2823
dodd.senate.gov/webmail

Senator Joseph Lieberman (D)
United States Senate
Washington DC 20510
(202) 224-4041
lieberman.senate.gov/contact/index.cfm

DELAWARE

Governor Ruth Ann Minner (D)
Tatnall Building, 3rd Floor
Dover, DE 19901
(302) 744-4101
gminner@state.de.us

Senator Joseph Biden (D)
United States Senate
Washington, DC 20510
(202) 224-5042
senator@biden.senate.gov

Senator Thomas Carper (D)
United States Senate
Washington, DC 20510
(202) 224-2441
carper.senate.gov/email-form.html

FLORIDA

Governor Jeb Bush (R)
The Capitol
400 S Monroe St
Tallahassee, FL 32399
(850) 488-4441
jeb.bush@myflorida.com

Senator Mel Martinez (R)
United States Senate
Washington, DC 20510
(202) 224-3041

Senator Bill Nelson (D)
United States Senate
Washington, DC 20510
(202) 224-5274
billnelson.senate.gov/contact/index.cfm#email

GEORGIA

Governor Sonny Perdue (R)
State Capitol Building
203 State Capitol
Atlanta, GA 30334
(404) 656-1776
www.gov.state.ga.us

Senator Saxby Chambliss (R)
United States Senate
Washington, DC 20510
(202) 224-3521
chambliss.senate.gov/webform.html

Senator Johnny Isakson (R)
United States Senate
Washington, DC 20510
(202) 224-3643

HAWAII

Governor Linda Lingle (R)
Hawaii State Capitol
Executive Chambers
Honolulu, HI 96813
(808) 586-0034
www.hawaii.gov/gov/

Senator Daniel Akaka (D)
United States Senate
Washington, DC 20510
(202) 224-6361
senator@akaka.senate.gov

Senator Daniel Inouye (D)
United States Senate
Washington, DC 20510
(202) 224-3934
inouye.senate.gov/webform.html

IDAHO

Governor Dirk Kempthorne (R)
700 W Jefferson, 2nd Floor
PO Box 83720
Boise, ID 83720
(208) 334-2100
www2.state.id.us/gov/ourgov/contact.htm

Senator Larry Craig (R)
United States Senate
Washington, DC 20510
(202) 224-2752
craig.senate.gov/webform.html

Senator Michael Crapo (R)
United States Senate
Washington, DC 20510
(202) 224-6142
crapo.senate.gov

ILLINOIS

Governor Rod Blagojevich (D)
207 State House
Springfield, IL 62706
(217) 782-0244
governor@state.il.us

Senator Richard Durbin (D)
United States Senate
Washington, DC 20510
(202) 224-2152
dick@durbin.senate.gov

Senator Barack Obama (D)
United States Senate
Washington, DC 20510
(202) 224-2854
obama.senate.gov/contact

INDIANA

Governor Mitchell Daniels (R)
State House, Room 206
Indianapolis, IN 46204
(317) 232-4567
www.in.gov/gov/contact/

Senator Evan Bayh (D)
United States Senate
Washington, DC 20510
(202) 224-5623
bayh.senate.gov/WebMail.html

Senator Richard Lugar (R)
United States Senate
Washington, DC 20510
(202) 224-4814
senator_lugar@lugar.senate.gov

IOWA

Governor Tom Vilsack (D)
State Capitol
Des Moines, IA 50319
(515) 281-5211
www.governor.state.ia.us

Senator Chuck Grassley (R)
United States Senate
Washington, DC 20510
(202) 224-3744
grassley.senate.gov/webform.htm

Senator Tom Harkin (D)
United States Senate
Washington, DC 20510
(202) 224-3254
harkin.senate.gov/contact/contact.cfm

KANSAS

Governor Kathleen Sebelius (D)
State Capitol, Ste. 212 S
Topeka, KS 66612
(785) 296-3232
governor@state.ks.us

Senator Sam Brownback (R)
United States Senate
Washington, DC 20510
(202) 224-6521
brownback.senate.gov/CMEmailMe.htm

Senator Pat Roberts (R)
United States Senate
Washington, DC 20510
(202) 224-4774
roberts.senate.gov/email_pat.html

KENTUCKY

Governor Ernie Fletcher (R)
700 Capitol Ave
Suite 100
Frankfort, KY 40601
(502) 564-2611
www.kentucky.gov/govmail/govcontact.aspx

Senator Jim Bunning (R)
United States Senate
Washington, DC 20510
(202) 224-4343
bunning.senate.gov/index.cfm

Senator Mitch McConnell (R)
United States Senate
Washington, DC 20510
(202) 224-2541
senator@mcconnell.senate.gov

LOUISIANA

Governor Kathleen Blanco (D)
PO Box 94004
Baton Rouge, LA 70804
(225) 342-0991
www.gov.state.la.us/contact/questions.aspx

Senator David Vitter (R)
United States Senate
Washington, DC 20510
(202) 224-4623
vitter.senate.gov/contact.cfm

Senator Mary Landrieu (D)
United States Senate
Washington, DC 20510
(202) 224-5824
landrieu.senate.gov/webform.html

MAINE

Governor John Baldacci (D)
#1 State House Station
Augusta, ME 04333
(207) 287-3531
governor@maine.gov

Senator Susan Collins (R)
United States Senate
Washington, DC 20510
(202) 224-2523
collins.senate.gov/low/contactemail.htm

Senator Olympia Snowe (R)
United States Senate
Washington, DC 20510
(202) 224-5344
olympia@snowe.senate.gov

MARYLAND

Governor Robert Ehrlich, Jr. (R)
100 State Circle
Annapolis, MD 21401
(410) 974-3591
governor@gov.state.md.us

Senator Barbara Mikulski (D)
United States Senate
Washington, DC 20510
(202) 224-4654
mikulski.senate.gov/mailform.htm

Senator Paul Sarbanes (D)
United States Senate
Washington, DC 20510
(202) 224-4524
sarbanes.senate.gov/pages/email.html

MASSACHUSETTS

Governor Mitt Romney (R)
Office of the Governor, Room 360
Boston, MA 02133
(617) 725-4000
GOffice@state.ma.us

Senator Edward Kennedy (D)
United States Senate
Washington, DC 20510
(202) 224-4543
senator@kennedy.senate.gov

Senator John Kerry (D)
United States Senate
Washington, DC 20510
(202) 224-2742
kerry.senate.gov/low/contact_email.html

MICHIGAN

Governor Jennifer Granholm (D)
P.O. Box 30013
Lansing, MI 48909
(517) 335-7858
www.michigan.gov/gov

Senator Carl Levin (D)
United States Senate
Washington, DC 20510
(202) 224-6221
levin.senate.gov/contact/index.cfm

Senator Debbie Stabenow (D)
United States Senate
Washington, DC 20510
(202) 224-4822
stabenow.senate.gov/email.htm

MINNESOTA

Governor Tim Pawlenty (R)
130 State Capitol
75 Rev Dr. Martin Luther King Jr Blvd
St. Paul, MN 55155
(651) 296-3391
tim.pawlenty@state.mn.us

Senator Mark Dayton (D)
United States Senate
Washington, DC 20510
(202) 224-3244
dayton.senate.gov/webform.html

Senator Norm Coleman (R)
United States Senate
Washington, DC 20510
(202) 224-5641
coleman.senate.gov/contact/index.cfm

MISSISSIPPI

Governor Haley Barbour (R)
PO Box 139
Jackson, MS 39205
(601) 359-3100
www.governor.state.ms.us

Senator Thad Cochran (R)
United States Senate
Washington, DC 20510
(202) 224-5054
cochran.senate.gov/contact.htm

Senator Trent Lott (R)
United States Senate
Washington, DC 20510
(202) 224-6253
senatorlott@lott.senate.gov

MISSOURI

Governor Matt Blunt (R)
Missouri Capitol Building, Room 216
Jefferson City, MO 65102
(573) 751-3222
constituentaffairs@mail.gov.state.mo.us

Senator Christopher Bond (R)
United States Senate
Washington, DC 20510
(202) 224-5721
bond.senate.gov/contactme.cfm

Senator Jim Talent (R)
United States Senate
Washington, DC 20510
(202) 224-6154
talent.senate.gov/contact/index.htm

MONTANA

Governor Brian Schweitzer (D)
State Capitol
Helena, MT 59620
(406) 444-3111
www.discoveringmontana.com
/gov2/css/default.asp

Senator Max Baucus (D)
United States Senate
Washington, DC 20510
(202) 224-2651
baucus.senate.gov/emailmax.html

Senator Conrad Burns (R)
United States Senate
Washington, DC 20510
(202) 224-2644
burns.senate.gov/index.cfm

NEBRASKA

Governor Mike Johanns (R)
P.O. Box 94848
Lincoln, NE 68509
(402) 471-2244
gov.nol.org/Johanns03/mail/govmail.htm

Senator Chuck Hagel (R)
United States Senate
Washington, DC 20510
(202) 224-4224
hagel.senate.gov/Email/contact.html

Senator Ben Nelson (D)
United States Senate
Washington, DC 20510
(202) 224-6551
bennelson.senate.gov/email.html

NEVADA

Governor Kenny C. Guinn (R)
Capitol Building
Carson City, NV 89701
(775) 684-5670
www.gov.state.nv.us/contact.htm

Senator John Ensign (R)
United States Senate
Washington, DC 20510
(202) 224-6244
ensign.senate.gov/contact_john

Senator Harry Reid (D)
United States Senate
Washington, DC 20510
(202) 224-3542
reid.senate.gov/email_form.cfm

NEW HAMPSHIRE

Governor John Lynch (D)
25 Capitol St.
Concord, NH 03301
(603) 271-2121
www.state.nh.us/governor/contact.html

Senator Judd Gregg (R)
United States Senate
Washington, DC 20510
(202) 224-3324
mailbox@gregg.senate.gov

Senator John Sununu (R)
United States Senate
Washington, DC 20510
(202) 224-2841
sununu.senate.gov/webform.html

NEW JERSEY

Governor Richard J. Codey (D)*
The State House, PO Box 001
Trenton, NJ 08625
(609) 292-6000
www.state.nj.us/governor/govmail.html

Senator Jon Corzine (D)
United States Senate
Washington, DC 20510
(202) 224-4744
corzine.senate.gov/contact.cfm

Senator Frank Lautenberg (D)
United States Senate
Washington, DC 20510
(202) 224-3224
lautenberg.senate.gov/webform.html

* Serving as Acting Governor until January 2006.

NEW MEXICO

Governor Bill Richardson (D)
State Capitol Building, Room 400
Santa Fe, NM 87501
(505) 476-2200
www.governor.state.nm.us

Senator Jeff Bingaman (D)
United States Senate
Washington, DC 20510
(202) 224-5521
senator_bingaman@bingaman.senate.gov

Senator Pete Domenici (R)
United States Senate
Washington, DC 20510
(202) 224-6621
domenici.senate.gov/contact/contactme.cfm

NEW YORK

Governor George Pataki (R)
State Capitol
Albany, NY 12224
(518) 474-8390
www.state.ny.us/governor

Senator Hillary Clinton (D)
United States Senate
Washington, DC 20510
(202) 224-4451
clinton.senate.gov/email_form.html

Senator Charles Schumer (D)
United States Senate
Washington, DC 20510
(202) 224-6542
schumer.senate.gov/webform.html

NORTH CAROLINA

Governor Michael F. Easley (D)
20301 Mail Service Center
Raleigh, NC 27699
(919) 733-4240
www.governor.state.nc.us

Senator Richard Burr (R)
United States Senate
Washington, DC 20510
(202) 224-3154
burr.senate.gov

Senator Elizabeth Dole (R)
United States Senate
Washington, DC 20510
(202) 224-6342
www.senate.gov/~dole/index.cfm

NORTH DAKOTA

Governor John Hoeven (R)
600 E Boulevard Ave., Dept 101
Bismarck, ND 58505
(701) 328-2200
governor@state.nd.us

Senator Kent Conrad (D)
United States Senate
Washington, DC 20510
(202) 224-2043
conrad.senate.gov/webform.html

Senator Byron Dorgan (D)
United States Senate
Washington, DC 20510
(202) 224-2551
senator@dorgan.senate.gov

OHIO

Governor Bob Taft (R)
77 South High St, 30th Fl
Columbus, OH 43215
(614) 466-3555
Governor.Taft@das.state.oh.us

Senator Mike DeWine (R)
United States Senate
Washington, DC 20510
(202) 224-2315
dewine.senate.gov

Senator George Voinovich (R)
United States Senate
Washington, DC 20510
(202) 224-3353
voinovich.senate.gov/contact/index.htm

OKLAHOMA

Governor Brad Henry (D)
State Capitol Building, Room 212
Oklahoma City, OK 73105
(405) 521-2342
governor@gov.state.ok.us

Senator James Inhofe (R)
United States Senate
Washington, DC 20510
(202) 224-4721
inhofe.senate.gov/contactus.htm

Senator Tom Coburn (R)
United States Senate
Washington, DC 20510
(202) 224-5754

OREGON

Governor Ted Kulongoski (D)
State Capitol Building, 900 Court St NE
Salem, OR 97301
(503) 378-4582
www.governor.state.or.us

Senator Gordon Smith (R)
United States Senate
Washington, DC 20510
(202) 224-3753
gsmith.senate.gov/webform.htm

Senator Ron Wyden (D)
United States Senate
Washington, DC 20510
(202) 224-5244
wyden.senate.gov/contact.html

PENNSYLVANIA

Governor Ed Rendell (D)
225 State Capitol Building
Harrisburg, PA 17120
(717) 787-2500
www.governor.state.pa.us

Senator Rick Santorum (R)
United States Senate
Washington, DC 20510
(202) 224-6324
santorum.senate.gov/emailrjs.html

Senator Arlen Specter (R)
United States Senate
Washington, DC 20510
(202) 224-4254
arlen_specter@specter.senate.gov

RHODE ISLAND

Governor Donald Carcieri (R)
The State House, Room 115
Providence, RI 02903
(401) 222-8170
rigov@gov.state.ri.us

Senator Lincoln Chafee (R)
United States Senate
Washington, DC 20510
(202) 224-2921
chafee.senate.gov/webform.htm

Senator Jack Reed (D)
United States Senate
Washington, DC 20510
(202) 224-4642
reed.senate.gov/form-opinion.htm

SOUTH CAROLINA

Governor Mark Sanford (R)
PO Box 12267
Columbia, SC 29211
(803) 734-2100
www.scgovernor.com/contact.asp

Senator Jim DeMint (R)
United States Senate
Washington, DC 20510
(202) 224-6121
demint.senate.gov

Senator Lindsey Graham (R)
United States Senate
Washington, DC 20510
(202) 224-5972
lgraham.senate.gov/email/email.htm

SOUTH DAKOTA

Governor Mike Rounds (R)
500 E Capitol Av
Pierre, SD 57501
(605) 773-3212
www.state.sd.us/governor

Senator John R. Thune (R)
United States Senate
Washington, DC 20510
(202) 224-2321

Senator Tim Johnson (D)
United States Senate
Washington, DC 20510
(202) 224-5842
johnson.senate.gov/contactpage/emailform.htm

TENNESSEE

Governor Phil Bredesen (D)
Tennessee State Capitol
Nashville, TN 37243
(615) 741-2001
phil.bredesen@state.tn.us

Senator Bill Frist (R)
United States Senate
Washington, DC 20510
(202) 224-3344
frist.senate.gov/index.cfm

Senator Lamar Alexander (R)
United States Senate
Washington, DC 20510
(202) 224-4944
alexander.senate.gov/contact.cfm

TEXAS

Governor Rick Perry (R)
PO Box 12428
Austin, TX 78711
(512) 463-2000
www.governor.state.tx.us/contact

Senator John Cornyn (R)
United States Senate
Washington, DC 20510
(202) 224-2934
cornyn.senate.gov/contact/index.cfm

Senator Kay Hutchison (R)
United States Senate
Washington, DC 20510
(202) 224-5922
hutchison.senate.gov/e-mail.htm

UTAH

Governor Jon Huntsman Jr. (R)
210 State Capitol
Salt Lake City, UT 84114
(801) 538-1000
www.governor.utah.gov/goca/form_governor.html

Senator Robert Bennett (R)
United States Senate
Washington, DC 20510
(202) 224-5444
bennett.senate.gov/e-mail_form.html

Senator Orrin Hatch (R)
United States Senate
Washington, DC 20510
(202) 224-5251
www.senate.gov/~hatch/index.cfm

VERMONT

Governor Jim Douglas (R)
190 State St Pavilion
Montpelier, VT 05609
(802) 828-3333
www.gov.state.vt.us

Senator James Jeffords (I)
United States Senate
Washington, DC 20510
(202) 224-5141
jeffords.senate.gov/contact-form.html

Senator Patrick Leahy (D)
United States Senate
Washington, DC 20510
(202) 224-4242
senator_leahy@leahy.senate.gov

VIRGINIA

Governor Mark R. Warner (D)
State Capitol, 3rd Floor
Richmond, VA 23219
(804) 786-2211
www.governor.state.va.us

Senator George Allen (R)
United States Senate
Washington, DC 20510
(202) 224-4024
allen.senate.gov/email.html

Senator John Warner (R)
United States Senate
Washington, DC 20510
(202) 224-2023
warner.senate.gov/contact/contactme.htm

WASHINGTON

Governor Christine Gregoire (D)
PO Box 40002
Olympia, WA 98504
(360) 902-4111
www.governor.wa.gov

Senator Maria Cantwell (D)
United States Senate
Washington, DC 20510
(202) 224-3441
cantwell.senate.gov/contact/index.html

Senator Patty Murray (D)
United States Senate
Washington, DC 20510
(202) 224-2621
murray.senate.gov/email/index.cfm

WEST VIRGINIA

Governor Joe Manchin III (D)
1900 Kanawha Blvd, E
Charleston, WV 25305
(888) 438-2731
www.state.wv.us/governor

Senator Robert Byrd (D)
United States Senate
Washington, DC 20510
(202) 224-3954
byrd.senate.gov/byrd_email.html

Senator John Rockefeller (D)
United States Senate
Washington, DC 20510
(202) 224-6472
senator@rockefeller.senate.gov

WISCONSIN

Governor Jim Doyle (D)
115 East State Capitol
Madison, WI 53702
(608) 266-1212
www.wisgov.state.wi.us/contact.asp

Senator Russell Feingold (D)
United States Senate
Washington, DC 20510
(202) 224-5323
russell_feingold@feingold.senate.gov

Senator Herb Kohl (D)
United States Senate
Washington, DC 20510
(202) 224-5653
kohl.senate.gov/gen_contact.html

WYOMING

Governor Dave Freudenthal (D)
State Capitol Building, Room 124
Cheyenne, WY 82002
(307) 777-7434
Governor@missc.state.wy.us

Senator Michael Enzi (R)
United States Senate
Washington, DC 20510
(202) 224-3424
senator@enzi.senate.gov

Senator Craig Thomas (R)
United States Senate
Washington, DC 20510
(202) 224-6441
thomas.senate.gov/html/contact.html

SOME FACTS ABOUT CANADA

Province/Territory	Capital	Population*	Flower	Land/Fresh Water (sq. mi.)	Total Area
Alberta	Edmonton	2,974,807	Wild Rose	248,000/7,541	255,541
British Columbia	Victoria	3,907,738	Pacific dogwood	357,216/7,548	364,764
Manitoba	Winnipeg	1,119,583	Prairie crocus	213,729/36,387	250,116
New Brunswick	Fredericton	729,498	Purple violet	27,587/563	28,150
Newfoundland & Labrador	St. John's	513,930	Pitcher plant	144,343/12,100	156,543
Northwest Territories	Yellowknife	37,360	Mountain avens	456,791/62,943	519,734
Nova Scotia	Halifax	908,007	Mayflower	20,593/752	21,345
Nunavut	Iqaluit	26,745	Purple saxifrage	747,537/60,648	808,185
Ontario	Toronto	11,410,046	White trillium	354,341/61,256	415,599
Prince Edward Island	Charlottetown	135,294	Lady's-slipper	2,185/0	2,185
Quebec	Quebec City	7,237,479	White garden lily	527,079/68,313	595,391
Saskatchewan	Regina	978,933	Western red lily	228,445/22,921	251,366
Yukon Territory	Whitehorse	28,674	Fireweed	183,163/3,109	186,272

*Based on the 2001 Canadian Census

PROVINCE & TERRITORY ABBREVIATIONS: CANADA

Alberta . . . . . AB
British Columbia . . . . . BC
Manitoba. . . . . MB
New Brunswick . . . . . NB
Newfoundland & Labrador . . . . . NF
Northwest Territories . . . . . NT
Nova Scotia . . . . . NS
Nunavut. . . . . NU
Ontario . . . . . ON
Prince Edward Island . . . . . PE
Quebec. . . . . QC
Saskatchewan . . . . . SK
Yukon Territory . . . . . YT

SOME FACTS ABOUT MEXICO

State	Abbreviation	Capital	Population*	Area (sq. mi.)
Aguascalientes	Ags.	Aguascalientes	944,285	2,156
Baja California	B.C.	Mexicali	2,487,367	27,655
Baja California Sur	B.C.S.	La Paz	424,041	27,979
Campeche	Camp.	Campeche	690,689	19,672
Chiapas	Chis.	Tuxtla Gutiérrez	3,920,892	28,732
Chihuahua	Chih.	Chihuahua	3,052,907	94,831
Coahuila	Coah.	Saltillo	2,298,070	58,067
Colima	Col.	Colima	542,627	2010
Distrito Federal	D.F.	Mexico City	8,605,239	573
Durango	Dgo.	Durango	1,448,661	47,691
Guanajuato	Gto.	Guanajuato	4,663,032	11,805
Guerrero	Gro.	Chilpancingo	3,079,649	24,887
Hidalgo	Hgo.	Pachuca	2,235,591	8058
Jalisco	Jal.	Guadalajara	6,322,002	31,152
México	Mex.	Toluca	13,096,686	8,268
Michoacán	Mich.	Morelia	3,985,667	23,202
Morelos	Mor.	Cuernavaca	1,555,296	1,917
Nayarit	Nay.	Tepic	920,185	10,547
Nuevo León	N.L.	Monterrey	3,834,141	25,136
Oaxaca	Oax.	Oaxaca	3,438,765	36,375
Puebla	Pue.	Puebla	5,076,686	13,126
Querétaro	Qro.	Querétaro	1,404,306	4,432
Quintana Roo	Q.R.	Chetumal	874,963	19,630
San Luis Potosí	S.L.P.	San Luis Potosí	2,229,360	24,417
Sinaloa	Sin.	Culiacán	2,536,844	22,582
Sonora	Son.	Hermosillo	2,216,969	70,484
Tabasco	Tab.	Villahermosa	1,891,829	9,783
Tamaulipas	Tamps.	Ciudad Victoria	2,753,222	30,734
Tlaxcala	Tlax.	Tlaxcala	962,646	1,555
Veracruz	Ver.	Jalapa	6,908,975	27,759
Yucatán	Yuc.	Mérida	1,658,210	14,868
Zacatecas	Zac.	Zacatecas	1,353,610	28,125

*Based on the 2000 Mexican Census

☆ The Teacher's Calendar, 2005–2006 ☆

CALENDAR INFORMATION FOR THE YEAR 2005

Time shown is Eastern Standard Time. All dates are given in terms of the Gregorian calendar.
(Based in part on information prepared by the Nautical Almanac Office, US Naval Observatory.)

ERAS	YEAR	BEGINS
Jewish*	5766	Oct 3
Chinese (Year of the Rooster)	4703	Feb 9
Japanese (Heisei)	17	Jan 1
Indian (Saka)	1927	Mar 22
Islamic (Hegira)**	1426	Feb 9

*Year begins at sunset. **Year begins at moon crescent.

RELIGIOUS CALENDARS—2005

Christian Holy Days

Epiphany . . . . Jan 6
Shrove Tuesday . . . . Feb 8
Ash Wednesday . . . . Feb 9
Lent . . . . Feb 9–Mar 26
Palm Sunday . . . . Mar 20
Good Friday . . . . Mar 25
Easter . . . . Mar 27
Ascension Day . . . . May 5
Whit Sunday (Pentecost) . . . . May 15
Trinity Sunday . . . . May 22
First Sunday in Advent . . . . Nov 27
Christmas Day . . . . Dec 25

Eastern Orthodox Church Observances

Great Lent begins . . . . Mar 14
Pascha (Easter) . . . . May 1
Ascension . . . . June 9
Pentecost . . . . June 19

Jewish Holy Days*

Purim . . . . Mar 25
Passover (1st day) . . . . Apr 24
Shavuot . . . . June 13–14
Tisha B'av . . . . Aug 14
Rosh Hashanah (New Year) . . . . Oct 4–5
Yom Kippur . . . . Oct 13
Succoth . . . . Oct 18–24
Chanukah . . . . Dec 26–Jan 2

*All Jewish holy days begin the previous day at sundown.

Islamic Holy Days**

Islamic New Year (1426) . . . . Feb 9
First Day of Ramadan (1426) . . . . Oct 3
Eid-Al-Fitr (1426) . . . . Nov 2

**All Islamic holy days begin at moon crescent.

CIVIL CALENDAR—USA—2005

New Year's Day . . . . Jan 1
Martin Luther King's Birthday (obsvd) . . . . Jan 17
Lincoln's Birthday . . . . Feb 12
Washington's Birthday (obsvd)/Presidents' Day . . . . Feb 21
Memorial Day (obsvd) . . . . May 30
Independence Day . . . . July 4
Labor Day . . . . Sept 5
Columbus Day (obsvd) . . . . Oct 10
General Election Day . . . . Nov 8
Veterans Day . . . . Nov 11
Thanksgiving Day . . . . Nov 24

Other Days Widely Observed in US—2005

Groundhog Day (Candlemas) . . . . Feb 2
St. Valentine's Day . . . . Feb 14
St. Patrick's Day . . . . Mar 17
Mother's Day . . . . May 8
Flag Day . . . . June 14
Father's Day . . . . June 19
National Grandparents Day . . . . Sept 11
Hallowe'en . . . . Oct 31

CIVIL CALENDAR—CANADA—2005

Victoria Day . . . . May 23
Canada Day . . . . July 1
Labor Day . . . . Sept 5
Thanksgiving Day . . . . Oct 10
Remembrance Day . . . . Nov 11
Boxing Day . . . . Dec 26

CIVIL CALENDAR—MEXICO—2005

New Year's Day . . . . Jan 1
Constitution Day . . . . Feb 5
Benito Juarez Birthday . . . . Mar 21
Labor Day . . . . May 1
Battle of Puebla Day (Cinco de Mayo) . . . . May 5
Independence Day* . . . . Sept 16
Dia de La Raza . . . . Oct 12
Mexican Revolution Day . . . . Nov 20
Guadalupe Day . . . . Dec 12

*Celebration begins Sept 15 at 11:00 PM

ECLIPSES—2005

Hybrid eclipse of the Sun . . . . Apr 8
Penumbral eclipse of the Moon . . . . Apr 24
Annular eclipse of the Sun . . . . Oct 3
Partial eclipse of the Moon . . . . Oct 17

SEASONS—2005

Spring (Vernal Equinox) . . . . Mar 20, 7:33 AM, EST
Summer (Summer Solstice) . . . . June 21, 2:46 AM, EDT
Autumn (Autumnal Equinox) . . . . Sept 22, 6:23 PM, EDT
Winter (Winter Solstice) . . . . Dec 21, 1:35 PM, EST

DAYLIGHT SAVING TIME SCHEDULE—2005

Sunday, Apr 3, 2:00 AM–Sunday, Oct 30, 2:00 AM—in all time zones.

☆ *The Teacher's Calendar, 2005–2006* ☆

CALENDAR INFORMATION FOR THE YEAR 2006

Time shown is Eastern Standard Time. All dates are given in terms of the Gregorian calendar.

(Based in part on information prepared by the Nautical Almanac Office, US Naval Observatory.)

ERAS	YEAR	BEGINS
Jewish*	5767	Sept 22
Chinese (Year of the Dog)	4704	Jan 29
Japanese (Heisei)	18	Jan 1
Indian (Saka)	1928	Mar 22
Islamic (Hegira)**	1427	Jan 30

*Year begins at sunset. **Year begins at moon crescent.

RELIGIOUS CALENDARS—2006

Christian Holy Days

Epiphany . . . . Jan 6
Shrove Tuesday . . . . Feb 28
Ash Wednesday . . . . Mar 1
Lent . . . . Mar 1–Apr 15
Palm Sunday . . . . Apr 9
Good Friday . . . . Apr 14
Easter . . . . Apr 16
Ascension Day . . . . May 25
Whit Sunday (Pentecost) . . . . June 4
Trinity Sunday . . . . June 11
First Sunday in Advent . . . . Dec 3
Christmas Day . . . . Dec 25

Eastern Orthodox Church Observances

Great Lent begins . . . . Mar 6
Pascha (Easter) . . . . Apr 23
Ascension . . . . June 1
Pentecost . . . . June 11

Jewish Holy Days*

Purim . . . . Mar 14
Passover (1st day) . . . . Apr 13
Shavuot . . . . June 2–3
Tisha B'av . . . . Aug 3
Rosh Hashanah (New Year) . . . . Sept 23–24
Yom Kippur . . . . Oct 2
Succoth . . . . Oct 7–12
Chanukah . . . . Dec 16–23

*All Jewish holy days begin the previous day at sundown.

Islamic Holy Days**

Islamic New Year (1427) . . . . Jan 30
First Day of Ramadan (1427) . . . . Sept 23
Eid-Al-Fitr (1427) . . . . Oct 23

**All Islamic holy days begin at moon crescent.

CIVIL CALENDAR—USA—2006

New Year's Day . . . . Jan 1
Martin Luther King's Birthday (obsvd) . . . . Jan 16
Lincoln's Birthday . . . . Feb 12
Washington's Birthday (obsvd)/Presidents' Day . . . . Feb 20
Memorial Day (obsvd) . . . . May 29
Independence Day . . . . July 4
Labor Day . . . . Sept 4
Columbus Day (obsvd) . . . . Oct 9
General Election Day . . . . Nov 7
Veterans Day . . . . Nov 11
Thanksgiving Day . . . . Nov 23

Other Days Widely Observed in US—2006

Groundhog Day (Candlemas) . . . . Feb 2
St. Valentine's Day . . . . Feb 14
St. Patrick's Day . . . . Mar 17
Mother's Day . . . . May 14
Flag Day . . . . June 14
Father's Day . . . . June 18
National Grandparents Day . . . . Sept 10
Hallowe'en . . . . Oct 31

CIVIL CALENDAR—CANADA—2006

Victoria Day . . . . May 22
Canada Day . . . . July 1
Labor Day . . . . Sept 4
Thanksgiving Day . . . . Oct 9
Remembrance Day . . . . Nov 11
Boxing Day . . . . Dec 26

CIVIL CALENDAR—MEXICO—2006

New Year's Day . . . . Jan 1
Constitution Day . . . . Feb 5
Benito Juarez Birthday . . . . Mar 21
Labor Day . . . . May 1
Battle of Puebla Day (Cinco de Mayo) . . . . May 5
Independence Day* . . . . Sept 16
Dia de La Raza . . . . Oct 12
Mexican Revolution Day . . . . Nov 20
Guadalupe Day . . . . Dec 12

*Celebration begins Sept 15 at 11:00 PM

ECLIPSES—2006

Penumbral eclipse of the Moon . . . . Mar 14–15
Total eclipse of the Sun . . . . Mar 29
Partial eclipse of the Moon . . . . Sept 7
Annular eclipse of the Sun . . . . Sept 22

SEASONS—2006

Spring (Vernal Equinox) . . . . Mar 20, 1:26 PM, EST
Summer (Summer Solstice) . . . . June 21, 8:26 AM, EDT
Autumn (Autumnal Equinox) . . . . Sept 23, 12:03 AM, EDT
Winter (Winter Solstice) . . . . Dec 21, 7:22 PM, EST

DAYLIGHT SAVING TIME SCHEDULE—2006

Sunday, Apr 2, 2:00 AM–Sunday, Oct 29, 2:00 AM—in all time zones.

2005 AMERICAN LIBRARY ASSOCIATION AWARDS FOR CHILDREN'S BOOKS

NEWBERY MEDAL
For most distinguished contribution to American literature for children published in 2004:
Cynthia Kadohata, author, *Kira-Kira* (Atheneum Books, 0-689-85639-3, $15.95 Ages 9–12)

Honor Books

Gary D. Schmidt, author, *Lizzie Bright and the Buckminster Boy* (Clarion Books, 0-618-43929-3 $15 Ages 12 & up)
Gennifer Choldenko, author, *Al Capone Does My Shirts* (G.P. Putnam's Sons, 0-399-23861-1, $15.99 Ages 9–12)
Russell Freedman, author, *The Voice That Challenged a Nation: Marian Anderson and the Struggle for Equal Rights* (Clarion Books, 0-618-15976-2, $18 Ages 9–12)

CALDECOTT MEDAL
For most distinguished American picture book for children published in 2004:
Kevin Henkes, author and illustrator, *Kitten's First Full Moon* (HarperCollins, 0-06-058828-4, $15.99 Ages 4–6)

Honor Books

Barbara Lehman, author and illustrator, *The Red Book* (Houghton Mifflin, 0-618-42858-5, $12.95 Ages 5–8)
E.B. Lewis, illustrator, *Coming On Home Soon*, written by Jacqueline Woodson (G.P. Putnam's Sons, 0-399-23748-8, $16.99 Ages 4–8)
Mo Willems, author and illustrator, *Knuffle Bunny: A Cautionary Tale* Hyperion Books, 0-7868-1870-0, $15.99 Ages 3–6)

CORETTA SCOTT KING AWARD FOR NARRATIVE
For outstanding books by African-American authors:
Toni Morrison, author, *Remember: The Journey to School Integration* (Houghton Mifflin, 0-618-39740-X, $18 Ages 9–12)

Honor Books

Shelia P. Moses, author, *The Legend of Buddy Bush* (Simon & Schuster, 0-689-85839-6, $15.95 Ages 12 & up)
Sharon G. Flake, author, *Who Am I Without Him* (Hyperion, 0-786-80693-1, $15.99 Ages 12 & up)
Marilyn Nelson, *Fortune's Bones: The Manumission Requiem* (Front Street, 1-9324-2512-8, $16.95 Ages 12 & up)

CORETTA SCOTT KING AWARD FOR ILLUSTRATION
For outstanding books by African-American illustrators:
Kadir Nelson, illustrator, *Ellington Was Not a Street*, written by Ntozake Shange (Simon & Schuster, 0-689-82884-5, $15.95 Ages 4–8)

Honor Books

Jerry Pinkney, illustrator, *God Bless the Child*, written by Billie Holiday and Arthur Herzog, Jr (HarperCollins, 0-06-028797-7, $16.99 Ages 6–10)
Leo and Diane Dillon, illustrators, *The People Could Fly: The Picture Book*, written by Virginia Hamilton (Random House, 0-375-82405-7, $16.95 Ages 7–12)

CORETTA SCOTT KING/JOHN STEPTOE NEW TALENT AWARD
For narrative:
Barbara Hathaway, author, *Missy Violet and Me* (Houghton Mifflin, 0-618-37163-X, $15 Ages 12 & up)
For illustration:
Frank Morrison, illustrator, *Jazzy Miz Mozetta*, written by Brenda C. Roberts (Farrar, Straus and Giroux, 0-374-33674-1, $16.50 Ages 4–8)

MICHAEL L. PRINTZ AWARD
For excellence in writing literature for young adults:
Meg Rosoff, author, *How I Live Now* (Wendy Lamb Books/Random House, 0-385-74677-6, $16.95 Ages 12 & up)

Honor Books

Kenneth Oppel, author, *Airborn* (HarperCollins, 0-06-053180-0 $16.99 Ages 12 & up)
Gary D. Schmidt, author, *Lizzie Bright and the Buckminster Boy* (Clarion Books, 0-618-43929-3 $15 Ages 12 & up)
Allan Stratton, author, *Chanda's Secrets* (Annick Press, Ltd, 155037835X, $8.95 Ages 12 & up)

ROBERT F. SIBERT AWARD
For most distinguished informational book for children published in 2004:
Russell Freedman, author, *The Voice That Challenged a Nation: Marian Anderson and the Struggle for Equal Rights* (Clarion Books, 0-618-15976-2, $18 Ages 9–12)

Honor Books

Barbara Kerley, author, *Walt Whitman: Words for America*, illustrated by Brian Selznick (Scholastic, Inc, 0-439-35791-8, $16.95 Ages 7–10)
Sy Montgomery, author, *The Tarantula Scientist*, illustrated by Nic Bishop (Houghton Mifflin, 0-618-14799-3, $18 Ages 7–12)
James Rumford, author, *Sequoyah: The Cherokee Man Who Gave His People Writing*, translated by Anna Sixkiller Huckaby (Houghton Mifflin, 0-618-36947-3, $16 Ages 5–8)

MARGARET A. EDWARDS AWARD
For lifetime achievement writing books for young adults:
Francesca Lia Block, recipient

LAURA INGALLS WILDER MEDAL
For an author or illustrator whose books, published in the United States, have made, over a period of years, a substantial and lasting contribution to literature for children:
Laurence Yep, recipient

MILDRED L. BATCHELDER AWARD
For the best children's book first published in a foreign language in a foreign country and subsequently translated into English for publication in the US:
Delacorte Press/Random House Children's Books, publisher, *The Shadows of Ghadames*, written by Joëlle Stolz, translated from French by Catherine Temerson (0-385-73104-3, $15.95 Ages 8–12)

Honor Books

Farrar, Straus and Giroux, publisher, *The Crow-Girl: The Children of Crow Cove*, written by Bodil Bredsdorff, translated from Danish by Faith Ingwersen (0-374-31247-8, $16 Ages 8–12)
A Richard Jackson Book, Atheneum Books for Young Readers, publisher, *Daniel Half Human and the Good Nazi*, written by David Chotjewitz, translated from German by Doris Orgel (0-689-85747-0, $17.95 Ages 12 & up)

ANDREW CARNEGIE MEDAL FOR EXCELLENCE IN CHILDREN'S VIDEO
Paul R. Gagne and Melissa Reilly, producers, *The Dot*, based on the book by Peter H. Reynolds (Weston Woods, $59.95 Gr. PreK–4)

MAY HILL ARBUTHNOT LECTURE AWARD
Russell Freedman, recipient

2004 AMERICAN LIBRARY ASSOCIATION AWARDS FOR CHILDREN'S BOOKS

NEWBERY MEDAL

For most distinguished contribution to American literature for children published in 2003:
Kate diCamillo, author, *The Tale of Despereaux*, illustrated by Timothy Basil Ering (Candlewick Press, 0-763-61722-9, $17.99 Ages 9–12)

Honor Books

Kevin Henkes, author, *Olive's Ocean* (Greenwillow Books/HarperCollins, 0-06-053543-1, $15.99 Ages 9–12)
Jim Murphy, author, *An American Plague: The True and Terrifying Story of the Yellow Fever Epidemic of 1793* (Clarion Books/Houghton Mifflin, 0-395-77608-2, $17 Ages 10 & up)

CALDECOTT MEDAL

For most distinguished American picture book for children published in 2003:
Mordicai Gerstein, author and illustrator, *The Man Who Walked Between the Towers,* (Roaring Brook Press/Millbrook Press, 0-7613-1791-0, $17.95 Ages 5–8)

Honor Books

Margaret Chodos-Irvine, author and illustrator, *Ella Sarah Gets Dressed* (Harcourt, Inc, 0-15-216413-8, $16 Ages 2–6)
Steve Jenkins and Robin Page, authors and illustrators, *What Do You Do with a Tail Like This?* (Houghton Mifflin, 0-618-25628-8, $15 Ages 4–8)
Mo Willems, author and illustrator, *Don't Let the Pigeon Drive the Bus* (Hyperion, 0-7868-1988-X, $12.99 Ages 4–8)

CORETTA SCOTT KING AWARD FOR NARRATIVE

For outstanding books by African-American authors:
Angela Johnson, author, *The First Part Last* (Simon & Schuster, 0-689-84922-2, $15.95 Ages 12 & up)

Honor Books

Sharon M. Draper, author, *The Battle of Jericho* (Atheneum, 0-689-84232-5, $16.95 Ages 12 & up)
Patricia C. and Fredrick L. McKissack, authors, *Days of Jubilee: The End of Slavery in the United States* (Scholastic, 0-590-10764-X $18.95 Ages 9 & up)
Jacqueline Woodson, author, *Locomotion* (Putnam, 0-399-23115-3, $15.99 Ages 9–12)

CORETTA SCOTT KING AWARD FOR ILLUSTRATION

For outstanding books by African-American illustrators:
Ashley Bryan, author and illustrator, *Beautiful Blackbird* (Atheneum, 0-689-84731-9, $16.95 Ages 3–7)

Honor Books

Colin Bootman, illustrator, *Almost to Freedom*, written by Vaunda Micheaux Nelson (Carolrhoda Books/Lerner Publishing Group, 1-575-05342-X, $15.95 Ages 6–10)
Kadir Nelson, illustrator, *Thunder Rose*, written by Jerdine Nolen (Harcourt, Inc, 0-152-16472-3, $16 Ages 5–8)

CORETTA SCOTT KING/JOHN STEPTOE NEW TALENT AWARD

For narrative:
Hope Anita Smith, author, *The Way a Door Closes*, illustrated by Shane W. Evans (Henry Holt, 0-8050-6477-X, $18.95 Ages 8–12)
For illustration:
Elbrite Brown, illustrator, *My Family Plays Music*, written by Judy Cox (Holiday House, 0-8234-1591-0, $16.95 Ages 5–8)

MARGARET A. EDWARDS AWARD

For lifetime achievement writing books for young adults:
Ursula K. LeGuin, recipient

MAY HILL ARBUTHNOT LECTURE AWARD

Richard Jackson, recipient
Editorial Director, Richard Jackson Books/Simon & Schuster

MICHAEL L. PRINTZ AWARD

For excellence in writing literature for young adults, for books published in 2003:
Angela Johnson, author, *The First Part Last* (Simon & Schuster, 0-689-84922-2, $15.95 Ages 12 & up)

Honor Books

Jennifer Donnelly, author, *A Northern Light* (Harcourt, Inc, 0-152-16705-6, $17 Ages 12 & up)
Helen Frost, author, *Keesha's House* (Farrar, Straus and Giroux, 0-374-34064-1, $16 Ages 12 & up)
K.L. Going, author, *Fat Kid Rules the World* (Putnam, 0-399-23990-1, $17.99 Ages 12 & up)
Carolyn Mackler, author, *The Earth, My Butt, and Other Big Round Things* (Candlewick Press, 0-763-61958-2, $15.99 Ages 12 & up)

ROBERT F. SIBERT AWARD

For most distinguished informational book for children published in 2003:
Jim Murphy, author, *An American Plague: The True and Terrifying Story of the Yellow Fever Epidemic of 1793* (Clarion Books/Houghton Mifflin, 0-395-77608-2, $17 Ages 10 & up)

Honor Books

Vicki Cobb, author, *I Face the Wind*, illustrated by Julia Gorton (HarperCollins, 0-688-17840-5, $15.99 Ages 3–7)

PURA BELPRÉ AWARD

For the Latino author whose work best portrays, celebrates and affirms Latino culture in a children's book:
Julia Alvarez, author, *Before We Were Free* (Knopf, 0-375-81544-9, $15.95 Ages 12 & up)

Honor Books

Nancy Osa, author, *Cuba 15*, (Delacorte Press, 0-385-73021-7, $15.95 Ages 12 & up)
Amada Irma Pérez, author, *My Diary From Here to There/Mi diario de aquí hasta allá* (Children's Book Press/Editorial Libros Para Niños, 0-8923-9175-8, $16.95 Ages 6–10)

For the Latino illustrator whose work best portrays, celebrates and affirms Latino culture in a children's book:
Yuyi Morales, author and illustrator, *Just a Minute: A Trickster Tale and Counting Book* (Chronicle Books, 0-8118-3758-0, $15.95 Ages 4–8)

Honor Books

Robert Casilla, illustrator, *First Day in Grapes*, written by L. King Pérez (Lee & Low Books, 1-58430-045-0, $16.95 Ages 4–8)
David Diaz, illustrator, *The Pot that Juan Built*, written by Nancy Andrews-Goebel (Lee & Low Books, 1-58430-038-8, $16.95 Ages 4–8)
Yuyi Morales, illustrator, *Harvesting Hope: The Story of Cesar Chavez*, written by Kathleen Krull (Harcourt, Inc, 0-152-01437-3, $17 Ages 6–9)

MILDRED L. BATCHELDER AWARD

For the best children's book first published in a foreign language in a foreign country and subsequently translated into English for publication in the US:
Walter Lorraine Books/Houghton Mifflin Co., publisher, *Run, Boy, Run*, written by Uri Orlev, translated from Hebrew by Hillel Halkin (0-618-16465-0, $15 Ages 10 & up)

Honor Book

Chronicle Books, publisher, *The Man Who Went to the Far Side of the Moon: The Story of Apollo 11 Astronaut Michael Collins*, written by Bea Uusma Schyffert, translated from Swedish by Emi Guner (0-8118-4007-7, $14.95 Ages 8–12)

ANDREW CARNEGIE MEDAL FOR EXCELLENCE IN CHILDREN'S VIDEO

Paul R. Gagne and Melissa Reilly, producers, *Giggle, Giggle, Quack?*, based on the book written by Doreen Cronin and illustrated by Betsy Lewin (Weston Woods, 1-55592-536-7, $60 Gr. 1–7)

CORETTA SCOTT KING AWARDS AND HONOR BOOKS, 1970–2003

The Coretta Scott King Awards have been presented annually by the Coretta Scott King Task Force of the American Library Association's Social Responsibilities Round Table since 1969. The Award commemorates the life and work of Dr. Martin Luther King Jr., and honors his widow, Coretta Scott King, for her courage and determination in continuing to work for peace and world brotherhood. They are given to an African-American author for an outstandingly inspirational and educational contribution published during the previous year. The separate award for an African-American illustrator was added in 1974. The original publisher of each work is listed in parentheses. Some titles may be out of print; check with your local library.

AWARDS FOR NARRATIVE

2003 WINNER: *Bronx Masquerade*, Nikki Grimes (Dial Books)

Honor Books
The Red Rose Box, Brenda Woods (G.P. Putnam's Sons)
Talkin' About Bessie: The Story of Aviator Elizabeth Coleman, Nikki Grimes, illustrated by E.B. Lewis (Scholastic)

2002 WINNER: *The Land*, Mildred D. Taylor (Dial Books)

Honor Books
Money Hungry, Sharon Flake (Jump at the Sun/Hyperion)
Carver: A Life in Poems, Marilyn Nelson (Front Street)

2001 WINNER: *Miracle's Boys*, Jacqueline Woodson (G.P. Putnam's Sons)

Honor Book
Let It Shine! Stories of Black Women Freedom Fighters, Andrea Davis Pinkney (Gulliver Books)

2000 WINNER: *Bud, Not Buddy*, Christopher Paul Curtis (Delacorte)

Honor Books
Francie, Karen English (Farrar, Straus and Giroux)
Black Hands, White Sails: The Story of African-American Whalers, Patricia C. and Frederick L. McKissack (Scholastic)
Monster, Walter Dean Myers (HarperCollins)

1999 WINNER: *Heaven*, Angela Johnson (Simon & Schuster)

Honor Books
Jazmin's Notebook, Nikki Grimes (Dial Books)
Breaking Ground, Breaking Silence: The Story of New York's African Burial Ground, Joyce Hansen and Gary McGowan (Henry Holt)
The Other Side: Shorter Poems, Angela Johnson (Orchard Books)

1998 WINNER: *Forged by Fire*, Sharon M. Draper (Atheneum)

Honor Books
Bayard Rustin: Behind the Scenes of the Civil Rights Movement, James Haskins (Hyperion)
I Thought My Soul Would Rise and Fly: The Diary of Patsy, a Freed Girl, Joyce Hansen (Scholastic)

1997 WINNER: *Slam*, Walter Dean Myers (Scholastic)

Honor Book
Rebels Against Slavery: American Slave Revolts, Patricia C. & Frederick L. McKissack (Scholastic)

1996 WINNER: *Her Stories*, Virginia Hamilton (Scholastic)

Honor Books
The Watsons Go to Birmingham—1963, Christopher Paul Curtis (Delacorte)
Like Sisters on the Homefront, Rita Williams-Garcia (Delacorte)
From the Notebooks of Melanin Sun, Jacqueline Woodson (Scholastic)

1995 WINNER: *Christmas in the Big House, Christmas in the Quarters*, Patricia C. & Frederick L. McKissack (Scholastic)

Honor Books
The Captive, Joyce Hansen (Scholastic)
I Hadn't Meant to Tell You This, Jacqueline Woodson (Delacorte)
Black Diamond: Story of the Negro Baseball League, Patricia C. & Frederick L. McKissack (Scholastic)

1994 WINNER: *Toning the Sweep*, Angela Johnson (Orchard)

Honor Books
Brown Honey in Broom Wheat Tea, Joyce Carol Thomas (HarperCollins)
Malcolm X: By Any Means Necessary, Walter Dean Myers (Scholastic)

1993 WINNER: *The Dark-Thirty: Southern Tales of the Supernatural*, Patricia A. McKissack (Knopf)

Honor Books
Mississippi Challenge, Mildred Pitts Walter (Bradbury)
Sojourner Truth: Ain't I a Woman?, Patricia C. & Frederick L. McKissack (Scholastic)
Somewhere in the Darkness, Walter Dean Myers (Scholastic)

1992 WINNER: *Now Is Your Time: The African American Struggle for Freedom*, Walter Dean Myers (HarperCollins)

Honor Book
Night on Neighborhood Street, Eloise Greenfield (Dial)

1991 WINNER: *The Road to Memphis*, Mildred D. Taylor (Dial)

Honor Books
Black Dance in America, James Haskins (Crowell)
When I Am Old With You, Angela Johnson (Orchard)

1990 WINNER: *A Long Hard Journey: The Story of the Pullman Porter*, Patricia C. & Frederick L. McKissack (Walker)

Honor Books
Nathaniel Talking, Eloise Greenfield, (Black Butterfly)
The Bells of Christmas, Virginia Hamilton (Harcourt)
Martin Luther King, Jr., and the Freedom Movement, Lillie Patterson (Facts on File)

1989 WINNER: *Fallen Angels*, Walter Dean Myers (Scholastic)

Honor Books
A Thief in the Village and Other Stories, James Berry (Orchard)
Anthony Burns: The Defeat and Triumph of a Fugitive Slave, Virginia Hamilton (Knopf)

1988 WINNER: *The Friendship*, Mildred L. Taylor (Dial)

Honor Books
An Enchanted Hair Tale, Alexis De Veaux (Harper)
The Tales of Uncle Remus: The Adventures of Brer Rabbit, Julius Lester (Dial)

1987 WINNER: *Justin and the Best Biscuits in the World*, Mildred Pitts Walter (Lothrop)

Honor Books
Lion and the Ostrich Chicks and Other African Folk Tales, Ashley Bryan (Atheneum)
Which Way Freedom, Joyce Hansen (Walker)

1986 WINNER: *The People Could Fly: American Black Folktales*, Virginia Hamilton (Knopf)

Honor Books
Junius Over Far, Virginia Hamilton (Harper)
Trouble's Child, Mildred Pitts Walter (Lothrop)

1985 WINNER: *Motown and Didi*, Walter Dean Myers (Viking)

Honor Books
Circle of Gold, Candy Dawson Boyd (Apple/Scholastic)
A Little Love, Virginia Hamilton (Philomel)

1984 WINNER: *Everett Anderson's Good-bye*, Lucille Clifton (Holt)

Special Citation
The Words of Martin Luther King, Jr., Coretta Scott King, compiler (Newmarket Press)

Honor Books
The Magical Adventures of Pretty Pearl, Virginia Hamilton (Harper)
Lena Horne, James Haskins (Coward-McCann)
Bright Shadow, Joyce Carol Thomas (Avon)
Because We Are, Mildred Pitts Walter (HarperCollins)

1983 WINNER: *Sweet Whispers, Brother Rush*, Virginia Hamilton (Philomel)

Honor Book
This Strange New Feeling, Julius Lester (Dial)

1982 WINNER: *Let the Circle Be Unbroken*, Mildred D. Taylor (Dial)

Honor Books
Rainbow Jordan, Alice Childress (Coward-McCann)
Lou in the Limelight, Kristin Hunter (Scribner)
Mary: An Autobiography, Mary E. Mebane (Viking)

1981 WINNER: *This Life*, Sidney Poitier (Knopf)

Honor Book
Don't Explain: A Song of Billie Holiday, Alexis De Veaux (Harper)

1980 WINNER: *The Young Landlords*, Walter Dean Myers (Viking)

Honor Books
Movin' Up, Berry Gordy (Harper)
Childtimes: A Three-Generation Memoir, Eloise Greenfield and Lessie Jones Little (Harper)
Andrew Young: Young Man With a Mission, James Haskins (Lothrop)
James Van Der Zee: The Picture Takin' Man, James Haskins (Dodd)
Let the Lion Eat Straw, Ellease Southerland (Scribner)

1979 WINNER: *Escape to Freedom*, Ossie Davis (Viking)

Honor Books
Benjamin Banneker, Lillie Patterson (Abingdon)
I Have a Sister, My Sister is Deaf, Jeanne W. Peterson (Harper)
Justice and Her Brothers, Virginia Hamilton (Greenwillow)
Skates of Uncle Richard, Carol Fenner (Random)

1978 WINNER: *Africa Dream*, Eloise Greenfield (Crowell)

Honor Books
The Days When the Animals Talked: Black Folk Tales and How They Came to Be, William J. Faulkner (Follett)
Marvin and Tige, Frankcina Glass (St. Martin's)
Mary McCleod Bethune, Eloise Greenfield (Crowell)
Barbara Jordan, James Haskins (Dial)
Coretta Scott King, Lillie Patterson (Garrard)
Portia: The Life of Portia Washington Pittman, The Daughter of Booker T. Washington, Ruth Ann Stewart (Doubleday)

1977 WINNER: *The Story of Stevie Wonder*, James Haskins (Lothrop)

1976 WINNER: *Duey's Tale*, Pearl Bailey (Harcourt)

1975 WINNER: *The Legend of Africana*, Dorothy Robinson (Johnson Publishing)

1974 WINNER: *Ray Charles*, Sharon Bell Mathis (Crowell)

1973 WINNER: *I Never Had It Made: The Autobiography of Jackie Robinson*, as told to Alfred Duckett (Putnam)

1972 WINNER: *17 Black Artists*, Elton C. Fax (Dodd)

1971 WINNER: *Black Troubador: Langston Hughes*, Charlemae Rollins (Rand McNally)

1970 WINNER: *Martin Luther King, Jr.: Man of Peace*, Lillie Patterson (Garrard)

AWARDS FOR ILLUSTRATION

2003 WINNER: *Talkin' About Bessie: The Story of Aviator Elizabeth Coleman*, E.B. Lewis, text by Nikki Grimes (Scholastic)

Honor Books
Rap a Tap Tap: Here's Bojangles—Think of That, Leo and Diane Dillon (Scholastic)
Visiting Langston, Bryan Collier, text by Willie Perdomo (Henry Holt)

2002 WINNER: *Goin' Someplace Special*, Jerry Pinkney, text by Patricia McKissack (Atheneum)

Honor Book
Martin's Big Words: The Life of Dr. Martin Luther King, Jr., Bryan Collier, text by Doreen Rappaport (Jump at the Sun/Hyperion)

2001 WINNER: *Uptown*, Bryan Collier (Henry Holt)

Honor Books
Freedom River, Bryan Collier (Jump at the Sun/Hyperion)
Only Passing Through: The Story of Sojourner Truth, R. Gregory Christie, text by Anne Rockwell (Random House)
Virgie Goes to School with Us Boys, E.B. Lewis, text by Elizabeth Fitzgerald Howard (Simon & Schuster)

2000 WINNER: *In the Time of the Drums*, Brian Pinkney, text by Kim L. Siegelson (Jump at the Sun/Hyperion)

Honor Books
My Rows and Piles of Coins, E.B. Lewis, text by Tololwa M. Mollel (Clarion Books)
Black Cat, Christopher Myers (Scholastic)

1999 WINNER: *i see the rhythm*, Michele Wood, text by Toyomi Igus (Children's Book Press)

Honor Books
I Have Heard of a Land, Floyd Cooper, text by Joyce Carol Thomas (Joanna Cotler Books/HarperCollins)
The Bat Boy and His Violin, E.B. Lewis, text by Gavin Curtis (Simon & Schuster)
Duke Ellington: The Piano Prince and His Orchestra, Brian Pinkney, text by Andrea Davis Pinkney (Hyperion)

1998 WINNER: *In Daddy's Arms I Am Tall: African Americans Celebrating Fathers*, Javaka Steptoe, text by Alan Schroeder (Lee & Low)

Honor Books
Ashley Bryan's ABC of African American Poetry, Ashley Bryan (Jean Karl/Atheneum)
Harlem, Christopher Myers, text by Walter Dean Myers (Scholastic)
The Hunterman and the Crocodile, Baba Waguè Diakitè (Scholastic)

1997 WINNER: *Minty: A Story of Young Harriet Tubman*, Jerry Pinkney, text by Alan Schroeder (Dial Books)

Honor Books
The Palm of My Heart: Poetry by African American Children, Gregorie Christie, edited by Davida Adedjouma (Lee & Low Books)
Running The Road To ABC, Reynold Ruffins, text by Denize Lauture (Simon & Schuster)
Neeny Coming, Neeny Going, Synthia Saint James, text by Karen English (BridgeWater Books)

1996 WINNER: *The Middle Passage: White Ships Black Cargo*, Tom Feelings (Dial Books for Young Readers)

Honor Books
Her Stories, Leo and Diane Dillon, text by Virginia Hamilton (Scholastic)
The Faithful Friend, Brian Pinkney, text by Robert San Souci (Simon & Schuster)

1995 WINNER: *The Creation*, James Ransome, text by James Weldon Johnson (Holiday House)

Honor Books
The Singing Man, Terea Shaffer, text by Angela Shelf Medearis (Holiday House)
Meet Danitra Brown, Floyd Cooper, text by Nikki Grimes (Lothrop, Lee & Shepard)

1994 WINNER: *Soul Looks Back in Wonder*, Tom Feelings, text edited by Phyllis Fogelman (Dial Books)

Honor Books
Brown Honey in Broom Wheat Tea, Floyd Cooper, text by Joyce Carol Thomas (HarperCollins)
Uncle Jed's Barbershop, James Ransome, text by Margaree King Mitchell (Simon & Schuster)

1993 WINNER: *The Origin of Life on Earth: An African Creation Myth*, Kathleen Atkins Wilson, retold by David A. Anderson/SANKOFA (Sights)

Honor Books
Little Eight John, Wil Clay, text by Jan Wahl (Lodestar)
Sukey and the Mermaid, Brian Pinkney text by Robert San Souci (Four Winds)
Working Cotton, Carole Byard, text by Sherley Anne Williams (Harcourt)

1992 WINNER: *Tar Beach*, Faith Ringgold (Crown)

Honor Books
All Night, All Day: A Child's First Book of African American Spirituals, Ashley Bryan (Atheneum)
Night on Neighborhood Street, Jan Spivey Gilchrist, text by Eloise Greenfield (Dial)

1991 WINNER: *Aida*, Leo and Diane Dillon, text by Leontyne Price (Harcourt)

1990 WINNER: *Nathaniel Talking*, Jan Spivey Gilchrist, text by Eloise Greenfield (Black Butterfly)

Honor Book
The Talking Eggs, Jerry Pinkney, text by Robert San Souci (Dial)

1989 WINNER: *Mirandy and Brother Wind*, Jerry Pinkney, text by Patricia McKissack (Knopf)

Honor Books
Under the Sunday Tree, Amos Ferguson, text by Eloise Greenfield (Harper)
Storm in the Night, Pat Cummings, text by Mary Stolz (Harper)

1988 WINNER: *Mufaro's Beautiful Daughters: An African Tale*, John Steptoe (Lothrop)

Honor Books
What a Morning! The Christmas Story in Black Spirituals, Ashley Bryan, selected by John Langstaff (Macmillan)
The Invisible Hunters: A Legend from the Miskito Indians of Nicaragua, Joe Sam, compiled by Harriet Rohmer, et al (Children's Press)

1987 WINNER: *Half a Moon and One Whole Star*, Jerry Pinkney, text by Crescent Dragonwagon (Macmillan)

Honor Books
Lion and the Ostrich Chicks and Other African Folk Tales, Ashley Bryan (Atheneum)
C.L.O.U.D.S., Pat Cummings (Lothrop)

1986 WINNER: *The Patchwork Quilt*, Jerry Pinkney, text by Valerie Flournoy (Dial)

Honor Book
The People Could Fly: American Black Folktales, Leo and Diane Dillon, text by Virginia Hamilton (Knopf)

1985: No award given

1984 WINNER: *My Mama Needs Me*, Pat Cummings, text by Mildred Pitts Walter (Lothrop)

1983 WINNER: *Black Child*, Peter Mugabane (Knopf)

Honor Books
All the Colors of the Race, John Steptoe, text by Arnold Adoff (Lothrop)
I'm Going to Sing: Black American Spirituals, Ashley Bryan (Atheneum)
Just Us Women, Pat Cummings, text by Jeanette Caines (Harper)

1982 WINNER: *Mother Crocodile; An Uncle Amadou Tale from Senegal*, John Steptoe, translated by Rosa Guy (Delacorte)

Honor Books
Daydreamers, Tom Feelings, text by Eloise Greenfield (Dial)

1981 WINNER: *Beat the Story Drum, Pum-Pum*, Ashley Bryan (Atheneum)

Honor Books
Grandmama's Joy, Carole Byard, text by Eloise Greenfield (Collins)
Count on Your Fingers African Style, Jerry Pinkney, text by Claudia Zaslavsky (Crowell)

1980 WINNER: *Cornrows*, Carole Byard, text by Camille Yarborough (Coward-McCann)

1979 WINNER: *Something on My Mind*, Tom Feelings, text by Nikki Grimes (Dial)

1978 WINNER: *Africa Dream*, Carole Bayard, text by Eloise Greenfield (Crowell)

1977–1975: No award given

1974 WINNER: *Ray Charles*, George Ford, text by Sharon Bell Mathis (Crowell)

NEWBERY MEDAL WINNERS AND HONOR BOOKS, 1933–2003

The Newbery Medal has been awarded annually since 1922 by the Association for Library Service to Children, a division of the American Library Association, to the author of the most distinguished contribution to American literature for children. It was named for eighteenth-century British bookseller John Newbery. The original publisher of each book is listed in parentheses. Some older titles may be out of print; check with your local library.

2003 WINNER: *Crispin: The Cross of Lead*, Avi (Hyperion)

Honor Books
The House of the Scorpion, Nancy Farmer (Atheneum)
Hoot, Carl Hiassen (Knopf)
Pictures of Hollis Woods, Patricia Reilly Giff (Random House)
A Corner of the Universe, Ann Martin (Scholastic)
Surviving the Applewhites, Stephanie Tolan (HarperCollins)

2002 WINNER: *A Single Shard*, Linda Sue Park (Clarion)

Honor Books
Everything on a Waffle, Polly Horvath (Farrar, Straus and Giroux)
Carver: A Life in Poems, Marilyn Nelson (Front Street)

2001 WINNER: *A Year Down Yonder*, Richard Peck (Dial)

Honor Books
Hope Was Here, Joan Bauer (G.P. Putnam's Sons)
The Wanderer, Sharon Creech (HarperCollins/Joanna Cutler Books)
Because of Winn-Dixie, Kate DiCamillo (Candlewick Press)
Joey Pigza Loses Control, Jack Gantos (Farrar, Straus and Giroux)

2000 WINNER: *Bud, Not Buddy*, Christopher Paul Curtis (Delacorte)

Honor Books
Getting Near to Baby, Audrey Couloumbis (G.P. Putnam's Sons)
26 Fairmount Avenue, Tomie dePaola (G.P. Putnam's Sons)
Our Only May Amelia, Jennifer L. Holm (HarperCollins)

1999 WINNER: *Holes*, Louis Sachar (Frances Foster)

Honor Book
A Long Way from Chicago, Richard Peck (Dial)

1998 WINNER: *Out of the Dust*, Karen Hesse (Scholastic)

Honor Books
Ella Enchanted, Gail Carson Levine (HarperCollins)
Lily's Crossing, Patricia Reilly Giff (Delacorte)
Wringer, Jerry Spinelli (HarperCollins)

1997 WINNER: *The View from Saturday*, E.L. Konigsburg (Atheneum)

Honor Books
A Girl Named Disaster, Nancy Farmer (Orchard Books)
Moorchild, Eloise McGraw (Simon & Schuster)
The Thief, Megan Whalen Turner (Greenwillow/Morrow)
Belle Prater's Boy, Ruth White (Farrar, Straus and Giroux)

1996 WINNER: *The Midwife's Apprentice*, Karen Cushman (Clarion)

Honor Books
What Jamie Saw, Carolyn Coman (Front Street)
The Watsons Go to Birmingham—1963, Christopher Paul Curtis (Delacorte)
Yolonda's Genius, Carol Fenner (Simon & Schuster)
The Great Fire, Jim Murphy (Scholastic)

1995 WINNER: *Walk Two Moons*, Sharon Creech (HarperCollins)

Honor Books
Catherine, Called Birdy, Karen Cushman (Clarion)
The Ear, the Eye and the Arm, Nancy Farmer (Jackson/Orchard)

1994 WINNER: *The Giver*, Lois Lowry (Houghton)

Honor Books
Crazy Lady, Jane Leslie Conly (HarperCollins)
Dragon's Gate, Laurence Yep (HarperCollins)
Eleanor Roosevelt: A Life of Discovery, Russell Freedman (Clarion Books)

1993 WINNER: *Missing May*, Cynthia Rylant (Jackson/Orchard)

Honor Books
What Hearts, Bruce Brooks (HarperCollins)
The Dark-Thirty: Southern Tales of the Supernatural, Patricia McKissack (Knopf)
Somewhere in the Darkness, Walter Dean Myers (Scholastic)

1992 WINNER: *Shiloh*, Phyllis Reynolds Naylor (Atheneum)

Honor Books
Nothing But The Truth: A Documentary Novel, Avi (Jackson/Orchard)
The Wright Brothers: How They Invented the Airplane, Russell Freedman (Holiday House)

1991 WINNER: *Maniac Magee*, Jerry Spinelli (Little, Brown)

Honor Book
The True Confessions of Charlotte Doyle, Avi (Jackson/Orchard)

1990 WINNER: *Number the Stars*, Lois Lowry (Houghton Mifflin)

Honor Books
Afternoon of the Elves, Janet Taylor Lisle (Jackson/Orchard)
Shabanu, Daughter of the Wind, Suzanne Fisher Staples (Knopf)
The Winter Room, Gary Paulsen (Jackson/Orchard)

1989 WINNER: *Joyful Noise: Poems for Two Voices*, Paul Fleischman (Harper)

Honor Books
In The Beginning: Creation Stories from Around the World, Virginia Hamilton (Harcourt)
Scorpions, Walter Dean Myers (Harper)

1988 WINNER: *Lincoln: A Photobiography*, Russell Freedman (Clarion)

Honor Books
After The Rain, Norma Fox Mazer (Morrow)
Hatchet, Gary Paulsen (Bradbury)

1987 WINNER: *The Whipping Boy*, Sid Fleischman (Greenwillow)

Honor Books
A Fine White Dust, Cynthia Rylant (Bradbury)
On My Honor, Marion Dane Bauer (Clarion)
Volcano: The Eruption and Healing of Mount St. Helens, Patricia Lauber (Bradbury)

1986 WINNER: *Sarah, Plain and Tall*, Patricia MacLachlan (Harper)

Honor Books
Commodore Perry in the Land of the Shogun, Rhoda Blumberg (Lothrop)
Dogsong, Gary Paulsen (Bradbury)

1985 WINNER: *The Hero and the Crown*, Robin McKinley (Greenwillow)

Honor Books
Like Jake and Me, Mavis Jukes (Knopf)
The Moves Make the Man, Bruce Brooks (HarperCollins)
One-Eyed Cat, Paula Fox (Bradbury)

1984 WINNER: *Dear Mr. Henshaw*, Beverly Cleary (Morrow)

Honor Books
The Sign of the Beaver, Elizabeth George Speare (Houghton)
A Solitary Blue, Cynthia Voigt (Atheneum)
Sugaring Time, Kathryn Lasky (Macmillan)
The Wish Giver: Three Tales of Coven Tree, Bill Brittain (HarperCollins)

1983 WINNER: *Dicey's Song*, Cynthia Voigt (Atheneum)

Honor Books
The Blue Sword, Robin McKinley (Greenwillow)
Doctor DeSoto, William Steig (Farrar)
Graven Images, Paul Fleischman (HarperCollins)
Homesick: My Own Story, Jean Fritz (Putnam)
Sweet Whispers, Brother Rush, Virginia Hamilton (Philomel)

1982 WINNER: *A Visit to William Blake's Inn: Poems for Innocent and Experienced Travelers*, Nancy Willard (Harcourt)

Honor Books
Ramona Quimby, Age 8, Beverly Cleary (Morrow)
Upon the Head of the Goat: A Childhood in Hungary 1939-1944, Aranka Siegal (Farrar)

1981 WINNER: *Jacob Have I Loved*, Katherine Paterson (Crowell)

Honor Books
The Fledgling, Jane Langton (Harper)
A Ring of Endless Light, Madeleine L'Engle (Farrar)

1980 WINNER: *A Gathering of Days: A New England Girl's Journal, 1830-1832*, Joan W. Blos (Scribner)

Honor Book
The Road from Home: The Story of an Armenian Girl, David Kherdian (Greenwillow)

1979 WINNER: *The Westing Game*, Ellen Raskin (Dutton)

Honor Book
The Great Gilly Hopkins, Katherine Paterson (Crowell)

1978 WINNER: *Bridge to Terabithia*, Katherine Paterson (Crowell)

Honor Books
Ramona and Her Father, Beverly Cleary (Morrow)
Anpao: An American Indian Odyssey, Jamake Highwater (Lippincott)

1977 WINNER: *Roll of Thunder, Hear My Cry*, Mildred D. Taylor (Dial)

Honor Books
Abel's Island, William Steig (Farrar)
A String in the Harp, Nancy Bond (Atheneum)

1976 WINNER: *The Grey King*, Susan Cooper (Atheneum)

Honor Books
The Hundred Penny Box, Sharon Bell Mathis (Viking)
Dragonwings, Laurence Yep (Harper)

1975 WINNER: *M. C. Higgins, The Great*, Virginia Hamilton (Macmillan)

Honor Books
Figgs & Phantoms, Ellen Raskin (Dutton)
My Brother Sam Is Dead, James Lincoln Collier & Christopher Collier (Four Winds)
The Perilous Gard, Elizabeth Marie Pope (Houghton)
Philip Hall Likes Me, I Reckon Maybe, Bette Greene (Dial)

1974 WINNER: *The Slave Dancer*, Paula Fox (Bradbury)

Honor Book
The Dark Is Rising, Susan Cooper (McElderry/Atheneum)

1973 WINNER: *Julie of the Wolves*, Jean Craighead George (Harper)

Honor Books
Frog and Toad Together, Arnold Lobel (Harper)
The Upstairs Room, Johanna Reiss (Crowell)
The Witches of Worm, Zilpha Keatley Snyder (Atheneum)

1972 WINNER: *Mrs. Frisby and the Rats of NIMH*, Robert C. O'Brien (Atheneum)

Honor Books
Incident At Hawk's Hill, Allan W. Eckert (Little, Brown)
The Planet of Junior Brown, Virginia Hamilton (Macmillan)
The Tombs of Atuan, Ursula K. LeGuin (Atheneum)
Annie and the Old One, Miska Miles (Little, Brown)
The Headless Cupid, Zilpha Keatley Snyder (Atheneum)

1971 WINNER: *Summer of the Swans*, Betsy Byars (Viking)

Honor Books
Knee Knock Rise, Natalie Babbitt (Farrar)
Enchantress From the Stars, Sylvia Louise Engdahl (Atheneum)
Sing Down the Moon, Scott O'Dell (Houghton)

1970 WINNER: *Sounder*, William H. Armstrong (Harper)

Honor Books
Our Eddie, Sulamith Ish-Kishor (Pantheon)
The Many Ways of Seeing: An Introduction to the Pleasures of Art, Janet Gaylord Moore (World)
Journey Outside, Mary Q. Steele (Viking)

1969 WINNER: *The High King*, Lloyd Alexander (Holt)

Honor Books
To Be a Slave, Julius Lester (Dial)
When Shlemiel Went to Warsaw and Other Stories, Isaac Bashevis Singer (Farrar)

1968 WINNER: *From the Mixed-Up Files of Mrs. Basil E. Frankweiler*, E. L. Konigsburg (Atheneum)

Honor Books
Jennifer, Hecate, Macbeth, William McKinley, and Me, Elizabeth, E. L. Konigsburg (Atheneum)
The Black Pearl, Scott O'Dell (Houghton)
The Fearsome Inn, Isaac Bashevis Singer (Scribner)
The Egypt Game, Zilpha Keatley Snyder (Atheneum)

1967 WINNER: *Up a Road Slowly*, Irene Hunt (Follett)

Honor Books
The King's Fifth, Scott O'Dell (Houghton)
Zlateh The Goat and Other Stories, Isaac Bashevis Singer (Harper)
The Jazz Man, Mary Hays Weik (Atheneum)

1966 WINNER: *I, Juan de Pareja*, Elizabeth Borton de Trevino (Farrar)

Honor Books
The Black Cauldron, Lloyd Alexander (Holt)
The Animal Family, Randall Jarrell (Pantheon)
The Noonday Friends, Mary Stolz (Harper)

1965 WINNER: *Shadow of a Bull*, Maia Wojciechowska (Atheneum)

Honor Book
Across Five Aprils, Irene Hunt (Follet)

1964 WINNER: *It's Like This, Cat*, Emily Neville (Harper)

Honor Books
Rascal: A Memoir of a Better Era, Sterling North (Dutton)
The Loner, Ester Wier (McKay)

1963 WINNER: *A Wrinkle in Time*, Madeleine L'Engle (Farrar)

Honor Books
Thistle and Thyme: Tales and Legends from Scotland, Sorche Nic Leodhas, pseud. (Leclaire Alger) (Holt)
Men of Athens, Olivia Coolidge (Houghton)

1962 WINNER: *The Bronze Bow*, Elizabeth George Speare (Houghton)

Honor Books
Frontier Living, Edwin Tunis (World)
The Golden Goblet, Eloise Jarvis McGraw (Coward)
Belling The Tiger, Mary Stolz (Harper)

1961 WINNER: *Island of the Blue Dolphins*, Scott O'Dell (Houghton)

Honor Books
America Moves Forward: A History for Peter, Gerald W. Johnson (Morrow)
Old Ramon, Jack Schaefer (Houghton)
The Cricket in Times Square, George Selden (Farrar)

1960 WINNER: *Onion John*, Joseph Krumgold (Crowell)

Honor Books
My Side of the Mountain, Jean Craighead George (Dutton)
America Is Born: A History for Peter, Gerald W. Johnson (Morrow)
The Gammage Cup, Carol Kendall (Harcourt)

1959 WINNER: *The Witch of Blackbird Pond*, Elizabeth George Speare (Houghton)

Honor Books
The Family Under The Bridge, Natalie Savage Carlson (Harper)
Along Came A Dog, Meindert Dejong (Harper)
Chucaro: Wild Pony of the Pampa, Francis Kalnay (Harcourt)
The Perilous Road, William O. Steele (Harcourt)

1958 WINNER: *Rifles for Watie*, Harold Keith (Crowell)

Honor Books
The Horsecatcher, Mari Sandoz (Westminster)
Gone-Away Lake, Elizabeth Enright (Harcourt)
The Great Wheel, Robert Lawson (Viking)
Tom Paine, Freedom's Apostle, Leo Gurko (Crowell)

1957 WINNER: *Miracles on Maple Hill*, Virginia Sorenson (Harcourt)

Honor Books
Old Yeller, Fred Gipson (Harper)
The House of Sixty Fathers, Meindert DeJong (Harper)
Mr. Justice Holmes, Clara Ingram Judson (Follett)
The Corn Grows Ripe, Dorothy Rhoads (Viking)
Black Fox of Lorne, Marguerite de Angeli (Doubleday)

1956 WINNER: *Carry On, Mr. Bowditch*, Jean Lee Latham (Houghton)

Honor Books
The Secret River, Marjorie Kinnan Rawlings (Scribner)
The Golden Name Day, Jennie Lindquist (Harper)
Men, Microscopes, and Living Things, Katherine Shippen (Viking)

1955 WINNER: *The Wheel on the School*, Meindert DeJong (Harper)

Honor Books
Courage of Sarah Noble, Alice Dalgliesh (Scribner).
Banner In The Sky, James Ullman (Lippincott)

1954 WINNER: *. . . And Now Miguel*, Joseph Krumgold (Crowell)

Honor Books
All Alone, Claire Huchet Bishop (Viking)
Shadrach, Meindert Dejong (Harper)
Hurry Home, Candy, Meindert Dejong (Harper)
Theodore Roosevelt, Fighting Patriot, Clara Ingram Judson (Follett)
Magic Maize, Mary & Conrad Buff (Houghton)

1953 WINNER: *Secret of the Andes*, Ann Nolan Clark (Viking)

Honor Books
Charlotte's Web, E. B. White (Harper)
Moccasin Trail, Eloise Jarvis McGraw (Coward)
Red Sails to Capri, Ann Weil (Viking)
The Bears on Hemlock Mountain, Alice Dalgliesh (Scribner)
Birthdays of Freedom, Volume 1, Genevieve Foster (Scribner)

1952 WINNER: *Ginger Pye*, Eleanor Estes (Harcourt)

Honor Books
Americans Before Columbus, Elizabeth Baity (Viking)
Minn of the Mississippi, Holling C. Holling (Houghton)
The Defender, Nicholas Kalashnikoff (Scribner)
The Light at Tern Rock, Julia Sauer (Viking)
The Apple and the Arrow, Mary & Conrad Buff (Houghton)

1951 WINNER: *Amos Fortune, Free Man*, Elizabeth Yates (Dutton)

Honor Books
Better Known as Johnny Appleseed, Mabel Leigh Hunt (Lippincott)
Gandhi, Fighter Without a Sword, Jeanette Eaton (Morrow)
Abraham Lincoln, Friend of the People, Clara Ingram Judson (Follett)
The Story of Appleby Capple, Anne Parrish (Harper)

1950 WINNER: *The Door in the Wall*, Marguerite de Angeli (Doubleday)

Honor Books
Tree of Freedom, Rebecca Caudill (Viking)
The Blue Cat of Castle Town, Catherine Coblentz (Longmans)
Kildee House, Rutherford Montgomery (Doubleday)
George Washington, Genevieve Foster (Scribner)
Song of The Pines: A Story of Norwegian Lumbering in Wisconsin, Walter & Marion Havighurst (Winston)

1949 WINNER: *King of the Wind*, Marguerite Henry (Rand McNally)

Honor Books
Seabird, Holling C. Holling (Houghton)
Daughter of the Mountain, Louise Rankin (Viking)
My Father's Dragon, Ruth S. Gannett (Random House)
Story of the Negro, Arna Bontemps (Knopf)

1948 WINNER: *The Twenty-One Balloons*, William Pène du Bois (Viking)

Honor Books
Pancakes-Paris, Claire Huchet Bishop (Viking)

Li Lun, Lad of Courage, Carolyn Treffinger (Abingdon)
The Quaint and Curious Quest of Johnny Longfoot, Catherine Besterman (Bobbs-Merrill)
The Cow-Tail Switch, and Other West African Stories, Harold Courlander (Holt)
Misty of Chincoteague, Marguerite Henry (Rand McNally)

1947 WINNER: *Miss Hickory,* Carolyn Sherwin Bailey (Viking)

Honor Books
Wonderful Year, Nancy Barnes (Messner)
Big Tree, Mary & Conrad Buff (Viking)
The Heavenly Tenants, William Maxwell (Harper)
The Avion My Uncle Flew, Cyrus Fisher (Appleton)
The Hidden Treasure of Glaston, Eleanor Jewett (Viking)

1946 WINNER: *Strawberry Girl,* Lois Lenski (Lippincott)

Honor Books
Justin Morgan Had a Horse, Marguerite Henry (Rand McNally)
The Moved-Outers, Florence Crannell Means (Houghton)
Bhimsa, the Dancing Bear, Christine Weston (Scribner)
New Found World, Katherine Shippen (Viking)

1945 WINNER: *Rabbit Hill,* Robert Lawson (Viking)

Honor Books
The Hundred Dresses, Eleanor Estes (Harcourt)
The Silver Pencil, Alice Dalgliesh (Scribner)
Abraham Lincoln's World, Genevieve Foster (Scribner)
Lone Journey: The Life of Roger Williams, Jeanetter Eaton (Harcourt)

1944 WINNER: *Johnny Tremain,* Esther Forbes (Houghton)

Honor Books
These Happy Golden Years, Laura Ingalls Wilder (Harper)
Fog Magic, Julia Sauer (Viking)
Rufus M., Eleanor Estes (Harcourt)
Mountain Born, Elizabeth Yates (Coward)

1943 WINNER: *Adam of the Road,* Elizabeth Janet Gray (Viking)

Honor Books
The Middle Moffat, Eleanor Estes (Harcourt)
Have You Seen Tom Thumb?, Mabel Leigh Hunt (Lippincott)

1942 WINNER: *The Matchlock Gun,* Walter Edmonds (Dodd)

Honor Books
Little Town on the Prairie, Laura Ingalls Wilder (Harper)
George Washington's World, Genevieve Foster (Scribner)
Indian Captive: The Story of Mary Jemison, Lois Lenski (Lippincott)
Down Ryton Water, Eva Roe Gaggin (Viking)

1941 WINNER: *Call It Courage,* Armstrong Sperry (Macmillan)

Honor Books
Blue Willow, Doris Gates (Viking)
Young Mac of Fort Vancouver, Mary Jane Carr (Crowell)
The Long Winter, Laura Ingalls Wilder (Harper)
Nansen, Anna Gertrude Hall (Viking)

1940 WINNER: *Daniel Boone,* James Daugherty (Viking)

Honor Books
The Singing Tree, Kate Seredy (Viking)
Runner of the Mountain Tops: The Life of Louis Agassiz, Mabel Robinson (Random House)
By the Shores of Silver Lake, Laura Ingalls Wilder (Harper)
Boy with a Pack, Stephen W. Meader (Harcourt)

1939 WINNER: *Thimble Summer,* Elizabeth Enright (Rinehart)

Honor Books
Nino, Valenti Angelo (Viking)
Mr. Popper's Penguins, Richard & Florence Atwater (Little, Brown)
Hello the Boat!, Phyllis Crawford (Holt)
Leader By Destiny: George Washington, Man and Patriot, Jeanette Eaton (Harcourt)
Penn, Elizabeth Janet Gray (Viking)

1938 WINNER: *The White Stag,* Kate Seredy (Viking)

Honor Books
Pecos Bill, James Cloyd Bowman (Little, Brown)
Bright Island, Mabel Robinson (Random House)
On the Banks of Plum Creek, Laura Ingalls Wilder (Harper)

1937 WINNER: *Roller Skates,* Ruth Sawyer (Viking)

Honor Books
Phebe Fairchild: Her Book, Lois Lenski (Stokes)
Whistler's Van, Idwal Jones (Viking)
The Golden Basket, Ludwig Bemelmans (Viking)
Winterbound, Margery Bianco (Viking)
The Codfish Musket, Agnes Hewes (Doubleday)
Audubon, Constance Rourke (Harcourt)

1936 WINNER: *Caddie Woodlawn,* Carol Ryrie Brink (Macmillan)

Honor Books
Honk, the Moose, Phil Stong (Dodd)
The Good Master, Kate Seredy (Viking)
Young Walter Scott, Elizabeth Janet Gray (Viking)
All Sail Set: A Romance of the Flying Cloud, Armstrong Sperry (Winston)

1935 WINNER: *Dobry,* Monica Shannon (Viking)

Honor Books
Pageant of Chinese History, Elizabeth Seeger (Longmans)
Davy Crockett, Constance Rourke (Harcourt)
Day On Skates: The Story of a Dutch Picnic, Hilda Von Stockum (Harper)

1934 WINNER: *Invincible Louisa: The Story of the Author of Little Women,* Cornelia Meigs (Little, Brown)

Honor Books
The Forgotten Daughter, Caroline Snedeker (Doubleday)
Swords of Steel, Elsie Singmaster (Houghton)
ABC Bunny, Wanda Gág (Coward)
Winged Girl of Knossos, Erick Berry (Appleton)
New Land, Sarah Schmidt (McBride)
Big Tree of Bunlahy: Stories of My Own Countryside, Padraic Colum (Macmillan)
Glory of the Seas, Agnes Hewes (Knopf)
Apprentice of Florence, Ann Kyle (Houghton)

1933 WINNER: *Young Fu of the Upper Yangtze,* Elizabeth Lewis (Winston)

Honor Books
Swift Rivers, Cornelia Meigs (Little, Brown)
The Railroad To Freedom: A Story of the Civil War, Hildegarde Swift (Harcourt)
Children of the Soil: A Story of Scandinavia, Nora Burglon (Doubleday)

CALDECOTT MEDAL WINNERS AND HONOR BOOKS, 1944–2003

The Caldecott Medal was named in honor of nineteenth-century English illustrator Randolph Caldecott, and is given to the illustrator of the most distinguished American picture book for children. It has been awarded annually since 1938 by the Association for Library Service to Children, a division of the American Library Association. The original publisher of each work is listed in parentheses. Some older titles may be out of print; check with your local library.

2003 WINNER: *My Friend Rabbit*, Eric Rohmann (Roaring Brook Press)

Honor Books
The Spider and the Fly, Tony diTerlizzi, based on a tale by Mary Howitt (Simon & Schuster)
Hondo & Fabian, Peter McCarty (Henry Holt)
Noah's Ark, Jerry Pinkney (North/South Books)

2002 WINNER: *The Three Pigs*, David Wiesner (Clarion)

Honor Books
Martin's Big Words: The Life of Dr. Martin Luther King, Jr., Bryan Collier, text by Doreen Rappaport (Jump at the Sun/Hyperion)
The Dinosaurs of Waterhouse Hawkins: An Illuminating History of Mr. Waterhouse Hawkins, Artist and Lecturer, Brian Selznick, text by Barbara Kerley (Scholastic)
The Stray Dog, Marc Simont (HarperCollins)

2001 WINNER: *So You Want to be President?*, David Small, text by Judith St. George (Philomel Books)

Honor Books
Casey at the Bat: A Ballad of the Republic Sung in the Year 1888, Christopher Bing, text by Ernest Lawrence Thayer (Handprint Books)
Click, Clack, Moo: Cows that Type, Betsy Lewin, text by Doreen Cronin (Simon & Schuster)
Olivia, Ian Falconer (Atheneum)

2000 WINNER: *Joseph Had a Little Overcoat*, Simms Taback (Viking)

Honor Books
Sector 7, David Wiesner (Clarion Books)
The Ugly Duckling, adapted and illustrated by Jerry Pinkney, based on the fairy tale by Hans Christian Andersen (Morrow)
When Sophie Gets Angry—Really, Really Angry, Molly Bang (Scholastic)
A Child's Calendar, Trina Schart Hyman, text by John Updike (Holiday House)

1999 WINNER: *Snowflake Bentley*, Mary Azarian, text by Jacqueline Briggs Martin (Houghton)

Honor Books
Duke Ellington: The Piano Prince and the Orchestra, Brian Pinkney, text by Andrea Davis Pinkney (Hyperion)
No, David!, David Shannon (Scholastic)
Snow, Uri Shulevitz (Farrar)
Tibet Through the Red Box, Peter Sis (Farrar)

1998 WINNER: *Rapunzel*, Paul O. Zelinsky (Dutton)

Honor Books
The Gardener, David Small, text by Sarah Stewart (Farrar)
Harlem, Christopher Myers, text by Walter Dean Myers (Scholastic)
There Was an Old Lady Who Swallowed a Fly, Simms Taback (Viking)

1997 WINNER: *Golem*, David Wisniewski (Clarion)

Honor Books
Hush! A Thai Lullaby, Holly Meade, text by Minfong Ho (Melanie Kroupa/Orchard Books)
The Graphic Alphabet, David Pelletier (Orchard Books)
The Paperboy, Dav Pilkey (Richard Jackson/Orchard Books)
Starry Messenger, Peter Sis (Frances Foster Books/Farrar, Straus and Giroux)

1996 WINNER: *Officer Buckle and Gloria*, Peggy Rathmann (Putnam)

Honor Books
Alphabet City, Stephen T. Johnson (Viking)
Zin! Zin! Zin! a Violin, Marjorie Priceman, text by Lloyd Moss (Simon & Schuster)
The Faithful Friend, Brian Pinkney, text by Robert D. San Souci (Simon & Schuster)
Tops & Bottoms, Janet Stevens (Harcourt)

1995 WINNER: *Smoky Night*, David Diaz, text by Eve Bunting (Harcourt)

Honor Books
John Henry, Jerry Pinkney, text by Julius Lester (Dial)
Swamp Angel, Paul O. Zelinsky, text by Anne Isaacs (Dutton)
Time Flies, Eric Rohmann (Crown)

1994 WINNER: *Grandfather's Journey*, Allen Say (Houghton)

Honor Books
Peppe the Lamplighter, Ted Lewin, text by Elisa Bartone (Lothrop)
In the Small, Small Pond, Denise Fleming (Holt)
Raven: A Trickster Tale from the Pacific Northwest, Gerald McDermott (Harcourt)
Owen, Kevin Henkes (Greenwillow)
Yo! Yes?, Chris Raschka (Orchard)

1993 WINNER: *Mirette on the High Wire*, Emily Arnold McCully (Putnam)

Honor Books
The Stinky Cheese Man and Other Fairly Stupid Tales, Lane Smith, text by Jon Scieszka (Viking)
Seven Blind Mice, Ed Young (Philomel Books)
Working Cotton, Carole Byard, text by Sherley Anne Williams (Harcourt)

1992 WINNER: *Tuesday*, David Wiesner (Clarion Books)

Honor Book
Tar Beach, Faith Ringgold (Random House)

1991 WINNER: *Black and White*, David Macaulay (Houghton)

Honor Books
Puss in Boots, Fred Marcellino, text by Charles Perrault, translated by Malcolm Arthur (Di Capua/Farrar)
"More More More," Said the Baby: Three Love Stories, Vera B. Williams (Greenwillow)

1990 WINNER: *Lon Po Po: A Red-Riding Hood Story from China*, Ed Young (Philomel)

Honor Books
Bill Peet: An Autobiography, Bill Peet (Houghton)
Color Zoo, Lois Ehlert (Lippincott)
The Talking Eggs: A Folktale from the American South, Jerry Pinkney, text by Robert D. San Souci (Dial)

Hershel and the Hanukkah Goblins, Trina Schart Hyman, text by Eric Kimmel (Holiday House)

1989 WINNER: *Song and Dance Man*, Stephen Gammell, text by Karen Ackerman (Knopf)

Honor Books
The Boy of the Three-Year Nap, Allen Say, text by Diane Snyder (Houghton)
Free Fall, David Wiesner (Lothrop)
Goldilocks and the Three Bears, James Marshall (Dial)
Mirandy and Brother Wind, Jerry Pinkney, text by Patricia C. McKissack (Knopf)

1988 WINNER: *Owl Moon*, John Schoenherr, text by Jane Yolen (Philomel)

Honor Book
Mufaro's Beautiful Daughters: An African Tale, John Steptoe (Lothrop)

1987 WINNER: *Hey, Al*, Richard Egielski, text by Arthur Yorinks (Farrar)

Honor Books
The Village of Round and Square Houses, Ann Grifalconi (Little, Brown)
Alphabatics, Suse MacDonald (Bradbury)
Rumpelstiltskin, Paul O. Zelinsky (Dutton)

1986 WINNER: *The Polar Express*, Chris Van Allsburg (Houghton)

Honor Books
The Relatives Came, Stephen Gammell, text by Cynthia Rylant (Bradbury)
King Bidgood's in the Bathtub, Don Wood, text by Audrey Wood (Harcourt)

1985 WINNER: *Saint George and the Dragon*, Trina Schart Hyman, retold by Margaret Hodges (Little, Brown)

Honor Books
Hansel and Gretel, Paul O. Zelinsky, retold by Rika Lesser (Dodd)
Have You Seen My Duckling?, Nancy Tafuri (Greenwillow)
The Story of Jumping Mouse: A Native American Legend, John Steptoe (Lothrop)

1984 WINNER: *The Glorious Flight: Across the Channel with Louis Bleriot*, Alice & Martin Provensen (Viking)

Honor Books
Little Red Riding Hood, Trina Schart Hyman (Holiday)
Ten, Nine, Eight, Molly Bang (Greenwillow)

1983 WINNER: *Shadow*, translated and illustrated by Marcia Brown, original French text by Blaise Cendrars (Scribner)

Honor Books
A Chair for My Mother, Vera B. Williams (Greenwillow)
When I Was Young in the Mountains, Diane Goode, text by Cynthia Rylant (Dutton)

1982 WINNER: *Jumanji*, Chris Van Allsburg (Houghton)

Honor Books
Where the Buffaloes Begin, Stephen Gammell, text by Olaf Baker (Warne)
On Market Street, Anita Lobel, text by Arnold Lobel (Greenwillow)
Outside Over There, Maurice Sendak (Harper)
A Visit to William Blake's Inn: Poems for Innocent and Experienced Travelers, Alice & Martin Provensen, text by Nancy Willard (Harcourt)

1981 WINNER: *Fables*, Arnold Lobel (Harper)

Honor Books
The Bremen-Town Musicians, Ilse Plume (Doubleday)
The Grey Lady and the Strawberry Snatcher, Molly Bang (Four Winds)
Mice Twice, Joseph Low (McElderry/ Atheneum)
Truck, Donald Crews (Greenwillow)

1980 WINNER: *Ox-Cart Man*, Barbara Cooney, text by Donald Hall (Viking)

Honor Books
Ben's Trumpet, Rachel Isadora (Greenwillow)
The Garden Of Abdul Gasazi, Chris Van Allsburg (Houghton)
The Treasure, Uri Shulevitz (Farrar)

1979 WINNER: *The Girl Who Loved Wild Horses*, Paul Goble (Bradbury)

Honor Books
Freight Train, Donald Crews (Greenwillow)
The Way to Start a Day, Peter Parnall, text by Byrd Baylor (Scribner)

1978 WINNER: *Noah's Ark*, Peter Spier (Doubleday)

Honor Books
Castle, David Macaulay (Houghton)
It Could Always Be Worse, Margot Zemach (Farrar)

1977 WINNER: *Ashanti to Zulu: African Traditions*, Leo & Diane Dillon, text by Margaret Musgrove (Dial)

Honor Books
The Amazing Bone, William Steig (Farrar)
The Contest, Nonny Hogrogian (Greenwillow)
Fish for Supper, M. B. Goffstein (Dial)
The Golem: A Jewish Legend, Beverly Brodsky McDermott (Lippincott)
Hawk, I'm Your Brother, Peter Parnall, text by Byrd Baylor (Scribner)

1976 WINNER: *Why Mosquitoes Buzz in People's Ears*, Leo & Diane Dillon, retold by Verna Aardema (Dial)

Honor Books
The Desert is Theirs, Peter Parnall, text by Byrd Baylor (Scribner)
Strega Nona, Tomie de Paola (Prentice-Hall)

1975 WINNER: *Arrow to the Sun*, Gerald McDermott (Viking)

Honor Book
Jambo Means Hello: A Swahili Alphabet Book, Tom Feelings, text by Muriel Feelings (Dial)

1974 WINNER: *Duffy and the Devil*, Margot Zemach, retold by Harve Zemach (Farrar)

Honor Books
Three Jovial Huntsmen, by Susan Jeffers (Bradbury)
Cathedral, David Macaulay (Houghton)

1973 WINNER: *The Funny Little Woman*, Blair Lent, text by Arlene Mosel (Dutton)

Honor Books
Anansi the Spider: A Tale from the Ashanti, adapted and illustrated by Gerald McDermott (Holt)
Hosie's Alphabet, Leonard Baskin, text by Tobias Hosea & Lisa Baskin (Viking)
Snow-White and the Seven Dwarfs, Nancy Ekholm Burkert, text translated by Randall Jarrell, retold from the Brothers Grimm (Farrar)
When Clay Sings, Tom Bahti, text by Byrd Baylor (Scribner)

1972 WINNER: *One Fine Day*, Nonny Hogrogian (Macmillan)

Honor Books
Hildilid's Night, Arnold Lobel, text by Cheli Duran Ryan (Macmillan)
If All the Seas Were One Sea, Janina Domanska (Macmillan)
Moja Means One: A Swahili Counting Book, Tom Feelings, text by Muriel Feelings (Dial)

1971 WINNER: *A Story, A Story*, Gail E. Haley (Atheneum)

Honor Books
The Angry Moon, Blair Lent, text by William Sleator (Atlantic)
Frog and Toad Are Friends, Arnold Lobel (Harper)
In the Night Kitchen, Maurice Sendak (Harper)

1970 WINNER: *Sylvester and the Magic Pebble*, William Steig (Windmill Books)

Honor Books
Goggles!, Ezra Jack Keats (Macmillan)
Alexander and the Wind-Up Mouse, Leo Lionni (Pantheon)
Pop Corn & Ma Goodness, Robert Andrew Parker, text by Edna Mitchell Preston (Viking)
Thy Friend, Obadiah, Brinton Turkle (Viking)
The Judge: An Untrue Tale, Margot Zemach, text by Harve Zemach (Farrar)

1969 WINNER: *The Fool of the World and the Flying Ship*, Uri Shulevitz, text by Arthur Ransome (Farrar)

Honor Books
Why the Sun and the Moon Live in the Sky, Blair Lent, text by Elphinstone Dayrell (Houghton)

1968 WINNER: *Drummer Hoff*, Ed Emberley, text by Barbara Emberley (Prentice Hall)

Honor Books
Frederick, Leo Lionni (Pantheon)
Seashore Story, Taro Yashima (Viking)
The Emperor and the Kite, Ed Young, text by Jane Yolen (World)

1967 WINNER: *Sam, Bangs & Moonshine*, Evaline Ness (Holt)

Honor Book
One Wide River to Cross, Ed Emberley, text by Barbara Emberley (Prentice Hall)

1966 WINNER: *Always Room for One More*, Nonny Hogrogian, text by Sorche Nic Leodhas (Holt)

Honor Books
Hide and Seek Fog, Roger Duvoisin, text by Alvin Tresselt (Lothrop)
Just Me, Marie Hall Ets (Viking)
Tom Tit Tot, Evaline Ness (Scribner)

1965 WINNER: *May I Bring a Friend?*, Beni Montresor, text by Beatrice Schenk de Regniers (Atheneum)

Honor Books
Rain Makes Applesauce, Marvin Bileck, text by Julian Scheer (Holiday)
The Wave, Blair Lent, text by Margaret Hodges (Houghton)
A Pocketful of Cricket, Evaline Ness, text by Rebecca Caudill (Holt)

1964 WINNER: *Where the Wild Things Are*, Maurice Sendak (Harper)

Honor Books
Swimmy, Leo Lionni (Pantheon)
All in the Morning Early, Evaline Ness, text by Sorche Nic Leodhas, (Holt)
Mother Goose and Nursery Rhymes, Philip Reed (Atheneum)

1963 WINNER: *The Snowy Day*, Ezra Jack Keats (Viking)

Honor Books
The Sun is a Golden Earring, Bernarda Bryson, text by Natalia M. Belting (Holt)
Mr. Rabbit and the Lovely Present, Maurice Sendak, text by Charlotte Zolotow (Harper)

1962 WINNER: *Once a Mouse*, Marcia Brown (Scribner)

Honor Books
Fox Went out on a Chilly Night: An Old Song, Peter Spier (Doubleday)
Little Bear's Visit, Maurice Sendak, text by Else H. Minarik (Harper)
The Day We Saw the Sun Come Up, Adrienne Adams, text by Alice E. Goudey (Scribner)

1961 WINNER: *Baboushka and the Three Kings*, Nicolas Sidjakov, text by Ruth Robbins (Parnassus)

Honor Book
Inch by Inch, Leo Lionni (Obolensky)

1960 WINNER: *Nine Days to Christmas*, Marie Hall Ets, text by Marie Hall Ets and Aurora Labastida (Viking)

Honor Books
Houses from the Sea, Adrienne Adams, text by Alice E. Goudey (Scribner)
The Moon Jumpers, Maurice Sendak, text by Janice May Udry (Harper)

1959 WINNER: *Chanticleer and the Fox*, Barbara Cooney, text adapted from Chaucer's *Canterbury Tales* by Barbara Cooney (Crowell)

Honor Books
The House that Jack Built: La Maison Que Jacques A Batie, written and illustrated by Antonio Frasconi (Harcourt)
What Do You Say, Dear?, Maurice Sendak, text by Sesyle Joslin (W.R. Scott)
Umbrella, written and illustrated by Taro Yashima (Viking)

1958 WINNER: *Time of Wonder*, written and illustrated by Robert McCloskey (Viking)

Honor Books
Fly High, Fly Low, written and illustrated by Don Freeman (Viking)
Anatole and the Cat, Paul Galdone, text by Eve Titus (McGraw-Hill)

1957 WINNER: *A Tree is Nice*, Marc Simont, text by Janice Udry (Harper)

Honor Books
Mr. Penny's Race Horse, written and illustrated by Marie Hall Ets (Viking)
1 is One, written and illustrated by Tasha Tudor (Walck)
Anatole, Paul Galdone, text by Eve Titus (McGraw-Hill)
Gillespie and the Guards, James Daugherty, text by Benjamin Elkin (Viking)
Lion, written and illustrated by William Pène du Bois (Viking)

1956 WINNER: *Frog Went A-Courtin'*, Feodor Rojankovsky, text by John Langstaff (Harcourt)

Honor Books
Play With Me, written and illustrated by Marie Hall Ets (Viking)
Crow Boy, written and illustrated by Taro Yashima (Viking)

1955 WINNER: *Cinderella, or the Little Glass Slipper*, Marcia Brown, text translated from Charles Perrault by Marcia Brown (Scribner)

Honor Books
Book of Nursery and Mother Goose Rhymes, Marguerite de Angeli (Doubleday)

Wheel On The Chimney, Tibor Gergely, text by Margaret Wise Brown (Lippincott)
The Thanksgiving Story, Helen Sewell, text by Alice Dalgliesh (Scribner)

1954 WINNER: *Madeline's Rescue*, written and illustrated by Ludwig Bemelmans (Viking)

Honor Books
Journey Cake, Ho!, Robert McCloskey, text by Ruth Sawyer (Viking)
When Will the World Be Mine?, Jean Charlot, text by Miriam Schlein (W. R. Scott)
The Steadfast Tin Soldier, Marcia Brown, text by Hans Christian Andersen, translated by M.R. James (Scribner)
A Very Special House, Maurice Sendak, text by Ruth Krauss (Harper)
Green Eyes, written and illustrated by A. Birnbaum (Capitol)

1953 WINNER: *The Biggest Bear*, written and illustrated by Lynd Ward (Houghton)

Honor Books
Puss in Boots, Marcia Brown, text translated from Charles Perrault by Marcia Brown (Scribner)
One Morning in Maine, written and illustrated by Robert McCloskey (Viking)
Ape in a Cape: An Alphabet of Odd Animals, written and illustrated by Fritz Eichenberg (Harcourt)
The Storm Book, Margaret Bloy Graham, text by Charlotte Zolotow (Harper)
Five Little Monkeys, written and illustrated by Juliet Kepes (Houghton)

1952 WINNER: *Finders Keepers*, Nicolas Mordvinoff, text by Will Lipkind (Harcourt)

Honor Books
Mr. T. W. Anthony Woo, written and illustrated by Marie Hall Ets (Viking)
Skipper John's Cook, written and illustrated by Marcia Brown (Scribner)
All Falling Down, Margaret Bloy Graham, text by Gene Zion (Harper)
Bear Party, written and illustrated by William Pène du Bois (Viking)
Feather Mountain, written and illustrated by Elizabeth Olds (Houghton)

1951 WINNER: *The Egg Tree*, written and illustrated by Katherine Milhous (Scribner)

Honor Books
Dick Whittington and his Cat, written and illustrated by Marcia Brown (Scribner)
The Two Reds, Nicolas Mordvinoff, text by Will Lipkind (Harcourt)
If I Ran the Zoo, written and illustrated by Dr. Seuss (Random House)
The Most Wonderful Doll in the World, Helen Stone, text by Phyllis McGinley (Lippincott)
T-Bone, the Baby Sitter, written and illustrated by Clare Turlay Newberry (Harper)

1950 WINNER: *Song of the Swallows*, written and illustrated by Leo Politi (Scribner)

Honor Books
America's Ethan Allen, Lynd Ward, text by Stewart Holbrook (Houghton)
The Wild Birthday Cake, Hildegard Woodward, text by Lavinia R. Davis (Doubleday)
The Happy Day, Marc Simont, text by Ruth Krauss (Harper)
Bartholomew and the Oobleck, written and illustrated by Dr. Seuss (Random House)
Henry Fisherman, written and illustrated by Marcia Brown

1949 WINNER: *The Big Snow*, written and illustrated by Berta & Elmer Hader (Macmillan)

Honor Books
Blueberries for Sal, written and illustrated by Robert McCloskey (Viking)
All Around the Town, Helen Stone, text by Phyllis McGinley (Lippincott)
Juanita, written and illustrated by Leo Politi (Scribner)
Fish in the Air, written and illustrated by Kurt Wiese (Viking)

1948 WINNER: *White Snow, Bright Snow*, Roger Duvoisin, text by Alvin Tresselt (Lothrop)

Honor Books
Stone Soup, written and illustrated by Marcia Brown (Scribner)
McElligot's Pool, written and illustrated by Dr. Seuss (Random House)
Bambino the Clown, written and illustrated by Georges Schreiber (Viking)
Roger and the Fox, Hildegard Woodward, text by Lavinia R. Davis (Doubleday)
Song of Robin Hood, Virginia Lee Burton, text edited by Anne Malcolmson (Houghton)

1947 WINNER: *The Little Island*, Leonard Weisgard, text by Golden MacDonald (Doubleday)

Honor Books
Rain Drop Splash, Leonard Weisgard, text by Alvin Tresselt (Lothrop)
Boats on the River, Jay Hyde Barnum, text by Marjorie Flack (Viking)
Timothy Turtle, Tony Palazzo, text by Al Graham (Welch)
Pedro, the Angel of Olvera Street, written and illustrated by Leo Politi (Scribner)
Sing in Praise: A Collection of the Best Loved Hymns, Marjorie Torrey, text selected by Opal Wheeler (Dutton)

1946 WINNER: *The Rooster Crows*, written and illustrated by Maude & Miska Petersham (Macmillan)

Honor Books
Little Lost Lamb, Leonard Weisgard, text by Golden MacDonald (Doubleday)
Sing Mother Goose, Marjorie Torrey, music by Opal Wheeler (Dutton)
My Mother is the Most Beautiful Woman in the World, Ruth Gannett, text by Becky Reyher (Lothrop)
You Can Write Chinese, written and illustrated by Kurt Wiese (Viking)

1945 WINNER: *Prayer for a Child*, Elizabeth Orton Jones, text by Rachel Field (Macmillan)

Honor Books
Mother Goose, Tasha Tudor (Oxford University Press)
In the Forest, written and illustrated by Marie Hall Ets (Viking)
Yonie Wondernose, written and illustrated by Marguerite de Angeli (Doubleday)
The Christmas Anna Angel, Kate Seredy, text by Ruth Sawyer (Viking)

1944 WINNER: *Many Moons*, Louis Slobodkin, text by James Thurber (Harcourt)

Honor Books
Small Rain: Verses From The Bible, Elizabeth Orton Jones, text selected by Jessie Orton Jones (Viking)
Pierre Pigeon, Arnold E. Bare, text by Lee Kingman (Houghton)
The Mighty Hunter, written and illustrated by Berta & Elmer Hader (Macmillan)
A Child's Good Night Book, Jean Charlot, text by Margaret Wise Brown (W. R. Scott)
Good-Luck Horse, Plato Chan, text by Chih-Yi Chan (Whittlesey)

INDEX

Aardema, Verna: Birth Anniv, Jun 6
Aaron, Hank: Birth, Feb 5
Aaron, Hank: Home Run Record: Anniv, Apr 8
Abdul-Jabbar, Kareem: Birth, Apr 16
Abolition Society Founded, First American: Anniv, Apr 14
Absolutely Incredible Kid Day, Mar 16
Abuse Prevention, Natl Child, Apr 1
Academy Awards, First: Anniv, May 16
Accession of Queen Elizabeth II: Anniv, Feb 6
According to Hoyle Day, Aug 29
Accordion Awareness Month, Intl, Jun 1
Ackerman, Diane: Birth, Oct 7
Ada, Alma Flor: Birth, Jan 3
Adams, Abigail: Birth Anniv, Nov 22
Adams, Ansel: Birth Anniv, Feb 20
Adams, John Quincy: Birth Anniv, Jul 11
Adams, John Quincy: Returns to Congress, Mar 4
Adams, John: Birth Anniv, Oct 30
Adams, Louisa Catherine Johnson: Birth Anniv, Feb 12
Adams, Richard: Birth, May 9
Adams, Samuel: Birth Anniv, Sep 27
Addams, Jane: Birth Anniv, Sep 6
Adler, David A.: Birth, Apr 10
Adoff, Arnold: Birth, Jul 16
Adopt-a-Shelter Cat Month, Jun 1
Adopt-a-Shelter Dog Month, Oct 1
Adoption Month, Natl (Pres Proc), Nov 1
Adoption Week, Natl, Nov 20
Adu, Freddy: Birth, Jun 2
Advent, First Sunday of, Nov 27
Affleck, Ben: Birth, Aug 15
Afghanistan
  Independence Day, Aug 19
  Islamic State's Victory Day, Apr 28
AFL Founded: Anniv, Dec 8
AFL-CIO Founded: Anniv, Dec 5
African-American History and Events
  African American History Month, Natl (Pres Proc), Feb 1
  African American Read-In, Feb 5
  Amistad Seized: Anniv, Aug 29
  Black History Month, Natl, Feb 1
  Black Page Appointed US House: Anniv, Apr 9
  Black Poetry Day, Oct 20
  Black Press Day, Mar 16
  Black Senate Page Appointed: Anniv, Apr 8
  Blacks Ruled Eligible to Vote: Anniv, Apr 3
  Bud Billiken Parade (Chicago, IL), Aug 13
  Civil Rights Act of 1964: Anniv, Jul 2
  Civil Rights Act of 1968: Anniv, Apr 11
  Civil Rights Bill of 1866: Anniv, Apr 9
  Crispus Attucks Day, Mar 5
  Desegregated, US Army First: Anniv, Jul 26
  Emancipation of 500: Anniv, Aug 1
  Escape to Freedom (F. Douglass): Anniv, Sep 3
  First American Abolition Society Founded: Anniv, Apr 14
  First Black Governor Elected: Anniv, Nov 7
  First Black Plays in NBA Game: Anniv, Oct 31
  First Black Serves in US House: Anniv, Dec 12
  First Black US Cabinet Member: Anniv, Jan 18
  First Natl Convention for Blacks: Anniv, Sep 15
  Frederick Douglass Speaks: Anniv, Aug 11
  Freedom Riders: Anniv, May 1
  Historically Black Colleges and Universities Week, Natl (Pres Proc), Sep 11
  Juneteenth, Jun 19
  King Wins Nobel Peace Prize: Anniv, Oct 14
  King, Martin Luther, Jr: Birth Anniv, Jan 15
  Kwanzaa Fest, Dec 26
  Little Rock Nine: Anniv, Sep 23
  Meredith (James) Enrolls at Ole Miss: Anniv, Sep 30
  Million Man March: Anniv, Oct 16
  Minority Scientists Showcase (St. Louis, MO), Jan 14
  Montgomery Boycott Arrests: Anniv, Feb 22
  Montgomery Bus Boycott Begins: Anniv, Dec 5
  NAACP Founded: Anniv, Feb 12
  Niagara Movement Founded: Anniv, Jul 11
  Ralph Bunche Awarded Nobel Peace Prize: Anniv, Dec 10
  Robinson Breaks MLB Color Barrier: Anniv, Apr 15
  Robinson Named First Black Manager: Anniv, Oct 3
  Rosa Parks Day, Dec 1
  Soul Food Month, Natl, Jun 1
  Stokes Becomes First Black Mayor in US: Anniv, Nov 13
  Tuskegee Airmen Activated: Anniv, Mar 22
  Wheatley, Phillis: Poetry Collection Published: Anniv, Sep 1
  With All Deliberate Speed: Anniv, May 31
African Freedom Day, May 25
Agassi, Andre: Birth, Apr 29
Agnew, Spiro: Birth Anniv, Nov 9
Agriculture
  Agriculture Day, Natl, Mar 20
  Agriculture Week, Natl, Mar 19
  Alabama Natl Fair, South (Montgomery, AL), Oct 7
  Alaska State Fair (Palmer, AK), Aug 25
  Arizona State Fair (Phoenix, AZ), Oct 6
  Arkansas State Fair (Little Rock, AR), Oct 7
  Bangor State Fair (Bangor, ME), Jul 28
  Big E (West Springfield, MA), Sep 16
  California State Fair (Sacramento, CA), Aug 19
  Colorado State Fair (Pueblo, CO), Aug 20
  Delaware State Fair (Harrington, DE), Jul 20
  Eastern Idaho State Fair (Blackfoot, ID), Sep 3
  Farm Animals Awareness Week, Natl, Sep 18
  Farm Safety Week, Natl (Pres Proc), Sep 18
  Farm-City Week, Natl (Pres Proc), Nov 18
  Florida State Fair (Tampa, FL), Feb 9
  Georgia National Fair (Perry, GA), Oct 7
  Grange Week, Apr 23
  Illinois State Fair (Springfield, IL), Aug 12
  Indiana State Fair (Indianapolis, IN), Aug 10
  Iowa State Fair (Des Moines, IA), Aug 11
  Kansas State Fair (Hutchinson, KS), Sep 9
  Kentucky State Fair (Louisville, KY), Aug 18
  Louisiana, State Fair of (Shreveport, LA), Oct 21
  Maryland State Fair (Timonium, MD), Aug 26
  Michigan State Fair (Detroit, MI), Aug 10
  Minnesota State Fair (St. Paul, MN), Aug 25
  Mississippi State Fair (Jackson, MS), Oct 5
  Missouri State Fair (Sedalia, MO), Aug 11
  Montana State Fair (Great Falls, MT), Jul 28
  Nebraska State Fair (Lincoln, NE), Aug 27
  Nevada State Fair (Reno, NV), Aug 24
  New Jersey State Fair/Sussex County Farm & Horse Show (Augusta, NJ), Aug 5
  New York State Fair (Syracuse, NY), Aug 25
  North Carolina State Fair (Raleigh, NC), Oct 14
  North Dakota State Fair (Minot, ND), Jul 21
  Ohio State Fair (Columbus, OH), Aug 3
  Oklahoma State Fair (Oklahoma City, OK), Sep 15
  Oregon State Fair (Salem, OR), Aug 26
  South Carolina State Fair (Columbia, SC), Oct 6
  South Dakota State Fair (Huron, SD), Sep 3
  State Fair (Albuquerque, NM), Sep 1
  Tennessee State Fair (Nashville, TN), Sep 9
  Texas, State Fair of (Dallas, TX), Sep 30
  Utah State Fair (Salt Lake City, UT), Sep 8
  Vermont State Fair (Rutland, VT), Sep 2
  Virginia, State Fair of (Richmond, VA), Sep 22
  Western Idaho Fair (Boise, ID), Aug 19
  Wisconsin State Fair (Milwaukee, WI), Aug 4
  Wyoming State Fair & Rodeo (Douglas, WY), Aug 13
Aguilera, Christina: Birth, Dec 18
Ahlberg, Allan: Birth, Jun 5
Ahlberg, Janet: Birth, Oct 21
Aichinger, Helga: Birth, Nov 29
AIDS Day, World (UN), Dec 1
AIDS First Noted: Anniv, Jun 5
Aiken, Clay: Birth, Nov 30
Aikman, Troy: Birth, Nov 21
Ailey, Alvin: Birth Anniv, Jan 5
Air Conditioning Appreciation Days, Jul 3
Akaka, Daniel: Birth, Sep 11
Akihito: Birth, Dec 23
Alabama
  Admission Day, Dec 14
  American Indian Heritage Day, Oct 10
  Battle of Mobile Bay: Anniv, Aug 5
  Confederate Memorial Day, Apr 24
  Natl Fair (Montgomery), Oct 7
  Riley, Bob: Birth, Oct 3
  Sessions, Jeff: Birth, Dec 24
  Shelby, Richard C.: Birth, May 6
Alamo: Anniv of the Fall, Mar 6
Alaska
  Admission Day, Jan 3
  Alaska Day, Oct 18
  Earthquake Strikes Alaska: Anniv, Mar 27
  Murkowski, Frank Hughes: Birth, Mar 28
  Murkowski, Lisa: Birth, May 22
  Natl Parks Established: Anniv, Dec 2
  Seward's Day, Mar 27
  State Fair (Palmer), Aug 25
  Stevens, Ted: Birth, Nov 18
Alba, Jessica: Birth, Apr 28
Albania: Independence Day, Nov 28
Alborough, Jez: Birth, Nov 13
Alcohol Awareness Month, Natl, Apr 1
Alcott, Louisa May: Birth Anniv, Nov 29
Aldrin, Buzz: Birth, Jan 20
Alexander, Lamar: Birth, Jul 30
Alexander, Lloyd: Birth, Jan 30
Alexander, Martha: Birth, May 25
Alger, Horatio, Jr: Birth Anniv, Jan 13
Algeria
  Independence Day, Jul 5
  Revolution Anniv, Nov 1
Ali, Muhammad: Birth, Jan 17
Ali, Muhammad: Clay Becomes Heavyweight Champ, Feb 25
Ali, Tatyana M.: Birth, Jan 24
Alice in Wonderland Published: Anniv, Nov 26
Aliki: Birth, Sep 3
All Fools' Day, Apr 1
All Hallows Day, Nov 1
All Hallows Eve, Oct 31
All Saints' Day, Nov 1
All Souls' Day, Nov 2
Allard, Harry: Birth, Jan 27
Allard, Wayne: Birth, Dec 2
Allen, Ethan: Birth Anniv, Jan 21
Allen, George: Birth, Mar 8
Allen, Marcus: Birth, Mar 26
Allen, Tim: Birth, Jun 13
Allergy/Asthma Awareness Month, Natl, May 1
All-Star Game, Major League Baseball First: Anniv, Jul 6
Almanack, Poor Richard's: Anniv, Dec 28
Almond, David: Birth, May 15
Alomar, Roberto: Birth, Feb 5
Alou, Moises: Birth, Jul 3
Alphabet Day (Korea), Oct 9
Alzheimer's Disease Month, Natl (Pres Proc), Nov 1
Ambrus, Victor: Birth, Aug 19
America Recycles Day, Nov 15
America the Beautiful Published: Anniv, Jul 4
American Assn of School Administrators: Conference on Education, Natl (San Diego, CA), Feb 23
American Council on Teaching of Foreign Languages Annual Conference (Baltimore, MD), Nov 18
American Education Week, Nov 13
American Education Week (Pres Proc), Nov 13
American Family Day in Arizona, Aug 7
American Federation of Labor Founded: Anniv, Dec 8
American Federation of Teachers Convention (San Francisco, CA), Jul 18
American History Essay Contest, Aug 1
American Indian Heritage Day (AL), Oct 10
American Indian Heritage Month, Natl (Pres Proc), Nov 1
American Library Assn Annual Conference (New Orleans, LA), Jun 22
American Library Assn Midwinter Mtg (San Antonio, TX), Jan 20
American Red Cross: Founding Anniv, May 21
American Samoa
  Flag Day, Apr 17
  White Sunday, Oct 9
American Teddy Bear Day, Natl, Nov 14
Americans with Disabilities Act: Anniv, Jul 26
America's First Department Store (Salt Lake City, UT), Oct 16
Amistad Seized: Anniv, Aug 29
Amundsen, Roald: Birth Anniv, Jul 16
Ancestor Appreciation Day, Sep 27
Ancona, George: Birth, Dec 4
Andersen, Hans Christian: Birth Anniv, Apr 2
Anderson, Laurie Halse: Birth, Oct 23
Andorra: National Holiday, Sep 8
Andrews, Julie: Birth, Oct 1
Anesthetic First Used in Surgery: Anniv, Mar 30
Angel Day, Be an, Aug 22
Angelou, Maya: Birth, Apr 4
Anglund, Joan Walsh: Birth, Jan 3
Angola
  Beginning of the Armed Struggle, Feb 4
  Independence Day, Nov 11
Animal Cruelty Prevention Month, Apr 1
Animals. See also Birds; Dogs; Horses
  Adopt-a-Shelter Cat Month, Jun 1
  Adopt-a-Shelter Dog Month, Oct 1
  Animal Cruelty Prevention Month, Apr 1
  Answer Your Cat's Question Day, Jan 22
  Balto: Sled Dog Hero: Death Anniv, Mar 14
  Be Kind to Animals Kids Contest Deadline, Apr 1
  Be Kind to Animals Week, May 7
  Cow Milked While Flying: Anniv, Feb 18
  Dog Week, Natl, Sep 18
  Elephant Appreciation Day, Sep 22
  Farm Animals Awareness Week, Natl, Sep 18
  First US Zoo: Anniv (Philadelphia, PA), Jul 1
  First Wild Animal with Artificial Lenses: Anniv, Jan 22
  Giraffe's Incredible Journey: Anniv, Jun 30
  Gorilla Born in Captivity, First: Anniv, Dec 22
  Jumbo the Elephant Arrives in America: Anniv, Apr 9
  Jumbo the Elephant: Death Anniv, Sep 15
  Keiko Returns to Iceland: Anniv, Sep 10
  Koko the Gorilla: Birth, Jul 4
  Last Great Buffalo Hunt: Anniv, Jun 25
  Marjan, The Lion of Kabul: Death Anniv, Jan 25
  Mule Day, Oct 26
  Pet Owners Independence Day, Apr 18
  Pet Week, Natl, May 7
  Pig Day, Natl, Mar 1
  Pony Penning, Chincoteague (Chincoteague Island, VA), Jul 26
  Rabbit Week, Natl, Jul 15
  Save the Rhino Day, May 1
  Sled Dogs Save Nome: Anniv, Feb 2
  Squid Battles Fishermen: Anniv, Oct 25
  Stubby Joins WWI Front Lines: Anniv, Feb 5
  Togo: Sled Dog Hero: Death Anniv, Dec 5
  Walk Your Pet Month, Jan 1
  Whale Awareness Day in MA, May 4
  White Cloud Birthday, Jul 10
  World Turtle Day, May 23
Annan, Kofi: Birth, Apr 8
Anno, Mitsumasa: Birth, Mar 20
Annunciation, Feast of, Mar 25
Anonymous Giving Week, Mar 19
Antarctic Ice Shelf Collapses: Anniv, Mar 7
Antarctica Made a Scientific Preserve: Anniv, Dec 1
Anthem Day, Natl, Mar 3
Anthony, Susan B.: Birth Anniv, Feb 15
Anthony, Susan B.: Fined for Voting: Anniv, Jun 6
Antietam, Battle of: Anniv, Sep 17
Antigua and Barbuda
  August Monday, Aug 1
  National Holiday, Nov 1
Antirabies Inoculation, First Successful: Anniv, Jul 6
Apache Wars Began: Anniv, Feb 4
Apartheid Law, South Africa Repeals Last: Anniv, Jun 17
Apgar, Virginia: Birth Anniv, Jun 7
Aphelion, Earth at, Jul 3
Apollo I: Spacecraft Fire: Anniv, Jan 27
Appert, Nicolas: Birth Anniv, Oct 23
Apple II Computer Released: Anniv, Jun 5
Apple, Margot: Birth, Mar 9
Appleseed, Johnny: Birth Anniv, Sep 26
Appleseed: Johnny Appleseed Day, Mar 11
April Fools' Day, Apr 1
Aquarius Begins, Jan 20
Aquatic: International Coastal Cleanup Day, Sep 17
Arab Oil Embargo Lifted: Anniv, Mar 13
Arab-Israeli War (Yom Kippur War), Oct 6
Arbor Day in Florida, Jan 20
Arbor Day, Natl, Apr 28
Archaeopteryx Fossil Discovery Announced: Anniv, Sep 30
Archeology
  Aztec Calendar Stone Discovery: Anniv, Dec 17
  Iceman Mummy Discovered: Anniv, Sep 19
  Inca Ice Maiden Discovered: Anniv, Sep 8
  Mary Rose Wreck Raised: Anniv, Oct 11
  Mayan Tomb of Pacal Discovered: Anniv, Jun 15
  Sutton Hoo Ship Burial Discovered: Anniv, May 11
Arches Natl Park: Anniv, Nov 12

Ardagh, Philip: Birth, Sep 11
Area Codes Introduced: Anniv, Nov 10
Argentina
  Death Anniversary of San Martin, Aug 17
  Flag Day, Jun 20
  Independence Day, Jul 9
  National Holiday, May 25
Aries Begins, Mar 21
Arizona
  Admission Day, Feb 14
  American Family Day, Aug 7
  Apache Wars Began: Anniv, Feb 4
  Grand Canyon Natl Park: Anniv, Feb 26
  Kyl, Jon: Birth, Apr 25
  McCain, John III: Birth, Aug 29
  Napolitano, Janet: Birth, Nov 29
  Petrified Forest Natl Park: Anniv, Dec 9
  PTA Convention, Natl (Phoenix), Jun 24
  State Fair (Phoenix), Oct 6
Arkansas
  Admission Day: Anniv, Jun 15
  Hot Springs Natl Park: Anniv, Mar 4
  Huckabee, Mike: Birth, Aug 24
  Lincoln, Blanche Lambert: Birth, Sep 30
  Pryor, Mark: Birth, Jan 10
  State Fair and Livestock Show (Little Rock), Oct 7
Armed Forces Day (Pres Proc), May 20
Armenia
  Armenia Christmas, Jan 6
  Armenian Martyrs Day, Apr 24
  National Day, Sep 21
Armistice Day, Nov 11
Armstrong, BJ: Birth, Sep 9
Armstrong, Jennifer: Birth, May 12
Armstrong, Lance: Birth, Sep 18
Armstrong, Louis: Birth Anniv, Aug 4
Armstrong, Neil Alden: Birth, Aug 5
Armstrong, William H.: Birth Anniv, Sep 14
Army Established: Anniv, Jun 14
Army First Desegregated, US: Anniv, Jul 26
Arnold, Benedict: Birth Anniv, Jan 14
Arnold, Caroline: Birth, May 16
Arnosky, Jim: Birth, Sep 1
Arquette, Courteney Cox: Birth, Jun 15
Arrington, LaVar: Birth, Jun 20
Art Education Assn Annual Convention, Natl (Boston, MA), Mar 4
Arthur TV Premiere: Anniv, Oct 7
Arthur, Chester A.: Birth Anniv, Oct 5
Arthur, Ellen: Birth Anniv, Aug 30
Arthur: Anniv, May 25
Articles of Confederation: Ratification Anniv, Mar 1
Arts and Crafts
  Craft Month, Natl, Mar 1
Arts, Fine and Performing; Art Shows
  Theater in North America, First Performance: Anniv, Apr 30
  Youth Art Month, Mar 1
Aruba: Flag Day, Mar 18
Ascension Day, May 25
Asch, Frank: Birth, Aug 6
Ash Wednesday, Mar 1
Ashabranner, Brent: Birth, Nov 3
Ashe, Arthur: Birth Anniv, Jul 10
Ashford, Evelyn: Birth, Apr 15
Ashura: Tenth Day (Islamic), Feb 9
Asian Pacific American Heritage Month (Pres Proc), May 1
Asimov, Isaac: Birth Anniv, Jan 2
Assassination of John F. Kennedy: Anniv, Nov 22
Assumption of the Virgin Mary, Aug 15
Astin, Sean: Birth, Feb 25
Astrology
  Aquarius, Jan 20
  Aries, Mar 21
  Cancer, Jun 21
  Capricorn, Dec 22
  Gemini, May 21
  Leo, Jul 23
  Libra, Sep 23
  Pisces, Feb 20
  Sagittarius, Nov 22
  Scorpio, Oct 23
  Taurus, Apr 20
  Virgo, Aug 23
Astronomy Day, May 6
Astronomy Week, May 1
AT&T Divestiture: Anniv, Jan 8
Atchison, David R.: Birth Anniv, Aug 11
Atlantic Charter Signing: Anniv, Aug 14
Atler, Vanessa: Birth, Feb 17
Atomic Bomb Dropped on Hiroshima: Anniv, Aug 6
Atomic Bomb Dropped on Nagasaki: Anniv, Aug 9
Atomic Bomb Tested: Anniv, Jul 16
Atomic Plant Begun, Oak Ridge: Anniv, Aug 1
Attack on America: Anniv, Sep 11
Attucks, Crispus: Day, Mar 5
Atwater, Richard: Birth Anniv, Dec 29
Atwood, Ann: Birth, Feb 12
Auch, Mary Jane: Birth, Nov 21
Audubon, John J.: Birth Anniv, Apr 26
Auschwitz Liberated by Soviets: Anniv, Jan 27
Ausmus, Brad: Birth, Apr 14
Austin, Stephen F.: Birth Anniv, Nov 3
Austin, Tracy: Birth, Dec 12
Australia
  Anzac Day, Apr 25
  Australia Day, Jan 26
  Canberra Day, Mar 20
  Commonwealth Formed: Anniv, Jan 1
  Picnic Day, Aug 1
  Proclamation Day, Dec 28
  Queen Elizabeth II's Official Birthday, Jun 12
  Sorry Day, May 26
Austria
  Krampuslauf, Dec 5
  National Day, Oct 26
  Silent Night, Holy Night Celebrations, Dec 24
Authors' Day, Natl, Nov 1
Autism Awareness Month, Natl, Apr 1
Automobile Speed Reduction: Anniv, Nov 25
Automobiles
  Buckle Up America! Week, May 22
  55 mph Speed Limit: Anniv, Jan 2
  First Automatic Toll Collection Machine: Anniv, Nov 19
  First Car Insurance: Anniv, Feb 1
  First License Plates: Anniv, Apr 25
  Longest Traffic Jam in History: Anniv, Feb 16
  Soap Box Derby, All-American (Akron, OH), Jul 30
Autumn Begins, Sep 22
Avi: Birth, Dec 23
Aviation; Air Shows; Airplane Fly-ins
  Aviation Day, Natl (Pres Proc), Aug 19
  Aviation History Month, Nov 1
  Aviation in America: Anniv, Jan 9
  Balloon Crossing of Atlantic: Anniv, Aug 17
  Civil Aviation Day, Intl, Dec 7
  Coleman, Bessie: Birth Anniv, Jan 26
  Earhart, Amelia: Disappears: Anniv, Jul 2
  First Balloon Flight Across English Channel: Anniv, Jan 7
  First Balloon Flight: Anniv, Jun 5
  First Complete Circle in an Airplane: Anniv, Sep 20
  First Concorde Flight: Anniv, Jan 21
  First Flight Attendant: Anniv, May 15
  First Ladies Take Flight: Anniv, Apr 20
  First Manned Flight (Balloon): Anniv, Oct 15
  First Man-Powered Flight: Anniv, Aug 23
  First Nonstop Flight of World/No Refueling: Anniv, Dec 23
  First Nonstop Transatlantic Flight: Anniv, Jun 14
  First Round-the-World Balloon Flight: Anniv, Mar 21
  Hindenburg Disaster: Anniv, May 6
  Lindbergh Flight: Anniv, May 20
  Lindbergh, Charles A.: Birth Anniv, Feb 4
  Montgolfier, Jacques: Birth Anniv, Jan 7
  Solo Transatlantic Balloon Crossing: Anniv, Sep 14
  Sound Barrier Broken: Anniv, Oct 14
  US Air Force Established: Anniv, Sep 18
  Wright Brothers Day (Pres Proc), Dec 17
  Wright Brothers' First Powered Flight: Anniv, Dec 17
Aylesworth, Jim: Birth, Feb 21
Azarian, Mary: Birth, Dec 8
Azerbaijan
  Day of the Martyrs, Jan 20
  Day of the Republic, May 28
Azzi, Jennifer: Birth, Aug 31
Babbitt, Natalie: Birth, Jul 28
Babysitters Day, Natl, May 13
Bach, Alice: Birth, Apr 6
Bach, Johann Sebastian: Birth Anniv, Mar 21
Backpack Safety America Month, Sep 1
Backyard Games Week, Natl, May 22
Baden-Powell, Robert: Birth Anniv, Feb 22
Badlands Natl Park: Anniv, Nov 10
Bagnold, Enid: Birth Anniv, Oct 27
Baha'i
  Baha'i New Year's Day: Naw-Ruz, Mar 21
  Race Unity Day, Jun 11
  World Religion Day, Jan 15
Bahamas
  Discovery Day, Oct 12
  Emancipation Day, Aug 1
  Independence Day, Jul 10
  Junkanoo, Dec 26
  Labor Day, Jun 2
Bahrain: Independence Day, Dec 16
Baisakhi (India), Apr 13
Baiul, Oksana: Birth, Nov 16
Baked Bean Month, Natl, Jul 1
Baker, Jeannie: Birth, Nov 2
Baker, Keith: Birth, Mar 17
Baker, Leslie: Birth, Jun 17
Baker, Vin: Birth, Nov 23
Balboa: Pacific Ocean Discovered: Anniv, Sep 25
Baldacci, John: Birth, Jan 30
Ballard, Dr. Robert: Birth, Jun 30
Ballet Introduced to the US: Anniv, Feb 7
Balloons, Hot-Air
  Aviation in America: Anniv, Jan 9
  Balloon Crossing of Atlantic: Anniv, Aug 17
  Balloons Around the World, Oct 5
  First Balloon Flight Across English Channel: Anniv, Jan 7
  First Balloon Flight: Anniv, Jun 5
  First Manned Flight: Anniv, Oct 15
  First Round-the-World Balloon Flight: Anniv, Mar 21
  Solo Transatlantic Balloon Crossing: Anniv, Sep 14
Ballpoint Pen Patented: Anniv, Jun 10
Balto: Sled Dog Hero: Death Anniv, Mar 14
Bang, Molly Garrett: Birth, Dec 29
Bangladesh
  Independence Day, Mar 26
  Martyrs' Day, Feb 21
  Solidarity Day, Nov 7
  Victory Day, Dec 16
Bank Opens in US, First: Anniv, Dec 31
Banks, Lynne Reid: Birth, Jul 31
Banned Books Week, Sep 24
Banneker, Benjamin: Birth Anniv, Nov 9
Bannister, Dr. Roger: Birth, Mar 24
Bar Code Introduced: Anniv, Jun 26
Barbados: Independence Day, Nov 30
Barbecue Month, Natl, May 1
Barber, Red: First Baseball Games Televised: Anniv, Aug 26
Barber, Tiki: Birth, Apr 7
Barbie Debuts: Anniv, Mar 9
Barbosa, Jose Celso: Birth Anniv, Jul 27
Barbour, Haley: Birth, Oct 22
Barbuda. See Antigua,
Barker, Clive: Birth, Oct 5
Barkley, Alben: Birth Anniv, Nov 24
Barkley, Charles: Birth, Feb 20
Barney & Friends TV Premiere: Anniv, Apr 6
Barnum, Phineas Taylor: Birth Anniv, Jul 5
Baron Bliss Day (Belize), Mar 9
Barracca, Debra: Birth, Dec 24
Barracca, Sal: Birth, Nov 10
Barrett, Brendon Ryan: Birth, Aug 5
Barrett, Ron: Birth, Jul 25
Barrie, J.M.: Birth Anniv, May 9
Barrier Awareness Day in Kentucky, May 7
Barron, T.A.: Birth, Mar 26
Barry, Dave: Birth, Jul 3
Barry, John: Death Anniv, Sep 13
Barrymore, Drew: Birth, Feb 22
Bartholdi, Frederic A.: Birth Anniv, Apr 2
Bartlett, John: Birth Anniv, Jun 14
Barton, Clara: Birth Anniv, Dec 25
Base, Graeme: Birth, Apr 6
Baseball History
  Babe Ruth Sets Home Run Record: Anniv, Sep 30
  Baseball First Played Under Lights: Anniv, May 24
  Baseball Hall of Fame, Natl: Anniv, Jun 12
  Bonds Breaks Home Run Record: Anniv, Oct 5
  Bronco League World Series (Monterey, CA), Aug 4
  Career Home Run Record: Anniv, Apr 8
  Designated Hitter Rule Adopted: Anniv, Jan 11
  First Games Televised: Anniv, Aug 26
  Hall of Fame Charter Members Elected: Anniv, Feb 2
  Little League World Series (Williamsport, PA), Aug 19
  Major League Baseball First All-Star Game: Anniv, Jul 6
  Major League's First Doubleheader: Anniv, Sep 25
  Maris Breaks Home Run Record: Anniv, Oct 1
  Mustang League World Series (Irving, TX), Aug 3
  Robinson Breaks MLB Color Barrier: Anniv, Apr 15
  Robinson Named First Black Manager: Anniv, Oct 3
  Yankee Stadium Opens: Anniv, Apr 18
Bashoff, Blake: Birth, May 30
Basketball
  Basketball Created: Anniv, Dec 1
  First Black Plays in NBA Game: Anniv, Oct 31
  First Women's Collegiate Game: Anniv, Mar 22
Bass, Lance: Birth, May 4
Bastille Day (France), Jul 14
Battier, Shane: Birth, Sep 9
Battle of Brandywine: Anniv, Sep 11
Battle of Britain Day (UK), Sep 15
Battle of Britain Week (UK), Sep 11
Battle of Lexington and Concord, Apr 19
Battle of Little Bighorn: Anniv, Jun 25
Baucus, Max: Birth, Dec 11
Bauer, Joan: Birth, Jul 12
Bauer, Marion Dane: Birth, Nov 20
Baum, L. Frank: Birth Anniv, May 15
Bawden, Nina: Birth, Jan 19
Bayh, Evan: Birth, Dec 26
Baylor, Byrd: Birth, Mar 28
Be an Angel Day, Aug 22
Be Kind to Animals Kids Contest Deadline, Apr 1
Be Kind to Animals Week, May 7
Be Kind to Humankind Week, Aug 25
Be Late for Something Day, Sep 5
Bean Month, Natl Baked, Jul 1
Bean Throwing Fest (Japan), Feb 3
Beanie Babies Introduced: Anniv, Jan 1
Beard, Amanda: Birth, Oct 29
Beasley, DaMarcus: Birth, May 24
Beatrix, Queen: Birth, Jan 31
Beatty, Patricia: Birth, Aug 26
Beaufort Scale Day, May 7
Becker, Boris: Birth, Nov 22
Beckham, David: Birth, May 2
Beddows, Eric: Birth, Nov 29
Bedell, Grace: Urges Abraham Lincoln To Grow Whiskers: Anniv, Oct 15
Beethoven, Ludwig van: Birth Anniv, Dec 16
Beethoven's Ninth Symphony Premiere: Anniv, May 7
Beggar's Night, Oct 31
Behn, Harry: Birth Anniv, Sep 24
Belarus
  Constitution Day, Mar 15
  Independence Day, Jul 3
Belfour, Ed: Birth, Apr 21
Belgium
  National Holiday, Jul 21
Belize
  Baron Bliss Day, Mar 9
  Columbus Day, Oct 12
  Commonwealth Day, May 24
  Garifuna Day, Nov 19
  Independence Day, Sep 21
  Saint George's Caye Day, Sep 10
Bell, Alexander Graham: Birth Anniv, Mar 3
Bell, Kendrell: Birth, Jul 2
Bellairs, John: Birth Anniv, Jan 17
Belle, Albert: Birth, Aug 25
Bemelmans, Ludwig: Birth Anniv, Apr 27
Ben-Gurion, David: Birth Anniv, Oct 16
Benin, People's Republic of: National Day, Aug 1
Bennett, Michael: Birth, Aug 13
Bennett, Richard Bedford: Birth Anniv, Jul 3
Bennett, Robert F.: Birth, Sep 18
Bennington Battle Day, Aug 16
Benson, Mildred Wirt: Birth Anniv, Jul 10
Bentley, Edmund Clerihew: Clerihew Day, Jul 10
Berenstain, Jan: Birth, Jul 26
Berenstain, Stan: Birth, Sep 29
Berg, Bjorn: Birth, Sep 17
Bergen, Candice: Birth, May 9
Berger, Barbara Helen: Birth, Mar 1
Berlin Airlift: Anniv, Jun 24
Berlin Wall Erected: Anniv, Aug 13
Berlin Wall Is Opened: Anniv, Nov 9
Berlin, Irving: God Bless America First Perf: Anniv, Nov 11
Bermuda
  Bermuda Day, May 24
  Peppercorn Ceremony, Apr 23
Berners-Lee, Tim: Birth, Jun 8
Bernstein, Leonard: Birth Anniv, Aug 25
Berra, Yogi: Birth, May 12
Better Hearing and Speech Month, May 1
Bettis, Jerome: Birth, Feb 16
Between the Lions TV Premiere: Anniv, Apr 3
Bhardwaj, Mohini: Birth, Sep 29

Bhutan
  Coronation Day, **Jun 2**
  National Day, **Aug 8**
Bial, Raymond: Birth, Nov 5
Bianco, Margery Williams: Birth Anniv, Jul 22
Bibby, Mike: Birth, May 13
Bible Week, Natl, Nov 20
Bichette, Dante: Birth, Nov 18
Bicycle
  Bike Month, Natl, **May 1**
  Bike to Work Day, Natl, **May 19**
Biden, Joseph R., Jr: Birth, Nov 20
Biel, Jessica: Birth, Mar 3
Bierhorst, John: Birth, Sep 2
Big Wind: Anniv, Apr 12
Biggio, Craig: Birth, Dec 14
Bill of Rights Day (Pres Proc), Dec 15
Bill of Rights Proposed: Anniv, Jun 8
Bill of Rights: Anniv, Dec 15
Bill of Rights: Anniv of First State Ratification, Nov 20
Billingsley, Franny: Birth, Jul 3
Bingaman, Jeff: Birth, Oct 3
Bingo's Birthday Month, Dec 1
Biographers Day, May 16
Biological Clock Gene Discovered: Anniv, Apr 28
Bird, Larry: Birth, Dec 7
Birds
  Bird Feeding Month, Natl, **Feb 1**
  Longest Human-Led Migration: Anniv, **Dec 3**
  Swallows Return to San Juan Capistrano, **Mar 19**
  Whooping Crane Fall Migration, **Sep 15**
  Whooping Crane Spring Migration, **Mar 1**
Birdseye, Clarence: Birth Anniv, Dec 9
Birdseye, Tom: Birth, Jul 13
Biscayne Natl Park: Anniv, Jun 28
Bjork, Christina: Birth, Jul 27
Black History Month, Natl, Feb 1
Black Maria Studio: Anniv, Feb 1
Black Nazarene, Feast of the (Philippines), Jan 9
Black Poetry Day, Oct 20
Black Press Day: Anniv of the First Black Newspaper, Mar 16
Black, Debbie: Birth, Jul 29
Blackbeard the Pirate (Edward Teach): Death Anniv, Nov 22
Blackmun, Harry A.: Birth Anniv, Nov 12
Blackwell, Elizabeth, Awarded MD: Anniv, Jan 23
Blagojevich, Rod: Birth, Dec 10
Blair, Bonnie: Birth, Mar 18
Blair, Tony: Birth, May 6
Blake, Jeff: Birth, Dec 4
Blanco, Kathleen: Birth, Dec 15
Bledel, Kimberly Alexis: Birth, Sep 16
Bledsoe, Drew: Birth, Feb 14
Blegvad, Erik: Birth, Mar 3
Blessing of Animals at the Cathedral (Mexico), Jan 17
Blizzard of '88, Great: Anniv, Mar 12
Block, Francesca Lia: Birth, Dec 3
Blondin, Charles: Conquest of Niagara Falls: Anniv, Jun 30
Bloom, Lloyd: Birth, Jan 10
Bloom, Orlando: Birth, Jan 13
Bloomberg, Michael: Birth, Feb 14
Bloomer, Amelia Jenks: Birth Anniv, May 27
Blos, Joan W.: Birth, Dec 9
Blue Ribbon Week, Natl (Child Abuse), Apr 3
Blueberries Month, Natl, Jul 1
Bluford, Guion S., Jr: Birth, Nov 22
Blumberg, Rhoda: Birth, Dec 14
Blume, Judy: Birth, Feb 12
Blunt, Matt: Birth, Nov 20
Bly, Nellie: Around the World in 72 Days: Anniv, Jan 25
Bly, Nellie: Birth Anniv, May 5
Boats, Ships, Things That Float
  First American to Circumnavigate Earth: Anniv, **Apr 10**
  Fulton Sails Steamboat: Anniv, **Aug 17**
  Safe Boating Week, Natl, **May 20**
  Safe Boating Week, Natl (Pres Proc), **May 19**
  Titanic Discovered: Anniv, **Sep 1**
  Titanic, Sinking of the: Anniv, **Apr 15**
Bocanegra, Carlos: Birth, May 25
Bodkin, Odds: Birth, Feb 14
Bodman, Samuel: Birth, Nov 26
Boer War: Anniv, Oct 12
Boggs, Wade: Birth, Jun 15
Boitano, Brian: Birth, Oct 22
Bolivar, Simon: Birth Anniv, Jul 24
Bolivia
  Independence Day, **Aug 6**
Bombing, Oklahoma City: Anniv, Apr 19
Bon Fest (Feast of Lanterns) (Japan), Jul 13
Bonaparte, Napoleon: Birth Anniv, Aug 15
Bond, Christopher S.: Birth, Mar 6
Bond, Felicia: Birth, Jul 18
Bond, Michael: Birth, Jan 13
Bond, Nancy: Birth, Jan 8
Bonds Breaks Home Run Record: Anniv, Oct 5
Bonds, Barry: Birth, Jul 24
Bonners, Susan: Birth, Apr 8
Bonsall, Brian: Birth, Dec 3
Bonza Bottler Day, Jan 1
Bonza Bottler Day, Feb 2
Bonza Bottler Day, Mar 3
Bonza Bottler Day, Apr 4
Bonza Bottler Day, May 5
Bonza Bottler Day, Jun 6
Bonza Bottler Day, Jul 7
Bonza Bottler Day, Aug 8
Bonza Bottler Day, Sep 9
Bonza Bottler Day, Oct 10
Bonza Bottler Day, Nov 11
Bonza Bottler Day, Dec 12
Booker, Marty: Birth, Jul 31
Books. See also Library/Librarians
  African American Read-In, **Feb 5**
  Appreciate a Dragon Day, **Jan 16**
  Arthur: Anniv, **May 25**
  Atlanta Book Fest (Atlanta, GA), **Sep 9**
  Authors' Day, Natl, **Nov 1**
  Baltimore Book Fest (Baltimore, MD), **Sep 23**
  Banned Books Week, **Sep 24**
  Bible Week, Natl, **Nov 20**
  Biographers Day, **May 16**
  Book Day (Spain), **Apr 23**
  Book It! Reading Incentive Program, **Oct 1**
  Book Month, Natl, **Oct 1**
  Canadian Children's Book Week, **Oct 29**
  Children's Book Day, Intl, **Apr 2**
  Children's Book Week, **Nov 14**
  Children's Literature Fest (Warrensburg, MO), **Mar 5**
  Copyright Law Passed: Anniv, **May 31**
  David McCord Children's Literature Fest (Framingham, MA), **Nov 3**
  Dictionary Day, **Oct 16**
  Fest of Books for Young People (Iowa City, IA), **Sep 10**
  First Dictionary of American English Published: Anniv, **Apr 14**
  Get Caught Reading Month, **May 1**
  Guadalajara Intl Book Fair, **Nov 26**
  Latino Book & Family Fest—Chicago (IL), **Nov 12**
  Latino Book & Family Fest—Houston (TX), **Oct 1**
  Latino Book & Family Fest—Los Angeles (CA), **Oct 16**
  Lord of the Rings: First Part Published: Anniv, **Jul 29**
  Multicultural Children's Book Fest (Washington, DC), **Nov 5**
  Norfolk Public Library Literature Fest (Norfolk, NE), **Jul 29**
  Paperback Books Introduced: Anniv, **Jul 30**
  Read Across America Day, **Mar 2**
  Reading Is Fun Week, **May 14**
  Return the Borrowed Books Week, **Mar 1**
  Southern Fest of Books (Nashville, TN), **Oct 7**
  Teen Read Week, **Oct 16**
  World Book and Copyright Day (UN), **Apr 23**
  Young Reader's Day, Natl, **Nov 8**
Boone, Bret: Birth, Apr 6
Boone, Daniel: Birth Anniv, Nov 2
Borden, Sir Robert Laird: Birth Anniv, Jun 26
Boreanaz, David: Birth, May 16
Borglum, Gutzon: Birth Anniv, Mar 25
Bosnia and Herzegovina
  Independence Day, **Mar 1**
  Natl Day, **Nov 25**
Boston Massacre: Anniv, Mar 5
Boston Public Library: Anniv, Apr 3
Boston Tea Party: Anniv, Dec 16
Botswana
  Independence Day, **Sep 30**
  Presidents Day, **Jul 17**
  Sir Seretse Khama Day, **Jul 1**
Boucher, Brian: Birth, Jan 2
Bounty, Mutiny on the: Anniv, Apr 28
Bourque, Ray: Birth, Dec 28
Bowman, Jessica: Birth, Nov 26
Boxer, Barbara: Birth, Nov 11
Boxing Day (United Kingdom), Dec 26
Boy Scouts of America Anniv Week, Feb 5
Boy Scouts of America Founded: Anniv, Feb 8
Boy Scouts: Baden-Powell, Robert: Birth Anniv, Feb 22
Boycott, Charles C.: Birth Anniv, Mar 12
Boys' Clubs Founded: Anniv, May 19
Bradbury, Ray: Birth, Aug 22
Bradford, William: Birth Anniv, Mar 19
Bradley, Shawn: Birth, Mar 22
Bradstreet: Anne Bradstreet Day, Sep 16
Brady Bunch TV Premiere, The: Anniv, Sep 26
Brady, Irene: Birth, Dec 29
Brady, Mathew: First Presidential Photograph: Anniv, Feb 14
Brady, Tom: Birth, Aug 3
Brahms, Johannes: Birth Anniv, May 7
Braille, Louis: Birth Anniv, Jan 4
Brain Awareness Week, Intl, Mar 13
Brand, Elton: Birth, Mar 11
Brandeis, Louis D.: Birth Anniv, Nov 13
Brandy: Birth, Feb 11
Branscum, Robbie: Birth Anniv, Jun 17
Brashear, Donald: Birth, Jan 7
Braxton, Carter: Birth Anniv, Sep 10
Brazil
  Carnival, **Feb 25**
  Discovery of Brazil Day, **Apr 22**
  Independence Day, **Sep 7**
  Independence Week, **Sep 1**
  Republic Day, **Nov 15**
  Tiradentes Day, **Apr 21**
Breakfast Week, Natl School, Mar 6
Breast Cancer Awareness Month, Natl (Pres Proc), Oct 1
Breathed, Berke: Birth, Jun 21
Breckinridge, John Cabell: Birth Anniv, Jan 21
Bredesen, Phil: Birth, Nov 21
Brees, Drew: Birth, Jan 15
Brendon, Nicholas: Birth, Apr 12
Brett, George: Birth, May 15
Brett, Jan: Birth, Dec 1
Breyer, Stephen G.: Birth, Aug 15
Bridwell, Norman: Birth, Feb 15
Brimner, Larry Dane: Birth, Nov 5
Brink, Carol Ryrie: Birth Anniv, Dec 28
British North America Act: Anniv, Mar 29
British Virgin Islands: Territory Day, Jul 1
Brittain, Bill: Birth, Dec 16
Broderick, Beth: Birth, Feb 24
Broderick, Matthew: Birth, Mar 21
Brodeur, Martin: Birth, May 6
Brokaw, Tom: Birth, Feb 6
Bronco League World Series (Monterey, CA), Aug 4
Brooklyn Bridge Opened: Anniv, May 24
Brooks, Aaron: Birth, Mar 24
Brooks, Bruce: Birth, Sep 23
Brooks, Garth: Birth, Feb 7
Brooks, Gwendolyn: Birth Anniv, Jun 7
Brooks, Walter R.: Birth Anniv, Jan 9
Brown, Curtis, Jr: Birth, Mar 11
Brown, Don: Birth, Oct 4
Brown, Jeff: Birth Anniv, Aug 20
Brown, Jesse Leroy: Birth Anniv, Oct 13
Brown, John: Birth Anniv, May 9
Brown, John: Raid Anniv, Oct 16
Brown, Kwame: Birth, Mar 10
Brown, Marc: Birth, Nov 25
Brown, Marcia: Birth, Jul 13
Brown, Margaret Wise: Birth Anniv, May 23
Brown, Tim: Birth, Jul 22
Brownback, Sam: Birth, Sep 12
Browne, Anthony: Birth, Sep 11
Browning, Elizabeth Barrett: Birth Anniv, Mar 6
Browning, Robert: Birth Anniv, May 7
Bruce, Isaac: Birth, Nov 10
Bruchac, Joseph: Birth, Oct 16
Brunell, Mark: Birth, Sep 17
Brunhoff, Jean de: Birth Anniv, Dec 9
Bryan, Ashley: Birth, Jul 13
Bryan, Zachery Ty: Birth, Oct 9
Bryant, Kobe: Birth, Aug 23
Buchanan, James: Birth Anniv, Apr 23
Buchenwald Liberation: Anniv, Apr 11
Buck, Pearl: Birth Anniv, Jun 26
Buckle Up America! Week, May 22
Buddha: Birth Anniv, Apr 8
Buddha: Birthday (China), May 5
Buehner, Caralyn: Birth, May 20
Buehner, Mark: Birth, Jul 20
Buffalo Bill (William F. Cody): Birth Anniv, Feb 26
Buffalo Hunt, Last Great: Anniv, Jun 25
Buffalo, Albino: White Cloud Birthday, Jul 10
Bugs Bunny's Debut: Anniv, Apr 30
Bulgaria
  Enlightenment and Culture Day, **May 24**
  Hristo Botev Day, **Jun 2**
  Liberation Day, **Mar 3**
  Saint Lasarus Day, **Apr 1**
  Unification Day, **Sep 6**
Bulla, Clyde Robert: Birth, Jan 9
Bullett, Vicky: Birth, Oct 4
Bullying: No Name-Calling Week, Jan 16
Bun Day (Iceland), Feb 27
Bunche, Ralph: Awarded Nobel Peace Prize: Anniv, Dec 10
Bunche, Ralph: Birth Anniv, Aug 7
Bunker Hill Day (MA), Jun 17
Bunning, Jim: Birth, Oct 23
Bunting, Eve: Birth, Dec 19
Buonarroti Simoni, Michelangelo: Birth Anniv, Mar 6
Burbank, Luther: Birth Anniv, Mar 7
Burch, Robert: Birth, Jun 26
Bure, Candace Cameron: Birth, Apr 6
Bure, Pavel: Birth, Mar 31
Bureau of Indian Affairs Established, Mar 11
Burger, Warren E.: Birth Anniv, Sep 17
Burk, Martha (Calamity Jane): Death Anniv, Aug 1
Burkina Faso
  Anniv of the 1966 Upheaval, **Jan 3**
  National Day, **Dec 11**
  Republic Day, **Aug 5**
  Revolution Day, **Aug 4**
Burleigh, Robert: Birth, Jan 4
Burnett, Frances Hodgson: Birth Anniv, Nov 24
Burnford, Sheila: Birth, May 11
Burningham, John: Birth, Apr 27
Burnquist, Bob: Birth, Oct 10
Burns, Conrad: Birth, Jan 25
Burns, Steven: Birth, Oct 9
Burr, Aaron: Birth Anniv, Feb 6
Burr, Aaron: Duel with Hamilton: Anniv, Jul 11
Burr, Richard: Birth, Nov 30
Burroughs, Edgar Rice: Birth Anniv, Sep 1
Bursting Day (Iceland), Feb 28
Burton, LeVar: Birth, Feb 16
Burton, Virginia Lee: Birth Anniv, Aug 30
Burundi
  Assassination of the Hero of the Nation Day, **Oct 13**
  Independence Day, **Jul 1**
Bush, Barbara Pierce: Birth, Jun 8
Bush, George H.W.: Birth, Jun 12
Bush, George W.: Birth, Jul 6
Bush, Jeb: Birth, Feb 11
Bush, Laura: Birth, Nov 4
Bushmiller, Ernie: Birth Anniv, Aug 23
Business: AT&T Divestiture: Anniv, Jan 8
Butcher, Susan: Birth, Dec 26
Butterfly, Monarch: Fall Migration, Aug 21
Butts, Alfred M.: Birth Anniv, Apr 13
Buy Nothing Day, Nov 25
Byars, Betsy: Birth, Aug 7
Bye, Karyn: Birth, May 18
Bynes, Amanda: Birth, Apr 3
Byrd, Robert C.: Birth, Nov 20
Cabbage Patch Kids Debuted: Anniv, Oct 7
Cabrillo Day (CA), Sep 28
Cadnum, Michael: Birth, May 3
Caduto, Michael J.: Birth, Dec 20
Cain, Dean: Birth, Jul 31
Caine, Michael: Birth, Mar 14
Calamity Jane (Martha Burk): Death Anniv, Aug 1
Caldecott, Randolph: Birth Anniv, Mar 22
Calder, Alexander: Birth Anniv, Jul 22
Calderon, Sila Maria: Birth, Sep 23
Calendar Adjustment Day: Anniv, Sep 2
Calendar Day, Gregorian, Feb 24
Calhoun, John C.: Birth Anniv, Mar 18
Calhoun, Mary: Birth, Aug 3
California
  Admission Day, **Sep 9**
  American Federation of Teachers Convention (San Francisco), **Jul 18**
  Boxer, Barbara: Birth, **Nov 11**
  Bronco League World Series (Monterey), **Aug 4**
  Cabrillo Day, **Sep 28**
  California Gold Discovery: Anniv, **Jan 24**
  Cesar Chavez Day, **Mar 31**
  Channel Islands Natl Park: Anniv, **Mar 5**
  Conference on Education, Natl (San Diego), **Feb 23**
  Disneyland Opened: Anniv, **Jul 17**
  Feinstein, Diane: Birth, **Jun 22**

Golden Gate Bridge Opened: Anniv, **May 27**
Lassen Volcanic Natl Park Established: Anniv, **Aug 9**
Latino Book & Family Fest—Los Angeles, **Oct 16**
Laura Ingalls Wilder Gingerbread Sociable (Pomona), **Feb 4**
Los Angeles Founded: Anniv, **Sep 4**
Mother Goose Parade (El Cajon), **Nov 20**
Pasadena Doo Dah Parade (Pasadena), **Nov 20**
Redwood Natl Park: Anniv, **Oct 2**
Rose Bowl Game (Pasadena), **Jan 1**
Schwarzenegger, Arnold: Birth, **Jul 30**
Science Teachers Assn Convention, Natl (Anaheim), **Apr 6**
Sequoia and Kings Canyon Natl Parks: Anniv, **Sep 25**
Southern California Earthquake: Anniv, **Jan 17**
State Fair (Sacramento), **Aug 19**
Swallows Return to San Juan Capistrano, **Mar 19**
Tournament of Roses Parade (Pasadena), **Jan 1**
Yosemite Natl Park: Anniv, **Oct 1**
Calmenson, Stephanie: Birth, Nov 28
Cambodia
Constitutional Declaration Day, **Sep 24**
Independence Day, **Nov 9**
Peace Treaty Day, **Oct 23**
Camby, Marcus: Birth, Mar 22
Camcorder Developed: Anniv, Jan 20
Cameron, Ann: Birth, Oct 21
Cameron, Kirk: Birth, Oct 12
Cameron, Mike: Birth, Jan 8
Cameroon
National Holiday, **May 20**
Volcanic Eruption: Anniv, **Aug 22**
Youth Day, **Feb 11**
Camp David Accord Signed: Anniv, Mar 26
Camp Fire USA Birthday Week, Mar 13
Camp Fire USA: Anniv, Mar 17
Camp Week, Natl Sign Up for Summer, Feb 1
Campanella, Roy: Birth Anniv, Nov 19
Campbell, Kim: Birth, Mar 10
Canada
Boxing Day, **Dec 26**
British North America Act: Anniv, **Mar 29**
Calgary Intl Children's Fest (Calgary, AB), **May 23**
Canada Day, **Jul 1**
Children's Book Week, **Oct 29**
Civic Holiday, **Aug 1**
CN Tower: Anniv, **Jun 26**
Constitution Act: Anniv, **Apr 18**
Drowning Prevention Day, Natl, **Jul 23**
English Colony in North America, First: Anniv, **Aug 5**
First Woman Canadian Prime Minister: Anniv, **Jun 25**
Halifax, Nova Scotia, Destroyed: Anniv, **Dec 6**
Klondike Eldorado Gold Discovery: Anniv, **Aug 31**
Labor Day, **Sep 5**
Maple Leaf Flag Adopted: Anniv, **Feb 15**
Martin, Paul: Birth, **Aug 28**
Newfoundland Discovery Day, **Jun 26**
Newfoundland Memorial Day, **Jul 3**
Newfoundland: Saint George's Day, **Apr 24**
Nunavut Independence: Anniv, **Apr 1**
Quebec Fete Nationale, **Jun 24**
Remembrance Day, **Nov 11**
Riel, Louis: Hanging Anniv, **Nov 16**
Thanksgiving Day, **Oct 10**
Victoria Day, **May 22**
Yukon Discovery Day, **Aug 15**
Canadian Pacific Railway: Transcontinental Completion Anniv, Nov 7
Cancer (Zodiac) Begins, Jun 21
Cancer Control Month (Pres Proc), Apr 1
Cancer in the Sun Month, Jun 1
Candlemas Day (Presentation of the Lord), Feb 2
Cannon, Janell: Birth, Nov 3
Cannon, Joe: Birth, Jan 1
Canseco, Jose, Jr: Birth, Jul 2
Cantwell, Maria: Birth, Oct 13
Cape Verde: National Day, Jul 5
Capitol Cornerstone Laid, US: Anniv, Sep 18
Capitol Reef Natl Park: Anniv, Dec 18
Capriati, Jennifer: Birth, Mar 29
Capricorn Begins, Dec 22
Captain Kangaroo TV Premiere: Anniv, Oct 3
Captain Kangaroo: see Keeshan, Bob: Birth Anniv, Jun 27
Car Trip: First US Transcontinental: Anniv, Jul 26
Caraway, Hattie: First Elected Woman Senator: Anniv, Jan 12
Carcieri, Donald: Birth, Dec 16
Career Home Run Record: Anniv, Apr 8
Carey, Mariah: Birth, Mar 27
Caribbean or Caricom Day, Jul 3
Caricom or Caribbean Day, Jul 3
Carle, Eric: Birth, Jun 25
Carlsbad Caverns Natl Park Established: Anniv (NM), May 14
Carlson, Nancy: Birth, Oct 10
Carlstrom, Nancy White: Birth, Aug 4
Carnegie, Andrew: Birth Anniv, Nov 25
Carnival, Feb 27
Carnival (Malta), Feb 25
Carnival (Port of Spain, Trinidad and Tobago), Feb 27
Carnival de Ponce (Ponce, PR), Feb 22
Carnival Season, Jan 6
Carnival Week (Milan, Italy), Feb 26
Carper, Tom: Birth, Jan 23
Carrey, Jim: Birth, Jan 17
Carroll, Charles: Birth Anniv, Sep 19
Carroll, Lewis: Birth Anniv, Jan 27
Carson, Christopher "Kit": Birth Anniv, Dec 24
Carson, Rachel: Birth Anniv, May 27
Carson, Rachel: Silent Spring Publication: Anniv, Apr 13
Carter, Aaron: Birth, Dec 7
Carter, Alan R.: Birth, Apr 7
Carter, Cris: Birth, Nov 25
Carter, David A.: Birth, Mar 4
Carter, Jimmy: Birth, Oct 1
Carter, Jimmy: Birthday, Oct 1
Carter, Nick: Birth, Jan 28
Carter, Robert III: Emancipation of 500: Anniv, Aug 1
Carter, Rosalynn Smith: Birth, Aug 18
Carter, Vince: Birth, Jan 26
Cartier, Jacques: Death Anniv, Sep 1
Carver, George Washington: Death Anniv, Jan 5
Carvey, Dana: Birth, Jun 2
Case, Steve: Birth, Aug 21
Caseley, Judith: Birth, Oct 17
Castile, Christopher: Birth, Jun 15
Castro, Fidel: Birth, Aug 13
Catalanotto, Peter: Birth, Mar 21
Catholic Educational Assn Convention/Expo, Natl (New Orleans, LA), Apr 18
Catholic Schools Week, Jan 29
Catlin, George: Birth Anniv, Jul 26
Catt, Carrie Lane Chapman: Birth Anniv, Jan 9
Cavoukian, Raffi: Birth, Jul 8
Caxton, William: Birth Anniv, Aug 13
CBS Evening News TV Premiere: Anniv, May 3
CD Player Debuts: Anniv, Oct 1
Cellophane Tape Patented: Anniv, May 27
Cellucci, A. Paul: Birth, Apr 24
Central African Republic
Boganda Day, **Mar 29**
Independence Day, **Aug 13**
National Day, **Dec 5**
Cezanne, Paul: Birth Anniv, Jan 19
Chad
African Freedom Day, **May 25**
Independence Day, **Aug 11**
Republic Day, **Nov 28**
Chafee, Lincoln: Birth, Mar 26
Challenger Space Shuttle Explosion: Anniv, Jan 28
Chalmers, Mary: Birth, Mar 16
Chamberlain, Wilt: Birth Anniv, Aug 21
Chambers, Aidan: Birth, Dec 27
Chambliss, Saxby: Birth, Nov 10
Chan, Jackie: Birth, Apr 7
Chang, Michael Te Pei: Birth, Feb 22
Channel Islands Natl Park: Anniv, Mar 5
Chanukah, Dec 26
Chao, Elaine: Birth, Mar 26
Chapman, John: Death Anniv: Johnny Appleseed Day, Mar 11
Character Counts Week, Natl (Pres Proc), Oct 16
Charles, Prince: Birth, Nov 14
Charles, Ray: Birth Anniv, Sep 23
Charlip, Remy: Birth, Jan 10
Chase, Chevy: Birth, Oct 8
Chasez, JC: Birth, Aug 8
Chastain, Brandi: Birth, Jul 21
Chauvin Day, Aug 15
Chavez, Cesar Estrada: Birth Anniv, Mar 31
Chavez, Eric: Birth, Dec 7
Check Your Batteries Day, Apr 2
Chelios, Chris: Birth, Jan 25
Chemistry Week, Natl, Oct 17
Cheney, Dick: Birth, Jan 30
Cheney, Lynne: Birth, Aug 14
Chernobyl Nuclear Reactor Disaster: Anniv, Apr 26
Cherokee Strip Day (OK), Sep 16
Cherry Month, Natl, Feb 1
Cherry, Lynne: Birth, Jan 5
Chesnut, Mary Boykin Miller: Birth Anniv, Mar 31
Chesnutt, Charles W.: Birth Anniv, Jun 20
Chess, Victoria: Birth, Nov 16
Chess: First Computer Victory over Human: Anniv, Feb 10
Chew, Ruth: Birth, Apr 8
Chiang Kai-Shek Day (Taiwan), Oct 31
Chicago Fire, Great: Anniv, Oct 8
Chicago Intl Children's Film Fest (Chicago, IL), Oct 27
Chief Joseph Surrender: Anniv, Oct 5
Chief Joseph: Death Anniv, Sep 21
Child Abuse Prevention Month, Natl, Apr 1
Child Abuse: Blue Ribbon Week, Natl, Apr 3
Child Health Day (Pres Proc), Oct 3
Child Safety Council, Natl: Founding Anniv, Nov 9
Childermas, Dec 28
Childhood Injury Prevention Week, Natl, Sep 1
Children
Absolutely Incredible Kid Day, **Mar 16**
Adoption Month, Natl (Pres Proc), **Nov 1**
Australia: Sorry Day, **May 26**
Babysitters Day, Natl, **May 13**
Child Abuse Prevention Month, Natl (Pres Proc), **Apr 1**
Child Vision Awareness Month, **Jun 1**
Childhood Depression Awareness Day, **May 2**
Children with Alopecia Day, **Apr 14**
Children's Book Day, Intl, **Apr 2**
Children's Book Week, **Nov 14**
Children's Day (FL), **Apr 11**
Children's Day (Japan), **May 5**
Children's Day (Korea), **May 5**
Children's Day (MA), **Jun 11**
Children's Day, Intl (People's Republic of China), **Jun 1**
Children's Day, Universal (UN), **Nov 20**
Children's Day/Natl Sovereignty (Turkey), **Apr 23**
Children's Good Manners Month, **Sep 1**
Children's Literature Fest (Warrensburg, MO), **Mar 5**
Children's Magazine Month, **Oct 1**
Children's Vision and Learning Month, **Aug 1**
Family Month, Natl, **May 14**
Firepup's Birthday, **Oct 1**
Innocent Children Victims of Aggression, Intl Day of, **Jun 4**
Japan: Shichi-Go-San, **Nov 15**
Key Club Intl Week, **Nov 7**
KidsDay, Natl, **Aug 7**
Safe Toys and Gifts Month, **Dec 1**
Stand for Children Day, **Jun 1**
Universal Children's Week, **Oct 1**
Young Achievers Month, **May 1**
Young Child, Week of the, **Apr 2**
Youth Day (Cameroon), **Feb 11**
Youth Day (Zambia), **Aug 1**
YWCA Week, Natl, **Apr 23**
Children's Craft Day, Natl, Mar 14
Children's Day of Broadcasting, Intl, Dec 11
Children's Literature Fest (Keene, NH), Oct 29
Children's Memorial Day, Natl, Dec 11
Children's Sunday, Jun 11
Childress, Alice: Birth, Oct 12
Chile
Independence Day, **Sep 18**
National Month, **Sep 1**
China, People's Republic of
Birthday of Lord Buddha, **May 5**
Chung Yeung Fest, **Oct 11**
Double 10th Day, **Oct 10**
Dragon Boat Fest, **May 31**
Fest of Hungry Ghosts, **Aug 19**
International Children's Day, **Jun 1**
Lantern Fest, **Feb 12**
Moon Fest or Mid-Autumn Fest, **Sep 18**
National Day, **Oct 1**
New Year, **Jan 29**
Qing Ming Fest, **Apr 5**
Sun Yat-Sen: Birth Anniv, **Nov 12**
Tiananmen Square Massacre: Anniv, **Jun 4**
Youth Day, **May 4**
Chincoteague Pony Penning (Chincoteague Island, VA), Jul 26
Chinese Nationalists Move to Taiwan: Anniv, Dec 8
Chinese New Year, Jan 29
Chirac, Jacques Rene: Birth, Nov 29
Chisholm, Shirley: Birth Anniv, Nov 30
Chlumsky, Anna: Birth, Dec 3
Chocolate, Debbi: Birth, Jan 25
Choi, Sook Nyul: Birth, Jan 10
Chorao, Kay: Birth, Jan 7
Chou En-Lai: Death Anniv, Jan 8
Chretien, Jean: Birth, Jan 11
Christelow, Eileen: Birth, Apr 22
Christmas
Armenian Christmas, **Jan 6**
Christmas, **Dec 25**
Christmas Eve, **Dec 24**
Christmas Greetings/First Radio Broadcast from Space: Anniv, **Dec 19**
Christmas Tree/Rockefeller Center (New York, NY), **Nov 29**
Navidades (Puerto Rico), **Dec 15**
Posadas (Mexico), **Dec 16**
Russian Christmas, **Jan 7**
Saint Nicholas Day, **Dec 6**
Silent Night, Holy Night Celebrations (Austria), **Dec 24**
Sinterklaas (Netherlands), **Dec 5**
Twelfth Night, **Jan 5**
Christopher, Matt: Birth Anniv, Aug 16
Chung Yeung Fest (China), Oct 11
Church, Charlotte: Birth, Feb 21
Churchill, Winston: Day, Apr 9
Ciardi, John: Birth Anniv, Jun 24
Cigarettes Reported Hazardous: Anniv, Jan 11
Cinco de Mayo (Mexico), May 5
Circuses; Circus Animals
Barnum, Phineas Taylor: Birth Anniv, **Jul 5**
Clown Week, Intl, **Aug 1**
Greatest Show on Earth: Anniv, **Mar 28**
Jumbo the Elephant Arrives in America: Anniv, **Apr 9**
Jumbo the Elephant: Death Anniv, **Sep 15**
Citizenship Day (Pres Proc), Sep 17
Civil Aviation Day, Intl, Dec 7
Civil Rights
Brown v Board of Education of Topeka: Anniv, **May 17**
Civil Rights Act of 1964: Anniv, **Jul 2**
Civil Rights Act of 1968: Anniv, **Apr 11**
Civil Rights Bill of 1866: Anniv, **Apr 9**
Freedom Riders: Anniv, **May 1**
Greensboro Sit-in: Anniv, **Feb 1**
King Wins Nobel Peace Prize: Anniv, **Oct 14**
Little Rock Nine: Anniv, **Sep 23**
March on Washington: Anniv, **Aug 28**
Marshall, Thurgood: Birth Anniv, **Jul 2**
Meredith (James) Enrolls at Ole Miss: Anniv, **Sep 30**
Montgomery Boycott Arrests: Anniv, **Feb 22**
Montgomery Bus Boycott Begins: Anniv, **Dec 5**
Rosa Parks Day, **Dec 1**
Rustin, Bayard: Birth Anniv, **Mar 17**
24th Amendment Ratified (Eliminated Poll Taxes), **Jan 23**
Voting Rights Act Signed: Anniv, **Aug 6**
With All Deliberate Speed: Anniv, **May 31**
Civil War, American
Amnesty Issued for Southern Rebels: Anniv, **May 29**
Battle of Antietam: Anniv, **Sep 17**
Battle of Gettysburg: Anniv, **Jul 1**
Battle of Mobile Bay: Anniv, **Aug 5**
Civil War Ending: Anniv, **Apr 9**
Davis, Jefferson: Inauguration: Anniv, **Feb 18**
Fort Sumter Shelled by North: Anniv, **Aug 17**
Grant Commissioned Commander: Anniv, **Mar 9**
Jefferson Davis Captured: Anniv, **May 10**
Johnson Impeachment Proceedings: Anniv, **Feb 24**
Lincoln Approves 13th Amendment (Freedom Day), **Feb 1**
Lincoln Assassination Anniv, **Apr 14**
Lincoln's Gettysburg Address: Anniv, **Nov 19**
Sherman Enters Atlanta: Anniv, **Sep 2**
South Carolina: Secession Anniv, **Dec 20**
Clark, Abraham: Birth Anniv, Feb 15
Clark, Barney: Artificial Heart Transplant: Anniv, Dec 2
Clark, Joe: Birth, Jun 5
Clark, William: Birth Anniv, Aug 1
Clarke, Bobby: Birth, Aug 13
Clarkson, Kelly: Birth, Apr 24
Clay (Muhammad Ali) Becomes Heavyweight Champ: Anniv, Feb 25
Clay, Cassius, Jr (Muhammad Ali): Birth, Jan 17
Clay, Henry: Birth Anniv, Apr 12
Clean (Green) Monday, Mar 6
Clean Air Act Passed by Congress: Anniv, Dec 17
Clean-Off-Your-Desk Day, Natl, Jan 9
Cleary, Beverly: Birth, Apr 12
Cleaver, Bill: Birth Anniv, Mar 24
Cleaver, Vera: Birth, Jan 6
Clemens, Roger: Birth, Aug 4

Clemens, Samuel (Mark Twain): Birth Anniv, Nov 30
Clemente, Roberto: Birth Anniv, Aug 18
Clements, Andrew: Birth, May 29
Clerc, Laurent: Birth Anniv, Dec 26
Clerc-Gallaudet Week, Dec 4
Clerihew Day, Jul 10
Cleveland, Esther: First White House Presidential Baby, Aug 30
Cleveland, Frances: Birth Anniv, Jul 21
Cleveland, Grover: Birth Anniv, Mar 18
Cleveland, Grover: Second Pres Inauguration: Anniv, Mar 4
Clifton, Lucille: Birth, Jun 27
Clijsters, Kim: Birth, Jun 8
Climo, Shirley: Birth, Nov 25
Clinton, George: Birth Anniv, Jul 26
Clinton, Hillary Rodham: Birth, Oct 26
Clinton, William Jefferson (Bill): Birth, Aug 19
Clinton, William: Impeachment Proceedings: Anniv, Dec 20
Cloning of an Adult Animal, First: Anniv, Feb 23
Clooney, George: Birth, May 6
Close, Glenn: Birth, Mar 19
Clown Week, Intl, Aug 1
Clymer, George: Birth Anniv, Mar 16
CN Tower: Anniv, Jun 26
CNN Debuted: Anniv, Jun 1
Coast Guard Day, Aug 4
Coastal Cleanup Day, Intl, Sep 17
Cobb, Ty: Birth Anniv, Dec 18
Cobb, Ty: Voted into Hall of Fame: Anniv, Feb 2
Coburn, Tom: Birth, Mar 14
Cochise: Death Anniv, Jun 8
Cochran, Jacqueline: Death Anniv, Aug 9
Cochran, Thad: Birth, Dec 7
Codey, Richard: Birth, Nov 27
Cody, William F. "Buffalo Bill": Birth Anniv, Feb 26
Coelacanth Discovered: Anniv, Dec 22
Coffey, Paul: Birth, Jun 1
Cohen, Sasha: Birth, Oct 26
Coin Flip for Benjamin Franklin's 300th Birthday, Jan 17
Coin Week, Natl, Apr 16
Coins Stamped "In God We Trust": Anniv, Apr 22
Cold War: Treaty Signed to Mark End: Anniv, Nov 19
Cole, Babette: Birth, Sep 10
Cole, Brock: Birth, May 29
Cole, Joanna: Birth, Aug 11
Coleman, Bessie: Birth Anniv, Jan 26
Coleman, Norm: Birth, Aug 17
Coles, Laveranues: Birth, Dec 29
Colfax, Schuyler: Birth Anniv, Mar 23
Colfer, Eoin: Birth, May 14
Collier, Christopher: Birth, Jan 29
Collier, James Lincoln: Birth, Jun 27
Collins, David R.: Birth, Feb 29
Collins, Eileen: Birth, Nov 19
Collins, Kerry: Birth, Dec 30
Collins, Stephen: Birth, Oct 1
Collins, Susan M.: Birth, Dec 7
Colombia
  Battle of Boyaca, Aug 7
  Cartagena Independence Day, Nov 11
  Independence Day, Jul 20
Colonies Become US: Anniv, Sep 9
Color TV Broadcast, First: Anniv, Jun 25
Colorado
  Admission Day, Aug 1
  Allard, Wayne: Birth, Dec 2
  Colorado Day, Aug 1
  Mesa Verde Natl Park: Anniv, Jun 29
  Owens, Bill: Birth, Oct 22
  Rocky Mountain Natl Park: Anniv, Jan 26
  Salazar, Ken: Birth, Mar 2
  State Fair (Pueblo), Aug 20
  Technology + Learning Conference (Denver), Oct 26
Coltrane, Robbie: Birth, Mar 30
Columbia Space Shuttle Disaster: Anniv, Feb 1
Columbus, Christopher
  Columbus Day (Observed), Oct 10
  Columbus Day (Traditional), Oct 12
  Columbus Day, Natl (Pres Proc), Oct 10
  Columbus Sails for New World: Anniv, Aug 3
  Columbus's Last Voyage to the New World: Anniv, Sep 18
  Discovery of Jamaica By: Anniv, May 4
Coman, Carolyn: Birth, Oct 28
Comaneci, Nadia: First Perfect Score in Olympic History: Anniv, Jul 18
Comet Crashes into Jupiter: Anniv, Jul 16
Comet, Closest Approach to Earth: Anniv, Feb 20
Comet, Halley's: Anniv of Last Perihelion, Feb 9
Comics; Comic Strips
  Bushmiller, Ernie: Birth Anniv, Aug 23
  Dick Tracy Strip Debuts: Anniv, Oct 4
  First Newspaper Strip: Anniv, Oct 18
  Funky Winkerbean: Anniv, Mar 27
  Garfield: Birthday, Jun 19
  Last Peanuts Strip: Anniv, Feb 13
  Odie: Birthday, Aug 8
  Outcault, Richard Fenton: Birth Anniv, Jan 14
  Peanuts Debuts: Anniv, Oct 2
  Schulz, Charles: Birth Anniv, Nov 26
  Segar, E.C.: Birth Anniv, Dec 8
Coming Out Day, Natl, Oct 11
Commodore Perry Day, Apr 10
Common Prayer Day (Denmark), May 12
Commonwealth Day (Belize), May 24
Commonwealth Day (United Kingdom), Mar 13
Communication Week, World, Nov 1
Communications: UN World Telecommunication Day, May 17
Communist Party Suspended, Soviet: Anniv, Aug 29
Community Education Day, Natl, Nov 15
Comoros: Independence Day, Jul 6
Compliment Day, Natl, Jan 25
Computer
  Apple II Computer Released: Anniv, Jun 5
  Eckert, J. Presper, Jr: Birth Anniv, Apr 9
  ENIAC Introduced: Anniv, Feb 14
  First Computer Chess Victory over Human: Anniv, Feb 10
  IBM PC Introduced: Anniv, Aug 12
  Internet Created: Anniv, Oct 29
  Macintosh Computer Released: Anniv, Jan 25
  Microsoft Releases Windows: Anniv, Nov 10
  Mouse Developed: Anniv, Dec 9
  Prime Number, Largest Found: Anniv, Nov 17
  Shareware Day, Intl, Dec 10
  Technology + Learning Conference (Denver, CO), Oct 26
  Typographic Smiley Face: Anniv, Sep 19
  UNIVAC: Anniv, Jun 14
  World Wide Web: Anniv, Aug 1
Concorde Flight, First: Anniv, Jan 21
Cone, David: Birth, Jan 2
Cone, Molly: Birth, Oct 3
Confederate Heroes Day, Jan 19
Confederate Memorial Day (AL, MS), Apr 24
Confederate Memorial Day (FL, GA), Apr 26
Confederate Memorial Day (NC, SC), May 10
Confederate Memorial Day/Jefferson Davis Day (KY, LA, TN), Jun 3
Confederation, Articles of: Ratification Anniv, Mar 1
Conference on Education, Natl (San Diego, CA), Feb 23
Conford, Ellen: Birth, Mar 20
Confucius: Birthday and Teachers' Day (Taiwan), Sep 28
Confucius: Birthday Observance (Hong Kong), Sep 30
Congo (Brazzaville)
  Day of National Reconciliation, Jun 10
  National Holiday, Aug 15
Congo (Kinshasa): Independence Day, Jun 30
Congress (House of Reps) First Quorum: Anniv, Apr 1
Congress Assembles (US), Jan 3
Congress First Meets in Washington: Anniv, Nov 21
Congress: First Mtg Anniv, Mar 4
Connecticut
  Connecticut Storytelling Fest (New London), Apr 28
  Dodd, Christopher J.: Birth, May 27
  Kids After Christmas (Mystic), Dec 26
  Lieberman, Joseph I.: Birth, Feb 24
  Ratification Day, Jan 9
  Rell, M. Jodi: Birth, Jun 16
Connolly, Peter: Birth, May 8
Conrad, Kent: Birth, Mar 12
Constantinople Falls to the Turks: Anniv, May 29
Constitution, US
  11th Amendment Ratified (States' Sovereignty), Feb 7
  12th Amendment Ratified (Electoral College Modified), Jun 15
  13th Amendment Ratified (Abolition of Slavery), Dec 6
  14th Amendment Ratified (Citizenship), Jul 9
  15th Amendment Ratified (Voting Rights), Feb 3
  16th Amendment Ratified (Income Tax), Feb 3
  17th Amendment Ratified (Direct Election of Senators), Apr 8
  18th Amendment Ratified (Prohibition), Jan 16
  19th Amendment Ratified (Women's Right to Vote), Aug 18
  20th Amendment Ratified (Inauguration, Congressional Opening Dates), Jan 23
  21st Amendment Ratified (Prohibition Repealed), Dec 5
  22nd Amendment Ratified (Two Term Limit), Feb 27
  23rd Amendment Ratified (DC Residents Right to Vote), Mar 29
  24th Amendment Ratified (Eliminated Poll Taxes), Jan 23
  25th Amendment Ratified (Presidential Succession, Disability), Feb 10
  26th Amendment Ratified (Voting Age to 18), Jun 30
  27th Amendment Ratified (No Midterm Congressional Pay Raises), May 19
  Bill of Rights: Anniv of First State Ratification, Nov 20
  Constitution Center Groundbreaking, Natl: Anniv, Sep 17
  Constitution of the US: Anniv, Sep 17
  Constitution Week (Pres Proc), Sep 17
  Constitution Week, Natl, Sep 17
  Constitutional Convention: Anniv, May 25
  Equal Rights Amendment Sent to States for Ratification, Mar 22
  Great Debate (Constitutional Convention): Anniv, Aug 6
  Presidential Succession Act: Anniv, Jul 18
  Religious Freedom Day, Jan 16
  Takes Effect: Anniv, Jul 2
  Women's Suffrage Amendment Introduced: Anniv, Jan 10
Construction Toy Month, Natl, Oct 1
Consumer Protection Week, Natl (Pres Proc), Feb 5
Continental Congress Assembly, First: Anniv, Sep 5
Cook, James: Birth Anniv, Oct 27
Cook, Rachael Leigh: Birth, Oct 4
Cooksey, Danny: Birth, Nov 2
Coolidge, Calvin: Birth Anniv, Jul 4
Coolidge, Grace Anna Goodhue: Birth Anniv, Jan 3
Cooney, Barbara: Birth Anniv, Aug 6
Cooney, Caroline B.: Birth, May 10
Cooney, Joan Ganz: Birth, Nov 30
Cooper, Cynthia: Birth, Apr 14
Cooper, Floyd: Birth, Jan 8
Cooper, James Fenimore: Birth Anniv, Sep 15
Cooper, Justin: Birth, Nov 17
Cooper, Susan: Birth, May 23
Cooperatives, UN Intl Day of, Jul 1
Copernicus, Nicolaus: Birth Anniv, Feb 19
Copland, Aaron: Birth Anniv, Nov 14
Copperfield, David: Birth, Sep 16
Copyright Law Passed: Anniv, May 31
Cormier, Robert: Birth Anniv, Jan 17
Cornyn, John: Birth, Feb 2
Corpus Christi: US Observance, Jun 18
Cortes Conquers Mexico: Anniv, Nov 8
Corzine, Jon: Birth, Jan 1
Cosby, Bill: Birth, Jul 12
Cosgrove, Margaret: Birth, Jun 3
Costa Rica
  Feast of Our Lady of the Angels, Aug 2
  Guanacaste Day, Jul 25
  Independence Day, Sep 15
Costas, Bob: Birth, Mar 22
Cote d'Ivoire
  National Day, Aug 7
Couch, Tim: Birth, Jul 31
Coughlin, Natalie: Birth, Aug 23
Council for Exceptional Children Annual Convention (Salt Lake City, UT), Apr 5
Council of Nicaea I: Anniv, May 20
Couric, Katie: Birth, Jan 7
Courtenay-Latimer, Marjorie: Birth Anniv, Feb 24
Cousins, Lucy: Birth, Feb 10
Cousteau, Jacques: Birth Anniv, Jun 11
Coville, Bruce: Birth, May 16
Cow Milked While Flying: Anniv, Feb 18
Cowboys, Frontier, Old West
  Battle of Little Bighorn: Anniv, Jun 25
  Burk, Martha (Calamity Jane): Death Anniv, Aug 1
  Cochise: Death Anniv, Jun 8
  Cody, William F. "Buffalo Bill": Birth Anniv, Feb 26
  Earp, Wyatt: Birth Anniv, Mar 19
  Geronimo: Death Anniv, Feb 17
  Gold Discovery, California: Anniv, Jan 24
  Last Great Buffalo Hunt: Anniv, Jun 25
  Oakley, Annie: Birth Anniv, Aug 13
  Sitting Bull: Death Anniv, Dec 15
Cowley, Joy: Birth, Aug 7
Craig, Helen: Birth, Aug 30
Craig, Larry E.: Birth, Jul 20
Crane, Whooping: Fall Migration, Sep 15
Crane, Whooping: Longest Human-Led Migration: Anniv, Dec 3
Crane, Whooping: Spring Migration, Mar 1
Crapo, Michael: Birth, May 20
Crater Lake Natl Park: Anniv, May 22
Creech, Sharon: Birth, Jul 29
Cresswell, Helen: Birth, Jul 11
Crews, Donald: Birth, Aug 30
Crispus Attucks Day, Mar 5
Croatia
  Antifascist Struggle Commemoration Day, Jun 22
  Homeland Thanksgiving Day, Aug 5
  National Day, May 30
Crocker, Ian: Birth, Aug 31
Crockett, Davy: Birth Anniv, Aug 17
Crossword Puzzle, First: Anniv, Dec 21
Cruise, Tom: Birth, Jul 3
Crutcher, Chris: Birth, Jul 17
Crystal, Billy: Birth, Mar 14
Cuba
  Anniv of the Revolution, Jan 1
  Beginning of Independence Wars Day, Oct 10
  Liberation Day: Anniv, Jan 1
  National Day, Jul 26
Cuckoo Dancing Week, Jan 11
Culkin, Macaulay: Birth, Aug 26
Culpepper, Daunte: Birth, Jan 28
Cummings, Pat: Birth, Nov 9
Cunningham, Randall: Birth, Mar 27
Curacao
  Curacao Day, Jul 26
  Kingdom Day and Antillean Flag Day, Dec 15
  Memorial Day, May 4
Curie, Marie Sklodowska: Birth Anniv, Nov 7
Curtis, Charles: Birth Anniv, Jan 25
Curtis, Christopher Paul: Birth, May 10
Curtis, Jamie Lee: Birth, Nov 22
Cusack, Ann: Birth, May 22
Cushman, Karen: Birth, Oct 4
Custer Battlefield Becomes Little Bighorn Battlefield, Nov 26
Custer, George: Battle of Little Bighorn: Anniv, Jun 25
Custodial Workers Day, Natl, Oct 2
Cutler, Jane: Birth, Sep 24
Cyprus
  Independence Day, Oct 1
Czech Republic
  Commemoration Day, Jul 6
  Foundation of the Republic, Oct 28
  Liberation Day, May 8
Czechoslovakia
  Czechoslovakia Ends Communist Rule: Anniv, Nov 29
  Czech-Slovak Divorce: Anniv, Jan 1
  Teacher's Day, Mar 28
D.A.R.E. Day, Natl (Pres Proc), Apr 13
D.A.R.E. Launched: Anniv, Sep 1
Dadey, Debbie: Birth, May 18
Daguerre, Louis: Birth Anniv, Nov 18
Dahl, Roald: Birth Anniv, Sep 13
Dairy Month, June, Jun 1
Dakides, Tara: Birth, Aug 20
Dakos, Kalli: Birth, Jun 16
Dalai Lama: Birth, Jun 6
Dallas, George: Birth Anniv, Jul 10
Damon, Matt: Birth, Oct 8
Dance
  Ailey, Alvin: Birth Anniv, Jan 5
  Ballet Introduced to US: Anniv, Feb 7
  Duncan, Isadora: Birth Anniv, May 27
  Graham, Martha: Birth Anniv, May 11
  Robinson, Bill "Bojangles": Birth Anniv, May 25
  Tap Dance Day, Natl, May 25
Daniels, Jeff: Birth, Feb 19
Daniels, Mitchell: Birth, Apr 7
Dare, Virginia: Birth Anniv, Aug 18
Darwin, Charles Robert: Birth Anniv, Feb 12
Daschle, Thomas: Birth, Dec 9
Daughters and Sons To Work Day, Take Our, Apr 27
D'Aulaire, Edgar Parin: Birth Anniv, Sep 30
D'Aulaire, Ingri: Birth Anniv, Dec 27
Davenport, Lindsay: Birth, Jun 8
David McCord Children's Literature Fest (Framingham, MA), Nov 3
Davis, Baron: Birth, Apr 13
Davis, Jefferson
  Birth Anniv, Jun 3
  Captured: Anniv, May 10
  Inauguration: Anniv, Feb 18
Davis, Jim: Birth, Jul 28
Davis, Stephen: Birth, Mar 1
Davis, Terrell: Birth, Oct 28
Davol, Marguerite W.: Birth, Jul 2
Dawes, Charles G.: Birth Anniv, Aug 27

Day of National Concern about Young People and Gun Violence, Oct 19
Day of Remembrance for Victims of Nazism (Germany), Jan 27
Day of the Five Billion: Anniv, Jul 11
Day of the Six Billion: Anniv, Oct 12
Day, Alexandra: Birth, Sep 7
Daylight Saving Time Begins, US, Apr 2
Daylight Saving Time Ends, US, Oct 30
Days of Prayer and Remembrance, Natl (Pres Proc), Sep 9
Dayton, Mark: Birth, Jan 26
D-Day: Anniv, Jun 6
de Angeli, Marguerite: Birth Anniv, Mar 14
De Forest, Lee: Birth Anniv, Aug 26
de Trevino, Elizabeth Borton: Birth, Sep 2
Deaf Awareness Week, Sep 18
Deaf Day, Mother, Father, Apr 30
Deaf History Month, Mar 13
Deaf, First School for: Anniv, Apr 15
Dean, Dizzy: Birth Anniv, Jan 16
Debate, Great (Over Constitution): Anniv, Aug 6
Deborah Samson Day (MA), May 23
Debussy, Claude: Birth Anniv, Aug 22
Decatur, Stephen: Birth Anniv, Jan 5
Declaration of Independence
Approval and Initial Signing: Anniv, **Jul 4**
First Public Reading: Anniv, **Jul 8**
Official Signing: Anniv, **Aug 2**
Resolution Anniv, **Jul 2**
DeClements, Barthe: Birth, Oct 8
Decoration Day (Memorial Day), May 29
Deem, James M.: Birth, Jan 27
Deepavali, Nov 1
DeFelice, Cynthia: Birth, Dec 28
Defenders Day, Sep 12
Degas, Edgar: Birth Anniv, Jul 19
Degen, Bruce: Birth, Jun 14
DeGroat, Diane: Birth, May 24
Del Negro, Janice: Birth, Jul 5
Delacre, Lulu: Birth, Dec 20
Delaware
Biden, Joseph R., Jr: Birth, **Nov 20**
Carper, Tom: Birth, **Jan 23**
Minner, Ruth Ann: Birth, **Jan 17**
Ratification Day, **Dec 7**
State Fair (Harrington), **Jul 20**
Delessert, Etienne: Birth, Jan 4
Demi: Birth, Sep 2
DeMint, Jim: Birth, Sep 2
Denali Natl Park Established: Anniv, Dec 2
Denmark
Common Prayer Day, **May 12**
Constitution Day, **Jun 5**
Midsummer Eve, **Jun 23**
Queen Margrethe's Birthday, **Apr 16**
Dental Drill Patent: Anniv, Jan 26
Dental Health Month, Natl Children's, Feb 1
Dental Hygiene Month, Natl, Oct 1
Dental School, First Woman to Graduate: Anniv, Feb 21
DePaola, Tomie: Birth, Sep 15
Department of Homeland Security Created: Anniv, Nov 25
Depression Awareness Day, Childhood, May 2
Desegregated, US Army First: Anniv, Jul 26
Desert Storm: Kuwait Liberated: Anniv, Feb 27
Desert Storm: Persian Gulf War Begins: Anniv, Jan 16
Designated Hitter Rule Adopted: Anniv, Jan 11
Desimini, Lisa: Birth, Mar 21
Desk Day, Natl Clean-Off-Your, Jan 9
Devers, Gail: Birth, Nov 19
Devil's Night, Oct 30
DeVito, Danny: Birth, Nov 17
Dewey, Jennifer Owings: Birth, Oct 2
Dewey, John: Birth Anniv, Oct 20
Dewey, Melvil: Birth Anniv, Dec 10
DeWine, Mike: Birth, Jan 5
Dia de la Raza (Mexico), Oct 12
Diabetes Assn Alert Day, American, Mar 28
Diabetes Month, Natl (Pres Proc), Nov 1
Diallo, Mamadou: Birth, Aug 28
Diamond, Hope, Mailed to Smithsonian: Anniv, Nov 8
Diana, Princess of Wales: Birth Anniv, Jul 1
Diaz, Cameron: Birth, Aug 30
DiCaprio, Leonardo: Birth, Nov 11
Dick Tracy Comic Strip Debuts: Anniv, Oct 4
Dickens, Charles: Birth Anniv, Feb 7
Dickinson, Emily: Birth Anniv, Dec 10
Dickinson, Peter: Birth, Dec 16
Dictionary Day, Oct 16
Didrikson, Babe: See Zaharias, Mildred Babe Didrikson, Jun 26
Diefenbaker, John: Birth Anniv, Sep 18
Diego, Jose de: Birth Anniv, Apr 16
Dien Bien Phu Falls: Anniv, May 7
Dillon, Barbara: Birth, Sep 2
Dillon, Corey: Birth, Oct 24
Dillon, Diane: Birth, Mar 13
Dillon, Leo: Birth, Mar 2
DiMaggio, Joe: Birth Anniv, Nov 25
Dinosaur Month, Intl, Oct 1
Dinosaurs
Archaeopteryx Fossil Discovery Announced: Anniv, **Sep 30**
Coelacanth Discovered: Anniv, **Dec 22**
Dinosaur Month, Intl, **Oct 1**
First Full-Size Replicas: Anniv, **Jun 10**
Jobaria Exhibited: Anniv, **Nov 13**
Sue Exhibited: Anniv, **May 17**
SuperCroc Discovered: Anniv, **Aug 30**
Disabilities
Americans with Disabilities Act: Anniv, **Jul 26**
Barrier Awareness Day in Kentucky, **May 7**
Clerc-Gallaudet Week, **Dec 4**
Deaf Awareness Week, **Sep 18**
Deaf History Month, **Mar 13**
Disability Day in Kentucky, **Aug 2**
Disability Employment Awareness Month, Natl (Pres Proc), **Oct 1**
Disabled Persons, Intl Day of, **Dec 3**
First School for Deaf: Anniv, **Apr 15**
Mother, Father Deaf Day, **Apr 30**
Disarmament Week, Oct 24
Dishonor List, New Year's, Jan 1
Disney World Opened: Anniv, Oct 1
Disney, Walt: Birth Anniv, Dec 5
Disneyland Opened: Anniv, Jul 17
Divac, Vlade: Birth, Feb 3
Diversity Awareness Month, Oct 1
Diwali, Nov 1
Dix, Dorothea L.: Birth Anniv, Apr 4
Djibouti: Independence Day, Jun 27
Doctors' Day, Mar 30
Dodd, Christopher J.: Birth, May 27
Dodge, Hazel: Birth, Mar 19
Dodge, Mary Mapes: Birth Anniv, Jan 26
Dodgson, Charles Lutwidge: See Carroll, Lewis, Jan 27
Dog Days, Jul 3
Dog Week, Natl, Sep 18
Dogs
Adopt-a-Shelter Dog Month, **Oct 1**
Balto: Sled Dog Hero: Death Anniv, **Mar 14**
Dog Week, Natl, **Sep 18**
Seeing Eye Created in America: Anniv, **Jan 29**
Sled Dogs Save Nome: Anniv, **Feb 2**
Stubby Joins WWI Front Lines: Anniv, **Feb 5**
Togo: Sled Dog Hero: Death Anniv, **Dec 5**
Dole, Elizabeth Hanford: Birth, Jul 29
Doll Fest (Japan), Mar 3
Dolphins Shield Swimmers from Great White Shark: Anniv, Oct 30
Domenici, Pete V.: Birth, May 7
Domestic Violence Awareness Month, Oct 1
Dominica: National Day, Nov 3
Dominican Republic
Independence Day, **Feb 27**
National Holiday, **Jan 26**
Restoration of the Republic, **Aug 16**
Donald Duck: Birth, Jun 9
Donate Life Month, Natl (Pres Proc), Apr 1
Donovan, Landon: Birth, Mar 4
Don't Step on a Bee Day, Jul 10
Doolittle, Eliza: Day, May 20
Dorgan, Byron L.: Birth, May 14
Dormition of Theotokos, Aug 15
Dorough, Howie: Birth, Aug 22
Dorros, Arthur: Birth, May 19
Dorsey, Thomas A.: Birth Anniv, Jul 1
Doty, Roy: Birth, Sep 10
Double 10th Day (China), Oct 10
Douglas, James: Birth, Jun 21
Douglas, William O.: Birth Anniv, Oct 16
Douglass, Frederick
Death Anniv, **Feb 20**
Escape to Freedom: Anniv, **Sep 3**
Frederick Douglass Speaks: Anniv, **Aug 11**
Doyle, Jim: Birth, Nov 23
Dragon Boat Fest (China), May 31
Dragonball Z TV Premiere: Anniv, Apr 26
Dragons: Appreciate a Dragon Day, Jan 16
Dragonwagon, Crescent: Birth, Nov 25
Draper, Sharon M.: Birth, Aug 21
Drew, Charles: Birth Anniv, Jun 3
Drinking Straw Patented: Anniv, Jan 3
Drowning Prevention Day, Natl (Canada), Jul 23
Drug Abuse/Illicit Trafficking, Intl Day Against (UN), Jun 26
Drum Month, Intl, Nov 1
Du Bois, W.E.B.: Birth Anniv, Feb 23
Du Bois, W.E.B.: Niagara Movement Founded: Anniv, Jul 11
Du Bois, William Pene: Birth Anniv, May 9
Ducky Fleet Sails the Pacific: Anniv, Jan 10
Duffey, Betsy: Birth, Feb 6
Duke, Patty: Birth, Dec 14
Dumb Week (Greece), Apr 9
Dunant, Jean Henri: Birth Anniv, May 8
Duncan, Isadora: Birth Anniv, May 27
Duncan, Lois: Birth, Apr 28
Duncan, Tim: Birth, Apr 25
Dunleavy, Mike: Birth, Sep 15
Dunn, Adam: Birth, Nov 9
Dunn, Shannon: Birth, Nov 26
Dunn, Warrick: Birth, Jan 5
Durbin, Richard J.: Birth, Nov 21
Duvoisin, Roger: Birth Anniv, Aug 28
Dygard, Thomas J.: Birth, Aug 10
Eager, Edward: Death Anniv, Oct 23
Earhart, Amelia: Birth Anniv, Jul 24
Earhart, Amelia: Disappears: Anniv, Jul 2
Earhart, Amelia: First Ladies Take Flight: Anniv, Apr 20
Earmuffs Patented: Anniv, Mar 13
Earnhardt, Dale, Jr.: Birth, Oct 10
Earp, Wyatt: Birth Anniv, Mar 19
Earth at Aphelion, Jul 3
Earth at Perihelion, Jan 4
Earth Day (Environment), Apr 22
Earth, First Picture of, From Space: Anniv, Aug 7
Earthquake
Earthquake Strikes Alaska: Anniv, **Mar 27**
Indian Earthquake, **Jan 26**
Japan Suffers Major Quake: Anniv, **Jan 17**
Mexico City Earthquake: Anniv, **Sep 19**
Missouri Earthquakes: Anniv, **Dec 6**
Most Powerful of the 20th Century: Anniv, **May 22**
San Francisco 1906 Earthquake: Anniv, **Apr 18**
San Francisco 1989 Earthquake: Anniv, **Oct 17**
Southern California: Anniv, **Jan 17**
Turkish Earthquake: Anniv, **Aug 17**
Earth's Rotation Proved: Anniv, Jan 8
Easley, Mike: Birth, Mar 23
East Coast Blackout: Anniv, Nov 9
East Timor: Independence: Anniv, May 20
Easter
Easter Even, **Apr 15**
Easter Monday, **Apr 17**
Easter Sunday, **Apr 16**
Easter Sundays Through the Year 2008, **Apr 16**
Holy Week, **Apr 9**
Orthodox Easter Sunday, **Apr 23**
Passion Week, **Apr 1**
Passiontide, **Apr 2**
White House Easter Egg Roll, **Apr 17**
White House Easter Egg Roll: Anniv, **Apr 2**
Easter Rising (Ireland), Apr 24
Eastman, P.D.: Birth, Nov 25
Easy-Bake Oven Debuts: Anniv, Feb 1
Eat Better, Eat Together Month, Oct 1
Eat What You Want Day, May 11
Eckert, Allan W.: Birth, Jan 30
Eckert, J. Presper, Jr: Birth Anniv, Apr 9
Eclipses
Lunar Eclipse, **Oct 17**
Lunar Eclipse, **Mar 14**
Solar Eclipse, **Oct 3**
Solar Eclipse, **Mar 29**
Ecuador
Battle of Pichincha Day, **May 24**
Day of Quito, **Dec 6**
Independence Day, **Aug 10**
Edelman, Marian Wright: Birth, Jun 6
Edens, Cooper: Birth, Sep 25
Ederle, Gertrude: Birth Anniv, Oct 23
Ederle, Gertrude: Swims English Channel: Anniv, Aug 6
Edison, Thomas Alva
Birth Anniv, **Feb 11**
Black Maria Studio: Anniv, **Feb 1**
Incandescent Lamp Demonstrated: Anniv, **Oct 21**
Record of a Sneeze: Anniv, **Feb 2**
Edmonds, Jim: Birth, Jun 27
Edmund Fitzgerald Sinking: Anniv, Nov 10
Education, Learning, Schools
American Education Week, **Nov 13**
American Education Week (Pres Proc), **Nov 13**
American Federation of Teachers Convention (San Francisco, CA), **Jul 18**
Art Education Assn Annual Convention (Boston, MA), **Mar 4**
Catholic Educational Assn Convention/Expo, Natl (New Orleans, LA), **Apr 18**
Catholic Schools Week, **Jan 29**
Chemistry Week, Natl, **Oct 17**
Children's Vision and Learning Month, **Aug 1**
Community Education Day, Natl, **Nov 15**
Conference on Education, Natl (San Diego, CA), **Feb 23**
Council for Exceptional Children (Salt Lake City, UT), **Apr 5**
Day of the Teacher/El Dia Del Maestro (CA), **May 10**
Education Assn Mtg, Natl (Orlando, FL), **Jun 30**
Education Goals, Natl: Anniv, **Feb 1**
Education of Young Children, Natl Assn for the, Conference (Washington, DC), **Dec 7**
Educational Bosses Week, Natl, **May 21**
Educational Support Personnel Day, Natl, **Nov 16**
Elementary School Principals, Natl Assn of, Annual Conference (San Antonio, TX), **Apr 1**
Family Sexuality Education Month, Natl, **Oct 1**
Field Trip Month, Natl Go on a, **Oct 1**
Froebel, Friedrich: Birth Anniv, **Apr 21**
Geographic Bee Finals, Natl (Washington, DC), **May 23**
Geographic Bee, Natl, Registration Deadline Approaching, **Oct 1**
Geographic Bee, School Level, Natl, **Nov 14**
Geographic Bee, State Level, Natl, **Mar 31**
Geographic Education, Natl Council for, Mtg (Birmingham, AL), **Oct 12**
Geography Awareness Week, Natl, **Nov 13**
Gifted Children Convention, Natl Assn (Louisville, KY), **Nov 9**
Historically Black Colleges and Universities Week, Natl (Pres Proc), **Sep 11**
Hooray for Year-Round School Day, **Jun 9**
Kindergarten Day, **Apr 21**
Library Week, Natl, **Apr 2**
Literacy Day, Intl (UN), **Sep 8**
Mathematics, Natl Council of Teachers of, Annual Mtg (St. Louis, MO), **Apr 26**
MENC Natl Conference (Salt Lake City, UT), **Apr 18**
Mentoring Month, Natl, **Jan 1**
Metric Week, Natl, **Oct 9**
Middle Level Education Month, Natl, **Mar 1**
Middle School Assn, Natl, Annual Conference (Philadelphia, PA), **Nov 3**
Museum Day, Intl, **May 18**
Music in Our Schools Month, **Mar 1**
Natl Council of Teachers of English Annual Convention (Pittsburgh, PA), **Nov 17**
Newspaper in Education Week, **Mar 6**
No Homework Day, **May 6**
NSSEA Ed Expo & School Equipment Show (Orlando, FL), **Mar 2**
One Hundredth Day of School, **Feb 7**
Paraprofessional Appreciation Day, **Apr 5**
Parents as Teachers Day, Natl, **Nov 8**
Project ACES Day, **May 3**
PTA Convention, Natl (Phoenix, AZ), **Jun 24**
PTA Founders' Day, Natl, **Feb 17**
PTA Teacher Appreciation Week, Natl, **May 1**
Public School, First in America: Anniv, **Apr 23**
Reading Is Fun Week, **May 14**
School Boards Assn Annual Conference, Natl (New Orleans, LA), **Apr 8**
School Counseling Week, Natl, **Feb 6**
School for Deaf Founded, First: Anniv, **Apr 15**
School Library Media Month, **Apr 1**
School Lunch Week, Natl, **Oct 9**
School Principals' Day, **May 1**
School Principals' Recognition Day (MA), **Apr 27**
School Success Month, Natl, **Sep 1**
School Support Staff Week, **May 21**
Science Teachers Assn Convention, Natl (Anaheim, CA), **Apr 6**
Social Studies, Natl Council for the, Annual Mtg (Kansas City, MO), **Nov 17**
Spelling Bee Finals, Natl (Washington, DC), **May 31**
Substitute Teacher Appreciation Week, **Sep 12**

Sullivan, Anne: Birth Anniv, **Apr 14**
Supervision and Curriculum Development, Assn for, Convention (Chicago, IL), **Mar 1**
Teacher Day, Natl, **May 9**
Teacher's Day (Czech Republic), **Mar 28**
Teacher's Day (FL), **May 19**
Teacher's Day (MA), **Jun 4**
Thank You, School Librarian Day, **Apr 5**
Truancy Law: Anniv, **Apr 12**
Tutor Appreciation Day, **Apr 8**
World Teachers' Day (UN), **Oct 5**
Educational Communications and Technology, Assn for, Annual Convention (Orlando, FL), Oct 18
Edwards, Julie Andrews: Birth, Oct 1
Edwards, Teresa: Birth, Jul 19
Egg Month, Natl, May 1
Egg Roll, White House Easter: Anniv, Apr 2
Egg Salad Week, Apr 16
Egielski, Richard: Birth, Jul 16
Egypt
Camp David Accord Signed: Anniv, **Mar 26**
National Day, **Jul 23**
Sinai Day, **Apr 25**
Ehlert, Lois: Birth, Nov 9
Ehrlich, Robert, Jr: Birth, Nov 25
Eid-al-Adha: Feast of the Sacrifice (Islamic), Jan 10
Eid-al-Fitr: Celebrating the Fast, Nov 4
Eiffel Tower: Anniv (Paris, France), Mar 31
Eiffel, Alexandre Gustave: Birth Anniv, Dec 15
Einstein, Albert: Atomic Bomb Letter Anniv, Aug 2
Einstein, Albert: Birth Anniv, Mar 14
Eisenberg, Hallie Kate: Birth, Aug 2
Eisenhower, Dwight David: Birth Anniv, Oct 14
Eisenhower, Mamie Doud: Birth Anniv, Nov 14
Eisner, Michael: Birth, Mar 7
El Salvador
Day of the First Shout for Independence, **Nov 5**
Day of the Soldier, **May 7**
Independence Day, **Sep 15**
Natl Day of Peace, **Jan 16**
Election Day, Nov 8
Electric Lighting, First: Anniv, Sep 4
Electricity: Incandescent Lamp Demonstrated: Anniv, Oct 21
Elementary School Principals, Natl Assn of, Annual Conference (San Antonio, TX), Apr 1
Elephants
Elephant Appreciation Day, **Sep 22**
Jumbo Arrives in America: Anniv, **Apr 9**
Jumbo: Death Anniv, **Sep 15**
Round-Up at Surin (Thailand), **Nov 19**
Eliot, John: Birth Anniv, Aug 5
Elizabeth I: Birth Anniv, Sep 7
Elizabeth II, Accession of Queen: Anniv, Feb 6
Elizabeth II: Birth, Apr 21
Ellerbee, Linda: Birth, Aug 15
Ellington, Duke: Birth Anniv, Apr 29
Elliott, Bill: Birth, Oct 8
Ellis Island Family History Day (New York, NY), Apr 17
Ellis Island Opened: Anniv, Jan 1
Ellis, Sarah: Birth, May 19
Ellsworth, Oliver: Birth Anniv, Apr 29
Elway, John: Birth, Jun 28
Emancipation Day (Texas), Jun 19
Emancipation of 500: Anniv, Aug 1
Emancipation Proclamation: Anniv, Sep 22
Emberley, Ed: Birth, Oct 19
Emmett, Daniel D.: Birth Anniv, Oct 29
Emoticon: See Typographic Smiley Face: Anniv, Sep 19
Employment (employers, occupations, professions)
Agriculture Day, Natl, **Mar 20**
Agriculture Week, Natl, **Mar 19**
Clown Week, Intl, **Aug 1**
Custodial Workers Day, Natl, **Oct 2**
Educational Bosses Week, Natl, **May 21**
Engineers Week, Natl, **Feb 19**
Introduce a Girl to Engineering Day, **Feb 23**
Labor Day (US, Canada), **Sep 5**
Nurses Day and Week, Natl, **May 6**
Peace Officer Memorial Day, Natl, **May 15**
Police Week, Natl, **May 14**
Printing Week, Intl, **Jan 15**
Shop/Office Workers' Holiday (Iceland), **Aug 1**
Take Our Daughters and Sons to Work Day, **Apr 27**
Weatherman's Day, **Feb 5**
Working Women's Day, Intl, **Mar 8**
Endangered Species Act: Anniv, Dec 28
Energy Education Week, Natl, Mar 20
Engdahl, Sylvia Louise: Birth, Nov 24
Engineers Week, Natl, Feb 19
England
Accession of Queen Elizabeth II: Anniv, **Feb 6**
Great Britain Formed: Anniv, **May 1**
Great Fire of London: Anniv, **Sep 2**
Guy Fawkes Day, **Nov 5**
Last Hurrah for British Hong Kong, **Jun 30**
Plough Monday, **Jan 9**
Saint George: Feast Day, **Apr 23**
Scotland Yard: First Appearance Anniv, **Sep 29**
English Colony in North America, First: Anniv, Aug 5
ENIAC Computer Introduced: Anniv, Feb 14
Ensign, John: Birth, Mar 25
Environmental
America Recycles Day, **Nov 15**
Arbor Day, Natl, **Apr 28**
Bike to Work Day, Natl, **May 19**
Biological Diversity, Intl Day for, **May 22**
Chernobyl Reactor Disaster: Anniv, **Apr 26**
Clean Air Act Passed by Congress: Anniv, **Dec 17**
Disaster Reduction, Natural, Intl Day For (UN), **Oct 12**
Earth Day, **Apr 22**
Endangered Species Act: Anniv, **Dec 28**
Environment Day, World (UN), **Jun 5**
Environmental Policy Act, Natl: Anniv, **Jan 1**
Exxon Valdez Oil Spill: Anniv, **Mar 24**
International Coastal Cleanup Day, **Sep 17**
Preservation of the Ozone Layer, UN Intl Day for, **Sep 16**
President's Environmental Youth Award Natl Competition, **Jul 31**
PTA Earth Week, Natl, **Apr 16**
Public Lands Day, Natl, **Sep 18**
Recreation and Parks Month, Natl, **Jul 1**
River of Words Poetry and Art Contest, **Feb 15**
Rivers Month, Natl, **Jun 1**
Save the Rhino Day, **May 1**
Sierra Club Founded: Anniv, **May 28**
Silent Spring Publication: Anniv, **Apr 13**
Sky Awareness Week, **Apr 23**
Water Pollution Control Act: Anniv, **Oct 18**
Water, World Day for (UN), **Mar 22**
Week of the Ocean, Natl, **Apr 2**
World Day to Combat Desertification and Drought, **Jun 17**
Enzi, Michael B.: Birth, Feb 1
Epiphany (Twelfth Day), Jan 6
Equatorial Guinea
Armed Forces Day, **Aug 3**
Constitution Day, **Aug 15**
Independence Day, **Oct 12**
Equinox, Autumn, Sep 22
Equinox, Spring, Mar 20
Erdrich, Louise: Birth, Jun 7
Erie Canal: Anniv, Oct 26
Erikson, Leif: Day (Iceland), Oct 9
Erikson, Leif: Day (Pres Proc), Oct 9
Eritrea: Independence Day, May 24
Erstad, Darin: Birth, Jun 4
Esposito, Phil: Birth, Feb 20
Esposito, Tony: Birth, Apr 23
Estes, Eleanor: Birth Anniv, May 9
Estonia
Baltic States' Independence Recognized: Anniv, **Sep 6**
Day of National Rebirth, **Nov 16**
Independence Day, **Feb 24**
Victory Day, **Jun 23**
Eta Aquarids Meteor Shower, Apr 21
Etch-A-Sketch Introduced: Anniv, Jul 12
Ethiopia
Adwa Day, **Mar 2**
Cross Day, **Sep 27**
New Year's Day, **Sep 11**
Patriots Victory Day, **May 5**
Timket, **Jan 19**
Etiquette Week, Natl, May 21
Etiquette: Children's Good Manners Month, Sep 1
Euro Introduced: Anniv, Jan 1
European Union: Schuman Plan Anniv, May 9
Evacuation Day (MA), Mar 17
Everett, Edward: Birth Anniv, Apr 11
Everett, Rupert: Birth, May 29
Everglades Natl Park: Anniv, Dec 6
Evert Lloyd, Chris: Birth, Dec 21
Ewing, Patrick: Birth, Aug 5
Exchange Club: Freedom Shrine Month, May 1
Exxon Valdez Oil Spill: Anniv, Mar 24
Ezer, Sarah: Birth, Feb 26
Fahrenheit, Gabriel D.: Birth Anniv, May 14
Fair, Lorrie: Birth, Aug 5
Fairbanks, Charles W.: Birth Anniv, May 11
Fall of the Alamo: Anniv, Mar 6
Family
Adoption Week, Natl, **Nov 20**
Ancestor Appreciation Day, **Sep 27**
Domestic Violence Awareness Month, **Oct 1**
Eat Better, Eat Together Month, **Oct 1**
Families, UN Intl Day of, **May 15**
Family Caregivers Month, Natl (Pres Proc), **Nov 1**
Family Day in Nevada, **Nov 25**
Family Health Month, **Oct 1**
Family Literacy Day, Natl, **Nov 1**
Family Month, Natl, **May 14**
Family Sexuality Education Month, Natl, **Oct 1**
Family Week, Natl, **May 7**
Family Week, Natl (Pres Proc), **Nov 20**
Family-Leave Bill: Anniv, **Feb 5**
Father-Daughter Take a Walk Together Day, **Jul 7**
Father's Day, **Jun 18**
Father's Day (Pres Proc), **Jun 18**
Frugal Fun Day, Intl, **Oct 1**
Grandparents' Day, Natl, **Sep 11**
Love the Children Day, **Mar 29**
Mother's Day, **May 14**
Moving Month, Natl, **May 1**
Parents as Teachers Day, Natl, **Nov 8**
School Success Month, Natl, **Sep 1**
Take Our Daughters and Sons to Work Day, **Apr 27**
Talk With Your Teen About Sex Month, Natl, **Mar 1**
Universal Children's Week, **Oct 1**
Visit Your Relatives Day, **May 18**
Farber, Norma: Birth Anniv, Aug 6
Farley, Walter: Birth Anniv, Jun 26
Farm Safety Week, Natl (Pres Proc), Sep 18
Farm-City Week, Natl (Pres Proc), Nov 18
Farmer, Nancy: Birth, Jul 9
Farragut, David: Battle of Mobile Bay: Anniv, Aug 5
Fasching (Germany, Austria), Feb 27
Fasching Sunday (Germany, Austria), Feb 26
Fast of Esther: Ta'anit Esther, Mar 13
Fast of Gedalya, Oct 6
Fat Tuesday (Mardi Gras), Feb 28
Father-Daughter Take a Walk Together Day, Jul 7
Father's Day, Jun 18
Father's Day (Pres Proc), Jun 18
Fatone, Joey: Birth, Jan 28
Faulk, Marshall: Birth, Feb 26
Favre, Brett: Birth, Oct 10
Fawkes, Guy: Day (England), Nov 5
Feast of Lanterns (Bon Fest) (Japan), Jul 13
Feast of St. Paul's Shipwreck (Valletta, Malta), Feb 10
Feast of the Immaculate Conception, Dec 8
Federal Communications Commission Created: Anniv, Feb 26
Fedorov, Sergei: Birth, Dec 13
Feelings, Tom: Birth, May 19
Feiffer, Jules: Birth, Jan 26
Feingold, Russell D.: Birth, Mar 2
Feinstein, Dianne: Birth, Jun 22
Fence Painting Contest: Natl Tom Sawyer (Hannibal, MO), Jul 1
Fermi, Enrico: Birth Anniv, Sep 29
Fernandez, Lisa: Birth, Feb 22
Ferris Wheel Day, Feb 14
Fiedler, Jay: Birth, Dec 29
Field Trip Month, Natl Go on a, Oct 1
Field, Sally: Birth, Nov 6
Fiji: Independence Day, Oct 10
Fillmore, Abigail P.: Birth Anniv, Mar 13
Fillmore, Caroline: Birth Anniv, Oct 21
Fillmore, Millard: Birth Anniv, Jan 7
Film
Academy Awards, First: Anniv, **May 16**
Black Maria Studio: Anniv, **Feb 1**
Bugs Bunny's Debut: Anniv, **Apr 30**
Chicago Intl Children's Film Fest (Chicago, IL), **Oct 27**
Donald Duck: Birth, **Jun 9**
First Movie Theater Opens, **Apr 23**
KidFilm Fest (Dallas, TX), **Jan 3**
Mickey Mouse's Birthday, **Nov 18**
Record of a Sneeze: Anniv, **Feb 2**
Star Wars Released: Anniv, **May 25**
Wizard of Oz First Released: Anniv, **Aug 25**
Fine, Anne: Birth, Dec 7
Finland
Flag Day, **Jun 4**
Independence Day: Anniv, **Dec 6**
Finley, Michael: Birth, Mar 6
Fire
Apollo Spacecraft Fire: Anniv, **Jan 27**
Fire Prevention Week, **Oct 9**
Fire Prevention Week (Pres Proc), **Oct 9**
Firepup's Birthday, **Oct 1**
Great Chicago Fire: Anniv, **Oct 8**
Great Fire of London: Anniv, **Sep 2**
Peshtigo (WI) Forest Fire: Anniv, **Oct 8**
Triangle Shirtwaist Fire: Anniv, **Mar 25**
Fireworks Safety Months, Jun 1
First American to Orbit Earth: Anniv, Feb 20
First Automatic Toll Collection Machine: Anniv, Nov 19
First Car Insurance: Anniv, Feb 1
Firsts
First Commercial Oil Well: Anniv, **Aug 27**
First Complete Circle in an Airplane: Anniv, **Sep 20**
First Computer Chess Victory over Human: Anniv, **Feb 10**
First Dictionary of American English Published: Anniv, **Apr 14**
First Elected Woman Senator: Anniv, **Jan 12**
First Flight Attendant: Anniv, **May 15**
First Full-Size Dinosaur Replicas: Anniv, **Jun 10**
First License Plates: Anniv, **Apr 25**
First Manned Private Spaceflight: Anniv, **Jun 21**
First McDonald's Opens: Anniv, **Apr 15**
First Movie Theater Opens: Anniv, **Apr 23**
First Newspaper Comic Strip: Anniv, **Oct 18**
First Perfect Score in Olympic History: Anniv, **Jul 18**
First Photographs in a Newspaper Report: Anniv, **Jul 1**
First Presidential Telecast: Anniv, **Apr 30**
First Radio Broadcast by a President: Anniv, **Jun 14**
First Roller Coaster Opens: Anniv, **Jun 13**
First Scheduled Radio Broadcast: Anniv, **Nov 2**
First Session of the Supreme Court: Anniv, **Feb 1**
First Televised Presidential Debate: Anniv, **Sep 26**
First US Census: Anniv, **Aug 1**
First US Income Tax: Anniv, **Mar 8**
First US Transcontinental Car Trip: Anniv, **Jul 26**
First Winter Olympics: Anniv, **Jan 25**
First Woman Supreme Court Justice: Anniv, **Sep 25**
Fiscal Year, US Federal, Oct 1
Fisher, Leonard Everett: Birth, Jun 24
Fisk, Carlton: Birth, Dec 26
Fitch, Sheree: Birth, Dec 3
Fitness, Physical, and Sports Month, Natl, May 1
Fitzgerald, John D.: Death Anniv, May 21
Fitzhugh, Louise: Birth Anniv, Oct 5
5-A-Day Month, Natl, Sep 1
Flag Act of 1818: Anniv, Apr 4
Flag Day (Pres Proc), Jun 14
Flag Day USA, Pause for Pledge, Natl, Jun 14
Flag Day: Anniv of the Stars and Stripes, Jun 14
Flag of Canada Day, Natl, Feb 15
Flag Week, Natl (Pres Proc), Jun 11
Fleischman, Paul: Birth, Sep 5
Fleischman, Sid: Birth, Mar 16
Fleming, Alexander: Birth Anniv, Aug 6
Fleming, Denise: Birth, Jan 31
Fleming, Ian: Birth Anniv, May 28
Fletcher, Ernie: Birth, Nov 12
Fleury, Theo: Birth, Jun 29
Flintstones TV Premiere: Anniv, Sep 30
Flood, Johnstown: Anniv, May 31
Florian, Douglas: Birth, Mar 18
Florida
Admission Day, **Mar 3**
Arbor Day, **Jan 20**
Biscayne Natl Park: Anniv, **Jun 28**
Bush, Jeb: Birth, **Feb 11**
Children's Day, **Apr 11**
Confederate Memorial Day, **Apr 26**
Disney World Opened: Anniv, **Oct 1**
Education Assn Mtg, Natl (Orlando), **Jun 30**
Educational Communications and Technology, Assn for, Annual Convention (Orlando), **Oct 18**
Everglades Natl Park: Anniv, **Dec 6**
Grandmother's Day, **Oct 9**
Juneteenth, **Jun 19**
Martinez, Mel: Birth, **Oct 23**
Nelson, Bill: Birth, **Sep 29**
NSSEA Ed Expo & School Equipment Show (Orlando), **Mar 2**
Pan-American Day, **Apr 14**
Pascua Florida Day, **Apr 2**
Patriot's Day, **Apr 19**

Poetry Day, **May 25**
Ponce de Leon Discovers Florida: Anniv, **Apr 2**
Retired Teacher's Day, **Nov 19**
Save the Florida Panther Day, **Mar 18**
State Day, **Apr 2**
State Fair (Tampa), **Feb 9**
Teacher's Day, **May 19**
TESOL Annual Conference (Tampa Bay), **Mar 15**
Flowers, Flower Shows
Flower Fest (Hana Matsuri, Japan), **Apr 8**
Lei Day (Hawaii), **May 1**
Poinsettia Day, **Dec 12**
Rose Month, Natl, **Jun 1**
Tournament of Roses Parade (Pasadena, CA), **Jan 1**
World's Largest, Smelliest Discovered by Science, **Aug 6**
Floyd, William: Birth Anniv, Dec 17
Flu Pandemic of 1918 Hits US: Anniv, Mar 11
Fonteyn, Margot: Birth Anniv, May 18
Food Allergy Awareness Month, Natl, Sep 1
Food and Beverage-Related Events and Observances
Appert, Nicholas: Birth Anniv, **Oct 23**
Baked Bean Month, Natl, **Jul 1**
Barbecue Month, Natl, **May 1**
Blueberries Month, Natl, **Jul 1**
Bun Day (Iceland), **Feb 27**
Cherry Month, Natl, **Feb 1**
Dairy Month, June, **Jun 1**
Eat Better, Eat Together Month, **Oct 1**
Eat What You Want Day, **May 11**
Egg Month, Natl, **May 1**
Egg Salad Week, **Apr 16**
First McDonald's Opens: Anniv, **Apr 15**
Food Fight, World's Largest: La Tomatina (Spain), **Aug 31**
Frozen Food Month, Natl, **Mar 1**
Hamburger Month, Natl, **May 1**
Honey Month, Natl, **Sep 1**
Hot Breakfast Month, Natl, **Feb 1**
Hot Dog Month, Natl, **Jul 1**
Ice Cream Cone: Birth, **Sep 22**
Ice Cream Day, Natl, **Jul 16**
June Is Turkey Lovers' Month, **Jun 1**
Mustard Day, Natl, **Aug 6**
North Carolina SweetPotato Month, **Feb 1**
Oatmeal Month, **Jan 1**
Peanut Butter Lovers' Month, **Nov 1**
Pecan Day, **Mar 25**
Popcorn Poppin' Month, Natl, **Oct 1**
Return Shopping Carts to the Supermarket Month, **Feb 1**
Rice God, Day of the (Chiyoda, Japan), **Jun 4**
Rice Planting Fest (Osaka, Japan), **Jun 14**
Salsa Month, Natl, **May 1**
Sandwich Day, **Nov 3**
School Breakfast Week, Natl, **Mar 6**
Soul Food Month, Natl, **Jun 1**
Vegetarian Day, World, **Oct 1**
Vegetarian Month, **Oct 1**
Vegetarian Resource Group's Essay Contest for Kids, **May 1**
World Food Day, **Oct 16**
World Food Day (UN), **Oct 16**
Football
Football League, Natl, Formed: Anniv, **Sep 17**
PSFCA East West All-Star Game (Altoona, PA), **Jun 24**
Rose Bowl Game (Pasadena, CA), **Jan 1**
Super Bowl (Detroit, MI), **Feb 5**
Foote, Adam: Birth, Jul 10
Forbes, Esther: Birth Anniv, Jun 28
Ford, Betty: Birth, Apr 8
Ford, Gerald R.: Birth, Jul 14
Ford, Gerald: Veep Day, Aug 9
Ford, Gerald: Vice President Sworn In: Anniv, Dec 6
Ford, Harrison: Birth, Jul 13
Foreign Languages, American Council on Teaching, Annual Conference (Baltimore, MD), Nov 18
Foreman, Michael: Birth, Mar 21
Forest Products Week, Natl (Pres Proc), Oct 16
Forsberg, Peter: Birth, Jul 20
Fort Sumter Shelled by North: Anniv, Aug 17
Fortas, Abe: Birth Anniv, Jun 19
Forten, James: Birth Anniv, Sep 2
Foster, Andrew "Rube": Birth Anniv, Sep 17
Foster, Jodie: Birth, Nov 19
Foster, Stephen: Birth Anniv, Jul 4
Foster, Stephen: Memorial Day (Pres Proc), Jan 13
Foucault, Jean: Earth's Rotation Proved: Anniv, Jan 8
Foudy, Julie: Birth, Jan 27
Foundation Day, Natl (Japan), Feb 11
Fox, Matthew: Birth, Jul 14
Fox, Mem: Birth, Mar 5
Fox, Michael J.: Birth, Jun 9
Fox, Paula: Birth, Apr 22
Fox, Vicente: Birth, Jul 2
Foxx, Jimmie: Birth Anniv, Oct 22
France
Armistice Day, **May 8**
Bastille Day, **Jul 14**
Eiffel Tower: Anniv (Paris), **Mar 31**
Francis, Ron: Birth, Mar 1
Francis, Steve: Birth, Feb 21
Frank, Anne, Diary: Last Entry: Anniv, Aug 1
Frank, Anne: Birth Anniv, Jun 12
Franklin, Benjamin
Birth Anniv, **Jan 17**
Franklin Prefers Turkey: Anniv, **Jan 26**
Poor Richard's Almanack: Anniv, **Dec 28**
Franklin, Benjamin: Coin Flip for 300th Birthday, Jan 17
Fraser, Brendan: Birth, Dec 3
Freedman, Russell: Birth, Oct 11
Freedom Day: Anniv, Feb 1
Freedom Riders: Anniv, May 1
Freedom Shrine Month, May 1
Freeman, Antonio: Birth, May 27
Freeman, Don: Birth Anniv, Aug 11
French and Indian War Ends: Anniv, Feb 10
French Polynesia: Hawaiki Nui Va'a Race, Oct 19
French West Indies
Concordia Day (St. Martin), **Nov 11**
Freudenthal, Dave: Birth, Oct 12
Friday the Thirteenth, Jan 13
Friedel, Brad: Birth, May 18
Friedman, Ina R.: Birth, Jan 6
Frisbee Introduced: Anniv, Jan 13
Frist, William: Birth, Feb 22
Fritz, Jean: Birth, Nov 16
Froebel, Friedrich: Birth Anniv, Apr 21
Frog Egg Rain: Anniv, Sep 19
Frost, Robert Lee: Birth Anniv, Mar 26
Frozen Food Month, Natl, Mar 1
Frugal Fun Day, Intl, Oct 1
Fuhr, Grant: Birth, Sep 28
Fuller, Melville Weston: Birth Anniv, Feb 11
Fulton, Robert: Sails Steamboat: Anniv, Aug 17
Funky Winkerbean: Anniv, Mar 27
Furcal, Rafael: Birth, Oct 24
G.I. Joe Introduced: Anniv, Feb 1
Gabon: National Day, Aug 17
Gag, Wanda: Birth Anniv, Mar 11
Gagne, Eric: Birth, Jan 7
Gagne, Simon: Birth, Feb 29
Gaiman, Neil: Birth, Nov 10
Galdone, Paul: Birth, Jun 2
Galeota, Michael: Birth, Aug 28
Galilei, Galileo: Birth Anniv, Feb 15
Gallagher, David: Birth, Feb 9
Gallaudet, Thomas Hopkins: Birth Anniv, Dec 10
Galveston, TX, Hurricane: Anniv, Sep 8
Gambia: Independence Day, Feb 18
Gambill, Jan-Michael: Birth, Jun 3
Game and Puzzle Week, Natl, Nov 20
Gandhi, Mohandas
Assassination Anniv, **Jan 30**
Birth Anniv, **Oct 2**
Makes Salt: Anniv, **Apr 6**
Gannett, Ruth Stiles: Birth, Aug 12
Gannon, Rich: Birth, Dec 20
Gantos, Jack: Birth, Jul 2
Garcia, Jeff: Birth, Feb 24
Garcia, Sergio: Birth, Jan 9
Gardam, Jane: Birth, Jul 11
Garden, Nancy: Birth, May 15
Gardiner, John Reynolds: Birth, Dec 6
Gardner, Randy: Birth, Dec 2
Garfield, James A.: Birth Anniv, Nov 19
Garfield, Leon: Birth Anniv, Jul 14
Garfield, Lucretia R.: Birth Anniv, Apr 19
Garfield: Birthday, Jun 19
Garner, Alan: Birth, Oct 17
Garner, Charlie: Birth, Feb 13
Garner, John Nance: Birth Anniv, Nov 22
Garnett, Kevin: Birth, May 19
Gasol, Pau: Birth, Jul 6
Gates of the Arctic Natl Park Established: Anniv, Dec 2
Gates, Bill: Birth, Oct 28
Gauguin, Paul: Birth Anniv, Jun 7
Gay and Lesbian Pride Month, Jun 1
Gedalya, Fast of, Oct 6
Gehrig, Lou: Birth Anniv, Jun 19
Geiger, Matt: Birth, Sep 10
Geisel, Theodor "Dr. Seuss": Birth Anniv, Mar 2
Geisert, Arthur: Birth, Sep 20
Gellar, Sarah Michelle: Birth, Apr 14
Geller, Uri: Birth, Dec 20
Gelman, Rita Golden: Birth, Jul 2
Gemini Begins, May 21
General Motors: Founding Anniv, Sep 16
Geographic Bee Finals, Natl (Washington, DC), May 23
Geographic Bee, Natl, Registration Deadline Approaching, Oct 1
Geographic Bee, School Level, Natl, Nov 14
Geographic Bee, State Level, Natl, Mar 31
Geographic Education, Natl Council for, Mtg (Birmingham, AL), Oct 12
Geography Awareness Week, Natl, Nov 13
George, Eddie: Birth, Sep 24
George, Jean Craighead: Birth, Jul 2
George, Kristine O'Connell: Birth, May 6
Georgia
Atlanta Book Fest (Atlanta), **Sep 9**
Chambliss, Saxby: Birth, **Nov 10**
Confederate Memorial Day, **Apr 26**
Isakson, Johnny: Birth, **Dec 28**
Jefferson Davis Captured: Anniv, **May 10**
National Fair (Perry), **Oct 7**
Oglethorpe, James: Birth Anniv, **Dec 22**
Perdue, Sonny: Birth, **Dec 20**
Ratification Day, **Jan 2**
Sherman Enters Atlanta: Anniv, **Sep 2**
Georgia (Europe): Independence Restoration Day, May 26
Geringer, Laura: Birth, Feb 23
German-American Day (Pres Proc), Oct 6
German-American Heritage Month, Oct 1
Germany
Berlin Airlift: Anniv, **Jun 24**
Berlin Wall Is Opened: Anniv, **Nov 9**
Buss und Bettag, **Nov 16**
Capital Returns to Berlin: Anniv, **Jul 6**
Day of Remembrance for Victims of Nazism, **Jan 27**
Kristallnacht: Anniv, **Nov 9**
Munich Fasching Carnival, **Jan 7**
Reunification Anniv, **Oct 3**
Totensonntag, **Nov 20**
Volkstrauertag, **Nov 13**
Germany Invades Poland: Anniv, Sep 1
Geronimo: Death Anniv, Feb 17
Gerry, Elbridge: Birth Anniv, Jul 17
Gershwin, George: Birth Anniv, Sep 26
Gershwin, Ira: Birth Anniv, Dec 6
Gerstein, Mordicai: Birth, Nov 24
Get a Different Name Day, Feb 13
Get Caught Reading Month, May 1
Gettysburg Address, Lincoln's: Anniv, Nov 19
Ghana
Independence Day, **Mar 6**
Republic Day, **Jul 1**
Revolution Day, **Jun 4**
Ghosts, Fest of Hungry (China), Aug 19
Gibbons, Gail: Birth, Aug 1
Giblin, James Cross: Birth, Jul 8
Gibson, Althea: Birth Anniv, Aug 25
Gibson, Josh: Birth Anniv, Dec 21
Gibson, Mel: Birth, Jan 3
Giff, Patricia Reilly: Birth, Apr 26
Gifted Children Convention, Natl Assn (Louisville, KY), Nov 9
Gilchrist, Brad: Birth, Oct 25
Gilchrist, Guy: Birth, Jan 30
Gilchrist, Jan Spivey: Birth, Feb 15
Gillom, Jennifer: Birth, Jun 13
Ginsburg, Ruth Bader: Birth, Mar 15
Ginza Holiday (Chicago, IL), Aug 19
Giovanni, Nikki: Birth, Jun 7
Gipson, Fred: Birth Anniv, Feb 7
Giraffe's Incredible Journey: Anniv, Jun 30
Girl Scouts
Girl Scout Leader's Day, **Apr 22**
Girl Scout Week, **Mar 12**
Girl Scouts Founding: Anniv, **Mar 12**
Girls and Women in Sports Day, Natl, Feb 9
Girls Incorporated Week, May 14
Giuliani, Rudolph: Birth, May 28
Glacier Bay Natl Park Established: Anniv, Dec 2
Glacier Natl Park: Anniv, May 11
Glaus, Troy: Birth, Aug 3
Glavine, Tom: Birth, Mar 25
Glenn, John: Birth, Jul 18
Goble, Paul: Birth, Sep 17
God Bless America First Performed: Anniv, Nov 11
Goddard Day, Mar 16
Goddard, Robert H.: Birth Anniv, Oct 5
Godden, Rumer: Birth Anniv, Dec 10
Goffstein, M.B.: Birth, Dec 20
Gold Discovery, California: Anniv, Jan 24
Gold Discovery, Klondike Eldorado: Anniv, Aug 31
Gold Star Mother's Day (Pres Proc), Sep 25
Goldberg, Whoopi: Birth, Nov 13
Goldblum, Jeff: Birth, Oct 22
Golden Gate Bridge Opened: Anniv, May 27
Golden Rule Week, Apr 1
Golden Spike Driving: Anniv, May 10
Golf
US Girls' Junior Chmpshp (Charlotte, NC), **Jul 17**
Zaharias, Mildred Babe Didrikson: Birth Anniv, **Jun 26**
Gomez, Scott: Birth, Dec 23
Gonzales, Tony: Birth, Feb 27
Good Friday, Apr 14
Good Morning America TV Premiere: Anniv, Nov 6
Goodall, Jane: Birth, Apr 3
Goode, Diane: Birth, Sep 14
Gooden, Dwight: Birth, Nov 16
Goodman, Benny: Birth Anniv, May 9
Goodman, John: Birth, Jun 20
Goof-Off Day, Intl, Mar 22
Gordon, Jeff: Birth, Aug 4
Gordon, Sheila: Birth, Jan 22
Gordon-Levitt, Joseph: Birth, Feb 17
Gore, Albert, Jr: Birth, Mar 31
Gorilla Born in Captivity, First: Anniv, Dec 22
Gorillas: Koko: Birth, Jul 4
Grace, Mark: Birth, Jun 28
Grace, Topher: Birth, Jul 19
Graf, Steffi: Birth, Jun 14
Graham, Lindsey: Birth, Jul 9
Graham, Martha: Birth Anniv, May 11
Grahame, Kenneth: Birth Anniv, Mar 8
Granato, Cammi: Birth, Mar 25
Grand Canyon Natl Park: Anniv, Feb 26
Grandma Moses Day, Sep 7
Grandmother's Day in Florida, Oct 9
Grandparents' Day, Natl, Sep 11
Grange Week, Apr 23
Granholm, Jennifer: Birth, Feb 5
Grant, Horace: Birth, Jul 4
Grant, Julia Dent: Birth Anniv, Jan 26
Grant, Ulysses S.
Birth Anniv, **Apr 27**
Commissioned Commander: Anniv, **Mar 9**
Grassley, Charles E.: Birth, Sep 17
Gray, Elizabeth: See Vining, Elizabeth: Birth Anniv, Oct 6
Gray, Robert, Circumnavigates the Earth: Anniv, Apr 10
Great (Holy) Week, Apr 9
Great American Grump Out, May 31
Great American Smokeout, Nov 17
Great Britain Formed: Anniv, May 1
Greatest Show on Earth Formed: Anniv, Mar 28
Greece
Dumb Week, **Apr 9**
Independence Day, **Mar 25**
Midwife's Day or Women's Day, **Jan 8**
Ochi Day, **Oct 28**
Greek Independence Day (Pres Proc), Mar 25
Green (Clean) Monday, Mar 6
Green, Ahman: Birth, Feb 16
Green, Trent: Birth, Jul 9
Greenberg, Jan: Birth, Dec 29
Greene, Bette: Birth, Jun 28
Greene, Rhonda Gowler: Birth, Oct 29
Greenfield, Eloise: Birth, May 17
Greensboro Sit-in: Anniv, Feb 1
Greenspan, Alan: Birth, Mar 6
Greenwich Mean Time Begins: Anniv, Sep 25
Gregg, Judd: Birth, Feb 14
Gregoire, Christine: Birth, Mar 24
Gregorian Calendar Adjustment: Anniv, Oct 4
Gregorian Calendar Day, Feb 24
Grenada
Emancipation Day, **Aug 1**
Independence Day, **Feb 7**
Grenadines and Saint Vincent: Independence Day, Oct 27

Gretzky, Wayne: Birth, Jan 26
Griese, Brian: Birth, Mar 18
Grieve, Ben: Birth, May 4
Griffey, Ken, Jr: Birth, Nov 21
Griffith, Yolanda: Birth, Mar 1
Grimes, Nikki: Birth, Oct 20
Grimm, Jacob: Birth Anniv, Jan 4
Grimm, Wilhelm: Birth Anniv, Feb 24
Groening, Matt: Birth, Feb 15
Grouch Day, Natl, Oct 15
Groundhog Day, Feb 2
Groundhog Day (Punxsutawney, PA), Feb 2
Gruelle, Johnny: Birth Anniv, Dec 24
Guadalajara Intl Book Fair, Nov 26
Guadalupe Hidalgo, Treaty of: Anniv, Feb 2
Guadalupe Mountains Natl Park: Anniv, Sep 30
Guadalupe, Day of Our Lady of, Dec 12
Guam
- Discovery Day, **Mar 6**
- Lady of Camarin Day, **Dec 8**
- Liberation Day, **Jul 21**
- Magellan Day, **Mar 6**

Guatemala
- Armed Forces Day, **Jun 30**
- Independence Day, **Sep 15**
- Kite Fest of Santiago Sacatepequez, **Nov 1**
- Revolution Day, **Oct 20**

Guinea: Independence Day, Oct 2
Guinea-Bissau
- Colonization Martyr's Day, **Aug 3**
- Independence Day, **Sep 24**
- Natl Heroes Day, **Jan 20**
- Readjustment Movement's Day, **Nov 14**

Guinn, Kenny: Birth, Aug 24
Gumbel, Bryant: Birth, Sep 29
Gun Violence, Day of National Concern about Young People and, Oct 19
Gurney, James: Birth, Jun 14
Guthrie, Woody: Birth, Jul 14
Gutierrez, Carlos: Birth, Nov 4
Gutman, Dan: Birth, Oct 19
Guy, Rosa: Birth, Sep 1
Guyana: National Day, Feb 23
Gwinnett, Button: Death Anniv, May 16
Gwynn, Tony: Birth, May 9
Haas, Jessie: Birth, Jul 27
Habitat Day, World (UN), Oct 3
Haddix, Margaret Peterson: Birth, Apr 9
Hagel, Chuck: Birth, Oct 4
Hague, Michael: Birth, Sep 8
Hahn, Hilary: Birth, Nov 27
Hahn, Mary Downing: Birth, Dec 9
Haim, Corey: Birth, Dec 23
Haiti
- Ancestors' Day, **Jan 2**
- Discovery Day: Anniv, **Dec 5**
- Flag and University Day, **May 18**
- Independence Day, **Jan 1**

Halcyon Days, Dec 14
Hale, Nathan: Birth Anniv, Jun 6
Haleakala Natl Park: Anniv, Sep 30
Haley, Alex Palmer: Birth Anniv, Aug 11
Haley, Gail E.: Birth, Nov 4
Halfway Point of 2006, Jul 2
Hall, Donald: Birth, Sep 29
Hall, Lynn: Birth, Nov 9
Halley, Edmund: Birth Anniv, Nov 8
Halley's Comet, Last Perihelion of: Anniv, Feb 9
Halley's Comet: Eta Aquarids Meteor Shower, Apr 21
Halley's Comet: Orionids Meteor Shower, Oct 15
Halloween
- Devil's Night, **Oct 30**
- Hallowe'en or All Hallow's Eve, **Oct 31**
- Magic Day, Natl, **Oct 31**
- Trick or Treat or Beggar's Night, **Oct 31**

Hamburger Month, Natl, May 1
Hamilton, Alexander: Birth Anniv, Jan 11
Hamilton, Alexander: Duel with Burr: Anniv, Jul 11
Hamilton, Scott: Birth, Aug 28
Hamilton, Virginia: Birth Anniv, Mar 12
Hamlin, Hannibal: Birth Anniv, Aug 27
Hamm, Mia: Birth, May 17
Hamm, Morgan: Birth, Sep 24
Hamm, Paul: Birth, Sep 24
Hammon, Jupiter: Birth Anniv, Oct 17
Hancock, John: Birth Anniv, Jan 23
Handel, George Frederick: Birth Anniv, Feb 23
Handford, Martin: Birth, Sep 27
Handwriting Day, Natl, Jan 23
Hangul (Korea), Oct 9
Hanks, Tom: Birth, Jul 9
Hannukah, Dec 26
Hansen, Joyce: Birth, Oct 18
Hanson, (Clarke) Isaac: Birth, Nov 17
Hanson, Jordan Taylor: Birth, Mar 14
Hanson, Zachary Walker: Birth, Oct 22
Happy Birthday to "Happy Birthday to You", Jun 27
Happy Day, I Want You to Be, Mar 3
Hardaway, Penny: Birth, Jul 18
Hardaway, Tim: Birth, Sep 1
Harding, Florence: Birth Anniv, Aug 15
Harding, Warren G.: Birth Anniv, Nov 2
Harding, Warren G.: First Radio Broadcast: Anniv, Jun 14
Harkin, Thomas R.: Birth, Nov 19
Harness, Cheryl: Birth, Jul 6
Harris, Ed: Birth, Nov 28
Harris, Joel Chandler: Birth Anniv, Dec 9
Harris, Rosemary: Birth, Feb 20
Harrison, Anna: Birth Anniv, Jul 25
Harrison, Benjamin: Birth Anniv, Aug 20
Harrison, Caroline L.S.: Birth Anniv, Oct 1
Harrison, Marvin: Bith, Aug 25
Harrison, Mary: Birth Anniv, Apr 30
Harrison, William Henry: Birth Anniv, Feb 9
Harry Potter: Birthday, Jul 31
Harry, Prince: Birth, Sep 15
Hart, John: Death Anniv, May 11
Hart, Melissa Joan: Birth, Apr 18
Haru-No-Yabuiri (Japan), Jan 16
Harvest Moon, Sep 17
Harvey, William: Birth Anniv, Apr 1
Hasek, Dominik: Birth, Jan 29
Haskins, James: Birth, Sep 19
Hastert, Dennis: Birth, Jan 2
Hatch, Annia: Birth, Jun 14
Hatch, Orrin Grant: Birth, Mar 22
Hatcher, Teri: Birth, Dec 8
Haugaard, Erik Christian: Birth, Apr 13
Hawaii
- Akaka, Daniel: Birth, **Sep 11**
- Annexed by US: Anniv, **Jul 7**
- Haleakala Natl Park: Anniv, **Sep 30**
- Hawaii Statehood: Anniv, **Aug 21**
- Inouye, Daniel Ken: Birth, **Sep 7**
- King Kamehameha I Day, **Jun 11**
- Lei Day, **May 1**
- Lingle, Linda: Birth, **Jun 4**
- Prince Jonah Kuhio Kalanianole Day, **Mar 26**

Hawaiki Nui Va'a Race, Oct 19
Hawk, Tony: Birth, May 12
Haydn, Franz Joseph: Birth Anniv, Mar 31
Hayes, Ira Hamilton: Birth Anniv, Jan 12
Hayes, Lucy: Birth Anniv, Aug 28
Hayes, Rutherford B.: Birth Anniv, Oct 4
Head Lice: Pediculosis Prevention Month, Natl, Sep 1
Health and Welfare
- Adoption Week, Natl, **Nov 20**
- AIDS Day, World (UN), **Dec 1**
- AIDS First Noted: Anniv, **Jun 5**
- Alcohol Awareness Month, Natl, **Apr 1**
- Allergy/Asthma Awareness Month, Natl, **May 1**
- Alzheimer's Disease Month, Natl (Pres Proc), **Nov 1**
- American Red Cross: Founding Anniv, **May 21**
- Anesthetic First Used in Surgery: Anniv, **Mar 30**
- Artificial Heart Transplant: Anniv, **Dec 2**
- Autism Awareness Month, Natl, **Apr 1**
- Backpack Safety America Month, **Sep 1**
- Better Hearing and Speech Month, **May 1**
- Breast Cancer Awareness Month, Natl (Pres Proc), **Oct 1**
- Cancer Control Month (Pres Proc), **Apr 1**
- Cancer in the Sun Month, **Jun 1**
- Child Health Day (Pres Proc), **Oct 3**
- Child Vision Awareness Month, **Jun 1**
- Childhood Depression Awareness Day, **May 2**
- Children with Alopecia Day, **Apr 14**
- Children's Dental Health Month, Natl, **Feb 1**
- Children's Vision and Learning Month, **Aug 1**
- Cigarettes Reported Hazardous: Anniv, **Jan 11**
- Dental Hygiene Month, Natl, **Oct 1**
- Diabetes Assn Alert Day, American, **Mar 28**
- Diabetes Month, Natl (Pres Proc), **Nov 1**
- Doctors' Day, **Mar 30**
- Donate Life Month, Natl (Pres Proc), **Apr 1**
- Family Caregivers Month, Natl (Pres Proc), **Nov 1**
- Family Health Month, **Oct 1**
- Family Sexuality Education Month, Natl, **Oct 1**
- 5-A-Day Month, Natl, **Sep 1**
- Flu Pandemic of 1918 Hits US: Anniv, **Mar 11**
- Food Allergy Awareness Month, Natl, **Sep 1**
- Great American Smokeout, **Nov 17**
- Health Education Week, Natl, **Oct 17**
- Heart Month, American, **Feb 1**
- Heart Month, American (Pres Proc), **Feb 1**
- Infection Control Week, Intl, **Oct 17**
- Insulin First Isolated: Anniv, **Jul 27**
- Lister, Joseph: Birth Anniv, **Apr 5**
- Mental Health Month, Natl, **May 1**
- Mental Retardation Awareness Month, Natl, **Mar 1**
- Mother, Father Deaf Day, **Apr 30**
- Nurses Day and Week, Natl, **May 6**
- Nutrition Month, Natl, **Mar 1**
- Orthodontic Health Month, Natl, **Oct 1**
- Pediatric Cancer Awareness Month, **Sep 1**
- Pediculosis Prevention Month, Natl, **Sep 1**
- Physical Fitness and Sports Month, Natl, **May 1**
- Poison Prevention Week, Natl, **Mar 19**
- Polio Vaccine: Anniv, **Apr 12**
- Population Day, World (UN), **Jul 11**
- Project ACES Day, **May 3**
- Red Cross Month, **Mar 1**
- Red Cross Month, American (Pres Proc), **Mar 1**
- Safe Boating Week, Natl, **May 20**
- Save Your Vision Month, **Mar 1**
- Save Your Vision Week (Pres Proc), **Mar 5**
- School Breakfast Week, Natl, **Mar 6**
- School Counseling Week, Natl, **Feb 6**
- School Lunch Week, Natl, **Oct 9**
- School Nurse Day, Natl, **May 10**
- Sleep Awareness Week, Natl, **Mar 27**
- Social Security Act: Anniv, **Aug 14**
- Stay Out of the Sun Day, **Jul 3**
- Stuttering Awareness Day, Intl, **Oct 22**
- Stuttering Awareness Week, Natl, **May 14**
- Successful Antirabies Inoculation, First: Anniv, **Jul 6**
- TB Bacillus Discovered: Anniv, **Mar 24**
- Vegetarian Month, **Oct 1**
- Vitamin C Isolated: Anniv, **Apr 4**
- Walk Our Children to School Day, Natl, **Oct 5**
- White Cane Safety Day (Pres Proc), **Oct 15**
- World AIDS Day (Pres Proc), **Dec 1**
- World Food Day (UN), **Oct 16**
- World Health Day (UN), **Apr 7**
- World Red Cross Day, **May 8**
- YMCA Healthy Kids Day, **Apr 1**
- Youth Month, Natl, **Nov 1**

Health, Physical Education, Recreation and Dance, American Alliance for, Natl Convention & Expo (Salt Lake City, UT), Apr 25
Hearne, Betsy: Birth, Oct 6
Heart Month, American (Pres Proc), Feb 1
Heineman, Dave: Birth, May 12
Heljduk, Milan: Birth, Feb 14
Heller, Ruth: Birth Anniv, Apr 2
Hello Day, World, Nov 21
Helms, Jesse: Birth, Oct 18
Helton, Todd: Birth, Aug 20
Henderson, Meredith: Birth, Nov 24
Henderson, Rickey: Birth, Dec 25
Hendricks, Thomas A.: Birth Anniv, Sep 17
Henin-Hardenne, Justine: Birth, Jun 1
Henkes, Kevin: Birth, Nov 27
Henman, Tim: Birth, Sep 6
Henry, Brad: Birth, Jul 10
Henry, Marguerite: Birth Anniv, Apr 13
Henry, Patrick: Birth Anniv, May 29
Henson, Jim: Birth Anniv, Sep 24
Henson, Matthew A.: Birth Anniv, Aug 8
Hentoff, Nat: Birth, Jun 10
Herman, Charlotte: Birth, Jun 10
Hermes, Patricia: Birth, Feb 21
Hernandez, Orlando: Birth, Oct 11
Hesse, Karen: Birth, Aug 29
Hest, Amy: Birth, Apr 28
Hewes, Joseph: Birth Anniv, Jan 23
Hewitt, Jennifer Love: Birth, Feb 21
Hewitt, Lleyton: Birth, Feb 24
Hey Arnold! TV Premiere: Anniv, Oct 9
Heyward, Thomas: Birth Anniv, Jul 28
Hiaasen, Carl: Birth, Mar 12
Hicks, Catherine: Birth, Aug 6
High School Activities Week, Natl, Oct 16
Highway Numbers Introduced: Anniv, Mar 2
Hildebrand, Sara: Birth, Sep 18
Hill, Eric: Birth, Sep 7
Hill, Grant: Birth, Oct 5
Hill, Mildred J. and Patty: Happy Birthday to "Happy Birthday to You", Jun 27
Hillary, Sir Edmund: Birth, Jul 20
Hilton, Paris: Birth, Feb 17
Hinamatsuri (Japan), Mar 3
Hindenburg Disaster: Anniv, May 6
Hingis, Martina: Birth, Sep 30
Hinske, Eric: Birth, Aug 5
Hinton, S.E.: Birth, Apr 22
Hirohito Michi-no-Miya, Emperor: Birth Anniv, Apr 29
Hiroshima Day, Aug 6
Hirschi, Ron: Birth, May 18
Hispanic
- Chavez, Cesar Estrada: Birth Anniv, **Mar 31**
- Cinco de Mayo (Mexico), **May 5**
- Clemente, Roberto: Birth Anniv, **Aug 18**
- Day of the Teacher/El Dia Del Maestro (CA), **May 10**
- Dia de la Raza (Mexico), **Oct 12**
- Hispanic Heritage Month, Natl (Pres Proc), **Sep 15**
- Latino Book & Family Fest—Chicago (IL), **Nov 12**
- Latino Book & Family Fest—Houston (TX), **Oct 1**
- Latino Book & Family Fest—Los Angeles (CA), **Oct 16**
- Posadas, **Dec 16**

Hissey, Jane: Birth, Sep 1
Historically Black Colleges and Universities Week, Natl (Pres Proc), Sep 11
Hitler, Adolf: Birth Anniv, Apr 20
Ho, Minfong: Birth, Jan 7
Hoban, Lillian: Birth Anniv, May 18
Hoban, Russell: Birth, Feb 4
Hobart, Garret A.: Birth Anniv, Jun 3
Hobbs, Lucy: First Woman to Graduate Dental School: Anniv, Feb 21
Hobbs, Will: Birth, Aug 22
Hoberman, Mary Ann: Birth, Aug 12
Hockey Mask Invented: Anniv, Nov 1
Hoeven, John: Birth, Mar 13
Hoff, Syd: Birth Anniv, Sep 4
Hoffman, Mary: Birth, Apr 20
Hoffman, Mat: Birth, Jan 9
Hogan, Hulk: Birth, Aug 11
Hogmanay (Scottish New Year), Dec 31
Hogrogian, Nonny: Birth, May 7
Holabird, Katherine: Birth, Jan 23
Holdsclaw, Chamique: Birth, Aug 9
Holi (India), Mar 18
Holiday Day, Make Up Your Own, Mar 26
Holiday, First US by Presidential Proclamation: Anniv, Nov 26
Holling, Holling C.: Birth Anniv, Aug 2
Hollyhock Fest (Kyoto, Japan), May 15
Holmes, Katie: Birth, Dec 18
Holmes, Oliver Wendell: Old Ironsides Saved by Poem: Anniv, Sep 16
Holmes, Priest: Birth, Oct 7
Holocaust Day (Israel), Apr 25
Holocaust Memorial Day (UK), Jan 27
Holt, Kimberly Willis: Birth, Sep 9
Holt, Torry: Birth, Jun 5
Holy Innocents Day, Dec 28
Holy See: National Holiday, Oct 22
Holy Thursday: See Maundy Thursday, Apr 13
Holy Week, Apr 9
Homeland Security Department Created: Anniv, Nov 25
Homestead Act: Anniv, May 20
Honduras
- Dia De Las Americas, **Apr 14**
- Francisco Morazan Holiday, **Oct 3**
- Hurricane Mitch: Anniv, **Oct 27**
- Independence Day, **Sep 15**

Honest Abe Awards: Natl Honesty Day, Apr 30
Honesty Day, Natl, Apr 30
Honey Month, Natl, Sep 1
Hong Kong
- Birthday of Confucius (Observance), **Sep 30**
- Last Hurrah for British, **Jun 30**
- Liberation Day, **Aug 29**

Hoodie-Hoo Day, Northern Hemisphere, Feb 20
Hooper, William: Birth Anniv, Jun 17
Hooray for Year-Round School Day, Jun 9
Hoover, Herbert Clark: Birth Anniv, Aug 10
Hoover, Lou H.: Birth Anniv, Mar 29
Hope Diamond Mailed to Smithsonian: Anniv, Nov 8
Hopkins, Lee Bennett: Birth, Apr 13
Hopkins, Stephen: Birth Anniv, Mar 7
Hopkinson, Francis: Birth Anniv, Sep 21

Horn, Joe: Birth, Jan 16
Horses
Chincoteague Pony Penning (Chincoteague Island, VA), Jul 26
Iron Horse Outraced by Horse: Anniv, Sep 18
Kentucky Derby (Louisville, KY), May 6
Kentucky State Fair (Louisville, KY), Aug 18
Horvath, Polly: Birth, Jan 30
Hossa, Marian: Birth, Jan 12
Hostos, Eugenio Maria: Birth Anniv, Jan 11
Hot Breakfast Month, Natl, Feb 1
Hot Dog Month, Natl, Jul 1
Hot Springs Natl Park: Anniv, Mar 4
Houdini Premieres His Greatest Escape: Anniv, Sep 21
Houdini, Harry: Birth Anniv, Mar 24
House of Representatives, First Black Serves in: Anniv, Dec 12
House of Representatives, US: First Quorum: Anniv, Apr 1
Housework Day, No, Apr 7
Houston, Sam: Birth Anniv, Mar 2
Houston, Whitney: Birth, Aug 9
Howard, Elizabeth Fitzgerald: Birth, Dec 28
Howard, Juwan: Birth, Feb 7
Howard, Ron: Birth, Mar 1
Howdy Doody TV Premiere: Anniv, Dec 27
Howe, Gordie: Birth, Mar 31
Howe, James: Birth, Aug 2
Hoyle, Edmund: Death Anniv, Aug 29
Hoyt-Goldsmith, Diane: Birth, Jul 1
Hubble Space Telescope Deployed: Space Milestone, Apr 25
Huckabee, Mike: Birth, Aug 24
Hughes, Charles E.: Birth Anniv, Apr 11
Hughes, Langston: Birth Anniv, Feb 1
Hull, Bobby: Birth, Jan 3
Hull, Brett: Birth, Aug 9
Human Relations
Be an Angel Day, Aug 22
Be Kind to Humankind Week, Aug 25
Black History Month, Natl, Feb 1
Communication Week, World, Nov 1
Diversity Awareness Month, Oct 1
Emancipation Proclamation: Anniv, Sep 22
Etiquette Week, Natl, May 21
Honesty Day, Natl, Apr 30
Human Rights Day (Pres Proc), Dec 10
Human Rights Day (UN), Dec 10
Human Rights Month, Universal, Dec 1
Human Rights Week (Pres Proc), Dec 10
I Want You to Be Happy Day, Mar 3
Joygerm Day, Natl, Jan 7
League of Nations: Anniv, Jan 10
Lost Penny Day, Feb 12
Make a Difference Day, Oct 22
No Name-Calling Week, Jan 16
Peace Corps Founded: Anniv, Mar 1
Pen-Friends Week Intl, May 1
Poverty, Intl Day for Eradication, Oct 17
Race Relations Day, Feb 14
Ralph Bunche Awarded Nobel Peace Prize: Anniv, Dec 10
Red Cross Day, World, May 8
Salvation Army Founder's Day, Apr 10
Salvation Army in US: Anniv, Mar 10
Stop the Violence Day, Natl, Nov 22
Thank You Days, Intl, Jan 11
Volunteer Week, Natl, Apr 23
World Day of Prayer, Mar 3
World Hello Day, Nov 21
Humbug Day, Dec 21
Humor, Comedy
Humor Month, Natl, Apr 1
Moment of Laughter Day, Apr 14
Humphrey, Hubert: Birth Anniv, May 27
Humphrey, Terin: Birth, Aug 14
Hungary
Anniv of 1956 Revolution, Oct 23
Hungary Declared Independent: Anniv, Oct 23
St. Stephen's Day, Aug 20
Hunt, Bonnie: Birth, Sep 22
Hunt, Charlotte: See Demi: Birth, Sep 2
Hunter, Mollie: Birth, Jun 30
Hunter, Torii: Birth, Jul 18
Hunter's Moon, Oct 17
Huntington, Samuel: Birth Anniv, Jul 3
Huntsman, Jon, Jr: Birth, Mar 26
Hurd, Thatcher: Birth, Mar 6
Hurricane
Atlantic, Caribbean and Gulf Hurricane Season, Jun 1
Galveston, TX: Anniv, Sep 8
Hurricane Andrew Hits American Coast: Anniv, Aug 24
Hurricane Mitch: Anniv, Oct 27
Hurricane Supplication Day (US Virgin Islands), Jul 24
Hurricane Thanksgiving Day (Virgin Islands), Oct 17
Hurwitz, Johanna: Birth, Oct 9
Hus, John: Commemoration Day (Czech), Jul 6
Hussein, Saddam: Operation Iraqi Freedom: Anniv, Mar 19
Hussein: King of Jordan: Birth Anniv, Nov 14
Hutchins, Hazel: Birth, Aug 9
Hutchins, Pat: Birth, Jun 18
Hutchison, Kay Bailey: Birth, Jul 22
Hyman, Trina Schart: Birth, Apr 8
I Want You to Be Happy Day, Mar 3
IBM PC Introduced: Anniv, Aug 12
Ice Cream Cone: Birth, Sep 22
Ice Cream Day, Natl, Jul 16
Iceland
August Holiday, Aug 1
Bun Day, Feb 27
Bursting Day, Feb 28
First Day of Summer, Apr 20
Independence Day, Jun 17
Leif Erikson Day, Oct 9
Shop and Office Workers' Holiday, Aug 1
Iceman Mummy Discovered: Anniv, Sep 19
Idaho
Admission Day, Jul 3
Craig, Larry: Birth, Jul 20
Crapo, Michael: Birth, May 20
Eastern Idaho State Fair (Blackfoot), Sep 3
Kempthorne, Dirk: Birth, Oct 29
Western Idaho Fair (Boise), Aug 19
Ides of March, Mar 15
Ig Nobel Prize Ceremony, Oct 6
Illinois
Admission Day, Dec 3
Blagojevich, Rod: Birth, Dec 10
Bud Billiken Parade (Chicago), Aug 13
Chicago Intl Children's Film Fest (Chicago), Oct 27
Durbin, Richard J.: Birth, Nov 21
Ginza Holiday: Japanese Cultural Fest (Chicago), Aug 19
Latino Book & Family Fest—Chicago, Nov 12
Obama, Barack: Birth, Aug 4
Reading Assn, Intl, Annual Convention (Chicago), Apr 30
Science Olympiad (Champaign-Urbana), May 19
State Fair (Springfield), Aug 12
Supervision and Curriculum Development, Assn for, Conference (Chicago), Mar 1
Immaculate Conception, Feast Of, Dec 8
Immigration: Ellis Island Opened: Anniv, Jan 1
Impeachment Proceedings, Clinton: Anniv, Dec 20
Impeachment Proceedings, Johnson: Anniv, Feb 24
Inane Answering Message Day, Natl, Jan 30
Inauguration Day, Old, Mar 4
Inca Ice Maiden Discovered: Anniv, Sep 8
Incandescent Lamp Demonstrated: Anniv, Oct 21
Income Tax Birthday, Feb 3
Income Tax Pay Day, Apr 15
Independence Day (Russia), Jun 12
Independence Day, US (Fourth of July), Jul 4
India
Baisakhi, Apr 13
Children's Day, Nov 14
Deepavali (Diwali), Nov 1
Earthquake, Jan 26
Gandhi, Mohandas: Birth Anniv, Oct 2
Holi, Mar 18
Independence Day, Aug 15
Republic Day: Anniv, Jan 26
Indiana
Admission Day, Dec 11
Bayh, Evan: Birth, Dec 26
Daniels, Mitchell: Birth, Apr 7
Lugar, Richard: Birth, Apr 4
State Fair (Indianapolis), Aug 10
Indonesia
Independence Day, Aug 17
Kartini Day, Apr 21
Infection Control Week, Intl, Oct 17
Inhofe, James M.: Birth, Nov 17
Inkpen, Mick: Birth, Dec 22
Inouye, Daniel Ken: Birth, Sep 7
Insulin First Isolated: Anniv, Jul 27
Internet Created: Anniv, Oct 29
Introduce a Girl to Engineering Day, Feb 23
Inventors' Month, Natl, Aug 1
Iowa
Admission Day, Dec 28
Fest of Books for Young People (Iowa City), Sep 10
Grassley, Charles E.: Birth, Sep 17
Harkin, Thomas R.: Birth, Nov 19
Iowa Storytelling Fest (Clear Lake), Jul 28
State Fair (Des Moines), Aug 11
Vilsack, Tom: Birth, Dec 13
Iran
Day of Oil, Natl, Mar 19
Fifteenth of Khordad, Jun 5
National Day, Feb 11
New Year, Mar 21
Yalda, Dec 21
Iraq
Iraq Invades Kuwait: Anniv, Aug 2
Kuwait Liberated: Anniv, Feb 27
Operation Iraqi Freedom: Anniv, Mar 19
Persian Gulf War Begins: Anniv, Jan 16
Ireland
Easter Rising, Apr 24
National Day, Mar 17
Irish Famine Begins: Anniv, Sep 9
Irish-American Heritage Month (Pres Proc), Mar 1
Irving, Washington: Birth Anniv, Apr 3
Irwin, Steve: Birth, Feb 22
Isaacs, Anne: Birth, Mar 2
Isakson, Johnny: Birth, Dec 28
Ishii, Kazuhisa: Birth, Sep 9
Ising, Rudolf C.: Birth Anniv, Aug 7
Isle of Man: Tynwald Day, Jul 5
Isle Royale Natl Park: Anniv, Apr 3
Ismail, Raghib: Birth, Nov 18
Isra al Mi'raj: Ascent of Prophet Muhammad, Sep 1
Israel
Camp David Accord Signed: Anniv, Mar 26
Yom Ha'atzma'ut (Independence Day), May 3
Yom Hashoah (Holocaust Day), Apr 25
Yom Ha'Zikkaron (Remembrance Day), May 2
Yom Yerushalayim, May 26
Italy
Carnival Week (Milan), Feb 26
Epiphany Fair, Jan 5
La Befana, Jan 6
Liberation Day, Apr 25
Palio Dei Balestrieri (crossbow), May 28
Republic Day, Jun 2
Victory Day, Nov 4
Wedding of the Sea (Venice), May 28
Iverson, Allen: Birth, Jun 7
Iwo Jima Day, Feb 23
Jackson, Alphonso: Birth, Sep 9
Jackson, Andrew: Birth Anniv, Mar 15
Jackson, Jermaine: Birth, Dec 11
Jackson, Jesse: Birth, Oct 8
Jackson, Michael: Birth, Aug 29
Jackson, Phil: Birth, Sep 17
Jackson, Rachel D.: Birth Anniv, Jun 15
Jackson, Reggie: Birth, May 18
Jackson, Thomas J. "Stonewall": Birth Anniv, Jan 21
Jacques, Brian: Birth, Jun 15
Jaeger, Andrea: Birth, Jun 4
Jaffe, Nina: Birth, Oct 10
Jagr, Jaromir: Birth, Feb 15
Jakub, Lisa: Birth, Dec 27
Jamaica
Discovery By Columbus: Anniv, May 4
Independence Achieved: Anniv, Aug 6
Independence Day Observed, Aug 1
Natl Heroes Day, Oct 17
James, Edgerrin: Birth, Aug 1
James, Jesse: Birth Anniv, Sep 5
Jamestown, VA: Founding Anniv, May 14
Jamison, Antawn: Birth, Jun 12
Janeczko, Paul: Birth, Jul 27
Japan
Atomic Bomb Dropped on Hiroshima: Anniv, Aug 6
Atomic Bomb Dropped on Nagasaki: Anniv, Aug 9
Autumnal Equinox Day, Sep 22
Bean Throwing Fest (Setsubun), Feb 3
Birthday of the Emperor, Dec 23
Bon Fest (Feast of Lanterns), Jul 13
Children's Day, May 5
Coming-of-Age Day, Jan 9
Constitution Memorial Day, May 3
Cormorant Fishing Fest, May 11
Culture Day, Nov 3
Day of the Rice God (Chiyoda), Jun 4
Doll Fest (Hinamatsuri), Mar 3
Flower Fest (Hana Matsuri), Apr 8
Foundation Day, Natl, Feb 11
Golden Week Holiday, May 4
Greenery Day, Apr 29
Ha-Ri-Ku-Yo (Needle Mass), Feb 8
Haru-No-Yabuiri, Jan 16
Health-Sports Day, Oct 10
Hiroshima Day, Aug 6
Hollyhock Fest (Kyoto), May 15
Japanese Era New Year, Jan 1
Kakizome, Jan 2
Labor Thanksgiving Day, Nov 23
Marine Day, Jul 20
Nanakusa, Jan 7
Newspaper Week, Oct 2
Respect for the Aged Day, Sep 15
Rice Planting Fest (Osaka), Jun 14
Shichi-Go-San, Nov 15
Snow Fest, Feb 8
Suffers Major Earthquake: Anniv, Jan 17
Tanabata (Star Fest), Jul 7
Vernal Equinox Day, Mar 20
Water-Drawing Fest, Mar 1
Japanese Internment (WWII): Anniv, Feb 19
Jarrell, Randall: Birth Anniv, May 6
Jarrett, Dale: Birth, Nov 26
Jay, John: Birth Anniv, Dec 12
Jazz and Blues
Jazz Day, Intl, May 27
Jefferson Davis Day (KY, LA, TN), Jun 3
Jefferson, Martha: Birth Anniv, Oct 19
Jefferson, Thomas: Birth Anniv, Apr 13
Jeffords, James: Birth, May 11
Jeffries, John: Weatherman's Day, Feb 5
Jemison, Mae: Birth, Oct 17
Jenkins, Steve: Birth, Mar 31
Jenner, Edward: Birth Anniv, May 17
Jennings, Jason: Birth, Jul 17
Jennings, Peter: Birth, Jul 29
Jeter, Derek: Birth, Jun 26
Jetsons TV Premiere: Anniv, Sep 23
Jewel: Birth, May 23
Jewish Heritage Week (Pres Proc), Apr 30
Jewish Observances
Auschwitz Liberated by Soviets: Anniv, Jan 27
Chanukah, Dec 26
Fast of Gedalya, Oct 6
Fast of Tammuz, Jul 13
Israel Yom Ha'atzma'ut (Independence Day), May 3
Israel Yom Yerushalayim, May 26
Kristallnacht: Anniv, Nov 9
Lag B'Omer, May 16
Liberation of Buchenwald: Anniv, Apr 11
Passover Begins, Apr 12
Pesach (Passover), Apr 13
Purim, Mar 14
Rosh Hashanah (New Year), Oct 4
Rosh Hashanah Begins, Oct 3
Shavuot, Jun 2
Shemini Atzeret, Oct 25
Simchat Torah, Oct 26
Sukkot Begins, Oct 17
Sukkot/Succoth/Feast of Tabernacles, Oct 18
Ta'anit Esther (Fast of Esther), Mar 13
Tu B'Shvat, Feb 13
Yom Hashoah/Holocaust Day (Israel), Apr 25
Yom Kippur, Oct 13
Yom Kippur Begins, Oct 12
Jinnah: see Pakistan: Birth of Qaid-i-Azam, Dec 25
Joan of Arc: Birth Anniv, Jan 6
Jobaria Exhibited: Anniv, Nov 13
Jobs, Steven: Birth, Feb 24
Johanns, Mike: Birth, Aug 18
John Carver Day (MA), Jun 25
John, Elton: Birth, Mar 25
Johnny Appleseed Day, Mar 11
Johnson, Andrew, Impeachment Proceedings: Anniv, Feb 24
Johnson, Andrew: Birth Anniv, Dec 29
Johnson, Angela: Birth, Jun 18
Johnson, Avery: Birth, Mar 25
Johnson, Charles, Jr: Birth, Jul 20
Johnson, Crockett: Birth Anniv, Oct 20
Johnson, Eliza M.: Birth Anniv, Oct 4
Johnson, Jack: Birth Anniv, Mar 31
Johnson, Keyshawn: Birth, Jul 22
Johnson, Lady Bird: Birth, Dec 22
Johnson, Lyndon B.: Birth Anniv, Aug 27
Johnson, Lyndon B.: Monday Holiday Law: Anniv, Jun 28

Johnson, Magic: Birth, Aug 14
Johnson, Nick: Birth, Sep 19
Johnson, Randy: Birth, Sep 10
Johnson, Richard M.: Birth Anniv, Oct 17
Johnson, Shannon: Birth, Aug 18
Johnson, Tim: Birth, Dec 28
Johnston, Tony: Birth, Jan 30
Johnstown Flood: Anniv, May 31
Jones, Andruw: Birth, Apr 23
Jones, Casey: Birth Anniv, Mar 14
Jones, Chipper: Birth, Apr 24
Jones, Cobi: Birth, Jun 16
Jones, Diana Wynne: Birth, Aug 16
Jones, Eddie: Birth, Oct 20
Jones, Hatty: Birth, Jul 21
Jones, Marcia Thornton: Birth, Jul 15
Jones, Marion: Birth, Oct 12
Joosse, Barbara: Birth, Feb 18
Jordan
Accession Day, Jun 9
Great Arab Revolt and Army Day, Jun 10
Independence Day, May 25
King Hussein: Birth Anniv, Nov 14
King's Birthday, Jan 30
Jordan, Michael: Birth, Feb 17
Joseph, Chief, Surrender: Anniv, Oct 5
Joseph, Curtis: Birth, Apr 29
Journalism
Around the World in 72 Days: Anniv, Jan 25
Children's Magazine Month, Oct 1
First American Daily Newspaper Published: Anniv, May 30
First American Newspaper: Anniv, Sep 25
First Magazine Published in America: Anniv, Feb 13
Japan: Newspaper Week, Oct 2
Newscurrents Student Editorial Cartoon Contest, Mar 1
Newspaper Carrier Day, Sep 4
Newspaper in Education Week, Mar 6
People Magazine: Anniv, Mar 4
Royall, Anne: Birth Anniv, Jun 11
Time Magazine First Published: Anniv, Mar 3
UN: World Press Freedom Day, May 3
USA Today First Published: Anniv, Sep 15
Joyce, William: Birth, Dec 11
Joygerm Day, Natl, Jan 7
Joyner-Kersee, Jackie: Birth, Mar 3
Juarez, Benito: Birth Anniv, Mar 21
Juggling Day, World, Jun 17
Jukes, Mavis: Birth, May 3
Jumbo the Elephant Arrives in America: Anniv, Apr 9
Jumbo the Elephant: Death Anniv, Sep 15
June Is Turkey Lovers' Month, Jun 1
Juneteenth, Jun 19
Junkanoo (Bahamas), Dec 26
Jupiter, Comet Crashes into: Anniv, Jul 16
Juster, Norton: Birth, Jun 2
Justice, US Dept of: Anniv, Jun 22
Kamehameha Day (HI), Jun 11
Kansas
Admission Day, Jan 29
Brownback, Sam: Birth, Sep 12
Literature Fest (Lawrence), Oct 18
Roberts, Pat: Birth, Apr 20
Salter Elected First Woman Mayor in US: Anniv, Apr 4
Sibelius, Kathleen: Birth, May 15
State Fair (Hutchinson), Sep 9
Kariya, Paul: Birth, Oct 16
Kasparov, Garry: Birth, Apr 13
Kasparov, Garry: First Computer Chess Victory: Anniv, Feb 10
Katmai Natl Park Established: Anniv, Dec 2
Kazakhstan
Constitution Day, Aug 31
Independence Day, Oct 25
Republic Day, Dec 16
Keanan, Staci: Birth, Jun 6
Keane, Bil: Birth, Oct 5
Keats, Ezra Jack: Birth Anniv, Mar 11
Keegan, Andrew: Birth, Jan 29
Keep Massachusetts Beautiful Month, May 1
Keeshan, Bob: Birth Anniv, Jun 27
Kehret, Peg: Birth, Nov 11
Keiko Returns to Iceland: Anniv, Sep 10
Keller, Helen: Birth Anniv, Jun 27
Kellogg, Steven: Birth, Oct 26
Kelly, Walt: Birth Anniv, Aug 25
Kemp, Shawn: Birth, Nov 26
Kempthorne, Dirk: Birth, Oct 29
Kenai Fjords Natl Park Established: Anniv, Dec 2
Kennedy Onassis, Jacqueline: Birth Anniv, Jul 28
Kennedy, Adam: Birth, Jan 10
Kennedy, Anthony M.: Birth, Jul 23
Kennedy, Edward Moore: Birth, Feb 22
Kennedy, John Fitzgerald
Assassination: Anniv, Nov 22
Birth Anniv, May 29
First Televised Presidential Debate: Anniv, Sep 26
John F. Kennedy Day in Massachusetts, Nov 27
Kennedy, Robert F: Birth Anniv, Nov 20
Kentucky
Admission Day, Jun 1
Barrier Awareness Day, May 7
Bunning, Jim: Birth, Oct 23
Confederate Memorial Day/Jefferson Davis Day, Jun 3
Disability Day, Aug 2
Fletcher, Ernie: Birth, Nov 12
Gifted Children Convention, Natl Assn (Louisville), Nov 9
Grandmother's Day, Oct 9
Kentucky Derby (Louisville), May 6
McConnell, Mitch: Birth, Feb 20
State Fair (Louisville), Aug 18
Kentucky Derby (Louisville, KY), May 6
Kenya
Jamhuri Day, Dec 12
Kenyatta Day, Oct 20
Madaraka Day, Jun 1
Kepes, Juliet A.: Birth Anniv, Jun 29
Kerns, Joanna: Birth, Feb 12
Kerr, Steve: Birth, Sep 27
Kerry, John F.: Birth, Dec 11
Ketchum, Liza: Birth, Jun 17
Key Club Intl Week, Nov 7
Key, Francis Scott: Birth Anniv, Aug 1
Key, Francis Scott: Star-Spangled Banner: Anniv, Sep 13
Kherdian, David: Birth, Dec 17
Kidd, Jason: Birth, Mar 23
KidFilm Fest (Dallas, TX), Jan 3
Kidman, Nicole: Birth, Jun 20
Kids After Christmas (Mystic, CT), Dec 26
Kids' Day, Kiwanis, Natl, Sep 24
Kids' Goal Setting Week, Nov 7
Kids Love a Mystery Month, Oct 1
KidsDay, Natl, Aug 7
Kilmer, Val: Birth, Dec 31
Kimmel, Eric A.: Birth, Oct 30
Kindergarten Day, Apr 21
King James Bible Published: Anniv, May 2
King Tut Tomb Discovery: Anniv, Nov 4
King, Coretta Scott: Birth, Apr 27
King, Martin Luther, Jr
Assassination Anniv, Apr 4
Birth Anniv, Jan 15
Birthday Observed, Jan 16
King Opposes Vietnam War: Anniv, Apr 4
March on Washington: Anniv, Aug 28
Martin Luther King, Jr Federal Holiday (Pres Proc), Jan 16
Wins Nobel Peace Prize: Anniv, Oct 14
King, Ronald Stacey: Birth, Jan 29
King, Stephen: Birth, Sep 21
King, W.L. MacKenzie: Birth Anniv, Dec 17
King, William R.: Birth Anniv, Apr 7
King-Smith, Dick: Birth, Mar 27
Kinsey-Warnock, Natalie: Birth, Nov 2
Kipling, Rudyard: Birth Anniv, Dec 30
Kiribati: Independence Day, Jul 12
Kirk, Daniel: Birth, May 1
Kirk, Jenny: Birth, Aug 15
Kirkpatrick, Chris: Birth, Oct 17
Kirsten, Samantha and Molly Debut: Anniv, Sep 15
Kite Fest of Santiago Sacatepequez (Guatemala), Nov 1
Kite Flying Day, Mar 27
Kiwanis
Key Club Intl Week, Nov 7
Kiwanis Kids' Day, Natl, Sep 24
Klause, Annette Curtis: Birth, Jun 20
Kleven, Elisa: Birth, Oct 14
Kliban, B(ernard): Birth Anniv, Jan 1
Kline, Suzy: Birth, Aug 27
Klondike Eldorado Gold Discovery: Anniv, Aug 31
Knight, Hilary: Birth, Nov 1
Knuckles Down Month, Natl, Apr 1
Kobuk Valley Natl Park Established: Anniv, Dec 2
Kohl, Herb: Birth, Feb 7
Koko the Gorilla: Birth, Jul 4
Komaiko, Leah: Birth, Jun 1
Konigsburg, E.L.: Birth, Feb 10
Koppel, Ted: Birth, Feb 8
Korea
Alphabet Day (Hangul), Oct 9
Children's Day, May 5
Chusok, Sep 18
Constitution Day, Jul 17
Korea, North and South, End War: Anniv, Dec 13
Korean War Armistice: Anniv, Jul 27
Korean War Began: Anniv, Jun 25
Memorial Day, Jun 6
National Day, Sep 9
National Foundation Day, Oct 3
Samiljol (Independence Movement Day), Mar 1
Tano Day, May 31
Liberation Day, Aug 15
Korman, Gordon: Birth, Oct 23
Kosciusko, Thaddeus: Birth Anniv, Feb 12
Kournikova, Anna: Birth, Jun 7
Krakatoa Eruption: Anniv, Aug 26
Krampuslauf (Austria), Dec 5
Kratt, Chris: Birth, Jul 19
Kratt, Martin: Birth, Dec 23
Kraus, Robert: Birth Anniv, Jun 21
Krayzelburg, Lenny: Birth, Sep 28
Kreis, Jason: Birth, Dec 29
Krementz, Jill: Birth, Feb 19
Kreuk, Kristin: Birth, Dec 30
Kristallnacht: Anniv, Nov 9
Kroll, Virginia: Birth, Apr 28
Krull, Kathleen: Birth, Jul 29
Krumgold, Joseph: Birth Anniv, Apr 9
Kulongoski, Ted: Birth, Nov 5
Kupets, Courtney: Birth, Jul 27
Kurban Bayram: See Eid-al-Adha, Jan 10
Kurri, Jari: Birth, May 18
Kurtz, Jane: Birth, Apr 17
Kuskin, Karla: Birth, Jul 17
Kutcher, Ashton: Birth, Feb 7
Kuwait
Iraq Invades Kuwait: Anniv, Aug 2
Kuwait Liberated: Anniv, Feb 27
Liberation Day, Feb 26
National Day, Feb 25
Kvasnosky, Laura McGee: Birth, Jan 27
Kwan, Michelle: Birth, Jul 7
Kwanzaa, Dec 26
Kyl, Jon: Birth, Apr 25
Kyrgyzstan: Independence Day, Aug 31
La Befana (Italy), Jan 6
La Farge, Oliver: Birth Anniv, Dec 19
Labonte, Bobby: Birth, May 8
Labor. See also Employment
AFL Founded: Anniv, Dec 8
AFL-CIO Founded: Anniv, Dec 5
Day of the Holy Cross, May 3
Labor Day, May 1
Labor Day (Bahamas), Jun 2
Labor Day (US, Canada), Sep 5
Lachey, Nick: Birth, Nov 9
Lackey, John: Birth, Oct 23
Laettner, Christian: Birth, Aug 17
Lafayette, Marquis de: Birth Anniv, Sep 6
Lag B'Omer, May 16
Lailat ul Qadr: (Islamic) Night of Power, Oct 25
Lake Clark Natl Park Established: Anniv, Dec 2
Lalas, Alexi: Birth, Jun 1
Landrieu, Mary L.: Birth, Nov 23
Landsgemeinde (Switzerland), Apr 30
Langton, Jane: Birth, Dec 30
Lantz, Walter: Birth Anniv, Apr 27
Lao People's Dem Repub: Natl Holiday, Dec 2
Larson, Gary: Birth, Aug 14
Lasek, Bucky: Birth, Dec 3
Laser Patented: Anniv, Mar 22
Lasky, Kathryn: Birth, Jun 24
Lassen Volcanic Natl Park Established: Anniv, Aug 9
Late for Something Day, Be, Sep 5
Lathrop, Julia C.: Birth Anniv, Jun 29
Latino Book & Family Fest—Chicago (IL), Nov 12
Latino Book & Family Fest—Houston (TX), Oct 1
Latino Book & Family Fest—Los Angeles (CA), Oct 16
Latvia
Baltic States' Independence Recognized: Anniv, Sep 6
Independence Day, Nov 18
John's Day (Midsummer Night Day), Jun 24
Lauber, Patricia: Birth, Feb 5
Lauer, Andrew: Birth, Jun 19
Lauer, Matt: Birth, Dec 30
Laura Ingalls Wilder Days (Pepin, WI), Sep 10
Laura Ingalls Wilder Fest (Mansfield, MO), Sep 17
Laura Ingalls Wilder Gingerbread Sociable (Pomona, CA), Feb 4
Laura Ingalls Wilder Pageant (De Smet, SD), Jul 7
Laura Ingalls Wilder Pageant (Walnut Grove, MN), Jul 7
Laurel and Hardy: Cuckoo Dancing Week, Jan 11
Laurier, Sir Wilfred: Birth Anniv, Nov 20
Lautenberg, Frank: Birth, Jan 23
Lavoisier, Antoine: Execution Anniv, May 8
Law Day (Pres Proc), May 1
Lawless, Lucy: Birth, Mar 29
Lawrence, Andrew: Birth, Jan 12
Lawrence, Jacob: Birth Anniv, Sep 7
Lawrence, Joey: Birth, Apr 20
Lawrence, Matthew: Birth, Feb 11
Lawson, Robert: Birth Anniv, Oct 4
Le Guin, Ursula K.: Birth, Oct 21
Leaf, Munro: Birth Anniv, Dec 4
League of Nations: Anniv, Jan 10
Leahy, Patrick J.: Birth, Mar 31
Leap Second Adjustment Time, Dec 31
Leap Second Adjustment Time, Jun 30
Lear, Edward: Birth Anniv, May 12
Leavitt, Mike: Birth, Feb 11
Lebanon
Independence Day, Nov 22
Lee, Francis Lightfoot: Birth Anniv, Oct 14
Lee, Harper: Birth, Apr 28
Lee, Richard Henry: Birth Anniv, Jan 20
Lee, Robert E.
Birth Anniv, Jan 19
Lee-Jackson Day, Jan 13
Lefleur, Guy: Birth, Sep 20
Legoland Opens: Anniv, Mar 20
Lei Day (Hawaii), May 1
Lemieux, Mario: Birth, Oct 5
L'Enfant, Pierre C.: Birth Anniv, Aug 2
L'Engle, Madeleine: Birth, Nov 29
Leno, Jay: Birth, Apr 28
Lenski, Lois: Birth Anniv, Oct 14
Lent, Mar 1
Lent, Blair: Birth, Jan 22
Lent, Orthodox, Mar 6
Leo Begins, Jul 23
Leonard, Justin: Birth, Jun 15
Leonardo Da Vinci: Death Anniv, May 2
Leonid Meteor Shower, Nov 15
Leopold, Aldo: Birth Anniv, Jan 11
Leslie, Lisa: Birth, Jul 7
Lesotho
Moshoeshoe's Day, Mar 12
National Day, Oct 4
Lester, Helen: Birth, Jun 12
Lester, Julius B.: Birth, Jan 27
Letter-Writing Week, Universal, Jan 8
Leutze, Emanuel: Birth Anniv, May 24
Levin, Carl: Birth, Jun 28
Levine, Gail Carson: Birth, Sep 17
Lewin, Ted: Birth, May 6
Lewis and Clark
Clark, William: Birth Anniv, Aug 1
Expedition Reaches the Pacific Ocean: Anniv, Nov 16
Expedition Sets Out: Anniv, May 14
Lewis, Meriwether: Birth Anniv, Aug 18
Sacagawea: Death Anniv, Dec 20
Lewis, C.S.: Birth Anniv, Nov 29
Lewis, Carl: Birth, Jul 1
Lewis, Francis: Birth Anniv, Mar 21
Lewis, Jamal: Birth, Aug 26
Lewis, Meriwether: Birth Anniv, Aug 18
Lewis, Rashard: Birth, Aug 8
Lewis, Shari: Birth Anniv, Jan 17
Liberia
Flag Day, Aug 24
J.J. Roberts Day, Mar 15
National Day, Jul 26
Thanksgiving Day, Nov 3
Liberty Day, Mar 23
Libra Begins, Sep 23
Library/Librarians
American Library Assn Annual Conference (New Orleans, LA), Jun 22
American Library Assn Midwinter Mtg (San Antonio, TX), Jan 20
Boston Public Library: Anniv, Apr 3
Intl Federation of Library Assns Annual Conference (Oslo, Norway), Aug 14

- Library Card Sign-up Month, Sep 1
- Library Lovers' Month, Feb 1
- Library of Congress: Anniv, Apr 24
- Library Week, Natl, Apr 2
- New York Public Library: Anniv, May 23
- Public Library Assn Conference (Boston, MA), Mar 21
- School Library Day, Intl, Oct 24
- School Library Media Month, Apr 1
- Teen Read Week, Oct 16
- Thank You, School Librarian Day, Apr 5

Libya
- American Bases Evacuation Day, Jun 11
- British Bases Evacuation Day, Mar 28
- Independence Day, Dec 24
- Revolution Day, Sep 1

Lieberman, Joseph I.: Birth, Feb 24
Liechtenstein: National Day, Aug 15
Limerick Day, May 12
Lincoln, Abraham
- Assassination Anniv, Apr 14
- Birth Anniv, Feb 12
- Emancipation Proclamation: Anniv, Sep 22
- Gettysburg Address: Anniv, Nov 19
- Lincoln Memorial Dedication: Anniv, May 30
- Urged To Grow Whiskers: Anniv, Oct 15

Lincoln, Blanche Lambert: Birth, Sep 30
Lincoln, Mary Todd: Birth Anniv, Dec 13
Lindbergh Flight: Anniv, May 20
Lindbergh, Charles A.: Birth Anniv, Feb 4
Lindgren, Astrid: Birth Anniv, Nov 14
Lindros, Eric: Birth, Feb 28
Lingle, Linda: Birth, Jun 4
Linz, Alex: Birth, Jan 3
Lion of Kabul: Death Anniv, Jan 25
Lionni, Leo: Birth Anniv, May 5
Lions Club Intl Peace Poster Contest, Oct 1
Lipinski, Tara: Birth, Jun 10
Lipnicki, Jonathan: Birth, Oct 22
Lisle, Janet Taylor: Birth, Feb 13
Lister, Joseph: Birth Anniv, Apr 5
Liszt, Franz: Birth Anniv, Oct 22
Literacy Day, Intl (UN), Sep 8
Literature
- Alice in Wonderland Published: Anniv, Nov 26
- American Poet Laureate Establishment: Anniv, Dec 20
- Anne Bradstreet Day, Sep 16
- Authors' Day, Natl, Nov 1
- Children's Book Day, Intl, Apr 2
- Children's Literature Fest (Warrensburg, MO), Mar 5
- David McCord Children's Literature Fest (Framingham, MA), Nov 3
- Eliza Doolittle Day, May 20
- Fest of Books for Young People (Iowa City, IA), Sep 10
- First Magazine Published in America: Anniv, Feb 13
- Harry Potter: Birthday, Jul 31
- Kids Love a Mystery Month, Oct 1
- Laura Ingalls Wilder Days (Pepin, WI), Sep 10
- Laura Ingalls Wilder Fest (Mansfield, MO), Sep 17
- Laura Ingalls Wilder Gingerbread Sociable (Pomona, CA), Feb 4
- Literature Fest (Lawrence, KS), Oct 18
- Poetry Month, Natl, Apr 1
- Reading Group Month, Natl, Oct 1
- Silent Spring Publication: Anniv, Apr 13
- Texas Book Fest (Austin, TX), Oct 28
- Virginia Hamilton Conference (Kent, OH), Apr 6
- Young People's Poetry Week, Apr 10

Literature Festival (Lawrence, KS), Oct 18
Lithgow, John: Birth, Oct 19
Lithuania
- Baltic States' Independence Recognized: Anniv, Sep 6
- Day of Statehood, Jul 6
- Independence Day, Feb 16

Little League Baseball World Series (Williamsport, PA), Aug 19
Little Rock Nine: Anniv, Sep 23
Littrell, Brian: Birth, Feb 20
Lively, Penelope: Birth, Mar 17
Livingston, Myra Cohn: Birth, Aug 17
Livingston, Philip: Birth Anniv, Jan 15
Livingston, Robert: Birth Anniv, Nov 27
Lizzie McGuire TV Premiere: Anniv, Jan 19
LL Cool J: Birth, Aug 16
Lloyd, Eric: Birth, May 19
Lloyd, Jake: Birth, Mar 5
Lobel, Anita: Birth, Jun 3
Lobel, Arnold: Birth Anniv, May 22
Lobo, Rebecca: Birth, Oct 6
Locust Plague of 1874: Anniv, Jul 20
Lodge, Bernard: Birth, Oct 19
Lofting, Hugh: Birth Anniv, Jan 14
Lofton, Kenny: Birth, May 31
Lohan, Lindsay: Birth, Jul 2
London, Jack: Birth Anniv, Jan 12
London, Jonathan: Birth, Mar 11
Lone Ranger TV Premiere: Anniv, Sep 15
Longfellow, Henry Wadsworth: Birth Anniv, Feb 27
Lopez, Steven: Birth, Sep 11
Lord of the Rings: First Part Published: Anniv, Jul 29
Los Angeles (CA) Founded: Anniv, Sep 4
Lost Penny Day, Feb 12
Lott, Trent: Birth, Oct 9
Louisiana
- Admissions Day, Apr 30
- American Library Assn Annual Conference (New Orleans), Jun 22
- Blanco, Kathleen: Birth, Dec 15
- Catholic Educational Assn Convention/Expo, Natl (New Orleans), Apr 18
- Confederate Memorial Day/Jefferson Davis Day, Jun 3
- Landrieu, Mary L.: Birth, Nov 23
- Louisiana Purchase Day, Dec 20
- School Boards Assn Annual Conference, Natl (New Orleans), Apr 8
- State Fair (Shreveport), Oct 21
- Vitter, David: Birth, May 3

Love the Children Day, Mar 29
Lovelace, Maud Hart: Birth Anniv, Apr 25
Lover's Day, Book Day and (Spain), Apr 23
Low, Juliet: Birth Anniv, Oct 31
Lowry, Lois: Birth, Mar 20
Loyalty Day (Pres Proc), May 1
Lucas, George: Birth, May 14
Lucid, Shannon: Birth, Jan 14
Luck: Open an Umbrella Indoors Day, Natl, Mar 13
Luenn, Nancy: Birth, Dec 28
Lugar, Richard G.: Birth, Apr 4
Luxembourg
- Burgsonndeg, Mar 5
- Ettelbruck Remembrance Day, Jul 6
- Liberation Ceremony, Sep 9
- National Holiday, Jun 23

Lynch, Chris: Birth, Jul 2
Lynch, John: Birth, Nov 25
Lynch, Thomas: Birth Anniv, Aug 5
Lyon, George Ella: Birth, Apr 25
Lyons, Mary: Birth, Nov 28
MacArthur Returns to the Philippines: Anniv, Oct 20
Macau Reverts to Chinese Control: Anniv, Dec 20
Macaulay, David: Birth, Dec 2
Macchio, Ralph: Birth, Nov 4
MacDonald, Amy: Birth, Jun 14
MacDonald, Betty: Birth Anniv, Mar 26
MacDonald, John A.: Birth Anniv, Jan 11
Macedonia, Former Yugoslav Republic of: National Day, Aug 2
Macintosh Computer Released: Anniv, Jan 25
MacKenzie, Alexander: Birth Anniv, Jan 28
MacLachlan, Patricia: Birth, Mar 3
Madagascar
- Independence Day, Jun 26
- National Holiday, Dec 30

Maddux, Greg: Birth, Apr 14
Madison, Dolly: Birth Anniv, May 20
Madison, James: Birth Anniv, Mar 16
Magazine, First Published in America: Anniv, Feb 13
Magellan, Ferdinand: Death Anniv, Apr 27
Magic Day, Natl, Oct 31
Magic: Houdini's Greatest Escape: Anniv, Sep 21
Magic: Robert-Houdin, Jean Eugene: Birth Anniv, Dec 6
Magna Carta Day, Jun 15
Maguire, Gregory: Birth, Jun 9
Mahy, Margaret: Birth, Mar 21
Mail: World Post Day (UN), Oct 9
Mail-Order Catalog: Anniv, Aug 18
Maine
- Admission Day, Mar 15
- Baldacci, John: Birth, Jan 30
- Bangor State Fair (Bangor), Jul 28
- Collins, Susan M.: Birth, Dec 7
- Patriot's Day, Apr 17
- Snowe, Olympia J.: Birth, Feb 21

Make a Difference Day, Oct 22
Make Up Your Own Holiday Day, Mar 26
Malawi
- Freedom Day, Jun 14
- John Chilembwe Day, Jan 16
- Martyr's Day, Mar 3
- Republic Day, Jul 6

Malaysia
- Freedom Day, Aug 31

Malcolm X: Birth Anniv, May 19
Maldives: National Day, Jul 26
Mali: Independence Day, Sep 22
Malone, Karl: Birth, Jul 24
Malone, Moses: Birth, Mar 23
Malta
- Carnival, Feb 25
- Feast of St. Paul's Shipwreck (Valletta), Feb 10
- Independence Day, Sep 21
- Republic Day, Dec 13

Manchin, Joe: Birth, Aug 24
Mandela, Nelson
- Arrest Anniv, Aug 4
- Birth, Jul 18
- Prison Release: Anniv, Feb 11

Manes, Stephen: Birth, Jan 8
Manet, Edouard: Birth Anniv, Jan 23
Mankiller, Wilma: Birth, Nov 18
Mann, Horace: Birth Anniv, May 4
Manning, Peyton: Birth, Mar 4
Man-Powered Flight, First: Anniv, Aug 23
Mantle, Mickey: Birth Anniv, Oct 20
Manushkin, Fran: Birth, Nov 2
Mao Tse-Tung: Birth Anniv, Dec 26
Maradona, Diego: Birth, Oct 30
Marathon, Days of: Anniv, Sep 2
Marbles: Natl Knuckles Down Month, Apr 1
Marbury, Stephon: Birth, Feb 20
Marcellino, Fred: Birth Anniv, Oct 25
Marco Polo: Death Anniv, Jan 8
Marconi, Guglielmo: Birth Anniv, Apr 25
Mardi Gras, Feb 28
Marine Corps Birthday, Nov 10
Marine War Memorial: Hayes, Ira: Birth Anniv, Jan 12
Maris Breaks Home Run Record: Anniv, Oct 1
Maris, Roger: Birth Anniv, Sep 10
Maritime Day, Natl, May 22
Maritime Day, Natl (Pres Proc), May 22
Marjan, The Lion of Kabul: Death Anniv, Jan 25
Marquette, Jacques: Birth Anniv, Jun 1
Marrin, Albert: Birth, Jul 24
Mars Climate Orbiter, Dec 11
Marsalis, Wynton: Birth, Oct 18
Marshall Islands: National Day, May 1
Marshall Plan: Anniv, Apr 3
Marshall, Donyell: Birth, May 18
Marshall, James: Birth Anniv, Oct 10
Marshall, John: Birth Anniv, Sep 24
Marshall, Thomas Riley: Birth Anniv, Mar 14
Marshall, Thurgood: Birth Anniv, Jul 2
Marti, Jose Julian: Birth Anniv, Jan 28
Martin, Andrea: Birth, Jan 15
Martin, Ann M.: Birth, Aug 12
Martin, Bill Jr.: Birth Anniv, Mar 20
Martin, Curtis: Birth, May 1
Martin, Jacqueline Briggs: Birth, Apr 15
Martin, Kenyon: Birth, Dec 30
Martin, Paul: Birth, Aug 28
Martin, Rafe: Birth, Jan 22
Martinez, Mel: Birth, Oct 23
Martinez, Pedro: Birth, Oct 25
Martinez, Victor: Birth, Feb 21
Martinmas, Nov 11
Martyrs' Day (Bangladesh), Feb 21
Martyrs' Day (Panama), Jan 9
Mary Rose Wreck Raised: Anniv, Oct 11
Maryland
- American Council on Teaching of Foreign Languages (Baltimore), Nov 18
- Baltimore Book Fest (Baltimore), Sep 23
- Defenders Day, Sep 12
- Ehrlich, Robert, Jr: Birth, Nov 25
- Maryland Day, Mar 25
- Mikulski, Barbara Ann: Birth, Jul 20
- Ratification Day, Apr 28
- Sarbanes, Paul S.: Birth, Feb 3
- State Fair (Timonium), Aug 26

Marzollo, Jean: Birth, Jun 24
Massachusetts
- Art Education Assn Annual Convention, Natl (Boston), Mar 4
- Big E (West Springfield), Sep 16
- Boston Public Library: Anniv, Apr 3
- Bunker Hill Day, Jun 17
- Children's Day, Jun 11
- David McCord Children's Literature Fest (Framingham), Nov 3
- Deborah Samson Day, May 23
- Evacuation Day, Mar 17
- First Women's Collegiate Basketball Game: Anniv, Mar 22
- John Carver Day, Jun 25
- John F. Kennedy Day, Nov 27
- Keep Massachusetts Beautiful Month, May 1
- Kennedy, Edward Moore: Birth, Feb 22
- Kerry, John F.: Birth, Dec 11
- Native American Day, Sep 16
- Patriot's Day, Apr 17
- Public Library Assn Conference (Boston), Mar 21
- Ratification Day, Feb 6
- Romney, Mitt: Birth, Mar 12
- Samuel Slater Day, Dec 20
- School Principals' Recognition Day, Apr 27
- State Constitution Day, Oct 25
- Student Government Day, Apr 7
- Teacher's Day, Jun 4
- Whale Awareness Day, May 4

Mastroeni, Pablo: Birth, Aug 29
Mathematics, Natl Council of Teachers of, Annual Mtg (St. Louis, MO), Apr 26
Mathis, Clint: Birth, Nov 25
Mathis, Sharon Bell: Birth, Feb 26
Matisse, Henri: Birth Anniv, Dec 31
Maundy Thursday (Holy Thursday), Apr 13
Mauritania: Independence Day, Nov 28
Mauritius: Independence Day, Mar 12
Mawlid al Nabi: Birthday of Prophet Muhammad, Apr 11
Maxwell, Gavin: Birth Anniv, Jul 15
May Day, May 1
Mayan Tomb of Pacal Discovered: Anniv, Jun 15
Mayer, Mercer: Birth, Dec 30
Mayflower Day, Sep 16
Mayne, William: Birth, Mar 16
Mays, Willie: Birth, May 6
Mazer, Harry: Birth, May 31
Mazer, Norma Fox: Birth, May 15
Mazowiecki, Tadeusz: Poland: Solidarity Founded, Aug 31
McAllister, Deuce: Birth, Dec 27
McArdle, Andrea: Birth, Nov 4
McAuliffe, Christa: Birth Anniv, Sep 2
McBride, Brian: Birth, Jun 19
McCaffrey, Anne: Birth, Apr 1
McCain, John III: Birth, Aug 29
McCartney, Paul: Birth, Jun 18
McClintock, Barbara: Birth, May 6
McConnell, Mitch: Birth, Feb 20
McCully, Emily Arnold: Birth, Jul 1
McDermott, Gerald: Birth, Jan 31
McDonald, Megan: Birth, Feb 28
McDonald's Opens in the Soviet Union: Anniv, Jan 31
McGovern, Ann: Birth, May 25
McGrady, Tracy: Birth, May 24
McGraw, Eloise Jarvis: Birth Anniv, Dec 9
McGuffey, William H.: Birth Anniv, Sep 23
McGwire, Mark: Birth, Oct 1
McKay, Hillary: Birth, Jun 12
McKean, Thomas: Birth Anniv, Mar 19
McKinley, Ida Saxton: Birth Anniv, Jun 8
McKinley, Robin: Birth, Nov 16
McKinley, William: Birth Anniv, Jan 29
McKissack, Fredrick: Birth, Aug 12
McKissack, Patricia: Birth, Aug 9
McLean, A.J.: Birth, Jan 9
McMillan, Bruce: Birth, May 10
McMullan, Kate: Birth, Jan 16
McNabb, Donovan: Birth, Nov 25
McNair, Steve: Birth, Feb 14
McNaughton, Colin: Birth, May 18
McPhail, David: Birth, Jun 30
Meddaugh, Susan: Birth, Oct 4
Medearis, Angela Shelf: Birth, Nov 16
Medical School for Women Opened: Anniv, Nov 1
Meltzer, Milton: Birth, May 8
Melville, Herman: Birth Anniv, Aug 1
Memorial Day (Observed), May 29
Memorial Day (Pres Proc), May 29
MENC Natl Conference (Salt Lake City, UT), Apr 18
Mental Health Month, Natl, May 1
Mental Retardation Awareness Month, Mar 1
Mentoring Month, Natl, Jan 1
Mercator, Gerhardus: Birth Anniv, Mar 5

Meredith (James) Enrolls at Ole Miss: Anniv, Sep 30
Merlin's Snug Hug for Kids, Nov 1
Merriam, Eve: Birth Anniv, Jul 19
Mesa Verde Natl Park: Anniv, Jun 29
Mesmer, Friedrich: Birth Anniv, May 23
Messier, Mark: Birth, Jan 18
Meteorological Day, World (UN), Mar 23
Meteors; Meteor Showers
  Eta Aquarids Meteor Shower, Apr 21
  Leonid Meteor Shower, Nov 15
  Orionids Meteor Shower, Oct 15
  Perseid Meteor Showers, Aug 9
Metric Conversion Act: Anniv, Dec 23
Metric System: Anniv, Apr 7
Metric Week, Natl, Oct 9
Mexico
  Aztec Calendar Stone Discovery: Anniv, Dec 17
  Benito Juarez: Birth Anniv, Mar 21
  Blessing of Animals at the Cathedral, Jan 17
  Cinco de Mayo, May 5
  Constitution Day, Feb 5
  Cortes Conquers Mexico: Anniv, Nov 8
  Day of the Dead, Nov 1
  Day of the Holy Cross, May 3
  Dia de la Candelaria, Feb 2
  Dia de la Raza, Oct 12
  Feast of the Radishes (Oaxaca), Dec 23
  Flag Day, Feb 24
  Guadalajara Intl Book Fair, Nov 26
  Guadalupe Day, Dec 12
  Independence Day, Sep 16
  Mexico City Earthquake: Anniv, Sep 19
  Posadas, Dec 16
  President's State of the Union Address, Sep 1
  Revolution Day, Nov 20
  San Isidro Day, May 15
  Treaty of Guadalupe Hidalgo (with US): Anniv, Feb 2
  Zapatista Rebellion: Anniv, Jan 1
Meyer, Carolyn: Birth, Jun 8
Mfume, Kweisi: Birth, Oct 24
Michaelmas, Sep 29
Michelangelo: Birth Anniv, Mar 6
Michelson, Albert: First US Scientist Receives Nobel: Anniv, Dec 10
Michigan
  Admission Day, Jan 26
  America's Thanksgiving Parade (Detroit), Nov 24
  Granholm, Jennifer: Birth, Feb 5
  Isle Royale Natl Park: Anniv, Apr 3
  Levin, Carl: Birth, Jun 28
  Month of the Young Child, Apr 1
  Stabenow, Debbie: Birth, Apr 29
  State Fair (Detroit), Aug 10
  Super Bowl (Detroit), Feb 5
Mickey Mouse Club TV Premiere: Anniv, Oct 3
Mickey Mouse's Birthday, Nov 18
Micronesia, Federated States of: Independence Day, Nov 3
Microsoft Releases Windows: Anniv, Nov 10
Mid-Autumn Fest, Sep 18
Middle Level Education Month, Natl, Mar 1
Middle School Assn, Natl, Annual Conference (Philadelphia, PA), Nov 3
Middleton, Arthur: Birth Anniv, Jun 26
Midori: Birth, Oct 25
Midsummer Day/Eve Celebrations, Jun 23
Midwife's Day (Greece), Jan 8
Mientkiewicz, Doug: Birth, Jun 19
Mighty Mouse Playhouse TV Premiere: Anniv, Dec 10
Mikita, Stan: Birth, May 20
Mikulski, Barbara Ann: Birth, Jul 20
Mikulski, Barbara: Polish American in the House: Anniv, Jan 4
Milano, Alyssa: Birth, Dec 19
Miles, Miska: Birth Anniv, Nov 14
Miller, Andre: Birth, Mar 19
Miller, Jeremy: Birth, Oct 21
Miller, Reggie: Birth, Aug 24
Miller, Shannon: Birth, Mar 10
Million Man March: Anniv, Oct 16
Million Mom March: Anniv, May 14
Milne, A.A.: Birth Anniv (Pooh Day), Jan 18
Minarik, Else Holmelund: Birth, Sep 13
Mineta, Norman: Birth, Nov 12
Ming, Yao: Birth, Sep 12
Minner, Ruth Ann: Birth, Jan 17
Minnesota
  Admission Day, May 11
  Coleman, Norm: Birth, Aug 17
  Dayton, Mark: Birth, Jan 26
  Laura Ingalls Wilder Pageant (Walnut Grove), Jul 7
  Pawlenty, Tim: Birth, Nov 1
  Schwan's USA Cup (Blaine), Jul 14
  State Fair (St. Paul), Aug 25
  Voyageurs Natl Park: Anniv, Apr 8
Minow, Newton: Vast Wasteland Speech: Anniv, May 9
Mint, US: Anniv, Apr 2
Miranda Decision: Anniv, Jun 13
Mirra, Dave: Birth, Apr 4
Mischief Night, Nov 4
Missing Children's Day, Natl, May 25
Mississippi
  Admission Day, Dec 10
  Barbour, Haley: Birth, Oct 22
  Cochran, Thad: Birth, Dec 7
  Confederate Memorial Day, Apr 24
  Lott, Trent: Birth, Oct 9
  Meredith (James) Enrolls at Ole Miss: Anniv, Sep 30
  State Fair (Jackson), Oct 5
Missouri
  Admission Day, Aug 10
  Blunt, Matt: Birth, Nov 20
  Bond, Christopher S.: Birth, Mar 6
  Children's Literature Fest (Warrensburg), Mar 5
  Earthquakes: Anniv, Dec 6
  Geographic Education, Natl Council for (Birmingham), Oct 12
  Laura Ingalls Wilder Fest (Mansfield), Sep 17
  Minority Scientists Showcase (St. Louis), Jan 14
  Missouri Day, Oct 19
  Social Studies, Natl Council for the, Annual Mtg (Kansas City), Nov 17
  State Fair (Sedalia), Aug 11
  Talent, Jim: Birth, Oct 18
  Teachers of Mathematics, Natl Council of, Annual Mtg (St. Louis), Apr 26
  Tom Sawyer Days, Natl (Hannibal), Jul 1
Missouri Compromise: Anniv, Mar 3
Mister Rogers' Neighborhood TV Premiere: Anniv, May 22
Mitchell, Beverley: Birth, Jan 22
Mitchell, Kel: Birth, Aug 25
Mitchell, Maria: Birth Anniv, Aug 1
Moceanu, Dominique: Birth, Sep 30
Mochizuki, Ken: Birth, May 18
Modano, Mike: Birth, Jun 7
Mohr, Nicholasa: Birth, Nov 1
Moldova
  Independence Day, Aug 27
  National Language Day, Aug 31
Molina, Bengie: Birth, Jul 20
Molitor, Paul: Birth, Aug 22
Mollel, Tololwa: Birth, Jun 25
Moment of Laughter Day, Apr 14
Monaco: National Holiday, Nov 19
Monaghan, Dominic: Birth, Dec 8
Monarch Butterfly Fall Migration, Aug 21
Mondale, Walter: Birth, Jan 5
Monday Holiday Law: Anniv, Jun 28
Monet, Claude: Birth Anniv, Nov 14
Money, Paper, Issued: Anniv, Mar 10
Mongolia
  National Holiday, Jul 11
  Republic Day, Nov 26
Monica: Birth, Oct 24
Monkey Trial: John T. Scopes Birth Anniv, Aug 3
Monopoly Invented: Anniv, Mar 7
Monroe Doctrine: Anniv, Dec 2
Monroe, Elizabeth K.: Birth Anniv, Jun 30
Monroe, James: Birth Anniv, Apr 28
Montana
  Admission Day, Nov 8
  Battle of Little Bighorn: Anniv, Jun 25
  Baucus, Max: Birth, Dec 11
  Burns, Conrad: Birth, Jan 25
  Schweitzer, Brian: Birth, Sep 5
  State Fair (Great Falls), Jul 28
Montana, Joe: Birth, Jun 11
Montessori, Maria: Birth Anniv, Aug 31
Montgolfier, Jacques: Birth Anniv, Jan 7
Montgolfier, Joseph M.: Birth Anniv, Aug 26
Montgomery Boycott Arrests: Anniv, Feb 22
Montgomery Bus Boycott Begins: Anniv, Dec 5
Montgomery, Lucy Maud: Birth Anniv, Nov 30
Month of the Young Adolescent, Oct 1
Montross, Eric Scott: Birth, Sep 23
Montserrat: Volcano Erupts: Anniv, Jun 25
Moody, Helen Wills: Birth Anniv, Oct 6
Moon Day (First Moon Landing), Jul 20
Moon Fest, Sep 18
Moon Phases
  First Quarter, Jan 6
  First Quarter, Feb 5
  First Quarter, Mar 6
  First Quarter, Apr 5
  First Quarter, May 5
  First Quarter, Jun 3
  First Quarter, Jul 3
  First Quarter, Aug 12
  First Quarter, Sep 11
  First Quarter, Oct 10
  First Quarter, Nov 8
  First Quarter, Dec 8
  Full Moon, Jan 14
  Full Moon, Feb 12
  Full Moon, Mar 14
  Full Moon, Apr 13
  Full Moon, May 13
  Full Moon, Jun 11
  Full Moon, Jul 10
  Full Moon, Aug 19
  Full Moon, Sep 17
  Full Moon, Oct 17
  Full Moon, Nov 15
  Full Moon, Dec 15
  Last Quarter, Jan 22
  Last Quarter, Feb 21
  Last Quarter, Mar 22
  Last Quarter, Apr 20
  Last Quarter, May 20
  Last Quarter, Jun 18
  Last Quarter, Jul 17
  Last Quarter, Aug 26
  Last Quarter, Sep 25
  Last Quarter, Oct 24
  Last Quarter, Nov 23
  Last Quarter, Dec 23
  New Moon, Jan 29
  New Moon, Feb 27
  New Moon, Mar 29
  New Moon, Apr 27
  New Moon, May 27
  New Moon, Jun 25
  New Moon, Jul 25
  New Moon, Aug 4
  New Moon, Sep 3
  New Moon, Oct 3
  New Moon, Nov 1
  New Moon, Dec 1
  New Moon, Dec 30
Moon, Harvest, Sep 17
Moon, Hunter's, Oct 17
Moon, Warren: Birth, Nov 18
Moore, Clement: Birth Anniv, Jul 15
Moore, Julianne: Birth, Dec 3
Mora, Pat: Birth, Jan 19
Moranis, Rick: Birth, Apr 18
Morazan, Francisco: Holiday (Honduras), Oct 3
Morocco: Youth Day, Jul 9
Morris, Ann: Birth, Oct 1
Morris, Lewis: Birth Anniv, Apr 8
Morris, Robert: Birth Anniv, Jan 31
Morse, Samuel F.: Birth Anniv, Apr 27
Morse, Samuel: Opens First US Telegraph Line: Anniv, May 24
Mortensen, Viggo: Birth, Oct 20
Morton, Levi P.: Birth Anniv, May 16
Moser, Barry: Birth, Oct 15
Moses, Edwin: Birth, Aug 31
Moses, Grandma: Day, Sep 7
Moshoeshoe's Day (Lesotho), Mar 12
Moss, Randy: Birth, Feb 13
Most, Bernard: Birth, Sep 2
Mother Goose Day, May 1
Mother Goose Parade (El Cajon, CA), Nov 20
Mother Language Day, Intl (UN), Feb 21
Mother Teresa: Birth Anniv, Aug 27
Mother, Father Deaf Day, Apr 30
Mother's Day, May 14
Mother's Day (Pres Proc), May 14
Mott, Lucretia: Birth Anniv, Jan 3
Mount Everest Summit Reached: Anniv, May 29
Mount Everest: First Woman To Climb: Anniv, May 16
Mount Pelee Eruption: Anniv, May 8
Mount Rainier Natl Park: Anniv, Mar 2
Mount Rushmore Completion: Anniv, Oct 31
Mount Saint Helens Eruption: Anniv, May 18
Mourning, Alonzo: Birth, Feb 8
Moving Month, Natl, May 1
Mowat, Farley: Birth, May 12
Moya, Carlos: Birth, Aug 27
Mozambique
  Armed Forces Day, Sep 24
  Heroes' Day, Feb 3
  Independence Day, Jun 25
Mozart, Wolfgang Amadeus: Birth Anniv, Jan 27
Muhammad: Isra al Mi'raj: Ascent of Prophet, Sep 1
Muhammad: Mawlid al Nabi: Birth of Muhammad, Apr 11
Muharram: See Islamic New Year, Jan 31
Mule Day, Oct 26
Mulgrew, Kate: Birth, Apr 29
Mummies
  Iceman Discovered: Anniv, Sep 19
  Inca Ice Maiden Discovered: Anniv, Sep 8
  King Tut Tomb Discovery: Anniv, Nov 4
Muniz, Frankie: Birth, Dec 5
Munoz-Rivera, Luis: Birth Anniv, Jul 17
Munro, Roxie: Birth, Sep 5
Munsch, Robert: Birth, Jun 11
Munsinger, Lynn: Birth, Dec 24
Muppet Show TV Premiere, The: Anniv, Sep 13
Muppets: Henson, Jim: Birth Anniv, Sep 24
Murkowski, Frank Hughes: Birth, Mar 28
Murkowski, Lisa: Birth, May 22
Murphy, Eddie: Birth, Apr 3
Murphy, Jim: Birth, Sep 25
Murray, Bill: Birth, Sep 21
Murray, Patty: Birth, Oct 11
Musburger, Brent: Birth, May 26
Museum Day, Intl, May 18
Musial, Stan: Birth, Nov 21
Music
  Aberdeen Intl Youth Fest (Aberdeen, Scotland), Aug 3
  Accordion Awareness Week, Intl, Jun 1
  America the Beautiful Published: Anniv, Jul 4
  Beethoven's Ninth Symphony Premiere: Anniv, May 7
  Calgary Intl Children's Fest (Calgary, AB, Canada), May 23
  Drum Month, Intl, Nov 1
  God Bless America First Performed: Anniv, Nov 11
  Happy Birthday to "Happy Birthday to You", Jun 27
  Jazz Day, Intl, May 27
  Music in Our Schools Month, Mar 1
  Opera Debuts in the Colonies: Anniv, Feb 8
  Piano Month, Natl, Sep 1
  Play-the-Recorder Month, Mar 1
  Pop Music Chart Introduced: Anniv, Jan 4
  Saxophone Day, Nov 6
  Stars and Stripes Forever Day, May 14
Muslim Observances
  Ashura: Tenth Day, Feb 9
  Eid-al-Adha: Feast of the Sacrifice, Jan 10
  Eid-al-Fitr: Celebrating the Fast, Nov 4
  Isra al Mi'raj: Ascent of Prophet Muhammad, Sep 1
  Lailat ul Qadr: The Night of Power, Oct 25
  Mawlid al Nabi: Birthday of Prophet Muhammad, Apr 11
  Muharram (New Year), Jan 31
  Rabi'l: Month of the Migration, Mar 31
  Ramadan: Islamic Month of Fasting, Oct 5
  Yawm Arafat: The Standing at Arafat, Jan 9
Mussina, Mike: Birth, Dec 8
Mustard Day, Natl, Aug 6
Mutiny on the Bounty: Anniv, Apr 28
Mutombo, Dikembe: Birth, Jun 25
Myanmar
  Independence Day, Jan 4
  Resistance Day, Mar 27
  Union Day, Feb 12
Myers, Mike: Birth, May 25
Myers, Walter Dean: Birth, Aug 12
NAACP Founded: Anniv, Feb 12
Nabokov, Evgeni: Birth, Jul 25
NAFTA Signed: Anniv, Dec 8
Naismith, James: Birth Anniv, Nov 6
Name Day, Get a Different, Feb 13
Namibia
  Heroes' Day, Aug 26
  Independence Day, Mar 21
Nanakusa (Japan), Jan 7
Napoli, Donna Jo: Birth, Feb 28
Napolitano, Janet: Birth, Nov 29
NASA Established: Anniv, Jul 29
National Bank, Chartered by Congress: Anniv, Feb 25

National Council of Teachers of English Annual Convention (Pittsburgh, PA), Nov 17
National Park Week (Pres Proc), Apr 16
Native-American
American Indian Heritage Day (AL), Oct 10
American Indian Heritage Month, Natl (Pres Proc), Nov 1
Apache Wars Began: Anniv, Feb 4
Battle of Little Bighorn: Anniv, Jun 25
Bureau of Indian Affairs Established, Mar 11
Chief Joseph Surrender: Anniv, Oct 5
Chief Joseph: Death Anniv, Sep 21
Cochise: Death Anniv, Jun 8
Crow Reservation Opened for Settlement: Anniv, Oct 15
Custer Battlefield Becomes Little Bighorn, Nov 26
Geronimo: Death Anniv, Feb 17
Hayes, Ira Hamilton: Birth Anniv, Jan 12
Last Great Buffalo Hunt: Anniv, Jun 25
Native American Day (MA), Sep 16
Native Americans Day in South Dakota, Oct 10
Native Americans Gain Citizenship: Anniv, Jun 15
Osceola: Death Anniv, Jan 30
Philip, King: Assassination: Anniv, Aug 12
Pocahontas: Death Anniv, Mar 21
Red Cloud: Death Anniv, Dec 10
Rights Recognized: Anniv, May 12
Sacagawea: Death Anniv, Dec 20
Sitting Bull: Death Anniv, Dec 15
Tecumseh: Death Anniv, Oct 5
Wounded Knee Massacre: Anniv, Dec 29
NATO Attacks Yugoslavia: Anniv, Mar 25
Nauru: National Day, Jan 31
Nautilus: First Nuclear-Powered Submarine Voyage: Anniv, Jan 17
Navy Day, Oct 27
Navy: Sea Cadet Month, Sep 1
Naylor, Phyllis Reynolds: Birth, Jan 4
Near Miss Day, Mar 23
Nebraska
Admission Day, Mar 1
Hagel, Chuck: Birth, Oct 4
Heineman, Dave: Birth, May 12
Nelson, Ben: Birth, May 17
Norfolk Public Library Literature Fest (Norfolk), Jul 29
State Fair (Lincoln), Aug 27
Nehru, Jawaharlal: Birth Anniv, Nov 14
Neither Snow Nor Rain Day: Anniv, Sep 7
Nelson, Ben: Birth, May 17
Nelson, Bill: Birth, Sep 29
Nelson, Thomas: Birth Anniv, Dec 26
Nepal
National Unity Day, Jan 11
Neptune Discovery: Anniv, Sep 23
Nesbit, E. (Edith): Birth Anniv, Aug 15
Ness, Evaline: Birth Anniv, Apr 24
Netherlands
Liberation Day, May 5
National Windmill Day, May 13
Prinsjesdag (Parliament opening), Sep 20
Queen's Birthday, Apr 30
Sinterklaas, Dec 5
Neufeld, John: Birth, Dec 14
Nevada
Admission Day, Oct 31
Ensign, John: Birth, Mar 25
Family Day, Nov 25
Guinn, Kenny: Birth, Aug 24
Reid, Harry: Birth, Dec 2
State Fair (Reno), Aug 24
Nevis: Independence Day, Sep 19
New Hampshire
Children's Literature Fest (Keene), Oct 29
Gregg, Judd: Birth, Feb 14
Lynch, John: Birth, Nov 25
Ratification Day, Jun 21
Sununu, John: Birth, Sep 10
New Jersey
Codey, Richard: Birth, Nov 27
Corzine, Jon: Birth, Jan 1
Lautenberg, Frank: Birth, Jan 23
New Jersey Day, Apr 17
New Jersey State Fair/Sussex County Farm & Horse Show (Augusta), Aug 5
Ratification Day, Dec 18
New Mexico
Admission Day, Jan 6
Bingaman, Jeff: Birth, Oct 3
Carlsbad Caverns Natl Park Established: Anniv, May 14
Domenici, Pete V.: Birth, May 7
Richardson, Bill: Birth, Nov 15
State Fair (Albuquerque), Sep 1
New Orleans, Battle of: Anniv, Jan 8
New Year
Chinese New Year, Jan 29
Hogmanay (Scotland), Dec 31
Iranian New Year (Persian), Mar 21
Japanese Era New Year, Jan 1
Muharram (Islamic New Year), Jan 31
Naw-Ruz (Baha'i New Year's Day), Mar 21
New Year's Day, Jan 1
New Year's Day (Ethiopia), Sep 11
New Year's Day (Gregorian), Jan 1
New Year's Day Observance (Russia), Jan 1
New Year's Dishonor List, Jan 1
New Year's Eve, Dec 31
Rosh Hashanah (Jewish), Oct 4
Sri Lanka: Sinhala and Tamil New Year, Apr 13
New York
Bloomberg, Michael: Birth, Feb 14
Brooklyn Bridge Opened: Anniv, May 24
Christmas Tree/Rockefeller Center (New York), Nov 29
Clinton, Hillary Rodham: Birth, Oct 26
Ellis Island Family History Day (New York), Apr 17
Great Blizzard of '88: Anniv, Mar 12
Macy's Thanksgiving Day Parade (New York), Nov 24
New York City Subway: Anniv, Oct 27
New York Public Library: Anniv, May 23
Pataki, George: Birth, Jun 24
Ratification Day, Jul 26
Saint Patrick's Day Parade (New York), Mar 17
Schumer, Charles E.: Birth, Nov 23
State Fair (Syracuse), Aug 25
New York Stock Exchange Established: Anniv, May 17
New Zealand
Anzac Day, Apr 25
Labor Day, Oct 24
New Zealand First Sighted by Europeans, Dec 13
Otago/Southland Provincial Anniv, Mar 23
Waitangi Day, Feb 6
Newbery, John: Birth Anniv, Jul 19
Newby, Marcia: Birth, Mar 8
Newscurrents Student Editorial Cartoon Contest, Mar 1
Newspaper in Education Week, Mar 6
Newspaper Week (Japan), Oct 2
Newspaper, First American: Anniv, Sep 25
Newton, Sir Isaac: Birth Anniv, Jan 4
Nez Perce: Chief Joseph Surrender: Anniv, Oct 5
Ng, Irene: Birth, Jul 30
Niagara Falls Runs Dry: Anniv, Mar 29
Niagara Falls, Charles Blondin's Conquest of: Anniv, Jun 30
Niagara Movement Founded: Anniv, Jul 11
Nicaragua
Independence Day, Sep 15
National Liberation Day, Jul 19
Nicholson, Jim: Birth, Feb 6
Nick at Nite TV Premiere: Anniv, Jul 1
Nickelodeon Channel TV Premiere: Anniv, Apr 2
Nieuwendyk, Joe: Birth, Sep 10
Niger
Independence Day, Aug 3
Republic Day, Dec 18
Nigeria: Independence Day, Oct 1
Night Out, Natl, Aug 2
Nightingale, Florence: Birth Anniv, May 12
Nixon, Pat: Birth Anniv, Mar 16
Nixon, Richard Milhous
Birth Anniv, Jan 9
First Televised Presidential Debate: Anniv, Sep 26
Resigns: Anniv, Aug 9
No Homework Day, May 6
No Housework Day, Apr 7
No Name-Calling Week, Jan 16
No Socks Day, May 8
Nobel Prize Ceremonies (Oslo, Norway/Stockholm, Sweden), Dec 10
Nobel Prize, First US Scientist Receives: Anniv, Dec 10
Nobel, Alfred: Birth Anniv, Oct 21
Nomo, Hideo: Birth, Aug 31
Norfolk Public Library Literature Fest (Norfolk, NE), Jul 29
North Atlantic Treaty Ratified: Anniv, Apr 4
North Carolina
Burr, Richard: Birth, Nov 30
Confederate Memorial Day, May 10
Dole, Elizabeth Hanford: Birth, Jul 29
Easley, Mike: Birth, Mar 23
Greensboro Sit-in: Anniv, Feb 1
North Carolina SweetPotato Month, Feb 1
Ratification Day, Nov 21
State Fair (Raleigh), Oct 14
US Girls' Junior (Golf) Chmpshp (Charlotte), Jul 17
North Cascades Natl Park: Anniv, Oct 2
North Dakota
Admission Day, Nov 2
Conrad, Kent: Birth, Mar 12
Dorgan, Byron L.: Birth, May 14
Hoeven, John: Birth, Mar 13
State Fair (Minot), Jul 21
Theodore Roosevelt Natl Park Established: Anniv, Apr 25
North Pole Discovered: Anniv, Apr 6
North Pole, Solo Trip to: Anniv, Apr 22
North, Sterling: Birth Anniv, Nov 4
Northern Hemisphere Hoodie-Hoo Day, Feb 20
Northern Ireland
Orangemen's Day, Jul 12
Saint Patrick's Day, Mar 17
Northern Pacific Railroad Completed: Anniv, Sep 8
Northwest Ordinance: Anniv, Jul 13
Norton, Gale: Birth, Mar 11
Norton, Mary: Birth Anniv, Dec 10
Noruz, Mar 21
Norway
Constitution or Independence Day, May 17
Intl Federation of Library Assns Annual Conference (Oslo), Aug 14
Midnight Sun at North Cape, May 14
Nobel Prize Awards Ceremony (Oslo), Dec 10
Saint Knut's Day, Jan 13
Nothing Day, Natl, Jan 16
NOW Founded: Anniv, Jun 30
Nowitzki, Dirk: Birth, Jun 19
NSSEA Ed Expo & School Equipment Show (Orlando, FL), Mar 2
Nuclear Power; Weapons
First Nuclear-Powered Submarine Voyage: Anniv, Jan 17
First Self-Sustaining Nuclear Chain Reaction: Anniv, Dec 2
Nuclear-Free World, First Step Toward a: Anniv, Dec 8
Three Mile Island Power Plant Accident: Anniv, Mar 28
Numeroff, Laura Joffe: Birth, Jul 14
Numismatics: Natl Coin Week, Apr 16
Nunavut Independence: Anniv, Apr 1
Nurses Day and Week, Natl, May 6
Nutrition Month, Natl, Mar 1
Nutt Day, Emma M., Sep 1
Nye, Bill: Birth, Nov 27
Nye, Naomi Shihab: Birth, Mar 12
Nylon Stockings: Anniv, May 15
Nyquist, Ryan: Birth, Mar 6
O.K. First Appearance in Print: Anniv, Mar 23
Oakley, Annie: Birth Anniv, Aug 13
Oatmeal Month, Jan 1
Obama, Barack: Birth, Aug 4
O'Brien, Anne Sibley: Birth, Jul 10
O'Brien, Austin: Birth, May 11
O'Brien, Robert C.: Birth Anniv, Jan 11
Ocean, Natl Week of the, Apr 2
O'Connor, Sandra Day: Birth, Mar 26
O'Connor, Sandra Day: First Woman Supreme Court Justice: Anniv, Sep 25
October War (Yom Kippur War), Oct 6
O'Dell, Scott: Birth Anniv, May 23
Odie: Birthday, Aug 8
O'Donnell, Chris: Birth, Jun 26
O'Donnell, Rosie: Birth, Mar 21
Ogden, Jonathan: Birth, Jul 31
Oglethorpe, James: Birth Anniv, Dec 22
O'Hara, Mary: Birth Anniv, Jul 10
O'Higgins, Bernardo: Birth Anniv, Aug 20
Ohio
Admission Day, Mar 1
DeWine, Mike: Birth, Jan 5
Ohio State Fair (Columbus), Aug 3
Soap Box Derby, All-American (Akron), Jul 30
Stokes Becomes First Black Mayor in US: Anniv, Nov 13
Storyteller of the Year Contest, Natl (Millersport), Oct 30
Taft, Bob: Birth, Jan 8
Virginia Hamilton Conference (Kent), Apr 6
Voinovich, George V.: Birth, Jul 15
Oil Embargo Lifted, Arab: Anniv, Mar 13
Oil: 55 mph Speed Limit: Anniv, Jan 2
Oil: First Commercial Oil Well: Anniv, Aug 27
O'Keeffe, Georgia: Birth Anniv, Nov 15
Oklahoma
Admission Day, Nov 16
Cherokee Strip Day, Sep 16
Coburn, Tom: Birth, Mar 14
Henry, Brad: Birth, Jul 10
Inhofe, James M.: Birth, Nov 17
Land Rush Begins, Apr 22
Oklahoma Day, Apr 22
State Fair (Oklahoma City), Sep 15
Oklahoma City Bombing: Anniv, Apr 19
Olajuwon, Hakeem: Birth, Jan 21
Old Inauguration Day, Mar 4
Old Ironsides Launched: Anniv, Oct 21
Old Ironsides Saved By Poem: Anniv, Sep 16
Older Americans Month (Pres Proc), May 1
Olerud, John: Birth, Aug 5
Oleynik, Larisa: Birth, Jun 7
Olsen, Ashley: Birth, Jun 13
Olsen, Mary-Kate: Birth, Jun 13
Olympics
First Modern Olympics: Anniv, Apr 6
First Perfect Score: Anniv, Jul 18
First Special Olympics: Anniv, Jul 20
First Winter Olympics: Anniv, Jan 25
Oman: National Holiday, Nov 18
Onassis, Jacqueline Kennedy: Birth Anniv, Jul 28
One Hundredth Day of School, Feb 7
100 Billionth Crayon Produced: Anniv, Feb 6
O'Neal, Shaquille: Birth, Mar 6
Open an Umbrella Indoors Day, Natl, Mar 13
Opera Debuts in the Colonies: Anniv, Feb 8
Operation Iraqi Freedom: Anniv, Mar 19
Oppel, Kenneth: Birth, Aug 31
Optimism Month, Mar 1
Orangemen's Day (Northern Ireland), Jul 12
Oregon
Admission Day, Feb 14
Crater Lake Natl Park: Anniv, May 22
Kulongoski, Ted: Birth, Nov 5
Smith, Gordon: Birth, May 25
State Fair (Salem), Aug 26
Wyden, Ron: Birth, May 3
Organic Act Day (US Virgin Islands), Jun 19
Organization of American States Founded: Anniv, Apr 30
Orgel, Doris: Birth, Feb 15
Orionids Meteor Shower, Oct 15
Orlev, Uri: Birth, Feb 24
Orr, Bobby: Birth, Mar 20
Orsi, Leigh Ann: Birth, May 15
Orthodontic Health Month, Natl, Oct 1
Orthodox Church; Eastern Orthodox Church
Ascension Day, Jun 1
Easter Sunday, Apr 23
Festival of All Saints, Jun 18
Lent, Mar 6
Palm Sunday, Apr 16
Pentecost, Jun 11
Osborne, Mary Pope: Birth, May 20
Osceola: Death Anniv, Jan 30
Osgood, Chris: Birth, Nov 26
Osment, Haley Joel: Birth, Apr 10
Osmond, Donny: Birth, Dec 9
Oswalt, Roy: Birth, Aug 29
Otfinoski, Steve: Birth, Jan 11
Outcault, Richard Fenton: Birth Anniv, Jan 14
Outrigger Canoes: Hawaiki Nui Va'a Race, Oct 19
Overseas Chinese Day (Taiwan), Oct 21
Owen, Michael: Birth, Dec 14
Owens, Bill: Birth, Oct 22
Owens, Jesse: Birth Anniv, Sep 12
Owens, Jesse: Greatest Day in Track and Field: Anniv, May 25
Owens, Terrell: Birth, Dec 7
Owl: First Wild Animal with Artificial Lenses: Anniv, Jan 22
Oxenbury, Helen: Birth, Jun 2
Paca, William: Birth Anniv, Oct 31
Pacific Ocean Discovered: Anniv, Sep 25
Pacing the Bounds (Liestal, Switzerland), May 22
Paige, Satchel: Birth Anniv, Jul 7
Paine, Robert Treat: Birth Anniv, Mar 11
Pak, Se Ri: Birth, Sep 28
Pakistan
Birthday of Qaid-i-Azam, Dec 25
Founder's Death Anniv (Qaid-i-Azam), Sep 11
Republic Day, Mar 23
Palm Sunday, Apr 9
Palm Sunday, Orthodox, Apr 16
Paltrow, Gwyneth: Birth, Sep 28
Pan Am Circles Earth: Anniv, Jan 6
Pan American Week (Pres Proc), Apr 9

Panama
  Assumes Control of Canal: Anniv, Dec 31
  First Shout of Independence, Nov 10
  Flag Day, Nov 4
  Independence Day, Nov 3
  Independence from Spain Day, Nov 28
  Martyrs' Day, Jan 9
Panama Canal Opens: Anniv, Aug 15
Pan-American Day (Pres Proc), Apr 14
Pan-American Day in Florida, Apr 14
Panic Day, Mar 9
Paper Money Issued: Anniv, Mar 10
Paperback Books Introduced: Anniv, Jul 30
Papua New Guinea: Independence Day, Sep 16
Paquin, Anna: Birth, Jul 24
Parades
  America's Thanksgiving Parade (Detroit, MI), Nov 24
  Bud Billiken Parade (Chicago, IL), Aug 13
  Macy's Thanksgiving Day Parade (New York, NY), Nov 24
  Mother Goose Parade (El Cajon, CA), Nov 20
  Mummers Parade (Philadelphia, PA), Jan 1
  Pasadena Doo Dah Parade (Pasadena, CA), Nov 20
  Saint Patrick's Day Parade (New York, NY), Mar 17
  Tournament of Roses Parade (Pasadena, CA), Jan 1
Paraguay
  Boqueron Day, Sep 29
  Independence Day, May 15
  National Heroes' Day, Mar 1
Paraprofessional Appreciation Day, Apr 5
Parent, Bernie: Birth, Apr 3
Parents as Teachers Day, Natl, Nov 8
Paris, Treaty of, Ends American Rev, Sep 3
Parish, Peggy: Birth, Jul 14
Park, Barbara: Birth, Apr 21
Parker, Charlie: Birth Anniv, Aug 29
Parker, Steve: Birth, Dec 7
Parker, Tony: Birth, May 17
Parker, Trey: Birth, May 30
Parks Month, Natl Recreation and, Jul 1
Parks, Rosa Lee: Birth, Feb 4
Parks, Rosa: Day, Dec 1
Partridge, Elizabeth: Birth, Oct 1
Pascal, Francine: Birth, May 13
Pascua Florida Day, Apr 2
Passion Week, Apr 1
Passiontide, Apr 2
Passover, Apr 13
Passover Begins, Apr 12
Passport Presentation (Russia), Jan 2
Pasteur, Louis: Birth Anniv, Dec 27
Pasteur, Louis: First Successful Antirabies Inoculation, Jul 6
Pataki, George: Birth, Jun 24
Patent Office Opens, US: Anniv, Jul 31
Patent, Dorothy Hinshaw: Birth, Apr 30
Paterson, Katherine: Birth, Oct 31
Paton Walsh, Jill: Birth, Apr 29
Patriot Day (Pres Proc), Sep 11
Patriot's Day (FL), Apr 19
Patriot's Day (MA, ME), Apr 17
Patterson, Carly: Birth, Feb 4
Pauley, Jane: Birth, Oct 31
Paulsen, Gary: Birth, May 17
Pause for Pledge (Natl Flag Day USA), Jun 14
Pawlenty, Tim: Birth, Nov 1
Payton, Gary: Birth, Jul 23
Peace
  Disarmament Week, Oct 24
  Lions Club Intl Peace Poster Contest, Oct 1
  Peace Corps Founded: Anniv, Mar 1
  Peace Officer Memorial Day (Pres Proc), May 15
  Peace Officer Memorial Day, Natl, May 15
  UN Intl Day of Peace, Sep 21
  World Hello Day, Nov 21
Peale, Charles Willson: Birth Anniv, Apr 15
Peanut Butter Lovers' Month, Nov 1
Peanuts Debuts: Anniv, Oct 2
Peanuts: Last Strip: Anniv, Feb 13
Pearl Harbor Day, Dec 7
Pearl Harbor Remembrance Day, Natl (Pres Proc), Dec 7
Pearson, Lester B.: Birth Anniv, Apr 23
Peary, Robert E.: Birth Anniv, May 6
Peary, Robert E.: North Pole Discovered: Anniv, Apr 6
Pecan Day, Mar 25
Peck, Richard: Birth, Apr 5
Peck, Robert Newton: Birth, Feb 17
Pediatric Cancer Awareness Month, Sep 1
Pediculosis Prevention Month, Natl, Sep 1
Pele Scores 1,000th Goal: Anniv, Nov 19
Pele: Birth, Oct 23
Pencil Patented: Anniv, Mar 30
Pen-Friends Week Intl, May 1
Penichiero, Ticha: Birth, Sep 18
Penn, John: Birth Anniv, May 6
Penn, William: Birth Anniv, Oct 14
Penn, William: Pennsylvania Deeded to: Anniv, Mar 4
Pennsylvania
  Battle of Gettysburg: Anniv, Jul 1
  First American Abolition Society Founded: Anniv, Apr 14
  First Natl Convention for Blacks: Anniv, Sep 15
  First US Zoo: Anniv (Philadelphia), Jul 1
  Groundhog Day in Punxsutawney, Feb 2
  Johnstown Flood: Anniv, May 31
  Little League Baseball World Series (Williamsport), Aug 19
  Middle School Assn, Natl, Annual Conference (Philadelphia), Nov 3
  Mummers Parade (Philadelphia), Jan 1
  Natl Council of Teachers of English Annual Convention (Pittsburgh), Nov 17
  Pennsylvania Deeded to William Penn: Anniv, Mar 4
  PSFCA East West All-Star Game (Altoona), Jun 24
  Ratification Day, Dec 12
  Rendell, Ed: Birth, Jan 5
  Santorum, Rick: Birth, May 10
  Specter, Arlen: Birth, Feb 12
Pentecost, Jun 4
People Magazine: Anniv, Mar 4
Peppercorn Ceremony (Bermuda), Apr 23
Perdue, Sonny: Birth, Dec 20
Perez, Tony: Birth, May 14
Perigean Spring Tides, Jan 29
Perigean Spring Tides, Feb 27
Perigean Spring Tides, Aug 19
Perihelion, Earth at, Jan 4
Perlman, Itzhak: Birth, Aug 31
Perlman, Rhea: Birth, Mar 31
Perrault, Charles: Birth Anniv, Jan 12
Perry, Matthew: Commodore Perry Day, Apr 10
Perry, Oliver H.: Birth Anniv, Aug 23
Perry, Rick: Birth, Mar 4
Perseid Meteor Showers, Aug 9
Persian Gulf War Begins: Anniv, Jan 16
Persian Gulf War: Kuwait Liberated: Anniv, Feb 27
Peru
  Day of National Honor, Oct 9
  Day of the Navy, Oct 8
  Independence Day, Jul 28
  Saint Rose of Lima Day, Aug 30
Pesach (Passover), Apr 13
Pesach (Passover) Begins, Apr 12
Pesci, Joe: Birth, Feb 9
Peshtigo Forest Fire: Anniv, Oct 8
Pestalozzi, Johann Heinrich: Birth Anniv, Jan 12
Pet Owners Independence Day, Apr 18
Pet Week, Natl, May 7
Peter and Paul Day, Jun 29
Peterson, Roger Tory: Birth Anniv, Aug 28
Petrified Forest Natl Park: Anniv, Dec 9
Petty, Richard: Birth, Jul 2
Pfister, Marcus: Birth, Jul 30
Phelps, Michael: Birth, Jun 30
Philip, King: Assassination Anniv, Aug 12
Philippines
  Ati-Atihan Fest, Jan 21
  Bataan Day: Anniv, Apr 9
  Bonifacio Day, Nov 30
  Feast of the Black Nazarene, Jan 9
  Fil-American Friendship Day, Jul 4
  Independence Day, Jun 12
  Mount Pinatubo Erupts in Philippines: Anniv, Jun 11
  Natl Heroes' Day, Aug 26
  Philippine Independence: Anniv, Mar 24
  Rizal Day, Dec 30
  Simbang Gabi, Dec 16
Phillips, Stone: Birth, Dec 2
Photo: First Presidential Photograph: Anniv, Feb 14
Photo: First Used in a Newspaper Report: Anniv, Jul 1
Physical Education, Recreation and Dance, American Alliance for Health, Natl Convention & Expo (Salt Lake City, UT), Apr 25
Physical Fitness and Sports Month, Natl, May 1
Piaget, Jean: Birth Anniv, Aug 9
Piano Month, Natl, Sep 1
Piazza, Mike: Birth, Sep 4
Picasso, Pablo: Birth Anniv, Oct 25
Piccard, Auguste: Birth Anniv, Jan 28
Piccard, Bertrand: See First Round-the-World Balloon Flight: Anniv, Mar 21
Piccard, Jean Felix: Birth Anniv, Jan 28
Piccard, Jeannette Ridlon: Birth Anniv, Jan 5
Pickett, Bill: Birth Anniv, Dec 5
Pickett's Charge: Battle of Gettysburg: Anniv, Jul 1
Pied Piper of Hamelin: Anniv, Jul 22
Pierce, Franklin: Birth Anniv, Nov 23
Pierce, Jane: Birth Anniv, Mar 12
Pierce, Meredith Ann: Birth, Jul 5
Pierce, Paul: Birth, Oct 13
Pierce, Tamora: Birth, Dec 13
Pig Day, Natl, Mar 1
Pilgrim Landing: Anniv, Dec 21
Pilkey, Dav: Birth, Mar 4
Pinkney, Andrea Davis: Birth, Sep 25
Pinkney, J. Brian: Birth, Aug 28
Pinkney, Jerry: Birth, Dec 22
Pinkwater, Daniel: Birth, Nov 15
Pinzon, Martin: Arrival Anniv, Mar 1
Piper, Watty: Birth Anniv, Sep 15
Pippen, Scottie: Birth, Sep 25
Pirate Day, Talk Like a, Sep 19
Pirate: Teach, Edward (Blackbeard): Death Anniv, Nov 22
Pisces Begins, Feb 20
Pitcher, Molly: Birth Anniv, Oct 13
Pitt, Brad: Birth, Dec 18
Pizarro, Francisco: Death Anniv, Jun 26
Planet Neptune Discovery: Anniv, Sep 23
Planet Pluto Discovery: Anniv, Feb 18
Planet Uranus Discovery: Anniv, Mar 13
Plastic Ducky Fleet Sails the Pacific: Anniv, Jan 10
Play Presented in North American Colonies, First: Anniv, Aug 27
Play-Doh Day, Natl, Sep 16
Playground Safety Day, Natl, Apr 27
Playground Safety Week, Natl, Apr 24
Play-the-Recorder Month, Mar 1
Pledge of Allegiance Recognized: Anniv, Dec 28
Pledge of Allegiance, Pause for (Natl Flag Day USA), Jun 14
Plough Monday (England), Jan 9
Plummer, Jake: Birth, Dec 19
Plushenko, Evgeny: Birth, Nov 3
Pluto Discovery, Planet: Anniv, Feb 18
Pocahontas: Death Anniv, Mar 21
Poe, Edgar Allan: Birth Anniv, Jan 19
Poe, Edgar Allan: Raven Published: Anniv, Jan 29
Poetry
  American Poet Laureate Establishment: Anniv, Dec 20
  Black Poetry Day, Oct 20
  Limerick Day, May 12
  Poetry Day in Florida, May 25
  Poetry Month, Natl, Apr 1
  Raven Published: Anniv, Jan 29
  Wheatley, Phillis: Poetry Collection Published: Anniv, Sep 1
  Young People's Poetry Week, Apr 10
Poinsett, Joel Roberts: Death Anniv, Dec 12
Poinsettia Day, Dec 12
Poison Prevention Week, Natl, Mar 19
Poison Prevention Week, Natl (Pres Proc), Mar 19
Pokemon Debuts: Anniv, Sep 28
Polacco, Patricia: Birth, Jul 11
Poland
  Constitution Day, May 3
  Independence Day, Nov 11
  Solidarity Founded Anniv, Aug 31
Police Week (Pres Proc), May 14
Police Week, Natl, May 14
Police: Peace Officer Memorial Day (Pres Proc), May 15
Police: Peace Officer Memorial Day, Natl, May 15
Polio Vaccine: Anniv, Apr 12
Polish American Heritage Month, Oct 1
Polish American in the House (Mikulski): Anniv, Jan 4
Polk, James: Birth Anniv, Nov 2
Polk, James: First Presidential Photograph: Anniv, Feb 14
Polk, Sarah Childress: Birth Anniv, Sep 4
Pompeii Destroyed by Vesuvius Eruption: Anniv, Aug 24
Ponce de Leon Discovers Florida: Anniv, Apr 2
Pooh Day (A.A. Milne: Birth Anniv), Jan 18
Poole, Josephine: Birth, Feb 12
Poor Richard's Almanack: Anniv, Dec 28
Pop Music Chart Introduced: Anniv, Jan 4
Popcorn Poppin' Month, Natl, Oct 1
Pope John Paul I: Birth Anniv, Oct 17
Pope John Paul II: Birth, May 18
Pope John XXIII: Birth Anniv, Nov 25
Pope Paul VI: Birth Anniv, Sep 26
Pope, Eddie: Birth, Dec 24
Pope, Elizabeth Marie: Birth, May 1
Population Day, World (UN), Jul 11
Population: Day of the Five Billion: Anniv, Jul 11
Population: Day of the Six Billion: Anniv, Oct 12
Porter, Connie: Birth, Jul 29
Portman, Natalie: Birth, Jun 9
Portugal
  Day of Portugal, Jun 10
  Independence Day, Dec 1
  Liberty Day, Apr 25
  Republic Day, Oct 5
Posadas (Mexico), Dec 16
Post Day, World (UN), Oct 9
Post, Emily: Birth Anniv, Oct 30
Postell, Ashley: Birth, Jun 9
Postmaster General Established, US: Anniv, Sep 22
Potter, Beatrix: Birth Anniv, Jul 28
Potter, Harry: Birthday, Jul 31
Potvin, Denis: Birth, Oct 29
Potvin, Felix: Birth, Jun 23
Poverty, Intl Day for Eradication, Oct 17
Poverty, War on: Anniv, Jan 8
POW/MIA Recognition Day, Natl (Pres Proc), Sep 15
Powell, Colin: Birth, Apr 5
Powell, Cristen: Birth, Mar 22
Powell, John Wesley: Birth Anniv, Mar 24
Powell, Lewis F., Jr: Birth Anniv, Sep 19
Powerpuff Girls TV Premiere: Anniv, Nov 18
Pratt, Kyla: Birth, Aug 12
Prayer
  National Day of Prayer (Pres Proc), May 4
  Supreme Court Bans School Prayer: Anniv, Jun 25
  World Day of Prayer, Mar 3
Preki: Birth, Jun 24
Prelutsky, Jack: Birth, Sep 8
Presentation of the Lord (Candlemas Day), Feb 2
Preservation Month, May 1
President First Occupies White House: Anniv, Nov 1
Presidential Inauguration Anniv, George Washington, Apr 30
Presidential Inauguration, G. Cleveland's Second: Anniv, Mar 4
Presidential Photograph, First: Anniv, Feb 14
Presidents' Day, Feb 20
President's Environmental Youth Award Natl Competition, Jul 31
Presley, Elvis: Birth Anniv, Jan 8
Priceman, Marjorie: Birth, Jan 8
Priesand, Sally: First Woman Rabbi in US: Anniv, Jun 3
Priestly, Joseph: Birth Anniv, Mar 13
Prime Meridian Set: Anniv, Nov 1
Prime Number, Largest Found: Anniv, Nov 17
Primeau, Keith: Birth, Nov 24
Prince Charles: Birth, Nov 14
Prince Harry: Birth, Sep 15
Prince Jonah Kuhio Kalanianole Day (HI), Mar 26
Prince William: Birth, Jun 21
Princess Diana: Birth Anniv, Jul 1
Pringle, Laurence: Birth, Nov 26
Printing Week, Intl, Jan 15
Prinze, Freddie, Jr: Birth, Mar 8
Probert, Bob: Birth, Jun 5
Procrastination: Be Late for Something Day, Sep 5
Prohibition Ratified: 18th Amendment: Anniv, Jan 16
Prohibition Repealed: 21st Amendment: Anniv, Dec 5
Project ACES Day, May 3
Provensen, Alice: Birth, Aug 14
Provensen, Martin: Birth Anniv, Jul 20
Pryor, Bonnie: Birth, Dec 22
Pryor, Mark: Birth, Jan 10
PTA Convention, Natl (Phoenix, AZ), Jun 24
PTA Earth Week, Natl, Apr 16
PTA Founders' Day, Natl, Feb 17
PTA Teacher Appreciation Week, Natl, May 1
Public Lands Day, Natl, Sep 18
Public Library Assn Conference (Boston, MA), Mar 21
Public Radio, Natl: Anniv, May 3
Public School, First in America: Anniv, Apr 23
Public Television Debuts: Anniv, Nov 3
Puerto Rico
  Barbosa, Jose Celso: Birth Anniv, Jul 27
  Calderon, Sila Maria: Birth, Sep 23
  Carnival de Ponce (Ponce), Feb 22
  Constitution Day, Jul 25
  Diego, Jose de: Birth Anniv, Apr 16

Discovery Day, Nov 19
Emancipation Day, Mar 22
Hostos, Eugenio Maria: Birth Anniv, Jan 11
Munoz-Rivera Day, Jul 17
Navidades, Dec 15
US Virgin Islands-Puerto Rico Friendship Day, Oct 10
Pujols, Albert: Birth, Jan 16
Pulaski, General Casimir: Memorial Day (Pres Proc), Oct 11
Pulaski, Casimir: Birth Anniv, Mar 4
Pulitzer, Joseph: Birth Anniv, Apr 10
Pullman, Philip: Birth, Oct 19
Punctuation Day, Natl, Aug 22
Purim, Mar 14
Purple Heart: Anniv, Aug 7
Putin, Vladimir: Birth, Oct 7
Puzzle Week, Natl Game and, Nov 20
Pyle, Howard: Birth Anniv, Mar 5
Qatar: Independence Day, Sep 3
Qing Ming Fest, Apr 5
Quackenbush, Robert: Birth, Jul 23
Quark, Physicists Discover Top: Anniv, Apr 23
Quayle, Dan: Birthday, Feb 4
Queen Elizabeth II's Official Birthday, Jun 12
Queen Latifah: Birth, Mar 18
Queen's Official Birthday/Trooping the Colour (United Kingdom), Jun 10
Rabbi, First Woman Rabbi in US: Anniv, Jun 3
Rabbit Week, Natl, Jul 15
Rabi'l: Month of the Migration, Mar 31
Race Relations Day, Feb 14
Race Unity Day, Jun 11
Racial Discrimination, Intl Day for Elimination of (UN), Mar 21
Radcliffe, Daniel: Birth, Jul 23
Radio
Children's Day of Broadcasting, Intl, Dec 11
Federal Communications Commission Created: Anniv, Feb 26
First Commercial: Anniv, Aug 28
First Public Broadcast: Anniv, Jan 13
First Scheduled Broadcast: Anniv, Nov 2
Public Radio, Natl: Anniv, May 3
Radio Broadcast by a President, First: Anniv, Jun 14
Transistor Invented: Anniv, Dec 23
Radishes, Feast of (Oaxaca, Mexico), Dec 23
Radium Discovered: Anniv, Dec 26
Radke, Brad: Birth, Oct 27
Radosavljevic, Preki: Birth, Jun 24
Rafalski, Brian: Birth, Sep 28
Raffi: Birth, Jul 8
Rafter, Patrick: Birth, Dec 28
Railroad
Canadian Pacific Railway: Completion Anniv, Nov 7
Golden Spike Driving: Anniv, May 10
Iron Horse Outraced by Horse: Anniv, Sep 18
New York City Subway: Anniv, Oct 27
Northern Pacific Railroad Completed: Anniv, Sep 8
Transcontinental US Railway Completion: Anniv, Aug 15
Rain of Frog Eggs: Anniv, Sep 19
Rainey, Joseph: First Black Serves in US House: Anniv, Dec 12
Raleigh, Sir Walter: Death Anniv, Oct 29
Ramadan: Islamic Month of Fasting, Oct 5
Ramirez, Manny: Birth, May 30
Randolph, Peyton: Death Anniv, Oct 22
Rankin, Jeannette: Birth Anniv, Jun 11
Ransom, Candice F.: Birth, Jul 10
Ransome, Arthur: Birth Anniv, Jan 18
Ransome, James: Birth, Sep 25
Raschka, Chris: Birth, Mar 6
Rashad, Ahmad: Birth, Nov 19
Raskin, Ellen: Birth, Mar 13
Rather, Dan: Birth, Oct 31
Rathmann, Peggy: Birth, Mar 4
Ratification Day, Jan 14
Raven Published: Anniv, Jan 29
Rawlings, Marjorie Kinnan: Birth Anniv, Aug 8
Rawls, Wilson: Birth Anniv, Sep 24
Read Across America Day, Mar 2
Read, George: Birth Anniv, Sep 18
Reader's Day, Natl Young, Nov 8
Reading
African American Read-In, Feb 5
Banned Books Week, Sep 24
Book It! Reading Incentive Program, Oct 1
Children's Book Week, Nov 14
Family Literacy Day, Natl, Nov 1
Get Caught Reading Month, May 1
Mother Goose Day, May 1
Read Across America Day, Mar 2
Reading Assn, Intl, Annual Convention (Chicago, IL), Apr 30
Reading Group Month, Natl, Oct 1
Reading Is Fun Week, May 14
Teen Read Week, Oct 16
Young Reader's Day, Natl, Nov 8
Reading Group Month, Natl, Oct 1
Reading Rainbow TV Premiere: Anniv, Jul 1
Reagan, Nancy: Birth, Jul 6
Reagan, Ronald: Birth Anniv, Feb 6
Recreation and Dance, American Alliance for Health, Physical Education, Natl Convention & Expo (Salt Lake City, UT), Apr 25
Recreation and Parks Month, Natl, Jul 1
Recycling: America Recycles Day (Pres Proc), Nov 15
Red Cloud: Death Anniv, Dec 10
Red Cross Day, World, May 8
Red Cross Month, Mar 1
Red Cross Month, American (Pres Proc), Mar 1
Redwood Natl Park: Anniv, Oct 2
Reece, Gabrielle: Birth, Jan 6
Reed, Jack: Birth, Nov 12
Reed, Walter: Birth Anniv, Sep 13
Reeder, Carolyn: Birth, Nov 16
Reef, Catherine: Birth, Apr 28
Reeve, Christopher: Birth Anniv, Sep 25
Reformation Day, Oct 31
Regular TV Broadcasts Begin: Anniv, Jul 1
Rehnquist, William Hubbs: Birth, Oct 1
Reid, Harry: Birth, Dec 2
Reinhard, Johan: Birth, Dec 13
Reiss, Johanna: Birth, Apr 4
Religious Freedom Day, Jan 16
Religious Freedom Day (Pres Proc), Jan 16
Rell, M. Jodi: Birth, Jun 16
Rembrandt: Birth Anniv, Jul 15
Remembrance Day (Canada), Nov 11
Rendell, Ed: Birth, Jan 5
Reno, Janet: Birth, Jul 21
Renoir, Pierre: Birth Anniv, Feb 25
Renteria, Edgar: Birth, Aug 7
Republican Symbol: Anniv, Nov 7
Resnik, Judith A.: Birth Anniv, Apr 5
Retired Teacher's Day in Florida, Nov 19
Retrocession Day (Taiwan), Oct 25
Retton, Mary Lou: Birth, Jan 24
Return Shopping Carts to the Supermarket Month, Feb 1
Return the Borrowed Books Week, Mar 1
Reunification of Germany: Anniv, Oct 3
Revere, Paul: Birth Anniv, Jan 1
Revere, Paul: Ride Anniv, Apr 18
Revolution, American
Battle of Brandywine: Anniv, Sep 11
Battle of Lexington and Concord, Apr 19
Bennington Battle Day, Aug 16
Boston Tea Party: Anniv, Dec 16
Cessation of Hostilities: Anniv, Jan 20
Evacuation Day (MA), Mar 17
Hale, Nathan: Birth Anniv, Jun 6
Henry, Patrick: Birth Anniv, May 29
Independence Day (US), Jul 4
Liberty Day, Mar 23
Paris, Treaty of: Signing Anniv, Sep 3
Paul Revere's Ride: Anniv, Apr 18
Shays Rebellion: Anniv, Aug 29
Washington Crosses the Delaware: Anniv, Dec 25
Yorktown Day, Oct 19
Yorktown Day (Yorktown, VA), Oct 19
Revolution, Russian: Anniv, Nov 7
Rey, H.A.: Birth Anniv, Sep 16
Rey, Margaret: Birth Anniv, May 16
Reyna, Claudio: Birth, Jul 20
Rhino Day, Save the, May 1
Rhode Island
Carcieri, Donald: Birth, Dec 16
Chafee, Lincoln: Birth, Mar 26
Children's Party at Green Animals (Newport), Jul 14
Ratification Day, May 29
Reed, Jack: Birth, Nov 12
Voters Reject Constitution: Anniv, Mar 24
Ricci, Christina: Birth, Feb 12
Rice, Condoleezza: Birth, Nov 14
Rice, Glen: Birth, May 28
Rice, Jerry: Birth, Oct 13
Richard, Adrienne: Birth, Oct 31
Richards, Todd: Birth, Dec 28
Richardson, Bill: Birth, Nov 15
Richardson, Joely: Birth, Jan 9
Richardson, Kevin: Birth, Oct 3
Richardson, Natasha: Birth, May 11
Richardson, Patricia: Birth, Feb 23
Richert, Nate: Birth, Apr 28
Richie, Nicole: Birth, Sep 21
Richmond, Mitch: Birth, Jun 30
Richter Scale Day, Apr 26
Richter, Conrad: Birth Anniv, Oct 13
Richter, Jason James: Birth, Jan 29
Ride, Sally Kristen: Birth, May 26
Riel, Louis: Hanging Anniv, Nov 16
Riley, Bob: Birth, Oct 3
Riley, Pat: Birth, Mar 20
Rimes, LeAnn: Birth, Aug 28
Rinaldi, Ann: Birth, Aug 27
Ringgold, Faith: Birth, Oct 8
Ripken, Cal, Jr: Birth, Aug 24
River of Words Environmental Poetry and Art Contest, Feb 15
Rivera, Mariano: Birth, Nov 29
Rivers Month, Natl, Jun 1
Robert-Houdin, Jean Eugene: Birth Anniv, Dec 6
Robert's Rules Day, May 2
Roberts, Julia: Birth, Oct 28
Roberts, Pat: Birth, Apr 20
Robeson, Paul: Birth Anniv, Apr 9
Robinet, Harriette Gillem: Birth, Jul 14
Robinson Crusoe Day, Feb 1
Robinson, Bill "Bojangles": Birth Anniv, May 25
Robinson, David: Birth, Aug 6
Robinson, Glenn: Birth, Jan 10
Robinson, Jackie
Birth Anniv, Jan 31
Breaks MLB Color Barrier: Anniv, Apr 15
Robinson, Larry: Birth, Jun 2
Robinson, Roscoe, Jr: Birth Anniv, Oct 11
Robot Enters World Lexicon: Anniv, Jan 25
Rockefeller, John D., IV (Jay): Birth, Jun 18
Rockefeller, Nelson Aldrich: Birth Anniv, Jul 8
Rockne, Knute: Birth Anniv, Mar 4
Rockwell, Anne: Birth, Feb 8
Rocky and His Friends TV Premiere: Anniv, Nov 19
Rocky Mountain Natl Park: Anniv, Jan 26
Roddick, Andy: Birth, Aug 30
Rodney, Caesar: Birth Anniv, Oct 7
Rodriguez, Alex: Birth, Jul 27
Rodriguez, Francisco: Birth, Jan 7
Rodriguez, Ivan: Birth, Nov 30
Rogers, Kenny: Birth, Nov 10
Roget, Peter Mark: Birth Anniv, Jan 18
Rohmann, Eric: Birth, Oct 26
Roker, Al: Birth, Aug 20
Rolen, Scott: Birth, Apr 4
Roller Coaster, First, Opens: Anniv, Jun 13
Roller Coaster. See Thompson, LaMarcus A: Birth Anniv, Mar 8
Roller Skating Month, Natl, Oct 1
Rollins, Jimmy: Birth, Nov 27
Roman Catholic: New Catechism: Anniv, Nov 16
Romania: National Day, Dec 1
Rome: Birthday (Italy), Apr 21
Romney, Mitt: Birth, Mar 12
Ronaldo: Birth, Sep 22
Röntgen, Wilhelm C.: Birth Anniv, Mar 27
Roop, Connie: Birth, Jun 18
Roop, Peter: Birth, Mar 8
Roosevelt, Alice: Birth Anniv, Jul 29
Roosevelt, Anna Eleanor: Birth Anniv, Oct 11
Roosevelt, Edith Kermit Carow: Birth Anniv, Aug 6
Roosevelt, Eleanor: First Ladies Take Flight: Anniv, Apr 20
Roosevelt, Franklin Delano
Birth Anniv, Jan 30
Death Anniv, Apr 12
Elected to Fourth Term: Anniv, Nov 7
First Presidential Telecast: Anniv, Apr 30
Roosevelt, Theodore: Birth Anniv, Oct 27
Root, Phyllis: Birth, Feb 14
Roots: Alex Palmer Haley: Birth Anniv, Aug 11
Rose Bowl Game (Pasadena, CA), Jan 1
Rose Month, Natl, Jun 1
Rose, Jalen: Birth, Jan 30
Rose, Pete: Birth, Apr 14
Roseanne: Birth, Nov 3
Rosen, Michael J.: Birth, Sep 20
Rosenbaum, Michael: Birth, Jul 11
Rosh Hashanah, Oct 4
Rosh Hashanah Begins, Oct 3
Rosman, MacKenzie: Birth, Dec 28
Ross, Betsy: Birth Anniv, Jan 1
Ross, Dave: Birth, Apr 2
Ross, Gayle: Birth, Oct 3
Ross, George: Birth Anniv, May 10
Ross, Nellie Tayloe: Wyoming Inaugurates First US Woman Gov: Anniv, Jan 5
Rounds, Mike: Birth, Oct 24
Rowling, J.K.: Birth, Jul 31
Roy, Patrick: Birth, Oct 5
Royall, Anne: Birth Anniv, Jun 11
Rugrats TV Premiere: Anniv, Aug 11
Ruiz, Carlos: Birth, Sep 15
Rumsfeld, Donald: Birth, Jul 9
Russia
Baltic States' Independence Recognized: Anniv, Sep 6
Boris Yeltsin Inaugurated: Anniv, Jul 10
Christmas Day, Jan 7
Constitution Day, Dec 12
Great October Socialist Revolution: Anniv, Nov 7
Independence Day, Jun 12
Labor Day, Intl, May 1
McDonald's Opens In the Soviet Union: Anniv, Jan 31
New Year's Day Observance, Jan 1
Passport Presentation, Jan 2
Soviet Communist Party Suspended: Anniv, Aug 29
Soviet Cosmonaut Returns to New Country: Anniv, Mar 26
Soviet Union Dissolved: Anniv, Dec 8
Victory Day, May 9
Women's Day, Intl, Mar 8
Rustin, Bayard: Birth Anniv, Mar 17
Ruth, George Herman
Babe Ruth Day: Anniv, Apr 27
Birth Anniv, Feb 6
Sets Home Run Record: Anniv, Sep 30
Voted into Hall of Fame: Anniv, Feb 2
Yankee Stadium Opens: Anniv, Apr 18
Rutherford, Ernest: Birth Anniv, Aug 30
Rutledge, Edward: Birth Anniv, Nov 23
Rutledge, John: Death Anniv, Jul 18
Rwanda
Genocide's Remembrance Day, Apr 7
Independence Day, Jul 1
Republic Day, Sep 25
Ryan, Meg: Birth, Nov 19
Ryan, Nolan: Birth, Jan 31
Rylant, Cynthia: Birth, Jun 6
Sabathia, C.C.: Birth, Jul 21
Sabatini, Gabriela: Birth, May 16
Sabin, Albert Bruce: Birth Anniv, Aug 26
Sabuda, Robert: Birth, Mar 8
Sacagawea: Death Anniv, Dec 20
Sachar, Louis: Birth, Mar 20
Sachs, Marilyn: Birth, Dec 18
Sadie Hawkins Day, Nov 5
Safe Kids Week, Natl, Apr 29
Safe Schools Week, America's, Oct 16
Safe Toys and Gifts Month, Dec 1
Safety
America's Safe Schools Week, Oct 16
Automobile Speed Reduction: Anniv, Nov 25
Buckle Up America! Week, May 22
Check Your Batteries Day, Apr 2
Child Safety Council, Natl: Founding Anniv, Nov 9
Childhood Injury Prevention Week, Natl, Sep 1
Crime Prevention Month, Natl, Oct 1
Day of National Concern about Young People and Gun Violence, Oct 19
Farm Safety Week, Natl (Pres Proc), Sep 18
Fire Prevention Week, Oct 9
Fire Prevention Week (Pres Proc), Oct 9
Firepup's Birthday, Oct 1
Fireworks Safety Months, Jun 1
Missing Children's Day, Natl, May 25
Night Out, Natl, Aug 2
Playground Safety Day, Natl, Apr 27
Playground Safety Week, Natl, Apr 24
Poison Prevention Week, Natl, Mar 19
Poison Prevention Week, Natl (Pres Proc), Mar 19
Safe Boating Week, Natl, May 20
Safe Boating Week, Natl (Pres Proc), May 19
Safe Kids Week, Natl, Apr 29
Safe Toys and Gifts Month, Dec 1
Safety Month, Natl, Jun 1
Safetypup's Birthday, Feb 12
School Bus Safety Week, Natl, Oct 16

  Walk Our Children to School Day, Natl, **Oct 5**
  Youth Sports Safety Month, Natl, **Apr 1**
Safety Pin Patented: Anniv, Apr 10
Saget, Bob: Birth, May 17
Sagittarius Begins, Nov 22
Saint Andrew's Day, Nov 30
Saint Aubin, Helen "Callaghan": Birth Anniv, Mar 13
Saint Augustine, Feast of, Aug 28
Saint Basil's Day, Jan 1
Saint Christopher: Independence Day, Sep 19
Saint Clare of Assisi: Feast Day, Aug 11
Saint David's Day (Wales), Mar 1
Saint Eustatius, West Indies: Statia and America Day, Nov 16
Saint Frances Xavier Cabrini: Birth Anniv, Jul 15
Saint Francis of Assisi: Feast Day, Oct 4
Saint George: Feast Day (England), Apr 23
Saint George's Day (Newfoundland, Canada), Apr 24
Saint Januarius: Feast Day, Sep 19
Saint Jerome, Feast of, Sep 30
Saint Joan of Arc: Feast Day, May 30
Saint John, Apostle-Evangelist: Feast Day, Dec 27
Saint Jude's Day, Oct 28
Saint Lasarus Day (Bulgaria), Apr 1
Saint Lawrence Seaway: Dedication Anniv, Jun 26
Saint Lucia: Independence Day, Feb 22
Saint Luke: Feast Day, Oct 18
Saint Nicholas Day, Dec 6
Saint Patrick's Day, Mar 17
Saint Patrick's Day (Northern Ireland), Mar 17
Saint Patrick's Day Parade (New York, NY), Mar 17
Saint Piran's Day, Mar 5
Saint Stephen's Day, Dec 26
Saint Swithin's Day, Jul 15
Saint Valentine's Day, Feb 14
Saint Vincent and the Grenadines: Independence Day, Oct 27
Saint Vincent De Paul: Feast Day, Sep 27
Saint-Exupery, Antoine de: Birth Anniv, Jun 29
Saint-Saens, Camille: Birth Anniv, Oct 9
Sakic, Joe: Birth, Jul 7
Salaam, Rashaan: Birth, Oct 8
Salazar, Ken: Birth, Mar 2
Salem Witch Hysteria Begins: Anniv, Mar 1
Salk, Jonas: Birth Anniv, Oct 28
Salmon, Tim: Birth, Aug 24
Salsa Month, Natl, May 1
Salter, Susanna, Elected First Woman Mayor in US: Anniv, Apr 4
Salvation Army Founder's Day, Apr 10
Salvation Army in US: Anniv, Mar 10
Samoa
  Anzac Day, **Apr 25**
  Natl Day, **Jun 1**
  White Sunday, **Oct 9**
Sampras, Pete: Birth, Aug 12
Samuelson, Joan Benoit: Birth, May 16
San Francisco 1906 Earthquake: Anniv, Apr 18
San Francisco 1989 Earthquake: Anniv, Oct 17
San Isidro Day (Mexico), May 15
San Jacinto Day (TX), Apr 21
San Marino: National Day, Sep 3
San Souci, Daniel: Birth, Oct 10
San Souci, Robert D.: Birth, Oct 10
Sandburg, Carl: Birth Anniv, Jan 6
Sandcastle Day, Aug 17
Sanders, Barry: Birth, Jul 16
Sanders, Deion: Birth, Aug 9
Sanders, Summer: Birth, Oct 13
Sanderson, Ruth: Birth, Nov 24
Sandler, Adam: Birth, Sep 9
Sandwich Day: John Montague: Birth Anniv, Nov 3
Sanford, Mark: Birth, May 28
Santa Lucia Day (Sweden), Dec 13
Santorum, Rick: Birth, May 10
Sao Tome and Principe: National Day, Jul 12
Sapp, Warren: Birth, Dec 19
Sarbanes, Paul S.: Birth, Feb 3
Sasaki, Kazuhiro: Birth, Feb 22
Sasaki, Sadako: Death Anniv, Oct 25
Saudi Arabia: Kingdom Unification, Sep 23
Savage, Ben: Birth, Sep 13
Savage, Fred: Birth, Jul 9
Savard, Denis: Birth, Feb 4
Save the Florida Panther Day, Mar 18
Save the Rhino Day, May 1
Save Your Vision Month, Mar 1
Save Your Vision Week (Pres Proc), Mar 5
Sawyer, Diane K.: Birth, Dec 22
Sax, Adolphe: Birth Anniv, Nov 6
Saxophone Day, Nov 6
Say, Allen: Birth, Aug 28
Scalia, Antonin: Birth, Mar 11
Scarry, Richard M.: Birth Anniv, Jun 5
Schaefer, Jack: Birth Anniv, Nov 19
Schenk de Regniers, Beatrice: Birth Anniv, Aug 16
Schilling, Curt: Birth, Nov 14
Schmidt, Mike: Birth, Sep 27
School Boards Assn Annual Conference, Natl (New Orleans, LA), Apr 8
School Bus Safety Week, Natl, Oct 16
School Counseling Week, Natl, Feb 6
School Library Day, Intl, Oct 24
School Library Media Month, Apr 1
School Lunch Week, Natl, Oct 9
School Lunch Week, Natl (Pres Proc), Oct 9
School Nurse Day, Natl, May 10
School Principals' Day, May 1
School Principals' Recognition Day (MA), Apr 27
School Spirit Season, Intl, Apr 30
School Support Staff Week, May 21
Schroeder, Alan: Birth, Jan 18
Schroeder, Gerhard: Birth, Sep 27
Schulz, Charles M.: Last Peanuts Strip: Anniv, Feb 13
Schulz, Charles M.: Peanuts Debuts: Anniv, Oct 2
Schulz, Charles: Birth Anniv, Nov 26
Schuman Plan Anniv: European Union, May 9
Schuman, William Howard: Birth Anniv, Aug 4
Schumann, Clara: Birth Anniv, Sep 13
Schumer, Charles E.: Birth, Nov 23
Schwan's USA Cup (Blaine, MN), Jul 14
Schwarzenegger, Arnold: Birth, Jul 30
Schweitzer, Brian: Birth, Sep 5
Schwikert, Tasha: Birth, Nov 21
Science
  Biological Clock Gene Discovered: Anniv, **Apr 28**
  Brain Awareness Week, Intl, **Mar 13**
  Camcorder Developed: Anniv, **Jan 20**
  Cellophane Tape Patented: Anniv, **May 27**
  Chemistry Week, Natl, **Oct 17**
  Cloning of an Adult Animal, First: Anniv, **Feb 23**
  Coelacanth Discovered: Anniv, **Dec 22**
  Earth's Rotation Proved: Anniv, **Jan 8**
  Energy Education Week, Natl, **Mar 20**
  First Self-Sustaining Nuclear Chain Reaction: Anniv, **Dec 2**
  First US Scientist Receives Nobel: Anniv, **Dec 10**
  Laser Patented: Anniv, **Mar 22**
  Metric System: Anniv, **Apr 7**
  Minority Scientists Showcase (St. Louis, MO), **Jan 14**
  Physicists Discover Top Quark: Anniv, **Apr 23**
  Radium Discovered: Anniv, **Dec 26**
  Science Olympiad (Champaign-Urbana, IL), **May 19**
  Science Teachers Assn Convention, Natl (Anaheim, CA), **Apr 6**
  Sky Awareness Week, **Apr 23**
  Vitamin C Isolated: Anniv, **Apr 4**
  X-Ray Discovery Day: Anniv, **Nov 8**
Science Teachers Assn Convention, Natl (Anaheim, CA), Apr 6
Scieszka, Jon: Birth, Sep 8
Scooby-Doo, Where Are You? TV Premiere: Anniv, Sep 13
Scopes, John T.: Birth Anniv, Aug 3
Scorpio Begins, Oct 23
Scotland
  Aberdeen Intl Youth Fest (Aberdeen), **Aug 3**
  Bannockburn Day, **Jun 24**
  Hogmanay, **Dec 31**
  Up Helly AA, **Jan 31**
Scotland Yard: First Appearance Anniv, Sep 29
Scott, Chad: Birth, Sep 6
Scott, Winfield: Birth Anniv, Jun 13
Scout Week, Girl, Mar 12
Scrabble Inventor: Butts, Alfred M.: Birth Anniv, Apr 13
Sea Cadet Month, Sep 1
Seattle Intl Children's Fest (Seattle, WA), May 15
Seau, Junior: Birth, Jan 19
Sebestyen, Ouida: Birth, Feb 13
Second Day of Christmas, Dec 26
Seeger, Pete: Birth, May 3
Seeing Eye Created in America: Anniv, Jan 29
Segar, E.C.: Birth Anniv, Dec 8
Sehorn, Jason: Birth, Apr 15
Selanne, Teemu: Birth, Jul 3
Selden, George: Birth Anniv, May 14
Seles, Monica: Birth, Dec 2
Senate Quorum, First: Anniv, Apr 6
Senate: Black Page Appointed: Anniv, Apr 8
Sendak, Maurice: Birth, Jun 10
Senegal: Independence Day, Apr 4
Senior Citizens
  Older Americans Month (Pres Proc), **May 1**
  Older Persons, Intl Day for, **Oct 1**
Sequoia and Kings Canyon Natl Parks: Anniv, Sep 25
Server, Josh: Birth, Apr 11
Sesame Street TV Premiere: Anniv, Nov 10
Sessions, Jeff: Birth, Dec 24
Seton, Elizabeth Ann: Birth Anniv, Aug 28
Setsubun (Japan), Feb 3
Seurat, Georges: Birth Anniv, Dec 2
Seuss, Dr.: Geisel, Theodor: Birth Anniv, Mar 2
Sewall, Marcia: Birth, Nov 5
Seward, William H.: Birth Anniv, May 16
Seward's Day (AK), Mar 27
Sewell, Anna: Birth Anniv, Mar 30
Sex Month, Natl Talk With Your Teen About, Mar 1
Sexuality Education Month, Natl Family, Oct 1
Seychelles: Constitution Day, Jun 18
Shakespeare, William: Birth and Death Anniv, Apr 23
Shamu: Birthday, Sep 26
Shannon, David: Birth, Oct 5
Shareware Day, Intl, Dec 10
Sharmat, Marjorie Weinman: Birth, Nov 12
Shatner, William: Birth, Mar 22
Shavuot, Jun 2
Shaw, Nancy: Birth, Apr 27
Shays Rebellion: Anniv, Aug 29
Shelby, Richard C.: Birth, May 6
Shelley, Mary Wollstonecraft: Birth Anniv, Aug 30
Shemini Atzeret, Oct 25
Shenandoah Natl Park: Anniv, Dec 26
Shepard, Alan: Birth Anniv, Nov 18
Sherman Enters Atlanta: Anniv, Sep 2
Sherman, James S.: Birth Anniv, Oct 24
Sherman, Roger: Birth Anniv, Apr 19
Sherman, William Tecumseh: Birth Anniv, Feb 8
Shopping Carts to the Supermarket Month, Return, Feb 1
Shopping Reminder Day, Nov 25
Shriver, Maria: Birth, Nov 6
Shrove Monday, Feb 27
Shrove Tuesday, Feb 28
Shrovetide, Feb 26
Shulevitz, Uri: Birth, Feb 27
Sibelius, Kathleen: Birth, May 15
Sierra Club Founded: Anniv, May 28
Sierra Leone
  Independence Day, **Apr 27**
  National Holiday, **Apr 19**
Sierra, Judy: Birth, Jun 8
Sikh: Baisakhi (India), Apr 13
Silent Spring Publication: Anniv, Apr 13
Silly Putty Debuts: Anniv, Mar 1
Silverstein, Shel: Birth Anniv, Oct 18
Silverstone, Alicia: Birth, Oct 4
Simchat Torah, Oct 26
Simon, Paul: Birth, Oct 13
Simon, Seymour: Birth, Aug 9
Simpson, Ashlee: Birth, Oct 3
Simpson, Jessica: Birth, Jul 10
Simpsons TV Premiere: Anniv, Dec 17
Sinai Day (Egypt), Apr 25
Sinbad: Birth, Nov 10
Singapore
  National Day, **Aug 9**
  Vesak Day, **May 10**
Singer, Isaac Bashevis: Birth Anniv, Jul 14
Singletary, Mike: Birth, Oct 9
Sis, Peter: Birth, May 11
Sisters' Day, Aug 7
Sitting Bull: Death Anniv, Dec 15
Skating: Natl Roller Skating Month, Oct 1
Sky Awareness Week, Apr 23
Skylab Falls to Earth, Jul 11
Slater, Samuel, Day (MA), Dec 20
Slavery: First American Abolition Society Founded: Anniv, Apr 14
Slayton, Donald "Deke" K.: Birth Anniv, Mar 1
Sleator, William: Birth, Feb 13
Sled Dogs Save Nome: Anniv, Feb 2
Sleep Awareness Week, Natl, Mar 27
Slinky Introduced: Anniv, Nov 26
Slobodkina, Esphyr: Birth Anniv, Sep 22
Slovakia
  Constitution Day, **Sep 1**
  Czech-Slovak Divorce: Anniv, **Jan 1**
  Natl Uprising Day, **Aug 29**
  St. Cyril and Methodius Day, **Jul 5**
Slovenia
  Independence Day, **Dec 26**
  Insurrection Day, **Apr 27**
  National Day, **Jun 25**
  Preseren Day, **Feb 8**
Small, David: Birth, Feb 12
Smallpox Vaccine Discovered: Anniv, May 14
Smith Day, Natl, Jan 6
Smith, Akili: Birth, Aug 21
Smith, Betty: Birth Anniv, Dec 15
Smith, Dean: Birth, Feb 28
Smith, Emmitt: Birth, May 15
Smith, Gordon: Birth, May 25
Smith, James: Death Anniv, Jul 11
Smith, Jedediah Strong: Birth Anniv, Jan 6
Smith, Jimmy: Birth, Feb 9
Smith, Kate: God Bless America First Perf: Anniv, Nov 11
Smith, Lane: Birth, Aug 25
Smith, Samantha: Death Anniv, Aug 25
Smith, Steve: Birth, Mar 31
Smith, Will: Birth, Sep 25
Smithsonian Institution Founded: Anniv, Aug 10
Smithsonian: Hope Diamond Mailed to: Anniv, Nov 8
Smits, Rik: Birth, Aug 23
Smokeout, Great American, Nov 17
Snow Fest (Japan), Feb 8
Snow, Eric: Birth, Apr 24
Snow, J.T.: Birth, Feb 26
Snow, John: Birth, Aug 2
Snowe, Olympia J.: Birth, Feb 21
Snyder, Zilpha Keatley: Birth, May 11
Soap Box Derby, All-American (Akron, OH), Jul 30
Sobieski, Leelee: Birth, Jun 10
Sobol, Donald: Birth, Oct 4
Soccer
  Pele Scores 1,000th Goal: Anniv, **Nov 19**
  Schwan's USA Cup (Blaine, MN), **Jul 14**
  World Cup Inaugurated: Anniv, **Jul 13**
Social Security Act: Anniv, Aug 14
Social Studies, Natl Council for the, Annual Mtg (Kansas City, MO), Nov 17
Solemnity of Mary, Jan 1
Solomon Islands: Independence Day, Jul 7
Solstice, Summer, Jun 21
Solstice, Winter, Dec 21
Sorbo, Kevin: Birth, Sep 24
Sorenstam, Annika: Birth, Oct 9
Soriano, Alfonso: Birth, Jan 7
Sosa, Sammy: Birth, Nov 12
Soto, Gary: Birth, Apr 12
Soul Food Month, Natl, Jun 1
Sound Barrier Broken: Anniv, Oct 14
Sousa, John P.: Birth Anniv, Nov 6
Sousa: Stars and Stripes Forever Day, May 14
Souter, David H.: Birth, Sep 17
South Africa
  Boer War: Anniv, **Oct 12**
  Day of Goodwill, **Dec 26**
  Family Day, **Apr 17**
  Freedom Day, **Apr 27**
  Heritage Day, **Sep 24**
  Human Rights Day, **Mar 21**
  Multiracial Elections: Anniv, **Apr 26**
  National Women's Day, **Aug 9**
  New Constitution: Anniv, **Nov 18**
  Reconciliation Day, **Dec 16**
  Repeals Last Apartheid Law: Anniv, **Jun 17**
  US Sanctions Lifted: Anniv, **Jul 10**
  Whites Vote to End Minority Rule: Anniv, **Mar 17**
  Youth Day, **Jun 16**
South Carolina
  Confederate Memorial Day, **May 10**
  DeMint, Jim: Birth, **Sep 2**
  Fort Sumter Shelled by North: Anniv, **Aug 17**
  Graham, Lindsey: Birth, **Jul 9**
  Ratification Day, **May 23**
  Sanford, Mark: Birth, **May 28**
  Secession Anniv, **Dec 20**
  State Fair (Columbia), **Oct 6**
South Dakota
  Admission Day, **Nov 2**
  Badlands Natl Park: Anniv, **Nov 10**
  Johnson, Tim: Birth, **Dec 28**
  Laura Ingalls Wilder Pageant (De Smet), **Jul 7**

Native Americans Day, **Oct 10**
Rounds, Mike: Birth, **Oct 24**
State Fair (Huron), **Sep 3**
Thune, John R.: Birth, **Jan 7**
Wind Cave Natl Park: Anniv, **Jan 3**
South Pole Discovery: Anniv, Dec 14
Southern Fest of Books (Nashville, TN), Oct 7
Space (excluding Space Milestones)
Apollo I: Spacecraft Fire: Anniv, **Jan 27**
Astronomy Day, **May 6**
Astronomy Week, **May 1**
Challenger Space Shuttle Explosion: Anniv, **Jan 28**
Closest Approach of a Comet to Earth: Anniv, **Feb 20**
Columbia Space Shuttle Disaster: Anniv, **Feb 1**
Comet Crashes into Jupiter: Anniv, **Jul 16**
Eta Aquarids Meteor Shower, **Apr 21**
First Man in Space: Anniv, **Apr 12**
First Picture of Earth: Anniv, **Aug 7**
First Woman in Space: Anniv, **Jun 16**
First Woman to Walk in Space, **Jul 17**
Last Perihelion of Halley's Comet: Anniv, **Feb 9**
Leonid Meteor Shower, **Nov 15**
NASA Established: Anniv, **Jul 29**
Near Miss Day, **Mar 23**
Orionids Meteor Shower, **Oct 15**
Radio Broadcast from Space, First: Anniv, **Dec 19**
Soviet Cosmonaut Returns to New Country: Anniv, **Mar 26**
Spiders Launched: Anniv, **Jul 28**
World Space Week (UN), **Oct 4**
Space Day, May 4
Space Milestones
Year 1 (1957)
Sputnik 1, **Oct 4**
Sputnik 2, **Nov 3**
Year 2 (1958)
Explorer 1, **Jan 31**
Christmas Greetings From Space, **Dec 19**
Year 3 (1959)
Luna 1, **Jan 2**
First Picture of Earth From Space, **Aug 7**
Luna 2, **Sep 12**
Year 4 (1960)
Echo 1, **Aug 12**
Sputnik 5, **Aug 19**
Year 5 (1961)
Project Mercury Test, **Jan 31**
Vostok 1, **Apr 12**
Freedom 7, **May 5**
Year 6 (1962)
Friendship 7, **Feb 20**
Telstar, **July 10**
Year 7 (1963)
Vostok 6, **June 16**
Year 9 (1965)
Voskhod 2, **Mar 18**
Gemini 4, **June 3**
Venera 3, **Nov 16**
Year 10 (1966)
Gemini 12, **Nov 11**
Year 12 (1968)
Apollo 8, **Dec 21**
Year 13 (1969)
Soyuz 4, **Jan 14**
Apollo 11, **July 16**
Moon Day, **July 20**
Year 14 (1970)
Osumi, **Feb 11**
Apollo 13, **Apr 11**
Space Rescue Agreement, **Oct 28**
Luna 17, **Nov 10**
Year 15 (1971)
Salyut, **Apr 19**
Mariner 9, **May 30**
Soyuz 11, **June 6**
Year 16 (1972)
Pioneer 10, **Mar 2**
Year 17 (1973)
Skylab, **May 14**
Year 19 (1975)
Apollo-Soyuz Linkup, **July 17**
Year 21 (1977)
Voyager 2, **Aug 20**
Voyager 1, **Sep 5**
Year 22 (1978)
Soyuz 28, **Mar 2**
Year 23 (1979)
Skylab Falls to Earth, **July 11**
Year 24 (1980)
Soyuz 37, **July 23**
Year 25 (1981)
Columbia STS-1, **Apr 12**
Year 26 (1982)
Kosmos 1383, **July 1**
Year 27 (1983)
NOAA 8, **Mar 28**
Challenger STS-7, **June 18**
Year 28 (1984)
Challenger STS-10, **Feb 3**
Soyuz T-12: First Woman Walks in Space, **July 17**
Discovery, **Aug 30**
Year 29 (1985)
Arabsat-1, **Feb 8**
Year 30 (1986)
Mir Space Station, **Feb 20**
Year 32 (1988)
Discovery, **Sep 29**
Year 33 (1989)
Atlantis, **May 4**
Year 34 (1990)
Hubble Space Telescope, **Apr 25**
Year 36 (1992)
Endeavour, **May 13**
Year 39 (1995)
Atlantis Docks with Mir, **June 29**
Record Time, **Mar 22**
Galileo, **Dec 7**
Year 41 (1997)
Mars Pathfinder, **July 4**
Mars Global Surveyor, **Sep 11**
Cassini, **Oct 15**
Year 42 (1998)
Lunar Explorer, **Jan 6**
Columbia Neurolab, **Apr 17**
Nozomi, **July 4**
Discovery: Oldest Man in Space, **Oct 29**
International Space Station Launch, **Dec 4**
Mars Climate Orbiter, **Dec 11**
Year 43 (1999)
Stardust, **Feb 7**
Columbia: First Female Commander, **July 23**
Year 44 (2000)
Endeavour Mapping Mission, **Feb 11**
Discovery STS-92: 100th Space Shuttle Flight, **Oct 11**
NEAR Orbits Asteroid, **Feb 14**
ISS Inhabited, **Nov 2**
Year 45 (2001)
100th Spacewalk, **Feb 14**
Mir Abandoned, **Mar 23**
Mars Odyssey, **Apr 7**
First Tourist in Space, **Apr 28**
Genesis, **Aug 8**
Helios, **Aug 13**
Year 48 (2004)
Mars Exploration Rover Spirit, **Jan 3**
First Manned Private Spaceflight, **June 21**
Spacek, Sissy: Birth, Dec 25
Spain
Book Day and Lover's Day, **Apr 23**
Constitution Day, **Dec 6**
La Tomatina, **Aug 31**
National Holiday, **Oct 12**
Spain Captures Granada: Anniv, **Jan 2**
Treaty of Paris Signed: Anniv, **Dec 10**
Spanish Flu: Pandemic of 1918 Hits US: Anniv, Mar 11
Spank Out Day USA, Apr 30
Speare, Elizabeth George: Birth Anniv, Nov 21
Spears, Britney: Birth, Dec 2
Special Olympics, First: Anniv, Jul 20
Specter, Arlen: Birth, Feb 12
Speech Month, Better Hearing and, May 1
Spelling Bee Finals, Natl (Washington, DC), May 31
Spellings, Margaret: Birth, Nov 30
Spiders in Space: Anniv, Jul 28
Spielberg, Steven: Birth, Dec 18
Spier, Peter: Birth, Jun 6
Spinelli, Jerry: Birth, Feb 1
Splurge Day, Natl, Jun 18
Spock, Benjamin: Birth Anniv, May 2
SpongeBob SquarePants TV Premiere: Anniv, Jul 17
Spooner, William: Birth Anniv, Jul 22
Spooner's Day, Jul 22
Sports, Physical Fitness and, Month, Natl, May 1
Sprewell, Latrell: Birth, Sep 8
Spring Begins, Mar 20
Springfield, Adam: Birth, Jan 30
Spyri, Johanna: Birth Anniv, Jul 12
Squid Battles Fishermen: Anniv, Oct 25
Sri Lanka
Independence Day, **Feb 4**
Natl Heroes Day, **May 22**
Sinhala and Tamil New Year, **Apr 13**
St. Laurent, Louis Stephen: Birth Anniv, Feb 1
Stabenow, Debbie: Birth, Apr 29
Stackhouse, Jerry: Birth, Nov 5
Staley, Dawn: Birth, May 4
Stamos, John: Birth, Aug 19
Stamps
Postage Stamps, First Adhesive US: Anniv, **Jul 1**
Stamp Collecting Month, Natl, **Oct 1**
Stand for Children Day, Jun 1
Standard Time Act, US: Anniv, Mar 19
Standing Bear: Native American Rights Recognized: Anniv, May 12
Stanley, Diane: Birth, Dec 27
Stanley, Jerry: Birth, Jul 18
Stanton, Elizabeth: Birth Anniv, Nov 12
Staples, Suzanne Fisher: Birth, Aug 27
Star Fest (Tanabata) (Japan), Jul 7
Star Trek TV Premiere: Anniv, Sep 8
Star Wars Released: Anniv, May 25
Stars and Stripes Forever Day, May 14
Star-Spangled Banner Inspired: Anniv, Sep 13
State Constitution Day (MA), Oct 25
State Dept Founded, US: Anniv, Jul 27
State Fairs. See Agriculture, Feb 9
Statue of Liberty: Dedication Anniv, Oct 28
Stay Out of the Sun Day, Jul 3
Steig, William: Birth Anniv, Nov 14
Steptoe, John: Birth, Sep 14
Stevens, John Paul: Birth, Apr 20
Stevens, Ted: Birth, Nov 18
Stevenson, Adlai: Birth, Oct 23
Stevenson, Alexandra: Birth, Dec 15
Stevenson, James: Birth, Jul 11
Stevenson, Robert L.: Birth Anniv, Nov 13
Stewart, Earnie: Birth, Mar 28
Stewart, Kordell: Birth, Oct 16
Stewart, Patrick: Birth, Jul 13
Stewart, Potter: Birth Anniv, Jan 23
Stewart, Sarah: Birth, Aug 27
Still, Valerie: Birth, May 14
Stilts: Walk on Stilts Day, Jul 27
Stine, R.L.: Birth, Oct 8
Stinson, Andrea: Birth, Nov 25
Stock Exchange, NY, Established: Anniv, May 17
Stock Market Crash (1929): Anniv, Oct 29
Stockings, Nylon: Anniv, May 15
Stockton, John Houston: Birth, Mar 26
Stockton, Richard: Birth Anniv, Oct 1
Stojakovic, Peja: Birth, Jun 9
Stojko, Elvis: Birth, Mar 22
Stokes, Carl: Becomes First Black Mayor in US: Anniv, Nov 13
Stone, Harlan Fiske: Birth Anniv, Oct 11
Stone, Lucy: Birth Anniv, Aug 13
Stone, Thomas: Death Anniv, Oct 5
Stookey, Paul: Birth, Nov 30
Stop the Violence Day, Natl, Nov 22
Story, Joseph: Birth Anniv, Sep 18
Storytelling
Calgary Intl Children's Fest (Calgary, AB, Canada), **May 23**
Connecticut Storytelling Fest (New London, CT), **Apr 28**
Corn Island Storytelling Fest (Louisville, KY), **Sep 8**
Iowa Storytelling Fest (Clear Lake, IA), **Jul 28**
Storyteller of the Year Contest, Natl (Millersport, OH), **Oct 30**
Storytelling Fest, Natl (Jonesborough, TN), **Oct 7**
Stoudamire, Damon: Birth, Sep 3
Stowe, Harriet Beecher: Birth Anniv, Jun 14
Stratemeyer, Edward L.: Birth Anniv, Oct 4
Strauss, Levi: Birth Anniv, Feb 26
Strawberry, Darryl: Birth, Mar 12
Street, Picabo: Birth, Apr 3
Strong, Rider: Birth, Dec 11
Strug, Kerri: Birth, Nov 19
Stubby Joins WWI Front Lines: Anniv, Feb 5
Studdard, Ruben: Birth, Sep 12
Student Government Day (MA), Apr 7
Stuttering Awareness Day, Intl, Oct 22
Stuttering Awareness Week, Natl, May 14
Submarine: Anniv of First Nuclear-Powered Voyage, Jan 17
Substitute Teacher Appreciation Week, Sep 12
Subway, New York City: Subway Anniv, Oct 27
Succoth, Oct 18
Sudan: Independence Day, Jan 1
Sue Exhibited: Anniv, May 17
Sukkot, Oct 18
Sukkot Begins, Oct 17
Sullivan, Anne: Birth Anniv, Apr 14
Sullivan, George: Birth, Aug 11
Summer Begins, Jun 21
Sun Yat-Sen: Birth Anniv, Nov 12
Sun Yat-Sen: Death Anniv, Mar 12
Sununu, John: Birth, Sep 10
Super Bowl (Detroit, MI), Feb 5
Super Mario Brothers Released: Anniv, Oct 1
SuperCroc Discovered: Anniv, Aug 30
Supervision and Curriculum Development, Assn for, Convention (Chicago, IL), Mar 1
Supreme Court
Bans School Prayer: Anniv, **Jun 25**
Breyer, Stephen G.: Birth, **Aug 15**
Brown v Board of Education of Topeka: Anniv, **May 17**
First Session of: Anniv, **Feb 1**
Ginsburg, Ruth Bader: Birth, **Mar 15**
Kennedy, Anthony M.: Birth, **Jul 23**
Miranda Decision: Anniv, **Jun 13**
O'Connor, Sandra Day: Birth, **Mar 26**
Rehnquist, William Hubbs: Birth, **Oct 1**
Rules for Bush: Anniv, **Dec 12**
Scalia, Antonin: Birth, **Mar 11**
Souter, David H.: Birth, **Sep 17**
Stevens, John Paul: Birth, **Apr 20**
Term Begins, **Oct 3**
Thomas, Clarence: Birth, **Jun 23**
With All Deliberate Speed: Anniv, **May 31**
Woman Presides Over: Anniv, **Apr 3**
Suriname: Independence Day, Nov 25
Sutcliffe, Rosemary: Birth Anniv, Dec 14
Sutherland, Catherine: Birth, Oct 24
Sutherland, Kiefer: Birth, Dec 21
Sutter, John A.: Birth Anniv, Feb 15
Sutton Hoo Ship Burial Discovered: Anniv, May 11
Suzuki, Ichiro: Birth, Oct 22
Swallows Return to San Juan Capistrano, Mar 19
Swaziland: Flag Day, Natl, Apr 25
Swaziland: Independence Day, Sep 6
Sweat, Lynn: Birth, May 27
Sweden
Feast of Valborg, **Apr 30**
Flag Day, **Jun 6**
Gustavus Adolphus Day, **Nov 6**
Linnaeus Day (Stenbrohult), **May 23**
Nobel Prize Awards Ceremony (Stockholm), **Dec 10**
Saint Knut's Day, **Jan 13**
Saint Martin's Day, **Nov 11**
Santa Lucia Day, **Dec 13**
Swimming and Diving
Ederle, Gertrude: Birth Anniv, **Oct 23**
First Woman Swims English Channel: Anniv, **Aug 6**
Swimming School Opens, First US, **Jul 23**
Switzerland
Berchtoldstag, **Jan 2**
Chalandra Marz, **Mar 1**
Confederation Day, **Aug 1**
Homstrom (Scuol), **Feb 5**
Landsgemeinde, **Apr 30**
Meitlisunntig, **Jan 8**
Morat Battle: Anniv, **Jun 22**
Pacing the Bounds (Liestal), **May 22**
Swoopes, Sheryl: Birth, May 25
Symone, Raven: Birth, Dec 10
Syria
Independence Day, **Apr 17**
Revolution Day, **Mar 8**
Ta'anit Esther (Fast of Esther), Mar 13
Taback, Simms: Birth, Feb 13
Tabaski: See Eid-al-Adha, Jan 10
Tabei, Junko: First Woman To Climb Mount Everest: Anniv, May 16
Tabernacles, Feast of: First Day, Oct 18
Taft, Bob: Birth, Jan 8
Taft, Helen Herron: Birth Anniv, Jan 2
Taft, William H.: Birth Anniv, Sep 15
Tafuri, Nancy: Birth, Nov 14
Taiwan
Cheng Cheng Kung Landing Day, **Apr 29**
Chiang Kai-Shek Day, **Oct 31**
Chinese Nationalists Move to Taiwan: Anniv, **Dec 8**

Confucius's Birthday and Teachers' Day, **Sep 28**
Constitution Day, **Dec 25**
Foundation Day, **Jan 1**
Overseas Chinese Day, **Oct 21**
Retrocession Day, **Oct 25**
Tomb-Sweeping Day, Natl, **Apr 5**
Two-Twenty-Eight Day, **Feb 28**
Youth Day, **Mar 29**
Tajikistan: Independence Day, Sep 9
Take Our Daughters and Sons to Work Day, Apr 27
Talent, Jim: Birth, Oct 18
Talk Like a Pirate Day, Sep 19
Talk With Your Teen About Sex Month, Natl, Mar 1
Tallarico, Tony: Birth, Sep 20
Tammuz, Fast of, Jul 13
Taney, Roger B.: Birth Anniv, Mar 17
Tanzania
Farmers' Day, **Aug 8**
Independence and Republic Day, **Dec 9**
Saba Saba Day, **Jul 7**
Union Day, **Apr 26**
Zanzibar Revolution Day, **Jan 12**
Tap Dance Day, Natl, May 25
Tate, Eleanor E.: Birth, Apr 16
Taurus Begins, Apr 20
Tax, Income, Pay Day, Apr 15
Taylor, Fred: Birth, Jan 27
Taylor, George: Death Anniv, Feb 23
Taylor, Lucy Hobbs: Birth Anniv, Mar 14
Taylor, Margaret S.: Birth Anniv, Sep 21
Taylor, Mildred: Birth, Sep 13
Taylor, Sydney: Birth Anniv, Oct 31
Taylor, Theodore: Birth, Jun 23
Taylor, Zachary: Birth Anniv, Nov 24
TB Bacillus Discovered: Anniv, Mar 24
Tchaikovsky, Peter Ilich: Birth Anniv, May 7
Teach Children to Save Day, Natl, Apr 25
Teach, Edward (Blackbeard): Death Anniv, Nov 22
Teacher Appreciation Week, Natl PTA, May 1
Teacher Day, Natl, May 9
Teacher, Day of the (El Dia Del Maestro) (CA), May 10
Teacher's Day (MA), Jun 4
Teacher's Day in Florida, May 19
Teachers' Day, Confucius's Birthday and (Taiwan), Sep 28
Teachers of Mathematics, Natl Council of, Annual Mtg (St. Louis, MO), Apr 26
Teague, Mark: Birth, Feb 10
Technology + Learning Conference (Denver, CO), Oct 26
Tecumseh: Death Anniv, Oct 5
Teddy Bear Day, Natl American, Nov 14
Teddy Bear: Anniv, Nov 18
Teen Read Week, Oct 16
Teflon Invented: Anniv, Apr 6
Tejada, Miguel: Birth, May 25
Telecommunication Day, World (UN), May 17
Telegraph Line, Morse Opens First US: Anniv, May 24
Telephone Operator, First: Emma M. Nutt Day, Sep 1
Telephone: Anniv, Mar 10
Television
Arthur Premiere: Anniv, **Oct 7**
Barney & Friends Premiere: Anniv, **Apr 6**
Between the Lions Premiere: Anniv, **Apr 3**
Brady Bunch Premiere: Anniv, **Sep 26**
Captain Kangaroo Premiere: Anniv, **Oct 3**
CBS Evening News Premiere: Anniv, **May 3**
Children's Day of Broadcasting, Intl, **Dec 11**
CNN Debuted: Anniv, **Jun 1**
Dragonball Z Premiere: Anniv, **Apr 26**
First Baseball Games Televised: Anniv, **Aug 26**
First Color Broadcast: Anniv, **Jun 25**
First Presidential Telecast: Anniv, **Apr 30**
First Televised Presidential Debate: Anniv, **Sep 26**
Flintstones Premiere: Anniv, **Sep 30**
Good Morning America Premiere: Anniv, **Nov 6**
Hey Arnold! Premiere: Anniv, **Oct 9**
Howdy Doody Premiere: Anniv, **Dec 27**
Jetsons Premiere: Anniv, **Sep 23**
Lizzie McGuire Premiere: Anniv, **Jan 19**
Lone Ranger Premiere: Anniv, **Sep 15**
Mickey Mouse Club Premiere: Anniv, **Oct 3**
Mighty Mouse Playhouse Premiere: Anniv, **Dec 10**
Mister Rogers' Neighborhood Premiere: Anniv, **May 22**
Muppet Show Premiere: Anniv, **Sep 13**
Nick at Nite Premiere: Anniv, **Jul 1**
Nickelodeon Channel Premiere: Anniv, **Apr 2**
Pokeman Debuts: Anniv, **Sep 28**
Powerpuff Girls Premiere: Anniv, **Nov 18**
Public Television Debuts: Anniv, **Nov 3**
Reading Rainbow Premiere: Anniv, **Jul 1**
Regular TV Broadcasts Begin: Anniv, **Jul 1**
Rocky and His Friends Premiere: Anniv, **Nov 19**
Rugrats Premiere: Anniv, **Aug 11**
Scooby-Doo, Where Are You? Premiere: Anniv, **Sep 13**
Sesame Street Premiere: Anniv, **Nov 10**
Simpsons Premiere: Anniv, **Dec 17**
SpongeBob SquarePants Premiere: Anniv, **Jul 17**
Star Trek Premiere: Anniv, **Sep 8**
The Wild Thornberries Premiere: Anniv, **Sep 1**
TV-Turnoff Week, Natl, **Apr 24**
Vast Wasteland Speech: Anniv, **May 9**
Walt Disney Premiere: Anniv, **Oct 27**
Wishbone Premiere: Anniv, **Oct 9**
World Television Day, **Nov 21**
Temperature, North America's Coldest Recorded: Anniv, Feb 3
Tennessee
Admission Day, **Jun 1**
Alexander, Lamar: Birth, **Jul 30**
Bredesen, Phil: Birth, **Nov 21**
Confederate Memorial Day/Jefferson Davis Day, **Jun 3**
Frist, William: Birth, **Feb 22**
Oak Ridge Atomic Plant Begun: Anniv, **Aug 1**
Southern Fest of Books (Nashville), **Oct 7**
State Fair (Nashville), **Sep 9**
Storytelling Fest, Natl (Jonesborough), **Oct 7**
Tenniel, John: Birth Anniv, Feb 28
Teresa, Mother: Birth Anniv, Aug 27
TESOL Annual Conference (Tampa Bay, FL), Mar 15
Testaverde, Vinny: Birth, Nov 13
Tet: See Chinese New Year, Jan 29
Texas
Admission Day, **Dec 29**
Alamo, Fall of the, **Mar 6**
American Library Assn Midwinter Mtg (San Antonio), **Jan 20**
Cornyn, John: Birth, **Feb 2**
Elementary School Principals, Natl Assn of, Annual Conference (San Antonio), **Apr 1**
Emancipation Day, **Jun 19**
Galveston Hurricane: Anniv, **Sep 8**
Guadalupe Mountains Natl Park: Anniv, **Sep 30**
Hutchison, Kay Bailey: Birth, **Jul 22**
Independence Day, **Mar 2**
Juneteenth, **Jun 19**
KidFilm Fest (Dallas), **Jan 3**
Latino Book & Family Fest—Houston, **Oct 1**
Mustang League World Series (Irving), **Aug 3**
Perry, Rick: Birth, **Mar 4**
San Jacinto Day, **Apr 21**
State Fair (Dallas), **Sep 30**
Texas Book Fest (Austin), **Oct 28**
Thailand
Birth of the Queen, **Aug 12**
Chakri Day, **Apr 6**
Chulalongkorn Day, **Oct 23**
Constitution Day, **Dec 10**
Coronation Day, **May 5**
Elephant Round-Up at Surin, **Nov 19**
King's Birthday and National Day, **Dec 5**
Songkran Fest, **Apr 13**
Thank God It's Monday! Day, Natl, Jan 9
Thank You Days, Intl, Jan 11
Thank You, School Librarian Day, Apr 5
Thanksgiving Day, Nov 24
Thanksgiving Day (Canada), Oct 10
Thanksgiving Day (Pres Proc), Nov 24
Thanksgiving Day Parade, Macy's (New York, NY), Nov 24
Thanksgiving Parade, America's (Detroit, MI), Nov 24
The Wild Thornberries TV Premiere: Anniv, Sep 1
Theater
Calgary Intl Children's Fest (Calgary, AB, Canada), **May 23**
First Play Presented in North American Colonies: Anniv, **Aug 27**
Laura Ingalls Wilder Pageant (De Smet, SD), **Jul 7**
Laura Ingalls Wilder Pageant (Walnut Grove, MN), **Jul 7**
Seattle Intl Children's Fest (Seattle, WA), **May 15**
Theater in North America, First Performance: Anniv, **Apr 30**
Theodore Roosevelt Natl Park Established: Anniv, Apr 25
Third World Day: Anniv, Apr 18
Thomas, Anthony: Birth, Nov 7
Thomas, Clarence: Birth, Jun 23
Thomas, Craig: Birth, Feb 17
Thomas, Frank: Birth, May 27
Thomas, Isiah: Birth, Apr 30
Thomas, Jane Resh: Birth, Aug 15
Thomas, Jonathan Taylor: Birth, Sep 8
Thomas, Joyce Carol: Birth, May 25
Thomas, Marlo: Birth, Nov 21
Thomas, Zach: Birth, Sep 1
Thompson, Jenny: Birth, Feb 26
Thompson, Kay: Birth Anniv, Nov 9
Thompson, Kenan: Birth, May 10
Thompson, LaMarcus A: Birth Anniv, Mar 8
Thompson, LaMarcus: First Roller Coaster: Anniv, Jun 13
Thompson, Tina: Birth, Feb 10
Thoreau, Henry David: Birth Anniv, Jul 12
Thornton, Matthew: Death Anniv, Jun 24
Thorpe, James: Birth Anniv, May 28
Three Kings Day, Jan 6
Three Mile Island Nuclear Power Plant Accident: Anniv, Mar 28
Thumb, Tom: Birth Anniv, Jan 4
Thune, John R.: Birth, Jan 7
Thurber, James: Birth Anniv, Dec 8
Tiananmen Square Massacre: Anniv, Jun 4
Tides, Perigean Spring, Aug 19
Tides, Perigean Spring, Jan 29
Tides, Perigean Spring, Feb 27
Till, Emmett: Death Anniv, Aug 28
Timberlake, Justin: Birth, Jan 31
Time Magazine First Published: Anniv, Mar 3
Time; Calendars
Daylight Saving Time Begins, US, **Apr 2**
Daylight Saving Time Ends, US, **Oct 30**
Leap Second Adjustment Time, **Dec 31**
Leap Second Adjustment Time, **Jun 30**
Prime Meridian Set: Anniv, **Nov 1**
Time Zone Plan, US Uniform: Anniv, **Nov 18**
US Standard Time Act: Anniv, **Mar 19**
Tin Can Patent: Anniv, Jan 19
Tinsley, Jamaal: Birth, Feb 28
Titanic Discovered: Anniv, Sep 1
Titanic, Sinking of the: Anniv, Apr 15
Titus, Eve: Birth, Jul 16
Tkachuk, Keith: Birth, Mar 28
Tobago
Emancipation Day, **Aug 1**
Independence Day, **Aug 31**
Spiritual Baptist Liberation Shouter Day, **Mar 30**
Togo
Independence Day, **Apr 27**
Liberation Day, **Jan 13**
Togo: Sled Dog Hero: Death Anniv, Dec 5
Tolerance, Intl Day for (UN), Nov 16
Tolkien, J.R.R.: Birth Anniv, Jan 3
Tolkien, J.R.R.: First Part of Lord of the Rings Published: Anniv, Jul 29
Toll Collection Machine, First Automatic: Anniv, Nov 19
Tom Sawyer Days, Natl (Hannibal, MO), Jul 1
Tomatina, La (Spain), Aug 31
Tomb-Sweeping Day, Natl (Taiwan), Apr 5
Tomlinson, LaDainian: Birth, Jun 23
Tompkins, Daniel D.: Birth Anniv, Jun 21
Tonga: Emancipation Day, Jun 4
Tourism Week, Natl, May 13
Tournament of Roses Parade (Pasadena, CA), Jan 1
Town Meeting Day (VT), Mar 7
Town Watch: Natl Night Out, Aug 2
Toys
Barbie Debuts: Anniv, **Mar 9**
Construction Toy Month, Natl, **Oct 1**
Easy-Bake Oven Debuts: Anniv, **Feb 1**
Etch-A-Sketch Introduced: Anniv, **Jul 12**
G.I. Joe Introduced: Anniv, **Feb 1**
Kirsten, Samantha and Molly Debut: Anniv, **Sep 15**
Monopoly Invented: Anniv, **Mar 7**
100 Billionth Crayon Produced: Anniv, **Feb 6**
Silly Putty Debuts: Anniv, **Mar 1**
Slinky Introduced: Anniv, **Nov 26**
Trachtenberg, Michelle: Birth, Oct 11
Track and Field: Jesse Owens' Remarkable Records: Anniv, May 25
Trade Week, World (Pres Proc), May 21
Trafalgar Weekend (United Kingdom), Oct 21
Traffic Jam, Longest in History: Anniv, Feb 16
Transatlantic Flight, First Nonstop: Anniv, Jun 14
Transatlantic Phoning: Anniv, Jan 7
Transcontinental Flight, First Scheduled: Anniv, Jan 25
Transfer Day (US Virgin Islands), Mar 31
Transistor Invented: Anniv, Dec 23
Transportation Week, Natl (Pres Proc), May 14
Trapini, Iza: Birth, Jan 12
Travers, Mary: Birth, Nov 7
Travers, P.L.: Birth Anniv, Aug 9
Treasury Dept, US: Anniv, Sep 2
Treaty of Guadalupe Hidalgo: Anniv, Feb 2
Triangle Shirtwaist Fire: Anniv, Mar 25
Trick or Treat Night, Oct 31
Trinidad and Tobago
Carnival (Port of Spain), **Feb 27**
Emancipation Day, **Aug 1**
Independence Day, **Aug 31**
Indian Arrival Day (Port of Spain), **May 30**
Spiritual Baptist Liberation Shouter Day, **Mar 30**
Trinity Sunday, Jun 11
Tripp, Valerie: Birth, Sep 12
Trivia Day, Jan 4
Truancy Law: Anniv, Apr 12
Truman, Bess: Birth Anniv, Feb 13
Truman, Harry S: Birth Anniv, May 8
Trust Your Intuition Day, May 10
Truth, Sojourner: Death Anniv, Nov 26
Tsunami, Highest Recorded in History: Anniv, Jul 9
Tu B'Shvat, Feb 13
Tubman, Harriet: Death Anniv, Mar 10
Tudor, Tasha: Birth, Aug 28
Tunis, John: Birth Anniv, Dec 7
Tunisia
Independence Day, **Mar 20**
Martyrs' Day, **Apr 9**
Republic Day, **Jul 25**
Women's Day, **Aug 13**
Tunnell, Michael O.: Birth, Jun 14
Turkey
Earthquake: Anniv, **Aug 17**
National Sovereignty/Children's Day, **Apr 23**
Republic Day, **Oct 29**
Victory Day, **Aug 30**
Youth and Sports Day, **May 19**
Turkey Lovers' Month, June Is, Jun 1
Turkmenistan
Independence Day, **Oct 27**
Neutrality Day, **Dec 12**
Revival and Unity Day, **May 18**
Turkoglu, Hedo: Birth, Mar 19
Turner, Megan Whalen: Birth, Nov 21
Turner, Ted: Birth, Nov 19
Turtle Day, World, May 23
Tuskegee Airmen Activated: Anniv, Mar 22
Tut, King: Tomb Discovery Anniv, Nov 4
Tutor Appreciation Day, Apr 8
Tuttle, Merlin: Birth, Aug 24
Tutu, Desmond: Birth, Oct 7
Tuvalu: National Holiday, Oct 1
Twain, Mark (Samuel Clemens): Birth Anniv, Nov 30
Twelfth Day (Epiphany), Jan 6
Twelfth Night, Jan 5
Twellman, Taylor: Birth, Feb 29
Tyler, John: Birth Anniv, Mar 29
Tyler, Julia G.: Birth Anniv, May 4
Tyler, Letitia Christian: Birth Anniv, Nov 12
Tynwald Day (Isle of Man), Jul 5
Typewriter, First: Anniv, Jun 23
Typographic Smiley Face: Anniv, Sep 19
Uchida, Yoshiko: Birth Anniv, Nov 24
Uganda
Independence Day, **Oct 9**
Liberation Day, **Apr 11**
Ukraine
Chernobyl Reactor Disaster: Anniv, **Apr 26**
Independence Day, **Aug 24**
Ukrainian Day, **Jan 22**
Umbrella Month, Natl, Mar 1
Umbrellas: Open an Umbrella Indoors Day, Natl, Mar 13
Underdog Day, Dec 16
Underwear Day, Natl, Aug 13
UNESCO: Anniv, Nov 4
UNICEF Anniv [UN], Dec 11
Union of Soviet Socialist Republics
Dissolved: Anniv, **Dec 8**
Saint Petersburg Name Restored: Anniv, **Sep 6**
United Arab Emirates: Independence Day, Dec 2
United Kingdom
Accession of Queen Elizabeth II: Anniv, **Feb 6**
Battle of Britain Day, **Sep 15**
Battle of Britain Week, **Sep 11**
Boxing Day, **Dec 26**
Commonwealth Day, **Mar 13**
Coronation Day, **Jun 2**

Holocaust Memorial Day, Jan 27
Trafalgar Weekend, Oct 21
Trooping the Colour/Queen's Official Birthday, Jun 10
United Nations
Biological Diversity, Intl Day for, May 22
Charter Signed: Anniv, Jun 26
Civil Aviation Day, Intl, Dec 7
Cooperatives, Intl Day of, Jul 1
Disabled Persons, Intl Day of, Dec 3
Disarmament Week, Oct 24
Drug Abuse/Illicit Trafficking, Intl Day Against, Jun 26
Families, Intl Day of, May 15
Human Rights Day, Dec 10
Innocent Children Victims of Aggression, Intl Day of, Jun 4
Intl Day For the Elimination of Violence Against Women, Nov 25
Literacy Day, Intl, Sep 8
Migrants Day, Intl, Dec 18
Mother Language Day, Intl, Feb 21
Natural Disaster Reduction, Intl Day for, Oct 12
Older Persons, Intl Day for, Oct 1
Peace, Intl Day of, Sep 21
Poverty, Intl Day for Eradication, Oct 17
Preservation of the Ozone Layer, Intl Day for, Sep 16
Racial Discrimination, Intl Day for Elimination of, Mar 21
Telecommunication Day, World, May 17
Tolerance, Intl Day for, Nov 16
UNESCO: Anniv, Nov 4
UNICEF Anniv, Dec 11
United Nations Day, Oct 24
United Nations Day (Pres Proc), Oct 24
United Nations General Assembly: Anniv, Jan 10
Universal Children's Day, Nov 20
Volunteer Day for Economic/Social Dvmt, Intl, Dec 5
Water, World Day for, Mar 22
Women's Rights and International Peace, Day for, Mar 8
World AIDS Day, Dec 1
World Book and Copyright Day, Apr 23
World Day to Combat Desertification and Drought, Jun 17
World Environment Day, Jun 5
World Food Day, Oct 16
World Habitat Day, Oct 3
World Health Day, Apr 7
World Health Organization: Anniv, Apr 7
World Meteorological Day, Mar 23
World Population Day, Jul 11
World Post Day, Oct 9
World Press Freedom Day, May 3
World Refugee Day, Jun 20
World Space Week, Oct 4
World Teachers' Day, Oct 5
World Television Day, Nov 21
Youth Day, Intl, Aug 12
United States (government and history)
Air Force Established: Anniv, Sep 18
Army Established: Anniv, Jun 14
Attack on America, Sep 11
Blacks Ruled Eligible to Vote: Anniv, Apr 3
Bureau of Indian Affairs Established, Mar 11
Capitol Cornerstone Laid: Anniv, Sep 18
Civil Rights Act of 1964: Anniv, Jul 2
Clinton Impeachment Proceedings: Anniv, Dec 20
Coins Stamped "In God We Trust": Anniv, Apr 22
Colonies Become US: Anniv, Sep 9
Congress Assembles, Jan 3
Congress First Meets in Washington: Anniv, Nov 21
Congress: First Meeting Anniv, Mar 4
Constitution of the US: Anniv, Sep 17
Days of Prayer and Remembrance, Natl (Pres Proc), Sep 9
Department of Defense Created: Anniv, Jul 26
Dept of Justice: Anniv, Jun 22
Dept of State Founded: Anniv, Jul 27
Family-Leave Bill: Anniv, Feb 5
Federal Communications Commission Created: Anniv, Feb 26
Female House Page, First: Anniv, May 14
55 mph Speed Limit: Anniv, Jan 2
First Census: Anniv, Aug 1
First Elected Woman Senator: Anniv, Jan 12
First US Income Tax: Anniv, Mar 8
Flag Amendment Defeated: Anniv, Jun 26
Independence Day, Jul 4
Japanese Internment: Anniv, Feb 19
Johnson Impeachment Proceedings: Anniv, Feb 24
Library of Congress: Anniv, Apr 24
NAFTA Signed: Anniv, Dec 8
Native American Rights Recognized: Anniv, May 12
Nuclear-Free World, First Step Toward a: Anniv, Dec 8
Operation Iraqi Freedom: Anniv, Mar 19
Paper Money Issued: Anniv, Mar 10
Peace Corps Founded: Anniv, Mar 1
Persian Gulf War Begins: Anniv, Jan 16
Philippine Independence: Anniv, Mar 24
Postmaster General Established: Anniv, Sep 22
President First Occupies White House: Anniv, Nov 1
Presidential Succession Act: Anniv, Jul 18
Ratification Day, Jan 14
Sanctions Against South Africa Lifted: Anniv, Jul 10
Senate Quorum: Anniv, Apr 6
Standard Time Act: Anniv, Mar 19
Supreme Court Bans School Prayer: Anniv, Jun 25
Treasury Department: Anniv, Sep 2
Treaty of Guadalupe Hidalgo (with Mexico): Anniv, Feb 2
Uniform Time Zone Plan: Anniv, Nov 18
US Capital Established at NYC: Anniv, Sep 13
US Enters WWI: Anniv, Apr 6
US Mint: Anniv, Apr 2
Vietnam Peace Agreement Signed: Anniv, Jan 27
WAAC: Anniv, May 14
War Department Established: Anniv, Aug 7
War of 1812: Declaration Anniv, Jun 18
War on Poverty: Anniv, Jan 8
Water Pollution Control Act: Anniv, Oct 18
White House Easter Egg Roll: Anniv, Apr 2
With All Deliberate Speed: Anniv, May 31
UNIVAC Computer: Anniv, Jun 14
Universal Human Rights Month, Dec 1
Universal Letter-Writing Week, Jan 8
Up Helly AA (Scotland), Jan 31
Uranus (planet) Discovery: Anniv, Mar 13
Urlacher, Brian: Birth, May 25
Uruguay
Artigas Day, Jun 19
Battle of Las Piedras Day, May 18
Constitution Day, Jul 18
Independence Day, Aug 25
US Air Force Academy Established: Anniv, Apr 1
US Air Force Established: Anniv, Sep 18
US House, Black Page Appointed: Anniv, Apr 9
US Military Academy Founded: Anniv, Mar 16
US Naval Academy Founded: Anniv, Oct 10
US Navy: Authorization Anniv, Oct 13
US Virgin Islands
Danish West Indies Emancipation Day, Jul 3
Hurricane Supplication Day, Jul 24
Hurricane Thanksgiving Day, Oct 17
Liberty Day, Nov 1
Natl Park Established: Anniv, Aug 2
Organic Act Day, Jun 19
Puerto Rico Friendship Day, Oct 10
Transfer Day, Mar 31
USA Today First Published: Anniv, Sep 15
USS Constitution Launched: Anniversary, Oct 21
USS Constitution Saved by Poem: Anniv, Sep 16
Utah
Admission Day, Jan 4
American Alliance for Health, Phys Ed, Recreation & Dance, Natl Convention & Expo (Salt Lake City), Apr 25
America's First Department Store (Salt Lake City), Oct 16
Arches Natl Park: Anniv, Nov 12
Bennett, Robert F.: Birth, Sep 18
Capitol Reef Natl Park: Anniv, Dec 18
Council for Exceptional Children Annual Convention (Salt Lake City), Apr 5
Hatch, Orrin: Birth, Mar 22
Huntsman, John, Jr: Birth, Mar 26
MENC Natl Conference (Salt Lake City), Apr 18
Pioneer Day, Jul 24
State Fair (Salt Lake City), Sep 8
Zion Natl Park: Anniv, Nov 19
Uzbekistan
Constitution Day, Dec 10
Independence Day, Sep 1
Valderrama, Carlos: Birth, Sep 2
Valentine's Day, Feb 14
Valenzuela, Fernando: Birth, Nov 1
Van Allsburg, Chris: Birth, Jun 18
Van Buren, Hannah Hoes: Birth Anniv, Mar 8
Van Buren, Martin: Birth Anniv, Dec 5
Van Der Beek, James: Birth, Mar 8
Van Dyke, Dick: Birth, Dec 13
Van Exel, Nick: Birth, Nov 27
Van Gogh, Vincent: Birth Anniv, Mar 30
Van Horn, Keith: Birth, Oct 23
Van Laan, Nancy: Birth, Nov 18
Van Leuween, Jean: Birth, Dec 26
VanCleave, Janice: Birth, Jan 27
Vanuatu: Independence Day, Jul 30
Vatican City: Independence Anniv, Feb 11
Vatican Council II: Anniv, Oct 11
VCR Introduced: Anniv, Jun 7
V-E Day, May 8
Veep Day, Aug 9
Vegetarian Day, World, Oct 1
Vegetarian Month, Oct 1
Vegetarian Resource Group's Essay Contest for Kids, May 1
Venezuela
Battle of Carabobo Day, Jun 24
Independence Day, Jul 5
Ventura, Jesse: Birth, Jul 15
Vermont
Admission Day, Mar 4
Douglas, James: Birth, Jun 21
Jeffords, James: Birth, May 11
Leahy, Patrick J.: Birth, Mar 31
State Fair (Rutland), Sep 2
Town Meeting Day, Mar 7
Verne, Jules: Birth Anniv, Feb 8
Verrazano Day, Apr 17
Vesey, Denmark: Death Anniv, Jul 2
Vespucci, Amerigo: Birth Anniv, Mar 9
Vesuvius Eruption Destroys Pompeii: Anniv, Aug 24
Veterans Day, Nov 11
Veterans Day (Pres Proc), Nov 11
Vick, Michael: Birth, Jun 26
Victoria Day (Canada), May 22
Victory in Europe Day, May 8
Video Games Day, Sep 12
Vietnam
Anniversary of the Founding of the Communist Party, Feb 3
Ho Chi Minh's Birthday, May 19
Independence Day, Sep 2
Liberation Day, Apr 30
Tet: See Chinese New Year, Jan 29
Vietnam War
Dien Bien Phu Falls: Anniv, May 7
King Opposes Vietnam War: Anniv, Apr 4
Vietnam Conflict Begins [with French]: Anniv, Aug 22
Vietnam Peace Agreement Signed: Anniv, Jan 27
Viking: Up Helly AA (Scotland), Jan 31
Villeneuve, Jacques: Birth, Apr 9
Vilsack, Tom: Birth, Dec 13
Vina, Fernando: Birth, Apr 16
Vining, Elizabeth Gray: Birth Anniv, Oct 6
Vinson, Fred M.: Birth Anniv, Jan 22
Violence Day, Natl Stop the, Nov 22
Violence, Intl Day For the Elimination of Against Women (UN), Nov 25
Violence, YWCA Week Without, Oct 16
Viorst, Judith: Birth, Feb 2
Virginia
Allen, George: Birth, Mar 8
Children's Fest (Norfolk), Oct 1
Chincoteague Pony Penning (Chincoteague Island), Jul 26
Lee-Jackson Day, Jan 13
Ratification Day, Jun 25
Shenandoah Natl Park: Anniv, Dec 26
State Fair (Richmond), Sep 22
Warner, John: Birth, Feb 18
Warner, Mark: Birth, Dec 15
Yorktown Day (Yorktown), Oct 19
Yorktown Victory Day, Oct 10
Virginia Company Expedition to America: Anniv, Dec 20
Virginia Hamilton Conference (Kent, OH), Apr 6
Virginia Plan Proposed: Anniv, May 29
Virgo Begins, Aug 23
Visit Your Relatives Day, May 18
Vitamin C Isolated: Anniv, Apr 4
Vitter, David: Birth, May 3
Vizquel, Omar: Birth, Apr 24
V-J Day (Announcement), Aug 14
V-J Day (Ratification), Sep 2
Voigt, Cynthia: Birth, Feb 25
Voinovich, George V.: Birth, Jul 15
Volcanoes; Volcanic Eruptions
Cameroon: Eruption: Anniv, Aug 22
Montserrat: Volcano Erupts: Anniv, Jun 25
Mount Pelee Eruption: Anniv, May 8
Mount Pinatubo Erupts in Philippines: Anniv, Jun 11
Mount Saint Helens Eruption: Anniv, May 18
Vesuvius Eruption Destroys Pompeii: Anniv, Aug 24
Volunteer Day for Economic/Social Dvmt, Intl (UN), Dec 5
Volunteer Week, Natl, Apr 23
Volunteer Week, Natl (Pres Proc), Apr 23
Volunteers: Make a Difference Day, Oct 22
von Steuben, Baron Friedrich: Birth Anniv, Sep 17
Vonnegut, Kurt, Jr: Birth, Nov 11
Vote: Blacks Ruled Eligible to Vote: Anniv, Apr 3
Voting Age Changed (26th Amendment): Anniv, Jun 30
Voting Rights Act Signed: Anniv, Aug 6
Voyageurs Natl Park: Anniv, Apr 8
Waber, Bernard: Birth, Sep 27
Waddell, Martin: Birth, Apr 10
Wadlow, Robert Pershing: Birth Anniv, Feb 22
Wagner, Honus: Birth Anniv, Feb 24
Wahlberg, Donnie: Birth, Aug 17
Wahlberg, Mark: Birth, Jun 5
Waitangi Day (New Zealand), Feb 6
Waite, Morrison R.: Birth Anniv, Nov 29
Waldseemuller, Martin: Remembrance Day, Apr 25
Wales: Saint David's Day, Mar 1
Walesa, Lech: Birth, Sep 29
Walesa, Lech: Solidarity Founded Anniv, Aug 31
Walk on Stilts Day, Jul 27
Walk Our Children to School Day, Natl, Oct 5
Walk Your Pet Month, Jan 1
Walker, Antoine: Birth, Aug 12
Walker, Larry: Birth, Dec 1
Walker, Madame C.J.: Birth Anniv, Dec 23
Wallace, Henry A.: Birth Anniv, Oct 7
Wallace, Karen: Birth, Apr 1
Wallace, Rasheed: Birth, Sep 17
Wallenberg, Raoul: Birth Anniv, Aug 5
Waller, Tisha: Birth, Dec 1
Walsh, Ellen Stoll: Birth, Sep 2
Walt Disney TV Premiere: Anniv, Oct 27
Walter, Mildred Pitts: Birth, Sep 9
Walters, Barbara: Birth, Sep 25
Walton, George: Death Anniv, Feb 2
Wang, Garrett: Birth, Dec 15
War of 1812: Declaration Anniv, Jun 18
War on Poverty: Anniv, Jan 8
Warmest US Winter on Record, Mar 20
Warner Weather Quotation: Anniv, Aug 24
Warner, John: Birth, Feb 18
Warner, Kurt: Birth, Jun 22
Warner, Mark: Birth, Dec 15
Warren, Earl: Birth Anniv, Mar 19
Washington
Admission Day, Nov 11
Cantwell, Maria: Birth, Oct 13
Gregoire, Christine: Birth, Mar 24
Mount Rainier Natl Park: Anniv, Mar 2
Murray, Patty: Birth, Oct 11
North Cascades Natl Park: Anniv, Oct 2
Seattle Intl Children's Fest (Seattle), May 15
Washington Crosses the Delaware: Anniv, Dec 25
Washington, Booker T.: Birth Anniv, Apr 5
Washington, Denzel: Birth, Dec 28
Washington, District of Columbia
District Establishing Legislation: Anniv, Jul 16
Education of Young Children, Natl Assn for the, Conference, Dec 7
Geographic Bee Finals, Natl, May 23
Invasion Anniv, Aug 24
Multicultural Children's Book Fest, Nov 5
Spelling Bee Finals, Natl, May 31
Washington Monument Dedicated: Anniv, Feb 21
Youth of the Year, Natl, Sep 21
Washington, George
Address to Continental Army Officers: Anniv, Mar 15
Birth Anniv, Feb 22
Birthday Observance (Legal Holiday), Feb 20
Crosses the Delaware: Anniv, Dec 25
Presidential Inauguration Anniv, Apr 30
White House Cornerstone Laid: Anniv, Oct 13
Washington, Martha: Birth Anniv, Jun 21
Water-Drawing Fest (Japan), Mar 1
Waterton-Glacier Intl Peace Park: Anniv, May 11
Watson, Clyde: Birth, Jul 25
Watson, Emma: Birth, Apr 15
Wayne, "Mad Anthony": Birth Anniv, Jan 1
Weather
Big Wind: Anniv, Apr 12
Meteorological Day, World (UN), Mar 23

North America's Coldest Recorded Temperature: Anniv, Feb 3
Warmest US Winter on Record, Mar 20
Warner Quotation: Anniv, Aug 24
Weatherman's Day, Feb 5
Weatherspoon, Teresa: Birth, Dec 8
Weaver, Robert C.: First Black US Cabinet Member: Anniv, Jan 18
Weaver, Will: Birth, Jan 19
Webber, Chris: Birth, Mar 1
Webster, Noah: Birth Anniv, Oct 16
Webster-Ashburton Treaty Signed: Anniv, Aug 9
Wechsler, Doug: Birth, Apr 2
Wedding of the Sea (Venice, Italy), May 28
Week of the Ocean, Natl, Apr 2
Wegman, William: Birth, Dec 2
Weights and Measures Day, May 20
Weiss, Michael: Birth, Aug 2
Weizmann, Chaim: Birth Anniv, Nov 27
Welfare. See Health and Welfare,
Welling, Tom: Birth, Apr 26
Wells, David: Birth, May 20
Wells, Ida B.: Birth Anniv, Jul 16
Wells, Rosemary: Birth, Jan 29
West Virginia
  Admission Day, Jun 20
  Byrd, Robert C.: Birth, Nov 20
  Manchin, Joe: Birth, Aug 24
  Rockefeller, John D., IV (Jay): Birth, Jun 18
  State Fair (Lewisburg), Aug 12
Weston, Martha: Birth, Jan 16
Whale Awareness Day (MA), May 4
What Do You Love About America Day, Nov 23
Wheatley, Phillis: Death Anniv, Dec 5
Wheatley, Phillis: Poetry Collection Published: Anniv, Sep 1
Wheeler, William A.: Birth Anniv, Jun 30
Whelan, Gloria: Birth, Nov 23
Whiner's Day, Natl, Dec 26
Whipple, William: Birth Anniv, Jan 14
White Cane Safety Day (Pres Proc), Oct 15
White Cloud Birthday, Jul 10
White House Cornerstone Laid: Anniv, Oct 13
White House Easter Egg Roll, Apr 17
White Sunday (Samoa and American Samoa), Oct 9
White, Byron R.: Birth Anniv, Jun 8
White, E.B.: Birth Anniv, Jul 11
White, Edward Douglass: Birth Anniv, Nov 3
White, Jaleel: Birth, Nov 27
White, Reggie: Birth, Dec 19
White, Ruth: Birth, Mar 15
Whitman, Walt: Birth Anniv, May 31
Whitmonday, Jun 5
Whitsunday, Jun 4
Whooping Cranes
  Fall Migration, Sep 15
  Longest Human-Led Migration: Anniv, Dec 3
  Spring Migration, Mar 1
Wick, Walter: Birth, Feb 23
Wiesner, David: Birth, Feb 5
Wiggin, Kate Douglas: Birth Anniv, Sep 28
Wilder, Gene: Birth, Jun 11
Wilder, L. Douglas: First Black Governor Elected: Anniv, Nov 7
Wilder, Laura Ingalls: Birth Anniv, Feb 7
Wildlife Week, Natl, Apr 16
Wilkins, Roy: Birth Anniv, Aug 30
Willard, Frances E.C.: Birth Anniv, Sep 28
Willard, Nancy: Birth, Jun 26
William the Conqueror: Death Anniv, Sep 9
William, Prince: Birth, Jun 21
Williams, Archie: Birth Anniv, May 1
Williams, Garth: Birth Anniv, Apr 16
Williams, Jay: Birth, Sep 10
Williams, Karen Lynn: Birth, Mar 22
Williams, Margery: See Bianco, Margery Williams: Birth Anniv, Jul 22
Williams, Natalie: Birth, Nov 30
Williams, Ricky: Birth, May 21
Williams, Robin: Birth, Jul 21
Williams, Serena: Birth, Sep 26
Williams, Venus: Birth, Jun 17
Williams, Vera B.: Birth, Jan 28
Williams, William: Birth Anniv, Apr 8
Willis, Bruce: Birth, Mar 19
Wilson, Blaine: Birth, Aug 3
Wilson, Edith: Birth Anniv, Oct 15
Wilson, Ellen L.: Birth Anniv, May 15
Wilson, Henry: Birth Anniv, Feb 16
Wilson, James: Birth Anniv, Sep 14
Wilson, Mara: Birth, Jul 24
Wilson, Woodrow: Birth Anniv, Dec 28
Wind Cave Natl Park: Anniv, Jan 3
Windmill Day, Natl (Netherlands), May 13
Winfrey, Oprah: Birth, Jan 29
Winkerbean, Funky: Anniv, Mar 27
Winslet, Kate: Birth, Oct 5
Winter Begins, Dec 21
Winter Solstice: Yalda (Iran), Dec 21
Winter, Jeanette: Birth, Oct 6
Winthrop, Elizabeth: Birth, Sep 14
Wisconsin
  Admission Day, May 29
  Christmas at the Top Museum (Burlington), Dec 26
  Doyle, Jim: Birth, Nov 23
  Feingold, Russell D.: Birth, Mar 2
  Kohl, Herb: Birth, Feb 7
  Laura Ingalls Wilder Days (Pepin), Sep 10
  State Fair (Milwaukee), Aug 4
Wishbone TV Premiere: Anniv, Oct 9
Wisniewski, David: Birth Anniv, Mar 21
Witches: Salem Hysteria Begins: Anniv, Mar 1
Witherspoon, John: Birth Anniv, Feb 5
Witt, Katarina: Birth, Dec 3
Wittlinger, Ellen: Birth, Oct 21
Wizard of Oz First Released: Anniv, Aug 25
Wojtyla, Karol: Pope John Paul II: Birth, May 18
Wolcott, Oliver: Birth Anniv, Nov 20
Wolf, Bernard: Birth, Feb 26
Wolf, Scott: Birth, Jun 4
Wolfe, James: Birth Anniv, Jan 2
Wolff, Josh: Birth, Feb 25
Wolff, Virginia Euwer: Birth, Aug 25
Women
  Around the World in 72 Days: Anniv, Jan 25
  Blackwell, Elizabeth, Awarded MD: Anniv, Jan 23
  Bloomer, Amelia Jenks: Birth Anniv, May 27
  Catt, Carrie Chapman: Birth Anniv, Jan 9
  English Channel, First Woman Swims: Anniv, Aug 6
  Equal Rights Amendment Sent to States for Ratification: Anniv, Mar 22
  Female House Page, First: Anniv, May 14
  First Elected Woman Senator: Anniv, Jan 12
  First To Climb Mount Everest: Anniv, May 16
  First US Woman Governor Inaugurated, Jan 5
  First Woman Canadian Prime Minister: Anniv, Jun 25
  First Woman in Space: Space Milestone, Jun 16
  First Woman Rabbi in US: Anniv, Jun 3
  First Woman Supreme Court Justice: Anniv, Sep 25
  First Woman to Graduate Dental School: Anniv, Feb 21
  First Woman to Walk in Space, Jul 17
  First Women's Collegiate Basketball Game: Anniv, Mar 22
  Girls and Women in Sports Day, Natl, Feb 9
  Intl Day For the Elimination of Violence Against Women (UN), Nov 25
  Medical School for Women Opened: Anniv, Nov 1
  Meitlisunntig (Switzerland), Jan 8
  Mott, Lucretia: Birth Anniv, Jan 3
  19th Amendment Ratified (Women's Right to Vote), Aug 18
  NOW Founded: Anniv, Jun 30
  Pocahontas: Death Anniv, Mar 21
  Royall, Anne: Birth Anniv, Jun 11
  Russia: Women's Day, Intl, Mar 8
  Salter Elected First Woman Mayor in US: Anniv, Apr 4
  Stanton, Elizabeth: Birth Anniv, Nov 12
  Stone, Lucy: Birth Anniv, Aug 13
  Susan B. Anthony Fined for Voting: Anniv, Jun 6
  Truth, Sojourner: Death Anniv, Nov 26
  WAAC: Anniv, May 14
  Willard, Frances E.C.: Birth Anniv, Sep 28
  Woman Presides Over US Supreme Court: Anniv, Apr 3
  Women's Equality Day, Aug 26
  Women's Equality Day (Pres Proc), Aug 26
  Women's History Month (Pres Proc), Mar 1
  Women's History Month, Natl, Mar 1
  Women's Rights and International Peace, Day for (UN), Mar 8
  Women's Rights Convention at Seneca Falls: Anniv, Jul 19
  Women's Suffrage Amendment Introduced: Anniv, Jan 10
  Working Women's Day, Intl, Mar 8
  YWCA Week, Natl, Apr 23
Wonder, Stevie: Birth, May 13
Wood, Don: Birth, May 4
Wood, Elijah: Birth, Jan 28
Wood, Grant: Birth Anniv, Feb 13
Wood, Kerry: Birth, Jun 16
Woodard, Alfre: Birth, Nov 8
Woodruff, Elvira: Birth, Jun 19
Woods, Tiger: Birth, Dec 30
Woodson, Carter Godwin: Birth Anniv, Dec 19
Woodson, Jacqueline: Birth, Feb 12
Woolworths Opened: Anniv, Feb 22
Working Women's Day, Intl, Mar 8
World AIDS Day (Pres Proc), Dec 1
World Communion Sunday, Oct 2
World Cup Inaugurated: Anniv, Jul 13
World Day of Prayer, Mar 3
World Food Day, Oct 16
World Health Organization: Anniv, Apr 7
World Juggling Day, Jun 17
World Religion Day, Jan 15
World Television Day, Nov 21
World Trade Week (Pres Proc), May 21
World War I
  Anzac Day, Apr 25
  Armistice: Anniv, Nov 11
  Battle of the Marne: Anniv, Jul 15
  Battle of Verdun: Anniv, Feb 21
  Begins: Anniv, Jul 28
  Stubby Joins Front Lines: Anniv, Feb 5
  Treaty of Versailles: Anniv, Jun 28
  US Enters: Anniv, Apr 6
World War II
  Atomic Bomb Dropped on Hiroshima: Anniv, Aug 6
  Atomic Bomb Dropped on Nagasaki: Anniv, Aug 9
  Atomic Bomb Tested: Anniv, Jul 16
  Auschwitz Liberated by Soviets: Anniv, Jan 27
  Battle of the Bulge: Anniv, Dec 16
  Begins: Germany Invades Poland: Anniv, Sep 1
  D-Day: Anniv, Jun 6
  Declaration Anniv, Sep 3
  Diary of Anne Frank: Last Entry: Anniv, Aug 1
  Germany's First Surrender: Anniv, May 7
  Germany's Second Surrender: Anniv, May 8
  Italy Surrenders: Anniv, Sep 3
  Iwo Jima Day, Feb 23
  Japanese Internment: Anniv, Feb 19
  Japan's Unconditional Surrender: Anniv, Aug 10
  Liberation of Buchenwald: Anniv, Apr 11
  MacArthur Returns to the Philippines: Anniv, Oct 20
  Oak Ridge Atomic Plant Begun: Anniv, Aug 1
  Paris Liberated: Anniv, Aug 25
  Pearl Harbor Day, Dec 7
  Pearl Harbor Remembrance Day, Natl (Pres Proc), Dec 7
  Roosevelt, Franklin D.: Death Anniv, Apr 12
  Russia: Victory Day, May 9
  Tuskegee Airmen Activated: Anniv, Mar 22
  V-E Day, May 8
  V-J Day (Announcement), Aug 14
  V-J Day (Ratification), Sep 2
  WAAC: Anniv, May 14
World Wide Web: Anniv, Aug 1
Wounded Knee Massacre: Anniv, Dec 29
Wozniak, Stephen: Birth, Aug 11
Wrangell-St Elias Natl Park Established: Anniv, Dec 2
Wrede, Patricia: Birth, Mar 27
Wright Brothers Day (Pres Proc), Dec 17
Wright Brothers' First Powered Flight: Anniv, Dec 17
Wright, Betty Ren: Birth, Jun 15
Wright, Frank Lloyd: Birth Anniv, Jun 8
Wright, Orville: Birth Anniv, Aug 19
Wright, Richard: Birth Anniv, Sep 4
Wright, Wilbur: Birth Anniv, Apr 16
Wyden, Ron: Birth, May 3
Wyoming
  Admission Day, Jul 10
  Enzi, Michael B.: Birth, Feb 1
  First US Woman Governor Inaugurated, Jan 5
  Freudenthal, Dave: Birth, Oct 12
  State Fair & Rodeo (Douglas), Aug 13
  Thomas, Craig: Birth, Feb 17
  Yellowstone Natl Park Established: Anniv, Mar 1
Wythe, George: Death Anniv, Jun 8
X-Ray Discovery Day: Anniv, Nov 8
Yagudin, Alexei: Birth, Mar 18
Yalda (Iran), Dec 21
Yamaguchi, Kristi: Birth, Jul 12
Yankee Stadium Opens, Apr 18
Yankovic, Al: Birth, Oct 23
Yates, Elizabeth: Birth Anniv, Dec 6
Yawm Arafat (Islamic): The Standing at Arafat, Jan 9
Yeager, Chuck: Birth, Feb 13
Yell "Fudge" at the Cobras in North America Day, Jun 2
Yellow Kid. See Outcault, Richard Fenton: Birth Anniv, Jan 14
Yellow Kid: First Newspaper Comic Strip: Anniv, Oct 18
Yellowstone Natl Park Established: Anniv, Mar 1
Yeltsin, Boris, Inaugurated Russian President: Anniv, Jul 10
Yeltsin, Boris: Birth, Feb 1
Yemen: Natl Day, May 22
Yep, Laurence: Birth, Jun 14
YMCA Healthy Kids Day, Apr 1
YMCA Organized: Anniv, Dec 29
Yolen, Jane: Birth, Feb 11
Yom Hashoah (Israel), Apr 25
Yom Kippur, Oct 13
Yom Kippur Begins, Oct 12
Yom Kippur War, Oct 6
Yorinks, Arthur: Birth, Aug 21
Yorktown Day, Oct 19
Yorktown Day (Yorktown, VA), Oct 19
Yorktown Victory Day (VA), Oct 10
Yosemite Natl Park: Anniv, Oct 1
Young Achievers Month, May 1
Young Adolescent, Month of the, Oct 1
Young Child, Month of the (MI), Apr 1
Young People's Poetry Week, Apr 10
Young, Cy: Birth Anniv, Mar 29
Young, Ed: Birth, Nov 28
Young, Steve: Birth, Oct 11
Yount, Robin: Birth, Sep 16
Youth Appreciation Week, Nov 14
Youth Art Month, Mar 1
Youth Day, Mar 29
Youth Day (Cameroon), Feb 11
Youth Day (People's Republic of China), May 4
Youth Day, Intl (UN), Aug 12
Youth Month, Natl, Nov 1
Youth of the Year, Natl (Washington, DC), Sep 21
Youth Sports Safety Month, Natl, Apr 1
Yugoslavia
  Civil War: Anniv, Jun 25
  NATO Attacks: Anniv, Mar 25
  Slovenia and Croatia Independence: Anniv, Jun 25
YWCA Week Without Violence, Oct 16
YWCA Week, Natl, Apr 23
Yzerman, Steve: Birth, May 9
Z Day, Jan 1
Zaharias, Mildred Babe Didrikson: Birth Anniv, Jun 26
Zaire: See Congo (Kinshasa), Jun 30
Zambia
  African Freedom Day, May 25
  Heroes Day, Jul 3
  Independence Day, Oct 24
  Unity Day, Jul 4
  Youth Day, Aug 1
Zelinsky, Paul O.: Birth, Feb 14
Zemach, Margot: Birth Anniv, Nov 30
Ziefert, Harriet: Birth, Jul 7
Zimbabwe
  African Freedom Day, May 25
  Heroes' Day, Aug 11
  Independence Day, Apr 18
Zion Natl Park: Anniv, Nov 19
Zion, Gene: Birth Anniv, Oct 5
Zip Codes Inaugurated: Anniv, Jul 1
Zipper Patented: Anniv, Apr 29
Zolotin, Adam: Birth, Nov 29
Zolotow, Charlotte: Birth, Jun 26
Zolotow, Ellen: see Dragonwagon, Crescent, Nov 25
Zoo: First US Zoo: Anniv (Philadelphia, PA), Jul 1
Zwerger, Lisbeth: Birth, May 26